THE LAW AND PRACTICE OF
MARINE INSURANCE AND AVERAGE

Associate Authors

BRIAN M. WALTHAM and JONATHAN LUX
Ince & Co., Solicitors
London, England

JOHN R. CUNNINGHAM
Campney & Murphy, Barristers & Solicitors
Vancouver, Canada

DEREK R. HENTZE
Senior Legal Officer, Caltex Australia Limited
Sydney, Australia

T. J. BROADMORE
Chapman Tripp Sheffield Young, Barristers & Solicitors
Wellington, New Zealand

CARTER QUINBY
Derby, Cook, Quinby & Tweedt, Attorneys at Law
San Francisco, California

MARTIN P. DETELS, JR.
Attorney at Law
Seattle, Washington

PAUL N. WONACOTT
Wood Tatum Mosser Brooke & Landis, Attorneys at Law
Portland, Oregon

THE LAW AND PRACTICE OF
MARINE INSURANCE
AND AVERAGE

VOLUME I

BY ALEX L. PARKS

Member of the Oregon State Bar
and the Bars of the United States District Court, District of Oregon;
Court of Appeals, Ninth Circuit; Court of Appeals, District of Columbia;
United States Supreme Court;
Member of the Maritime Law Association of the United States; Associate
Member of the Association of Average Adjusters of the United States;
Adjunct Professor (Admiralty and Insurance),
Willamette University College of Law

CORNELL MARITIME PRESS
Centreville, Maryland

Library of Congress Cataloging in Publication Data

Parks, Alex Leon, 1925–
The law and practice of marine insurance and average.

Includes index.
1. Insurance, Marine—United States.   2. Average
(Maritime law)   3. Insurance, Marine.   I. Title.
KF1135.P35   1987   346'.086   87-13667
ISBN 0-87033-368-2   342.686

Manufactured in the United States of America
First edition

CONTENTS : VOLUME I

FOREWORD

Once again the prolific pen of Alex Parks has produced a major text on a vital part of the maritime law. "Pen" is, of course, used only figuratively; Mr. Parks is able to type at incredible speed, and now uses a highly sophisticated word processor for his writings. Judging from the quantity and quality of his output—the first and second editions of *The Law of Tug, Tow, and Pilotage,* this work on marine insurance and average, numerous law review articles and seminar papers, and the start of a forthcoming text on collision law—his thought processes must be as rapid and effective as his fingers.

The past half century has witnessed the publication of a sizable number of scholarly texts on particular subjects of maritime law, including collision, carriage of goods by water, salvage, seamen, maritime personal injury, and charter parties. In the marine insurance field, Leslie Buglass's *Marine Insurance and General Average in the United States* is a valuable handbook for average adjusters, marine insurance brokers, and marine claims managers, and has proved to be useful to admiralty attorneys as well. The papers delivered at the Tulane University Admiralty Law Institute's Symposiums on the Hull Policy and the P & I Policy have likewise been of considerable value to admiralty attorneys and others concerned with marine insurance and average, as have the chapters on marine insurance included in Gilmore and Black's *The Law of Admiralty* and Mr. Parks's *The Law of Tug, Tow, and Pilotage.* Until publication of this two-volume work, however, the law of marine insurance has not been the subject of a definitive American legal text since Parsons's *Marine Insurance* was published in 1868, a year after publication of the fifth edition of the classic *Phillips on Insurance.*

In the more than a century that has intervened since then, the maritime law has undergone profound changes, not the least of which have been in the marine insurance area. In the 1860s, protection and indemnity insurance was a very new concept, invented in response to the needs of shipowners suddenly faced with exposure to the burdensome risks that came with steam propulsion and iron and steel ship construction. The great codification of the English law of marine insurance embodied in the Marine Insurance Act, 1906 was still four decades away. There was no Jones Act, and the seaworthiness warranty to which seamen are now entitled was unknown; seamen's injuries caused by the fault of employers or fellow crew members were left uncompensated, except for the allowance of "wages, maintenance and cure." Workmen's compensation for longshoremen and other maritime workers was unheard of. There was no Harter Act or Carriage of Goods Act regulating carriage of cargo under ocean bills of lading. There was no Suits in Admiralty Act or Public Vessels Act permitting actions against the government for damages caused by, or salvage services rendered to, government-owned vessels. The development of the maritime law in all of these areas required corresponding development in marine insurance and the law that governs it.

The need for an up-to-date American text giving exhaustive treatment to the law of marine insurance—a subject closely interrelated with every other branch of the maritime law—was therefore readily apparent, and the need has been amply filled by Mr. Parks's work. Every significant phase of the subject has been fully treated. The early chapters thoroughly cover the basic principles of marine insurance law, such as the nature of the insurance contract, the rules governing construction of the policy, insurable interests, and warranties. Subsequent chapters treat particular subjects in depth, including, among others, the Inchmaree Clause, actual and constructive total loss, sue and labor, and the Running Down Clause. More than 200 pages are devoted to protection and indemnity insurance. Other topics covered include products liability and direct actions—concepts wholly unknown in the days of Phillips and Parsons.

The numerous documents and forms included as appendices have never before been collected in a single volume. Among them are the British Marine Insurance Act, 1906; the Rules of Practice of the American and British Average Adjusters' Associations; the 1974 York-Antwerp Rules (including a comparison with the 1950 Rules); and Lloyd's Standard Form of Salvage Agreement (LOF 1980). There are no less than 21 American and 52 English and Canadian insurance forms, a substantial number of which are not easy to come by, especially for busy admiralty practitioners. They, and others concerned with marine insurance and average, will be happy to find these documents and forms in one place, saving them the task of searching through a number of texts and stationers' catalogs for the right ones.

As he did in *The Law of Tug, Tow, and Pilotage,* Mr. Parks has cited hundreds of American, English, and Commonwealth decisions, the most significant of which are discussed in depth. Indeed, it is doubtful that any English language marine insurance decision of any account has been omitted. In collecting the English and Commonwealth decisions he has had the able assistance of colleagues in Canada, England, Australia, and New Zealand.

It is by no means an exaggeration to state that Mr. Parks's work is a major contribution to American maritime legal literature. It is certain to find a place in the libraries of all those whose work demands a thorough understanding, not only of the basic principles of marine insurance and average, but also of the practical application of those principles to hull, cargo, P & I, and other types of marine insurance contracts.

This writer concluded his foreword to the second edition of *The Law of Tug, Tow, and Pilotage* by expressing the gratitude of all of us who are engaged in the field of maritime law for Mr. Parks's efforts in the preparation of that volume. Again, we can all be thankful to him for laboring so diligently and effectively to produce an even more valuable work on maritime law.

NICHOLAS J. HEALY

PREFACE

The last exhaustive work on marine insurance in the United States was *Phillips on Insurance* (5th ed., 1867). Not only are the two volumes of Phillips's text out of print, the cited cases necessarily antedate the publication date of 1867, and since that time the number of decisions by American courts, both state and federal, directly involving marine insurance have been relatively enormous.

Many excellent source materials on marine insurance have been published in the United States in recent years, the most notable of which are a number of articles in the *Journal of Maritime Law & Commerce,* and, of course, the outstanding Tulane University Admiralty Law Institute volumes on the Hull Policy (1967) and the P & I Policy (1969).

By contrast, a number of excellent texts on marine insurance have been published in Great Britain. First in order of precedence must come Arnould, *Law of Marine Insurance and Average,* 16th ed., by Sir Michael J. Mustill and Jonathan C. B. Gilman (London: Stevens, 1981). In addition, one must mention the fine volumes such as *Templeman on Marine Insurance,* 5th ed., by R. J. Lambeth (Plymouth, England: Macdonald and Evans Ltd., 1981); *Marine Insurance,* 3rd ed., by E. R. Hardy Ivamy (London: Butterworths, 1979); and *Marine Insurance Claims,* 2nd ed., by J. Kenneth Goodacre (London: Witherby & Co. Ltd., 1981).

While a number of American decisions are cited in Arnould, that monumental work understandably concentrates on decisions in Great Britain. Thus, the emphasis of that work (and the other volumes mentioned above) is on English law in the field of marine insurance. By contrast, the *primary emphasis* in this text is on the law of marine insurance and average in the United States. Every effort, however, has been made to include all of the important decisions in Great Britain as well as in the Commonwealth nations because, after all, true marine insurance as it is practiced today originated in England, and it would be a foolish lawyer indeed who failed to recognize this.

In the preface to the first edition of his fine volume on the subject [*Marine Insurance and General Average in the United States,* 2nd ed. (Centreville, MD: Cornell Maritime Press, Inc., 1981)], Leslie J. Buglass acknowledged his debt to the marine insurance writers on both sides of the Atlantic. As he so correctly put it, without the durable foundation laid by these men (and many others) the marine insurance profession would be indescribably poorer. I fully subscribe to what he said there.

My objectives in producing this text were manifold:

(1) To produce a practical text keyed to the needs of insurance brokers, average adjusters, marine insurance executives, and, of course, the bench and bar in the United States, in Great Britain, and in other places in the world where the English marine insurance system and principles prevail

(2) To include, insofar as possible, all the relevant case citations, including discussion and citations of general maritime interest that have an impact upon the liabilities underwriters seek to cover in their policies (for example, the coverage under the Running Down Clause would not be understandable without a basic knowledge of the principles of collision law, nor would the coverage afforded under P & I club rules be intelligible without a basic understanding of the general maritime principles applicable to liabilities which those rules purport to cover)

(3) To give case citations in a fashion most useful to the bench and bar; i.e., by reference to the standard case reports such as the Federal Reporter system, Lloyd's Reports, reports from the various Commonwealth nations, and most importantly, to American Maritime Cases, which are frequently available not only to American lawyers but also to solicitors and barristers in the United Kingdom and the Commonwealth nations

(4) To include in the Appendices all the most common marine insurance policy forms; the York-Antwerp Rules; Lloyd's Open Form; the Marine Insurance Act, 1906; and other relevant material of value to the practitioner, the goal being to provide to all practitioners, wherever located, a quick and ready reference to basic source materials without having to refer to other texts or sources

(5) To emphasize the tremendous importance of the Marine Insurance Act, 1906 to American lawyers. While that act has never been adopted in the United States, its provisions reflect the common law of marine insurance as it existed in England in 1906—and in large measure the marine insurance law of the United States as of that date. With a few exceptions (notably the relationship among brokers, underwriters, and assureds), it could rightfully be called the "Restatement of the Law of Marine Insurance."

In undertaking this task, I felt obligated to seek the assistance of those whom I consider experts in the United States, the United Kingdom, Canada, Australia, and New Zealand. In this I have been fortunate indeed. I owe the deepest debt of gratitude to the following people, whom I am happy to acknowledge: Brian M. Waltham and Jonathan Lux of Ince & Co., Solicitors, London, England; John R. Cunningham of Campney & Murphy, Barristers and Solicitors, Vancouver, British Columbia; Derek R. Hentze, Senior Counsel, Caltex Australia, Ltd., Sydney, Australia;

Thomas J. Broadmore of Chapman Tripp Sheffield Young, Wellington, New Zealand; Martin P. Detels, Jr., of Seattle, Washington; Carter Quinby of Derby, Cook, Quinby & Tweedt, San Francisco, California; and Paul N. Wonacott of Wood, Tatum, Mosser, Brooke & Landis, Portland, Oregon. They did not merely assist; they coauthored in many instances. For that reason, it will be observed that they are shown in the capacity of associate authors on the title page.

However, I bear full responsibility for any errors of style, format, and content that appear in the text. To the extent to which the text is accurate, understandable, and helpful, the associate authors deserve full credit; to the extent to which it is not, I plead *mea culpa*. Reponsibility for the errors that inevitably creep into any text is mine, and none of those named bears any onus because of them.

If the text proves of value, it will also be due in large measure to the assistance and—most of all—the encouragement received from my friends in the law profession and in the insurance industry. Notable among these are Nicholas J. Healy of Healy & Baillie, New York City; William Tetley, Q.C., Faculty of Law, McGill University, Montreal, Canada; Geoffrey Brice, Q.C., London, England; David W. Taylor, Hill Dickinson & Co., London, England; Daniel F. Knox, Guy C. Stephenson, and Paul N. Daigle of Schwabe, Williamson, Wyatt, Moore & Roberts, Portland, Oregon, and Seattle, Washington; David R. Owen of Semmes, Bowen & Semmes, Baltimore, Maryland; Gene Sause of Gene Sause & Co., Portland, Oregon; Douglas Parks of Emery & Karrigan, Portland, Oregon; Dean D. Dechaine of Miller, Nash, Weiner, Hager & Carlsen, Portland, Oregon; and James D. Hurst of Durham & Bates, Inc., Portland, Oregon.

Special tribute must be paid to my partners at Parks, Allen, Livingston & Grief, Portland, Oregon, for their assistance, patience, and indulgence in permitting me to spend so much time on the writing of the text, and especially to C. Kent Roberts, William P. Horton, and Paul Burton for their assistance in the tedious and unrewarding task of proofreading much of the text.

I am especially indebted to Jacquelin Jurkins and the staff of the Multnomah County Law Library, Portland, Oregon. The library is outstanding; their efforts, cooperation, and assistance went far beyond the bounds of duty. I must also mention with gratitude the availability of American Maritime Cases, that invaluable aid to all maritime lawyers in the United States and elsewhere.

Last, but not least, my full appreciation goes to my late wife, Jean, without whose assistance, understanding, and forbearance this text would never have been commenced, and to Valerie Macaree whose encouragement and assistance were unflagging.

I will also repeat the plea I advanced in the preface to the first edition of my text, *The Law of Tug, Tow, and Pilotage*: the subject is a vast one and the number of citations almost too voluminous. Any author's pride must be subordinate to the need for accuracy. Consequently, any notations of errors will be gratefully received and duly corrected in future supplements.

ALEX L. PARKS

TABLE OF CASES

F.2d 769 (2d Cir.), 1933 AMC 323, cert.den. 289 U.S. 759 (1933): 520, 533

Societa Commerciale Italiana de Navigazone v. Maru Navigation Co., 280 U.S. 334 (4th Cir. 1922): 600

Societe d'Avances Commerciales v. Merchants Marine Ins. Co., [1923] 16 Ll.L.Rep. 374, (1924) 20 Ll.L.Rep. 74, C.A.: 425, 426

Societe Belge des Betons Societe Anonyme v. London & Lancashire Ins. Co., Ltd., (1938) 2 All E.R. 305, 158 L.T. 352: 342, 307

Societe Maritime Caledonienne v. The Cythera, [1965] 2 Lloyd's Rep. 454: 644, 645

Soc. Nouvelle d'Armement v. Spillars and Bakers Ltd., [1917] 1 K.B. 865, 86 L.J.K.B. 406: 502

Socony Mobil Oil Co. v. West of England Ship Owners Mutual Insurance Ass'n (London), [1984] 2 Lloyd's Rep. 1119

Soelberg v. Western Assur. Co., 119 F. 23 (9th Cir. 1902): 461

Soileau v. Nicklos Drilling Co., 302 F.Supp. 119 (W.D. La. 1969): 893, 1065

Soil Mechanics v. Empire Mut. Ins. Co., 285 N.Y.S.2d 391, 1968 AMC 491 (St. N.Y.): 122, 125, 944

Solet v. M/V Capt. H.V. Dufresne, 303 F.Supp. 980, 1970 AMC 571 (E.D. La.): 846

Solly v. Whitmore, (1821) 106 E.R. 1110: 48

Solomon v. Miller, (1865) 2 W.W. & A'B 135 (Vic.Sup.Ct.Aus.): 187, 770

Sontag v. Galer, 181 N.E. 182 (Mass. 1932): 1042

Sorenson v. Boston Ins. Co., 20 F.2d 640, 1927 AMC 1288 (4th Cir.), cert.den. 275 U.S. 555: 267, 417, 426

Sosnow v. Storatti Co., 1945 AMC 645 (St. N.Y.): 1094

South British Fire & Marine Insce. Co. of New Zealand v. Da Costa, (1906) 1 K.B. 456: 196, 787

Southern Cotton Oil Co. v. Mer-

chants' & Miners' Transp. Co., 179 F. 113 (S.D.N.Y. 1910): 1101

Southern Cross Fisheries Ltd. v. New Zealand Fisheries Ltd. (The Newfish I), [1970] N.Z.L.R. 873 (N.Z.): 644, 645

Southern Farm Bureau Cas. Ins. v. Daniel, 440 S.W.2d 582 (Ark. 1969): 1041, 1043

Southern Pacific Co. v. Jensen, 244 U.S. 205: 763

Southern Pac. S.S. Co. v. New Orleans Coat etc., 43 F.2d 177, 1930 AMC 1593 (E.D. La.): 656

Southern Surety Co. v. Equitable Surety Co., 84 Okla. 23, 202 P. 295 (St. Okla. 1921): 1142

Southlands, 37 F.2d 474, 1930 AMC 337 (5th Cir.): 78, 296

Southport Fisheries, Inc. v. Saskatchewan Gov't Ins. Office, 161 F. Supp. 81, 1959 AMC 1280 (E.D.N.C.): 134, 279, 311, 315

Southwark, 191 U.S. 1 (1903): 261, 519

Soya G.M.B.H. Kommanditgesellschaft v. White (The Corfu Island), [1980] 1 Lloyd's Rep. 491, aff'd [1982] 1 Lloyd's Rep. 136 (C.A.), aff'd [1983] 1 Lloyd's Rep. 122, H.L.: 22, 65, 350, 794, 811

Sparkes v. Marshall, (1836) 132 E.R. 293: 185, 188

Sparrow v. Mutual B.L. Ins. Co., F.Cas. 13,214 (D. Mass. 1873): 159

Spence v. Mariehamns R/S, 766 F.2d 1504, 1986 AMC 685 (11th Cir. 1985): 883

Spence v. Union Marine Ins. Co., (1868) L.R. 3 C.P. 427, 18 L.T. 632: 791

Spiller, Admx v. Lowe, 328 F.Supp. 54, 1971 AMC 2661 (W.D. Ark.): 695

Spinks v. Chevron Oil Co., 507 F.2d 216 (5th Cir. 1975), reh.den., opinion clarified 546 F.2d 675, 1979 AMC 1165: 862, 863, 868

Spinney v. Ocean Mutual Marine Ins. Co., (1890) 17 S.C.R. 326 (Can.): 44, 237

Spinney's (1948) Ltd. et al. v. Royal

THE LAW AND PRACTICE OF
MARINE INSURANCE AND AVERAGE

CHAPTER I

INTRODUCTION

History

Marine Insurance is a difficult and complex subject. Yet its importance in maritime affairs cannot be overemphasized. Without exception, it pervades every single sphere of maritime activities and, absent marine insurance protection, maritime commerce could come to a standstill.

The origins of marine insurance are lost in obscurity. Although hard evidence is lacking that marine insurance as we know it today was practiced prior to the twelfth century, general average has existed at least since the days of the Rhodians (circa 900 B.C.) and a system of indemnity known as bottomry followed somewhat later.[1]

The Rhodian law provided that "in order to lighten a ship merchandise is thrown overboard, that which has been given for all shall be replaced by the contribution of all." The Marine Insurance Act, 1906, Sec. 66(2) defines general average as follows:

> There is a general average act where any extraordinary sacrifice or expenditure is voluntarily and reasonably made or incurred in time of peril for the purpose of preserving the property imperilled in the common adventure.

See discussion *infra*. Accurately speaking, of course, general average exists wholly independently of marine insurance and is not, technically, a part of marine insurance except to the extent that the rights and liabilities arising out of a general average situation are covered today or directly affected by the provisions of marine insurance policies.

In the early days of seafaring, merchants usually traveled with their goods. When an emergency arose, common prudence often suggested

---

1. Raymond Flower and Michael Wynn Jones in their *Lloyd's of London* (Newton Abbott: David & Charles, 1974) intimate that the Romans developed bottomry into insurance, citing, *inter alia*, Suetonius with respect to Emperor Claudius accepting personal responsibility for merchants' losses in the corn trade, and Cicero writing to Sallust in 50 B.C. asking him to underwrite some cash in transit from Laodicia to Rome. J. A. Park, in his classic work, *Marine Insurance* (3d ed., 1796), citing ancient as well as contemporary writers, demolishes any such theory and ascribes the advent of "true" marine insurance to the merchants of North Italy at the close of the twelfth or the beginning of the thirteenth century. William Gow in his text *Marine Insurance* (4th ed., 1913) seemingly agrees. As he notes, quoting the Florentine historian Villani, when the Jews were expelled by Philip Augustus from France in 1182, they adopted some system of insurance of their properties. Certainly, by the time of Villani's death (1348) insurance was an established practice in northern Italy.

that someone's goods should be thrown overboard, or "jettisoned" in order to save the ship and the other cargo aboard it. Naturally, no one wanted their particular goods to be sacrificed. To avoid quarrels when valuable time was being lost, the practice grew up of apportioning the value of the jettisoned cargo among the shipowner and the other cargo owners according to the value of their respective interests. That this practice was sound and equitable is proven by the fact that general average still exists today as a part of the law of every maritime nation and marine insurance policies routinely provide coverage for general average losses and sacrifices. It will be recognized that, in a sense, general average is a system of indemnity whereby the various parties to a venture contribute rateably to indemnify another party to the same venture upon principles of common equity.

"Bottomry" represents another system of indemnity which has existed for many centuries. Essentially, bottomry was nothing more than a shipowner borrowing money in order to carry out a seafaring venture, pledging his vessel as security for the loan. Under this system, the shipowner took out a loan, conditioned upon repayment only if the vessel arrived safely. If the vessel was lost, the shipowner was relieved of the obligation of repaying the loan. The agreement was termed a "bottomry bond." "Respondentia," on the other hand, was a like loan upon like conditions with the cargo as security. The rate of interest charged upon such bonds represented not only the use of the money loaned but also compensation for the risk of loss of the money which was loaned. It will be seen that bottomry and respondentia really are the reverse of the present system of marine insurance; i.e., in the case of bottomry and respondentia, the loan is repaid only if the vessel and cargo arrive safely, whereas in marine insurance, the loss is paid only if the vessel and cargo do not arrive safely and in an undamaged condition. Bottomry and respondentia are unheard of in modern days, having been totally supplanted by marine insurance.

It seems undisputed that true marine insurance originated with the Lombard merchants in northern Italy in the twelfth century who regularly insured their maritime ventures.[2] As the Lombards extended their interests northward, they came into contact with the Hansa merchants of northern Europe who by then were organized into the Hanseatic League,

---

2. Flower and Jones in *Lloyd's of London* (note 1, *supra*) document the existence of some 400 marine insurance policies among the papers of a Florentine merchant, Francesco di Marco Datini. Datini may have uttered the first commentary on underwriters when he wrote his wife regarding the untrustworthiness of underwriters: "For when they insure it is sweet to them to take the monies; but when disaster comes it is otherwise and each man draws his rump back and strives not to pay."

Of more modern vintage in the province of commentary on underwriters is James A. Quinby's delightful little poem entitled "No Doubt" reading:

probably one of the most powerful cartels which ever existed. The League compiled the "Laws of Wisby," a sea code which originated probably in the early fourteenth century and contains references to abuses in the issuance of bottomry bonds, but nothing concerning marine insurance.

It seems very probable that eventually the members of the Hanseatic League adopted the system of marine insurance brought northward by the Lombards. Meanwhile, the other Continental nations were not slow to follow. According to Gow, the firmness of the hold of marine insurance and the reality of its growth can best be seen in the various ordinances and codes in which were compiled in more or less systematic form the insurance usages which had developed in the various commercial centers.[3] The most notable of these were:

The Ordinances of Barcelona, 1434, 1458, 1461 and 1484
The Ordinances of Florence, 1523
The Ordinances of Burgos, 1538
The Ordinances of Bilbao, 1560
Le Guidon de la Mer, Rouen, between 1556 and 1584, published in 1671 by Cleirac
The Ordinance of Middleburg, 1600
The Ordinances of Rotterdam, 1604, 1635, and 1655
Us et Coutumes de la Mer, by Cleirac of Rouen, 1656
Ordonnance de la Marine, 1681, of Louis XIV

It appears that the Hansa merchants introduced marine insurance into England. As the English kings were constantly in debt from their martial affairs abroad, they found it expedient to borrow from the Hansa

---

"I have studied all the clauses in my cargo policy
    And there comes into my mind a growing doubt,
For the very things the underwriter ought to guarantee
    Seem to be the things I'm warranted without.
There is happy indecision as to whom I notify
    When my goods are sunk or injured in a crash,
But one thing's set to catch the eye in glaring letters plain and high,
    The premium is payable in cash.
I can't quite get it clear about those perils of the seas;
    Or exactly what is meant by F.P.A.
Or why they have to mention 'thieves' and later say to me
    That theft's a thing for which they cannot pay.
But when I'm worn and troubled as to what these phrases are
    And I fear I'll never, never understand,
One item shines afar like a bright and guiding star—
    The premium's due and owing on demand."
[Reprinted by kind permission of James A. Quinby from his volume of poems, *The Street and the Sea*, copyright, 1971]

3. *Marine Insurance*, by William Gow (London: McMillan & Co., Ltd., 1913).

merchants who, by then, were established in the Steelyard, a collection of buildings in which they lived and housed their merchandise. For a time, these merchants practically controlled the overseas trade of England. However, overwhelming success inevitably breeds envy and to this maxim the Hansa merchants were not immune. Notwithstanding their entrenched position with the monarchy, the native merchants finally succeeded in driving them out.

Meanwhile, the Lombard traders were not idle and invaded England about the middle of the thirteenth century. Not only did the Lombards lend money to the English kings, they were also the fiscal agents of the pope. They, too, incurred the wrath of the natives, so much so that they petitioned King Henry IV to grant them a section of the City of London where they could build their homes and conduct their trade with some degree of security. This the king did, probably in return for some financial favor. The area thus granted became known as Lombard Street, which became famous in the history of marine insurance. To this day, the Lloyd's form of policy, first adopted in 1779 (reproduced in the First Schedule, Marine Insurance Act, 1906) reads in part:

> And it is agreed by us, the insurers, that this writing or policy of assurance shall be of as much force and effect as the surest writing or policy of assurance heretofore made in Lombard Street, or in the Royal Exchange, or elsewhere in London.

By the close of the fifteenth century, the Lombards had captured much of the overseas trade of England. They, too, incurred the enmity of the local merchants. Several Acts of Parliament were enacted to curb their activities. During the reign of Queen Elizabeth, they were gradually leaving England for greener pastures in the Continental countries. By the time of their departure, the practice of marine insurance in England was well established.[4]

---

4. The earliest reference to a marine insurance policy in the records of the Court of Admiralty appears to be *Broke v. Maynard*. File 27, No. 147, in 1547, reproduced in Select Pleas in the Court of Admiralty, Vol. II, A.D. 1547-1602, Selden Society. The case report involved a suit on a marine cargo policy in which the defense was that part of the goods were salved and that the underwriter had had no notice of abandonment and had received no part of the goods. There was also an allegation of deviation. One year later, in *Cavalchant v. Maynard*, File 18, No. 131-132, the policy was admitted, and also the loss, but the suit was defended upon the ground that "if any of the goods so assured should happen to fall to any wreck or mischance and yet some part of the same happen to be saved, that part or portion of the saved goods which should be so saved and rescued should be divided equally between the assurers rateably according to their proportion or at least accounted for and by some means certified to the assurers before any assurance could be demanded of them, they not being bound by the nature and condition of the contract of assurance but only for that part or portion that is specified." The policy was in Italian, with the underwriters' subscriptions being in English. The first policy in English appears to have been litigated in *Salizar v. Blackman*, File 29, No. 45, (1555), Vol. II, p. 49, Select Pleas in the Court of Admiralty, A.D. 1547-1602, Selden Society. The classic form of the perils clause seems to have first surfaced

The Italian origin of English marine insurance policies is amply demonstrated by comparing the old English form with the wording in the Ordinance of Florence of 1523, and the term "policy" is clearly derived from the Italian *polizza,* meaning a promise or undertaking. There were no insurance companies as such in the sixteenth century. Underwriting was done by private individuals. In 1570, Sir Thomas Gresham founded the Royal Exchange which for the first time gave to merchants a place to congregate instead of in Lombard Street.

The first statute of the English Parliament relating to marine insurance was enacted in 1601. The preamble read in part:

Whereas it ever hathe bene the policie of this realme by all good meanes to comforte and encourage the merchante, therebie to advance and increase the general wealthe of the realme, her majesties customes and strengthe of shippinge, which consideracion is nowe the more requisite because trade and traffique is not at this presente soe open as at other tymes it hathe bene; And whereas it has bene tyme out of mynde an usage amongste merchantes, both of this realme and of forraine nacyons, when they make any great adventure (speciallie into remote partes) to give some consideracion of money to other persons (which commonlie are in noe small number) to have from them assurance made of their goodes, merchandizes, ships and things adventured, or some parte thereof, at suche rates and in such sorte as the parties assurers and the parties assured can agree, which course of dealinge is commonlie termed a policie of assurance; by means of whiche policie of assurance it comethe to passe that upon the losse or perishinge of any shippe there followethe not the undoinge of any man, but the losse lighteth rather easily upon many, than heavilie upon fewe, and rather upon them that adventure not, than upon those who do adventure, whereby all merchantes, speciallie those of the younger sorte, are allured to venture more willingly, and more freely.

The statute was designed to erect a particular court for the trial of insurance causes in a summary manner and to that end the statute ordained that a commission should issue yearly, directed to the Judge of Admiralty, the Recorder of London, two doctors of the civil law, two common lawyers, and eight merchants. Park reports that in *Came v. Moy,* 2 Sidersin 121, it was held that it was no bar to an action upon a policy to say

---

in *Whyte v. Besswicke,* File 37, No. 74, (1563), where the goods were insured against " . . . the danger of the sea from fire and water, men of war, enemies, corsairs, pirates, thieves, letters of mart, barratry of masters and mariners, jettisons, retainment by king or prince or by any by their authority or by any other person or persons whomsoever and from all other perils and dangers whatsoever." See, also, the text of the 1613 policy on the Tiger, Tanner MS No. 74, folio 32, Bodleian Library, Oxford.

that the plaintiff had sued the defendant for the same cause in the court erected by the statute of Elizabeth and that his suit was dismissed. The insurance court, whatever the reasons, fell into disuse and no commissions were appointed for many years. Park is probably correct in his statement that litigants preferred the courts of the common law where witnesses could be examined *viva voce* and where juries could observe the witnesses.

There being no insurance companies in those days, business was conducted very informally by simply hawking a policy around the city for subscription by anyone with the private means to take a share of the risk in return for a portion of the premium. A merchant with a ship to insure would request an "insurance office" to obtain coverage. The proprietor of the insurance office acted as a broker, taking the policy from one wealthy merchant to another until the risk was finally covered. The broker's skill lay chiefly in ensuring that policies were underwritten only by men of sufficient financial integrity to meet their share of a claim—to the full extent, if need be, of their personal fortunes.

Lloyd's of London

It was against this background that Lloyd's Coffee House made its appearance in Tower Street.[5] Very little is known either about Edward Lloyd or his coffee house. It was one of many similar establishments and, apart from occasional references in contemporary newspapers, the record is blank. The first mention of Lloyd's appears in a London Gazette of the late 1680s where an advertisement offers a guinea reward for information about stolen watches, claimable from "Mr. Edward Lloyd's Coffee House in Tower Street."

It is very probable that, from the first, Edward Lloyd encouraged a clientele of ships' captains, merchants, shipowners and the like, and provided a meeting place where the latest gossip could be heard. Moreover, at a time when communications were chancy, Lloyd gained a reputation for trustworthy shipping news. This was one of the basic ingredients of successful underwriting and perhaps more than any other factor, ensured that Lloyd's Coffee House eclipsed its rivals and became the recognized place for obtaining marine insurance.

Apparently, Edward Lloyd took no part in underwriting, contenting himself with providing congenial surroundings and facilities for his patrons to do business until his death in 1713. Lloyd's chief bequest to posterity was his name and the coffee house which bore it.

---

5. Much of the discussion of Lloyd's which follows was taken from the publication issued by Lloyd's entitled *Lloyd's, A Sketch History*.

Until 1720 there was nothing to suggest that underwriting was carried on exclusively in any one place. In that year, however, Parliament (over strenuous opposition of the individual underwriters) pased an act which granted charters to two incorporated companies, the Royal Exchange Assurance and the London Assurance Company, and, at the same time, prohibited the writing of marine insurance by any other corporation or business partnership. The Act deliberately excluded "private and particular persons" from its scope and Lloyd's can be fairly said to owe its future existence to this omission. The two companies thus received a monopoly, *as corporations,* of insuring ships and their cargos. However, the volume of their business was small and, in the early years, rather unsuccessful.

For the next hundred years, while the two corporations struggled, Lloyd's prospered. It soon became apparent that the monopoly of the two companies was rather more a protection for Lloyd's than a hindrance as it prevented the formation of other corporations engaged in marine underwriting. In 1769, a number of the more reputable underwriters at Lloyd's became disturbed at the wagering policies which were being written by some habitues of the coffee house and withdrew, setting up a rival establishment in nearby Pope's Head Alley devoted strictly to marine insurance. It led rapidly to the establishment of a properly constituted society out of which evolved the business institution of today.

New Lloyd's Coffee House, as it was called, soon proved to be too small. In 1771 a committee was elected to find new quarters and seventy-nine merchants, underwriters, and brokers each paid £100 into the Bank of England for this purpose.

Three years later rooms were rented by the committee in the Royal Exchange and "New Lloyd's" left the coffee-house era for good. Although everyone still referred to "Lloyd's Coffee House" for many years to come, there is no doubt that it immediately took on the appearance of a place of business rather than one of recreation. Thus, modern Lloyd's was born.

During the next century, the society of underwriters at Lloyd's evolved step by step, gradually assuming its present-day form. Membership was regulated and the elected committee given increased authority. This development culminated in 1871 with an Act of Parliament granting incorporation which was amended in 1911, 1925, and in 1951 to meet the changing requirements of insurance.

The hundred years from the election of the first committee was a testing and formative period for Lloyd's during which it survived the strain of both the American War of Independence and a twenty-year war with France. Due to the efforts of Nathan Rothschild (in behalf of his brother-in-law, Benjamin Gompertz) the insurance company monopoly was finally rescinded in 1824. From 1824 onward, Lloyd's also faced competition from the newly emancipated insurance companies. Rather than being weakened, Lloyd's emerged stronger than ever.

The corporation of Lloyd's today does not accept insurance any more than did Edward Lloyd, nor does it assume liability for the insurance business transacted by its members. Nevertheless, it maintains a close watch on their financial standing and lays down strict regulations regarding membership. It provides the market with premises and a variety of supporting services such as claims settling, policy signing and the gathering of intelligence, which are administered by the Committee of Lloyd's.

Lord Mansfield and his Contribution

It will be remembered that the insurance court established by Parliament in 1601 languished for lack of business as merchants and underwriters preferred the regular law courts, or, in the alternative, arbitration. Legal proceedings, as Park has noted, were subject to great vexations and oppressions. If the underwriters refused payment, it was usual for the insured to bring a separate action against each of the underwriters on the policy, and to proceed to trial on all. The multiplicity of trials was oppressive, both to the insurers and the insured, and the insurers, if they had any real point to try, were put to an enormous expense before they could obtain any decision on the question which they wished to have decided.

Lord Mansfield changed all that sort of thing. By imposing a consolidation rule, which grew into general use, underwriters could litigate one case with one underwriter, with the result being binding on all the underwriters subscribing.

William Murray, Lord Mansfield, presided in the Court of King's Bench from 1756 to 1788. His influence upon the whole of commercial law in England, and particularly that of marine insurance, was incalculable. As Park notes, prior to the ascension of Lord Mansfield, the whole of the case was left generally to the jury without any minute statement from the bench as to the principles of law on which insurance was established. As the verdicts were general, it was almost impossible to determine from the reports upon what grounds the case was decided. Even if a doubt arose on a point of law, and the case was reversed upon that point, it was afterwards argued in private in the chambers of the judge who tried the cause and by his single decision the parties were bound. Thus, whatever his opinion might have been, it never was promulgated to the world and could never be the rule of decision in any future case.

Lord Mansfield introduced a different mode of proceeding. In his statement of the case to the jury, he enlarged upon the rules and principles of law applicable to that case and left it to the jury to make an application of those principles to the facts in evidence before them. Consequently, if a general verdict were given, the grounds on which the jury proceeded could be more easily ascertained. Moreover, if any real diffi-

culty occurred in point of law his lordship advised the counsel to consent
to a special case. In the special case, the facts were either admitted by the
parties, or if disputed, were proved and then the judge would take the
opinion of the jury upon all of the facts, reserving the question of law to
be decided elsewhere. These cases were afterwards argued, not before
the judge in private, but in open court before all the judges of the bench
from which the record came. Thus, important questions were not hastily
decided but the parties had their case seriously considered by the whole
court, the decision became notorious to the world, and it was recorded for
a precedent of law arising from the facts found, and served as a rule to
guide the opinions of future judges.

As Gow observes, Lord Mansfield's decision and dicta are the founda-
tions of English insurance law, and through the acceptance of them by
eminent American judges they lie at the base of the American decisions.
Lord Mansfield took full advantage of all he could gather from all the
continental ordinances and codes existing in his day and accepted his legal principles largely from those sources. He freely used special mercantile jurors to whom he carefully expounded the law. It is a lasting tribute
to his genius that many of his decisions are now codified in the Marine
Insurance Act, 1906.

That Act, a veritable masterpiece of legislative draftsmanship, was
first introduced as a bill in Parliament in 1894 by Lord Herschell (then
Lord Chancellor). It was again introduced in 1895, 1896, 1899, and 1901.
It finally was enacted in 1906 as 6 Edw. 7, Ch. 41, entitled "An Act to cod-
ify the Law relating to Marine Insurance."

As Chalmers (the draftsman of the Act) noted, in his first edition of
the digest relating to the Act, published in 1901, the object of the bill was
to reproduce as exactly as possible the existing law without making any
attempt to amend it. Chalmers said, in his introduction to the first edition
of the digest:[6]

> The law of marine insurance rests almost entirely upon common
> law. Only a few isolated points are dealt with by statute. The reported
> cases are very numerous, being over 2,000 in number. On some points
> there is a plethora of authority. On other points of apparently equal
> importance the decisions are meagre and not always satisfactory.
> Some important questions are still untouched by authority and the
> rule depends on recognized commercial usage. . . .

The memorandum attached to the bill in 1901 stated in part:

---

6. Chalmer's introduction to the first edition will be found reproduced in *Chalmers' Marine Insurance Act, 1906* (8th ed. by E. R. Hardy Ivamy, London: Butterworths, 1976). This
little volume is a classic and should be in the library of every underwriter, broker, and admiralty lawyer involved in the field of marine insurance.

In dealing with rules of law, which may be modified by the stipulations of the parties, it is to be borne in mind that the certainty of the rule laid down is of more importance than its theoretical perfection. As J. Willes said in 1786, "In all commercial transactions the great object is certainty: it will therefore be necessary for the Court to lay down some rule, and it is of more consequence that the rule should be certain than whether it is established one way or the other." (*Lockyer v. Offley*, 1 T.R. at p. 259. See, too, *Sailing Ship Blairmore v. Macredie*, [1898] A.C. at p. 597, per Lord Halsbury.) What mercantile men require is a clear rule to provide for cases where the parties have either formed no intention or have failed to express it clearly. Where the rule of law is certain, the parties know when to stipulate and what to stipulate for.

Marine Insurance in the United States

Not surprisingly, in the early history of the colonies, American risks were placed with British underwriters. However, underwriting of marine risks did begin around 1759 in New York City and in other seacoast cities offices were opened.

In 1792, the Insurance Company of North America was incorporated in Philadelphia, to which a charter was granted by the Pennsylvania Assembly in 1794. The company is still in existence. During the next two decades the insurance market developed in common with the merchant marine. The War of 1812 almost destroyed the American merchant marine and, along with it, the insurance business. The clipper ships provided new impetus but the War Between the States again almost destroyed all the markets. The Merchant Marine Act of 1920 encouraged collective action between marine insurance companies and with this encouragement the forerunner of the American Hull Insurance Syndicate was organized.[7]

On more than one occasion, the U. S. Supreme Court has stated that there are special reasons for keeping in harmony with the marine insurance laws of England and to "accord respect to established doctrines of English maritime law."[8]

---

7. For further information on the development of marine insurance companies in the United States, see *Marine Insurance*, by William D. Winter (3rd ed., New York: McGraw-Hill Book Company, Inc., 1952).

8. *Standard Oil Company of New Jersey v. U. S.*, 340 U.S. 54, 1950 AMC 365 (1950); *Queen Ins. Co. v. Globe & Rutgers Fire Ins. Co.*, 262 U.S. 487, 1924 AMC 107; *Calmar S.S. Coro. v. Scott*, 345 U.S. 427, 1953 AMC 952. See, also, *Rensselaer*, 1925 AMC 1116 (NYM); *Honeybrook*, 6 F.2d 736 (CA-2), 1925 AMC 717; *Eastern Prince—U.S.S. Roustabout*, 56 F.Supp. 275 (W.D. Wash.), 1944 AMC 727, 77 Ll.L.Rep. 431, 173 F.2d 955 (CA-9), 1950 AMC 377; *Armar.* 1954 AMC 1674 (NYM). In *Eastern Prince—U.S.S. Roustabout. supra*, the court stated that where

However, in 1955 the Supreme Court decided *Wilburn Boat v. Fireman's Fund Ins. Co.*[9] Until that decision, marine insurance cases were clearly governed by maritime law. See *De Lovio v. Boit*,[10] where Justice Story, sitting on circuit, seized the opportunity for claiming under federal admiralty law the power to hear and decide marine insurance cases, and cases cited *supra*.

Wilburn cast the law of marine insurance into a state of turmoil. Because the case is so important, the facts should be closely considered.

The Wilburn brothers were the owners of a small houseboat being operated on Lake Texoma, an inland lake between Oklahoma and Texas. They sold the boat to a corporation in which they were the sole stockholders, the boat was mortgaged, and, instead of being used for private pleasure purposes, it had been chartered and used to carry passengers for hire. The insurance policy issued by the defendant insurance company contained warranties that (1) the insurance would be void in case the policy or the insured interest was sold, assigned, transferred, or pledged without the previous consent in writing of the underwriters; (2) that the vessel would be used solely for private pleasure purposes during the currency of the policy; and (3) that the vessel would not be hired or chartered unless permission was granted by the underwriters by endorsement on the policy.

The boat was destroyed by fire while moored in the lake. The corporate owner brought suit on the policy in a Texas state court. The action was removed to the Federal court on grounds of diversity.

The assured contended that under Texas law the claimed policy breaches were immaterial unless they contributed to the loss. The insurance company contended for a strict or literal compliance with the warranties in accordance with maritime law. The trial court held that the assured could not recover because the established admiralty rule required literal fulfillment of every policy warranty and that a breach of any warranty bars recovery even though the breach in no way contributed to the loss. The court of appeals affirmed. The pronouncements of the trial court and the court of appeals as to the law of warranties in marine insurance cases were unquestionably correct.

The Supreme Court reversed, dividing three ways. The majority reversed and remanded with instructions to apply appropriate state law; Justice Frankfurter concurred with the result but disagreed on the reasoning; Justices Reed and Burton dissented.

---

there were English decisions clearly applicable, no good purpose would be served by extending discussion to the problem of *causa proxima* because "if there is an authoritative English decision on the facts of the case in question that decision concludes the matter."

9. *Wilburn Boat v. Fireman's Fund Ins. Co.*, 348 U.S. 310 (1955), 1955 AMC 467.

10. *De Lovio v. Boit*, 7 F.Cas. No. 418, 3776.

Although the court recognized its historic rule-making function in admiralty matters, it refused to formulate a warranties rule, stating that making a choice of rules involved policy considerations which congress was peculiarly suited to make. Justice Reed, in dissenting, correctly noted that all prior decisions supported the necessity of a uniform rule in marine insurance cases above all else and urged that sound judicial policy dictated that American marine insurance law be kept in harmony with that of Great Britain.

An eminent text writer states that *Wilburn* left the admiralty bar in a "state of utter confusion."[11] Gilmore & Black characterized the solution as "nightmarish."[12]

What have the courts done in light of *Wilburn?* Maritime law was never intended as an all-inclusive and definitive system. The interplay between state law and federal law has always recognized that state law could supplement the maritime law where not otherwise inconsistent and antagonistic to its characteristic features.[13]

If a trend after *Wilburn* can be discerned it is that *Wilburn* will be restricted to marine insurance cases. Moreover, the tendency appears to be to restrict it to cases involving policy warranties.[14] *Wilburn* has been used to justify application of state statutes.[15]

On the other hand, *Wilburn* appears to have little effect on parol contracts.[16]

11. Baer, *Admiralty Law of the Supreme Court* (3d ed., Charlottesville, Va.: The Michie Company, 1979).

12. *The Law of Admiralty* (2d ed., St. Paul, Minn.: The Foundation Press, 1975).

13. See *Kossick v. United Fruit Co.*, 365 U.S. 731 (1961), 1961 AMC 833; *San Patrick*, 286 F.Supp. 1007 (S.D.N.Y.), 1968 AMC 2636; *Walker & Sons v. Valentine*, 431 F.2d 1235 (CA-5), 1970 AMC 2261, (Watchman Clause of American Institute Tug form valid, whether under maritime or state principles, or an amphibious mixture of both); *Princess Cruises v. Bayly, Martin & Fay*, 373 F.Supp. 762 (N.D. Cal.), 1974 AMC 433; *Martin & Robertson v. Orion Ins. Co.*, 1971 AMC 515 (St. Cal.) (California direct action statute applicable). Note, however, *Groban v. Pegu*, 331 F.Supp. 883 (S.D.N.Y.), 1972 AMC 460, where the question of existence of an insurable interest under general maritime law or under state law was questioned but not decided.

14. *Indemnity Insurance Company of North America v. California Stevedore and Ballast Company*, 307 F.2d 513 (CA-9 1962), 1962 AMC 2507; *United States Fire Insurance Co. v. Gulf States Marine and Mining Company*, 262 F.2d 565 (CA-5 1959), 1959 AMC 397.

15. *Employers Mutual Liability Ins. Co. v. Pacific Inland Navigation Co.*, 358 F.2d 719 (1966), 1967 AMC 1855-1856 (typewritten clauses under Washington law control over printed clauses); *Beckham v. Reed.* 217 F.Supp. 749 (1963), 1963 AMC 2429 (strong state policy); *Taylor v. Fishing Tools, Inc.*, 274 F.Supp. 666 (1967), 1968 AMC 782; *In re Independent Towing Company*, 242 F.Supp. 950 (1965), 1965 AMC 818 (direct action statutes); *Navegacion Goya v. Mutual Boiler*, 411 F.Supp. 929 (S.D.N.Y.), 1972 AMC 650 (state law governs but federal rules control as to which state has the most significant relationship); *Irwin v. Eagle Star Ins.*, 455 F.2d 827 (CA-5), [1973] 2 Lloyd's Rep. 489, 1973 AMC 1184 (state law governs the sinking of a Florida yacht, owned by a Florida resident, in Florida waters and issued by a Florida-based marine insurance broker, discussing *Wilburn* and *Kossick*); *Liman, Trustees v. Amer. S.S. Owners*, 299 F.Supp. 106 (S.D.N.Y.), 1969 AMC 1669.

16. *Kossick v. United Fruit Co., supra;* (repair cases) *Booth Steamship v. Meier, et al*, 262 F.2d 310, 1959 AMC 1974; (indemnification cases) *Indemnity Ins. Co. of North America v. California*

And courts are continuing to apply maritime principles to marine insurance cases, notwithstanding *Wilburn*.[17]

Rule in Great Britain and the Commonwealth Nations

The English law of marine insurance, developed over the centuries on a case-by-case basis, was finally codified as noted heretofore in the Marine Insurance Act, 1906, which became effective on January 1, 1907. Inasmuch as it embodies most but not all the legal principles of marine insurance, its extremely concise yet general language can only be applied successfully in light of the cases from which it evolved. The general rule being that the language of a statute must be given its natural meaning, resort being had to prior cases only in instances of doubt or ambiguity (*Bank of England v. Vagliano Bros.*, [1891] A.C. 107), the language is first examined without any presumptions, then resort is had to the previous law for construing provisions or words which have previously acquired a technical meaning or are of doubtful import.[18]

This principle, in fact, is expressly set forth in the Act, Sec. 91(2), reading:

> The rules of the common law including the law merchant, save in so far as they are inconsistent with the express provisions of this Act, shall continue to apply to contracts of marine insurance.

Stevedore and Ballast Co., supra; U.S. Fire Ins. Co. v. Gulf States Marine and Mining Company, 262 F.2d 565 (1959), 1959 AMC 397; and (stevedoring contracts) *McCross v. Ratnakar Shipping Co.*, 265 F.Supp. 827 (D. Md. 1967), 1967 AMC 291.

17. *Koninklyke Nederlansche, etc., v. Strachen Shipping Co.*, 301 F.2d 741 (CA-5 1962), 1964 AMC 1925; *McCross v. Ratnaker Shipping Co., supra, Indemnity Insurance Co. of North America v. California Stevedore and Ballast Co., supra, Bell v. Tug Shrike*, 332 F.2d 330 (CA-4 1964), 1964 AMC 2396; *Ludwig Mowinckels Rederi v. Commercial Stevedoring Co.*, 256 F.2d 227 (CA-2 1958), 1959 AMC 545; *Alcoa S.S. Co. v. Charles Ferran & Co.*, 383 F.2d 46 (CA-5 1967), 1967 AMC 2578; *Litwinowicz v. Weyerhaeuser S.S. Co.*, 179 F.Supp. 812 (D.D. Pa. 1959), 1960 AMC 2175; *Crosson v. Stoomvart*, 409 F.2d 865 (CA-2), 1969 AMC 1363; *Tugboat Underwriting v. Brittingham, Extx.*, 1971 AMC 805 (St. Md.); Alcoa S.S. v. Ferran & Co., 443 F.2d 250 (CA-5), 1971 AMC 116; Stanley Scott v. Makah Development, 496 F.2d (CA-9), 1974 AMC 934; *N.W. Marine v. U. S.*, 497 F.2d 652 (Ct.Cl.), 1974 AMC 1304; *Carroll v. Prot. Marine Ins.*, 512 F.2d 4 (CA-1), 1975 AMC 1633 (cause of action for tortious interference held cognizable in admiralty); *Stuyvesant Ins. v. Butler*, 1976 AMC 1182 (St. Fla.) (where ambiguity exists, the court will look to maritime law to resolve the ambiguity); *Wells Fargo v. London S. S. Owners*, 408 F.Supp. 626 (S.D.N.Y.), 1976 AMC 592; *Landry v. Steamship Mut. Underwriting Ass'n.*, 177 F.Supp. 143 (D.C. Mass.), 1960 AMC 54, 281 F.2d 484 (CA-1), 1960 AMC 1650 (where it said: "The court is not aware of any pertinent difference between British and American law"); *Northwestern Mutual L.I. Co. v. Linard*, 498 F.2d 556 (CA-2), [1974] 2 Lloyd's Rep. 398, 1974 AMC 877 ("Great weight is to be given to English decisions in the field of marine insurance"); and *Lenfest v. Coldwell*, 525 F.2d 717 (CA-2), 1975 AMC 2489 (American courts look to British law for meaning and definition in the field of marine insurance).

18. *Richards v. Forestal Land, Timber & Railways Co., Ltd.*, (1942) A.C. 50; *British & Foreign Marine Ins. Co., Ltd. v. Samuel Sandy & Co.*, (1916) 1 A.C. 650; and *British & Foreign Marine Ins. Co. v. Gaunt. (1921)* 2 A.C. 41.

Statutory enactments in Canada, Australia, and New Zealand parallel the provisions of the Act. Consequently, for practical purposes, cases in one jurisdiction are equally applicable in others.

Comity in the English-Speaking Jurisdictions

It has been said (erroneously it is believed) that the Marine Insurance Act, 1906, is not applicable in the United States. Technically this is true as the Act has not been enacted by the congress as part of the organic law of the United States. However, dating from the ratification of the Constitution, American courts have held that the "common law" has been adopted in the United States insofar as not overriden by specific statutory enactments. The Act, almost in its entirety, is but a codification of the "common law" of marine insurance. See the comments of Chalmers quoted, *supra*, from his introduction to the first edition of the digest. Consequently, at the least those decisions upon which each section of the Act is predicated *a fortiori* are, and certainly should be, highly persuasive authority in the courts of the United States.

Comity is not a one-way street. If great weight is to be given by the United States courts to English decisions in the field of marine insurance then, by the same token, American decisions on marine insurance ought to be given careful consideration by the English and Commonwealth courts. And this is the case. For example, in *Cory v. Burr*,[19] L. J. Brett said:

> If I thought that there were American authorities clear on this point I do not say I would not follow them but I would try to do so, for I agree with Chancellor Kent that, with regard to American insurance law, it is most advisable that the law should, if possible, be in conformity with what it is in all countries. I must therefore add that, although American decisions are not binding on us in this country, I have always found those on insurance law to be based on sound reasoning and to be such as ought to be carefully considered by us and with an earnest desire to endeavor to agree with them.[20]

---

19. *Cory v. Burr*, 9 A.B.D. 463, (on appeal, (1883) 8 App.Cas. 393, H.L.).
20. The above language was quoted with approval by J. Macdonald in *Cunningham v. St. Paul Fire. etc. Ins. Co.*, (1914) 16 D.L.R. 39 (Can.). See, also, *Berry v. Confederation Life Ass'n*, (1927) 1 D.L.R. 127, rev'd on a matter of interpretation (1927) 3 D.L.R. 945; *Fingard v. Merchants Casualty Ins. Co.*, (1928) 2 W.R.R. 609 (Man.Can.); *Emperor Goldmining Co., Ltd. v. Switzerland General Ins. Co., Ltd.*, [1964] 1 Lloyd's Rep. 248 (SC N.S.W. Aus.) (quoting from American decisions on the Sue and Labor Clause); and *Prudent Tankers Ltd. v. Dominion Insurance Co., Ltd. (The Caribbean Sea)*, [1980] 1 Lloyd's Rep. 338, where J. Goff referred to numerous American decisions on the Inchmaree Clause. The foregoing list is not all-inclusive, and is intended for illustrative purposes only. There are many, many decisions, not only in the field of marine insurance but also in admiralty cases generally, where the courts have

The volume of marine insurance litigation in the United States now exceeds that of Great Britain and the Commonwealth nations by a considerable extent. One can only hope, in light of the truly remarkable similarities in decisions from all the English-speaking nations, that decisions from one jurisdiction will be heavily relied upon in all other jurisdictions, and that uniformity and certainty will thereby be promoted for all concerned. Additional source references on marine insurance are cited in the accompanying footnote.[21]

---

relied upon and cited with approval decisions from the other English-speaking jurisdictions. A good example is *The Eurymedon*, (1975) A.C. 154, P.C., where the Privy council freely cited cases from Australia and the United States.

21. Buglass, *Marine Insurance Claims* (Centreville, Md.: Cornell Maritime Press, Inc., 1963); Buglass, *General Average and the York/Antwerp Rules* (Centreville, Md.: Cornell Maritime Press, Inc., 1974); Buglass, *Marine Insurance and General Average in the United States* (2nd ed., Centreville, Md.: Cornell Maritime Press, Inc., 1980); Gilmore and Black, *The Law of Admiralty* (2nd ed., St. Paul, Minn.: The Foundation Press, Inc., 1975); J. A. Park, *A System of the Law of Marine Insurances* (3rd ed., London: J. Butterworth, 1796); John Duer, *Law and Practice of Marine Insurance*, 2 vols. (New York, 1845, 1846); Willard Phillips, *Treatise on the Law of Insurance*, 2 vols. (New York: Hurd & Houghton, 1867); Theophilus Parsons, *Law of Marine Insurance and General Average;* William Gow, *Marine Insurance* (London: Macmillan & Co., Ltd., 1913); William D. Winter, *Marine Insurance, Its Principles and Practice* (New York: McGraw-Hill Book Company, Inc., 1952); Templeman & Greenacre, *Marine Insurance, Its Principles & Practice* (5th ed., Macdonald & Evans, London: 1981); Howard Hurd, *The Law and Practice of Marine Insurance*, (London: Sir Isaac Putnam & Sons, Ltd., 1952); Victor Dover, *A Handbook to Marine Insurance*, (London: Witherby & Co., Ltd.,); Arnould, *The Law of Marine Insurance and Average*, (16th ed., by Sir Michael J. Mustill and Jonathan C.B. Gilman, London: Stevens & Sons Ltd., 1981); E. R. Hardy Ivamy, *Marine Insurance* (3rd ed., London: Butterworths, 1979); *Chalmers' Marine Insurance Act, 1906* (8th ed.), E. H. Ivamy, (London: Butterworths, 1976); J. Kenneth Goodacre, *Marine Insurance Claims* (2d ed., London: Witherby & Co. Ltd., 1981); Admiralty Law Institute, "A Symposium on the Hull Policy," *Tulane Law Review*, Vol. 41, No. 2, (1967); Admiralty Law Institute, "A Symposium on the P & I Policy," *Tulane Law Review*, Vol. 43, No. 3, (1969); American Maritime Cases, Fifth-Year Digests, 1923-1982, "Marine Insurance."

CHAPTER II

THE CONTRACT

Historical

Modern marine insurance law, although affected by custom and usage in the industry, primarily developed through case law and various treatises of textwriters. This is still true in the United States, although in England the case law up to 1906 was codified in the Marine Insurance Act, 1906. As noted heretofore,[1] that Act to a very major degree is a "restatement" of English marine insurance law (and to a major extent American marine insurance law) up to 1906. Consequently, the statutory sections of that Act, being based upon decisional law, are highly persuasive in the courts of the United States.

Elements of a Contract

As in any contract, there are fundamental elements in every contract of marine insurance which must be present. These are:

(1) The parties to the contract must be legally competent to enter into the contract;

(2) There must be an insurable interest upon which the contract can operate;[2]

(3) The contract must be supported by consideration; i.e., an undertaking by the underwriter to indemnify the insured and an undertaking by the insured to pay for that indemnification—that is, to pay the "premium";[3]

(4) The minds of the parties must meet upon the terms of the bargain; and

(5) The agreement, or contract, must have a legal purpose.[4]

---

1. See Chapter I, Introduction.
2. As to "insurable interest," see Chapter VII, *infra.*
3. As to "premium," see Chapter VI, *infra.*
4. As to "lawful purpose," see Chapter XI, subheading "Warranty of Legality," *infra.*

Definition of Marine Insurance

Phillips, in his *Treatise on the Law of Insurance*, 1867, Sec. 1, defined insurance as follows:

Insurance is a contract whereby, for a stipulated consideration, one party undertakes to indemnify the other against damage or loss on a certain subject by certain perils.

The Marine Insurance Act, 1906, Sec. 1, defines a contract of marine insurance as follows:

A contract of marine insurance is a contract whereby the insurer undertakes to indemnify the assured, in manner and to the extent thereby agreed, against marine losses, that is to say, the losses incident to a marine adventure.

As to "risks," the Act provides in Sec. 2:

(1) A contract of marine insurance may by its express terms, or by usage of trade, be extended so as to protect the assured against losses on inland waters or on any land risk which may be incidental to any sea voyage.[5]

(2) Where a ship in course of building, or the launch of a ship or any adventure analogous to a marine adventure, is covered by a policy in the form of a marine policy, the provisions of this Act, in so far as applicable shall apply thereto, but, except as by this section provided nothing in this Act shall alter or affect any rule of law applicable to any contract of insurance other than a contract of marine insurance as by this Act defined.[6]

The Act defines a "marine adventure" and "maritime perils" as follows in Sec. 3:

---

5. Originally, marine insurance related only to maritime perils. To meet the needs of modern commercial trade, policies were extended to cover additional risks arising on inland waters and on land which were incidental to sea voyages. A good example of the extension of a marine policy to land risks incidental to a sea voyage will be found in the "warehouse to warehouse" clause, frequently included in cargo policies.

6. Coverage for shipbuilders, commonly called "Builder's Risk" forms, are common in the industry. See the American Institute Builder's Risk Form reproduced in the Appendix. This subject is discussed in detail in Chapter XXII, *infra*. Mutual insurance against liabilities, that is, Protection and Indemnity insurance ("P & I"), falls within the scope of the Act. See *Compania Maritima San Basilio S.A. v. Oceanus Mutual Underwriting Association (Bermuda) Ltd. (The Eurysthenes)*, [1976] 2 Lloyd's Rep. 171. See, also, Chapter XXI, Protection and Indemnity.

(1) Subject to the provisions of this Act, every lawful marine adventure may be the subject of a contract of marine insurance.
(2) In particular there is a marine adventure where—

(a) Any ship goods or other moveables are exposed to maritime perils. Such property is in this Act referred to as "insurable property";
(b) The earning or acquisition of any freight, passage money, commission, profit, or other pecuniary benefit, or the security for any advances, loan, or disbursements, is endangered by the exposure of insurable property to marine perils;
(c) Any liability to a third party may be incurred by the owner of, or other person interested in or responsible for, insurable property, by reason of maritime perils.

"Maritime perils" means the perils consequent on, or incidental to, the navigation of the sea, that is to say, perils of the seas, fire, war perils, pirates, rovers, thieves, captures, seizures, restraints and detainments of princes and peoples, jettison, barratry, and any other perils, either of the like kind or which may be designated in the policy.

Definition of Terms

The formal instrument by which the contract of marine insurance is evidenced is called a "policy."[7] The underwriter, sometimes called the "assurer," or "insurer," in consideration of the payment of a sum certain called the "premium," undertakes to indemnify the person desiring the insurance coverage, called the "insured," or "assured," against loss or damage caused by certain specified perils called "maritime perils."

The term "average," which appears frequently in the field of marine insurance, and is so mystifying to the uninitiated, unquestionably comes from the French word "averie." The term as used in marine insurance simply means loss or damage. Simple or *particular* average means damage incurred by or for one part of the concern, which that part must bear alone.[8]

The term "particular average" is defined in Sec. 64(1) of the Act as:

A particular average loss is a partial loss of the subject-matter insured, caused by a peril insured against, and which is not a general average loss.

---

7. See Chapter III, The Policy.
8. *The Copenhagen* (1799), 1 Ch. Rob. 289.

Phillips (Sec. 1422) defines the term as:

A particular average is a loss borne wholly by the party upon whose property it takes place, and is so called in distinction from a general average for which divers parties contribute.

"General average," by contrast, is sometimes used to denote the loss to be borne in common by all the interests involved, and sometimes to denote the contribution to be paid by each separate party involved, in proportion to his interest.[9]

Other terms, such as "barratry," "detainments of princes and peoples," "perils of the seas," "thieves," etc., will be found defined in later portions of this text under the appropriate headings.

Marine Insurance—A Contract of Indemnity

In theory, a contract of marine insurance is a contract of indemnity. In practice, however, the extent and amount of indemnity are matters of agreement between the parties.[10] For example, in an unvalued policy on goods in the ordinary form and without any special provisions, the assured may well receive an amount less than his actual loss.[11] By contrast, under a valued policy, where the valuation of the subject-matter is treated, in general, as conclusive against both parties (in the absence of fraud), the amount received by the assured could either exceed or not equal the actual loss. Where there is a total loss, and the assured has expended sums under the Sue and Labor Clause,[12] he may receive more than a full indemnity, as is also the case with respect to unvalued policies on vessels when the freight is also insured. Moreover, in policies on freight the assured stands to recover more than mere indemnity since in the case of a loss he is entitled to be paid the gross freight without any deduction for expenses which would have been incurred after the loss in order to earn the freight.[13]

Any opportunity for net gain to the assured through the receipt of insurance proceeds in excess of the actual loss he has sustained offends the principle of indemnity. It is readily apparent that there are two principal evils involved in violating the principle of indemnity. The first is that such a contract is an inducement to wagering, and the second is the inherent inducement to the assured to destroy his own property.

9. See Chapter XVII, General Average.
10. See *Goole and Hull Steam Towing Co. Ltd. v. Ocean Marine Ins. Co. Ltd.* (1927) 29 Ll.L.Rep. 242, K.B.D.; *Irving v. Manning* (1847) 1 H.L. Cas. 287, 9 E.R. 766, H.L.
11. See Chapter XX, Particular Average, "Cargo Policies."
12. See Chapter XVIII, Sue and Labor Clause.
13. See *Robertson v. Nomikos* [1939] A.C. 371, H.L.

Consequently, the possession of an insurable interest by the assured in the subject-matter of the insurance is essential and goes to the very heart of the right to recover on the contract.[14] Absent such an interest, the assured is not injured and this is so even though there has been a total loss of the subject-matter insured.[15]

Insured Interest Must be Exposed to a Fortuitous Risk

It is not sufficient to recover on a contract of marine insurance that the assured merely have an insurable interest; that interest must be exposed to a risk of loss from a peril insured against during the currency of the marine adventure for which the contract was written, and any ensuing loss must be fortuitous. Marine insurance was never intended to indemnify the assured against all loss or damage which might occur to his property or interest, but only those losses which are fortuitous and beyond the control of the assured. For example, unless otherwise specifically covered, the usual policy will not cover losses that are inevitable or expectable by reason of the nature of the subject-matter insured such as inherent vice, improper packing, or delay.[16] This principle is confirmed in Sec. 55(2) of the Marine Insurance Act, reading:

> Unless the policy otherwise provides, the insurer is not liable for ordinary wear and tear, ordinary leakage and breakage, inherent vice or nature of the subject-matter insured, or for any loss proximately caused by rats or vermin, or for any injury to machinery not proximately caused by maritime perils.

Moreover, the risk of loss must act upon the subject-matter insured after the policy takes effect or the risk underwritten in the policy commences or "attaches." If the loss occurs before the risk attaches, no matter what it may be, that loss is not covered. A perfect example is *Fuerst Day v.*

---

14. See *Lucena v. Craufurd* (1805) 127 E.R. 630, H.L., 127 E.R. 858 (1808).

15. See Chapter VII, Insurable Interest. As will be seen, this does not mean an actual loss of something the assured *possesses;* it is sufficient if the assured is deprived of a legitimate expectation of gain, such as profit to be realized by consummation of a commercial transaction. See *Hooper v. Robinson*, 98 U.S. 528 (1878); *Groban v. Pegu*, 331 F.Supp. 883, 1972 AMC 460 (S.D.N.Y.).

16. See Chapter XV, Proximate Cause, under "Ordinary Wear and Tear, Inherent Vice, etc." There is, however, nothing which prevents underwriters from agreeing to cover risks which would otherwise be excluded by reason of "inherent vice." See *Soya G.M.B.H. Kommanditgesellschaft v. White (The Corfu Island)*, [1980] 1 Lloyd's Rep. 491. *aff'd* [1982] 1 Lloyd's Rep. 136 (C.A.), *aff'd* [1983] 1 Lloyd's Rep. 122, H.L., where the policy insured against, *inter alia*, heat, sweat, and spontaneous combustion, known collectively as the "HSSC Clauses," for damage to a cargo of soya beans. See, also, *Blackshaws (Pty) Ltd. v. Constantia Insurance Co. Ltd.*, [1983] S.A. (1) 120, A.D. (So. Afr.) 1984 AMC 637 (defective packing of a container constitutes "inherent vice").

Orion Insurance Co.[17] where a c. & f. purchaser insured, on all risks terms, drums of "essential" oils which he had purchased in Indonesia. When he took delivery of the drums they were found to contain water, with only a thin layer of oil floating on the top. The assured's difficulty, of course, was to prove that the fraud had occurred during the currency of the policy; i.e., while the shipment was in transit. It was rather difficult to imagine the oil—if it ever was in the drums—could have been siphoned off and replaced with water during the transit and, accordingly, the court found that the assured had failed to establish that the fraud occurred after the drums of oil had commenced their transit.

From the foregoing, it will be seen that in every contract of marine insurance, the assured must have an insurable interest in the subject matter and that interest must be exposed to a risk of loss, damage, or detriment by a maritime peril. The requirement of an insurable interest is the factor which distinguishes a true contract of marine insurance from a mere wager.

Wagering policies were not invalid at common law in most jurisdictions. They were declared void by statute in England in 1745 by the Act of 19 Geo. 2, c. 37, which prohibited wager policies on British ships and their cargoes. That act was repealed by the Marine Insurance Act, 1906, Sec. 4 of which deals with wager policies as follows:

(1) Every contract of marine insurance by way of gaming or wagering is void.

(2) A contract of marine insurance is deemed to be a gaming or wagering contract—

(a) Where the assured has not an insurable interest as defined by this Act, and the contract is entered into with no expectation of acquiring such an interest; or

(b) Where the policy is made "interest or no interest," or "without further proof of interest than the policy itself," or "without benefit of salvage to the insurer," or subject to any other like term:

Provided that, where there is no possibility of salvage, a policy may be effected without benefit of salvage to the insurer.

The 1745 Act was held not to apply to foreign vessels; there is no such limitation in the Marine Insurance Act, 1906, and consequently, as Sec. 4 so clearly states, every marine insurance by way of gaming or wagering within the meaning of that section is void.

It will be noted that Sec. 4(1) merely declares such policies to be void; it does not declare them to be illegal. However, a later statute, the Marine

17. [1980] 1 Lloyd's Rep. 656.

Insurance (Gambling Policies) Act, 1909, makes them illegal, and prescribes certain criminal penalties.

Nevertheless, it has always been the practice of underwriters in both England and the United States to accept risks on such terms.[18] Such policies are called "honour" policies and are frequently referred to as P.P.I (policy proof of interest), or F.I.A. (full interest admitted).[19] Such policies are frequently used to insure uncertain or non-quantified interests such as "disbursements" of vessel owners. Such "disbursements" would embrace such items as increased value, commissions, profits, disbursements, freight (including chartered freight or anticipated freight), and the like. Thus, P.P.I policies are utilized to further a commercial purpose where, although the assured may have an insurable interest, it would be difficult or impossible to authenticate that interest. The AIH form (1977), as in nearly all hull forms, contains a Disbursements clause reading:

It is a condition of this Policy that no additional insurance against the risk of Total Loss of the Vessel shall be effected to operate during the currency of this Policy by or for account of the Assured, Owners, Managers, Operators or Mortgagees except on the interests and up to the amounts enumerated in the following Sections (a) to (g), inclusive, and no such insurance shall be subject to P.P.I, F.I.A. or other like term on any interests whatever excepting those enumerated in Section (a); provided always and notwithstanding the limitation on recovery in the Assured clause a breach of this condition shall not afford Underwriters any defense to a claim by a Mortgagee who has accepted this Policy without knowledge of such breach:

---

18. However, in England, the assured runs the risk of having his policy declared void by the courts. See *Gedge et al v. Royal Exchange Assurance Corp.* (1900) 2 Q.B. 221, 5 Com. Cas. 229, 16 T.L.R. 344 (void); *In re London County Commercial Re-insurance Office* (1922) 10 Ll.L. Rep. 100, 370, 2 Ch. 399 (void); *Cheshire & Co. v. Vaughn Bros. & Co.* (1919) 3 Ll.L. Rep. 213 (void); *Edwards & Co. Ltd. v. Motor Union Ins. Co.* (1922) 11 Ll.L.Rep. 170 (void). In the United States, "honor" policies are not prima facie void; however, the insurer may avoid liability by establishing that, in fact, the assured had no insurable interest. *Republic of China v. National Union F. I. Co.*, 163 F.Supp. 812, 1958 AMC 1529, [1958] 2 Lloyd's Rep. 578 (D., Md.); *Hall v. Jefferson Ins. Co.*, 279 F.2d 892 (S.D.N.Y., 1921). Interestingly, in *Buchanan v. Faber* (1899) 4 Com. Cas. 223, although the policy contained a clause which constituted a policy proof of interest, the court by agreement of and at the request of the parties, agreed to try the case as if the clause did not exist.

19. The English practice seems to be that the P.P.I. clause is not affixed to the policy but either is pinned on to the policy or separated from a component part by a line perforation; the assured at his option may detach it if he wishes. A common form of the P.P.I. clause reads:

This slip is no part of the policy, and is not to be attached thereof, but is to be considered as binding in honour on the underwriters; the Assured however having permission to remove it from this policy should they so desire.

In the event of claim it is hereby agreed that this Policy shall be deemed sufficient proof of interest.

Full interest admitted.

(a) *Disbursements, managers' commissions, profits or excess or increased value of hull and machinery, and/or similar interests however described, and freight (including chartered freight or anticipated freight) insured for time.* An amount not exceeding in the aggregate 25% of the Agreed Value.

(b) *Freight or hire, under contracts for voyage.* An amount not exceeding the gross freight or hire for the current cargo passage and next succeeding cargo passage (such insurance to include, if required, a preliminary and an intermediate ballast passage) plus the charges of insurance. In the case of a voyage charter where payment is made on a time basis, the amount shall be calculated on the estimated duration of the voyage, subject to the limitation of two cargo passages as laid down therein. Any amount permitted under this Section shall be reduced, as the freight or hire is earned, by the gross amount so earned. Any freight or hire to be earned under the form of Charters described in (d) below shall not be permitted under this Section (b) if any part thereof is insured as permitted under said Section (d).

(c) *Anticipated freight if the vessel sails in ballast and not under charter.* An amount not exceeding the anticipated gross freight on next cargo passage, such amount to be reasonably estimated on the basis of the current rate of freight at time of insurance, plus the charges of insurance. Provided, however, that no insurance shall be permitted by this Section if any insurance is effected as permitted under Section (b).

(d) *Time charter hire or charter hire for series of voyages.* An amount not exceeding 50% of the gross hire which is to be earned under the charter in a period not exceeding 18 months. Any amount permitted under this Section shall be reduced as the hire is earned under the charter by 50% of the gross amount so earned but, where the charter is for a period exceeding 18 months, the amount insured need not be reduced while it does not exceed 50% of the gross hire still to be earned under the charter. An insurance permitted by this Section may begin on the signing of the charter.

(e) *Premiums.* An amount not exceeding the actual premiums of all interest insured for a period not exceeding 12 months (excluding premiums insured as permitted under the foregoing Sections but including, if required, the premium or estimated calls on any Protection and Indemnity or War Risks and Strikes insurance) reducing pro rata monthly.

(f) *Returns of Premium.* An amount not exceeding the actual returns which are recoverable subject to "and arrival" or equivalent provision under any policy of insurance.

(g) *Insurance irrespective of amount against:* Risks excluded by the War, Strikes and Related Exclusions clause; risks enumerated in the American Institute War Risks and Strikes clauses; and General Average and Salvage Disbursements.

It will be noted that the Disbursements Clause therefore:

(1) Prohibits additional insurances against total loss of the vessel except as permitted in sections (a) through (g) of the clause;

(2) Section (a) permits total loss only insurance without proof of interest but limits such insurance to 25% of the agreed (or insured) value; i.e., section (a) limits insurance which could be effected on P.P.I. or F.I.A. terms to 25%;

(3) Insurances permitted under sections (b) through (g), inclusive, are all subject to proof of interest;

(4) Insurances permitted under sections (b) through (g), inclusive, may be effected (subject to the limitation in each individual section) in addition to the 25% total loss insurance permitted on P.P.I. or F.I.A. terms under section (a).

Clearly, the Clause prevents vessel owners from insuring for a low valuation under the hull policy and then placing other total loss insurance on P.P.I. terms for disproportionate amounts relative to the agreed valuation in the hull policy. Other insurances on freight, etc., for which the assured can prove an insurable interest are not limited. Thus, only the non-quantifiable total loss insurance on disbursements, etc. (where the assured may find it difficult to prove an interest), are limited or controlled relative to the agreed valuation in the basic hull policy.

Most open cargo policies contain a clause relating to insurable interest reading substantially as follows:

> To cover all shipments consigned to, or shipped by the Assured, or consigned to or shipped by others for the account or control of the Assured and in which the Assured may have an insurable interest, but excluding shipments sold by the Assured on f.o.b.; f.a.s.; cost and freight or similar terms whereby the Assured is not obligated to furnish Ocean Marine Insurance and excluding shipments purchased by the Assured on terms which include insurance to final destination; also to cover all shipments which the Assured may be instructed to insure provided such instructions are given in writing prior to sailing of vessel and before any known or reported loss or accident.

It is imperative from the standpoint of cargo insurance that the various types of contracts for the sale of goods be fully understood. At the risk of oversimplification, these contract terms may be defined as follows:

F.O.B. (Free on board). Where the terms of purchase are such that the buyer is not liable for the goods until they are actually loaded on board the vessel, the seller's price being one which covers all expenses up to and including delivery of the goods upon the vessel provided for, or by, the buyer at the port of origination. The insurable interest in the goods while they are being moved from the factory or warehouse to the vessel remains with the seller until the goods are lifted over the side of the vessel; from that point onward, the purchaser has an insurable interest.

F.A.S. (Free alongside). The seller quotes a price which includes delivery of the goods alongside the vessel and within reach of the vessel's loading tackle. Thus, the purchaser's insurable interest does not come into being until the goods are so delivered and the seller's insurable interest ceases at that point.

C.& F. (Cost and freight). The seller quotes a price which includes the cost of transportation (freight) to the port or place of destination. Either the seller prepays the freight or permits the buyer, after having paid actual charges, to deduct them from the price.[20]

Under such a contract, the seller does not furnish the buyer with marine insurance. It is up to the buyer to effect his own insurance. It will also be seen that the seller is without insurance from the time the shipment leaves the seller's plant or warehouse until title passes to the buyer. However, the seller can protect himself by procuring "contingency" insurance which only is effective when ownership of the goods remains with the seller. It has happened that the buyer arranges marine insurance under his own policy with a Warehouse-to-Warehouse clause. Unless the seller is named on the buyer's policy as an additional assured, he is without insurance despite the Warehouse-to-Warehouse clause. In short, it is the responsibility of the seller to arrange insurance coverage from the time his goods leave his plant or warehouse and during the period he retains title, or he takes the risk of loss until title passes to the buyer.

To the contrary, an actual ownership interest is not necessary in order to qualify as an "insurable interest." The assured need not have title to or legally enforceable *in rem* rights in the property insured to have an insurable interest. If any economic advantage from the continued existence or pecuniary loss from destruction or damage of the insured property result to the assured, he has an insurable interest.[21] Stated in another fashion, any person has an insurable interest in property, by the existence of which he will gain an advantage, or by the destruction of which he will suffer a loss, whether has or has not any title in, or lien upon, or possession of the property itself.[22] This includes goods under an f.o.b. contract, prior to

20. See *Madeirense Do Brasil, S.A. v. Stulman-Emrick Lumber Co.*, 147 F.2d 399, 402 (2nd Cir.).

21. *Groban et al v. S.S. Pegu*, 331 F.Supp. 883, 1972 AMC 460 (S.D.N.Y., 1971).

22. *Harrison v. Fortlage*, 161 U.S. 57, 65 (1896); *Hagan v. Scottish Union & National Insurance Co.*, 186 U.S. 423 (1902).

the delivery of the goods to the f.o.b. carrier.[23]

In theory, if goods are shipped f.o.b., both the risk and title pass to the buyer upon loading but, after shipment, if the buyer rejects the goods, the risk reverts to the seller and he may have no insurance coverage.

C.I.F. (Cost, insurance, freight). The price fixed covers the cost of the goods, insurance, and freight.[24]

Under such a contract, it is the obligation of the seller to provide the buyer with a policy that covers the shipment from the time the buyer has an insurable interest until the buyer's interest ceases. It is incumbent upon the seller, therefore, to insure for his own account until such time as the buyer has an insurable interest. In essence, the buyer under a c.i.f. contract is supposed to receive a policy which has been arranged by the seller and in practice the policy may be effected in the name of the buyer or the seller but if the latter it is incumbent upon the seller to transfer the policy by endorsing it appropriately or assigning the proceeds thereof. Obviously, it is also incumbent upon the buyer to ascertain prior to shipment what kind of policy the seller intends to procure and upon what terms and conditions.

Every lawful maritime adventure may be the subject of a contract of marine insurance. Section 3 of the Marine Insurance Act, 1906, states that there is a marine adventure where:

> (a) Any ship, goods or other moveables are exposed to maritime perils. Such property is in this Act referred to as "insurable property";
> (b) The earning or acquisition of any freight, passage money, commission, profit, or other pecuniary benefit, or the security for any advances, loan, or disbursements, is endangered by the exposure of insurable property to maritime perils.
> (c) Any liability to a third party may be incurred by the owner of, or other person interested in or responsible for, insurable property, by reason of maritime perils.

The principal subjects of marine insurance; i.e., cargo, freight and ship, are defined by Rules for Construction of Policy, numbers 15 through 17, as follows:

> The term "ship" includes the hulls, materials and outfit, stores and provisions for the officers and crew, and, in the case of vessels engaged

---

23. *Curacao Trading Co. v. Federal Ins. Co.*, 50 F.Supp. 441, 1942 AMC 1079 (S.D.N.Y.), *aff'd* 137 F.2d 911, 1943 AMC 1050 (2nd Cir.), cert. den. 321 U.S. 765 (1943).

24. *National Wholesale Grocery Co. v. Mann*, 251 Mass. 238, 146 N.E. 791; *A. Klipstein & Co. v. Dilsizian*. 273 F. 473 (2nd Cir.); *Columbia Bagging & Tie Co. v. Steel Union Co.*, 43 Ga. App. 126, 158 S.E. 459.

in a special trade, the ordinary fittings requisite for the trade, and also, in the case of a steamship, the machinery, boilers, and coals and engine stores, if owned by the assured.

The term "freight" includes the profit derivable by a shipowner from the employment of his ship to carry his own goods or moveables, as well as freight payable by a third party, but does not include passage money.

The term "goods" means goods in the nature of merchandise, and does not include personal effects or provisions and stores for use on board.

In the absence of any usage to the contrary, deck cargo and living animals must be insured specifically, and not under the general denomination of goods.

Frequent references will be found in the Act to the term "usage" and equally frequent references in the reported decisions relating to marine insurance. The Act has this to say about "usage" in Section 87:

(1) Where any right, duty, or liability would arise under a contract of marine insurance by implication of law, it may be negatived or varied by express agreement, or by usage, if the usage be such as to bind both parties to the contract.

(2) The provisions of this section extend to any right, duty, or liability declared by this Act which may be lawfully modified by agreement.

As Phillips states (Sec. 36), under American law:

. . . the place where the insurance is made . . . affects its construction, since every contract must be construed in reference to the customs and usages of the country, and even the port where it is entered into, as well as by the subject-matter to which it relates, and the surrounding circumstances. Such customs and usages are in effect included in the contract, and . . . have a material bearing in respect to the character and extent of the risks and perils included in the insurance.[25]

For example, the reference to "usage" in respect of deck cargo found in Section 87 of the Act is well illustrated by *Gaunt v. British and Foreign Marine Insurance Co. Ltd.*[26] In that case, a cargo of wool was shipped on deck during a coasting voyage. There existed a trade usage to carry such cargoes on deck. The court held that it was not necessary to insure the wool as deck cargo specifically. The court stated, in part:

---

25. See Chapter IV, Principles of Construction, under subheading "Usage."
26. [1920] 1 K.B. 903, C.A., *aff'd* [1921] 2 A.C. 41, 7 Ll.L. Rep. 62, H.L.

The underwriter is bound to know of the existence of such usages, and the description of particular goods as of the class to which such a usage applies gives him the information that the goods will or may be carried on deck. If there is such a usage there is no reason for requiring a statement that goods which fall within it are in fact to be carried on deck as the mere description of the goods gives the necessary intimation.

In *Goodman v. Fireman's Fund*,[27] the policy on a yacht covered "all risks" and contained a special typed clause which warranted that the yacht would be laid up and out of commission from October 1 until May 1. The assured undertook to do the lay-up work himself but, unfortunately, omitted to drain the seawater cooling system and, more importantly, did not close the port and starboard sea valves which permitted seawater to enter the cooling system. The cooling system included two filters encased in plastic cylindrical jackets and, because the sea valves remained open and the sea water lines were not drained, the water remained in the filters.

The plastic filter jackets broke during the course of the winter, due to freezing of water in the filters, and the breaking of the filter jackets permitted water in the cooling system to flow into the hull through the broken jackets. Indeed, water continued to enter the system through the open valves and to flow through the broken jackets in such volume that the yacht sank at its moorings.

At first instance, the assured was denied recovery on grounds that insofar as the loss was caused by the freezing of water in the cooling system, it was excluded from coverage; that the loss was not covered by the "all risks" clause of the policy; and that the provision insuring against negligence of the master—the Inchmaree Clause—did not apply.

On appeal, it was held that the Inchmaree Clause did apply and that the predominant "efficient" cause of the sinking was not the freezing of water in the cooling system but negligence of the assured in failing to close the intake valves. However, the assured nonetheless failed to recover because it was held that he had breached his express warranty that the yacht would be laid up during the time specified and it was not laid up in accordance with the custom in Chesapeake Bay which at the very least required that the sea valves be closed as a part of the winterizing program.

The *forms* by which marine insurance contracts are written are discussed in detail in Chapter III, The Policy. The *manner* in which such contracts are construed is covered in depth in Chapter IV, Principles of Construction.

---

27. 600 F.2d 1040, 1979 AMC 2534 (4th Cir.).

CHAPTER III

THE POLICY

In General

The policy is the basic instrument in a contract of marine insurance. Section 22 of the Marine Insurance Act, 1906 provides:

Subject to the provisions of any statute, a contract of marine insurance is inadmissible in evidence unless it is embodied in a marine policy in accordance with this Act. The policy may be executed and issued either at the time when the contract is concluded or afterward.[1]

A contract of marine insurance is deemed to be concluded when the proposal of the assured is accepted by the insurer, whether the policy be then issued or not; and for the purpose of showing when the proposal was accepted, reference may be made to the "slip" or covering note or other customary memorandum of the contract.[2]

The two statements, at first blush, appear mutually contradictory. However, the contradiction is more apparent than real. Section 89 of the Act reads:

Where there is a duly stamped policy,[3] reference may be made, as heretofore, to the slip or covering note in any legal proceeding.

Thus, clearly under English law the slip was a contract of marine insurance but, equally clearly, prior to 1970 it was not a "policy" which could be sued upon.[4]

---

1. See, also, *Royal Exchange Assur. Corp. v. Vega* [1902] 2 K.B. 384, C.A.; *Re Norwich Equitable Fire Ins. Soc., Royal Ins. Co.'s Claim No. 9* (1887) 57 L.T. 241; *Jones v. Provincial Ins. Co.* (1858) 16 U.C.R. 477 (Can.). This is the English and Commonwealth rule, as modified or ameliorated by the Finance Act 1959 which, by virtue of its provisions that repealed subsections (2) to (5) of Section 23 of the Act, seemingly renders a "slip policy" a "marine policy" as that term is used in Section 22. The American rule differs in the sense that an oral contract of insurance may be sued upon. See discussion *infra*.
2. This is an exact quote of Section 21 of the Act.
3. The words "duly stamped" may now be ignored by virtue of the Finance Act 1970 (Eliz. 2 1970 c. 24) which abolished all stamp duties.
4. In *Ionides v. Pacific Mar. Ins. Co.* (1871) L.R. 6 Q.B. 674, at 684-685, *aff'd* on appeal (1872) L.R. 7 Q.B. 517, Ex. Ch., Lord Blackburn said, in part:
    The slip is in practice, and according to the understanding of those engaged in marine insurance, the complete and final contract between the parties, fixing the terms of the insurance and the premium and neither party can, without the assent of the other, deviate from the terms thus agreed on without a breach of faith, for which he would suffer severely in his credit and future business.

Subsequent to the repeals of the Finance Act, 1959, the practice has arisen in the English market for the slip to be treated as a policy, or "slip policy" as it is known, by attaching the slip to a slip policy form signed by or on behalf of the underwriters.

A slip, as the name implies, is merely a slip of paper setting forth the basic terms of the risk in outline or abbreviated form.[5] The slip is then submitted to the underwriter who, if he is willing to subscribe to the risk, initials the slip. If the underwriter is willing to accept only a part of the risk, he inserts before his initials the sum he is willing to underwrite.

An "open slip" is precisely what the name implies; i.e., the underwriter agrees by initialing the slip that he is prepared to bear, either at a fixed premium or a premium "to be arranged", the risk of loss up to a certain amount (but not beyond that amount) by whatever vessels may be engaged to transport it. As shipments are made and the underwriter is notified of them, such shipments are termed insurances "off slip" and, eventually, policies are issued in respect of them.

In the United States, a policy is merely evidence of the contract of insurance and oral contracts of insurance are upheld. There need not be an express and precise agreement on each of the terms, which terms may be shown by and implied from the acts of the parties, including previous dealings, and from all the attending circumstances.[6] Where there is an

---

A "cover note" is a form of slip and of similar import; i.e., a memorandum of the contract arrived at and issued to the broker or assured by an underwriter accepting the risk.

Whether termed a cover note or a slip, it did constitute a memorandum of what the parties agreed upon, or a framework upon which the policy itself could be constructed, although merely initialing the slip did not create a *legal* obligation to issue a policy. See *Clyde Marine Ins. Co. v. Renwick & Co.* [1924] S.C. 113. Certainly, the slip could be used for the purpose of rectifying the policy. *Symington & Co. v. Union Ins. Soc. of Canton (No. 2)* [1928] 34 Com.Cas. 233; *Eagle Star and British Dominion Ins.Co. v. Reiner* [1927] 43 T.L.R. 259. However, absent a claim for rectification, the slip could not contradict the terms of the policy. *Empress Assur. Corp. v. Bowring* [1905] 11 Com.Cas. 107; *British and Foreign Marine Ins. Co. v. Sturge* (1897) 2 Com.Cas. 244.

It must be emphasized, however, that since the enactment of the Finance Act, 1959 and the Finance Act, 1970, the slip has been exempted from stamp duty and presumably may now be sued upon for the express purpose of procuring the issuance of a policy conforming to the terms of the slip. Compare *Home Marine Ins. Co. Ltd. v. Smith* (1898) 2 Q.B. 351, 3 Com.Cas. 201 (slip could not be stamped as a policy and therefore was not a valid contract of marine insurance; consequently it was binding in honor only and could not be enforced as a contract to issue a policy) with *Bhugwandass v. Netherlands India Sea & Fire Ins. Co. of Batavia* (1888) 14 A.C. 83 (P.C.) (no revenue laws similar to Stamp Act existed at the time of trial; "open cover" enforced as a covenant to insure).

5. Apparently, the ordinary perils to be insured against are usually not specified in the slip issued by English underwriters but, through expertise in the trade, it can usually be determined from a perusal of the slip what the perils and the terms and conditions of the insurance were intended to be. See *Symington & Co. v. Union Ins. Soc. of Canton* [1928] 34 Com. Cas. 23 and *Edwards v. Aberayon Mutual Ship Ins. Soc.* (1875) 1 Q.B.D. 563.

6. *Great Amer. Ins. v. Maxey*, 193 F.2d 151, 1952 AMC 36 (5th Cir.); *McBride v. Home Ins. Co.*, 105 F.Supp. 116 (E.D.,La.). See, also, *Audubon v. Excelsior Ins. Co.*, 27 N.Y. 216 (1863) and *Western Mass. Ins. Co. v. Duffey*, 2 Kan. 347 (1864).

agreement to insure, the insurer is held bound even though the policy itself may not be issued until after the loss occurs and that fact is known to the parties.[7]

It is, of course, the duty of insurance companies to make the policies issued by them accord with and not depart from the terms of their proposal form and to express both documents in clear and unambiguous terms.[8]

Even under American law, the duration of an oral contract of insurance is limited to the time reasonably necessary for the insurer or its agent to issue a written policy. See, for example, *Epstein v. Great American*,[9] where eight months elapsed between an alleged oral binder and the loss of the assured's yacht, and the assured—himself a licensed insurance broker—was held chargeable with knowledge that marine insurance policies are issued only after an application has been accepted by the underwriter and that in this instance no insurance policy had ever been issued by the defendant insurance company. The court also noted that the assured has the burden of proving that a valid contract of insurance exists, such burden being substantially greater with respect to an unusual type of policy.[10]

In the United States, a "binder" occupies a position analogous to a "slip" and is an agreement to issue a policy of insurance in the usual and ordinary form. Thus, a binder to "fully insure" for $10,000 on a trip policy is satisfied by an ordinary and usual form of trip policy for the full amount named.[11]

The subject of binders can become somewhat convoluted and confusing. For example, in *Suraga*,[12] the insurance was first made on a binder which referred to a policy, and was later evidenced by a "certificate" which referred to the same policy. The certificate did not state all the terms of the risk on its face, including a one-year for suit clause. Suit was brought by the party insured under the binder. Distinguishing *Phoenix Ins. Co. v. DeMonchy*,[13] the court held the assured to be bound by the one-year for suit clause.

Binders may also be "provisional." For example, in *Morris & Cummings v. Fireman's Fund Ins. Co.*,[14] one of the participating underwriters wrote on

---

7. *National Bulk Carriers v. U. S.*, 148 F.2d 462, 1945 AMC 415 (3rd Cir.); *Mead v. Davison* (1835) 111 E.R. 428.

8. *Braund v. Mutual Life & Citizens Assur. Co., Ltd.* [1926] N.Z.L.R. 529 (N.Z.).

9. 392 S.W. 2d 331 (St., Tenn.), 1965 AMC 854.

10. See, also, *Seven Provinces Ins. Co. v. Commerce & Industry Ins. Co.*, 65 F.R.D. 674 (D.,Mo., 1975), where 15 months was held to be an unreasonable time for a provisional binder on reinsurance to remain outstanding.

11. *Atlantic*, 1928 AMC 1723, 143 A. 165 (St., Conn.); *Insurance Co. v. Mordecai*, 63 U.S. 111 (1859); *Woodruff v. Columbus Ins. Co.*, 56 La. 697 (1850); Phillips, Sec. 15.

12. 37 F.2d 461, 1930 AMC 328 (2nd Cir.).

13. [1929] All E.R. 531, H.L.

14. 36 F.2d 36, 1929 AMC 1534 (S.D.N.Y.).

the face of the application: "Binding. Attached date to be advised. Rate to be advised. Provisional," and it was verbally agreed with the agent of the assured that the insurance would not be effective until the agent should obtain the remainder of the risk from the other companies. The court held that the notation did not constitute a contract to issue a policy nor an absolute binder pending further negotiations. See, also, *American Eagle F. I. Co. v. Eagle Star Ins. Co.*,[15] where a condition inserted in longhand in a provisional binder was held to govern the whole contract although not restated in the final binder, and *Egremont Castle*[16] where it was held that a failure to notify the prospective underwriters of a loss material to the risk while binders were under consideration was a breach of *uberrimae fides* and delivery of provisional binders by the broker for the assured to the underwriters with essential elements—date, term, and risk—yet to be supplied, did not constitute a valid contract of insurance.

In *Allied Chemical v. Gulf Atlantic*,[17] it was held that a cargo underwriter's letter, waiving subrogation against the carrier under a private contract of affreightment, was a part of the policy even though the latter was never formally amended before the loss. Consequently, it was held to be a bar to recovery by the shipper against the carrier for damage to the insured cargo.

In the absence of a waiver of a policy term that the broker is the assured's agent, any oral or collateral warranties by the broker are ineffective to create liability on the part of the underwriter. Thus, in *Curacao Tr. Co. v. Federal Ins. Co.*,[18] it was held that the broker's authority to sign various types of binders did not warrant an inference that he was empowered to convert a policy against physical loss into a guarantee of a warehouseman's honesty. In that case, a warehouse company having gone into bankruptcy, it appeared that there were more receipts for cocoa bags outstanding than there were bags in the warehouse. On tracing the delivery of each bag, it appeared that all existing bags were allocated to receipts issued prior to the issuance of plaintiff's warehouse receipt. Plaintiff thereupon sued under his all-risk policy, alleging a loss by "nondelivery." The defendant underwriter's motion for summary judgment was granted on the grounds that the fraudulently issued receipts did not give the plaintiff any insurable interest in any cocoa and the non-delivery risk stated in the policy was not an indemnity against the non-existence of the cocoa but was a risk of the merchandise and contemplated only a loss of the merchandise; i.e., non-delivery by reason of fraud of the warehouseman was not a risk contemplated in the policy.

15. 216 F.2d 176, 1954 AMC 1263 (9th Cir.).
16. 272 N.Y.S. 792, 1934 AMC 1317 (NYM).
17. 244 F.Supp. 2, 1965 AMC 776 (E.D.,Va.).
18. 137 F.2d 911, 1943 AMC 1050 (2d Cir.).

One who agrees to insure but does not do so is liable as an underwriter would be had the appropriate policy been obtained.[19]

Assignment of Policies

Under English law, a policy is somewhat akin to a negotiable instrument in the sense that the assured must produce the policy in order to claim on it. It is not, however, strictly speaking, a negotiable instrument as the transferee takes subject to any equities affecting the assignor.

Section 15 of the Act reads:
Where the assured assigns or otherwise parts with his interest in the subject-matter insured, he does not thereby transfer to the assignee his rights under the contract of insurance, unless there be an express or implied agreement with the assignee to that effect.

But the provisions of this section do not affect a transmission of interest by operation of law.[20]

However, Section 15 of the Act must be read in conjunction with Section 51, which reads:

Where the assured has parted with or lost his interest in the subject-matter insured, and has not, before or at the time of so doing, expressly or impliedly agreed to assign the policy, any subsequent assignment of the policy is inoperative.

---

19. *Barryton-Freedom*, 42 F.2d 561, 1931 AMC 148 (S.D.N.Y.), modified 54 F.2d 282, 1931 AMC 1878 (2d Cir.); *Calcasieu Chemical Corp. v. Canal Barge Co.*, 404 F.2d 1227, 1969 AMC 114 (5th Cir.). See, also, *Hampton Roads Carriers v. Boston Ins. Co.*, 150 F.Supp. 338, 1958 AMC 425 (D.,Md.) (broker held personally liable to the insured for procuring absolute physical loss coverage where he was to have procured total loss only, with the result that a constructive total loss was not covered); *Slade, Inc. v. Samson Towing Company*, 327 F.Supp. 555, 1971 AMC 2342 (E.D.,Tex.) (provision in a charter that the owner of a tow would obtain liability insurance against any negligence of the tug; the owner of the tow failed to do so and was precluded from recovery against the tug for losses which would have otherwise been covered by the insurance); *Twenty-Grand Offshore, Inc. v. West India Carriers, Inc.*, 492 F.2d 679, 1974 AMC 2254 (5th Cir.) (towage contract under the terms of which the owners of the tug and of the tow were each to have fully insured their respective vessels and obtained in each of the policies a waiver of subrogation and a designation of the other party as an additional assured; the owner of the tow failed to have the tug owner or its tug named as an additional assured and to obtain a waiver of subrogation. Held: no recovery by the tow owner against the tug owner). See, also, Chapter V, Agents and Brokers.
  The same rule appears to obtain in England. See *Parry v. Great Ship Co.* (1863) 122 E.R. 568 (shipowner was to insure for the benefit of a prospective mortgagee but did not do so); *Mallough v. Barber* (1815) 171 E.R. 49; *Yuill & Co. v. Robson* [1908] 1 K.B. 270, C.A.; *Dickson & Co. v. Devitt* [1916] 86 L.J.K.B. 315; *Fraser v. B.N. Furman (Productions) Ltd.* [1967] 3 All E.R. 57; *Smith v. Lascelles* (1788) 100 E.R. 101; *Callander v. Oelrichs* (1838) 132 E.R. 1026, 6 Scott 761; *Park v. Hammond* (1815) 171 E.R. 110.
  20. See *North of England Oil Cake Co. v. Archangel Mar. Ins. Co.* (1875) L.R. 10 Q.B. 249; *Yangtze Ins. Ass'n v. Lukmanjee* [1918] A.C. 585, P.C.

Provided that nothing in this section affects the assignment of a policy after loss.

So, if the loss has already occurred, and the claim against the underwriter has matured, so that nothing remains to be done under the policy but to pay the claim, the claim itself may be assigned without transferring the interest in the policy.[21] This presupposes, of course, that the assignor had an insurable interest in the subject-matter of the policy at the time of the assignment.[22]

The rules with respect to assignability of a policy under English law are well expressed in Section 50 of the Act, reading:

(1) A marine policy is assignable unless it contains terms expressly prohibiting assignment. It may be assigned either before or after loss.

(2) Where a marine policy has been assigned so as to pass the beneficial interest in such policy, the assignee of the policy is entitled to sue thereon in his own name; and the defendant is entitled to make any defense arising out of the contract which he would have been entitled to make if the action had been brought in the name of the person by or on behalf of whom the policy was effected.[23]

(3) A marine policy may be assigned by endorsement thereon or in other customary manner.

Policies frequently preclude an assignment without the consent of the underwriters. See, for example, Clause 5 of the new Institute Time Clauses (Hulls, 1/10/83) reading:[24]

No assignment of or interest in this insurance or in any moneys which may be or become payable thereunder is to be binding on or

---

21. *Swan & Cleland's Graving Dock & Slipway Co. v. Maritime Ins. Co. & Crowshaw* [1907] 1 K.B. 116; *Lloyd v. Flemino* (1872) L.R. 7 Q.B. 299; *J. Aron & Co. v. Miall* (1928) 34 Com. Cas. 18; *Baker v. Adam* (1910) 15 Com. Cas. 227.

22. See, for example, *North of England Oil Cake Co v. Archangel Mar. Ins. Co.* (1875), *supra*, n. 20. And in *Powels v. Innes* (1843) 152 E.R. 695, a part owner of a vessel, after being insured but before a loss, sold his interest in the vessel to a third party without purporting to transfer the policy along with the interest or reserving any right to keep the policy alive for the purchaser's benefit. Held: no recovery. See, also, *Cram v. Sun Ins. Office*, 254 F.Supp. 702, 1966 AMC 2201 (E.D.,S.C.).

23. See, for example, *Liman, Trustee v. United Kingdom*, 297 F.Supp. 577, 1971 AMC 727 (S.D.N.Y.), where P & I underwriters were held entitled to set off against a bankrupt's trustee their claims for unpaid calls and premiums; *Pickersgill v. London and Prov. Mar. Ins. Co.* [1912] 3 K.B. 614, where the underwriter successfully defended on the ground of a nondisclosure by the assured assignor; and *Bank of N. S. Wales v. South British Ins. Co.* (1920) 4 Ll.L.Rep. 266, where the assignor was an alien enemy. The right of set-off or defense must arise, however, under the policy which was assigned and not under other policies. *Baker v. Adam* (1910) 15 Com. Cas. 227.

24. The new Institute Time Clauses (Hulls, 1/10/83) and the new Lloyd's policy form and Cargo Clauses are discussed in considerable detail, *infra*, under the subheading, "Form of the Policy."

recognized by the Underwriters unless a dated notice of such assignment or interest signed by the Assured, and by the assignor in case of subsequent assignment, is endorsed on the Policy and the Policy with such endorsement is produced before payment of any claim or return of premium thereunder.

Clause 22 of the old Institute Time Clauses (Hulls) was substantially identical as was Clause 14 of the Institute Time Clauses (Freight).

Under both American and English practice, hull policies invariably contain a "change of ownership" clause under which (unless underwriters agree in writing), the policies automatically terminate at the time of change of ownership, flag, management, charter, requisition, or classification.[25]

The loss experience of a shipowner is one of the main factors in rating a hull renewal. Consequently, when a vessel is sold or transferred to new management, underwriters usually prefer to cancel the policy. This correctly reflects the "moral hazard" involved in insuring for a period of time, at an agreed value, a vessel which could be sunk by a new owner about whom the underwriters probably know nothing.[26]

The American form also differs from the English form in another respect which is the inclusion in American policies of a "Loss Payee" clause. In the AIH form this reads:

> Loss, if any (excepting claims required to be paid to others under the Collision Liability Clause) payable to . . . . or order.

Under the Loss Payee Clause, losses must be paid to the party or parties named therein unless they voluntarily waive payment in favor of others either directly or by an assignment of the proceeds.[27] By contrast, un-

---

25. See the AIH form of policy (June, 1977) reproduced in the Appendix. In the new Institute Time Clauses (Hulls), 1/10/83), also reproduced in the Appendix, the clause is denominated the "Termination" Clause. In any event, the clauses are substantially identical.

26. See *Lemar Towing v. Fireman's Fund*, 471 F.2d 609, 1973 AMC 1843 (5th Cir.) where it was held that there had been no breach of the management warranty where the same two men retained direction and control of the insured tug while acting as controlling stockholders and officers of separate corporate entities; *Prudent Tankers Ltd. v. The Dominion Ins. Co. (The Caribbean Sea)*, [1980] 1 Lloyd's Rep. 338 (relating in part to classification of the vessel); and *Taylor v. Commercial Union*, 614 F.2d 160, 1982 AMC 1815 (8th Cir.) (tower's liability policy did not by its terms provide coverage to a corporate successor of an individually owned towing service, but the underwriter was held estopped from asserting that defense by its own conduct). Compare, however, *Whiteman v. Rhode Island Ins. Co.*, 78 F.Supp. 624, 1949 AMC 111 (E.D.,La.) where it was held that a transfer of management was a breach of the warranty against transfer of interest. See, also, *Cram v. Sun Ins. Office*, 254 F.Supp. 702, 1966 AMC 2201 (S.D.,S.C.).

27. See, in this connection, *Reliable Marine Boiler Repair, Inc. v. Frank B. Hall, Inc. et al*, 325 F.Supp. 58, 1971 AMC 1941 (S.D.N.Y.) where the loss payee was held estopped from

der English practice, the policy is a document of title and, in the absence of specific instructions from the assureds in the policy, losses can only be paid to them. Moreover, the policy must be actually produced and the payment of the claim endorsed thereon.

See discussion, *infra*, Chapter XXVII, under heading "Right to Sue as Assignee".

Form of Assignment

Assignment under English law is usually effected by endorsement and delivery. In this connection, it will be recalled that Section 50(3) of the Act states that a policy may be assigned by endorsement thereon "or in other customary manner." In *Baker v. Adam*,[28] the policy was simply handed over to the purported assignee with the knowledge and concurrence of the assured. The court held that insofar as the Act was concerned, that mode did not constitute a sufficient assignment. However, in *J. Aron Co. v. Miall*,[29] the policy was endorsed in blank by the brokers and by an agent of the seller and this mode was held to be in the customary manner. See *Sadafi v. Western Assur. Co.*,[30] where the court was not satisfied that there was a sufficient intent to assign and held there was no indorsement. See, also, *Amalgamated General Finance Co. v. C. E. Golding & Co., Ltd.*,[31] where there was no actual assignment as required by Section 50 but the assured pled an assignment under the Law of Property Act, 1925, Sec. 136 based upon an exchange of letters between the assured and the brokers in which the brokers agreed to pay the policy proceeds to the assignee [plaintiff] of the assured. The contention failed.

What the Policy Must Specify

Originally, Section 23 of the Act read as follows:

A marine policy must specify:

(1) The name of the assured, or of some person who effects the insurance on his behalf;

---

subsequently revoking payment orders authorizing underwriters to pay a repairer for repairs effected to the insured vessel and the repairer had gone forward with the repairs in reliance upon the assignment of the insurance proceeds by way of the payment orders. See, also, *Loveland v. East West Towing et al*, 415 F.Supp. 596, 1978 AMC 2293 (S.D.,Fla.) ("change of management" does not refer to crew but rather to surrender of control).

28. (1910) 15 Com. Cas. 227.
29. (1928) 34 Com. Cas. 18.
30. (1933) 46 Ll.L.Rep. 140, K.B.D.
31. [1964] 2 Lloyd's Rep. 163.

(2) The subject-matter insured and the risk insured against;

(3) The voyage, or period of time, or both, as the case may be, covered by the insurance;

(4) The sum or sums insured;

(5) The name or names of the insurers.

All of the foregoing requirements, except the first, were repealed by Sec. 30(5) of the Finance Act 1959, 8th Schedule, Part II.

However, Section 24 of the Act requires that the policy must be signed by or on behalf of the insurer.[32] It reads:

(1) A marine policy must be signed by or on behalf of the insurer, provided that in the case of a corporation the corporate seal may be sufficient, but nothing in this section shall be construed as requiring the subscription of a corporation to be under seal.

(2) Where a policy is subscribed by or on behalf of two or more insurers, each subscription, unless the contrary be expressed, constitutes a direct contract with the assured.

The policy, however, would not be complete and intelligible if the subject matter to be insured, the risks insured against, the term of the insurance, and the amount insured were not also included. In practice, the policy forms invariably contain the items mentioned in Section 23. Moreover, as will be seen, subsequent sections of the Act are quite specific regarding the necessity of various items. For example, Section 26 requires that the subject-matter insured shall be designated in the policy with reasonable certainty and Section 31 provides that where an insurance is effected at a premium to be arranged, and no arrangement is made, a reasonable premium is payable.

Form of the Policy

Section 30 of the Act states simply:

(1) A policy may be in the form in the First Schedule to this Act.

(2) Subject to the provisions of this Act, and unless the context of the policy otherwise requires, the terms and expressions mentioned in the First Schedule to this Act shall be construed as having the scope and meaning in that schedule assigned to them.

---

32. See *Tyser v. Shipowners' Syndicate (Reassured)* [1896] 1 Q.B. 135. But see generally *Lieberman v. Atlantic Mutual*, 1964 AMC 413 (St., Wash.), in which three individuals were insured as "d/b/a a partnership." The court held that the policy insured only the partnership and not the individuals.

It is to be emphasized that use of the policy in the form shown in the First Schedule is wholly permissive and not mandatory. The form is, of course, the old classic Lloyd's S. G. policy which was revised and confirmed in 1779 in the form set out in the First Schedule (excepting the Waiver Clause, which was added in 1874).

The form was in use generally for many years by underwriters in England and the Commonwealth nations. Not surprisingly, many of the so-called "developing nations" have used adaptations of the form.[33] The American forms rather closely track with the "perils clause" in the old S. G. form but are generally tailored to more specific uses.

The English practice has been to use the old form but to append one or more specific clauses, many of which are sponsored by the Institute of London Underwriters, such as the "Institute Voyage Clauses", the "Institute Time Clauses", the "Institute War Risks Clauses", and the "Institute Cargo Clauses"—of which there were three sets—All Risks, W.A. (With Average) and F.P.A. (Free of Particular Average).

The archaic language in the old form has been severely criticized over the years by the courts. At times, the language used has been almost vituperative.[34] Although the language admittedly is archaic, the theory seemed to be that because nearly all the terms and phraseology had been discussed and construed over several hundred years, uncertainty would be promoted if changes were made. In short, the attitude has been that those in the industry would

> . . . rather bear those ills we have than fly to others that we know not of.

As will be seen, the old form has been replaced with new forms of policies which are discussed in detail, *infra*. However, a familiarity with the old form (and the accompanying Institute Clauses) is highly desirable—indeed necessary—if one is to understand how the new forms developed and how they are likely to be judicially construed.

The old form may be dissected and broken down into its component parts as follows:

(1) The name of the assured or his agent.[35]

---

33. See, for example, *Amin Rasheed Shipping Corp. v. Kuwait Ins. Co. (The Al Wahab)*, [1983] 2 Lloyd's Rep. 365, H.L., where the policy was issued in Kuwait using substantially all the standard English marine form. The court held that English law was to be applied in construing the policy but the assured was relegated to the Kuwaiti courts for a decision.

34. For example, see *Le Cheminant v. Pearson* (1812) 128 E.R. 372 ("a very strange instrument"); *Brough v. Whitmore* (1791) 100 E.R. 976 ("an absurd and incoherent instrument"); *City Stores v. Sun Insurance*, 357 F. Supp. 1113, 1973 AMC 44 (S.D.N.Y.)("so prolix, diffuse and confused that it is a mystery how business can be conducted with such a verbal mishmash").

35. See Chapter V, Agents and Brokers, and Chapter VII, Insurable Interest.

(2) Insurance placed "lost or not lost."[36]
(3) Voyage or term insured.[37]
(4) Subject-matter insured.[38]
(5) Name of the master.[39]
(6) Duration of the risk.[40]
(7) Liberty to touch and stay.[41]
(8) Valuation clause.[42]
(9) Perils clause.[43]
(10) Sue and Labor Clause.[44]
(11) Waiver Clause.[45]
(12) Promise to insure.[46]
(13) Premium.[47]
(14) The Memorandum.[48]
(15) Subscription, sum insured, and date.[49]

Types of Policies

Before discussing the new London hull and cargo clauses, it is well to define the various *types* of policies. Section 25(1) of the Marine Insurance Act, 1906, defines voyage, time, and "mixed" policies as follows:[50]

Where the contract is to insure the subject-matter "at and from," or from one place to another or others, the policy is called a "voyage policy," and where the contract is to insure the subject-matter for a definite period of time the policy is called a "time policy." A contract for both voyage and time may be included in the same policy.

36. See Chapter IV, Principles of Construction.
37. See Chapter IV, Principles of Construction.
38. See Chapter VII, Insurable Interest, and Chapter VIII, Subject Matter and Description Thereof.
39. See Chapter X, Disclosures, and Chapter XI, Warranties.
40. See Chapter IV, Principles of Construction; Chapter XIII, Frequent Coverages and Exclusions.
41. See Chapter IV, Principles of Construction.
42. See Chapter IX, Measure of Insurable Value.
43. See Chapter XII, Perils of the Seas.
44. See Chapter XVII, Sue and Labor Clause.
45. See Chapter XVII, Sue and Labor Clause.
46. See Chapter IV, Principles of Construction, and Chapter V, Agents and Brokers.
47. See Chapter VI, The Premium.
48. See Chapter IV, Principles of Construction; Chapter XVI, Actual and Constructive Total Loss; and Chapter XX, Particular Average.
49. See Chapter IV, Principles of Construction, and Chapter IX, Measure of Insurable Value.
50. The section is reproduced as amended by the Finance Act 1959; i.e., subsection (2) which invalidated time policies made for more than twelve months was repealed.

In addition to voyage, time, and "mixed" policies, there are mixed land and sea policies, floating policies, open policies, valued policies, and unvalued policies, all of which are discussed, *infra*.

Voyage Policies

Section 42 of the Act reads:

(1) Where the subject-matter is insured by a voyage policy "at and from" or "from" a particular place, it is not necessary that the ship should be at that place when the contract is concluded, but there is an implied condition that the adventure shall be commenced within a reasonable time, and that if the adventure be not so commenced the insurer may avoid the contract.[51]

(2) The implied condition may be negatived by showing that the delay was caused by circumstances known to the insurer before the contract was concluded, or by showing that he waived the condition.[52]

The terms "from" and "at and from" have a particular significance as will be seen from the Rules of Construction of Policy in the First Schedule of the Act. Rule 2 reads:

Where the subject-matter is insured "from" a particular place, the risk does not attach until the ship starts on the voyage insured.[53]

Rule 3 covers the term "at and from" and reads:

(a) Where a ship is insured "at and from" a particular place and she is at that place in good safety when the contract is concluded, the risk attaches immediately.[54]

---

51. *Dewolf v. Archangel Ins. Co.* (1874) L.R. 9 Q.B. 415 (floating policy on cargo; vessel was so delayed in departing that the risk was converted from a summer risk to a winter risk . . . a material variance); *Smith v. Automobile Ins. Co.*, 108 Conn. 349, 143 A. 165 (1928) (policy does not attach where written "from" a port until the vessel leaves that port; thus a loss by sinking while loading cargo is not covered); see, generally, *Mey v. South Carolina Ins. Co.*, 5 S.C.L. 329; *Nelson v. Sun Marine Ins. Co.*, 71 N.Y. 453 (1877); *Union Ins. Co. v. Tysen*, 3 Hill (N.Y.) 118 (1842). *Unreasonable delay:* The vessel should not unreasonably delay her sailing. If she does so without a reasonable excuse or for some reason connected with the purpose of the voyage insured, the underwriters cannot be held. *Columbia Ins. Co. v. Catlett*, 25 U.S. 383 (1827); *Patrick v. Ludlow*, 3 Johns. 10 (N.Y., 1802); *Settle & Bacon v. St. Louis P. M. & F. Ins. Co.*, 7 Mo. 379 (1842); *Grant v. King*, 170 E.R. 682 (1802).

52. It would appear that this proposition was somewhat doubtful before passage of the Act.

53. See *Pittegrew v. Pringle*, 110 E.R. 186 (1832); *Smith v. Automobile Ins. Co.* (1928), *supra*, n. 51; *Seamans v. Loring*, F.Cas. No. 12,583 (1816); *Sea Insurance Co. v. Blogg* (1898) 2 Q.B. 398; *Mersev Mutual Underwriting Ass'n v. Poland* (1910) 15 Com. Cas. 210; *Colonial Ins. Co. of N. Z. v. Adelaide Mar. Ins. Co.* (1886) 12 App. Cas. 128, P.C., affirming 18 S.A.L.R. 84, 6 A.L.T. 71 (Aus.).

54. The "safety" contemplated is physical safety and not safety from political dangers. *Bell v. Bell* 170 E.R. 1223 (1810). See, for example, *Parmeter v. Cousins*, 170 E.R. 1141 (1809),

(b) If she is not at that place when the contract is concluded, the risk attaches as soon as she arrives there in good safety, and, unless the policy otherwise provides, it is immaterial that she is covered by another policy for a specified time after arrival.[55]

(c) Where chartered freight is insured "at and from" a particular place, and the ship is at that place in good safety when the contract is concluded, the risk attaches immediately. If she be not there when the contract is concluded, the risk attaches as soon as she arrives there in good safety.[56]

(d) Where freight other than chartered freight is payable without special conditions, and is insured "at and from" a particular place, the risk attaches *pro rata* as the goods or merchandise are shipped; provided that if there be cargo in readiness which belongs to the shipowner, or which some other person has contracted with him to ship, the risk attaches as soon as the ship is ready to receive such cargo.[57]

Where the port of departure is altered, although the place of departure is stipulated in the policy, the risk does not attach. By the same token, where the destination is specified in the policy and the ship, instead of sailing for that destination, sails for any other destination, the risk does not attach. These principles are set forth in Sections 43 and 44 of the Act, reading:

---

where the vessel arrived at port leaky and not fit to take in the cargo. After coming to anchor, she was driven out to sea again and wrecked after having been at anchor for more than 24 hours. It was held that the risk had not commenced. Compare, however, where the insurance is effected "lost or not lost." See, also, *Maritime Ins. Co. v. Alianza Ins. Co. of Santander* (1907) 2 K.B. 661, and *M'Lanahan v. Universal Ins. Co.*, 26 U.S. 129 (1828).

55. *Haughton v. Empire Mar. Ins. Co.* (1866) L.R. 1 Ex. Ch. 206; *Seamans v. Loring*, F.Cas. No. 12,538 (C.C., Mass., 1816).

56. See *Foley v. United Fire & Mar. Ins. Co. of Sydney* (1870) L.R. 5 C.P. 153; *Hart v. Delaware Ins. Co.*, F.Cas. No. 6150 (1809); *Adams v. Warren Ins. Co.*, 39 Mass. 163 (1839); *McGaw v. Ocean Ins. Co.*, 40 Mass. 403 (1839). Chartered freight is the price paid the shipowner as charter money under a contract of affreightment; freight *per se* is merely the compensation for the carriage of goods in a ship. See *Thompson v. Taylor* (1795) 101 E.R. 657; *Davidson v. Willasey* (1813) 105 E.R. 117; *Barber v. Fleming* (1869) L.R. 5 Q.B. 59; *Horncastle v. Suart* (1806) 103 E.R. 155; *McKenzie v. Shedden* (1810) 170 E.R. 1208.

57. See *Scottish Shire Line v. London and Prov. Mar. Ins. Co.* (1912) 17 Com. Cas. 240; *Williamson v. Innes* (1831) 131 E.R. 311, N.P.; *Montgomery v. Eggington* (1789) 100 E.R. 621; *Patrick v. Eames* (1813) 3 Camp. 441, N.P.; *Jones v. Neptune Mar. Ins. Co.* (1872) L.R. 7 Q.B. 702; *The Copernicus* [1896] P. 237; *M'Gaw v. Ocean Ins. Co.*, 40 Mass. 405 (1839); *Gordon v. American Ins. Co.*, 4 Denio 360 (N.Y., 1847); *Hart v. Delaware Ins. Co.*, F.Cas. No. 6150; *De Longuemere v. New York Fire Ins. Co.*, 10 Johns. 119 (N.Y., 1813); *Patapsco Ins. Co. v. Briscoe*, 7 Gill & J. 293 (Md., 1835); *Wolcott v. Eagle Ins. Co.*, 21 Mass. 429 (1827); *Cole v. Louisiana Ins. Co.*, 2 Mart. N.S. 165 (1824); *Robinson v. Manufacturers Ins. Co.*, 42 Mass. 143 (1840).

43. Where the place of departure is specified in the policy, and the ship instead of sailing from that place sails from any other place, the risk does not attach.[58]

44. Where the destination is specified in the policy, and the ship, instead of sailing for that destination, sails for any other destination, the risk does not attach.[59]

Compare the above sections with Section 45, reading:

(1) Where, after the commencement of the risk, the destination of the ship is voluntarily changed from the destination contemplated in the policy, there is said to be a change of voyage.

(2) Unless the policy otherwise provides, where there is a change of voyage, the insurer is discharged from liability as from the time of change, that is to say, as from the time when the determination to change it is manifested; and it is immaterial that the ship may not in fact have left the course of the voyage contemplated by the policy when the loss occurs.

It is apparent that three differing states of fact are possible; i.e., (1) the vessel sails on a voyage which is not comprehended in the policy; (2) the vessel sails on the voyage contemplated but afterwards voluntarily changes its destination; and (3) the vessel sails on the intended voyage but by an unauthorized route.[60] In the first illustration, the policy is void *ab initio* and the risk never attaches. In the second, the policy attaches but by reason of the change of voyage, the risk may be avoided. In the third, there is a "deviation" as will be seen from the terms of Section 46 of the Act:

(1) Where a ship, without lawful excuse, deviates from the voyage contemplated by the policy, the insurer is discharged from liability as from the time of deviation, and it is immaterial that the ship may have regained her route before any loss occurs.[61]

---

58. *Way v. Modigliani* (1787) 2 T.R. 30; *Mount v. Larkins* (1831) 131 E.R. 342 (departure unreasonably delayed); *Vallance Northland Nav. Co. v. Amer. Mer. Mar. Ins. Co.*, 212 N.Y.S. 541 (1926); *Martin v. Delaware Ins. Co.*, F.Cas. No. 9161 (1808); *Spinney v. Ocean Mutual Marine Ins. Co.* (1890) 17 S.C.R. 326 (Can.).

59. *Simon, Israel & Co. v. Sedgwick* [1893] 1 Q.B. 303, C.A.; *Sellar v. McVicar* (1804) 127 E.R. 365; *Woolridge v. Boydell* (1778) 99 E.R. 14; *Talcott v. Marine Ins. Co.*, 2 Johns. 130 (N.Y., 1807); *McFee v. South Carolina. Ins. Co.*, 13 S.C.L. 503 (S.C., 1823); *New York Firemen's Ins. Co. v. Lawrence*, 14 Johns. 45 (N.Y., 1816). And see *Rickards v. Forestal Land, Timber & Railwavs Co.. Ltd.* [1941] 3 All E.R. 62, H.L.

60. For cases involving the first illustration, see note 58 *supra;* for those involving the second illustration, see note 59 *supra*. Policies, however, frequently contain clauses authorizing a change in voyage at a premium "to be arranged."

61. *Elliot v. Wilson* (1776) 2 E.R. 320, H.L.; *Hartley v. Buggin* (1781) 99 E.R. 527 (it is not necessary to constitute a deviation that the risk be increased); *Burns v. Holmwood* (1856) 27 L.Y.O.S. 66; *Way v. Modigliana* (1787) 2 T.R. 30; *The Indrapura*, 171 F. 292 (D., Ore., 1909);

(2) There is a deviation from the voyage contemplated by the policy[62]

(a) Where the course of the voyage is specifically designated by the policy, and that course is departed from; or

(b) Where the course of the voyage is not specifically designated by the policy, but the usual and customary course is departed from.[63]

(3) The intention to deviate is immaterial; there must be a deviation in fact to discharge the insurer from his liability under the contract.[64] It will be seen that it can be a rather difficult task to distinguish between an intention to deviate and a change of voyage. If the former, the underwriter is not discharged; if the latter, the policy may be avoided. It would appear that the true test is whether the port of destination specified in the policy remains the final place of intended destination. If it is, then an intention formed before sailing of putting into other ports or of taking an intermediate voyage while enroute does not constitute a "change of voyage."[65]

The doctrine of "deviation" also applies in the law relating to carriage of goods by sea, although the original strictness of the doctrine in the latter has been somewhat ameliorated by the Hague Rules and the respective Carriage of Goods by Sea Acts adopted by nearly all maritime nations.

Subsection (2) of Section 46 must be read in conjunction with Section 47 of the Act, reading:

Maryland Ins. Co. v. Le Roy, 11 U.S. 26 (1812); *Winthrop v. Union Ins. Co.,* F.Cas. No. 17901 (1807); *Burgess v. Equitable M. Ins. Co.,* 126 Mass. 70 (1898); *Natchez Ins. Co. v. Stanton,* 10 Miss. 340 (1844).

62. *Beatson v. Haworth,* (1796) 101 E.R. 686; *Gairdner v. Senhouse* (1810) 128 E.R. 7; *Hearne v. New England M. Ins. Co.,* 87 U.S. 488 (1874); *Burgess v. Equitable M. Ins. Co.,* 126 Mass. 70 (1878); *Child v. Sun Mar. Ins. Co.,* 3 Sandford Rep. 26 (1846).

63. *Davis v. Garrett* (1830) 130 E.R. 1456; *Morrison v. Shaw, Saville & Albion Co.* [1916] 2 K.B. 783, C.A.; *Turner v. Protection Ins. Co.,* 25 Me. 515 (1846); *Wiggin v. Amory,* 13 Mass. 117 (1816); *Brazier v. Clap,* 5 Mass. 1 (1809); cf. *Frenkel v. MacAndrews & Co., Ltd.* (1929) A.C. 545, H.L.; *The Indian City* [1930] 3 All E.R. 444, H.L.

64. *Hewitt v. London General Ins. Co.* (1925) 23 Ll.L. Rep. 243; *Thellusson v. Ferguson* (1780) 99 E.R. 231; *Middlewood v. Blakes* (1797) 101 E.R. 911; *Foster v. Wilmer* (1746) 93 E.R. 1162; *Simpson S. S. Co. v. Premier Underwriting Ass'n* (1905) 10 Com.Cas. 198; *Reed v. Weldon* (1869) 12 N.B.R. 458 (Can.); *Lee v. Grav,* 7 Mass. 348 (1811); *Marine Ins. Co. v. Tucker,* 7 U.S. 357 (1806); *North British & Marine Ins. Co. v. Baars,* 255 F. 625 (5th Cir., 1919); *Maryland Ins. Co. v. Woods,* 10 U.S. 29 (1810); *Hobart v. Norton,* 25 Mass. 159 (1829); *Winter v. Delaware M. S. Ins. Co.,* 30 Pa. 334 (1858).

65. Compare *Tusker v. Cunningham* (1819) 4 E.R. 32, H.L. and *Heselton v. Allnutt* (1813) 105 E.R. 18 with *Thames & Mersey Mar. Ins. Co. v. Van Laun* [1917] 2 K.B. 48 and *Hewitt v. London General Ins. Co.* (1925) 23 Ll.L. Rep. 243.

(1) Where several ports of discharge are specified by the policy, the ship may proceed to all or any of them, but, in the absence of any usage or sufficient cause to the contrary, she must proceed to them, or such of them as she goes to, in the order designated by the policy. If she does not, there is a deviation.[66]

(2) Where the policy is to "ports of discharge" within a given area, which are not named, the ship must, in the absence of any usage or sufficient cause to the contrary, proceed to them, or such of them as she goes to, in their geographical order. If she does not, there is a deviation.[67]

It should be noted that to revisit a port is to deviate.[68] Moreover, the risk insured must not be materially varied by voluntary action on the part of the assured. For example, in *African Merchants Co. v. British & Foreign Marine Insurance Co.*,[69] a ship was insured "at and from Liverpool to the west and/or south-west coast of Africa, during her stay and trade there, and back to a port of discharge in the United Kingdom." Upon arrival in Africa, the vessel discharged her outward cargo and then loaded the homeward cargo. However, in order to carry out a salvage venture, and upon orders of her owners, she stayed a month in Cabenda Bay. During her stay, she was driven from her moorings by a tornado and was a total loss. The delay was held to be a deviation which avoided the policy.

Unreasonable Delay. Section 48 makes it very clear that any unreasonable delay in prosecuting the voyage varies the risk and discharges the underwriter. It reads:

> In the case of a voyage policy, the adventure insured must be prosecuted throughout its course with reasonable dispatch, and, if without lawful excuse it is not so prosecuted, the insurer is discharged from liability as from the time when the delay becomes unreasonable.[70]

---

66. *Marsden v. Reid* (1803) 102 E.R. 716; *Beatson v. Haworth* (1791) *supra*, n. 62; *Kane v. Columbian Ins. Co.*, 2 Johns 264 (N.Y., 1807); *Cross v. Shutliffe*, 2 Bay (S.C.) 220 (S.C., 1799); *Hale v. Mercantile Ins. Co.*, 23 Mass. 121 (1828); *Marine Ins. Co. v. Stras*, 15 Va. 408 (1810).

67. *The Dunbeth* [1897] P. 133; *Houston v. New England Ins. Co.*, 22 Mass. 89 (1827); *Kane v. Columbian Ins. Co.*, 2 Johns 264 (N.Y., 1807).

68. *Deblois v. Ocean Ins. Co.*, 33 Mass. 303 (1835).

69. (1873) L.R. 8 Ex. Ch. 154.

70. *Mount v. Larkins* (1831) 131 E.R. 342, subsequent proceedings, (1832) 8 Bing. 195; *Hamilton v. Sheddon* (1837) 150 E.R. 1051; *African Merchants Co. v. British & Foreign Marine Ins. Co.* (1873) L.R. 8 Ex. 154, 1 Asp. M.L.C. 558; *Pearson v. Commercial Union Assur. Co.* (1876) 1 App. Cas. 498; *Motteau v. London Assur. (Governor & Co.)* (1739) 26 E.R. 343; *Chitty v. Selwyn & Martyn* (1742) 26 E.R. 617; *Palmer v. Fenning* (1833) 131 E.R. 685; *Hyderabad (Deccan) Co. v. Willoughby* (1899) 2 Q.B. 530; *DeWolf v. Archangel Ins. Co.* (1874) 43 L.J.Q.B. 147; *Palmer v. Marshall* (1832) 131 E.R. 415; *Grant v. King* (1802) 170 E.R. 682; *Suydam v. Marine Ins. Co.*, 2 Johns. 138 (N.Y., 1807); *Earl v. Shaw*, 1 Johns. 313 (N.Y., 1800); *Himely v. South Carolina Ins. Co.*, 8 S.C.L. 154 (S.C. 1817); *Seamans v. Loring*, F. Cas. No. 12,538 (C.C., Mass., 1816); *Burgess v. Equitable Mar. Ins. Co.*, 126 Mass. 70 (Mass., 1878); *Martin v. Delaware Ins. Co.*, F. Cas. No.

The law in the United States is the same.[71]
Whether the voyage has been prosecuted with reasonable dispatch is a question of fact. See Section 88 of the Act reading:

Where by this Act any reference is made to reasonable time, reasonable premium, or reasonable diligence, the question what is reasonable is a question of fact.[72]

Deviation or delay in prosecuting the voyage may, however, be excused in certain circumstances. Section 49 of the Act reads:

(1) Deviation or delay in prosecuting the voyage contemplated by the policy is excused—

(a) Where authorized by any special term in the policy,[73] or
(b) Where caused by circumstances beyond the control of the master and his employer,[74] or
(c) Where reasonably necessary in order to comply with an express or implied warranty,[75] or
(d) Where reasonably necessary for the safety of the ship or subject-matter insured,[76] or
(e) For the purpose of saving human life, or aiding a ship in distress where human life may be in danger,[77] or

---

9161 (C.C. Pa., 1808); *Settle v. St. Louis P. M. F. & L. Ins. Co.*, 7 Mo. 379 (Mo., 1842); *Oliver v. Maryland Ins. Co.*, 11 U.S. 487 (1813); *Natchez Ins. Co. v. Stanton*, 10 Miss. 340 (Miss., 1844); *Augusta I. & Bkg. Co. v. Abbott*, 12 Md. 348 (Md., 1858); *Kingston v. Girard*, 4 U.S. 274 (Pa., 1803)

71. See Phillips, Sec. 1002, and cases cited *supra*, n. 70.

72. *Motteau v. London Assur. (Governor & Co.)* (1739) 26 E.R. 343; *Phillips v. Irving* (1844) 135 E.R. 136; *Columbia Ins. Co. v. Catlett*, 25 U.S. 383 (1827).

73. *Puller v. Glover* (1810) 104 E.R. 49; *Hyderabad (Deccan) Co. v. Willoughby, supra*, n. 70; *Naylor v. Taylor* (1829) 109 E.R. 267; *Andrews v. Mellish* (1814) 128 E.R. 782, Ex. Ch.; *Leathly v. Hunter*, (1831) 131 E.R. 200, Ex. Ch.; *Rucker v. Allnutt* (1812) 104 E.R. 849; *Seccomb v. Provincial Ins. Co.*, 92 Mass. 305 (Mass., 1865); *Columbian Ins. Co. v. Catlett* (1827), *supra*, n. 72; *Child v. Sun Marine Ins. Co.*, 3 Sandford Rep. 26 (N.Y., 1846).

74. *Rickards v. Forestal Land, Timber and Railways Co.* [1941] 3 All E.R. 62, H.L.; *Delaney v. Stoddart* (1785) 99 E.R. 950; *Elton v. Brogden* (1747) 93 E.R. 1171; *Scott v. Thompson* (1805) 127 E.R. 429; *Schroeder v. Thompson* (1817) 129 E.R. 185; *Burgess v. Equitable Marine Ins. Co.*, 126 Mass. 70 (Mass., 1878); *Robinson v. Marine Ins. Co.*, 2 Johns. 88 (N.Y., 1806); *Graham v. Commercial Ins. Co.*, 11 Johns. 352 (N.Y., 1814); *Campbell v. Williamson*, 2 S.C.L. 237 (S.C., 1800); *Snowden v. Phoenix Ins. Co.*, 3 Binn. 457 (Pa., 1811).

75. *Bouillon v. Lupton* (1863) 143 E.R. 726; *Motteau v. London Assur. (Governor & Co)* (1739), *supra*, n. 72; *Phillips v. Irving* (1844) 135 E.R. 136; *Turner v. Protection Ins. Co.*, 25 Me. 515 (Me., 1846); *Akin v. Mississippi M. & F. Co.*, 4 Mart. N.S. 661 (La.,   ); *Taylor v. Lowell*, 3 Mass. 331 (Mass., 1807); *Merchants Ins. Co. v. Clapp*, 28 Mass. 56 (Mass., 1831); *Wiggin v. Amory*, 13 Mass. 118 (Mass., 1816).

76. *Phelps v. Hill* [1891] 1 Q.B. 605, C.A.; *Thomas v. Royal Exchange Assur.* (1814) 145 E.R. 1375; *Clason v. Simmonds* (1741) 101 E.R. 687; *Raine v. Bell* (1808) 103 E.R. 547; *Hall v. Franklin Ins. Co.*, 26 Mass. 466 (Mass., 1830); and see cases cited *supra*, n. 75.

77. *Scaramanga v. Stamp* (1880) 49 L.J.Q.B. 674; *The Orbona* (1853) 164 E.R. 93; *Lawrence v. Sydebotham* (1805) 102 E.R. 1204; *Goyon v. Pleasants*, F. Cas. No. 5647 (1814); *Reade v. Com-*

(f) Where reasonably necessary for the purpose of obtaining medical or surgical aid for any person on board the ship,[78] or (g) Where caused by the barratrous conduct of the master or crew, if barratry be one of the perils insured against.[79]

(2) When the cause excusing the deviation or delay ceases to operate, the ship must resume her course, and prosecute her voyage with reasonable dispatch.[80]

Policies frequently contain a liberty to "touch and stay," but such liberty is not, in and of itself, sufficient authorization to deviate. Rule 6, First Schedule, provides in this respect:

In the absence of any further license or usage, the liberty to touch and stay "at any port or place whatsoever" does not authorize the ship to depart from the course of her voyage from the port of departure to the port of destination.[81]

Phillips states the rule (Sec. 1007) as:

A general liberty to touch at a port or at ports, without specifying them, will justify touching only for the purposes of the voyage.[82]

From the relative antiquity of the cases cited under this heading, it will be apparent that voyage policies are not in vogue and have not been for some time. However, in the interest of completeness, it has been felt necessary to set forth the cases which have construed such policies.

"Held Covered" Clause. Although a deviation permits the underwriter to avoid the policy, this is not the case where the policy contains a "held cov-

---

mercial Ins. Co., 3 Johns. 352 (N.Y., 1808); *Mason v. The Blaireau,* 6 U.S. 240 (1804); *The Henry Ewbank,* F. Cas. No. 6376 (1833); *Williams v. Box of Bullion,* F.Cas. No. 17717 (D., Mass., 1843); *Perkins v. Augusta I. & Bkg. Co.,* 76 Mass. 312 (Mass., 1858); *Herman v. Western F. & M. Ins. Co.,* 13 La. 523 (La.,); see, also, 46 U.S.C. 728 (U.S. Salvage Act, 1912) and Maritime Conventions Act, 1911, Sec. 6, as respects the statutory duty of a master to assist persons in danger.

78. *Perkins v. Augusta I. & Bkg. Co, supra,* n. 77.

79. *Ross v. Hunter* (1790) 100 E.R. 879; *O'Connor v. Merchants Marine Ins. Co.* (1889) 16 S.C.R. 331 (Can.) (not necessary that barratry should be expressly excepted in a marine policy to relieve the underwriters of liability for such a loss); *Burgess v. Equitable M. Ins. Co.,* 126 Mass. 70 (Mass., 1878). And see Rule 11, First Schedule to Marine Insurance Act, 1906.

80. *Lavabre v. Wilson, Bize v. Fletcher, Lavabre v. Walter* (1779) 99 E.R. 185; *Delaney v. Stoddart* (1785), *supra,* n. 74; *Harrington v. Halkeld* (1778) 2 Park 639; *Graham v. Commercial Ins. Co.,* 11 Johns. 352 (N.Y., 1814).

81. *Gairdner v. Senhouse* (1810) 128 E.R. 7; *Leathly v. Hunter* (1831) 131 E.R. 200; *Solly v. Whitmore* (1821) 106 E.R. 1110; *Hammond v. Reid* (1820) 106 E. R. 865; *Williams v. Shee* (1813) 170 E.R. 1449, N.P.

82. See *Burgess v. Equitable Marine Ins. Co.* (1878), *supra,* n. 79; *Kettell v. Wiggin,* 13 Mass. 68 (Mass., 1816); *Seccomb v. Provincial Ins. Co.* (1865), *supra,* n. 73; *Robertson v. Columbian Ins. Co.,* 8 Johns. 491 (N.Y., 1811).

ered" clause such as will be found in the AIH form of policy (June, 1977) and the assured brings himself within the scope of the clause. The clause reads: The Vessel is held covered in case of any breach of conditions as to cargo, trade, locality, towage or salvage activities, or date of sailing, or loading or discharging cargo at sea, provided (a) notice is given to the Underwriters immediately following receipt of knowledge thereof by the Assured and (b) any amended terms of cover and any additional premium required by Underwriters are agreed to by the Assured.

A like clause appeared in the old Institute Clauses, Hull and Freight and a rather more simple version in the old Institute Cargo Clauses (F. P. A.).

The new Institute Cargo Clauses (A, B, and C) are rather more specific in terminology. For example, under all three forms, "held covered" language appears in several distinct clauses. Clause 8, the Transit Clause, provides:

This insurance shall remain in force (subject to termination as provided for above and to the provisions of Clause 9 below) during delay beyond the control of the Assured, any deviation, forced discharge, reshipment or transhipment and during any variation of the adventure arising from the exercise of a liberty granted to shipowners or charterers under the contract of affreightment.

The first portion of Clause 9, referred to above, the "Termination of Contract of Carriage Clause," emphasizes the importance, by italicized language, of prompt notice to underwriters. It reads in part:

If owing to circumstances beyond the control of the Assured either the contract of carriage is terminated at a port or place other than the destination named therein or the transit is otherwise terminated before delivery of the goods as provided for in Clause 8 above, then this insurance shall also terminate *unless prompt notice is given to the Underwriters and continuation of cover is requested when the insurance shall remain in force, subject to an additional premium if required by the Underwriters,* either . . .

Clause 10, entitled the "Change of Voyage Clause," covers the situation where the destination is changed by the assured. It reads:

Where, after attachment of this insurance, the destination is changed by the Assured, *held covered at a premium and on conditions to be arranged subject to prompt notice being given to the Underwriters.*

Lastly, as if to make assurance doubly sure, all three forms (A, B, and C) conclude with the emphasized admonition:

NOTE: It is necessary for the Assured when they become aware of an event which is "held covered" under this insurance to give prompt notice to the Underwriters and the right to such cover is dependent upon compliance with this obligation.

The new Institute Time Clauses (Hulls, 1/10/83) covers the subject in Clause 3, entitled "Breach of Warranty," which reads:

Held covered in case of any breach of warranty as to cargo, trade, locality, towage, salvage services or date of sailing, provided notice be given to the Underwriters immediately after receipt of advices and any amended terms of cover and any additional premium required by them be agreed.

The similarity of the held covered clause in the new Institute Hull form to the comparable clause in the AIH (June, 1977) form will be appreciated.

All of the held covered clauses, it will be noted, require immediate notice to the underwriters and payment of an additional premium, if required. If no notice is given, or the notice is not timely, the assured is precluded from the benefit of the clauses.[83]

The held covered clause protects a vessel owner from the harsh results of an inadvertent failure to comply with specified warranties in the policy, provided the breach is not wilful, the insured gives prompt notice of the breach, and agrees to pay an additional premium, if required. The fact that the assured became aware of the breach for the first time only after the loss occurred does not in and of itself prevent recovery.[84] Generally speaking, once a loss has occurred, and notice has been given, but there is nothing practicable which can be done on receipt of the notice by underwriters, the notice is given in sufficient time.[85]

In *Tinkerbell*,[86] the held covered clause in a hull policy held the insured covered in the advent of any inadvertent breach of warranty as to "cargo, trade, locality or date of sailing." The clause was held not applicable to a breach of a winter lay-up warranty wherein the assured had warranted that his vessel would be "laid-up and out of commission" from October 1 to April 1. The court noted that the lay-up warranty was not concerned with location but only with condition; i.e., had the vessel been winterized

---

83. *Bristol S. S. Corp. v. London Assurance*, 404 F.Supp. 749, 1976 AMC 448 (S.D.N.Y.); cf. *Mentz Decker & Co. v. Maritime Insurance Co.* (1910) 1 K.B. 132; *Hewitt v. London General Ins. Co., Ltd.* (1925) 23 Ll.L.Rep. 243, K.B.D.; see, also, *Thames & Mersey Marine Ins. Co. Ltd. v. Van Laun & Co.* [1905] [1917] 2 K.B. 48 n., 14 Asp. M.L.C. 14, n.; *Hood v. West End Motor Car Packing Co.*, (1917) 2 K.B. 38, 14 Asp. M.L.C. 12.

84. *Tinkerbell*, 533 F.2d 496, 1976 AMC 799 (9th Cir.); *Hewitt v. London General Insurance Co., Ltd.* (1925), *supra*, n. 83; see, also, *Chartered Bank of India v. Pac. Marine Ins. Co.* [1923] 2 D.L.R. 612, *aff'd* [1923] 4 D.L.R. 942 (Can., C.A.).

85. *Hewitt, supra*, n. 83.

86. 533 F.2d 496, 1976 AMC 799 (9th Cir.).

in accordance with local custom. There, the insured had entrusted his vessel to another with instructions to lay her up by October 1, but unbeknownst to the insured, mechanical difficulties had delayed the winter lay-up with the result that the vessel was totally lost in a storm on October 20.

A held covered clause covering a *variation* of the risk does not cover an *alteration* of that risk. See *Alluvials Mining Machinery Co. v. Stowe*,[87] where oil was actually shipped on deck at the shipper's risk but this fact was not disclosed to the underwriter when the insurance was effected. Hence, the nondisclosure voided the policy.[88]

What is a "reasonable" premium is a question of fact. See, Section 88, Marine Insurance Act, quoted *supra*. The rule for ascertainment of an extra premium was laid down in *Greenock S. S. Co. v. Maritime Ins. Co., Ltd.*,[89] to the effect that the parties must assume that a breach was known to them at the time when it happened, and ascertain what it then would have been reasonable to charge.

See, generally, Chapter VI, The Premium, and Section 31 of the Act, reading:

(1) Where an insurance is effected at a premium to be arranged, and no arrangement is made, a reasonable premium is payable.

(2) Where an insurance is effected on terms that an additional premium is to be arranged in a given event, and that event happens but no arrangement is made, then a reasonable additional premium is payable.

Voyage Policies on Goods. Generally speaking, under such policies the risk on goods attaches when they are loaded,[90] but the risk may attach earlier if the policy contains a "craft" clause or a "warehouse to warehouse" clause.

---

87. (1922) 10 Ll.L.Rep. 96.

88. Where the voyage on which the vessel sailed was not the voyage which was insured, the policy never attaches and any held covered clause in it would be ineffective. See, for example, *Simon Israel & Co. v. Sedgwick* (1893) 2 Q.B. 303, 7 Asp. M.L.C. 245.

89. [1903] 1 K.B. 367. And see *Mentz, Decker & Co. v. Maritime Ins. Co.*, [1910] 1 K.B. 132, and *Murray Oil Co. v. Hanover F.I. Co.*, 24 N.Y.S. 2d 763, 1941 AMC 1496 (N.Y.A.D.), modifying 24 N.Y.S.2d 101, 1940 AMC 1567.

90. The old Lloyd's S. G. form expressed the commencement of risk on goods as being "from the loading thereof." Rule 4, First Schedule to the Act, states:

Where goods or other moveables are insured "from the loading thereof," the risk does not attach until such goods or moveables are actually on board and the insurer is not liable for them in transit from the shore to the ship. See *Rucker v. London Assur. Co.* (1784) 126 E.R. 1368; followed in *Hurry v. Royal Exchange Assur. Co.* (1801) 170 E.R. 619, N.P.; *Richards v. Marine Ins. Co.*, 3 Johns. 307 (N.Y., 1808); *Vredenburg v. Gracie*, 4 Johns. 444 (N.Y., 1809).

Thus, goods on board a vessel when she enters the port of loading, having been loaded at an anterior port, are not covered. *Robertson v. French* (1803) 102 E.R. 779; *Langhorn v. Hardy* (1812) 128 E.R. 477; *Rickman v. Carstairs* (1833) 110 E.R. 931.

Under the old method of insuring in the English market, specific Institute Cargo clauses were appended to the Lloyd's S. G. form. Under the new Marine Policy Form, it is incumbent upon the underwriters to fill in the various blanks (see Appendix). One of the blanks to be filled in is: "Voyage or Period of Insurance." Presumably, appropriate language will be used to indicate at which point the risk begins. But, all three of the new cargo forms (A, B, and C) contain a Transit Clause, a Termination of Contract of Carriage Clause, a Change of Voyage Clause, and a Forwarding Charges Clause, each of which is discussed *infra*. Unless those specific clauses are physically deleted, or deleted by a specific endorsement, they would apply to the basic coverages. Consequently, under the new Marine Policy form, forms A, B, and C automatically include the more expanded coverages for cargo.

Nonetheless, the earlier cases relative to when the risk begins are instructive with respect to how the new policy language may be interpreted, In summary, the rules for construction are:

So long as the port of departure *(terminus a quo)* and port of destination *(terminus ad quem)* remain unchanged, an intention to deviate existing before the voyage begins has no effect on the policy attaching.[91] See, for example, *Hewitt v. London General Ins. Co., Ltd.*,[92] where there was an intent to deviate before the voyage began. The assurers paid on their policy and sued the reinsurers on the policy of insurance (which was subject to the same terms as the original policy). The court held that the intent to deviate was immaterial.[93]

Where the intention of the parties as expressed in the policy warrants a different interpretation with respect to when the risk attaches than "from the loading thereof," the courts construe the language in accordance with the expressed intention. For example, in *Gladstone v. Clay*,[94] the phrase used was "on board the ship wheresoever," and the expansion by the use of "wheresoever" was held to cover goods previously loaded at an anterior port.

Interestingly, where the policy is to attach "from the loading thereof," it can be made to attach to goods loaded at an anterior port by the expedient—not too practical in this era of high stevedoring costs—of discharg-

---

The rules applicable to policies on ships apply with respect to policies on goods insofar as the risk not attaching where the vessel sails from a place not specified in the policy, or sails for a different port of destination, or "deviates" after the voyage commences. See discussion, *supra*, with respect to Sections 43, 44, and 45 of the Marine Insurance Act. As to deviation, see discussion, *supra*, with respect to Sections 46 and 47.

91. Section 46, Marine Insurance Act, 1906.

92. (1925) 23 Ll.L.Rep. 243, K.B.D.

93. The American cases are to the same effect. See *Thompson v. Alsop*, 1 Root 64 (Conn., 1789); *Winter v. Delaware. Etc., Inc. Co.*, 30 Penn. St. 334 (Pa., 1858); *M'Fee v. South Carolina Ins. Co.*, 2 M'Cord So. C. 503 (S.C., 1823).

94. (1813) 105 E.R. 156.

ing the cargo onto the wharf and reloading.[95] However, simply hoisting the cargo on deck and then restowing it in the vessel will not qualify as this does not amount to a loading on board.[96]

An interesting point arose in *Cory & Sons v. Friedlander*,[97] where a clause in the policy read:

> The policy to pay the loss of such portion of the cargo as does not reach the destination of the said ship.

The assured contended that the clause extended the risk covered so as to make the underwriters liable for any part of the cargo which it could be proved did not reach the port of destination. The assurer contended that the loss had to fall within the risks specified in the body of the policy.

Upon arrival, the cargo was short 260 tons of briquettes out of a cargo of 1,301 tons loaded at the port of departure. The evidence indicated from the tally counts that every briquette loaded was actually discharged. The court was of a mind that a mistake in counting had been made and, therefore, the assured did not bear the burden of proving their case.

Compare *Curacao Tr. Co. v. Federal Ins. Co.*,[98] discussed *supra*, where the court held that the policy did not cover a shortage arising out of fraud of the warehouseman but only a shortage by reason of loss of the merchandise due to perils of the sea.

"Craft" Clauses. In the former Institute Cargo Clauses (F. P. A.), a "craft" clause was included reading:

> Including transit by craft, raft or lighter to or from the vessel. Each craft, raft or lighter to be deemed a separate insurance. The Assured are not to be prejudiced by any agreement exempting lightermen from liability.

Comparable clauses in American cargo policies are very similar and in many instances identical.

In the absence of such a clause, and a failure on the part of the assured to disclose to the underwriter that such an agreement with a lighterman was entered into, there is a concealment of a material fact which vitiates the policy.[99]

It should be emphasized that the lighterage must be the actual termination of the voyage insured and not merely for the purpose of storing

---

95. *Nonnen v. Kettlewell* (1812) 104 E.R. 1055.
96. *Murray v. Columbia Ins. Co.*, 11 Johns. 302 (N.Y., 1814).
97. (1922) 10 Ll.L.Rep. 40, K.B.D.
98. 137 F.2d 911, 1943 AMC 1050 (2d Cir.).
99. *Tate v. Hyslop* (1885) 15 Q.B.D. 368.

the goods temporarily in lighters or for the purpose of transhipping from one vessel to another for an onward voyage.[100]

A craft clause does not cover loss of cargo due to decay during a delay for repairs to the vessel necessitated by injuries received before any cargo is put on board.[101]

The risk while on a craft includes such risk as is usual for the purpose of loading or landing the cargo by lighters or other craft at the particular port in question.[102]

In *Thames & Mersey Marine Ins. Co. v. Pacific Creosoting Co.*,[103] a cargo policy was held to imply no warranty on the part of the assured of the seaworthiness of a lighter used in discharging cargo at the end of the voyage.

Warehouse to Warehouse, or "Transit" Clauses. It is almost universal today in cargo policies to extend the limits of coverage beyond those of the ordinary cargo policy by adding a "warehouse to warehouse," or a "transit" clause.

The new Institute Cargo clauses, A, B, and C contain a "Transit Clause" (Clause 8) with a "Termination of Contract of Carriage Clause" (Clause 9). The two clauses are identical in all three forms and do not differ too significantly from the prior Institute Cargo Clauses (F.P.A.). In that prior form, the usual warehouse to warehouse clause was incorporated in what was termed the "Transit Clause" and that clause, together with Clause 2 (Termination of Adventure Clause) is essentially the counterpart of the new Clauses 8 and 9 in the new forms.

The new "Transit Clause" and the "Termination of Contract of Carriage Clause" read as follows:

8. Transit Clause.

8.1 This insurance attaches from the time the goods leave the warehouse or place of storage at the place named herein for the commencement of the transit, continues during the ordinary course of transit and terminates either

8.1.1 on delivery to the Consignees' or other final warehouse or place of storage at the destination named herein,

---

100. See *Lindsay Blee Imports, Ltd. v. Motor Union Ins. Co., Ltd.* (1930) 37 Ll.L.Rep. 220 (goods merely stored in lighters), and *Houlder v. Merchants Marine Ins. Co.* (1886) 17 Q.B.D. 354 (goods transhipped from one vessel upon its arrival in port to another vessel for an ongoing voyage).

101. *Bluefield F. & S. S. Co. v. Western Assur. Co.*, 265 F. 221 (5th Cir., 1920).

102. See *Hurry v. Royal Exchange Assur.* (1901) 126 E.R. 1367 where the goods were transported by boats from Cronstadt to St. Petersburg.

103. 223 F. 561 (9th Cir., 1915).

8.1.2 on delivery to any other warehouse or place of storage, whether prior to or at the destination named herein, which the Assured elect to use either

8.1.2.1 for storage other than in the ordinary course of transit or

8.1.2.2 for allocation or distribution, or

8.1.3 on the expiry of 60 days after completion of discharge overside of the goods hereby insured from the oversea vessel at the final port of discharge,

whichever shall first occur.

8.2 If, after discharge overside from the oversea vessel at the final port of discharge, but prior to termination of this insurance, the goods are to be forwarded to a destination other than that to which they are insured hereunder, this insurance, whilst remaining subject to termination as provided for above, shall not extend beyond the commencement of transit to such other destination.

8.3 This insurance shall remain in force (subject to termination as provided for above and to the provisions of Clause 9 below) during delay beyond the control of the Assured, any deviation, forced discharge, reshipment or transhipment and during any variation of the adventure arising from the exercise of a liberty granted to shipowners or charterers under the contract of affreightment.

9. Termination of Contract of Carriage Clause. If owing to circumstances beyond the control of the Assured either the contract of carriage is terminated at a port or place other than the destination named therein or the transit is otherwise terminated before delivery of the goods as provided for in Clause 8 above, then this insurance shall also terminate *unless prompt notice is given to the Underwriters and continuation of cover is requested when the insurance shall remain in force, subject to an additional premium if required by the Underwriters,* either

9.1 until the goods are sold and delivered at such port or place, or, unless otherwise specially agreed, until the expiry of 60 days after arrival of the goods hereby insured at such port or place, whichever shall first occur, or

9.2 if the goods are forwarded within the said period of 60 days (or any agreed extension thereof) to the destination named herein or to any other destination, until terminated in accordance with the provisions of Clause 8 above.

It must be emphasized that, although the transit clause protects the goods insured beyond the limits fixed in the ordinary form of cargo policy, it does not enlarge the perils insured against, even though the goods may be covered while in transit on land. That is, unless the loss or damage occurs by reason of one of the included perils in the policy form, there is no coverage.

Although the clause is rather broadly drawn, it does not represent the extreme limits to which underwriters are willing to go in the insurance of cargo. For example, policies have been written so broadly as to encompass the risk of loss of raw materials from the mining site to ultimate destination, crops still growing in the fields and wool from "sheep's back."[104]

There are many cases interpreting the scope of the warehouse to warehouse, or transit, clauses. The following, although not an exhaustive compilation, will give the "flavor" of the decisions:

In *Ocean Marine Ins. Co. v. Lindo,*[105] under a warehouse to warehouse clause in the policy, it was held that the risk did not terminate when the cargo (cotton) was deposited in the custom house. Compare, however, *Safadi v. Western Assur. Co.,*[106] where the court reached an opposite conclusion because the evidence showed that the cargo (cotton goods) were left in a customs warehouse for ten weeks because the assured did not want to pay for them and purposely delayed.

In *Industrial Waxes, Inc. v. Brown,*[107] the underwriters were held liable under a broadly drawn transit clause where the damage occurred while the goods were delayed in customs awaiting release of American dollars, the court noting that where neither the open cover contract for a Lloyd's policy nor the certificate of insurance contained a restriction on the period during which the insured goods might be held in customs and a delay in customs was so common, such a delay would not discharge the underwriter. In *Commercial Trading v. Hartford Fire Ins. Co.,*[108] the coverage was to continue until the cargo was "unloaded at port of destination." The cargo was put in trucks furnished by the named assured meat importer, but the shipowner's representatives failed to first demand and receive from the named assured copies of order bills of lading covering the cargo. The court held that the policy was still in force where the loss occurred from misdelivery without first obtaining the order bills of lading. In *Dunbar Molasses Corp. v. Home Ins. Co. of New York,*[109] a policy insuring molasses in bulk, including risk of "loading and unloading," and accident to "conveyance" was held to cover a loss by escape from a broken

104. See, for example, *Gaunt & Co. v. British & Foreign Ins. Co.* [1921] 2 A.C. 41, H.L.
105. 30 F.2d 782, 1928 AMC 1335 (9th Cir., 1928).
106. (1933) 46 Ll.L.Rep. 140, K.B.D.
107. 160 F.Supp. 230, 1958 AMC 2391 (S.D.N.Y.), rev'd 258 F.2d 800 (2d Cir.).
108. 466 F.2d 1239, 1972 AMC 2495 (5th Cir.).
109. 3 F.Supp. 296 (S.D.N.Y., 1933).

section of the pipeline leading from the storage tank to a valve at the dock.

In *Phetteplace v. British & Foreign Marine Ins. Co.*,[110] the policy covered all shipments of oil from foreign ports to Philadelphia to Boston, or "via port or ports, and at and thence to Providence, with privilege of transhipment, including risk of craft to and from the ship or vessel; such craft to be considered a separate risk." The policy also covered "leakage amounting to five per cent on each barrel, over ordinary leakage, which is agreed to be 2 per cent." Other provisions of the policy were the usual perils clause and "not liable for particular average for leakage unless occasioned by stranding or collision with another vessel." It was held that the policy authorized oil shipped from Mediterranean ports to Philadelphia or Boston to be carried overland from either place to Providence—this being the shortest and safest route—and hence that the underwriter was liable for leakage under the policy although there was nothing to show whether it occurred on land or water.

In *Hamdi & Ibrahim Mango Co. v. Reliance Ins. Co.*,[111] the parties to a warehouse to warehouse insurance with war risks clauses attached, covering shipments of motor vehicles to Haifa in Palestine and then overland to Amman from port of shipment to port of discharge, amended the insurance certificates by substitution of "via Beirut" for "via Haifa." All negotiations were completed before the shipments arrived in Haifa. While in Haifa, the shipments were lost or destroyed due to "warlike operations" when still in course of shipment. It was held that the underwriter was obliged to cover the goods until reaching Amman via Beirut and the goods when laded in Haifa were still in the process of transhipment and expressly within the coverage of the war risks clauses. However, the storage and transportation costs resulting from the changed routing were held to be for the account of the assured.

However, in *Brammer Corp. v. Holland-American Ins. Co.*,[112] the goods had been removed and separated from the manufacturing area of the building by placing them in a shipping area where they were turned over to the control of a trucker. The trucker, for its own convenience, left the goods in the shipping area for a period of time during which they were damaged. It was held that the goods were not "in transit" and thus not within the coverage of the marine cargo policy which contained a warehouse to warehouse clause.

In *Greene v. Cheatham*,[113] under an open cargo policy containing a warehouse to warehouse clause, the assured was authorized to issue cer-

110. 23 R.I. 26, 49 A. 33 (R.I., 1901).

111. 291 F.2d 437, 1961 AMC 1987 (2d Cir.).

112. 228 N.Y.S.2d 512, 1962 AMC 1584 (N.Y.,1961).

113. 293 F.2d 933, 1961 AMC 2549 (2d Cir.), on remand, 316 F.2d 730, 1963 AMC 123 (2d Cir.).

tificates delineating the scope of coverage. It did so, with respect to frozen fish fillets, noting in the certificates " . . . from warehouse at any port or ports, place or places in the United Kingdom to warehouse at any port or ports, place or places in the World." The certificates provided coverage to the plaintiff consignees. After arrival in the United States, customers of the plaintiff rejected the shipment on grounds that some of the contents of the packages was "bad." At first instance, the trial court had held that the policy covered the overland transportation from the manufacturer's plant in Grimsby. The court of appeal reversed and remanded for further evidence as to the assured's extrinsic purpose and intent in the language used in the certificates. On remand, the court found that the fish had spoiled either while enroute overland to shipside or while being unloaded from lorries into the vessels, and that the assured had intended the certificates to provide cover during this period of time. However, the plaintiff consignees failed to notify the underwriter for a period of five months and on this ground the complaint was dismissed.[114]

Margo Manufacturing Corp. v. American Motorists Ins. Co., et al[115] involved an open cargo policy with a warehouse to warehouse clause. The liability limitation in the policy was $750,000. Goods worth in excess of $873,000 were destroyed by fire while in one of the warehouses. Plaintiff assured accepted in settlement $647,500 but later sued to recover the entire loss, contending that the settlement was void or voidable because principles of co-insurance did not apply; i.e., if plaintiff had a claim to a liquidated sum, the release was not supported by any consideration. The policy contained no co-insurance clause. The court held that the policy being a marine policy, under both English and American law no explicit clause was necessary to compel application of the principle of co-insurance. Thus, the plaintiff could not recover.

In *Shaver Transportation Co. v. Travelers Ins. Co.,*[116] the cargo policy was written on F. P. A. conditions covering a shipment of caustic soda in a barge under a contract of affreightment. The barge had previously been used for the transportation of tallow. The barge owner had the interior of the barge cleaned of all tallow residue, but, inadvertently, the cleaning contractor failed to cleanse the barge's intake lines of tallow residue. When the caustic soda was pumped from shoreside storage tanks into the barge, the tallow residue in the barge's intake lines contaminated the entire cargo. The cargo policy provided coverage for both the towing com-

---

114. The importance of early and careful inspection of goods by cargo receivers was also emphasized in *Castle & Cook Foods v. S. S. Tobias Maersk,* 491 F.Supp. 1305 (S.D.N.Y., 1980). See, also, *Folger Coffee Co. v. M/V Medi Sun,* 492 F.Supp. 988 (E.D.,La., 1980) (delay in removing coffee from a warehouse infested by rats).
115. 1978 AMC 1274 (S.D.N.Y.).
116. 481 F.Supp. 892, 1980 AMC 393 (D., Ore.).

pany and the shipper and contained a very broad warehouse to warehouse clause. Upon arrival at destination, the consignee refused to accept the shipment because of the contamination. In a suit on the cargo policy, emphasizing that the proximate cause of the loss was contamination—a peril not covered in the policy—the court held that the warehouse to warehouse clause did not enlarge the perils insured against even though the contamination occurred during the movement from shoreside tanks into the barge's holds.

The English form of warehouse to warehouse clause originally expressed the commencement of the risk as being "at port of shipment, unless otherwise stated."[117] Probably as a consequence of the decision in *Traders, supra,* the clause was amended to read: "at the place named in the policy for the commencement of the transit."[118]

In *Allgar Rubber Estates, Ltd. v. National Benefit Assurance Co., Ltd.,*[119] involving a policy on rubber from time of entry at the receiving house on the rubber plantation until safe delivery was taken by the purchaser in England, it was held that a delay of eight months in taking delivery, during which time the rubber was destroyed in a fire in a warehouse at destination, was not unreasonable.

In *Safadi v. Western Assurance Co.,*[120] the assured assignee of the policy purposely delayed in taking delivery of the goods for business reasons and the goods were destroyed by fire while in a customs warehouse. It was held the assured could not recover as the delay was not one arising from circumstances beyond the control of the assured.

In *Ide & Christie v. Chalmers & White,*[121] the court held that the usual Lloyd's policy includes a warehouse to warehouse clause; consequently, where the insuring conditions were that the policy would contain the "usual" Lloyd's conditions, but the policy risk was expressed to terminate on quays or warehouses or wharves within the limits of the port, it was held the policy did not conform to the contract to insure.

In *G. H. Renton & Co., Ltd. v. Black Sea and Baltic Gen. Ins. Co., Ltd.,*[122] timber was insured under the Timber Trade Federal Insurance Clauses of which one clause provided coverage for risks of non-delivery from the time of leaving the mill, etc., until "discharged at the port of destination;

---

117. See *In re Traders & Gen. Ins. Ass'n, Ltd.* (1924) 18 Ll.L.Rep. 450 and *Symington & Co. v. Union Ins. Soc. of Canton, Ltd.* (1928) 30 Ll.L.Rep. 280, 31 Ll.L.Rep. 179, C.A.
118. American policies are similarly claused and coverage starts when the goods leave the warehouse at the place named in the policy for the commencement of the transit. *Hillcrea Export & Import Co. v. Universal Ins. Co.,* 110 F.Supp. 204, 1953 AMC 799 (S.D.N.Y.), *aff'd* 212 F.2d 206, 1954 AMC 878 (2d Cir.); *Plata American Trading, Inc. v. Lancashire,* 214 N.Y.S. 2d 43, 1958 AMC 2329 (N.Y., 1958).
119. (1922) 10 Ll.L.Rep. 564, K.B.D.
120. (1933) 46 Ll.L.Rep. 140, K.B.D.
121. (1900) 5 Com.Cas. 212.
122. (1941) 1 All E.R. 149, K.B.D.

and whilst in transit by land and/or water to final destination there or in the interior." Upon arrival in London, and pursuant to the general custom there, the timber was discharged from the ship to the quay alongside and there stacked without regard to marks or description. Later, the timber was sorted and stored in a shed. Sometime later, the timber was counted whereupon it was found that some timbers were missing. The court held that the risk had terminated when the timber was discharged onto the quayside. Certainly, if the goods cease to be "in transit," they will no longer be covered by the policy even though not then delivered to final destination.[123]

The Marine Insurance Act, Sec. 59, expressly covers a transhipment by reason of necessity. It reads:

> Where, by a peril insured against, the voyage is interrupted at an intermediate port or place, under such circumstances as, apart from any special stipulation in the contract of affreightment, to justify the master in landing and re-shipping the goods or other moveables, or in transhipping them and sending them on to their destination, the liability of the insurer continues, notwithstanding the landing or transhipment.[124]

Unless some provision of the contract of affreightment is included in the policy, such as a "liberties" clause, the underwriter usually is not concerned with the affreightment contract.[125]

The cases on protection during land transit are fairly numerous.[126] Compare, however, *Wingate v. Foster*[126a] where the policy contained a special clause to protect salvage pumps. The salvage pumps were put aboard the salved vessel which later sank. It was held that there was a deviation as

123. See *Bartlet and Partners v. Meller*, [1961] 1 Lloyd's Rep. 487; *Deutsch-Australische Dampschiffs-gesellschaft v. Sturge* [1913] 109 L.T. 905, 12 Asp. M.L.C. 453; *Westminster Fire Office v. Reliance Marine Ins. Co.* (1903) 19 T.L.R. 668, C.A.; *Brammer Corp. v. Holland-American Ins. Co.*, 228 N.Y.S. 2d 512, 1962 AMC 1584 (N.Y., 1961); *Fireman's Fund Ins. Co. v. Service Transp. Co.*, 466 F.Supp. 934 (D., Md., 1979); *St. Maurice Valley Paper Co. v. Continental Ins. Co.*, 13 F.Supp. 346, aff'd 85 F.2d 1018 (2d Cir.); *Crew Levick Co. v. Brit. & For. Mar. Ins. Co. of Liverpool*, 103 F. 48 (1896); *Wiggins Teape Australia Pty., Ltd. v. Baltica Ins. Co., Ltd.* [1970] 2 N.S.W.R. 77 (Aus.); *Leaders Shoes (Aust.) Pty., Ltd. v. National Ins. of N. Z., Ltd.* [1968] 1 N.S.W.R. 344 (Aus.) ("transit" not concluded when loaded upon a lorry at destination and thereafter some of the goods were stolen).
124. *Oliverson v. Brightman, Bold v. Rotherham* (1846) 115 E.R. 1066; *Australian Agriculture Co. v. Saunders* (1875) L.R. 10 C.P. 668; *Plantamour v. Staples* (1781) 99 E.R. 507; *Houlder v. Merchants Marine Ins. Co.* (1886) 17 Q.B.D. 354; c.f. *Bold v. Claxton* (1850) 16 L.T.O.S. 7; *Betesh v. Fire Ass'n of Philadelphia*, 187 F.2d 526 (2d Cir., 1951).
125. See *Neale & Wilkinson v. Rose* (1898) 3 Com.Cas. 236.
126. *Rodoconachi v. Elliott* (1874) 31 L.T. 239; *Simon, Isreal & Co. v. Sedgwick* [1893] 1 Q.B. 303; *Schloss Bros. v. Stevens* [1906] 2 K.B. 665 (policy covered "all risks by land and by water"); *Hyderabad (Deccan) Co. v. Willoughby* [1899] 2 Q.B. 530; *Richardson v. C.P.R.* (1914) 7 O.W.N. 458, 20 D.L.R. 580 (Can.) (on appeal, new trial ordered).
126a. (1878) 2 Q.B. 582, C.A.

the policy comprehended the pumps would be insured while in transit on board the salving vessel, while engaged in salvaging operations, and for the return journey—but only while on the salving vessel.

"All Risks" Coverage

Cargoes are frequently insured against "all risks." Although the precise wording in policies may vary (as will be readily seen from the cases), the wording found in the old Institute Cargo Clauses (All Risks), Clause 5, is relatively standard. Clause 5 reads:

> This insurance is against all risks of loss or damage to the subject-matter insured but shall in no case be deemed to extend to cover loss, damage or expense proximately caused by delay or inherent vice or nature of the subject-matter insured. Claims recoverable hereunder shall be paid irrespective of percentage.

A typical American all risks clause reads:

> Against all risks of physical loss or damage from any external cause irrespective of percentage, but excluding, nevertheless, the risks of war, strikes, riots, seizure, detention, and other risks excluded by the F. C. & S. Warranty and the S. R. & C. C. Warranty in this policy, excepting to the extent that such risks are specifically covered by endorsement.

The new Institute Cargo Clauses (A) are rather more specific in the exclusions as well as in the breadth of those exclusions. The new clauses in this respect read:

> 1. This insurance covers all risks of loss of or damage to the subject-matter insured except as provided in Clauses 4, 5, 6, and 7 below.

Clauses 4, 5, 6, and 7 appear in the new form under the heading "Exclusions" and read as follows:

> 4. In no case shall this insurance cover
>
> 4.1 loss damage or expense attributable to wilful misconduct of the Assured
> 4.2 ordinary leakage, ordinary loss in weight or volume, or ordinary wear and tear of the subject-matter insured
> 4.3 loss damage or expense caused by insufficiency or unsuitability of packing or preparation of the subject-matter insured (for the purpose of this Clause 4.3 "packing" shall be deemed to include stowage in a container or liftvan but only when such stowage is carried out prior to attachment of this insurance or by the Assured or their servants)

4.4 loss damage or expense caused by inherent vice or nature of the subject-matter insured

4.5 loss damage or expense proximately caused by delay, even though the delay be caused by a risk insured against (except expenses payable under Clause 2 above)

4.6 loss damage or expense arising from insolvency or financial default of the owners managers charterers or operators of the vessel

4.7 loss damage or expense arising from the use of any weapon of war employing atomic or nuclear fission and/or fusion or other like reaction or radioactive force or matter.

5.

5.1 In no case shall this insurance cover loss damage or expense arising from unseaworthiness of vessel or craft unfitness of vessel craft conveyance container or liftvan for the safe carriage of the subject-matter insured, where the Assured or their servants are privy to such unseaworthiness or unfitness, at the time the subject-matter is loaded therein.

5.2 The Underwriters waive any breach of the implied warranties of seaworthiness of the ship and fitness of the ship to carry the subject-matter insured to destination, unless the Assured or their servants are privy to such unseaworthiness or unfitness.

6. In no case shall this insurance cover loss damage or expense caused by

6.1 war civil war revolution rebellion insurrection, or civil strife arising therefrom, or any hostile act by or against a belligerent power

6.2 capture seizure arrest restraint or detainment (piracy excepted), and the consequences thereof or any attempt thereat

6.3 derelict mines torpedoes bombs or other derelict weapons of war.

7. In no case shall this insurance cover loss damage or expense

7.1 caused by strikers, locked-out workmen, or persons taking part in labour disturbances, riots or civil commotions

7.2 resulting from strikes, lock-outs, labour disturbances, riots or civil commotions

7.3 caused by any terrorist or any person acting from a political motive.

It will be seen that the new Institute Cargo Clauses (A), while stating coverage in rather broad terms, also exclude coverage in equally broad terms. Of particular interest is the exclusion in paragraph 4.6 with respect to loss, damage, or expense "arising from insolvency or financial default of the owners managers charterers or operators of the vessel." It has long been the belief in the London market (and the belief of American attorneys experienced in the marine insurance field) that under an all risks policy, the assured would be covered for loss, damage, or expense proximately caused by the insolvency or financial default of the shipowner or operator of the carrying vessel.[127] Exclusion 4.6 of the new form makes "assurance doubly sure" that under the new form no coverage is provided with respect to such risks of insolvency or financial default.

Notwithstanding the all-inclusive nature of the words "all risks," not all risks are covered, only those arising from *fortuitous accident or casualty* resulting in damage or loss attributable to an external cause. However, where all risks are covered, the plaintiff discharges the burden of proof when he proves that the loss was caused by some event covered by the general expression and he is not bound to go further and prove the *exact* nature of the accident or casualty which, in fact, occasioned the loss.[128] This does not mean, however, that the plaintiff can rest upon his laurels if the underwriter comes forward and presents theories which would account for the loss being due to normal transit risks. In that event, the plaintiff must satisfy the trier of fact that the theories are neither right nor logical.[129]

An all risks clause covers risks, not certainties, and purports to cover losses only from extraordinary and fortuitous casualties of the sea; losses occasioned by the ordinary circumstances of a voyage are not indemnified.[130]

---

127. See, in this connection, *London and Provincial Leather Processes, Ltd. v. Hudson*, (1939) 2 K.B. 724, 109 L.J.K.B. 100 (dressing firm to which skins were sent for processing went bankrupt; subcontractors retained them under a lien for payment; German administrator in bankruptcy then seized other skins belonging to the plaintiff/assured. Held: wrongful conversion a covered peril).

128. *British and Foreign Marine Ins. Co. v. Gaunt* [1921] A.C. 41, H.L.; *Theodorou v. Chester* [1951] 1 Lloyd's Rep. 204, K.B.D.

129. *Theodorou v. Chester, supra,* n. 128.

130. *Anders v. Poland*, 181 So.2d 879, 1966 AMC 1867 (La.,App.); *British and Foreign Marine Ins. Co. v. Gaunt, supra,* n. 128; *Berk (F. W.) & Co., Ltd. v. Style* [1955] 3 All E.R. 625, [1955] 2 Lloyd's Rep. 382 (inherent vice in bags used to ship kieselguhr); *Greene v. Cheatham*, 293 F.2d 933, 1961 AMC 2549 (2d Cir.) (does not include an undisclosed event existing prior to coverage or the consummation during the period of coverage of an indwelling fault in the goods existing prior to inception of coverage).

The cases involving all risks policies are exceedingly numerous.[131] Attention is specifically directed to such cases as *Victoria Overseas Trading Co., Pty., Ltd. v. Southern Pacific Ins. Co., Ltd.*,[132] where the all risks policy was on a shipment of ashtrays and was endorsed with a clause "including breakage." The ashtrays were packed in cardboard containers which was the usual way to package such cargoes. Approximately one-third of the ashtrays were broken or damaged in transit and the underwriter denied liability. The court held that the endorsement "including breakage" rendered the underwriter liable for breakage caused by ordinary, as well as extraordinary, circumstances of handling. In addition, the assured was awarded the amount claimed for checking and salving the undamaged portion of the shipment.

In *Overseas Commodities, Ltd. v. Style*,[133] tins of pork were insured under an all risks policy including inherent vice; nonetheless, the court held that the underwriters could not have intended to cover loss by inherent vice developing anytime in the future since such pork products necessarily contained their own seeds of ultimate destruction if not consumed within a limited period of time.

In *Curacao Tr. Co. v. Federal Ins. Co.*,[134] there was a non-delivery of cargo by reason of fraud on the part of a warehouseman. The court held

---

131. See *Jacob v. Gaviller* (1902) 87 L.T. 26; *British and Foreign-Marine Ins. Co. v. Gaunt, supra*, n. 128; *Schloss v. Stevens* [1906] 2 K.B. 665; *In re National Benefit Assurance Co., Ltd. (Application of H.L. Sthry)* (1933) 45 Ll.L.Rep. 147, Ch. D.; *Nakasheff v. Continental Ins. Co.*, 89 F.Supp. 87, 1954 AMC 986 (S.D.N.Y.); *Bershad Int. Corp. v. Commercial Union*, 1960 AMC 2446 (N.Y., Sup., 1960); *Wigle v. Aetna Casualty & Surety*, 177 F.Supp. 932, 1959 AMC 2270 (E.D.,Mich.); *Mellon v. Federal Ins. Co.*, 14 F.2d 997 (S.D.N.Y., 1915); *Morrison Grain Co. v. Utica Mut. Ins. Co.*, 632 F2d 424, 1982 AMC 658 (5th Cir.); *Mayeri v. Glens Falls Ins. Co.*, 85 N.Y.S. 2d 370 (N.Y., 1948); *Norwich Union Fire Ins. Soc. v. Board of Commissioners*, 141 F.2d 600 (5th Cir., 1944); *Aetna Ins. Co. v. Sachs*, 186 F.Supp. 105 (E.D.,Mo., 1960); *Gillespie & Co. v. Continental Ins. Co.*, 176 N.Y.S. 2d 146, 1958 AMC 2437 (N.Y., 1958); *Berkshire Chemicals v. Lloyds*, 337 N.Y.S. 2d 701 (App. Div., 1972), *aff'd* 356 N.Y.S. 2d 295 (N.Y., 1974); *C.H. Leavell & Co. v. Fireman's Fund Ins. Co.*, 372 F.2d 784 (9th Cir., 1967); *Quattrociocchi v. Albany Ins.*, 1983 AMC 1152 (N.D.,Cal); *Heindl-Evans v. Reliance Ins. Co.*, 1980 AMC 2823 (E.D.,Va.); *Nautilus v. Edinburgh Ins.*, 673 F2d 1314, 1982 AMC 696 (4th Cir.); *Northwestern v. Chandler*, 1982 AMC 1631 (N.D.,Cal); *Consolidated Int'l v. Falcon*, 1983 AMC 270 (S.D.N.Y.); *I. Q. Originals v. Boston Old Colony*, 185 AD (2d) 21, 1983 AMC 580 (St.,N.Y.); *Fruehauf v. Royal Exchange*, 704 F2d 1168, 1984 AMC 1194 (9th Cir.); *Grand Reserve v. Hartford Fire*, 1984 AMC 1408 (N.D., Ill.); *Redna Marine Corp. v. Poland*, 46 F.R.D. 81, 1969 AMC 1809 (S.D.N.Y.); *Ajiba Coussa v. Westchester Fire Ins. Co.*, 1962 AMC 1805 (S.D.N.Y.); *Goldman v. Rhode Island Ins. Co.*, 100 F.Supp. 196 (E.D.,Pa., 1951); *General American Transp. Co. v. Sun Ins. Office, Ltd.*, 239 F. Supp. 844 (E.D., Tenn., 1965), *aff'd* 369 F.2d 906 (6th Cir., 1966); *Contractors Realty v. I.N.A.*, 469 F.Supp. 1287, 1979 AMC 1864 (S.D.N.Y.); *Teneria etc. v. Home Ins. Co. et al*, 136 N.Y.S.2d 574, 1955 AMC 328 (N.Y., 1954); *Essex House v. St. Paul F. & M. Ins. Co.*, 404 F.Supp. 978 (S.D., Ohio, 1975); *Atlantic Lines, Ltd. v. American Motorists*, 547 F.2d 11, 1976 AMC 2522 (2d Cir.); *Chute v. North River Ins. Co.*, 214 N.W. 473, 1927 AMC 1285 (St., Minn.); *Cyclops Corp. v. Home Ins. Co.*, 352 F. Supp. 931 (W.D., Pa., 1973); *Employers Casualty Co. v. Holm*, 393 S.W. 2d 363 (St., Tex., 1965); *Petrofina (U.K.) Ltd. v. Magnaload Ltd.*, [1983] 2 Lloyd's Rep. 91 (non-marine).

132. [1964-65] N.S.W.R. 824 (Aus.).

133. [1958] 1 Lloyd's Rep. 546.

134. 137 F.2d 911, 1943 AMC 1050 (2d Cir.).

that such fraud was not a risk contemplated in an all risks policy.

In *Mathis v. Hanover Ins. Co.*,[135] the all risks policy was on a yacht. Proof by the plaintiff/assured that the vessel was afloat and in good condition just prior to the sinking raised a presumption that the sinking was caused by some extraordinary occurrence.

However, in *Nevers v. Aetna Ins. Co.*,[136] it was held that an all risks policy on a yacht did not warranty the *quality* of an owner's title and the owner was not covered when he lost his vessel by reason of a defective title.

In *Bertie Kay*,[137] it was held that a hull policy covering "perils of the seas" and "all other perils, losses and misfortunes" did not convert the policy into an all risks policy.

And, in *Caballero v. Travelers F. I. Co.*,[138] where the policy was on an all risks basis on hosiery, coverage was denied because the assured breached an express warranty to ship by air for a portion of the journey.

Attention is called to Sec. 55(2) (c) of the Marine Insurance Act, 1906, reading:

> Unless the policy otherwise provides, the insurer is not liable for ordinary wear and tear, ordinary leakage and breakage, inherent vice or nature of the subject-matter insured, or for any loss proximately caused by rats or vermin, or for any injury to machinery not proximately caused by maritime perils.

The policy did otherwise provide in *De Monchy v. Phoenix Ins. Co. of Hartford*,[139] where the certificate of insurance on barrels of turpentine had a provision reading "to pay leakage from any cause in excess of 1 per cent." Liability was denied on the grounds that "leakage" meant visible leakage on the outside of the barrels at the time of discharge. The House of Lords held otherwise. And the policy did "otherwise provide"in *Soya G.M.B.H. Kommanditgesellschaft v. White (The Corfu Island)*[140] where the policy insured against, *inter alia*, heat, sweat, and spontaneous combustion, known collectively as the "HSSC Clauses," for damage to a cargo of soya beans. The cargo arrived in a damaged condition. The underwriters defended on the grounds that the cargo had been shipped in such a condition that it was unable to withstand the ordinary incidents of the voyage from Indonesia to Europe; i.e., the cargo was inherently vicious and therefore not covered because of Sec. 55(2) (c) of the Act. The defense failed on the facts, the judge considering that underwriters had not estab-

---

135. 127 Ga. App. 89, 192 S.E. 2d 510 (St.,Ga., 1972).
136. 14 Wash. App. 906, 546 P.2d 1240 (St.,Wash., 1976).
137. 106 F.Supp. 244, 1952 AMC 1812 (E.D.N.C.).
138. 1951 AMC 1825 (NYM).
139. (1929) 34 Ll.L.Rep. 201, H.L.
140. [1980] 1 Lloyd's Rep. 491, *aff'd* [1982] 1 Lloyd's Rep. 136 (C.A.); *aff'd* [1983] 1 Lloyd's Rep. 122, H.L.

lished inherent vice and the damage was not, therefore, inevitable. However, interestingly, the court at first instance was obviously prepared to hold that as long as it was established that the damage was not inevitable, the HSSC Clauses would cover the loss, even if the damage to the cargo had been proximately caused by inherent vice in the cargo. That is, the express coverage against heat, sweat, and spontaneous combustion was a sufficient expression of intent to override the contrary provisions of the inherent vice exclusion of Section 55 of the Act. Contrast, however, *Nakasheff v. Continental Ins. Co.*,[141] where the policy was held not to cover leakage of cargo by expansion due to heat while in the lawful custody of the collector of customs who had detained it because of an under-declaration of value at the time of entry.

Goodman v. Fireman's Fund Ins. Co.,[142] contains a valuable and instructive discussion of proximate causation under a yacht all risks policy. In that case, a yacht insured against all risks sank during lay-up in winter months because the assured negligently failed to drain the seawater cooling system. As a consequence, the piping system froze and broke, permitting water to enter the hull. The policy contained an exclusion against damage caused by freezing.

The court held that the proximate cause of the sinking was the negligence of the owner (an insured peril) which caused an uninsured peril (freezing). Thus, the proximate cause of the loss was the insured peril because it was the predominant cause. The court said, in part:

> When two or more causes combine to cause a loss, one of which is insured against while the other is not, the loss is not insured unless the covered cause is the predominant efficient cause of the loss . . . We think plaintiff's negligence was the predominant efficient cause of the sinking. While freezing was an intervening cause in the series of events, it was not unforeseeable.

However, the court denied recovery because the assured violated the lay-up warranty in failing to close the sea valves as a part of the winterizing program, something which was found to have been a custom in the Chesapeake Bay region.

Voyage Policies on Ships

The rules and decisions with respect to the inception of the risk on vessels under a voyage policy have been discussed earlier under the heading

---

141. 89 F.Supp. 87, 1954 AMC 986 (S.D.N.Y.). See, also, *Traders and General Ins. Ass'n. v. Bankers and General Ins. Co.* [1921] 9 Ll.L.Rep. 223, involving a reinsurance policy containing a clause insuring against "leakage in excess of 2 per cent over trade ullage."
142. 600 F.2d 1040, 1979 AMC 2534 (4th Cir.).

"Voyage Policies." The termination of the risk on a vessel, under the old Lloyd's standard form, read: "when she hath moored at anchor twenty-four hours in good safety." Consequently, the ship must be moored and must have then been in "good safety" before the twenty-four hours begins to run.

The risk on a vessel under a policy to a place generally, without any provision as to her safety there, terminates on the vessel being safely anchored at her port of destination in the usual place and manner.[143] Thus, a ship insured to Havana came to anchor near the Morro Castle at the entrance of the harbor where all vessels are obligated to wait until they are visited by the health officers and those from the customs house. It is not, however, considered a place of safety nor do vessels discharge their cargo there. After remaining there for more than one day, and before the ship had been visited and admitted to entry, she was wrecked. It was held that the risk had not terminated.[144] Whether or not a vessel has "arrived" is a question of fact.[145] Being moored in safety is to have the opportunity of unloading. Consequently, in *Waples v. Eames*[146] where a vessel was ordered into quarantine within twenty-four hours of her arrival in London whereupon her crew deserted her and she did not get out of quarantine until eighteen days later, it was held that the risk continued during the quarantine and thereafter until she should have been moored twenty-four hours in safety after the expiration of the quarantine.

The intention of the parties as to the last port of discharge governs.[147] However, the parties may also agree upon a new or substituted port of discharge.[148]

Mooring in good safety means moored in physical safety. A vessel arriving in a sinking condition which thereafter sinks is not moored "in good safety."[149] Safe arrival and being moored in good safety may comprehend arrival and anchoring at a port which is an open roadstead where vessels must anchor and discharge part of their cargo by lighters in order to reduce their drafts sufficiently to go to an inner basin. Thus, a

143. *Bill v. Mason*, 6 Mass. 313 (Mass., 1810); *Lindsay v. Janson* (1859) 157 E.R. 1016; *Dickey v. United Ins. Co.*, 11 Johns. 358 (N.Y., 1814); *Zacharie v. Orleans Ins. Co.*, 5 Mart. N.S. 637 (La., 1827); *Stone v. Marine Ins. Co. Ocean, Ltd. of Gothenburg* (1876) 45 L.J.Q.B. 361; *Samuel v. Royal Exchange Assurance* (1828) 108 E.R. 987; *Moore v. Taylor* (1834) 110 E.R. 1117; *Cruickshank v. Janson* (1810) 127 E.R. 1093; *Whitwell v. Harrison* (1848) 154 E.R. 433; *Marten v. Vestey Bros. of Nome, Alaska v. Maritime Ins. Co.*, 156 F. 710 (W.D.,Wash, 1907); *Standard Oil Co. of N.J. v. St. Paul F. & M. Ins. Co.*, 59 F.Supp. 470, opinion supplemented 64 F.Supp. 230 (S.D.N.Y., 1945); *Crocker v. Sturge* (1897) 1 Q.B. 330.
144. *Dickey v. United Ins. Co.*, 11 Johns. 358 (N.Y., 1814).
145. *Lindsay v. Janson* (1859) 157 E.R. 1016.
146. (1745) 93 E.R. 1158.
147. *Brown v. Vigne* (1810) 104 E. R. 110.
148. *Stone v. Marine Ins. Co. Ocean Ltd of Gothenburg* (1876) 45 L.J.Q.B. 361; *Kynance Sailing Ship Co. v. Young* (1911) 104 L.T. 397; *Crocker v. Sturge* (1897) 1 Q.B. 330.
149. *Shawe v. Felton* (1801) 102 E.R. 310.

loss after such arrival and before moving to the inner basin is not covered.[150] But in *Meigs v. Mutual Marine Ins. Co.*,[151] the vessel could not come into the wharf which was her place of final destination because of insufficient depth of water. After being lightened and while proceeding into the wharf, she was lost due to a peril insured against. It was held that the policy covered as merely reaching the harbor was not arriving; she must reach the particular place or point which was the ultimate destination.

The good safety clause may take different forms and often is extended beyond the twenty-four hours time period. See, for example, *Lidgett v. Secretan*,[152] where the risk was extended to thirty days after arrival with the usual twenty-four hour mooring clause. The vessel arrived in port having sustained damage at sea. Unloading her cargo took a number of days after which she was removed to drydock for repairs. After thirty days had expired, she was lost by fire. It was held that the underwriters were discharged as she had been moored in good safety for more than twenty-four hours—although in a damaged condition—and more than thirty days had elapsed before her loss.[153]

Voyage Policies on Freight

The rules and decisions with respect to the inception of the risk on freight have been discussed earlier under the general heading "Voyage Policies." As noted, the term "freight" includes freight due under a bill of lading as well as chartered freight and the shipowner's profit from the carriage of his own goods.

Policies on freight continue to cover until the contract of carriage has been completed, broken up, or abandoned. That is, for so long as the goods remain in the custody of the shipowner and exposed to perils insured under the policy.[154] When the freight has been earned, the underwriter has no further interest in it.[155]

---

150. *Bramhall v. Sun Marine Ins. Co.*, 104 Mass. 510 (Mass.).
151. 56 Mass. 439 (Mass., 1870). See, also, *Mariatigui v. Louisiana Ins. Co.*, 28 La. 65 (La., 1835).
152. (1870) 22 L.T. 272.
153. See, also, *Gambles v. Ocean Marine Ins. Co. of Bombay* (1876) 45 L.J.Q.B. 366; *Cornfoot v. Royal Exchange Assur. Corp.* [1904] 1 K.B. 50; *Mercantile Marine Ins. Co. v. Titherington* (1864) 122 E.R. 1015; *Carapanayoti & Co., Ltd. v. Comptoir Commercial Andre & Cie, S.A.* [1971] 1 Lloyd's Rep. 327.
154. *Atty v. Lindo* (1805) 127 E.R. 415.
155. *Patapsco Ins. Co. v. Biscoe*, 7 Gill & J. 293 (Md., 1835); *Mayo v. Marine F. & M. Ins. Co.*, 4 Mass. 374 (Mass., 1808).

There is no impediment to insuring freight for only a part of a voyage.[156] Moreover, freight may be and frequently is insured under a time policy.[157]

Under English practice (but not under American law), freight is not granted if the entire voyage is not performed; i.e., part payment of freight or freight *pro rata itineris peracti* is not made predicated upon part performance of the voyage. This does not preclude, however, a cargo owner from agreeing voluntarily to receiving his cargo short of destination upon payment of an agreed amount of partial freight.[158] In fact, this is frequently done by a cargo owner in order to obtain possession of his cargo inasmuch as the vessel owner has a right to retain possession for a reasonable period of time if a possibility exists of forwarding them to destination and thus earning the freight.

Where the vessel is a total or constructive total loss, the master has a duty to earn the freight by seeking another vessel to carry the goods to destination, but if another vessel cannot be found in the vicinity, or the expense of forwarding by another vessel would exceed the freight which would have been earned had the voyage been completed, then the underwriters are liable for the whole loss of freight.[159]

Since the shipowner is responsible only for the transportation of the cargo, the freight will be due on its delivery at the port of destination even though the cargo may be diminished in value by decay or damage from insured perils, and even though it may have become of no value on arrival at the port of destination so long as it is delivered in *specie;* i.e., articles of the same kind as shipped and not mere remains of its destruction or decay.[160]

Where the master or shipowner voluntarily relinquishes the cargo to the shipper and thus has no claim against the cargo owners for freight earned, the underwriter on freight is discharged. Consequently, the risk on freight is terminated by the master's action in prematurely giving up the voyage and delivering the cargo at an intermediate port.[161]

---

156. *Taylor v. Wilson* (1812) 104 E.R. 867; *Gordon v. American Ins. Co. of New York*, 4 Den. 360 (N.Y., 1847).

157. See *Michael v. Gillespy* (1857) 140 E.R. 562.

158. *The Mohawk*, 75 U.S. 153, 19 L.ed. 406 (1868); *The Joseph Farwell*, 31 F. 844 (D.,Ala., 1887); *M'Gaw v. Ocean Ins. Co.*, 40 Mass. 405 (Mass., 1839); *Teasdale v. Charleston Ins. Co.*, 4 S.C.L. 190 (S.C., 1807); *Merchants M. Ins. Co. v. Butler*, 20 Md. 41 (Md., 1862); *Hurtin v. Union Ins. Co.*, F.Cas. No. 6942 (Pa., 1806); *McKibbin v. Peck*, 39 N.Y. 262 (N.Y., 1868). And see *Herbert v. Hallett*, 3 Johns. 93 (N.Y., 1802); *Griswold v. New York Ins. Co.*, 1 Johns. 205 (N.Y., 1806).

159. *Hugg v. Augusta Ins. & Banking Co. of City of Augusta*, 48 U.S. 595 (1849); *Lockwood v. Atlantic M. Ins. Co.*, 47 Mo. 50 (Mo., 1870); *Willard v. Millers & M. Ins. Co.*, 24 Mo. 561 (Mo., 1857); *Jordan v. Warren Ins. Co.*, F.Cas. No. 7524.

160. *Hugg v. Augusta Ins. & Banking Co. of City of Augusta*, 48 U.S. 595 (1849).

161. *Jordan v. Warren Ins. Co.* (1840) *supra; Lord v. Neptune Ins. Co.*, 76 Mass. 109 (Mass., 1857); *Griswold v. New York Ins. Co.* (N.Y., 1806), *supra; M'Gaw v. Ocean Ins. Co.* (Mass., 1839)

For further cases on freight insurance, see Chapter VII, Insurable Interest; Chapter XVIII, Actual and Constructive Total Loss; Chapter XX, Sue and Labor Clause; and Chapter XXII, Particular Average.

Time Policies

Time policies on vessels are much more common than voyage policies. The attaching of the policy and the duration of the risk depend upon the terms of the policy; e.g., "from midnight, January 1st, 1979 to midnight, December 31st, 1979." Frequently, the policy contains a "continuation" clause such as will be found in the AIH form, June 2, 1977, reading:

> Should the Vessel at the expiration of the Policy, be at seas, or in distress, or at a port of refuge or call, she shall, provided previous notice be given to the underwriters, be held covered at a pro rata monthly premium to her port of destination.

An identical clause appears (Cl. 4) in the old Institute Time Clauses (Hull), and in the new London Hull clauses.

It has been held that a P & I policy is a species of time policy.[162] Consequently, Sec. 39(5) of the Marine Insurance Act was held to apply. That subsection reads:

> In a time policy there is no implied warranty that the ship shall be seaworthy at any stage of the adventure, but where, with the privity of the assured, the ship is sent to sea in an unseaworthy state, the insurer is not liable for any loss attributable to seaworthiness.

As Buglass points out,[163] the American rule as to a warranty of seaworthiness in a time policy differs, although the difference may be more semantical than real. The overall subject, and the differences between the English rule and American rule are discussed in depth in Chapter XI, Warranties, under subheading "Warranty of Seaworthiness," *infra*.

There are many diverse types of time policies on vessels, the most widely used of which is probably the American Institute Hull Clauses (June 2, 1977), reproduced in the Appendix. Until recently, the most widely used English form was the Institute Time Clauses (Hulls, 1/10/70), reproduced in the Appendix, but these have now been supplanted by the

---

supra; Allen v. Mercantile M. Ins. Co., 44 N.Y. 437 (N.Y., 1871); *Clark v. Massachusetts F. & M. Ins. Co.*, 19 Mass. 104 (Mass., 1824); *Moss v. Smith* (1850) 137 E.R. 827.

162. *Compania Maritima San Basilio S.A. v. Oceanus Mutual Underwriting Ass'n. (Bermuda) Ltd., (The Eurysthenes)*, [1976] 2 Lloyd's Rep. 171, C.A.

163. Buglass, *Marine Insurance and General Average in the U. S., (2d)*, Cornell Maritime Press, Inc., 1981

new London Clauses (10/1/83) also reproduced in the Appendix and used solely in conjunction with the new MAR policy form.[164]

Moreover, there are special types of time policies, such as Builder's Risks, Shipbuilders' and Repairers' Risks, and policies covering products liability.[165]

For a more detailed discussion and interpretation of time policies see Chapter IV, Principles of Construction; Chapter XI, Warranties; Chapter XV, Additional Insurance (Disbursements Clause); Chapter XX, Sue and Labor Clause; Chapter XXI, Running Down Clause; Chapter XXII, Particular Average.

Mixed Policies

Section 25, Marine Insurance Act, quoted *supra*, expressly provides that a contract of both voyage and time may be included in the same policy. Thus, a policy could read so as to insure a vessel from Portland, Oregon to Valdez, Alaska for two months.[166]

Mixed Land and Sea Policies

Section 2, Marine Insurance Act, provides:

(1) A contract of marine insurance may, by its express terms or by usage of trade, be extended so as to protect the assured against losses on inland waters or on any land risk which may be incidental to any sea voyage.

(2) Where a ship in course of building, or the launch of a ship, or any adventure analogous to a marine adventure, is covered by a policy in the form of a marine policy, the provisions of this Act, in so far as applicable, shall apply thereto; but, except as by this section provided, nothing in this Act shall alter or affect any rule of law applicable to any contract of insurance other than a contract of marine insurance as by this Act defined.

---

164. Among the policies in rather current use in the United States will be found: American Hulls (Pacific), 1938 [with varying coverages]; Barge Hull Form, 1955; California Fishing Vessels (1974); American Institute Hull Clauses (January 18, 1970); Taylor, 1953 (Rev. 70); SP-39 C; Tug Form No. 1706; Tug/Barge Form (1979), Pacific Coast; Yacht (May, 1947), No. 1804; Yacht Form, All Risk, No. 3054, and innumerable special clauses for attachment to standard hull policy forms, such as Collision Clauses, A,B, C, and D, and Liner Negligence Clause (May 1, 1964), American Hull Insurance Syndicate.

165. See discussion, *infra*, Chapter XXIV.

166. See, in this connection, *Wilson v. Boag* (1957) S.R. (N.S.W.) 384, 74 W.N. 160 (Aus.); [1965] 2 Lloyd's Rep. 564 (policy held to a "time policy" and not a "mixed" policy), and *Dimock v. N.B. Marine Assur. Co.* (1848) 5 N.B.R. 654 (C.A., Can.).

For illustrations of policies falling within the scope of subsection (1), see discussion, *supra,* under heading "Craft Clause" and "Warehouse to Warehouse Clause." An illustration of subsection (2) will be found in *James Yachts Ltd. v. Thames & Mersey Marine Ins. Co., Ltd. et al (B.C.,S.Ct.),*[167] in which the Canadian Marine Insurance Act (identical in all material respects to the Marine Insurance Act, 1906) was held to apply in construing a shipbuilders' and repairers' liability policy.

Floating Policies

Section 29 of the Marine Insurance Act, 1906, describes floating policies as follows:

(1) A floating policy is a policy which describes the insurance in general terms, and leaves the name of the ship or ships and other particulars to be defined by subsequent declaration.

(2) The subsequent declaration or declarations may be made by endorsement on the policy, or in other customary manner.

(3) Unless the policy otherwise provides, the declarations must be made in the order of despatch or shipment. They must, in the case of goods, comprise all consignments within the terms of the policy, and the value of the goods or other property must be honestly stated, but an omission or other erroneous declaration may be rectified even after loss or arrival, provided the omission or declaration was made in good faith.

(4) Unless the policy otherwise provides, where a declaration of value is not made until after notice of loss or arrival, the policy must be treated as an unvalued policy as regards the subject-matter of that declaration.

Floating policies in England were approved by the courts as early as 1794.[168] According to Phillips (Sec. 438 et seq.), they have been utilized in the United States since Independence.

As Buglass notes,[169] most insurances on cargo in the United States are written under "open" policies or "open" covers, which are not quite the same as floating policies described in Sec. 29. Floating policies describe the insurance in general terms, leaving the particulars to be defined by subsequent declarations; they differ from open policies in that they are effected for a specific amount which is drawn upon until exhausted. Open policies, unlike floating policies, are usually stated for a specific period of time and remain in force indefinitely until cancelled. Individual

---

167. [1977] 1 Lloyd's Rep. 206 (Can.)
168. *Kewley v. Ryan* (1794) 126 E.R. 586.
169. Buglass, *supra,* n. 163.

successive shipments are reported or declared, the assured having automatic coverage (within the terms, conditions, and limitations stated in the open policy).

The Stamp Act was responsible for the prevalence of floating policies in England as that act required that a fixed sum be stated on which the correct stamp duty could be charged. There being no such requirement in the United States, the open policy from the outset became prevalent.

Blackburn, J. described the practices applicable to floating policies very well in *Ionides v. Pacific Ins. Co.*,[170] where he said:

> The contract of an underwriter who subscribes a policy on goods by ship or ships to be declared is that he will insure any goods of the description specified which may be shipped on any vessel answering the description, if any there be, in the policy, on the voyage specified in the policy, to which the assured elects to apply the policy. The object of the declaration is to earmark and identify the particular adventure to which the assured elects to apply the policy. The assent of the assurer is not required to this, for he has no option to reject any vessel which the assured may select, nor is it necessary that the declaration should do more than identify the adventure, and so prevent the possible dishonesty of a party insured, who might intend to apply the policy to particular goods, so that they should be at the risk of the assurers, and he should come on them if there was a loss; and then, when those goods had arrived safely, to pretend that he intended to apply the policy to another set of goods still subject to the risk.

There are, however, cardinal principles to be observed in floating policies. For example, the assured must declare every shipment; he is not entitled to "pick and choose" as to which shipments he wishes coverage.[171] Obviously, the policy covers goods lost before the assured could make a declaration.[172]

As Sec. 29(3) notes, an omission to declare or an erroneous declaration may be rectified even after loss or arrival provided the omission or declaration was made in good faith.[173]

---

170. (1871) L.R. 6 Q.B. 674, aff'd (1872) L.R. 7 Q.B. 517 (Ex.Ch.).

171. *Dunlop Bros. v. Townend* (1919) 24 Com.Cas. 201; Phillips, Sec. 438; *Bartlett and Partners v. Mellor* [1961] 1 Lloyd's Rep. 487.

172. *E. Carver Co. v. Manufacturers' Ins. Co.*, 72 Mass. 215 (Mass., 1856). If the assured were required to declare before the loss, or lose the benefit of the policy, the coverage would frequently be ineffectual since it was placed when no more particular description could have been given. From necessity, therefore, the assured is permitted to declare his interest after he receives news of a loss. See, also, *Stephens v. Australasian Ins. Co.*, (1872) 27 L.T. 585.

173. *Robinson v. Touray* (1811) 170 E.R. 1340, N.P.; *Imperial Marine Ins. Co. v. Fire Ins. Corp., Ltd.* (1879) 48 L.J.Q.B. 424; *Stephens v. Australasian Ins. Co.* (1872), *supra; Harman v. Kingston* (1811) 170 E.R. 1337, N.P.; *Gledstanes v. Royal Exchange Assur.* (1864) 122 E.R. 1026.

Moreover, the declaration should be made at the earliest possible time and this requirement may, and often is, incorporated in the policy.[174]

Sec. 29(4) correctly states the existing law; i.e., that unless the policy otherwise provides, where a declaration of value is not made until after notice of loss or arrival, the policy must be treated as an unvalued policy as regards the subject-matter of that declaration.[175]

Fraud in the declaration renders the policy voidable. This was clearly established in *Rivaz v. Gerussi*.[176] In that case the assured systematically and fraudulently undervalued shipments under earlier policies and concealed this from the underwriters on successive, and later, policies. It was held that the underwriter was entitled to have the later policies set aside and cancelled. Being fraudulent, there was no return of premium.

Generally speaking, where more than one floating policy has been placed in effect, one is stated to be succeeded by another. Where this occurs, the shipments are declared under the first, or initial policy, until it is exhausted and then fall under the later, or successive, policy. Where, however, there is no "succeeding" provision, the assured may issue declarations on either policy.[177]

Open Policies

Most "open" policies are, in reality, usually forms of time policies, as they generally cover all goods (as defined in the policy) for a stipulated period of time shipped on specified conveyances.[178]

As with other marine insurance policies, the intent of the parties in expressing the extent of coverage and terms governs.[179] For example, in

174. In *Union Ins. Soc. of Canton v. Wills* (1916) 1 A.C. 281, such a requirement was held to be a promissory warranty and a failure to declare was held to defeat recovery on the part of the assured. See, also, *Davies v. National Fire and Marine Ins. Co. of New Zealand* (1891) A.C. 485.

175. *Union Ins. Soc. of Canton v. Wills* (1916), *supra*, n. 174; *Gledstanes v. Royal Exchange Assur.* (1864), *supra*, n. 173; *Ionides v. Pacific Ins. Co.* (1871) *supra*, n. 170.

176. (1880) 6 Q.B.D. 222, C.A.

177. *Henchman v. Offley* (1782) 99 E.R. 577. See, also, *Villa do Porto*, 1958 AMC 229 (Arb.), where the assured was considered to have declared under both policies.

178. See *Insurance Co. of North America v. Bernard*, 226 N.Y.S. 524, 222 App.Div. 512 (N.Y., 1928).

179. See *Rand v. Morse*, 289 F. 339 (6th Cir., 1923) (having paid for the goods and acquired title thereto and right of possession, each buyer under a c.i.f. contract in turn is protected against loss by the insurance policy procured by the seller); *Forster v. Ins. Co. of N. A.*, 139 F.2d 875, 1944 AMC 131 (2d Cir., 1943) (open policy insuring merchandise consisting principally of "fur cuttings," did not limit coverage to fur cuttings alone but indicated intent to extend such coverage to other articles used or dealt in, in the assured's business; consequently, the assured could not recover premiums paid on such policies on the ground that the policies failed to cover shipments which were not fur cuttings; nor could the insurer retain the premiums as the declaration was made twelve days after safe arrival and no risk was ever assumed); *Ocean Marine Ins. Co. v. Lindo*, 30 F.2d 782 (9th Cir., 1928) (policy covering goods in transit "until safely deposited in . . . warehouse at destination," covered loss in a

Marine Ins. Co., Ltd. v. Walsh Upstill Coal Co.,[180] the application for insurance covered: "Sundry coal cargoes, belonging to them (the assured) and as agents, at risk," etc. A policy of insurance issued, stating that it was made "as per said contract." It was held that the policy covered only such cargoes shipped by the assured as belonged to it as owner and such as were shipped by it as agent, and in which it had some pecuniary interest at risk.

In *Crossell v. Mercantile Mut. Ins. Co.*,[181] an insurance certificate, issued under an open marine policy, described the goods as "shipped on board of the Great Western Steamship Company." A shipment was made on a

---

customs house notwithstanding intended reshipment); *Groban v. Pegu*, 456 F.2d 685, 1972 AMC 460 (2d Cir.) (where only a single shipment was involved, goods remained covered by a marine extension clause even though transit was interrupted by a delay in the course of transit beyond the assured consignee's control); *Brammer Corp. v. Holland-American Ins. Co.*, 228 N.Y.S. 2d 512 (N.Y., 1962) (open cargo policy with warehouse to warehouse clause; goods delivered to trucker and thereafter damaged held not to be "in transit"); *Greene v. Cheatham*, 293 F.2d 933, 1961 AMC 2549 (2d Cir.) (assured's execution of certificates of insurance under an open policy, with any loss to be payable to purchasers, made the entire open policy applicable to shipments only to the extent embraced within reasonable interpretation of assured's intent as found in language used in the certificates); *Atlas Assur. Co., Ltd. v. Harper Robinson Shipping Co.*, 508 F.2d 1381, 1975 AMC 1381 (9th Cir., 1975) (marine cargo underwriter could not be subrogated to the claims of consignees against a carrier when the cargo damage under an open policy was caused by stevedores and the cargo was shipped on an FIO basis by the shipper who had procured the insurance); *IHC v. Affiliated F. & M. Ins. Co.*, 451 F.2d 758 (10th Cir., 1971) (assured warranted to declare a 25 percent invoice value of shipment to the carrier; held: not an affirmative warranty but a promissory warranty and thus the breach of the promissory warranty did not void the policy as a whole but only defeated the assured's right of recovery against the assurer for a particular loss); *Rosa v. Ins. Co. of State of Pa. (The Belle of Portugal)*, 421 F.2d 390, 1970 AMC 30, [1970] 2 Lloyd's Rep. 386 (9th Cir.) (errors and omissions clauses in an open marine cargo policy applied to excuse the failure of the assured to report extent of cargo taken aboard; failure was due to curtailed sending capacity of the ship's radio, resulting from heavy rain conditions); *Harlem*, 223 N.Y.S. 559, 1927 AMC 1088 (NYM) (report of shipment under an open policy was not made within 72 hours as provided in the policy; the underwriter's agent wrote on the report "warranted conditions as to reporting complied with"; held: not a waiver of such conditions by the underwriter; *Keresaspa*, 215 N.Y.S. 854, 1924 AMC 836 (NYM) (consignee not bound by one-year limit on time for suit under open policy both because the limit was not mentioned in the separate certificate covering the cargo consigned to him and because the underwriter's conduct during the investigation, negotiation and litigation amounted to a waiver thereof); *Hebron*, 34 Ga. App. 825, 1926 AMC 373 (St.,Ga.) (underwriter issued the assured a certificate in which there was a statement that the underwriter insured a certain cargo "under policy No. 7"; when properly identified, the policy was enforceable as part of the contract); *Slavenburg Co. v. Boston Ins. Co.*, 332 F.2d 990, 1964 AMC 1120 (2d Cir.) (insured failed to comply with open policy's reporting clause, thereby forfeiting any claim it might have had under the policy); *Larsen v. Ins. Co. of N. A.*, 252 F.Supp. 458, 1965 AMC 2576 (W.D.,Wash.) (two special free from particular average clauses stamped in red ink immediately under the names of particular vessels in an open cargo policy construed to apply only to the particular vessels named and not the vessel involved in the loss).

180. 68 Ohio St. 469, 68 N.E. 21 (St.,Ohio, 1903).
181. 19 F. 24 (D., Minn., 1884).

vessel not owned by that company but chartered by it and placed upon its line as one of its vessels. It was held that the insurance covered.

In *Transatlantic Shipping Co. v. St. Paul Fire & Marine Ins. Co.*,[182] the open policy provided cover only for cargo stored under the main deck or in structures "built in the frame of the vessel." The poop, forecastle and bridge spaces were held to be structures built in the frame of the vessel, but not officers' quarters, consisting of houses fixed to the bridge deck by angle plates and angle irons and set inboard at least six inches from the side of the vessel.

In *Camors v. Union Mar. Ins. Co.*,[183] a warranty in an open policy stipulated that all risks should be reported to the underwriter as soon as known to the assured. It was the custom of the assured to notify promptly of the arrival of a cargo and settlement would be made at the end of the month. An epidemic prevailed and the assured failed to make a prompt report of risks on account of the sickness of his clerks. It was held that the failure to report was a breach of the warranty giving to the underwriter the option of vacating the policy entirely and not merely as to the risks not reported. See, however, *Callahan v. Orient Ins. Co.*,[184] where a provision in an open policy, "shipments to be reported to the agents of said company," was not construed to mean all shipments made by the assured where it was well known to the assurer's agents that the assured did not insure all shipments and previous policies contained no express agreement to report all shipments.

As in floating policies, an open policy enables the merchant to insure his goods shipped to a foreign port when he is not advised of the particular ship on which the goods are to be laden and cannot name it in the policy.[185] Moreover, again as in floating policies, unless a certain amount is stipulated and expressed in the contract of insurance as the value of the property upon which the risk is taken, then it is necessary that proof be made of the market value of the goods in case of loss, and such a policy of insurance is denominated an open policy.[186] An open policy does not attach unless the ship on which the goods are laden is seaworthy.[187] But, it is now customary—indeed practically universal—for cargo policies to contain a "seaworthiness admitted" clause which is nothing more than a recognition that the shipper of goods has no control over the vessel on which his goods are laden. There is, however, no implied warranty in a cargo policy that the goods are seaworthy for the voyage, and, where the vessel was seaworthy when the voyage commenced and the cargo was in

---

182. 298 F. 551, *aff'd* 9 F.2d 720 (2d Cir., 1925).
183. 28 So. 926, 104 La. 349 (St.,La., 1900).
184. 63 F. 830 (N.D., Ohio, 1894).
185. *Orient Mutual Ins. Co. v. Wright*, 64 U.S. 401 (1859), 68 U.S. 456 (1863).
186. *Williams v. Continental Ins. Co.*, 24 F. 767 (D., Minn., 1885).
187. *Orient Mutual Ins. Co. v. Wright, supra*, n. 185.

good condition when received, the underwriter is liable for a loss during the voyage resulting from external causes.[188]

Most cargo policies provide simply that: "The seaworthiness of the vessel as between the assured and underwriters is hereby admitted." The new Institute Cargo Clauses (A, B, and C) take a slightly different approach. Under the "Exclusions" portions of those clauses, the language is as follows:

> 5.1 In no case shall this insurance cover loss damage or expense arising from unseaworthiness of vessel or craft, unfitness of vessel craft conveyance container or liftvan for the safe carriage of the subject-matter insured, where the Assured or their servants are privy to such unseaworthiness or unfitness, at the time the subject-matter insured is loaded therein.
>
> 5.2 The Underwriters waive any breach of the implied warranties of seaworthiness of the ship and fitness of the ship to carry the subject-matter insured to destination, unless the Assured or their servants are privy to such unseaworthiness or unfitness.

The usual practice under an open policy is to issue the primary policy to the assured and then grant to him the right to issue "certificates" thereunder, describing in abbreviated form the extent of coverage and naming the parties insured or to be insured. The certificate (which is not itself a policy), must be read with the policy which it only overrules where inconsistent.[189]

Where the policy insured the assured "for whom it may concern," and also authorized the holder of the policy to issue certificates thereunder, upon the issuance of the certificates and their transfer to a consignee, the certificates in essence become a complete and independent contract between the underwriter and the holder of the certificate, and the holder of the certificate is an assured in direct contractual right.[190]

Generally speaking, where the certificate refers to the open policy and the certificate does not itself recite the risks, etc., nor purport to be a policy, the assured accepts the certificate subject to the conditions contained

---

188. *Pacific Creosoting Co. v. Thames & Mersey Ins. Co.*, 223 F. 561 (9th Cir., 1914).

189. *Royster Guano Co. v. Globe & Rutgers*, 168 N.E. 834, 1930 AMC 11 (N.Y., 1930). See, also, *Zacharias v. Rhode Island Ins. Co.*, 213 F.2d 840, 1954 AMC 1522 (5th Cir.) where it was held that an open policy to insure "as agreed" was not ambiguous; the agreement is found in and limited by the certificate; *Swedish Rys. v. Dexter & Carpenter*, 299 F.Supp. 99, 1924 AMC 908 (S.D.N.Y.) (tender of American broker's certificate as to placing coverage in London instead of tendering a complete policy satisfied the requirement of "insurance" in a c.i.f. sales contract); *Hallfried*, 22 F. Supp. 454, 1927 AMC 1682 (S.D.N.Y.) (tender of certificate instead of an actual policy is sufficient compliance with insurance term of a c.i.f. contract under the custom of the Port of New York).

190. *Gishun Maru*, 228 F. 912, 1923 AMC 474 (N.D.,Ohio).

in the policy. Consequently, a provision in the policy limiting time for suit is valid and enforceable even though the limitation is not contained in the certificate.[191]

Where the open policy binds the underwriter to protect cargo improperly stowed through inadvertence or without the knowledge of the assured, the underwriter is obliged, after knowledge of a loss of cargo improperly stowed on deck, to issue riders and pay for such loss, as the payment does not waive any rights of the underwriters as against the vessel.[192] But a cargo underwriter in issuing a certificate of insurance under an open policy for goods described "as per bill of lading," does not thereby warrant that the statements in the bill of lading as to the condition of the goods are true.[193]

It will readily be seen that situations involving "double insurance" can easily occur where the shipper insures under an open policy and the consignee likewise insures under a different policy. For example, in *Davis Yarn Co. v. Brooklyn Yarn Dye Co.,*[194] Davis shipped yarn to Brooklyn for processing. Brooklyn insured with Commercial against risk of damage to yarn entrusted to it for processing, with a clause reading that "whenever insured's customers have other insurance in force covering the property, this insurance is to be considered excess insurance." Davis had a floater policy with Sentinel covering the goods while in transit and at processing plants, with a similar "other insurance" clause. A windstorm damaged the roof of Brooklyn's plant, destroying some piping, and sprinkler system water and rain damaged Davis's yarn. Each underwriter claimed that it was not liable because there was "other insurance." The court rejected the proposition that because the loss was covered by two policies, the plaintiff could recover upon neither, and further held that Commercial's policy was more specific in coverage than the floater policies and was therefore intended to create a primary liability to which the floater policies were supplementary and secondary.

Open policies, like floating policies, may be rectified after loss. In *Black Gull (Fire)*,[195] the plaintiff importer declared a value of $52,000 under its open cargo policy in respect of a shipment lost at sea in a fire. The plaintiff might properly have declared also the freight and 10 percent, or

191. *Corsicana*, 252 N.Y. 69, 168 N.E. 832, 1930 AMC 7 (N.Y., 1930); *Suruga*, 37 F.2d 461, 1930 AMC 328 (2d Cir.) (distinguishing *Phoenix Ins. Co. v. De Monchy* (1929) 34 Ll.L.Rep. 201, H.L.); *Hart v. Automobile Ins. Co.,* 246 N.Y.S. 586, 1931 AMC 24 (NYM); *Royster Guano Co. v. Globe & Rutgers* (1930), *supra,* n. 189. Compare, however, *Keresaspa* (1924), *supra,* n. 179.

192. *Southlands*, 37 F.2d 474, 1930 AMC 337 (5th Cir.).

193. *Fernandez v. Golodetz*, 55 F.Supp. 1003, 1944 AMC 699 (S.D.N.Y.).

194. 56 N.E. 2d 564, 1943 AMC 116 (NYM).

195. 278 F.2d 439, 1960 AMC 1566 (2d Cir.).

$5,945 more than it did declare. The underwriters forwarded their check for $52,000 which the importer negotiated. Subsequently, the importer brought a civil action to recover the $5,945. The court held that (1) since the check was not tendered "in full and final payment," negotiating it did not constitute an accord and satisfaction; (2) the action was not time-barred by a policy provision requiring suit within 12 months after the consignee received notice of arrival of the goods as the carrier had sent the consignee only a notice of "expected arrival" and the goods were lost at sea; (3) the insured need not show that the cargo was in good condition when loaded on the vessel as the entire purpose of providing the basis of value in the policy was to preclude the necessity of such a showing; and (4) since the assured admitted that back premiums were owing, the underwriter would be credited with the sums due even though the issue was not raised by the pleadings.[196]

It should be emphasized that co-insurance principles apply to marine insurance policies even in the absence of a co-insurance clause and this is equally true under open cargo policies.[197]

Although an open policy may be payable to "whom it may concern," where the certificate issued provides for only the forwarders of the cargo being beneficiaries, the certificate governs.[198] But where there is no limitation, the open policy will cover all who have an insurable interest.[199]

Although unvalued policies such as open policies are not frequently found in English jurisprudence, see *Berger and Light Diffusers Pty., Ltd. v. Pollock*,[200] where steel injection moulds were insured on a voyage from Australia to England. On arrival, the moulds were found to be damaged by rust by reason of being submerged in water after a pipe in the vessel's hold had fractured. The court held, *inter alia*, that although a contract of open cover existed between the assured's brokers and the underwriters, the existence of that contract did not relieve the assured of his duty under Sec. 18(1) of the Marine Insurance Act, 1906, to disclose all material circumstances known to him, and the duty to disclose contained between the issuance of a "cross-slip" and the "signing slip." Notwithstanding the assured had stated the value of the goods as £20,000 and the proof showed a value of £4,316, it was held that the underwriters had failed to prove that the alleged overvaluation was material.

196. *The Black Gull* litigation is also found at 1956 AMC 1267; 1958 AMC 277, 1773; 1959 AMC 648; 1960 AMC 163, 170, 175, 249, 375, 377, 2388; 1962 AMC 1205.
197. *Margo Manufacturing v. Chamlin*, 1978 AMC 1274 (S.D.N.Y.).
198. *The Sidney*, 23 F. 88 (S.D.N.Y.), appeal dismissed 139 U.S. 331 (1885).
199. *Canadian Co-op v. John Russell*, 68 F.2d 901, 1934 AMC 7 (2d Cir.) (insurance on cargo "for account of whom it may concern," held to cover a shipowner who paid the premium as per charter party; hence the underwriter, after paying a loss to cargo under loan receipts, was held barred to maintain a subrogation action against the shipowner).
200. [1973] 2 Lloyd's Rep. 442, Q.B.D.

Valued Policies

Section 27 of the Marine Insurance Act describes "valued" policies concisely:

(1) A policy may be either valued or unvalued.

(2) A valued policy is a policy which specifies the agreed value of the subject-matter insured.

(3) Subject to the provisions of this Act, and in the absence of fraud, the value fixed by the policy is, as between the insurer and insured, conclusive of the insurable value of the subject intended to be insured, whether the loss be total or partial.

(4) Unless the policy otherwise provides, the value fixed by the policy is not conclusive for the purpose of determining whether there has been a constructive total loss.

It is customary, in American and English policies, to stipulate that in ascertaining whether a vessel is a constructive total loss, the insured value shall be taken as the repaired value. See Clause 17 of the old Institute Time Clauses (Hull), Clause 19 of the new Institute Time Clauses (Hull), and Lines 134-135 of the AIH (June 2, 1977) form.

As subsection (3) above so clearly states, subject to the provisions of the Act, *and in the absence of fraud,* the value fixed in the policy as between the insurer and the insured is conclusive. An agreed value, honestly arrived at, settles the true value. In its practical operation, it is a stipulation for liquidated damages. American and English law do not differ in this respect.[201]

---

201. *Bruce v. Jones* (1863) 158 E.R. 1094; *Irving v. Manning* (1847) 9 E.R. 766; *North of England Iron S. S. Ins. Ass'n. v. Armstrong* (1870) 39 L.J.Q.B. 81; *Papadimitriou v. Henderson* (1939) 64 Ll.L.Rep. 345, K.B.D.; *Barker v. Janson* (1868) 17 L.T. 473; *Woodside v. Globe Marine Ins. Co.* (1896) 1 Q.B. 105; *The Main* (1894) P. 320; *General Shipping and Forwarding Co. v. British Gen. Ins. Co., Ltd.* (1923) 15 Ll.L.Rep. 175, K.B.D.; *Thames & Mersey Mar. Ins. Co. v. Pitts, Son & King* (1893) 1 Q.B. 476; *Marine Ins. Co. of Alexandria v. Hodgson,* 10 U.S. 206 (1810); *The Potomac,* 105 U.S. 630 (1881); *Booth-American Shipping Co. v. Importers' & Exporters' Ins. Co.,* 9 F.2d 304 (2d Cir., 1926); *St. Paul F. & M. Ins. Co. v. Pure Oil Co.,* 63 F.2d 771, 1933 AMC 502; *Gulf Refining Co. v. Atlantic Mut. Ins. Co.,* 279 U.S. 708 (1929); *The St. Johns,* 101 F. 469 (S.D.N.Y., 1900); *Ursula Bright S. S. Co. v. Amsinck,* 115 F. 242 (S.D.N.Y., 1902); *Almirante,* 304 U.S. 430, 1938 AMC 707; *New York & Cuba Mail S. S. Co. v. Royal Exchange Assur.,* 154 F. 315 (2d Cir., 1907); *Lenfest v. Coldwell,* 525 F.2d 717, 1975 AMC 2489 (2d Cir.); *Groban v. Pegu,* 456 F.2d 685, 1972 AMC 460 (2d Cir., 1971); *Zack Metal Co. v. Federal Ins. Co.,* 284 N.Y.S. 2d 582, 1967 AMC 125 (N.Y., 1966); *Orange,* 337 F.Supp. 1161, 1972 AMC 627 (S.D.N.Y.); *Greyhound,* 1931 AMC 1940 (overvaluation of sixteen times; held: assured's complaint dismissed); *Helmville Ltd. v. Yorkshire Ins. Co. (The Medina Princess),* [1965] 1 Lloyd's Rep. 361; *Disrude v. Comm. Fish.,* 570 P.2d 963, 1978 AMC 261 (St.,Ore.); *Perez v. Los Fresnos State Bank,* 512 S.W. 2d 796 (St.,Tex., 1974); *Rosenthal v. Poland,* 337 F.Supp. 1161 (S.D.N.Y., 1972).

To illustrate, in *General Shipping and Forwarding Co. v. British Gen. Ins. Co., Ltd.*,[202] the vessel was insured for £2,000 in a policy where she was valued at £5,000. In fact, her market value was considerably less than the insured value. The court held that the claim succeeded, noting that the underwriters had as much information concerning the vessel as the assured did and that underwriters seem to prefer overvaluation of hull and machinery.

In *Disrude v. Comm. Fish.*,[203] the hull policy recited that the agreed valuation was $25,000. After the vessel was insured, the insured owner made improvements to it bringing its value up to about $45,000. The vessel was damaged and the insured brought suit for a partial loss in the sum of $25,000 as the cost of repairs equalled or exceeded that amount. The underwriters contended that since the insured vessel was worth $45,000 at the time of the damage, they should only be required to pay 25/45ths of the cost of repairs. The court held that the policy was a valued policy and in the absence of fraud (and none was alleged) the agreed value and not the actual value at the time of loss governed. It will be noted that the insured sued for a partial loss rather than a constructive total loss. See, in this connection, *International Navigation Co. v. Atlantic Mutual Ins. Co.*[204]

In *The Main*,[205] the assured procured a valued policy on freight in the sum of £5,500. Due to an accident, the ship was detained during which time freight rates declined drastically. On her departure, the amount of freight payable was considerably less than the agreed value of freight in the policy. Upon a total loss, the underwriters contended that payment should be made only upon the actual freight at risk. The court held the parties bound by the valuation in the policy.

It should be noted, however, that with respect to freight the valuation in the policy may be "opened" if the vessel does not carry all of the goods but only a part.[206]

It should be emphasized, however, that if the subject-matter is fraudulently overvalued with the intent to cheat the underwriters, the contract may be voided.[207] There may also be a non-disclosure which amounts to a suppression of material fact in which case the policy is voidable by the underwriters.[208]

---

202. (1923) 15 Ll.L.Rep. 175, K.B.D.
203. 570 P.2d 963, 1978 AMC 261 (St.,Ore.).
204. 100 F. 304, *aff'd* 108 F. 988 (2d Cir., 1901).
205. (1894) P. 320.
206. *Williams v. North China Ins. Co.* (1876) 35 L.T. 884; *Forbes v. Aspinall* (1811) 104 E.R. 394; *Alsop v. Commercial Ins. Co.*, F.Cas. No. 262 (lst Cir., 1833). But see *Griswold v. Union Mut. Ins. Co.*, F.Cas. No. 5,840.
207. *Haigh v. De La Cour* (1812) 170 E.R. 1396.
208. *Ionides v. Pender* (1874) 43 L.J.Q.B. 227; *Thames and Mersey Mar. Ins. Co. v. Gunford Ship Co.* (1911) A.C. 529; *Slattery v. Mance* [1962] 1 Q.B. 676. See, also, cases cited in footnote 201 and Chapter X, Disclosures and Representations.

The rules are different where there are general average expenses. The same is true with respect to salvage charges. That is, the underwriter is obligated to pay the valuation in the policy (or proportionately thereto) since the contributing values of the interests involved and the amounts of contributions are determined independently of the valuation in the policy. Thus, if the vessel is valued in the policy at less than her value as that value is set forth in the general average statement, the underwriter is obliged to pay only an amount which bears the same ratio to the vessel's contribution as the valuation in the policy bears to the valuation in the general average statement.[209]

The American Institute Hulls form (June 2, 1977) contains a most important clause bearing on payment under the policy. It reads:

> When the contributory value of the Vessel is greater than the Agreed Value herein, the liability of the Underwriters for General Average contribution (except in respect to amounts made good to the Vessel), or Salvage, shall not exceed that proportion of the total contribution due from the Vessel which the amount insured hereunder bears to the contributory value; and if, because of damage for which the Underwriters are liable as Particular Average, the value of the Vessel has been reduced for the purpose of contribution, the amount of such Particular Average damage recoverable under this Policy shall first be deducted from the amount insured hereunder, and the Underwriters shall then be liable only for the proportion which such net amount bears to the contributory value.

The parenthetical expression, "except in respect to amounts made good to the Vessel," makes it clear that general average sacrifices are not affected by the clause and are recoverable in full regardless of any underinsurance. In the absence of the clause, underwriters would be liable for the full general average contribution attaching to the vessel (that is, both sacrifices and expenses) regardless of any underinsurance.[210] Thus, at the risk of oversimplification, the clause relates to general average *expenses*— not sacrifices; in the case of underinsurance, the underwriter pays proportionately; if the contributory value of the vessel is reduced by particular average damage claims for which the same underwriters are liable, then again the underwriters are liable only proportionately; and any deductible average must be taken into consideration.[211]

---

209. *Balmoral S. S. Co. v. Marten* (1901) 2 K.B. 896, *aff'd* (1902) A.C. 511, H.L.; *Gulf Refining Co. v. Atlantic Mutual Ins. Co.*, 279 U.S. 708 (1930).

210. *International Navigation Co. v. Atlantic Mut. Ins. Co.*, 100 F. 304, *aff'd* 108 F. 988 (2d Cir., 1901).

211. A comparison of the above clause with Section 73 of the Marine Insurance Act, 1906, will reveal from whence the American underwriters derived the clause. Sec. 73 reads:

However, any underinsurance of the vessel under hull and machinery policies can be ameliorated insofar as liability for general average expenses is concerned by taking out insurance on "Excess Liabilities."[212]

Unvalued Policies

Section 28, Marine Insurance Act, defines an unvalued policy as:

An unvalued policy is a policy which does not specify the value of the subject-matter insured, but, subject to the limit of the sum insured, leaves the insurable value to be subsequently ascertained, in the manner hereinbefore specified.

Unvalued policies are quite rare in modern day insurance on hulls and machinery. For the most part, they will be encountered only with respect to policies on goods of which the form of "open policy" is a classic example, although occasionally freight policies will be unvalued.

With respect to insurable value, see Chapter IX, Measure of Insurable Value. As to the meaning of indemnity, see Sections 68 through 71, Marine Insurance Act, 1906. With respect to underinsurance, see Section 81 of the Act.

Comparative Analysis of Old and New Institute Cargo Clauses

The genesis of the new Institute Cargo Clauses unquestionably was action on the part of the United Nations Committee on Trade and Development (UNCTAD).[213] That report stated in part with reference to the old Lloyd's S. G. form:

---

(1) Subject to any express provision in the policy, where the assured has paid, or is liable for, any general average contribution, the measure of indemnity is the full amount of such contribution if the subject-matter liable to contribution is insured for its full contributory value; but if such subject-matter be not insured for its full contributory value, or if only part of it be insured, the indemnity payable by the insurer must be reduced in proportion to the underinsurance, and where there has been a particular average loss which constitutes a deduction from the contributory value, and for which the insurer is liable, that amount must be deducted from the insured value in order to ascertain what the insurer is liable to contribute.

(2) Where the insurer is liable for salvage charges the extent of his liability must be determined on the like principle.

212. See discussion, *infra*, Chapter XIX, Running Down Clause.

213. Report by the UNCTAD secretariat, "Legal and Documentary Aspects of the Marine Insurance Contract," TD/B/C.4ISL/27, 27 November 1978. See, also, "Report of the Working Group on International Shipping Legislation on its Seventh Session, Trade and Development Board, Committee on Shipping, Tenth Session, UNCTAD, TD/B/C.4/219, TD/B/C4/ISL/32, 26 January 1981.

The immortalisation of an antiquated and obscurely worded document as being immune from any improvement is excessive and unnecessary . . . the unyielding resistance to any change of the S. G. form is unfounded.[214]

Not content with this slashing attack on the policy form itself, UNCTAD has concluded that the use of a national regime (and here UNCTAD is referring to the English insurance market) as a de facto international legal regime presents problems with its continued use on an indefinite basis, noting that it is not the result of an internationally representative forum, but is rather a legal regime created in a national context and designed to meet national needs. Thus, UNCTAD concluded, neither developing countries, nor any others, whether socialist or developed market-economy countries, have had a say in its original structure or its continued development; hence, the "national character" of this marine insurance legal regime inhibits it from successfully serving as a truly international legal base for marine insurance contracts adaptable to all members of the international community.[215]

One may well ponder the effect these rather startling pronouncements had upon Lloyd's and the Institute of London Underwriters. Aside from what one may assume was probably a reaction of instant hostility and rejection, underwriters in London moved rapidly, predictably, and certainly to counter UNCTAD's move to its own perception of "international uniformity," without proper weight being given to the preeminence of the English underwriters in marine insurance coverage worldwide.

Thus, as respects cargo (and, as will be seen, hull insurance as well), the time-honored Lloyd's S. G. policy form has been replaced by a sheet of paper containing sub-headings and blank spaces to be filled in with such vital information as the policy number, name of assured, vessel, voyage or period of insurance, subject-matter insured, agreed value (if any),

---

214. *Ibid.*, Para 245.

215. This startling conclusion was reached despite the fact that shippers from the so-called "developing" nations seem to be quite happy to pay the London market handsome premiums and endure slightly harsher terms merely because that market provides efficient service and prompt claims handling—something which experience has demonstrated does not always characterize the state-owned/controlled marine insurance concerns operating in the developing countries; despite the fact that insurance companies in most developing countries were using, almost word for word, the S. G. form and Institute Clauses, and despite the fact that redrafting insurance clauses does not always improve comprehensibility. See, for example, *Amin Rasheed Shipping Corp. v. Kuwait Ins. Co. (The Al Wahab),* [1983] 2 Lloyd's Rep. 365 (H.L.) where the policy was issued in Kuwait using substantially all the standard English marine forms; held: English law was to be applied to construe the policy but the assured was relegated to the Kuwaiti courts for a decision on the merits).

amount insured, premium, clauses and endorsements to be attached, and a "catch-all": special conditions and warranties.[216]

There are now three new sets of cargo clauses to replace the existing "All Risks," W.A. (with average), and F.P.A. (free of particular average) clauses. These are known, presumably for lack of better titles, simply as the "A," "B," and "C" clauses. These are not, however, mirror images of the old "All Risks," "With Average," and "Free of Particular Average" clauses under new labels, but reflect a decidedly new approach.

At the risk of over-simplification, it is fairly accurate to state that the "A" clauses cover, essentially, all risks with the caveat that, as everyone knows, an all risks policy does not cover all risks, but only those which are fortuitous. Thus, Clause 1 of the "A" form covers all risks of loss of or damage to the subject-matter insured except as provided in Clauses 4, 5, and 6, which are clearly denominated as "Exclusions." Moreover, the intention is to cover physical loss or damage and not economic loss or consequential loss, however those terms may be defined.

To predict how the courts will interpret and apply the new cargo clauses, and what the underwriters will do when the clauses have been in force for some time and their impact is felt in the market, is obviously a difficult task. Perhaps the best way of approaching it would be to comment on some omissions in the new clauses of words which were included in the old policy forms.

For example, neither the "B" nor "C" forms includes, under the named perils sections, the phrase "all other perils, losses and misfortunes that have or shall come to the hurt, detriment, or damage of the said goods, and merchandises, and ship, etc., or any part thereof."

Will the ejusdem generis rule be applied when a loss occurs which does not fit neatly into the description of the named perils in those forms?

Search as one may in the "C" form (providing the least extensive coverage), there is no mention of the incursion of seawater into the vessel, craft, hold, conveyance, container, etc., although this particular peril will be found among the "named perils" in the "B" form. What, for example, would the court in *Davidson v. Burnand*[217] hold with respect to a total loss of cargo under the new form "C"? In that case, while the vessel was loading, her draft was increased to the point where a discharge pipe was brought below the surface of the water. The water flowed down the pipe, and some valves having been negligently left open, flowed thence into the hold and damaged the goods. Under the old S. G. form, the court held

---

216. The new Lloyd's Marine Policy Form, the new Cargo Clauses, and the new Hull Clauses are reproduced in the Appendix.

217. (1868) L.R. 4 C.P. 117.

that the loss was "similar" in kind to one happening from "perils of the seas."

In *Jones v. Nicholson*,[218] the master, who was a part owner of the ship, fraudulently sold the cargo. There, the underwriters were held liable under the heading of barratry as well as under the words "all other perils." In *Canada Rice Mills, Ltd. v. Union Marine & Gen. Ins. Co.*,[219] the damage was occasioned to the cargo of rice, not by incursion of seawater, but by the closing of ventilators to prevent such incursion. There, the underwriters were held liable for a loss by "perils of the sea" as well as under the general words.

Attention is directed to *Shell International Petroleum Co., Ltd. v. Gibbs (The Salem)*,[220] where at first instance it was held that the sale of the oil cargo by the master and some of the crew was a "taking at sea." "Takings at sea" has now disappeared from Forms "B" and "C." Even if that peril were considered as falling within the new perils named, Clause 4.8 of the "Exclusions" in the "B" and "C" forms would eliminate coverage for " . . . deliberate damage to or deliberate destruction of the subject-matter insured or any part thereof by the wrongful act of any person or persons." It will be noted, of course, that Clause 4.8 in the "B" and "C" forms now removes all liability for arson, scuttling, any form of sabotage, or other malicious acts aimed at the subject-matter insured. Moreover, since the "B" and "C" forms do not include perils of the seas as such, rainwater damage and theft are not included as covered risks, although rainwater damage may be included in certain causes of loss mentioned in Risk Clause 1.

To illustrate, the carrying vessel encounters a vicious storm such that the vessel is badly battered and the cargo rendered completely worthless by sea water entering the holds. No fire or explosion ensues, nor is the vessel stranded, grounded, sunk, or capsized. The vessel was not in collision with anything; no general average sacrifice was made or attempted, and no cargo was jettisoned. In short, the cargo was rendered worthless (the cost of reconditioning and sale would exceed its value) by the incursion of seawater. Under Form "C" there is no coverage even though the cargo was clearly destroyed by a peril of the sea and there was a constructive total loss.

218. (1854) 156 E.R. 342.
219. (1940) 4 All E.R. 169, (1941) A.C. 55, 67 Ll.L.Rep. 549 (P.C.).
220. [1981] 2 Lloyd's Rep. 316, K.B.D.; [1982] 1 All E.R. 225, C.A.; aff'd [1983] 1 Lloyd's Rep. 342 (H.L.). The term "taking at sea" was held by the Court of Appeal and affirmed by the House of Lords not to comprehend dishonest takings by the crew or shipowner. In light of *The Salem, Nishina Trading Co., Ltd. v. Chiyoda*, (1969) 1 Lloyd's Rep. 293, C.A. must be deemed to be overruled. Also, *The Mandarin Star*, [1969] 2 Q.B. 449 was expressly overruled in its holding that takings at sea covered wrongful misappropriation by a bailee. However, since form "A" is on an "all risks" basis and no exclusion appears in that form with respect to "wrongful acts of any person or persons," one must presume that coverage would have been provided for the loss of the oil aboard the *Salem*.

In *Montoya v. London Assurance Co.*,[221] during the course of a voyage, a vessel loaded with hides and tobacco shipped large quantities of seawater. On the termination of the voyage, it was discovered that the seawater had rendered the hides putrid and that the putrefaction had imparted an ill flavor to the tobacco, rendering it worthless. In that case, the court ruled that the loss was due to a peril of the sea. Under Form "C" this result would not follow, notwithstanding the fact that the tobacco was a total loss.

Take this illustration. It is desired to insure a cargo of antique furniture from Belgium to the United Kingdom; the furniture is stored in a warehouse in Antwerp and is purchased F.O.B. the warehouse by the prospective insured, who places insurance on the furniture under Form "A" (all risks). The insured then employs an independent contracting company (which specializes in packing antique furniture) to pack the furniture in containers for shipment to the United Kingdom. The independent contracting firm performs its function in a grossly negligent manner and, as a consequence, the furniture is badly damaged enroute by heavy weather.

Clause 4.3 of the "Exclusions" eliminates coverage for loss, damage, or expense arising from insufficiency or unsuitability of packing or preparation of the subject-matter insured and, for the purpose of that clause, "packing" is deemed to include stowage in a container or liftvan, but only when such stowage is carried out prior to attachment of the insurance or by the assured or their servants.

Query: Is the damage to the furniture covered by Form "A"? It will be observed that the packing of the container occurred after the attachment of the insurance and was carried out by an independent contractor, not by the assured or their *servants*.[222]

As a further example, suppose that a cargo is insured under new Form "A." The vessel arrives in Vancouver, Washington, U. S. A., just after the first major eruption of Mt. St. Helens. The master, professing that the safety of his vessel was imperiled by the possibility of further eruptions, discharges all of the cargo to the dock, purportedly under the "Liberties" or "Caspiana" clause of the bills of lading, and the vessel hurriedly departs. The consignees, at considerable expense, tranship the cargo from Vancouver, Washington to Vancouver, British Columbia via truck, as the ultimate destination of the cargo was the latter. Enroute from Vancouver,

---

221. (1851) 6 Exch. 451, 155 E.R. 620.

222. Elsewhere in the policy, there are references to the "Assured or their servants *or agents*." The language in Clause 4.3 refers only to the "Assured or their *servants*." The answer devolves on a narrow distinction between the assured's "servant" and the term "agent." Is an independent contractor in these circumstances an agent, or a servant, or neither?

Washington to Vancouver, British Columbia, one of the trucks is over-turned and the cargo damaged.

Under Form "A," the Transit Clause would extend coverage to the cargo while enroute during the overland portion of the transit and under Clause 12, the Forwarding Charges Clause, underwriters would be obli-gated to reimburse the assured for any extra charges properly and rea-sonably incurred in storing and forwarding the cargo to the destination to which it was insured;. i.e., Vancouver, B.C.[223]

The same result would obtain with respect to coverage on Form "B," as one of the specifically named perils includes "volcanic eruption."

Form "C" does not include volcanic eruption as one of the risks. As-suming, for purposes of discussion, that the master's fear that further vol-canic eruptions constituted a danger to his ship and the fear was real, not fanciful, and that his reliance upon the "Caspiana" clause was not mis-placed, Form "C" would *not* provide coverage, as the operation of the For-warding Charges Clause is dependent upon the "operation of a risk cov-ered by this insurance."

Comparison of the Old and New Institute Time Hull Clauses and the American Institute Hull Clauses

The new Hull Clauses, officially termed "Institute Time Clauses, Hulls," are indeed very new. A draft was not issued by London underwriters until February 1, 1983 and prior to that time it was impossible to obtain any idea of what the new clauses were to contain. A veil of secrecy surrounded them, and the work of the Committee was impenetrable. The new Hull Clauses and the new Institute War and Strikes Clauses, Hull-Time are reprinted in the Appendix.

Before launching into a discussion of the new clauses, it would be wise to consider the specific improvements and changes which the UNCTAD report recommended with respect to hull insurance.[224] The report sum-marized the suggested improvements,[225] of which the following is a condensation:

1. Develop regulations relating to brokers requiring minimum stan-dards of compentency and financial responsibility;

2. Eliminate the rule voiding policies written on a P. P. I. basis;[226]

3. Amend the rule that all, even innocent, nondisclosure or misrepre-

---

223. Subject, of course, to Clause 9, "Termination of Contract of Carriage Clause," re-quiring prompt notice to underwriters.

224. TD/B/C./4/ISL/27, 20 November, 1978, hereinafter called the "Report."

225. Report, 64-66.

226. P.P.I. (policy proof of interest) policies have no legal standing under English law, although they are valid under American law to the extent to which the assured can prove an

sentations of material information at the time of making the insurance contract enables the insurer to avoid liability, even as to damage caused by an event completely unconnected with the nondisclosure or misrepresentation;

4. Revise the antiquated S. G. form, including revision of the Perils Clause to make it more comprehensible in the modern day context, as well as eliminating war risk terminology and combine the Perils Clause with other appropriate Institute so that the designated risks appear in one unified Risks Clause. Alter the method of granting insurance, from an enumeration of named perils to an "all risks" grant of cover with specific exceptions, and facilitate the method of granting war risk insurance, to the end that insurance coverage is easier to understand and interpret;

5. Draft a temporary payment clause for situations where two or more insurers dispute liability for a loss;

6. Amend the rule making the agreed value in the policy binding on determination of rights of the parties to recoveries from third parties, in order to eliminate the resulting inequitable preference given insurers when the actual value of the insured property is greater than the agreed value;

7. Include an "agreement to be bound" clause in all policies written on a co-insurance basis to avoid the assured having to sue each insurer individually in the event of a dispute. All international insurances where the assured and insurers are situated in different countries should contain a jurisdiction clause stipulating a mutually convenient jurisdiction;

8. Eliminate the discriminatory aspects of the Joint Hull Formula;

9. Make available the "All Risks" cover contained in the Liner Negligence Clause to all shipowners who are prepared to pay the appropriate premium. The Inchmaree and Liner Negligence Clauses should also be redrafted to make their intended effect easier to understand;

10. Reduce the difficulties in the use of "all claims, each accident" deductibles, such as when there are particularly large deductibles as well as deductibles applicable to heavy weather damage and to sue and labor expenses. Use special clauses to assist in the application of the concept of "each accident or occurrence;"

11. Eliminate "Co-insurance" clauses as inappropriate in a standard hull policy;

---

insurable interest. Nevertheless, it has always been the practice of underwriters in the English-speaking world to accept risks on such terms, although they are binding in honor only. They are, as it were, a commercial convenience in situations where, although the assured may have an insurable interest, it would be difficult and time-consuming to prove that interest. See *The Sephie*, 9 F.2d 304, 1926 AMC 447 (2d Cir.); *The Governor*, 1923 AMC 741 (W.D., Wash.); *Republic of China v. National Union Fire Ins. Co.*, 163 F.Supp. 812, 1958 AMC 1529 (D.,Md.).

12. Eliminate the rule reducing the indemnity payable for general average contributions, salvage charges, and sue and labor expenses where the agreed value is less than the actual value of the insured subject;

13. The collision liability coverage in the Running Down Clause should permit the fixing of an independent limit on the insurer's liability instead of automatically tieing this limit to the agreed value in the policy;

14. Eliminate two inequitable provisions in the Tender Clause relating to payment of an allowance for lost time while additional tenders are required by the insurer, and imposing a penalty for noncompliance with the terms of the Clause where the assured is prevented from doing so by circumstances beyond his control;

15. Insert a "payment on account" clause in hull policies;

16. Amend the clause in standard hull policies denying a shipowner a "co-insurer" status to the extent of his deductible, thereby denying him proportional rights to participate in third party recoveries and instead giving the insurer preference in such recoveries;

17. Develop a standard clause granting coverage for physical damage resulting from delay caused by a peril insured against; and

18. Prohibit the use of "subrogation" forms assigning to insurers the assured's rights of action against third parties in return for payment of an insurance claim.

Analysis of the New Hull Clauses

Keeping in mind that the new "MAR" form is really nothing more than a sheet of paper upon which the most vital information is to be entered, such as the policy number, name of assured, vessel, voyage or period of insurance, subject-matter insured, agreed value, if any, amount insured, premium, the clauses and endorsements to be attached, and any "special conditions and warranties" are to be noted, the new hull clauses actually contain the basic terms of coverage. In this sense, the new MAR form is substantially identical to almost all the blank spaces which must be filled in on page 1 of the American Institute Hulls (1977) form.

Navigation/Adventure Clause. In the new hull form, this is termed the "Navigation" clause; in the AIH (1977) form it is termed the "Adventure" clause. In the old Institute Hulls Clauses, it is Clause 3. All three clauses are substantially identical, except that the new Navigation clause contains an additional paragraph which eliminates coverage for claims for loss or damage after a vessel sails with the intention of being "broken up" for scrap or "sold for being broken up," unless previous notice is given to underwriters and any amended terms of cover, adjustment of the insured value, and additional premiums required have been agreed.

The inclusion of the new paragraph is quite understandable when one considers that in this era of large deductibles, the owner of an aged ship may well forego repairs if he knows that in a relatively short time he is going to sell the vessel for scrap anyway. Thus, it can easily happen that when the time policy was written the vessel's value as an operating entity was much more than her end value as scrap. Nevertheless, underwriters are bound by the agreed value in the policy and should the vessel be lost on her final voyage to the scrap yard, underwriters will have made a rather handsome gift to the assured. Therefore, Clause 1.3 restricts coverage to the "market" value of the vessel as scrap, unless the assured gives prior notice so that reasonable terms can be arranged.

It should be observed that no mention is made in the clause regarding sue and labor expenses should the vessel sustain a casualty enroute to the scrap yard. Referring to Clause 13 relating to the duty of the assured to sue and labor, would the "reasonableness" of the assured's effort be measured by the scrap value or the insured value? In construing the clauses in para materia, it would seem that the reasonableness of the expense should be measured against the scrap value. Suppose, however, that the efforts are considerable and extend over a period of time such that the expenses incurred exceed the scrap value but are under the insured value. Clause 13.6 states that the sum recoverable under Clause 13 shall be in addition to the loss otherwise recoverable but shall not exceed the insured value. Clearly, this could be the source of a problem which, ultimately, is bound to surface.

It should also be noted that Clause 1.3 speaks in terms of the vessel sailing (with or without cargo) with an intention of being broken up. An "intention" is highly subjective. Upon whom will the burden of proof rest in proving that the owner did, or did not, have such an intention and how much evidence will underwriters demand before being satisfied that a vessel is not actually on a scrapping voyage?

In fairness to underwriters, it must be mentioned that the moral hazard involved in insuring a vessel for a relatively large amount when it is destined for the scrap yard is simply too great to be borne in these times, with ships sinking in incredible good weather, in calm seas, and invariably in the deepest portion of the water being traversed. As one astute observer has noted, Murphy's Law applies and if a vessel can sink, it will sink. The corollary is that the depth of the water in which it sinks is in direct ratio to the shipowner's financial impecuniosity.

Continuation/Duration of Risk Clause. This clause simply provides that should the vessel at the expiration of the policy be at sea, or in distress, or at a port of refuge or of call, she shall, provided previous notice is given to underwriters, be held covered, at a pro rata premium, to her port of destination. The clause is identical in the new hull clauses, the AIH (1977) form, and in the old Institute Hull form.[227]

Breach of Warranty Clause. This clause provides simply that the vessel is held covered in case of any breach of conditions as to cargo, trade, locality, towage or salvage activities, or date of sailing, provided notice is given immediately following receipt of knowledge by the assured, and any amended terms of cover and any additional premium are agreed to by the assured. It is substantially identical in the new hull form, the AIH form and the old Institute Hull form.[228]

A subsidiary question occurs here. Is loading or discharging cargo at sea a breach as to "trade"? If so, the penalty to the assured will be found in Clause 1.2 (of the Navigation/Adventure Clause) which provides that underwriters will not be responsible for "ranging damage" to the insured vessel, or for any liability to the other vessel involved, unless they have been given previous notice and any amended terms of cover and any additional premium required by them have been agreed.

Termination/Change of Ownership Clause. In the new hull clauses, this is called the "Termination" clause; in the AIH form it is called "Change of Ownership"; in the old Institute Hull form it is denominated Clause 6. In any event, the language is substantially identical and provides (subject to deferral of termination in certain events) that the insurance terminates if there is a change in the vessel's classification, ownership, flag, charter, management, etc.

It will be noted here that an entirely new clause has been introduced; i.e., 4.1 which provides for automatic termination if the vessel's classification is changed, or her existing class is not maintained. This applies, of course, unless the vessel is at sea in which case termination is deferred until arrival at the next port. Here, much will depend upon the rules of the respective classification society and it must be assumed that underwriters will demand proof of the circumstances.

It is only common sense that the loss experience of a shipowner is one of the major factors in rating a hull renewal. Consequently, when a vessel

---

227. In this connection, see *Robertson v. Royal Exchange Assur. Corp.*, (1924) 20 Ll.L.Rep. 17, where it was held that an owner was entitled to invoke the clause when he gave notice of abandonment on the grounds that the vessel was a constructive total loss, and that underwriters, by declining notice of abandonment, recognized that the owner still had an insurable interest.

228. In connection with the judicial construction of the clause, see *The Tinkerbell,* 533 F.2d 496, 1976 AMC 99 (9th Cir.); *Harris v. Glens Falls Ins. Co.,* 493 P.2d 861, 1972 AMC 138 (St.,Cal.); *Liberian Ins. Agency v. Mosse,* [1971] 2 Lloyd's Rep. 560; *Kalmbach Inc. v. Insurance Co. of State of Pa.,* 529 F.2d 552 (9th Cir., 1976); *Bristol Steamship Corp. v. London Assurance and H. O. Linard,* 1976 AMC 448 (S.D.N.Y.); *Fed. Bus. Development Bank v. Commonwealth Ins. Co., Ltd. et al (The Good Hope),* [1983] 2 C.C.L.I. 200 (S.C. of B.C., 1983).

is sold or transferred to new management, underwriters usually prefer to cancel the policy. This correctly reflects the "moral hazard" involved in insuring for a period of time, at an agreed value, a vessel which could be sunk by a new owner about whom the underwriters probably know nothing.[229]

Assignment Clause. This clause precludes assignment of the policy or of moneys due thereunder unless a dated notice of the assignment, signed by the assured, is endorsed on the policy and the policy is produced before payment of a claim. This reflects the more stringent conditions relating to assignment of policies under English marine insurance law than will be found under American law.

The language in the new hull form and in the old Institute Hull form is substantially identical. There is no comparable clause in the AIH form.[230]

Perils Clause. The "perils" clause of the new hull form is a radical departure from past practice under the old S. G. form. In the AIH (1977) form, the perils clause follows rather closely the old perils clause in the Lloyd's S. G. form. However, in the new hull clauses, the London market seems to have taken to heart at least one recommendation of the UNCTAD secretariat; i.e., the antiquated form should be revised to make it more comprehensible, eliminate war risk terminology, and combine it with other

---

229. See *Lemar Towing v. Fireman's Fund*, 471 F.2d 609, 1973 AMC 1843 (5th Cir.) (no breach of the clause where the same two men retained direction and control of a tug while acting as controlling stockholders and officers of separate corporate entities); *Taylor v. Commercial Union*, 614 F.2d 160, 1982 AMC 1815 (8th Cir.) (tower's liability policy did not by its terms provide coverage to a corporate successor of an individually owned towing service, but underwriter held estopped to deny coverage by reason of its own conduct); *Prudent Tankers Ltd. v. The Dominion Ins. Co. (The Caribbean Sea)*, [1980] 1 Lloyd's Rep. 338 (relating, in part, to the classification of the vessel); *Vinnie's Market v. Canadian Marine*, 1978 AMC 977 (D.Mass.) (termination for non-payment of premium); *U. S. Fire Ins. Co. v. Cavanaugh*, 1983 AMC 1261 (SD,Fla.) (hiring a new master who agreed to comply with the owner's instructions as to fishing locations—but who disobeyed—not a breach of the "change of interest" warranty); *Fed. Bus. Development Bank v. Commonwealth Ins. Co., Ltd. (The Good Hope)*, [1983] 2 C.C.L.I. 200 (S.C. of B.C., 1983); *Palmdale Ins. Ltd. v. R. P. & I Baxter Pty. Ltd.*, [1982] 2 ANZ Ins. Cas. 60-479 (Aus.,N.S.W.) (assured owner chartered his vessel without participation by his mortgagee; warranty against chartering held breached both as to the owner and the mortgagee and recovery denied); *Pindos Shipping Corp. v. Raven (The Mata Hari)*, [1983] 2 Lloyd's Rep. 449, Q.B.D. (policy subject to a condition "warranted class maintained"; the yacht was not in class at the time of the loss and had never been maintained in class. Rectification of the policy was denied as was recovery under the policy); *Norwest Refrigeration v. Bain Dawes et al*, [1983] 2 ANZ Ins. Cas. 60-507 (Aus., W.A.) (policy warranted free of liability if the vessel did not have a current harbor board certificate of seaworthiness [note the similarity to "classification"]); *Parfait v. Central Towing*, 660 F2d 608, 1982 AMC 698 (5th Cir.) (sale of all stock in a closely held tug-owning corporation and election of new directors and officers voided the policy under the "change of management" clause).

230. See *Rayner v. Preston* (1881) 50 L.J. Ch. 472, and *Samuel & Co. v. Dumas*, [1924] A.C. 431, (1928) 18 Ll.L.Rep. 211.

Institute Clauses (such as the "Inchmaree" Clause) so that the designated risks appear in one unified clause.

In doing so, several changes are immediately apparent. For example, the designated risks are not followed by the general words ". . . and of all other perils, losses and misfortunes, etc." On the face of it, the words are very wide, amounting almost to all risks coverage. The criticism has been made by commentators (including the UNCTAD secretariat) that they are misleading to assured, because, of course, the apparent breadth of the general words is limited in several ways. That is:

1. By the Rules of Construction to the Marine Insurance Act (Schedule, Rule 12) which states that the general words "include only perils similar in kind to the perils specifically mentioned in the policy;"

2. It does not enable an assured to recover in respect of a peril which is specifically excluded by other words in the policy or clauses.[231]

3. The general words only apply to the standard S. G. perils; not, for instance, to the additional perils covered by the Inchmaree Clause.

The efficacy of the general words may be said to have been truly demonstrated in very few cases;[232] in all the others, the general words were treated as an additional, or alternative, reason for the decision that there was coverage.[233]

For example, in *Cullen v. Butler,*[234] the ship and goods were sunk at sea by another ship firing upon her, mistaking her for an enemy. Although the loss was not one occasioned by "enemies," the court held that it was sufficiently "like" that peril as to be brought within the general words. Lord Ellenborough explained the principle in the following words:

> The extent and meaning of the general words have not yet been the immediate subject of any judicial construction by our courts of law. As

---

231. *Republic of Bolivia v. Indemnity Mutual Marine,* (1909) 1 K.B. 785.

232. *Cullen v. Butler,* (1815) 105 E.R. 119; *Phillips v. Barber,* (1821) 106 E.R. 1151; *West Indian Telegraph v. Home & Colonial,* (1880) 6 Q.B. 51; *Symington v. Union Insurance,* (1928) 3 C.C. 28; *The Lapwing,* (1940) 66 Ll.L.Rep. 174; *Feinberg v. Ins. Co. of N. A.,* 260 F2d 523, 1959 AMC 11 (lst Cir.).

233. *Butler v. Wildman,* (1820) 106 E.R. 708 (throwing overboard of Spanish dollars to prevent capture by enemy held *ejusdem generis* with jettison); *Jones v. Nicholson,* (1854) 156 E.R. 342 (sale of cargo by master, a part owner of the cargo, held *ejusdem generis* with barratry); *Palmer v. Naylor,* (1854) 156 E.R. 492 (murder of master and taking over the vessel by emigrants aboard as passengers held *ejusdem generis* with piracy). See *Sun Fire Office v. Hart,* (1899) 14 A.C. 98, P.C.; *Republic of Bolivia v. Indemnity Mutual Marine,* (1909) 1 K.B. 785; *Davidson v. Burnand,* (1868) 19 L.T. 782; *Thames & Mersey Marine Ins. Co. Ltd. v. Hamilton, Fraser & Co.,* (1887) 12 A.C. 484; *The Knight of St. Michael,* (1898) P. 30; *Samuel P. & Co. Ltd. v. Dumas,* [1924] A.C. 431; *Canada Rice Mills, Ltd. v. Union Marine & General Ins. Co., Ltd.,* [1940] A.C. 55; *O'Connor v. Merchants Marine Ins. Co.,* (1889) 20 N.S.R. 514, 16 S.C.R. 331 (Can.); *Miskofski v. Economic Ins. Co.,* 43 D.L.R. (2d) 281 (Can.); *Taylor v. Dunbar,* (1869) L.R. 4 C.P. 206; *Stott (Baltic Steamers, Ltd.) v. Marten,* [1916] 1 A.C. 304; *S. S. Knutsford, Ltd. v. Tillmans & Co.,* [1908] A.C. 406.

234. (1815) 105 E.R. 119.

they must, however, be considered as introduced into the policy in furtherance of the objects of marine insurance and may have the effect of extending a reasonable indemnity to many cases not distinctly covered by the special words, they are entitled to be considered as material and operative words, and to have due effect assigned to them in the construction of this instrument; and which will be done by allowing them to comprehend and cover other cases of marine damage of the like kind with those which are specially enumerated and occasioned by similar causes.

In *Phillips v. Barber*,[235] the vessel was put in a graving dock for repairs. While in the graving dock, she was thrown over by violent winds and was bilged and sustained considerable damage. Her damage was held to be *ejusdem generis* with stranding and the assured recovered. Without the general words, it is doubtful the assured would have recovered. However, it would appear that under the new hull clauses, the assured could bring himself within Clause 6.1.7 and claim for damage caused by "contact with . . . dock or harbour equipment or installation."

In *West Indian Telegraph v. Home & Colonial*,[236] a steamer was wrecked after an explosion in her boiler. It was held that this was *ejusdem generis* with "fire." The point is unlikely to arise now, as "explosion" is expressly covered in the new clauses.

In *Symington v. Union Insurance*,[237] the damage to cargo was due to its jettison into the sea following a fire on the quay. However, jettison and fire are now expressly covered in the new clauses and one would not expect a different decision today.

In *The Lapwing, sub nom Baxendale v. Fane*,[238] the master of the vessel docked it so as to allow it to sit on a dangerous bottom. The loss was held to be *ejusdem generis* with stranding. She had been so docked as a consequence of the negligence of the manager of the ship repair company. Under the new clauses, even without the general words, it would appear that the assured could recover, either under contact with a "dock or harbour installation" (6.1.7) or "negligence of repairers" (6.2.5).

In *Feinberg v. Ins. Co. of N. A.*,[239] a yacht tied up in a marina was moved from its location, personal items aboard were stolen, and the yacht severely damaged by vandalism; it was held that physical damage to the yacht, coupled with the theft of the personal items, was *ejusdem qeneris* with theft. Without the general words, the damage to the yacht would clearly have not been covered.

---

235. (1821) 106 E.R. 1151.
236. (1880) 6 Q.B. 51.
237. (1928) 3 C.C. 28.
238. (1940) 66 Ll.L.Rep. 174.
239. 260 F.2d 523, 1959 AMC 11 (1st Cir.).

A distinguished commentator believes that there has been no diminution in coverage by deletion of the general words.[240] He stated:

The deletion of the general words was in the interest of clarity and to remove ambiguity which the antiquated terminology produced. It was not intended by Underwriters to diminish cover, and it is to be expected that the English Courts will approach the matter on this basis. Analysis of the cases show that the old instances would be recoverable under the new Clauses without the need for general words. It is to be hoped that this may lay the ghost of any contention that there has been a significant diminution of cover by their deletion.

Another equally distinguished commentator has this to say:[241]

I think the true position was that Underwriters were able to accept many claims which came very near, but not precisely, within the specified perils, and thus the real benefit was in the disputes avoided, particularly in the case of "perils of the seas." Many practitioners felt this would be a rather limited term without the general words, and it will be seen that in the end Underwriters were prevailed upon to add the words "rivers, lakes or other navigable waters" so as to avoid any arguments about which waters were intended to be covered.

Notwithstanding the preeminence of these noted commentators, unfortunately not all underwriters will be aware of their views and it is confidently predicted that not only will the question arise (probably in the American courts) but the decision, or decisions, will come down on the side of no coverage.

In the new hull form, the perils clause is divided into two distinct parts. The first part, Paragraphs 6.1 through 6.1.8, sets forth the stated perils; i.e., perils of the seas, fire, violent theft by persons from outside the vessel, jettison, piracy, breakdown of or accident to nuclear installations or reactors, contact with aircraft or similar objects, land conveyance, dock or harbor equipment or installation, and earthquake, volcanic eruption, or lightning. These last three named perils were formerly included in the Inchmaree Clause; their position in the new hull form reflects different placement.[242]

---

240. Donald O'May, of Ince & Co., London. who assisted the various committees of Lloyd's with respect to new clauses and the meetings with UNCTAD.

241. J. K. Goodacre, Chairman, U. K. Society of Average Adjusters, Address to the Membership, October 27, 1983.

242. Note that "perils of the seas" has been expanded by addition of the words "rivers lakes or other navigable waters." The point has arisen in the United States and it has been squarely held that as applied to inland watercraft, the words "perils of the seas," standing alone, are synonymous with "perils of the river." See *Continental Ins. Co. v. Patton-Tully Transp. Co.,* 212 F2d 543, 1954 AMC 889 (5th Cir.); *Russell Mining v. Northwestern F. & M. Ins. Co.,* 207 F.Supp. 162, 1963 AMC 130 (E.D.,Tenn.), *aff'd* 322 F2d 440, 1963 AMC 2358 (6th

The second part, Paragraph 6.2 through 6.3, is obviously modeled on the old Inchmaree Clause. After enumerating the perils (i.e., accidents in loading, discharging, or shifting cargo or fuel; explosions; bursting of boilers, breakage of shafts, or any latent defect in the machinery or hull; negligence of repairers or charterers, provided such repairers or charterers are not assured, and barratry), Paragraph 6.2.6 concludes with this proviso:

> Provided such loss or damage has not resulted from want of due diligence by the Assured, Owners or Managers.

Consequently, coverage for the perils enumerated in Paragraghs 6.2 through 6.2.6 is provided so long as the assured, owners, and managers can demonstrate the exercise of due diligence.

It is not entirely clear from a reading of the clauses whether it was intended that the proviso also applies to the perils specified in Paragraphs 6.1 through 6.1.8, but the author is informed by reliable sources in the London market that the intent was that the proviso would apply only to the perils specified in Paragraphs 6.2 through 6.2.6.

It will be noted that all of the "perils" listed in Clause 6 have been preceded by the words "This insurance covers loss of or damage to the subject-matter insured *caused by* . . . ." Reference to the old form of Inchmaree Clause will disclose that the perils mentioned in that clause were preceded by the words " . . . directly caused by . . . ." Of course, the basic perils in the old S. G. form were simply mentioned as those which the underwriters were "contented to bear." The question naturally arises as to whether the changes alter the manner in which the policy is to be construed.

The answer appears to be in the negative. This is so because the basic perils in the policy have always been subject to the doctrine of proximate cause which is set forth in Section 55(1) of the Marine Insurance Act reading:

> Subject to the provisions of this Act, and unless the policy otherwise provides, the insurer is liable for any loss proximately caused by a peril insured against, but, subject as aforesaid, he is not liable for any loss which is not proximately caused by a peril insured against.

Moreover, there appears to be no real difference in meaning between the word "directly" and the word "proximately" when used to qualify the cause.[243]

Cir.); *Shaver Forwarding Co. v. Eagle Star Ins. Co.*, 172 Or. 91, 129 P2d 769, 1943 AMC 1178, 177 Or. 410, 162 P2d 789 (1945); *Prohaska v. St. Paul Fire & Marine Ins. Co.*, 270 F. 91 (5th Cir., 1921).

243. *Coxe v. Employer's Liability Assurance Corp. Ltd.*, [1916] 2 K.B. 629: *Oei v. Foster and Eagle Star Ins. Co., Ltd.*, [1982] 2 Lloyd's Rep. 170.

It is interesting to note that "barratry," which was formerly a part of the old classic perils clause, now appears in what was formerly the Inchmaree Clause. The intent here presumably was to make the "want of due diligence" proviso applicable to barratry.[244] This is a decidedly new approach and could serve to relieve underwriters from liability where the loss is occasioned by barratry of the master, officers, or crew and the shipowner/assured has "turned a blind eye" to the qualifications of the master and crew who were hired. It may be expected that in the future under the new hull clauses underwriters will closely scrutinize what the shipowner/assured did or did not do in terms of hiring an honest and competent master and crew. A "blind eye" will not suffice.[245]

It seems probable that the foregoing was drafted in the fashion it was in light of such cases as *Astrovlanis Compania Naviera S. A. v. Linard (The Gold Sky)*,[246] and *Piermay Shipping Co., S. A. v. Chester (The Michael)*.[247]

As noted above, the UNCTAD report criticized the fact that the limitations in the Inchmaree Clause are not easily detectable in the old format. For example, it was early decided that the term "latent defect" did not include a latent defect by reason of an error in design.[248] Moreover, early decisions clearly established that under the Inchmaree Clause, replacement or repair of the defective part causing the damage was not recoverable.[249]

The new hull clauses (Paragraphs 6.2 through 6.2.6) do not clarify the foregoing. For example, if the draftsmen of the clauses had wished, both these points could have been clarified by drafting 6.2.3 to read:

> Bursting of boilers, breakage of shafts, or any latent defect (other than error in design), excluding however, the cost and expense of replacing or repairing the defective part.[250]

---

244. Of course, underwriters still have a defense to those perils not coming under the proviso if they can show wilful misconduct on the part of the assured. Section 55(2) (a), Marine Insurance Act.

245. See *Compania Maritima San Basilio S.A. v. Oceanus Mutual Underwriting Association (Bermuda) Ltd. (The Eurysthenes)*, [1976] 2 Lloyd's Rep. 171.

246. [1972] 2 Lloyd's Rep. 187.

247. [1979] 1 Lloyd's Rep. 55.

248. *Jackson v. Mumford*, (1902) 8 Com.Cas. 61. But compare the recent decision of *Prudent Tankers Ltd. v. The Dominion Ins. Co. (The Caribbean Sea)*, [1980] 1 Lloyd's Rep. 338, where the loss of the vessel was held to have been caused by a latent defect when fatigue cracks developed due to a *combination* of poor design and the effect of the ordinary working of the vessel.

249. See *Ocean Steamship Co. v. Faber*, (1907) 97 L.T. 466 (C.A.); *Hutchins Bros. v. Royal Exchange Assur. Corp.*, (1911) 2 K.B. 398; *The Rensselaer*, 1925 AMC 1116 (St.,N.Y.); *National Bulk Carriers v. American Marine Hull Ins. Synd.*, 1949 AMC 340 (Arb.); *Ferrante v. Detroit Fire & Marine Ins. Co.*, 125 F.Supp. 621, 1954 AMC 2026 (D., Cal.).

250. The AIH (1977) form has long contained a specific clause in this respect which mentions, parenthetically, "excluding the cost and expense of replacing or repairing the defective part."

In at least one area, clarification seems to have been achieved. That is, the term "thieves" appears as one of the perils in the old perils clause.[251] But the term was defined in Rule for Construction 9 of the Marine Insurance Act, 1906, as not covering clandestine theft or theft committed by one of the ship's company, whether crew or passengers. Paragraph 6.1.3 now reads "violent theft by persons from outside the vessel." Consequently, anyone reading the new clauses should now be fully apprised that only theft with violence from persons outside the vessel is covered.

However, the addition for the first time of the Strikes Exclusion Clause (Clause 24) in an English hull policy may and probably will occasion some problems with respect to coverage for thieves and piracy under Clause 6. This is so because the Strikes Exclusion Clause excludes claims caused by persons taking part in "riots."

Under English law, the term "riot" is a term of art which, by legal definition, may well embrace acts which would popularly be thought of as "piracy" or "assailing thieves." For example, in *London & Lancashire Fire Ins. Co. v. Bolands*,[252] four armed men entered a bakery, held up the employees with guns and took a considerable amount of cash. The policy provided coverage against loss of cash by burglary, housebreaking, and theft, but excluded loss directly or indirectly caused by, or happening through, or in consequence of, riots. The court held that the circumstances in which the money was stolen constituted a riot within the legal definition of the term and the exclusion was applied. The court acknowledged that an uninstructed layman would probably not think of the word "riot" in such circumstances and would think it something a bit more noisy. But, as the term was emphatically one of art, the definition already arrived at for it would be applied.[253]

As a consequence, it would appear that coverage is provided under Clause 6 for violent thieves and piratical thieves but riotous thieves would be excluded. The exclusion is paramount—the language preceding the Strikes Exclusion and the other exclusions specifically provides that those clauses shall be paramount and shall override anything contained in the policy inconsistent therewith—and in no case would the insurance cover loss, damage, liability, or expense caused by persons taking part in riots.

---

251. The term "assailing thieves" is used in the AIH (1977) form, and refers to acts of obtaining access to property by force. It includes persons who break into and steal property from a vessel; it is not limited to thieves using violence against the person, as in robbery. See *Swift v. American Universal Ins. Co.*, 1966 AMC 269 (St.,Mass.); *Goodman v. U. S. Fire Ins. Co.*, 1967 AMC 1853 (St.,N.Y.); *The Orange*, 337 F.Supp. 1161, 1972 AMC 627 (S.D.N.Y.); *Bobley v. California Union Ins. Co.*, 1976 AMC 216 (St.,N.Y.).
252. [1924] A.C. 836, (1924) 19 Ll.L.Rep. 1 (H.L.).
253. See *Field and Others v. The Receiver of Metropolitan Police*, [1907] 2 K.B. 853; *The Andreas Lemos*, [1982] 2 Lloyd's Rep. 483. Compare, however, *Pan American World Airways v. Aetna Casualty & Surety Co.*, F2d , [1975] 1 Lloyd's Rep. 77 (Cir.) and *Ford Motor Co. of Canada Ltd. v. Prudential Assur. Co. Ltd.*, (1958) 14 D.L.R. (2d) 7 (Can., Ont.)

Yet, so long as there are three or more thieves, the very nature of the crime would seem to provide all the necessary ingredients of a riot under English law.

Pollution Hazard Clause. The AIH (1977) form has a clause denominated "Deliberate Damage (Pollution Hazard)." Essentially, it provides coverage for loss or damage to the vessel *directly caused* by governmental authorities to prevent or mitigate a pollution hazard, provided such act of the governmental authorities did not result from a want of due diligence by the assured. Clause 7 of the new hull clauses is almost identical. No such clause appears in the old Institute Time Hulls Clauses.

Collision Clause. The classic English form of collision clause has always been limited to three-fourths of the total liability incurred by the insured by reason of a collision of the insured vessel with another vessel. The theory behind the limitation was to place some of the burden on the assured and to provide an incentive or inducement to employ non-negligent officers and crews.[254]

By contrast, the American form of collision clause (exemplified by the Collision Clause in the AIH (1977) form), provides coverage for four-fourths (100 percent) of the vessel owner's liability for collision with another ship or vessel. With this exception, the Collision Clause in the old Institute form is almost identical with the Collision Clause in the AIH (1977) form.

The three-fourths Collision Liability Clause (Clause 8) in the new hull form contains slightly different wording than will be found in the AIH (1977) form and the old Institute form. At first glance, the different wording would not appear to alter significantly the legal effect of the clause, but this conclusion may be more apparent than real. For example, the old language provides that if there is a collision with another vessel and the assured shall in consequence thereof "become liable to pay and shall pay by way of damages" underwriters will respond. The new language makes it very clear that the duty of the underwriters is only to *indemnify* the assured for three-fourths of any sum or sums "paid by the assured to any other person or persons by reason of the assured becoming legally liable by way of damages." In light of the American and English cases, the effect of the new language probably does not differ, although the new language does appear more clear and concise.

Under the old Institute form of the clause, the underwriters' liability could not exceed their "proportionate part of three-fourths of the *value* of the vessel . . . insured." Under the new form (Clause 8.2.2), the under-

---

254. The Collision Clause is discussed in detail in Chapter XIX, Running Down Clause, *infra.*

writers' liability does not exceed their proportionate part of three-fourths of "the *insured value*" of the vessel. The simple word "value" could be construed to mean market value, which might greatly exceed the "insured value." By amending the clause to read "insured value," it is made crystal clear that underwriters are liable only for their proportionate oart of the insured value and not the market value.

Clause 8.2 of the new form provides that the indemnity to be paid shall be "in addition to" the indemnity provided by other terms and conditions of the overall policy. Thus, it is made quite clear that the collision clause coverage is supplementary to the other coverages. Conceivably, therefore, underwriters could be held liable for a very substantial claim for particular average under other applicable provisions of the policy, and could also be required to pay up to three-fourths of the insured value under the collision clause. This was not clear in the old Institute form of the clause, although court decisions had arrived at the same result. In terms of clarity, for the benefit of an unsophisticated assured, this is a decided improvement.

The "Exclusions" under the collision clause in the AIH (1977) form and the old Institute form have long been identical. They exclude liability of underwriters for sums which the assured shall pay for:

(a) removal or disposal of obstructions, wrecks, cargoes or any other thing whatsoever under statutory powers or otherwise;

(b) injury to real or personal property of every description; (c) discharge, spillage, emission or leakage of oil, petroleum products, chemicals or other substances of any kind or description whatsoever;

(d) cargo or other property on or the engagements of the vessel; and

(d) loss of life, personal injury or illness.

Under "Exclusions" in the new hull form now appear the old exclusions found in the old Institute form, *plus* the pollution exclusion has been slightly broadened.

It should be noted that it has long been established under both American and English cases that the liabilities contemplated by the collision clause are those arising from "tort" rather than out of contracts under which liability may be assumed.[255] For example, in *Furness, Withy & Co. Ltd. v. Duder, supra*, a tug was damaged by the vessel in its tow, the tow being responsible for the cost of repairs under a provision in the towage

---

255. See, for example, *Furness, Withy and Co. Ltd. v. Duder*, (1936) 55 Ll.L.Rep. 52; *Hall Bros. S. S. Co. v. Young*, (1939) 63 Ll.L.Rep. 143 (C.A.); *Tug Claribel*, 341 F2d 956, 1965 AMC 535 (5th Cir.); *Harbor Towing Co. v. Atlantic Mutual Ins. Co.*, 189 F2d 409, 1951 AMC 1070 (4th Cir.); *The Narco and The Lolita*, 258 F2d 718, 1958 AMC 2404 (5th Cir.), modified 1961 AMC 1999, 286 F2d 600 (5th Cir.).

contract, although the sole negligence was on the part of the tug. The assured was unable to secure reimbursement from the underwriters under the clause.[256] In *Hall Bros. S. S. Co. v. Young, supra,* the assured was compelled by French law to pay for damages sustained by a French pilot boat which collided with the assured's vessel although no fault was imputed to the latter. The court held, in essence, that payment was made because of French law and not by reason of the collision liability *per se.*

It is also interesting to note the difference in the wording of the exclusions proviso. In the old Institute form the proviso reads:

> Provided always that this clause shall in no case extend or be deemed to extend to any sum which the Assured may become *liable to pay* or *shall pay* for or in respect of:

The exclusions proviso in the new hull clause reads:

> Provided always that this Clause 8 shall in no case extend to any sum which the Assured *shall pay* for or in respect of . . . .

This raises an interesting question. Inasmuch as the new collision clause in the new hull form now provides for an indemnity for three-fourths of any sum or sums *paid* by the assured, and the exclusions proviso again refers to sums which the assured *shall pay,* what is the result if the assured is held liable for a collision but becomes insolvent . . . and consequently does not pay?

In England, the Third Parties (Rights Against Insurers) Act, 1930, provides, in essence, that where an assured becomes bankrupt and, be-

---

256. The applicability to the U. K. Standard Towing Conditions is readily apparent. By contrast, under the AIH (1977) form, the shipowner's coverage is not jeopardized. The Pilotage and Towage Clause in the main body of the AIH form reads:

This insurance shall not be prejudiced by reason of any contract limiting in whole or in part the liability of pilots, tugs, towboats, or their owners when the Assured or the agent of Assured accepts such contract in accordance with established local practice.

Where in accordance with such practice, pilotage or towage services are provided under contracts requiring the Assured or the agent of the Assured:

(a) to assume liability for damage resulting from collision of the Vessel insured with any other ship or vessel, including the towing vessel; or

(b) to indemnify those providing the pilotage or towage services against loss or liability for any such damages,

it is agreed that amounts paid by the Assured or Surety pursuant to such assumed obligations shall be deemed payments "by way of damages to any other person or persons" and to have been paid "in consequence of the Vessel being at fault" within the meaning of the Collision Liability clause in this Policy to the extent that such payments would have been covered if the Vessel had been legally responsible in the absence of any agreement. Provided always that in no event shall the aggregate amount of liability of the Underwriters under the Collision Liability clause, including this clause, be greater than the amount of any statutory limitation of liability to which owners are entitled or would be entitled if liability under any contractual obligation referred to in this clause were included among liabilities subject to such statutory limitations.

fore or after the event, liability is incurred, his rights against the insurer under the insurance contract in respect of the liability shall be transferred to and vest in the third party to whom the liability is so incurred. It will be interesting to see whether the change in policy language, requiring that the assured actually *pay* such sums (rather than merely become "liable to pay") will be construed so as to relieve underwriters of obligations under the Third Parties (Rights Against Insurers) Act, 1930.

Moreover, should vessels owned by residents of Louisiana or Puerto Rico be insured under the new hull clauses, would the Direct Action statutes in those two jurisdictions apply so as to impose liability upon underwriters where the assured is bankrupt, has incurred liability for a collision, but has actually *paid* nothing?

Sistership Clause. This clause provides coverage (under the new form as well as the old Institute form) where the insured vessel comes into collision with or receives salvage services from another vessel belonging wholly or in part to the same owners or under the same management.

In the AIH form, sistership clauses appear in two different places. One such clause appears in the middle of the Collision Clause and applies to collisions; another similarly worded clause appears in the General Average and Salvage Clause and, of course, applies to salvage, towage, or assistance rendered by a sistership.

The English forms of this clause provide for a reference of the claim to a sole arbitrator to be agreed upon between underwriters and the assured; the AIH form also provides for referral to three arbitrators if the parties cannot agree on a sole arbitrator.

There do not appear to be any cases in England or the Commonwealth nations dealing with the sistership clauses. Interestingly, there are two leading American cases interpreting the clause which appear to have been overlooked by the English commentators. These are *The Augusta-The Detroit*,[257] and *The Ariosa and The D-22*,[258] and are discussed fully in Chapter XIX, the Running Down Clause.

Attention is also directed to *The Industry*,[259] where a collision took place between two vessels, owned by the same company, but insured by separate underwriters. Only one of the vessels sustained damage. The hull underwriters on the damaged vessel paid the loss in full under a loan receipt, thereafter claiming contribution from the other vessel's under-

---

257. 290 F2d 685, 1923 AMC 754, 1923 AMC 816, 1924 AMC 872, *aff'd* 5 F2d 773, 1925 AMC 756 (4th Cir.).
258. 144 F2d 262, 1944 AMC 1035 (2d Cir.), *cert. den.* 323 U.S. 797 (1944).
259. 1939 AMC 717 (Arb).

writers. It was held that the paying underwriters were entitled to contribution either as assignee of the owner or in their own right.

In *Bushey & Sons v. Tugboat Underwriting*,[260] the court held that the arbitration provision in the sistership clause obligated the underwriters to arbitrate claims arising out of a collision between a tug and a barge owned by separate corporations, where the underwriters were aware that each owning corporation was a wholly owned subsidiary of the same parent corporation and all were named assureds in the policy.

Tender Clause. In the new hull clauses, the old Tender Clause is denominated as the "Notice of Claim and Tenders" and is Clause 10 of the policy form. Under it, of course, the underwriters are entitled to notice of loss or damage and may dictate the port to which the vessel is to go to effect repairs. Inasmuch as the standard used to determine underwriters' liability is that of the "reasonable cost of repairs," the selection of the port of repair can be highly important. It is expected that the assured will take tenders at first instance, but the Tender Clause allows the underwriters to veto the assured's choice, to take their own tenders, or to require the taking of further tenders.

There have been very slight modifications to the language of the clause in the new hull policy but the net effect appears to be the same. An interesting change appears in the second paragraph of Clause 10.3, relating to due credit being given against the allowance for any amounts recovered in respect of fuel and stores and wages and maintenance of the master, officers, and crew, or any member thereof. In the old Institute form this was tied to amounts allowed in general or particular average; in the new form, the term used is "including general average."

It must be emphasized that if, *but only if*, the underwriters do require the taking of further tenders, a tender so taken is approved and accepted by the underwriters, and the assured in turn promptly accepts the tender after notification of underwriters' approval, the clause provides for an allowance of 30 percent per annum on the insured value of the vessel with respect to the time lost by the taking of such tenders.

If, however, the underwriters subsequently decide to rely on one of the earlier tenders taken by the assured, no allowance is made. Moreover, the clause imposes a penalty of 15 percent of the total claim for failure to comply literally with its terms. No exception is made for extenuating circumstances. Although underwriters may sometimes agree to an *ad hoc* waiver of the penalty, no firm assurance is given that this will be done.

General Average and Salvage Clause. Under both English and American law, the indemnity payable by underwriters for general average and sal-

260. 1975 AMC 392 (S.D.N.Y.).

vage charges is predicated upon the "contributory" values involved, rather than what the "Agreed Value" (AIH) or the "insured value" (English) may be. Thus, if the vessel is valued at $2 million for insurance purposes and is insured for that amount, but at the time of the casualty giving rise to a general average or salvage situation, is worth, say, $4 million, underwriters' liability is only for the proportion that the insured value bears to the actual value. This has sometimes come as a shock to an unsophisticated assured.[261]

The new clause does not really clarify the situation, except that it does make it clear that it only covers the vessel's *proportion* of salvage, salvage charges, and/or general average, *reduced in respect of any under-insurance.* In another respect it also provides a little more guidance to an assured. Clause 11.4 provides that no claim under the clause shall in any case be allowed where the loss was not incurred to avoid or in connection with the avoidance of a peril insured against. Although this is nothing more than a statement of what the law already is, it may be helpful to some. The comparable clause in the AIH form is worded somewhat differently, but the net effect appears to be substantially the same.

It should be noted that in revising this clause, the draftsmen ignored the recommendation of the UNCTAD secretariat.

Deductible Clause. Under both the English forms (new and old) and the AIH (1977) form, the deductible (whatever it may be) is applied to the aggregate of all claims (including claims under the Sue and Labor Clause and Collision Clause) *arising out of each separate accident.* The "separate accident" concept is difficult to apply and has occasioned problems. There is one exception in both forms, and that is in treating heavy weather damage (including contact with ice) occurring during a single passage between two successive ports as though it was due to one accident.

Under the old, as well as the new form, the underwriters receive all of any recovery from third parties up to the amount they have paid, and only when this is exceeded will the assured receive any of the recovery to offset his deductible. This is inequitable, as the underwriters are, after all, in the business of insuring risks and should not merit such preferential treatment.

Moreover, any interest included in recoveries is apportioned between the assured and the underwriters, notwithstanding that by the addition of interest the underwriters may receive a larger sum than they have paid. Keeping in mind that the policy is really one of indemnity, and that under

261. However, it is possible for the assured to protect himself where the insured value is lower than the contributory value by obtaining special insurance, such as the Institute Excess Liabilities Clause (Hulls) to cover his liability to pay the excess general average contribution, etc.

subrogation principles underwriters are entitled to recoup only that which they have paid and no more, it seems rather inequitable to allow themselves a greater recovery.

In the old Institute form (Clause 11), the underwriters could deduct 10 percent from the net claim when crew negligence contributed to the loss of or damage to boilers, machinery, etc. The clause does not appear in the AIH (1977) form and the Canadian market has dropped the use of it. The clause was grossly unfair in many instances involving large values and came under severe criticism in the UNCTAD report. It is refreshing to find that the clause does not appear in the new form.

The UNCTAD report also severely criticized the application of the deductible to sue and labor claims except where the claim is for a total or constructive total loss. It will be recalled that the Sue and Labor Clause (discussed hereinafter) requires the assured to sue and labor to avert or minimize damages, which is, of course, also to the underwriters' advantage. Where the assured has done so, it seems inequitable to apply a deductible to sums which he has paid or incurred in an effort to save the vessel and actually operates as a disincentive to make such efforts. For example, suppose that a vessel is worth $1 million; the policy contains a $50,000 deductible; the vessel sustains an insured casualty, and by the expenditure of $45,000, the assured is able to save the vessel from becoming a total or constructive total loss. Application of the deductible to the assured's claim results in the assured bearing the whole expense.

Notwithstanding the UNCTAD criticism, the deductible clause in the new form still continues to apply to sue and labor claims. The inequity, if such it is, also appears in the AIH form and American underwriters seemingly are oblivious to the UNCTAD criticism.

Duty of Assured (Sue and Labor). Under the old S. G. form, the Sue and Labor Clause merely recited that "it shall be lawful" for the assured to sue and labor. The AIH form uses the phrase "lawful *and necessary.*" The clause in the new form forthrightly states that it shall be the "duty" of the assured to sue and labor. Since this is the law anyway, it is well that the new clause properly informs the assured.

It is, however, a definite improvement to find the Sue and Labor Clause prominently displayed in the body of the new hull clauses, rather than having to refer back to the old S. G. form where it was literally buried in closely packed lines of type. In this respect, the new hull form follows the American practice, under which the Sue and Labor Clause is a part of the formal hull policy.

Despite the UNCTAD criticism, the new clause perpetuates the restriction on recoveries under the policy to that proportion which the insured or agreed value bears to the "sound" value; i.e., the assured is penalized by under-insurance even though such under-insurance may not have been his fault at all, and may have arisen by virtue of a dramatic increase in vessel values *after* the inception of the policy. The AIH form does not differ significantly in effect from the new clause although the wording is slightly different.

New for Old Clause. It was formerly the practice that when repairs were effected, the underwriter was responsible for the cost of replacing or repairing the old material. Thus, the practice developed of deducting "new for old," usually one-third. The New for Old Clause in the new form merely duplicates the comparable clause in the old Institute form and the AIH form, but with somewhat more clarity. The old Institute clause states that "average" is payable without deduction, new for old. The AIH form states that "general and particular" average is payable without deduction. The new clause simply uses the phrase "claims." The legal effect is the same.

Bottom Treatment Clause. Both the old Institute form and the AIH form provide that the expense of sighting the vessel's bottom after stranding will be paid if reasonably incurred especially for that purpose, even though no damage is found, and no claim is payable in any case in respect of painting or scraping the vessel's bottom.

The new Bottom Treatment Clause in the new form is considerably more explicit and provides coverage for scraping, gritblasting, and/or other surface preparation, or painting of the ship's bottom, but only *as to new work or surfaces.*

Wages and Maintenance Clause. This clause, which appears in the old Institute form, the new hull form, and in the AIH form, excludes claims (other than in general average) for wages and maintenance of the master, officers, and crew, except when incurred solely for the necessary removal of the vessel from one port to another for repairs, or for trial trips, and then only while the vessel is underway.

The wording of the clause in the new form is more precise but the net effect is the same. The AIH form is somewhat more generous in that it allows for overtime or similar extraordinary payments to the master and crew incurred in shifting the vessel for tank cleaning or repairs, or while specifically engaged in these activities, either in port or at sea.

Agency Commission Clause. This is totally new and will not be found either in the old Institute form or the AIH form. It reads:

> In no case shall any sum be allowed under this insurance either by way of remuneration of the Assured for time and trouble taken to obtain and supply information or documents or in respect of the com-

missions or charges of any manager, agent, managing or agency company or the like, appointed by or on behalf of the Assured to perform such services.

The new Agency Clause was apparently added to the new form to reflect that in hull claims there are often three surveys; i.e., one for the owner, one for the underwriters, and one for the vessel's classification society. In practice, the fees of the owner's surveyor and those of the classification society are paid by the underwriters if the basic claim is otherwise covered under the policy.

The object of the clause appears to be to preclude reimbursement to owners for services which are performed by their own personnel. Such services normally take a great deal of time and effort for which the owner usually receives only his out-of-pocket expenses. If, however, the owner creates an "agency" or "management" company which is a separate entity and that entity performs the services, claims a commission, etc., it can be treated as a direct charge against the underwriters. The manner in which the clause is worded indicates that underwriters will no longer be responsible either for the expenses (direct) of the owner or for indirect expenses paid to any agency or management company appointed by or on behalf of the assured to perform such services.

Unrepaired Damage Clause. Great uncertainty exists under English law with respect to the amount to be paid for damage to a vessel which remains unrepaired at the time a claim is made on underwriters. Reference must necessarily be made to Section 69 of the Marine Insurance Act, 1906, as interpreted by the various court decisions.[262]

The uncertainty involves such questions as whether the agreed value in the policy should be taken into account in determining the depreciation, whether the estimated cost of repairs should include the estimated cost of drydocking, and at what time the estimated repairs should be considered.

The clause in the new form should assist in resolving some of the uncertainties. It spells out that the measure of indemnity for claims for unrepaired damage shall be the reasonable depreciation in the *market value* of the vessel at the time the insurance terminates, resulting from such unrepaired damage, but not exceeding the reasonable cost of repairs. In no case shall the underwriters be liable for more than the insured value of

---

262. In this connection, see *Irvin v. Hine*, [1949] 2 All E.R. 1089, 83 Ll.L.Rep. 162; *Helmville Ltd. v. Yorkshire Ins. Co. (The Medina Princess)*, [1965] 1 Lloyd's Rep. 361; *Pitman v. Universal Mar. Ins. Co.*, (1882) 9 Q.B.D. 192, 4 Asp. M.L.C. 544, C.A.; *Aitchison v. Lohre*, (1879) 4 A.C. 755, 4 Asp. M.L.C. 168 (H.L.); *Compania Maritime Astra S.A. v. Archdale (The Armar)*, 1954 AMC 1674, [1954] 2 Lloyd's Rep. 95 (St.,N.Y.); and *Delta Supply Co. v. Liberty Mutual Ins. Co.*, 211 F.Supp. 429, 1963 AMC 1540 (S.D.,Tex.).

the vessel at the time the insurance terminates, nor are underwriters liable for unrepaired damage in the event of a subsequent total loss sustained during the period covered by the policy or any extension thereof.

This new clause should also be read *in para materia* with Clause 1.3 of the Navigation Clause, which provides:

> In the event of the Vessel sailing (with or without cargo) with the intention of being (a) broken up, or (b) sold for breaking up, no claim shall be recoverable under this insurance in respect of loss or damage to the Vessel occurring subsequent to such sailing unless previous notice has been given to the Underwriters and any amended terms of cover, adjustment of the insured value and additional premium required by them have been agreed. Nothing in this Clause 1.3 shall exclude claims under Clause 8 [Collision] and/or 11 [General Average and Salvage].

Unfortunately, left unanswered in the new language is whether the proportion of depreciation thus arrived at when the reasonable depreciation in market value is determined is applied to the insured value. If the insured value and the market value are the same, no problem arises; the difficulty comes when the insured value and the market value differ.[263]

Constructive Total Loss Clause. The old Institute clause has been expanded in the new form by adding a sentence reading: "In making this determination [whether cost of recovery and/or repair exceeds insured value], only the cost relating to a single accident or sequence of damages arising from the same accident shall be taken into account." This additional sentence is already included in the AIH form and it appears that the clause in the new form may well have been modelled upon the comparable AIH clause.

As noted heretofore, the problem engendered in applying the concept of "separate accident or occurrence" has not been resolved.

Freight Waiver Clause. This clause appears in the old Institute form and in the AIH form, and has been carried over into the new form. It simply provides that in the event of a total or constructive total loss no claim is to be made by underwriters for freight, whether or not notice of abandonment has been given.

Disbursements Warranty Clause. The purpose of this clause is to prevent shipowners from insuring a vessel against all risks for a comparatively low figure, and then making up the total loss value (or overinsuring) at a

---

263. See, in this connection, the formula applied in *Delta Supply Co. v. Liberty Mutual Ins. Co., supra,* note 262.

lower rate of premium by a series of insurances on interests which are ancillary to the hull insurance. The clause therefore limits the amount of such ancillary or supplementary insurance to the percentages specified in the clause. For example, the clause limits additional insurance on disbursements, managers' commissions, profits or excess or increased value of hull and machinery, and/or similar interests, and freight to 25 percent of the insured value. It should be noted that no restriction is placed on risks excluded by war, strikes, and related perils, nor on general average and salvage disbursements.

The Disbursements Warranty Clause in the new form follows precisely the wording in the old Institute clause on the same subject. The American form differs slightly in language but the net effect is the same.

Returns for Lay-Up and Cancellation Clause. This clause provides for the return of the whole or a proportionate part of the premium if the policy is cancelled by agreement, or if the vessel is laid up, as provided in the clause. The language in the new form is almost identical to that of the old Institute clause. The language of the AIH form does not differ significantly.

War, Strikes, Malicious Acts, and Nuclear Exclusion. Both the AIH form and the old Institute form contain exclusions which are paramount and which supersede and override anything contained in the policy inconsistent therewith. These are, of course, the exclusions relating to war risks, capture, seizure, arrest, restraint or detainment, and the like. While the AIH form contained an exclusion relating to strikes, riots, and civil commotions, the old Institute form did not contain this exclusion. The new form more closely follows the American pattern and, for the first time, strikes, riots, civil commotions, etc., are excluded. Aside from the problem which may be encountered with respect to "riots" under English law, and about which comment has been made, the language of the new form is rather clear and precise and some clarity has been achieved.

Miscellaneous. The old Institute form contained a "Grounding" clause which, in essence, provided that groundings in certain areas (such as the Panama Canal, Suez Canal, Manchester ship canal, etc., certain rivers, bars, etc.) were not to be deemed strandings. Comparable language appears in the earlier AIH form but has since been deleted. The clause is no longer needed and has been correspondingly deleted in the new form.

Attention is specifically directed to the single sentence appearing at the top of the new form, directly under the title. It reads: "This insurance is subject to English law and practice." Thus, unless deleted for use in foreign markets, such as the United States, English law will be applied by the courts. Where the English law is more restrictive or perhaps more "harsh" than the law of the foreign country—such as the consequences attendant upon a breach of warranty—use of the form could occasion problems. This should prove to be particularly important to brokers in foreign jurisdictions who overlook the significance of the sentence.

Conclusions. Unquestionably, the new London hull form is much superior in clarity and precision to the old system, under which the old S. G. form provided the basis for coverage with various Institute clauses attached. Whether greater or additional coverages are provided is somewhat debatable. Moreover, new restrictions have been added. And, lastly, many of the recommendations and/or observations of the UNCTAD secretariat have been ignored. Whether the new London policy forms will prove to be a suitable international vehicle rather than a revised national "regime" system remains to be seen. In any event, should the new London forms achieve substantial acceptance—and it appears certain that they will in the English and Commonwealth market—the legal profession may well be one of the principal beneficiaries as it will be many years before some of the new language can be judicially construed and doubts laid to rest.

CHAPTER IV

PRINCIPLES OF CONSTRUCTION

Contract Principles Generally Govern

Policies of insurance are governed by the same laws and principles of construction as other written contracts.[1] Although in written commercial contracts it may be necessary to go out of the instrument itself to interpret it more frequently than in many other contracts, the instrument itself is generally conclusive of the rights and liabilities of the parties and its provisions are not subject to being controlled or superseded by preliminary negotiations, communications, or verbal agreements.[2] True, but it must always be remembered that nearly all of the law of marine insurance is primarily involved with interpretation of the terms of the insurance contract itself[3]—a narrow and somewhat restricted area of contract law generally.

It must also be remembered that in the United Kingdom, and for the most part in the Commonwealth nations, the marine insurance law is of general and universal application. That is, a principle of marine insurance law enunciated by the Queen's Bench division and the appellate courts will generally be followed in all other English and Commonwealth jurisdictions. This universality of principle is, unfortunately, not always the case in the United States because of the impact of the U. S. Supreme Court's decision in *Wilburn Boat Co. v. Fireman's Fund Ins. Co.*[4] As noted in Chapter I, Introduction, *Wilburn* stands for the following propositions; i.e., a uniform federal rule of marine insurance law will be applied by all courts if there is such uniformity. If not, the federal courts should either formulate such a rule or apply state law, depending upon whether or not the particular issue involved reasonably requires national uniformity or can be better left to local law and custom. Thus, a commonly accepted principle of marine insurance law in England and the United States may be altered or changed if there exists a state statute which is inconsistent with that commonly accepted principle. For example, see *Irwin v. Eagle*

---

1. *Robertson v. French*, (1803) 102 E.R. 779; *Goix v. Low*, 1 Johns. N.Y. 341; *Mumford v. Hallett*, 1 Johns. 433 (N.Y., 1806); *Graves v. Boston Mar. Ins. Co.*, 6 U.S. 419 (1805).
2. *Bell v. Western Marine & Fire Ins. Co.*, 5 Rob. 423 (La.); *Eyre v. Marine Ins. Co.*, 6 Whart. 249 (St. Pa. 1841); *Reliance Marine Ins. Co. v. Duder*, [1913] 1 K.B. 265. This is but another way of saying that extrinsic evidence is not admissible to contradict, vary, or add to the terms of a written contract.
3. *Kulukundis v. Norwich Union Fire Ins. Soc.*, [1937] 1 K.B. 1.
4. 348 U.S. 310, 1955 AMC 467 (1955).

Star Ins. Co.,[5] where it was held that state law governs the sinking in Florida waters of a Florida yacht, owned by a Florida resident and issued by a Florida-based marine insurance broker.

Intention

As in all commercial documents, marine insurance policies are to be construed so as to give effect to the intention of the parties, such intention to be gathered in the first instance from the words of the instrument, but interpreted, if necessary, by the surrounding circumstances.[6] The language is to be taken in its plain and ordinary sense and the court is not to speculate on some supposed meaning which the parties have not expressed.[7] If the words are plain, the court should not construe them so as to make a new contract for the parties, and any doubt or difficulty in construction must not be fanciful; it must be real.[8] However, notwithstanding the generality of the foregoing, the policy must be construed as a whole.[9] Thus, it is improper to take words out of context and they must be construed together with all the words of the contract. In short, it must be given a "commercially reasonable" interpretation.[10]

As will be seen, the use of the old Lloyd's S.G. form for both ship and goods and freight, with inconsistent phrases frequently not being struck out, occasioned a great deal of trouble for the courts. This problem should now be alleviated or at least ameliorated with the use of the new

5. 455 F.2d 827, 1973 AMC 1184 (5th Cir.).
6. *Carr v. Montefiore*, (1864) 122 E.R. 833, Ex. Ch.; *Robertson v. French, supra*, n. 1; *Goix v. Low, supra*, n. 1; *Mumford v. Hallett, supra*, n. 1; *Sleght v. Rhinelander*, 1 Johns. 192 (N.Y., 1806); *Stuyvesant Ins. v. Butler*, 314 So.2d 567, 1976 AMC 1182 (St.,Fla.); *Shore v. Wilson*, (1842) 9 Cl. & Fin. 355; *Reliance Marine Ins. Co. v. Duder, supra*, n. 2.
7. *Haughton v. Empire Marine Ins. Co.*, (1866) L.R. 1 Exch. 204; *Lawrence v. Aberdein*, (1821) 106 E.R. 1133; *Scottish Metropolitan Assur. Co. Ltd. v. Stewart*, (1923) 15 Ll.L. Rep. 55; *Wall v. Howard Ins. Co.*, 14 Barb. 383 (N.Y., 1852); *Benedict v. Ocean Ins. Co.*, 31 N.Y. 389 (N.Y., 1865).
8. *Gyles v. Mutual Benefit Health & Accident Ass'n*, [1940] 4 D.L.R. 801 (Can.); *Kruger v. Mutual Benefit Health & Accident Ass'n*, [1944] 1 D.L.R. 638 (Can.); *Robertson v. French, supra*, n. 1; *Birrell v. Dryer*, (1884) 9 A.C. 345; *Hart v. Standard Marine Ins. Co., Ltd.*, (1889) 22 Q.B.D. 499; *Grey v. Auber*, (1862) 1 New Rep. 33, *sub nom Aubert v. Gray*, 122 E.R. 65, Ex. Ch.; *Banks v. Wilson*, (1873) R.E.D. 210 (Can.); *American Employers Ins. Co. v. St. Paul Fire & Marine Ins. Co.*, 594 F.2d 973, 1979 AMC 1478 (4th Cir.).
9. *Robertson v. French, supra*, n. 1; *Tatham, Bromage & Co. v. Burr*, [1898] A.C. 382; *Marten v. Vestey*, [1920] A.C. 307; *Moody v. Surridge*, (1798) 2 Esp. 633, N.P.; *Wilson v. Merchants Mar. Ins. Co.*, (1872) 9 N.S.R. 81 (Can.); *Cunard S.S. Co. v. Marten*, [1903] 2 K.B. 511; *Hydarnes S.S. Co. v. Indemnity Mut. Mar. Assur. Co.*, [1895] 1 Q.B. 500; *Elderslie v. Borthwick*, [1905] A.C. 93; *Monterey - Dixie*, 1929 AMC 336, 250 N.Y. 322 (St.,N.Y.); *Minnie R.*, 49 F.2d 121, 1931 AMC 995 (5th Cir.); *Shamrock No. 25*. 9 F.2d 57, 1926 AMC 433 (2d Cir.); *Western Assurance Co. of Toronto v. Poole*, [1903] 1 K.B. 376; *Parfait v. Jahnke Service*, 347 F.Supp. 485, 1973 AMC 753 (ED,La.), *rev'd* 484 F.2d 296, 1973 AMC 2447 (5th Cir.).
10. See discussion, *infra*, "Commercial Interpretation."

London cargo clauses, the "MAR" form, and the new London hull clauses.

But application of the "plain and ordinary sense" rule provides only a *prima facie* meaning if, as sometimes happens, apparently very clear words are latently ambiguous or do not upon a closer examination really bear out their apparent meaning. The *prima facie* meaning is only conclusive when it is unambiguous, when not contradicted by the context in which it is used, and when consistent with the extrinsic circumstances.[11]

Moreover, the rule has always been that extrinsic evidence may be given if the contract is not clear as to what the subject matter is; i.e., there is a latent ambiguity which may be cleared up in this fashion. For example, in *Stuyvesant Ins. v. Butler*,[12] a clause in the policy excluded liability "in respect to minors." The court held that the word "minor" was ambiguous because it was not defined in terms of a specific age, justifying resort to the parlance of the maritime industry where the minimum age for seamen is 17 (U. S. Navy), 16 (U. S. federal law), and 15 (I.L.O. Convention). Stating that the ambiguity should be resolved against the insurer and in favor of the insured, the court held that the policy provided coverage for injuries to an inexperienced 17-year-old deckhand. Further examples are given, *infra*, under "Illustrative Interpretations When Applying Principles of Construction."

Written v. Printed Clauses

Although full effect must be given in a policy to both printed and written words, if it is possible, greater weight is to be accorded to a written clause than to a printed one because " . . . the part that is specially put into a particular instrument is naturally more in harmony with what the parties are intending than the other, although it must not be used so as to reject the other, or to make it have no effect."[13] Thus, written words prevail over printed words, even though the latter may not be stricken from the policy.[14]

---

11. See *Shore v. Wilson, supra,* n. 6.
12. 314 So.2d 567, 1976 AMC 1182 (St.,Fla.). See, also, *Burges v. Wickham,* (1863) 33 L.J.Q.B. 17; *Reardon Smith Line v. Black Sea & Baltic Gen. Ins. Co.,* [1939] A.C. 562; *Irving v. Richardson,* (1831) 2 B. & Ad. 193; *Macdonald v. Longbottom,* (1859) 1 E. & E. 977; *Kelloch v. S. & H.,* 473 F.2d 767, 1973 AMC 948 (5th Cir.) (term "whilst diving" held to include entire diving operation, in and out of the water, and therefore it covered injury to a diver's helper who slipped on the deck while assisting the diver in his descent).
13. *Joyce v. Realm Marine Ins. Co.,* (1872) L.R. 7 Q.B. 580.
14. *Robertson v. French, supra,* n. 1; *Dudgeon v. Pembroke,* (1877) 2 A.C. 284; *Haughton v. Ewbank,* (1814) 171 E.R. 29, N.P.; *Hydarnes S.S. Co. v. Indemnity Mutual Mar. Assur. Co.,* [1895], *supra,* n. 9; *Lord v. Grant,* (1875) 10 N.S.R. 120 (Can.); *Meagher v. Home Ins. Co.,* (1861) 11 C.P. 328 (Can.); *Searle v. New Zealand Ins. Co.,* (1884) 3 N.Z.L.R. 148 (S.C.,N.Z.); *Givens v. Baloise Marine Ins. Co.,* (1958) 13 D.L.R. (2d) 416, *rev'd* (1959) 17 D.L.R. (2d) 7 (Can.); *Atlantic Basin*

Interestingly, written clauses are given a stricter construction than printed clauses for the reason that the parties themselves have introduced them as being applicable to that particular adventure. A common illustration is where the parties have entered into written stipulations seeking either to enlarge or restrict the coverage given by the policy, and these are appended to the policy by way of endorsements.[15]

Commercial Interpretation

The rule is well settled that clauses in a marine insurance policy will not be given effect when they are inconsistent with the very purpose of the insurance. Thus, in *Western Assur. Co. of Toronto v. Poole*,[16] a printed Sue and Labor Clause was not deleted even though the policy contained an exclusion as to "salvage charges." It was held that this obviated the underwriters' obligation to contribute in sue and labor charges. In *Cunard S.S. Co. v. Marten*,[17] even though the printed policy form contained a suing and laboring clause which had not been deleted, it was held inapplicable to a policy insuring a carrier's liabilities. As the court noted:

It is obviously necessary in every case to consider carefully the description of the risk or special kind of indemnity expressed in the written words of the policy in order to ascertain whether any particular clause of the printed form applies to the insurance effected by the policy. It is most unusual to find that the superfluous or inapplicable words have been struck out of the printed form.[18]

In *Hydarnes S.S. Co. v. Indemnity Mutual Marine Assur. Co.*,[19] a printed portion of the policy provided that the insurance should commence upon

---

Iron Works v. American Ins. Co., 219 N.Y.S. 84, 1927 AMC 319 (St.,N.Y.); *Vigilant*, 1927 AMC 1411 (S.D.N.Y.); *Dudley*, 1928 AMC 1806 (St.,N.Y.); *Minnie R.*, 49 F.2d 121, 1931 AMC 995 (5th Cir.); *Atlantic Lighterage Co. v. Continental Ins. Co.*, 75 F.2d 288, 1935 AMC 305 (2d Cir.); *Bobley v. California Union Ins. Co.*, 1976 AMC 216 (St.,N.Y.); *Morrison Mill Co. v. Queen Ins. Co.*, [1925] 1 D.L.R. 1159 (Can.); *Belcher v. Southern Ins. Co., Ltd.*, (1872) 2 N.Z.C.A. 59 (N.Z.); *Bluewaters Inc. v. Boag*, 320 F.2d 833, 1964 AMC 71 (lst Cir.), [1963] 2 Lloyd's Rep. 218; *Linton Harris v. Glens Falls Ins. Co.*, 493 P2d 861, 1972 AMC 138 (St.,Cal.); *Hagan v. Scottish Union & National Ins. Co.*, 186 U.S. 423 (1902); *Vancouver Lumber Co. v. Home Ins. Co.*, 68 F.2d 1019 (2d Cir., 1934); *Independence Indemnity Co. v. W.J. Jones & Sons.* 64 F.2d 312 (9th Cir., 1933); *The Halo*, 52 F.2d 136 (2d Cir., 1931); *Fireman's Fund Ins. Co. v. Globe Nav. Co.*, 236 F. 618 (9th Cir., 1916); *Royal Exch. Assur. v. Graham & Morton Transp. Co.*, 166 F. 32 (7th Cir., 1908); *Mercantile Marine Ins. Co. v. Titherington*, (1864) 122 E.R. 1015; *Techni-Chemicals Products Co., Ltd. v. South British Ins. Co., Ltd.*, [1977] 1 N.Z.L.R. 311.
15. See, for example, *Bluewaters, Inc. v. Boag, supra*, n. 14.
16. [1903] 1 K.B. 376.
17. [1903] 2 K.B. 511.
18. In *Connors Marine v. Northwestern Fire*, 88 F.2d 637, 1937 AMC 344 (2d Cir.), the court commented unfavorably on the use of "riders" to supersede all the printed terms of a policy.
19. [1895] 1 Q.B. 500.

the freight and goods . . . from the loading of the goods at Montevideo. A written portion described the insurance as being on "freight of meat at and from Montevideo." After arriving at Montevideo, the vessel refrigeration equipment broke down and she was unable to load her cargo and the freight was lost. The underwriters contended that by virtue of the printed words, the freight never came on at risk, while the assured contended that the printed clause was never intended to apply to the freight. The assured complained that it was well known to the underwriters that no frozen meat could be shipped at Montevideo and this was not denied by the underwriters. As the policy was one being used for insurance of ship, cargo, and freight, any portion of it inapplicable to freight should be stricken, and the assured was granted recovery.

In *Bluewaters, Inc. v. Boag*,[20] a standard printed form of British hull policy was issued at lower than normal rates. Attached to it was the Institute form labeled "American Institute Time (Hulls)" at the top of which was typed "in so far as applicable." The typed portion of the policy provided for coverage against total and/or constructive total loss. The Institute printed clause included collision or "running down" coverage. The court of appeal held that the policy covered total or constructive total loss only, and not collision, stating:

> Irrespective of whether or not the rider provides additional coverage it was not, as appellant seeks to suggest, an independent contract. Rather, the policy and the rider constitute, together, a single agreement. *Washburn & Moen Mfg. Co. v. Reliance Marine Ins. Co.* (1900) 179 U.S. 1. It is difficult to understand how appellant can argue otherwise in view of the fact that the rider itself commences, "To be attached to and form a part of the Policy . . . ." While there might be an inference arising from its physical attachment that the entire rider was included, this inference alone does not create an ambiguity, to be construed in favor of the insured, if there is an express provision negativing that inference.
>
> In the case at bar, the words "in so far as applicable" at the top of the rider, coinciding with the same words in the policy itself, of necessity indicate that not the entire rider, but only the "applicable" parts of it, were within the agreement.
>
> Appellant's initial difficulty is that it shows nothing in the policy to which the separate purported collision coverage is applicable. Hence that provision would seem, in terms, not to have been incorporated. In addition to this apparent failure to incorporate, we think it clear that any undertaking such as collision coverage was plainly denied by the typewritten provisions in the policy . . . . It follows that the appellees'

20. 320 F.2d 833, 1964 AMC 71 (1st Cir.), [1963] 2 Lloyd's Rep. 218.

undertaking consisted of, and only of, the total loss of vessel provisions contained in the policy itself and those conditions or provisions of the rider that related to that coverage. Cf. *Otago Farmers' Cooperative Ass'n of New Zealand v. Thompson,* [1910] 2 K.B. 145.

Still another area exists in which, in order to give the contract a proper commercial interpretation, the court should imply a term if this is necessary to give business efficacy to the contract. That is, the court should add a term, not to explain what the parties actually intended but what as reasonable men they should have intended. An example is the incorporation into the insurance contract of an implied warranty which, although not expressed by the parties, must certainly have been intended by them had their minds focused on the question. Thus, in every voyage policy there is an implied warranty that at the commencement of the voyage the ship shall be seaworthy for the purpose of the particular adventure insured. While this principle is incorporated into statute in England by the Marine Insurance Act, 1906, Section 39, it is a matter of decisional law in the United States. Therefore, even though a voyage policy may be silent as to the warranty, the courts should, and do, imply a warranty that she be seaworthy when she breaks ground.[21]

Another illustration is where a statute applies and the parties must have contracted with reference to the existence of the statute. Thus, in *Richelieu & O. Nav. Co. v. Boston Marine Ins. Co.,*[22] a Canadian steamer, navigating Canadian waters between two Canadian ports was held bound to comply with a statute of Canada regulating the navigation of her waters. Consequently, an American insurance company, providing a policy upon the steamer, was held to have contemplated the requirements of the statute.

Technical Words

Although words may have an ordinary meaning and, generally speaking, terms are to be construed in their "plain, ordinary meaning," evidence may be introduced to show that they have a peculiar and different meaning (i.e., a technical meaning not ordinarily associated with ordinary language such as in the insurance trade), so long as such an interpretation does not disregard the intention of the parties.[23]

21. See cases cited in Chapter XI, Warranties, *infra.*
22. 136 U.S. 408, 34 L.ed. 398, 10 S.Ct. 934 (1886).
23. *Beacon Life & Fire Assur. Co. v. Gibb,* (1862) 15 E.R. 630, P.C.; *Carr v. Montefiore,* (1864) *supra,* n. 6; *Haughton v. Empire Marine Ins. Co.,* (1866) *supra,* n. 7; *Thomson v. Weems,* (1884) 9 A.C. 671, H.L.; *Scott v. Bourdillion,* (1806) 127 E.R. 606 (rice is not corn); *Hoskins v. Pickersgill,* (1783) 99 E.R. 623 (ship's furniture—fishing tackle); *Hart v. Standard Marine Ins. Co., Ltd.,* (1899) *supra* n. 8 (iron—steel); *Polpen Shipping Co., Ltd. v. Commercial Union Assur. Co., Ltd.,*

A general dictionary of the English language is not authority to override the particular meaning which a word has been shown to derive from mercantile usage.[24]

Technical words are, consequently, frequently interpreted by the aid of usage.[25]

Geographical Terms

In construing a policy, the words must be taken to have been used in their popular or commercial sense; i.e., as applying to what would be understood by shippers, shipowners, and underwriters.[26] Thus, policies are to be construed according to the course of trade and the methods usual at the place.[27] Consequently, evidence of the mercantile meaning associated with such terms is admissible and effect will be given to such meaning.[28]

[1943] 1 All E.R. 162, 1943 AMC 438 (flying boat not a "ship or vessel"); *Quinlivan v. Northwestern Fire & Marine Ins. Co.*, 37 F.2d 29 (2d Cir., 1930) (elbow pipe on a dredge was "machinery"); *Moores v. Louisville Underwriters*, 14 F. 226 (6th Cir., 1882) (raft insured by a cargo policy and in charge of a towboat held to be a "vessel"); *Connors Marine Co., Inc. v. Northwestern Fire & Marine Ins. Co.*, 88 F.2d 637, 1937 AMC 344 (2d Cir.) (pontoons are not "hulls").

24. *Haughton v. Gilbart*, (1836) 173 E.R. 307.

25. See discussion, *infra*, under "Usage." See, for example, *Otago Farmers' Cooperative Ass'n of New Zealand v. Thompson*, (1910) 2 K.B. 145 (term "warranted free from particular average & loss unless caused by stranding, sinking, burning or collision" well understood among underwriters to mean "all loss" not embraced within the enumerated class of perils covered. Hence, there was no recovery on arrival of a cargo of meat unfit for consumption from causes not involving a stranding, sinking, burning, or collision), and *Steinhoff v. Royal Canadian Ins. Co.*, (1877) 42 U.C.R. 307 (Can.) (definition of "barge" as used in the policy). Also, see *Pelly v. Royal Exchange Assur. Co.*, (1757) 97 E.R. 343; *Brough v. Whitmore*, (1791) 100 E.R. 976; *Aitchison v. Lohre*, (1879) 4 A.C. 755.

26. *Hunter v. Northern Marine Ins. Co.*, (1888) 13 A.C. 717, H.L. (meaning of phrase "in port"); *Colonial Ins. Co. v. New Zealand v. Adelaide Marine Ins. Co.*, (1886) 18 S.A.L.R. 84, 6 A.L.T. 71, 12 A.C. 128 (meaning of phrase "at and from").

27. *Stewart v. Bell*, (1821) 106 E.R. 1179; *Wall v. Howard Ins. Co.*, 14 Barb. 383 (N.Y., 1852); *Astor v. Union Ins. Co.*, 7 Cow. 202 (N.Y., 1827); *Seccomb v. Provincial Ins. Co.*, 92 Mass. 305 (Mass., 1865); *Mobile Marine Ins. Co. v. McMillan & Son*, 27 Ala. 77 (Ala., 1855).

28. *Maritime Ins. Co., Ltd. v. Alianza Ins. Co. of Santander*, [1907] 2 K.B. 660; *Constable v. Noble*, (1810) 127 E.R. 1134; *Brown v. Tayleur*, (1835) 111 E.R. 777; *Uhde v. Walters*, (1811) 3 Camp. 15, N.P.; *Payne v. Hutchinson*, (1810) 127 E.R. 1135; *Cruickshank v. Janson*, (1810) 127 E.R. 1093; *Sea Ins. Co. of Scotland v. Gavin*, (1829) 5 E.R. 206, H.L.; *St. Paul Fire & Marine Ins. Co. v. Troop*, (1896) 26 S.C.R. 5 (Can.); *Gerow v. Providence Washington Ins. Co.*, (1889) 28 N.B.R. 435, *aff'd* 17 S.C.R. 387 (Can.); *Re Terra Nova Mut. Marine Ins. Co. and Blackwood*, [1952] I.L.R. 403 (Can., Nfld.); *Wilson v. Merchants' Marine Ins. Co.*, (1872) 9 N.S.R. 81 (Can.); *Hart v. Boston Marine Ins. Co.*, (1894) 26 N.S.R. 427, C.A. (Can.); *Sleght v. Rhineland*, 1 Johns. 192 (N.T., 1806); *Coit v. Commercial Ins. Co.*, 7 Johns. 385 (N.Y., 1842); *Eyre v. Marine Ins. Co.*, 5 Watts & S. 116 (Pa., 1842); *Dow v. Whetton*, 8 Wend. 160 (N.Y., 1831); *De Longuemere v. New York Fire Ins. Co.*, 10 Johns. 120 (N.Y., 1813); *Gracie v. Marine Ins. Co.*, 3 U.S. 32 (1814).

Illustrative of the interpretations given to geographical terms are the following: inland waters;[29] "North River";[30] "Atlantic Coast waters of the United States";[31] "waters of the Mexican Gulf";[32] "port";[33] "while within the United Kingdom";[34] "Pacific";[35] extent of geographical coverage;[35a] "while cruising; while at moorings";[35b] "sent to sea."[35c]

Usage

Section 87(1) of the Marine Insurance Act states:

Where any right, duty or liability would arise under a contract of marine insurance by implication of law, it may be negatived or varied by express agreement, or by usage, if the usage be such as to bind both parties to the contract.

Usage cannot contradict an express term in the policy but it does permit the introduction of extrinsic evidence to explain ambiguities or even to add to the policy so long as the usage is not inconsistent with the express terms,[36] and is general and notorious in the insurance business or in

29. *Alexander, Ramsey & Kerr v. National Union Fire Ins. Co.*, 104 F.2d 1006 (2d Cir., 1939); *Simon v. Switzerland General Ins. Co.*, 238 So.2d 257 (La.,App., 1970); *Fulton v. Ins. Co. of N.A.*, 136 F. 183 (S.D.N.Y., 1904).

30. *Hastorf v. Greenwich Ins. Co.*, 132 F. 122 (S.D.N.Y., 1904).

31. *St. Paul Fire & Marine Ins. Co. v. Knickerbocker Steam Towing Co.*, 93 F. 931 (1st Cir., 1899).

32. *Mannheim Ins. Co. v. Charles Clarke & Co.*, 157 S.W. 291 (St., Tex., 1913).

33. *Maritime Ins. Co. Ltd. v. Alianza Ins. Co. of Santander*, [1907] *supra*, n. 28 (as meaning a place or places at which the vessel might arrive with some object other than merely passing on her way to some other point); *Constable v. Noble*, (1810) *supra*, n. 28; *Brown v. Tayleur*, (1835) 111 E.R. 777; *Hunter v. Northern Marine Ins. Co.*, (1888) 13 A.C. 717, H.L.; *Cockey v. Atkinson*, (1819) 106 E.R. 434 (open roadstead the usual place of loading and unloading held to be a "port"); *Gerow v. Providence Washington Ins. Co.*, (1889), *supra*, n. 28 (open roadstead held to be a "port"); *Troop v. St. Paul Fire & Marine Ins. Co.*, (1895) *supra*, n. 28.

34. *Navigators & General Ins. Co., Ltd. v. Ringrose*, [1962] 1 All E.R. 97 (Channel Islands not within the United Kingdom).

35. *Royal Exchange Assur. Corp. v. Todd*, (1892) 8 T.L.R. 669.

35a. *Wilson v. Boag*, (1957) S.R. (N.S.W.) 384, 74 W.N. 160.

35b. *Marine Ins. Co. Ltd. v. Clifton*, (1906) N.Z.L.R. 206).

35c. *Cooper v. Phoenix Prudential Australia Ltd.*, (1983) 2 ANZ Ins. Cas. 60-526.

36. *Salvador v. Hopkins*, (1765) 97 E.R. 1057; *Hall v. Janson*, (1855) 119 E.R. 183; *Blackett v. Royal Exchange Assur. Co.*, (1832) 149 E.R. 106; *Provincial Ins. Co. of Canada v. Leduc*, (1874) 43 L.J.P.C. 49; *Marine Ins. Co. Ltd. v. Grimmer*, [1944] 77 Ll.L.Rep. 461, C.A.; *McGivern v. Provincial Ins. Co.*, (1858) 9 N.B.R. 64 (Can.); *Miller v. Tetherington*, (1862) 158 E.R. 758, Ex. Ch.; *Ronaghan v. Canada West Ins. Co.*, (1957) 22 W.W.R. (Can.) (words construed in their ordinary meaning unless an artificial meaning has been acquired which is peculiar to the business or trade involved); *Foley v. Norwich Union Fire Ins. Soc.*, (1888) 40 N.S.R. 624 (Can.) (policy contained a condition making it void if gunpowder was kept on the premises; evidence of usage to keep gunpowder cannot vary the express language of the policy); *Eisenhaur v. Nova Scotia Marine Ins. Co.*, (1892) 24 N.S.R. 205 (Can.) (custom of small schooners in the coasting trade to keep close to shore so as to make harbor in bad weather); *St. Paul Fire & Marine Ins. Co. v. Troop*, (1896), *supra*, n. 28 (word "port" construed in its

the particular trade to which the policy relates.[37]

Thus, a usage may explain, modify, or qualify the words used in a policy but it may never be permitted to nullify or expunge them.

The principle is difficult to apply as it is not always easy to determine whether the usage being contended for constitutes a contradiction or an amplification.

Judicial tests for the application of the principle have been developed, however, which assist in arriving at a correct result. That is, the usage must be certain,[38] it must be uniformly acted upon,[39] it must have existed under such circumstances, or for such a length of time, as to have become generally well known to all persons concerned in or about the branch of trade to which it relates so as to warrant a presumption that contracts are

popular sense as understood in the trade); *Sun Ins. Office v. Scott*, 284 U.S. 117 (1931); *St. Paul Fire & Marine Ins. Co. v. Balfour*, 168 F. 212 (9th Cir., 1909); *Aetna Ins. Co. v. Sacramento-Stockton S.S. Co.*, 273 F. 55 (9th Cir., 1921); *Transatlantic Shipping Co. v. St. Paul Fire & Marine Ins. Co.*, 9 F.2d 720 (2d Cir., 1925); *Tidmarsh v. Wash. F. & M. Ins. Co.*, Fed.Cas. No. 14,024 (1st Cir., 1827); *Hancox v. Fishing Ins. Co.*, Fed.Cas. No. 6,013 (1st Cir., 1838); *Winthrop v. Union Ins. Co.*, Fed.Cas. No. 17,901 (3d Cir., 1807); *Ocean S.S. Co. v. Aetna Ins. Co.*, 121 F. 882 (S.D.,Ga., 1903); *Hazleton v. Manhattan Ins. Co.*, 12 F. 159 (D.C.,Ill., 1882); *Ruger v. Fireman's Fund Ins. Co.*, 90 F. 310 (S.D.N.Y., 1898); *Compania de Navegacion, Int., S.A. v. Fireman's Fund Ins. Co.*, 277 U.S. 66 (1926); *Hearn v. New England Mut. Ins. Co.*, Fed.Cas. No. 6,301 (1st Cir., 1870); *Orient Mut. Ins. Co. v. Wright*, 68 U.S. 456 (1863).

37. *Salvador v. Hopkins*, (1765) *supra*, n. 36; *Gabay v. Lloyd*, (1825) 107 E.R. 927 (usage commonly prevailing at Lloyd's not known to assured and therefore not binding upon him); *Matveieff & Co. v. Crossfield*, (1903) 8 Com.Cas. 120 (custom at Lloyd's that premiums due underwriters are set off against losses due the broker not known to assured and therefore not binding); *Warren v. Swiss Lloyd's Ins. Co.*, (1893) 9 V.L.R. 397 (Aus.) (strong evidence must be given that insurer knew of usage when issuing policy); *Brit. & For. Marine Ins. Co., Ltd. v. Gaunt*, [1921] 2 A.C. 41, H.L.(custom proved that usage existing in the trade that bales of wool would be carried as deck cargo); *Noble v. Kennoway*, (1780) 99 E.R. 326 (Newfoundland fishing trade presumed to be known to underwriter; if he does not know of it, he should inform himself); *Acme Wood Flooring Co., Ltd. v. Marten*, (1904) 90 L.T. 313 (assured not having knowledge of Lloyd's custom not bound by it); *Universo Ins. Co. of Milan v. Merchants' Marine Ins. Co., Ltd.*, [1897] 2 Q.B. 93 (custom upheld that underwriter does not look to assured for payment of premium but to broker who effected the coverage); *Spooner v. Western Assur. Co.*, (1876) 38 U.C.Q.B. 62 (Can.) (following *Noble v. Kennoway, supra*); *Hennessy v. New York Mut. Marine Ins. Co.*, (1863) 5 N.S.R. 259 (Can.); *Merchants' Marine Ins. Co. v. Rumsey*, (1884) 9 S.C.R. 577 (Can.); *St. Paul Fire & Marine Ins. Co. v. Troop*, (1896) *supra*, n. 28; *Gerow v. Providence Wash. Ins. Co.*, (1889) *supra*, n. 28; *Rogers v. Mechanics' Ins. Co.*, Fed.Cas. No. 12,016 (1st Cir., 1841); *Hearn v. Equitable Safety Ins. Co.*, Fed.Cas. No. 6,300 (1st Cir., 1872); *Donnell v. Columbian Ins. Co.*, Fed.Cas. No. 3,987 (1st Cir., 1836); *Lanasse v. Travelers Ins.*, 450 F.2d 580, 1972 AMC 818 (5th Cir.).

38. The usage must have quite as much certainty as the written contract itself. *Nelson v. Dahl*, (1879) 12 Ch. D. 568; *Rogers v. Mechanics' Ins. Co.*, *supra*, n. 37; *Leach v. Perkins*, 17 Me. 462 (St.,Me., 1840); *Trott v. Wood*, 1 Gallison's Rep. 443 (U.S., 1813).

39. To be uniform, it must be generally accepted throughout the mercantile community or in the particular trade where it is claimed to be applicable, and be so well settled that all persons engaged in the trade must be considered as having contracted with reference to it. *Trott v. Wood, supra*, n. 38; *Bartlett v. Pentland*, (1830) 109 E.R. 632.

made with reference to it,[40] it must be reasonable,[41] and it must be legal.[42]

With respect to legality, it should be apparent that a number of customs which originated at Lloyd's (in the absence of some existing principle of law at that time) have since become enshrined in law by virtue of various provisions of the Marine Insurance Act, 1906. For example, see *Palmer v. Blackburn*,[43] involving the payment of gross freight on an unvalued policy on freight, which was embodied as a rule by Section 16(2) of the Act.

While occasional instances will not constitute a usage of which the parties are presumed to have notice, a usage may either be local and confined to the particular place where the contract is made, or it may be coextensive with a district or territory, or even be general with respect to the subject matter. For example, in *Globe & Rutgers Fire Ins. Co. of New York v. David Moffat Co.*,[44] a New York fire policy was to expire at noon on a specified day. The property insured was in Virginia. It was held that parol evidence was admissible to show the custom of Virginia for the purpose of determining whether the parties intended the time to be governed by standard or solar time. But in *Child v. Sun Mut. Ins. Co.*,[45] a policy underwritten in New York on a Rhode Island ship and cargo, for a whaling voyage in the Pacific, was held not to be governed by the usage of Nantucket as to similar voyages, and in *Mason v. Franklin Fire Ins. Co.*,[46] a fire policy on a vessel that was being built in Baltimore was held not to be subject to the usages of other ports in the United States. See, also, *Bartlett v. Pentland*.[47] Local usages generally prevail over general usages,[48] and there is no impediment to a usage being applied which is of comparatively recent origin so long as it is general and notorious.[49]

A usage may be binding upon a party even though he may not have known about it, if it has become so generally well known to all persons engaged in that particular trade or business that he ought to have in-

---

40. That is, it must be "notorious." See *Smith v. Wright*, (1803) 1 Caines 43 (St., N.Y.); *Nelson v. Dahl*, (1879) *supra*, n. 38; *Renner v. Bank of Columbia*, 22 U.S. 531 (1824).

41. *Ougier v. Jennings*, (1800) 170 E.R. 1037; *Macy v. Whaling Ins. Co.*, 9 Metc. 354 (Mass., 1845); *Leach v. Perkins*, (1840) *supra*, n. 38; *Seccomb v. Provincial Ins. Co.*, 10 All. 305 (St.,Mass., 1865); *Baltimore Bank & Trust Co. v. U.S. Fidelity & G. Co.*, 436 F.2d 743 (8th Cir., 1971).

42. *Homer v. Dorr*, 10 Mass. 26 (St.,Mass., 1813); *Bryant v. Commonwealth Ins. Co.*, 6 Pick. 131 (St.,Mass., 1828); *Barney v. Coffin*, 3 Pick. 115 (St.,Mass., 1825); *Robertson v. Western F. & M. Ins. Co.*, 19 La. 227 (St.,La., 1841); *Ougier v. Jennings*, (1800) *supra*, n. 41; *McGregor v. Ins. Co. of Penn.*, 1 Wash. C.C. 39 (U.S., 1803); *Eyre v. Marine Ins. Co.*, 6 Whart. 249 (St.,Pa., 1841).

43. (1822) 130 E.R. 25.

44. 154 F. 13 (2d Cir., 1907).

45. 3 Sandf. 26 (St.,N.Y., 1849).

46. 12 Gill & J. 468 (St.,Md., 1842).

47. (1830) 109 E.R. 632.

48. *Baltimore Merchants' Ins. Co. v. Wilson*, 2 Md. 217 (St., Md., 1852); *British & Foreign Mar. Ins. Co. v. Gaunt*, [1921] 2 A.C. 41; *Da Costa v. Edmunds*, (1815) 171 E.R. 46.

49. *Winsor v. Dillaway*, 4 Metc. 221 (St.,Mass., 1842); *Noble v. Kennoway*, (1780) *supra*, n. 37; *Rumball v. Metropolitan Bank*, (1877) 2 O.B.D. 194.

formed himself about it. That is, in such circumstances, it was his concern to inform himself about it and not the duty of the other party to inform him.[50]

Usage at Lloyd's

While usages at Lloyd's are generally binding on the underwriters, they are not binding on others unless the usages either can be proven to have been actually known by the others, or that they should have known about them from their course of dealings.[51]

Usage of Average Adjusters

While it might be thought that the rules and practices of average adjusters would be usages which would be binding, such is not the case, and such rules and practices are not binding unless expressly incorporated in the policy.[52] As a consequence of *Atwood v. Sellar* and *Svendson v. Wallace*, the Association of Average Adjusters altered their rules with respect to outward and inward port charges and warehousing and reloading expenses in general average.

Contra Proferentem Rule

An important rule of construction is the application of the maxim *verba chartarum fortius accipiuntur contra proferentem*, under which documents and words are, when ambiguous, construed most strongly against the interest of the party responsible for them. The maxim is generally applied where there is an ambiguity which cannot be resolved by any other rule of construction, although it is more proper to say that it may only be decisive if all the other indicia by which the instrument is being construed are "in equipoise."[53]

50. *Rogers v. Mechanics' Ins. Co.*, (1841) *supra*, n. 38; *Noble v. Kennoway*, (1780) *supra*, n. 37; *Mollett v. Robinson*, (1872) L.R. 7 C.P. 84, (1875) L.R. 7 H.L. 802.

51. *Gabay v. Lloyd's*, (1825) 107 E.R. 927; *Matveieff & Co. v. Crossfield*, (1903) 51 W.R. 365; *Acme Wood Flooring Co., Ltd. v. Marten*, (1904) 90 L.T. 313; *Bartlett v. Pentland*, (1830) 109 E.R. 632.

52. *Atwood v. Sellar*, (1880) 4 Q.B.D. 342, 5 Q.B.D. 286; *Svendson v. Wallace*, (1885) 11 Q.B.D. 616, 13 Q.B.D. 69, 10 A.C. 404.

53. *Notman v. Anchor Assur. Co.*, (1859) 140 E.R. 1170; *Fowkes v. Manchester & London Life Assur. & Loan Ass'n*, (1863) 122 E.R. 343; *Thomson v. Weems*, (1884) 9 A.C. 671, H.L.; *Fitton v. Accidental Death Ins. Co.*, (1864) 144 E.R. 50; *Metal Scrap & By-Products, Ltd. v. Federated Conveyors, Ltd.*, [1953] 1 Lloyd's Rep. 221; *Blackett v. Royal Exchange Assur. Co.*, (1832), *supra*, n. 36; *Smith v. Accident Ins. Co.*, (1870) 22 L.T. 861; *Cornish v. Accident Ins. Co.*, (1889) 23 Q.B.D. 453, C.A.; *Re Etherington and Lancashire & Yorkshire Accident Ins. Co.*, [1909] 1 K.B. 591, [1908-10] All E.R. 581, C.A.; *Mowat v. Boston Marine Ins. Co.*, (1896) 26 S.C.R. 47 (Can.); *Boyle v. Yorkshire Ins. Co., Ltd.*, [1925] 2 D.L.R. 596, 56 O.L.R. 564; *Froelick v. Continental Casualty Co.*,

Application of the maxim has generally taken the form of construing the policy most strongly against the underwriters. This appears to be particularly true under American cases.[54]

However, in recent years, the trend seems to be to analyze more carefully which party was, in fact, primarily responsible for the words used in the policy and to apply the maxim accordingly. Thus, in *Edward A. Ryan*,[55] the assured was held responsible for the words used, and in *A/S Ocean v. Black Sea and Baltic Gen. Ins. Co.*,[56] the court noted that an ambiguous clause in a policy must not necessarily be construed against the underwriters, "it being left for determination in each case as regards any special provision in the policy whether the insured or the insurer are to be considered the 'proferentes' within the maxim." And, in a landmark decision, the Fifth Circuit in *Eagle Leasing v. Hartford Fire*,[57] construed an ambiguous provision so as to deny the assured a recovery of attorneys' fees for the defense of a suit brought by the owner of a vessel which allegedly collided with a hulk owned by the assured after expiration of the policy period, even though the hulk had sunk during the policy period. In that case, a P & I policy had been concocted especially for the fleet of the assured corporation, which was of immense size, carrying insurance with annual premiums in six figures, managed by sophisticated businessmen, and represented by legal counsel on the same professional level as counsel for the underwriters. The court did not apply the maxim, but rather, construed the policy provisions to give a reasonable meaning that most closely comported with the probable intentions of the parties and which was most reasonable from a business point of view. The court noted that in substance the authorship of the policy was attributable to both parties alike, citing *Canton Ins. Office, Ltd. v. Independent Transportation Co.*[58]

Thus, it appears well settled that when the words were selected by both parties during the process of negotiation, the maxim does not apply. See also, *Birrell v. Dryer.*[59]

In instances where the policy is most often prepared in accordance with a slip, the wording of which is devised initially by the broker (who is

---

[1956] 18 W.W.R. 529 (Can.); *Papas v. General Accident, Fire & Life Assur. Corp., Ltd.*, [1916] C.P.D. 619 (S.Af.); *J.P. Porter & Sons, Ltd. v. Western Assur. Co.*, [1938] 1 D.L.R. 619 (N.S.,C.A., Can.); *Stuyvesant Ins. Co. v. Butler*, 314 So.2d 567, 1976 AMC 1182 (St.,Fla.); *Soil Mechanics v. Empire Mut. Ins. Co.*, 285 NYS2d 391, 1968 AMC 491 (St.,N.Y.); *Shelley v. Nationwide Mutual*, 213 Pa.Sup. Ct. 218, 1968 AMC 2305 (St.,Pa.); *Larson Construction v. Oregon Auto*, 450 F.2d 1193, 1971 AMC 2484 (9th Cir.).

54. *Hartford Fire Ins. Co. v. First National Bank of Kansas City*, 95 U.S. 673 (1877); *American Steamship Co. v. Indemnity Mut. Marine Ins. Co.*, 108 F. 421 (1901); *Hagan v. Scottish Ins. Co.*, 186 U.S. 423 (1901).

55. 2 F.Supp. 489, 1933 AMC 350 (E.D.N.Y.).

56. [1935] 51 Ll.L.Rep. 305.

57. 540 F.2d 1257, 1978 AMC 604 (5th Cir.).

58. 217 F. 213 (9th Cir., 1914).

59. (1884) 9 A.C. 345.

considered to be the agent of the assured), it would appear that the "proferentes" should be the assured rather than the assurer.

However, it is clear that the insurer must at its peril make its policy exclusions and exceptions clear and unmistakable; otherwise, coverage exists, all ambiguities being most strongly construed against it.[60] As the court said in *Blackett v. Royal Exchange Assur. Co.*:[61]

> The rule of construction as to exceptions is that they are to be taken most strongly against the party for whose benefit they are introduced. The words in which they are expressed are considered as his words; and if he do not use words clearly to express his meaning, he is the person who ought to be the sufferer.

In this instance, the underwriter has the burden of proving lack of coverage; i.e., that the exclusionary and exceptions clauses definitely exclude a particular risk.[62]

Causa Proxima

Another rule of construction is that marine policies only cover losses proximately caused by the perils insured against; that is, losses where an insured peril is the proximate or dominant cause rather than the remote or indirect cause.[63]

---

60. See, for example, *Mayronne M. & C. Co. v. T.W. Drilling Co.*, 168 F.Supp. 800, 1959 AMC 403 (S.D.,La.); *Parfait v. Jahncke Service*, 484 F.2d 296, 1973 AMC 2447 (5th Cir.); *Ruffalo's v. National Ben-Franklin*, 243 F.2d 949, 1957 AMC 1233 (2d Cir.); *Petros M. Nomikos, Ltd. v. Robertson*, (1939) 64 Ll.L.Rep. 45, H.L.; *Palmer v. Warren Insurance Co.*, 1 Story 360 (U.S., 1840); *A/S Ocean v. Black Sea and Baltic Gen. Ins. Co.*, [1935] *supra*, n. 56; *Forestal Land, Timber and Railways Co., Ltd. v. Rickards*, [1941] 70 Ll.L.Rep. 173, H.L.; *Donnell v. Columbia Ins. Co.*, 2 Sumn. C.C. 366 (U.S., 1836); *Gulf Oil v. Margaret*, 441 F.Supp. 1, 1978 AMC 868, *aff'd* 565 F.2d 958 (5th Cir., 1978).
    61. (1832) 149 E.R. 106, at 109.
    62. *Ruffalo's v. National Ben-Franklin, supra*, n. 60; *Blackett v. Royal Exchange Assur. Co., supra*, n. 60; *Harris v. Olympus T. & T. Co.*, 516 F2d 922, 1975 AMC 2146 (5th Cir.).
    63. *Thames & Mersey Marine Ins. Co. Ltd. v. Hamilton, Fraser & Co.*, (1887) 12 App. Cas. 484; *Grant, Smith & Co. and McDonnell Ltd. v. Seattle Construction & Dry Dock Co.*, [1920] A.C. 162, [1918-19] All E.R. 378; *Ballantyne v. Mackinnon*, [1896] 2 Q.B. 455; *Dudgeon v. Pembroke*, (1874) L.R. 9 Q.B., 2 App. Cas. 284; *Leyland Shipping Co. v. Norwich Union Fire Ins. Society*, (1917) 1 K.B. 873, (1918) A.C. 350; *The Coxwold*, (1942) A.C. 291, 2 All E.R. 6; *Shaver Transportation Co. v. Travelers Indemnity Co.*, 471 F.Supp. 892, 1980 AMC 393 (D.,Ore.); *Techni-Chemicals Products Co., Ltd. v. South British Ins. Co., Ltd.*, [1977] 1 N.Z.L.R. 311; *Shell International Petroleum Co., Ltd. v. Gibbs (The Salem)*, [1983] 2 A.C. 375, H.L.; *Athens Maritime Enterprises Corp. v. Hellenic Mutual War Risks Association (Bermuda) Ltd. (The Andreas Lemos)*, [1982] 2 Lloyd's Rep. 483; *Rhesa Shipping Co. v. Edmunds et al (The Popi M)*, [1983] 2 Lloyd's Rep. 235, *rev'd* by House of Lords [1985] 2 Lloyd's Rep. 1. See, also, Sec. 55(1) of the Marine Insurance Act, 1906, reading:
    Subject to the provisions of the Act, and unless any policy otherwise provides, the insurer is liable for any loss proximately caused by a peril insured against, but, subject as

Ejusdem Generis

This rule is concerned with the meaning to be given to general words added to special words in order to amplify the latter. The rule is discussed fully in Chapter XII, "Perils of the Seas," under the heading, "All Other Perils, Losses, and Misfortunes." See, also, Rule 12, Schedule 1, Rules of Construction of Policy, Marine Insurance Act, 1906, reading:

The term "all other perils" includes only perils similar in kind to the perils specifically mentioned in the policy.

Illustrative Interpretations When Applying Principles of Construction

While not intended to be all-inclusive, the following cases will illustrate how the foregoing principles of construction have been applied by the courts.

In *Polpen Shipping Co., Ltd. v. Commercial Union Assurance Co., Ltd.*,[64] the plaintiff's motor vessel was insured, *inter alia,* against loss by collision by plaintiff's vessel with "any other ship or vessel." The vessel dragged its anchor and collided with a flying boat belonging to His Majesty's government which was also at anchor. The court held that a flying boat was not a "ship or vessel" within the meaning of the policy, stating that a ship or vessel is a hollow structure intended to be used in navigation, that is, to do its real work on the seas and other waters, and capable of free and ordered movement thereon from one place to another.[65]

In *Kelloch v. S. & H.*,[66] the term "whilst diving," as used in a salvage company's liability insurance policy, was held to include the entire diving operation in and out of the water and the policy therefore covered injury to a diver's helper who slipped on the deck while assisting the diver in his descent.

---

aforesaid, he is not liable for any loss which is not proximately caused by a a peril insured against.
The subject of proximate cause is discussed fully in Chapter XV, "Proximate Cause."
64. [1943] 1 All E.R. 162, 74 Ll.L.Rep. 157, 1943 AMC 438.
65. In the same context, see *Conners Marine v. Northwestern Ins.*, 16 F.Supp. 626, 1936 AMC 1061 (S.D.N.Y.) (pontoons not "vessels"); *Halvorsen v. Aetna Ins. Co.*, 1954 AMC 1996 (St.,Wash.) (log rafts not "vessels"); and *Soil Mechanics v. Empire Mut. Ins. Co.*, 285 N.Y.S. 2d 391, 1968 AMC 491 (St., N.Y.) (raft or float used to mount soil boring equipment not a "water craft" within the watercraft exclusion). See, also, *Moores v. Louisville Underwriters*, 14 F. 226 (5th Cir., 1882) and *Morrison Mill Co. v. Queens Ins. Co.*, [1925] 1 D.L.R. 1159 (Can.).
66. 473 F.2d 767, 1973 AMC 948 (5th Cir.).

In *Rowe, Admr. v. U.S.F. & G.*,[67] the court held that prospective purchasers of a motorboat, injured in a collision during a demonstration ride for which they paid nothing, were not "passengers for a charge" under an exclusion to that effect in the policy.

In *Stuyvesant Ins. v. Butler*,[68] a clause in a marine insurance policy excluded liability "in respect to minors." The court held that the word "minors" was ambiguous because it was not defined in terms of a specific age, justifying resort to the parlance of the maritime industry where the minimum age for seamen is 17 (U. S. Navy), 16 (U. S. federal law), and 15 (I.L.O. Convention). Stating that the ambiguity should be resolved against the insurer and in favor of the assured, the court held that the policy provided coverage for injuries to an inexperienced 17 year old deckhand.

In *Gulf Oil v. Dean Marine Divers*,[69] there was a policy provision purporting to exclude damage to property used by or in the "care, custody and control" of the assured. The court held that the provision was not sufficiently explicit to defeat coverage where the assured's use of a third party's property was merely temporary and incidental to the work being performed. But, see *Monari v. Surfside Boat Club*,[70] construing the phrase "property as to which the insured . . . is exercising physical control" and denying coverage.

In *Shelley v. Nationwide Mutual*,[71] the personal accident insurance policy involved covered injuries to the insured "while riding as a passenger . . . on any water conveyance operated under a license for the transportation of passengers for hire." The wife of the insured owner of a 37 foot cabin cruiser, licensed to carry up to six passengers for hire, was injured during a pleasure share-the-expense outing with her husband and several friends. The court, stating that any ambiguity in the policy must be resolved in favor of the assured, held that the wife's injuries were covered.

Where a homeowner's liability policy excluded coverage with respect to boating accidents if the boat had (1) an inboard motor exceeding 50 horsepower, and (2) an outboard motor exceeding 24 horsepower, the court held that the insurer must nonetheless defend in an accident involving use of a 120-horsepower inboard-outboard motor, as the third type of motor, i.e., an inboard-outboard combination, was not referred to in the exclusions clause.[72]

---

67. 375 F.2d 215, 1968 AMC 374 (4th Cir.).
68. 314 So. 2d 567, 1976 AMC 1182 (St.,Fla.).
69. 323 F.Supp. 679, 1972 AMC 1570 (E.D.,La.).
70. 469 F.2d 9, 1973 AMC 56 (5th Cir.).
71. 1968 AMC 2305 (St.,Pa.).
72. *Guarantee Mutual v. Middlesex Mutual*, 339 A.2d 6, 1975 AMC 2327 (St., N.H.). See, also, *Martenson v. Massie*, 1975 AMC 2418 (St.,N.H.).

In *Trinidad Corp. v. American S.S. Owners Mut. P & I Ass'n*,[73] the insured vessel ran into a dredge's pipeline and pontoon, forcing the pontoons into another vessel and causing damage to the pipeline, pontoons, and the other vessel. It was held that the collison did not occur to the dredge itself and the loss consequently fell within the scope of the P & I policy, which, in that instance, covered liability for damage to "any fixed or moveable object or property, except another vessel or craft" and not under the hull policy's Running Down Clause.

In *Steinhoff v. Royal Canadian Ins. Co.*,[74] the policy upon a vessel described it as a "steam barge," and was warranted "free from any contribution for loss by jettison or property laden on deck of any sail vessel or barge." There was nothing else in the policy as to the vessel carrying a deck load. It was held that the "barge" mentioned in the policy did not mean the insured vessel, nor did it refer to a "steam barge."

In *Maritime Ins. Co., Ltd. v. Alianza Ins. Co. of Santander*,[75] a ship was insured while at "port or ports, place or places in New Caledonia." While on her way to a port at that island, she struck upon a reef and was damaged. The court held that the words "port or ports" occurring in conjunction with "place or places" mean a place or places at which the vessel might arrive with some object other than that of merely passing on her way to some other point; the vessel was not, therefore, "at a port or ports, place or places in New Caledonia" within the meaning of the policy and the insurers were not liable. With respect to definitions of the term "port," see cases cited under "Geographical Terms," *supra*.

In *Board of Management of Agricultural Bank of Tasmania v. Brown*,[76] a vessel, in consideration of an additional premium, was held covered "for the period 5th September 1950 to 5th November 1950, inclusive, whilst engaged in pile driving and salvage work." On October 24, 1950, while not engaged in pile driving and salvage work, she went aground and became a constructive total loss. It was held on a proper construction of the policy, the liability of the insurer was increased generally during the period named and not merely while the vessel was engaged in pile driving and salvage work.

In *Driftwood Lands & Timber Ltd. v. U.S. Fire Ins. Co. of New York*,[77] the insured was covered against, *inter alia*, damage caused to any dock by a barge owned by the insured. The insured also owned a tug. While the tug was towing the barge, the employees of the insured were negligent such that the barge struck the dock and damaged it. The court held that the damage was not covered as it was intended that the insured would be cov-

---

73. 229 F.2d 57, 1956 AMC 1464 (2d Cir.), *cert den.* 351 U.S. 966.
74. (1877) 42 U.C.R. 307 (Can.).
75. [1907] 2 K.B. 660, 10 Asp. M.L.C. 579.
76. (1957) 97 C.L.R. 503, 31 A.L.J. 865 (H.C.,Aus.).
77. [1955] 1 D.L.R. 176, *aff'd* [1955] 1 D.L.R. 176, C.A., 1955 AMC 884.

ered only in its capacity as owner of the barge and not as to the negligence of its employees while operating a tug.

In *J.P. Porter & Sons, Ltd. v. Western Assur. Co.*,[78] the policy was endorsed to permit the owner of a dredge and scow to proceed to Halifax "in tow of two approved tugs." The dredge was towed by one approved tug and the scow by another. During the tow, the scow was damaged. In an action to recover for the cost of repairs, the court held that the words "in tow of two approved tugs" were ambiguous and should be construed against the insurer so as to permit separate towing.

In *Belcher v. Southern Ins. Co., Ltd.*,[79] the blank in the body of a printed form of policy was filled in with the words, in writing, "On colonial produce as per bill of lading. Warranted free from average unless general." In the conditions in the printed memorandum following, certain provisions were made about wool and cotton, and then the following printed words occurred: "and all other goods or merchandise, except livestock, are warranted free from average unless general, or the ship be wrecked." The ship was wrecked and the assured sued for a partial loss. The court held that the written and printed matter could not be taken as cumulative, but must be treated as being so discrepant that the written matter must prevail as expressing the immediate intention of the contracting parties; therefore, the assured could not recover for a partial loss of the goods consequent on the vessel being wrecked.

Gulf Oil v. Margaret,[80] involved damages to an oil pipeline owned by Gulf Oil caused by a drilling barge owned by Odeco, and doing work for Shell Oil Co. Shell Oil Co. had been named as an additional assured on several policies covering the drilling barge and its owner. The dispute between the parties was over which policies covered and, if so, which of the policies were primary and which were excess. One of the applicable policies contained an endorsement defining the term "insured" as meaning the named insured and others to whom the named insured was obligated by virtue of a written contract to provide insurance such as was afforded by the policy " . . . but only with respect to operations by or in behalf of or facilities used by the Named Insured." The underwriters on that policy contended that this definition restricted coverage to situations where the named assured (Odeco) had been at fault. All parties had stipulated that Odeco was free from fault and that Shell Oil was solely at fault. Shell Oil contended that the cited language merely limited coverage to damages incurred while Shell and Odeco were performing their respective obligations under the drilling contract, regardless of who was at fault. The court held that the policy provided coverage on grounds, *inter alia*, that

---

78 [1938] 1 D.L.R. 619 (Can.).
79. [1872] 2 N.Z.C.A. 59 (N.Z.).
80. 441 F.Supp. 1, 1978 AMC 868, *aff'd per curiam* 565 F.2d 958 (5th Cir.).

the underwriter had the burden of proof when it sought to avoid liability under an exclusion, which burden it did not carry, as well as construing the policy most strongly against the insurer who was responsible for the language used.

In *Emmco Ins. Co. v. Southern Terminal & Transport Co.*,[81] the underwriter insured under three policies a towing and barging concern which it knew was engaged in the business of towage. The P & I policy provided coverage for "liability for loss of, or damage to, any other vessel or craft . . . caused by collision with the vessel named herein, insofar as such liability would not be covered by full insurance under the [companion policies]." The companion policies were an AIH policy insuring barges and an AIH tug form (Tug Syndicate 1953) on the insured tugs. The P & I policy also contained an exclusion reading:

> Notwithstanding anything to the contrary contained in this policy, no liability attaches to the Assurer:

> For any loss, damage, expense or claim arising out of or having relation to the towage of any other vessel or craft . . . .

A tug belonging to the assured, while towing a barge, was involved in a collision in which the barge and other vessels were damaged by reason of the negligence of the towing tug. The underwriter paid a portion of the loss under the Running Down Clause of the Tug Hull policy but refused to pay any sums under the P & I policy because of the towing exclusion.

At first instance, the court found that it was the intent of the parties to supplement the coverage under the Tug Syndicate policy with coverage under the P & I policy. Thus, by one policy coverage was specifically granted and by another specifically excluded. The court thereupon found that an ambiguity existed which could not be reconciled, and, construing the policy liberally to carry out the intent of the parties, held that the underwriters could not claim the benefit of the exclusion. The trial court was reversed, the appeals court holding that there was not an irreconcilable ambiguity and that in the absence of such ambiguity, it was not at liberty to cancel entirely the explicit exclusion in the P & I policy and thus convert the policy to one indiscriminately covering all towing activities of the assured, whether they be insured barges or not.[82]

Regrettably, the case appears to have been tried upon a motion for summary judgment rather than after a trial in which evidence could have

---

81. 333 So.2d 80 (St.,Fla., 1976).

82. The appeals court apparently was of the erroneous impression that the barge was owned by the assured but was not "scheduled"; i.e., noted on the schedule insuring the barges. Actually, as disclosed by a petition for reconsideration filed on behalf of the assured, the barge was owned by a third party. The court was unimpressed and adhered to its decision.

been adduced as to what the respective parties intended. It seems incomprehensible that the assured did not intend by procuring the P & I policy to cover its excess liabilities over and above the coverage provided by the Running Down Clause in the Tug Syndicate policy. Indeed, the case would seem to be a proper one for reformation.

In *Techni-Chemicals Products Co., Ltd. v. South British Ins. Co., Ltd.*,[83] the plaintiff insured a shipment of edible oils under an all risks cargo policy containing a warehouse-to-warehouse clause. Originally, the oils were to be shipped in drums or strong tin. Plaintiff sought and obtained an extension of the policy to cover shipment in bulk. The extension was not embodied in the policy by way of an endorsement but was set forth in memoranda by representatives of the plaintiff and the defendant underwriters. The memorandum prepared by the underwriters' representative noted that there was no coverage for contamination unless there was an external fortuity. The memorandum continued: "In particular, we would not be covering loss, etc. incurred from the edible oils having passed through dirty pumps and connecting equipment, etc. or stored in an unclean ship's tank."

When the tanker arrived in New Zealand, the oil was transshipped by a trucking firm which delivered a considerable quantity of the oil to the wrong destination where it was mixed and contaminated with other types of oil already in the shore tanks. The plaintiff assured brought suit. Defendants contended that the quoted phrase in the memorandum was a limitation of coverage; that the proximate cause of the loss was contamination and that there was no external fortuity. The court held otherwise, holding that the written words of the memorandum prevailed over the printed provisions of the policy; that the qualifying words in the memorandum were not merely illustrative because of the use of the phrase "in particular"; that the limiting words only applied to the specific instances named; and that the act of the trucking company in delivering to the wrong destination and into tanks already containing other types of oil was the proximate cause of the loss and an "external fortuity."

In *Navegacion Goya v. Mutual Boiler*,[84] the policy contained a "London following" clause, requiring the American companies insuring 15 percent of the risk to "follow" the lead underwriters in London in the settlement, etc., of claims. The London underwriters paid their 85 percent of the claim whereupon the American underwriters refused to do so, asserting defenses of breach of warranty and misrepresentation. In over-

---

83. [1977] 1 N.Z.L.R. 311 (N.Z.).
84. 411 F.Supp. 929, 1972 AMC 650 (S.D.N.Y.). See, however, *Armadoro Occidental S.A. & Ors v. Horace Mann Insurance Co.*, [1977] 2 Lloyd's Rep. 406, C.A., involving the construction of the "follow London" clause with a New York "suable clause." The court held that the "follow London" clause was of paramount importance and indicated that the contract was to be construed, interpreted, and applied according to English law.

ruling a motion for summary judgment, the court held that the "London following" clause was ambiguous and involved an issue of fact as to the intent of the parties.

Amin Rasheed Shippinq Corp. v. Kuwait Ins. Co. (The Al Wahab)[85] involved a marine policy, issued in Kuwait by a Kuwaiti insurance company but on a form using substantially all the standard English marine form. The insured vessel was confiscated by the Saudi Arabian authorities and the insured gave notice of abandonment which was rejected. The insured obtained leave to serve proceedings upon the Kuwaiti insurance company in Kuwait and the Kuwaiti company sought to set aside the proceedings on grounds that the court had no jurisdiction to give leave for such service, or, alternatively, that the court should exercise its discretion against permitting such service on the ground that Kuwait and not England was the proper forum for trial of the action. The House of Lords held that it was not possible to interpret the policy or determine the respective rights of the parties except by reference to the Marine Insurance Act, 1906; the English rules of conflict of law applied and the proper law of the contract embodied in the policy was English law. Although it was held that the court had jurisdiction to order service of the writ in Kuwait, there was no reason to believe that justice either could not be obtained in the Kuwaiti court or could only be obtained at excessive cost, delay, or inconvenience and, therefore, the matter should be tried in Kuwait but with English law being applicable.

Shell International Petroleum Co., Ltd. v. Gibbs (The Salem)[86] involved the proper construction of the term "taking at sea." In that case, most of a vessel's oil cargo was misappropriated and sold by the master and crew and the vessel was eventually scuttled. The term "taking at sea" was held not to comprehend dishonest takings by the crew or charterer. The misappropriation actually took place in a harbor in South Africa when the oil in the vessel was pumped ashore and thus, technically, could not be deemed a "taking at sea." In so ruling, *Nishina Trading Co., Ltd. v. Chiyoda* was expressly overruled in its holding that a taking at sea covered wrongful misappropriation by a bailee.[87]

In *Edinburgh Assur. v. R.L. Burns,*[88] the court was confronted with the task of construing the term "actual total loss" in connection with a drilling platform damaged by a typhoon. The drilling platform was held to be an actual total loss although physical remains still existed as it had ceased to be "a thing of the kind insured."

The proper construction of the term "constructive total loss" was in-

---

85. [1983] 2 Lloyd's Rep. 365, H.L.
86. [1983] 2 A.C. 374, H.L., [1983] 1 Lloyd's Rep. 342, H.L.
87. [1969] 2 Q.B. 449.
88. *Edinburgh Assur. v. R.L. Burns,* 669 F.2d 1269, 1982 AMC 2532 (9th Cir.).

volved in *Owners of the Ship Bamburi v. Compton.*[89] There, the insured vessel
was detained from moving from an Iraqi port because of the Iraqi-Iran
war, and the crew was evacuated. The court held in essence that the
owners would be unlikely to recover the vessel within a reasonable time
which, in the view of the court, was a period of twelve months. The war
risk underwriters were consequently held liable.

The proper construction of the term "perils of the seas" constantly
gives rise to interesting and difficult cases. One of the most fascinating is
Case Existological Laboratories, Ltd. v. Foremost Ins. Co. (The Bamcell II).[90]
There, the court was confronted with a question of coverage with respect
to the unexpected sinking of a specially contrived barge or floating platform which was actually designed to be sunk deliberately. The vessel was a
converted scow. As converted, it could be partially submerged at the stern
so as to allow a module to be drifted off its deck or received on deck. A
longitudinal bulkhead divided the midships and after sections into two
compartments. There was a total absence of any bottom under the midships and after compartments, leaving them wholly open to the sea. The
concept was that air would be pumped into the open compartments from
the top so as to provide a cushion of compressed air lying between the
underside of the deck and the level of seawater inside the compartments.
Without the cushion of compressed air, the vessel would inevitably sink
like a rock—and that is precisely what happened when a new employee
negligently left open a valve so that the air in the compartments was displaced by water.

At first instance, the assured failed in his contention that the loss was
caused by a "peril of the sea." However, the court of appeals reversed,
holding that an act is not negligent in itself but only in relation to a foreseeable risk of harm. If that foreseeable risk of harm is a peculiarly marine risk, then the act, coupled with its foreseeable consequence, is a fortuitous accident of the seas. Thus, it was the risk of the vessel sinking that
made the failure to close the deck valves a negligent omission when there
was a duty to act. When that negligent omission was coupled with its foreseeable consequence, the proximate cause of the loss was a peril of the
seas and, as such, was covered by the policy. The Supreme Court of Canada affirmed.[91]

89. [1982] 1 Lloyd's Rep. 312.
90. 1981 AMC 881 (Sup. Ct., B.C.), reversed [1982] 133 D.L.R.(3d) 727 (Ct. of Appeal),
reversal affirmed [1984] 48 B.C.L.R. 273, [1983] 1 S.C.R. 47 (Can.)
91. What is a "peril of the seas" is discussed fully in Chapter XII, "Perils of the Seas,"
and the relevant cases cited. Attention is specifically directed to *Rhesa Shipping Co., S.A. v.
Edmunds et al (The Popi M),* [1983] 2 Lloyd's Rep. 235, *rev'd* [1985] 2 Lloyd's Rep. 1, H.L.,
where there was a sudden inrush of water through shell plating in the engine room which
suddenly opened up; had not the crew also been negligent, the vessel would probably have
not sunk. The trial judge was unable to state whether or not the vessel was or was not "seaworthy," but nonetheless awarded judgment to the vessel owner. The court of appeals af-

Words and terms in policies construed in other representative cases are: sinking;[92] stranding;[93] latent defect;[94] marine perils;[95] fish and oil;[96] bodily injury as not including "death";[97] maintenance of watercraft;[98] occurrence;[99] completed operations;[100] owner;[101] on advances;[102] legal liability;[103] towers liability;[104] "of and in" as embracing a naphtha launch carried on a yacht;[105] bilging;[106] lying between piers;[107] structures built in the frame of a vessel;[108] docked;[109] foreign;[110] underwater damage;[111] in

---

firmed, but the House of Lords reversed, holding that the evidence was in equipoise and the owner had failed to bear the burden of proof. See, also, *Skandia Ins. Co. Ltd. v. Skoljarev*, [1979] 26 A.L.R. 1 (H.C.,Aus.); *Gregoire v. Underwriters at Lloyds*, 1982 AMC 2045 (D.,Alaska); *Visscher Enterprises Pty. Ltd. v. Southern Pacific Ins. Co., Ltd.*, [1981] Qd. R. 561 (Aus.). Compare *Nickerson & Sons Ltd. v. I.N.A. (The J.E. Kenny)*, 49 N.R. 321, [1983] C.C.L.I. 78 (Can.).

92. *Bryant and May v. London Assurance*, (1886) 2 T.L.R. 591; *John C. Jackson Ltd. v. Sun Ins. Office Ltd.*, [1962] S.C.R. 412 (Can.) (term "sinking" does not embrace a vessel taking on water whereby the cargo was damaged but the vessel did not, in fact, sink).

93. See, under subheading Strandings and Groundings in Chapter XII, "Perils of the Seas," and *Rudolph v. British & Foreign Marine Ins. Co.*, (1898) 30 N.S.R. 380, *aff'd* 28 S.C.R. 607 (Can.).

94. See, under appropriate subheading, Chaoter XVI, "Inchmaree Clause."

95. *Staples v. Great Amer. Ins. Co.*, [1941] S.C.R. 213, 8 I.L.R. 98, [1941] 2 D.L.R. 1; *Hanover Ins. Co. v. Sonfield*, 386 S.W.2d 160 (St.,Tex., 1965) (term does not embrace a yacht falling from a trailer when the towing automobile struck a bridge abutment).

96. *Thomas v. St. John's Marine Ins. Co.*, (1863) 4 Nfld L.R. 754 (Can.) (words "fish and oil" written in margin of policy narrowed down the words "goods and merchandises" contained in the body of the policy).

97. *Mid-Century Ins. v. Hauck*, 1974 AMC 2154 (St.,Cal., Sy.).

98. *Parfait v. Jahncke Service*, 484 F.2d 296, 1973 AMC 2247 (5th Cir.); *Grigsby v. Coastal Marine*, 412 F.2d 1011, 1969 AMC 1513 (5th Cir.).

99. *Newark Ins. Co. v. Continental Casualty Co.*, 363 N.Y.S.2d 327, 1975 AMC 307, 46 A.D.2d 514 (St., N.Y.); *Barge BW 1933 Fire*, 1968 AMC 2738 (Arb.).

100. *Home Ins. Co. v. Doe*, 1976 AMC 382 (St.,La.).

101. *Tugboat Underwriting v. Brittingham, Extx*, 262 Md. 134, 1971 AMC 805 (St.,Md.) (bareboat charterer as owner *pro hac vice* is an "owner"). See, also, *Offshore Logistics v. Mutual Marine*, 462 F.Supp. 485, 1981 AMC 1154 (E.D.,La.); *Continental v. Bonanza*, 706 F.2d 1365, 1983 AMC 2059 (5th Cir.) ; *Baltimore Dry Docks & Ship Building Co. v. New York & P.R.S.S. Co.*, 258 F. 934, *aff'd* 262 F. 485 (4th Cir.).

102. *B.A. Assur. Co. v. Law & Co.*, (1892) S.C.R. 325 (Can.); *Providence Washington v. Bowring*, 50 F. 613 (2d Cir., 1892).

103. *Monterey-Dixie*, 1929 AMC 336 (St., N.Y.).

104. *Atlantic Lighterage Co. v. Continental Ins. Co.*, 75 F.2d 288, 1935 AMC 305 (2d Cir.).

105. *Dennis v. Home Ins. Co.*, 136 F. 481 (S.D.N.Y., 1905).

106. *Ellery v. Merchants Ins. Co.*, 20 Mass. 45 (St.,Mass., 1825).

107. *Huntley v. Providence Washington Ins. Co.*, 79 N.Y.S. 35, 77 App.Div. 197 (St., N.Y.).

108. *Transatlantic Shipping Co. v. St. Paul F. & M. Ins. Co.*, 298 F. 551, *aff'd* 9 F.2d 720 (2d Cir., 1925).

109. *Snare & Triest Co. v. St. Paul F. & M. Ins. Co.*, 258 F. 425 (2d Cir., 1919).

110. *Re Terra Nova Mut. Marine Ins. Co. and Blackwood*, [1952] I.L.R. 403 (Can.) (foreign held to mean "external" to Newfoundland where the insurance company was local in character).

111. *Young v. Dale & Co.*, [1968] I.L.R. 1-200 (Can.) (included damages other than mere damage to the hull).

tow of two approved tugs;[112] "shifting" of cargo;[113] breakage of machinery;[114] as property may appear;[115] unpaid and/or collect freight;[116] hulls;[117] ratings of vessels;[118] "shipped on board";[119] raft;[120] demise charter;[121] "any peril";[122] risk of loading and unloading and accident to conveyance;[123] trial trips;[124] "risk" of harbor;[125] breakdown of motor generators or other electrical machinery;[126] "waterborne";[127] other like perils;[128] "towage";[129] "vermin" as used in an all risk policy;[130] within the continental limits of the United States;[131] accidents in hauling or launching or

112. *J.P. Porter & Sons, Ltd. v. Western Assur. Co.*, [1938] 1 D.L.R. 619 (Can.).

113. *Phoenix Assur. Co. v. Letellier*, (1925) 40 Q.K.B. 254 (Can.) (shifting means "moving about" and does not connote moving from one side of the vessel to another).

114. *New Castle Terminal Co. v. Western Assur. Co.*, 5 F.Supp. 890 (D., Md., 1934) (does not include "damage" occasioned by port propeller striking submerged piling); *Quinlivan v. Northwestern Fire and Mar. Ins. Co.*, 37 F.2d 29 (2d Cir., 1930).

115. *Graves & Barnwell v. Boston Mar. Ins. Co.*, 6 U.S. 419 (1805) (without a clause stating the insurance to be for the benefit of all concerned, the policy does not cover the interest of another joint owner).

116. *New Orleans & South American S.S. Co. v. W.R. Grace & Co.*, 26 F.2d 967 (2d Cir., 1928) (does not cover obligation to pay freight).

117. *Connors Marine Co. v. Northwestern F. & M. Ins. Co.*, 88 F.2d 637, 1937 AMC 344 (2d Cir.) (word "hulls" refers to cargo-bearing hulls and not tugs used for towage).

118. *Orient Mut. Ins. Co. v. Wright*, 68 U.S. 456 (1863) (means determination of relative state or condition).

119. *Croswell v. Mercantile Mut. Ins. Co.*, 19 F. 24 (8th Cir., 1884) (embraces being on board a ship chartered by the shipowner).

120. *Moores v. Louisville Underwriters*, 14 F. 226 (6th Cir., 1882) (raft is not ordinarily a vessel but where insured by a cargo policy and in charge of a towboat, construed as a vessel).

121. *O'Donnell v. Latham*, 525 F.2d 650 (5th Cir., 1976).

122. *In re Gulf & Midlands Barge Line, Inc.*, 509 F.2d 713 (5th Cir., 1975) (includes perils associated with the seas, including damage by collision whether caused by negligence or not).

123. *Dunbar Molasses Corp. v. Home Ins. Co.*, 3 F.Supp. 296, 1933 AMC 842 (S.D.N.Y.) (covers loss by escape from a broken section of pipeline leading from a storage tank to a valve at the dock).

124. *Wheeler v. Aetna Ins. Co.*, 68 F.2d 30 (2d Cir., 1933).

125. *Britannia Shipping Corp. v. Globe & Rutgers Fire Ins. Co.*, 249 N.Y.S. 908 (St.,N.Y., 1931) (theft of tug moored to a pier in a harbor held not a loss by "risk of harbor").

126. *Russell Min. Co. v. Northwestern F. & M. Ins. Co.*, 322 F.2d 440, 1963 AMC 2358 (6th Cir.) (turning off switch to electric pumps used to keep barge afloat not a "breakdown").

127. *Nichols & Thompson Core Drilling Co. v. Homeland Ins. Co.*, 148 F.Supp. 260 (D., Ida., 1947) (exclusion of loss while waterborne held ambiguous; policy covered loss of equipment dumped into river when drilling platform capsized).

128. *Southport Fisheries, Inc. v. Saskatchewan Gov't Ins. Office*, 161 F.Supp. 81, 1959 AMC 1280 (E.D.N.C.) (spiteful injury to fishing nets by acid being thrown upon them not covered). See, also, cases cited in Chapter XII, "Perils of the Seas."

129. *Crain Bros., Inc. v. Hartford Ins. Co.*, 149 F.Supp. 663, 1958 AMC 1468 (D., Pa., 1957) (means delivery of a tow to an apparently safe berth which is ostensibly secure).

130. *Sincoff v. Liberty Mut. F. Ins. Co.*, 230 N.Y.S.2d 13, 183 N.E.2d 899 (St.,N.Y., 1962) (vermin does not include damage by carpet beetles).

131. *Snyder v. Motorists Mut. Ins. Co.*, 2 Ohio App.2d 19, 206 N.E.2d 227, 1965 AMC 1791 (St., Ohio) (term so ambiguous as to be beyond reasonable definition).

moving in shipyards;[132] change of interest . . . under new management;[133] "laid up";[134] "satisfactory condition survey";[135] and "sent to sea";[136] "warranted class maintained";[137] "rejection clause";[138] "barratry";[139] "piracy."[140]

Reasonable Expectations Doctrine

In recent years, courts have increasingly relied upon what has been termed the "reasonable expectations doctrine" to grant recovery to assureds even though policy provisions may well be clear and unambiguous in limiting, denying, or excluding coverage. Professor Robert E. Keeton, a noted author and professor in the field of insurance (and now a United States district judge), has described the doctrine in the following terms:

The objectively reasonable expectations of applicants and intended beneficiaries regarding the terms of insurance contracts will be hon-

---

132. *Walker v. Reliance Ins. Co.*, 340 F.Supp. 206, 1972 AMC 1769 (E.D.,Mich.) (does not protect against sinking of yacht due to shipyard's failure to reinsert drain plugs removed at time of winter lay-up).

133. *Heindl-Evans v. Reliance Ins. Co.*, 1980 AMC 2823 (E.D.,Va.); *U.S. Fire Ins. Co. v. Cavanaugh*, 1983 AMC 1261 (S.D.,Fla.) (mere hiring a fishing boat master to operate and maintain the vessel did not constitute a "change of management"); *Lemar Towing v. Fireman's Fund*, 471 F.2d 609, 1973 AMC 1843 (5th Cir.) (no change of management where the same two men retained direction and control of vessel while acting as controlling stockholders and officers of separate corporate entities).

134. *Tinkerbell*, 533 F.2d 496, 1976 AMC 799 (9th Cir.) (lay-up is not concerned with location but only with "condition"; i.e., that the vessel had been winterized and laid up in accordance with local custom); *Harris v. Glen Falls*, 493 P.2d 861, 1972 AMC 138 (St.,Cal.) (vessel did not cease to be "laid up" merely because it went on short trial trip); *Yacht Braemar*, 125 F.Supp. 677, 1955 AMC 384 (D.,R.I.) (vessel was "laid up" according to local custom); *Gehrlein's v. Travelers Ins. Co.*, 1957 AMC 1029 (S.D.N.Y.) (vessel did not cease to be "laid up" by being moved from its berth to a painting berth in the same boatyard); *Eamotte v. Employers Commercial Union Ins. Co.*, 1976 AMC 204 (St.,N.Y.) (wet storage found to be acceptable lay-up practice in the local area); *Federal Business Development Bank v. Commonwealth Ins. Co. Ltd. et al (The Good Hope)*, [1984] 2 C.C.L.I. 200 (Can.) (defining geographical area where compliance with lay-up warranty was sufficient).

135. *M. Almojil Establishment v. Malayan M. & G. Underwriters Ltd. (The Al-Jubail IV)*, [1982] 2 Lloyd's Rep. 637 (Singapore).

136. *Cooper v. Phoenix Prudential Australia Ltd.*, [1983] 2 ANZ Ins. Cas. 60-526 (Aus.).

137. *Pindos Shipping Corp. v. Raven (The Mata Hari)*, [1983] 2 Lloyd's Rep. 449, Q.B.D.

138. *Snyder International, Inc. v. Dae Han Fire & Mar. Ins. Co., Ltd.*, 1981 AMC 2685 (D.,Mass.).

139. *Piermay Shipping Co. v. Chester (The Michael)*, [1979] 2 Lloyd's Rep. 7; *Allied Chemical - Piermay*, 1978 AMC 773 (Arb.); *Fishing Fleet v. Trident*, 598 F.2d 925, 1980 AMC 583 (5th Cir.); *Nautilus v. Edinburgh Ins.*, 673 F.2d 1314, 1982 AMC 696 (4th Cir.). And see cases cited under the subheading of Barratry, Chapter XII, "Perils of the Seas."

140. *Athens Maritime Enterprises Corp. v. Hellenic Mutual War Risks Association (Bermuda) Ltd. (The Andreas Lemos)*, [1982] 2 Lloyd's Rep. 483, [1983] 1 All E.R. 590, Q.B.D. (clandestine theft does not amount to piracy and does not become piracy because the thieves subsequently used force in order to escape). See, also, cases cited under same subheading in Chapter XII, "Perils of the Seas."

ored even though painstaking study of the policy provisions would
have negated those expectations.

Further, Keeton says:

First, as an ideal this principle incorporates the proposition that policy language will be construed as laymen would understand it and not
according to the interpretation of sophisticated underwriters . . . .
An important corollary of the expectations principle is that insurers
ought not to be allowed to use qualifications and exceptions from
coverage that are inconsistent with the reasonable expectations of a
policyholder having an ordinary degree of familiarity with the type of
coverage involved. This ought not to be allowed even though the insurer's form is very explicit and unambiguous, because insurers know
that ordinarily policyholders will not in fact read their policies. Policy
forms are long and complicated and cannot be fully understood without detailed study; few policyholders ever read their policies as carefully as would be required for moderately detailed understanding.
Moreover, the normal processes for marketing most kinds of insurance do not ordinarily place the detailed policy terms in the hands of
the policyholder until the contract has already been made . . . .

Illustrations of the application of the doctrine—perhaps it would be
more accurate to term it a newly developing "principle of construction"—
will be found in such cases as *Kievit v. Loyal Protective Life Ins. Co.*,[141] *Prudential Life Ins. Co. v. Lamme*,[142] *Allen v. Metropolitan Life Ins. Co.*,[143] *Gerhardt
v. Continental Ins. Co.*,[144] and *Lewis v. Aetna Ins. Co.*[145]

All of the foregoing illustrative cases involve non-maritime policies except *Lewis v. Aetna Ins. Co.* In that case, the plaintiffs were the owners of a
sports cruiser on which the defendant issued a yacht policy. The cruiser
was found sunk in its boathouse. It was raised and repairs commenced.
Plaintiff brought an action for the cost of repairs and a verdict was returned in their favor. The trial court set the verdict aside and entered
judgment for defendant.

On appeal, the Oregon Supreme Court noted that the evidence
showed that the cruiser sank because of leaks in its hull. The issue was
whether from this evidence alone the jury could infer that the leaks were
caused by a "latent defect" within the meaning of the Inchmaree Clause
in the policy. The majority of the court held that when it had been found
that a vessel was seaworthy and did not sink because of negligent mainte-

141. 34 N.J. 475, 170 A.2d 22 (St., N.J., 1961).
142. 83 Nev. 146, 425 P.2d 346 (St.,Nev., 1967).
143. 44 N.J. 294, 208 A.2d 638 (St.,N.J., 1965).
144. 48 N.J. 291, 225 A.2d 328 (St.,N.J., 1966).
145. 505 P.2d 914 (St.,Ore., 1972).

nance, the jury may infer the vessel sank because of a latent defect even though there was no direct evidence that a latent defect caused the loss.

Two justices concurred, in essence espousing application of the "reasonable expectations" principle enunciated by Professor Keeton.[146] The concurring opinion stated in part:

> . . . We would reach an unreasonable result if we denied the plaintiff policyholders the coverage which they reasonably assumed they had purchased because they cannot explain an inexplicable sinking [Citing *Kievit v. Loyal Protective Life Ins. Co., supra*].

Whatever may be one's feeling regarding such a liberal principle of construction, more and more courts are relying upon it and it is alive and well in the United States.[147] It may be logical and proper to apply the principle in construing standard form yacht policies where the assureds are unsophisticated and might well not understand the policy terms even if they read them. It most certainly would be an egregious example of improper application of the basic principles of judicial construction to resort to the reasonable expectations principle where both the assured and assurer are knowledgeable, sophisticated, and represented by competent counsel such as was the case in *Eagle Leasing v. Hartford Fire*.[148]

Small Print

The vice of using inordinately small print in a policy is amply demonstrated in *Koskas v. Standard Marine Ins. Co., Ltd.*[149] and *Greet v. Citizens Ins. Co.*[150] In both instances, the underwriters were denied the benefit of the small print.

---

146. R. Keeton, "Insurance Law Rights at Variance with Policy Provisions," *Harv. L.Rev.*, 83 (1970): 961.
147. See *Rodman v. State Farm Mutual Ins. Co.*, 208 N.W.2d 903 (St.Iowa, 1973); *C. & J. Fertilizer, Inc. v. Allied Mut. Ins. Co.*, 227 N.W.2d 169 (St.,Iowa, 1975); *Century Bank v. St. Paul Fire & Marine Ins. Co.*, 4 Cal.3d 319, 482 P.2d 193 (St.,Cal., 1971); *Gyler v. Mission Ins. Co.*, 10 Cal.3d 216, 514 P.2d 1219 (St.,Cal., 1973).
148. 540 F.2d 1257, 1978 AMC 604 (5th Cir.).
149. (1926) 42 T.L.R. 123, *aff'd* 137 L.T. 165, C.A.
150. (1880) 27 Gr. 121, 5 A.R. 596 (Can.).

CHAPTER V

AGENTS AND BROKERS

Relationship in General

Surprisingly, neither the legal commentators nor the courts have developed and expounded to any major degree the fundamental distinctions between agents and brokers as those terms are used in the field of marine insurance. For the most part, it appears that the marine insurance fraternity fully understands the distinctions and, consequently, conducts its business accordingly without feeling any compelling need for technical explanations or definitions.

A few American cases have touched upon the distinctions, noting that insurance brokers are ordinarily employed by the person seeking insurance, as distinguished from insurance agents who are, generally speaking, employed by insurance companies to solicit and write insurance by and in the name of the insurance company.[1] The term "broker" in English marine insurance law has a well-settled meaning. He is clearly the agent of the assured, and in effecting insurance with an underwriter upon instructions from his principal, the assured, owes no duty to the underwriters.[2] The same rule obtains in the United States insofar as true brokers are concerned.[3]

---

1. *American Cas. Co. v. Ricas*, 179 Md. 627, 22 A.2d 484 (1941); *Mooney v. Underwriters at Lloyds*, 54 Ill.App. 2d 237, 204 N.E.2d 51 (1964), *rev'd* on other grounds, 33 Ill.2d 566, 214 N.E. 2d 283 (1965); *Universal Ins. Co. v. Manhattan Motor Line*, 82 Cal.App.2d 425, 186 P.2d 437 (1947); *Osborn v. Ozlin*, 310 U.S. 53 (1940); *Morris McGraw Wooden Ware Co. v. German F. Ins. Co.*, 126 La. 32, 52 So. 183 (1910); *Karam v. St. Paul F. & M. Ins. Co.*, 265 So.2d 821 (La.App., 1972), *aff'd* 281 So.2d 728 (1973), 72 ALR3rd 697; *Chicago v. Barnett*, 404 Ill. 136, 88 N.E.2d 477 (1949); *Assiniboia Corp. v. Chester*, 355 A.2d 873 (St.,Del., 1974), *aff'd* 355 A.2d 880 (St.,Del., 1976); *Ross v. Thomas*, 45 Ill.App.3d 705, 360 N.E.2d 126 (1977); *McFarlane v. Demco, Inc.*, 546 P.2d 625 (St., Okla., 1976); *Lynn v. West City*, 36 Ill.App.3d 561, 345 N.E.2d 172 (1976); *Dudley v. Inland Mut. Ins. Co.*, 330 F.2d 112 (4th Cir., 1963); *Seamans v. Knapp-Stout & Co.*, 89 Wis. 171, 61 N.W. 757 (1895); *United Firemen's Ins. Co. v. Thomas*, 82 F. 406, *aff'd* 92 F. 127 (7th Cir., 1899); *Port of Portland v. Water Quality Ins. Syndicate et al*, 549 F.Supp. 233, 1984 AMC 2019 (D., Ore., 1982).

2. *Empress Assur. Corp., Ltd. v. C.T. Bowring & Co., Ltd.*, (1905) ll Com.Cas. 107; *Glasgow Assur. Corp., Ltd. v. William Symondson & Co.*, (1911) 104 L.T. 254. But if the broker makes an actively misleading statement, then the underwriter may have an action against him under *Hedley Byrne v. Heller*, (1964) A.C. 465, where Lord Morris pointed out that if someone possessed of a special skill undertakes the assistance of another person who relies upon such skill, a duty of care will arise. If a person is so placed that others could reasonably rely upon his skill or ability to make a careful inquiry and that person allows his information to be passed on to another person who will place reliance upon it, a duty of care will arise. As Lord

Impact of Statutory Provisions

In the United States, some of the states have enacted statutory provisions that may impact upon the definition of agent or broker. These statutes customarily provide that any person performing specified acts in relation to insurance, such as soliciting or taking applications for insurance or making or causing to be made any contract of insurance for an insurance company, will be regarded as an agent of the insurance company and not of the assured.

A true broker frequently solicits or takes applications for insurance. However, he does so as an independent contractor with the goal of later placing the coverage with an acceptable underwriter *on behalf of the assured*. An uncritical application of a state statute providing that anyone who solicits or takes applications for insurance shall be deemed to be the agent of the underwriter, without recognition that the statute was actually intended to apply only to agents who are specifically appointed by insurance companies to solicit or take applications for those particular companies, can only lead to confusion and error.

A classic illustration of the foregoing can be found in the state of Oregon Insurance Code (ORS Chapters 731 to 752, inclusive), and specifically ORS 744.165, reading:

> Any person who solicits or procures an application for insurance shall in all matters relating to such application for insurance and the

---

Reid said, a reasonable man, knowing that he is being trusted or that his skill and judgment are being relied upon, must accept some responsibility for his answer being given carefully. Hedley Byrne was relied upon in this respect in *Cherry Ltd. v. Allied Ins. Brokers, Ltd.*, [1978] 1 Lloyd's Rep. 274.

3. *Ruby (Hurona)*, 18 F.2d 948, 1927 AMC 714 (2d Cir.); *Yellowtail*, 22 F.Supp. 545, 1938 AMC 499 (S.D.,Cal.); *Portsmouth*, 54 F.Supp. 2, 1944 AMC 384 (D.,Md.); *Beidler v. Universal Ins. Co.*, 134 F.2d 828, 1943 AMCC 345 (2d Cir.); *Curacao Tr. Co. v. Fed. Ins. Co.*, 137 F.2d 911, 1943 AMC 1050 (2d Cir.); *Whiteman v. Rhode Is. Ins. Co.*, 78 F.Supp. 624, 1949 AMC 111 (E.D.,La.); *Centennial Ins. Co. v. Parnell*, 1956 AMC 406 (St.,Fla.); *Voges v. Travelers F. I. Co.*, 1954 AMC 457 (St.,N.Y.); *Schooner Dartmouth v. Piper*, 1966 AMC 1877 (St.,Mass.); *Hauser v. American Central Ins. Co.*, 216 F.Supp. 318, 1964 AMC 526 (E.D.,La.); *Pyne v. Trans-Atlantic Marine*, 1972 AMC 274 (D.,Mass.); *Arkwright-Boston v. Bauer*, 1978 AMC 1570 (S.D.,Tex.) (knowledge of insureds' broker not imputed to excess insurer); *Vinnie's Market v. Canadian Marine*, 441 F.Supp. 341, 1978 AMC 977 (D.,Mass.) (delivery of policy to broker constitutes delivery to the assured); *Edinburgh Assur. v. R.L. Burns*, 479 F.Supp. 138, 1980 AMC 1261 (C.D.,Cal.), *aff'd* and modified, 669 F.2d 1269, 1982 AMC 2532 (9th Cir.). See, also, *Ruby S.S. Corp. v. Commercial Union Assur. Co.*, (1932) 44 Ll.L.Rep. 263, C.A., also reported at 1933 AMC 469. The practice, in some parts of the United States, in referring to all brokers as "agents" is clearly a misnomer. See, however, *U.S. Pipe & Foundry Co. v. Northwestern Agencies, Inc.*, 284 Or. 167, 585 P.2d 691 (1978), where a broker's receipt of premium and issuance of a certificate of insurance was held binding on the insurer, and *Contractor's Realty Co., Inc. v. Ins. Co. of North America*, 469 F.Supp. 1287, 1979 AMC 1864 (S.D.N.Y.), where the broker's knowledge of breakdowns of a vessel prior to placing insurance was not revealed to the insurer; the broker's knowledge was, however, imputed to the insurer.

policy issued in consequence thereof be regarded as the agent of the insurer issuing the policy and not the agent of the insurer. Any provisions in the application and policy to the contrary are invalid and of no effect whatever.

By contrast, the term "agent" is defined in ORS 731.062 as follows:

"Agent" means a person *appointed by an insurer* to solicit applications for insurance or to negotiate insurance on its behalf, and, if authorized so to do by the insurer, to effect and countersign insurance policies. [Emphasis supplied]

Moreover, ORS 744.165 is immediately preceded by ORS 744.155 requiring, *inter alia,* each insurer appointing an agent in the state to file, in writing with the insurance commissioner, notice of the appointment specifying the class or classes of insurance or sub-classes thereof to be transacted by the agent for the insurer.

Taking into consideration the legislative history of the present Insurance Code of Oregon, noting the provisions of the predecessor code (which was amended in 1967), and construing the provisions of the new code *in para materia,* leads inevitably to the conclusion that the legislature intended when the new code was adopted in 1967 only to establish in ORS 744.165 that true agents, who are appointed by specific insurers as their denominated agents in the state, are to be treated as agents of the insurer. Certainly, the legislature could not have intended that ORS 744.165 would be applicable to true brokers who frequently place insurance with alien or foreign insurers and whose duties and functions constitute them unquestionably as agents of the assured in accordance with the general rule. Yet, the unfortunate and somewhat ambiguous wording of ORS 744.165, standing alone, would lead the uninitiated to assume that all agents and brokers in Oregon, all of whom "solicit and procure applications for insurance," are agents for the insurer.

The proper interpretation of the Oregon statute came before the courts in *Port of Portland v. Water Quality Ins. Syndicate et al.*[4] There, the port employed a well-known insurance agency on a yearly contract to place and monitor its entire insurance program. The port's dredge sank and caused pollution in the harbor. The case presented the question of whether notice to the agency's representative of the sinking and potential pollution claim was notice to the defendant insurance companies whose policies presumptively provided coverage for the cleanup expenses. The port, basing its arguments on ORS 744.165 quoted above, took the position that the agency was the agent of the insurers and that notice to the

4. 549 F.Supp. 233, 1984 AMC 2019 (D.,Ore., 1982).

agency representative was therefore notice to the defendant under-writers. The court disagreed, stating:

> I hold that they are not [agents of the insurers]. While the agents in question fall within the literal ambit of ORS 744.165, and while that statute can create an agency relationship where none existed before [citing cases], the agents here served on yearly contracts as the employees of the *insured*. To apply the statute blindly would allow the insurer to give notice to the insurer merely by informing its own employees of a loss. These agents would be agents of *both* insurer and insured and the agency relationship would lose whatever meaning it has. This would stretch ORS 744.165 beyond the limited facts of the *Paulson* holding and do violence to the legitimate expectations of an insurer to receive notice of loss. The fundamental fact remains that Cole and James are not "intermediaries" at all, but the contract employees of the insured, and ORS 744.165 does not apply.

It is incumbent, therefore, when confronted with a statute that on its face seemingly makes any agent the agent of an insurer, to analyze carefully the statute and other statutory provisions accompanying it. It is doubtful that any legislature has the power by mere fiat to transmute a true broker, who in legal intendment and by common law principles is an agent for the assured, into an agent, whose actions can bind the insurer. Although the validity and constitutionality of such statutes have been upheld by the courts, this has been on grounds not involving the primary distinctions between agents and brokers.[5]

Practice in Placing Coverage by Brokers

Edinburgh Assur. Co. v. R.L. Burns[6] contains a fascinating and factually accurate exposition of the methods used in placing marine insurance coverages in the London market by or through American brokers. In that case, American Pacific International (API), a corporation engaged in oil and gas exploration, and the R.L. Burns Corporation (Burns), formed a joint venture to purchase the *Gatto*, a self-contained, three-legged, mobile, and self-elevating offshore drilling platform that had sustained a casualty in the Mozambique Channel off Madagascar, as a consequence of which its owners were paid as for a constructive total loss. API and Burns believed the drilling rig could be salvaged but desired insurance to cover

---

5. See Annotation, 19 ALR2d 950, 962 (1950); cf. *Cateora v. British Atlantic*, 282 F.Supp. 167, 1968 AMC 2160 (S.D.,Tex.); *Gilbert v. U.S. Fire Ins. Co.*, 49 Wis.2d 193, 181 N.W.2d 527 (1970).

6. 479 F.Supp. 138, 1980 AMC 1261, modified in part 669 F.2d 1269, 1982 AMC 2532 (9th Cir.).

the risks attendant on the proposed salvage project. They approached Emett & Chandler, a firm of insurance brokers in Los Angeles, to place the insurance. It soon became apparent that total loss only insurance was the only cover that could be placed. This Emett & Chandler placed through Hogg Robinson in London on the basis of "actual total loss only [meaning irretrievably lost]."

It appears that the insurance cover was finally placed and confirmed on or about October 29, 1975. On January 14, 1976, a typhoon developed in the vicinity of Mozambique Channel, and by January 30, 1976, the rig had toppled over completely and appeared to be so damaged as to be totally unsalvageable. The insureds thereupon filed claim on their policy for actual total loss.

One of the principal issues in the case was whether the Los Angeles brokers and Hogg Robinson in London were agents of the insurers or insureds. In the course of ruling, the court developed at considerable length the trade practices involved in the placement of coverage in the London market. The court said, in part:

> Lloyd's was originally an association of underwriters in London with a management committee. It was incorporated in 1871 by an Act of Parliament. The Corporation of Lloyd's provides a physical site for the sale of insurance by underwriters that are members of the Corporation, together with support and incidental services to member underwriters. Lloyd's corporate committee, elected by members from among their number, administers matters of common interest to members. For example, the committee manages the affairs of the corporation, maintains the premises where insurance is sold and the facilities there. It directs accountancy, intelligence and newspaper services. An office under its direction prepares individual insurance policies based upon the terms upon which insurers and insureds contract. Another office handles policy claims evaluations referred to it. Yet another office examines the credentials of insurance brokers who seek the right to place insurance at Lloyd's.
>
> The Corporation of Lloyd's never sells insurance itself and is not at risk on the insurance sold on the floor at Lloyd's. Rather, the underwriter members subscribe to cover all or part of a proposed placement of insurance, at their own election. Numbers of individual underwriters, many in England but others scattered throughout the world, have joined together to form syndicates. Syndicates may have anywhere from two or three to hundreds of members. The individual members are known as the "names" on that syndicate. These syndicates are the entities which subscribe on behalf of their members to cover risks and percentage parts of risks. The actual potential liability of a given name depends upon his percentage share of the syndicate

of which he is a member, as well as the percentage of the risk to which his syndicate has subscribed.

Purchase and sale of insurance takes place on the floor of the underwriting room at Lloyd's and also in the offices of individual insurance companies in London. The underwriting market at Lloyd's consists of the syndicates; a syndicate or group of syndicates is in turn managed by an underwriting agency. An underwriting agency employs a management staff, and maintains a box on the floor at Lloyd's with a representative. This representative is an underwriter, who evaluates, negotiates, and decides on proposed placements of insurance brought by brokers for the consideration of the syndicate or syndicates he represents. The underwriting agent contracts for the liability of his syndicate or syndicates, and assumes no risk himself except insofar as he is a name himself on the syndicate.

The recognized custom and usage of the London insurance market is that the broker is the agent of the potential assured for most purposes, including the placement of insurance. The potential assured is recognized as the broker's client. The recognized role of the broker is to obtain the best possible terms and quotation he can from the market for his client. In addition, the brokers in the London insurance market generally serve as coordinators of all parts of the insurance, negotiation, placement, claims presentation, and sometimes payment. Only brokers who have been approved by the Committee of Lloyd's are permitted to place risks with Lloyd's underwriters. Such brokers are known as "Lloyd's brokers." Because an applicant for insurance from Lloyd's must act through a Lloyd's broker, there will often be at least one other broker in the picture. An applicant for insurance may deal with an outside broker not a Lloyd's broker, who then must contact a Lloyd's broker. In the instant case, the applicant API used the services of Emett & Chandler in Los Angeles to arrange the insurance transaction through Hogg Robinson, a Lloyd's broker in London.

The underwriter agent, or underwriter, sits at his box on the floor waiting for brokers to approach him with possible insurance risks. The broker provides for the underwriter's consideration a document known as a broker's slip, which contains the details of the risk which the broker is trying to insure. The broker negotiates with the underwriter to obtain the latter's agreement to both the insurance terms and the rate of premium. The underwriter who structures the transaction with the broker and settles on terms becomes known as the lead underwriter. The lead underwriter's syndicate is called the market lead or leader of the market for that particular risk. The lead underwriter then subscribes his syndicate to a particular percentage of the risk, for example, five percent. The underwriter places his initials on the broker's slip together with the particular percentage to which he is subscribing. By placing his initials on the slip, the underwriter considers that he has created an insurance contract between the individual members of the syndicate and the insured.[a]

The broker, having obtained the agreement of one underwriter to terms and premium, as well as a subscription to a percentage of the risk, retains the slip and approaches other syndicates or insurance companies both on the floor at Lloyd's and in the outside offices of insurance companies. The broker presents the slip to them for them to consider whether they desire to subscribe to the agreement as constituted between the broker and the lead underwriter. Each subsequent underwriter may express no interest, may agree to the terms on the same premium rate, require a higher premium rate, or require different terms. In the last two cases, underwriters who had already subscribed would be informed of new terms and their obligations normally amended to conform. In any event, the underwriter who agrees to subscribe his syndicate places his syndicate initials and the percentage of risk he desires to cover on the slip, and the broker moves on to other underwriters. In this manner, the broker moves around the insurance market, both at Lloyd's and among the insurance companies, until he has obtained underwriters' commitments subscribing to one hundred percent of the risk on the slip. At that stage, the broker can confirm to the applicant for insurance or his contact with the application that the risk is fully subscribed, or "completed."

Once the broker has succeeded in completing the slip, that is, has obtained one hundred percent coverage, he retains the slip and returns it to his office. Participating underwriters on the risk receive a copy of that part of the slip containing terms and conditions for their files. From the information on the slip, the broker's policy department prepares the policy, using the appropriate printed forms and completing them with the appropriate terms and conditions from the slip. The completed policy and slip are then forwarded to the Lloyd's Policy Signing Office, and if companies members of the Institute of London Underwriters are involved, to the Institute's Policy Department. Both the Lloyd's office and the Policy Department check the policy against the information on the slip to ensure that the policy reflects the terms and conditions on the slip. At these offices as well a list of the syndicates or companies at risk, compiled pursuant to the slip, is appended. Marine insurance policies are generally issued with a sig-

---

(a). The broker may negotiate the terms and premium with a company underwriter initially, and in such an event an insurance company is the market lead. The market sometimes recognizes both a lead underwriter at Lloyd's and a lead company underwriter. The broker, in any event, may circulate the slip among both Lloyd's syndicates and insurance companies until the risk is fully subscribed.

nificant time lag after the signing of the slip. In order for an insured to have some evidence of the insurance placed during the period after the slip is completed but before the policy is issued, brokers may furnish the insured with a cover note memorializing the fact of insurance. Brokers consider the cover note a contract between them and the insured indicating that they have placed the insurance.

The broker also has responsibilities in the event that the insured makes a claim. His role is to present his client's claim, and present it in the best way possible, to underwriters. If the insured makes a claim, the broker endorses the policy with details of the claim and submits it to the underwriters for their consideration. Often the market lead mong the underwriters handles the claim, and other insurers follow the lead unless they have a major disagreement. Alternatively, the claim may be handled by the Lloyd's Underwriters claims office, a central facility maintained by Lloyd's as a service to members. The broker presents the claim to an underwriter or to the claims office, depending upon instructions from the insured. If the underwriter or claims office does not agree to pay the claim, it may state its objections or raise questions, and the broker transmits the questions to the insured. In the event that the claim is accepted, the claim may be processed through accounting arrangements that exist between underwriters and brokers in the London market, and in such a case the broker transmits a check in the agreed amount to the insured. Alternatively, Lloyd's may transmit funds directly to the insureds. For example, insureds in the United States may be paid through a financial arrangement centered in New York.

As the court noted, the placement of insurance by the assured in the London market followed the customary pattern of such transactions. On that basis, the court found specifically that Emett & Chandler and Hogg Robinson were agents of the assured in the placement of the coverage.

The court next considered which was the proper law to apply. In so doing, the court said, in part:

> Considering the agency relationships in fact and the circumstances of the insurance placement in issue; and reviewing and weighing all the evidence of the parties' intent, based upon contemporaneous understandings and nearly contemporaneous expressions, which are suggestive, together with the drawing of reasonable inferences, this court finds that the intent of the parties was that the English law definition of actual total loss apply to the policy term.[7]

---

7. See Chapter XVI, "Actual and Constructive Total Loss," for a discussion of the court's ruling on the question of whether or not the rig was an actual total loss.

The assureds contended that the parties had contracted on the basis of the presence of a "U.S. service of suit clause" in the insurance binder prepared and delivered by its Los Angeles brokers and on the basis of the customary inclusion of such clauses in Lloyd's broker's slips for insureds in the United States. The court held, on the basis of a preponderance of the evidence, that API and Burns had not shown either that there was a contract for United States law to apply via a U.S. service of suit clause, or that such clauses were considered in the market as a provision for choice of U.S. law to govern disputes.

On the question of agency, the court concluded that as between API and Hogg Robinson and the underwriters, the English rule applied under which insurance brokers are the agents of the assured, citing *Anglo-African Merchants, Ltd. v. Bayley*,[8] and *Rozanes v. Bowen*.[9] As between the assured and the Los Angeles brokers and between the latter and the underwriters, the court concluded that California law applied under which the broker is the agent for the assured and not the underwriters, citing Section 33 of the California Insurance Code.

There is nothing, of course, to prevent the broker from acting as an agent for both parties. In fact, so long as the premium as well as the policy remains in the hands of the broker, he is considered a common agent for the assured and the underwriter.[10]

The underwriter in the London market, who often does not know the assured, looks to the broker for payment of the premium, and the broker,

8. [1971] 1 Q.B. 311.

9. (1928) 32 Ll.L.Rep. 98, C.A.

10. *Shee v. Clarkson,* (1810) 104 E.R. 199. Whether the broker is an agent for the assured or the assurer is a question of fact to be determined from the evidence. It is not the label given him by the parties but the manner in which he acts. *Fredman v. Consolidated F. & M. Ins. Co.,* 104 Minn. 76, 116 N.W. 221 (1908). As *Arff v. Star F. Ins. Co.,* 125 N.Y. 57, 25 N.E. 1073 (1890) points out, the following inquiries are relevant: (1) Was the broker at the time of effecting the insurance actually or ostensibly connected with the insurer and employed by it, or was he acting independently of any employment by the company? (2) From whom did the broker's express or implied authority to do the act in question originally proceed? (3) Was the act one that the broker was expressly authorized to do, or was it a usual and necessary means to accomplish the execution of the authority conferred? (4) Was the act done independently of the original employment, and if so, for whom, or at whose instance? (5) Which party could the broker hold directly responsible for his remuneration at the time the act in question was done? (6) Was there any limitation on the broker's ostensible authority, of which the person dealing with him was, or ought to have been, cognizant? (7) Was there any ratification by the ostensible principal of the claimed authorized act?

See, also, *North & South Trust Co. v. Berkeley,* [1971] 1 All E.R. 980 and the discussion, *infra,* relating to that case.

Generally speaking, there would appear to be no objection to an agent representing both parties to the transaction in matters in which the interests of the two principals are not incompatible or conflicting, or where the two principals consent to the agency with full knowledge of the material facts relating to the transaction. *Dibble v. Northern Assur. Co.,* 70 Mich. 1, 37 N.W. 704 (1888); *Phoenix Ins. Co. v. State,* 76 Ark. 180, 88 S.W. 917 (1905); *Warren v. Franklin F. Ins. Co.,* 161 Iowa 440, 143 N.W. 554 (1913); *Hodges v. Mayes,* 240 Ga. 643, 242 S.E.2d 160 (1978); *Anno.* 83 ALR 298, 309 (1933).

in turn, looks to the assured. He is, in essence, with respect to premiums, a "middleman" between the assured and the underwriter.[11]

The Marine Insurance Act, 1906, has specific provisions which relate to the functions of brokers. These are:

52. Unless otherwise agreed, the duty of the the assured or his agent to pay the premium, and the duty of the insurer to issue the policy to the assured or his agent, are concurrent conditions, and the insurer is not bound to issue the policy until payment or tender of the premium.[12]

53.(1) Unless otherwise agreed, where a marine policy is effected on behalf of the assured by a broker, the broker is directly responsible to the insurer for the premium, and the insurer is directly responsible to the assured for the amount which may be payable in respect of losses, or in respect of returnable premium.[13]

(2) Unless otherwise agreed, the broker has, as against the the assured, a lien upon the policy for the amount of the premium and his charges in respect of effecting the policy; and where he has dealt with the person who employs him as a principal, he has also a lien on the policy in respect of any balance on any insurance account which may

---

11. *Power v. Butcher*, (1829) 109 E.R. 472.

12. The term "unless otherwise agreed" also brings into play usage, inasmuch as usage is an implied term of the agreement. In this connection, see Sec. 87(1) of the Act, reading: Where any right, duty, or liability would arise under a contract of marine insurance by implication of law, it may be negatived or varied by express agreement, or by usage, if the usage be such as to bind both parties to the contract.

See, also, *Universo Ins. Co. of Milan v. Merchants Marine Ins. Co.*, [1897] 2 Q.B. 93 and *Xenos v. Wickham*, (1866) 16 L.T. 800. American law and practice differ. Normally, in the United States, the assured is responsible for payment of the premium; placement of insurance by the broker does not raise any implication that the broker will furnish credit to the assured. *Ruby*, 18 F.2d 948, 1927 AMC 714 (2d Cir.). See, also, *Hurona*, 44 Ll.L.Rep. 263, 1933 AMC 469 (K.B.) (companion case in England; insurance effected with English underwriters by brokers in New York. The assured failed to pay the premiums, whereupon the brokers cancelled the policies. Held: broker has implied authority to cancel the policies where authority to do so was conferred upon him by American law). See Arnould, Sec. 159. Note, however, *Griffith & Sprague v. Bayly, Martin & Fay, Inc.*, 71 Wn.2d 679, 430 P.2d 600 (St.,Wash., 1967) where the broker was held liable to pay the premium where he had expressly agreed to do so.

13. *Universo Ins. Co. of Milan v. Merchants Marine Ins. Co.*, (1897), *supra*, n. 12; cf. *Sweeting v. Pearce*, (1859) 29 L.J.C.P. 265 (payment of a loss where the policy was left in the hands of the broker and the assured was unfamiliar with Lloyd's usages). Phillips (Sec. 1882) states that the agent who has effected a policy is authorized to receive payment of a loss under it, after the loss has become payable; payment will therefore discharge the underwriters if the agent then has the policy and the underwriters have had no notice of the revocation of his authority or reason to suppose it to have been revoked, citing *Erick v. Johnson*, 6 Mass. 193 (1810). However, modern American practice is to include a "loss payee" clause in the policies. No underwriter would be safe in paying the agent or broker without at least including the names of the loss payees on the settlement drafts.

be due to him from such person, unless when the debt was incurred he had reason to believe that such person was only an agent.[14]

54. Where a marine policy effected on behalf of the assured by a broker acknowledges the receipt of the premium, such acknowledgment is, in the absence of fraud, conclusive as between the insurer and the assured, but not as between the insurer and the broker.[15]

It should be noted that premiums paid on an illegal insurance or by mistake may, in certain instances, be recoverable, as may losses paid by underwriters under a mistake of fact. Thus, where the underwriter, by mistake, pays a loss to a broker to which the assured is not entitled, the underwriter may recover it back as money had and received provided that the broker has not, in fact, paid it over to the assured. A mere accounting credit is not sufficient; the money must actually be paid or the liability irrevocably incurred.[16] Moreover, in such circumstances, the broker has no lien upon the moneys.[17]

---

14. *Fisher v. Smith*, (1878) 4 App.Cas. 1, H.L., citing, *inter alia*, Phillips (Sec. 1909), where that noted authority stated: "The agent who effects a policy for his principal and advances the premium, or becomes responsible for it, and retains the policy in his hands, has a lien upon it for his commission and the premium until the same are paid to him, or he is supplied with funds for the payment, whether his immediate superior is the assured himself, or an intermediate agent; and in the latter case, whether the intermediate agency was known, or not known, to the sub-agent claiming the lien." See *Spring v. South Carolina Ins. Co.*, 21 U.S. 268 (1823); *Jarvis v. Rogers*, 15 Mass. 389 (1819); *Moody v. Webster*, 20 Mass. 424 (1826); *Foster v. Hoyt*, 2 Johns. 327 (St.,N.Y., 1801); *McKenzie v. Nevius*, 22 Me. 138 (1892); *Millick v. Peterson*, F.Cas. No. 9,601 (1807). See, also, *Near East Relief v. King, Chasseur & Co., Ltd.*, [1930] 36 Ll.L.Rep. 91, *Dixon v. Stansfeld*, (1850) 138 E.R. 160; *Westwood v. Bell*, (1815) 171 E.R. 111; *Montagu v. Forwood*, (1893) 2 Q.B. 350; *Maanss v. Henderson*, (1801) 102 E.R. 130; *Mann v. Forrester*, (1814), 171 E.R. 20, N.P.; *Snook v. Davison*, (1809) 170 E.R. 1134 N.P.; *Lanyon v. Blanchard*, (1811) 170 E.R. 1264 N.P.; *Fairfield Shipbuilding & Engineering Co., Ltd. v. Gardner, Etc.*, (1911) 104 L.T. 288. English cases may be resorted to as authority in the United States where a usage is established insofar as those cases do not conflict with established local rules of law. *Insurance Co. of Pa. v. Smith*, 3 Whart. 520 (Pa., 1838); *Taylor v. Lowell*, 3 Mass. 331 (1807); *Millick v. Peterson*, (1807) *supra*.   See, generally, Arnould, Secs. 185 through 190, inclusive.

15. *Universo Ins. Co. of Milan v. Merchants Marine Ins. Co.*, *supra*, and *Xenos v. Wickham*, *supra*. In the United States, there does not appear to be any material distinction between such an acknowledgment in a policy of insurance and in other instruments such as a deed of conveyance. The prevailing doctrine thus is that though it estops the grantor from alleging want of consideration, it is only *prima facie* evidence of payment, which may be rebutted. *Tyler v. Carlton*, 7 Me. 175 (1830); *Belden v. Seymour*, 8 Conn. 304 (1831); *M'Crea v. Purmont*, 16 Wend. 460 (St.,N.Y., 1836); *Bowen v. Bell*, 20 Johns. 338, (N.Y., 1823); *Sheldon v. Atlantic etc. Ins. Co.*, 26 N.Y. 460 (1863). This is especially so in reference to a third party or a question of mistake or fraud. *Mellick v. Peterson* (1807), *supra; Wilkinson v. Scott*, 17 Mass. 249 (1821); *Clapp v. Tirrell*, 20 Pick. 247 (Mass., 1838). It should be conclusive, however, in favor of an assignee, for value, from the assured, without notice. Compare, however, *O'Keefe & Lynch of Can. Ltd. v. Toronto Ins. & Vessel Agency Ltd.*, [1926] 4 D.L.R. 477, and *Mannheim Ins. Co. v. Hollander*, 112 F. 549 (1901), holding the assured liable to the underwriter for a premium on insurance effected by a broker.

16. *Buller v. Harrison*, (1777) 98 E.R. 1243, K.B.; *Scottish Metropolitan Assur. Co. v. P. Samuel & Co.*, [1923] 1 K.B. 348.

17. See *Scottish Metropolitan*, *supra*, n. 16.

See, generally, Arnould, Sections 166 and 183, and discussion, *infra,* Chapter XXVI, "Mistake and Reformation."

Assured Bound by Representations of the Broker

It should be emphasized that the assured is bound by the acts and representations of his broker, because the broker is the agent of the assured. The Marine Insurance Act, 1906 provides in Section 20(1) as follows:

> Every material representation made by the assured or his agent to the insurer during the negotiations for the contract, and before the contract is concluded, must be true. If it be untrue the insurer may avoid the contract.

Section 19 of the Act provides:

> Subject to the provisions of the preceding section as circumstances which need not be disclosed where an insurance is effected for the assured by an agent, the agent must disclose to the insurer:
>
> (a) Every material circumstance which is known to himself, and an agent to insure is deemed to know every circumstance which in the ordinary course of business ought to be known by, or to have been communicated to, him; and
> (b) Every material circumstance which the assured is bound to disclose, unless it comes to his knowledge too late to communicate.

For example, in *Russell v. Thornton*[18] plaintiff was the agent of foreign owners of a vessel. He was instructed to effect a time policy on the vessel, and employed a firm of brokers to do so. Prior to effecting the insurance, the plaintiff received a communication from the master of the vessel informing him that the vessel had been aground and had made her way in a sinking state to a port of refuge. The plaintiff communicated the letter to the brokers but they did not communicate it to the insurer. Subsequently, the vessel was lost. The court held that the concealment of the information received from the master was concealment of a material fact which vitiated the policy.

In *Blackburn v. Haslam,*[19] the plaintiffs, underwriters in Glasgow, employed there a firm of brokers to reinsure a ship which was overdue. The brokers received information tending to show that the ship, as was the fact, was lost. Without communicating this information to the plaintiffs, they telegraphed in the plaintiffs' name to their own London agents, stat-

---

18. (1860) 158 E.R. 58, Ex.Ch.
19. (1888) 21 Q.B.D. 144.

ing the rate of premium which the plaintiffs were prepared to pay. Communications followed between the plaintiffs and the London agents. The London agents, through a firm of London insurance brokers, effected a policy of reinsurance at a higher rate of premium. It was held that the policy was void on the ground of concealment of material facts by the agents of the assureds.

See, also, *Yellowtail,*[20] and cases cited in Chapter X, Disclosures and Representations.

It is immaterial that the assured is innocent.[21] Fraud of the agent, even though the assured had no actual knowledge of it, vitiates the policy.[22]

"Voluntary" Agent

An undertaking to insure by a purported "agent" in and of itself imposes a duty to procure such insurance, although there is authority to the effect that one who gratuitously undertakes to procure insurance for another is not liable for his omission to do so. Compare, for example, *Heaphy v. Kimball*[23] with *Lawrence v. Francis.*[24]

The rule may be stated as follows: when a person voluntarily and without consideration undertakes to effect insurance for another, he is liable for any negligence in doing so if he takes any steps toward performance of his undertaking.[25] However, if the person voluntarily promising, without any kind of consideration, never takes any steps whatever toward the performance of his promise, he is not liable.[26]

Rights, Duties, and Liabilities of Agents and Brokers

The rights, duties, and liabilities of agents and brokers are, of course, governed by the general principles of the law of agency. Moreover, those rights, duties and liabilities may be affected by the general course of business in marine insurance insofar as that has been settled by custom and usage.

Agents may be created either expressly or by implication arising out of the relationship in which they stand to the their principals. In this connec-

---

20. 22 F.Supp. 545, 1938 AMC 499 (S.D.,Cal.).
21. *Bella S.S. Co. v. Insurance Co. of N.A.,* 290 F. 992 (D.,Md.), *aff'd* 5 F.2d 570 (4th Cir., 1925).
22. *Davis Schofield Co. v. Reliance Ins. Co.,* 109 Conn. 686, 145 A. 42 (1st Cir., 1929).
23. 293 Mass. 414, 200 N.E. 551 (1936).
24. 223 Ark. 584, 267 S.W.2d 306 (1954).
25. *Wallace v. Telfair,* (1780) 100 E.R. 102.
26. *Thorne v. Deas,* 4 Johns. 84 (St.,N.Y., 1809).

tion, it should be noted that ratification by subsequent adoption by the assured, of insurance effected by a person without prior authority from the assured, is a species of express authorization, after the fact, so to speak.[27]

Perplexing questions arise, however, with respect to whether a particular person has authority, by implication, to insure. Agents to procure insurance are special agents, not general, and persons dealing with an agent are bound to ascertain the scope of the agent's authority.[28]

The question whether a person has authority, by implication, to act as another's agent to insure, to give notice of abandonment, to accept payment of losses, etc., generally arises where the person stands in a particular relationship to the person or entity for whom or for which he purports to act; e.g., a part owner of a vessel, a consignee of goods, one partner in a partnership, the master of a vessel, etc.

Generally speaking, a ship's husband has not, merely as such, the authority to insure.[29] Neither does a supercargo have such authority, although he may possess the authority by reason of the particular circumstances involved.[30] Again, generally speaking, a partner does have such authority.[31] A consignor or commission agent ordinarily does not have authority to insure in the absence of express orders, but an established course of dealings between the principal and agent or the usage of a particular port or trade may confer an implied authority.[32] A ship's master, as such, is not authorized to insure, although in a disaster, by the exigency of the circumstances, he may be considered to be invested with a general authority as agent of the parties for the management of the ship and cargo; e.g. as in bottomry of the vessel by the master in an emergency, bottomry being considered a species of insurance.[33]

The discussion which follows is limited to true marine insurance agents and brokers who have been given express authority to insure; that is, the owner of property retains or employs an agent or broker to insure his property for him and to otherwise act on his behalf in connection with insurance implications arising therefrom.

Generally speaking, and whether the authorization or direction is express or arises from implication, the agent or broker has certain well-defined duties. These are: he must carry out his principal's instructions; in

27. See, for example, *Hanley v. Royal Exchange Assur. Corp.*, 33 B.C.R. 163, [1924] 1 D.L.R. 197, *rev'd* on other grounds but affirmed on this point, [1924] 3 D.L.R. 860, C.A. (Can.).
28. *Smith v. Firemen's Ins. Co.*, 104 F.2d 546 (7th Cir., 1939); *Curtis v. Zurich G.A. & L. Ins. Co.*, 108 Mont. 275, 89 P.2d 1038 (1939).
29. *French v. Backhouse*, (1771) 98 E.R. 431.
30. See *De Forest v. Fulton Ins. Co.*, 1 Hall 84 (St.,N.Y.,1828).
31. *Hooper v. Lusby*, (1814) 171 E.R. 22, N.P.; *Robinson v. Gleadow*, (1835) 132 E.R. 62, C.P.
32. See Phillips, Sec. 1858.
33. *The Ship Fortitude; Haven, Claimant*, 9 F.Cas. No. 479 (D.,Mass., 1838).

doing so, he must use proper care and skill; and he must complete the transaction. These are discussed in detail *seriatim*.

Duty to Carry Out Instructions

If a broker, of whatever description, proceeds in the execution of an order to procure insurance, he is bound to follow the instructions of his principal according to the construction which he can reasonably be presumed to put upon them by an attentive examination.[34] He cannot claim as a defense that the principal ought to have examined the policy to see if he received full protection.[35] If it is impracticable for him to follow the instructions given him, he should at once notify his principal.[36]

The principal should, however, make his instructions explicit and clear. If they are ambiguous and susceptible of two interpretations, and the broker in good faith acts upon his interpretation, he is not liable to his principal if, in fact, it turns out that his principal interpreted his instructions differently.[37]

Moreover, the broker is entitled to use some degree of discretion if the circumstances warrant it, and if the discretion exercised is sound and honest, the broker is not liable.[38] Thus, where the practice is in doubt, or

---

34. *Glaser v. Cowie*, (1813) 105 E.R. 20; *Weare v. Burnett*, (1850) 7 L.T. 24; *Strong and Pearl v. S. Allison & Co.*, Ltd., (1926) 25 Ll.L.Rep. 504; *Dickson & Co. v. Devitt*, (1916) 21 Com.Cas. 291; *Moore v. Mourgue*, (1776) 98 E.R. 1197; *Yuill & Co. v. Robson*, [1908] 1 K.B. 270; *Mallough v. Barber*, (1815) 4 Camp. N.P.; *Park v. Hammond*, (1816) 128 E.R. 1127; *Maydew v. Forrester*, (1814) 128 E.R. 831; Leverick v. Meigs, 1 Cowp. 645 (St.,N.Y., 1824); *Ela v. French*, 11 N.H. 356 (1840); *French v. Reed*, 6 Binn. 307 (Pa., 1814); *Raydon Engineering Corp. v. Church*, 337 Mass. 652, 151 N.E.2d 57 (1958); *Romeo v. Bimco Industries, Inc.*, 57 App.Div.2d 947, 395 N.Y.S.2d 93 (N.Y., 1977); *Shapiro v. Amalgamated T. & Sav. Banks*, 283 Ill.App. 243 (Ill., 1935); *Ogden & Co. v. Reliance Fire Sprinkler*, [1975] Lloyd's Rep. 52 (Aus.).

35. *Dickson & Co. v. Devitt*, (1916) *supra*, n. 34; *Hampton Roads Carriers v. Boston Ins. Co.*, 150 F.Supp. 338, 1958 AMC 425 (D.,Md.); *Shapiro v. Amalgamated T. & Sav. Bank*, (1935) *supra*, n. 34; *Israelson v. Williams*, 166 App.Div. 25, 151 N.Y.S. 679 (N.Y., 1915); *General Accident Fire & Life Assur. Corp. Ltd v. J.H. Minet & Co., Ltd.*, (1942) 74 Ll.L.Rep. 1 (cover note); *Everett v. Hogg, Robinson & Gardner Mountain (Insurance) Ltd.*, [1973] 2 Lloyd's Rep. 217.

36. *Callendar v. Oelrichs*, (1838) 132 E.R. 1026; *DeTastett v. Crousillat*, F.Cas. No. 3,828 (Pa.,1807); *Rider v. Lynch*, 42 N.J. 465, 201 A.2d 561 (N.J., 1964); *Sea Fever v. Hartford Fire*, 1983 AMC 1276 (D.,Mass.) (broker failed to obtain a standard commercial hull policy and did not notify the assured of the policy's special provisions); *Norlympia Seafoods Ltd. v. Dale & Co. (The Ultra Processor No. 1)*, Civil No. C805280, Vanc.,B.C. Register (not yet reported) (broker negligent in failing properly to advise his assured of lack of cover and placement of 25% of the loss of profits coverage in a fringe market instead of Lloyd's and I.L.U. companies); *Haeubner v. Can-Do*, 666 F.2d 275, 1984 AMC 1214 (5th Cir., 1982) (broker has the duty to use due diligence to obtain the desired coverage and to advise his client promptly if such coverage is not available; the assured wanted a particular warranty deleted from its P & I policy and the broker neither obtained it nor advised the client that it had not been obtained).

37. *Ireland v. Livingston*, (1872) L.R. 5 H.L. 395; *DeTastett v. Crousillat*, (1807) F.Cas. No. 3,828 (Pa.,1807); *Rundle v. Moore*, 3 Johns. 36 (N.Y., 1802); *Winne v. Niagara F. Ins. Co.*, 91 N.Y. 185 (N.Y., 1883); *Fomin v. Oswell*, (1813) 3 Camp. 357, N.P.

38. *Liotard v. Graves*, 3 Caines 225 (N.Y., 1805); *Greenleaf v. Moody*, 95 Mass. 363 (1866).

there is no known or certain usage, or the law is uncertain or disputed, the broker is not liable where he uses a sound and honest discretion.[39] Nor is he liable when he procures insurance on the usual terms in the trade.[40]

Duty to Use Proper Skill and Care

As Phillips notes (Section 1884), a greater knowledge and skill in matters of insurance are required of a professional insurance broker than in a general mercantile agent and correspondent. A professional insurance broker is bound to know the usages of the place where he practices his business, and he must exercise such reasonable skill and ordinary diligence as may fairly be expected from a person in his profession. In short, he must act with proper skill and care.[41]

For example, in *Turpin v. Bilton*,[42] the broker was instructed to procure insurance but did not do so within a reasonable time. It was held that his duty not only was to use proper care and diligence but, in all events, to insure as requested.

39. *Comber v. Anderson*, (1808) 1 Camp. 523, N.P.; *Mechanics Bank v. Merchants Bank*, 47 Mass. 13 (1843); *Greenleaf v. Moody*, (1866) *supra* n. 38; *Liotard v. Graves*, (1805) *supra* n. 38; Duer, Vol. 2, Sec. 214. See, also, *United Mills Agencies Ltd. v. R.E. Harvey, Bray & Co.*, [1952] 1 All E.R. 225, where the instructions given were inadequate.

40. *Silverthorne v. Gillespie*, (1852) 9 U.C.Q.B. 414, C.A. (Can.).

41. *Wake v. Atty*, (1812) 128 E.R. 422; *Park v. Hammond*, (1816) 128 E.R. 1127; *Mallough v. Barber*, (1815) 4 Camp. 150, N.P.; *Turpin v. Bilton*, (1843), 134 E.R. 641; *Chapman v. Walton*, (1833) 131 E.R. 827; *Mayde v. Forrester*, (1814) 128 E.R. 831; *Dickson & Co. v. Devitt*, (1916) 21 Com.Cas. 291; *Sanches v. Davenport*, 6 Mass. 258 (1810); *Shepard v. Davis*, 42 App.Div. 462, 59 N.Y.S. 456; *Scharles v. N. Hubbard, Jr. & Co.*, 74 Misc. 72, 131 N.Y.S. 848 (1911); *Orfanos v. California Ins. Co.*, 29 Cal.App.2d 75, 84 P.2d 233 (1938); *Rider v. Lynch*, (N.Y., 1964) *supra; Lowitt v. Pearsall Chemical Corp.*, 242 Md. 245, 219 A.2d 67 (1965); *Butler v. Scott*, 417 F.2d 471 (10 Cir., 1969); *Hampton Roads Carriers v. Boston Ins. Co.*, 150 F.Supp. 338, 1958 AMC 425 (D.,Md.); *Cateora v. British Atlantic*, 282 F.Supp. 167, 1968 AMC 2160 (S.D.,Tex.); *Gazija v. Jerns Co.*, 530 P.2d 685, 1975 AMC 975 (St.,Wash.); *Morton v. Browne*, 438 F.2d 1205, 1971 AMC 1144 (1st Cir.); *Desgagnes v. Antonin Belleau Inc.*, [1970] L.L.R. 1-348 (Can.); *Perkins v. Wash. Ins. Co.*, 4 Cowp. 645 (N.Y., 1825); *Ela v. French*, (1890), *supra; Sea Fever v. Hartford Fire*, 1983 AMC 1276 (D.,Mass.); *L.B. Martin Construction Ltd. v. Gaglardi, Lauze et al*, 91 D.L.R.3d 393 (Can.); *McCann v. Western Farmers Mut. Ins. Co.*, 87 D.L.R.3d 135. In *Hardt v. Brink*, 192 F.Supp. 879 (W.D.,Wash., 1969), a broker was held to the duty of advising the assured of potential liability under a lease and of recommending appropriate insurance; this included the affirmative duty to ask the assured for the lease, examine it, and discover the need for insurance. In *W.R. Chamberlain & Co. v. Northwestern Agencies, Inc.*, 42 Or.App. 125, 600 P.2d 438 (1979), *rev'd* on other grounds, 289 Or. 201, 611 P.2d 652, a broker who obtained only 85% coverage on a subscription hull policy was held to have breached his duties. In *Haeubner v. Can-Do* (5th Cir., 1982), *supra*, n. 36, the client asked his broker to see to it that a particular warranty was deleted from his P & I policy; the broker neither obtained the deletion nor did he advise the client that it had not been obtained. Held: The broker was negligent and liable. And see *Princess Cruises v. Bayly, Martin & Fay*, 373 F.Supp. 762, 1974 AMC 433 (N.D.,Cal.), where plaintiff's complaint joined an admiralty cause of action against the brokers for alleged failure to procure marine insurance. The court exercised its discretion to assert pendent jurisdiction since only one "constitutional case" was involved. See, also, *McNealy v. Pennine Ins. Co., Ltd.*, [1978] 2 Lloyd's Rep. 18.

42. (1843) 134 E.R. 641.

In *Hampton Roads Carriers v. Boston Ins. Co.*,[43] the broker agreed to procure total loss insurance on a barge. Instead, he procured absolute total loss which specifically excluded constructive total loss. He was held personally liable to the assured for the amount of the constructive total loss.[44] In *Gazija v. Jerns Co.*,[45] the assured owned two fishing vessel whose fishing gear was insured under separate policies. He told his broker to transfer one of the policies to another insurance company but the broker erroneously applied the premiums to keep the first policy alive and cancelled the other policy. When the vessel formerly covered by the latter policy sank, the underwriters refused to pay on the grounds that it had been cancelled. The broker was held liable.

In *Cateora v. British Atlantic*,[46] the Texas agent placed the coverage with a British P & I club which was not authorized to do business in Texas, and the underwriters refused to defend the shipowner against a seaman's personal injury claim. The agent was held liable on the basis that he knew or should have known that the underwriters were insolvent and failed to notify the assured of that fact.

In *Park v. Hammond*,[47] a merchant at Malaga wrote to a broker in London instructing him to insure goods from Gibraltar to Dublin, indicating that he himself would take the risk of the goods from Malaga to Gibraltar Bay. Instead of insuring the goods from Gibraltar to destination, the broker effected the insurance in the common printed form reading "beginning the adventure upon the said goods and merchandise from the loading thereof aboard the same ship." The ship sailed from Malaga but because of the plague at Gibraltar did not touch there and was later lost off the coast of Ireland. The underwriters refused to pay be-

---

43. 150 F.Supp. 338, 1958 AMC 425 (D.,Md.).
44. One does not have to be an insurance broker to be held liable for a failure to insure. See *Smith v. Price*, (1862) 2 F. 748, N.P.; *Barryton-Freedon*, 42 F.2d 561, 1931 AMC 148, modified 54 F.2d 282, 1931 AMC 1878, where a charterer agreed to insure the vessel under a charter but failed to do so; *Calcasieu Chem. Corp. v. Canal Barge Co.*, 404 F.2d 1227, 1969 AMC 114 (7th Cir.), involving the same sort of failure on the part of a cargo owner. In *Norwest Refrigeration Services Pty. Ltd. v. Bain Dawes (W.A.) Pty Ltd.*, (1984) 3 ANZ Ins. Cas. 60-582 (H.C., Aus.), the plaintiff assured was a member of a fishing cooperative. The cooperative instructed a broker to obtain cover for the assured's vessel by adding it to the cooperative's fleet policy. The fleet policy provided that coverage was excluded if no current certificate of survey had been issued. The assured was never informed of the exclusion, and his vessel did not have a current certificate. The court held that the cooperative had a duty to exercise proper care to ensure that insurance of the type requested was actually procured or that the assured was warned of the limitations that would be contained in any insurance cover arranged; i.e., the cooperative either knew or should have been aware that its member did not have a current certificate of survey. The court expounded upon the duties of a "gratuitous agent" at considerable length. The broker whom the cooperative employed to obtain the coverage was exonerated from liability.
45. 530 P.2d 685, 1975 AMC 975 (St.,Wash.)
46. 282 F.Supp. 167, 1968 AMC 2160 (S.D.,Tex.).
47. (1816) 128 E.R. 1127.

cause the risk had not been insured against, whereupon the plaintiff sued the defendant broker for negligence. The court held that it was the duty of the broker to state correctly the facts in the policy, which he did not do, as the broker was bound to know the applicable law and to act accordingly.

In *Sea Fever v. Hartford Fire*,[48] the broker was held liable for procuring other than a standard commercial hull policy without notifying the assured of its special provisions, which excluded collision liabilities during a lay-up period. In *Norlympia Seafoods Ltd. v. Dale & Co. (The Ultra Processor No. 1)*,[49] the broker was found liable for failure to advise his assured of lack of cover and placement of 25 percent of the loss of profits coverage in a fringe market instead of Lloyd's and I.L.U. companies.

Clearly, however, an assured who sues his broker for negligent failure to obtain the requested insurance coverage has the duty of proving that the loss would have been covered by insurance had the broker obtained the coverage requested.[50] Although the broker may be sued for breach of contract or negligent default in the performance of a duty imposed by contract at the election of the principal, since the allegations of a breach of contract, or negligent performance of a contract are affirmative allegations on the part of the principal, he has the burden of proof.

Duty to Complete Transaction

While a broker cannot be compelled by his principal to procure insurance, if he receives instructions concerning placement from his principal and does not dissent, he is liable because, in effect, he has deprived his principal of the opportunity of obtaining coverage elsewhere.[51] It is not clear whether a broker is obligated to take extra steps to effect insurance if it cannot be effected in the usual way, such as by going outside the geo-

---

48. 1983 AMC 1276 (D.,Mass.)

49. Civil No. C805280, Vanc. Register (Can., B.C.), not yet reported.

50. *Pacific Dredging v. Hurley*, 397 P.2d 819, 1964 AMC 836 (St., Wash.); *Eleanor (Insurance)*, 250 F.2d 943, 1958 AMC 299 (1st Cir.); *Heller-Mark & Co. v. Kassler & Co.*, 544 P.2d 995, 37 Colo. App. 267 (St.,Colo., 1976) (insured must establish both causation and damages); *National Boat v. John Doe Ins.*, 1979 AMC 2274 (Md.,Fla.)

51. *Smith v. Lascelles*, (1788) 100 E.R. 101; *Thorne v. Deas*, 4 Johns. 84 (N.Y., 1809); *Kingston v. White*, F.Cas. No. 7,823 (Pa., 1822); *French v. Reed*, 6 Binn. 308 (Pa., 1814); *Aresto v. National B.F.F. Ins. Co.*, 133 A.2d 304 (Pa., 1957); *Ezell v. Associates Capital Corp.*, 518 S.W.2d 232 (Tenn., 1974); *Porter v. Utica Mut. Ins. Co.*, 359 So.2d 1234 (La.App., 1978); *Trinity Universal Ins. Co. v. Burnett*, 560 S.W.2d 440 (Tex.Civ.App., 1977); *Corlett v. Gordon*, (1813) 170 E.R. 1450; *Wallace v. Telfair*, (1786) 100 E.R. 102; *Turpin v. Bilton*, (1843) 134 E.R. 641; *Weare v. Barnett*, (1850) 7 L.T. 24.

If the broker's principal is a foreign merchant and the broker is asked to place coverage, in circumstances giving rise to the foreign merchant's right to expect that his instructions will be complied with, a total failure by the broker to comply with those instructions without notice to his principal subjects the broker to liability. *Smith v. Lascelles*, (1788) 100 E.R. 101.

graphical limits of his particular sphere of business.[52] Certainly, it is the duty of the broker, after having accepted the responsibility for procuring the insurance, not to delay unreasonably in doing so.[53]

Moreover, the broker is liable if he fails to give prompt notice of his refusal or inability to procure the requested insurance.[54]

Although a broker is liable when he places a risk in a company which is insolvent if proper diligence and inquiry would have revealed the insolvency,[55] he is not liable where the underwriter was solvent at the time the coverage was placed but subsequently became insolvent.[56]

It is not clear whether a broker who is under a continuing duty to keep his principal's property insured, and who learns that the underwriter with whom he placed coverage has become insolvent, is under a duty to insure promptly with another underwriter. It has been so held.[57]

A broker who has received the premium from his principal is liable if he fails to remit it to the underwriter and the policy is cancelled.[58] If the

52. *Smith v. Calogan*, (1788) 100 E.R. 102, N.P.; *Sanches v. Davenport*, 6 Mass. 258 (1810).

53. *Turpin v. Bilton*, (1843) *supra*, n. 51; and see *Gulf-Tex Brokerage, Inc. v. McDade & Associates*, 433 F.Supp. 1015 (S.D.,Tex., 1977), where it was held that the broker had a duty to keep the assured informed of progress being made on the assured's request for an extension of trading limits, and the broker knew that the vessel had left port for a destination beyond the trading limits.

54. *Smith v. Lascelles*, (1788) *supra; DeTastett v. Crousillat*, F.Cas. No. 3,828 (Pa., 1807); *Karam v. St. Paul F. & M. Ins. Co.*, 265 So.2d 821, aff'd 281 So.2d 728 (La., 1973); *Wiles v. Mullinax*, 267 N.C. 392, 148 S.E.2d 229 (N.C., 1966); *Rider v. Lynch*, 42 N.Y. 465, 201 A.2d 561 (N.Y., 1964); *Gibbs v. Allstate Ins. Co.*, 386 S.W.2d 606 (Tex., 1965); *Callander v. Oelrichs*, (1838) 132 E.R. 1026; *National Bank of Commerce v. Royal Exchange Assur. of America, Inc.*, 455 F.2d 892 (6th Cir., 1972); *Caperonis v. Underwriters at Lloyds*, 25 N.C. App. 119, 212 S.ED.2d 532 (N.C., 1975); *Jonas v. Bank of Kodiak*, 162 F.Supp. 751 (D.,Alaska, 1958). In *Clary Insurance Agency v. Doyle*, 620 P.2d 194 (Alaska, 1980), the Alaska Supreme Court upheld a punitive damage award of $190,000 (twice the compensatory damage award) where the evidence showed that the broker, after an initial failure to obtain insurance, failed upon discovery thereof to acknowledge the error to the assured and continued to act as though the assured was covered.

55. *Smith v. Price*, (1862) 175 E.R. 1258; *Shepard v. Davis*, 42 App. Div. 462, 59 N.Y.S. 456 (N.Y., 1899); *Scharles v. N. Hubbard & Co.*, 74 Misc. 72, 131 N.Y.S. 848 (1911); *Bordelon v. Herculean Risks, Inc.*, 241 So.2d 766 (La.App., 1970); *Cateora v. British Atlantic*, 1968 AMC 2160 (S.D.,Tex.).

56. *Curacao v. Stake*, 61 F.Supp. 181, 1945 AMC 790 (S.D.N.Y.); *Beckman v. Edwards*, 59 Wash. 411, 110 P. 6 (1910); *Eastham v. Stumbo*, 212 Ky. 685, 279 S.W. 1109 (1926); *Vann v. Downing*, 10 Pa. Co. 59 (1891); *Kane Ford Sales, Inc. v. Cruz*, 119 Ill.App. 2d 102, 255 N.E.2d 90 (1970); *Williams-Berryman Ins. Co. v. Morphis*, 249 Ark. 786, 461 S.W.2d 577 (1971); *Pierce Enterprises of Louisiana, Inc. v. Jacob Towing, Inc.*, 340 So.2d 693 (La.App., 1976); *Gettins v. Scudder*, 71 Ill. 86 (1873); *National Boat v. John Doe Ins.*, 1979 AMC 2274 (M.D.,Fla.) (since defendant broker acted reasonably and prudently in selecting a reputable underwriter to insure plaintiff's fishing boat, it is not responsible when the underwriter becomes insolvent and can not pay plaintiff's hull claim).

57. *Diamond v. Duncan*, 109 Tex. 256, 172 S.W. 1100 (1915).

58. *Robinson v. Oliver*, 171 App.Div. 349, 156 N.Y.S. 896 (1916); *Thomas v. Funkhouse*, 91 Ga. 478, 18 S.E. 312 (1893); *Criswell v. Riley*, 5 Ind.App. 496, 30 N.E. 1101, aff'd 32 N.E. 814 (1892).

contract between the broker and his principal calls for the broker to advance the premiums due, he is liable to his principal if he fails to do so.[59]

Defenses of the Broker

Obviously, a broker is not liable to an assured for failing to procure insurance where there is no binding contract obligating him to do so. There must be a "meeting of the minds" between the assured and the broker.[60] Nor is the broker liable to the assured for failure to procure a policy when, in fact, if he had procured one the potential insured would not have been entitled to recover under the policy.[61] Moreover, the broker may assert every defense which the underwriters themselves might have set up in an action on the policy, such as illegality, breach of policy warranties, or fraud. Expressions of opinion by a broker as to the legal effect of the language in the policy are not warranties or affirmations of fact but merely expressions of opinion.[62]

---

59. *Criswell v. Riley, supra* n. 58.

60. See discussion *supra.* See, also, *Ireland v. Livingston,* (1872) L.R. 5 H.L. 395; *De Tastett v. Crousillat,* F.Cas. No. 3,828 (Pa., 1807); *Rundel v. Moore,* 3 Johns. 36 (N.Y., 1802); *Winne v. Niagara F. Ins. Co.,* 91 N.Y. 185 (N.Y., 1883); *Fomin v. Oswell,* (1813) 170 E.R. 1410; *Fasce v. Clark,* 12 Wash.2d 300, 121 P.2d 357 (1942); *United Mills Agencies, Ltd. v. R.E. Harvey, Bray & Co.,* [1952] 1 All E.R. 225; *Luther v. Coal Operators Cas. Co.,* 379 Pa. 113, 108 A2d 691 (1954); *Stockberger v. Meridian Mut. Ins. Co.,* 395 N.E.2d 1272 (Ind.App., 1979); *Eedy v. Stephens,* [1976] L.L.R. 1-735 (B.C.,Can.); *River Barges, Inc. v. M/V Jessie Brent,* 377 F.Supp. 1052 (D.,Miss., 1974).

61. *Pacific Dredging v. Hurley,* 397 P.2d 819, 1964 AMC 836 (Wash.); *Eleanor (Insurance),* 250 F.2d 943, 1958 AMC 299 (1st Cir.); *Heller-Mark & Co. v. Kassler & Co.,* 544 P.2d 995, 37 Colo.App. 267 (1976) (assured must establish both causation and damages); *Florida Waterways v. Oceanus Mutual,* 1977 AMC 70 (M.D.,Fla.); *Keddie v. Beneficial Ins. Inc.,* 580 P.2d 955 (Nev., 1978) (assured failed to notify broker that the vessel to be insured was a commercial fishing vessel; application was for a yacht policy which would not have covered in any event); *Wake v. Atty,* (1812) 128 E.R. 422; *Curacao v. Stake,* 61 F.Supp. 181, 1945 AMC 790 (S.D.n.Y.) (broker gave an opinion as to coverage; had the assured had an insurable interest in the goods, which turned out not to have been the case, the assured would have been covered); *Stinson v. Cravens, Dargan and Co.,* 579 S.W.2d 298 (Tex., 1979).

62. *Webster v. De Tastett,* (1797) 101 E.R. 908 (illegality); *Cheshire (T.) & Co. v. Vaughn Bros. & Co.,* [1920] 3 K.B. 240 (brokers were negligent yet the policy obtained by them was in accordance with their instructions in a form which rendered the policy void as a p.p.i. policy under the Marine Insurance Act, 1906; plaintiffs could not in any event have recovered); *O'Connor v. B.D.B. Kirby & Co.,* [1971] 1 Lloyd's Rep. 454, C.A. (failure of assured to check proposal form before signing it); cf. *Glaser v. Cowie,* (1813) 170 E.R. 1410; *Hauser v. American Central Ins. Co.,* 216 F.Supp. 318, 1964 AMC 526 (E.D.,La.); *Curacao v. Stake,* (1945) *supra; Schooner Dartmouth v. Piper,* 1966 AMC 1877 (D.,Mass.). Compare *Sarginson Bros. v. Keith Moulton & Co., Ltd.,* (1942) 73 Ll.L.Rep. 104 (expression of opinion); *Florida Waterways v. Oceanus Mutual,* 1977 AMC 70 (M.D.,Fla.) (broker negligent *per se* but assured unable to prove any loss).

Duties of Broker after Effecting a Policy

The duties of a broker after effecting a policy are, of course, governed by the terms of his agreement with the assured. Some assureds prefer, after the policy has been placed, to handle all subsequent matters themselves. In other instances, the assured may wish the broker to continue to act as his representative in matters relating to the policy, such as giving notice of abandonment, collecting the proceeds of the policy after a loss, or cancellation of the policy. Where the broker's duties continue, he is, of course, bound to protect the interests of his principal in all matters arising out of the contract of insurance.[63]

Assuming that the broker's duties are so broadly encompassing that he must collect the sums insured, he must use all reasonable diligence to effect a settlement and compel the underwriters to pay over the sums due.[64]

A more difficult question is posed where the broker receives no express instructions as to notice of abandonment and he is left to his own discretion as to doing so. As a practical matter, if he is in a position to confer with his principals and obtain express authority, he should do so. If he cannot do so, and he has the policy in his hands, he would no doubt be held to a duty to act in behalf of his principals by giving notice of abandonment where the circumstances require it.[65]

In the absence of express authority from his principal, it would appear that a broker has no authority to cancel a policy.[66]

---

63. *Xenos v. Wickham*, (1863) L.R. 2 H.L. 296.
64. *Bousfield v. Creswell*, (1810) 2 Camp. 545, N.P.; see, also, *Williams Torrey & Co. v. Knight, The Lord of the Isles*, (1894) P. 342.
65. See *Comber v. Anderson* (1808), *supra*, and *Merchants Marine Ins. Co. v. Barrs*, (1888) 15 S.C.R. 185 (Can.)
66. *Xenos v. Wickham, supra*, n. 63; compare, however, the situation in which a broker acts as a general agent in insuring and keeping property insured, or who is authorized to exercise his own discretion in regard to what underwriters and forms of policies he may employ in keeping his principal's property insured. In these instances, it appears that the broker has authority to cancel policies. See, for example, *Great American Ins. Co. v. D.W. Ray & Son*, 15 S.W.2d 233 (Tex., 1919); *La France Workshop Lampshade Co. v. Fire Ass'n of Phila.*, 112 P.Sup. 599, 171 A. 127, 129 (Pa., 1934); *Paccione v. Home Indemn. Co.*, 244 App.Div. 339, 279 N.Y.S. 271 (1935), *aff'd* 273 N.Y. 643, 8 N.E.2d 35 (1937); *Belk's Dept. Store v. George Washington F. Ins. Co.*, 208 N.C. 267, 180 S.E. 63 (1935); *Holbrook v. Institutional Ins. Co.*, 369 F.2d 236 (7th Cir., 1966); *Bituminous Casualty Corp. v. Aetna Ins. Co.*, 461 F.2d 730 (8th Cir., 1972). Thus, a mistaken cancellation constitutes negligence. *Gazija v. Jerns Co.*, 530 P.2d 682, 1975 AMC 975, *aff'd* 86 Wn2d. 215, 543 P.2d 338 (Wash., 1975). Moreover, the broker cannot accept notice of cancellation from the underwriters. *Wisconsin Barge Line, Inc. v. Coastal Marine Transport, Inc.*, 414 F.2d 872 (5th Cir., 1969). Policies sometimes contain a "broker's cancellation clause" which gives to the broker express authority to cancel in the event of non-payment of premium by giving notice to the assured and the insurer. *Vinnie's Market v. Canadian Marine*, 441 F.Supp. 314, 1978 AMC 977 (D.,Mass.). It has been held that if the broker

In *United Mills Agencies Ltd. v. R.D. Harvey Bray & Co.*,[67] the question was presented as to whether the broker had a duty to notify his principals of the terms of a cover note as soon as possible, although in practice it was customary to do so. The court held that he did not.

Dual Representation by a Broker of Both Assured and Assurer

Generally speaking, an agent or broker owes the duty of undivided loyalty and cannot represent both the assured and the assurer, unless such dual capacity is known to both parties with full knowledge of the facts and is acceded to either before the acts are done by the agent or subsequently ratified.[68] Thus, where the assured and the assurer have knowledge of the agent's dual representation and concur that it is appropriate for him so to act, and if the agent acts in good faith, there is no impediment to the agent acting for both parties.[69] Moreover, where the broker's duties are purely ministerial and not fiduciary, there would appear to be no impediment to acting for both parties.[70]

It is entirely possible for brokers to find themselves in a hybrid situation involving conflicts that can be most awkward. See, for example, *Anglo African Merchants v. Bayley*[71] and *North & South Trust Co. v. Berkeley*.[72] In *North & South*, plaintiffs asked a local agent of Lamberts, who were Lloyd's brokers, to place coverage on goods then in transit. Lamberts placed the risk with Lloyd's underwriters, including the defendant who was a member of the leading syndicate on the policy. There being a shortage, plaintiffs asked Lamberts to effect an early settlement. Underwriters rejected the claim, and plaintiff refused to accept the rejection. Underwriters then

---

has authority to cancel, he has a duty to notify an additional assured. *Wisconsin Barge Line, Inc. v. Coastal Marine Transport, supra.* But, it has also been held that the duty of notification does not extend to a loss payee. *Federal Deposit Ins. Corp. v. Timbalier Towing Co., Inc.*, 497 F.Supp. 912, 1980 AMC 2695 (E.D., Ohio, 1979).

67. [1952] 1 All E.R. 225. See, also, *W.R. Chamberlain & Co. v. Northwestern Agencies, Inc.*, 42 Or.App. 125, 600 P.2d 438 (1979), *rev'd on other grounds*, 289 Or. 201, 611 P.2d 652 (1980), where the court held that the broker's duty to exercise due care may encompass a duty to obtain the cover note and verify coverage.

68. See, for example, *John Conlon Coal Co. v. Westchester F. Ins. Co.*, 16 F.Supp. 93 (M.D.,Pa., 1936); *Copeland v. Mercantile Ins. Co.*, 23 Mass. 198 (1828); *New York C. Ins. Co. v. National P. Ins. Co.*, 14 N.Y. 85 (1856).

69. See *Home Ins. Co. v. Campbell Mfg. Co.*, 79 F.2d 588 (4th Cir., 1935); *Sparrow v. Mutual B.L. Ins. Co.*, F.Cas. No. 13,214 (D.,Mass., 1873); *New Zealand Ins. Co. v. Larson Lumber Co.*, 13 F.2d 374 (7th Cir., 1926).

70. *Kansas City L. Ins. Co. v. Elmore*, 226 S.W. 709 (Tex., 1920); *Gelczis v. Preferred A. Ins. Co.*, 12 N.Y. Misc. 232, 171 A. 144 (1934); *Shee v. Clarkson*, (1810) 104 E.R. 199 (so long as the premium remains in the hands of a broker as well as the policy, he is a common agent for assured and underwriter).

71. [1969] All E.R. 421.

72. [1971] 1 All E.R. 980.

asked Lamberts to instruct a firm of assessors to investigate the circumstances of plaintiffs' claim, which was done. A report was rendered in due course to underwriters. Plaintiffs commenced an action against the underwriters, whereupon the latter raised issues of fraud and non-disclosure. During the course of the action, plaintiffs demanded access to the assessors' report, which underwriters refused. At issue was the question of plaintiffs' right to inspect the report or copies thereof.

The court held that Lamberts in placing the cover had been acting as agents for the plaintiffs and that Lamberts breached their duty to plaintiffs by failing to obtain their consent to their acquiring a second principal (i.e., the underwriters) in procuring the assessors' report, even though that was in accordance with a long-standing practice at Lloyd's to use the broker who placed the cover as their channel of communications with the assessors. But, the court also held that Lamberts need not divulge the report because it had been procured for underwriters and not in the service of the plaintiffs. Accordingly, the plaintiffs were denied access to the report.

The decision is somewhat curious in that the court appeared to be saying that it would have ordered disclosure of the report (in effect preferring the first principals' interests to those of the second principals) but for the fact that neither the underwriters nor the brokers could be imputed with knowledge that they were acting in a wrongful manner. This is rather strange reasoning in view of the previous decision in *Anglo African Merchants v. Bayley*. The court did say, however, that its rationale would not apply in future cases. This particular hybrid situation is unlikely to arise, or if it does, to be condoned in the future.[73] Any broker who permits himself to be placed in such a dual capacity runs the risk of being found negligent in his duties to the assured.

Lloyd's Agents

Lloyd's for many years has appointed agents in all the principal ports of the world. Their duty is to report general shipping news as well as departures and arrivals of vessels and casualties which come to their attention. These are agents of Lloyd's and not the individual underwriters. Lloyd's agents, as such, have no authority to adjust losses, accept abandonments, or to receive notice of abandonments. A Lloyd's agent is one whose cooperation will facilitate the adjustment of loss or average, but not one who has the authority to settle the loss himself.[74]

---

73. There is an interesting review of these two cases in 35 M.L.R. 78 (January, 1972).
74. *Crake v. Marryat*, (1823) 107 E.R. 175; *Vacuum Oil Co. v. Union Ins. Soc. of Canton, Ltd.*, (1926) 25 Ll.L.Rep. 546, C.A.; *Wilson v. Salamandra Assur. Co. of St. Petersburg*, (1903) 88 L.T. 96, 8 Com.Cas. 192 (knowledge of Lloyd's agents at port of discharge cannot be taken to be the knowledge of an individual underwriter at Lloyd's).

Right and Procedure for Recovery

A policy is for the benefit of the person properly entitled to it. Consequently, the principal may sue on the policy even though made in the name of his broker.[75] Conversely, an agent who insures for another with the latter's authority may sue in his own name.[76] But a broker who insures without authority cannot bind his principal to pay the premium.[77]

A broker cannot, as agent, dispute the claim of his only known principal for whom he has effected insurance on the ground that other persons are interested in it, their claims being a matter between themselves and the principal.[78]

A broker must exercise caution in attempting to obligate his principal for premiums. For example, in *Wilson v. Avec Audio-Visual Equipment, Ltd.*,[79] the broker effected policies for his principals and, after doing so, and within about one and one-half months the underwriters went bankrupt and were compulsorily wound up. The broker asked his principals to pay him the premiums so he in turn could pay the liquidators. Four months after the policies were taken out, the principals wrote advising they were prepared to pay the premiums from the inception of the policies until the underwriters went bankrupt but nothing in respect of the period after that. Upon the direction of the liquidator, the broker paid the entire premium. In a suit by him against his principals for the premium, the court held that he had failed to prove that he had rendered himself personally liable and that the case was merely one of an agent choosing, apparently because he was under a mistaken belief as to his legal position, to assume a personal liability and, having done so, in turn seeking to make his principal liable. The court also noted that even if the broker had initially had authority to pay the premium on behalf of his principals, that authority was revoked by the letter of refusal to pay.

In at least one case, it has been held that a broker could recover *future* lost commissions where the assured breached a firm contract permitting the broker to place insurance on the assured's fleet for two years. The broker was held entitled to recover the commissions he would have received from placing the insurance for the following two years.[80]

---

75. *Anchor Marine Ins. Co. v. Allen*, (1886) 13 Q.L.R. 4, C.A. (Can.); *Browning v. Prov. Ins. Co.*, (1873) L.R. 5 P.C. (Can.).
76. *Prov. Ins. v. Leduc*, (1873) L.R. 6 P.C. 244.
77. *Millar (for Victoria F. & L. Ins. Co.) v. Roddam*, 8 N.S.W.S.C.R. (1) 319 (Aus.).
78. *Roberts v. Ogilvie*, (1821) 147 E.R. 89; *Bell v. Jutting*, (1817) 1 Moore, C.P. 155.
79. [1974] 1 Lloyd's Rep. 81, C.A.
80. *Johnson & Higgins v. Harper Transp. Co.*, 228 F. 730 (D.,Mass., 1915) *rev'd* on other grounds, 244 F. 936 (1st Cir., 1917).

The Law Applicable to Claims by or Against Marine Insurance
Brokers

The law applicable to claims by or against marine insurance brokers is
that, generally speaking, which applies to all marine insurance contracts.[81] That is, in the absence of a state statute which is directly applicable, federal maritime law applies. In determining which law applies, the
federal choice of law rules requires application of the law of the state or
nation with the most significant contacts with the insurance contract.[82]
There is, however, no impediment to the parties to a marine insurance
contract agreeing that English law will apply, or the law of a particular
state.[83] Merely because there is a "London following" clause in an American policy, issued in New York, that does not mean nor imply that English
substantive law applies.[84]

Although marine insurance policies are clearly maritime contracts
and claims arising from them are unquestionably within maritime jurisdiction,[85] if the policy is on a vessel which has been withdrawn from navigation and thus not within maritime or admiralty jurisdiction, there is an
exception.[86] And, it must always be remembered that under the "savings
to suitors" clause (28 U.S.C. 1333), admiralty jurisdiction is non-exclusive
and state courts have concurrent jurisdiction; i.e., an action can be
brought *in personam* in state courts or as a civil action in the federal courts
so long as independent jurisdictional grounds exist—diversity of citizen-
ship and the requisite jurisdictional amount.

It must also be remembered that a contract to procure marine insurance on a vessel or cargo is a non-maritime contract and outside admiralty

81. See Chapter I, "Introduction," discussing the *Wilburn Boat* decision (*Wilburn Boat
Co. v. Fireman's Fund Ins. Co.*, 348 U.S. 310, 1955 AMC 467).
82. *Healy Tibbetts Constr. Co. v. Foremost Ins. Co.*, 482 F.Supp. 830, 1980 AMC 1600
(N.D.,Cal.); *Edinburgh Assur. Co. v. R.L. Burns Corp.*, 479 F.Supp. 138, 1980 AMC 1261, modified 669 F.2d 1269, 1982 AMC 2532 (9th Cir.).
83. *Eastern Prince—U.S.S. Roustabout*, 56 F.Supp. 275, 1944 AMC 727 (W.D.,Wash.), 173
F.2d 955, 1950 AMC 377 (9th Cir.), 77 Ll.L.Rep. 431; *Disrude v. Commercial Fishermen's Ins.
Exchange*, 280 Or. 245, 570 P.2d 963, 1978 AMC 261 (Or., 1978) (English law applied pursuant to policy provisions); *Edinburgh Assur. Co. v. R.L. Burns Corp.*, supra, n. 82.
84. See *Navegacion Goya, S.A. v. Mutual Boiler & Mach. Ins. Co.*, 411 F.Supp. 929, 1977
AMC 175 (S.D.N.Y.). See, also, *Amin Rasheed S. Corp. v. Kuwait Ins. Co. (The Al Wahab)*, [1983]
2 Lloyd's Rep. 365, H.L., where the shipowners secured an order granting leave to serve
process on the defendant underwriters in Kuwait. The House of Lords held that the proper
law of the contract (which tracked almost completely with the standard Lloyd's form) was
that of England but that venue could and should have been laid in Kuwait. See, also, the
excellent article by Adrian Briggs, 3 LMCLQ 360 (1985), "Forum Non Conveniens: An
Update."
85. Id., n. 81.
86. *Frank B. Hall & Co. v. S.S. Seabreeze Atlantic*, 432 F.Supp. 1205 (S.D.N.Y., 1976); cf.
Jeffcott v. Aetna Ins. Co., 129 F.2d 582, 1942 AMC 1021 (2d Cir.).

jurisdiction, on the theory that such arrangements are anterior or pre-liminary to the formation of the actual marine insurance contract.[87]

In *Stanley T. Scott & Co., Inc. v. Makah Development Corp.*,[88] the Ninth Circuit held that admiralty jurisdiction extends to a broker's action to re-cover premiums advanced for marine insurance from a defaulting as-sured. The critical issue in *Scott* involved the characterization of the agreement between the assured and the broker: (1) whether it was inte-grally related to and arose out of the marine insurance policy (which clearly was a maritime contract), or (2) whether it was a mere contract to procure insurance (which is not a maritime contract). Justice Wallace en-tered a vigorous dissent to the majority's ruling that admiralty jurisdiction extended to the broker's action.[89] It would appear on balance that the ma-jority decision was correct inasmuch as the policy had been issued and the broker had correlative duties to perform *after* the issuance of the policy.

87. *Warner v. The Bear*, 126 F.Supp. 529, 1955 AMC 1123 (D.,Alaska); cases cited in the dissent in *Stanley T. Scott and Co., Inc. v. Makah Development Corp.*, 496 F.2d 525, 1974 AMC 934 (9th Cir.). See, also, *Home Ins. Co. v. New York Merchants' Transp. Co.*, 16 F.2d 372, 1926 AMC 1045 (9th Cir.) (action for fraud in procuring an insurance policy).

88. Id., n. 87.

89. In *Frank B. Hall and Co., Inc. v. S.S. Seabreeze Atlantic*, 432 F.Supp. 1205 (S.D.N.Y., 1976), the view of the *Scott* majority was specifically rejected. See "Admiralty Jurisdiction in Broker's Action for Premium," 10 *J. Maritime Law & Commerce* 563 (1979).

CHAPTER VI

THE PREMIUM

In General

All contracts require consideration. In contracts of marine insurance, the consideration for the "promise" of the underwriter is the payment of a "premium" by the assured.

Section 31 of the Marine Insurance Act, 1906, expresses the law quite well:

(1) Where an insurance is effected at a premium to be arranged, and no arrangement is made, a reasonable premium is payable.

(2) Where an insurance is effected on the terms that an additional premium is to be arranged in a given event, and that event happens but no arrangement is made, then a reasonable additional premium is payable.[1]

The AIH form (June, 1977) recognizes in lines 67 to 69 the possibility of an additional premium being payable as follows:

The Vessel is held covered in case of any breach of conditions as to cargo, trade, locality, towage or salvage activities, or date of sailing, or loading or discharging cargo at sea, provided (a) notice is given to underwriters immediately following receipt of knowledge thereof by the Assured and (b) any amended terms of cover and any additional premium required by the Underwriters are agreed to by the Assured.

By contrast, Clause 3 of the new London hulls clauses provides:

Held covered in case of any breach of warranty as to cargo, trade, locality, towage, salvage services or date of sailing, provided notice be given to the Underwriters immediately after receipt of advices and any amended terms of cover and any additional premium required by them be agreed.

What is a "reasonable" premium is a question of fact. In this connection, see Section 88 of the Marine Insurance Act, 1906, reading:

---

1. There does not appear to be any direct or express decision which was relied upon in formulating Sec. 31. However, it does accord with mercantile understanding and may, by analogy, be likened to a "reasonable price" under contracts of sales of goods.

Where by this Act any reference is made to reasonable time, reasonable premium, or reasonable diligence, the question what is reasonable is a question of fact.

The rule for ascertainment of an extra premium was laid down in *Greenock S.S. Co. v. Maritime Insurance Co., Ltd.*[2] to the effect that the parties must assume that a breach was known to them at the time when it happened, and ascertain what it would have then been reasonable to charge.[3]

The subject of what the word "arranged" means in terms of premium arose in *Liberian Insurance Agency Inc. v. Mosse.*[4] There, a consignment of enamelware, described as packed in wooden cases, was insured on all risks conditions. It was not disclosed to the underwriter that the consignment consisted of a job lot containing a high proportion of "seconds," some of which had been overpainted and with a large proportion packed in export cartons instead of wooden cases.

Findings having been made to this effect, and the court having concluded that there was non-disclosure, the assured's fall-back position was the clause of the policy reading:

Held covered at a premium to be arranged in case of change of voyage or of any omission or error in the description of the interest, vessel or voyage.

The policy (based upon the then version of the Institute Cargo Clause, all risks) also contained a note stating:

It is necessary for the assured when they become aware of an event which is "held covered" under this insurance to give prompt notice to the Underwriters and the right to such cover is dependent upon compliance with this obligation.

The assured contended that, as there was a discrepancy between the description of the cargo as insured and that found as a fact by the court, he could avail himself of the held covered clause to extend the coverage and thereby resolve the discrepancy.

It will be noted that the held covered clause involved referred only to a premium to be arranged and not to conditions to be arranged. Justice Donaldson said, in part:

I understand the word "arranged" to mean "agreed or, in default of agreement, fixed by an arbitrator or by the court." But I think there

---

2. [1903]1 K.B. 367, *aff'd* 2 K.B. 657, [1900-3] All E.R. Rep. 834, 9 Asp. M.L.C. 462, C.A.

3. See, also, *Mentz, Decker & Co. v. Maritime Ins. Co.*, [1910] 1 K.B. 132, 11 Asp. M.L.C. 339.

4. [1977] 1 Lloyd's Rep. 560.

has to be a further limitation. The clause cannot contemplate a situation in which the only premium which could be "arranged" was 100 per cent of the sum insured. So some upper limit to the new premium must be contemplated.

In considering what would or would not constitute a reasonable premium which would trigger the operation of the clause, the court said, in part:

> This can be relatively high if the risk is high, but it will not be in the same class as, for example, rates of premium for reinsurance cover after a casualty has in fact occurred. Still less will it approach 100 per cent of the sum insured.

Continuing, he said:

> I can summarise the application of the held covered clause as follows: (i) The Assured seeking the benefit of the clause must give prompt notice to underwriters of his claim to be held covered as soon as he learns of the facts which render it necessary for him to rely upon the clause. (ii) It is no obstacle to the operation of the clause that it will defeat underwriters' right to avoid the contract for non-disclosure or misdescription. (iii) The Assured cannot take advantage of the clause if he has not acted in the utmost good faith. (iv) The clause does not contemplate any alteration in the terms of the insurance other than in respect of premium. (v) The clause only applies if the premium to be arranged would be such as could properly be described as a reasonable commercial rate.

The court concluded from the evidence that no underwriter would have quoted a reasonable commercial rate of premium on all risks conditions for such a risk, and the held covered clause consequently failed to provide any protection.

The held covered clause, of course, protects an assured from the harsh results of an inadvertent failure to comply with specified warranties of the policy, provided the breach is not wilful, the assured gives prompt notice of the breach and agrees to pay an additional premium. The fact that the assured became aware of the breach for the first time only after the loss occurred does not in and of itself prevent recovery.[5]

In *Tinkerbell, supra,* although recognizing that the insured was not barred from recovery when he learned of the breach after the loss, the court held that the held covered clause was not applicable to a breach of a win-

---

5. *Tinkerbell,* 533 F.2d 496, 1976 AMC 799 (9th Cir.); *Mentz, Decker & Co. v. Maritime Ins. Co.,* [1910] 1 K.B. 132, 11 Asp. M.L.C. 339; *Chartered Bank of India v. Pacific Marine Ins. Co.,* [1923] 2 D.L.R. 612, *aff'd* [1923] 4 D.L.R. 942 (Can., C.A.). See, also, *Stad v. Union Ins. Soc. of Canton, Ltd., et al,* No. 1958/65, SupCrt., B.C. (Can.) (otherwise unreported).

ter lay-up warranty in which the assured warranted that his vessels would be "laid up and out of commission" from October 1 to April 13. The court stated that a lay-up warranty was not concerned with location but only with condition, i.e., whether the vessel had been winterized in accordance with local custom. There, the assured had entrusted his vessel to another with instructions to lay her up by October 1, but unbeknownst to the assured mechanical difficulties had delayed the winter lay-up with the result that the vessel was totally lost in a storm on October 20.

The importance of prompt notice to the underwriter cannot be overemphasized. The protection afforded by a held covered clause is clearly subject to an implied condition that notice must be given to the underwriter within the shortest reasonable time after the facts become known to the assured.[6]

For example, in *Hood v. West End Motor Car Packing Co.*, a car was shipped from London to Messina and was insured under a policy in the usual form (which did not cover the risk of carriage on deck). The policy, however, incorporated a held covered clause which covered any omission or error in the description of the interest, vessel, or voyage. The terms of shipment included a clause "with liberty to carry on deck at shipper's risk." The bill of lading stated that the car had been shipped "on deck." On arrival, it was found that the car was so damaged by seawater as to be worthless. No notice had been given to the underwriters before the loss was discovered that the car had been carried on deck, and the issue before the court was whether or not notice was necessary. The court said, in part:

> It is said that there was an omission or error in the description of the interest. It is a fatal objection to the soundness of that contention that it has been held by the House of Lords in *Thames & Mersey Marine Insurance Co. v. Van Laun*, affirming a judgment of Kennedy, J., that in such a case it is an implied term of the contract that the assured will not be covered unless within a reasonable time after knowing of the omission or error he has given notice thereof to the underwriter. That case lays it down that it is an implied term of the contract that notice must be given by or on behalf of the assured to the underwriter within the shortest reasonable time after his knowledge of the error. There is in such cases a tendency on the part of the assured to wait in order to see what may turn up, and he often omits to pay the extra premium until a loss has actually occurred. It is to meet that tendency that this implied term is introduced into the contract.

---

6. *Hood v. West End Motor Car Packing Co.*, (1917) 2 K.B. 38, 14 Asp. M.L.C. 12; *Thames & Mersey Marine Ins. Co., Ltd. v. Van Laun*, (1917) 23 Com.Cas. 104, (1918) 23 Com.Cas. 104.

It was held that the assured could not take advantage of the protection, if any, afforded by the clause.

In *Bristol Steamship Corp. v. London Assurance and H.O. Linard*,[7] it was held that the movement of a vessel under a port risk policy from the prescribed port area without notice to the underwriters constituted a material deviation which discharged them from liability. Twelve days after the port risk coverage was renewed on the vessel "at Hirohata, Japan," the vessel was moved some forty miles to Osaka for a drydocking survey, and while at Osaka she was damaged. The court noted that the "held covered at premium to be agreed" clause in the port risk policy was inapplicable in the absence of any proof that the parties agreed upon a premium for coverage at a port other than the one named in the policy.

There is, of course, a major distinction between a "variation" of a voyage and a "variation" of the risk. Clearly, the precise language of the held covered clause being construed must be carefully scrutinized. Compare, for example, *Alluvials Mining Machinery Co. v. Stowe*[8] with *Hewitt v. London General Ins. Co., Ltd.*[9]

In *Alluvials Mining*, barrels of kerosene were shipped from the United Kingdom to mines in Nigeria. The policy of insurance contained a held covered clause reading:

> Held covered on premium to be arranged in case of deviation or change or other variation of risk by reason of the exercise of any liberty granted to the shipowner or charterer, etc.

It was part of the terms of shipment arranged by the assured that the cargo would be carried as deck cargo. Only about ten percent of the cargo arrived at destination. The assured contended that the clause quoted above applied upon the payment of an additional premium. The underwriter defended on the ground that there had been no variation of "risk" within the meaning of the clause.

Judgment was given for the underwriter. The court observed:

> In order to come within this clause it is necessary to decide if the risk which arises from the peril of being loaded on deck and carried on deck was a variation of the risk by reason of the exercise of any liberty granted to the shipowner. It seems to me there was no variation of risk on this voyage at all, because the risk from the start to the end of the contract of carriage was a risk of goods to be loaded on deck.
> . . . Thus from the very commencement of the contractual relations between the plaintiffs and the shipowners there was a consent on the

---

7. 404 F. Supp. 749, 1976 AMC 448 (S.D.N.Y.). See, also, *Canton Insurance Office, Ltd. v. Independent Transportation Co.*, 217 F. 213 (9th Cir., 1914) and cases discussed therein.
8. (1922) 10 Ll.L.Rep. 96, K.B.D.
9. (1925) 23 Ll.L.Rep. 243, K.B.D.

part of the plaintiffs and an agreement between the parties that the goods were to be carried on deck, and there was never any variation of that risk from the beginning of the transaction to the end. There was not, in my judgment, a variation in the risk at all; or, rather, there was no variation of the risk by reason of the exercise of any liberty granted to the shipowner. There was no liberty granted the shipowner in the contract of affreightment to carry these goods on deck, in the sense of the words that he was free to carry them on deck, because it was part of the contract to carry on deck. . . . The facts in this case do not show any exercise of liberty to vary that risk within the meaning of the words.

In *Hewitt*, a cargo of nitrates was insured for a voyage to France via the Panama Canal. The policy contained a clause reading:

In the event of the voyage being changed or of any deviation from the terms of this policy, the same to be held covered at premium to be arranged hereafter.

The primary cargo insurers reinsured the risk under a reinsurance policy reciting that it was subject to the same terms, clauses, and conditions as in the original policy.

The vessel called at Colon in transiting the Panama Canal. There, she was ordered to go to New Orleans which she did, deviating in order to get to that port. Some weeks later, she sailed from New Orleans and was lost with all her cargo. Among the issues involved in an action brought by the original underwriters against the reinsurers, was whether the reinsurers were entitled to the payment of an additional premium.

Applying *Greenock S.S. Co. v. Maritime Insurance Co., Ltd.,* the court stated:

The evidence as to the usual course of a voyage to France from Colon was very slight. It depends upon the bunkering capacity of the vessel in question and the price of coal at various ports which might be used to provide the coal. A steamer might go to a coaling port on the Atlantic seaboard of the U. S. or to the French West Indies. So in view of all the evidence and although the putting in to New Orleans was clearly a deviation, it was not in my opinion at all a serious one. It is said to have lengthened the voyage by some 500 miles. The voyage was 5,000 miles so the lengthening was in my opinion not more than ten percent of the total. The policy subscribed by defendants permits of much greater variations in the voyage than this without any change of premium. It was stated and not denied that upon the original policy no extra premium was asked in respect of the deviation, because it was considered that the deviation did not cause any material addition to the risk.

It will be observed that a question can easily arise as to whether the underwriter is compelled to hold covered cargo that is shipped on deck but not originally declared by the shipper/assured as being so shipped. If the cargo is one that the underwriter would normally assume would be carried under deck but is, in fact, shipped on deck, the phrase "omission or error in the description of the interest" would not appear to protect the shipper/assured because the omission or error was one in the description of the *risk* rather than that of "interest."

The words used in the new London Institute Cargo Clause (A) warrant mention. Clause 8.3 provides:

> This insurance shall remain in force (subject to termination as provided for above and to the provisions of Clause 9 below) during delay beyond the control of the Assured, any deviation, forced discharge, reshipment or transshipment and during any variation of the adventure arising from the exercise of a liberty granted to shipowners or charterers under the contract of affreightment.

Clause 9 provides, in part:

> If owing to circumstances beyond the control of the Assured either the contract of carriage is terminated at a port or place other than the destination named therein or the transit is otherwise terminated before delivery of the goods as provided for in Clause 8 above, then this insurance shall also terminate *unless prompt notice is given to the Underwriters and continuation of cover is requested when the insurance shall remain in force, subject to an additional premium if required by the Underwriters,* either
>
>> 9.1 until the goods are sold and delivered at such port or place, or, unless otherwise specially agreed, until the expiry of 60 days after arrival of the goods hereby insured at such port or place, whichever shall first occur, or
>> 9.2 if the goods are forwarded within the said period of 60 days (or any agreed extension thereof) to the destination named herein or to any other destination, until terminated in accordance with the provisions of Clause 8 above.

Clause 10 relates to a change of destination by the assured and reads:

> Where, after attachment of this insurance, the destination is changed by the Assured, *held covered at a premium and on conditions to be arranged subject to prompt notice being given to the Underwriters.*[10]

---

10. The emphasis shown by italicizing in Clause 9 appears in the original and as also emphasized in Clause 10. The purpose, obviously, is to attract the attention of the assured to the requirement. Further emphasis is given by the inclusion of a "note," also italicized, at the

Again, it should be noted that the phrase "any variation of the adventure" which appears in Clause 8.3 would presumably not cover a variation of the *risk* where a shipowner exercises a liberty to carry on deck cargo which he had originally contracted to carry under deck.[11]

In practice, it would seem that the difficulty could be overcome by appropriate language such as "in and/or over" deck with such limitations on cover as usually apply to on-deck shipments; i.e., coverage on F.P.A. conditions including jettison and washing overboard.

Time for Payment of the Premium

Section 52 of the Marine Insurance Act provides:

> Unless otherwise agreed, the duty of the assured or his agent to pay the premium, and the duty of the insurer to issue the policy to the assured or his agent, are concurrent conditions, and the insurer is not bound to issue the policy until payment or tender of the premium.[12]

In keeping with the general rule, delivery of a policy to the assured's broker—who is as a general rule an agent of the assured—constitutes delivery to the assured.[13] Moreover, the acceptance of a partial premium after cancellation under an automatic termination provision in the policy amounts to a waiver of any prior cancellation and a reinstatement of the policy. However, later non-payment and subsequent mailing of a cancellation notice effectively cancels the policy.[14]

Liability for Payment of the Premium

In England, unless otherwise agreed, where a policy is effected by a broker, the broker is directly responsible to the insurer for the premium and

---

bottom of the policy reading:

> It is necesary for the Assured when they become aware of any event which is "held covered" under this insurance to give prompt notice to the Underwriters and the right to such cover is dependent upon compliance with this obligation.

11. See *Alluvials Mining, supra,* n. 8.

12. Compare *Burges v. Wickham,* (1863) 33 L.J.Q.B. 17. An error in the premium can, of course, be corrected by a subsequent endorsement on the policy. *Mildred v. Maspons,* (1883) 8 App.Cas. 874, 5 Asp. M.L.C. 182, H.L. A marine policy, like every other legal document, is deemed incomplete and revocable until delivery to, or for the benefit of, the person entitled to it. Delivery is presumed on very scant evidence. See *Xenos v. Wickham,* (1866) L.R. 2 H.L. 296. The word "agreed" as used in Sec. 52 includes a binding usage because usage is binding as being an implied term of the agreement. See Chap. IV, "Principles of Construction."

13. *Tarleton v. De Veuve,* 113 F.2d 290 (9th Cir.), *cert. denied,* 312 U.S. 691 (1940); *Michaelson v. Franklin Fire Ins. Co.,* 252 Mass. 336, 147 N.E. 851 (1924); *Vinnie's Market v. Canadian Marine,* 441 F.Supp. 341, 1978 AMC 977 (D., Mass.).

14. *Vinnie's Market, supra,* n. 13. However, see *Osborne v. The Queen,* [1984] I.L.R. 1-1724 (Can.), where it was held that since there was no contractual provision for automatic termination, the insurer could only terminate coverage by giving written notice prior to a loss.

the insurer is directly responsible to the assured for the amount which may be payable in respect of losses, or in respect of returnable premium.[15] Under English law, it is a well-recognized practice in marine insurance for the broker to treat himself as responsible to the underwriter for the premium; by a fiction he is deemed to have paid the underwriter, and to have borrowed from him the money with which he pays.[16]

The rule in the United States is otherwise, as the assured is responsible for payment of the premium. The fundamental difference is well illustrated by two cases brought by the same plaintiff in the United States and in England. In *Ruby Steamship Corp. Ltd. v. Commercial Union Assurance Company,* [17] the court stated in part:

> It is necessary here to state the difference between English and American underwriting. In England by long practice the underwriter acknowledges in the policy, often contrary to the facts, that the assured has paid the premium, and cannot thereafter claim for it on the assured.

The court said further:

> It naturally follows by English law that the assured being supposed to have paid the premium, his contract with the underwriter cannot be cancelled by the broker without the authority of the assured, because he has not received the premium from the assured [citing *Xenos v. Wickham*, L.R. 2 H.L. 296].

In that instance, the insurance had been procured by the assured, a Canadian company, through a New York broker who then placed the coverage in London through a Lloyd's broker. This naturally raised a question as to which law was applicable to the employment of the New York broker. The court applied New York law and stated:

> In the case of an American assured on a policy underwritten through an American broker, there is no contractual liability of the broker to the underwriter for premium; The latter looks to the insured. The broker has no further duties after he has effected the policy.

In the event, the court held that the New York broker was entitled to rescind the contract of employment and cancel the policies.

---

15. See 53(1) Marine Insurance Act, 1906. See, also, *Universo Ins. Co. of Milan v. Merchants' Marine Ins. Co.*, [1897] 2 Q.B. 205, *aff'd* [1897] 2 Q.B. 93, C.A.; cf. *Matveieff v. Crossfield*, (1903) 8 Com.Cas. 120.
    16. Id., n. 15.
    17. 46 Ll.L.Rep. 265 (1933).

In the American litigation, *Ruby Steamship Corporation v. Johnson &*
Higgins,[18] the court considered the case of *Xenos v. Wickham* but decided,
contrary to English practice, that an American broker placed in such a
position could effect cancellation of the policy without the consent of the
assured. Nonetheless, it was held that the American broker was responsible to the English broker for the premium since the latter was bound under English law to pay the premium to the underwriter. The Second Circuit felt that the English principle that as between an insurer and insured
the policy is fully paid, precluding cancellation without consent of the assured, was inequitable. The court said, in part:

> Clearly, in property of this kind, the broker's right as against the
> insured to cancel the policies and obtain the return of the pro rata
> premium or credit advanced by him is the only effective method of
> foreclosing the lien. And in our judgment, the reservation of a right so
> to cancel is fairly and properly to be implied as the understanding of
> the parties to such a contract in which, by their agreement, the pre-
> miums are to be paid in advance by the insured to the broker.

The Marine Insurance Act, 1906, is even more explicit with respect to
the relationship between the broker and the underwriter. Section 54
provides:

> Where a marine policy effected on behalf of the assured by a broker
> acknowledges the receipt of the premium, such acknowledgment is, in
> the absence of fraud, conclusive as between the insurer and the as-
> sured, but not as between the insurer and the broker.

Practice in the English Market

Although Section 52 of the Act provides that the insurer is not obliged to
issue a policy until the premium is paid, in practice, when the insurance
cover is placed through a broker, the insurer does not obtain immediate
payment but, instead, looks to the broker to credit him with the premium
"in account."

The practice in the market is that premiums are subject to brokerage
and discount of varying percentages.[19] Lloyd's underwriters customarily
settle their accounts with the brokers on a quarterly basis, with checks
being issued for balances due on the eighth of the month following the

---

18. 18 F.2d 948, 1927 AMC 714 (2d Cir.). See, also, *Mannheim Ins. Co. v. Hollander*, 111 F.
549 (1901).

19. See, in this connection, *Baring v. Stanton*, (1876) 3 Ch.D. 502; *Glasgow Assurance
Corp. v. Symondson*, (1911) 16 Com.Cas. 109; *Green v. Tughan*, (1913) 30 T.L.R. 64.

end of each quarter.[20] The practice between brokers and underwriters has no bearing on the right of an assured to payment of a claim; the claim is usually paid by the broker to the assured as soon as the account has been settled with the underwriter.

There seems to be no settled practice or custom with respect to accounts between brokers and assureds, although in general premiums for any particular month are due and payable on the eighth day of the succeeding month. Losses are generally payable upon receipt of the funds from the underwriter, or, if merely credited to the broker's account, paid by the broker within seven days after settlement with the underwriter.

On hull insurances on large vessels, where the premium may be very substantial, special arrangements are frequently made by which the premium is paid in installments. Here, it is customary to provide that the policy may be cancelled if any installment is not paid in a timely fashion. Moreover, many hull policies provide that all unpaid installments are immediately due and payable in the event of a total loss.[21]

As noted heretofore, the mercantile custom in England has been that the underwriter cannot sue the assured directly for the premium, nor can he set off unpaid premiums where he is sued by the assured for losses falling under the policy. This principle or custom was aptly described in *Powell v. Butcher*,[22] where it was said:

> According to the ordinary course of trade between the assured, the broker and the underwriter, the assured does not in the first instance pay the premium to the broker, nor does the latter pay it to the underwriter. But, as between the assured and the underwriter, the premiums are considered as paid. The underwriter, to whom, in most instances, the assured are unknown, looks to the broker for payment, and he to the assured. The latter pays the premiums to the broker only, who is a middleman between the assured and the underwriter. But he is not merely an agent; he is a principal to receive the money from the assured, and to pay it to the underwriters.

In light of the foregoing, it is not surprising that, as a general rule, the assured is liable to the broker for premiums whether they were or were not paid over to the underwriter, because the premiums are, as between the broker and the underwriter, considered as having been paid. Correspondingly, the broker has a right to recover immediately against the as-

---

20. The practice appears to differ where there is a total loss; in that case, the broker may claim payment within seven days after settlement, but if he does so, the premium is due to the underwriter in that current month.

21. See, for example, lines 38-39 of the AIH (1977) form which provides that ". . . full annual premium shall be considered earned and immediately due and payable in the event of Total Loss of the Vessel."

22. 8 L.J.K.B. (o.s.) 217.

sured as money paid for his benefit.[23] The same principles apply with respect to return premiums, and such premiums can immediately be recovered by the assured from the underwriter as money had and received.[24] But, as Section 54 so clearly provides, an acknowledgment in the policy of receipt of premium is conclusive only in the absence of fraud.[25]

Return Premiums

The right of an assured to a return of premium may, and usually is, set out in the policy. Section 83 of the Act provides:

> Where the policy contains a stipulation for the return of the premium, or a proportionate part thereof, on the happening of a certain event, and that event happens, the premium, or, as the case may be, the proportionate part thereof, is thereupon returnable to the assured.

Various policy provisions will be found that provide for return premiums. For example, lines 40-54 of the AIH (1977) form provide:
Premium returnable as follows:

> Pro rata daily net in the event of termination under the Change of Ownership Clause;
> Pro rata monthly net for each uncommenced month if it be mutually agreed to cancel this Policy;
> For each period of 30 consecutive days the Vessel may be laid up in port for account of the Assured, _____ cents percent. net not under repair, _____ cents percent. net under repair;

provided always that

> (a) a Total Loss of the Vessel has not occurred during the currency of this Policy;
> (b) in no case shall a return for lay-up be allowed when the Vessel is lying in exposed or unprotected waters or in any location not approved by the Underwriters;
> (c) in the event of any amendment of the annual rate, the above rates of return shall be adjusted accordingly;
> (d) in no case shall a return be allowed when the Vessel is used as a storage ship or for lightering purposes.

23. Id.
24. *Xenos v. Wickham, supra,* n. 12.
25. See *Foy v. Bell,* (1911) 3 Taunt. 493.

If the Vessel is laid up for a period of 30 consecutive days, a part only of which attaches under this Policy, the Underwriters shall pay such proportion of the return due in respect of a full period of 30 days as the number of days attaching hereto bears to 30. Should the lay-up period exceed 30 consecutive days, the Assured shall have the option to elect the period of 30 consecutive days for which a return is recoverable.

The comparable "returns for lay-up and cancellation" clause (Clause 22 of the new London hull clauses) does not differ significantly, although the language is slightly different in some particulars.

The meaning of the term "laid up in port" was considered in *North Shipping Co. v. Union Mar. Ins. Co.*[26] There, it was held that the term did not apply to a period during which the insured vessel was employed in bunkering warships at a particular port where such acts necessitated keeping steam up and proceeding from her moorings to get alongside the warships. The court noted that the evidence established a custom that the term did cover various operations in port which might occur in the normal course of discharging cargo.

In *Gorsedd S.S. Co. v. Forbes,*[27] it was held that the assured was entitled to a return of part of the premium paid, under a stipulation that it would be returned should the vessel be employed in a specified trade during the "whole currency of this policy," and it was so employed.

In *Hunter v. Wright,*[28] the premium was returnable if the vessel was "sold or laid up." After being laid up for a time, the vessel was again employed during the currency of the policy. It was held that the term did not include a temporary laying up.

In *Pyman v. Marten,*[29] the premium was returnable if the vessel was sold or placed under new management. The vessel was captured, and the assured claimed for a return of the premium. It was held that a capture did not satisfy the condition stipulated, and recovery was denied.

Where there is no stipulation in the policy, there are two general rules which were laid down in *Tyrie v. Fletcher*[30] by Lord Mansfield. As to the first, he said:

> . . . the first is that where the risk has not been begun, whether this be owing to the fault, pleasure, or will, of the assured, or any other cause, the premium shall be returned, because a policy of insurance is a contract of indemnity; the underwriter receives a premium for running the risk of indemnifying the assured, and, to whatever cause it

26. (1919) 35 T.L.R. 292.
27. (1900) 5 Com.Cas. 413.
28. (1830) 109 E.R. 615.
29. (1906) 13 Com.Cas. 64.
30. (1777) 98 E.R. 1927.

may be owing, if he do not in fact run the risk, the consideration for which the premium was put into his hands fails, and therefore he ought to return it.

The second rule is that once an entire risk has commenced, there is no apportionment or return of premium. Although the premium is estimated and the risk, of course, depends upon the nature and extent of the voyage, once the voyage commences even for a short space of time the risk is run.[31]

Section 82 of the Marine Insurance Act, 1906, provides:

Where the premium, or a proportionate part thereof is, by this Act, declared to be returnable,

(a) If already paid, it may be recovered by the assured from the insurer; and
(b) If unpaid, it may be retained by the assured or his agent.[32]

Section 84 of the Act rather explicitly sets forth the rules with respect to return of premium where there is a failure of consideration. It reads:

(1) Where the consideration for the payment of the premium totally fails, and there has been no fraud or illegality on the part of the assured or his agents, the premium is thereupon returnable to the assured.[33]

(2) Where the consideration for the payment of the premium is apportionable and there is a total failure of any apportionable part of the consideration, a proportionate part of the premium is, under the like conditions, thereupon returnable to the assured.

(3) In particular—

(a) Where the policy is void, or is avoided by the insurer as from the commencement of the risk, the premium is returnable, provided that there has been no fraud or illegality on the part of the assured; but if the risk is not apportionable, and has once attached, the premium is not returnable:
(b) Where the subject-matter insured, or part thereof, has never been imperilled, the premium, or, as the case may be, a proportionate part thereof, is returnable:

Provided that where the subject-matter has been insured "lost or not lost" and has arrived in safety at the time when the contract is concluded, the premium is not returnable unless, at such time, the insurer knew of the safe arrival:

31. Id.
32. *Shee v. Clarkson*, (1810) 12 East 507.
33. See *Bradford v. Symondon*, (1881) 7 Q.B.D. 456. See, also, 2 Phillips s. 1826.

(c) Where the assured has no insurable interest throughout the currency of the risk, the premium is returnable, provided that this rule does not apply to a policy effected by way of gaming or wagering:

(d) Where the assured has a defeasible interest which is terminated during the currency of the risk, the premium is not returnable:

(e) Where the assured has over-insured under an unvalued policy, a proportionate part of the premium is returnable:

(f) Subject to the foregoing provisions, where the assured has over-insured by double insurance, a proportionate part of the several premiums is returnable:

Provided that, if the policies are effected at different times, and any earlier policy has at any time borne the entire risk, or if a claim has been paid on the policy in respect of the full sum insured thereby, no premium is returnable in respect of that policy, and where the double insurance is effected knowingly by the assured no premium is returnable.

Clearly, Section 84(1) requires a return of premium regardless of neglect or fault on the part of the insured, *but only if there has been no fraud or illegality on his part or that of his agents.* In this connection, in *Intermunicipal v. Gore,*[34] the assured misrepresented the identity of his ship manager. The court held that the misrepresentation was material and fraudulent where it was made to induce underwriters to take on the risk. As the misrepresentation was fraudulent, the policy was void *ab initio* and entitled the underwriters not only to disclaim liability but also to retain the whole prepaid premium.[35]

As Section 84(3)(b) of the Act notes, where the subject matter insured, or part thereof, has never been imperilled, the premium or a proportionate part thereof is returnable. For example, it has been held that if the ship was unseaworthy at the time the risk was to have commenced, the risk never attached and the premium is returnable.[36] In short, in any instance in which the risk does not attach and the underwriter was therefore never exposed to any liability for payment of a loss, the premium is returnable.[37]

---

34. 1980 AMC 1540 (Can. Fed. Ct.).

35. See, also, *Feise v. Parkinson,* (1812) 128 E.R. 482.

36. *Scriba v. Insurance Co. of N.A.,* F.Cas. No. 12560 (D., Pa. 1807).

37. See, for example, *Porter v. Bussey,* 1 Mass. 436 (1805); *Taylor v. Lowell,* 3 Mass. 331 (1807); *Merchants Ins. Co. v. Clapp,* 28 Mass. 56 (1831); *Jones v. St. Paul F. & M. Ins. Co.,* 118 F.2d 237 (5th Cir., 1941); *Henkle v. Royal Exchange Assur. Co.,* (1749) 27 E.R. 1055; *Meyer v. Gregson,* (1785) 99 E.R. 879; *Long v. Allen,* (1785) 99 E.R. 879; *Marine Ins. Co. v. Tucker,* 7 U.S. 357, 2 L.ed 466 (1806); *Commonwealth Ins. Co. v. Whitney,* 32 Mass. 21 (1840); *Penniman v. Tucker,* 11 Mass. 66 (1814); *Robertson v. United Ins. Co.,* 2 Johns Cas. 191 (N.Y., 1801); *Murray v.*

It naturally follows that premiums paid on an illegal insurance or by mistake can be recovered. For example, in *Edgar v. Fowler*,[38] it was held that no action could be maintained by the assignees of a bankrupt underwriter against the brokers for recovery of premiums since no premium moneys had actually been paid to the brokers by the assured. As Lord Ellenborough remarked, in the case of illegal transactions, money may always be stopped while *in transitu* to the person entitled to receive it.[39]

With respect to the right of set-off as between underwriter and broker under English law, see Arnould, Sections 175-86.[40]

Lien for Premium

The law is well settled in the United States that there is no lien against a vessel on account of unpaid insurance premiums.[41] However, the admiralty court may enforce, in an *in rem* proceeding, a state-created lien for insurance premiums, as neither the general maritime law nor the federal Maritime Lien Act, 1920, has ever provided a lien for unpaid insurance premiums.[42]

Under British law, a broker has a lien on the policy while it remains in his possession for the premium and commissions due. The right to a claim *in rem* against the vessel itself does not appear to exist under British law.[43] It should be noted, however, that in most modern policies in the United States and in Great Britain as well cancellation clauses are incor-

---

Columbian Ins. Co., 2 Johns Cas. 168 (1802); *Lawrence v. Ocean Ins. Co.*, 11 Johns Cas. 241 (N.Y., 1814); *Forbes v. Church*, 3 Johns Cas. 159 (N.Y., 1802); *Horneyer v. Lushington*, (1812) 104 E.R. 761; *Taylor v. Sumner*, 4 Mass. 55 (1808); *Toppan v. Atkinson*, 2 Mass. 365 (1807); *Boehm v. Bell*, (1799) 101 E.R. 1318; *Martin v. Sitwell*, (1691) 89 E.R. 509; *Forster v. Ins. Co. of N.A.*, 139 F.2d 875, 1944 AMC 131 (2d Cir.). See, also, *In Re London County Commercial Re-Insurance Office, Ltd.*, (1922) 10 Ll.L.Rep. 370

38. (1803) 3 East 222.

39. See, also, *Tenant v. Elliott*, (1797) 1 B. & P. 3; *Nicholson v. Gouch*, (1865) 5 E. & B. 999; *Edwards v. Motor Union Ins. Co.*, [1922] 2 K.B. 249; *De Mattos v. Benjamin*, (1894) 64 L.J.Q.B. 248. By the same token, moneys paid to a broker by mistake are recoverable by the underwriter so long as the broker has not paid it over to the assured. *Buller v. Harrison*, (1777) 2 Cowp. 565; *Scottish Metropolitan Assur. Co. v. Samuel*, [1923] 1 K.B. 348.

40. Arnould, *Law of Marine Insurance and Average*, 16th ed., 1981.

41. *Ruby (Hurona)*, 18 F.2d 948, 1927 AMC 714 (2d Cir.); *Man of War*, 1923 AMC 187 (D.,Mass.); *West of England v. Patriarch*, 491 F.Supp. 539, 1981 AMC 423 (D.,Mass.).

42. *Grow v. Loraine K.*, 310 F.2d 547, 1963 AMC 2044 (6th Cir.). Among the states which grant a lien for unpaid premiums is numbered Oregon which, in 1981, amended its old Boat Lien Act to provide for a lien such as was involved in *Grow, supra*. See ORS 783.010 *et seq.* In terms of priority, however, such state-created liens come well after all other true maritime liens.

43. *The Aifanourios*, [1980] 2 Lloyd's Rep. 403. However, Sec. 22(2)(r) of the Canadian Federal Court Act applies to marine insurance, and Sec. 43 appears to give jurisdiction *in rem* to claims for unpaid marine insurance premiums. Such a lien appears to exist in Quebec. See *Zabarovalna S. Triglav v. Terrasses Jewellers, Inc.*, [1983] 1 S.C.R. 283 (Can.), at p. 297.

porated in the policies permitting cancellation for non-payment of premiums.

In a perhaps analogous case, *The Acrux*,[44] an action was brought *in rem* against a vessel for unpaid social insurance premiums payable by the owners of the vessel on behalf of the officers and crew of the vessel. The action was brought in England by an Italian corporation claiming a statutory right *in rem* for the premiums by virtue of Italian law. The court rejected the contention, stating:

> There are no provisions in any statute to which my attention has been called which specifically give a right to any person, including the Minister of Pensions and National Insurance to sue *in rem* for unpaid insurance contributions either as wages or as a form of civil debt.

The court then applied the law of the *lex fori* and would give effect to the lien only as it might exist under English law—and no such lien existed. The decision appears to foreshadow *Bankers Trust v. Todd Shipyards (The Halcyon Isle)*,[45] applying the *lex fori* to a mortgage lien being foreclosed in a Singapore court.

As noted above, in the United States the broker assumes no responsibility for the payment of the premium. The situation may well be different when, as frequently happens, an American broker places coverage through an English broker, who is, of course, responsible to the underwriter for the premium. This was the situation in *Ruby Steamship Corporation v. Johnson & Higgins*, discussed *supra*. Thus, while the American broker was liable to pay the English broker since the latter was bound under English law to pay the underwriter, the American broker had another remedy in that he could cancel the policy without the consent of the assured and even in the absence of a cancellation clause in the policy.

Return of Premium—Defense by Underwriter

Under American law, a return of premium is not a condition precedent to assertion by an underwriter of a defense of breach of warranty by the assured.[46] Nor is tender of return of premium necessary before suit in order to recover money over-paid on a policy loss.[47]

44. [1965] 1 Lloyd's Rep. 565.
45. [1981] A.C. 221 (P.C., 1980 AMC 1221.
46. *Poulos v. Fireman's Fund Ins. Co.*, 1962 AMC 1979 (St., N.Y.).
47. *St. Paul F. & M. Ins. Co. v. Pure Oil Co.*, 1933 AMC 502 (2d Cir.).

Insurable Interest in Premium

Section 13 of the Marine Insurance Act, 1906, provides:

> The assured has an insurable interest in the charges of any insurance which he may effect.[48]

This rule naturally follows in order that the assured may be fully indemnified in the event of a loss. Otherwise, the assured would not be made whole as respects the charges for the insurance, i.e., the premium he has to pay.

As a practical matter, in cargo insurance the premium is usually included in the insurance value of the cargo. So, if the cargo is sold on c.i.f. terms (cost, insurance, freight), the cargo is normally valued for insurance purposes at the c.i.f. value plus a certain percentage, usually around ten percent.

It should also be noted that under nearly all hull policies, the shipowner is permitted to procure "additional insurance." In the new London hull policy, this provision is denominated under Clause 21 as the "disbursements warranty." Under the AIH (1977) form, it is termed "additional insurances" (lines 210-38). The effect under both is essentially the same; i.e., the shipowner may effect insurance on freight insured for time and on disbursements for a total sum up to 25 percent of the insured value of the vessel; the amount on disbursements, however, included in that 25 percent being limited to ten percent. Premiums, reducing *pro rata* monthly, and returns of premium subject to "and arrival," may also be insured.

The court, in *Conners Marine v. British and Foreign*,[49] had occasion to consider the automatic reducing and reinstatement clause in a tugboat policy also containing a collision clause. It was held that where the face amount had been reduced to zero by payment of a collision loss, the assured became obligated to pay a further premium and the full initial premium as well, in order to restore the original face amount of the policy.

In *Portsmouth*,[50] the court had occasion to construe the term "pro rata monthly premium" as used in the "continuation" clause of the AIH form; i.e., if the policy is extended by notice given under the clause and the risk as so extended attaches for any part of the month after the original expiration date of the policy, the whole of a month's premium becomes due and payable; the amount of the monthly premium so payable is that pro-

---

48. *Usher v. Noble*, (1810) 12 East 639.
49. 1938 AMC 645 (St.,N.Y.).

portion of the whole premium which the month bears to the whole time period of the policy.

Miscellaneous

Where an underwriter has a claim for additional premiums, that claim must be timely made. For example, in *Hamdi & Ibrahim v. Reliance Ins. Co.*,[51] the underwriter failed to assert claims for additional premiums either at the trial court level or on appeal; it was held that the claim was waived, especially where more than a simple mathematical calculation was involved.

In *Baja California*,[52] the plaintiff, through a broker, insured three lots of cargo under an open policy against war risks, the name of the vessel and sailing dates being unknown because secret. After the insurances were effected, plaintiff caused them to be cancelled and applied for similar insurance under the federal government's cargo war risk insurance scheme at a lower rate. In the meantime, unknown to the parties, the vessel had sailed and had been attacked and sunk. The managers of the government scheme declined the application because the vessel was not in "good safety" at the time of the application. Plaintiff thereupon sued on his policies, claiming mistake or seeking reformation. It was held that the policies had been cancelled; there was no mistake nor any basis for reformation.

Although under American law a contract for the sale of a vessel is not cognizable in admiralty, new agreements made in connection with the performance of the contract of sale may be. Thus, in *Munson Line v. Vervliet*,[53] it was held that the court had jurisdiction to hear and determine the effect of an agreement by which insurance premiums were to be arranged and paid by the seller and extended to the buyer at the latter's request.

50. 54 F.Supp. 2, 1944 AMC 384 (D.,Md.).
51. 291 F.2d 437, 1961 AMC 1987 (2d Cir.).
52. 60 F.Supp. 995, 1945 AMC 461 (S.D.N.Y.).
53. 39 F.Supp. 945, 1941 AMC 959 (E.D.N.Y.).

CHAPTER VII

INSURABLE INTEREST

In General

It is important to recognize that whether or not the assured has an insurable interest is a matter which is to be considered independently of the terms of the particular policy. Since insurance is, in essence, a contract of indemnity, it is the existence of an insurable interest which distinguishes indemnity from mere gaming or wagering contracts—which are interdicted by Section 4, Marine Insurance Act, 1906. The law in the United States does not differ significantly, although life insurance policies appear to fit into a totally different category, and the absence of an insurable interest under a life policy seems to occasion no difficulty.

The definition of insurable interest in Section 5 of the Marine Insurance Act, 1906, is clear, concise, and to the point:

(1) Subject to the provisions of this Act, every person has an insurable interest who is interested in a marine adventure.

(2) In particular, a person is interested in a marine adventure where he stands in any legal or equitable relation to the adventure or to any insurable property at risk therein, in consequence of which he may benefit by the safety or due arrival of insurable property, or may be prejudiced by its loss, or by damage thereto, or by the detention thereof, or may incur liability in respect thereof.

Generally speaking, it would seem that anyone holding any type of title to, or security interest in, a maritime adventure has an insurable interest in it. For example, the charterer of a tugboat, having the vessel in his possession and being liable for its preservation or value to whomever had legal right of ownership, has an insurable interest even though the charter might be void on account of the dissolution of the owning partnership.[1]

In *Hooper v. Robinson,*[2] the leading case on the subject in the United States, the court had this to say about insurable interest:

A right of property in a thing is not always indispensable to an insurable interest. Injury from its loss or benefit from its preservation to accrue to the assured may be sufficient, and a contingent interest thus

---

1. *Washington State Bear,* 220 P.2d 754 (St.,Wash.), 1924 AMC 620.
2. *Hooper v. Robinson,* 98 U.S. 528 (1878).

arising may be made the subject of a policy. In the law of marine insurance, insurable interests are multiform and very numerous. The agent, factor, bailee, carrier, trustee, consignee, mortgagee, and every other lien-holder, may insure to the extent of his own interest in that to which such interest relates; and by the clause, "on account of whom it may concern," for all others to the extent of their respective interests, where there is previous authority or subsequent ratification. Numerous as are the parties of the clauses named, they are but a small portion of those who have the right to insure.

In *Lucena v. Craufurd*,[3] the court explained insurable interest as follows:

> A man is interested in a thing to whom advantage may arise or prejudice happen from the circumstances which may attend it; . . . and whom it importeth that its condition as to safety or other quality should continue. Interest does not necessarily imply a right to the whole or part of the thing, nor necessarily and exclusively that which may be the subject of privation, but the having some relation to, or concern in, the subject of the insurance; which relation or concern, by the happening of the perils insured against, may be so affected as to produce a damage, detriment or prejudice to the person insuring. And where a man is so circumstanced with respect to matters exposed to certain risks and dangers as to have a moral certainty of advantage or benefit but for those risks and dangers, he may be said to be interested in the safety of the thing. To be interested in the preservation of a thing is to be so circumstanced with respect to it as to have benefit from its existence, prejudice from its destruction.[4]

The presumption is in favor of an insurable interest, if possible, "for . . . after underwriters have received the premium, the objection that there was no insurable interest is often, as nearly as possible, a technical objection and one which has no real merit, certainly not as between the assured and the insurer."[5]

An insurable interest must in all cases at the time of the loss be an interest, legal or equitable, and not merely an expectation, however probable.[6] The assured must have an interest in the subject matter insured at the time of the loss, although he need not be interested when the insurance is effected, subject to the qualification (as set forth in Section 6) that

---

3. *Lucena v. Craufurd*, (1806) 2 Bos. & P.N.R. 269, H.L.

4. *Wilson v. Jones*, (1867) L.R. 2 Exch. 139; *Seagrave v. Union Marine Insce. Co.*, (1866) L.R. 1 C.P. 305; *Moran, Galloway & Co. v. Uzielli*, (1905) 2 K.B. 555; *Groban v. Pegu*, 331 F.Supp. 883 (S.D.N.Y. 1972), 1972 AMC 460.

5. *Stock v. Inglis*, (1884) 12 Q.B.D. 564, C.A., on appeal *sub nom.*, *Inglis v. Stock*, (1885) 10 App. Cas., H.L.

6. *Moran, Galloway & Co. v. Uzielli, supra.*

where the subject matter is insured, "lost or not lost," the assured may recover although he may not have acquired his interest until after the loss, unless at the time of effecting the contract of insurance the assured was aware of the loss and the insurer was not.[7] In accordance with general principles, the loss in issue must, of course, fall on the assured.[8]

Although neither a shareholder nor a simple creditor of a corporation has any insurable interest in any particular asset of the company,[9] if the policy is properly claused, a shareholder can have an insurable interest.[10]

The interest need not be one vested in possession; an expectancy, coupled with existing title to that out of which the expectancy arises, may be a sufficient insurable interest.[11] This is true, however, as respects freight only insofar as the freight is not repayable in case of loss.[12] But an anticipated commission, or profit expected out of a sale of goods not yet contracted for at the time of loss, is not an insurable interest.[13]

Section 8, Marine Insurance Act, 1906, makes it clear that a partial interest is insurable.[14]

Types of Insurable Interests

There are many varied types of insurable interests. For example:

Defeasible or Contingent Interest

A defeasible interest is one which may be undone or rendered void. For example, captors under English law have an insurable interest in property captured in time of war but with its attendant liabilities; i.e., a liability to be ordered to restore the property and pay costs.[15]

7. Sec. 6, Marine Insurance Act, 1906; *Anderson v. Morice*, (1875) L.R. 10 C.P. 609, *aff'd* (1876), 1 App. Cas. 713, H.L. See, also, *Ada*, 1925 AMC 393 (N.Y.A.D.), *rev'd* on other grounds, 1926 AMC 1 (N.Y. Ct. App.).

8. *Sutherland v. Pratt*, (1843) 11 M.W. 296; *Reinhart Co. v. Joshua Hoyle & Sons, Ltd.*, (1960) 2 Lloyd's Rep. 483, varied (1961), 1 Lloyd's Rep. 346, C.A.

9. *Macaura v. Northern Assce. Co.*, (1925) A.C. 619, (1925) All E.R. Rep. 51.

10. *Wilson v. Jones, supra*. See, also, *Seaman v. Enterprise F. & M. Ins. Co.*, 18 F. 250 (CA Mo. 1883).

11. *Welded Tube v. Hartford Fire*, 1973 AMC 555 (E.D. Pa.); Marine Insurance Act, 1906, Sec. 12.

12. *Santa Christina*, 26 F.2d 967 (CA-9), 1928 AMC 1074.

13. *Stockdale v. Dunlop*, (1840) 151 E.R. 391.

14. *Stock v. Inglis, supra; Wilson v. Jones, supra; Ebsworth v. Alliance Mar. Ins.*, (1873) L.R. 8 C.P. 596, *rev'd* by consent, (1874) 43 L.J.C.P. 394, N., Ex. Ch.

15. Marine Insurance Act, 1906, Secs. 7(1) and 7(2); *Sparkes v. Marshall*, (1836) 132 E.R. 293; *Colonial Ins. Co. of New Zealand v. Adelaide Ins. Co.*, (1886) 12 App. Cas. 128, P.C. (wheat covered as soon as loaded aboard); *Crowley v. Cohen*, (1832) 110 E.R. 172; *Hill v. Scott*, (1895) 2 Q.B. 713, C.A.; *Stephens v. Australasian Insce Co.*, (1872) L.R. 8 C.P. 18 (declaration under an open cargo policy amended after loss to rectify mistake in not declaring when shipped on deck and subsequently jettisoned); *Briggs v. Merchant Traders' Assocn.*, (1849) 13 Q.B. 167, 116

Interest in Profits

One having a reasonable expectation of profits from a marine adventure may take out insurance to protect such profits, but such profits must be insured as such and policies upon a loss of cargo or upon freight will not cover a loss of profits.[16]

Interest in Ship

Clearly, one owning a vessel, or an interest therein, has an insurable interest. And this is true even though he may have chartered it upon terms and conditions which would enable him to recover from the charterer the full value of the vessel in the event of a loss. This principle is embodied in Section 14(3) of the Marine Insurance Act, 1906, reading:

> The owner of insurable property has an insurable interest in respect of the full value thereof, notwithstanding that some third person may have agreed, or be liable, to indemnify him in case of loss.[17]

Interest in Freight

The term "freight" includes the profit derivable by a shipowner from the employment of his ship to carry his own goods or movables, as well as

---

E.R. 1227 (insurance effected to cover "average expenses" payable by reason of salvage services having been rendered; vessel and cargo later lost); *Piper v. Royal Exchange Assurance,* (1932) 44 Ll.L.Rep 103 (purchaser of vessel abroad has contingent interest in vessel's arrival even though vessel at seller's risk until arrival in England); *Stirling v. Vaughn,* (1809) 11 East 428.

16. *Leonard v. Bosch,* 71 A. 1134 (St. N.J.); *Stockdale v. Dunlop, supra* (assured must either be the owner of goods or must have entered into a binding contract to purchase); *Barclay v. Cousins,* (1802) 102 E.R. 478 (profits of a cargo employed in trade on the coast of Africa); *Lucena v. Craufurd, supra; Grant v. Parkinson,* (1781) 99 E.R. 515; *Hodgson v. Glover,* (1805) 102 E.R. 1308 (necessary under a valued policy on goods to prove that some profit would be realized); *Eyre v. Glover,* (1812) 104 E.R. 1071 (under open policy, burden on assured to show amount of profit had goods arrived); *Wilson v. Jones, supra* (policy on profits to be derived from laying of Atlantic cable); *Patapsco Ins. Co. v. Coulter,* 28 U.S. 222 (1830) (profit on sale of goods).

17. *Hobbs v. Hannam,* (1811) 3 Camp. 93, N.P. (shipowner has insurable interest in chartered vessel even though charterer covenants to indemnify him in case of loss); *Piper v. Royal Exchange Assurance,* (1932) 44 Ll.L.Rep. 103, K.B.D. (seller of a yacht located in Norway was at the risk of the seller until the yacht arrived in London; purchaser procured a hull policy on the yacht prior to sailing from Norway; underwriters paid for damage sustained en route and counterclaimed later for recoupment on grounds of no insurable interest in the purchaser. Held: underwriters succeeded; purchaser had no insurable interest in the yacht at time damage sustained); *WPL Marine Services, Inc. v. Woods-Tucker Aircraft & Marine Leasing Corp.,* 361 So.2d 1304 (St. La.). (Under charter of a vessel, owner entitled to a stipulated loss

freight payable by a third party, but does not include passage money. Section 90, Schedule 1, Rule 16, Marine Insurance Act, 1906. This does not mean, however, that passage money cannot be insured specifically.[18]

Anticipated freight may also be insured and will include, in the case of a chartered vessel, not only the charter hire but the full amount expected to be earned during the period of the insurance.[19] This is true even though the formal charter party has not been drafted and executed, so long as the parties are in agreement upon its terms.[20]

A charterer may have an insurable interest in freight because a loss of the cargo results in a loss of bill of lading freight, certainly to the extent of the excess of freight over charter hire.[21] Dead freight is, of course, insurable.[22] The builder of a vessel, to whom part of the purchase price is owed, has an insurable interest in the freight.[23] Insurance effected upon "charges of the said assured upon said cargo or any portion thereof" includes freight.[24]

The insurable interest in chartered freight commences when the ship begins the voyage which it must make in order to acquire an inchoate interest in the freight.[25]

Cockburn, C. J., in *Barber v. Flemming, supra,* put it nicely:

> From the moment that a vessel is chartered to go from Port A to Port B, and at Port B to take a cargo and bring it home to England, or to take it to any Port, which I will call Port C, for freight, the shipowner having got such a contract, has an interest unquestionably in earning the freight secured to him by the charter; and having such an interest it is manifest that that interest is insurable; and he loses the freight and benefit of his charter just as much by the ship being disabled on a voyage to the Port at which the cargo is to be loaded, and from which it is to be bought, as he would lose it by the disaster arising from the perils

value; insurance procured by charterer exceeded that value. Upon a total loss, charterer entitled to the excess over amount payable to owner.)

18. *Flint v. Flemyng,* (1830) 109 E.R. 704; *Driscoll v. Millville Marine Ins. Co.,* (1883) 23 N.B.R. 160, *on appeal,* 2 S.C.R. 183 (Can.); *Truscott v. Christie,* (1820) 2 Brod. & B. 320.

19. *Papadimitriou v. Henderson,* (1939) 3 All E.R. 908; *Robertson v. Petros M. Nomikos, Ltd.,* (1939) 2 All E.R. 723, (1939) A.C. 371; *Ins. Co. of Valley of Va. v. Mordecai,* 63 U.S. 111 (1860); *Roanoke,* 1924 AMC 790 (CA-9).

20. *Roanoke, supra,* n. 19.

21. *Asfar & Co. v. Blundell,* (1895) 2 Q.B. 196, (1896) 1 Q.B. 123, C.A.; *Aylde v. Union Marine Ins. Co.,* (1874) 10 N.S.R. 205 (C.A.) (Can.). And see *Solomon v. Miller,* (1865) 2 W.W. & A'B 135 (Aus.).

22. *Puller v. Staniforth,* (1809) 102 E.R. 993.

23. *Queen Insce. Co. of America v. Hoffar-Beeching Shipyards, Inc.,* (1932) 3 W.W.R. 240, 46 B.C.R. 233 (Can.).

24. *Gulf & Southern S.S. Co., Inc. v. British Traders Insce. Co., Ltd.,* (1930) 1 K.B. 451, (1929) All E.R. 601.

25. *Foley v. United Fire etc. Ins. Co. of Sydney,* (1870) L.R. 5 C.P. 155; *Rankin v. Potter,* (1873) L.R. 6 H.L. 83; *Barber v. Flemming,* (1869) L.R. 5 Q.B. 59.

insured against between the Port of loading and the Port of discharge. It is therefore an appreciable tangible interest, and I entertain no doubt that it can be insured.

It appears that the insurable interest in bill of lading freight commences when the cargo has been contracted for, although none of it has been loaded onto the vessel at the time of the loss.[26]

In line with the basic principle that insurance is a contract of indemnity, Blackburn, J., in *Barber v. Flemming, supra,* concluded that an insurable interest in freight commenced when expense was incurred to earn the freight. The present editors of Arnould are clearly of the view that the shipowner's insurable interest in freight should commence as soon as the shipowner makes a contract pursuant to which, in the normal course of events, he will earn freight. They point out (paragraph 336):

> . . . the principle of indemnity was long ago departed from in insurance on freight when the right of the assured to recover in all cases the gross rate was recognized, and it is now clearly possible to recover for a loss of freight when little or no expense has been incurred by the assured.

Interest in Advance Freight

In the case of advance freight, the person advancing the freight has an insurable interest insofar as such freight is not repayable in case of loss.[27] The terms of the agreement under which the freight was advanced govern whether or not it is repayable in event of loss.[28]

Interest in Charges of Insurance

The assured has an insurable interest in the charges of any insurance which he may effect.[29] Customarily, the charges of insurance are made up of the premium paid and the brokerage if paid by the assured.

Interest of Vendor and Purchaser

When the property in a ship or vessel passes to the purchaser, he has an insurable interest.[30] The insurable interest of a vendor ceases, of course,

26. *Warre v. Miller,* (1825) 4 B. & C.R. 538.

27. Sec. 12, Marine Insurance Act, 1906. *Allison v. Bristol Mar. Ins. Co.,* (1876) 1 App. Cas. 209.

28. *Allison v. Bristol Mar. Ins. Co., supra; Watson & Co. v. Shankland,* (1873) 2 Asp. M.L.C. 115, H.L.

29. Sec. 13, Marine Insurance Act, 1906. *Usher v. Noble,* (1810) 104 E.R. 249.

30. *Sparkes v. Marshall,* (1835-42) E.R. Rep. 597; *Inglis v. Stock,* (1885) 10 App. Cas. 263,

upon the property passing, but it must be recognized that the parties may agree that the property shall pass but that the risk shall remain in the vendor during the transit. Again, the unpaid vendor has a lien on the goods, and there is no doubt that the vendor has an insurable interest in these events.[31] Title to goods sold c.i.f. generally passes to the purchaser upon delivery to the carrier unless the goods are sold against presentation of negotiable instruments.[32] Thus, the risk passes to the c.i.f. purchaser on shipment but the property will not generally pass to him until tender of the documents and payment of the price. It would appear that both a c.i.f. seller and a c.i.f. purchaser would have an insurable interest in the goods at least until such time as the documents have been negotiated to the c.i.f. purchaser against payment. Thereafter, the vendor would have no insurable interest.

It was held in *Clay v. Harrison*[33] that if the seller of goods exercises his right of stoppage *in transitu*, the vendee thereupon has no insurable interest. But query: since stoppage *in transitu* does not now rescind the contract, the validity of *Clay v. Harrison* may be doubted. It has been the position, at least since the passage of the sale of goods acts in the various countries, that stoppage *in transitu* does not affect the property in the goods; i.e., a contract of sale is not rescinded by the mere exercise by an unpaid seller of his right of lien or retention or stoppage *in transitu*. Thus, the vendor by stopping the goods *in transitu* does not thereby regain title to the property.[34] Accordingly, the position is analogous to that between a mortgagor and mortgagee; i.e., the unpaid seller has an insurable interest to the extent of his vendor's lien, and the purchaser has an insurable interest in the full value of the goods.

To be sure, it is often difficult to ascertain the exact moment when the risk of loss passes from the vendor to the vendee. Clearly, the terms of the contract should govern. The true test is *a fortiori* has the risk passed to the buyer at the time of the loss. See Section 7(2), Marine Insurance Act, 1906, reading:

> In particular, where the buyer of goods has insured them, he has an insurable interest, notwithstanding that he might, at his election, have rejected the goods, or have treated them as at the seller's risk, by reason of the latter's delay in making delivery or otherwise.[35]

5 Asp. M.L.C. 422, H.L.; *Colonial Ins. Co. of New Zealand v. Adelaide Marine Ins. Co.,* (1896) S.A.L.R. 84, 12 App. Cas. 128.

31. *Outram v. Smith,* (1876) 11 N.S.R. (2 R. & C.) 187 (Can.); *Seagrave v. Union Marine Ins. Co.,* (1886) L.R. 1 C.P. 305; *Pugh v. Wylie,* (1876) 11 N.S.R. 177 (C.A.) (Can.).

32. *York-Shipley v. Atlantic Mutual Ins. Co.,* 474 F.2d 8, 1973 AMC 584 (5th Cir.).

33. (1829) 109 E.R. 388.

34. *United States Steel Products Co. v. Great Western Railway,* (1916) 1 A.C. 189.

35. *Anderson v. Morice,* (1876) 1 App. Cas. 713, H.L.; *Harlem,* 1927 AMC 1088 (N.Y.M.) (coal sold f.o.b. buyer's barge, seller to tow it to destination and buyer having right to reject on inspection; barge sank after being loaded. Held: seller had no insurable interest) *Eu-*

Interest of Trustee

A trustee holding legal title for the beneficiary of the trust may insure to the full value of the subject matter.[36] Both the trustee and the beneficiary have an insurable interest.[37] An equitable interest is insurable.[38]

Interest of Consignee

Section 14(2) ofo the Marine Insurance Act, 1906, states

> A mortgagee, *consignee*, or other person having an interest in the subject matter insured may insure on behalf and for the benefit of other persons interested as well as for his own benefit.[39]

Where the named consignee in a bill of lading was engaged in a joint venture with a co-plaintiff, both had an insurable interest in the goods as soon as they were identified for shipment.[40] Under a policy insuring "for the account of whom it may concern," the consignee in a bill of lading acquired an insurable interest in the goods, and the policy covers, as well, any person whom the consignee intends to be insured.[41]

Interest of "Other Person"

Ascertaining the insurable interest of an "other person" can be troublesome and often complex. For example, in *O'Donnell Towing & Transp. Company v. Marine Transit Corp. and Globe and Rutgers Fire Ins. Co.*,[42] the plaintiff towboat owner entered into a joint venture with Marine Transit

---

patoria—San Juan, 30 F.2d 782 (CA-9), 1929 AMC 540 (assignment of bills of lading does not divest assured of insurable interest where title to goods was not to pass until delivery of them to assignee); *Plata Amer. v. Lancashire*, 1957 AMC 1417 (N.Y.M.).

36. *Lucena v. Craufurd, supra; Ebsworth v. Alliance Marine Insce. Co.*, (1873) L.R. 8 C.P. 596, *rev'd* by consent, (1874) 43 L.J.C.P. 394, N., Ex. Ch.

37. *Ex. p. Houghton, Ex. p. Gribble*, (1810) 34 E.R. 97.

38. *Clark v. Scottish Imperial Ins. Co.*, (1879) 4 S.C.R. 192 (Can.); *Esperanza*, 1930 AMC 293 (CA-2); *Ada*, 1924 AMC 468 (N.Y.M.); *Regent*, 57 F.Supp. 242 (E.D.N.Y.), 1945 AMC 25; *Hurona*, 224 Ap. 531, 231 NYS 503 (N.Y.A.D.), 1929 AMC 258 (contract purchaser of vessel).

39. This provision merely enunciates the law as decided in *Hibbert v. Carter*, (1787) 99 E.R. 1355; *Hill v. Secretan*, (1798) 126 E.R. 924; and *Wolff v. Horncastle*, (1798) 126 E.R. 924.

40. *Welded Tube v. Hartford Fire*, 1973 AMC 555, (E.D. Pa.).

41. *Welded Tube v. Hartford Fire, supra*. And see, generally, *Seagrave v. Union Marine Insce. Co., supra; Stockdale v. Dunlop, supra; Ebsworth v. Alliance Marine Insce. Co., supra; Sutherland v. Pratt*, (1843) 152 E.R. 1092 (pledgee of bills of lading entitled to sue in own name); *Moran, Galloway & Co. v. Uzielli, supra; Cusack v. Mutual Ins. Co.*, (1862) 6 L.C. Jur. 97, 10 R.J.R.Q. 194 (Can.).

42. *O'Donnell Towing & Transp. Company v. Marine Transit Corp. and Globe and Rutgers Fire Ins. Co.*, 264 NY 101, 190 NE 165, 1934 AMC 762.

Corporation to transport grain in barges owned by the latter. Marine Transit was to insure the cargo with carrier's liability insurance, to cover the interests of the plaintiff and itself in the cargo, and the legal liability of each of them. Premium costs were to be borne equally by the two parties.

A loss occurred; the shipper brought suit against the plaintiff towboat company, and recovered. The plaintiff paid the judgment with funds received from another insurance policy covering the operations of the tug, and then brought suit on the policy Marine Transit had procured.

The policy was issued to Marine Transit "on account of whom it may concern." The court assumed, without deciding, that the policy covered and was intended to cover the plaintiff but found that typewritten riders on the policy limited coverage to a deficiency where there was prior insurance. As there was prior insurance that was paid in full, the plaintiff was held not entitled to recovery. In discussing the clause "on account of whom it may concern," the court stated that it would be applied to the interest of the party for whose benefit it was intended by the person who procured or odered the insurance, but that the term would not carry the benefit of the policy to a risk or interest not fairly within the contemplation of the parties to the policy.

In *Santa Christina*,[43] the court stated that it could look to the surrounding circumstances to ascertain whether the person claiming the benefits of the policy was such a person as those effecting the policy had in contemplation. In this instance, freight was payable in any event, and it was therefore held that the shipowner had no insurable interest in the freight. In *Dudley*,[44] the court stated that the phrase "for whom it may concern" embraced the interests of any person whatever who might ultimately appear to be concerned, and included any person within that category who subsequently ratified or adopted it.

In *F.A. Lowery and Lowery Sisters*,[45] a canal operator of a chartered tug and barges contracted with the tug owner that the charterer would provide legal liability insurance for both owner and charterer. A barge was sunk in a collision, and its cargo was lost. The charterer became insolvent and did nothing, and the tug was held liable *in rem* for the cargo loss. The court held that to be covered by a policy issued for the account of whom it may concern, it must appear that the person claiming the benefit of the insurance had an insurable interest in the subject matter covered by the insurance; that the tug owner had no insurable interest in the charterer's "legal liability as carrier," and that since this was the subject matter of the insurance the tug owner was not protected by the phrase "for

---

43. *Santa Christina*, 26 F.2d 967 (CA-9), 1928 AMC 1074.
44. *Dudley*, 1928 AMC 1806 (N.Y.M.).
45. *F.A. Lowery and Lowery Sisters*, 70 F.2d 324 (CA-2), 1934 AMC 581.

whom it may concern." The court recognized, in effect, that it was the intention of the charterer to cover the legal liability of the tug owner, but unfortunately its declaration to the insurer did not have the effect of extending coverage to a new subject matter not included within the terms of the policy.

In *Chateaugay v. Eastern Tr. Co.*,[46] the shipowner placed and paid for cargo insurance "for whom it may concern." The court held that the shipowner had an insurable interest in cargo on his vessel.[47]

In *Sephie*,[48] the court held a charterer to have an insurable interest where the charter party provided for a gross hire and the charterer collected freight, both being payable in advance and to be irrevocably retained irrespective of the loss of the vessel. The underwriter there had insured "disbursements and/or profits on freight" without knowing of the charterer's relation to the vessel.

In *Ruth*,[49] a carrier procured insurance on goods being carried "for account of themselves, loss, if any, payable to assured." The goods were damaged by a peril excepted by the bill of lading. Although holding that the carrier had an insurable interest, the court noted that the carrier could collect only for its special loss; i.e., its liability to the shipper under the bill of lading, and there being no liability under that instrument, the carrier could not collect from the underwriters.

The intent at the time of negotiation of the policy governs the identity of persons insured under the clause "for whom it may concern," and where there was no intent to include the owner of the vessel after termination of the charter, insurance procured by the charterer does not extend to the owner.[50]

A ship repairer has an insurable interest in a vessel under repair sufficient to support insurance against liability for injury to third parties.[51]

A policy covering cargo in a warehouse against risk of "non-delivery" was held to be limited to protection against physical loss from any external cause and did not include protection against loss resulting from the issuance of spurious warehouse receipts; i.e., the non-delivery risk stated in the policy was not an indemnity insurance against the non-existence of the cargo, and the holder of fraudulently issued warehouse receipts did not have an insurable interest in the non-existent cargo.[52]

---

46. *Chateaugay v. Eastern Tr. Co.*, 12 F.Supp. 753 (E.D.N.Y.), 1935 AMC 1320.
47. *Canadian Co-op v. John Russell*, 1934 AMC 7 (CA-2).
48. *Sephie*, 9 F.2d 304 (CA-2) 1926 AMC 447.
49. *Ruth*, 287 F. 464 (CA-9), 1923 AMC 357.
50. *Greenbrae*, 1935 AMC 221 (Cal.St.).
51. *Monterey—Dixie*, 1928 AMC 1690 (N.Y.A.D.).
52. *Curacao Tr. Co. v. Fed. Ins. Co.*, 137 F.2d 911 (CA-2), 1943 AMC 1050. See, also, *Plata American Trading v. Lancashire, supra.*

In *Yellowtail*,[53] the court held that the clause in a policy "as their interest may appear" postulates the assureds' respective interests at the time of loss and not as of the time the policy was issued, and, consequently, their respective right to the proceeds of the policy upon total loss of the vessel depends wholly upon the contract of insurance (maritime mortgage and lien claimants).

The importance of having an insurable interest was demonstrated in the *Sucre—Tamare*.[54] In that case, the *Sucre* was time chartered to the Creole Co., and the vessel's hull and P & I policies endorsed to include the interest of the Creole Co. as time charterer. The vessel was damaged in a collision with the *Tamare*, the latter being solely at fault. The *Sucre's* underwriters having paid for the repairs, claim was made for the repair costs and detention loss against the *Tamare* which, it so happened, was demise chartered to the Creole Co. There being an identity of interest, the arbitrator held that the underwriters on the *Sucre* had waived their subrogation rights against the Creole Co. by extending their policies to cover the interests of the Creole Co. as time charterer of the *Sucre*.

In *The Narco and The Lolita*,[55] the court held that a demise charterer of a tug had an insurable interest in the owner's running down risk insurance. The decision is difficult to understand and must be construed in the light of the specific language in the Running Down Clause.

Willamette-Western v. Columbia-Pacific[56] involved an interesting interplay between a waiver of subrogation and an insurable interest. There, the owner of a floating crane chartered it. The owner's hull policy had a provision in it waiving subrogation against "charterers," of which the charterer was unaware. After a loss while in the care and custody of the charterer, the hull underwriters paid the owner on loan receipts, whereupon the owner brought suit against the charterer. The court held that the owner was not entitled to recover since this would constitute "indirect subrogation" and permit the underwriters to escape the effect of the waiver provision.

In *Boston Old Colony v. Charles Orland Co.*,[57] involving a suit by a cargo underwriter against its assured for premiums allegedly due on shipments, the court held that an insurable interest in the goods must be proved and there was no such interest where the defendant acted only as a broker who had not been instructed by his principals to insure their goods and whose brokerage commission was not contingent upon their safe delivery.

53. *Yellowtail*, 104 F.2d 131 (CA-9), 1939 AMC 1278.
54. *Sucre—Tamare*, 1950 AMC 493 (Arb.).
55. *The Narco and The Lolita*, 258 F.2d 718, 1958 AMC 2404, modified 286 F.2d 600 (CA-5), 1961 AMC 1999.
56. *Willamette-Western v. Columbia-Pacific*, 466 F.2d 1390 (CA-9), 1972 AMC 2128.
57. *Boston Old Colony v. Charles Orland Co.*, 1975 AMC 2066 (N.Y.M.).

Because a tug owner might be found negligent in operating a towed barge belonging to a third party, the court, in *N.Y. & L.B.R.R. v. U.S.*,[58] held that the tug owner had a sufficient insurable interest in the barge to justify it being included as a named assured in the barge owner's P & I policy.[59]

The importance of arranging proper coverage for an insurable interest is aptly demonstrated in *Sample No. 1*,[60] where a tug owner and a barge owner each had its hull policies endorsed so that the other was named as an additional assured, but the tug owner was not named as an additional assured on the policy covering cargo on the barge. When the tug negligently stranded the barge, resulting in damage to the cargo, cargo underwriters sued the tug. Since the negligence was that of the tug, the tug's underwriters were compelled to respond in damages. Had the tug owner secured a waiver of subrogation from the cargo underwriters or been named as an additional assured on the cargo policy (assuming proper notification to the underwriters that the purpose of so doing was to waive subrogation), he would have been protected.[61]

It cannot, however, be too strongly emphasized that it is the obligation of the assured to notify the underwriters of any other party having a material interest in the insured venture who is insisting upon protection by way of the insurance coverage, as this materially changes the underwriters' risk. In this connection, see Section 18(1) and (2), Marine Insurance Act, 1906, reading:

> (1) Subject to the provisions of this section, the assured must disclose to the insurer, before the contract is concluded, every material circumstance which is known to the assured, and the assured is deemed to know every circumstance which, in the ordinary course of

---

58. *N.Y. & L.B.R.R. v. U.S.*, 1976 AMC 2253 (S.D.N.Y.).

59. *Merchants' Marine Ins. Co. v. Barss*, (1888) 15 S.E.R. 185, *aff'ming* 26 N.B.R. 339 ("whom it may concern"; open to plaintiff to show an insurable interest and that it was intended that he be included); *Merchants' Marine Ins. Co. v. Rumsey*, (1884) 9 S.C.R. 577, *aff'ming* 16 N.S.R. 220 (plaintiffs joint venturers providing charterers with cargo held to have insurable interest); and *York-Shipley v. Atlantic Mutual*, 474 F.2d 8 (CA-5), 1973 AMC 584 (title to goods shipped c.i.f. passes to buyer upon their delivery to carrier, and seller ceases to have an insurable interest).

60. *Sample No. 1*, 262 F.2d 565 (CA-5) 1959 AMC 397, *Rel pro* 1956 AMC 1799.

61. For illustrations of where proper coverage was placed with respect to insurable interests, see *Twenty Grand Offshore v. West India Carriers*, 492 F.2d 679 (CA-5), 1974 AMC 2254; *Hartford Fire v. Port Everglades*, 454 F.2d 276 (CA-5), 1972 AMC 316; *Fluor Western v. G. & H. Offshore*, 447 F.2d 35 (CA-5), 1972 AMC 406. But, compare *Brittingham v. Tugboat Underwriting*, 1971 AMC 1639 (St. Md.) (barge demise chartered to tug owner not covered by a policy which excludes vessels "owned by" the tug owner), and *Dow Chemical Co. V. Thomas Allen*, 349 F.Supp. 1354 (E.D. La.), 1974 AMC 781 (tug's P & I named the barge owner as an additional assured for liability "in respect" of the tug; policy afforded no coverage to a barge owner whose liability arose from its negligence in ordering dangerous navigation by the tug).

business, ought to be known by him. If the assured fails to make such disclosure, the insurer may avoid the contract.

(2) Every circumstance is material which would influence the judgment of a prudent insurer in fixing the premium, or determining whether he will take the risk.

Interest of Master and Crew

The master or any member of the crew of a ship has an insurable interest in respect of his wages.[62] This is statutory, it being doubted in older cases that a seaman could insure his wages. But the effects of a master could always be insured.[63]

Reinsurance

Reinsurance is a perfect example of a contingent interest, and is specifically covered by the Marine Insurance Act, 1906, Section 9, reading:

(1) The insurer under a contract of marine insurance has an insurable interest in his risk, and may reinsure in respect of it.

(2) Unless the policy otherwise provides, the original assured has no right or interest in respect of such reinsurance.

Under the common law, reinsurance was valid, but from 1745 to 1864 in England was prohibited by statute. It appears to have always been recognized as valid in the United States.[64] A policy of reinsurance attaches from the time of the original policy although effected later.[65]

Interestingly, the policy need not state that it is a reinsurance,[66] but this is subject to the qualification that there may be circumstances where a failure to mention that the policy is by way of reinsurance amounts to non-disclosure, such as, for instance, where the primary assured is known by the reassured but not by the reinsurer to be a "special risk." Nor is notice of abandonment to the reinsurer required in the event of a constructive total loss.[67]

The classic language in a policy of reinsurance reads: "being a reinsurance subject to the same clauses and conditions as the original policy,

---

62. Sec. 11, Marine Insurance Act, 1906.
63. *Anstey v. Ocean Mar. Ins. Co.*, (1913) 88 L.J.K.B. 218.
64. Phillips, *Law of Insurance*, Sec. 377.
65. *Marine Insurance Co. Ltd. v. Grimmer*, (1944) 2 All E.R. 197, C.A.
66. Sec. 26(2), Marine Insurance Act, 1906. *Mackenzie v. Whitworth*, (1875) 45 L.J.Q.B. 233, C.A.
67. Sec. 62(9), Marine Insurance Act, 1906; *Uzielli v. Boston Mar. Ins. Co.*, (1884) 15 Q.B. 11; and see *Aronsen, Inc. v. Compton*, 495 F.2d 674 (CA-2), 1974 AMC 480, (1974) 1 Lloyd's

and to pay as may be paid."[68] As might be expected, interpretation of the clause has given rise to much litigation.[69]

Yukon[70] involved an interesting intermixture of covered versus non-covered perils under a policy of reinsurance. In that case, a collision occurred between the insured vessel and another. The crew abandoned and went aboard the other vessel, which refused to tow the disabled vessel to shallow water. Shortly after the collision, a fire broke out aboard the abandoned vessel, and explosion occurred, and it sank. The reinsurer insured in respect of loss "in consequence of fire only." The court held that the dominating and efficient cause of the vessel's loss was the fire and, as the damage from collision could not be segregated from the loss by fire, the reinsurer was held liable.

All the defenses available to the original underwriter against the assured are available to the reinsurer.[71] This includes the right of a rein-

---

Rep. 590, and *British Dominions Gen. Ins. Co. v. Duder,* (1915) 2 K.B. 394, (1914-15) All E.R. 176, C.A. (criticizing *Uzielli* and holding that reinsurers are entitled to take advantage of a compromise effected by the original underwriters, but must also pay their proportion of the expenses incurred in securing the compromise).

68. *Charlesworth v. Faber,* (1900) 5. Com. Cas. 408.

69. For example, *Eddystone Marine Insce. Co., Ex P. Western Insce. Co.,* (1892) 2 Ch. 423, and; *Allemannia F. Ins. Co. of Pittsburgh v. Firemen's Ins. Co. of Baltimore,* 209 U.S. 326 (1907) (payment by original insurer not a condition precedent to recovery by the original insurer against the reinsurer); *Hicks v. Poe,* 269 U.S. 118 (1925) (liability of reinsurer under a participation contract not affected by insolvency of original insurer or inability of the latter to fulfill its own contracts with the original insured); *Chippendale v. Holt,* (1895) 65 L.J.Q.B. 104; and *Marten v. S.S. Owners' Underwriting Assocn.,* (1902) 71 L.J.K.B. 718 (reinsurer not bound to pay such sum as the original underwriter might have paid, whether liable or not); *Firemen's Fund Insce. Co. v. Western Australian Insce. Co., Ltd., and Atlantic Insce. Co. Ltd.,* (1927) All E.R. 243 (original policy did not contain admission of seaworthiness of vessel but policy of reinsurance did; cargo loss was occasioned by unseaworthiness—reinsurers not liable); *Assicurazioni Generali of Trieste v. Royal Exchange Assce. Corpn.,* (1897) 13 T.L.R. 307, *sub nom General Insce. Co., Ltd. of Trieste v. Royal Exchange Assce. Corpn.,* 2 Com. Cas. 144 (original policies contained lighterage clause specifying that each craft or lighter deemed a separate insurance; policy of reinsurance warranted free from all average; partial loss occurred; held, loss covered by the policy); *Reliance Insce. Co. v. Duder,* (1913) 1 K.B. 265, C.A. (three policies of original insurance; reinsurer contended that his policy related only to the third policy and not the other two; held, policy covered all three); cf. *Janson v. Poole,* (1915) 84 L.J.K.B. 1543; *Insce. Co. of North America v. North China Insce. Co.,* (1898) 15 T.L.R. 101, 4 Com. Cas. 67, C.A. (reinsurance of excess liability per named steamer lines; goods intended for named steamer line shipped by tramp steamer; loss not covered); *South British Fire & Marine Insce. Co. of New Zealand v. Da Costa,* (1906) 1 K.B. 456 (policy covering risk of craft, each craft deemed a separate insurance; loss on one craft below limit of reinsurance; loss covered); *Street v. Royal Exchange Assce.,* (1914) 111 L.T. 235, C.A. (compromise of an alternative claim for total or partial loss where reinsurance applied only to total or constructive losses; held covered); *Bergens Dempskibs Assce. Forening v. Sun Insce. Office, Ltd.,* (1930) 37 Ll.L.Rep. 175 (meaning of "arranged" total loss; artificial total loss arrived at by agreement not covered); *Gurney v. Grimmer,* (1932) 44 Ll.L.Rep. 189, C.A. (meaning of "compromised or arranged total loss"); *Marine Insce. Co. Ltd. v. Grimmer, supra* (meaning of term "and/or steamers"). See, also, Chalmers, *Marine Insurance Act, 1906,* Ivamy, 8th ed., fn. 1, p. 17.

70. *Yukon,* 1939 AMC 111 (Arb.).

71. *National Marine Insce. Co. of Australasia v. Halfey,* (1879) 5 V.L.R. 226 (Aus.); *China Traders' Insce. Co. v. Royal Exchange Assce. Corpn.,* (1898) 2 Q.B. 187, C.A.

surer (who had agreed to settle upon representation that the vessel had clearly been stranded and burnt) to contest the claim if facts were concealed which constituted a material misrepresentation and vitiated the assent to settlement.[72] The reinsurer when called upon to perform under his policy is entitled to require the reassured first to show that a loss of the kind reinsured has in fact happened and, secondly, that the reassured has sustained loss and, thirdly, that the reassured has taken all proper and businesslike steps to have the amount of it fairly and carefully ascertained.[73]

In *Western Assce Co., supra,* the vessel was reinsured against the risk of total or constructive total loss only, and provided no claim to attach for "salvage charges." The policy of reinsurance was on the standard Lloyd's form containing the usual printed suing and laboring clause. The vessel stranded. The probable cost of refloating, taking her to a port of repair, and effecting repairs exceeded the agreed value of the vessel but in fact was less than the real repaired value. Consequently, the owners elected not to give notice of abandonment. The ship was refloated and repaired and its owners recovered from the original underwriters 107 percent of their loss (total of expenses of refloating and repairing). The original underwriters then sued the reinsurer for the full amount, either as a constructive total loss or in the alternative for the proportion of the suing and laboring charges. The court held that there had been no constructive total loss as no notice of abandonment had been given, and no recovery could be had for suing and laboring charges as the policy of reinsurance expressly excluded "salvage charges," notwithstanding that the printed suing and laboring clause had not been physically deleted. The decision was cited and followed in *Insurance Company of North America v. U.S. Ins. Co.,*[74] in which the court said in part:

> While the "follow the fortune" clause is certainly a broad one, it is clear the reinsurer is liable only for "a loss of the kind reinsured" (*Western Assurance Co. of Toronto v. Poole, supra*). To determine what type of loss was reinsured, we must turn to the original insurance contract. Construction of the latter contract reveals that it covered "shipments," "voyages," "connecting consignees" and goods while "in transit." The examination before trial . . . makes it crystal clear that the bagging process was not necessary to the transit of the cargo . . . .
>
> The stoppage and bagging of the cargo at Gulfport was an interruption in the transit of the goods and created a shore risk not insured under plaintiff's original insurance contract.

---

72. *The Keresan,* 1927 AMC 577 (N.Y.A.D.).
73. *Western Assce. Co. of Toronto v. Poole,* (1903) 1 K.B. 376.
74. *Insurance Company of North America v. U.S. Ins. Co.,* 332 N.Y.S.2d 520, 1971 AMC 1891.

In essence, the reinsurer stands in the shoes of the original insurer. This right carries over to the extent that the reinsurer also stands in the shoes of the original assured. For example, in the *Gloria*,[75] a cargo reinsurer who had paid its proportion of the loss to the assured was permitted to intervene in proceedings by which the vessel owner was attempting to limit its liability for the cargo loss.

Although the reinsurer must "follow the fortune" of the original underwriter, it does not follow that he is liable for all costs incurred by the latter.[76] Nor is there liability on the reinsurer for the original underwriter's expenses in defending against an unsuccessful action by the assured.[77]

In the absence of inquiry, the original underwriter need not disclose the name of the assured to the reinsurer.[78]

Interest of Mortgagor and Mortagee

Clearly, both the mortgagor and mortgagee have an insurable interest in the subject insured. The Marine Insurance Act, 1906, Section 14(1) reads:

(1) Where the subject matter insured is mortgaged, the mortgagor has an insurable interest in the full value thereof, and the mortgagee has an insurable interest in respect of any sum due or to become due under the mortgage.[79]

Sub-section (2) of Section 14 provides that a mortgagee, *inter alia,* having an interest in the subject matter insured, may insure on behalf and for the benefit of other persons interested as well as for his own benefit.[80]

---

75. *Gloria*, 46 F.2d 925 (CA-5), 1931 AMC 1048.

76. *Versicherungs Und Transport A.G. Daugava v. Henderson and Campbell*, (1934) 39 Com. Cas. 154, *aff'd.* (1934) All E.R. 626, 49 Ll.L.Rep. 252, C.A. (reinsurer not liable for expenses of original underwriter in litigating assured's claim and later settling).

77. *Scottish Metropolitan Assce. Co., Ltd. v. Groom*, (1924) 20 Ll.L.Rep. 44, C.A. See, also, *Amer. Eagle F.I. Co. v. Eagle Star Ins. Co.*, 216 F.2d 176 (CA-9), 1954 AMC 1263. (Reinsurers were held not liable for the original insurer's expenses in attempting to salvage cargo and unsuccessfully prosecuting a libel against the negligent towing tug. The fact that the reinsurers, without prejudice, paid the original cargo loss was not construed as an admission of liability where the original insurer need not have paid.)

78. *Glasgow Assce. Corp. v. Symondson*, (1911) 104 L.T. 254. (The case is interesting in that it describes how reinsurance is written.)

79. This sub-section expresses the substance of *Irving v. Richardson*, (1831) 109 E.R. 1115, and *North British & Mercantile Insce. Co. v. London, Liverpool & Globe Insce. Co.*, (1877) 5 Ch. D. 569, C.A. See, also, *Crawford v. St. Lawrence Insce. Co.*, (1851) 8 U.C.Q.B., C.A., (Can.); *Troop v. Mosier*, (1876) 1 R.E.D. 189, C.A., (Can.); *West v. Seaman*, (1885) Cout. S.C. 723, Cass. S.C. 388, *aff'ming* 17 N.S.R. 207; and *White v. Mann*, 26 Me. 361, (1846).

80. *Richardson v. Home Insce. Co.*, (1871) 21 C.P. 291 (Can.); *West v. Seaman, supra; Irving v. Richardson, supra; Levy & Co. v. Merchants Marine Insce. Co.*, (1885) 52 L.T. 263.

A transfer of title to a vessel, although absolute in form, may in fact be intended as a mortgage and be treated as such.[81] Consequently, the vendor/mortgagor has an insurable interest.

What is the extent of a mortgagee's interest under the policy if the loss is a direct result of an act or omission on the part of the mortgagor-insured which voids the policy? The answer lies in whether the mortgagee's rights are derivative in nature; i.e., flow from act of the mortgagor, or arise independently from direct placement of coverage in the mortgagee's own right. Under general insurance principles, where the loss payee clause simply recites that the loss is payable to the mortgagor or mortgagee "as their respective interests may appear," the mortgagee is simply an appointee of the insurance fund, whose right of recovery is no greater than the right of the mortgagor (24 ALR3d 435), and the same appears to apply in admiralty.[82] Consequently, if the mortgagor-insured breaches the policy's conditions and the policy is voided, the mortgagee stands in no better position than the mortgagor-insured and cannot recover.[83]

On the other hand, compare *Small v. U.K. Marine Mut. Insce. Assocn.*,[84] where the insurance was effected by the ship's husbands for the mortgagor as well as for the mortgagee. The court said, in part:

> The interests of a mortgagor and mortgagee of shares in a ship are distinct and antagonistic interests. The mortgagee does not claim his interest in the ship through the mortgagor but has a distinct interest of his own. If the mortgagee is never in possession of the ship and the captain and the crew are bound to obey the mortgagor's orders, and the ship goes to the bottom, the mortgagee can sue on the policy made on his behalf. The acts of a captain, who is not the mortgagee's captain, are so far as the mortgagee is concerned, the acts of a stranger. If a stranger does some wrongful act in consequence of which the ship is lost, the proximate cause of the loss is a peril of the sea. The wrongful act of the stranger is the *causa causans*, but the peril of the sea is the *causa proxima*; and if therefore, a captain, who is a stranger to the mortgagee is guilty of some criminal act, which brings about the loss

---

81. *Alston v. Campbell*, (1779) 2 E.R. 325, H.L.; *Hutchison v. Wright*, (1858) 53 E.R. 706; *Ward v. Beck*, (1863) 143 E.R. 265; *Millidge v. Stymest*, (1864) 11 N.B.R. (6 All.) 164 (Can.).

82. *Minnie R.*, 49 F.2d 121 (CA-5), 1931 AMC 995. Decided prior to *Wilburn*. Language with respect to supremacy of admiralty law over conflicting state statutes must be treated with caution.

83. *Graham Joint Stock Shipping Co. Ltd. v. Merchants Marine Insce. Co. Ltd.*, (1924) A.C. 294, (1924) All E.R. 66, *aff'ming* S.C. *sub nom Samuel (P) & Co. Ltd. v. Dumas, Graham Joint Stock Shipping Co., Ltd. v. Merchants Marine Insce. Co. Ltd.*, (No. 2), (1923) 1 K.B. 592, C.A. (loss under hull policy).

84. *Small v. U.K. Marine Mut. Insce. Assocn.*, (1897) 2 Q.B. 311, C.A.

of the ship, the mortgagee's right to recover is not affected. Such a captain cannot be guilty of barratry against the mortgagee.

And see *Samuel (P) & Co. Ltd. v. Dumas,*[85] where a separate insurance against loss of freight by war risks was effected on account of the mortgagee and the ship was scuttled by the master and crew. Although the court held that the loss by scuttling was not included in the general words of the policy, and action therefore failed, it was also stated that:

> . . . On the facts, there was evidence upon which the trial judge could find that the interest of the mortgagee in the policy was *not by way of assignment from the owner,* but was original, and, consequently, the mortgagee was not affected by the fraud of the owner . . . .

(The distinction between the *Graham Joint Stock Shipping Co.* case, *supra,* and *Samuel (P) & Co. Ltd., supra,* should be carefully observed, as both appeals arose from the same case in the court of appeals. In the former, the hull cover was held to be derivative, and the mortgagee was bound because not "independently insured"; in the latter, the insurance on freight was held not to be derivative but was "independent," and the mortgagee was not bound by the wrongful conduct of the master and crew.)

In the United States, breach of warranty endorsements is not uncommon in marine policies (particularly at the instance of the federal government), whereby underwriters agree that the interest of the mortgagee in the policy will not be impaired or invalidated by reason of any act or neglect of the mortgagor, owner, master, agent, or crew of the vessel insured, admitting the seaworthiness of the vessel as between the underwriters and the mortgagee and denying to underwriters the right to cancel the policy without prior written consent of the mortgagee. Such endorsements usually entail the payment of an additional premium.

A difference between United States and English practice exists with respect to assignment of policies or interests therein. Attention is, however, directed to *Swan & Cleland's Graving Dock & Slipway Co. v. Maritime Insce. Co. & Croshaw,*[86] where, *after* a loss, the mortgagor assigned his interest in a policy to the mortgagee, the court stating that the mortgagee could sue and recover if, at the date of the assignment, the policy had expired so that nothing remained to be done under it but to pay the claim.

See, also, *Wineco,*[87] where a water carrier placed an open cargo policy "as freighters, forwarders, bailees, common carriers," all for the account

---

85. *Samuel (P) & Co. Ltd. v. Dumas,* (1924) A.C. 431, (1924) All E.R. 66, *aff'ming sub nom Samuel (P) & Co. Ltd. v. Merchants Marine Insce. Co., Ltd.,* (No. 2), (1923) K.B. 592, C.A.
86. *Swan & Cleland's Graving Dock & Slipway Co. v. Maritime Insce. Co. & Croshaw,* (1907) 1 K.B. 116.
87. *Wineco,* 1938 AMC 254 (N.Y.M.).

of "whom it may concern," and the underwriters paid a loss under the policy to the water carrier. The court held, in the absence of special notice or special equities, that neither the underwriters nor the broker through whom the loss was paid was responsible for a conversion of the insurance payment by the water carrier.

CHAPTER VIII

SUBJECT MATTER AND DESCRIPTION THEREOF

Introduction

A description of the subject matter of the insurance is required both from the nature of an insurance contract and from the universal practices of insurance. The subject matter is generally described as being so much "on ship," "on goods," "on freight," "on profits on goods," etc. If no property or interest which answers the description in the policy is at risk, the policy will not attach, although the assured may have property (or an insurable interest) at risk of equal or greater value, the reason being that the underwriters have not entered into a contract to indemnify the assured for any loss on that other property or interest.[1]

Section 26, Marine Insurance Act, 1906, deals with description of the subject matter and reads:

(1) The subject-matter insured must be designated in a marine policy with reasonable certainty.

(2) The nature and extent of the interest of the assured in the subject-matter insured need not be specified in the policy.

(3) Where the policy designates the subject-matter insured in general terms, it shall be construed to apply to the interest intended by the assured to be covered.

(4) In the application of this section regard shall be had to any usage regulating the designation of the subject-matter.

The same Act defines some of the terms which are customarily used in describing the subject matter. For example,

Freight

Rule 16, Rules for Construction of Policy, First Schedule, Marine Insurance Act, 1906, reads:

The term "freight" includes the profit derivable by a shipowner from the employment of his ship to carry his own goods or moveables,

---

1. *Mackenzie v. Whitworth*, (1875) 45 L.J.Q.B. 233, 3 Asp. M.L.C. 81, C.A.

as well as freight payable by a third party, but does not include passage money.[2]

Section 90 of the Act provides in part:

"Moveables" means any moveable tangible property, other than the ship, and includes money, valuable securities, and other documents.[3]

Ship

Rule 15 of Rules for Construction states:

The term "ship" includes the hull, materials and outfit, stores and provisions for the officers and crew, and, in the case of vessels engaged in a special trade, the ordinary fittings requisite for the trade, and also, in the case of a steamship, the machinery, boilers, and coals and engine stores, if owned by the assured.[4]

Goods

Rule 17 of Rules for Construction reads:

The term "goods" means goods in the nature of merchandise, and

2. *Flint v. Flemyng,* (1830) 109 E.R. 704; *Denoon v. Home and Colonial Assur. Co.,* (1872) L.R. 7 C.P. 341, 1 Asp. M.L.C. 309; *The Roanoke,* 298 F. 1, 1924 AMC 790 (9th Cir.); *The Sephie,* 9 F.2d 304, 1926 AMC 447 (2d Cir.); *Robinson v. Manufacturers' Ins. Co.,* 42 Mass. 143 (St.,Mass., 1840).

3. *The Pomeranian,* [1895] P. 349 (live cattle); *Sleigh v. Tyser,* [1900] 2 Q.B. 333 (live cattle); *Baring Brothers & Co. v. Marine Ins. Co.,* (1894) 10 T.L.R. 276 (stock certificates).

4. However, the word "hull" in a policy on hull and machinery does not cover coal, engine room and deck stores, provisions and cabin stores, port expenses and advances, or premiums. *Roddick v. Indemnity Mutual Marine Ins. Co.,* [1895] 2 Q.B. 380, C.A.; *Dennis v. Home Ins. Co.,* 136 F. 481 (D.C.N.Y., 1905) (naphtha launch considered to be "of and in" the hull of a yacht);*Connors Marine Co. v. Northwestern Fire & Marine Ins. Co.,* 88 F.2d 637, 1937 AMC 344 (2d Cir.) (term "hulls" in legal liability policy covers cargo-bearing hulls but not tugs used for towing; pontoons taken into possession for transportation not covered under term "hulls"); *Voges v. Travelers Fire Ins. Co.,*130 N.Y.S.2d 51 (St.,N.Y.) (term "hull, etc.," does not cover wooden structure used to protect a yacht while stored on land).

As to "provisions," see *Robertson v. Ewer,* (1786) 1 T.R.127; *Brough v. Whitmore,* (1791) 4 T.R. 206; *New Liverpool Eastham Ferry & Hotel Co. v. Ocean Accident & Guarantee Corporation,* (1929) 35 Com.Cas. 37.

The term "outfit" generally denotes the stores and provisions put on board the ship for the use of officers and crew. See *Hill v. Patten,* (1807) 8 East 373; *Forbes v. Aspinall,* (1811) 13 East 323. As applied to a whaling voyage, the term was construed to mean the fishing supplies of the ship put on board for that purpose, i.e., lances, harpoons, etc., in short, all the equipment necessary for making the catch, preparing it, and returning it to port. *Hill v. Patten, supra.* See, also, *Gale v. Laurie,* (1826) 108 E.R. 58.

"Furniture," in a time policy on a vessel employed in the grain trade, was construed to cover separation cloths and dunnage mats utilized in the proper carriage of grain cargoes. *Hogarth v. Walker,* (1899) 2 Q.B. 401, *aff'd* (1900) 2 Q.B. 283, C.A.

does not include personal effects or provisions and stores for use on board.

In the absence of any usage to the contrary, deck cargo and living animals must be insured specifically, and not under the general denomination of goods.[5]

Not only does the term "usage" refer to a usage of the trade, but where the subject matter insured consists of goods, not only are the goods insured but also the "adventure" itself. See *British and Foreign Marine Ins. Co. v. Samuel Sanday & Co.*,[6] where it was stated:

> There are many things that may be at risk, and in respect of which insurance may be effected . . . ship, goods, freight, profits, and so on. There are also familiar even antique, expressions constantly being used from long ago in marine policies, and continued because they are well understood in the business, or have been interpreted by Judges. This section says that regard is to be had to any usage regulating the designation of the subject-matter assured. The words of the policy have for generations been understood and held by Judges to designate not merely the goods but also the adventure. So far from abrogating this designation of subject-matter I should have thought the Act took pains to preserve it and others like it. I will merely in a sentence refer to s. 91(2) of the Act which preserves the rules of the Common Law, including the law merchant, save in so far as they are inconsistent with the express provisions of the Act.

It should be emphasized that where the goods are specified in the policy, they must fairly comport with the description given, or else the policy will not attach. This is demonstrated in *Overseas Commodities v. Style*,[7] where cases of tinned pork were insured under an all risks policy prescribing that each case had to bear a particular mark. Some of the cases did not bear that mark and, as to these, underwriters were not held liable.

An insurance upon "cargo" means cargo which is put aboard a vessel for the purposes of commerce. Thus, as Rule 17 states, the term "goods" does not embrace personal effects.[8] However, personal effects may be covered if shipped as cargo. For example, in *Duff v. Mackenzie*,[9] a master

---

5. The term "usage" in Rule 17 refers to a usage of the trade and not a usage of the business of insurance. *British and Foreign Mar. Ins. Co. v. Gaunt*, [1921] All E.R. 447, [1921] 2 A.C. 41 (usage proved in the trade to carry bales of wool as deck cargo and underwriter held liable even though he did not know of the usage). See cases cited under heading of "Usage," Chap. IV, "Principles of Construction."

6. [1916-17] All E.R. 134, H.L. See, also, *Rickards v. Forestal Land Timber & Rys. et al.*, [1942] A.C. 50.

7. [1958] 1 Lloyd's Rep. 546, Q.B.D.

8. *Brown v. Stapyleton*, (1827) 4 Bing. 119; *Hill v. Patten, supra*, n. 4.

9. (1857) 3 C.B. (N.S.) 16, 26 L.J.C.P. 313, 140 E.R. 643.

insured his clothes, instruments, charts, etc., as "master's effects" and they were held covered, and in *Wilkinson v. Hyde*,[10] it was held that a policy on goods covered an emigrant's outfit.

As Rule 17 also notes, in the absence of a usage to the contrary, deck cargo must be insured specifically. This is so because deck cargo is generally considered to be exposed to a greater hazard than goods normally carried in the ordinary way; i.e., below deck. However, if they are generally carried on deck as a general custom of the particular trade, such as on barges in inland waterways traffic, the underwriter is presumed to be knowledgeable with respect to such usage and is considered to have undertaken the risk of the goods being carried on deck.[11]

The applicability of Rule 17 to goods carried in containers carried on deck is questionable. The advent of containerization has literally caused a revolution in the transportation of cargo by water, and the ramifications are still unknown for the most part. But the decisions thus far make it possible to derive certain conclusions. For example, it clearly appears that even though containers may be transported on land as well as sea, they are integral to a steamship company's cargo operations. Hence, container leasing agreements are maritime contracts for the breach of which the lessor is entitled to invoke admiralty attachment procedures and remedies.[12] When a container is transferred from one carrier to another, the signature of the receiving carrier on the interchange receipt is as much a certification of the container's condition as the signature of the initial carrier.[13]

Containers—On-Deck Carriage

It must be emphasized that the American courts have shown little reluctance in extending the doctrine of deviation to non-geographical breaches of a contract of carriage. Such non-geographical deviations, occasionally termed "quasi-deviations," have frequently included the unauthorized carriage of goods on deck pursuant to a clean bill of lading.[14]

---

10. (1858) 140 E.R. 649.

11. *Apollinaris Co. v. Norddeutsche Ins. Co.*, [1904] 1 K.B. 252 (inland voyages by canal or river). See, also, *Da Costa v. Edmunds*, (1815) 4 Camp. 142, 1 Phillips, s. 406 *et seq.*

12. *Integrated Containers v. Starlines*, 476 F.Supp. 119, 1980 AMC 736 (S.D.N.Y.); *CTI Container v. Oceanic*, 682 F.2d 377, 1982 AMC 2541 (2d Cir.); *Star Shipping v. Star Lines*, 1981 AMC 2959 (D.,N.J.).

13. *G.H. Mooney, Ltd. v. Farrell*, 616 F.2d 619, 1980 AMC 505 (2d. Cir.).

14. See *St. Johns Corp. v. Companhia General*, 263 U.S. 119 (1923), where the Supreme Court said, in part:

> The clean bill of lading amounted to a positive representation . . . that the goods would go under deck. By stowing the goods on deck the vessel broke her contract, exposed them to greater risk than had been agreed, and thereby directly caused the loss. She accordingly became liable as for a deviation, cannot escape by reason of the relieving

The impact of "custom" with respect to "on-deck" stowage was considered in *Encyclopedia Britannica, Inc. v. Hong Kong Producer*,[15] where cartons of encyclopedias were shipped aboard the defendant's vessel in containers. Unknown to the plaintiff-shipper, several of the containers were stowed on deck. The carrier had issued a "short form" bill of lading which did not mention on-deck carriage but incorporated by reference the carrier's regular bill of lading, which contained a provision authorizing on-deck carriage. Noting that the short form bill of lading was issued after delivery of the containers to the vessel, and that there was thus no prior opportunity for the shipper to demand under-deck stowage, the court held that the on-deck stowage was an unreasonable deviation as the shipper was entitled to assume that he would receive under-deck stowage. The principal defense of the carrier was that on-deck stowage was authorized by a custom of the port. The court concluded that the carrier had failed to prove the alleged custom.

The carrier fared better in *Du Pont de Nemours Int'l, S.A. v. S.S. Mormacvega*,[16] where the shipper was seeking recovery of damages for the loss overboard of the container which contained his goods. As in *Encyclopedia Britannica*, a clean bill of lading had been issued, and the shipper and consignee were unaware that the containers had been stowed on deck. The vessel had been specially designed to carry containers on deck and, therefore, if there were a deviation, it could not be an unreasonable one in view of the special design.

The court recognized that technological innovation and vessel design could sometimes justify on-deck stowage and held that, in the circumstances, particularly in view of the special construction of the vessel and the type of cargo involved, on-deck stowage was "excusable, justifiable and therefore reasonable within the meaning of Section 4(4) of Cogsa." Existing case law was interpreted to mean that stowage on deck would be an unreasonable deviation only when the ship's hold was the ordinary and contemplated stowage area.[17]

---

clauses inserted in the bill of lading for her benefit, and must account for the value at destination.

Of more recent vintage, see *Captain v. Far Eastern S.S. Co.*, 1979 AMC 2210 (Sup.Ct., B.C., Can.), where five vans of household goods, carried under the defendant carrier's under-deck bill of lading, were damaged by rain during open storage at an intermediate port. The court held that the carrier's failure to provide covered storage at the intermediate port precluded reliance on clauses disclaiming liability and constituted a "fundamental breach" of the contract of carriage.

15. 422 F.2d 7 (2d Cir., 1969), *cert. den.* 397 U.S. 964 (1970), 1969 AMC 1741. See, also, *Jones v. Flying Clipper*, 116 F.Supp. 387, 1954 AMC 259.

16. 493 F.2d 97 (2d Cir., 1974), 1974 AMC 67.

17. For a general discussion of the subject of deviation, see Morgan, "Unreasonable Deviation under Cogsa," 9 *J.Mar. L. & Com.* 481 (1978), and Whitehead, "Deviation: Should the Doctrine Apply to On-Deck Carriage?" 6 *Maritime Lawyer* 37 (1981).

Logically and reasonably, on-deck stowage should be considered reasonable and proper on vessels specially designed and equipped to carry containers on deck. Shippers of containers aboard specially designed container ships should be slow to claim deviation. Issuance of an on-deck bill of lading, of course, removes the on-deck cargo from the protection of Cogsa, and on-deck bills of lading are generally not acceptable to financial institutions under letters of credit.

Containers—Are They Insured under Hull and Cargo Insurance?

Arnould states:[18]

> . . . Where the containers are owned or hired by the owner of the carrying vessel, they will as a rule be covered by specific wording in the hull policy or by separate insurance. In such a case, they would plainly not be covered by a policy on goods. Conversely, in cases where the containers are provided by the persons interested in the cargo, they may be covered by the goods policy, but it is believed that it is not the practice to treat the policy as covering containers or similar articles of transport having a commercial value of their own which is essentially distinct from the value of the goods unless the policy is expressly worded so as to provide such cover.

However, the U. S. Supreme Court has equated containers (in the context of the Longshoremen's and Harbor Workers' Act) as being a "modern substitute for the hold of the vessel." *Northeast Marine Terminal Co. v. Caputo.*[19] There, the injured longshoreman was injured while "stripping" or removing the contents of a container while it was on a pier some distance from the ship from which it had been unloaded. The issue was whether the amended Act covered an employee injured while working ashore. Quoting from the decision below, the court said, in part:

> . . . Stripping a container . . . is the functional equivalent of sorting cargo discharged from a ship; stuffing a container is part of the loading of the ship even though it is performed on the shore and not in the ship's cargo holds.

The issue was raised peripherally in *Holland v. Sea-Land Services, Inc.,*[20] where a longshoreman was injured while driving a "hustler" used

---

18. Arnould, *Law of Marine Insurance and Average,* ed. M. J. Mustill and J. C. B. Gilman, (16th ed., 1981).
19. 432 U.S. 249, 1977 AMC 1037 (1977).
20. 655 F.2d 556, 1981 AMC 2474 (4th Cir.).

to transport containers, which were mounted on trailers, from storage on land to the pier for loading aboard a vessel. While making a turn, the hustler tipped over and injured him. After receiving compensation under the Act from his employer, he filed suit against Sea-Land Services, the shipowner, claiming it was a third party tortfeasor subject to maritime law. At trial, the plaintiff suggested that because the container was an "appurtenance" to a vessel, jurisdiction was conferred under the Admiralty Extension Act, 46 U.S.C. 740. The plaintiff did not, however, bring an action against the vessel; the defendant was sued as the operator of the terminal "and not as the owner of any particular vessel." As this basis of jurisdiction was not presented to the district court and was not addressed in the parties' briefs, the court refused to consider it on appeal.

The cases are not consistent with respect to whether a policy on "goods" covers the packing container. For example, in *Brown v. Fleming*,[21] the policy covered cases of whiskey. The court held that the straw in which the bottles were packed as well as the labels on the bottles were part of the subject matter insured. In *Berk v. Style*,[22] the policy was on 100 tons of kieselguhr which was shipped in paper bags. The bags were defective and ripped during transit. In holding that there was no coverage by reason of "inherent vice," the court necessarily concluded that the bags were insured as well as the kieselguhr. In *Blackshaws (Pty.) Ltd. v. Constantia Ins. Co.*,[23] the South African appellate division held that defective packing of cargo within a container constituted inherent vice under the applicable marine cargo policy.

To the contrary, in *Vacuum Oil Co. v. Union Ins. Soc. of Canton*,[24] a policy covering 10,000 tins of petroleum was held to cover only the petroleum and not the tins, and in *Lysahgt v. Coleman*,[25] a policy on galvanized iron was held not to cover the damaged packing cases in which the iron had been packaged.

Profits as Subject Matter Insured

Insurance on anticipated profits is common both in England and the United States. As was stated in *Barclay v. Cousins*:[26]

> As insurance is a contract of indemnity, it cannot be said to be extended beyond what the design of such species of contract will em-

21. 7 Com.Cas. 245.
22. [1955] 2 Lloyd's Rep. 383.
23. [1983] 1 AD 120, 1984 AMC 637 (So.Af.).
24. (1925) 24 Ll.L.Rep. 188.
25. [1895] 1 Q.B. 49.
26. (1802) 102 E.R. 478.

brace, if it be applied to protect men from those losses and disadvantages which but for the perils insured against the assured would not suffer; and in every maritime adventure the adventurer is liable to be deprived, not only of the things immediately subjected to the perils insured against, but also of the advantages to be derived from the arrival of those things at their destined port. If they do not arrive, his loss is not merely that of his goods . . . but of the benefits which, were his money employed in an undertaking not subject to the perils, he might obtain without more risk than the capital itself would be liable to; and if when the capital is subject to the risks of maritime commerce it be allowable for the merchant to protect that by insuring it, why may he not protect those advantages he is in danger of losing by their being subjected to the same risks? It is surely not an improper encouragement of trade to provide that merchants, in case of adverse fortune, should not only lose the principal adventure, but that that principal should not, in consequence of such bad fortune, be totally unproductive; and that men of small fortunes should be encouraged to engage in commerce by their having the means of preserving their capitals entire.

It will be recalled that Section 26(3) of the Marine Insurance Act provides that where the policy designates the subject matter in general terms, it shall be construed to apply to the *interest intended by the assured to be covered*. The term "interest" is somewhat broader than the term "insurable interest." As was noted in *Dunlop Bros. & Co. v. Townsend*,[27] it is construed to apply to the pecuniary or insurable interest which the assured intended to be covered, whether that interest be that of the owner or whether it be that of a person who has made advances, or of a person who is interested in the safe arrival of the goods by reason of the commission which he shall get on the sale; and, of course, the policy applies to a case where a person takes out a floating policy not to cover any pecuniary interest of his own, but to cover the liabilities and interest of persons on whose behalf he is instructed to insure.

The word "interest," standing alone, also appears in the held covered clasues of the Institute Cargo Clauses and speaks in terms of " . . . any omission or error in the description of the interest, vessel or voyage." There too, it has been held that the word "interest" means more than merely "insurable interest."[28]

Obviously, however, a policy insuring profits cannot cover a loss of profit on goods not shipped. Consequently, whether insured under a valued or an unvalued policy, the assured must prove that some profit would

27. [1918-19] All E.R. 575.
28. *Hewitt Bros v. Wilson*, (1915) 113 L.T. 304, C.A.

have been realized by the sale of his goods on arrival at destination.[29] Moreover, for there to be an obligation on the part of the underwriter to pay for lost profits, the profits must have been exposed to a peril which is covered by the policy. This was the holding in *M'Swiney v. Royal Exchange Assur. Co.*,[30] where the assured bought several thousand bags of rice and placed insurance on profits on the rice loaded in or to be loaded in the carrying vessel. After a portion of the bags had been loaded aboard, the vessel was disabled by a peril of the sea and the rice loaded aboard spoiled. It was held that the policy covered only the rice loaded aboard as the rice still ashore had not been exposed to any peril enumerated in the policy. The court did point out, however, that it would have been possible for the assured to have recovered for the lost profit on the portion left ashore had the policy been properly claused.

Commissions

Commissions are a species of profits and, therefore, may be insured, and these would seem to include brokerage commissions which a shipbroker expects to earn under his contract.[31] But to be recoverable, they must be specifically named. Generally speaking, profits and commissions are not covered by a policy on goods and merchandise.[32]

Clearly, a charterer can insure his expected profit.[33] There is some authority for the proposition that a shipowner may insure the profit which he expects to make from the use of his vessel, but this would seem to be true only where the shipowner has contracted in advance for a booking of cargo such that there would be an actual contract for the freight to be earned.[34] In *Faris v. Newburyport Mar. Ins. Co.*,[35] the policy was some-

---

29. The law may be different in the United States. See *Patapsco Ins. Co. v. Coulter*, 28 U.S. 222 (1830); Phillips, Sec. 318. There appears to be a presumption that some profit would have been made had the goods arrived.

30. (1849) 14 Q.B. 634. See, also, *Halhead v. Young*, (1856) 25 L.J.Q.B. 290, involving the inability to transport goods from an intermediate port when the vessel was totally lost on the first leg of the voyage from the first port of loading to the intermediate port.

31. See *Buchanan v. Faber*, (1899) 4 Com.Cas. 223; *Barclay v. Cousins, supra*, n. 26.

32. *Lucena v. Craufurd*, (1806) 2 B. & P.N.R. 269; *Maurice v. Goldsborough Mort & Co.*, [1939] A.C. 542; *Tom v. Smith*, 3 Caines 245 (1805, N.Y.); *Connecticut Fire Ins. Co. v. W.H. Roberts Lumber Co.*, 119 Va. 479, 89 S.E. 945 (1916). *cf. Holbrook v. Brown*, 2 Mass. 280 (1807, Mass.).

33. *Asfar v. Blundell*, [1895] 2 Q.B. 196, [1896] 1 Q.B. 123, C.A.; *Continental Grain Co. v. Twitchell*, (1945) 61 T.L.R. 291, C.A.; *Smith & Scaramanga v. Fenning*, (1898) 3 Com.Cas. 75; *Robinson v. Manufacturers Ins. Co.*, 42 Mass. 143 (1840); *Hart v. Delaware Ins. Co.*, F.Cas. No 6150 (1809); *M'Gaw v. Ocean Ins. Co.*, 40 Mass. 405 (1839); *Silloway v. Neptune Ins. Co.*, 78 Mass. 73 (1858).

34. *Papadimitriou v. Henderson*, (1939) 55 T.L.R. 1035; *Manchester Liners v. Brit. & For. Mar. Ins. Co.*, (1901) 7 Com.Cas. 26.

35. 3 Mass. 476 (1807).

what unusual in that it was claused to cover cargo or freight, "both or either to the amount insured." The court held that the coverage was not on either type of risk at the election of the assured, and that if only one of the species of property was at risk, it only was covered; but if both were at risk, each was covered proportionately to the assured's interest in each.

Miscellaneous

For many years, seamen's wages were not insurable in England, the reason apparently being that if seamen could insure their wages they might be tempted not to exert their best efforts for the preservation of their vessel. This was changed by the Merchant Shipping Act, 1854, and the Marine Insurance Act, 1906, provides in Section 11 that the master or any member of the crew of a ship has an insurable interest in respect of his wages. Even when seamen were precluded from insuring their wages, they were nonetheless privileged to insure goods which they might have shipped aboard their vessel.[36] And the master was always allowed to insure his wages, commissions, or any interest he might have in the vessel as a part owner.[37]

Disbursements

"Disbursements" are a very common subject of insurance, and rightly so. Policy provisions insuring disbursements are used to insure nebulous interests as commissions, profits, "increased value" (total loss insurance on a vessel in addition to the agreed or insured value), and the like. They are, unquestionably, of great commercial utility where, although the assured may have an insurable interest, it would be difficult to quantify it. The AIH form of hull policy (1977), like most hull policies, contains a disbursements clause, entitled "Additional Insurances," which covers such interests as disbursements, managers' commissions, profits or excess of increased value of hull and machinery, freight (including chartered or anticipated freight) insured for time, freight or hire under contracts for voyage, anticipated freight if the vessel sails in ballast and not under charter, time charter hire or charter hire for a series of voyages, premiums on insurance, return premiums, and risks excluded by the war, strikes, and related exclusions clause, risks enumerated in the American Institute war risks and strikes clauses, and general average and salvage disbursements.[38]

36. *Galloway v. Morris*, 3 Yeates R. 445 (1802, Pa.).
37. *King v. Glover*, (1806) 2 B. & P.N.R. 206; *Hawkins v. Twizell*, (1856) 25 L.J.Q.B. 160.
38. For the precise wording of the additional insurances clause, see the AIH (1977) form reproduced in the Appendix.

As a matter of practice, disbursements insurance is intended to permit a shipowner to recover additional sums beyond the amount for which he has specifically insured his vessel and freight. As a practical matter, this simply increases the insurance on the vessel without increasing the valuation of the vessel as specified in the hull policy. It will be seen that an unlimited right to insure disbursements to any particular amount could be an open invitation to a shipowner for the fraudulent casting away of his vessel. Consequently, the object of including a disbursements clause in a hull policy is to limit the amount of coverage procured to a moderate proportion of the whole amount insured. Thus, a shipowner is prevented from insuring under his hull policy at a low valuation and then effecting other total loss insurance for greatly disproportionate amounts as compared to the agreed valuation under the hull policy.[39] A review of the additional insurances clause in the AIH (1977) hull form will reveal, for example, that under Section (a) of the clause, total loss only insurance effected without proof of interest is limited to 25 percent of the agreed value. Insurances allowed under sections (b) through (g) are subject to proof of interest but, subject to the limitation in each section, they may be effected in addition to the 25 percent total loss insurance permitted under Section (a).

Liability Insurance

There is, of course, no impediment to a shipowner insuring against liabilities which may arise out of the operation of his vessel such as loss of life, personal injury, damage to property, damage to cargo in circumstances in which the shipowner cannot limit his liability, etc. The collision or "Running Down Clause" contained in nearly all hull policies provides coverage for certain liabilities arising out of collision, and most of the remaining liabilities are covered under P & I policies. For example, the usual form of collision clause covers only liabilities arising out of collision with another *vessel*. As might be expected, the question as to what is a "vessel" has arisen in a variety of contexts.[40] Even more decisions have been generated under P & I policies insuring liabilities of the "owner" of the vessel where the vessel is actually under charter. For example, in *Con-*

---

39. See, as a matter of historical interest, *Currie v. Bombay Ins. Co.*, (1869) L.R. 3 P.C. 72; *Chellew v. Royal Commission on the Sugar Supply*, [1921] 2 K.B. 627 (insurance on general average expenditures); *Thames & Mersey Mar. Ins. Co. v. Gunford Ship Co.*, [1911] A.C. 529; *Moran v. Uzielli*, [1905] 2 K.B. 555; *Lawther v. Black*, (1900) 6 Com.Cas. 5; *Price v. Maritime Ins. Co.*, [1901] 2 K.B. 412; *Anderson v. Marten*, [1907] 2 K.B. 248; *Brown v. Merchants' Mar. Ins. Co.*, 152 F. 411 (1907); *International Nav. Co. v. Atlantic Mut. Ins. Co.*, 100 F. 304 (S.D.N.Y.), *aff'd* 108 F. 987 (2d. Cir., 1901).

40. See Chap. XIX, "Running Down Clause."

tinental v. Bonanza,[41] the vessel's time charterer was named as an additional assured in the vessel owner's P & I policy. The vessel sank and became a "wreck." The court held that since the time charterer had no "ownership" interest in the vessel, it had no duty as an "owner" to remove the wreck, and the P & I club was held not liable to reimburse the charterer for its costs of removing the wreck from its leased underwater property. In *Farmers Home v. I.N.A.*,[42] a policy insuring a yacht owner against liabilities for bodily injury arising by reason of his "interest" in the vessel was held to be ambiguous and was construed to cover injury to a guest who fell through an opening in a pier while assisting another guest to disembark. In *Offshore Logistics v. Mutual Marine*,[43] it was held that a bareboat charterer is an owner *pro hac vice* and, as such, was covered by a P & I policy insuring the charterer's liability as an "owner." In *St. Paul Fire v. Vest*,[44] the P & I underwriter on a barge was held not liable for wreck removal expenses where the barge sank solely because of the negligence of the towing tug. From the foregoing, it will be readily seen that the description of the subject matter of insurance can be vitally important.

41. 706 F.2d 1365, 1983 AMC 2059 (5th Cir.).
42. 1979 AMC 2549 (St.,Wash.).
43. 462 F.Supp. 485, 1981 AMC 1154 (E.D.,La.).
44. 500 F.Supp. 1365, 1982 AMC 450 (N.D.,Miss.).

CHAPTER IX

MEASURE OF INSURABLE VALUE

Section 16, Marine Insurance Act, 1906, sets forth the measure of insurable value as follows:

> Subject to any express provision or valuation in the policy, the insurable value of the subject-matter insured must be ascertained as follows:
>
> (1) In insurance on ship, the insurable value is the value at the commencement of the risk, of the ship, including her outfit, provisions and stores for the officers and crew, money advanced for seamen's wages, and other disbursements (if any) incurred to make the ship fit for the voyage or adventure contemplated by the policy, plus the charges of insurance upon the whole;
>
> The insurable value, in case of a steamship, includes also the machinery, boilers, and coals and engine stores if owned by the assured, and, in the case of a ship engaged in a special trade, the ordinary fittings requisite for that trade;
>
> (2) In insurance on freight, whether paid in advance or otherwise, the insurable value is the gross amount of the freight at the risk of the assured, plus the charges of insurance;
>
> (3) In insurance on goods and merchandise, the insurable value is the prime cost of the property insured, plus the charges of and incidental to shipping and the charges of insurance upon the whole;
>
> (4) In insurance on any other subject-matter, the insurable value is the amount at the risk of the assured when the policy attaches, plus the charges of insurance.

Taking the above categories *seriatim,* it must be remembered that, in practice, nearly all policies are valued policies. Therefore, as respects vessels, it would appear that only where fraud is asserted in connection with valuation so that the valuation is not conclusive, would the amount of the insured value become particularly relevant.[1]

---

1. Sec. 27(3) of the Act provides that, subject to the provisions of the Act, and in the absence of fraud, the value fixed by the policy is, as between the insurer and assured, conclusive as to the insurable value of the subject intended to be insured, whether the loss be total or partial. With respect to a non-disclosure of an overvaluation, see Sec. 18 of the Act, and Chap. X, "Disclosures and Representations." See, also, *Irvin v. Hine,* [1949] 2 All E.R. 1089, K.B.; *Barker v. Janson,* (1868) 17 L.T. 473, 3 Mar. L.C. 28; *The Main,* [1894] P. 320, 7 Asp. M.L.C. 424; *Watson v. Ins. Co. of N.A.,* Fed.Cas. No. 17,286 (C.C.,Pa.,1811); *Aetna Ins. Co. v. United Fruit Co.,* 1938 AMC 707, 304 U.S. 430 (1937); *The St.Johns,* 101 F. 469 (S.D.N.Y, 1900).

Where, however, a vessel is insured under an unvalued policy, the value of the vessel is that which she is worth at the port where the voyage commences, including stores, money advanced for seamen's wages, etc.[2] Under such a policy, the assured is entitled to recover the actual value of the vessel and not its cost to the assured.[3]

It would seem that valuing the vessel when and where the voyage commences would rather favor the assured, particularly as he can insure his freight also. But it has the advantage of certainty, whereas attempting to value the vessel at some other time would be extremely difficult.

The definition of "ship" prior to the passage of the Marine Insurance Act, 1906, was considerably less extensive than under the Act.[4] It would seem that in the absence of some countervailing custom, the meaning of "outfit" and "ordinary fittings" would be governed by the provisions of the Act, rather than by the earlier cases. See, for example, *Gale v. Laurie*.[5]

Sub-section (2) of Section 16 merely restates the law as it existed before the Act.[6]

Sub-section (3) is perfectly straightforward. The value of the goods is, therefore, their value aboard the vessel at the port of loading plus commissions and insurance premiums.[7] The phrase "prime cost" means the prime cost to the assured at or about the time of shipment, or at any rate at some time when the prime cost can be reasonably deemed to represent their value to their owner at the time of shipment.[8]

From the foregoing it will be seen that the assured is not entitled to recover for any estimated profit he might have made on the sale of the goods insured.[9]

---

2. *Forbes v. Aspinall*, (1811) 104 E.R. 394; *Shawe v. Felton*, (1801) 102 E.R. 310; *Snell v. Delaware Ins. Co.*, 4 U.S. 430 (1806); *Carson v. Marine Ins. Co.*, Fed.Cas. No. 2,465 (C.C.,Pa., 1811); *Peninsula & O.S.S. Co. v. Atlantic Mut. Ins. Co.*, 194 F. 84 (3d Cir., 1911).

3. *Snell v. Delaware Ins. Co.*, *supra*, n. 2.

4. See *Roddick v. Indemnity Mut. Mar. Ins. Co.*, [1895] 2 Q.B. 380, 8 Asp. M.L.C. 24, C.A., and cases cited in Chap. III, "The Policy," and Chap. IV, "Principles of Construction."

5. (1826) 108 E.R. 58.

6. *Forbes v. Aspinall*, (1811) 104 E.R. 394; *Palmer v. Blackburn*, (1822) 130 E.R. 25; *U.S. Shipping Co. v. Empress Assur. Corp.*, [1907] 1 K.B. 259, *aff'd* [1908] 1 K.B. 115 (rule of gross freight applies to charterer as well, and any hire saved could not be deducted from the amount recoverable on the policy). And see *Thames & Mersey Marine Ins. Co., Ltd. v. Gunford Ship Co.*, [1911] A.C. 529 at p. 549, 12 Asp. M.L.C. 49.

7. See *Usher v. Noble*, (1810) 104 E.R. 249; *Berger and Light Diffusers Pty. Ltd. v. Pollock*, [1973] 2 Lloyd's Rep. 442, Q.B.D.; *Williams v. Atlantic Assurance Co., Ltd.*, [1933] 1 K.B. 81, C.A. Compare *Groban v. Pegu*, 331 F.Supp. 883, 1972 AMC 460 (S.D.N.Y.) and *Zack Metal v. Federal Ins. Co.*, 1968 AMC 1384 (St.,N.Y.). In *Groban*, before shipment the importer had resold the goods for $48,000 but paid only $19,000 for them. The "invoice value" for cargo insurance purposes was held to be correctly stated at $48,000. In *Zack Metal*, it was held that where goods have a fluctuating market value, cargo underwriters' liability should be computed by deducting the amount for which the goods were sold in a damaged condition from their sound market value on the date of that sale, not from their sound value at some other and earlier date.

8. *Williams v. Atlantic Assurance Co., Ltd.*, *supra*, n. 7.

9. *Usher v. Noble*, (1810) 104 E.R. 249.

CHAPTER X

DISCLOSURES AND REPRESENTATIONS

A marine insurance policy is unquestionably "*uberrimae fidei*"—of the utmost good faith—and may be avoided by the injured party where the other fails to exercise the utmost good faith required. The Marine Insurance Act, 1906, Section 17, states the universal rule succinctly:

A contract of marine insurance is a contract based upon the utmost good faith, and, if the utmost good faith is not observed by either party, the contract may be avoided by the other party. The court in *The Papoose*[1] said in part:

The marine insurance contract is *uberrimae fidei* . . . requiring the highest degree of good faith. That standard can hardly be complied with by concealing from the assurer a current survey report which shows that the vessel is unseaworthy at the time of the application, particularly when the assurer is given an earlier report showing the vessel seaworthy . . . .[2]

The principle embodied in Section 17 would seem to apply to every kind of insurance, not merely marine insurance.[3]

The burden of proof is upon the underwriters when they raise the defense of concealment or non-disclosure.[4] As to the *nature* of the proof which underwriters must adduce, see discussion *infra*.

1. 409 F.2d 974, 1969 AMC 781 (5th Cir.).
2. See *Carter v. Boehm*, (1766) 97 E.R. 1162; *Brownlie v. Campbell*, (1880) 6 App.Cas. 925, H.L.; *Seaton v. Heath, Seaton and Burnand*, (1899) 1 Q.B. 782, C.A., on appeal *sub nom. Seaton v. Burnand, Burnand v. Seaton*, [1900] A.C. 135, H.L.; *Elkin v. Janson*, (1845) 153 E.R. 274; *McLanahan v. Universal Ins. Co.*, 26 U.S. 170 (1828); *Sun Mutual Ins. Co. v. Ocean Ins. Co.*, 107 U.S. 485 (1883); *Hauser v. Amer. Central Ins. Co.*, 216 F.Supp. 318, 1964 AMC 526 (E.D.,La.); *Pacific Queen*, 307 F.2d 700, 1962 AMC 1845 (9th Cir.); [1963] 2 Lloyd's Rep. 201; *The Keresan*, 1927 AMC 577 (St.,N.Y.); *Egremont Castle*, 1934 AMC 1317 (St.,N.Y.); *Connors Marine v. British & Foreign*, 1938 AMC 1317 (St.,N.Y.); *Bella*, 5 F.2d 570, 1925 AMC 751 (4th Cir.); *Mahoney v. Providence Ins. Co.*, (1869) 12 N.B.R. 633 (Can., C.A.);*Hancock v. Equitable Life Ins. Co. of Canada*, [1941] 1 W.W.R. 464 (Can.); *Lavigne v. Poland*, (1944) 11 I.L.R. 65 (Can.); *Visscher Enterprises Pty. Ltd. v. Southern Pacific Ins. Co., Ltd.*, [1981] Qd. R. 561 (Aus.); *Itobar Pty. Ltd. v. Mackinnon and Commercial Ins. Co.*, (1985) 3 ANZ Ins. Cas. 60-610 (Aus.); *Claude Ogden & Co. v. Reliance Fire Sprinkler Co. et al*, [1973] 2 N.S.W.L.R. 7 (Aus.); *Intermunicipal Realty v. Gore Mut. Ins. Co.*, 1980 AMC 1540 (Can.F.Ct.); *Sea Fever v. Hartford Fire*, 1983 AMC 1276 (D.,Mass.); *Allden v. Raven (The Kylie)*, [1983] 2 Lloyd's Rep. 444; *CTI International, Inc. v. Oceanus Mutual Underwriting Ass'n (Bermuda) Ltd.*, [1984] 1 Lloyd's Rep. 476; *A/S Ivarans v. P.R. Ports Authority*, 617 F.2d 903, 1982 AMC 2493 (1st Cir.).
3. *Australia and New Zealand Bank, Ltd. v. Colonial and Eagle Wharves, Ltd.: Boag (Third Party)*, [1960] 2 Lloyd's Rep. 241.
4. *Williams v. Atlantic Assur. Co., Ltd.*, [1933] 1 K.B. 81, 43 Ll.L.Rep. 177, C.A.; *Visscherij Maatschappij Nieuw Onderneming v. Scottish Metropolitan Assur. Co., Ltd.*, (1922) 10 Ll.L.Rep.

The rules with respect to what must be disclosed are set forth with clarity in Section 18, Marine Insurance Act, 1906. That section expresses also the weight of authority in the United States. Section 18 reads in its entirety:

(1) Subject to the provisions of this section, the assured must disclose to the insurer, before the contract is concluded, every material circumstance which is known to the assured, and the assured is deemed to know every circumstance which, in the ordinary course of business, ought to be known by him. If the assured fails to make such disclosure, the insurer may avoid the contract.

(2) Every circumstance is material which would influence the judgment of a prudent insurer in fixing the premium, or determining whether he will take the risk.

(3) In the absence of inquiry the following circumstances need not be disclosed, namely:

(a) Any circumstance which diminishes the risk;

(b) Any circumstance which is known or presumed to be known to the insurer. The insurer is presumed to know matters of common notoriety or knowledge, and matters which an insurer in the ordinary course of his business, as such, ought to know;

(c) Any circumstance as to which information is waived by the insurer;

(d) Any circumstance which it is superfluous to disclose by reason of any express or implied warranty;

(4) Whether any particular circumstance, which is not disclosed, be material or not is, in each case, a question of fact.

(5) The term "circumstance" includes any communication made to, or information received by, the assured.

Section 18 must be read in conjunction with Sections 19 and 20. Section 19 relates to disclosures by an agent effecting insurance and reads:

Subject to the provisions of the preceding section as to circumstances which need not be disclosed where an insurance is effected for the assured by an agent, the agent must disclose to the insurer:

(a) Every material circumstance which is known to himself, and an agent to insure is deemed to know every circumstance which

579, C.A.; *Davies v. National Fire & Marine Ins. Co. of New Zealand*, [1891] A.C. 485, P.C.; *Western Fin. Corp. Ltd. v. London & Lancashire Guar. & Acc. Co. of Canada*, [1928] 3 D.L.R. 592, [1928] 2 W.W.R. 454 (Can.); *Stecker v. Amer. Home F.A. Co.*, 1949 AMC 1949 (St.,N.Y.); *Visscher Enterprises Pty. Ltd. v. Southern Pacific Ins. Co. Ltd*, [1981] Qd. R. 561.

in the ordinary course of business ought to be known by, or to have been communicated to, him; and

(b) Every material circumstance which the assured is bound to disclose, unless it come to his knowledge too late to communicate it to his agent.

Section 20 covers representations pending the negotiation of the insurance contract, and reads:

(1) Every material representation made by the assured or his agent to the insurer during the negotiations for the contract, and before the contract is concluded, must be true. If it be untrue the insurer may avoid the contract.

(2) A representation is material which would influence the judgment of a prudent insurer in fixing the premium, or determining whether he will take the risk.

(3) A representation may be either a representation as to a matter of fact, or as to a matter of expectation or belief.

(4) A representation as to a matter of fact is true, if it be substantially correct, that is to say, if the difference between what is represented and what is actually correct would not be considered material by a prudent insurer.

(5) A representation as to a matter of expectation or belief is true if it be made in good faith.

(6) A representation may be withdrawn or corrected before the contract is concluded.

(7) Whether a particular representation be material or not is, in each case, a question of fact.

The similarity between Section 18 and Section 20 is obvious. The former may be characterized as "sins of omission"; the latter as "sins of commission." The results are essentially the same.

The cases with respect to the disclosure of facts which the assured ought to know are rather numerous.[5] The language of the court in *Proudfoot v. Montefiore*[6] is instructive:

---

5. See *Northwestern S.S. Co. v. Maritime Ins. Co.*, 161 F. 166 (9th Cir., 1908); *Muller v. Globe & Rutgers Ins. Co., etc.*, 246 F. 759 (2d Cir., 1917); *Proudfoot v. Montefiore*, (1867) L.R. 2 Q. B. 511; *Blackburn, Low & Co. v. Vigors*, (1887) 12 App.Cas. 531; *Ionides v. Pender*, (1874) L.R. 9 Q.B. 531; *Cauto*, 49 F.2d 720, 1931 AMC 1044; *Albany Ins. Co. v. Wisniewski*, 579 F.Supp. 1004, 1985 AMC 689 (D., R.I.); *Visscher Enterprises Pty. Ltd. v. Southern Pacific Ins. Co. Ltd.*, [1981] Qd. R. 561 (Aus.); *CTI International Inc. v. Oceanus Mutual Underwriting Ass'n (Bermuda) Ltd.*, [1984] 1 Lloyd's Rep. 476, C.A. See, also, cases cited note 1, *supra*, and the non-marine case of *Khoury v. Gov't. Ins. Office of New South Wales*, (1984) 58 A.L.J.R. 502 (H.C., Aus.), where the High Court held that the ordinary duty of a person seeking insurance—in this instance a houseowner's and householder's policy—to disclose to the insurer facts material to the risk

The insurer is entitled to assume, as the basis of the contract between him and the assured, that the latter will communicate to him every material fact of which the assured has, or, in the ordinary course of business, ought to have knowledge; and the latter will take the necessary measures, by the employment of competent and honest agents, to obtain, through the ordinary channels of intelligence in use in the mercantile world, all due information as to the subject-matter of the insurance. This condition is not complied with where, by the fraud or negligence of the agent, the party proposing the insurance is kept in ignorance of a material fact, which ought to have been made known to the underwriter, and through such ignorance fails to disclose it.

The case is interesting in that it involved an agent whose duty it was to communicate with his principal, the assured. The agent deliberately abstained from telegraphing news of a stranding of the vessel to his principal who, thereupon, insured the vessel in ignorance of the casualty. The act of the agent in failing to communicate with his principal was imputed to his principal. Compare, however, *Mercantile Mut. Ins. Co. v. Folsom*[7] and *General Interest Ins. Co. v. Ruggles.*[8] In the former, the master of the vessel which was lost could have telegraphed news of the loss to the assured but did not do so. The policy was nonetheless held to be in force. In the latter, the master of the vessel which was lost, wilfully and with a fraudulent design to enable the owner to make insurance after a total loss, failed to communicate news of the loss, whereupon the owner, in good faith, placed coverage. The court held that the non-disclosure did not render the policy void or preclude the owner from a recovery under it.

In *Cauto,*[9] the assured had insured two cases of silk goods as silk and two cases of cotton goods as cotton but shipped all four on bills of lading invoices as cotton. One case of silk and one case of cotton were lost enroute. The court held that the failure to reveal to the underwriter that the silk was being misdescribed to the ocean carrier was a breach of the duty to disclose. The underwriter was, however, held liable for the loss of the cotton which had not been misdescribed. In passing, the court observed that concealment consists of the suppression by the insured of any fact or circumstance which the underwriter does not know or is not legally presumed to know and which is material to the risk, or which could possibly influence the mind of a prudent and intelligent insurer in determining whether he would accept the risks or what his premium would be if he

---

was a duty arising at common law and did not flow from an implied term or condition of the contract of insurance.

6. Note 5, *supra.*
7. 85 U.S. 237 (1873).
8. 25 U.S. 408 (1825).
9. 49 F.2d 720, 1931 AMC 1044.

decided to accept it. The court further stated that such a concealment avoids the insurance contract whether it be due to *fraud, negligence, accident,* or *mistake.*

In *Keresan,*[10] the assured failed to state the nature of the cargo (lily of the valley pips), the existence of a prolongation clause, and the date of sailing. The cargo was simply described as merchandise and its perishable nature was not disclosed. The court, noting that Sections 17 and 18 of the Marine Insurance Act, 1906, were a "fair codification of the case law and custom" on the point, held there was a breach of the duty to disclose, and voided the policy.

In *Fireman's Fund v. Wilburn Boat,*[11] on remand from the U. S. Supreme Court, the Fifth Circuit held that, under Texas law, a mistake or concealment material to a marine risk, whether it be wilful or contractual, or results from mistake, negligence, or voluntary ignorance, voids the policy.

In *Neubros Co. v. Northwestern National Ins. Co.,*[12] the policy was vitiated because the assured breached its affirmative duty to reveal to underwriters that the barge being insured was structurally incapable of carrying a full load.

In *Bella,*[13] the shipowner's brokers, in answer to an inquiry by underwriters as to the apparently excessive valuation of the ship, made false statements as to the amount of profits being made in its operation. The court held the misrepresentation was material as a matter of law, and voided the policy.

In *Tremaine v. Phoenix Ins. Co.,*[14] a failure to disclose that the vessel was unseaworthy and sunk and in need of repairs was held to be material in an application to renew and extend the insurance and was a complete defense to underwriters.

In *Kerr v. Union Marine Ins. Co.,*[15] the time of sailing of the insured vessel was misrepresented in response to a direct question in the application form. The court held that in such circumstances it would be conclusively presumed that the answer was material to the risk.[16]

In *Albany Ins. v. Wisniewski,*[17] the applicant represented that his decommissioned navy hydrofoil had been subjected to a "Lloyd's survey," was in excellent condition, and had a fair market value in excess of $2 million. In fact, the vessel was "broken down, scruffy and largely un-

---

10. 1927 AMC 577 (St.,N.Y.).

11. 300 F.2d 631, 1962 AMC 1593 (5th Cir.).

12. 1972 AMC 2443 (E.D.N.Y.).

13. 5 F.2d 570, 1925 AMC 751 (4th Cir.).

14. 1935 AMC 753 (St.,Cal.). See, also, *Hamblett v. City Ins. Co.,* 36 F. 118 (D.,Pa., 1888).

15. 130 F. 415 (2d Cir., 1904), *cert. den.* 194 U.S. 635 (1904).

16. By contrast, in *McLanahan v. Universal Ins. Co.,* 26 U.S. 170 (1828), an accidental concealment of time of sailing was held not material.

17. 579 F.Supp. 1004, 1985 AMC 689 (D.,R.I.).

marketable," and was worth less than $1/20$th of the alleged value. The court held that an applicant for marine insurance is bound, even absent inquiry, to reveal every fact within his knowledge material to the risk, and any distortion of the facts gives the insurer a right to rescind. On the facts, the insurer was held entitled to rescind.

In *Papoose*,[18] the owners of a 70-foot wooden vessel failed to provide the underwriters with a recent survey showing the vessel to be unseaworthy. The court held the policy to be void for non-disclosure. In *Hauser v. American Central Ins. Co.*,[19] the vessel owner deliberately and falsely stated that a butane stove on board a wooden shrimper had been removed when, in fact, it had not. The court voided the policy. In *Pacific Queen*,[20] the policy was held void for failure to disclose an increase in the capacity of the ship's fuel tanks.[21] In *James Yachts Ltd. v. Thames & Mersey Marine Ins. Co. et al*,[22] the assured boat builder failed to disclose to the insurer that a permit to carry on business at the premises had been refused by the local authorities, and that the business was practically bankrupt. The court held that there had been a non-disclosure of material facts, and that the assured's behavior in carrying on the boat building business was a breach of the implied warranty of legality. The assurers were held entitled, therefore, to avoid liability on the policy.

The duty to disclose is one imposed upon the assured. Merely remaining silent, even though innocently, as to a material fact is sufficient to

---

18. 409 F.2d 974, 1969 AMC 781, [1970] 1 Lloyd's Rep. 178.
19. 216 F.Supp. 318, 1964 AMC 526 (E.D.,La.).
20. 307 F.2d 700, 1962 AMC 1845 (9th Cir.).
21. See, also, *Anglo-African Merchants Ltd. and Exmouth Clothing Co. Ltd. v. Bayley*, [1969] 1 Lloyd's Rep. 268 (shipment of unused 20-year-old army surplus jerkins misrepresented by brokers as new men's clothes); *Perry v. British America Fire & Life Ass. Co.*, (1838) U.C.R. 330 (Can.) (misrepresentation that the vessel had not sailed when, in fact, it had sailed); *Baxter v. New England Ins. Co.*, F.Cas. No. 1,127 (1822, 1st Cir.); *Eisenhaur v. Providence Washington Ins. Co.*, (1887) 20 N.S.R. 48 (Can.) (assured misrepresented that the vessel was still loading, whereas he knew in fact that vessel had already sailed and that another vessel which had sailed about the same time had been involved in very rough weather); *Bailey v. Ocean Mut. Marine Ins. Co.*, (1891) 19 S.C.R. 153 (Can.) (representation that the vessel would be towed "up and back" the river on its proposed voyage; the vessel was lost while steaming under its own power); *Brooks-Scanlon O'Brien Co. v. Boston Ins. Co.*, [1919] 2 W.W.R. 129, 47 D.L.R. 93 (Can.,B.C.) (assured represented that scows would be towed singly and they were not; coverage denied); *Egremont Castle*, 1934 AMC 1317 (St.,N.Y.) (underwriters were considering the plaintiff's brokers' binders when an explosion occurred on the vessel but which was not reported to underwriters; held, a failure so to notify was a breach of *uberrimae fides*); *Dalglish v. Jarvie*, (1850) 42 E.R. 89 (failure to disclose information which may influence the rate of premium, although the assured does not know for a fact that such information would influence the rate of premium, vitiates the policy); *Liberian Ins. Co. v. Mosse*, [1977] 2 Lloyd's Rep. 560 (enamelware described, but cups and plates in wooden cases actually consisted of goods touched up by overpainting; many were packed in cartons instead of wooden cases, and the cargo lot was an end of stock or job lot purchase at a low price; held, non-disclosure by the assured).
22. [1977] 1 Lloyd's Rep. 206 (Can.).

avoid the policy.[23] Moreover, failure on the part of an assured to disclose a material fact known to his agent will be imputed to the assured and the policy may be voided.[24] The *bona fides* of the assured really has very little to do with the question, if, in fact, his agent wrongfully fails to disclose that which ought to have been disclosed. Even an honest mistake by the assured will avail him nothing.[25]

Whether or not there is a disclosure by the assured to the insurer of all circumstances known to him and unknown to the insurer which materially affect the risk is a question of fact.[26] The question as to what must be disclosed is one of degree, depending upon the circumstances of each case.[27]

What is a "Material" Circumstance?

Keeping in mind that sub-section 2 of Section 18 specifies that every circumstance is material which would influence the judgment of a prudent insurer in fixing the premium, or in determining whether he will take the risk, what have the courts found to be material? For example, in *Tate v. Hyslop*,[28] the failure of an assured to inform underwriters that he had entered into a contract with a lighterman whereby the lighterman would be liable only for negligence was held to be a material circumstance vitiating the policy.

In *Scottish Shire Line Ltd. v. London & Provincial Marine & General Ins. Co., Ltd.*,[29] the non-disclosure of the date of arrival of a vessel carrying perishable Hobart apples was held material. In *Rivas v. Gerussi*,[30] the assureds systematically and fraudulently undervalued shipments under an open policy, resulting in a finding that the policies should be set aside and cancelled. In *Harrower v. Hutchison*,[31] the court held that it was material

---

23. *Bates v. Hewitt*, (1867) L.R. 2 Q.B. 595.

24. *Berger and Light Diffusers Pty. Ltd. v. Pollock*, [1973] 2 Lloyd's Rep. 442. See, also, *Proudfoot v. Montefiori*, (1867) L.R. 2 Q.B. 511.

25. *Macdowell v. Fraser*, (1779) 99 E.R. 170; *Journay v. Railway Messengers Assur. Co.*, [1924] 1 D.L.R. 308, 50 N.B.R. 501 (Can.); *Cauto*, 49 F.2d 720, 1931 AMC 1044 (2d Cir.); *Dennistoun v. Lillie*, (1821) 4 E.R. 579, H.L.

26. *Northwestern S.S. Co. v. Maritime Ins. Co.*, 161 F. 166 (9th Cir., 1908); *Alexander v. National Union Fire Ins. Co.*, 104 F.2d 1006, 1939 AMC 923 (2d Cir.); *Ionides v. Pender*, (1874) L.R. 9 Q.B. 531; *Babatsikos v. Car Owners' Mutual Ins. Co., Ltd.*, [1970] V.R. 297, [1970] 2 Lloyd's Rep. 314 (Aus.); *Lindenau v. Desborough*, (1828) 108 E.R. 1160; *Evenden v. Merchants' Casualty Ins. Co. (No. 1)*, [1935] 2 W.W.R. 484, 5 F.L.J. 21 (Can.); *Davies v. National Fire & Marine Ins. Co. of New Zealand*, [1891] A.C. 485, P.C.

27. *Mann Macneal & Steeves Ltd. v. Capital & Counties Ins. Co., Ltd.* [1921] 2 K.B. 300, 15 Asp. M.L.C. 225.

28. (1885) 15 Q.B.D. 368, 5 Asp. M.L.C. 407, C.A.

29. 3 K.B. 51, 12 Asp. M.L.C. 253.

30. (1880) 6 Q.B.D. 222, 4 Asp. M.L.C. 377, C.A.

31. (1870) L.R. 5 Q.B. 584.

that the assured failed to communicate that the vessel was going to another place to complete her loading. In the *Papoose*,[32] the assured did not disclose that the master had reported that the vessel had unusual vibrations, that after repairs she leaked excessively, and that a surveyor had reported she was unfit for duty offshore.[33]

Where an unusual risk is involved, the policy does not cover that risk unless the assured brings it to the attention of the insurer in such a way that the mind of the underwriter was directed toward it.[34]

Although Lloyd's List is *prima facie* evidence against an underwriter as to what the List contains, this does not mean that an underwriter is bound to carry in his head all that is contained in the List relative to a vessel in which he has no interest, rather than holding the owner of the ship bound to disclose it, as this would put a difficult and needless burden upon the underwriter.[35] Consequently, although information may be contained in the List and thus available to the underwriter, if material it is also the duty of the owner to disclose it.[36]

---

32. 409 F.2d 974, 1969 AMC 781 (5th Cir.), [1970] 1 Lloyd's Rep. 178.

33. Other instances of circumstances not disclosed being held to be material are: *Hood v. West End Motor Car Packing Co.*, [1917] 2 K.B. 38, 14 Asp. M.L.C. 12, C.A. (failure to notify underwriters that a car in a packing case was being carried on deck); *London General Ins. Co. v. General Marine Underwriters Ass'n*, [1921] 1 K.B. 104, 4 Ll.L.Rep. 382, C.A. (loss to cargo occurred and the casualty slip containing that information was sent to underwriters who failed to read the slip and reinsured the cargo; held, non-disclosure of material information); *Uzielli v. Commercial Union Ins. Co.*, (1865) 12 L.T. 399 (after application for insurance but before the terms were agreed upon, owner learned that his vessel had put into an intermediate port for repairs but failed to notify the underwriters of this fact); *Mahoney v. Provincial Ins. Co.*, (1869) 12 N.B.R. 633, C.A. (owner of a vessel bound for St. Thomas learned of a violent storm in the vicinity of that island and failed to disclose that fact to underwriters at the time the coverage was placed); *Moses v. Delaware Ins. Co.*, F.Cas. No. 9,872 (3rd Cir., 1806) (failure to communicate news of a hurricane in the vicinity of the vessel); *Greenhill v. Federal Ins. Co.*, [1927] 1 K.B. 65, 17 Asp. M.L.C. 62 (cargo of celluloid shipped partly on deck and exposed for a considerable period of time on an open quay); *Allden v. Raven (Kylie)*, [1983] 2 Lloyd's Rep. 444, Q.B.D.. (non-disclosure by the assured that he had been convicted earlier of handling stolen goods and that the vessel had been built from a kit); *Intermunicipal Realty v. Gore Mut. Ins. Co.*, 1980 AMC 1540 (Can., F.Ct.) (misrepresentation as to the identity of the assured's ship manager was material and fraudulent where it was made to induce underwriters to take on the risk; the fraudulent misrepresentation not only voided the policy *ab initio* but entitled underwriters to retain the whole prepaid premium); *A/S Ivarans v. P.R. Ports Authority*, 617 F.2d 903, 1982 AMC 2493 (1st Cir.) (pier owner sued for indemnity from the reinsurer of its insolvent primary insurer; held, primary insurer's knowledge of two prior incidents of vessel damage resulting from improper maintenance of the pier could not be imputed to the reinsurer).

34. *Cheshire (T) & Co. v. Thompson*, (1919) 24 Com.Cas. 198, C.A.

35. *Mackintosh v. Marshall*, (1843) 152 E.R. 739; *Morrison v. Universal Marine Ins. Co.*, (1872) L.R. 8 Exch. 40; *rev'd on other grounds*, (1873) L.R. 8 Exch. 197, Ex.Ch.; *London General Ins. Co. v. General Marine Underwriters' Ass'n, Ltd.*, (1920) 3 K.B. 23, 3 Ll.L.Rep. 199, *aff'd* (1921) 1 K.B. 104, 4 Ll.L.Rep. 382.

36. See, also, *McFaul v. Montreal Inland Ins. Co.*, (1845) 2 U.C.Q.B. 59 (Can.,C.A.); *Eisenhaur v. Providence Washington Ins. Co.*, (1887) 20 N.S.R. 48 (Can.); *N.S. Marine Ins. Co. v. Stevenson*, (1894) 23 S.C.R. 137; *Neubros Co. v. Northwestern National Life Ins. Co.*, 1972 AMC

Disclosure Not Necessary

On the other hand, as sub-section 3 of Section 18 of the Act so clearly states, it is not necessary to disclose:

(a) Any circumstance which diminishes the risk.[37]

(b) Any circumstance which is known or presumed to be known to the insurer, and, in this respect, the insurer is presumed to know matters of common notoriety or knowledge, and matters which an insurer in the ordinary course of his business, as such, ought to know.[38]

Attention is specifically directed to those cases involving alleged misrepresentations by the assured to underwriters as to the value of a vessel for insurance purposes. It appears that in those instances in which the assured has prevailed, either the information concerning valuation was not considered material or the underwriters either knew, or should have known, that the valuation was not excessive or that the vessel was not undervalued, as the case might be.[39] For example, in *Orange*,[40] the assured got a fantastic bargain in buying a historic ferryboat for only $2,850. Basing his figures on reconstruction costs less straight line depreciation, rather than on sale prices of similar vessels, a U. S. Salvage Association surveyor found a market value of $100,000, and the vessel was insured for that amount at Lloyd's. Later the ferryboat was boarded by thieves who inflicted considerable damage to it. The insured owner finally made claim for a constructive total loss.

2443 (E.D.N.Y.); *Navegacion Goya v. Mutual Boiler,* 411 F.Supp. 929, 1972 AMC 650 (S.D.N.Y.); *Dennistoun v. Lillie,* (1821) 4 E.R. 579, H.L.

37. *Carter v. Boehm,* (1766) 97 E.R. 1162.

38. *Anne Quinn Co. v. American Manufacturers' Mutual,* 369 F.Supp. 1312, 1974 AMC 655 (S.D.N.Y.) (trade usage to overload grain vessels bunkering at Freeport, Bahamas, enroute from U.S. ports to the Far East); *De Costa v. Edmunds,* (1815) 4 Camp. 142 (trade usage); *British & Foreign Marine Ins. Co. v. Gaunt,* [1921] 2 A.C. 41 (trade usage to carry bales of wool on deck); *Freeland v. Glover,* (1806) 103 E.R. 177 (disclosure of a letter which referred to an earlier letter detailing the condition of the vessel and its crew; underwriters failed to ask to examine the first letter); *Anthony D. Nichols,* 49 F.2d 927, 1931 AMC 562 (2d Cir.) (underwriter's surveyor reported vessel to be equipped with a gasoline pump, hoister, and launch; estoppel raised against the underwriter as to the presence of gasoline aboard the vessel); *Companion,* 35 F.2d 956, 1930 AMC 502 (9th Cir.) (hull policy was erroneously issued naming the charterer as the owner, although underwriter knew the name of the real owner); *Wash Gray,* 277 U.S. 66, 1928 AMC 923 (1928) (the existence of a clause exculpating the tug from responsibility "in any way for loss or damage" was not disclosed to underwriters; held to be immaterial, as the clause would not have relieved the tug of the consequences of its own negligence in any event); *Rose and Lucy,* 249 F.Supp. 991, 1965 AMC 1953 (D.,Mass.) (agent of underwriter relied upon a survey of his own rather than any alleged misrepresentations of owner).

39. *Hodgson v. Marine Ins. Co. of Alexandria,* 9 U.S. 100 (1809).

40. 337 F.Supp. 1161, 1972 AMC 627 (S.D.N.Y.).

At the trial, the evidence demonstrated that there was considerable publicity in the general area regarding the assured's purchase of the ferryboat at such a ridiculously low price. Moreover, the court found as a fact that there was a substantial historical value of the ferryboat plus a rather considerable commercial potential for use in chartering and as a commercial floating restaurant. The court sustained the valuation and held the policy was not voided for failure to disclose a material fact, i.e., the purchase price of the vessel.

By contrast, in *King v. Aetna Ins. Co. (The Greyhound)*,[41] a vessel purchased for $2,500 was insured for $40,000 without there being a disclosure to underwriters of the purchase price. In addition, the assured placed two additional policies of $10,000 and $5,000 with other insurance companies and was refused a third additional policy of $15,000 because he refused to divulge the purchase price.

One week after the binder was issued the vessel was totally destroyed by fire. Underwriters defended upon the basis of concealment of the purchase price. In upholding the defense, the court observed that concealment of an overvaluation so excessive as to make the risk speculative vitiates the policy, and that a valuation sixteen times what she had just cost the insured made the risk speculative because the insured had less incentive to protect her than he would have had if he had paid a price somewhere near commensurate with the stated value.

In *Helmville Ltd. v. Yorkshire Ins. Co. (The Medina Princess)*,[42] the vessel was insured for a total of £350,000. At the time of sustaining damage, it had a value of about £65,000 and, in addition, the assured had taken out freight and disbursements policies for an additional £75,000. A claim was made for a constructive total loss which, if allowed, would have brought the assured a total of £425,000. The claim was denied but on grounds other than overvaluation. In his decision, the judge said:

> There is no legal objection to a ship with a low market value being insured on hull and machinery on a high agreed value, where such an agreement accords with the wishes of both parties to the transaction. This was undoubtedly so in the present case. The plaintiffs wished for a high value, the cost of obtaining which was not very much greater than the cost of obtaining insurance on a lower value. Underwriters also wanted a high value, for insurance on a high value enabled their premium income to be maintained without the necessity for an increase in the actual rate per cent of premium.

---

41. 54 F.2d 253, 1931 AMC 1940 (2d Cir.). See, also, *Btesh v. Royal Ins. Co.*, 49 F.2d 720, 1931 AMC 1044 (2d Cir.), and *Hauser v. American Central Ins. Co.*, 216 F.Supp. 318, 1964 AMC 526 (E.D.,La.).
42. [1965] 1 Lloyd's Rep. 361.

In summary, it appears that the policy is voidable if an overvaluation is for the purpose of defrauding the underwriters and proof is adduced to this effect.[43] But a non-disclosure amounting to suppression of material fact vitiates the policy.[44]

In any event, however, the knowledge of the underwriter must be as complete as that of the assured, and if it is not, then the assured has a duty to disclose.[45]

It is not, under Section 18, necessary to disclose:

(c) Any circumstance as to which information is waived by the insurer.[46]

Mann, McNeal, and Steeves v. Capital and Counties Ins. Co.[47] illustrates the foregoing perfectly. In that case, the insureds insured the hull and machinery of a wooden auxiliary vessel for a voyage from the United States to France and return. The vessel was lost by fire on its return voyage from France to the United States. Underwriters defended on the ground of non-disclosure of the fact that the vessel was carrying as part of its cargo 100,000 gallons of petrol in 2,500 drums. The evidence indicated that the carriage of petrol in drums was not an unusual occurence in trade from the United States to France and that the vessel normally would carry petrol and oil for its own engines. It was held that the underwriters had waived disclosure by not making inquiry as to the nature of the cargo and thus could not avoid the contract.

The practice of underwriters, however, in accepting risks or not making inquiries on particular points cannot affect the duty of the assured to disclose, or be received as evidence of waiver in any particular case.[48] In short, waiver is not to be lightly presumed.[49]

---

43. *Haigh v. De la Cour*, (1812) 3 Camp. 319, N.P.
44. *Ionides v. Pender*, (1874) L.R. 9 Q.B.; *Gooding v. White*, (1913) 29 T.L.R. 312. See, also, *Hoff Trading Co. v. Union Ins. Soc. of Canton, Ltd.*, (1929) 34 Ll.L.Rep. 85, C.A., where the court stated that where an assured proposes a valuation based upon what he believes to be a reasonable prospect of appreciation, he must make it plain to the insurer that the value stated is not immediate but speculative, and if this disclosure is not made to the insurer, the insurance will be void even though the statement of value by the assured did not amount to a conscious and deliberate overvaluation.
45. *Sun Mut. Ins. Co. v. Ocean Ins. Co.*, 107 U.S. 485 (1882); *Moses v. Delaware Ins. Co.*, F.Cas. No. 9,872 (3rd Cir., 1806).
46. *Carter v. Boehm*, (1766) 97 E.R. 1162; *Property Ins. Co., Ltd. v. National Protector Ins. Co., Ltd.*, (1913) 108 L.T. 104; *Freeland v. Glover*, (1806) 103 E.R. 177); *Mann, Macneal & Steeves Ltd. v. Capital Counties Ins. Co. Ltd.*, [1921] 2 K.B. 300, 15 Asp. M.L.C. 225; *Herring v. Jansen*, (1895) 1 Com.Cas. 177; *Centiere Meccanico Brindisino v. Janson*, [1912] 3 K.B. 452, C.A.; *Court v. Martineau*, (1782) 99 E.R. 591; *The Bedouin*, [1894] P. 1, 7 Asp. M.L.C. 391, C.A.
47. [1921] 2 K.B. 300, 15 Asp. M.L.C. 225.
48. *Thames and Mersey Marine Ins. Co., Ltd. v. Gunford Ship Co., Ltd.*, [1911] A.C. 529, 12 Asp. M.L.C. 49.
49. *Greenhill v. Federal Ins. Co.*, [1927] 1 K.B. 65, 17 Asp. M.L.C. 62.

(d) Any circumstance which it is superfluous to disclose by reason of any express or implied warranty.[50] The logic of this principle is compelling; surely there is no necessity of disclosing a fact or circumstance which would be deemed to be embraced in and an ingredient of an express or implied warranty.

(4) Whether any particular circumstance, which is not disclosed, be material or not is, in each case, a question of fact.[51] Expert testimony is admissible with respect to the materiality of facts which have not been disclosed.[52]

Keeping in mind that sub-section 2 of Section 18 of the Act provides that every circumstance is material which would influence *the judgment of a prudent insurer* in fixing the premium or determining whether he will take the risk, a rather difficult question is presented with respect to the judgment of the *particular* insurer and whether or not he would have been influenced by the fact not disclosed. Recent decisions are somewhat conflicting on this point.

In *Zurich General Accident and Liability Ins. Co. v. Morrison,*[53] Lord Justice Mackinnon had this to say:

> . . . what is material is that which would have influenced the mind of a prudent insurer in deciding whether to accept the risk or fix the premium, and if this be proved, it is not necessary further to prove that the mind of the actual insurer was so affected. In other words, the assured could not rebut the claim to avoid the policy because of a material representation by a plea that the particular insurer concerned was so stupid, ignorant or reckless that he could not exercise the judgment of a prudent insurer and was, in fact, unaffected by anything the assured has represented or concealed.

---

50. *Thames and Mersey Marine Ins. Co. v. Gunford Ship Co., Ltd.,* [1911] A.C. 529, 12 Asp. M.L.C. 49 (master had not been to sea in 22 years; held superfluous to disclose this fact because of the implied warranty of seaworthiness); *Haywood v. Rodgers,* (1804) 102 E.R. 957 (unnecessary to disclose the necessity of having the ship surveyed because of her bad character inasmuch as the assured impliedly warranted the vessel to be seaworthy in any event). See, also, *Boak v. Merchants' Marine Ins. Co.,* (1876) 10 N.S.R. (1 R. & C.) 288, *aff'd* 1 S.C.R. 110 (Can.), and *Standard Marine Ins. Co. v. Whalen Pulp & Paper Co.,* (1922) 64 S.C.R. 90, 68 D.L.R. 269.

51. See discussion *supra.*

52. *Scottish Shire Line v. London and Provincial Mar. Ins. Co.,* [1912] 3 K.B. 51; 81 L.J.K.B. 1066; *Richards v. Murdock,* (1830) 109 E.R. 546; *Ionides v. Pender,* (1874) L.R. 9 Q.B. 531; *Thames and Mersey Mar. Ins. Co. v. Gunford Ship Co., Ltd.,* [1911] A.C. 529, 12 Asp. M.L.C. 49; *Hoff Trading Co. v. Union Ins. Soc. of Canton, Ltd.,* (1929) 34 Ll.L.Rep. 85. There are, however, conflicting earlier decisions. See, for example, *Durrell v. Bederley,* (1816) Holt, N.P. 283, and *Campbell v. Richards,* (1833) 2 L.J.K.B. 204, 110 E.R. 1001. However, admission of such evidence now seems to be common practice.

53. [1942] 2 K.B. 53.

In *Berger and Light Diffusers Pty. Ltd. v. Pollock*,[54] Mr. Justice Kerr took a rather more "subjective" approach in stating that the court, in deciding whether a policy can be avoided for non-disclosure, must determine as

> . . . a question of fact whether by applying the standard of the judgment of a prudent insurer, the insurer in question would have been influenced in fixing the premium or taking the risk . . . .

The question arose again in *Visscher Enterprises Pty. Ltd v. Southern Pacific Ins. Co. Ltd.*[55] In that case, there was a hole in the aft engine room bulkhead which the owner had cut around the propeller shaft. An engine room fire ruptured a rubber coupling in the raw water line which admitted seawater for cooling the engines. Water rushed into the engine room, and the hole around the propeller shaft allowed water to enter the adjoining compartment in sufficient quantities to cause the ship to founder. There were other holes in the bulkhead through which bilge lines ran, and the bilge lines were also fitted with rubber couplings which would have been destroyed by the fire. The court found that because of the fire these couplings would have been destroyed and the hold would have been flooded in any event, whether the hole around the propeller was there or not.

One ground of defense by underwriters was that the existence of the hole around the propeller shaft was a material circumstance which ought to have been disclosed. There was a great deal of evidence as to whether the existence of the hole would have influenced the judgement of a prudent insurer. The trial court found that, on the facts, a prudent insurer would not have been influenced by it and, in reaching his conclusion, took into account that the defendant insurer itself would not (as he found) have been influenced in determining whether to take the risk had the disclosure been made. He also took into account the failure of the defendant insurer to give any evidence of how knowledge of the hole would have affected its behavior. The full court affirmed, stating in part:

> [E]vidence as to the practice of the particular insurer may in some cases be relevant and admissible . . . at least in cases where the question of materiality is not obvious evidence of experts as to insurance practice generally is admissible. . . . [I]n such doubtful cases it is desirable for the particular insurer to give evidence itself as to whether it would have been influenced had it known of the undisclosed circumstances.

It will thus be seen that *Visscher* stands for the proposition that the defense of non-disclosure will not be available to an insurer who would not,

---

54. [1973] 2 Lloyd's Rep. 442.
55. [1981] Qd.R. 561.

in fact, have been influenced by the information withheld, even if prudent insurers would have been so influenced. It also points up the danger to insurers of failing to give evidence on this issue in a doubtful case.

The point surfaced again in *Itobar Pty. Ltd. v. Mackinnon and Commercial Ins. Co., PLC*,[56] where the alleged non-disclosure involved a failure of the assured to disclose that the vessel's master had been convicted of a number of criminal offenses. The trial court felt constrained to follow the decision in *Visscher*, although noting that the law prevailing in Queensland now differed from that of the United Kingdom as a result of the decision in *Container Transport International, Inc. v. Oceanus Mutual Underwriting Association (Bermuda) Ltd*,[57] where Kerr, L. J., confessed that he regarded himself as having been "wrong" in the view he earlier had taken in *Berger and Light Diffusers Pty. Ltd. v. Pollock.*

The court of appeal in *Container Transport* squarely held that in determining whether there had been a non-disclosure within the section, the yardstick is the prudent insurer and not the particular insurer, and that there was no requirement that the particular insurer should have been induced to take the risk or charge a lower premium than he would otherwise have done as a result of the non-disclosure. The court also added that the very choice of a "prudent underwriter" as the yardstick indicated that the test intended was one which could be sensibly answered in relation to prudent underwriters in general. In the event, the court held that the underwriter had established both misrepresentation and concealment of material facts as to which there had been no waiver by the underwriter.

(5) The term "circumstance" includes any communication made to, or information received by, the assured.[58]

A representation as to a matter of fact is true if it is substantially correct.[59] That is, if the difference between what is represented and what is actually correct would not be considered material by a prudent insurer.[60]

There is a fundamental distinction, however, between the non-disclosure of a circumstance considered material and a representation as to a matter of expectation or belief if made in good faith. In the former, the non-disclosure enables the insurer to avoid the policy; in the latter, it does

---

56. (1985) 3 ANZ Ins. Cas. 60-610 (Aus.).

57. [1984] 1 Lloyd's Rep. 476.

58. *Morrison v. Universal Marine Ins. Co.*, (1872) L.R. 8 Exch. 40, *rev'd* on other grounds, (1873) L.R. 8 Exch. 197, Ex.Ch.; *Rivaz v. Gerussi*, (1880) 6 Q.B.D. 222, 4 Asp. M.L.C. 377, C.A. (an apparently well-founded rumor, although it may later turn out to have been incorrect, must be disclosed to underwriter); *The Papoose*, 409 F.2d 974, 1969 AMC 781 (5th Cir.) (*inter alia*, the assured failed to disclose to insurers that the master had reported to him that the vessel had unusual rhythmic vibrations).

59. *Pawson v. Watson*, (1778) 98 E.R. 1361.

60. *Macdowell v. Frazer*, (1779) 99 E.R. 170.

not. Compare, in this instance, *Cauto*[61] with *Anderson v. Pacific Mar. Ins. Co.*[62]

As might be logically expected, a representation may be withdrawn or corrected before the insurance contract is concluded.[63]

Duty to Disclose until Contract Concluded

The placement of insurance coverage frequently involves considerable negotiation, search for appropriate markets by the broker, analysis of the risk by the prospective underwriters, and discussions with respect to the premium to be charged. These negotiations and discussions may take considerable time, during which new information may come to the attention of the broker and assured which bears materially on the risk. In such circumstances, the assured and his broker have a duty to disclose to underwriters such new information until such time as the *contract of insurance is concluded.*

For example, in *Berger & Light Diffusers Pty. Ltd. v. Pollock,*[64] the insurance was accepted under a "cross slip" which was to be eventually supplemented by further information. It was held that there was a continuing duty of disclosure between the date of the "cross slip" and the "signing slip."

In *Rallod Transp. Co. v. Continental Ins. Co.,*[65] a steamship agent sought and procured legal and contractual liability insurance from the defendant underwriter. An oral contract of insurance was formed as of noon, February 13, 1979. A formal written policy was issued on February 14, 1979. The steamship agent was subsequently sued by a company which had chartered vessels to the agent's principal who defaulted in the payment of the charter hire. The suit against the broker was to enforce a contractual lien on freights which the agent presumably had in its possession. When sued, the agent sought protection under its policy with the defendant underwriter. The underwriter defended on the grounds that the steamship agent had concealed information material to the execution of the contract of insurance; i.e., information which had come to the agent's attention prior to the completion of the contract of insurance.

The trial court held that the assured's duty of full disclosure continued until the policy was issued on February 14, 1979. On appeal, the Ninth Circuit reversed, noting that all the cases relied upon by the trial

61. 49 F.2d 720, 1931 AMC 1044 (2d Cir.).
62. (1872) L.R. 7 C.P. 65, 1 Asp. M.L.C. 220.
63. *Edwards v. Footner,* (1808) 1 Camp. 530; see Sec. 20(6) of the Act, where this principle has been put into statutory language.
64. [1973] 2 Lloyd's Rep. 442.
65. 727 F.2d 851 (9th Cir., 1984).

court involved contracts of insurance which were not deemed concluded until the actual issuance of policies. There being no dispute that an oral contract of insurance had been concluded at noon on February 13, 1979, and that oral contracts of insurance are valid under the law of the jurisdiction, the case was remanded for findings of fact as to what the steamship agent knew or should have known as of noon on February 13, 1979.

CHAPTER XI

WARRANTIES

A. Express Warranties

The Marine Insurance Act, 1906, defines a warranty as follows in Section 33:

(1) A warranty, in the following sections relating to warranties, means a promissory warranty, that is to say, a warranty by which the assured undertakes that some particular thing shall or shall not be done, or that some condition shall be fulfilled, or whereby he affirms or negatives the existence of a particular state of facts.

(2) A warranty may be express or implied.

(3) A warranty, as above defined, is a condition which must be exactly complied with whether it be material to the risk or not. If it be not so complied with, then, subject to any express provision in the policy, the insurer is discharged from liability as from the date of the breach of warranty, but without prejudice to any liability incurred by him before that date.

Section 34 applies to warranties generally and relates to excuses for non-compliance.

It reads:

(1) Non-compliance with a warranty is excused when, by reason of a change in circumstances, the warranty ceases to be applicable to the circumstances of the contract, or when compliance with the warranty is rendered unlawful by any subsequent law.[1]

(2) Where a warranty is broken, the assured cannot avail himself of the defence that the breach has been remedied, and the warranty complied with, before loss.

(3) A breach of warranty may be waived by the insurer.

Section 35 deals with express warranties in particular. It reads:

(1) An express warranty may be in any form of words from which the intention to warrant is to be inferred.

(2) An express warranty must be included in, or written upon, the policy, or must be contained in some document incorporated by reference into the policy.

---

1. See discussion *infra*.

(3) An express warranty does not exclude an implied warranty, unless it be inconsistent therewith.

Contained in a Policy

Obviously, nothing could be considered as an express warranty unless it is somehow incorporated in, or expressly referred to so as to effect an incorporation in, the policy.[2]

Such an incorporation may be expressed almost any way one chooses so long as it conveys the thought that incorporation is intended.[3] Section 35(2) of the Act explicitly recognizes this principle.

What Amounts to a Warranty

Any form of language from which an intention to warrant may be inferred will suffice to constitute a warranty.[4] However, using the word "warranted" in the policy does not necessarily mean that what follows is a true warranty. Although it may be, and often is, equivalent to a condition precedent, it may also indicate merely an exception to the overall coverage provided by the policy such as, for example, "warranted free of capture and seizure."[5] Merely labeling a statement a warranty does not make it so. The typical hull policy contains a number of clauses which begin with the word "warranted" which are not true warranties at all, of which the F. C. & S. warranty mentioned above is a good example. On the other hand, policies can contain clear warranties. For example, see the private pleasure warranty involved in *Reliance Ins. Co. v. The Escapade*[6] which reads:

> Warranted by the Assured that the vessel shall not be used for private pleasure purposes and shall not be hired or chartered, etc.

The yacht grounded while under charter. Although the underwriter could have avoided the policy, its action in insisting that the assured take

---

2. In *Pawson v. Barnevelt*, (1779) 1 Doug. 12 and *Bize v. Fletcher*, it was held that something attached to the policy but not contained within the written language could not be considered as a warranty. These decisions were followed in *Higginson v. Dall*, 13 Mass. 96 (1816) and *Goddard v. East Texas Fire Ins. Co.*, 67 Tex. 69 (1886), but none represents the law as it is viewed today.

3. See *Kenyon v. Berthon*, (1778) 1 Doug. 12; *Blackhurst v. Cockel*, (1789) 3 T.R. 360.

4. *Yorkshire Ins. Co. Ltd. v. Campbell*, [1917] A.C. 218; *Union Ins. Co. of Canton Ltd. v. Wills*, [1916] A.C. 281. There are, in fact, cases in which merely describing the vessel as, for example, "a Danish brig" amounts to an express warranty that the vessel insured has the national character ascribed to it in the policy. See *Baring v. Claggett*, (1802) 3 B. & P. 201. The principle operates the same in the United States. Phillips, *Marine Insurance*, Sec. 757.

5. *Roberts v. Anglo-Saxon Ins. Ass'n Ltd.*, (1926) 26 Ll.L.Rep. 154.

6. 280 F.2d 482, 1961 AMC 2410 (5th Cir.).

steps to save the yacht and to authorize salvage operations was held to create an estoppel.[7]

Certain it is that statments of fact contained in a policy are almost invariably construed as warranties and, as such, must be literally complied with. Thus, in the words of Section 35(1) of the Act, an "intention to warrant is to be inferred" from any such statements of fact.

It is also clear that a warranty may be either a condition precedent or a condition subsequent.[8] There is, of course, a material distinction between a warranty and a representation. A representation may be equitably and substantially answered; a warranty is a condition or contingency which, unless performed, abrogates the contract. It is immaterial for what purpose a warranty is introduced, but, being inserted, the contract does not exist unless it be literally complied with.[9]

A warranty may also be either express or implied, but, as the Act notes (Section 35(3)), an express warranty does not exclude an implied warranty unless it is inconsistent therewith. This merely reflects the common law prior to enactment of the Act.[10] As used in marine policies, it is a representation or undertaking that something exists, or that something will be done or not done.

For example, in *Scow No. 12*,[11] the policy contained a warranty that the scow would be towed by an approved tug with a full crew. A mate was missing from the tug's crew, and his absence was held to be a breach of the warranty. In *Kron v. Hanover Fire Ins. Co.*,[12] there was a provision that gasoline or explosives would not be kept aboard a tug without permission being endorsed on the policy; gasoline was kept on board without the underwriters' permission or knowledge and an explosion occurred. The court held that compliance with the warranty was a condition precedent to imposing liability on the underwriters. In *Harlem*,[13] there was a warranty that a watchman would be kept on board an insured barge at all times. The watchman left the vessel to get his supper, during which time a loss occurred. The court held the condition was breached and denied recovery.

In *Henjes v. Aetna Ins. Co.*,[14] the warranty was that the tug would not proceed in certain coastal waters with more than one vessel in tow. The

7. To the same effect, see *Provincial Ins. Co. of Canada v. Leduc*, (1874) L.R. 6 P.C. 244, where underwriters took possession, made repairs, and detained the vessel for an unreasonable period of time, resulting in a constructive acceptance of abandonment.

8. *Union Ins. Soc. of Canton v. Wills & Co.*, [1916] A.C. 281, P.C.

9. *De Hahn v. Hartley*, (1786) 99 E.R. 1130.

10. *Sleigh v. Tyser*, (1900) 2 Q.B. 333, 9 Asp. M.L.C. 97; *Quebec Marine Ins. Co. v. Commercial Bank of Canada*, (1870) L.R. 3 P.C. 234, 17 E.R. 1, P.C.

11. 1929 AMC 425 (W.D.,Wash.), aff'd 35 F.2d 862, 1930 AMC 557 (9th Cir.).

12. 246 N.Y.S.2d 848, 1964 AMC 1467 (St.,N.Y.).

13. 1927 AMC 1088; see, also, *The Silk*, 1931 AMC 1348 (St.,N.Y.).

14. 132 F.2d 715, 1943 AMC 27 (2d Cir.).

master combined the tug and barge with two other tugs and barges to make up a combined flotilla handled by three tugs. The combined tow got into difficulty during a storm and the insured tug was lost endeavoring to retrieve a barge which had gone adrift. The court held that the policy did not cover.

In *Lighter No. 176,*[15] a barge which had been laid up for some time was purchased from the government and insured for a sea voyage. The movement did not start until approximately a month after the policy attached. The court held that there was no "deviation" since there was nothing in the policy to indicate that time was important and no representations had been made as to the time of the proposed movement.

In *Wilson, Harraway & Co. v. National Fire & Marine Ins. Co. of New Zealand,*[16] the warranty was that the vessel would be towed in and out of a certain port. It was held that a non-compliance therewith was not excused by a barratrous act of the master, as the warranty was absolute. Compare, however, *U.S. Fire v. Cavanaugh,*[17] where the proximate cause of a fishing boat's loss was barratry of the master (an insured peril) even though the master's deliberate act and wilful misconduct resulted in a breach of the vessel owner's warranty that the vessel would not be operated beyond certain prescribed geographical limits. The vessel owner recovered his full loss, plus interest and fees.

In a policy of insurance, *prima facie* all the words which the policy contains except parts of the general form inapplicable to the particular transaction, are words of contract. Words qualifying the subject matter of the insurance are words of warranty which must be complied with, whether material to the risk or not. In considering whether words were intended by the parties to be a warranty, regard must be had to the nature of the transaction and the known course of business and forms in which similar transactions are carried out.[18]

Exact and Literal Compliance Necessary

Under English and Commonwealth law, a warranty must be exactly complied with whether the warranty is material to the risk or not. If not complied with and the breach is not waived by the underwriter, the underwriter is discharged from liability as of the date of the breach but without prejudice to any liability incurred under the policy prior to the breach.[19]

---

15. 1929 AMC 554 (St.,Md.).

16. (1886) 4 N.Z.L.R. 343 (S.C., N.Z.).

17. 732 F.2d 832, 1985 AMC 1001 (11th Cir.).

18. *Yorkshire Ins. Co. Ltd. v. Campbell,* (1917) A.C. 218, 115 L.T. 644, P.C.

19. *Pawson v. Watson,* (1778) 98 E.R. 1361; *De Hahn v. Hartley,* (1786) 99 E.R. 1130; *Blackhurst v. Cockell,* (1789) 100 E.R. 620; *Moore v. Provincial Ins. Co.,* (1873) 23 C.P. 383 (Can.); *Wilson, Harraway & Co. v. National Fire & Marine Ins. Co. of New Zealand,* (1886) 4 N.Z.L.R.

A mere intention to breach a warranty without actually doing so is not a breach of the warranty.[20]

A strict performance of the warranty is not dispensed with by an unavoidable necessity preventing it. For example, in *Colby v. Hunter*,[21] there was a warranty that the ship was in port A on a given antecedent day. It was held that it was not sufficient that she was safe in some other port than A on the day in question; the meaning of the warranty was that she was safe in the port of A.[22]

In *Beacon Life Etc. Assur. Co. v. Gibb*,[23] a policy of fire insurance was written on a vessel using an ordinary form of fire policy. The policy contained a condition that if more than twenty pounds of gunpowder was upon the "premises" at any time when a loss occurred, the loss would not be made good. The ship burned at a time when she was carrying about 100 pounds of gunpowder. Holding that the word "premises" obviously meant the vessel itself, and that there had been a wilful violation of the condition, the court relieved the insurer from liability although the violation was not shown to have caused the loss.

Other examples of express warranties which have been judicially construed are: *Roddick v. Indemnity Mutual Ins. Co.*[24] (hull and machinery policy warranted 50 percent uninsured; the assured procured an honor policy covering "disbursements"; the insurers refused to pay; held, the warranty was not breached, as disbursements are not embraced within the term "hull and machinery"); *Overseas Commodities, Ltd. v. Style*[25] (a warranty that tins would be marked for verification so as to identify the date of manufacture; substantial numbers of the tins were not so marked; held, no recovery); *Ocean Trawling Co. Pty. Ltd. v. Fire and All Risks Ins. Co.*,

343 (S.C.,N.Z.); *Newcastle Fire Ins. Co. v. Macmorran*, (1815) 3 Dow. 255; *Yorkshire Ins. Co. v. Campbell*, [1917] A.C. 218.

20. *Simpson S.S. Co. v. Premier Underwriting Ass'n*, (1905) 92 L.T. 730, 10 Asp. M.L.C. 126 (the assured intended to breach the warranty but the vessel was lost prior to the point where the breach would have taken place).

21. (1827) 3 C. & P. 7, Mood & M. 81, N.P.

22. See, also, *Hore v. Whitmore*, (1778) 98 E.R. 1360; *Nelson v. Salvador*, (1829) Dan & Ll. 219, Mood. & M. 309; *Ridsdale v. Newnham*, (1815) 105 E.R. 681 (the ship was warranted to sail on or before October 28th but did not sail until October 30th; held, no compliance with the warranty); *Pittegrew v. Pringle*, (1832) 110 E.R. 186 (the insured vessel crossed a bar without ballasting; it was held that until she was ballasted, there was not "sailing," and she was not ready for sea within the terms of the policy); *Graham v. Barras*, (1834) 110 E.R. 1065 (the ship was to sail by September 1; she actually sailed on September 2d because of the lack of a full crew; held, warranty not complied with); *Duncan & Co. v. British America Ins. Co.*, (1871) 1 P.E.I. 370 (Can.) (ship did not sail by the day named in the policy; underwriters not liable); *Warren v. Thomas*, (1851) 3 Nfld. L.R. 168 (Can.) (the ship did not break ground by the date named; held, no coverage). Clearly, a date stipulated in the application that the vessel will sail on a particular day is construed as a warranty that she will sail on that particular day. *Royal Canadian Ins. Co. v. Pugh*, (1887) 20 N.S.R. (8 R. & G.) 133, 8 C.L.T. 378 (Can.).

23. (1862) 15 E.R. 630.

24. (1895) 2 Q.B. 380, 8 Asp. M.L.C. 24, C.A.

25. (1958) 1 Lloyd's Rep. 546.

Ltd.[26] (a statute required inspection of vessels' machinery at least once each year; a survey was performed, but no certificate was issued; held, insurer liable where the certificate was not issued merely because of departmental delay); *Sea Ins. Co. v. Blogg*[27] (vessel completed loading on the evening of February 29th and departed the wharf to lie in the stream until the following morning; policy was warranted to sail "on or after March 1"; it was held that the act of leaving the wharf did not constitute a sailing, and the policy therefore attached); *Hart v. Standard Marine Ins. Co.*[28] (policy was warranted "no iron, or ore, or phosphate cargo, exceeding the net registered tonnage"; a quantity of steel exceeding the net registered tonnage was shipped; held, warranty breached); *Birrell v. Dryer*[29] (policy was warranted "no St. Lawrence between October 1 and April 1"; vessel had navigated the Gulf of St. Lawrence during the prohibited period and was lost enroute home; held, warranty breached, as the words "St. Lawrence" included both the river and the gulf); *Cochrane v. Fisher*[30] (policy was warranted "not to sail for British North America after August 15"; on August 15, the vessel was ready for sea, had cleared customs, and was warped part of the way down the harbor but was detained by inclement winds until August 17th; held, warranty not breached); *Union Ins. Soc. of Canton v. George Wills & Co.*[31] (open cargo policy required declarations as to shipments of goods "as soon as possible after sailing of vessel to which interest attaches"; declarations were made but not as soon as possible; the underwriters were relieved of liability, as the warranty had been breached); *Staples v. Great American Ins. Co.*[32] (warranty for private pleasure use only; held, warranty breached when the owner permitted others to use the vessel for their own purposes); *Palmer v. Fenning*[33] (unreasonable delay in sailing); *Spinney v. Ocean Mut. Marine Ins. Co.*[34] (unreasonable delay in sailing); *Robertson v. Pugh*[35] (failure to leave harbor on date specified in the warranty); *James Duncan & Co. v. B.A. Ins. Co.*[36] (failure to sail when warranted); *Provincial Ins. Co. v. Connolly*[37] (vessel warranted to go out of the harbor under tow but did not do so); *Troop v. Union Ins. Co.*[38] (warranty as to restricted waters was breached); *Campbell v. Can. Ins.*

26. (1965) W.A.R. 65 (W.S.Sup.Crt., Aus.).
27. (1898) 2 Q.B. 398, 8 Asp. M.L.C. 412.
28. (1889) 22 Q.B.D. 499, 6 Asp. M.L.C. 368, C.A.
29. (1884) 9 App.Cas. 345, 5 Asp. M.L.C. 267, H.L.
30. (1835) 149 E.R. 1307.
31. (1916) A.C. 281, 13 Asp. M.L.C. 233, P.C.
32. (1939) 4 D.L.R. 798 (Can.).
33. (1833) 131 E.R. 685.
34. (1890) 17 S.C.R. 326.
35. (1888) 15 S.C.R. 706.
36. (1871) 1 P.E.I. 370, Peters 243 (Can.).
37. (1879) 5 S.C.R. 258 (Can.).
38. (1893) 32 N.B.R. 135, C.A. (Can.).

Union[39] (loss occurred in prohibited port); *Owen v. Ocean Mut. Marine Ins. Co.*[40] (warranty as to not sailing in Gulf of St. Lawrence breached); *O'Leary v. Pelican Ins. Co.*[41] (breach of warranty as to loading and use of certain waters); *Richard S.S. Co. v. China Mut. Ins. Co.*[42] (breach of warranty as to restricted waters); *Robertson v. Stairs*[43] (breach of warranty not to sail in prohibited waters); *Taylor v. Moran*[44] (breach of warranty in attempting to enter a forbidden port); *Simons v. Gale*[45] (breach of warranty to make all arrangements for conversion of the vessel at the inception of the insurance); *Laurent Gendron Ltd. v. Union Ins. Soc. of Canton, Ltee*[46] (breach of lay-up warranty); *Yangtze Ins. Ass'n v. Indemnity Mut. Marine Assur. Co.*[47] (warranty not to carry "contraband of war" applicable to goods only and not to the transportation of military officers of a belligerent state as passengers on board a neutral ship); *Aktieselkabet Grenland v. Janson*[48] (warranty against carrying mining timber; vessel carried timber which could have been used in mines although this was not the primary purpose; German governnment seized the cargo as contraband; held, decision of the German government was not binding as to the meaning of the term "mining timber" in the warranty, and the assured recovered).

An interesting point arose in *General Ins. Co. Ltd. of Trieste v. Cory.*[49] A time policy on hull and machinery of a vessel valued at £12,000 contained a provision "warranted £2,400 uninsured." The owner effected time policies to the total amount of £9,600, one of the policies being effected with a syndicate to the amount of £5,000. During the term of the policies, the syndicate stopped payment, and eventually a large majority of the members became bankrupt. The owner, estimating correctly that the syndicate could not respond for more than £2,000, took out further policies for £3,000. The ship was lost, and the total amount the owner could recover under the most favorable circumstances was less than £9,600. It was held in the circumstances that effecting more insurance than the warranty permitted was not a breach of the warranty.

In *Samuel (P) & Co., Ltd. v. Dumas*,[50] the policy contained the usual F. C. & S. Clause and also under the then current Institute Time Clauses a warranty that "the amount insured on account of assured" on (*inter alia*)

39. (1887) 12 N.S.R. 21 (C.A.,Can.).
40. (1885) 18 N.S.R. 495 (C.A.,Can.).
41. (1889) 29 N.B.R. 51 (C.A., Can.).
42. (1907) 42 N.S.R. 240 (Can.).
43. (1875) 10 N.S.R. 345 (C.A.,Can.).
44. (1885) 11 S.C.R. 347 (Can.).
45. [1958] 2 All E.R. 504, [1958] 2 Lloyd's Rep. 1, P.C.
46. [1964] 1 Lloyd's Rep. 220 (Exch. Que., Admiralty Dist.).
47. [1908] 2 K.B. 504, 11 Asp. M.L.C. 138, C.A.
48. (1918) 35 T.L.R. 135.
49. (1897) 1 Q.B. 335.
50. [1924] A.C. 431, 16 Asp. M.L.C. 305, H.L.

freight should not exceed a certain amount. A separate insurance was effected against loss of freight by war risks only in a sum exceeding the amount allowed by the warranty. The court held there was a breach of the warranty. In the United States, prior to the decision in *Wilburn Boat Co. v. Fireman's Fund Ins. Co.*,[51] and in many instances after the *Wilburn Boat* decision, the courts adhered to the English rule and held that a breach of warranty vitiated the policy. *Wilburn* has been characterized as an anomaly and should, when properly understood and construed, be applicable only where there is a countervailing state statute which conflicts with the English rule as to warranties.

The difference in the application of the warranty rules may be described as follows. Under *Wilburn,* where a state statute requires that the breach of warranty must contribute to the loss, the state statute will govern; where the state statute does not so provide, a mere violation of the warranty is sufficient to void the policy even though the loss may not be attributable to the breach.[52] See, for example, *Continental Sea Foods, Inc. v. New Hampshire Fire Ins. Co.*[53] In that case, the policy contained a warranty requiring that the shipment (shrimp) be inspected by government authorities in the country of origin. At the time, there was no such inspection facility in the country of origin (Pakistan) authorized to issue a certificate of inspection. Notwithstanding that performance of the warranty was totally impossible, under New York law a strict literal compliance was required and the assured did not recover.[54]

Clearly, the tendency has been to restrict *Wilburn* to cases involving policy warranties, and even here the courts are far from consistent. To say that the American courts appear to be reluctant to follow *Wilburn* unless constrained to do so is to understate the case.[55]

Prior to *Wilburn,* warranties were held breached in a rather considerable number of cases. For example, in *Gelb v. Automobile Ins. Co.*,[56] a lay-up warranty that the vessel would be laid up and out of commission during the winter was held not satisfied by leaving the boat moored at a boatyard where, in that area, the custom was to haul out such vessels. In *Kane v. Aetna Ins. Co.*,[57] a warranty to lay up the vessel from October 1 to April 1

---

51. 348 U.S. 310, 1955 AMC 467 (1955).

52. It is not precisely accurate to say that breach of a warranty *voids* a policy, inasmuch as a breach of warranty may be waived. In essence, it is merely a breach of a *condition* which, if not waived, discharges the underwriter from liability. And Sec. 34(3), Marine Insurance Act, 1906, expressly provides that a breach of warranty may be waived by the insurer.

53. 1964 AMC 196 (S.D.N.Y.).

54. See, also, *Fidelity Phoenix Ins. Co. v. Chicago Title & Trust Co.*, 12 F.2d 573 (7th Cir., 1926) and *Castleton*, 19 F.Supp. 767, 1937 AMC 1247 (D.C.N.Y.).

55. See discussion, Chap. I, subheading "Marine Insurance in the United States."

56. 168 F.2d 774, 1948 AMC 1257 (2d Cir.).

57. 1955 AMC 2346 (St.,N.J.).

was held breached by leaving the boat in a basin which was not a winter storage yard.[58]

On the other hand, in the following cases antedating *Wilburn Boat*, it was held that there was no breach of warranty: *Merchants' Mut. Ins. Co. v. Allen*[59] (overinsurance of freight not a breach of warranty by the owner not to insure his interest in the vessel; also, Gulf of Mexico considered part of the "Atlantic Ocean"); *St. Paul Fire & Marine Ins. Co. v. Knickerbocker Steam Towing Co.*[60] (warranty against any other insurance exceeding $50,000; assured took out another policy, which provided, however, that it was subordinate to any prior insurance; it was held that as the second policy could only take effect upon suspension of the prior policy, there was at no time insurance in an amount in excess of that permitted); *Gross v. New York & T.S.S. Co.*[61] (policy contained a clause against double insur-

---

58. For other cases, see *Great Western Ins. Co. v. Thwing*, 80 U.S. 672, 20 L.ed. 607 (1871) (carriage of goods weighing more than the vessel's registered tonnage even though carried as dunnage); *St. Paul Fire & Marine Ins. Co. v. Snare & Triest Co.*, 269 F. 603 (2d Cir., 1920) (bottom of scow not seen or examined, in violation of warranty to drydock); *Calbreath v. Gracy*, F.Cas. No. 2,296 (3d. Cir., 1805) (vessel and cargo warranted American but claimed as Spanish property; *Schwartz v. Ins. Co. of N. America*, F.Cas. No. 12,504 (3d Cir., 1811) (breach of warranty of neutrality); *Thames & Mersey Ins. Co. v. O'Connell*, 86 F. 150 (9th Cir., 1898) (vessel lost while proceeding in a prohibited area); *Scow No. 12*, 32 F.2d 271, 1929 AMC 425, aff'd 35 F.2d 862, 1930 AMC 557 (9th Cir., 1929) (tug had no mate, in violation of statute); *New Haven Steam Sawmill Co. v. Security Ins. Co.*, 9 F. 779 (1st Cir., 1881) (breach of voyage limits); *Hearn v. New England Mut. Mar. Ins. Co.*, 87 U.S. 488 (1872) (one port of loading warranted; vessel loaded in two ports); *Providence Washington Ins. Co. v. Brummelkamp*, 58 F. 918 (2d Cir., 1893) (voyage outside permitted limits); *James G. Shaw*, 27 F.Supp. 988, 1928 AMC 1253 (E.D.N.Y.) (loss occurred outside trading limits); *Libbie*, 73 F.2d 3, 1934 AMC 1557 (9th Cir., 1934) (breach of trading warranty); *Whiteman v. Rhode Island Ins. Co.*, 78 F.Supp. 624, 1949 AMC 111 (E.D.,La.) (transfer of management a breach of the warranty against change of interest); *Caballero v. Travelers Ins. Co.*, 1951 AMC 1825 (St., N.Y.) (shipment was to be made partly by water and partly by air; air transportation proved to be impossible and the shipment was made by truck; held, warranty breached); *Mohegan*, 1926 AMC 50 (St.,N.Y.) (warranty to sail on a fixed date breached, as the vessel left its pier without clearance papers and with a defective rudder); *Sylvia Victory*, 9 F.2d 720, 1926 AMC 83 (2d Cir.) (warranted underdeck stowage; cargo carried on deck instead); *Norland*, 12 F.2d 573, 1926 AMC 787 (7th Cir.) (warranted a passenger vessel; vessel did not have the requisite watertight bulkheads, nor was it licensed to carry passengers); *Red Top Brewing v. Mazzoti*, 202 F.2d 481, 1953 AMC 309 (2d Cir.) (warranty requiring inspection and a certificate thereof; certificate produced was inadequate); *Royster Guano Co. v. Globe & Rutgers*, 1930 AMC 11 (St.,N.Y.) (warranty that trips must be approved by a named surveyor; no proof adduced that the named surveyor actually performed the survey); *Maxwell Textile Co. v. Globe & Rutgers*, 1928 AMC 1669 (St.,N.Y.) (warranty against releasing carrier from common law liability; declaration by shipper had the effect of so releasing; held, warranty breached). And in the following cases, a breach was found of the warranty that a watchman had to be aboard. *Dauntless*, 1928 AMC 1430 (St.,N.J.); *Minnie R.*, 1931 AMC 995 (5th Cir.); *Castleton*, 19 F.Supp. 767, 1937 AMC 1247 (S.D.N.Y.); *Shamrock No. 25*, 9 F.2d 57, 1926 AMC 433 (2d Cir.); *Jarvis T. & T. Co. v. Aetna Ins. Co.*, 82 N.E.2d 577, 1949 AMC 108 (St.N.Y.); *Continental Ins. Co. v. Patton-Tully*, 212 F.2d 543, 1954 AMC 889 (5th Cir.); *Harlem*, 1927 AMC 1088 (St. N.Y.); *Silk*, 1931 AMC 1348 (St. N.Y.).

59. 121 U.S. 67, 122 U.S. 376 (1887).

60. 93 F. 931 (1st Cir., 1899).

61. 107 F. 516 (D.C.N.Y., 1901)

ance; both consignee and consignor insured the same shipment of wool, neither being aware that the other had insured; held, no breach of warranty, as the interests of the two assureds were different); *Alexander Ramsey & Kerr v. National Union Fire Ins. Co.*[62] (policy confined a dredge to inland and coastwise waters; dredge was laid up in a drainage canal near the Everglades in the interior of the state of Florida; "inland waters" held to embrace even non-navigable inland waters); *Northwestern S.S. Co. v. Maritime Ins. Co.*[63] (no violation of warranty by stopping at an intermediate port for provisions and coal even though the delay resulted in the vessel's capture); *Anthony D. Nichols*[64] (policy covering while on "inland and coastwise waters of the U.S. and West Indies and waters tributary thereto" held to cover loss off the coast of Yucatan; the words relate to localities, not voyages, and a transitory diversion outside the policy limits held immaterial); *The Indrapura*[65] (vessel went into drydock with cargo aboard; found to be in acceptance with a general custom of the port).

There are, of course, after *Wilburn Boat*, numerous cases where express warranties have been found to have been breached. Typical examples are *Miss Esmeralda, (Grounding)*[66] where the use of a two-man crew where a three-man crew was required was held to be a breach of an express warranty; *Rosenberg v. Maritime Ins. Co.*,[67] where there was a breach of the trading warranty, among others; *Capital Coastal v. Hartford Fire (The Christie)*,[68] where there was a special warranty that a named individual would be captain of the vessel and an unapproved captain was acting when the loss occurred; *R. & W. Boat Rentals v. Penna. Ins. Co.*,[69] where the warranty was that the vessel would be confined to inland waters and the vessel was lost while being towed 10 miles off the Louisiana coast; *Continental Sea Foods, Inc. v. New Hampshire Fire Ins. Co.*,[70] where the warranty was that the assured would obtain an inspection certificate from the country of origin covering a cargo of shrimp but it was impossible to do so as there was no certification authority in the country of origin.

In *Tinkerbell*,[71] the assured had warranted that his vessel would be laid up and out of commission in a certain port from October 1 to April 1. The assured instructed the master to lay her up by October 1, but unbeknownst to him, the master put into another (and less protected) port

---

62. 104 F. 1006 (2d Cir.).
63. 161 F. 166 (9th Cir., 1908).
64. 49 F.2d 927, 1931 AMC 562 (D.C.N.Y.).
65. 238 F. 853 (D. Ore., 1916).
66. 441 F.2d 141, 1971 AMC 1134 (5th Cir.).
67. 1968 AMC 1609 (St.,Fla.).
68. 378 F.Supp. 163, 1974 AMC 2039, [1975] 2 Lloyd's Rep. 100 (E.D.,Va.).
69. 1972 AMC 1783 (St.,La.).
70. 1964 AMC 196 (S.D.N.Y.).
71. 533 F.2d 496, 1976 AMC 799 (9th Cir.).

where the vessel was lost during a violent storm on October 20. Upon learning of the loss, the owner sought to establish coverage by paying an additional premium under the "held covered" clause and, in addition, claimed recovery under the Inchmaree Clause on grounds of negligence of the master. The court, recognizing that the fact that the assured became aware of the loss only after it had occurred did not, in and of itself, prevent recovery, nonetheless held that the lay-up warranty was not concerned with location but only with *condition;* i.e., had the vessel been winterized and laid up in accordance with local custom, and denied recovery.

A somewhat similar interpretation was made of the lay-up warranty in *Goodman v. Fireman's Fund Ins. Co.*[72] There, the lay-up warranty was to the effect that the vessel would be laid up and out of commission from October 1 to May 1. The assured undertook to lay up the vessel himself but unfortunately did so negligently by failing to drain the seawater cooling system. The policy also contained an exclusion for loss or damage by reason of, *inter alia,* "ice and/or freezing." During the winter the water froze in the cooling system, ruptured the system, and the vessel sank. At first instance, the trial court held that the loss was thus excluded and that the Inchmaree Clause did not apply. On appeal, the Fourth Circuit held that since the predominant proximate clause of the loss was the assured's negligence, rather than the freezing, the policy would cover under the Inchmaree Clause, but further held that because the assured had failed to close the sea valves as part of the winterizing, contrary to custom in the area, he had breached his warranty as to lay-up and the insurer was relieved of liability.[73]

By contrast, in the "lay-up warranty" cases, in *Harris v. Glens Falls,*[74] the California Supreme Court held that a yacht policy, which provided that the assured warranted that the insured vessel be "laid up and out of commission in Sausalito" during the currency of the policy (but with leave to sail, tow, and be towed, and to go on trial trips) was ambiguous in that it covered trial trips within specified waters but failed to specify any waters, thus providing coverage for the sinking of the vessel approximately three miles out to sea on a trial trip.

---

72. 600 F.2d 1040, 1979 AMC 2534 (4th Cir.).

73. See, also, *St. Paul Fire & Marine Ins. Co. v. Ebe,* C83-14M (W.D.,Wash., 1984) (not yet reported), where the vessel was enroute from one port to another to be laid up at the latter port but was lost during the voyage and after the lay-up period had commenced. And in *Sea Fever v. Hartford Fire,* 1983 AMC 1276 (D.,Mass), the vessel owner was not entitled to recover for collision damage occurring during a lay-up period even though he was unaware that his hull insurance policy contained a warranty that the vessel would not be operated during that period. The court noted, however, that the broker would be liable for a breach of fiduciary duty in obtaining other than a standard commercial hull policy without notifying the assured of its special provisions.

74. 493 P.2d 861, 6 Cal (2d) 699, 100 Cal.Rptr. 133, 1973 AMC 1025 (St.,Cal.), reversing 1972 AMC 138 (St.Cal.).

In *Kalmbach, Inc. v. Ins. Co. of State of Pennsylvania*,[75] the policy provided that the two vessels (a tug and barge) were to be laid up after October 31, 1966. However, the assureds decided to make an additional trip from Adak to Attu in the Aleutians, and their broker arranged an amendment of the Navigation Warranty which provided, in part, that the vessel was "warranted returned to Adak Island by the end of November and laid up during the balance of the Policy term." The endorsement also provided that the extension of movement was subject to the approval of one Captain Logan and further subject to a satisfactory long range weather forecast. Such approval was not obtained nor a long range weather forecast. The vessels were lost enroute from Adak to Attu.

The underwriter conceded that had not the "extension of movement" endorsement contained the necessity for the above "approvals," the policy would have covered. It contended, however, that the language was inserted as a warranty or condition to liability, and that since the warranty was not fulfilled, the extension did not become effective.

The court questioned the meaning of the extension endorsement, noting, among other things such imperfections as: (1) upon whom was the burden of securing the captain's approval; (2) when was the approval to be delivered; (3) to whom was the approval to be delivered, etc. etc. Then the court stated:

> Assuming, however, that the language of the challenged provision is sufficiently clear to constitute a condition or a warranty we, nonetheless, hold that the "held covered" clause in the body of the policy controls. There is no challenge to the outright grant of an extension of time to the end of November in the October indorsement. The "held covered" clause means that the vessels remained covered even " . . . in the event of *any* breach of *warranty*, or *deviation* from the *conditions* . . . " of the policies. While it is true that appellee [the underwriter] could have worded the restrictive endorsement so as to modify or even eliminate the "held covered" clause by using language such as, "the held covered clause of the policy is not applicable to these warranties and conditions" or "this policy is null and void if these warranties and conditions are breached," or similar language that would clearly indicate that the broad language in the "held covered" clause would not be applicable in these circumstances, the fact remains that appellee failed to use such language.

In the event, the court held that the "held covered" clause overrode the provisions of the subsequent endorsement and that the assured could recover. The decision illustrates the lengths to which a modern-day court

---

75. 529 F.2d 552 (9th Cir.1976).

will go in utilizing the held covered clause in aid of an assured who is otherwise without a remedy.

In *Yacht Braemar*,[76] the policy contained a warranty that the yacht would be laid up from November 1 to May 1. The yacht sank while moored in a slip on November 25. It was the custom at that particular yacht basin to leave some boats tied up until December 15th. Upon the custom being proved, the court held that the warranty had not been breached, distinguishing *Gelb v. Automobile Ins. Co., supra.* In *Gehrlein's v. Travelers Ins. Co.*,[77] it was held that the lay-up warranty was not breached by moving the vessel from its lay-up berth to a painting berth in the same boatyard. In *Eamotte v. Employers Union Ins. Co.*,[78] the yacht owner's application for theft insurance did not indicate whether his yacht would be laid up afloat or ashore. It was held that the warranty was not breached by winterizing the boat and leaving it in the water at a boatyard where evidence established that "wet storage" was the accepted lay-up practice in the area in question.

In *Federal Business Development Bank v. Commonwealth Ins. Co. Ltd. et al. (The Good Hope)*,[79] the policy contained a warranty reading: "Warranted vessel laid up at the north foot of Columbia Street." At the north foot of Columbia Street there was a large public dock. After being laid up, the vessel had been moved from the public dock to one or two other locations that were clearly not at the north foot of Columbia Street, before finally being moored to the temporary float where she was when she stranded and subsequently fell over on her side. The temporary float was close to the public dock at the north foot of Columbia Street.

Underwriters contended, *inter alia*, that the lay-up (or "trading warranty" as the court termed it) had been breached. The court disagreed, holding that the warranty as expressed described *where* and not *how* the vessel was to be laid up, and that as the vessel had been laid up in the general geographical area of the waters described, the assured had complied with the warranty at the time the loss occurred. The underwriters further submitted that the prior breaches of the warranty entitled them to avoid the policy on the grounds that the warranty was a Section 34 warranty. The court disagreed, holding that the warranty was not a Section 34 warranty and the underwriters were therefore not discharged from liability when the geographical limits were first exceeded.

In *MacDonald v. Liverpool & London & Globe Ins. Co.*,[80] the vessel was warranted "laid up and out of commission" from October 1st to April 1st.

---

76. 125 F.Supp. 677, 1955 AMC 384 (D.R.I.).
77. 1957 AMC 1029 (S.D.N.Y.).
78. 1976 AMC 204 (St.,N.Y.).
79. [1984] 2 C.C.L.I. 200 (Can.).
80. (1978) 22 N.B.R.(2d) 172, 39 A.P.R. 172 (Can.).

The yacht burned on October 6th at its moorings while waiting to be stored on dry land for the winter. The court held that the warranty clause meant that the vessel's sailing would end on the specified day of October 1st and that the vessel would be taken from the water a reasonable time thereafter. As a reasonable time had not elapsed when the vessel burned, the assured recovered.

It is impossible to describe all the different kinds of warranties which parties to the insurance contract have inserted in their policies. An important example of such warranties is one restricting the navigational limits within which the vessel may ply, either in terms of a geographical limit or during certain periods, or both. The following are considered to be representative of the body of law on this subject.[81]

Trading Limits Warranty

One of the leading cases on this subject is *Birrell v. Dryer*.[82] There, the policy contained a clause: "Warranted no St. Lawrence between October 1 and April 1." The loss occurred after the vessel had left the St. Lawrence gulf. Although the Court of Sessions in Scotland had held that the warranty applied only to the St. Lawrence River and that the warranty was ambiguous, the House of Lords reversed, holding there was no ambiguity and that the whole of the St. Lawrence navigational area, both river and gulf, was a forbidden area.[83]

In the *Eleanor*,[84] the policy warranty provided that the vessel would engage in "day fishing only, out of Gloucester, Mass." The vessel occasionally, after fishing all day, would not put back into Gloucester but would drop anchor within a harbor more convenient for the next day's fishing. The court held that the warranty was not breached.

In *U.S. Fire Ins. Co. v. Cavanaugh*,[85] the policy contained a trading limits warranty to Cape Hatteras, North Carolina, to Brownsville, Texas, and not farther than 150 miles offshore. The owners hired a captain who agreed that he would maintain the vessel, and would only fish it in the area covered by the trading limits warranty. Instead, he navigated the vessel outside the trading warranty, put it aground, and it became a total loss. The court found that the proximate cause of the loss was the barratry of the master even though his deliberate and wilful misconduct resulted in a breach of the trading warranty. Judgment was awarded to the assured.

81. A rather considerable number of cases in this category have already been cited in connection with the general propositions of law relating to express warranties, *supra*.

82. (1884) App.Cas. 345.

83. To the same effect, see *Provincial Ins. Co. of Canada v. Leduc*, (1874) L.R. 6 P.C. 224. See, also, *Colledge v. Harty*, (1851) 20 L.J.Ex.146.

84. 234 F.2d 491, 1956 AMC 1400 (1st Cir.).

85. 732 F.2d 832, 1985 AMC 1001 (11th Cir.).

In *Alexander Ramsey & Kerr v. National Union Fire Ins. Co.*,[86] the policy confined a dredge to inland and coastwise waters. The dredge was laid up in a drainage canal near the Everglades in the interior of Florida. The court held that the term "inland waters" embraced even non-navigable inland waters.

In *Anthony D. Nichols*,[87] the policy covered while on "inland and coastwise waters of the U.S. and West Indies and waters tributary thereto." The vessel was lost off the coast of Yucatan. The court held that the words related to localities, not voyages, and a transitory diversion outside the policy limits was held to be immaterial.

In *Rosenberg v. Maritime Ins. Co.*,[88] the vessel was warranted confined to the inland waters of the state of Kentucky, including the Ohio River. It was found sunk at the dock in Miami, Florida. Coverage was, of course, denied on this ground as well as others.[89]

Certificates of Seaworthiness

Not uncommonly, policies will be encountered where the assured warrants either that the vessel will not be operated without a "certificate of

---

86. 104 F.1006 (2d Cir.).

87. 49 F.2d 927, 1931 AMC 562 (D.C.N.Y.).

88. 1968 AMC 1609 (St.,Fla.).

89. Other cases involving breaches of trading warranties or allegations thereof on the part of underwriters are: *R & W. Boat Rentals v. Penna. Ins. Co.*, 1972 AMC 1783 (St.,La.) (warranty that vessel would be confined to inland waters was found breached where the vessel was lost while being towed 10 miles off the Louisiana coast); *Troop v. Union Ins. Co.*, (1893) 32 N.B.R. 135, C.A. (Can.) (warranty breached); *Owen v. Ocean Mut. Mar. Ins. Co.*, (1885) 18 N.S.R. 495 (C.A.,Can.); *O'Leary v. Pelican Ins. Co.*,(1889) 29 N.B.R. 51 (C.A.,Can.) (warranty breached); *Richard S.S. Co. v. China Mut. Ins. Co.*, (1907) 42 N.S.R. 240 (Can.) (warranty breached); *Thames & Mersey Ins. Co. v. O'Connell*, 86 F. 150 (9th Cir., 1898); *Providence Washington Ins. Co. v. Brummelkamp*, 58 F. 918 (2d Cir., 1893); *James G. Shaw*, 27 F.Supp. 988, 1928 AMC 1253 (E.D.N.Y.) (warranty breached); *Libbie*, 73 F.2d 3, 1934 AMC 1557 (9th Cir., 1934) (warranty breached); *Snyder v. Motorists Mut. Ins. Co.*, 1965 AMC 1791, 206 N.E. (2d) (St.,Ohio) (warranty found ambiguous as to what was embraced within the "limits of the continental United States" and recovery allowed); *Winter v. Employers Fire Ins. Co.*, 1962 AMC 1972, [1962] 2 Lloyd's Rep. 320 (St.,Fla.) (almost identical with *Snyder, supra*); *Stad v. Union Ins. Society of Canton, Ltd. et al.*, (S.C. of B.C., No. 1958/65, Can. unreported) (trading warranty held breached but the held covered clause operated to protect him; recovery granted). And see, also, *Navigators & General Ins. Co. v. Ringrose*, [1962] 1 W.L.R. 173 and *Wilson v. Boag*, (1957) S.R. (N.S.W.) 384, 74 W.N. 160 [1956] 2 Lloyd's Rep. 564 (Aus.), involving the question of coverage of vessels "while within" a specified area. In the latter, the loss occurred while the vessel was "within" the prescribed area although engaged in a trip which would have taken her outside that area; in the former, the question was whether the phrase "within the United Kingdom" would extend coverage farther than territorial waters. The point was not decided, but it was held that the Channel Islands did not fall within the expression, while in *Wilson v. Boag* coverage was found to exist. Note that provisions of this type are not so much warranties as they are "conditions." In effect, they define the parameters of the cover. Thus, a departure from the specified area does not prevent recovery when the vessel returns to the area.

seaworthiness" or that the vessel will be surveyed and inspected by an approved surveyor and a certificate issued by the surveyor attesting to the seaworthiness of the vessel.

For example, in *Royster Guano Co. v. Globe & Rutgers*,[90] there was a warranty that the trips would be approved by a named surveyor; no proof was adduced that the named surveyor actually performed the survey, and coverage was denied. In *Ocean Trawling Co. Pty. Ltd. v. Fire and All Risks Ins. Co., Ltd.*,[91] a local statute required inspection of vessels' machinery at least once each year; a survey was performed, but no certificate was issued because of delays on the part of the governmental department. It was held that the underwriters could not escape liability where the certificate was not issued merely because of departmental delay.

In *The Al Jubail IV*,[92] underwriters insisted upon a warranty that an approved surveyor would inspect the vessel not only for its physical condition but for its suitability for the intended voyage. The vessel was surveyed, but apparently the surveyor did not touch upon the suitability of the vessel for the intended voyage nor was he "approved" within the meaning of the warranty. It was held that the compliance with the warranty was a condition precedent to coverage, and the assured failed to recover.

In *Pindos Shipping Corp. v. Raven (The Mata Hari)*,[93] the policy was subject to a condition that "warranted class maintained"; the vessel was not in class at the time of the loss and had never been classed. Rectification of the policy was denied, as was recovery.

In *Norwest Refrigeration v. Bain Dawes et al.*,[94] the assured applied for coverage through his fishing cooperative and the cooperative sent the request on through its broker. The vessel was merely added to the cooperative's fleet policy, which was warranted free of liability if the vessel(s) did not have a current harbor board certificate of seaworthiness. The cooperative and the broker were aware of the warranty, but the assured was not. The vessel was lost at a time when it did not have a current certificate. The assured/owner sued the cooperative and the broker. Judgment was awarded against the cooperative but not the broker.

In *Westlake v. White, et al.*,[95] the plaintiff obtained a policy on his vessel through a broker who dealt with a Lloyd's representative. The policy contained a warranty that the vessel would have a current and valid survey certificate issued by the Maritime Services Board. The plaintiff discussed the absence of the certificate with the broker before the insurance was

90. 1930 AMC 11 (St.,N.Y.).
91. [1965] W.A.R. 65 (Aus.).
92. [1982] 2 Lloyd's Rep. 637 (Singapore).
93. [1983] 2 Lloyd's Rep. 449, Q.B.D.
94. [1983] 2 ANZ Ins. Cas. 60-507 (W. Aus.).
95. [1984] 3 ANZ Ins. Cas. 60-616 (N.S.W., Aus.).

placed, but the broker did not advise him that there would be no coverage without the certificate. The vessel was lost and the plaintiff sued the Lloyd's representative and the broker. Judgment was entered against the broker for breach of duty in not advising the plaintiff/assured of the consequences of the lack of a certificate.

Such warranties are also found in cargo policies. For example, in *Red Top Brewing v. Mazzoti*,[96] the warranty required inspection of the cargo and the issuance of a certificate; the certificate which was produced was inadequate and coverage was denied. The strictness with which such warranties have been construed is amply demonstrated in *Continental Sea Foods, Inc. v. New Hampshire Fire Ins. Co.*,[97] where the warranty required an inspection certificate from the country of origin. That country had no inspection facilities and could issue no certificate. Notwithstanding the impossibility of compliance, the warranty was enforced and the assured did not recover.

Change of Interest or Change of Management

The AIH form (1977), as is the case with many forms of hull policies, contains a clause entitled "Change of Ownership." Essentially, the clause provides that in the event of any change of ownership or flag, or if the vessel is placed under new management, or chartered on a bareboat basis, or the class of the vessel is changed, then unless underwriters agree in writing, the policy terminates.[98]

As one might expect, cases have arisen construing the clause. One of the leading American cases is *Lemar Towing v. Fireman's Fund.*[99] In that case, it was held that there had been no breach of the clause where, although title to the vessel was transferred, the same two men retained direction and control of the tug while acting as controlling shareholders and officers of separate corporate entities.

In *U.S. Fire v. Cavanaugh*,[100] a boat captain was hired for a single voyage during which, by reason of the captain's barratry, the vessel was lost. Underwriters contended that there had been a change of management. The court held that since the common fishing boat practice permitted a boat captain to be hired for single fishing trips, there had been no breach of the warranty.

By contrast, in *Whiteman v. Rhode Island Ins. Co.*,[101] the owner, while his policy was in force, contracted to sell it to another who was to have imme-

---

96. 202 F.2d 481, 1953 AMC 309 (2d Cir.).
97. 1964 AMC 196 (S.D.N.Y.).
98. The subject is discussed in considerable detail in Chap. III, "The Policy," and various forms of such clauses are set forth.
99. 471 F.2d 609, 1973 AMC 1843 (5th Cir.).
100. 732 F.2d 832, 1985 AMC 1261 (11th Cir.).
101. 78 F.Supp. 624, 1949 AMC 111 (E.D.La.).

diate possession. The transfer was held to be a breach of the warranty, voiding the policy.

Private Pleasure Warranties

Yacht policies frequently contain a warranty that the yacht will be used only for private pleasure purposes. Where a clear breach of the warranty is demonstrated, the courts are not at all disposed to award coverage to the assured/yacht owner.[102] However, a reasonable interpretation is often given to policies containing such warranties. For example, in *Travelers Indemnity v. Gulf Weighing*,[103] the boat captain, who had the owner's authority to use the yacht on personal fishing trips, agreed to take a party on a fishing expedition, expecting some payment by way of sharing expenses. It was held that there was no charter agreement between the parties and the policy covered. And in *Caribbean Enterprises—Continental Ins. Co.*,[104] the warranty was that passengers would not exceed six while under charter. The corporate charterer entertained 30 non-paying guests on a cruise. The court held that an element of hire or consideration moving from the person transported was necessary if he was to be a "passenger," and therefore the policy covered.

Burden of Proof as to Breach

The burden of proving a breach of warranty is on the underwriter, and this is so even where compliance is expressed as a condition precedent to recovery under the policy.[105] Moreover, the defense of breach of warranty must be affirmatively and specially pleaded to be available.[106]

Exceptions to Rule that Nothing Excuses Non-Compliance with Warranty

The Marine Insurance Act, 1906, recognizes two exceptions to the rule that nothing excuses non-compliance with a warranty. Thus, Section 34(1) of the Act provides:

> Non-compliance with a warranty is excused when, by reason of a change of circumstances, the warranty ceases to be applicable to the circumstances of the contract, or when compliance with the warranty is rendered unlawful by and subsequent law.

---

102. See, for example, *Wilburn Boat Co. v. Fireman's Fund Ins. Co.*, 348 U.S. 310, 1955 AMC 467 (1955), where, on remand to the Fifth Circuit, it was found that the owners of the houseboat had used it—not for private pleasure puposes—but for hire.
103. 353 F.Supp. 335, 1974 AMC 2478 (E.D.,La.).
104. 1973 AMC 635 (Arb.).
105. See *Bond Air Services, Inc. v. Hill*, [1955] 2 Q.B. 417.
106. See *Helen L.*, 1937 AMC 1170 (St.,Wash.), citing *Ferrandi v. Bankers Life Association*, 51 Wash. 442, 99 P. 6.

For example, suppose that the owner of a vessel warrants in the policy that the vessel will sail in convoy. However, before the vessel sails, the war ceases and peace is declared. The reason for the warranty having been nullified, there is no occasion to comply with it and the necessity to do so vanishes. This is simple logic; it must be presumed that the parties when they contracted contemplated that the state of affairs then existing would continue, but if the reason for so contracting ceases, then the necessity for compliance likewise vanishes. The maxim is, of course, *cessante ratione, cessat lex.*

By a parity of reasoning, if a subsequent law renders it unlawful to comply with a warranty, then non-compliance is excused. For example, suppose that a P & I policy is warranted not to employ more than three seamen aboard (thus limiting the potential claims that might be asserted by seamen on board). Subsequently, an act is passed by Congress requiring not less than six seamen on vessels of that class. Compliance with the warranty would, consequently, be unlawful. This situation must be distingished from one in which compliance with the warranty was unlawful at the time the policy was issued; should that be the case, the policy would be void on grounds of its illegality.

Warranty of Neutrality

Section 36 of the Marine Insurance Act, 1906, expresses the universal law with respect to warranties of neutrality in the following words:

(1) Where insurable property, whether ship or goods, is expressly warranted neutral, there is an implied condition that the property shall have a neutral character at the commencement of the risk, and that, so far as the assured can control the matter, its neutral character shall be preserved during the risk.

(2) Where a ship is expressly warranted "neutral," there is also an implied condition that, so far as the assured can control the matter, she shall be properly documented, that is to say, that she shall carry the necessary papers to establish her neutrality, and that she shall not falsify or suppress her papers, or use simulated papers. If any loss occurs through breach of this condition the insurer may avoid the contract.

See, for example, *Woolmer v. Muilman,*[107] where the property did not have a neutral character at the commencement of the risk, and the policy was held vitiated, even though the loss happened in a mode not affected by the falsity of the warranty.[108]

---

107. (1763) 96 E.R. 243.
108. See, also, *Eden v. Parkison,* (1781) 99 E.R. 468; *Baring v. Claggett,* (1802) 3 B. & P. 201; *Barker v. Blakes,* (1808) 103 E.R. 581; *Tyson v. Gurney,* (1789) 100 E.R. 686.

As the section states, a forfeiture of neutrality by the wilful act of the assured, or of the master, after the commencement of the voyage, is a breach of the warranty.[109]

The law in the United States does not differ. In *Schwartz v. Ins. Co. of N.A.*,[110] the court stated that the meaning of the warranty of neutrality was that the property insured was neutral in fact and would be so in appearance and conduct; that the property belonged to neutrals; that it would be so documented as to prove its neutrality; and that no act of the assured or his agents would be done which would compromise its neutrality. The court further held that the insurance was forfeited where the risk was varied or increased by conduct inconsistent with the duties of neutrality.

In *Calbreath v. Gracy*,[111] the court held that it was a breach of the warranty of neutrality where the vessel and cargo were warranted American but was navigated and claimed as being Spanish and all evidence proving the neutrality of the vessel and cargo was concealed from her captors.

Where a vessel is condemned by a foreign court, and it can be discerned on the face of the judgment of the foreign court that the grounds were belligerent property, the warranty has been breached even though the rules of evidence differed from those of the country under whose flag the vessel travelled.[112]

However, all or a portion of the warranty may be waived. For example, see *Bell v. Bromfield*,[113] where the policy on goods gave leave to carry simulated papers. The ship and goods were American, but the vessel carried simulated British papers and was captured by Denmark, then at war with Great Britain, and was condemned on the ground of having false papers. The insurer was held liable.

If a vessel is guilty of any conduct which by the international rules of law renders her subject to capture by a hostile power, the warranty is breached; but merely failing to observe a foreign regulation or ordinance not having the sanction of international law or treaty does not result in a breach of the warranty.[114]

There is, however, no implied warranty as to the nationality of a ship, or that her neutrality will not be changed during the risk. See Section 37, Marine Insurance Act, 1906.[115]

109. *Garrels v. Kensington*, (1799) 101 E.R. 1361.

110. F.Cas. No. 12,504 (3rd Cir., 1811). See, also, *Phoenix Ins. Co. v. Pratt*, 2 Birm. 308 (1810).

111. F.Cas. No. 2,296 (3rd Cir., 1805). See, also, *Maryland Ins. Co. v. Woods*, 10 U.S. 29 (1810) and *Livingston v. Maryland Ins. Co.*, 10 U.S. 274 (1810).

112. *Bolton v. Gladston*, (1809) 127 E.R. 1008. *Contra*, if the grounds of the sentence appear and do not show a breach of neutrality. *Salucci v. Johnson*, (1785) 99 E.R. 852. To the same effect, see *Vasse v. Ball*, 2 U.S. 270 (1797).

113. (1812) 104 E.R. 822.

114. *Bird v. Appleton*, (1800) 8 T.R. 562; *Pollard v. Bell*, (1800) 8 T.R. 434.

115. *Dent v. Smith*, (1869) L.R. 4 Q.B. 414.

Warranty of Good Safety

Where the subject matter insured is warranted "well" or "in good safety" on a particular day, it is sufficient if it be safe at any time during the day.[116]

Section 38 of the Act must be read in conjunction with Section 18 with respect to disclosure of facts known to the assured before the contract of insurance is concluded. Also, Schedule 1, Rule 1 of the Act applies. It reads:

> Where the subject-matter is insured "lost or not lost," and the loss has occurred before the contract is concluded, the risk attaches unless, at such time, the assured was aware of the loss, and the insurer was not.[117]

Express Warranties in Policies

The discussion, *supra*, has already covered certain express warranties which appear in standard policies such as "trading limits," the "laid up" warranty, "change of interest or change of management" warranty, etc. It is timely to consider other express warranties which are commonly found in policies.

For example, the new London Institute Time Clauses (Hulls) (24/1/83) form provides in paragraph 1.1 as follows:

> The vessel is covered subject to the provisions of this insurance at all times and has leave to sail or navigate with or without pilots, to go on trial trips and to assist and tow vessels or craft in distress, *but it is warranted* that the Vessel shall not be towed, except as is customary or to the first safe port or place when in need of assistance, or undertake towage or salvage services under a contract previously arranged by the Assured and/or Owners and/or Managers and/or Charterers. This Clause 1.1 shall not exclude customary towage in connection with loading and discharging. [Emphasis supplied]

---

116. Sec. 38, Marine Insurance Act, 1906. See, also, *Blackhurst v. Cockell*, (1789) 100 E.R. 620; *Anchor Marine Ins. Co. v. Keith*, (1884) 9 S.C.R. 483 (Can.); *Colby v. Hunter*, (1827) 3 C. & P. 7, Mood & M. 81, N.P.; *Alexander, Ramsey & Kerr v. National Union Fire Ins. Co.*, 104 F.2d 1006, 1939 AMC 923 (2d Cir.) (dredge laid up in a short spur off a drainage canal was in "good safety" at the time the policy attached), and *Kohne v. Ins. Co. of N.A.*, F.Cas. No. 7,920 (3rd Cir., 1804) (omission to mention that the voyage from a second port had commenced at the time the insurance attached held to be immaterial where the vessel was in "good order" at the time of departure from the first port).

117. See *Mead v. Davidson*, (1835) 111 E.R. 428; *Marine Ins. Co. v. Grimmer*, [1944] 2 All E.R. 197, 77 Ll.L.Rep. 461, C.A.; *Gledstanes v. Royal Exchange Assur. Corp.*, (1864) 34 L.J.Q.B. 30.

The warranty portion of Clause 1.1 is perfectly clear and needs no elaboration.

By contrast, the AIH form (1977) is to the contrary and provides:

> This insurance shall not be prejudiced by reason of any contract limiting in whole or in part the liability of pilots, tugs, towboats, or their owners when the Assured or the agent of the Assured accepts such contract in accordance with established local practice.

> Where in accordance with such practice, pilotage or towage services are provided under contracts requiring the Assured or the agent of the Assured:

> (a) to assume liability for damage resulting from collision of the Vessel insured with any other ship or vessel, including the towing vessel, or

> (b) to indemnify those providing the pilotage or towage services against loss or liability for any such damages, it is agreed that amounts paid by the Assured or Surety pursuant to such assumed obligations shall be deemed payments "by way of damages to any other person or persons" and to have been paid "in consequence of the vessel being at fault" within the meaning of the Collision Liability clause in this Policy to the extent that such payments would have been covered if the Vessel had been legally responsible in the absence of any agreement. Provided always that in no event shall the aggregate amount of liability of the Underwriters under the Collision Liability clause, including this clause, be greater than the amount of any statutory limitation of liability to which owners are entitled or would be entitled if liability under any contractual obligation referred to in this clause were included among the liability subject to such statutory limitations.

As noted above, Clause 1.1 of the new London Institute Time (Hulls) form is warranted free of liability for towage and salvage services. Clause 2 of the new Institute war and strikes clause (Hulls) expressly incorporates by reference various clauses of the Institute Time (Hulls) form, including Clause 1.1. However, paragraph 2 of Clause 2 is a "held covered" provision by which the assured is held covered "in case of breach of warranty as to towage or salvage services," provided notice be given to the underwriters *immediately* after receipt of advices and any additional premium required by them to be agreed. The word "immediately" has been interpreted as meaning that the assured must give notice "with all reasonable speed" considering the circumstances of the case if coverage is to be maintained.[118]

---

118. See *Re Coleman's Depositories*, [1907] 2 K.B. 798; *Liberian Ins. Agency Ins. v. Mosse*, [1977] 2 Lloyd's Rep. 560; *R. v. Berkshire Justices*, (1878) 4 Q.B.D. 469.

B. Implied Warranties

Four sections of the Marine Insurance Act, 1906, deal with implied warranties.[119] These are Sections 37, 39, 40, and 41.

Taking these, not in the order given, Section 41 covers the warranty of legality and reads:

> There is an implied warranty that the adventure insured is a lawful one, and that, so far as the assured can control the matter, the adventure shall be carried out in lawful manner.

Where a voyage is illegal, an insurance upon such a voyage is invalid.[120] The warranty amounts to a stipulation that the trade in which the insured will engage shall be lawful to the purpose of protecting the property insured, and that it shall not become unlawful by the misconduct or neglect of the assured.[121]

For example, in *Pipon v. Cope*,[122] through the negligence of the owner the crew were enabled barratrously to carry smuggled goods on board the vessel, whereupon it was seized as forfeited. The underwriters were held not liable. Compare *Cory v. Burr*,[123] where the master barratrously smuggled goods aboard the ship. The policy covered barratry but was warranted free from capture and seizure. Spanish authorities seized the vessel, and proceedings were instituted for her condemnation and confiscation. The assured incurred expenses in attempting to procure her release and sought recovery under the policy. The court held that the loss was imputed to capture and seizure and not to the barratry.[124]

The privity of the assured with respect to the illegality is all-important. For example, in *Cunard v. Hyde*,[125] cargo was loaded on deck in contravention of the Customs Consolidation Act of 1853. The assured was

---

119. Secs. 33 and 34 of the Act deal with warranties in general, whether express or implied.

120. *Redmond v. Smith*, 135 E.R. 183; *Gray v. Sims*, F.Cas. No. 5,729 (C.C.,Pa.,1814).

121. *Smith v. Delaware Ins. Co.*, F.Cas. No. 13,035, *rev'd* 11 U.S. 434 (1811).

122. (1808) 1 Camp. 434, N.P.

123. (1883) 8 App.Cas. 393.

124. Contrast *Fishing Fleet v. Trident*, 598 F.2d 925, 1980 AMC 583 (5th Cir.), where a fishing vessel master committed barratry when he fraudulently attempted to sell the vessel, lied to the owner about her catch, and disappeared after the vessel sank. The court held that the subsequent seizure of the vessel by Mexican authorities did not fall under the F. C. & S. Clause, as the vessel's constructive total loss occurred through barratry committed prior to the seizure. But, in *Nautilus v. Edinburgh Ins.*, 673 F.2d 1314, 1981 AMC 2082 (4th Cir.), the master committed barratry by transporting marijuana, for which the vessel was seized by governmental authorities. The proximate cause of the loss was held to be the governmental seizure. See, also, the excellent article "Barratry: The Scuttler's Easy Route to the Golden Prize," *LMCLQ* 3 (1982) 388.

125. (1859) 121 E.R. 1.

well aware of the loading and the breach of the statute. Recovery under the policy was denied. In *Wilson v. Rankin*,[126] the master, without the knowledge of the owner, stowed a portion of the cargo on deck and sailed without any certificate from the clearing officer that all the cargo was below deck, contrary to the Consolidation Act. Recovery was allowed under the policy. See, also, *Dudgeon v. Pembroke*,[127] where a policy effected by an innocent assured was held valid when the master wrongfully carried passengers without the vessel having a certificate authorizing such carriage.

A seemingly harsh result occurs where insurance is effected on foreign property and war subsequently breaks out between the respective countries of the assured and assurer, as the insurance is thereby rendered void.[128] But where seizure occurs before a declaration of war, even though in contemplation of war and in order to use the property to support the anticipated war, the insurance is good.[129]

Apparently little notice seems to be taken with respect to foreign revenue laws, and a breach thereof does not necessarily vitiate the insurance.[130] Even though a voyage may be in technical breach of the supposed laws of a foreign nation, it has been held that the insurance was not vitiated where the foreign laws were systematically and practically ignored.[131] However, the mere possibility of illegality with respect to a later portion of the voyage does not vitiate the policy, as it may be presumed that the master would abandon that possibility before performing it.[132]

The American cases do not differ significantly. For example, in *Maryland Ins. Co. v. Woods*,[133] the vessel sailed for a port in the West Indies knowing the same to be blockaded and was warned off. In *Clark v. Protection Ins. Co.*,[134] the vessel was insured for a voyage from the United States to Liverpool and took on board a chain cable smuggled by another vessel. The cable was lost enroute to Liverpool by perils of the sea. The court held that insurance on the chain cable was good, the title being in the owner of the vessel and no illegality attached to the voyage on which it was

---

126. (1865) L.R. 1 Q.B. 162, 122 E.R. 1173.

127. (1877) 2 App.Cas. 284, H.L.

128. *Gamba v. LeMesurier*, (1803) 102 E.R. 887; *Ex parte Lee*, (1806) 33 E.R. 218, L.C.; *Brandon v. Curling*, (1803) 102 E.R. 888; *Kellner v. LeMesurier*, (1803) 102 E.R. 883.

129. *Janson v. Driefontein Consolidated Mines, Ltd.*, [1902] A.C. 484.

130. *Plance v. Fletcher*, (1779) 99 E.R. 165.

131. *Fracis, Times & Co. v. Sea Ins. Co.*, (1898) 79 L.T. 28. But, see *Regazzoni v. K.C. Sethia (1944) Ltd.*, [1957] 3 All E.R. 286, H.L., holding that if there is any legality in the commencement of an integral voyage and insurance is effected on a latter portion of the voyage, which, if taken by itself, would be illegal, the illegality taints the entire voyage and the assured cannot recover on the policy. See, also, *Marryat v. Wilson*, (1799) 126 E.R. 993, and *Bird v. Appleton*, (1800) 101 E.R. 1547.

132. *Sewell v. Royal Exchange Assur. Co.*, (1813) 128 E.R. 568. With respect to illegality tainting a shipment of cargo, see *Pieschell v. Allnut*, (1813) 128 E.R. 543, and *Keir v. Andrade*, (1816) 128 E.R. 1128.

133. 10 U.S. 29 (1810).

134. F.Cas. No. 2,832 (C.C., Mass., 1840).

used. A mere liability to forfeiture does not void coverage or prevent a recovery for a loss by an independent peril. In *Fitzsimmons v. Newport Ins. Co.*,[135] the insured vessel, warranted to be American, cleared for a blockaded port without knowledge of the blockade and persisted in an attempt to enter the port even after having been warned off. It was held that such conduct was not a breach of the blockade which would preclude recovery against underwriters, notwithstanding the condemnation of the vessel by the British Admiralty Court as a lawful prize. In *Gray v. Sims*,[136] it was held that if the trade in which a vessel is to be engaged during the voyage be contrary to the laws of the country or the laws of nations, a policy upon the ship, as well as one on the cargo, is void.

In *Maritime Ins. Co. v. M.S. Dollar S.S. Co.*,[137] the vessel was insured for war risks only on a voyage from San Francisco to Vladivostok during the war between Russia and Japan, with express liberty to the assured to run the blockade, and the vessel carried false clearance papers showing her destination to be a Japanese port. The vessel was seized and condemned by the Japanese authorities on the ground of carrying false papers. This was held to be no defense to an action on the policy under either English or American law.

Under English law, neutrals are entitled to carry on trade with a belligerent, subject to the latter's right of capture. Consequently, carriage of contraband on voyages is not illegal, and policies thereon are not void.[138]

Although Section 41 speaks in terms of an "implied warranty," this would appear to be inept language, as illegality voids the policy and cannot be waived, whereas a warranty can be waived.[139] See, also, *Gedge v. Royal Exchange Assur. Corp.*,[140], where the court on its own motion refused to enforce a policy which was illegal even though the insurers did not plead or rely thereon.

In *Scow No. 12*,[141] it was held that a tug having no mate on board violated an applicable manning statute. Consequently, the insurer on cargo which was lost by reason of the sinking of the scow under tow was released from liability. Compare, however, *Pacific Queen Fisheries v. Atlas Assur. Co.*[142] There, a fishing vessel being used in the gill net fishery in Alaska became a total constructive loss as a consequence of a gasoline explosion while the vessel was docked. The trial court held that the hull policy was void *ab initio* because the owners had increased the vessel's gasoline carry-

---

135. 8 U.S. 185 (1808).
136. F.Cas. No. 5,729 (C.C.,Pa., 1814).
137. 177 F. 127 (9th Cir., 1910).
138. *Caine v. Palace Steam Shipping Co.*, [1907] 1 K.B. 670, C.A.
139. See Sec. 34(3) of the Act.
140. [1900] 2 Q.B. 214, 9 Asp. M.L.C. 57.
141. 32 F.2d 271, 1929 AMC 425, *aff'd* 35 F.2d 862 (9th Cir.).
142. 1962 AMC 575, *aff'd* 307 F.2d 700, 1962 AMC 1845 (9th Cir.), [1963] 2 Lloyd's Rep. 201.

ing capacity without disclosing that fact to the underwriters, and because, in effect, the owners had sent her to sea in an unseaworthy condition. In addition, the trial court concluded (*in dictum*) that the vessel violated the Tanker Act but that this violation was not of such a character as to render the entire venture or voyage an illegal one. As the trial court put it, the hauling of gasoline in bulk was not the primary purpose of the voyage but merely an incident thereof. The court of appeal declined to rule on the question, affirming on the basis that the other findings of the trial court were not "clearly erroneous" and because of a question as to whether or not the bulk gasoline carried by the vessel would come within the term "fuel or stores" which were exempted from the provisions of the Tanker Act. It will be seen that the trial court's ruling comes very close to saying that the legality warranty is not breached unless the primary purpose of the voyage was to violate the law and comes perilously close to rendering *Scow No. 12, supra,* obsolete *sub silentio.*

Warranty of Seaworthiness

The implied warranty of seaworthiness is unquestionably the most important warranty of all. Under English law, there is an implied warranty of seaworthiness in a voyage policy (Section 39, Marine Insurance Act, 1906), but there is no implied warranty of seaworthiness in a time policy. However, under a time policy where, with the privity of the assured, the ship is sent to sea in an unseaworthy state, the insurer is not liable for any loss attributable to such unseaworthiness.

Section 39 of the Act reads in its entirety:

(1) In a voyage policy there is an implied warranty that at the commencement of the voyage the ship shall be seaworthy for the purpose of the particular adventure insured,

(2) Where the policy attaches while the ship is in port, there is also an implied warranty that she shall, at the commencement of the risk, be reasonably fit to encounter the ordinary perils of the port.

(3) Where the policy relates to a voyage which is performed in different stages, during which the ship requires different kinds of or further preparation or equipment, there is an implied warranty that at the commencement of each stage the ship is seaworthy in respect of such preparation or equipment for the purposes of that stage.

(4) A ship is deemed to be seaworthy when she is reasonably fit in all respects to encounter the ordinary perils of the seas of the adventure insured.

(5) In a time policy there is no implied warranty that the ship shall be seaworthy at any stage of the adventure, but where, with the privity of the assured, the ship is sent to sea in an unseaworthy state, the insurer is not liable for any loss attributable to unseaworthiness.

The cases are legion establishing that in a voyage policy, the law implies a warranty on the part of the assured which amounts to a positive undertaking—an absolute condition—that the vessel at the commencement of the voyage is seaworthy.[143]

What Is Compliance with the Implied Warranty?

A vessel under a voyage policy is seaworthy when she is in a fit state "as to repairs, equipment, and crew, and in all other respects, to encounter the ordinary perils of the voyage insured at the time of sailing upon it."[144] However, seaworthiness is a relative state and not necessarily an absolute one. Whether a vessel is seaworthy must be determined as a matter of fact, dependent upon the particular voyage and the risks to be encountered. See, for example, *Reed v. Philps*,[145] where the court said that the vessel is bound to be sufficiently seaworthy at the inception of the voyage to make it without repairs, in the absence of any damage from extraordinary perils of the seas. In *Burges v. Wickham*,[146] the vessel had been built for navigating the Ganges River, and on this account was generally unfit for ocean navigation. However, everything was done that could possibly be done by temporary appliances to render a vessel of her type as strong as she could be made to withstand the perils of the voyage insured, and the underwriters were so informed. The court held that the warranty must be taken to be limited to the capacity of the vessel, and, therefore, was satis-

---

143. For the derivation of the rule see *Christie v. Secretan*, (1799) 8 T.R. 192, and *Wedderburn v. Bell*, (1807) 1 Camp. 1, N.P. Representative cases involving voyage policies are: *Dixon v. Sadler*, (1839) 5 M. & W. 405; *Gibson v. Small*, (1852) 4 H.L.Cas. 353 (if insured "at and from," the vessel must be seaworthy for the ordinary risks in port to comply with the "at" portion of the clause, and must be seaworthy for the intended voyage, wherever that may be, under the "from" portion of the clause); *Biccard v. Shepherd*, (1861) 15 E.R. 383; *Bouillon v. Lupton*, (1863) 143 E.R. 726; *Quebec Marine Ins. Co. v. Commercial Bank of Canada*, (1870) 17 E.R. 1, P.C.; *Turnbull v. Janson*, (1877) 3 Asp. M.L.C. 433, C.A.; *Greenock Steamship Co. v. Maritime Ins. Co.*, [1903] 1 K.B. 367, *aff'd* [1903] 2 K.B. 657, C.A.; *Northumbrian Shipping Co., Ltd. v. E. Timm & Son Ltd.*, [1939] 2 All E.R. 648, H.L.; *Daniels v. Harris*, (1874) L.R. 10 C.P. 1 (cargo policy); *The Vortigern* [1899] P. 140 (contract of affreightment); *Kynance Sailing Ship Co. v. Young*, (1911) 104 L.T. 397, 11 Asp. M.L.C. 596; *Forshaw v. Chabert*, (1870) L.R. 3 P.C. 234 (innocence of the assured is immaterial; the warranty is breached even though the unseaworthiness was remedied before the loss); *The Thorsa*, (1916) 22 Com.Cas. 218, C.A.; *Hoffman & Co. v. British General Ins. Co., Ltd.*, (1922) 10 Ll.L.Rep. 434; *White v. Newfoundland Marine Ins. Co.*, (1864) 5 Nfld. L.R. 27 (Can.); *Rogerson v. Union Marine Ins. Co.*, (1870) 5 Nfld. L.R. 359 (Can.); *Reed v. Philps*, (1870) 13 N.B.R. 171 (Can.); *Lemelin v. Montreal Assur. Co.*, (1873) 1 Q.L.R. 337; *Bell v. Miller*, (1877) Knox 331 (Aus.); *Wilkie v. Geddes*, (1815) 3 E.R. 988, H.L. (to comply with warranty, not only must the hull be tight, staunch, and seaworthy but, in addition, the ground tackle must be adequate and proper); *Douglas v. Scougall*, (1816) 3 E.R. 1161; *Cross v. B.A. Ins. Co.*, (1877) 22 L.C. Jur. 10, C.A.; *McLanahan v. Universal Ins. Co.*, 26 U.S. 170 (1828); *Hazard's Admr. v. New England Marine Ins. Co.*, 33 U.S. 557; *Richelieu & O. Nav. Co. v. Boston Marine Ins. Co.*, 136 U.S. 408 (1886) *Merchants' Mut. Ins. Co. v. Allen*, 121 U.S. 67 (1883).

144. *Dixon v. Sadler*, (1839) 151 E.R. 172, *aff'd* (1841) 11 L.J. Ex. 435, Ex.Ch.

145. (1870) 13 N.B.R. 172 (Can.).

146. (1863) 33 L.J.Q.B. 17.

fied if, at the commencement of the risk, the vessel was made as seaworthy as she was capable of being made, although it might not make her as fit for the voyage as would have been usual and proper if the venture had been one of sending out an ordinary seagoing vessel.[147] Compare, however, *Turnbull v. Janson*,[148] where in a similar situation the jury found that the vessel, built for river navigation but engaged on an ocean voyage, had not been made as seaworthy as she might have been by ordinary available means and she was therefore unseaworthy.

In *Wedderburn v. Bell*,[149] the court laid down the rule that the assured is bound to prove not only that the ship was tight, staunch, and strong, but that she was manned with a sufficient crew to navigate her on the voyage insured, and properly equipped with sails and other stores. These are conditions precedent to the policy attaching and, if not complied with, so that the peril is enhanced, from whatever cause and though no fraud was intended on the part of the assured, the insurer is relieved of liability.[150]

The warranty extends, of course, to fitness of equipment and appliances, and a failure to have proper equipment or stores is a breach of the warranty.[151]

It was held at one time that where a voyage is to be accomplished in stages, the vessel is unseaworthy for failure to take on board a pilot where pilotage is compulsory.[152] This was subsequently overruled in *Dixon v. Sadler*.[153]

The vessel must at the commencement of the voyage be fit for her intended voyage *and cargo;* i.e., the vessel must be "cargoworthy." A ship may be fit to carry a cargo not subject to being dissolved by seawater and yet not be seaworthy for a perishable cargo such as soda in barrels.[154] In

---

147. To the same effect, see *Clapham v. Langton*, (1864) 122 E.R. 1001, Ex.Ch. and *Wash Gray*, 277 U.S. 66, 1928 AMC 923 (1928).

148. (1877) 36 L.T. 635, 3 Asp. M.L.C. 433, C.A.

149. (1807) 1 Camp. 1, N.P.

150. See, also, to the same effect with respect to the necessity of a proper and sufficient crew, *Phillips v. Headlan*, (1831) 109 E.R. 1184; *Biccard v. Shepherd*, (1861) 15 E.R. 383; *Forshaw v. Chabert*, (1821) 129 E.R. 1243; *Thomas (M) & Son Shipping Co. Ltd. v. London & Provincial Marine & General Ins. Co.*, (1914) 30 T.L.R. 595, C.A.; *Tait v. Levi*, (1811) 104 E.R. 686; *Gillespie v. British America Fire & Life Assur. Co.*, (1849) 7 U.C.R. 108 (Can.); *Holly*, 11 F.2d 495, 1926 AMC 578 (3rd Cir.); *Uriel*, 1924 AMC 103 (W.D.,Wash.); *Lemar Towing v. Fireman's Fund, supra; Miss Esmeralda (grounding), supra;* and *Hazard's Adm'r v. New England Marine Ins. Co.*, 33 U.S. 557.

151. *Wedderburn v. Bell, supra; Wilkie v. Geddes*, (1815) 3 E.R. 988, H.L. (defective anchors); *Quebec Marine Ins. Co. v. Commercial Bank of Canada*, (1870) 17 E.R. 1, P.C. (defective boiler); *Greenock S.S. Co. v. Maritime Ins. Co.*, (1903) 2 K.B. 657, 9 Asp. M.L.C. 463 (insufficient coal); *Aetna Ins. Co. v. Florida Towing Co.*, 37 F.Supp. 781, 1941 AMC 1405 (S.D.,Fla.) (leaking transom plate); *Ideal Cement Co. v. Home Ins. Co.*, 210 F.2d 9937, 1954 AMC 663 (S.D.,Ala.) (leaky seams); *McAllister v. Ins. Co. of N.A.*, 244 F.2d 867, 1957 AMC 1774 (2d Cir.) (improper caulking).

152. *Law v. Hollingsworth*, (1797) 101 E.R. 909.

153. (1839) 151 E.R. 172, *aff'd sub nom. Sadler v. Dixon*, (1841) 8 M. & W. 895.

154. *Castles v. Irving*, (1840) 8 L.T. 767.

Sleigh v. Tyser,[155] the policy on a cargo of cattle provided that the fittings of the vessel were to be approved by a Lloyd's surveyor, and they were, in fact, approved. During the voyage, a large number of the cattle died, owing partly to the insufficiency of the appliances for ventilation and partly to an insufficient number of cattlemen appointed to attend them. It was held that the ship was unseaworthy in both respects, the implied warranty of seaworthiness not being excluded by the requirement as to the approval of the fittings. In *Daniels v. Harris,*[156] the policy covered wine in casks, on or under deck. The wine on deck was badly stowed, and the ship was unable to withstand the bad weather she encountered except by jettisoning the deck cargo. As to herself and the deck cargo, the vessel was in no danger. The court held that in a policy on cargo, the implied warranty of seaworthiness cannot be considered to contemplate the destruction, in order to save the ship on an ordinary voyage, of the very cargo which was the subject matter of the insurance.

The affreightment cases aptly illustrate the principle, and their rationale may be applied to insurance cases. In *Tattersall v. National S.S. Co.,*[157] the vessel had just previously carried a cargo of cattle with hoof and mouth disease. The vessel was not disinfected after that voyage, and on a subsequent voyage with a cargo of cattle, some of the cattle contracted the disease. The vessel was held to be unseaworthy.

The cargo may be so badly stowed as to affect the seaworthiness of the vessel. In *Kopitoff v. Wilson,*[158] iron armor plates were badly stowed and, as a consequence during heavy weather, went through the side of the ship, causing her loss. The vessel was found to be unseaworthy by reason of the bad stowage. The rule appears to be that bad stowage which affects nothing but the cargo damaged by it and nothing more but still leaves the ship seaworthy for the venture, may impose liability upon the shipowner under the bill of lading, depending upon its terms, but does not render the vessel unseaworthy.[159]

Section 40 of the Marine Insurance Act, 1906, bears directly on the subject. It reads:

(1) In a policy on goods or other moveables there is no implied warranty that the goods or moveables are seaworthy.

(2) In a voyage policy on goods or other moveables there is an implied warranty that at the commencement of the voyage the ship is not only seaworthy as a ship, but also that she is reasonably fit to carry the

155. [1900] 2 Q.B. 333, 9 Asp. M.L.C. 97.
156. (1874) L.R. 10 C.P. 1, 2 Asp. M.L.C. 413.
157. (1884) 12 Q.B. 297, 5 Asp. M.L.C. 206.
158. (1876) 1 Q.B.D. 377, 3 Asp. M.L.C. 163.
159. See *Elder Dempster v. Paterson Zochonis,* [1924] A.C. 522, 16 Asp. M.L.C. 351, H.L., in which bad stowage crushed casks of palm oil, but this was not found to have rendered the vessel unseaworthy.

goods or other moveables to the destination contemplated in the policy.

Koebel v. Saunders[160] illustrates sub-section 1. In that case, involving the carriage of coconut oil, the insurer was relieved of liability by reason of inherent vice of the cargo. In *Stanton v. Richardson*[161] (an affreightment case), the vessel was unfit to carry a cargo of wet sugar, although the vessel itself was perfectly seaworthy, an illustration of sub-section 2 of Section 40.

A word of caution is in order. A vessel may obviously be seaworthy as respects the hull underwriters and yet unseaworthy as between the shipper of the cargo and the shipowner.[162]

The American cases do not differ from the English and Commonwealth decisions. See, for example, *The Sylvia*,[163] where the Supreme Court stated concisely:

> The test of seaworthiness is whether the vessel is reasonably fit to carry the goods which she has undertaken to transport.

And in *The Southwark*,[164] the Supreme Court said:

> As seaworthiness depends not only on the vessel being staunch and fit to meet the perils of the sea, but upon its character in reference to the particular cargo to be transported, it follows that the vessel must be able to transport the cargo which it is held out as fit to carry or it is not seaworthy in that respect.

In *The Sagamore*,[165] the court was even more precise:

> A vessel may be perfectly seaworthy for cargo carrying purposes around the harbor, and not be seaworthy for oceanic voyages; and she may be seaworthy for the carriage of a load of lumber, and not be seaworthy for a load of steel rails.[166]

---

160. (1864) 144 E.R. 29. See, also, Sec. 55 (2)(c) of the Act.
161. (1875) 33 L.T. 193.
162. Compare *Kopitoff v. Wilson, supra,* with *Elder Dempster v. Paterson Zochonis, supra.* See, also, *Kuehne & Nagel v. Baiden,* 1974 AMC 1373, [1975] 1 Lloyd's Rep. 331 (St.,N.Y.) involving a charterer's liability policy. In that case, automobiles were transported on deck from Poland to Colombia and outturned in a damaged condition. The carrier agreed to forgo its claim for freight if the consignee would not press its claim on the basis of the carrier's failure to stow the cargo under deck. The carrier then sued its liability underwriters to recover the amount of the freight as representing settlement of the cargo claim. Held: the underwriters were entitled to summary judgment, as the policy did not cover liability for deck stowage.
163. 171 U.S. 462 (1898).
164. 191 U.S. 1 (1903).
165. 300 F. 701, 1924 AMC 961 (2d Cir.).
166. See, also, *Briton,* 70 F.2d 146, 1934 AMC 667 (6th Cir.); *S.C.L. No. 9,* 37 F.Supp. 386, 1939 AMC 1323 (E.D.,Pa.) (improper loading); *Lotz v. Elsie M.,* 1951 AMC 1311 (S.D.,Tex.) (barge overloaded); *Dick Towing Co. v. Leo,* 202 F.2d 850, 1953 AMC 498 (5th Cir.)

Cargo policies, it should be noted, almost universally contain a "sea-worthiness admitted" clause by which the cargo underwriters admit the seaworthiness of the vessel on which the goods are carried, thus negating the effect of the implied warranty as to cargo interests. But the admission runs only between the cargo underwriters and the cargo owners—not between the cargo underwriters and the shipowner.

Voyage in Different Stages. Where the voyage is conducted in stages, the vessel must be seaworthy for each stage. This is true under both insurance cases and affreightment cases.[167]

In *Bouillon, supra,* the court held that in descending the Rhone River the vessel must be seaworthy for the Rhone; and from Marseilles to Galatz (a sea voyage), she must be ready for the sea. That is, the different stages of the voyage required different equipment, one being sufficient for a river voyage and the other being necessary for an ocean voyage. In *Greenock, supra,* the vessel sailed from the first port with an insufficient supply of coal for that stage and as a consequence some of the vessel's fittings and part of the cargo were consumed as fuel. The warranty of seaworthiness was broken by the failure of the vessel to carry sufficient fuel for that particular stage. The same situation was involved in *The Vortigern, supra.* In the latter, the court specifically noted that there was no difference between the implied warranty of seaworthiness which attaches under a marine policy at the commencement of the voyage and the case of a shipowner under a contract of affreightment. *Northumbrian, supra,* establishes that the stage of the voyage must be ascertained prior to departure; fuel being available at intermediate ports cannot be considered.[168]

Lighters. There is no implied warranty that the lighters into which the cargo is put after conclusion of the voyage are seaworthy.[169]

(explosive substance left in rake tank of a gasoline barge); *New Orleans T. & M. Ry. Co. v. Union M.I. Co.,* 286 F.2d 32, 1923 AMC 183 (5th Cir.) (barge took on water when partially loaded by reason of seams opening up in hot weather). And, see *Texaco, Inc. v. Universal Marine, Inc.,* 400 F.Supp. 311, 1976 AMC 226 (E.D.,La.), where the court pointed out the fundamental distinction between the duty owed by a shipowner to cargo interests versus the duty owed by him to his hull underwriters.

167. See Sec. 39(3), Marine Insurance Act, 1906, and *Bouillon v. Lupton,* (1864) 143 E.R. 726; *Quebec Marine Ins. Co. v. Commercial Bank of Canada,* (1870) 17 E.R. 1, P.C.; *Greenock S.S. Co. v. Maritime Ins. Co.,* (1903) 2 K.B. 657, C.A.; *The Vortigern,* [1899] P. 140, C.A.; *Northumbrian Shipping Co., Ltd. v. E. Timm & Son, Ltd.,* [1939] 2 All E.R. 648, [1939] A.C. 397; *Thin & Sinclair v. Richards & Co.,* (1892) 2 Q.B. 141, C.A.

168. For additional cases, see *Reed v. Page,* (1927) 1 K.B. 743, C.A.; *McIver & Co. Ltd. v. Tate Steamers, Ltd.,* (1903) 1 K.B. 362, C.A.; *The Makedonia,* (1962) 2 All E.R. 614, [1962] 1 Lloyd's Rep. 316; *Whybrow & Co. Pty Ltd. v. Howard Smith Co.,* (1913) 17 C.L.R. 1 (Aus.); *Canadian S.S. Lines v. Grain Growers Export Co.,* (1919) 59 S.C.R. 643, 52 D.L.R. 680 (Can.).

169. *Lane v. Nixon,* (1866) L.R. 1 C.P. 412; *Thames & Mersey Marine Ins. Co. v. Pacific Creosoting Co.,* 233 F. 561 (9th Cir., 1915).

Waiver of Warranty. Section 34 of the Marine Insurance Act, 1906, reads:

(1) Noncompliance with a warranty is excused when, by reason of a change of circumstances, the warranty ceases to be applicable to the circumstances of the contract, or when compliance with the warranty is rendered unlawful by any subsequent law.[170]

(2) Where a warranty is broken, the assured cannot avail himself of the defense that the breach has been remedied, and the warranty complied with, before loss.

(3) A breach of warranty may be waived by the insurer.

Prior to the Act, the law was well settled that an assured could not breach a warranty and then remedy it before loss and still recover.[171] In *Forshaw,* the master of a ship on a voyage from Cuba to Liverpool departed Cuba with ten crewmen, two of whom had to be dropped off at Jamaica and two crewmen procured there as substitutes. The court held the vessel to be unseaworthy when departing Cuba by reason of a shortage of crew and the subsequent remedy of that condition by procuring substitute crewmen was immaterial. In *Quebec Marine,* the vessel sailed with a defective boiler which was not apparent until she got to sea. Upon discovering the defect, she was put about and returned to port, where the boiler was repaired. After being detained for some days, she proceeded to sea and, encountering bad weather, was lost. The implied warranty of seaworthiness having been breached, the subsequent remedial action in correcting the defect was to no avail.

Sub-section 3 of Section 34 simply confirms that a breach of warranty may be waived.[172] Subject to that qualification, it is only reasonable that a warranty or condition may be waived as any party to a contract may voluntarily forgo the benefit of reliance upon a contractual term. If the action is voluntary and expressly shows an intent to forgo a benefit, it is a waiver; on the other hand, conduct inconsistent with insistence upon the contractual term generally is called an estoppel. For example, in *Weir v. Aberdeen,*[173] the vessel sailed in an unseaworthy state by reason of being overloaded. This was discovered before any loss occurred, and the ship put into port, where a portion of the cargo was discharged. An application to underwriters to go into the port to effect the partial discharge was made and granted. Subsequently, the vessel was lost. The warranty as to seaworthiness was held to have been waived.

In *Provincial Ins. Co. of Canada v. Leduc,*[174] the underwriters were held estopped to rely on a breach of trading warranty where their conduct con-

---

170. The interpretation of this sub-section is discussed *supra.*
171. *De Hahn v. Hartley,* (1786) 99 E.R. 1130; *Quebec Marine Ins. Co. v. Commercial Bank of Canada,* (1870) L.R. 3 P.C. 234, 17 E.R. 1, P.C.; *Forshaw v. Chabert,* (1821) 129 E.R. 1243.
172. As noted before, however, the warranty of legality can never be waived.
173. (1819) 106 E.R. 383.
174. (1874) L.R. 6 P.C. 244, 2 Asp. M.L.C. 538, P.C.

stituted an acceptance of abandonment after a constructive total loss. A perfect example of estoppel appears in *Reliance Ins. Co. v. The Escapade*,[175] where the underwriters were held estopped to deny coverage on a yacht for violation of a private pleasure warranty when they insisted that the assured incur salvage expenses by using a salvor of the underwriters' choice.

It is clear, however, that a waiver will not be lightly presumed.[176]

It should be observed that the "seaworthiness admitted" clause found in most cargo policies (such as are found in the Institute Cargo Clauses) is a species of "waiver" of the implied warranty of seaworthiness.

No Implied Warranty of Seaworthiness in a Time Policy. Sub-section 5 of Section 39 of the Act bears repeating. It reads:

> (5) In a time policy there is no implied warranty that the ship shall be seaworthy at any stage of the adventure, but where, with the privity of the assured, the ship is sent to sea in an unseaworthy state, the insurer is not liable for any loss attributable to unseaworthiness.

Sub-section 5 is merely declaratory of the common law, and expresses the gist of a great many decisions.[177]

---

175. 280 F.2d 482, 1961 AMC 2410 (5th Cir.). See, also, *Daneau v. Laurent Gendron, Ltee: Union Ins. Soc. of Canton, Ltd.*, [1964] 1 Lloyd's Rep. 220 (Can.) (alleged breach of a lay-up warranty; underwriters actively participated in, and in some respects actually directed and approved, the time, place, and manner of lay-up); *Samuel (P) & Co. Ltd. v. Dumas*, [1924] A.C. 431 (breach of warranty not to insure freight in excess of a certain amount; underwriters knowingly participated in writing such excess insurance and were held estopped to deny coverage); *Stuyvesant Ins. v. Leloup Shrimp*, 333 F.Supp. 233, 1972 AMC 1286 (S.D.,Tex.) (underwriter estopped to deny coverage where it undertook to defend insured in a collision case without notifying him that a court finding of failure to provide a seaworthy vessel would constitute a breach of the assured's warranty). See, also, *Kahman & McMurry v. Aetna Ins. Co. of Hartford, Conn.*, 242 F. 20 (5th Cir., 1918) and *Sholes v. Continental Casualty Co.*, 196 So.2d 680 (St.,La., 1967).

176. See, for example, *New Orleans etc. Ry. v. Union M.I. Co.*, 286 F.2d 32, 1923 AMC 183 (5th Cir.) (warranty of seaworthiness not waived by a policy requirement that the vessel have a certificate of inspection from the board of underwriters); *Libbie*, 73 F.2d 3, 1934 AMC 1557 (5th Cir.) (silence of underwriters after notice that a vessel had been moved in violation of a warranty does not constitute a waiver of the breach of warranty); *Reisman v. N.H. Fire Ins. Co.*, 312 F.2d 17, 1963 AMC 1151 (5th Cir.) (agent of the insurer noted oysters and barnacles on the hull of a houseboat and suggested that she be hauled and painted; such action did not render the insurer liable when the loss of the vessel was caused by worms in her bottom); *Sleigh v. Tyser*, (1900) 2 Q.B. 333, 9 Asp. M.L.C. 97 (implied warranty of seaworthiness not waived where the policy required that the fittings and conditions be approved by a Lloyd's agent surveyor). See, also, *Capital Coastal Corp. v. Hartford Fire Ins. Co.*, 378 F.Supp. 163, 1974 AMC 2039 (E.D.,Va.), [1975] 2 Lloyd's Rep. 100, where the court found that the underwriters did not waive the warranty that a certain captain would be employed on the insured tug.

177. *Gibson v. Small*, (1853) 10 E.R. 499, H.L.; *Jenkins v. Haycock*, (1853) 14 E.R. 134, P.C.; *Thompson v. Hopper*, (1856) 119 E.R. 828; *Michael v. Tredwin*, (1856), 139 E.R. 1191; *Fawcus v. Sarsfield*, (1856) 119 E.R. 836; *Biccard v. Shepherd*, (1861) 15 E.R. 383, P.C.; *Dudgeon v. Pembroke*, (1877) 2 App.Cas. 284; *Thomas (M) & Son Shipping Co. Ltd. v. London & Provincial Marine & General Ins. Co., Ltd.*, (1914) 30 T.L.R. 595, C.A.; *Thomas v. Tyne & Wear S.S. Freight*

By way of illustration, in *Michael v. Tredwin, supra,* the vessel was lost and the insurer pleaded that the ship was not at the time of sailing, or at any time on the day of sailing, or at any time during the continuance of the risk, seaworthy. The court held that the plea was no answer to the action inasmuch as the policy was, in substance, a time policy.

By contrast, in *Thomas (M) & Son Shipping Co., Ltd., supra,* the vessel was held to be unseaworthy inasmuch as she was sent on her voyage with an insufficient crew with the privity of the assured's managing owner. As the loss was attributable to the insufficient crew, the policy did not cover.

In *Thomas v. Tyne & Wear S.S. Freight Ins. Ass'n, supra,* the ship was insured under a time policy. At the time she was sent to sea, she was unseaworthy in two respects; i.e., her hull was in an unfit state for the voyage, and her crew was insufficient. The assured knew of the insufficiency of the crew but not of the unfitness of the hull. The ship was lost on the voyage by reason of her unseaworthiness in respect of the unfitness of the hull. As the assured was not privy to the unfit hull, the policy covered—a perfect illustration of the proviso in sub-section 5.[178]

In *Phoenix Ins. Co. v. Anchor Ins. Co., supra,* payment of the loss was contested on the ground that the vessel was unseaworthy in that she proceeded on a voyage with only one anchor after having passed a port where a she could have replaced the anchor which was lost. The court held that, the policy being a time policy, there was no implied warranty of seaworthiness and no evidence that the vessel was unseaworthy merely because she had only one anchor, nor was it clear from the evidence that the stranding of the vessel was caused by the absence of the second anchor.

In *The Eurysthenes, supra,* the vessel was entered in a P & I club for Class 1 risks. The vessel was stranded while carrying cargo, and the cargo interests made claims against the shipowner. The shipowner then sued on the policy, and the defendant P & I club defended on the grounds that the vessel was unseaworthy with the privity of the assured. The question was squarely presented as to whether or not sub-section 5 applied to P & I policies. The question was answered in the affirmative, the court of appeal further adding that it was necessary to prove knowledge and con-

---

Ass'n, [1917] 1 K.B. 938, 14 Asp. M.L.C. 87; *Harocopus v. Mountain,* (1934) 49 Ll.L.Rep. 267; *Frangos v. Sun Life Ins. Office, Ltd.,* (1934) 49 Ll.L.Rep. 354; *Compania Maritime San Basilio, S.A. v. Oceanus Mutual Underwriting Ass'n (Bermuda) Ltd., (The Eurysthenes),* [1976] 3 All E.R. 243, [1976] 3 W.L.R. 265, C.A. [1976] 2 Lloyd's Rep. 171, C.A.; *Porter & Sons Ltd. v. Western Assur. Co.,* [1938] 1 D.L.R. 619 (Can.); *White v. Newfoundland Ins. Co.,* (1864) 5 Nfld. L.R. 27 (Can.); *Pacific Coast Coal Freighters Ltd. v. Westchester Fire Ins. Co. of New York, Pacific Coast Coal Freighters Ltd. v. Western Assur. Co.,* [1926] 4 D.L.R. 963, *aff'd* [1927] 2 D.L.R. 590 (Can.); *Phoenix Ins. Co. v. Anchor Ins. Co.,* (1884) 4 O.R. 524 (Can.); *Wilson v. Boag,* (1957) S.R. (N.S.W.) 384 (Aus.); *Bell v. Miller,* (1877) Knox 331 (Aus.); *Mountain v. Whittle,* [1921] 1 A.C. 615, [1921] 6 Ll.L.Rep. 378, H.L.

178. See, also, *Mountain v. Whittle,* [1921] 1 A.C. 615.

currence on the part of the shipowner personally in the ship being sent to sea in an unseaworthy condition but that this did not necessarily amount to wilful misconduct.

Compare, however, *Martin & Robertson v. Orion Ins. Co.*,[179] in which it was held that a charterer's liability policy, insuring against liabilities ordinarily covered by P & I club terms, was not subject to an implied warranty of seaworthiness and covered the liability of the charterer for loss of cargo due to unseaworthiness of the vessel with the owner's privity.[180]

The American Rule—Time Policies. The American rule with respect to implied warranties of seaworthiness in time policies, certainly in the Fifth Circuit and possibly in the Second Circuit, seemingly implies a warranty of seaworthiness in time policies as of the very moment of attachment. Unlike the English rule with respect to voyage policies (which limits the warranty to the commencement of the voyage, or to commencement of successive stages when the voyage is conducted in stages), the American rule seems to take it further to extend, in point of time, a sort of negative, modified warranty. It is not that the vessel shall continue absolutely to be kept in a seaworthy condition, or even that she be so at the inception of each voyage, or before departure from each port during the policy period. Rather, it is stated in the negative that the owner, from bad faith or neglect, will not knowingly permit the vessel to break ground in an unseaworthy condition. And, unlike a breach of warranty of continuing seaworthiness, which voids the policy altogether, the consequence of a violation of the "negative" burden imposed by the American rule is merely a denial of liability for loss or damage *proximately caused by such unseaworthiness.* In such time policies it is only where, *with the privity of the assured,* the ship is sent to sea in an unseaworthy condition that the insurer is not liable for any loss attributable to that unseaworthiness.[181]

It is not clear whether, under the American rule, there is an implied warranty of seaworthiness in a time policy where the vessel is at sea when the risk attaches.[182]

Evolution of the American Rule. American courts appear to have considered from the outset that a warranty of seaworthiness was to be implied in both voyage and time policies.[183]

179. 1971 AMC 515 (St.,Cal.).

180. See, also, *Export S.S. Corp. v. American Ins. Co.*, 26 F.Supp. 79, 1938 AMC 1556, 106 F.2d 9, 1939 AMC 1095, *cert. den.* 309 U.S. 686 (1939), and *Stewart v. Wilson*, (1843) 152 E.R. 1089.

181. *Spot Pack*, 242 F.2d 385, 1957 AMC 655 (5th Cir.).

182. *New York & P.R. S.S. Co. v. Aetna Ins. Co.*, 204 F. 255 (2d Cir., 1913).

183. See *Barnewall v. Church*, 1 Caines 217 (1803); *Paddock v. Franklin Ins. Co.*, 11 Pick. (Mass.) 227 (St.,Mass., 1831); *Adderley v. American Mut. Ins. Co. of Baltimore*, F.Cas. No. 75 (D.,Md., 1847); *Depeyre v. Western Mar. & Fire Ins. Co.*, 2 Rob. 457 (St.,La., 1842); *McDowell v.*

In 1888, the U. S. Supreme Court decided *Union Ins. Co. of Phila-delphia v. Smith*,[184] in which the following rule was stated:

In the insurance of a vessel by a time policy, the warranty of sea-worthiness is complied with if the vessel be seaworthy at the commencement of the risk, and the fact that she subsequently sustains damage, and is not properly refitted at an intermediate port, does not discharge the insurer from subsequent risk or loss, provided such loss be not the consequence of the omission. A defect of seaworthiness, arising after the commencement of the risk, and permitted to continue from bad faith or want of ordinary prudence or diligence on the part of the insured or his agents, discharges the insurer from liability for any loss which is the consequence of such bad faith or want of prudence or diligence; but does not affect the contract of insurance as to any other risk or loss covered by the policy, and not caused or increased by such particular defect.

The case, however, is of questionable legal precedent (as several courts have noted) because there the time policy contained an express exception for losses due to unseaworthiness. Thus, the quoted language is really *dictum* which was unnecessary to the facts then before the court.[185]

In *New York, New Haven and Hartford R.R. Co. v. Gray*,[185] Judge Frank of the Second Circuit distinguished many of the cases mentioned above as being *obiter dicta* and, in essence, ignored both elements of the rule enunciated in *Union Ins. Co. v. Smith, supra.* (It should be recognized, however, that in *New York, New Haven* the policy expressly provided that it would be subject to English law.)

Incredibly, in the same year, the Second Circuit decided *McAllister Lighterage Line v. Ins. Co. of N.A.*[187] In that case, the insured scow was unseaworthy and was moored to a pier at the time of the policy inception. Judge Lombard (who had been a member of the panel in *New York, New Haven*), citing *Union Ins. Co. v. Smith* and *Henjes v. Aetna*, held that there is

---

General Mut. Ins. Co., 7 La.Ann. 84 (St.,La., 1852); *Jones v. Ins. Co.*, F.Cas. No. 7,470 (E.D.,Pa., 1852); *Hoxie v. Home Ins. Co.*, 32 Conn. 21 (St.,Conn.,1864). But, compare *Merchants Ins. Co. v. Morrison*, 62 Ill. 242 (St.,Ill., 1871), which followed the English decision of *Thompson v. Hooper*, 119 E.R. 828.

184. 124 U.S. 405 (1888).

185. See *The Traffic*, 1928 AMC 174 (St.,N.Y.,1927) (question "still open" as to whether there is an implied warranty of seaworthiness in a time policy); *Sorenson & Neilson v. Boston Ins. Co.*, 1926 AMC 241, *rev'd* on other grounds 1927 AMC 1288 (4th Cir.); *New York & P.R. S.S. Co. v. Aetna Ins. Co.*, 204 F. 255 (2d Cir., 1913); *Zillah*, 1929 AMC 166 (St., Minn., 1928); *Rendezvous*, 1936 AMC 25 (St.,Wis., 1935); *Plummer v. Ins. Co. of N.A.*, 95 A. 605, 114 Me. 128 (St.,Me., 1915); *Companion*, 1929 AMC 693 (W.D.,Wash.); *Henjes v. Aetna Ins. Co.*, 132 F.2d 715, 1943 AMC 27 (2d Cir.).

186. 240 F.2d 460, 1957 AMC 616 (2d Cir.) *cert. den.* 353 U.S. 966.

187. 244 F.2d 867, 1957 AMC 1774 (2d Cir.).

implied in every policy of hull insurance a covenant of seaworthiness. The decision in *New York, New Haven* was not even mentioned.[188]

In the Fifth Circuit, there are a number of cases, many of which were written by Judge John R. Brown.[189]

A careful analysis of the decisions of Judge Brown in *Spot Pack, Sea Pak,* and *The Papoose, supra,* indicates that the answers to several questions still remain somewhat unclear. For example:

1. Is there an implied warranty in a time policy under the American rule that at the time of attachment of the insurance that the vessel is seaworthy when the vessel is not in port, or not in a port having repair facilities? While the rather broad language of the decisions would seem to indicate that there is, it is submitted that no case has arisen in the Fifth Circuit in which the court has been called upon to decide the precise question. *The Papoose* involved a vessel which was in a condition of "spectacular unseaworthiness" but also was in port at the time of attachment. By contrast, in *The Natalie,*[190] the distinguished arbitrator held that where a vessel was in a foreign port without repair facilities, the poicy attaching at that time was not subject to the implied warranty. The Fifth Circuit did not find it necessary to decide the question in *Lemar Towing, supra,* because, again, the vessel was in port, had been recently put in a shipyard for repairs, and no contention was made by underwriters that the vessel was unseaworthy at the inception of the policy. In *Miss Esmeralda, supra,* the policy contained an express warranty which, in its terms, did not significantly differ from the so-called "American rule." The insured vessel was normally fished with a three-man crew and departed port on her last voyage with only a two-man crew. On the facts, the court held that, at the time the casualty occurred and in the circumstances then existing, the vessel required a three-man crew and was thus unseaworthy by reason of an insufficient crew at the time of the casualty. Moreover, the vessel departed port with only a two-man crew with the knowledge of one of the owners. In *Lemar Towing,* the court found that the crew was incompetent at the com-

---

188. As recently as 1972, in *Neubros Corp. v. Northwestern Insurance Co.,* 359 F.Supp. 310, 1972 AMC 2443 (E.D.N.Y.), the trial court completely ignored *New York, New Haven,* stating in part, "It is well established that the warranty of seaworthiness attaches to a time hull policy at the time the policy becomes effective," citing, *inter alia, Henjes.*

189. *Saskatchewan Government Ins. Office v. Spot Pack (The Spot Pack),* 242 F.2d 385, 1957 AMC 655 (5th Cir.); *Tropical Marine Products v. Birmingham Fire Ins. Co. of Pennsylvania (The Sea Pak),* 247 F.2d 116, 1957 AMC 1946 (5th Cir.); *The Papoose,* 409 F.2d 974, 1969 AMC 781 (5th Cir.), [1970] 1 Lloyd's Rep. 178. See, also, of more recent vintage, *Lemar Towing Co. v. Fireman's Fund Ins. Co.,* 471 F.2d 609, 1973 AMC 1843 (5th Cir.); *Miss Esmeralda (grounding),* 441 F.2d 141, 1971 AMC 1134 (5th Cir.); and *D.J. McDuffie, Inc. v. Old Reliable Fire Ins. Co.,* 1979 AMC 595 (E.D.,La.), *aff'd* 608 F.2d 145, 1980 AMC 1886 (5th Cir.), *cert.den.* 449 U.S. 830, 1981 AMC 2099 (1980).

190. 1959 AMC 2379 (Arb.).

mencement of the voyage, thus rendering the vessel unseaworthy at that and subsequent times, and that such unseaworthiness proximately resulted from the owner's neglect in failing to determine the qualifications and experience of the crew to man the vessel for its intended voyage before its commencement. In *D.J.McDuffie, supra,* the evidence was clear that the vessel was unseaworthy upon leaving port, with the owners being aware of that unseaworthiness. It must therefore be concluded that the question is still an open one in the Fifth Circuit.

2. What does the word "neglect" mean in the requirement that the owner "from bad faith or *neglect,* will not knowingly permit the vessel to break ground in an unseaworthy condition"? Would mere negligence on the part of the shipowner in letting the vessel go to sea in an unseaworthy state enable the underwriter to escape liability? Or, must the owner be aware of the unseaworthiness before the policy can be avoided?

Although the Fifth Circuit does not appear to have made a square holding on the point, language in *Sea Pak* appears to infer that the correct meaning of the word "neglect" is that the owner who knows his vessel is unseaworthy will not negligently (or in bad faith) permit her to break ground.

This is the holding in other jurisdictions. For example, in *The Eurysthenes,*[191] Lord Denning opined that the term "privity" as used in Section 39(5) meant that to disentitle the shipowner, he must have knowledge not only of the facts constituting the unseaworthiness but also knowledge *that those facts rendered the vessel unseaworthy.*

In *Visscher Enterprises Pty. Ltd. v. Southern Pac. Ins. Co. Ltd.,*[192] the insurer defended on ground of the existence of a hole in the engine room bulkhead which ought to have been disclosed by the assured. The assured knew of the existence of the hole but did not realize the implications of it as it related to the seaworthiness of his vessel. Citing *The Eurysthenes,* the court held for the assured.

A similar question was involved in *Gregoire v. Underwriters at Lloyd's.*[193] In that case, the insured vessel capsized and sank in moderate seas in Cook Inlet, Alaska. Ultimately, the underwriters relied upon alleged evidence that the vessel was overloaded with crab pots when it left port and that this was the reason the vessel capsized and sank. In motions for summary judgment by both parties, the court was confronted with three issues: (1) was the vessel unseaworthy when it left port; (2) did the owner know it was unseaworthy; and (3) whether a warranty of seaworthiness is

---

191. [1976] 3 All E.R. 243, [1976] 2 Lloyd's Rep. 171, C.A.
192. [1981] Qd.R. 561 (Aus.).
193. 1982 AMC 2045 (D.,Alaska).

to be implied in every time hull policy. Holding that the first two issues presented questions of fact which could not be resolved on summary judgment, the court proceeded to analyze the cases with respect to the implied warranty of seaworthiness—the so-called American rule. The court said, in part:

> The owner's duty of care to ensure the seaworthiness of vessel at the time it breaks ground. Most of the confusion surrounding the second part of the American rule springs from the ambiguous language "the Owner, from bad faith or neglect, will not knowingly permit the vessel to break ground in an unseaworthy condition" (citing *Spot Pack*). The unfortunate juxtaposition of "neglect" and "knowingly" leaves it unclear whether the standard being proposed requires actual knowledge of the unseaworthy condition of the vessel by the owner as in the English rule, or whether the owner's mere negligence is enough. Later language in the *Spot Pack* opinion, however, makes it clear that it is the English position that is being adopted.

After analyzing the American cases on the subject, the court said further:

> . . . Since the great majority of the decided cases in this country are consistent with the English Rule, it should be applied in this case. I, therefore, hold that in a time hull policy of marine insurance there is no implied warranty that a vessel will not break ground in an unseaworthy condition. Where, however, the owner of a vessel or those in privity with him send their vessel to sea knowing it to be unseaworthy, the insurer is not liable for damages proximately caused by the unseaworthiness.

Logic and reason, as well as the greater weight of the decisions, support the proposition that the insured vessel must be in a seaworthy condition at the inception of the policy if, at that time, she is in port. This might well not have been true in times past when communications were chancy and months might elapse before an owner might be informed that his vessel in, for example, a foreign port was in need of repairs. Today, with almost instantaneous communications between vessel masters and vessel owners, and the ease and facility of air travel and shipment by which competent personnel and parts can reach the vessel without delay, there is no reason why the owner should not be held to the implied warranty, regardless of which port the vessel might be in at the inception of the policy.

Moreover, it is submitted that, in keeping with the principle enunciated in *The Eurysthenes* and *Visscher*, before an owner should be disentitled to coverage, he must be shown to have knowledge—not only of the facts which may constitute unseaworthiness—but also knowledge that those facts do, in fact, render his vessel unseaworthy. Otherwise, he has not "knowingly" permitted his vessel to break ground in an unseaworthy condition.[194]

194. The author wishes to express his indebtedness in having available to him, in connection with the discussion of the American rule, the excellent article entitled "The Implied Warranty of Seaworthiness in Time Policies: The American View," by Russell W. Pritchett, in [1983] 2 *Lloyd's Maritime and Commercial Law Quarterly* 195.

CHAPTER XII

THE PERILS CLAUSE

Introduction

The venerable "perils" clause in the old Lloyd's S.G. form was settled in its present form in 1779, but the clause dates from a much earlier period (as can be seen in Chapter I, "Introduction") and reads as follows:

> Touching the adventures and perils which we, the assurers, are contented to bear and do take upon us in this voyage: they are of the seas, men of war, fire, enemies, pirates, rovers, thieves, jettisons, letters of mart and countermart, surprisals, takings at sea, arrests, restraints, and detainments of all kings, princes, and people, of what nation, condition or quality soever, barratry of the master and mariners, and of all other perils, losses, and misfortunes, that have or shall come to the hurt, detriment, or damage of the said goods, and merchandises, and ship etc. or any part thereof . . . .

As is noted in Chapter III, "The Policy," under "Comparative Analysis of Old and New Institute Cargo Clauses," Lloyd's has responded to criticisms of UNCTAD by amending the basic policy form. As a consequence, the old perils clause is a thing pretty much of the past in the London market, and the new Institute Time Clauses (Hull) (1/10/83) itemizes (in paragraph 6) the revised "perils" clause which the London market anticipates will be used in the future with respect to hull coverages. The new perils clause in the Institute Cargo Clauses (A), (B), and (C) will be found in paragraph 1 of those forms.

Nonetheless, the American market and other markets continue to use the old perils clause, or variants thereof, and for many years to come the decisions rendered under the old perils clause will govern the construction of the same (or substantially identical) terms in the new London forms. This is so because there does not appear to have been any intention on the part of the draftsmen of the new London clauses that basic definitions would be changed. Moreover, the Marine Insurance Act, 1906, applies with all vigor to the new clauses, and that Act contains a host of definitions which follow decisions rendered prior to the passage of the Act. For example, there is no evidence whatever that the definition of the term "stranding" was intended to be changed by the use of the new London clauses, and the same holds true for the remainder of the perils which formerly appeared in the old perils clause but which now appear in itemized form in the new clauses.

Perils of the Seas

"Perils of the seas" means precisely what the phrase states; i.e., the peril must be "of the seas" and not merely "on the seas."[1] As applied to inland watercraft, it is synonymous with "perils of the river."[2] The term includes losses which are of an extraordinary nature or arise from some irresistible force which cannot be guarded against by the ordinary exertions of human skill and prudence. It is something which is accidental, unexpected, or fortuitous and not something which is normal, ordinary, and usual in nature.[3]

1. *Wilson, Sons, & Co. v. Xantho (Cargo Owners)*, (1887) 12 A.C. 503; *Cary v. Home Ins. Co.*, 199 App.Div. 122, *aff'd* 235 N.Y. 296, 139 N.E. 274, 1923 AMC 438 (St.,N.Y.); *Murray v. N.S. Marine Ins. Co.*, (1875) 10 N.S.R. 24 (Can., C.A.). But insurance against perils of the seas includes perils in a port. *Hill v. Union Ins. Soc.*, (1927) 61 O.L.R. 201, (1927) 4 D.L.R. 718 (Can., C.A.).

2. *Continental Ins. Co. v. Patton-Tully Transp. Co.*, 212 F.2d 543, 1954 AMC 889 (5th Cir.). And see *Russell Mining v. Northwestern F. & M. Ins. Co.*, 207 F.Supp. 162, 1963 AMC 130 (E.D.,Tenn.), *aff'd* 322 F.2d 440, 1963 AMC 2358 (6th Cir.), where the court stated, in effect, that an insurer who writes a standard marine policy covering a barge used on an inland lake may not be heard to say that the policy's salty Elizabethan language has no application to an unmanned, moored barge on a freshwater inland lake, as the words of the policy, being the words of the insurer, are most strongly construed against it. See, also, *Shaver Forwarding Co. v. Eagle Star Ins. Co.*, 172 Or. 91, 139 P.2d 769, 1943 AMC 1178, 177 Or. 410, 162 P.2d 789 (1945), and *Prohaska v. St. Paul F. & M. Ins. Co.*, 270 F. 91 (5th Cir., 1921).

3. *Hamilton, Fraser & Co. v. Pandorf*, (1887) 12 A.C. 518; *Wash Gray*, 277 U.S. 66, 1928 AMC 923; *Continental Ins. Co. v. Patton-Tully*, (1954) *supra*, n. 2; *Dwyer v. Providence Washington Ins. Co.*, 1958 AMC 1488 (St.,Ga.); *Hazard's Adm'r v. New England Marine Ins. Co.*, 33 U.S. 557 (1834); *Mountain v. Whittle*, (1921) 1 A.C. 615, 6 Ll.L.Rep. 378, H.L.; *Arbib v. 2nd Russian Ins. Co.*, 294 F. 811, 1924 AMC 16 (2d Cir.); *Western Assur. Co. of Toronto, Canada v. Shaw*, 11 F.2d 495, 1926 AMC 578 (3rd Cir.); *Moores v. Louisville Underwriters*, 14 F. 226 (W.D.,Tenn., 1882); *George W. Clyde*, 12 F.2d 733, 1926 AMC 807 (7th Cir.); *Union Marine Ins. Co. v. Charles D. Stone & Co.*, 15 F.2d 937, 1927 AMC 7 (7th Cir.); *Lighter No. 176*, 1929 AMC 554 (St.,Md.); *Marion Logging Co. v. Utah Home Fire Ins. Co.*, (1956) 5 D.L.R. 2d 700 (Can.); *Murray v. N.S. Marine Ins. Co.*, (1875), *supra* n. 1. See, however, *Olympia Canning Co. v. Union Marine Ins. Co.*, 10 F.2d 72, 1926 AMC 181 (9th Cir.), holding that the fortuity required need not be something extraordinary or irresistible so long as it is something more than inevitable. See, also, *The Peerless*, 1927 AMC 104 (NYAD), in which the court held that to constitute a peril of the sea, it is not necessary that there should be the action of the sea, wind, or waves, violent or otherwise, but a truly accidental occurrence, peculiar to the sea, such as the entry of seawater through the seams of a vessel or through a hole in her hull, neither happening through design. And in *The Panamanian*, 50 F.Supp. 986, 1943 AMC 976 (S.D.N.Y.), the court characterized the casualty as being "the result of a fortuitous entry of the sea water; that it was an event which might and did happen, not one which must happen." The court continued by stating:

> At most we have at bar a situation where undiscovered wear and tear made the jamming of the valve possible—not certain; and the jamming of the valve made the incursion of water into the hotwell possible, not certain; and the incursion of water into the hotwell made the flooding of the vessel possible, not certain. What we have, therefore, is a loss through perils of the sea.

The case of *Samuel (P) & Co., Ltd. v. Dumas*[4] appears to establish the rule in England that the mere incursion of seawater is a peril of the sea unless deliberately permitted to enter the vessel. In the United States, the court of appeals, Second Circuit, arrived at the same conclusion in *New York, New Hampshire & H. R.R. Co. v. Gray.*[5] The decision is more explicable when one realizes that the policy involved in the *Gray* case was one written and delivered in England and that English law applied—although the court does not seem to have focused on that fact. *Spooner & Son v. Connecticut Fire Ins. Co.*[6] expressly followed *Gray* in holding that, where a crane barge engaged in a delicate salvage operation collapsed because of swells caused by a passing freighter, the loss was caused by a peril of the sea. Compare, however, *Western Assur. Co. v. Shaw,*[7] where the passing of steamers along the Delaware River was held to be a "normal" occurrence and the swells contributed to the sinking of an unseaworthy barge. The question seems to hinge upon whether or not the swells are encountered in the ordinary course of the vessel's use.

Rule 7, Rules for Construction of Policy, contained in the first schedule of the Marine Insurance Act, 1906, states the rule as follows:

> The term "perils of the seas" refers only to fortuitous accidents or casualties of the seas. It does not include the ordinary action of the winds and waves.

In England, the expression "perils of the seas" appears to have the same meaning in a marine policy as it has in a bill of lading or charter. This seems also to be the rule in the United States, although there is language in *Spooner* and *Gray* which is at variance.[8] The burden of proof is, however, totally different in insurance cases from that in affreightment cases, and this difference, if not appreciated, can lead to confusion and difficulties.[9]

It is difficult to formualte a precise definition of the term. In *Duche & Sons v. Brocklebank & Cunard,*[10] Judge Chase said:

> A multiplication of definitions will result only in a multiplication of words without serving any useful purpose. The difficult task is not to

4. (1924) A.C. 431, (1924) All E.R. 66. See, also, *Canada Rice Mills, Ltd. v. Union Mar. & Gen. Ins. Co., Ltd.,* (1941) A.C. 55.

5. 240 F.2d 460, 1957 AMC 616 (2d Cir.).

6. 314 F.2d 753, 1963 AMC 859 (2d Cir.).

7. 273 U.S. 698, 71 L.ed. 846 (1926).

8. See, for example, *Reisman v. New Hampshire Fire Ins. Co.,* 312 F.2d 17, 1963 AMC 1151 (5th Cir.); *Jones Lumber Co. v. Roen S.S. Co.,* 157 F.Supp. 304, 1957 AMC 2419 (W.D.N.Y.); and *The Arlington,* (1943) S.C.R. 179, (1943) 2 D.L.R. 193, 1943 AMC 388. The leading English cases are: *Hamilton, Fraser & Co. v. Pandorf* (1887), *supra; Wilson, Sons & Co. v. Xantho (Cargo Owners)* (1887), *supra; Sassoon v. Western Assur. Co.,* (1912) A.C. 561.

9. *Texaco v. Universal Marine,* 400 F. Supp. 311, 1976 AMC 226 (E.D.,Va.).

10. 40 F.2d 418, 1930 AMC 717 (2d Cir.).

define in general terms a peril of the sea, but to determine whether some established facts and circumstances fall within a sound definition.

In the *Warren Adams*,[11] the definition was:

> . . . all marine casualties resulting from the violent action of the elements, as distinguished from their natural, silent influence upon the fabric of the vessel; casualties which may, and not consequences which must, occur.

In *The Guilia*,[12] the definition was:

> Perils of the seas are understood to mean those perils which are peculiar to the sea, and which are of extraordinary nature or arise from irresistible force or overwhelming power, and which cannot be guarded against by the ordinary exertion of human skill and prudence.

Judge Hough, in *The Rosalie*,[13] stated it vividly, in oft-quoted language:

> It . . . means something so catastrophic as to triumph over those safeguards by which skillful and vigilant seamen usually bring ship and cargo to port safely.

Judge Learned Hand, in *The Naples Maru*,[14] in referring to Judge Hough's language, said:

> That meant nothing more, however, than that the weather must be too much for a well-found vessel to withstand.

In *Lighter No. 176* (1929), *supra,* the court stated that a peril of the sea need not be something catastrophic in nature but was something arising from the violent action of the elements without rather than from a weakness within the vessel.

Lord Bramwell, in *Hamilton, Fraser & Co. v. Pandorf & Co.* (1887), *supra,* defined the term as follows:

> . . . every accidental circumstance not the result of ordinary wear and tear, delay, or of the act of the assured, happening in the course of the navigation of the ship, and incidental to the navigation, and causing loss to the subject-matter of the insurance.

He then quoted from another definition given by Lopes, L. J.:

---

11. 74 F.413 (2d Cir., 1896). Note the similarity of expression also used in *Wilson, Sons & Co. v. Xantho* (1887), *supra;* and *The Panamanian* (1943), *supra.*
12. 218 F. 744 (2d Cir., 1914).
13. 264 F. 285 (2d Cir., 1920).
14. 106 F.2d 32, 1939 AMC 1087 (2d Cir.).

. . . in a seaworthy ship damage to goods caused by the action of the sea during transit not attributable to the fault of anybody.

Loss Held Not to Be Caused by a Peril of the Sea

What, then, have been held to be perils of the sea? Or perhaps the inquiry more properly is: What have been held *not* to be perils of the sea?

The action of worms eating holes in the bottom of a ship is not a peril of the sea.[15] Neither is the chemical action of salt water as distinguished from violence of the waves.[16] Nor is a loss arising from rats eating a hole in a ship's bottom,[17] although the action of rats in eating a hole in a ship's pipe thus allowing the incursion of seawater into the cargo is such a peril.[18]

The bursting of the air chamber in a donkey engine is not a peril of the sea.[19] Neither is mere leakage from casks, not occasioned by a shifting of the cargo from a gale.[20] Merely encountering heavy seas in a locality and at a time of the year when they might be expected is not a peril of the sea.[21] Tides or the action of the tides may or may not be, depending upon whether or not the action was extraordinary or unexpected.[22]

But in *Thompson v. Whitmore*,[23] the ship was beached to be cleaned and repaired in the normal fashion and the tide came in and knocked the supports away, thereby causing her to heel over and suffer damage. The loss was held not to be due to a peril of the sea. To the same effect, see *Magnus v. Buttemer*,[24] where the vessel took ground in the normal course of events when the tide ebbed.

The injuries sustained by live animals caused by the rolling and pitching of the vessel were held to be due to perils of the seas in *Gabay v. Lloyd*, and in *Lawrence v. Aberdein*,[25] but death of live animals by reason of a failure to provide sufficient provisions for them to withstand an extraor-

---

15. *Rohl v. Parr*, (1796) 1 Esp. 445, N.P.; *Hazard's Adm'r v. New England Marine Ins. Co.* (1834), *supra*.

16. *Paterson v. Harris*, (1861) 121 E.R. 740, where imperfect insulation permitted seawater to disable a transatlantic telegraph cable.

17. *Hunter v. Potts*, (1815) 4 Camp. 203, N.P.

18. *Hamilton, Fraser & Co. v. Pandorf & Co.* (1887), *supra*.

19. *Thames & Mersey Marine Ins. Co., Ltd. v. Hamilton, Fraser & Co.*, (1887) 12 A.C. 484.

20. *Crofts v. Marshall*, (1836) 7 C. & P. 597, N.P.

21. *The Gulnare*, 42 F. 861 (5th Cir., 1890).

22. See, for example, *Potter v. Suffolk Ins. Co.*, Fed.Cas. No. 11,339 (1st Cir., 1835), where the loss occurred by reason of the ebbing of the tide, extraordinary in nature, and *Fletcher v. Inglis*, (1819) 106 E.R. 382, where the vessel grounded in a harbor, the bed of which was hard and uneven, and the ebbing of the tide was accompanied by a heavy swell.

23. (1810) 128 E.R. 90. See, also, *Phillips v. Barber*, (1821) 106 E.R. 1151, and *Rowcroft v. Dunmore*, (1801) 128 E.R. 91.

24. (1852) 138 E.R. 720.

25. (1825) 107 E.R. 927; (1821) 106 E.R. 1133.

dinary delay in the voyage due to bad weather was held not to be a peril of the sea.[26]

In *Taylor v. Dunbar*,[27] meat shipped at Hamburg for London was delayed on the voyage by tempestuous weather, and solely by reason of the delay the meat became putrid and was thrown overboard. The court held this was not a peril of the sea. Compare, however, *Lanasa Fruit Steamship and Importing Company, Inc. v. Universal Insurance Company (The Smaragd)*,[28] where the delay was caused by a stranding during which time the cargo spoiled. The U. S. Supreme Court held that the proximate cause was a peril of the seas; i.e., the stranding.

Other cases holding that the loss was not due to perils of the seas are where rats damaged a cargo of cheese;[29] sums paid to another vessel with which the insured vessel collided;[30] ship scuttled by strangers;[31] damage to a cargo of opium due to the rotten condition of the hull, permitting water to enter;[32] unseaworthy vessel; cost of repairs at an intermediate port held not recoverable;[33] capsize of a drydock, the design not being suitable for the work intended;[34] departure with insufficient supply of coal, necessitating salvage charges not recoverable against the assurer, as the cause of loss was unseaworthiness and not a peril of the sea;[35] heavy weather experienced enroute, and the cargo arrived in a damaged condition; assured failed to prove that the damage was caused by seawater;[36]

---

26. *Tatham v. Hodgson*, (1796) 101 E.R. 756.

27. (1869) L.R. 4 C.P. 206.

28. 302 U.S. 55, 1938 AMC 1. The decision has been harshly criticized as not being in accord with principle, and, as a consequence, American cargo policies now expressly provide for an exception with respect to losses by reason of delay notwithstanding that the delay may have been caused by a peril insured against. The English rule has always been to that effect. See Sec. 55(2)(b) of the Marine Insurance Act, 1906, reading:

> Unless the policy otherwise provides, the insurer on ship or goods is not liable for any loss proximately caused by delay, although the delay be caused by a peril insured against.

See, also, *Pink v. Fleming*, (1890) 25 Q.B.D. 396.

29. *Laveroni v. Drury*, (1852) 8 Exch. 166.

30. *De Vaux v. Salvador*, (1836) 111 E.R. 845. This case led to the adoption of the Running Down Clause. While clearly a "collision" is a peril of the sea (see *Gen. Mut. Ins. Co. v. Sherwood*, 55 U.S. 351 (1847), *and the hull underwriter must pay for damage to the insured vessel even though caused by negligence of the master or crew*, the coverage under the hull policy does not extend to the payment of damages to the other vessel in collision. Nor is there any liability on the hull udnerwriter for damages for detention of the insured vessel while undergoing repairs due to a collision. *Shelbourne v. Law Investment Corp.*, (1898) 2 Q.B. 626. The Running Down Clause provides such coverage and is discussed in depth in Chapter XXI, *infra*.

31. *Miskofski v. Economic Ins. Co.*, (1964) 45 W.W.R. 395, 43 D.L.R. 2d 281 (Can.).

32. *Sassoon (E.D.) & Co. v. Western Assur. Co.*, (1912) A.C. 561, (1911-13) All E.R. 438.

33. *Faucus v. Sarsfield*, (1856) 119 E.R. 836.

34. *Grant, Smith & Co. & McDonnell Ltd. v. Seattle Constr. & Drydock Co.*, (1920) A.C. 162, (1918-19), All E.R. 378.

35. *Ballantyne v. MacKinnon*, (1896) 2 Q.B. 455, C.A.

36. *Micelli v. Union Marine Ins. Co., Ltd.*, (1938) 60 Ll.L.Rep. 275, C.A.

loss due to inadequate packing of the cargo and not a sea peril;[37] water
entering the vessel through a torpedo hole; held a war risk and not a peril
of the sea;[38] evidence as consistent with defects in the casks, bad stowage,
etc., as with heavy weather;[39] failure of proof as to damage by seawater;[40]
vessel sent to sea with insufficient crew with knowledge of the assured;[41]
perishable goods lost by reason of delay caused by a collision;[42] loss of
freight occasioned by detention in ice; the delay was caused by the inevitable course of nature;[43] vessel in a weakened condition owing to want of
due diligence of the assured;[44] wear and tear and the action of worms; not
a peril of the seas;[45] ship sank at a dock; failure of proof by the assured as
to the cause;[46] incursion of seawater held not a peril of the sea where the
vessel was overloaded because of want of due diligence on the part of the
owner;[47] ship put into port by reason of stress of weather, whereupon the
master landed and sold the cargo; held, the loss was not due to a peril of
the sea, since the goods could have been forwarded to destination.[48]

The American cases holding the loss not to be due to a peril of the sea
are very numerous. For example, worm damage to a vessel's hull is not a
sea peril;[49] nor is encountering heavy seas at an expectable time of the
year.[50] Other American cases holding the loss not due to perils of the seas
are where shipways collapsed, allowing the vessel to sink;[51] a lighter
damaged by an explosion of dynamite on a nearby vessel;[52] barge sinking
at a dock by reason of hot sun opening up her seams;[53] capsizing of a
leaky scow with improperly stowed cargo;[54] cargo found wet and
damaged by fresh water, not seawater;[55] barge sinking as a result of the

37. *Gee & Garnham Ltd. v. Whittal*, (1955) 2 Lloyd's Rep. 562.
38. *Leyland Shipping Co. v. Norwich Union Ins. Co.*, (1918) A.C. 350.
39. *N.E. Neter & Co. v. Licenses and Gen. Ins. Co., Ltd.*, (1944) 1 All E.R. 341, 77 Ll.L.Rep.
202.
40. *Cobb and Jenkins v. Volga Ins. Co., Ltd.*, (1920) 4 Ll.L.Rep. 130, K.B.D.
41. *Thomas (M) & Son, Shipping Co., Ltd. v. London & Prov. Mar. and Gen. Ins. Co., Ltd.*,
(1914) 30 T.L.R. 595, C.A. See, also, *Wood v. Associated Nat. Ins. Co. Ltd.*, [1984] 1 Qd.R. 507
(Aus.).
42. *Pink v. Fleming*, (1890) 25 Q.B.D. 396, C.A.
43. *Great Western Ins. Co. v. Jordan*, (1886) 14 S.C.R. 734 (Can.).
44. *Atlantic Freighting Co. v. Prov. Ins. Co.*, (1956) 5 D.L.R.2d 164 (Can.).
45. *Coons v. Aetna Ins. Co.*, (1868) 18 U.C.C.P. 305 (Can.,C.A.).
46. *Marion Logging Co. v. Utah Home Fire Ins. Co.*, (1956) 5 D.L.R.2d 700 (Can.).
47. *Coast Ferries, Ltd. v. Coast Underwriters, Ltd. (The Brentwood)*, (1974) 48 D.L.R.3d 310
(S.C.,Can.).
48. *Ross v. Miller*, (1863) 2 S.C.R. 329 (Aus.).
49. *Hazard's Adm'r v. New England Marine Ins. Co.*, 33 U.S. 557 (1834).
50. *The Gulnare*, 42 F. 861 (5th Cir., 1890).
51. *Prohaska v. St. Paul F. & M. Ins. Co.*, 265 F. 430 (E.D.,La., 1920).
52. *Listers Agricultural Chemical Works v. Home Ins. Co.*, 202 F. 1011 (D.C.N.Y., 1912).
53. *New Orleans T. & M. Ry. Co. v. Union Marine Ins. Co.*, 286 F. 32, AMC 183 (5th Cir.).
54. *Cary v. Home Ins. Co.*, 1923 AMC 438, 199 App.Div. 122, *aff'd* 235 N.Y. 296, 139 N.E.
274.
55. *Hebron*, 1926 AMC 373 (St.,Ga.).

rolling of unshored boilers, held not a peril of the seas;[56] vessel having defective rivets and plates around a newly installed side port;[57] damage to cargo caused by improper stowage rather than a grounding;[58] sea connection left open after a launching held not due to a peril of the sea;[59] feeling a "jolt" on board a barge while underway found not to warrant a finding of striking a submerged object;[60] vessel unseaworthy by reason of improper cutting of holes in its hatch-leaves, allowing water to enter;[61] leak in exhaust outlet, toilet valve, and seams not a sea peril;[62] weather and seas such as might reasonably be expected and therefore there was no sea peril;[63] vessel found holed in three places but assured failed to show a sea peril;[64] failure of proof as to a sea peril: cases holding a presumption of loss by perils of the seas where there is an unexplained sinking disapproved;[65] pre-existing crack in a vessel's ribs held not a sea peril;[66] vessel damaged by collapse of a sea crane being used to hoist her;[67] displacement wave from a passing tugboat held not a peril of the river;[68] insufficient evidence to show that the cause was a sea peril, the vessel being found unseaworthy in several respects;[69] newly caulked barge found to have a deficient 18-inch section of old oakum;[70] unexplained sinking while under tow with no proof of negligent towage;[71] vessel sinking because of packing around a driveshaft becoming loose held not a sea peril;[72] acid thrown by unknown persons on fishing nets which were appurtenant to the insured vessel; held, not a sea peril nor *ejusdem generis* therewith;[73] omissions of owner and friends aboard the cause of a sinking but not a sea peril;[74] loss by reason of high seas and heavy, but not unexpectable, March weather not a fortuitous accident and thus not a sea peril;[75] failure of a yacht owner to close a gooseneck valve, causing his yacht to sink not a sea peril;[76] flooding of a ship's hold because of failure

56. *Holly*, 11 F.2d 495, 1926 AMC 578 (3d Cir.).
57. *George W. Clyde*, 12 F.2d 733, 1926 AMC 807 (7th Cir.).
58. *Redman*, 43 F.2d 361, 1930 AMC 1896, (5th Cir.).
59. *Rendezvous*, 1936 AMC 25 (St.,Wis.).
60. *Dreifus Co. v. Diamond P. & Transp. Co.*, 7 F.Supp. 363, 1934 AMC 720 (E.D.,Pa.).
61. *Material Service*, 96 F.2d 923, 1938 AMC 842 (7th Cir.).
62. *Fine v. American Eagle Ins. Co.*, 1942 AMC 96 (NYM).
63. *Admiral-Cleveco*, 154 F.2d 605, 1946 AMC 933 (7th Cir.).
64. *Mettler v. Phoenix Assur. Co.*, 107 F.Supp. 194, 1952 AMC 1734 (E.D.N.Y.).
65. *Bertie Kay*, 106 F.Supp 244, 1952 AMC 1812 (E.D.N.Y.).
66. *Glover v. Philadelphia F. & M. Ins. Co.*, 1956 AMC 1210 (St.,Md.).
67. *Lind v. Boston Ins. Co.*, 1953 AMC 1047 (St.,Wash.).
68. *Continental Ins. Co. v. Patton-Tully*, 212 F.2d 543, 1954 AMC 889 (5th Cir.).
69. *Sundin v. Birmingham F. I. Co.*, 1957 AMC 281 (S.D.,Tex.).
70. *McAllister v. Ins. Co. of N.A.*, 244 F.2d 867, 1957 AMC 1774 (2d Cir.).
71. *Ideal Cement Co. v. Home Ins. Co.*, 210 F.2d 939, 1954 AMC 663 (5th Cir.).
72. *Dwyer v. Providence-Washington Ins. Co.*, 1958 AMC 1488 (St.,Ga.).
73. *Southport Fisheries v. Saskatchewan*, 161 F.Supp. 81, 1959 AMC 1280 (E.D.N.C.).
74. *Yacht Rowdy*, 177 F.Supp. 932, 1959 AMC 2270 (E.D.,Mich.).
75. *Anders v. Poland*, 1966 AMC 1867 (St.,La.).
76. *King v. Liverpool & London & Globe*, 1964 AMC 532 (N.Y.M.).

of a pipe caused by electrolysis or corrosion not a sea peril;[77] 50-mile winds and 12-15-foot waves on Lake Erie in November not a sea peril;[78] failure of proof by the assured where there was an unexplained sinking;[79] failure of assured to make cockpit drains fast not a sea peril;[80] dredge in tow sank from unexplained causes and the assured failed to call available eyewitnesses;[81] sinking by reason of wormy bottom;[82] sinking because of holes in an exhaust line, which holes had been in existence for some time;[83] loss due to unseaworthiness rather than a sea peril held a breach of warranty case;[84] sinking due to unseaworthiness rather than a sea peril;[85] hole in a rubber hose which caused vessel to sink held not a sea peril, as no proof offered by the assured as to the cause of the hole;[86] sinking at a dock from an open sea valve not a peril of the sea;[87] sinking from deteriorated metal fastenings in the hull not a sea peril;[88] unexplained sinking coupled with a failure to abandon as a constructive total loss; underwriters' surveyor precluded from making a formal survey;[89] jam nut securing the stuffing box came loose, but the assured contended waves from a passing vessel caused the propeller to turn and the nut to come off; held not a sea peril;[90] an explosion occurring in unexplained circumstances, causing the sinking of the vessel, held not a sea peril;[91] the sinking of a barge while under tow in calm water not a peril of the seas;[92] results of normal wear and tear and corrosive effects of seawater not a "latent defect" and not a peril of the seas;[93] unexplained sinking in fair weather and calm seas with no probable explanation of the reason; assured failed to bear burden of proof.[94]

77. *Larsen v. Ins. Co. of N.A.*, 252 F.Supp. 458, 1965 AMC 2576 (W.D.,Wash.).

78. *Jones Lumber Co. v. Roen S.S. Co.*, 270 F.2d 456, 1960 AMC 46 (2d Cir.).

79. *Coburn v. Utah Home Fire Ins.*, 233 Or. 20, 375 P.2d 1022, 1963 AMC 410 (St.,Ore.).

80. *Commercial Union v. Foster*, 1965 AMC 393 (St.,Tex.).

81. *Pacific Dredging Co. v. Hurley*, 1965 AMC 836 (St.,Wash.).

82. *Reisman v. N.H. Fire Ins. Co.*, 312 F.2d 17, 1963 AMC 1151 (5th Cir.).

83. *Adequate*, 305 F.2d 944, 1963 AMC 116 (9th Cir.).

84. *Papoose*, 409 F.2d 974, 1969 AMC 781 (5th Cir.), [1970], 1 Lloyd's Rep. 178.

85. *Capital Coastal v. Hartford Fire (The Christie)*, 378 F.Supp. 163, 1974 AMC 2039 (E.D.,Va.), [1975], 2 Lloyd's Rep. 100.

86. *Wood v. Great American*, 1968 AMC 1815A (E.D.,Wis.).

87. *Commercial Union v. Daniels*, 343 F.Supp. 674, 1973 AMC 452 (S.D.,Tex.).

88. *Sipowicz v. Wimble (The Green Lion)*, 370 F.Supp. 442, 1975 AMC 524 (S.D.N.Y.), [1974] 1 Lloyd's Rep. 593.

89. *College Point D. & S. v. National Union Fire*, 392 F.Supp. 277, 1976 AMC 1873 (S.D.N.Y.).

90. *Vining v. Security Ins. Co. of New Haven*, 252 So.2d 754 (St.,La.).

91. *Northwestern Mutual Life Ins. Co. v. Linard (The Vainqueur)*, 498 F.2d 556, 1974 AMC 877 (2d Cir.), [1974] 2 Lloyd's Rep. 398.

92. *McDuffie v. Old Reliable*, 1979 AMC 595.

93. *Parente v. Bayville Marine Inc. et al.*, 1974 AMC 1399 (N.Y.A.D.), [1975] 1 Lloyd's Rep. 333.

94. *Nickerson & Sons Ltd. v. I.N.A. (The J.E. Kenny)*, (1983) C.C.L.I. 78 (Can.).

Loss Held Due to Perils of the Seas

English Cases. There are, of course, numerous cases in which the assured has prevailed on a claim of loss by reason of a peril of the sea. Examples are: grounding in a harbor by reason of a heavy swell;[95] injuries to animals by rolling and pitching of the vessel;[96] incursion of seawater into the hull where rats ate a hole in the ship's pipe;[97] foundering of a vessel following a collision;[98] cargo of rice damaged by heat when ventilators were closed to prevent the incursion of seawater during heavy weather;[99] insured vessel run down by another vessel through gross negligence;[100] insured vessel in collision with wreck of a vessel torpedoed a short time before; held, the hostile act of torpedoing was not the proximate cause of the loss;[101] loss of insured vessel occasioned by being negligently towed;[102] ship stranded and totally lost; cargo underwriters held liable when cargo on board was subsequently plundered;[103] vessel sinking because of a collision;[104] vessel damaged by ice and thereafter prematurely abandoned by master and crew;[105] crewmen sent ashore to make fast new lines impressed by a press gang before the lines could be made fast, and the ship went ashore and was lost;[106] submarine being broken up for scrap sank because of negligence of the wrecking crew;[107] vessel being towed shipped water by reason of tempestuous seas;[108] ship caught in unseasonable ice necessitating transshipment of goods by rail at greater cost;[109] seawater damaged hides being carried aboard which, becoming putrid, imparted a nauseous flavor to tobacco stored nearby;[110] engineer intending to ballast vessel opened the wrong valve by mistake, flooding the cargo—

---

95. *Fletcher v. Inglis,* (1819) 106 E.R. 382.
96. *Gabay v. Lloyd,* (1825) 107 E.R. 927; *Lawrence v. Aberdein,* (1821) 106 E.R. 1133.
97. *Hamilton, Fraser & Co. v. Pandorf,* (1887) 12 A.C. 518.
98. *Wilson, Sons & Co. v. Xantho (Cargo Owners),* (1887) 12 A.C. 503.
99. *Canada Rice Mills, Ltd. v. Union Marine & Gen. Ins. Co., Ltd.,* (1940) 4 All E.R. 169, (1941) A.C. 55.
100. *Smith v. Scott,* (1811) 128 E.R. 276.
101. *France (William) Fenwick & Co., Ltd. v. North of England Prot. & Ind. Ass'n,* (1917) 2 K.B. 522.
102. *Mountain v. Whittle,* (1921) 1 A.C. 615.
103. *Hahn v. Corbett,* (1824) 130 E.R. 285; *Bondrett v. Hentigg,* (1816) Holt, N.P. 149.
104. *Reischer v. Borwick,* (1894) 2 Q.B. 548, C.A.
105. *Lind v. Mitchell,* (1928) 98 L.J.K.B.. 120, 32 Ll.L.Rep. 70, C.A.
106. *Hodgson v. Malcolm,* (1806) 127 E.R. 656.
107. *Cohen, Sons & Co. v. National Benefit Assur. Co., Ltd.,* (1924) 40 T.L.R. 347, 18 Ll.L.Rep. 199.
108. *Hagedorn v. Whitmore,* (1816) 1 Stark. 157, N.P.
109. *Popham v. St. Petersburg Ins. Co.,* (1904) 10 Com.Cas. 31.
110. *Montoya v. London Assurance,* (1851) 155 E.R. 620.

an affreightment case;[111] wind force of ten and over for five days during a period of nine days in winter in the North Atlantic—an affreightment case;[112] cargo of grain damaged by heat from the engine room when ventilators were closed during a storm of exceptional severity—an affreightment case;[113] while loading a deck load of timber, the ship took an unexpected list and a portion of the cargo was lost—an affreightment case.[114]

In *Rhesa Shipping Co., S.A. v. Edmunds et al (The Popi M)*,[115] the trial court held that the assured's contention that his vessel had hit a submerged submarine was inherently improbable, but on a balance of probabilities that explanation would be accepted as a "peril of the sea." The trial judge confessed that he was unable to declare that the vessel was or was not unseaworthy. The court of appeal affirmed on the basis of an unexplained incursion of seawater. An application for leave to appeal to the House of Lords was filed. The House of Lords reversed.

In *N. Michalos & Sons Maritime S.A. v. Prudential Assur. Co. Ltd. et al. (The Zinovia)*,[116] the insured vessel went aground. She was subsequently determined to be a constructive total loss. The underwriters claimed she had been cast away by a Mr. Kouvaris, whom the owners had hired to join the vessel at an intermediate port. The owners denied the allegation and contended that if it had been cast away, it was without their knowledge or connivance and contrary to their interest. The court held that underwriters had failed to bear the burden of proof as to their contentions but that the owners had shown that the vessel's loss was proximately caused by a peril of the sea; i.e., grounding by reason of negligent navigation and subsequent pounding on the bottom.

Commonwealth Cases. Goods shipped in good condition found to be damaged by seawater after the vessel encountered a sudden storm;[117] sails torn through an accident while attempting to moor;[118] sea peril made operative by reason of negligence of the crew;[119] heavy weather damage to cargo and vessel;[120] vessel foundered at sea;[121] vessel foundered in a severe storm shortly after leaving port;[122] unexplained disap-

---

111. *Blackburn v. Liverpool, Brazil and River Plate Steam Nav. Co.*, (1902) 1 K.B. 290.
112. *W.P. Wood & Co. v. Hanseatisch*, (1930) 37 Ll.L.Rep. 144.
113. *The Thrunscoe*, (1897) P. 301.
114. *The Stranna*, (1938) 1 All E.R. 458, (1938) P. 69.
115. [1983] 2 Lloyd's Rep. 235, *aff'd* court of appeal, July, 1984.
116. [1984] 2 Lloyd's Rep. 264.
117. *Creedon & Avery Ltd. v. North China Ins. Co., Ltd.*, (1917) 36 D.L.R. 359, (1917), 3 W.W.R. 33 (Can.).
118. *Hill v. Union Ins. Soc.*, (1927) 61 O.L.R. 201, (1927), 4 D.L.R. 718 (Can.,C.A.).
119. *Cross v. Allan*, (1880) 3 L.N. 47 (Can.).
120. *Murray v. N.S. Marine Ins. Co.*, (1875) 10 N.S.R. 24 (Can.,C.A.).
121. *Morrison v. N.S. Marine Co.*, (1896) 28 N.S.R. 346 (Can.,C.A.).
122. *Parrish & Heimbecker Ltd. and Ins. Co. of N.A. v. Burke Towing & Salvage Co.*, (1943) S.C.R. 179, (1943), 2 D.L.R. 193, 1943 AMC 388 (Can.).

pearance of a vessel; held, presumption that foundering caused the loss;[123] vessel under charter sustained an accident and went into an inter-mediate port for repairs; cargo was perishable, and charterer terminated the charter and took possession of cargo; vessel owner claimed under the freight policy;[124] repairs rendered necessary by reason of a stranding;[125] vessel while entering coastal waters felt a "bump"; later, water entered the engine room and the vessel sank while being towed to a port of refuge; held, peril of the seas;[126] unexplained sinking in smooth water shortly after leaving port; held, peril of the seas;[127] stranding a peril of the sea;[128] vessel grounded and fell over on her starboard side; later, she was beached to ascertain the extent of repairs and again fell over, this time on her port side; held, the latter casualty was occasioned by a peril of the sea;[129] vessel leaked badly shortly after leaving port;[130] shortly after leav-ing port, vessel sank in a sea which, though subject to a considerable swell, was calm;[131] vessel bumped along the bottom from shoal to shoal until she got to sea; held, a "stranding" and a peril of the sea.[132]

In *Skandia Ins. Co. Ltd. v. Skoljarev*,[133] the insured vessel sank shortly after leaving port in seas which were relatively calm. The court found the vessel to be seaworthy and that there was no negligence on the part of the master and crew. The court then applied the presumption that if a ship which is seaworthy sinks in smooth water and there is no evidence as to the cause, the casualty is attributable to a peril of the sea.

In *Case Existological Laboratories Ltd. v. Foremost Ins. Co.*,[134] a specially contrived barge inexplicably sank. The special barge was actually de-signed to be sunk deliberately in order partially to submerge it so as to allow a module to be drifted off its deck or received on deck. The concept was that air would be pumped into the mid-section of the barge (which

---

123. *Pac. Coast Coal Freighters Ltd. v. Westchester Fire Ins. Co.*, (1926) 3 W.W.R. 356, (1926) 4 D.L.R. 963 (Can.).

124. *Musgrave v. Mannheim Ins. Co.*, (1899) 32 N.S.R. 405 (Can.,C.A.).

125. *Steinhoff v. Royal Can. Ins. Co.*, (1877) 42 U.C.Q.B. 307 (Can.,C.A.).

126. *Suo v. Openshaw Simmons Ltd. et al.*, (1978) Sup.Crt. B.C. No. C762797/76 (not yet reported).

127. *Reynolds v. North Queensland Ins. Co.*, (1896) 17 L.R. (N.S.W.) 121, 13 W.N. 1 (Aus.); *W. Langley & Sons Ltd. v. Australian Prov. Assur. Ass'n, Ltd.*, (1924) 24 S.R. (N.S.W.) 280, 41 W.N. 46 (Aus.).

128. *Board of Management of Agricultural Bank of Tasmania v. Brown*, (1957) 97 C.L.R. 503, 31 A.L.J. 865 (Aus.).

129. *Cobcroft v. National Marine Ins. Co. of S. Australia*, (1871) 11 S.C.R. (N.S.W.) 40 (Aus.).

130. *Emperor Goldmining Co., Ltd. v. Switzerland Gen. Ins. Co., Ltd.*, (1964) N.S.W.R. 1243, [1964] 1 Lloyd's Rep. 348 (Aus.).

131. *Skandia Insurance Co., Ltd. v. Skoljarev and Another*, (1979) 26 A.L.R. 1 (H.C.,Aus.).

132. *Rudolf v. Brit. & Foreign Marine Ins. Co.*, (1898) 30 N.S.W. 380, *aff'd* 28 S.C.R. 607 (Can.).

133. [1979] 26 A.L.R. 1 (H.C.,Aus.).

134. 1981 AMC 881 (Sup.Ct., B.C.), *rev'd* [1982] 133 D.L.R. (3d) 727 (B.C., Ct. of Ap-peal), reversal *affirmed* by Supreme Court of Canada,, [1984] 48 B.C.L.R. 273.

was open to the sea) so as to provide a cushion of air lying between the underside of the deck and the level of seawater inside the compartments. Without the cushion of air, the vessel would inevitably sink like a rock—which is precisely what happened when a new employee negligently left open a valve so that the air in the compartments was displaced by seawater. The court held that the negligent act constituted a foreseeable risk of harm—a peculiarly marine risk—and that act, coupled with the foreseeable consequence, a sinking, was an accident of the seas.

In *Visscher Enterprises Pty Ltd. v. Southern Pac. Ins. Co. Ltd.*,[135] there was a hole in an engine room bulkhead. The assured knew of it but did not realize its implications as it related to the seaworthiness of his vessel. When water entered the vessel through a broken pipe in the engine room, it entered other portions of the vessel through the hole in the bulkhead and the vessel sank, becoming a total loss. The court held that the sinking was a "peril of the sea."

In *Williams v. The Queen*,[136] the vessel struck a submerged, unidentified object and the crew heard a distinct "thump." An inspection revealed nothing, and there was no water found in the bilges. The following morning water was discovered entering the engine room from a leak in a sea intake pipe leading into the vessel. The pipe subsequently ruptured and the vessel sank. The court held that the loss was proximately caused by a peril of the seas; i.e., a fortuitous fracturing of the sea intake pipe which led to the incursion of seawater in circumstances which could not have been foreseen.

In *Gould v. Cornhill Ins. Co. Ltd.*,[137] a vessel sank in moderately rough weather. The court held that exactly what caused the sinking was "unknown" but that there was no evidence that it was the result of unseaworthiness. It was, therefore, a peril of the sea.

With respect to the meaning of the term "perils of the seas" in New Zealand jurisprudence, see *Wanganui Herald Newspaper Co., Ltd. v. Coastal Shipping Co., Ltd*,[138] and *W.A. McLaren & Co., Ltd. v. New Zealand Ins. Co., Ltd*,[139] both involving missing ships.

United States Cases. The American cases holding that the loss was due to a peril of the seas are exceedingly numerous. See, for example, *Potter v. Suffolk Ins. Co.*,[140] where an extraordinary ebbing tide caused a grounding; *General Mutual Ins. Co. v. Sherwood*,[141] loss due to a sea peril even

---

135. [1981] Qd. R. 561 (Aus., 1980).
136. No. T-106-83, Fed. Ct. of Canada, Trial Div., April 25, 1984 (not yet reported).
137. (1984) 1 D.L.R. (4th) 183 (Can.).
138. (1929) N.Z.L.R. 305.
139. (1929) N.S.L.R. 437.
140. Fed.Cas. No. 11,339 (1st Cir., 1835).
141. 55 U.S. 351 (1852).

though the master did not use due care to avoid the peril; *Bullard v. Roger Williams Ins. Co.*,[142] heavy cross seas, although common in the voyage insured; *Seaman v. Enterprise Fire & Marine Ins. Co.*,[143] vessel damaged while making a landing; *The Natchez*,[144] vessel grounded and found to be leaking badly; to keep her from sinking she was beached; thereafter, the river rose rapidly and destroyed her; *American-Hawaiian S.S. Co. v. Bennett & Goodall*,[145] an unexpected striking and grounding of a vessel in tidal waters arising from the negligence of the vessel's crew; *New York & P.R. S.S. Co. v. Aetna Ins. Co.*,[146] breaking of propeller blades where the propeller was new and no latent defect was found therein; *Queen Ins. Co. of America v. Globe & Rutgers Fire Ins. Co.*,[147] collision at sea *prima facie* considered a marine peril; *John L. Roper Limber Co. v. Portsmouth Fisheries, Inc.*,[148] sinking of a dredge being towed at night; *Arbib & Houlberg v. Second Russian Ins. Co.*,[149] leakage of water into a vessel during a storm which also damaged cargo; *Tornado*,[150] river steamer being towed sprang a leak and sank; the preponderance of evidence was as to her prior seaworthiness for river purposes and compliance with underwriters' requirements as to voyage; *Wash Gray*,[151] choppy sea and waves approximately four or five feet high and a 25-mile-per-hour wind held to be extraordinary condition as to an inland tug being towed in the open sea and which sprang a leak and sank; *Helen L.*,[152] breaking of a bell-pull resulted in a wrong engine maneuver and a consequent series of accidents; *Lanasa Fruit S.S. & Importing Co., Inc. v. Universal Ins. Co. (The Smaragd)*,[153] vessel stranded, and consequent delay due to the stranding caused the cargo to spoil; *Olympia Canning Co. v. Union Marine Ins. Co.*,[154] overturning of a vessel under the impulse of tidal and river currents; *Hecht, Levis & Kahn v. New Zealand Ins. Co.*,[155] a "sea peril" is the same in a cargo policy as in a bill of lading and includes great storms, even though expectable; *Boston Ins. Co. v. Dehydrating Process Co.*,[156] sinking of barge at a sheltered berth in calm weather where the owner was able to rebut presumption of unseaworthiness; *New York, New Hampshire & H. R.R. Co. v. Gray*,[157] otherwise unex-

142. Fed.Cas. No. 2,122 (1st Cir., 1852).
143. 21 F. 788 (8th Cir., 1884)
144. 42 F. 169 (D.,La., 1890).
145. 207 F. 510 (9th Cir., 1913).
146. 204 F. 255 (2nd Cir., 1913).
147. 263 U.S. 487.
148. 269 F. 586 (3d Cir., 1919).
149. 294 F. 811, 1924 AMC 16 (2d Cir.).
150. 2 F.2d 137, 1925 AMC 197 (3d Cir.).
151. 277 U.S. 66, 1928 AMC 923.
152. 1937 AMC 1170 (St.,Wash.).
153. 302 U.S. 556, 1938 AMC 1.
154. 10 F.2d 72, 1926 AMC 181 (9th Cir.).
155. 1941 AMC 1185 (S.D.N.Y.).
156. 204 F.2d 441, 1953 AMC 1364 (1st Cir.).
157. 240 F.2d 460, 1957 AMC 616 (2d Cir.).

plained incursion of seawater into a carfloat held a "sea peril"; *M/V Tuna Fish,*[158] fishing vessel struck a submerged object and sank while being towed to a repair yard; *Harding v. Amer. Univ. Ins. Co.,*[159] striking a submerged object, even though not a collision under the policy and not covered under the collision clause, was nonetheless a loss falling under the perils clause; *Starr v. Aetna,*[160] seams of a scow opened when the scow grounded on a falling tide at a dock where the bottom was ordinarily soft; *Cherokee,*[161] a heavy storm drove vessel ashore; *Wong v. Utah Home Fire Ins. Co.,*[162] action of a tidal wave; *Celestina Arias,*[163] oil pump broke down while vessel was at sea; while vessel was being towed to port, the samson post pulled loose, whereupon vessel sank; *Spooner & Son v. Connecticut Fire,*[164] a crane barge engaged in delicate salvage operations collapsed because of swells from a passing freighter; *Juno-Drill Barge 58,*[165] a barge being towed collided with an unknown floating object; *Belle of Portugal,*[166] fire on board a vessel caused by negligence of a shoreside electrician; *Carter Tug v. Home Insurance,*[167] negligence of pilot and deckhand in failing to take any action to stop flow of water into an inland tug, which foundered and sank; *Neptune Lines v. Hudson Valley,*[168] wooden scow sank because of assured charterer's negligent failure to pump it out; held, sinking was fortuitous because regular pumping and due care would have prevented it; *Joseph H. (stranding),*[169] negligence of the master stranded the vessel; *Parkhill-Goodloe v. Home Ins.,*[170] sinking of an otherwise seaworthy barge was proximately caused by the negligence of a night watchman in failing to make a proper inspection of the bilges and in disconnecting a portable pump;[171] *Continental Ins. v. Hersent,*[172] barge capsized as result of a storm of gale proportions, the taking on of water which caused a list, and the sliding of a crane and boom toward the listing side.[173]

158. 242 F.2d 513, 1957 AMC 805 (5th Cir.).
159. 1962 AMC 2423 (St.,Fla.).
160. 285 F.2d 106, 1961 AMC 342 (2d Cir.).
161. 157 F.Supp. 414, 1958 AMC 381 (E.D.,Va.).
162. 167 F.Supp. 230, 1960 AMC 649 (D.,Haw.).
163. 261 F.2d 490, 1959 AMC 135 (5th Cir.).
164. 314 F.2d 753, 1963 AMC 859 (2d Cir.).
165. 1966 AMC 2172 (S.D.,Tex.).
166. 421 F.2d 390, 1970 AMC 30 (9th Cir.), [1970] 2 Lloyd's Rep. 386. Arguably, this is not a "sea peril" case, as the court sidestepped the issue and actually held the loss covered as being due to the separate peril of fire.
167. 345 F.Supp. 1193, 1972 AMC 498 (S.D.,Ill.).
168. 1973 AMC 125 (S.D.N.Y.).
169. 411 F.Supp. 496, 1976 AMC 1565 (S.D.N.Y.).
170. 1976 AMC 951 (M.D.,Fla.).
171. For cases involving "unexplained sinking," see the same heading under discussion of the Inchmaree Clause, *infra.*
172. 1978 AMC 234 (2d Cir.).
173. See, also, *Starbuck v. Phoenix Ins. Co.,* 45 N.Y.S. 995, 19 App. Div. 139 (St.N.Y., 1897) (water entered a watertight compartment through an open deadlight); *McNally v. Ins. Co. of*

In summary, on the definition of perils of the seas in a marine insurance policy, it would be well to quote the pungent remarks of Scrutton, L. J., who said, in the course of his speech in the court of appeals in *P. Samuel & Co. v. Dumas* (1922), 13 Ll.L.Rep. 503:

> The expression is not happy; it is not clear what kind of "accident or casualty" is not fortuitous, or what is an intentional accident. I imagine the draughtsman took "fortuitous" from the judgment of Lord Halsbury in *Hamilton, Fraser & Co. v. Pandorf & Co.* (12 A.C. at p. 524) and "accident or casualty" from the judgment of Lord Herschell in *The Xantho* (12 A.C. at p. 509) and combined the two, without any very intelligent idea of why he did so. But it is clear that there must be a peril, an unforeseen and evitable accident, not a contemplated and inevitable result; and it must be of the seas, not merely on the seas. The ordinary action of the winds and waves is "of the seas," but not a "peril."

Presumption When a Ship Is Missing

Section 58, Marine Insurance Act, 1906, states the rule succinctly:

North America, 63 N.Y.S. 125, 31 Misc.Rep. 61 (St.N.Y., 1900) (stream entering the harbor caused a vessel to list and be damaged); *Crescent Ins. Co. v. Vicksburg, Y & S.R. Packet Co.*, 69 Miss. 208, 13 So. 254, 30 Am.St. Rep. 537 (1891) (vessel careened by reason of negligence of those unloading her, and her cargo was thrown into the river); *American-Hawaiian S.S. Co. v. Bennett & Goodall*, 207 F. 510 (9th Cir., 1913) (loss by stranding or collision is a peril of the sea even though arising from the negligence of the master or crew); *Aetna Ins. Co. v. Sacramento-Stockton S.S. Co.*, 273 F. 55 (9th Cir., 1921) (peril of the sea need not be extraordinary in the sense of being catastrophic or necessarily the result of uncommon causes; and severe storms, rough seas, and even fogs may be comprised in perils of the seas); *Clinchfield Fuel Co. v. Aetna Ins. Co.*, 121 S.C. 305, 114 S.E. 543 (St.,S.C., 1922) (perils of the seas not limited to extraordinary perils but embrace storms and the action of the winds and the seas); *Charles Clarke & Co. v. Mannheim Ins. Co.*, 210 S.W. 528 (St.,Tex. App., 1919) (loss or damage is not prevented from being a peril of the sea by the cooperation of other causes such as acts or omissions of the owner of his agent amounting to negligence but not amounting to fraud or design); *Hillman Transp. Co. v. Home Ins. Co.*, 268 Pa. 547, 112 A. 108 (St.,Pa., 1920) (any accident occurring during the operation of the vessel not falling within the exceptions must be deemed within the terms of the policy if by a reasonable construction it can be held to be an unavoidable danger); *Kelly, Weber & Co. v. Franklin Fire Ins. Co.*, 43 F.2d 361 (D.,La., 1930) (grounding of a vessel during a heavy fog held to be a peril of the sea); *James A. McAllister & Co. v. Western Assur. Co. of City of Toronto*, 218 N.Y.S. 658, 218 App.Div. 564 (St.,N.Y., 1927) (water entering through an opening in a vessel's seams); *Compania Transatlantica Centro-Americana, S.A. v. Alliance Assur. Co. (The Panamanian)*, 50 F.Supp. 986, 1943 AMC 976 (S.D.N.Y.) (port vapor discharge valve jammed while open, setting up a siphon-like action which flooded the engine room); *INA v. Lanasa Shrimp*, 726 F.2d 688, 1984 AMC 2915 (11th Cir.) (unexplained disappearance of a ship found to have been seaworthy upon departure from port); *Inland Rivers Service Corp. v. Hartford Fire Ins. Co.*, 66 Ohio St. 2d 32, 418 N.E.2d 1381 (St.,Ohio, 1981) (damage to moored vessel by striking a sharp object constitutes a peril of the sea).

Where the ship concerned in the adventure is missing, and after the lapse of a reasonable time no news of her has been received, an actual total loss may be presumed.

And Section 88 of the Act provides:

Where by this Act any reference is made to reasonable time, reasonable premium, or reasonable diligence, the question what is reasonable is a question of fact.

Section 58 is merely declaratory of the common law as it was before the adoption of the Act.[174] The case of *Munro, Brice & Co. v. War Risks Ass'n*[175] reviews the previous cases in detail.

The point has usually arisen when the vessel is missing during time of war. For example, in *Compania Maritima of Barcelona v. Wishart*,[176] the hull policy on the S.S. *Pelayo* contained the usual F. C. & S. and hostilities clause. On November 17, 1916, she left the Tyne for Barcelona and was never heard of again. It was proven that when she left port she was seaworthy, and that the weather on her proposed route was very severe. There was no evidence of any submarine casualties having taken place on her route between November 17 and 21, nor was there any evidence of floating mines or mine fields in the area in question. Holding that although certainty was unattainable, the law demanded that an inference be drawn from the facts that she was lost by foundering and not by a peril excluded by the hostilities clause.

By contrast, in *Munro, Brice & Co. v. War Risks Ass'n* (1920), *supra*, the sailing vessel *Inveramsay* was declared missing during a voyage from the United States to the United Kingdom during World War I. The evidence did not indicate any violent or severe weather during the period of her voyage, but to the contrary, enemy submarines had been very active in the area. It was held that the legitimate inference was that the loss had been due to enemy action and that, inasmuch as the policy was on F. C. & S. terms, there would be no recovery.

In *Compania Martiartu v. Royal Exchange Ass'n*,[177] the ship sailed and was never heard of again. The owner presented some evidence that the

---

174. See *Green & Brown*, (1743) 93 E.R. 1126; *Koster v. Reed*, (1826) 108 E.R. 359; *Houstman v. Thornton*, (1816) Holt 242, N.P.; *Brown v. Neilson*, 1 Caines N.Y. 525 (1804); *Cambreling v. M'Call*, 2 Dall. Penn. 128 S.C. (1797); *Gordon v. Bowne*, 2 Johns. N.Y. 150 (1807). Phillips states the American rule as follows (Sec. 1496):

If a ship has not been heard from for so long a time, as to be a ground of presumption that it has perished by perils of the seas, a total loss may be recovered on ship, cargo, or freight, without abandonment.

See, also, *INA v. Lanasa Shrimp*, 726 F.2d 688, 1984 AMC 2915 (11th Cir.) (unexplained disappearance of a ship found to have been seaworthy upon departure from port).

175. (1920) 3 K.B. 94, 2 Ll.L.Rep. 2, C.A.
176. (1918) 87 L.J.K.B. 1027, 23 Com.Cas. 264.
177. (1923) 1 K.B. 650, 28 Com.Cas. 76, C.A., *aff'd* (1924) A.C. 850, H.L.

loss was by a peril of the sea, whereupon the underwriters presented evidence that the disappearance was probably due to a scuttling. The evidence having left the court in some doubt as to which case the loss was attributable, the assured failed to recover.[178]

In summary, where the assured proves a loss there is a presumption that it was caused by a peril of the sea. However, the underwriter may rebut the presumption by showing that, on balance, the probability preponderated in favor of another cause either not embraced within the named perils or specifically excluded. But where the policy is on war risks only, the burden of proof rests with the assured to prove by a preponderance of the evidence that the loss was occasioned by a war peril.

Strandings and Groundings

A "stranding" is very important in marine insurance for two reasons: a stranding is one of the commonly accepted perils of the sea and thus a basis for coverage. It also satisfies one of the conditions for paying a partial loss under a policy on F.P.A. terms which is a different concept altogether and involves the memorandum clause under the old Institute forms.

Whether or not a stranding has taken place is essentially a question of fact, and a precise definition is rather difficult. It implies a stoppage of the vessel's progress and a "resting" for a longer or shorter period of time.[179] In *Wells v. Hopwood*,[180] the court defined the term as:

> Where a vessel takes the ground in the ordinary and usual course of navigation and management in a tide river or harbour, upon the ebbing of the tide or from natural deficiency of water, so that she may float again upon the flow of tide or increase of water, such an event shall not be considered a stranding within the sense of the memoran-

---

178. For other war risks cases, and the burden of proof imposed upon war risk underwriters, see *MacBeth & Co. v. King*, (1916) 86 L.J.K.B. 1004; *British & Burmese Steam Navigation Co., Ltd. v. Liverpool & London War Risks Ins. Ass'n, Ltd.*, (1917) 34 T.L.R. 140, *Euterpe S.S. Co.,Ltd. v. North of England Prot. & Indemnity Ass'n, Ltd.*, (1917) 33 T.L.R. 540; *Zachariessen v. Importers' & Exporters' Marine Ins. Co.*, [1924] 18 Ll.L.Rep. 98, C.A.; *General Steam Navigation Co. v. Commercial Union Assur. Co.*, (1915) 31 T.L.R. 630; *Scottish Ins. Co., Ltd. v. British Fishing Vessels Mutual War Risk Ass'n, Ltd.*, [1944] 78 Ll.L.Rep. 70. See, also, *Pomares v. Minas Marine Ins. Co.*, (1875) 16 N.B.R. (3 Pug.) 245 (Can.) and *Pacific Coast Coal Freighters Ltd. v. Westchester Fire Ins. Co.*, (1926) 3 W.W.R. 356, 38 B.C.R. 20, (1926) 4 D.L.R. 963, *aff'd* (1927) 1 W.W.R. 878, 38 B.C.R. 315, (1927) 5 D.L.R. 590 (C.A., Can.); *Pan American Airways v. Aetna Casualty and Surety Co. et al.*, [1974] 1 Lloyd's Rep. 207 (S.D.N.Y., 1983), [1975] 1 Lloyd's Rep. 77 (2d Cir.); *The Athos*, [1983] 1 Lloyd's Rep. 127; *The Mitera*, [1969] 1 Lloyd's Rep. 359; *Ope Shipping v. Allstate*, 687 F.2d 639, 1983 AMC 22 (2d Cir.) (real efficient cause of loss of vessels was not barratry of the crews but rather the Nicaraguan civil war, an excluded peril); *Home Ins. Co. v. Davila*, 212 F.2d 731 (2d Cir.).
179. *Honeybrook*, 6 F.2d 736, 1925 AMC 717 (2d Cir.).
180. (1832), 110 E.R. 8.

dum. But when the ground is taken under any extraordinary circumstances of time or place, by reason of some unusual or accidental occurrence, such an event shall be considered a stranding within the meaning of the memorandum.[181]

In *Magnus v. Buttemer*,[182] the vessel was damaged by taking the ground on the falling of the tide, in a harbor in a spot where she was properly placed for the purpose of unloading. The court held it not to be a grounding and that to make underwriters liable, the injury must be the result of something fortuitous or accidental occurring in the course of the voyage.

In *Rayner v. Godmond*,[183] the vessel was on a canal. To repair the canal, the water was drawn off. Although the ship was placed in the most secure location that could be found, when the water was drawn off the vessel stranded by accident upon some piles, the location of which was not previously known. As the accident did not happen in the ordinary course of a voyage, it was held to be a stranding.

In *Union Marine Ins. Co. v. Borwick*,[184] the policy insured against "risk of loss or damage through collision with (*inter alia*) piers, or stages, or similar structures." In a storm two vessels insured under the policy drifted onto the toe of a breakwater consisting of a sloping bank of stones or boulders. The vessels were driven broadside onto the bank, their keels being the parts which struck the boulders. It was held to be a collision and not a mere stranding.

An intentional operation causing damage is not a grounding.[185]

Held Not to Be a Stranding

The following are examples in which it was held there was no stranding.

A vessel struck a rock, remaining there for a minute and a half; held,

---

181. To the same effect, see *Liverpool & Great Western Steam Co. v. Phoenix Ins. Co.*, 129 U.S. 397 (1889), and *Corcoran v. Gurney*, (1853) 118 E.R. 507. See, also, *Granite State Minerals v. American Ins.*, 435 F.Supp. 159 (D.,Mass., 1877).

182. (1852) 138 E.R. 720.

183. (1821) 106 E.R. 1175.

184. (1895) 2 Q.B. 279.

185. *Louis O'Donnell—Scipio*, 1933 AMC 316 (Arb.), a tug stranded its tow without damage on a well-known shoal which blocked a canal for 500 yards. The tug then proceeded to drag its tow across the shoal by main force, thereby damaging it. Recovery was denied because the operation causing the damage was intentional and not fortuitous. See, also, *Thompson v. Whitmore*, (1810) 128 E.R. 90, where the vessel was deliberately hove down on a beach within a tideway in order to be repaired. It was bilged and damaged. Recovery was denied, as there was not a stranding. However, in *De Mattos v. Saunders*, (1872) L.R. 7 C.P. 570, a vessel in distress and being towed was intentionally run on a bank, and it was held to be a stranding.

not a stranding although the injury received ultimately proved fatal;[186] a vessel under a pilot took the ground and, afterwards, being moored to a quay, took the ground again on the ebbing of the tide, fell over on her side, and damaged herself and her cargo;[187] a motorboat sustained damage when the engine exploded because the propeller struck an underwater cable;[188] upon the ebbing of the tide, a vessel took the ground as it was intended she should; however, in doing so, she struck against some hard substance by which two holes were made in her bottom, damaging the cargo;[189] a policy insuring against loss of a vessel by grounding or stranding does not cover a loss by the sinking of the vessel in deep water;[190] a deliberate stranding by the master with the knowledge and consent of the owner is not a "stranding," and thus not a peril of the seas;[191] use of a two-man crew where three were needed held to be a breach of the express warranty of seaworthiness, thereby suspending policy coverage for what was otherwise a stranding.[192]

Held to Be a Stranding

The following are examples in which strandings were held to have occurred.

Striking and resting upon a rock;[193] striking a rock and remaining there for a space of fifteen or twenty minutes;[194] a collision causing a grounding;[195] while in harbor, the vessel grounded; subsequently, she leaked badly; held, loss not attributable to inherent weakness but to striking some hard substance when she grounded;[196] a vessel aground was voluntarily scuttled to save her from a storm that arose several hours after the grounding;[197] vessel went aground on an uncharted mudflat during a heavy fog;[198] vessel forced aground by winds and remained there for

---

186. *M'Dougle v. Royal Exchange Assur. Co.*, (1816) 105 E.R. 921.
187. *Hearne v. Edmunds*, (1819) 129 E.R. 772.
188. *Cohen v. Agricultural Ins. Co.*, 1961 AMC 2408 (St.,N.Y.).
189. *Kingsford v. Marshall*, (1832) 131 E.R. 470.
190. *Baker-Whiteley Coal Co. v. Marten*, (1910) 26 T.L.R. 314.
191. *Padre Island (Stranding)*, 1970 AMC 600, [1971] 2 Lloyd's Rep. 431.
192. *Miss Esmeralda (Grounding)*, 441 F.2d 141, 1971 AMC 1134 (5th Cir.). Attention is also directed to *Hoffman v. Marshall*, (1835) 132 E.R. 150, where the policy covered risk of craft to and from the ship, with the cargo being insured on F.P.A. conditions unless the ship be stranded. After the goods were put upon a lighter, it stranded and sank. Held: The underwriters were not liable.
193. *Strong v. Sun Mut. Ins. Co.*, 31 N.Y. 103 (St.,N.Y., 1865).
194. *Baker v. Towry*, (1816) 1 Stark 436, N.P.
195. *Richelieu & Ontario Nav. Co. v. Boston Ins. Co.*, 136 U.S. 408 (1890).
196. *Potter v. Suffolk Ins. Co.*, Fed.Cas. No. 11,339 (1st Cir., 1835).
197. *Northwestern Transp. Co. v. Boston Marine Ins. Co.*, 41 F. 793 (E.D.,Mich., 1890).
198. *Kelly, W. & Co. v. Franklin Fire Ins. Co.*, 42 F.2d 361 (E.D.,La., 1930).

some time although no damage was done;[199] vessel under command of a pilot was fastened to the end of a pier by a rope to the shore and when the tide ebbed the vessel fell over on her side and bilged;[200] during a voyage, a vessel was forced to take shelter in a harbor and in entering the harbor struck upon an anchor and was in danger of sinking; consequently, she was hauled with warps higher up the harbor where she took the ground;[201] under stress of weather a vessel was run to the tidal harbor, where she grounded in consequence of low water;[202] vessel being brought into a tidal basin by a pilot could not get next to the quay by reason of insufficient water, whereupon she was left where she was but later when the tide ebbed pitched down by the head into a hole whose existence was not known prior to the accident; held, the taking of the ground was accidental and unforeseen;[203] vessel in distress was put aground deliberately;[204] crewmen sent ashore to secure a vessel were caught by a press gang and were carried away; as a consequence, the vessel went ashore and was lost;[205] vessel grounded on bed of harbor, which was hard and uneven when the tide ebbed;[206] vessel in a graving dock was thrown over on her side by violent wind and bilged; loss held to be *ejusdem generis* with stranding;[207] vessel negligently docked so as to sit on a dangerous bottom; held, *ejusdem generis* with stranding;[208] vessel proceeding to Le Havre diverted because of war, proceeded to Falmouth pursuant to suggestions of British warship; on her arrival at Falmouth, a British trawler signalled "follow me"; in doing so, she grounded on a shoal; held, the grounding was a marine peril and not a war peril;[209] a yacht in custody of a U. S. Marshal moved from deep to shallow water when there was a small hole in her side about 12-14 inches above the waterline; low tides caused her to be grounded and to lean toward the hole, allowing water to enter; held, loss occasioned by perils of the seas being due to the grounding and not inevitable because of the presence of the hole.[210]

199. *Harman v. Vaux*, (1813) 3 Camp. 429, N.P.
200. *Carruthers v. Sydebotham*, (1815) 105 E.R. 764.
201. *Barrow v. Bell*, (1825) 107 E.R. 1234.
202. *Falkner v. Gurney*, (1853) 1 W.R. 120.
203. *Letchford v. Oldham*, (1880) 5 Q.B.D. 538.
204. *Russell & Erwin Mfg. Co. v. Lodge*, (1890) 6 T.L.R. 353.
205. *Hodgson v. Malcolm*, (1906) 127 E.R. 656.
206. *Fletcher v. Inglis*, (1819) 106 E.R. 382.
207. *Phillips v. Barber*, (1821) 106 E.R. 1151.
208. *The Lapwing*, (1940) P. 112.
209. *Petter*, 56 F.Supp. 470, 1945 AMC 109 (S.D.N.Y.).
210. *Duet*, 264 F.Supp. 865, 1967 AMC 1144 (D.,Ore.). See, also, *American Hawaiian S.S. Co. v. Bennett & Goodall*, 207 F. 510 (9th Cir., 1913); *Newark Ins. v. Continental Cas.*, 1975 AMC 307 (St., N.Y.); *Lanasa Fruit Steamship and Importing Company, Inc. v. Universal Ins. Company (The Smaragd)*, 1938 AMC 1, 302 U.S. 556; *Wells v. Hopwood*, (1832) 110 E.R. 8; *Corcoran v. Gurney*, (1853) 118 E.R. 507; *Rayner v. Godmond*, (1821) 106 E.R. 1175; *De Mattos v. Saunders*, (1872) L.R. 7 C.P. 570; *Steinhoff v. Royal Can. Ins. Co.*, (1877) 42 U.C.Q.B. 397, (Can., C.A.).

It should be observed that some charter agreements permit grounding in harbors or waters where groundings are customary.[211] Also, certain insurance policies recognize that where groundings in certain areas are customary, they do not constitute strandings. See Clause 13, Institute Time Clauses (hulls), where groundings in the Panama Canal, Suez Canal, Manchester Ship Canal, River Mersey about Rock Ferry Slip, River Plate (above a certain line), the Danube or Demerra rivers, or on the Yenikale Bar are not considered strandings. An earlier version of the AIH form (1964) followed along the same lines, but the new AIH policy (1977) deletes such language inasmuch as the voyage franchise clause has been replaced by a deductible average clause.

Fire, Lightning, and Earthquake

"Fyer" was mentioned as one of the covered perils in the *Tiger* policy in 1613. One of the earlier reported cases appears to be *Gordon v. Rimmington*,[212] in which Lord Ellenborough noted that if a ship is destroyed by fire, it is of no consequence that the fire was occasioned by common accident or by lightning or by an act done in duty to the state, nor does it make any difference whether the ship was destroyed by third persons, subjects of the king, or by the captain and crew acting with loyalty and good faith; the fire is still the *causa causans*. In that case, the vessel was set on fire by her captain and crew to prevent her from falling into the hands of an enemy privateer.

That the fire was caused by the negligence of the master or crew is immaterial, although this point was a troublesome question for some time.[213] Fire caused by a collision is covered.[214]

In an unusual case involving a freight policy, coals which began to heat were unloaded in part and sold, as the continuation of the voyage with the

---

211. Charter parties usually also provide that the vessel shall always lie "safely afloat." Unless specific permission is granted to ground, no charterer would be safe in permitting a grounding.

212. (1807) 1 Camp. 123, N.P.

213. *Busk v. Royal Exchange Assur. Co.*, (1818) 106 E.R. 294; *Waters v. Merchants' Louisville Ins. Co.*, 36 U.S. 213 (1837); *Patapsco Ins. Co v. Coulter*, 28 U.S. 222 (1830); *Columbia Ins. Co. v. Laurence*, 10 Pet. 507, 35 U.S. 507 (1836); *Spot Pack*, 242 F.2d 385, 1957 AMC 655 (5th Cir.); *Belle of Portugal*, 421 F.2d 390, 1970 AMC 30 [1970] 2 Lloyd's Rep. 386. Coverage otherwise existing may, however, be lost if the assured breaches a warranty or fails to disclose all material facts to the assurer. See *Alexander v. National Union Ins. Co.*, 104 F.2d 1006, 1939 AMC 923 (2d Cir.); *Kron v. Hanover Fire Ins. Co.*, 1965 AMC 282 (St.,N.Y.); *Pacific Queen*, 307 F.2d 700, 1962 AMC 1845 (9th Cir.); *Hauser v. Amer. Central Ins. Co.*, 216 F.Supp. 318, 1964 AMC 526 (E.D.,La.). Nor does coverage embrace a fire caused by inherent vice. *Boyd v. Dubois*, (1811) 3 Camp. 133, N.P.; *Pirie & Co. v. Middle Dock Co.*, (1881) 44 L.T. 426; *Providence Wash. Ins. Co. v. Adler*, 65 Md. 162 (St.,Md., 1885).

214. *Howard Fire Ins. Co. v. Norwich & N.Y. Transp. Co.*, 79 U.S. 194 (1870); *Western Massachusetts Ins. Co. v. Norwich & N.Y. Transp. Co.*, 79 U.S. 201 (1870).

smouldering coal aboard could have imperilled ship and cargo. Recovery was allowed for the lost freight on the theory that imminent danger of fire existed, or if not a loss by fire, it was a loss *ejusdem generis* covered by the general words "all other losses and misfortunes."[215]

Illustrative decisions involving fire and explosion will be found in the accompanying footnote.[216]

---

215. *The Knight of St. Michael*, (1898) P. 30. But the mere apprehension or fear of a fire, however reasonable it may have been, is not a peril by fire. See *Watson v. Fireman's Fund Ins. Co.*, (1922) 2 K.B. 355.

216. *Eugenia J. Kiacakis*, 1923 AMC 305 (S.D.N.Y.) (damage due to a general average act of flooding a hold to extinguish a fire was held covered to the extent of the ship's contribution in general average); *Daniel J. Dugan*, 1928 AMC 492 (E.D.N.Y.) (the assured and assurer intended to insure against fire, but through mistake or inadvertence a rider containing no reference to "fire" was attached; the rider stated that it was a total substitute for the original policy; vessel was destroyed by fire; policy reformed and recovery granted); *Pacific Queen*, 307 F.2d 700, 1962 AMC 1845 (9th Cir.) (fishing vessel rendered a constructive total loss by reason of a gasoline explosion while docked; held, hull insurance void *ab initio* because owners failed to disclose increased gasoline carrying capacity and extra-hazardous methods of carriage); *Staff Jennings v. Fireman's Fund Ins. Co.*, 218 F.Supp. 112, 1963 AMC 2659 (D.,Ore.) (pleasure yacht destroyed by an engine fuel explosion-fire of unknown cause, where evidence indicates vessel was operating normally immediately prior thereto; judgment entered for assured); *Belle of Portugal*, 421 F.2d 390, 1968 AMC 30, [1970] 2 Lloyd's Rep. 386 (9th Cir.) (fire caused by negligence of a shoreside electrician; recovery granted); *Kuljis v. Union Marine & General Ins. Co.*, 70 F.2d 231, 1933 AMC 1232 (9th Cir.) (insurer cannot avoid liability under fire coverage on a vessel destroyed by fire, on ground that the phrase "perils of the sea" is limited to operation of natural phenomena arising at sea); *Watson v. Firemen's Fund Ins. Co.*, (1922) 2 K.B. 355, 12 Ll.L.Rep.133 (under mistaken assumption of fire, captain caused steam to be turned into the hold to extinguish the supposed fire and so damaged the cargo; the cargo owners claimed against the insurers for general average; held, the peril being non-existent, there was no general average loss); *Symington & Co. v. Union Ins. Soc. of Canton*, (1928) All E.R. Rep. 346, 31 Ll.L.Rep. 179, C.A. (cork insured under cargo policy containing a warehouse-to-warehouse clause caught fire on a jetty while awaiting shipment; the authorities jettisoned a portion and poured sea water on remainder, causing a large portion to be lost or damaged; held, there being an existing fire and imminent peril, damage caused by the water was a proximate consequence of fire and recoverable under the general words); *Anthony D. Nichols*, 49 F.2d 927, 1931 AMC 562 (1st Cir.) (underwriters' surveyor's report indicated that vessel was equipped with a gasoline pump, hoister, and launch, and the presence of gasoline on board was deemed to have been known when the risk was accepted; an estoppel was thus raised when fire later occurred); *Companion*, 32 F.2d 353, 1929 AMC 693 (9th Cir.) (captain of insured vessel poured what he thought was kerosene in the galley stove to kindle a fire; the kerosene turned out to have been gasoline which caused an explosion, resulting in fire which destroyed the vessel; coverage affirmed); *Doromar*, 223 F.2d 844, 1955 AMC 1531 (5th Cir.) (insured vessel sailed from Miami to the Panama Canal, a four-day voyage, with a complement of only three men and no one in the engine room for three hours before a fire broke out in the engine room; held, underwriters failed to sustain the burden of proving that the vessel was unseaworthy at commencement of voyage); *Spot Pack*, 242 F.2d 385, 1957 AMC 655 (5th Cir.) (vessel departed port with a repaired electrical circuit breaker on board but not installed; a sudden engine room fire destroyed vessel completely; recovery was allowed even though master and crew were negligent); *American Mail v. Tokyo Marine*, 270 F.2d 499, 1959 AMC 2220 (9th Cir.) (ship's captain was notified that a ship's smoke detector indicated slight smoke coming from a cargo of barley being loaded; loading continued, and a smothering agent was not applied until three days later; cargo insurer in a subrogation suit was allowed full recovery for fire damage); *Kron v. Hanover Fire Ins. Co.* 1965 AMC 282 (St.,N.Y.) (tug damaged by fire where gasoline

Once the assured has shown that the loss was due to a fire, he has made out a *prima facie* case, and the onus is on the insurer to show on a balance of probabilities that the fire was caused by or connived at by the assured.[217]

Custom and usage in the trade may extend the parameters of coverage. See *Pelly v. Royal Exchange Assur. Co.*,[218] where the destruction of ship's rigging stored ashore in accordance with the usage of the Chinese trade was held to be a loss by fire.

Jettison

As the word implies, jettison includes an intentional throwing overboard of any part of the vessel or cargo for a good and prudent reason, with the intention of preserving the vessel or cargo. *The Gratitudine*.[219] But a throwing overboard of goods in a panic without justification or reason is not a jettison. *Notara v. Henderson*.[220]

In a rather extraordinary case,[221] the master of a Spanish ship insured at Lloyd's, in order to prevent a quantity of dollars from falling into the hands of an enemy, by whom he was about to be attacked, threw the dollars into the sea. His vessel was captured immediately afterwards. In an action on the policy, the court held that it was a loss by jettison, that term in a policy of insurance signifying any throwing overboard of the cargo for a justifiable reason, and that, if not a jettison in the strictest sense, it was something of the same kind and therefore came within the words "all other losses and misfortunes."

The coverage with respect to jettison is without reference to any right to a general average contribution; i.e., the insured can recover directly against the assurer under the policy for the subject matter jettisoned, and the assurer can then subrogate with respect to any sums recoverable as general average.[222]

---

was on board in violation of terms of policy; recovery denied); *London Assur. Corp. v. Great Northern Transit Co.*, (1899) 29 S.C.R. 577 (Can.) (ordinary fire policy insured a vessel while running on inland waters during navigation season; vessel was destroyed by fire while laid up during navigation season; held, no recovery).

217. *Slattery v. Mance*, (1962) 1 All E.R. 525, [1962] 1 Lloyd's Rep. 60.

218. (1757) 97 E.R. 343.

219. (1801) 165 E.R. 450.

220. (1872) L.R. 7 Q.B. 225.

221. *Butler v. Wildman*, (1820) 106 E.R. 708. But, compare, *Shaver Transportation Co. v. Travelers Ind.*, 481 F.Supp. 892, 1980 AMC 393 (D.,Ore.), where the orderly discharge and sale of contaminated cargo to a salvage company in lieu of simply dumping it overboard at considerably less cost was held not to be *ejusdem generis* with "jettison."

222. *Dickenson v. Jardine*, (1868) L.R. 3 C.P. Subject, of course, to the *caveat* that if the jettison involves deck cargo the applicable policy provides coverage with respect to deck cargo. See discussion, *infra*.

In *Dyson v. Rowcroft*,[223] the policy covered fruit under the usual memorandum. During the course of the voyage, the fruit was damaged by seawater so that it became rotten and offensive. On the vessel's arrival at an intermediate port, the governmental authorities there prohibited the landing of the cargo. The ship was too much damaged by heavy weather to proceed on its voyage and it was sold, the cargo necessarily being thrown overboard. The assured recovered for a total loss.

Compare, however, *Taylor v. Dunbar*,[224] in which meat shipped was delayed on the voyage by bad weather and solely by reason of the delay became putrid and was necessarily thrown overboard. It was held that the loss was one from inherent vice and not a peril of the sea.

The second paragraph of Rule 17, Rules for Construction of Policy, Marine Insurance Act, reads as follows:

> In the absence of any usage to the contrary, deck cargo and living animals must be insured specifically, and not under the general denomination of goods.

Article 1(c) of the Hague Rules defines goods as "goods, wares, merchandise and articles of every kind whatsoever except . . . cargo which by the contract of carriage is stated as being carried on deck and is so carried." Thus, neither the ship nor cargo are subjected to the rules, nor can they benefit by them if the bill of lading on its face provides for carriage on deck and the cargo is, in fact, carried on deck.

Prior to the Hague Rules, the law appears to have been that if it was the custom of the trade to carry the specific goods on deck, it was not necessary that the bill of lading specify deck carriage. Notwithstanding loose expressions by some courts that the custom of the trade may govern, the Hague Rules clearly specify otherwise, and where the carriage is pursuant to the rules, the rules would appear to govern.

The problem frequently arises where a clean bill of lading is issued but the cargo is nonetheless carried on deck. For example, in *The Southlands*,[225] the vessel carried the cargo (lumber) on deck under a clean bill of lading. A portion of the cargo was jettisoned and a portion swept overboard by storms. There having been a "deviation," the bill of lading contract was displaced and the vessel became liable as an insurer. And see *The Idefjord*,[226] where the court held that carrying the goods on deck, knowing that that fact was not marked on the bills of lading, was a fraud upon anyone who might innocently pay value for the bills. Also, in *Fairhaven*,[227]

---

223. (1803) 127 E.R. 257.
224. (1869) L.R.. 4 C.P. 206.
225. 37 F.2d 474, 1932 AMC 337 (5th Cir.).
226. 114 F.2d 262, 1940 AMC 1280 (2d Cir.).
227. 1923 AMC 481 (N.D.,Cal.).

the goods were stowed on the bridge deck in violation of the under deck terms and later jettisoned. It was held that the carrier, having been deprived of the right to a general average contribution by general law and by the applicable York-Antwerp Rules, was liable for the loss proximately caused by such stowage.

See *Gibb v. McDonnell*,[228] in which the court held that goods stowed under deck were not liable for general average contributions with respect to deck cargo that was jettisoned. Moreover, the circumstances of the loss (the vessel was deliberately stranded) did not give rise to a general average situation. See, also, to the same effect, *Grouselle v. Ferrie*.[229]

In light of the Hague Rules which, of course, all the major maritime nations have adopted in whole or in part, it would seem most unlikely that there could be any proof adduced as to any custom or usage of the trade with respect to deck cargo which would avail the owner of the cargo. If deck cargo is not insured specifically as such, and the custom of the trade is in effect barred by the express terms of the Hague Rules, the question should not arise.[230]

Pirates

A pirate is one who plunders indiscriminately for his own ends and not one who is simply operating against the property of a particular state for a public end; i.e., the end of establishing a government. Such an act may be illegal, it may be criminal, but it is not piracy within the meaning of a policy of marine insurance. Stated in another fashion, it may be piracy within the meaning of the doctrines of international law but it is not piracy within the meaning of a marine insurance policy. *Bolivia Republic v. Indemnity Mutual Marine Assur. Co., Ltd.*[231]

In that case, goods were shipped from a port near the mouth of the Amazon River to a place far inland upon a tributary in a remote territory belonging to the Republic of Bolivia. The policy specifically insured against pirates but contained an F. C. & S. Clause. The goods consisted of provisions and stores belonging to the Bolivian government and were intended for Bolivian troops engaged in establishing the authority of that government in the remote territory. Certain malcontents, mostly Brazilians, determined not to permit the establishment of Bolivian authority, fitted out an expedition for the purpose of resisting the Bolivian troops and establishing an independent republic. The expedition seized the in-

228. (1850) 7 U.C.Q.B. 356 (C.A.,Can.).
229. (1843) 6 O.S. 454 (C.A.,Can.).
230. For an excellent discussion of the problem of on-deck carriage, see Wm. Tetley, *Marine Cargo Claims*, chap. 29 (2d ed.), 1978.
231. (1909) 1 K.B. 785, (1908-10) All E.R. 260.

sured goods. The assured claimed under the policy for a loss through pirates. The court held that the term "pirates" in its popular sense meant persons who plunder indiscriminately for their own private gain and not persons who operate against the property of a particular state for a public political end, and, therefore, the loss was not due to pirates.[232]

In *Palmer v. Naylor*,[233] coolie emigrants murdered the captain and part of the crew and forcibly took over the vessel. It was held to be an act of piracy and, if not a piratical act, one *ejusdem generis* with piracy.[234]

See, generally, *Banque Monetaca and Carystuiaki v. Motor Union Ins. Co., Ltd.*,[235] where the policy covered capture, seizure, or arrest but not piracy; the vessel was seized by a brigand who was virtually controlling, as a dictator, the region in which the seizure took place. The wrongful act was held to be a seizure and capture rather than piracy.

In *Rickards v. Forestal Land, Timber and Railways Co., Ltd.*,[236] the master of the insured vessel (which was German) scuttled it to avoid capture. It was held not to be piracy, as the scuttling was pursuant to the orders of the German government.

In *Dean v. Hornby*,[237] the insured vessel was seized by pirates but later recaptured by a British war vessel and sent back by a prize crew. As a consequence of bad weather, she was damaged and put into a port of refuge, where she was sold. It was held that there was a total loss by the piratical seizure, the owners from the time of the seizure until commencement of the action not having had either actual possession of the vessel or the means of obtaining it.

In the *Britannia Shipping Co. v. Globe & Rutgers*,[238] a tug was moored to a pier in a harbor from which it was taken and stolen. The assured

---

232. See *Mauran v. Alliance Ins. Co.*, 73 U.S. 1 (1867), holding that a seizure by a *de facto* government, whether a lawful one or not, is not piracy, and *Dole v. New England Mut. Marine Ins. Co.*, Fed.Cas. No. 3,966 (1st Cir., 1864), to the same effect.

233. (1854) 156 E.R. 492, Ex.Ch.

234. Rule 8, Rules for Construction of Policy, Marine Insurance Act, states:
The term "pirates" includes passengers who mutiny and rioters who attack the ship from the shore.

235. (1923) 14 Ll.L.Rep. 48, K.B.D. Compare, however, *Nesbitt v. Lushington*, (1792) 100 E.R. 1300, where a mob seized the vessel, which later stranded, and forced the captain to sell the cargo at a very low price. Held: The value of the portion sold was not recoverable under any policy terms.

236. (1942) A.C. 50, (1941) 3 All E.R. 62.

237. (1854) 118 E.R. 1008.

238. 1930 AMC 1722, 244 NYS 720, *aff'd* 249 NYS 908, 232 App.Div. 801 (St.,N.Y.). See, also, *Athens Maritime Enterprises Corporation v. Hellenic Mutual War Risks Association (Bermuda) Ltd. (The Andrea Lemos)*, [1983] 2 W.L.R. 425, Q.B.D. There, while the vessel was lying anchored in territorial waters of Bangladesh, armed men boarded and stole equipment. However, the armed men left the vessel after an alarm was sounded, although the ship's crew was threatened by force prior to their leaving. Held: Clandestine theft does not amount to piracy and does not become piracy merely because the thieves subsequently use force to effect an escape.

claimed, *inter alia*, on the ground of piracy. The court held that the theft of a vessel in a harbor was not piracy because not on the "high seas."

Thieves and Assailing Thieves

In the Lloyd's policy (S.G.), the term is simply "thieves." This is so because it was established at an early date in England that coverage for theft related only to losses by theft from outside a vessel during which force and violence occurred, and theft or embezzlement by the crew was not covered. In any event, this is clearly stated in Rule 9, Rules for Construction of Policy, Marine Insurance Act, reading:

> The term "thieves" does not cover clandestine theft, or a theft committed by any one of the ship's company, whether crew or passengers.

As the American courts were divided on the proper interpretation of the term "thieves,"[239] the AIH form uses the phrase "assailing thieves," which limits coverage to losses resulting from acts of obtaining access to property by force. It includes persons who break into and steal property from a vessel; it is not limited to thieves using violence against the person, as in robbery.[240] Moreover, it would clearly appear to preclude larceny or theft committed by members of the crew or passengers, and should be distinguished from "pilferage," which appears to comprehend a secret theft of a small part only, rather than the whole.[241] It would also appear that the term "thieves" as used in a bill of lading should be given the same construction as in a marine insurance policy.[242]

Acts of vandalism being plainly dissimilar to acts of assailing thieves, damage caused by acts of vandals is not covered by a policy embracing, *inter alia*, "assailing thieves."[243]

In *Orange*,[244] an action against underwriters for a constructive total loss of a vessel resulting from extensive damage caused by thieves, it was held that since the vessel had been moored in a reasonably safe place in the harbor and the shipowner was not negligent for failure to hire watchmen, the policy covered.

---

239. See *Atlantic Ins. Co. v. Storrow*, 5 Paige 293 (St.,N.Y., 1835); *Kent's Comm.*, vol. 3, p. 303; *Parsons*, vol. 1, p. 564 (1868, ed.); *Phillips*, Sec. 1106.

240. *Swift v. American Universal Ins. Co.*, 1966 AMC 269, 212 N.E.2d 448 (St.,Mass.). See, also, *Lafabrique de Produits Chimiques Societe Anonyme v. F.N. Large*, (1922) 13 Ll.L.Rep. 269, K.B.D.

241. *Goldman v. Ins. Co. of North America*, 194 App.Div. 266, aff'd 232 N.Y. 623 (1922); *Ruffalo's v. Nat. Ben-Franklin*, 1957 AMC 1233. And under a specific perils policy, the burden of proving a loss by theft is on the assured. *Gulf Ventures III, Inc. v. Glacier Gen. Assur. Co.*, 584 F.Supp. 882 (E.D.,La., 1984).

242. *Taylor v. Liverpool and Great Western Steam Co.*, (1874) L.R. 9 Q.B. 546.

243. *Goodman v. U.S. Fire Ins. Co.*, 1967 AMC 1853 (St.,NYM).

244. 337 F.Supp. 1161, 1972 AMC 627 (S.D.N.Y.).

In *Bobley v. California Union Ins. Co.*,[245] the policy was on the "hull and contents" of a houseboat and contained the standard marine perils clause, including "assailing thieves," but specifically excluded loss by "theft" or "mysterious disappearance." In the assured's suit to recover for jewelry stolen from the houseboat, the court held (in denying the insurer's motion for summary judgment) that the insurer had failed to establish as a matter of law that (1) the theft exclusion applied and (2) the word "contents" referred only to what pertains to the hull. The court further held that the proper construction of the terms warranted resort to extrinsic evidence.

In *Feinberg v. Ins. Co. of N.A.*,[246] a yacht policy covered "theft of the entire yacht . . . and all other perils, losses and misfortunes." The yacht was left moored at a marina where she lay in range of a floodlight to discourage marauders; there was no night watchman in attendance. The following morning, she was discovered 90 feet away, tied to a different float out of range of the floodlight, in a sinking condition, her seacock having been removed. Items of furnishings and personal property had been removed. The district court held that the moving and scuttling did not permanently deprive the owner of his vessel so as to make out a "theft" within the meaning of the policy. The court of appeal reversed, holding that under relevant Massachusetts decisions the loss was "very much like a theft." The coverage of "all other perils" was not without meaning and covered the loss. The decision does not seem to be in accord with the principles enunciated in the English cases, as the facts also disclosed a stealthy entrance into an unoccupied vessel without the necessary element of violence. See, for example, *S. Felicione & Sons Fish Co. v. Citizens Casualty Co. of New York*,[247] where a madman came aboard the vessel in an intoxicated condition, murdered the captain and one of the crew, and then sank the vessel. The court held that the loss of the vessel did not fall within the provision of the policy insuring against "assailing thieves."

Many cargo policies now contain a "theft, pilferage and non-delivery" clause whereby these risks are expressly covered.[248]

---

245. 1976 AMC 216 (NYM).
246. 260 F.2d 523, 1959 AMC 11 (1st Cir.).
247. 430 F.2d 136 (5th Cir.), *cert. den.* 401 U.S. 939.
248. It was held in *Middows v. Robertson*, (1940) 67 Ll.L.Rep. 484 that the term "non-delivery" did not create an additional risk but merely affected the burden of proof. See, also, *Federman v. American Ins. Co.*, 1935 AMC 1224 (St.,N.Y.); *Haddad v. Reliable M.L. Ins. Co.*, 1948 AMC 1673; *Starlight Fabrics v. Glens Falls Ins. Co.*, 1948 AMC 1416 (St.,N.Y.); *Kessler Export Co. v. Reliance Ins. Co.*, 1962 AMC 2429; *Ruffalo's v. Nat. Ben-Franklin, 1957 1233 (2d Cir.); Federation Ins. Co. of Canada v. Coret Accessories, Inc.*, 1968 AMC 1796, [1968] 2 Lloyd's Rep. 109 (Can.); *Champion International v. Arkwright*, 1982 AMC 2496 (S.D.N.Y.) (shipowner converted the assured's goods but the assured was successful in repossessing them and having them delivered to the consignee; however, expenses were incurred by the assured in doing so, for which assured was entitled to recovery under the policy as sue and labor expenses, etc.).

Barratry of Master and Mariners

Rule 11, Rules for Construction of Policy, Marine Insurance Act, 1906, defines barratry with great precision:

> The term "barratry" includes every wrongful act wilfully committed by the master or crew to the prejudice of the owner, or, as the case may be, the charterer.

The definition of the term in American cases does not differ.[249]

While the term comprehends all wrongs done by the master or crew against the interests of the owner, it does not include errors of judgment or ordinary negligence,[250] and it is axiomatic that connivance of the owner in the wrongful act, or gross negligence on the part of the owner whereby the act is permitted, bars recovery for barratry.[251]

In *National Union F.I. Co. v. Republic of China* (1958), *supra*, six vessels (sold by the United States to the Nationalist Chinese government) were lost when the masters and crews defected and took their vessels with them

---

The London Institute Theft, Pilferage, and Non-Delivery (Insured Value) Clause reads:

 (A) It is hereby agreed that this Policy covers the risk of Theft and/or Pilferage irrespective of percentage. No liability for loss to attach hereto unless notice of survey has been given to Underwriters' Agents within 10 days of the expiry of risk under the Policy.

 (B) It is hereby agreed that this Policy covers the risk of Non-Delivery of an entire package for which the liability of the Shipowner or other Carrier is limited, reduced or negatived by the Contract of Carriage by reason of the value of the goods.

 Underwriters to be entitled to any amount recovered from the Carriers or others in respect of such losses (less cost of recovery if any) up to the amount paid by them in respect of the loss.

 249. See *Patapsco Ins. Co. v. Coulter*, 28 U.S. 222 (1830); *New Orleans Ins. Co. v. E.D. Albro Co.*, 112 U.S. 506 (1884); *National Union F.I. Co. v. Republic of China*, 151 F.Supp. 211, 1957 AMC 915 (D.,Md.), modified 254 F.2d 166, 1958 AMC 751 (4th Cir.), [1958] 1 Lloyd's Rep. 351; *Padre Island (Stranding)*, 1970 AMC 600 (S.D.,Tex.), [1971] 2 Lloyd's Rep. 431; *Commercial Trading v. Hartford F.I. Co.*, 466 F.2d 1239, 1972 AMC 2495 (5th Cir.), [1974] 1 Lloyd's Rep. 179; *Crousillat v. Ball*, 4 U.S. 294 (1803); *Williams v. Suffolk Ins. Co.*, Fed.Cas. No. 17,738 (1st Cir., 1838); *Marcardier v. Chesapeake Ins. Co.*, 12 U.S. 39 (1814); *Waters v. Merchants' Louisville Ins. Co.*, 36 U.S. 213 (1837); *Gulf Ventures III, Inc. v. Glacier Gen. Assur. Co.*, 584 F.Supp. 882 (E.D.,La., 1984).

 250. *Wolff v. Merchants Ins. Co.*, (1892) 31 N.B.R. 577 (Can.); *Wilson, Harraway & Co. v. National Fire and Marine Ins. Co. of New Zealand*, (1886) N.Z.L.R. 343 (S.C.); *Crowell v. Geddes*, (1862) 5 N.S.R. 184 (C.A.,Can.); *Phyn v. Royal Exchange Assur. Co.*, (1789) 101 E.R. 1101; *Bradford v. Levy*, (1825) 2 C. & P. 137 Ry. & M. 331, N.P.; *Todd v. Ritchie*, (1816) 1 Stark 240, N.P.; *Commercial Trading v. Hartford F.I. Co.*, 466 F.2d 1239, 1972 AMC 2495 (5th Cir.), [1974] 1 Lloyd's Rep. 179; *Williams v. Suffolk Ins. Co..*, Fed.Cas. No. 17,738 (1st Cir., 1838); *Gulf Ventures III, Inc. v. Glacier Gen. Assur. Co.*, 584 F.Supp. 882 (E.D.,La., 1984).

 251. *Vallejo v. Wheeler*, (1774) 98 E.R. 1012; *Pipon v. Cope*, (1808) 1 Camp. 434, N.P.; *Banque Francaise de Syrie v. Providence Washington Ins. Co.*, 1927 AMC 1602 (SDNY); *Padre Island (Stranding)*, 1970 AMC 600 (S.D.,Tex.), [1971] 2 Lloyd's Rep. 431; *Banco de Barcelona v. Union Marine Ins. Co., Ltd.*, (1925) 134 L.T. 350, 22 Ll.L.Rep. 209; *Piermay Shipping Co., S.A. v. Chester (The Michael)*, [1979] 2 Lloyd's Rep. 1, C.A.

to the aid of the Chinese Communist government. The district court re-jected the contention that masters and mariners who change sides in a civil war cannot be considered to have committed barratry, holding that the characterization of an act as barratrous is independent of the motives which provoked the act. "Barratry cannot be modified by patriotism." Thus, the proximate cause of the loss was barratry—a risk covered by the marine and war risk insurance, and not a capture and seizure—a risk ex-cluded from coverage. The court of appeals modified by holding that a seventh vessel—which the district court had held was "seized"—was like-wise lost through barratry. The decision of the court of appeals reviews in detail the English decisions on barratry and is highly commended.

The interplay of a claim of loss by perils of the seas with a claim by underwriters of scuttling was involved in *Piermay Shipping Co., S.A. v. Chester (The Michael)* (1979), *supra*. In that case, the vessel's engines stop-ped, and she was drifting helpless in heavy seas and strong winds. By the time salvage tugs reached her and put a line aboard, it was noticed that the engine room was flooding. Shortly afterwards, the towline was re-leased without orders and for no apparent reason. Thereafter, there was a blackout throughout the vessel, apparently due to water rising to the level of the generators. The crew panicked and abandoned ship. There being no portable pumps available on the assisting tugs, the master also aban-doned ship, and the crew and the master were taken aboard the salvaging tugs. Meanwhile, the vessel sank and was a total loss. The owner claimed, *inter alia,* for loss by barratry, it being common ground between the par-ties that the vessel had been deliberately sunk by one Komiseris, an engi-neer.[252] The defendant underwriters defended on the ground that the vessel had been deliberately sunk by Komiseris with the knowledge and consent of the owners.[253]

At first instance, Kerr, J., held that to establish a loss by barratry in-volved establishing both a deliberate sinking and the absence of the owners' consent, but if the court was left in doubt whether the owners consented or not then the claim failed; and common sense required that the owners had to satisfy the court on a clear balance of probability that Komiseris had sunk the vessel without their knowledge or consent. On the basis of the evidence as he viewed it, he held that Komiseris sank the vessel deliberately and without any consent or foreknowledge on the part

252. Compare the facts in *Astrovlanis Compania Naviera, S.A. v. Linard (The Gold Sky),* [1972] 2 Lloyd's 187. See, also, the excellent article "Barratry: The Scuttler's Easy Route to the Golden Prize," [1982] 3 *LMCLQ* 383.

253. Alternatively, the underwriters contended that the owners' initial claim for a loss by perils of the seas had been put forward fraudulently or recklessly on the ground that the owners then knew or strongly suspected that the vessel had, in fact, been deliberately sunk by Komiseris. The owners denied all knowledge.

of the owners. The claim for barratry thus succeeded. On appeal, it was held that there was no ground for disturbing the trial judge's conclusion that the owners had successfully and satisfactorily discharged the burden of proving lack of complicity in the sinking on a "clear balance of probabilities."

The remarks of Roskill, L. J. concerning the function of an appellate court are illuminating. He said, in part:

> It is . . . clear that no trial judge can make himself immune from the due process of judicial review by an Appellate Court by seeking to rely upon the demeanour of witnesses when other evidence relevant to his evaluation of their demeanour points strongly the other way. But an Appellate Court must always be very slow to disturb the judgment of a Judge who both saw and heard the witnesses in a case where he, unlike the Appellate Court, must clearly be in a much better position to determine where the truth lies . . . . A trial judge must always test his impression of the veracity of a witness based on a demeanour against other evidence in the case which may point the other way. There is no doctrine of judicial infallibility for trial judges . . . . Clearly if a trial Judge fails to take proper advantage of his position in seeing and hearing the witnesses an Appellate Court will be more ready to interfere. But even then it will be very slow indeed to do so unless his failure to take advantage of his position is clearly shown . . . .

In *Commercial Trading v. Hartford F.I. Co.* (1972), *supra*, the plaintiff insured a cargo of meat for a voyage from Costa Rica to Tampa, with the defendant insurers, under a marine insurance policy in which the perils insured against included, *inter alia*, "criminal barratry of the Master and Mariners." The goods were delivered by the master to a third party who did not produce all the outstanding bills of lading, and not to the plaintiffs who were the consignees. The third party went bankrupt, and the plaintiffs thereupon claimed an indemnity from the defendant underwriters on the grounds that the goods had been lost (a) by criminal barratry of the master, or (b) by a like peril within the general words of the policy. At first instance, the trial court dismissed the claims. On appeal, it was held that the plaintiffs had failed to prove a loss by criminal barratry, because (a) criminal barratry could be committed by the master only against the shipowners, (b) there was considerable doubt whether in the present case the act had been committed by the master since he had done nothing more than follow the directions of the shipowners' general agent, and (c) there was no criminal intent to defraud or in any way harm the shipowners. The court also held that it was unnecessary to decide whether the goods were lost by a "like" peril.

In *Fishing Fleet v. Trident*,[254] a fishing vessel master attempted fraudulently to sell the vessel in Mexican waters, lied to the owner about her shrimp catch, and disappeared after the vessel sank. Subsequently, the Mexican government raised the vessel and sold it at judicial sale. In a suit on the policy, the court held that the proximate cause of the loss of the vessel was the barratrous acts of the master and did not relieve the underwriters of liability under the policy's "free of capture and seizure" clause, where the constructive total loss of the vessel had already resulted from the barratry of the master prior to the seizure. The vessel owner's failure to notify the underwriters of a "suspicion" that the vessel had been intentionally scuttled did not amount to concealment and misrepresentation, and the owner fulfilled his duty of minimizing the loss under the sue and labor clause by travelling to Mexico to ascertain the location of the vessel, contacting embassy officials for assistance and, on learning of the vessel's sinking, hired marine surveyors to investigate.

In *Isbell Enterprises, Inc. v. Citizens Cas. Co. of New York*,[255] a member of the crew of a fishing vessel who did not have authority to do so took the vessel to sea in rough weather; the vessel went aground, and sank. It was held that for an act to constitute barratry it must be fraudulent or criminal, wilful, and against the interests of the owner of a vessel. Under that definition, the acts of the crew member were held to be barratrous.

In *Wharton v. Home Ins. Co.*,[256] the master provisioned and fueled the vessel for an illegal drug run instead of a shrimping trip as authorized by the owner. Thereafter, he deliberately sailed the vessel beyond the hull policy's navigational limits and it was lost at sea. The court held that the master committed barratry while at Key West, a port within the marine insurance policy's navigational limits, when he engaged in extraordinary preparations for the illegal drug run, and that this was the proximate cause of the loss of the vessel.

In *U.S. Fire Ins. Co. v. Cavanaugh*,[257] it was held that the proximate cause of a fishing vessel's loss was barratry by the master in operating the vessel beyond the navigational limits of the policy whereupon it was lost on a reef, even though such acts were a breach of the vessel owner's warranty that the vessel would not be operated outside of prescribed geographical limits.

By contrast, in *Ope Shipping v. Allstate*,[258] the court held that the "real efficient cause" of the loss of Nicaraguan vessels to the shipowners was not barratry by their crews in sailing to ports friendly to the Sandinista revo-

254. 598 F.2d 925, 1980 AMC 583 (5th Cir.).
255. 431 F.2d 409 (5th Cir., 1969).
256. 724 F.2d 427, 1984 AMC 937 (4th Cir.).
257. 1983 AMC 1261 (S.D.,Fla., 1982).
258. 687 F.2d 639, 1983 AMC 22 (2d Cir.).

lutionary party, but rather the Nicaraguan civil war, an excluded peril under the policy's war, strikes, and related exclusions clause.

In *Nautilus v. Edinburgh Ins. Co., Ltd.*,[259] a vessel was seized in Colombian territorial waters for carrying marijuana. It was held that although the master's unauthorized deviation to Colombia constituted barratry, the proximate cause of the loss was the governmental seizure (reviewing cases).

It must be recognized that barratrous acts are frequently committed by a master engaging in smuggling ventures for his own account or in deliberate and fraudulent violations of laws and regulations.[260]

The master of a ship who is also part owner may commit barratry of the goods. That is, barratry is cheating which may be done by a part owner but not by a sole owner.[261]

It should be noted that barratry is not an exculpating cause of loss under Cogsa. For example, in *Intercontinental Prop. Lim. Procs.*,[262] a mentally disturbed seaman's wilful scuttling of the carrying vessel was held not to be a defense to the carrier under the "Q" clause of Cogsa, Section 4(2), since the seaman was the carrier's servant. Whether the servant's wrongful act must be within the scope of his employment was discussed but not decided. In *Allied Chemical—Piermay*,[263] involving a voyage charter party incorporating Cogsa, it was held that the shipowner failed to sustain its burden of proving either that its vessel was intentionally sunk by her engineer without the collusion of the shipowner or that the loss during Force 8 weather resulted from a sea peril.

Interestingly, the origin of the word "barratry" seemingly is lost in the mists of antiquity. The term "barrattier" appears in Dante's *Inferno*, meaning one who purchases offices in church or state.

Takings at Sea

Any "taking at sea," whether by capture or seizure, conversion or otherwise, falls within the phrase. For example, a ship sunk before a declara-

---

259. 510 F.Supp. 1092, 1981 AMC 2082 (D.,Md.), *aff'd* 1983 AMC 696 (4th Cir.).

260. *Havelock v. Hancill*, (1789) 100 E.R. 573 (smuggling); *Goldschmidt v. Whitmore*, (1811) 128 E.R. 202 (breach of blockade); *Knight v. Cambridge*, (1724) 88 E.R. 165 (leaving port to evade paying dues); *Australasion Ins. Co. v. Jackson*, (1875) 13 S.C.R. (N.S.W.) 196, *aff'd* 33 L.T. 286, 3 Asp. M.L.C. 26 (P.C.) (kidnapping native laborers); *Earle v. Rowcroft*, (1806) 103 E.R. 292 (trading with the enemy); *Ross v. Hunter*, (1790) 100 E.R. 879 (deviation by master for fraudulent purposes); *Mentz, Decker & Co. v. Maritime Ins. Co.*, (1910) 1 K.B. 132 (deviation); *Wharton v. Home Ins. Co.*, 724 F.2d 472, 1984 AMC 937 (4th Cir.). It should be noted, in this connection, that barratry is specifically eliminated from the new AIH policy (1977) and in the future will fall under the war risks policies and endorsements.

261. *Jones v. Nicholson*, (1854) 156 E.R. 342; *Marcardier v. Chesapeake Ins. Co.*, 12 U.S. 39 (1818); *Moore v. Graham*, (1868) 5 W.W. & A.B. (L) 229 (Vic. Sup. Ct., Aus.).

262. 1979 AMC 1680 (4th Cir.).

263. 1978 AMC 773 (Arb.).

tion of war;[264] capture by a privateer after collusion between the two masters;[265] seizure of a ship by mistake;[266] a wrongful seizure;[267] ship driven by stress of weather on an enemy coast and there captured;[268] seizure by sanitary authorities of a foreign state;[269] seizure of a vessel by Vietnamese customs officials, followed by confiscation of the vessel by a special court;[270] seizure by emigrants aboard vessel.[271]

Prior to the decision of the court of appeal in *Nishina Trading Co. Ltd. v. Chiyoda Fire and Marine Ins. Co. Ltd. (The Mandarin Star)*,[272] it had been established law that the peril of "takings at sea" was synonymous with "seizure" or "capture." The decision in *The Mandarin Star* was to the effect that it included the risk of a shipowner wrongfully appropriating goods on the ship. However, in *Shell International Petroleum Co. Ltd. v. Gibbs (The Salem)*,[273] the House of Lords expressly overruled *The Mandarin Star* and held that no standard marine policy covers wrongful misappropriation of a cargo by a shipowner. In that case, most of a vessel's oil cargo was misappropriated by the master and crew with the knowledge (and presumably connivance) of the charterer/owner. The misappropriation occurred while the vessel was off the harbor at Durban, where it pumped off approximately 180,000 tons of oil to tank farms ashore. The vessel left and was deliberately sunk by the crew off the coast of Africa with some 15,000 tons of cargo still aboard it. The House of Lords held, *inter alia*, that there was no barratry in that the shipowner was privy to the loss of the cargo, nor was there a "taking at sea," as the loss occurred in port. However, the loss of the 15,000 tons which went down with the ship was held to be a peril of the sea under the relevant policies.

Arrests, Restraints, and Detainments

Rule 10, Rules for Construction of Policy, Marine Insurance Act, 1906, reads:

> The term "arrests, etc. of kings, princes and people" refers to political or executive acts and does not include a loss caused by riot or civil commotion.

264. *Goss v. Withers*, (1758) 97 E.R. 511.
265. *Arcangelo v. Thompson*, (1811) 2 Camp. 620, N.P.
266. *Dean v. Hornby*, (1854) 118 E.R. 1108.
267. *Lozano v. Janson*, (1859) 121 E.R. 61.
268. *Green v. Emslie*, (1794) Peake 213, N.P.
269. *Miller v. Law Accident Ins. Co.*, (1903) 1 K.B. 712.
270. *Panamanian Oriental S.S. Corp. v. Wright*, [1970] 2 Lloyd's Rep., 356, Q.B.D., *reversed* on other grounds in (1971) 1 Lloyd's Rep.487, C.A.
271. *Kleinwort v. Shepard*, (1859) 120 E.R. 977.
272. (1969) 2 All E.R. 776, [1969] 1 Lloyd's Rep. 293, C.A.
273. [1983] 2 A.C. 375, [1983] 1 Lloyd's Rep. 342, H.L.

Since the word "people" means the ruling power or the power of the country *per se*, detention of a ship by a mob is not a loss falling within the phrase.[274] Compare, however, *Societe Belge des Betons Societe Anonyme v. London & Lancashire Ins. Co., Ltd.*,[275] where workers having the support of the Popular Executive Committee of Valencia, Spain, then the *de facto* and *de jure* government of Valencia, seized the insured vessel. The distinction lies in the constituency of the group seizing. In the first case, it was a mob, pure and simple. In the latter, the workers were given at least the guise of legitimacy by reason of the connection with the *de facto* and *de jure* governmental committee.

"Restraints of princes" covers every case of interruption or loss arising by reason of lawful authority.[276] But it relates only to unusual inter-

274. *Nesbitt v. Lushington*, (1792) 100 E.R. 1300. Nor is a diversion on instructions of a governmental shipowner (Brazilian government agency) in order to obtain was risk insurance from the United States War Shipping Administration. *Baker Castor Oil Co. v. Insurance Company of North America*, 157 F.2d 3, 1946 AMC 1115 [1945] 78 Ll.L.Rep. 240.

275. (1938) 2 All E.R. 305. See, also, *Pape, Williams & Co. v. Home Ins. Co.*, 1944 AMC 51, (2d Cir.) (seizure by "Labor Committee" at Barcelona, Spain).

276. *Russell v. Nieman*, (1864) 17 C.B.N.S. 163. See, also, *Sanday & Co. v. British & Foreign Marine Ins. Co., Ltd.*, (1915) 2 K.B. 781, (1916) 1 A.C. 650; *Associated Oil Carriers, Ltd. v. Union Insurance Soc. of Canton, Ltd.*, (1917) 2 K.B. 184. In the *Sanday* case, British vessels were enroute from South America with cargo consigned to Hamburg, Germany, when World War I erupted. Because of the prohibitions against trading with the enemy, the voyages were rendered illegal, and the vessels put into British ports, where the cargo was sold. This aborted the voyages, and there was a constructive total loss of the insured venture, which was held to be recoverable under the policies. This led directly to the introduction of the Frustration Clause, discussed *infra* in Chapter XIII. Similar cases arose during World War II, where German vessels were, shortly before hostilities commenced, in various foreign ports or enroute back to Germany. The German government ordered such vessels to take refuge in neutral ports and then get to Germany if possible, or to be scuttled if they could not avoid capture. In 1940 three test cases were brought, all of which were heard and determined together. See *Middows Ltd. v. Robertson and Other Test Cases*, (1941) 70 Ll.L.Rep. 193, H.L. (involving the vessels *Minden*, *The Halle*, and *The Wangoni*). In each instance, the House of Lords held that there had been a restraint of princes inasmuch as the masters had acted on orders of the German government.

See, also, *Miller v. Law Accident Ins. Soc.*, (1903) 1 K.B. 712 (landing of cattle prohibited by local municipal law where the cattle had hoof and mouth disease); *Rodocanachi v. Elliott*, (1874) 31 L.T. 239 (goods insured were covered for overland transit through Paris, but upon arrival the German army had invested the city so that the goods could not be forwarded, whereupon the assured gave notice of abandonment; held, restraint of princes within the meaning of the policy); *Green v. Young*, (1702) 92 E.R. 61 (government laid an embargo upon a vessel, seized her and converted her into a fireship); *Robinson Gold Mining Co. v. Alliance Insurance Co.*, (1901) 2 K.B. 919 (goods and ships in a blockaded port); *Intermondale Trading Co. v. North River Ins. Co.*, 100 F.Supp. 128, 1951 AMC 936 (S.D.N.Y.) (vessel transporting insured tires was detained by British officials at Gibraltar because it was suspected that the ship was also carrying illegal refugees bound for Palestine; the detention, held to be the principal cause of whatever losses were sustained, was found to fall within the F. C. & S. exemption); *Resin Coatings Corp. v. Fidelity & Casualty Co. of New York*, 489 F.Supp. 73 (S.D.,Fla., 1980) (F. C. & S Clause held to bar recovery for losses due to seizure by Saudi Arabian customs officials); *Blaine Richards & Co., Inc. v. Marine Indemnity Insurance Co. of North America*, 653 F.2d 1051, 1981 AMC 1 (2d Cir.) (scope of F. C. & S. Clause includes risk of detention by civil authorities in time of peace; "hold" placed by the U.S. Food & Drug Administration on possibly contaminated foodstuffs constituted a "seizure" or "detention," although there was no adverse possession of the goods by the government).

ferences by lawful authority and does not embrace, as Rule 10 specifically notes, a loss occasioned by ordinary judicial process during the course of litigation.[277] Use of physical force is not necessary, because, by implication, every command of a sovereign is assumed to be capable of being enforced by physical compulsion if necessary. However, an arrest or seizure by an official or agency of a government does not take on the status of "ordinary judicial process" merely because a court may later order the vessel condemned or confiscated.[278] An example of ordinary judicial process is a case where a vessel is arrested for security for the payment of a maritime lien and later sold by court decree.

An arrest is to be distinguished from a capture. In the former, there is a temporary detention with the intent to liberate or restore the property later, or pay the value thereof; the latter comprehends a design on the part of the captor to appropriate the ship or goods permanently and have it condemned as a prize.[279] There is also a distinction between an arrest and a detainment. In *Thompson v. Read*,[280] the court observed that an arrest operates immediately on the subject matter arrested as does a detainment, since it presupposes the subject detained to be in the hands of the detainer. But there may be a restraint where the subject matter is not in the hands of the restrainer. For example, neutrals are often accosted and ordered into port for the purpose of investigation. An embargo may be a detainment as well as a restraint. But a blockade may be a restraint without arrest or detainment.

The clause is to be interpreted in the disjunctive; i.e., either an arrest, a detainment, or a restraint may take place, and the clause thereupon becomes operative. Consequently, where there is a blockade (which is neither an arrest nor a detainment but a mere restraint), the clause applies.[281] An embargo is also a species of restraint, there being, however, a

---

277. *Crew Widgery & Co. v. Great Western S.S. Co.*, (1887) W.N. 161; *Lancastrian*, 1927 AMC 1196 (NYCt.Ap.). In the latter, the underwriters were held not liable for decay of a cargo of lemons due to delay in releasing the vessel from civil arrest after a collision.

278. *Panamanian Oriental S.S. Corp. v. Wright*, (1970) *supra*. As to the definitions of "malicious damage," "usurped power," "civil war," "rebellion," "insurrection," and "civil commotion," see *Spinney's (1948) Ltd. et al. v. Royal Insurance Co. Ltd.*, [1980] 1 Lloyd's Rep. 406, where groups of persons, acting in concert, looted and destroyed the insured premises and stocks therein as a part of the disturbances in 1976 in Beirut, Lebanon. The court held that such acts constituted "civil commotion assuming the proportions of or amounting to a popular uprising." Specifically, the court noted that a "civil commotion" does not have to involve a revolt against the government, although the disturbance has to have sufficient cohesion to prevent the disturbance from being the work of a mindless mob. Moreover, the turbulence and collapse of public order attendant upon the civil commotion permitted and encouraged the acts of looting and vandalism and were sufficient to establish that the loss was occasioned indirectly (if not directly) by, through, or in consequence of the civil commotion.

279. *Richardson v. Maine Fire & Marine Ins. Co.*, 6 Mass. 102 (1809).

280. 12 Serg. & R. 440 (Pa.Sup.Ct., 1820).

281. *Olivera v. Union Ins. Co.*, 16 U.S. 183 (1818).

distinction between an embargo laid on during time of peace and an embargo declared during hostilities.[282]

It is not necessary that there be a justifiable and lawful cause of seizure and condemnation in order to bring the case within the exceptions contained in the F. C. & S. Clause. It is sufficient if the seizure is made *bona fide* upon reasonable grounds and probable cause.[283] In *Powell v. Hyde*,[284] the Russians by mistake fired on an English ship thinking she was Turkish, and sank her. The policy contained an F. C. & S. Clause. Even though war between Russia and England was not declared until a few days later, it was held that the exception extended to any seizure whereby the vessel was lost, whether legal or altogether illegal and contrary to the law of nations.

In the absence of an F. C. & S. Clause, when the ruling authorities of a state deprive the assured of the use of his property by an act which is not an act of war, the assured may nonetheless recover.[285]

It is instructive in this context to compare *Rickards v. Forestal Land, Timber and Railways Co., Ltd.,*[286] with *Atlantic Maritime Co., Inc. v. Gibbon.*[287] In the former, a cargo was insured on a German vessel. The vessel arrived at Rio de Janeiro shortly before war was declared between Great Britain and Germany. Shortly thereafter, the German government gave orders for all German vessels to take refuge in neutral ports, or return to Germany, or, as a last resort, to be scuttled. The vessel later sailed but was scuttled off the Faroe Islands to avoid capture by a British warship. Because the German master was acting pursuant to orders of the German government, the court held the loss to be one due to a "restraint of princes." The policy also contained Clause 2(c) of the Institute War Clauses (the Frustration Clause) reading:

> This policy is warranted free of any claim based upon loss of, or of frustration of, the insured voyage or adventure caused by arrests, re-

---

282. *Aubert v. Gray*, (1862) 122 E.R. 65. And see *Janson v. Driefontein Consolidated Mines, Ltd.*, (1902) A.C. 484, where subjects of a foreign nation insured treasure with British underwriters against capture during transit from the foreign nation to Great Britain. The foreign government seized the treasure and thereafter war was declared between that nation and Great Britain. Recovery was allowed, the court noting that the important date was the seizure before the declaration of war even though the seizing power made the seizure in contemplation of war and in order to use the treasure in support of the war. See, also, *Odlin v. Ins. Co. of Pennsylvania*, Fed.Cas. No. 10,433 (3d Cir, 1808) where the court held a domestic embargo, not imposed during time of war, to be a loss within the meaning of the clause "arrests, restraints and detainments of princes."

283. *Magoun v. New England Marine Ins. Co.*, Fed.Cas. No. 8,961 (1st Cir., 1840); *Bradshaw v. Neptune Ins. Co.*, Fed.Cas. No. 1,793 (1st Cir., 1839).

284. (1855) 119 E.R. 606. See, also *Cory v. Burr*, (1883) 8 A.C. 393.

285. *Robinson Gold Mining Co. v. Alliance Ins. Co.*, (1901) 2 K.B. 918; *Sanday & Co. v. British & Foreign Marine Ins. Co., Ltd.*, (1916) *supra*.

286. (1941) 3 All E.R. 62, (1942) A.C. 350.

287. (1953) 2 All E.R. 1086, [1953] 2 Lloyd's Rep. 294, C.A.

straints or detainments of Kings, Princes, Peoples, Usurpers or persons attempting to usurp power.

The court further held that the policy covered the goods themselves from destruction while the Frustration Clause only excepted "claim[s] based upon loss of, or frustration of, the . . . adventure"—and not the actual loss of the goods.

In *Atlantic Maritime, supra,* the policy was on freight to be earned on a voyage from Taku Bar, the port for Tientsin, China, to Japan. While the vessel was at anchor, she was approached by a Chinese Nationalist destroyer and, in effect, told that there was going to be trouble and "if you are present you may get hurt; if you do, we cannot help it." At that time, the surrounding territory was controlled by the Chinese Communists. There was gunfire in the vicinity, and a Chinese ship in the harbor was shelled and sunk. The master departed without loading any cargo and later loaded a cargo of lumber in British Columbia for carriage to the east coast of the United States. After his departure, several ships arrived at Taku Bar and loaded small quantities of cargo without molestation. In a suit on the freight policy, a majority of the court of appeal held that the freight was lost by reason of restraint of princes but denied recovery on the ground that the Frustration Clause relieved underwriters of the obligation of paying.

The subject of war risks insurance is covered in Chaprer XIII.

Letters of Mart and Countermart

Although the perils clause ostensibly insures with respect to letters of mart and countermart, this peril is non-existent today, privateering having been abolished under the laws of nations by the Declaration of Paris, 1856.[288]

All Other Perils, Losses, and Misfortunes

At first blush, it would seem that this phrase is so comprehensive and all-encompassing that it would cover losses from any source whatever. But this is not the case. Rule 12, Rules for Construction of Policy, states the principle succinctly:

---

288. Such letters were formerly issued to privateers by sovereign nations to enable their subjects to obtain restitution and indemnity for articles seized by subjects of other states. In the absence of such letters, the "privateer" would simply be a "pirate."

The term "all other perils" includes only perils similar in kind to the perils specifically mentioned in the policy.

Thus, to come within the general words, the peril must be *ejusdem generis* with those specifically enumerated. Lord Ellenborough in *Cullen v. Butler*,[289] explained the principle in the following cogent terms:

> The extent and meaning of the general words have not yet been the immediate subject of any judicial construction in our courts of law. As they must, however, be considered as introduced into the policy in furtherance of the objects of marine insurance and may have the effect of extending a reasonable indemnity to many cases not distinctly covered by the special words, they are entitled to be considered as material and operative words, and to have due effect assigned to them in the construction of this instrument; and which will be done by allowing them to comprehend and cover other cases of marine damage of the like kind with those which are specially enumerated and occasioned by similar causes.

The case which occasioned this language involved a policy of insurance in common form where the ship and goods were sunk at sea by another ship firing upon her, mistaking her for an enemy. Although the loss was not one occasioned by "enemies," it was sufficiently "like" that peril to be brought within the general words.

Lord Watson in *Sun Fire Office v. Hart*,[290] explained the canon of construction of *ejusdem generis* as follows:

> It is a well known canon of construction, that when a particular enumeration is followed by such words as "or other," the latter expression ought, if not enlarged by the context, be limited to matters *ejusdem generis* with those specifically enumerated. The canon is attended with no difficulty, except in its application. Whether it applies at all, and if so, what effect should be given to it, must in every case depend upon the precise terms, subject matter, and context of the clause under construction.

Southport Fisheries v. Saskatchewan Government Ins. Office,[291] illustrates the point quite well. In that case, unknown persons threw acid on fishing nets and they were totally destroyed. The hull and tackle of the fishing vessels were covered under a policy similar to the usual Lloyd's policy. In an action on the policy, the court held that the damage was occasioned by a spiteful injury to property rather than a peril to which maritime ven-

---

289. (1816) 105 E.R. 119.
290. (1889) 14 A.C. 98.
291. 161 F.Supp. 81, 1959 AMC 1280 (E.D.N.C.).

tures are exposed. In other words, the peril of acid being thrown on the nets was not one peculiar to maritime activity. The court said, in part:[292]

> Turning to the listed perils in order to define their common quality it is noted that circumstances attendant upon maritime commerce render vessels notoriously defenseless against losses effected by fire, lightning and earthquake. Loss by jettison is a risk certainly peculiar to the sea. Excepting jettison, the man-caused perils set forth in the policies are more likely to befall mariners, as opposed to others, because historically a ship's physical location and total lack of communication has limited its security to that derived from its own resources, thus increasing the possibility of successful warfare or plunder against the same. In short, an examination of the perils set forth in the policies discloses that each has become particularly feared by the maritime world because circumstances surrounding maritime commerce increase the likelihood of loss from such risks . . . . In the Court's opinion it is the sole ingredient essential in order to qualify a risk as a "like peril" within the coverage of the policy.

Perhaps the leading case on the point is *Thames & Mersey Marine Ins. Co. v. Hamilton, Fraser & Co.*[293] In that case, a donkey engine was being used in pumping water into the main boilers when, owing to a valve being closed which ought to have been kept open, water was forced into and split open the air chamber of the donkey pump. The closing of the valve was either accidental or due to the negligence of an engineer and was not due to ordinary wear and tear. The assured contended that the loss was due to "other like perils" as those contained in the principal portion of the perils clause. In holding that the loss was not covered by the policy, the court noted that the general words, following a specific enumeration, must be limited to perils *ejusdem generis* with those specified and that they must be construed with reference to the scope and purpose of a marine insurance policy. Lord Macnaghten said in part in his speech:

> Your Lordships were asked to draw the line and to give an exact and authoritative definition of the expression "perils of the sea" in connection with the general words. For my part I decline to attempt any such task. I do not think it is possible to frame a definition which would include every case proper to be included, and no other. I think that each case must be considered with reference to its own circumstances, and that circumstances of each case must be looked at in a broad com-

---

292. It is to be noted that the American form of policy uses the phrase "all other *like* Perils, Losses and Misfortunes . . . ." The addition of the word "like" contributes nothing, as the canon of *ejusdem generis* would imply the word "like" in any event.

293. (1887) 12 App.Cas. 484.

mon sense view and not be the light of strained analogies and fanciful resemblances.

Lord Herschell said, in part:

> . . . It is, I think, impossible to say that this is damage occasioned by a cause similar to "perils of the sea" on any interpretation which has ever been applied to that term. It will be observed that Lord Ellenborough limits the operation of the clause to "marine damage." By this I do not understand him to mean only damage which has been caused by the sea, but damage of a character to which a marine adventure is subject. Such an adventure has its own perils, to which either it is exclusively subject or which possess in relation to it a special or peculiar character. To secure an indemnity against these is the purpose and object of a policy of marine insurance.[294]

In the following cases, the peril was found to be *ejusdem generis* with one of the perils specifically enumerated:

De Vaux v. J'Anson[295] (vessel broke to pieces by reason of the accidental giving way of her tackle and shoring devices in being moved out of an artificial dock); *Phillips v. Barber*[296] (ship by the violence of wind and weather was thrown over while in a graving dock and was bilged); *Butler v. Wildman*[297] (master of a ship, in order to prevent a quantity of dollars from falling into hands of the enemy, by whom he was about to be attacked, threw the same into the sea and was immediately afterwards captured; held, a loss by jettison and if not jettison in the strict sense, something of the same kind); *The Knight of St. Michael*[298] (cargo of coal enroute from Newcastle, N.S.W., to Peru became so heated as to imperil the cargo and ship; a large portion of the cargo was discharged at an intermediate port, entailing a consequent loss of a portion of the freight; held, if not a loss by fire, it was a loss *ejusdem generis* covered by the general words); *Baxendale v. Fane (The Lapwing)*[299] (negligent berthing of vessel by an acting pilot such that the vessel was damaged by sitting on a block of wood and afterwards on some baulks of timber; held, negligent docking was a fortuitous circumstance which entitled assured to recover for a loss due to a peril *ejusdem generis* with a peril of the sea, namely stranding) *Palmer v. Taylor*,[300] (coolies aboard as passengers murdered master and some members of the crew; held, if not a piratical act, one *ejusdem generis*, and there-

---

294. It is to be emphasized that it was the decision in *Thames & Mersey* which was the genesis of the Inchmaree Clause. See Chapter XIV, "The Inchmaree Clause."
295. (1839) 5 Bing. N.C. 519, 132 E.R. 1200.
296. (1821) 106 E.R. 1151.
297. (1820) 106 E.R. 708.
298. (1898) P. 30, 3 Com.Cas. 62.
299. (1940) P. 112, 19 Asp. M.L.C. 363.
300. (1854) 156 E.R. 492, Ex.Ch.

fore within the general words); *Boehm v. Combe*[301] (goods lost as a consequence of the fraud and negligence of servants of the carrier; held, barratry was large enough to cover the risk even though the loss was not, strictly speaking, due to barratry); *Davidson v. Burnand*[302] (policy on goods; while vessel was loading, her draft was increased to the point where a discharge pipe was brought below surface of water; water flowed down the pipe and, some valves having negligently been left open, flowed thence into the hold and damaged the goods; held, a loss similar in kind to one happening from perils of the sea); *Caldwell v. St. Louis P. Ins. Co.*[303] (collision); *Citizens Ins. Co. v. Glasgow*[304] (explosion); *British A. Ins. Co. v. Joseph*[305] (explosion); *Ellery v. New England Ins. Co.*[306] (vessel blown over in graving dock after discharge of cargo); *Jones v. Nicholson*[307] (master, who was a part owner of the ship, fraudulently sold the cargo; underwriters liable both under "barratry" and also the words "all other perils"); *Babbit v. Sun M. Ins. Co.*[308] (mob of citizens of the Confederacy took possession of ship and cargo); *Symington & Co. v. Union Ins. Soc. of Canton*[309] (fire broke out on a jetty while cork was stored there awaiting shipment; to prevent spread of the fire, part of the cork was jettisoned and seawater thrown on the remainder; held, loss was *ejusdem generis* with "fire" and "jettison"); *Canada Rice Mills, Ltd. v. Union Marine & Gen. Ins. Co., Ltd.*[310] (damage to rice cargo, caused not by incursion of seawater but by closing of ventilators to prevent such incursion, was a loss by perils of the sea and also under the general words); *Feinberg v. Ins. Co. of N.A.*[311] (yacht damaged by vandalism coupled with theft of personal items; held, damage to yacht a loss *ejusdem generis* with "theft"). The latter decision does not seem in accord with the English cases, as the facts disclosed a stealthy entrance into an unoccupied vessel without the necessary element of violence. In *Nishina Trading Co., Ltd. v. Chiyoda Fire and Marine Ins. Co., Ltd.*,[312] the master of the vessel did not discharge the cargo at the port of destination but, instead, pledged it at another port to secure a loan to pay delinquent freight; the court held the loss fell within the general words as *ejusdem generis* with a "taking at sea"; the decision was, however, overruled by *Shell Oil Co. v. Gibbs, supra*, n. 273.

301. (1813) 105 E.R. 347.
302. (1868) L.R. 4 C.P. 117.
303. 1 La.Ann. 85 (1846).
304. 9 Mo. 411 (St.,Mo.).
305. 9 L.C.R. 448 (Can., 1857).
306. 25 Mass. 14 (1829).
307. (1854) 156 E.R. 342.
308. 23 La.Ann. 314 (1871).
309. (1928) 97 L.J.K.B. 646, 31 Ll.L.Rep. 179, C.A.
310. (1940) 4 All E.R. 169, (1941) A.C. 55, 67 Ll.L.Rep. 549, P.C.
311. 260 F.2d 523, 1959 AMC 11 (1st Cir.).
312. [1969] 1 Lloyd's Rep. 293.

In the following cases, the contention that the loss was *ejusdem generis* with a named peril was rejected:

Thames & Mersey Marine Ins. Co. v. Hamilton, Fraser & Co. (1887) *supra* (bursting of air chamber of donkey pump); *Southport Fisheries v. Saskatchewan Government Ins. Office* (1959) *supra* (acid thrown on fishing nets); *Moses v. Sun M. Ins. Co.*[313] (sale and consumption of cargo of provisions at an intermediate port); *Powell v. Gudgeon*[314] (sale of part of a cargo to defray the expense of repairing the ship); *Stott (Baltic) Steamers, Ltd. v. Marten*[315] (ship's tackle broke as it was lowering a boiler into a hold; held, loss not covered by the general words); *Jackson v. Mumford*[316] (breaking of a connecting rod held not *ejusdem generis* with "breakage of shafts" in Inchmaree Clause); *Field S.S. Co. v. Burr*[317] (vessel involved in collision; water entered cargo, which was rendered putrid and had to be discharged by order of authorities; in a claim on the hull policy, recovery was denied for loss of cargo and costs and charges incurred in discharging and disposing of it; the loss was not covered by the general words); *Taylor v. Dunbar*[318] (meat shipped was delayed by tempestuous weather and solely by reason of delay became putrid and was jettisoned; held, not a loss by perils of the sea, or within the general words); *O'Connor v. Merchants' Marine Ins. Co.*[319] (general words not sufficient to entitle assured to recovery for an act of barratry where barratry was not specifically mentioned in the policy as one of the risks insured against); *Commercial Trading Co., Inc. v. Hartford Fire Ins. Co.*[320] (under the criminal barratry clause of an open cargo policy, the peril must be "like" criminal barratry, and to be "like" criminal barratry must at least include a moral characteristic to take the omissions of the master in delivering goods to a person not holding the bill of lading out of the category of negligence, ignorance, or stupidity); *Bolivia Republic v. Indemnity Mutual Marine Assur. Co., Ltd.*[321] (seizure of goods by armed expedition composed of malcontents held not *ejusdem generis* with "pirates"); *Samuel (P) & Co., Ltd. v. Dumas*[322] (scuttling of ship by master and crew with connivance of owner but without connivance or complicity on the part of the mortgagee; held, loss by scuttling not included within the general words); *Shaver Transportation Co. v. Travelers Ins. Co.*[323] (discharge of contaminated caustic soda into tank trucks and sale

313. 1 Duer 159 (St.,N.Y., Sup.Ct., 1852).
314. (1816) 105 E.R. 1100.
315. (1916) 1 A.C. 304, 21 Com.Cas. 114, H.L.
316. (1904) 20 T.L.R. 172, 9 Com.Cas. 114, C.A.
317. (1899) 1 Q.B. 579, 4 Com.Cas. 106, C.A.
318. (1869) L.R. 4 C.P. 206.
319. (1889) 20 N.S.R. 514, 9 C.L.T. 209, *aff'd* 16 S.C.R. 331 (Can.).
320. 466 F.2d 1239, 1972 AMC 2495 (5th Cir.), [1974] Lloyd's Rep. 179.
321. (1909) 1 K.B. 785, 14 Com.Cas. 156, C.A.
322. (1923) 1 K.B. 592, C.A., *aff'd* (1924) A.C. 431, (1924) All E.R. Rep. 66.
323. 481 F.Supp. 892, 1980 AMC 393 (D.,Ore.).

thereof to a chemical salvor to prevent sinking of barge not *ejusdem generis* with "jettison").

It must be emphasized that the term "all other perils" is significant by its absence from the new London hull and cargo clauses. Moreover, the new policy forms do not include the peril "takings at sea." In fact, Clause 4.8 of the exclusions in the B and C cargo forms eliminates coverage " . . . for deliberate damage to or deliberate destruction of the subject-matter insured or any part thereof *by the wrongful act of any person or persons.*"Now that the old "perils" clause is a thing of the past in English policies, and the new policy forms are on a named perils basis, will the *ejusdem generis* rule be applied when a loss occurs which does not fit neatly into the description of the "named perils" in the new forms?[324]

Loss by a Combination of Causes

A loss by a combination of causes, a loss by a single cause amounting to more than one of the perils insured by the policy, and a loss by a combination of causes where one is excepted, are discussed under the general heading of "proximate cause." See Chapter XV, "Proximate Cause," *infra.*

---

324. For example, in *Prohaska v. St. Paul Fire & Marine Ins. Co.*, 265 F. 430, *aff'd* 270 F. 91, *cert.den.* 41 S.Ct. 623, 256 U.S. 702, 65 L.Ed. 1179 (E.D.,La., 1920), it was held that a marine policy insuring against loss from unavoidable dangers of rivers, fires, and jettisons, with no clause extending the risk to analogous dangers, does not cover a loss caused by a peril *ejusdem generis*.

CHAPTER XIII

FREQUENT COVERAGES AND EXCLUSIONS

War Risks

The traditional "perils" clause includes many war-oriented risks such as "Men-of-War . . . Enemies . . . Letters of Mart and Countermart, Surprisals, Takings at Sea, Arrests, Restraints and Detainments of all Kinds, Princes and Peoples, etc." It is, therefore, not surprising that the underwriters became highly nervous about their exposure to grave liabilities in the series of wars in which all nations have been engaged in the last five hundred years. For example, in 1780, at the battle of Cape St. Vincent, a British convoy of 63 merchant ships met up with the combined fleets of France and Spain. Only eight ships escaped unmolested. The effect on underwriters at Lloyd's was nearly catastrophic.

As a practical expedient, the underwriters found it necessary to "split-off" these wartime risks and such war perils are now excluded from coverage under the perils clause in the AIH form by the "free of capture and seizure" clause, abbreviated F. C. & S. Clause, and the War Exclusion Clause (Clause 23) in the new London Institute Time Clauses (hulls) (1983). If war risks are to be covered, they must be covered by the use of separate clauses such as the new Institute War and Strike Clauses. The clauses limit the scope of the risks which would otherwise be covered under the perils clause; i.e., war risk coverage is not as broad as if the free of capture and seizure clause were merely deleted so that the full scope of the perils clause could come into play.

There was no F. C. & S. Clause in the form of policy originally set forth in the First Schedule of the Marine Inaurance Act, 1906. Initially, when the clause was desired to be used by underwriters, it was affixed adhesively to the form of policy. Subsequently, the clause was set forth in the printed form itself. Consequently, unless the clause is deleted, the risks enumerated therein are not covered. If not deleted, it supersedes all the perils enumerated in the policy as to which its terms are antagonistic.[1] If deleted, the risks covered are those mentioned in the perils clause.[2]

---

1. See *Robinson Gold Mining Co. v. Alliance Marine & General Ins. Co. Ltd.*, (1901) 2 K.B. 918, 6 Com.Cas. 244.

2. *Britain S.S. Co. v. The King (The Petersham)*, (1919) 2 K.B. 670, 14 Asp. M.L.C. 507. In short, it is as if the F. C. & S. warranty were not included in the policy from its beginning. Later, separate policies were issued which, in effect, incorporated the marine policy and then stated its coverage as limited to the risks which would be covered by the marine policy but for the F. C. & S. Clause. Subsequently, additional perils were added such as "persons

The derivation of the clauses in use today is instructive and helpful. From 1916 to 1937, the standard F. C. & S. Clause read:

> Warranted free of capture, seizure, arrest, restraint, or detainment, and the consequences thereof or of any attempt thereat (piracy excepted), and also from all consequences of hostilities or war-like operations whether before or after declaration of war.

It was amended in 1937 and again in 1942, the latter amendment being as a consequence of the decision of the House of Lords in *Yorkshire Dale Steamship Co., Ltd. v. Minister of War Transport (The Coxwold)*.[3]

From 1942 until the recent 1983 revisions, the clause in English policies read:

> Warranted free of capture, seizure, arrest, restraint or detainment, and the consequences thereof or of any attempt thereat; also from the consequences of hostilities or warlike operations, whether there be a declaration of war or not; but this warranty shall not exclude collision, contact with any fixed or floating object (other than a mine or torpedo), stranding, heavy weather or fire unless caused directly (and independently of the nature of the voyage or service which the vessel concerned or, in the case of a collision, any other vessel involved therein, is performing) by a hostile act by or against a belligerent power; and for the purpose of this warranty "power" includes any authority maintaining naval, military or air forces in association with a power.
>
> Further warranted free from the consequences of civil war, revolution, insurrection, or civil strife arising therefrom, or piracy.

The net effect of one exclusion, followed by the reinclusion of certain risks, is exemplified in *The Portmar*,[4] which occasioned an opportunity for levity by Justice Frankfurter, as follows:

> . . . Construing such conglomerate provisions requires a skill not unlike that called for in the decipherment of obscure palimpsest texts . . . nor have we any Elder Brethren of Trinity House to help us.

---

acting maliciously." The new London Institute War and Strikes Clauses appear to have abandoned, in form at least, this general approach. Instead, they specify the list of risks which are covered without regard to them having been included or excluded from the marine policy. The 1983 revisions have separated the exclusions into four groups: war, strikes, malicious acts, and nuclear risks. The war risks coverages and exclusions are grouped for easy comparison. Another change in the 1983 revisions has been to place the insurance on the basis of "loss of or damage to the vessel" rather than simply to list the perils and depend upon the terms of the incorporated marine policy (or by implication the Marine Insurance Act, 1906) to quantify the indemnity afforded.

3. (1942) A.C. 691, 73 Ll.L.Rep. 1, 1942 AMC 1000.
4. 345 U.S. 427, 1954 AMC 558 (1953).

The practice in the English market was to delete the F. C. & S. Clause and attach the Institute War Clauses. In *Panamanian Oriental S.S. Corp. v. Wright*,[5] Mocatta, J., said in reference to this practice:

It is probably too late to make an effective plea that the traditional methods of insuring against ordinary marine risks and what are called war risks should be radically overhauled. The present method, certainly as respects war risks insurance, is tortuous and complex in the extreme. It cannot be beyond the wit of underwriters and those who advise them in this age of law reform to devise more straightforward and easily comprehended terms of cover.

This, apparently, is what underwriters have tried to achieve with the new forms.[6]

For example, Exclusions 23.1, 23.2, and 23.3 of the marine form are repeated verbatim as perils covered by the new war clauses 1.1, 1.2, and 1.3. (It sould be noted that 23.2 includes a parenthetical phrase emphasizing that loss of the vessel by piracy or barratry is marine in nature and not excluded as a seizure or capture, etc.)

Exclusions 24.1 and 24.2 of the marine form are specifically covered by war perils clauses 1.4 and 1.5. Clause 1.5 also includes loss or damage caused by "any person acting maliciously or from a political motive" and thus provides coverage which would otherwise be excluded by Exclusions 25.1 and 25.2 of the marine form.

The new war risk form does not provide any coverage for the nuclear risk exclusion set forth in Exclusion 26.

The new war risk form does include coverage for an additional peril, i.e., Clause 1.6 relating to "confiscation or expropriation." Formerly, if confiscations or expropriations occurred as a consequence of a war peril, they would have been covered. They are now covered explicitly, subject to the terms of the Detainment Clause and Exclusions 4.1.4 through 4.1.6.

Prior versions of the War Clauses referred to "hostilities (whether war be declared or not)," and "warlike operations." This occasioned many disputes making it necessary to assess the proximate causes of losses in order to make a distinction between marine and war casualties. These decisions are discussed *infra*.

---

5. [1970] 2 Lloyd's Rep. 365, Q.B., reversed on another ground, [1971] 2 All E.R. 1028, [1971] 1 Lloyd's Rep. 487, C.A.

6. The author wishes to express his sincere appreciation for the assistance available to him in writing this portion of the text from the report of the Sub-Committee on Hulls of the Committee on Marine Insurance, General Average and Salvage of the Maritime Law Association of the United States, the author of which was Sheldon A. Vogel. The report was available in manuscript form at the time this chapter was prepared which was indeed fortunate, as the overall effect and proper interpretation of the new London clauses is still a matter of some conjecture.

Clause 3 of the new War Clauses, denominated "Detainment," did not appear in earlier versions of the War Clauses.[7] However, Section 60 of the Marine Insurance Act defining a constructive total loss would be applicable and, with respect to ships, sub-section (2)(i) is of aid. That sub-section, in relevant part, provides that " . . . there is a constructive total loss where the assured is deprived of his ship . . . by a peril insured against, and (a) it is *unlikely* that he can recover the ship . . . ." Prior to the passage of the 1906 Act, the test appeared to be that of the uncertainty of the recovery, but the courts have been consistent in their interpretation of the word "unlikely" as meaning that the shipowner would be unlikely to recover his vessel *within a reasonable time.*[8]

The new Detainment Clause reads quite clearly and simply:

> 3. In the event the Vessel shall have been the subject of capture seizure arrest restraint detainment confiscation or appropriation, and the Assured shall thereby have lost the free use and disposal of the Vessel for a continuous period of 12 months then for the purpose of ascertaining whether the Vessel is a constructive total loss the Assured shall be deemed to have been deprived of the possession of the Vessel without any likelihood of recovery.

It will be observed that the new clause uses the phrase "free use and disposal" of his vessel. The precise intention for the use of this phrase is not known.

Blocking and Trapping

The new clauses make no mention of losses by "blocking or trapping," but it appears that the London market offers, along with the new War and Strikes Clauses, at no additional premium, a clause providing that the term "restraint" in the War Clauses will be deemed to include:

> . . . the inability of the vessel to sail from any port, canal, waterway or other place to the high seas for a continuous period of 12 months as a result of the closure of the connecting channel of all vessels of such

7. As Mr. Vogel has pointed out, the principle was often achieved by adding the Institute Detainment Clause (1.1.70) to the War Clauses. That wording provided that, if the assured shall have been deprived of the "use and disposal of his vessel" for a continuous period of twelve months by reason of one of the war perils (e.g., capture, seizure, arrest, restraint, or detainment), he shall be deemed to have been "deprived of the possession of his vessel without any likelihood of recovery" for the purposes of determining if the vessel is a Constructive Total Loss.

8. See *Polurrian S.S. Co., Ltd. v. Young*, [1915] 1 K.B. 922, 84 L.J.K.B. 1034; *Hall v. Hayman*, [1912] 2 K.B. 5, 81 L.J.K.B. 509; *Marstrand Fishing Co. v. Beers*, [1936] 56 Ll.L.Rep. 163.

size or draft . . . provided that such closure has arisen through the blockage of the waterway by a warlike act or act of national defense.

Why the phrase "warlike act or act of national defense" was used is not known. It is possible that it was derived from the case of *Owners of the ship Bamburi v. Compton.*[9] There, the vessel sailed to an Iraqi port with a load of cement. It commenced unloading on September 22, 1980. On the same day, Iraq invaded Iran and all movements of all vessels in Iraqi waters were prohibited although neither government asserted any right to the vessel. On September 30 and again on October 14, 1981, slightly over one year later, the owners gave notice of abandonment and the question was whether the vessel was a constructive total loss under the war risks policy covering it. It was held that (1) the proximate cause of the vessel remaining at the Iraqi port was restraint or detainment of people and a peril insured against under the policy; (2) on the facts the owners had been wholly deprived of the free use of their vessel since all movements of the ship had been prohibited; and (3) the owners would be "unlikely" to recover their vessel within a reasonable time which, in the opinion of the court, was a period of 12 months from the date of the notice of abandonment.

Exclusions

The new Exclusions Clause, Clause 4, reads:
This insurance excludes

4.1 loss damage liability or expense arising from

4.1.1 any detonation of any weapon of war employing atomic or nuclear fission and/or fusion or other like reaction or radioactive force or matter, hereinafter called a nuclear weapon of war
4.1.2 the outbreak of war (whether there be a declaration of war or not) between any of the following countries: United Kingdom, United States of America, France, the Union of Soviet Socialist Republics, the People's Republic of China
4.1.3 requisition or pre-emption
4.1.4 capture seizure arrest restraint detainment confiscation or expropriation by or under the order of the government or any public or local authority of the country in which the Vessel is owned or registered
4.1.5 arrest restraint detainment confiscation or expropriation under quarantine regulations or by reason of infringement of any customs or trading regulations

9. [1982] Com.L.R. 31.

4.1.6 the operation of ordinary judicial process, failure to provide security or to pay any fine or penalty or any financial cause

4.2 loss damage liability or expense covered by the Institute Time Clauses—Hull (date) (including 4/4ths Collision Clause) or which would be recoverable thereunder but for Clause 12 thereof,

4.3 any claim for any sum recoverable under any other insurance on the Vessel or which would be recoverable under such insurance but for the existence of this insurance,

4.4 any claim for expenses arising from delay except such expenses as would be recoverable in principle in English law and practice under the York-Antwerp Rules 1974.

It will be seen that the exclusionary sentence has four principal clauses. The first now excludes "loss, damage, *liability* or expense" arising from eight named occurrences. In the previous version, the word "liability" occurred only in the clause excluding coverage of any loss which would be covered by the "standard form of English marine policy including 4/4ths Collision liability." This clause reappears in the new form with the description of the new policy updated to the new Institute Time Clauses (hulls) form.

The nuclear weapons exclusion formerly referred to "hostile" detonations; the word "hostile" has been deleted so that any such detonation is now excluded.

Keeping in mind that confiscation and expropriation have now been added to the perils clause in the new War Clauses, they necessarily have been excluded with respect to orders of the government or under quarantine regulations or for violations of customs or trading regulations—the word "trading" being new.

Although the Marine Insurance Act, 1906, made it clear that "restraint, etc." did not include the operation of ordinary judicial process, it will be noted that the new form specifically excludes restraint by way of ordinary judicial process as well as loss from failure to provide security or to pay any fine or penalty or any financial cause—all matter falling within the ambit of ordinary judicial process.

The exclusion with respect to claims arising from delay except as to claims recoverable in general average reflects an updating to accommodate the 1974 York-Antwerp Rules.

Termination

The only change in the Termination Clause from the earlier version is to shorten the period of time for notice from 14 to 7 days. Cancellation by giving notice is still a condition. However, the insurance can be reinstated if the underwriters and the assured agree as to a new rate of premium and/or condition and/or warranties prior to the expiration of the 7 days.

Automatic termination of coverage still occurs, whether or not notice is given, if there is a detonation of any nuclear weapon of war, upon the outbreak of war between any of the major powers, and upon a requisitioning for title or use.

By contrast, American practice is to combine the F. C. & S. Clause with exclusions with respect to strikes, riots, and civil commotions. As a consequence, the AIH (June, 1977) form contains a clause entitled "War, Strikes and Related Exclusions" reading as follows:

The following conditions shall be paramount and shall supersede and nullify any contrary provisions of the Policy. The Policy does not cover any loss, damage or expense cause by, resulting from, or incurred as a consequence of:

(a) Capture, seizure, arrest, restraint or detainment or any attempt thereat; or

(b) Any taking of the Vessel, by requisition or otherwise, whether in time of peace or war and whether lawful or otherwise; or

(c) Any mine, bomb or torpedo not carried as cargo on board the Vessel; or

(d) Any weapon of war employing atomic or nuclear fission and/or fusion or other like reaction or radioactive force or matter; or

(e) Civil war, revolution, rebellion, insurrection, or civil strife arising therefrom, or piracy, or

(f) Strikes, lockouts, political or labor disturbances, civil commotions, riots, martial law, military or usurped power; or

(g) Malicious acts or vandalism, unless committed by the Master or Mariners and not excluded elsewhere under this War Strikes and Related Exclusions clause; or

(h) Hostilities or warlike operations (whether there be a declaration of war or not) but this subparagraph (h) shall not exclude collision or contact with aircraft, rockets or similar missiles, or with any fixed or floating object, or stranding, heavy weather, fire or explosion unless caused directly by a hostile act by or against a belligerent power which act is independent of the nature of the voyage or service which the Vessel concerned or, in the case of a collision, any other Vessel involved therein, is performed. As used herein, "power" includes authority maintaining naval, military or air forces in association with a power.

If war risks or other risks excluded by this clause are hereafter insured by indorsement on this Policy, such endorsement shall supersede the above conditions only to the extent that the terms of such endorsement are inconsistent therewith and only while such endorsement remains in force.

As noted above, for a time war risks coverage was simply provided by deleting the F. C. & S. Clause; it is now written as a separate contract by attaching a rider to the basic policy. It must, therefore, be construed in relationship to the policy to which it is attached.[10]

During World War I, most of the merchant vessels of Great Britain were requisitioned by the Admiralty under the terms of a charter party known as T.99 which, in essence, provided that the Crown was to bear the risks of war and marine risks were to be borne by the underwriters. Much litigation arose of whether losses were due to marine risks or war risks. The trend of the English courts at that time appears to have been to give a liberal interpretation to what was a marine risk where merchant vessels were involved in carrying commercial cargos to commercial ports.

Britain S.S. Co. v. R. (The Petersham)[11] and *British India Steam Navigation Co. v. Green et al (The Matiana)*[12] illustrate the foregoing. In the former, the vessel while carrying a cargo of iron ore collided with a neutral vessel and sank. Both vessels were navigating without lights pursuant to admiralty instructions. In the latter case, while sailing in convoy and while zigzagging on a course prescribed by the naval escort, the vessel struck a reef. Both losses were held to have been due to marine risks. By contrast, in *Commonwealth Shipping Rep. v. P. & O. Branch Service (The Geelong)*,[13] the *Geelong,* sailing under requisition and carrying general merchandise, collided with the *Bonvilston,* also under requisition, carrying ambulance wagons and other stores from a base in Alexandria, and the *Geelong* was lost. Both vessels were under naval orders, sailing at high speed without lights. The loss was held to have been due to a warlike operation. The distinction seems to have been that the *Bonvilston* was transporting goods as a part of a military operation and from one war base to another.

World War II gave rise to a further spate of cases involving war risks, the most important of which was *Yorkshire Dale S.S. Co. v. Minister of War Transport (The Coxwold).*[14] There, the merchant vessel *Coxwold,* requisitioned by the minister of war transport, and while sailing in convoy and

---

10. See, for example, *Stoomvart Maatschappij Sophie H. v. Merchants' Marine Ins. Co.,* (1919) 89 L.J.K.B. 834, 14 Asp. M.L.C. 497, H.L., where, in addition to the F. C. & S. Clause, the policy also covered "loss . . . through explosions, riots, or other causes of whatever nature arising either on shore or otherwise howsoever." The vessel struck a mine and was lost. In a suit to recover, the court held that the F. C. & S. Clause governed and applied to all warlike acts.
11. [1919] 1 K.B. 575, [1919] 2 K.B. 670, [1921] A.C. 99.
12. [1919] 1 K.B. 632, [1919] 2 K.B. 670, [1921] 1 A.C. 99.
13. [1923] A.C. 191.
14. [1942] 2 All E.R. 6, [1942] A.C. 691.

admittedly engaging in a warlike operation (conveyance of war materials), stranded. There was no negligence on the part of the ship, the stranding being due to a variety of causes, including a deviation pursuant to naval orders coupled with an unexpected tidal set. It was held that the proximate cause of the stranding was the warlike operation. See, also, *Ocean S.S. Co. Ltd. v. Liverpool and London War Risks Ass'n, Ltd.*[15]

It appears the market was rather surprised by the *Coxwold* decision and, as a consequence, the F. C. & S. Clause was amended to exclude from its operation collision, stranding, etc. (other marine risks) unless *caused directly, and independently of, the nature of the voyage concerned, by a hostile act or against a belligerent power.* Thus, under the earlier form, a loss not directly caused by a hostile act was not a war risk but a marine risk.[16]

As Haehl has noted,[17] the method used to insure war and other related risks excluded from the hull policy by the F. C. & S. Clause is "curious." In effect, the F. C. & S. Clause is deleted and the Institute War Risks Clauses are attached. At that time the Institute War Risk Clause excluded arrest, restraints, or detainments, etc. As to this, Haehl noted:

> Arrest, restraint or detainment, like capture, seizure and any taking of the vessel, are the only risks described in the F. C. & S. Clause which are not repeated in the "deemed to include" Risks in the War Risks Clause. Presumably, these are not repeated because the Adventures and Perils Clause of the hull policy includes these traditional war perils either expressly or by clear implication, and the first phrase of the War Risks Clause therefore covers them.

But the end result is not always so simple. For example, in *The Portmar*,[18] there was an excluding warranty against government seizure (by Great Britain or its allies), which had a savings clause attached, limiting its operation if the vessel were not condemned. In that case, the loss occurred during detainment under United States and Australian orders but without any condemnation. The risk was (1) included in the hull policy; (2) excluded by the F. C. & S. Clause; (3) re-included by the War Risks Clause, and would have been (4) re-excluded by the "British seizure" warranty in the War Risks Clause had it not been for the fact that the last exclusion was nullified by the savings clause.

War risks coverage, of course, has its limitations. Generally speaking, risks of loss arising out of outbreak of a major war, a prior hostile act by

---

15. [1947] 63 T.L.R. 594, [1948] A.C. 243.

16. See, generally, 1943 AMC 130, "New British Free of Capture & Seizure Clause—1942."

17. Harry L. Haehl, Jr., The Hull Policy: Coverages and Exclusions Frequently Employed: F. C. & S., War Risks, S. R. & C. C., Automatic Termination, Cancellations, 41 *Tulane Law Review*, 2, (February 1967).

18. 345 U.S. 427, 1954 AMC 558 (1953).

one of the "major war" nations resulting in such a war within ninety days thereafter, and delay or demurrage are excluded. Also, there is a specific limitation with respect to arrest, restraints, or detainments; condemnation is required before the vessel can be abandoned after capture, seizure, or detainment; and claims based upon loss or frustration of the voyage are excluded. Moreover, no form of seizure, restraint, or taking of the vessel is insured if done by the U.S. government or the government of the vessel's ownership or registry or of any country empowered to requisition it.

Commercial underwriters have always been understandably wary of war risk insurance. Consequently, after the onset of World War II, the respective governments entered the field.[19]

Generally speaking, the same risks were insured as in private insurance and the same rules were applied to determine whether particular losses were covered.[20]

Because of the confusion which ensued during World War II with respect to allocation of losses between the marine and war perils, after lengthy negotiations an Overall War-Marine Risk Settlement Agreement was reached between the War Shipping Administration of the United States and the American and British underwriters.[21] The compromise disposed of literally hundreds of major cases which, if it had been necessary to litigate them, would have been an almost impossible task.

Historically, as already observed, marine risks have been separated from war risks and this principle has been uniformly followed.[22] And, as has already been noted, automatic termination and cancellation provisions are included in the war risks coverages which permit underwriters to terminate such risks on very short notice.

Initially, the courts seemed inclined to veer toward holding losses to be marine risks unless the proximate cause was clearly due to war or a

---

19. In 1940, the U. S. Maritime Commission was authorized to provide insurance and re-insurance against war risks. See 54 Stat. 689, 690 (1940).

20. Haehl, n. 16, *supra,* citing *Standard Oil Co. v. U.S. (The Llama),* 267 U.S. 76, 1925 AMC 323 (1925).

21. See 1945 AMC 1014 where the agreement is set forth. A schedule attached to the agreement sets forth definitions and includes a complete dissertation of the principles upon which the settlement was based, with amplifying discussion of the American and British decisions. The settlement disposed of over 400 cases, of which all but 62 were major casualties, 256 being collisions. Of the major cases, 266 were accepted as marine risks, 63 were war risks, and 13 collision cases were divided under special terms. Of the 62 lesser fueling, bumping, and surging cases, 20 were war risks, 10 were marine risks, and 32 were divided on the basis of mutual fault.

22. As early as the Civil War in the United States, the federal government, by one means or another, has assumed war risks on merchant vessels. See *Baker v. U.S. (Schooner Manhasset),* 3 Ct. Cl. 76 (1867); *Mauran v. Alliance Ins. Co.,* 73 U.S. 1 (1868); *Clyde v. U.S.,* 9 Ct. Cl. 184 (1873); *Morgan v. U.S.,* 81 U.S. 531 (1872); *Standard Oil Co. v. U.S. (The Llama),* 267 U.S. 76 (1925), 1925 AMC 323.

warlike risk.[23] However, beginning in the 1920s a trend began to develop holding such losses due to war risks.[24] This trend culminated in *The Coxwold*, and, as already noted, resulted in the amendment to the F. C. & S. Clause which, in effect, reinstituted the emphasis on marine perils.[25]

Although the U. S. Supreme Court has noted that there are "special reasons for keeping in harmony with the marine insurance laws of England, the great field of this business,"[26] that Court has not always been so impressed with the desireability of "uniformity" as one might wish.[27] Nonetheless, if a trend can be discerned in recent years, it would appear that the decision in *Wilburn Boat* may well have lost some of its vitality and, hopefully, the principle of uniformity will continue to merit judicial approbation.[28]

Hostilities

What are hostilities? Lord Wrenbury in *The Petersham*[29] defined the term as follows:

> All the decisions have, I think, proceeded, and in my judgment have rightly proceeded, upon the footing that the word "hostilities" does not mean "the existence of a state of war," but means "acts of hostility,"

---

23. *Britain S.S. Co. v. R. (The Petersham)* (1921), *supra; British India Steam Navigation Co. v. Green (The Matiana)*, (1921), *supra; Morgan v. U.S.* (1872), *supra; Ionides v. Universal Marine Ins. Co.*, 143 E.R. 445 (1863); *Larchgrove v. R.*, (1919) 1 Ll. L. Rep. 408, 498.

24. See *Adelaide S.S. Co. v. R. (The First Warilda)*, [1923] A.C. 292, H.L.; *Commonwealth Shipping Rep. v. P. & O. Branch Service (The Geelong)*, [1923] *supra; Liverpool & London War Risks Ins. Ass'n Ltd. v. Marine Underwriters of the S.S. Richard de Larrinaga*, [1921] 2 A.C. 141; *Ard Coasters v. Attorney General*, [1921] 2 A.C. 141.

25. See 1943 AMC 130 with the accompanying note which lists some of the English decisions which were "neutralized" by the new clause. And, following *The Coxwold*, attention is directed to *Athel Line Ltd. v. Liverpool and London War Risks Ins. Ass'n Ltd*, (1946) 79 Ll.L.Rep. 18, 62 T.L.R. 81, C.A.; *Ocean Steamship Co., Ltd. v. Liverpool & London War Risks Ins. Ass'n, Ltd.*, (1947) 81 Ll.L.Rep. 1, 63 T.L.R. 594, H.L.; *Willis Steamship Co., Ltd. v. United Kingdom Mutual War Risks Ass'n Ltd.*, (1947) 80 Ll.L.Rep. 398; *Costain-Blankevoort (U.K.) Dredging Co. v. Davenport (Inspector of Taxes)*, [1979] 1 Lloyd's Rep. 395. In *Costain-Blankevoort*, the court had occasion to consider the F. C. & S. Clause as amended in 1943. In that case, a dredge while dredging a harbor was sunk through the explosion of shells dumped in the harbor at the end of World War II. Although the case involved a dredging contractor's taxable status, the point at issue was whether the loss was due to a war risk, defined in the taxing regulations as a risk excluded by the F. C. & S. Clause. Mr. Justice Walton held that the loss of the dredge was not a consequence of a warlike operation, since the disposal of war materials after the conclusion of the war was an act of pacification rather than a warlike operation. Moreover, he opined that the dumped shells fell within the expression "fixed or floating objects (other than a mine or torpedo)" as used in the clause.

26. See *Queen Ins. Co. v. Globe & Rutgers Fire Ins. Co. (The Napoli)*, 263 U.S. 487, 1924 AMC 107 (1924).

27. See *Wilburn Boat Co. v. Fireman's Fund Ins. Co.*, 348 U.S. 310, 1955 AMC 467.

28. See discussion on decisions after *Wilburn Boat* in Chapter I, "Introduction."

29. [1921] 1 A.C. 99.

or (to use the noun substantive which follows) "operations of hostility."
The sentence may be read "all consequences of operations of hostility
(of war), or operations warlike (similar to operations of war) whether
before or after declaration of war." To attribute to the word the longer
meaning viz "all consequence of the existence of a state of war" would
give the expression a scope far beyond anything which one can con-
ceive as intended. To define the meaning of "operation" in this connection is, no doubt, a matter of great difficulty, and for the purpose
of these cases is not, I think, necessary.[30]

Warlike Operations

The U. S. Supreme Court has declared that the term "warlike operations
is broader and relates generally to operations in time of war.[31] In *Clan
Line Steamers, Ltd. v. Liverpool & London War Risks Ins. Ass'n, Ltd.*, Justice
Atkinson said of warlike operations:[32]

The conclusion at which I have arrived from a careful examination
of the authorities to which I have referred is that a warlike operation is
one which forms part of an actual or intended belligerent act or series
of acts by combatant forces; that part may be performed preparatory

---

30. In *Liverpool & London War Risks Ins. Ass'n, Ltd. v. Marine Underwriters of the S.S.
Richard de Larrinaga*, [1921] 2 A.C. 141, the court noted that operations in war and operations of war are not necessarily the same thing. See, for example, *Atlantic Mutual Ins. Co. v. R.
(The Tennyson)*, [1919] 1 K.B. 307 (fire and explosion aboard a vessel caused by bombs placed
on board by an enemy agent—a hostile act); *Leyland Shipping Co. v. Norwich Union Fire Ins.
Soc. (The Ikaria)*, [1918] A.C. 350 (merchant vessel torpedoed, taken to port where she later
sank—a hostile act); and *Stoomvart Maatschappij Sophie H. v. Merchants' Marine Ins. Co., Ltd.*,
(1919) 89 L.J.K.B. 834, 14 Asp. M.L.C. 497, H.L. (vessel struck a mine—a hostile act).
    31. *Queen Ins. Co. v. Globe & Rutgers Fire Ins. Co. (The Napoli)*, 263 U.S. 487, 1924 AMC
107 (1924). See, also, *Panama Transp. Co. v. U.S. (Esso Balboa—Mobilgas)*, 155 F.Supp. 699,
1957 AMC 1898 (S.D.N.Y.). See *Harrisons, Ltd. v. Shipping Controller*, [1920] 1 K.B. 122; *Clan
Line Steamers, Ltd. v. Board of Trade (The Clan Matheson)*, [1929] A.C. 514. The Overall War-
Marine Risk Settlement Agreement, 1945 AMC 1014, 1034, defined the term to mean "any
action of the enemy itself . . . seeking to capture, or damage or destroy any vessels or cargo,
as by means of bombs, torpedoes, mines or shells, or any similar action against the enemy.
Any loss resulting directly from the 'hostilities' as so defined shall be a war risk," citing *The
Coxwold, supra.*
    32. [1942] 2 All E.R. 367, K.B.D. See, also, *Pan American World Airways, Inc. v. Aetna
Casualty and Surety Co. et al*, 505 F.2d 989 (2d Cir., 1974), [1975] 1 Lloyd's Rep. 77 (plaintiff's
aircraft while on a scheduled flight from Brussels to New York was hijacked by two men,
members of the Popular Front for the Liberation of Palestine (PFLP), who ordered the aircraft to Beirut where it was loaded with explosives and then flown to Cairo where it was
blown up and totally destroyed; held, the policy exclusion of warlike operations did not
extend to hijacking of any aircraft by a political group; i.e., the term "warlike operations"
could not be extended to include infliction of intentional violence of political groups, neither employed by nor representing any government, where the avowed pupose was not co-
ercion and conquest but the striking of spectacular blows for propaganda effect.).

to the actual act or acts of belligerency, but there must be a connection sufficiently close between the act in question and the belligerent act or acts to enable a tribunal to say with at least some modicum of common sense . . . that it formed part of acts of belligerency. If military equipment is being taken in a ship to a place behind the fighting front from which the forces engaged, or about to be engaged on that front, may be supplied, that ship may beyond any question be said to be taking part in a warlike operation. If a ship is bringing home such equipment after it has been employed on a fighting front, or had been lying available for and at the service of a fighting front, again beyond question, in view of the decisions, she is taking part in a military operation.

Clearly, ships of war engaged in a mission for their governments are engaged in warlike operations.[33]

Equally clearly, ships requisitioned by or under the control of governments and employed in duties relating to the fighting forces or as merchantmen navigating under special conditions necessitated by war are also engaged in warlike operations.[34]

33. *Britain S.S. Co. v. R. (The Petersham)*, [1919] 1 K.B. 575, [1919] 2 K.B. 670, [1921] A.C. 99; *Ard Coasters, Ltd. v. Attorney General*, [1921] 2 A.C. 141 (destroyer patrolling for enemy submarines); *British & Foreign S.S. Co. v. R. (The St. Oswald)*, [1918] 2 K.B. 879; *Liverpool & London War Risks Ins. Ass'n Ltd. v. Marine Underwriters of the S.S. Richard de Larrinaga*, [1921] 2 A.C. 141, 7 Ll.L.Rep. 151, H.L. (warship proceeding to her station to assume duties as a convoy escort); *British India Steam Navigation Co. v. Green et al (The Matiana)*, [1921] 1 A.C. 99, 4 Ll.L.Rep. 245 (warship convoying merchantmen); *Caroline (Owners) v. War Risk Underwriters*, [1921] 7 Ll.L.Rep. 56, K.B.D. (armed trawler leading a convoy blew up as a result of a mine or torpedo and two other vessels came into collision in the confusion); *Hain S.S. Co., Ltd. v. Board of Trade*, [1929] A.C. 534, 34 Ll.L.Rep. 197 (U. S. mine layer returning to the United States with mines aboard collided with another vessel shortly after the Armistice; held, engaged in a "warlike operation"); *Adelaide S.S. Co. v. The Crown (No. 1)*, [1923] A.C. 292, 14 Ll.L.Rep. 341, H.L. (hospital ship requisitioned by the admiralty collided with another vessel); *Link v. General Ins. Co. (Eastern Prince—Roustabout)*, 56 F.Supp. 275 (W.D., Wash.), 1944 AMC 727, 77 Ll.L.Rep. 431, *aff'd* 173 F.2d 955, 1948 AMC 438 (9th Cir.) (U. S. naval tanker collided with a Canadian merchant vessel).

34. *Adelaide S.S. Co. v. The Crown (No. 1)*, [1923] A.C. 292; *Commonwealth Shipping Rep. v. P. & O. Branch Service (The Geelong)*, [1923] A.C. 91; *Atlantic Trasport Co. v. The Crown and Elders & Fyffes v. The Crown*, [1922] 9 Ll.L.Rep. 370; *Standard Oil Co. v. U.S. (The Llama)*, 267 U.S. 76, 1925 AMC 323 (American steamer stopped off the Orkneys by a British naval officer and four ratings were placed on board. While enroute, on a route approved by the British naval officer, she stranded; held, a war risk); *Calmar S.S. Corp. v. Scott (The Portmar)*, 345 U.S. 427, 1953 AMC 952 (vessel under charter to the United States was directed in her movements by the U. S. Navy; while in Darwin, Australia, she was sunk by Japanese bombs; held, a war risk); *Battat v. Home Ins. Co.*, 56 F.Supp. 967, 1946 AMC 1249 (N.D.,Cal.) (Norwegian ship subject to British navy orders; the ship, pursuant to such orders and the master's own judgment, put back into port where the plaintiff's cargo was sold at a loss; held, a war risk). See, also, *Hamdi & Ibrahim v. Reliance Ins. Co.*, 291 F.2d 427, 1961 AMC 1987 (2d Cir.), where cargo underwriters agreed, in consideration of an extra premium, to amend a cargo policy so as to cover routing of the goods via Beirut instead of via Haifa. The goods were lost while awaiting transportation at Haifa due to what the court called "warlike operations" and the cargo underwriters were held liable. Attention is also directed to *Santo Domingo*, 272 F.Supp. 540, 1968 AMC 250 (S.D.N.Y.), and *Flota Mercante v. American Manufac-*

Difficulties arise when peaceful merchantmen pursuing a commercial voyage are involved in collisions with vessels engaged in warlike operations. The American and English decisions are not in the least in accord. For example, in *Adelaide S.S. Co. v. Attorney General (The Warilda)*,[35] the vessel was requisitioned by the admiralty as a hospital ship, and while carrying wounded soldiers and proceeding at full speed without lights, collided with a merchantman. The House of Lords held that the collision was the result of a warlike operation notwithstanding that the sole cause of the collision was negligent navigation on the part of the requisitioned vessel. But, in *Standard Oil Co. v. U.S. (The John Worthington)*,[36] the collision was between a tanker and a minesweeper then engaged in sweeping mines off New York harbor. Negligent navigation on the part of both vessels contributed to the collision. The tanker was covered by a government war risks policy and its owner contended that the government was responsible as a matter of law. The Supreme Court, in affirming the court of appeals, declined to follow the English precedents although giving lip service to the principle of according "respect to established doctrines of English maritime law." Essentially, the Supreme Court agreed with the court of appeals that the warlike phase of the minesweeper's operation was not a proximate cause of the collision. At the same time, the Supreme Court also decided *Libby, McNeil & Libby v. U.S. (The David Branch)*,[37] involving a stranding of a merchant vessel demise chartered to the United States and manned by a civilian crew. It was held that the stranding was a marine peril and not a war risk as the cause was the helmsman turning the wheel the wrong way. Other factors, such as high speed and an erratic compass rendered so by demagnetization of the ship, were held to be conditions and not causes.

However, where the collision with a vessel on a warlike operation is the consequence of the sole negligence of a private merchantman, it would appear that the loss falls upon the marine underwriters.[38]

---

turers, 312 F.Supp. 57, 1970 AMC 1678 (S.D.N.Y.), involving loss of vessels by U. S. Army gunfire directed against Dominican rebels who had seized the vessels.

35. [1923] A.C. 292. See, also, *Mazarakis Bros. v. Furness, Withy & Co.,* [1924] 18 Ll.L.Rep. 152; *Link v. General Ins. Co. (Eastern Prince—Roustabout),* n. 33, *supra; Muller v. Globe & Rutgers Fire Ins. Co. of City of New York,* 246 F. 759 (2d Cir., 1917).

36. 340 U.S. 54, 1951 AMC 1, [1951] 2 Lloyd's Rep. 36.

37. 340 U.S. 71, 1951 AMC 14.

38. See, also, *Queen Ins. Co. of America v. Globe & Rutgers Fire Ins. Co. (The Napoli),* 263 U.S. 487, 1924 AMC 107; *Petter,* 59 F.Supp. 470, 1945 AMC 109 (S.D.N.Y.) (Norwegian freighter was warned off the coast of France and urged to go to Falmouth. While approaching Falmouth, she was accosted by a British trawler who signaled her to "follow me"; in so doing, she stranded on a shoal, damaging both ship and cargo; held, in a suit on the cargo policy, to be a marine risk and not a war risk); *Sea Pride,* 1945 AMC 1456 (Arb.) (fishing vessel while entering harbor collided with a submarine net or a dolphin supporting it; held, the sole cause of the collision was negligent navigation on the part of the fishing vessel and, therefore, a marine peril); *Halifax Ins. Co. v. Mehdi Dilmolghani & Co.,* 92 F.Supp. 747, 1950

A clear distinction must, however, be drawn with respect to voyages being performed by merchantmen under the altered conditions necessitated by war, such as navigation without lights or proceeding in convoy. As Templeman on Marine Insurance notes,[39] the fact of a merchantman operating at night without lights does not of itself constitute a warlike operation. They are merely pursuing their peaceful errands as merchantmen; the incident of navigating with lights obscured is with a view to evading enemy warships or submarines. It therefore follows that a collision occurring between merchantmen consequent on their being navigated under these conditions is a marine risk and not a war risk; it is merely a consequence of a peaceful voyage having to be performed under conditions rendered necessary for safety by the existence of a state of war.[40]

While in convoy, merchantmen are deemed to be proceeding on a "peaceful" voyage, albeit under altered conditions, although the escorting vessels are, perforce, engaged in warlike operations. Consequently, in most instances, a collision between two merchantmen while proceeding in convoy would be a marine risk and not a war risk.[41]

Instances can and do occur, however, where damage or loss to merchantmen resulted from altered circumstances deemed sufficient to convert what would normally be considered a marine risk into a war risk. For example, in *Muller v. Globe & Rutgers Fire Ins. Co. of City of New York*,[42] the vessel grounded and sank while proceeding in accordance with directions from a belligerent war vessel in an area in which the aids to navigation had been removed for belligerent purposes. The grounding and sinking were held to be a war risk with the court expressly basing its decision upon the prior and continuing restraint on the vessel through the control of a naval officer placed on board.

AMC 1120 (S.D.N.Y.) (cargo loss in a collision between two merchant vessels in a wartime anchorage at the north end of Cape Cod Canal at night; held, loss due to a marine peril); *Esso Charleston (War Risk Ins.),* 221 F.2d 805, 1955 AMC 1191 (2d Cir.) (two vessels collided at the entrance of the submarine net at Casablanca where traffic was controlled by the U.S. Navy; held, the vessels were not engaged in a "warlike operation" and therefore were not covered by the war risk insurance policy); *Esso Balboa—Mobilgas,* 155 F.Supp. 699, 1957 AMC 1898 (S.D.N.Y.) (dominant effective cause held to be faulty navigation, i.e., failure to allow for the effect of a 2-knot current, and not a war risk).

39. *Templeman on Marine Insurance,* (5th ed.), R. J. Lambert (McDonald & Evans, 1981). Unquestionably one of the best texts available on marine insurance.

40. *Britain S.S. Co. v. R. (The Petersham),* [1921] 1 A.C. 99; *Queen Ins. Co. of America v. Globe & Rutgers Fire Ins. Co. (The Napoli),* 263 U.S. 487, 1924 AMC 107 (1924); *Halifax Ins. Co. v. Mehdi Dilmoghani & Co.,* 92 F.Supp. 747, 1950 AMC 1220 (S.D.N.Y.); *Esso Charleston (War Risk Ins.),* 221 F.2d 805, 1955 AMC 1191 (2d Cir.); *Morgan v. U.S.,* 81 U.S. 531 (1872).

41. See n. 40, *supra,* and *British India Steam Navigation Co. v. Green at al (The Matiana),* [1921] A.C. 99; *Christ, Adm'r v. U.S.,* 163 F.2d 145, 1947 AMC 932 (3rd Cir.) (in the absence of any evidence that a vessel was actually *ordered* to join a convoy, the practical necessity of doing so will not be considered to be a "restraint."

42. 246 F. 759 (2d Cir., 1917).

In *Hindustan S.S. Co. v. Admiralty Commissioners,*[43] a steamer was under requisition to the Admiralty. It was originally engaged to carry a cargo of steam coal to Malta, but on arrival there the coal was not discharged and the vessel took on a further load of oil and naval stores. She was then ordered on to Tenedos where she was used as a supply ship for a submarine flotilla. Notwithstanding several warnings by the master that a danger of spontaneous combustion existed because of the coal on board, the coal was kept on board for more months. Finally, a fire did break out due to spontaneous combustion. The court held that since the vessel had been engaged in a warlike operation, the loss by fire was a war risk.

In *Caroline v. War Risk Underwriters,*[44] a collision occurred between two merchantmen who were scattering in convoy following an explosion of an armed trawler and the subsequent dropping of depth charges by escorting vessels. The collision and subsequent sinking of one of the merchantmen was held to be a war risk.[45]

In summary, it is instructive to compare the cases holding the loss to be due to warlike operations[46] with those holding the loss to be due to

---

43. [1921] 8 Ll.L.Rep. 230.

44. [1921] 7 Ll.L.Rep. 56.

45. *Henry & McGregor v. Marten & North of England Protection & Indemnity Ass'n,* (1918) 34 T.L.R. 504 (master of a merchantman came across a semi-submerged object and thinking it to be a submarine, rammed it in order to destroy it; held, a war risk); *Standard Oil Co. v. U.S. (The Llama),* 267 U.S. 76, 1925 AMC 323 (American steamer boarded by a British naval officer and ratings and ordered into Kirkwall; while enroute on a course approved by the naval officer, she stranded on a submerged reef and was lost; held, a war risk); *The Ada,* 241 N.Y. 197, 149 N.E. 830, 1925 AMC 393 (St.,N.Y.) (Swedish neutral steamer enroute from Sweden to New York was detained in English waters and compelled to make an extra North Sea voyage with Engish cargo during which voyage it was torpedoed by a German submarine; held, proximate cause of the loss was a war risk, the torpedoing).

46. *Liverpool and London War Risks Ins. Ass'n v. Marine Underwriters of S.S. Richard de Larrinaga,* [1921] 7 Ll.L.Rep. 151, H.L.; *Hindustan Steam Shipping Co. v. Admiralty Commissioners,* (1921) 8 Ll.L.Rep. 230, K.B.D.; *Attorney General v. Ard Coasters,* (1921) 2 A.C. 141, H.L.; *Adelaide S.S. Co. v. The Crown (The Warilda),* (1923) 14 Ll.L.Rep. 341, H.L.; *Board of Trade v. Hain S.S. Co.,* (1929) A.C. 534, H.L.; *Peninsula and Oriental Branch Service v. Commonwealth Shipping Representative (The Geelong),* (1922) 13 Ll.L.Rep. 230, H.L.; *Athel Line Ltd. v. Liverpool and London War Risks Ins. Ass'n, Ltd.,* (1946) 79 Ll.L.Rep. 18, 62 T.L.R. 81, C.A.; *Mazarakis Bros. v. Furness, Withy & Co.,* (1924) 18 Ll.L.Rep. 152, C.A.; *Ocean Steamship Co. Ltd. v. Liverpool and London War Risks Ins. Ass'n, Ltd.,* (1947) 81 Ll.L.Rep. 1, 63 T.L.R. 594, H.L.; *Yorkshire Dale S.S. Co. v. Minister of War Transport (The Coxwold),* [1942] A.C. 691; *Eagle Oil Transport Co. v. Board of Trade,* (1925) 23 Ll.L.Rep. 301, K.B.D.; *Atlantic Transport Co. v. R. (The Maryland),* (1921) 9 Ll.L.Rep. 370, K.B.D.; *Charente S.S. Co. v. Director of Transports,* (1922) 10 Ll.L.Rep. 514, C.A.; *Muller v. Globe & Rutgers Fire Ins. Co. of City of New York,* 246 F. 759 (2d Cir., 1917); *Standard Oil Co. v. U.S. (The Llama),* 267 U.S. 76, 1925 AMC 323; *The Ada,* 241 N.Y. 197, 149 N.E. 830, 1925 AMC 393 (St.,N.Y.); *Link v. General Ins. Co. (Eastern Prince—Roustabout),* 56 F.Supp. 275, 1944 AMC 727 (W.D.,Wash.), 77 Ll.L.Rep. 431, *aff'd* 173 F.2d 955, 1948 AMC 438 (9th Cir.); *Calmar S.S. Corp. v. Scott (The Portmar),* 345 U.S. 427, 1953 AMC 952; *Battat v. Home Ins. Co.,* 56 F.Supp. 967, 1946 AMC 1249 (N.D.,Cal.); *Caroline v. War Risk Underwriters,* [1921] 7 Ll.L.Rep. 56; *Hamdi & Ibrahim v. Reliance Ins. Co.,* 291 F.2d 437, 1961 AMC 1987 (2d Cir.); *Santo Domingo,* 272 F.Supp. 540, 1968 AMC 250 (S.D.N.Y.); *Flota Mercante v. American Manufacturers,* 312 F.Supp. 57, 1970 AMC 1678 (S.D.N.Y.); *Northwestern S.S. Co. v. Maritime Ins. Co.,* 161 F. 166 (9th Cir., 1908); *International Dairy Engineering v. American Home,* 1971

marine risks,[47] keeping in mind, however, the different emphasis resulting from the amendment of the F.C. & S. Clause in 1943 as a consequence of *The Coxwold.*

Consequences of Hostilities or Warlike Operations

It will be remembered that the former F.C. & S. Clause in the Institute Time Clauses (hulls) was warranted free of " . . . the *consequences* of hostilities or warlike operations, whether there be a declaration of war or not." The AIH form (1977) echoed in part this language but there the language is somewhat more expansive, reading: "This Policy does not cover any loss, damage or expense caused by, resulting from, or incurred as a *consequence of* . . . hostilities or warlike operations (whether there be a declaration of war or not) . . . ." The new London clauses use the terminology "caused by," and the phrase "consequences of" does not appear.

Likewise, under the old War Risks Clauses and under the wording of the AIH (1977) form, the assured was bound to prove that the loss occurred as a *consequence* of hostilities or warlike operations. In short, the question was simply one of proximate causation. Any incident that might be remotely attributed to a state of war did not necessarily occur as a consequence of a state of war. In this context, the remarks of Viscount Simon

---

AMC 1001 (N.D.,Cal.); *Ope Shipping v. Allstate Ins.,* 687 F.2d 639, 1983 AMC 22 (2d Cir.) (the "real efficient cause" of the loss of Nicaraguan vessels to shipowners was not barratry by their crews in sailing to ports friendly to the Sandinista revolutionary party, but rather the Nicaraguan civil war, an excluded peril under the policy's War, Strikes and Related Exclusions Clause).

47. *Admiralty Commissioners v. Brynawel S.S. Co.,* (1923) 17 Ll.L.Rep. 89, K.B.D.; *Clan Line Steamers, Ltd. v. Liverpool and London War Risks Ins. Ass'n, Ltd.,* [1942] 73 Ll.L.Rep. 165; *Clan Line Steamers, Ltd. v. Board of Trade (The Clan Matheson),* (1929) A.C. 514; *Harrison's Ltd. v. Shipping Controller,* [1920] 4 Ll.L.Rep. 429, C.A.; *Moor Line v. King and United Kingdom Mutual War Risks Ass'n,* (1920) 4 Ll.L.Rep. 286, K.B.D.; *Wynnstay S.S. Co. v. Board of Trade,* (1925) 23 Ll.L.Rep. 278; *Larchgrove (Owners) v. R.,* (1919) 1 Ll.L.Rep. 408, 498; *Britain S.S. Co. v. R. (The Petersham),* [1921] A.C. 99, H.L.; *Ocean S.S. Co., Ltd. v. Liverpool and London War Risks Ins. Ass'n, Ltd.,* [1947] 63 T.L.R. 594, [1948] A.C. 243; *British Indian Steam Navigation Co. v. Green, et al (The Matiana),* [1921] A.C. 99; *Willis S.S. Co., Ltd. v. United Kingdom Mutual War Risks Ass'n, Ltd.,* (1947) 80 Ll.L.Rep. 398; *Morgan v. U.S.,* 81 U.S. 531 (1872); *Panama Transp. Co. v. U.S. (Esso Balboa—Mobilgas),* 155 F.Supp. 699, 1957 AMC 1898 (S.D.N.Y.); *Esso Charleston (War Risks Ins.),* 221 F.2d 805, 1955 AMC 1191 (2d Cir.); *Esso Manhattan (Split Ship),* 1953 AMC 1152 (S.D.N.Y.); *Queen Ins. Co. of America v. Globe & Rutgers Fire Ins. Co. (The Napoli),* 262 U.S. 487, 1924 AMC 107; *Petter,* 59 F.Supp. 470, 1945 AMC 109 (S.D.N.Y.); *Sea Pride,* 1945 AMC 1456 (Arb.); *Halifax Ins. Co. v. Mehdi Dilmoghani & Co.,* 92 F.Supp. 747, 1950 AMC 1220 (S.D.N.Y.); *Standard Oil Co. v. U.S. (The John Worthington),* 340 U.S. 54, 1951 AMC 1; *Libby, McNeil & Libby v. U.S. (The David W. Branch),* 340 U.S. 71, 1951 AMC 14; *Christ, Adm'r v. U.S.,* 163 F.2d 145, 1947 AMC 932 (3rd Cir.); *Costain-Blankevoort (U.K.) Dredging Co., Ltd. v. Davenport (Inspector of Taxes),* [1979] 1 Lloyd's Rep. 395; *Pan American World Airways, Inc. v. Aetna Casualty and Surety Co., et al,* 505 F.2d 989, [2d Cir., 1974], [1975] 1 Lloyd's Rep. 77 (aircraft case); *American Airlines, Inc. v. Hope: Banque Sabbag S.A.A. v. Hope,* [1974] 2 Lloyd's Rep. 301, H.L. (aircraft case).

in *Yorkshire Dale S.S. Co., Ltd. v. Minister of War Transport (The Coxwold)*, *supra*, are instructive. He said, in part:

> It is not correct to say that, because a vessel is engaged in a warlike operation, therefore everything that happens to her during her voyage is proximately caused by a warlike operation or is a proximate consequence of a warlike operation. Neither is it correct to say that because the accident is a kind which arises from a marine risk (e.g. stranding or collision), therefore the particular accident can in no circumstances be regarded as the consequence of a warlike operation. The truth lies between these two extremes. It seems to me that there is no abstract proposition, the application of which will provide the answer in every case, except this: one has to ask oneself what was the effective and predominant cause of the accident that happened, whatever the nature of that accident may be. It is well settled that a marine risk does not become a war risk merely because the conditions of war may make it more probable that the marine risk will operate and the loss will be caused. It is for this reason that sailing without lights, or sailing in convoy, are regarded as circumstances which do not in themselves convert marine risks into war risks. But where the facts as found by the Judge establish that the operation of a war peril is the "proximate" cause of the loss in the above sense, then the conclusion that the loss is due to war risk follows.

The U. S. Supreme Court first had occasion to construe the phrase "all consequences . . . of hostilities or warlike operations" in *Queen Ins. Co. v. Globe & Rutgers Fire Ins. Co.*, *supra*. In that case, two insurance policies had been issued—one an ordinary marine policy and the other a war risk policy. The court of appeal, feeling obliged to follow the construction of the phrase adopted by the English courts, held that a loss by collision between two vessels sailing in convoy and without lights in time of war was a marine risk and not a loss due to "warlike operations." The Supreme Court affirmed, noting (per Justice Holmes) that "there are special reasons for keeping in harmony with the marine insurance law of England."

In 1950, the phrase again came before the Court in *Standard Oil Co. v. U.S. (The John Worthington)*, *supra*, discussed heretofore. The court of appeals refused to follow the English cases and found, contrary to the trial court, that the warlike phase of the minesweeper's operation was not a proximate cause of the collision. The Supreme Court affirmed. It is noteworthy that Justice Black, writing for the majority, saw fit to point out that the English cases relied upon by the shipowner (among which was *The Coxwold*) had occasioned a revision of the policy provisions resulting in the amended F. C. & S. Clause which sought to avoid the effect of those decisions.

In *Ocean S.S. Co., Ltd. v. Liverpool and London War Risks Ins. Ass'n, Ltd. (The Priam)*,[48] the vessel was carrying cargo, the majority of which consisted of war stores some of which was carried on deck. As a consequence of heavy weather, some of the deck cargo shifted, damaging the hatch covers and allowing seawater to enter the hold. Notwithstanding the entry of seawater, a high speed was maintained together with the zigzagging because of fear of enemy submarines, resulting in further damage to the vessel. The House of Lords, in effect, segregated the damages, holding that the damage to the hatches and covers and due to the flooding of the hold was the consequence of warlike operations. The remainder of the damage to the vessel was held due to heavy weather, aggravated by the manner in which the vessel was navigated during war conditions. Lord Porter commented in his speech:

> . . . Where the ship is struck and injured by the sea, in substance it is not the movement of the vessel, but the motion of the sea which causes the damage. The doctrine has never been extended to cover mere sea damage without more. Possibly, it may cover a case where the ship is pressed into the sea for war purposes. No such act was done in the present case, and damage caused by the force of wind is not, in my view, war damage even though it would not have occurred if the vessel had not zigzagged or kept her speed, provided, of course, that her action in doing so did not differ from that which a ship carrying an ordinary mercantile cargo would undertake in the conditions of war.

A further illustration is *Willis S.S. Co., Ltd. v. United Kingdom Mutual War Risks Ass'n, Ltd.*,[49] in which the insured vessel, carrying war stores, arrived at port on her outward voyage with damage to her tailshaft. The shaft was found to be misaligned. Repairs were made before the vessel commenced her homeward voyage. During the repairs, it was found that the lining in the tailshaft was excessively worn. The assured contended that excessive wearing was due to having to maintain an excessive speed during heavy weather which, in turn, caused excessive vibration and the consequent misalignment of the shaft. The court held that the damage to the shaft was not due to the alleged war risk but instead was due to a faulty lining of the tailshaft. The court said, in part:

> . . . If I were satisfied that the maneuvering of the ship as one of the essential parts of the warlike operation had been responsible, though even only responsible by contributing in causing excessive vibration, and that the true cause of the damage was not solely due to the defective [lining], I should on the authorities have been bound to find in

48. [1947] 81 Ll.L.Rep. 1, 63 T.L.R. 594, H.L.
49. [1947] 80 Ll.L.Rep. 398.

favour of the plaintiffs, but on the facts I have found I am of the opinion that the action fails.

It is readily apparent that the American courts have always been reluctant to attribute losses to war risks if the losses can possibly be brought under the heading of marine risks. A recent and notable exception in which the court had occasion to consider the phrase "caused directly . . . by a hostile act by or against a belligerent power" is *International Diary Engineering v. American Home*,[50] where the plaintiff's property in South Vietnam was destroyed by fire caused by an aerial parachute flare dropped by the U. S. military forces in connection with operations against Viet Cong forces. The court held that the loss was caused directly by a hostile act by or against a belligerent power within the meaning of the F.C. & S. Clause even though the property was not located in a combat area, and even though the flare may have been negligently dropped, noting that a hostile act does not lose its hostile character because it is negligently carried out nor need it involve the use of a weapon designed to inflict harm.

Negligence

Even before the amendment resulting as a consequence of the *Coxwold* decision, the effect of negliqence on war risk coverage had been considered.[51] Unless negligence was the real proximate cause of the casualty, it seems to have made little difference. Where negligence has contributed, it has been only when the cause was one arising from warlike operations rather than marine risks.[52]

Burden of Proof—War Risks versus Marine Risks

Normally, where a vessel simply disappears and her fate is unknown, the loss is presumed to be due to maritime perils.[53] Consequently, the burden

---

50. 1971 AMC 1001.

51. See paragraphs 2(a), 3, and 4 of the principles in Schedule A of the Overall War-Marine Risk Settlement Agreement, 1945 AMC 1014, 1031-33, and Note, 51 Yale L.J. 674 (1942).

52. *Standard Oil Co. v. U.S. (The John Worthington)*, 178 F.2d 488 (2d Cir., 1949, dictum); *International Dairy Engineering v. American Home, supra; Adelaide S.S. Co. v. Attorney General (The Warilda)*, (1923) A.C. 292, 14 Ll.L.Rep. 549; *Mazarakis Bros. v. Furness, Withy & Co.*, (1924) 18 Ll.L.Rep. 152; *British India Steam Navigation Co. v. Green et al (The Matiana)*, (1919) 1 K.B. 632, 24 Com.Cas. 156 (dictum, Bailhache, J.).

53. See Sec. 58 of the Marine Insurance Act, 1906, reading:
Where the ship concerned in the adventure is missing, and after a lapse of a reasonable time no news of her has been received, an actual total loss may be presumed.
See, also, Chapter XII, "The Perils Clause," and Chapter XVI, "The Inchmaree Clause."

would lie upon the underwriter to prove on the balance of probabilities that the loss was due to a cause falling within an exceptions clause or warranty, such as the F. C. & S. Clause.[54] But, where the assured is claiming under the war risks clause, he has the affirmative burden of the issue and thus the burden of proving on a balance of probabilities that the loss was caused by a war risk.[55] In the last analysis, the question is one of fact.

Compare, for example, *Munro Brice & Co. v. Marten*[56] with *Compania Maritime of Barcelona v. Wishart*.[57] In the former, a seaworthy vessel sailing through an area in which enemy submarines were known to be operating simply disappeared. Holding that it was improbable that she had foundered due to bad weather, the court of appeal held her loss due to a war risk, and denied recovery inasmuch as the marine policy contained an F. C. & S. Clause. In the latter, a vessel carrying a cargo of coal left the Tyne in November 1917 bound for Barcelona and was never spoken again. There was evidence of exceptionally bad weather in the North Sea shortly after her departure which had resulted in loss and damage to other vessels in the area. Though there was no direct evidence of the cause of her loss, the court held that the inference, having regard to the state of the weather, was that she was lost due to a marine peril.[58]

---

54. *Ruffalo's v. National Ben-Franklin*, 1957 AMC 1233 (2d Cir.); *Mayronne M. & C. Co. v. T-W Drilling Co.*, 168 F.Supp. 800, 1958 AMC 403 (E.D.,La.); *Re National Benefit Ins. Co., Ltd.*, (1933) 45 Ll.L.Rep. 147.

55. *Ocean S.S. Co., Ltd. v. Liverpool and London War Risks Ins. Ass'n, Ltd. (The Priam)*, [1947] 63 T.L.R. 594, [1948] A.C. 243, H.L.

56. (1920) 2 Ll.L.Rep. 2, C.A.

57. (1918) 23 Com.Cas. 264.

58. Other examples are: *Moitrovitch Bros. & Co. v. Merchants' Marine Ins. Co., Ltd.*, (1923) 14 Ll.L.Rep. 25 (vessel overdue; debris picked up in area in which submarines were known to be operating; held, war peril); *General Steam Navigation Co., Ltd. v. Janson*, (1915) 31 T.L.R. 630, K.B.D. (*The Oriole*, a seaworthy vessel, left port in January, 1915, and was last seen off Dungeness on the same day that two other vessels had been torpedoed off Le Havre; several of her life buoys were later picked up as well as a bottle containing a message, "*Oriole* torpedoed . . . sinking"; held, a war peril); *British and Burmese Steam Navigation Co. v. Liverpool and London War Risks Ass'n, Ltd., etc.*, (1917) 34 T.L.R. 140 (seaworthy vessel sailing in 1917 through an area in which other vessels had been lost by war risks was not heard of again; no wireless message was ever received and the disappearance was sudden; held, war peril); *De Marco and Gazan v. Scottish Metropolitan Assur. Co.*, (1923) 14 Ll.L.Rep. 173, 220 (vessel insured under a war risk policy while enroute felt a "thud" all over and one of her hatches was blown off, whereupon she sank; evidence was adduced as to the presence of mines in the vicinity as well as the over-insurance of the vessel and cargo; held, assured failed to prove she was lost by a war peril); *Euterpe S.S. Co., Ltd. v. North of England Protecting and Indemnity Ass'n, Ltd.*, (1917) T.L.R. 540, K.B.D. (vessel off the coast of England in January 1917 was simply never heard of again; no distress signals were given and no debris or bodies were found; held, war peril); *United Scottish Ins. Co., Ltd. v. British Fishing Vessels Mutual War Risks Ass'n, Ltd. (The Braconbush)*, (1944) 78 Ll.L.Rep. 70, K.B.D. (underwater explosion occurred in January 1942 when the vessel was off the coast of England; the vessel vibrated and later sank; held: a war risk); *MacBeth & Co. v. King*, (1916) 32 T.L.R. 581 (vessel was proceeding through an area in which there was a possibility that mines from an English minefield had gone adrift as well as German mines and submarines in the area; she simply disappeared; held, war peril).

Strikes, Riots and Civil Commotions Clause

As noted earlier, American practice is to combine the F. C. & S. Clause with the Strikes, Riots and Civil Commotions Clause. The word "war" in a policy of insurance includes civil war unless the context makes it clear that a different meaning should be given to the word.[59]

The effect of the Strikes, Riots and Civil Commotions Clause is to exempt the underwriters from liability for loss or damage caused by strikes, lockouts, political or labor disturbances, civil commotions, riots, martial law, military or usurped power, or malicious acts or vandalism (unless committed by the master or mariners), and not excluded elsewhere under the War, Strikes and Related Exclusions Clause.

Under American practice, the American Institute Hull War Risks and Strikes Clauses are attached to the standard American Institute Hull Clauses to reinstate the like coverage excluded by the War, Strikes and Related Exclusions Clause. As will be seen, the War Risks and Strikes Clause incorporates additional risks to those excluded under the policy by the War, Strikes and Related Exclusions Clause. The current AIH War Risks and Strikes Clause reads:

> This insurance, subject to the exclusions set forth herein,[60] covers only those risks which would be covered by the attached Policy (including collision liability) in the absence of the War, Strikes and Related Exclusions Clause contained therein but which are excluded thereby and which risks shall be construed as also including:
>
> 1. Any mine, bomb or torpedo not carried as cargo on board the vessel;
> 2. Any weapon of war employing atomic or nuclear fusion or other like reaction or radioactive force or matter;
> 3. Civil war, revolution, rebellion, insurrection, or civil strike arising therefrom;

---

59. *Pesquerias y Secaderos de Bacalao de Espansa, S.A. v. Beer*, (1949) 82 Ll.L.Rep. 501, 514.
60. The exclusions mentioned are:
(a) Any hostile detonation of any weapon of war described above in paragraph (2);
   (b) Outbreak of war (whether there be a declaration of war or not) between any of the following countries: United States of America, United Kingdom, France, The Union of Soviet Socialist Republics or the People's Republic of China;
   (c) Delay or demurrage;
   (d) Requisition or preemption;
   (e) Arrest, restraint or detainment under customs or quarantine regulations or similar arrests, restraints or detainments not arising from actual or impending hostilities;
   (f) Capture, seizure, arrest, restraint, detainment, or confiscation by the Government of the United States or of the country in which the Vessel is owned or registered.

4. Strikes, lockouts, political or labor disturbances, civil commotion, riots, martial law, military or usurped power, malicious acts or vandalism to the extent only that such risks are covered by the attached Policy;[61]

5. Hostilities, or warlike operations (whether there be a declaration of war or not) but this paragraph (5) shall not include collision or contact with aircraft, rockets or similar missiles, or with any fixed or floating object, or stranding, heavy weather, fire or explosion unless caused directly by or against a belligerent power which act is independent of the nature of the voyage or service which the Vessel concerned or, in the case of a collision, any other vessel involved therein, is performed. As used herein, "power" includes any authority maintaining naval, military or air forces in association with a power.

The new London War and Strikes Clauses adopts the same approach as the American practice.

The term "civil commotions" was defined in the non-marine case *Levy v. Assicurazione Generali* to mean:[62]

> . . . a stage between a riot and a civil war. It has been defined to mean an insurrection of the people for general purposes, though not amounting to rebellion; but it is probably not capable of any precise definition. The element of turbulence or tumult is essential; an organized conspiracy to commit criminal acts, where there is no tumult or disturbance until after the acts, does not amount to civil commotion. It is not, however, necessary to show the existence of any outside organization at whose instigation the acts were done.

The term came under consideration in *Spinney's Ltd. v. Royal Ins. Co., Ltd.*,[63] which involved claims under various policies for loss or damage arising out of episodes of internal political strife accompanied by violence and destruction on a large scale in Beirut, Lebanon. These involved breaking into the assureds' premises in Beirut and looting. Virtually all the stock in trade were taken, and the whole of furniture and fittings taken away with the remainder being smashed. The internal structures of the building were damaged and some damage by fire occurred.

Although the terms of the various policies differed in some degree, substantially the assureds were covered for riot and strike damage defined as (subject to certain exclusions) "loss or damage . . . directly caused

---

61. Since the words "malicious acts or vandalism" are qualified by the words "to the extent only that such risks are not covered by the attached policy," barratry, even though malicious in nature, would continue to be covered by the marine policy.

62. (1940) 67 Ll.L.Rep. 174.

63. [1980] 1 Lloyd's Rep. 406.

by: 1. The act of any person taking part with others in any disturbance of the public peace . . . not being an occurrence mentioned in Condition 6 of the Special Conditions."

The special conditions stated in part:

> This insurance does not cover any loss or damage occasioned by or through or in consequence directly or indirectly of any of the following occurrences: (a) . . . civil war; (b) . . . civil commotion assuming the proportions of or amounting to a popular rising . . . insurrection, rebellion, revolution, military or usurped power or any act of any person acting on behalf of or in connection with an organization with activities directed towards the overthrow by force of the Government de jure or de facto or to the influencing of it by terrorism or violence . . . .

A malicious damage endorsement was attached which stated, in essence, that the term "malicious damage" meant loss of or damage directly caused by the malicious act of any person not being an act amounting to or committed in connection with an occurrence mentioned in Special Condition 6 of the riot and strike endorsement.

The battle lines were thus drawn. The underwriters contended that although *prima facie* the losses fell within the cover conferred by the policy, they were relieved from liability by one or more of the exceptions contained in the policy.[64]

J. Mustill held:

(1) The issue was not whether the events were recognized in the United Kingdom as amounting to a civil war in the sense in which that term was used in public international law but whether there was a civil war within the meaning of the policy. Consequently, a pronouncement by the U. K. secretary of state would not decide the matter one way or the other;

(2) As to the exception of civil war, the expression "civil" war was part of contemporary speech and there was no point in calling up the ancient doctrine of constructive treason as the test would not provide a conclusive answer; i.e., it would be possible to commit treason without approaching anywhere near to the waging of civil war;

---

64. The policy also contained a "reverse burden" clause under which it was provided that if the underwriters alleged that by reason of the provisions of the special conditions any loss or damage was not covered by the policy, the burden of proving that such loss or damage was covered would be upon the assured. The court held, in this connection, that a mere assertion or allegation that the loss was excluded and challenging the plaintiffs to prove to the contrary would not suffice but, to the contrary, the underwriters must produce evidence from which it could reasonably be argued that (a) a state of affairs existed or an event had occurred falling within an exception and (b) the excepted peril directly or indirectly caused the loss.

(3) To bring the exception into play, the words "civil war" must be given their ordinary and literal meaning which were the same and meant a war which had the special characteristics of being civil; i.e., internal rather than external since without that there was a war, not simply internal strife on a massive scale. A decision involved three questions: (a) Was the conflict between opposing "sides"? (b) What were the objects of the "sides" and how did they go about promoting them? and (c) What was the scale of the conflict and its effect upon public order and the life of the inhabitants?

(4) At the time of the losses, there were no "sides" which could be identified as being engaged in a civil war enough, though the fighting was serious;

(5) As to whether the loss was "occasioned by . . . usurped power," one test is whether the acts amounted to constructive treason, it being unnecessary to show that the events amounted to a rebellion or the acts of a *de facto* government. In the event, the usurpation consisted of the arrogation to itself by the mob of a law-making and law-enforcing power, which properly belonged to the sovereign; consequently, there was no reason why the test should not be applied in the present case;

(6) Those participating in the event (trained militia and armed civilians) had a sufficiently warlike posture, organization, and universality of purpose to constitute them a usurped power;

(7) There was no causal connection, either direct or indirect, between an alleged invasion of a Palestinian brigade and the losses;

(8) The events which occurred constituted neither a rebellion nor an insurrection;

(9) Neither the exceptions of hostilities nor warlike operations applied;

(10) As to the exception covered by "civil commotion assuming the proportions of or amounting to a popular rising," the events did constitute a state of civil commotion as well as assuming the proportions of a popular rising;

(11) As there was some evidence for the assertion that the losses were occasioned directly or indirectly by, through or in consequence of the civil commotion, and the plaintiffs did not rebut it, the claims of all the plaintiffs failed and would be dismissed.

In *Pape, Williams & Co. v. Home Ins. Co.*,[65] goods were seized by the "Labor Committee" at Barcelona during the Spanish Civil War in 1936. The court held it was a loss by riot, civil commotion, or usurped power, although no resistance or bloodshed was shown. The court said, in effect, that the right of recovery under the policy which thereupon accrued could not be destroyed by a later ratification of the seizure by the Catalan

65. 139 F.2d 231, 1944 AMC 51 (2d Cir.).

government. Compare, however, *Societe Belge des Betons Societe Anonyme v. London & Lancashire Ins. Co., Ltd.,*[66] involving similar facts where a similar seizure by a similar group was held to be a "restraint."

Malicious Acts

The term "persons acting maliciously" is, of course, broad enough to cover sabotage since all sabotage is malicious.[67] But the term does not cover a shipowner pledging cargo as security for a loan under the mistaken belief that he has a valid lien on the cargo.[68]

Riots

In *Field et al v. The Receiver of Metropolitan Police,*[69] referred to with approval by the House of Lords in *Thomas Boggan v. The Motor Union Ins. Co., Ltd.,*[70] the court stated that to constitute a riot, five elements were necessary: (1) a number of persons not less than three; (2) a common purpose; (3) execution or inception of the common purpose; (4) an intent on the part of the number of persons to help one another, by force if necessary, against any person opposing them in the execution of the common purpose; and (5) force or violence, not merely used in and about the common purpose, but displayed in such a manner as to alarm at least one person of reasonable firmness and courage.[71]

Arrests, Restraints, and Detainments

The subject of primary cover under the old perils clause for arrests, restraints, and detainments is discussed in Chapter XII, "The Perils Clause," as is the operation of the F. C. & S. Clause upon such perils. By way of illustration, however, see *Blaine Richards v. Marine Indemnity Ins. Co. of America et al.*[72] In that case, a shipment of beans from Europe was de-

66. [1938] 2 All E.R. 305, 158 L.T. 352.
67. See, for example, *Atlantic Mutual Ins. Co. v. King,* (1919) 24 Com.Cas. 107.
68. *Nishina Trading Co., Ltd. v. Chiyoda Fire and Marine Ins. Co., Ltd.,* [1969] 1 Lloyd's Rep. 293. That case must be deemed overruled as to its primary holding as to takings at sea by *Shell International v. Gibbs (The Salem),* [1983] 1 Lloyd's Rep. 342, H.L., but that decision appears to have no effect on the ruling as to malicious acts.
69. [1907] 76 L.J.K.B. 1015, 23 T.L.R. 736, [1907] 2 J.B. 853.
70. (1923) 16 Ll.L.Rep. 65, H.L.
71. Compare *Pan American World Airways, Inc. v. Aetna Casualty & Surety Co.,* 505 F.2d 989 (2d Cir.), [1975] 1 Lloyd's Rep. 77. In that case, the court held that the underwriters could not rely upon an exclusion of riots as there was not a multitude creating an uproar or tumult.
72. 635 F.2d 1051, 1981 AMC 1 (2d Cir.).

tained by the Food and Drug Administration upon arrival in the United States because the beans had been treated with Phostoxin, a fumigant widely used in Europe but not approved by the U. S. Food and Drug Administration. The detention notice gave the consignee ten days in which to respond. Six weeks later, the consignee made application for permission to segregate, clean, and rebag the beans which were found with Phostoxin residue. The plan was approved. The FDA then released 9,387 "clean" bags, and agreed to the reconditioning and release of the remaining 1,013 bags. Aside from the money spent on reconditioning, the plaintiff consignee lost money when the original sales contracts for the beans were cancelled, and the beans had to be sold at a lower price.

The plaintiff assured held two marine insurance policies. The first insured the cargo against "all risks of physical loss or damage from any external cause." This policy, however, included a standard F. C. & S. Clause which excluded from coverage all losses due to "capture, seizure, arrest, restraint, detainment, confiscation, preemption, requisition or nationalization, and the consequences thereof or any attempt thereat, whether in time of peace or war and whether lawful or otherwise." It also included a delay clause excluding coverage of claims "for loss of market or for loss, damage or deterioration arising from delay, whether caused by a peril insured against or otherwise." The second policy was a war risk policy which generally insured against those risks excluded by the F. C. & S. Clause. This policy, however, excluded damages caused by either "seizure or destruction under quarantine or customs regulations" or "delay, deterioration and/or loss of market."

The plaintiff consignee brought suit, claiming that the loss occurred by reason of improper fumigation, a fortuitous external event which resulted in the physical loss of the beans during the period of detention and in the cancellation of its sales contracts. The underwriters defended on the grounds, inter alia, that (1) the damage did not arise during the period of coverage of the policies; (2) that the damages related to "inherent" or "internal" defects in the shipped goods; (3) that the suit was for damages solely due to delay; and (4) that the damages fell under the exceptions noted above. The trial court held that recovery was barred under the F. C. & S. Clause in the all risks policy and under the customs regulations exclusion in the war risk policy. He held that the F. C. & S. Clause was not limited to exclusions of perils of a warlike nature but applied as well to risk of detention by civil authorities.

The court of appeals held that although the F. C. & S. Clause may have originally been inserted in marine policies to protect the underwriters against the risks of war, the clause also included the risk of detention by civil authorities in time of peace. Therefore, the "hold" placed by the FDA on possibly contaminated foodstuffs constituted a seizure or detention even though there was no adverse possession of the goods by the government; i.e., although FDA regulations were not technically U. S. customs regulations, detention due to regulations concerning imported foods should be regarded as customs regulations. Noting that prior cases had consistently applied the F. C. & S. Clause to detention by civil authorities,[73] the court held that such an interpretation was consistent with the general purposes of the clause, which were to exclude from coverage losses arising from unforeseeable actions of sovereign states against the insured vessel or its cargo.

However, the assured argued strongly that even if the detention fell within the exceptions, the proximate cause of its losses was not the detention itself but the improper fumigation with Phostoxin, supporting this submission by asserting that *but for* the improper fumigation, the FDA detention would not have occurred and none of the losses would have been sustained.[74]

On this submission, the appeals court said in part:

> We do not agree that proximate cause in insurance matters is to be determined by resort to "but for" causation. As this Circuit has noted, "the horrendous niceties of the doctrine of so-called 'proximate cause,' employed in negligence suits, apply in a limited manner only to insurance policies." *New York, New Haven & Hartford R. Co. v. Gray*, 1957 AMC 616, 620, 240 F.2d 460, 465 (2d Cir., 1957). Instead, in such cases we have looked at the reasonable understanding of the parties as to the meaning of their insurance agreements. Cf. *Bird v. St. Paul Fire & Marine Ins. Co.*, 224 N.Y. 47, 120 N.E. 86 (1918) (Cardozo, J.) ("The question is not what men ought to think of as a cause. The question is what do they think of as a cause.")
>
> . . . Instead, in accord with the reasonable understandings and expectations of the parties, we must attempt to ascertain what the Supreme Court has referred to as the "predominant and determining" or the "real efficient" cause of the loss. . . . Determination of proximate cause in these cases is thus a matter of applying common sense and reasonable judgment as to the sources of the losses alleged.

---

73. Citing *Intermondale Trading Co. v. North River Ins. Co.*, 100 F.Supp. 128, 1951 AMC 936 (S.D.N.Y.); *Nakasheff v. Continental Ins. Co.*, 1954 AMC 986 (S.D.N.Y.); and *Resin Coatings Corp. v. Fidelity & Casualty Co. of New York*, 489 F.Supp. 73 (S.D.,Fla., 1980). The court distinguished *Flota Mercante Dominicana v. American Manufacturers Mut. Ins. Co.*, 272 F.Supp. 540, 1968 AMC 250 (S.D.N.Y.), which held that the sinking of a ship by U. S. forces did not constitute a seizure or detention, by noting that in so holding the court quite properly relied upon the common sense understanding of those terms.

74. The assured cited in support of its contention that the proximate cause of the loss should be traced to events prior to detention, *Fishing Fleet, Inc. v. Trident Ins. Co., Ltd.*, 598 F.2d 925, 1980 AMC 583 (5th Cir.). However, the court noted that in *Fishing Fleet*, the court had found that the insured ship was a total constructive loss *prior to seizure*. Thus, *Fishing Fleet* had no relevance where the loss claimed was the loss of insured goods during the seizure or detention itself.

Observing that there were two possible theories of "physical loss or damage" to the beans, the appeals court affirmed in part, reversed in part, and remanded to the trial court, stating:

To conclude, on remand the district court must determine whether any of the bean were "damaged" by contamination with Phostoxin such that contracts were cancelled due to such contamination or whether cancellation was merely the result of delay. If delay was the only cause, then no "damage" to the beans existed when sold, and Blaine Richards cannot recover for the losses sustained upon resale at a lesser price. Damages for reconditioning however, could be assessed and awarded. The insurers are free, nonetheless, to raise other objections not based upon the exemptions discussed here, such as whether the losses were brought about by "internal" or "external" causes and whether the policy of insurance here in question was in force at the time of fumigation, which might preclude recovery altogether.

Attention is also directed to *Continental Sea Foods v. N.H. Fire Ins. Co.*,[75] where the assured procured a rejection insurance endorsement covering a shipment of frozen shrimp from Pakistan to New York. On arrival, the U. S. customs rejected the shrimp due to decomposition. The policy also contained an express warranty that the assured would obtain an inspection and certification of pre-shipment quality and packing by a "proper Government authority." Instead, no such government authority existed in Pakistan. Notwithstanding that it was impossible for the assured to comply with the warranty, the court held that the breach thereof defeated recovery.[76]

In *Fishing Fleet, Inc. v. Trident Ins. Co.*,[77] a fishing vessel captain committed barratry when he fraudulently attempted to sell the vessel, lied to the owner about her catch, and disappeared after the vessel sank. It was held that a seizure by the Mexican authorities did not fall under the F. C. & S. Clause because the vessel's constructive total loss occurred through barratry committed prior to the seizure.

---

75. 1964 AMC 196 (S.D.N.Y.).

76. See, also, *Berns & Koppstein, Inc. v. Orion Ins. Co.*, 170 F.Supp. 707, 1960 AMC 1379, [1960] 1 Lloyd's Rep. 276 (rejection insurance endorsements insure against acts of government, not the presence of putrid substance); *Tavares v. Glens Falls Ins. Co.*, 300 P.2d 102 (St.,Cal.) (loss of fishing vessel due to fine levied by a foreign country for passage of the vessel through its territorial waters without a permit was a loss resulting from violation of a law and was not excluded from coverage by an F. C. & S. Clause); *Sciarrino v. Glens Falls Ins. Co.*, 308 N.Y.S.2d 165, 62 Misc.2d 223 (St., N.Y., 1970) (F. C. & S. Clause in a pleasure craft policy did not exempt underwriters from liability for loss of a cruiser which was stolen and which, while in police custody, sank on two separate occasions and which was finally destroyed by the U. S. Army Corps of Engineers as a hazard to navigation).

77. 598 F.2d 925, 1980 AMC 583 (5th Cir.).

In *Nautilus v. Edinburgh Ins.*,[78] it was held that although the master committed barratry by transporting marijuana, the proximate cause of the loss of the insured vessel was a government seizure.

And, in *Ope Shipping v. Allstate*,[79] it was held that the "real efficient cause" of a loss of Nicaraguan vessels to their owners was not barratry by their crews in sailing them to ports friendly to the Sandinista revolutionary party, but rather the Nicaraguan civil war, an excluded peril under the F. C. & S. Clause.

Theft, Pilferage, and Non-Delivery (Insured Value) Clause

Merchants frequently insure their goods either under "All Risks" conditions, or arrange to have attached to their policies the Institute Theft, Pilferage and Non-Delivery (Insured Value) Clause, reading:

(A) It is hereby agreed that this Policy covers the risk of Theft and/or Pilferage irrespective of percentage. No liability for loss to attach hereto unless notice of survey has been given to Underwriters Agents within 10 days of the expiry of the risk under the Policy.

(B) It is hereby agreed that this Policy covers the risk of non-delivery of an entire package for which the liability of the Shipowner or other Carrier is limited, reduced or negatived by the Contract of Carriage by reason of the value of the goods.

Underwriters to be entitled to any amount recovered from the Carriers or others in respect of such losses (less cost of recovery, if any) up to the amount paid by them in respect of the loss.

The decisions with respect to theft are discussed in Chapter XII, "The Perils Clause, under the heading "Thieves and Assailing Thieves."

As Mullins notes,[80] pilferage is petty theft or sneak thievery. It is not covered by the word "thieves" in the clause which specifies perils insured against as the intention of that word is to cover only when some violence is involved. Many American policies make this quite clear by prefixing the word "assailing" to the word thieves.[81] In *Cleveland Twist Drill Co. (Great*

---

78. 673 F.2d 1314, 1982 AMC 2082 (4th Cir.).

79. 687 F.2d 639, 1983 AMC 22 (2d Cir.).

80. *Marine Insurance Digest*, Hugh A. Mullins (Cornell Maritime Press, Inc., 1959).

81. The term was adverted to in *Nishina Trading Co., Ltd. v. Chiyoda Fire & Marine Ins. Co., Ltd.*, [1968] 2 Lloyd's Rep. 47 (dictum, per Donaldson, J.), as referring to a further theft and "probably" the taking of a small part of the goods rather than all the goods. Clandestine theft does not amount to piracy and does not become piracy because the thieves subsequently used force to escape. *Athens Marine Enterprises v. The Hellini Mutual War Risks Ass'n*, [1983] 1 All E.R. 590, Q.B.D.

Britain) Ltd. v. Union Ins. Soc. of Canton,[82] the policy covered cases of twist drills from warehouse to warehouse against risks, including pilferage, but excluding non-delivery or mis-delivery. On arrival, two cases had been partially rifled, six cases were missing totally, and eight cases had been completely rifled. Although admitting liability for the cases partially or completely rifled, the underwriter denied liability with respect to the cases which were totally missing. It was held that it was a reasonable inference that the disappearance of the cases was due to the same cause as the disappearance of the contents of the other cases, and, therefore, the assured succeeded in his action.

It will be remembered that Rule For Construction No. 9 of the schedule to the Marine Insurance Act specifically provides that the term "thieves" does not embrace clandestine theft. However, where the policy expressly covers theft and pilferage, *a fortiori* secret theft and pilferage are covered. Thus, secret theft as well as robbery by violence would be covered. In *Goldman v. Insurance Company of North America,*[83] the court defined the term "pilferage" as meaning a theft made in secret and the taking of a small part rather than the whole. Generally speaking, the term seems to be understood as meaning the theft of a part or the whole of the contents of a package.

"Short delivery" and "mis-delivery" are terms which, by their very nature, are difficult to distinguish from theft or pilferage. If an article during the course of shipment is stolen then it will not be available for delivery at destination. If the policy covers "short delivery," then it is usually sufficient for the assured to prove delivery in good condition to the ocean carrier and a failure to make delivery at destination without otherwise specifying or having to prove that the missing article was stolen or simply lost. For example, in *Federation Ins. Co. v. Coret Accessories, Inc.,*[84] the cargo underwriter paid a claim for a shipment of handbags which were not delivered at destination. The claim was paid under a loan receipt. Subsequently, the goods were found but delivery of the goods was refused on the ground that they were seasonal and, as they had arrived late, could not be used. It was held that the loss was caused by delay and since the policy excluded loss of market by delay, the assured was not entitled to recover. Hence, the money paid under the loan receipt had to be repaid to the underwriter.

---

82. (1925) 23 Ll.L. Rep. 50, C.A.; non-delivery envisages *physical loss* of the merchandise and non-delivery by reason of fraud of a warehouseman is not a risk comprehended with the term. *Curacao Tr. Co. v. Federal Ins. Co.,* 137 F.2d 911, 1943 AMC 1051 (2d Cir.); *Nieschlag v. Atlantic Mutual,* 1942 AMC 391 (2d Cir.).
83. 194 App.Div.266, 232 N.Y. 623 (St., N.Y., 1922).
84. [1968] 2 Lloyd's Rep. 109 (Can.), 1968 AMC 1796.

The meaning of the term was considered in *Middows Ltd. v. Robertson et al*,[85] involving the loss of cargo which was being carried by German vessels at the outbreak of World War II. The cargo owners contended that if all else failed, certainly their cargo was covered because non-delivery was a risk specifically covered in the policies. The court disagreed and said, in part:

> Another alternative contention of the plaintiffs was that in the circumstances there was a "non-delivery" of the cargo and that "non-delivery" was a peril insured against. In truth, the policy does include a type slip in the terms I have already quoted, that is to say, "including damage by hook, oil, sweat, heat, freshwater and other cargo (liquid or solid), theft, pilferage and non-delivery," etc. But these general words "non-delivery" following enumerated perils insured against cannot be divorced from what has gone before and treated as intended to denominate an entirely new risk. They are limited by the context in which they are found. Such words in such a context are to construed not as creating a new or further risk but as affecting the burden of proof. Where such words occur in such a context the insured need not prove loss by theft or pilferage; it is enough if he proves non-delivery and gives prima facie proof that the goods were not lost in any other way than by theft or pilferage. . . . But the case I am deciding is not one of mere non-arrival plus evidence sufficient to establish prima facie that it could have been a matter of theft or pilferage and that the loss is not otherwise reasonably to be accounted for. It is not a case which on its facts has anything to do with "non-delivery" when those words are applied in the context in which they occur. The words "non-delivery" do not therefore assist the plaintiff.

Leakage and Breakage

It will be remembered that under Section 55(2)(c) of the Act, the underwriter is not liable, *unless the policy otherwise provides*, for ordinary leakage and breakage. Consequently, if either risk is to be insured, it must be by special language in the policy. In *De Monchy v. Phoenix Ins. Co. of Hartford*,[86] the policy on a shipment of barrels containing turpentine was claused " to pay leakage from any cause, in excess of one per cent." The policy also contained a formula for ascertaining leakage by comparing the gross shipped and delivered weights using a conversion factor for the difference in gallons and weight in kilograms. Although the House of

---

85. (1940) 67 Ll.L.Rep. 484.
86. (1929) 34 Ll.L.Rep. 201, H.L.

Lords noted that the method of ascertaining the loss might be somewhat inaccurate (it made no allowance for atmospheric pressure and variations in temperature) it was held the term "leakage" meant any stealthy escape either through a small hole which might be discernable or through the pores of the material of which the barrels were composed, noting that turpentine has great powers of penetration and, having penetrated, leaves no sign or external mark.[87]

In *Victoria Overseas Trading Co., Pty. Ltd. v. Southern Pacific Ins. Co., Ltd.*,[88] an all risks policy on a shipment of ashtrays was endorsed with a clause "including breakage." The ashtrays were packed in cardboard containers which was the usual way to pack such items. Approximately one-third of the ashtrays were broken or damaged in transit and the underwriter denied liability. The court held that the endorsement "including breakage" rendered the underwriter liable for breakage caused by ordinary, as well as extraordinary, circumstances in handling. In addition, the assured was awarded the amount claimed for checking and salving the undamaged portion of the shipment.

Contrast *Nakasheff v. Continental Ins. Co.*,[89] where the policy was held not to cover leakage of cargo by expansion due to heat while in the lawful custody of the collector of customs who had lawfully detained it because of an under-declaration of value at the time of entry.

In *Phetteplace v. British & Foreign Marine Ins. Co.*,[90] the policy covered shipments of oil from foreign ports to Philadelphia or Boston, and thence to Providence with privilege of transshipment. The policy was also endorsed to cover "leakage amounting to five percent on each barrel, over ordinary leakage, which is agreed to be two percent." It was held that the policy authorized that the oil be shipped overland to Providence—this being the shortest and most direct route—and hence the underwriter was liable for leakage under the policy though there was nothing to show whether it occurred on land or water.

Where the policy is claused such that it clearly covers leakage, the underwriter is likewise liable for any deterioration of the remaining contents during the insured voyage directly resulting from the leakage. For example, wine might go bad when exposed to air in partially empty casks.[91]

An all risks policy would include, of course, the risk of leakage but clearly would cover only for the extra leakage caused fortuitously and not

---

87. In *Traders and General Insurance Ass'n v. Bankers and General Ins. Co.*, [1921] 9 Ll.L.Rep. 223, the policy included language with respect to "leakage in excess of 2 per cent. over trade ullage."

88. [1964-65] N.S.W.R. 824 (Aus.).

89. 89 F.Supp. 87, 1954 AMC 986 (S.D.N.Y.).

90. 23 R.I. 26, 49 Atl. 33 (St., Rhode Is., 1901).

91. *Maignen & Co. v. National Benefit Assur. Co.*, (1922) 10 Ll.L.Rep. 30.

for normal leakage, as such leakage would be a certainty and not a risk.[92] It is important to keep in mind that marine insurance policies cover normal losses only where the express language of the policies so provides. Thus, a non-fortuitous loss which would normally occur in any event without regard to a fortuitous event is not contemplated by the underwriters as being covered.

The Inchmaree Clause

The Inchmaree Clause is discussed in depth in Chapter XVI, *infra*. It provides, of course, coverage for perils above and beyond those embraced in the standard perils clause.

The Running Down Clause

The Running Down Clause is discussed in detail in Chapter XXI, *infra*. It, too, provides coverage which is not embraced within the standard perils clause.

Heat, Sweat, and Spontaneous Combustion

As discussed heretofore, Section 55(2)(c) provides that unless the policy otherwise provides, the underwriter is not liable for inherent vice or nature of the subject-matter insured. As a result, loss or damage caused by reason of the operation of natural forces such as heat, sweat (condensation of moisture), or spontaneous combustion would not normally be covered. However, this would not prevent underwriters from agreeing, where the policy is properly claused, from agreeing to insure such perils. This was the case in *Soya G.m.b.H. Kommanditgesellschaft v. White (The Corfu Island)*,[93] where a cargo of soya beans was insured under an open policy against the risks of heat, sweat, and spontaneous combustion for a voyage from an Indonesian port to Antwerp. The cargo arrived in a heated condition. The cargo owners recovered, heat and sweat being risks but not known certainties where the goods had been shipped with a moisture content well below 13 percent. Apparently, the evidence demonstrated

---

92. *Dodwell & Co., Ltd. v. British Dominions General Ins. Co.*, (1918), extract from judgment reported at [1955] 2 Lloyd's Rep. 391; *F.W. Berk v. Style*, [1955] 2 Lloyd's Rep. 383 (reviewing cases).
    93. [1982] 1 Lloyd's Rep. 136, C.A.

that where the moisture content of soya beans was between 12 and 14 percent, heating might or might not occur.

All Risks Coverage

As noted heretofore,[94] it is quite common for cargo policies to be written on an all risks basis. Such coverage is considerably more expanded than that found in the old Lloyd S.G. policy or in the usual American policies. But, it must be remembered that the loss or damage, to be recovered, must be fortuitous, i.e., a risk and not a certainty. Moreover, such policies do not cover loss or damage proximately caused by delay, or inherent vice or nature of the subject-matter insured.

Exceptions

As discussed, *supra*, the Marine Insurance Act, 1906, provides that the underwriter is not liable for certain perils among which are: delay,[95] ordinary wear and tear,[96] inherent vice,[97] losses not proximately caused by a peril insured against,[98] wilful misconduct of the assured,[99] ordinary leakage and breakage,[100] losses proximately caused by rats or vermin,[101] and any injury to machinery not proximately caused by maritime perils.[102]

Frequently, policies expressly mention the exceptions, and, of course, perils insured against under the perils clause are often expressly excluded by such clauses as the F. C. & S. Clause. Moreover, as already discussed, the perils of strikes, riots, and civil commotions are often excluded by the Strikes, Riots and Civil Commotions Clause.

In addition, the memorandum clause[103] excludes liability for partial losses of goods if such losses fall within the specified classes, unless such losses are ones falling within general average or the ship sinks, strands,

---

94. See Chap. III, "The Policy," and subheading "All Risks Coverage."
95. See discussion, *infra*, this chapter.
96. See discussion, *infra*, Chap. XV, "Proximate Cause."
97. See discussion, *infra*, Chap. XV, "Proximate Cause." See, also, *Blackshaws (Pty) Ltd. v. Constantia Ins. Co.*, [1983] 1 A.D. 120 (So.Af.), 1984 AMC 637.
98. See discussion, *infra*, this chapter and discussion, Chap. XV, "Proximate Cause," "Loss Must Relate Directly and Proximately to a Peril Insured Against."
99. See discussion, *infra*, Chap. XV, "Proximate Cause."
100. See discussion, *infra*, Chap. XV, "Proximate Cause."
101. See discussion, *infra*, Chap. XV, "Proximate Cause," and Chap. XIV, "The Inchmaree Clause."
102. See discussion, *infra*, Chap. XV, "Proximate Cause," and Chap. XIV, "The Inchmaree Clause."
103. See discussion, *infra*, Chap. XX, "Particular Average."

grounds, or burns.[104] Moreover, the underwriter is not liable for partial losses which do not amount to the percentage specified in the memorandum clause.[105] If the policy contains an F.P.A. warranty, the underwriter is liable only in case of the total loss of the subject-matter insured.[106]

Some policies, particularly including protection & indemnity policies, frequently contain "excess" clauses whereby any loss falling within their ambit is not covered.[107]

The liability of underwriters under freight policies is frequently excluded if the charterer cancels the charter pursuant to rights given to him to do so under a "cancelling" clause.[108]

Moreover, the various undertakings of the underwriters may be qualified by express "warranties" (perhaps more properly termed "conditions") whereby the underwriters are relieved of liability if the assured does or does not do certain acts or carry out certain specified duties.[109]

War risk policies frequently contain a "frustration" clause which operates to free the underwriters of any claim based upon frustration of the insured voyage.[110]

Loss Caused by Delay

Section 55(2)(b) of the Act states:

> Unless the policy otherwise provides, the insurer on ship or goods is not liable for any loss proximately caused by delay, although the delay be caused by a peril insured against.

The Institute Time Clauses (freight) provide in part:

> Warranted free from any claim consequent on loss of time whether arising from a peril of the sea or otherwise.

The new London Institute Cargo Clauses (A), (B), and (C) provide that in no case shall the insurance cover:

> 4.5 loss damage or expense proximately caused by delay, even though the delay be caused by a risk insured against (except expenses payable under Clause 2 [general average] above).

A typical American cargo policy (manuscript form) provides:

---

104. See Chap. IV, "Principles of Construction," Chap. XVI, "Actual and Constructive Total Loss," under subheading "Damage to Cargo," and Chap. XX, "Particular Average."
105. See n. 104 above.
106. See discussion, *infra*, Chap. XX, "Particular Average."
107. See discussion, *infra*, Chap. XXIII.
108. See discussion, *infra*.
109. See discussion, *infra*.
110. See discussion, *infra*.

This insurance shall in no case be deemed to extend to cover loss, damage or expense proximately caused by delay.[111]

Unfortunately, the leading case in the United States on "delay" not only is directly opposed to Section 55(2)(b) of the Act, but so disconcerted the marine insurance industry that as a consequence a clause is almost invariably inserted in cargo policies reaffirming the principle that the insurer is not liable for any loss proximately caused by delay, even though the delay may have been caused by a peril insured against.[112]

In that case, the plaintiff was the owner of a cargo of bananas on board the *Smargagd*. The vessel stranded and before she could be refloated, the entire cargo of bananas became overripe and rotted, causing a total loss. The question before the Supreme Court was: Is there coverage when a marine peril, *viz.*, stranding, so delays the voyage that the cargo becomes a total loss? The Court answered in the affirmative, holding that the stranding was the proximate cause of the loss.

It will be observed that Section 55(2)(b) speaks only in terms of "ship or goods," and there is no mention of "freight." Clearly, the result of delay, by reason of a peril insured against, could give rise to a claim recoverable under a freight policy.[113] But, the proximate cause of the loss of freight by reason of delay must be a peril insured against and not the operation of a charter provision allowing the charterer to avoid the payment of hire in certain circumstances; i.e., the election of the charterer to put the vessel "off-hire" by reason of a "cesser" clause.[114] Moreover, practically all freight policies contain a Time Penalty Clause such as Clause 8, Institute Time Clauses (freight).[115]

---

111. Note the similarity of expression between the American clause and the wording of Clause 4.4 of the new London Institute Cargo Clauses.

112. *Lanasa Fruit Steamship and Importing Company v. Universal Ins. Co. (The Smaragd)*, 302 U.S. 556, 1938 AMC 1 (1938).

113. See *Jackson v. Union Marine Ins. Co.*, (1874) 31 T.L.R. 789, 2 Asp. M.L.C. 435, Ex.Ch.; *The Bedouin*, (1894) 69 L.T. 782, 10 T.L.R. 70; *The Alps*, (1893) 68 L.T. 624, 9 T.L.R. 285. It has been said that the Time Penalty Clause in the Institute form was introduced as a consequence of the decision in *Jackson v. Union Marine Ins. Co.*

114. See, for example, *Mercantile S.S. Co. Ltd. v. Tyser*, (1881) 7 Q.B.D. 73; *Inman S.S. Co. v. Bischoff*, (1882) 7 App.Cas. 670, H.L.; *Manchester Lines, Ltd. v. British & Foreiqn Marine Ins. Co., Ltd.*, (1901) 86 L.T. 148, 7 Com.Cas. 26; *Bensaude & Co. v. Thames & Mersey Marine Ins. Co.*, (1897) A.C. 609.

115. Cases construing Clause 8, or language similar thereto, include *Bensaude & Co. v. Thames & Mersey Marine Ins. Co., supra*, n. 114; *Turnbull, Martin & Co. v. Hull Underwriters' Ass'n*, (1900) 2 Q.B. 402; *Russian Bank for Foreign Trade v. Excess Ins. Co.*, (1918) 2 K.B. 123, *aff'd* on other grounds, (1919) 1 K.B. 39, C.A.; *Atlantic Maritime Co., Inc. v. Gibbon*, [1953] 2 Lloyd's Rep. 294, C.A. (dictum that the clause did not apply in the particular circumstances involved); *Naviera de Canaris, S.A. v. Nacional Hispanica Aseguradora, S.A.*, [1977] 1 All E.R. 625, [1978] A.C. 873, [1977] 1 Lloyd's Rep. 457, H.L.

Ship

Field S.S. Co. v. Burr[116] is a classic example of a vessel being delayed by a peril insured against where the shipowner failed to recover his expenses from underwriters for wages and provisions for his crew during a detention for repairs. In that case, the vessel was involved in a collision whereby a hole was knocked in her bottom. Water and mud came through the hole and caused the cargo (cotton seed) to become rotten and offensive. At considerable expense, the vessel owner was compelled to cleanse his vessel of the offensive cargo which, in turn, occasioned a delay during which he had to pay wages and procure provisions. His expenses could not, of course, be classified as *damage to the vessel itself*—the subject matter of the insurance—and hence were not recoverable from hull underwriters.[117]

Where a ship is damaged and repairs are not timely effected with the result that the vessel becomes a constructive total loss, the excessive damage resulting from delay is not recoverable.[118]

Cargo

There are a number of cases holding that losses caused by delay in connection with cargo are not recoverable.[119] Moreover, the excessive damage resulting from delay is not recoverable.[120]

Losses Not Proximately Caused by Perils Insured Against

This subject is treated in considerable detail in Chapter XV, "Proximate Cause." It must be emphasized in this connection that a loss, to be recoverable under the policy, must relate *directly* and *proximately* to a peril insured against. If it does not, then it is not a loss to which the underwriters must respond.[121]

---

116. 68 L.J.Q.B. 426, 8 Asp. M.L.C. 529. See, also, *Barge J. Whitney, Asphalt Incident*, 1968 AMC 995 (Arb.), involving expenses incurred in discharging solidified asphalt from a barge which could not be unloaded when the interior heating coil system became inoperative. See, also, *Shelbourne v. Law Investment & Ins. Corp.*, (1898) 2 Q.B. 626, 8 Asp. M.L.C. 445.

117. This is not to say that wages and provisions during detention for repairs in a port of refuge may not be recovered on other grounds; e.g., as general average, or particular average, or (in certain circumstances), under the Running Down Clause which provides covered for demurrage to a third party's vessel.

118. *St. Margaret's Trust Ltd v. Navigators & General Ins. Co. Ltd*, [1949] 82 Ll.L.Rep. 752.

119. See, for example, *Pink v. Fleming*, (1890) 25 Q.B.D. 396, 6 Asp. M.L.C. 554, C.A.; *Taylor v. Dunbar*, (1869) L.R. 4 C.P. 206.

120. *Federation Ins. Co. of Canada v. Coret Accessories, Inc.*, [1968] 2 Lloyd's Rep. 109, 1968 AMC 1796 (Can.).

121. See cases cited Chap. XV, "Proximate Cause," *infra*, as well as *Fuerst Day Lawson, Ltd. v. Orion Ins. Co., Ltd.*, [1980] 1 Lloyd's Rep. 656, Q.B.D., where a cargo of oil in drums

Losses Falling within an "Excess" Clause or Only in Excess of a Stipulated Deductible

At least one British P & I club provides in its rules that claims will be paid in specified cases only in the amount by which the loss exceeds an amount stipulated in the rules.[122] A well-known American P & I policy, by contrast, stipulates that claims will be paid subject to a deductible named therein.[123] The net effect is, of course, the same.

Cancellation of Charters—Freight Policies

In re Jamison & Newcastle S.S. Freight Ins. Ass'n,[124] the policy of insurance on freight contained a provision: "No claim arising from the cancelling of any charter . . . shall be allowed." The vessel was delayed by perils of the sea; no agreement to set aside the charter was made, but the voyage contemplated by the charter became manifestly impossible. In a suit on the policy, it was held that the charter had not been cancelled within the meaning of the provision and the assured was entitled to recover. It will be seen that the cancellation must arise from some *agreement* between the parties and, if no such agreement is made, the charter is not cancelled as that term was used in the policy. Any other interpretation would render such a policy of little value to an assured.

But if the real proximate cause of the loss of the freight is the exercise of an option to cancel, then the loss would be due to cancellation and not to an insured peril, even though that insured peril caused a delay which resulted in the cancellation.[125]

---

was insured against all risks and on arrival the drums were found to contain water with only slight traces of oil. It was quite apparent that the shipper had been defrauded and that there was never any oil in the drums prior to loading aboard ship. The court held for the underwriters because the assured had failed to discharge the burden of proof that *oil in drums* had ever started on their transit.

122. See, for example, Rule 35 of the Rules of the United Kingdom Mutual Steamship Assurance Association (Bermuda) Ltd.

123. The American Steamship Owners Mutual Protection and Indemnity Association, Inc., form of policy (reproduced in the Appendix) provides for a deductible (to be typed in) under paragraphs 1, 2, 4-10, 12, and 13. No deductible is specified in the SP-23 (revised) form. The AIH (hulls, 1977) form of hull policy provides for a deductible to be typed in at line 30.

124. [1895] 2 Q.B. 90, 72 L.T. 648.

125. Compare *Jackson v. Union Marine Ins. Co.,* (1874) 31 L.T. 789, with *Mercantile S.S. Co. v. Tyser,* (1881) 5 Asp. M.L.C. 6, and *Inman S.S. Co. v. Bischoff,* (1882) 7 App. Cas. 670.

Conditions Imposed Precedent to Liability

The underwriter may qualify his undertaking to insure and if a loss occurs which falls within the ambit of the qualification, the underwriter is relieved of liability.

Here, a clear distinction should be drawn between true *promissory warranties* (that is, as mentioned in Section 33 of the Marine Insurance Act, 1906, a warranty by which the assured undertakes that some particular act shall or shall not be done, or that some condition shall be fulfilled, or whereby he affirms or negatives the existence of a particular state of facts), and an exceptions clause in which the underwriter is exempted from liability only for those losses caused by the excepted peril. In the former, the underwriter is relieved of liability for all losses merely upon the breach of the warranty, whether or not the loss was proximately caused by the breach; in the latter, the underwriter is relieved of liability only with respect to those losses proximately caused by the excepted peril.[126] The mere fact that an exceptions clause may begin with the words "warranted free . . . " does not mean that the condition imposed is a true warranty. To the contrary, it may be (and often is) merely a condition.

Among such exceptions will be found various trading or locality restrictions,[127] stipulations as to the master or crew,[128] provisions prohibit-

---

126. While this statement is true as respects English marine insurance law, it is concededly an oversimplification as respects American marine insurance law. This is so because of the decision of the U. S. Supreme Court in *Wilburn Boat Co. v. Fireman's Fund Ins. Co.*, 348 U.S. 310, 1955 AMC 467, discussed in Chap. I, "Introduction," in which the Supreme Court said, in essence, that the answer to the question may be dependent upon state law. See, also, Chap. X, "Disclosures and Representations," and Chap. XI, "Warranties."

127. For example, the Institute Trading Warranties (see Appendix) proscribe operations in various specified waters, such as not north of, or south of, certain latitudes in the Atlantic and Pacific Oceans and the Baltic and Bering Seas. See, also, *Birrell v. Dryer*, (1884) 9 App.Cas. 345 (policy warranted "no St. Lawrence between October 1 and April 1"; held, warranty broken when the vessel was navigating the Gulf of St. Lawrence during the prohibited period and was lost); *Mountain v. Whittle*, [1921] All E.R. 626, H.L. (houseboat insured under a time policy "whilst anchored in a creek off Netley . . . with liberty to shift, including all risks of docking, etc."; while being towed to a yard where she could be docked and cleaned, she foundered; held, the "docking" clause must be construed as extending the policy to cover a voyage to a dock); *Providence Washington Ins. Co. v. Brummelkamp*, 58 F. 918 (2d Cir., 1893) (voyage outside the permitted limits). Numerous other cases involving trading warranties will be found in Chap. XI, "Warranties," *supra*.

128. See, for example, *Capital Coastal Corp. v. Hartford Fire Ins. Co.*, 378 F.Supp. 163, 1974 AMC 2039 (E.D.,Va.), [1975] 2 Lloyd's Rep. 100; *Scow No. 12*, 1929 AMC 425 (W.D.,Wash.), *aff'd* 35 F.2d 862, 1930 AMC 557 (9th Cir.) (warranty that a scow would be towed by an approved tug with a full crew; a mate was missing and the absence thereof was held to be a breach of warranty); *Russell v. Provincial Ins. Co., Ltd.*, [1959] 2 Lloyd's Rep. 275, Q.B.D. (warranted free of any claim for any loss caused by the inexperience of the person in control; held, on the evidence, the persons in control were experienced). See, also, numerous other like cases cited in Chap. XI, "Warranties."

ing the towing of the insured vessel or the towing of other vessels by the insured vessel,[129] lay-up requirements,[130] and carriage of deck cargo.[131]

Frustration Clause

Clause 15 of the Institute Time Clauses (freight) provides, in part, that should the clause (F. C. & S.) be deleted, Clause 16 becomes operative. Clause 16 reads:

Warranted free of any claim based upon loss of, or by arrests, restraints or detainment of Kings, Princes Peoples Usurpers or persons attempting to usurp power.

Clause 3.7 of the Institute War Clauses (cargo) (1/1/82) excludes:

. . . any claim based upon loss of or frustration of the voyage or adventure.

The Frustration Clause was adopted as a consequence of *Sanday & Co. v. British & Foreign Marine Insurance Co., Ltd.*,[132] where the underwriters were held liable for a loss by "restraint of princes" with respect to shipments of grain which could not be delivered to their destination in Germany due to the outbreak of World War I. Although the grain still existed *in specie* and was under the control of the assured, the insured venture was lost or "frustrated." The effect of the introduction of the Frustration Clause was to exclude liability for losses based upon frustration of the venture but the clause had no effect upon the *physical* loss of the subject matter of the insurance for which liability under the policy still existed.[133]

---

129. See, for example, *Emmco Ins. Co. v. Southern Terminal and Transp. Co.*, 333 So2d 80 (Fla., D.C.A.) (prohibition in a P & I policy issued to a commercial towing company as to towing other vessels; damage occurred during such towing; held, no coverage notwithstanding that the underwriter knew that the assured was a company engaged in towing as a commercial venture). *Florida Waterway Properties, Inc. v. The Oceanus Mutual Underwriting Association (Bermuda) Ltd., et al,* 1977 AMC 70 (M.D., Fla.) (underwriter not required to indemnify the assured for amounts paid in settlement of collision claims where the policy contained a specific exception for risks covered under the tug syndicate form); *Russell v. Provincial Ins. Co., supra,* n. 128, and cases cited in Chap. XI, "Warranties," *supra,* and Chap. XXI, "Protection and Indemnity," *infra.*

130. See, for example, *Tinkerbell,* 533 F.2d 496, 1976 AMC 799 (9th Cir.) (lay-up warranty not concerned with location but only with condition; failure to winterize the vessel and lay it up in accordance with local custom defeated recovery by the assured). See, also, cases cited in Chap. XI, "Warranties," *supra.*

131. See, for example, *Leopold Walford (London), Ltd. v. National Benefit Assur. Co., Ltd.,* (1921) 7 Ll.L.Rep. 39, K.B.D., where the floating policy contained a provision that the policy was to pay in respect of cargo carried on deck for which bills of lading were issued as being under deck. There was a failure of the assured cargo owner to prove that the goods were carried on the terms of an under-deck bill of lading.

132. (1916) 1 A.C. 650.

133. *Forestal Land, Timber and Railways Co., Ltd. v. Rickards,* [1942] A.C. 50, [1941] 70 Ll.L.Rep. 173, H.L.

In *Atlantic Maritime Company, Inc. v. Gibbon*,[134] the vessel left the vicinity of Taku Bar off Tientsin, China, pursuant to orders of a Chinese Nationalist destroyer, and was destroyed during the civil war then raging in that country between the Nationalists and the Communists. The assured rather ingeniously contended that the claim under the policy could be based exclusively on the civil war and the Frustration Clause would not then apply as civil war was not one of the perils enumerated in the clause which would bring it into play. However, the court of appeal held that the real and proximate cause of the loss was restraint of princes even though arising out of the civil war. As the court pointed out, the claim could not effectively be formulated otherwise than by alleging the prohibition or restraint and that restraint of princes would seldom if ever occur other than in association with another or others of the various perils insured against.

Cancellation Clause

War Risks insurances invariably include a cancellation clause whereby coverage is automatically cancelled upon the happening of certain events. Clause 5 of the new London Institute War and Strikes Clauses (Hulls-Time) (1/6/82) discussed *supra* is a typical example.

The American War Risks Clauses are very similar in language and effect.

Automatic Termination and Cancellation

The AIH form (June, 1977) provides for automatic termination of the policy in the event of:

(1) Any change, voluntary or otherwise, in the ownership or flag of the vessel;
(2) The vessel being placed under new management;
(3) The vessel being chartered on a bareboat basis or requisitioned for charter on that basis;
(4) A change, cancellation or withdrawal of a vessel's class.

However, if the vessel has sailed, either with cargo or in ballast, the automatic termination is deferred until arrival at a final port of discharge or at the port of destination. Moreover, in the event of an involuntary temporary transfer, such automatic termination does not occur until fifteen days after the transfer.

---

134. [1953] 2 Lloyd's Rep. 294, C.A.

The insurance does not inure to the benefit of any transferee or charterer of the vessel and if a loss occurs between the time of change or transfer and deferred automatic termination, the underwriters are subrogated to the rights of the assured.

The term "new management" refers only to the transfer of management of the vessel from one firm or corporation to another and does not apply to internal changes within the offices of the assured.[135] Automatic termination is also provided for when the assurer has paid a total loss.[136]

Clause 4 of the new London Institute Time Clauses (hulls) is very similar to the language of the AIH form, quoted above, and the net effect seems to be the same.[137] The AIH (June, 1977) form also provides for cancellation in the event of non-payment of premium. The clause (lines 55-58) provides:

> In event of non-payment of premium 30 days after attachment, or of any additional premium when due, this Policy may be cancelled by the Underwriters upon 10 days written or telegraphic notice sent to the Assured at his last known address or in care of the broker who negotiated this Policy. Such proportion of the premium, however, as shall have been earned up to the time of cancellation shall be payable. In the event of Total Loss of the Vessel occurring prior to any cancellation or termination of this Policy full annual premium shall be considered earned.

135. See *Whiteman v. Rhode Island Ins. Co.*, 78 F.Supp. 624, 1949 111 (E.D.,La.) and *Lemar Towing v. Fireman's Fund*, 471 F.2d 609, 1973 AMC 1843 (5th Cir.) (no breach of the warranty clause where the same two men retained direction and control of the tug while acting as controlling shareholders and officers of separate corporate entities). In *U.S. Fire Ins. Co. v. Cavanaugh*, 1983 AMC 1261 (S.D.,Fla.), the policy on a fishing vessel contained the usual warranty relating to "change of interest." The policy also contained a trading limits warranty. The owners hired a captain who agreed that he would maintain the vessel properly and would only fish it in the area covered by the trading limits warranty. Instead, he navigated the vessel outside the trading warranty, put it aground, and it became a constructive total loss. Underwriters claimed a breach of the warranty with respect to a change of interest and the warranty as to trading limits. The court held that the owners had exercised due diligence in hiring what appeared to be a competent master; that the practice of hiring a paid captain was common in the industry; and that such practice did not constitute a change of management. See, also, *Palmdale Ins. Ltd. v. R.P. & I. Baxter Pty. Ltd.*, [1982] 2 ANZ Ins. Cas. 60-479 (N.S.W., Aus.), where the policy contained warranty not to charter the vessel; the assured owner chartered the vessel without the knowledge or participation of his mortgagee; held, warranty breached both as to the owner and the mortgagee and recovery under the policy denied.

136. AIH (June, 1977), line 25.

137. The phrase used therein, "transferred to new management," was judicially construed in *Pyman v. Marten*, (1907) 13 Com.Cas. 64. In that case the insured vessel was, during the Russo-Japanese War, on a voyage from Port Talbot to Vladivostok with a cargo of coal. She was seized by the Japanese, taken into Yokosuka, and subsequently condemned as a prize. In a suit by the shipowner for a pro rata return of premium, the court held that the ship was not transferred to new management within the meaning of the policy and, therefore, the shipowner was not entitled to a return of premium. Moreover, the court held that the ship was lost by capture and the F. C. & S. warranty applied.

A very similar clause was involved in *Vinnie's Market v. Canadian Marine.*[138] In that case, a fishing vessel was insured for $65,000 hull and disbursements and $300,000 P & I. The vessel owner's brokers retained possession of the policy.

The brokers repeatedly attempted to persuade the vessel owner to pay the premium. Eventually, some two months plus after the inception date of the policy, the vessel owner sent a partial payment but did not execute and return a promissory note (which had been sent to him to secure the balance due). Finally, a month later, the brokers sent a letter by certified mail to the vessel owner, with the policy to be null and void on the fifth day after the notice was mailed.

Meanwhile, the vessel had been sent to fish in waters off Honduras. Upon arrival, the master and crew discovered that the waters were too shallow for the vessel and its gear to be used in the type of fishing to which they were accustomed, whereupon the vessel was anchored securely in shallow water and the master and crew returned home to Massachusetts.

The notice of cancellation became effective on September 9, 1974, by virtue of its terms. On September 19, 1974, Hurricane Fifi struck the area off Honduras and the vessel was totally destroyed. In a suit on the policy, the vessel owner contended that he had never received the letter of cancellation but, based on the evidence, the court found to the contrary. The policy having been effectively cancelled prior to the casualty on September 19th, 1974, the court found the vessel to have been uninsured.

The policy also contained another clause which provided, in essence, that in the event of non-payment of premium within sixty days after the date of attachment, the policy would automatically terminate upon the sixtieth day and that no further notice of termination or cancellation would be necessary. Based on this clause, the underwriters contended that the policy was cancelled as of the sixtieth day. However, on this submission, the court held that the acceptance of a partial premium payment had the effect of reinstating the policy and amounted to a waiver.

Additional Insurances (Disbursements Clause)

Obviously, the placement of insurance in excess of the agreed value of a vessel could pose a moral hazard if the assured could gain more from the loss of the vessel than to preserve her intact. For that reason, hull policies commonly contain an express warranty, the effect of which is to limit the amount of insurance which an owner may procure. In the absence of such a limitation, an owner could insure his vessel at a very low figure, with the underwriter being compelled to pay particular average claims up to the

138. 441 F.Supp. 341, 1978 AMC 977 (D.,Mass.)

full limit of the sum insured.[139] Moreover, the underwriter could be compelled to pay for a constructive total loss up to the amount insured. If, in the meantime, the owner has procured total loss insurance (actual or constructive) through other underwriters for the balance, he could obtain full insurance at a lower cost.[140]

Although limiting the amount of additional insurance which may be procured, the disbursements clause also permits an assured to effect additional insurances up to the limits prescribed without fear of the underwriters attempting to avoid the policy by claiming a non-disclosure.

In the AIH (June, 1977) form will be found a clause entitled "Additional Insurances," the opening paragraph of which reads:

It is a condition of this Policy that no additional insurance against the risk of Total Loss of the Vessel shall be effected to operate during the currency of this Policy by or for the account of the Assured, Owners, Managers, Operators or Mortgagees except on the interests and up to the amounts enumerated in the following Section (a) to (g), inclusive, and no such insurance shall be subject to P.P.I., F.I.A. or other like term on any interest whatever excepting those enumerated in Section (a); provided always and notwithstanding the limitation on recovery in the Assured clause a breach of this condition shall not afford Underwriters any defense to a claim by a Mortgagee who has accepted this Policy without knowledge of such breach.

There then follow Sections (a) to (g) which permit, in general terms, insurance on:

Disbursements, managers' commissions, profits or excess or increased value of hull and machinery, and freight (including chartered freight or anticipated freight), but not exceeding 25% of the agreed value of the vessel; freight or hire, under contract for voyage; anticipated freight if the vessel sails in ballast and not under charter; time charter hire or charter hire for a series of voyages; premiums actually paid for all interest insured for a period not exceeding 12 months; returns of premiums; and insurance to cover risks excluded by war,

---

139. See Marine Insurance Act, 1906, Sec. 69(1).

140. Subject, however, to the qualification that the owner should disclose to the underwriters on the policy with the low valuation that he has procured additional insurance and his failure to do so may entitle the underwriters to avoid the policy on grounds of non-disclosure. For example, in *Thames & Mersey Marine Ins. Co. Ltd. v. Gunford Ship Co.*, [1911] A.C. 529, the vessel was insured largely in excess of the amount which represented the fair value of the vessel and the freight was likewise insured in an excessive amount. In addition, a valued "honor" policy on disbursements was also procured. Recovery was denied on grounds that the excessive over-valuation was a material fact which should have been disclosed to underwriters insuring the vessel. See, also, *Gulfstream Cargo Ltd. v. Reliance Ins. Co.*, 409 F.2d 974, 1969 AMC 781 (5th Cir., 1969); *King v. Aetna Ins. Co.*, 54 F.2d 253, 1931 AMC 1940 (2d Cir., 1931).

strikes and related exclusions and General Average and Salvage Disbursements.

While the primary function of the additional insurances clause is clearly to preclude insuring a vessel for all risks at a comparatively low figure, and then overinsuring at a lower rate of premium on a total loss basis, it does permit a vessel owner to procure insurance against perils which could beset his vessel—or his pocketbook—and which might otherwise be difficult to quantify.[141]

141. See, generally, *Currie v. Bombay Native Ins. Co.*, (1869) 16 E.R. 740; *Roddick v. Indemnity Mutual Marine Ins. Co.*, (1895) 2 Q.B. 380, C.A.; *Lawther v. Black*, (1900) 17 T.L.R. 597, C.A.; *Price v. Maritime Ins. Co.*, [1901] 2 K.B. 412, C.A.; *Cunard v. Nova Scotia Marine Ins. Co.*, (1897) 29 N.S.R. 409 (Can.); *McLeod v. Universal Marine Ins. Co.*, (1896) 33 N.B.R. 447 (Can.); *Hall v. Janson*, (1855) 119 E.R. 183; *Brown v. Jerome*, 298 F. 1 (9th Cir., 1924); *Booth-American Shipping Co. v. Importers' & Exporters' Ins. Co.*, 9 F.2d 304, 1924 AMC 1047 (2d Cir., 1926); *Lenfest v. Coldwell*, 525 F.2d 717, 1975 AMC 2489 (2d Cir.); *International Nav. Co. v. Atlantic Mutual Ins. Co.*, 100 F. 304 (S.D.N.Y, 1907); *Moran, Galloway & Co. v. Uzielli*, [1905] 2 K.B. 555, 10 Com.Cas. 203.

CHAPTER XIV

THE INCHMAREE CLAUSE

History

This clause, of inestimable value to assureds, takes its name from that of the vessel involved in *Thames & Mersey Marine Ins. Co., Ltd. v. Hamilton, Fraser & Co.*[1] In that case, a donkey engine was being used to pump water into the main boilers when, owing to a valve being closed which ought to have been kept open, water was forced into and split open the air chamber of the donkey pump. The closing of the valve was either accidental or due to the negligence of an engineer and was not due to ordinary wear and tear. The assured contended that the loss was due to "other like perils" as those contained in the principal portion of the classic "perils clause." In holding that the loss was not covered by the policy, the court noted that the general words, following a specific enumeration, must be limited to perils *ejusdem generis* with those specified and that they must be construed with reference to the scope and purpose of a marine policy. Basically, the decision simply held that the loss was not a type to which a maritime venture is subject.[2]

The decision so completely vindicated the underwriters that a special clause, which came to be known as the Inchmaree Clause, was specially developed to give shipowners protection against losses in similar situations. It first appeared in the first edition of the Institute Time Clauses in 1889 and read as follows:

> This Insurance also specially to cover loss or damage to hull or machinery through the negligence of the Master Mariners Engineers or Pilots or through explosions bursting of boilers breakage of shafts or through any latent defect in the hull or machinery provided such loss or damage has not resulted from want of due diligence by the owners of the ship or any of them or by the Manager.

1. 12 App. Cas. 484, H.L.
2. In so holding, the court specifically overruled an earlier decision of the court of appeal holding that the wreck of a steamer caused by an explosion in her boiler under ordinary pressure of steam in moderate weather was within the coverage of the usual perils clause. *West India Telegraph Co. v. Home and Colonial Ins. Co.*, (1880) 6 Q.B.D. 51, C.A., which cited a similar American decision in *Perrin v. Protection Ins. Co.*, 11 Ohio 147 (1842).

The clause through the years has been greatly expanded in the American market. The latest American version (AIH, 1977) reads:

6. Perils

6.1 This insurance covers loss or damage to the subject matter insured caused by
6.1.1 perils of the seas rivers lakes or other navigable waters
6.1.2 fire, explosion
6.1.3 violent theft by persons from outside the vessel
6.1.4 jettison
6.1.5 piracy
6.1.6 breakdown of or accident to nuclear installations or reactors
6.1.7 contact with aircraft or similar objects, falling therefrom, land conveyance, dock or harbour equipment or installation
6.1.8 earthquake volcanic eruption or lightning.
6.2 This insurance covers loss of or damage to the subject-matter insured caused by
6.2.1 accidents in loading discharging or shifting cargo or fuel
6.2.2 bursting of boilers breakage of shafts or any latent defect in the machinery or hull
6.2.3 negligence of Masters Officers Crew or Pilots
6.2.4 negligence of repairers or charterers provided such repairers or charterers are not an Assured hereunder
6.2.5 barratry of Master Officers or Crew, provided such loss or damage has not resulted from want of due diligence by the Assured, Owners or Managers.
6.3 Master Officers Crew or Pilots not be be considered Owners within the meaning of this Clause 6 should they hold shares in the Vessel.   The clause through the years has been greatly expanded in the American market. The latest American version (AIH, 1977) reads:

Subject to the conditions of this Policy, this insurance also covers loss of or damage to the Vessel directly caused by the following:
Accidents in loading, discharging or handling cargo, or in bunkering;
Accidents in going on or off, or while on drydocks, graving docks, ways, gridirons or pontoons;

---

3. See the address by D.V. Moore, "The Inchmaree Clause," 1956, *From the Chair* (1978) The Association of Average Adjusters and Lloyd's of London Press Ltd.

Explosions on shipboard or elsewhere;

Breakdown of motor generators or other electrical machinery and electrical connections thereto, bursting of boilers, breakage of shafts, or any latent defect in the machinery or hull (excluding the cost and expense of replacing or repairing the defective part);

Breakdown of or accidents to nuclear installations or reactors not on board the insured Vessel;

Contact with aircraft, rockets or similar missiles, or with any land conveyance;

Negligence of Charterers and/or Repairers, provided such Charterers and/or Repairers are not an Assured hereunder;

Negligence of Masters, Officers, Crew or Pilots; provided such loss or damage has not resulted from want of due diligence by the Assured, the Owners or Managers of the Vessel, or any of them. Masters, Officers, Crew or Pilots are not to be considered Owners within the meaning of this clause should they hold shares in the Vessel.

The clause first came before the English courts in *Jackson v. Mumford*.[4] In that case, the engine of a torpedo-boat destroyer was damaged as a result of a connecting rod breaking. The assured contended that the breaking of a connecting rod should be considered *ejusdem generis* with breakage of shafts and that the rod broke by reason of a latent defect. The court rejected these contentions, finding that the breaking was due to a weakness in design and that the clause was not intended to cover the erroneous judgment of the designer as to effect of the strain which his machinery would have to resist.

In 1902, the clause had come before an American court in *Cleveland & B. Transit Co. v. Insurance Co. of N.A.*[5] In that case, a crack was discovered in the bedplate of a vessel's engine. Although temporary repairs were made, new cracks developed as a result of the first crack and after additional temporary repairs the bedplate was removed. The cause of the initial crack was imperfect casting of two metals of different temperature commonly known as a "cold shot." This was found to be a latent defect which had existed prior to the effective date of the policy which might never have manifested itself had it not been for stress in the engine from water getting into the cylinders.

Referring to language of Lord Selbourne in *West India,* which had been disapproved in *Thames & Mersey,* the court concluded that it was reasonable to assume that the scriveners of the clause had intended to cover losses of the type described by Lord Selbourne and that in England recovery would have been allowed for replacing the defective part. It is clear that the decision is not in accord with subsequent English cases and has

4. (1904) 9 Com.Cas. 114, C.A.
5. 115 F. 431 (D.C.N.Y., 1902).

been expressly overruled in subsequent American cases. See, for example, *Mellon v. Federal Ins. Co.*,[6] in which the court referred to the case and said in part:

. . . it may well be doubted whether Judge Adams would have reached the conclusion he did, if the weight of authority and the persuasive arguments which have been presented here had been available at a time when the Inchmaree Clause was comparatively new, and when but few cases had arisen in respect of its interpretation.

It is, of course, well settled now that the clause does not cover the cost of replacing the defective part but only the consequential damage resulting to other parts of the machinery or hull by reason of the defect, and language expressly incorporating this principle was inserted in later American versions of the clause.[7]

The decision in *Ferrante et al v. Detroit F. & M. Ins. Co., supra,* is particularly interesting, involving as it did an effort on the part of the assured to bring the loss under that portion of the clause relating to negligence of masters, officers, and crew while the underwriter endeavored with equal diligence to bring the loss under the latent defect portion of the clause. At stake was the cost of replacing the broken crankshaft. If the assured's contention prevailed the cost was covered; if the underwriter prevailed the assured got nothing; i.e., the cost of replacing the crankshaft was in excess of $10,000 while the consequential damage to other parts of the vessel amounted to only slightly in excess of $1,000—which was below the 3 percent franchise clause in the policy.

The court resolved the issue in favor of the assured, holding that the shaft broke because of the engineer's failure to give proper attention to the lubrication of the engine. In doing so, it was pointed out that even before the express exclusion relating to the cost of the defective part was inserted in the clause, both English and American courts (with one exception) had refused to construe the clause as covering the defective part. In the view of the court, the parenthetical exclusion was inserted to make doubly clear the meaning of the clause where latent defects were involved. (The absence of the parenthetical exclusion in the English clause is of no significance in light of the English cases.)

---

6. 14 F.2d 997 (D.C.N.Y., 1926) *sub nom El Mundo,* 1926 AMC 1449.

7. See *Oceanic Steamship Co. v. Faber,* (1907) 13 Com.Cas. 28, C.A.; *Rensselaer,* 125 Misc. 395, 211 N.Y.S. 348, 1925 AMC 1116; *Scindia Steamships (London) Ltd. v. London Assur.,* (1937) 3 All E.R. 895, 56 Ll.L.Rep. 136; *Hutchins Bros. v. Royal Exchange Assur. Corp.,* (1911) 16 Com.Cas. 242, C.A.; *National Bulk Carriers v. American Marine Hull Ins. Synd.,* 1949 AMC 340 (Arb.); *Ferrante et al v. Detroit F. & M. Ins. Co.,* 125 F.Supp. 621, 1954 AMC 2026 (D., Cal.); *Mellon v. Federal Ins. Co., sub nom El Mundo,* 14 F.2d 997, 1926 AMC 1449 (D.C.N.Y.); *J.L. Fisheries Ltd. v. Boston Ins. Co.,* (1969) 69 D.L.R. 2d 18 (N.S.,Can.); *MacColl and Pollock, Ltd. v. Indemnity Mutual Marine Assurance,* (1930) 47 T.L.R. 27; *Thibert v. Union Ins. Soc.,* 1951 AMC 1661 (Arb.).

What Is a Latent Defect

It is important to consider how the latent defect clauses have been interpreted by the courts in determining what is and what is not a "latent defect." In *Hutchins Bros. v. Royal Exchange Assur. Corp.*,[8] the builders had put into the vessel a stern frame which contained a fracture which had been concealed and painted over. It was not discoverable by a reasonable inspection until, during the currency of the policy, it became visible owing to ordinary wear and tear of the vessel. The cost of a new frame was disallowed. The court said (per L. J. Scutton):

> The only damage is . . . the latent defect itself, which by wear and tear has become patent . . . .The latent defect did not arise during the currency of the policy . . . .The underwriter does not insure against ordinary wear and tear and its consequences.

On appeal, L. J. Fletcher Moulton said:

> It was not loss or damage caused by a latent defect, but a latent defect itself. To hold that the clause covers it would be to make the underwriters not insurers, but guarantors, and to turn the clause into a warranty that the hull and machinery are free from latent defects, and, consequently to make all such defects reparable at the expense of the underwriters. There are no words in the clause which would warrant such an interpretation. . . .

To the same general effect, see *MacColl & Pollack Ltd. v. Indemnity Mutual Marine Assur. Co. Ltd.*,[9] where the plaintiffs, who were marine engineers, contracted to fit a steamer with a new intermediate pressure cylinder, but the cylinder, when tried under steam, failed, and a second one having also been found to be defective, plaintiffs had to fit a third. In an action on their policy, plaintiffs failed, the court holding that the mere existence of a latent defect was not a casualty and the cost of replacing a thing which had a latent defect was not recoverable as loss or damage due to latent defect.

In *Sipowicz v. Wimble (The Green Lion)*,[10] the court defined a latent defect as follows:

> A latent defect is a defect which a reasonably careful inspection would not reveal. *Reisman v. New Hampshire Fire Ins. Co.*, 1963 AMC 1151, 1156, 312 F.2d 17, 20 (5th Cir., 1963). It is not a gradual deteriora-

8. (1911) 16 Com.Cas. 242, C.A.
9. (1930) 47 T.L.R. 27.
10. 370 F.Supp. 442, 1975 AMC 524 (D.C.N.Y.), (1974) 1 Lloyd's Rep. 593.

tion but rather a defect in the metal itself. *Waterman S.S. Corp. v. U.S.S.R. & M. Co.*, 1946 AMC 997, 155 F.2d 687, 691 (5th Cir.), cert. denied 329 U.S. 761, 1946 AMC 1730 (1946). In *Tropical Marine, supra,* the court stated that the classic meaning of the term "latent defect" was as follows:

A latent defect is one that could not be discovered by any known or customary test, . . . and . . . is a hidden defect and generally involves the material out of which the thing is constructed as distinguished from the results of wear and tear.

It is a "hidden defect" . . . not manifest, but hidden or concealed, and not visible and apparent; a defect hidden from knowledge as well as from sight; . . . a defect which reasonably careful inspection will not reveal; one which could not have been discovered by inspection . . . by any known and customary test. 1957 AMC at 1953, 247 F.2d at 121.

In *Sipowicz,* the 27-year-old vessel sank at her moorings because deteriorated metal fastenings which secured the keel and keelson to the hull had weakened and had allowed a separation to occur, thus permitting water to enter the hull. The fastenings and metal assisting frames had deteriorated from age, wear, and lack of maintenance but were not shown to be inherently defective in their original construction. The court held that the loss did not occur from a latent defect.

In *National Bulk Carriers v. American Marine Hull Ins. Synd.,*[11] a thermometer tube fell into the gear train, damaging the teeth. After repairs were effected, other teeth in other gears also broke. The thermometer tube was held in place by a machine screw tensioned by a spring steel washer to prevent it from backing out. The arbitrator held that the reasonable inference was that the dislodging of the spring steel washer was due to a defect in material or its tempering and allowed recovery. In doing so, he defined a latent defect as a "concealed defect, a defect that is not discoverable by ordinary practicable means."

In *Thibert v. Union Ins. Soc.,*[12] another arbitration case, a cam roller and pin in the engine of a tug broke. The pin and cam became wedged in the engine but were apparently ground up and destroyed. The engine had operated less than 1,000 hours, and the evidence showed that a cam roller ordinarily requires no maintenance for 6,000 hours. These facts, plus the generally good condition of the machinery, led the arbitrator to conclude that in the absence of evidence to the contrary, a latent defect was the most reasonable inference to be made.

The Sea Pak (Tropical Marine Products, Inc. v. Birmingham Fire Insurance Company of Pennsylvania),[13] cited in *Sipowicz, supra,* contains such a

---

11. 1949 AMC 340 (Arb.).
12. 1951 AMC 1661 (Arb.).
13. 247 F.2d 116, 1957 AMC 1946 (5th Cir.).

pungent and pithy analysis of the latent defect clause and its interplay with seaworthiness that it warrants special mention. In that case, a 71-foot wooden-hull fishing vessel sprang an unexpected leak a few days after leaving port while fishing in August in calm protected waters in the Bahamas. Before she could reach harbor, her engine became flooded and she eventually sank after experiencing rough seas. When the vessel started leaking, an inspection had revealed that the water was coming from underneath a refrigerated space in the forward part of the vessel. Because of the construction of the interior of the vessel, the bilge underneath this area was inaccessible. The underwriter contended that the vessel was unseaworthy and that the proviso in the Inchmaree Clause had been breached in that the assured had not exercised due diligence to make the vessel seaworthy immediately prior to the developing of the leak. Judge Brown, in his inimitable style, demolished this contention in the following language:

Indeed, far from voiding the policy, it was as to just such unseaworthiness that the policy was meant to apply. The Inchmaree Clause insures against damage or loss occasioned by latent *defects* in machinery or hull. Of course, a defect in machinery or a defect in a hull means that the vessel is thereby unseaworthy since, with such defect, the machinery or hull cannot comply with the classic definition of "reasonably suitable" for the purposes intended (citations omitted). The only limitation on this is that the defect be latent and one not known or discoverable by the owner or one in privity with him. This is so because . . . the phrase "Provided such loss or damage has not resulted from want of due diligence by the Assured, the Owners, or Managers of the Vessel" does not include acts of the master or crew members merely imputed on notions of *respondeat superior.*

Here, of course, the owner was in the United States and on this record all was left to the master. There is no evidence that the nonresident owner had personal knowledge of this condition, whatever existed, or the necessity for any detailed drydocking, bottom inspection, scraping or repainting. . . .

The defect was certainly latent in a practical sense. The court found that there is "no explanation as to what caused the leak." And all are unanimous that it was and could not be determined. As the leak was increasing, the master and engineer had determined that it had to be coming from that part of the hull in way of the freezer compartment. There was positively no means of checking the inside of the hull in this space and, of course, lying at anchor eight miles from port, there were no facilities established for a worthwhile inspection or repair over the side.

Since cases should be decided on practicalities and not theoreticals, the fact that this record stands uncontradicted that the hull did not leak in any way, at this place, or in this quantity prior to departure from port August 9, or on any one of the intervening days up to the afternoon of August 12, demonstrates also that . . . there is no basis for concluding that the defect could then have been discovered.

And if the matter is approached from that viewpoint that the Shipowner, without the benefit of any presumptions, must affirmatively establish that the particular defect was latent within the classic meaning of the term, the result is the same. Since the Underwriter's assertion of unseaworthiness is a claim that the hull was defective, it was either latent or not latent. If it was not discoverable prior to departure for sea by all known and customary tests, it was latent and covered by the policy. If, on the other hand, it is claimed that the proof showed that it was discoverable by prudent inspections, or that the proof failed to show that prudent inspection could not have revealed it, the result is that the defect was one which in prudence ought to have been discovered. On this hypothesis, it was the Master who should have discovered it. . . . The Master's failure in carrying out this duty to this Shipowner was negligence and, under the Inchmaree clause, this too was specifically covered.

If the defect could have been discovered the resulting unseaworthiness was due to the Master's negligence; if it was not discoverable by him or Shipowner, it was latent. Either way the Underwriter turns, the loss is within his expanded coverage.

With all due respect to the illustrious Judge Brown, he seems to be saying that an unexplained defect may amount to a latent defect. This proposition does not appear to be sustainable under English law where it is for the assured to discharge the onus of proving that the loss was due to a peril insured against, i.e., a latent defect. The same criticism can be levied with respect to many of the American cases holding that the fact finder may conclude that a latent defect existed where a seaworthy ship sinks from unascertained causes. See, for example, *Lewis v. Aetna Ins. Co.*[14]

In what promises to be a landmark decision, Goff, J., in *Prudent Tankships Ltd., S.A. v. The Dominion Ins. Co., Ltd. (The Caribbean Sea)*[15] held that the mere fact that the historical reasons for a defect in hull or machinery was defective design would not of itself preclude recovery under the In-

---

14. 264 Or. 314, 505 P.2d 914 (St.,Ore., 1973). See, also, discussion, *infra*, "Unexplained Sinkings."
15. [1980] 1 Lloyd's Rep. 338.

chmaree Clause, thereby overruling (at least inferentially) *Jackson V. Mumford, supra.*

In that case, the vessel lightly took the ground during a passage through a dredged channel from Lake Maracaibo. Subsequently, while off the coast of Nicaragua in the Pacific Ocean, with mild weather and seas, the vessel sank due to entry of seawater into her engine room. The owners claimed under their insurance policy, which incorporated the American Institute (hulls) clauses, and specifically the Inchmaree Clause, asserting that the loss was caused by the grounding which damaged the sea suction valve, or, alternatively, that the failure of the valve was due to a latent defect therein, and that the loss was due to the negligence of the master and crew in the navigation of the vessel; i.e., the grounding. The underwriters defended on the grounds that they were relieved of liability because the vessel was sent to sea in an unseaworthy state; or that the assureds breached the provisions of the American Institute (hulls) clauses relating to keeping the vessel in class, and that if the failure occurred in the sea valve it was caused by ordinary wear and tear or by defect in design and therefore was not a peril insured against.

The court held that the vessel did take the ground on her passage up the dredged channel but that the grounding had no causative effect on the casualty; that the casualty was not attributable to ordinary wear and tear in that the defect upon which the owners relied consisted of the fatigue cracks in the wedge-shaped nozzle that were attributable to (1) the manner in which the nozzle was designed and (2) the effect upon the nozzle of the ordinary working of the vessel, the result of this combination being that the fracture opened up a significant period of time before the end of the life of the vessel and therefore recovery for the loss of the vessel consequent upon such a fracture was not excluded by Section 55(2)(c) of the Marine Insurance Act, 1906 (ordinary wear and tear excluded), but was due to a latent defect.

Mr. Justice Goff said in part:

> . . . At all events, however this case is to be interpreted [here Justice Goff was referring to *Jackson v. Mumford*], neither the decision nor the dictum on which Mr. Kentridge relied, has in my judgment the effect of excluding a defect in hull or machinery from the cover provided by the Inchmaree clause merely because the historical reason for such defect was defect in design.

> . . . The present case is one where defective (though not negligent) design has had the effect that defects would inevitably develop in the ship as she traded; if such defects develop and have the result that a fracture occurs and the ship sinks, such a loss is not in my judgment caused by ordinary wear and tear and so is not excluded by s. 55 (2) (c) of the Act.

I am also satisfied that the defect in the present case, consisting as it did of the fatigue cracks in the wedge-shaped nozzle, constituted a latent defect.

Mr. Justice Goff then cited with approval *Brown v. Nitrate Producers S.S. Co.*,[16] defining a latent defect as one which could not be discovered on such an examination as a reasonably careful skilled man would make, and stated:

> ... I therefore conclude on that test, that the loss of the ship in the present case was directly caused by a latent defect in the hull, within the cover provided by the Inchmaree Clause; and it follows that the owners are entitled to recover . . . .[17]

An American court in *National Sugar Refining Co. v. M/S Las Villas*,[18] a cargo case, also held that a design defect was a latent defect. In that case, there was damage to cargo when water entered the hold of a ship which was laden with a cargo of sugar. The water entered through a defective bilge suction valve which, although closed, nonetheless permitted entry of the water. The court stated, in part:

> There was no way that a visual or manual inspection of the valve, short of actually dismantling the valve itself, could disclose or reveal the defect in the valve. After dismantling the valve, it was discovered that the valve's stem, stopper, and guide were improperly fitted and/or *designed* and that the valve was thus defective. [Emphasis added]

Subsequently, the court also stated:

> A latent defect is a defect which is not apparent and which would not be discoverable upon reasonable inspection. It may be a defect in design or a defect in the material used to make or fabricate an object. In this case, improper design was used in the manufacture of the suction valve involved. The improper design was not apparent upon visual inspection, nor was it discoverable by any reasonable inspection that might have been performed. This faulty design which caused the malfunctioning of the valve was a latent defect not discoverable by due diligence.[19]

---

16. (1937) 58 Ll.L.Rep. 188.

17. On the submission of underwriters that the vessel's class was changed, cancelled, or withdrawn, in violation of the terms of the American Institute Hulls Clauses, Mr. Justice Goff ruled negatively on the ground that as the time for performance of the requiremer t of a survey at the nearest port had not yet arrived at the time of the vessel's sinking, there was no breach of the requirement and the ship never lost her class under the rule.

18. 225 F.Supp. 686 (E.D.,La., 1964).

19. The court cited *Sociedad Armadora A.P. v. 5,020 L/T of Raw Sugar*, 122 F.Supp. 892 (E.D.,Pa., 1954), *aff'd* 223 F.2d 417 (3rd Cir., 1955), in support of its view, but that case

As Tetrault has noted,[20] it is difficult in principle to distinguish defects in design from other latent defects and hard to see why underwriters should pay for the consequential damage resulting from a foundaryman's concealed mistake but not the mistake of a naval architect, though the latter is no more patent to the owner than is the former.

It is notable that Justice Goff, in *The Caribbean Sea, supra,* quoted from *Parente v. Bayville Marine Inc.*[21] but declined to follow it and other American cases which have a rather more strict standard as to what constitutes a latent defect, i.e., one which cannot be discovered by any known and customary test. Rather, Justice Goff adopted the more practical test in *Brown v. Nitrate Producers S.S. Co.,*[22] which defined a latent defect as one which could not be discovered on such an examination as a reasonably careful, skilled man would make.[23]

Who Has the Duty of Inspecting

Irrespective of which definition is deemed to apply, who must do the inspecting? If the "reasonable man/reasonably prudent inspection" standard applies, there are obviously critical differences between a "reasonable manufacturer's" inspection, a "reasonable shipyard's" inspection, a "reasonable classification" inspection, a "reasonable owner's" inspection, and a "reasonable crew's" inspection. What may be reasonable from the

---

merely held that a visual inspection of a valve in a cargo space prior to loading was an adequate exercise of due diligence.

20. Tetrault, "The Inchmaree Clause," 41 *Tulane Law Review* 2, 1967: Admiralty Law Institute: A Symposium on the Hull Policy. Tetrault calls attention to an example presenting the problem of distinguishing an error in design from a latent defect, in the case of Liberty ships which in the late 1940s were splitting their tailshafts and dropping their propellers at an alarming rate until it was found that their normal cruise RPM was in phase with the harmonic characteristics of their hulls; the troublemaking resonant vibration was cured by reducing the engine speed from 76 RPM to 66 RPM and substituting larger propellers to maintain efficiency. Mr. Tetrault's article is highly commended.

21. 1974 AMC 1399, [1975] 1 Lloyd's Rep. 333 (St.,N.Y.).

22. (1937) 58 Ll.L.Rep. 188.

23. This was the definition adopted in *Reisman v. New Hampshire Fire Ins. Co.,* 312 F.2d 17, 1963 AMC 1151 (5th Cir.), and *National Sugar Refining Co. v. M/S Las Villas, supra,* among others. By contrast, in the *Carib Prince,* 63 F. 266 (E.D.N.Y., 1894), *aff'd* 68 F. 254 (2d Cir., 1895), *rev'd* on other grounds, 170 U.S. 655 (1898); *Tropical Marine Products v. Birmingham Fire Ins. Co. (The Sea Pak),* 247 F.2d 116, 1957 AMC 1946 (5th Cir.), cert den. 355 U.S. 903 (1957); and *Waterman S.S. Corp. v. United States Smelting, Refining & Mining Co.,* 155 F.2d 687, 1946 AMC 1730 (5th Cir.), cert den. 329 U.S. 761, among others, a latent defect was defined as one which could not be discovered *by any known and customary test.* In *Mellon v. Federal Ins. Co.,* 14 F.2d 997, 1926 AMC 1449 (S.D.N.Y.), the court seemingly approved both definitions. Obviously, the two are rather different. In *Parente, supra,* quoted by Justice Goff, the trial court had charged the jury that a latent defect was any defect not discoverable through ordinary use and maintenance. On appeal, it was held that there must be a defect or flaw not discoverable *by any ordinary test.*

standpoint of a highly sophisticated manufacturer may well be grossly unreasonable from the standpoint of an inexperienced yachtsman.[24]

As McAuliffe points out, the courts have not considered fully the separate and differing standards for the numbers and types of inspections which apply to manufacturers, fabricators, repairers, classification societies, shipyards, shipowners, and crews.[25] For example, in *American Shops, Inc. v. Reliance Ins. Co.*,[26] the underwriters contended that the loss was due to a literal disintegration of the engine in the insured yacht, caused by maldistribution of the stress and strain as a result of the separation of a counterweight from the shaft while the engine was in operation. Testimony of the yacht owner and another eyewitness was to the effect that the damage was caused by an inherent defect in the forging of a steel motor counterweight. The court held that the loss occurred through "explosions, bursting of boilers, breakage of shafts, or through . . . latent defect in the machinery" without in the least differentiating among the four possible causes.

In *Reliance Ins. Co. v. Brickenkamp*,[27] the court had before it a casualty which resulted from the manner in which a water pump and generator were positioned relative to one another in the assembly of a motor boat. The trial court found that the rubber hoses between the exhaust elbows and the pipes going out of the transom of the boat were burned in half, allowing water to enter the hull. The holes in the rubber exhaust hoses were caused by the loss of cooling water circulation to the engine, which, in turn, resulted from a water pump failure, which failure was a result of a drive belt slipping. The cause of the belt slipping was a maladjustment of the generator, which adjustment draws the belt tight on the water pump. There was nothing physically or mechanically wrong with the water pump, with the engine, with the generator, or with the belt, the only difficulty being that the generator was improperly adjusted which permitted the belt to be too loose and thereby slip on the water pump, causing a shortage of cooling water to the engine, and consequently overheating of the exhaust gasses and the burning of the exhaust hoses. The motor boat had been used by its purchaser (the assured) for only about twenty hours when it sank.

The majority of the court concluded:

> The condition which ultimately caused the sinking of the vessel in the instant case was not a latent defect, but it was, as shown by the

---

24. This important distinction is the subject, in depth, of an article by William C. McAuliffe, Jr., "The Concept of Latent Defect in Marine Insurance," 11 *Journal of Maritime Law & Commerce* 4 (July 1980).

25. McAuliffe, *op.cit.*, n. 24, *supra*.

26. 26 N.J. Super. 145, 97 A.2d 513 (Essex Co. Ct., 1953).

27. 147 So.2d 200, 1963 AMC 792 (Fla.Dist.Ct.App.).

record, one that was difficult to see or find. If the condition had been one on deck it would have been seen readily, but merely because it was difficult of ascertainment does not draw it into the category of a latent defect.

The dissent by White, J., seems better reasoned. He said in part:

A latent defect has been defined as one which is not ascertainable by known customary test. The majority cites this definition with approval but does not apply it from the standpoint of the insured owner or purchaser. In some contexts latent defects have been defined also as those which could have been discovered had due diligence been exercised. . . . In this connection it would seem that due diligence is that care which an ordinary *owner or purchaser* would exercise under the circumstances . . . not the care that would be expected of a trained factory technician or skilled mechanic. . . . In order to come fully within the definition of "latent" the defect must be hidden from *knowledge* as well as sight. . . . Apparently it was found in the trial court that the misaligned or maladjusted generator was a part of the machinery insured, that the defect existed at the time of the purchase and was not apparent to the insured through observance of the customary test with reference to the functioning of the water pump.

The applicable test was described by an expert witness as being one of starting the engine up and observing whether water came out of the exhaust, thus indicating that the water pump was functioning. *This test was, in fact, performed by the assured, and he saw water coming out of the exhaust,* thus indicating proper functioning.

The dissent also stated:

The conclusion reached by the majority appears to hinge on the assumption that if the engine had been positioned above deck the defect certainly would have been discovered by the plaintiff. In my opinion, however, the evidence was sufficient to support the conclusion that the defect could well have been missed even if the engine were above deck and completely within the plaintiff's vision.

By contrast, in *The Prussia*,[28] a cargo case, the court reached an opposite result from the majority in *Brickenkamp* on a rather comparable set

---

28. 93 F. 837 (2d Cir., 1899). For cases involving defects in the component parts of a vessel, see the "rivet" cases. *The Cameronia*, 38 F.2d 522 (E.D.N.Y., 1930); *The Carib Prince*, 63 F. 266 (E.D.N.Y., 1894), *aff'd* 68 F. 254 (2d Cir., 1895), *rev'd* on other grounds, 170 U.S. 655 (1898); *Brown v. Nitrate S.S. Co.*, (1937) 58 Ll.L.Rep. 188. In the *Carib Prince*, the court found that there was a defect in the rivet arising from the fact that the quality of the iron had been injured by too much hammering at the time it was annealing so that it became brittle and weak, a latent defect which was not discovered and not discoverable, at that time or subsequently, by the exercise of all known and customary tests and methods of examination which

of circumstances. In that case, a new vessel was carrying a cargo of meat. The meat spoiled during the voyage due to the failure of a refrigeration unit. The failure of the unit was due to the presence of a leather washer in the unit which must have been left in the unit by the inadvertence of the employees of the manufacturer when assembling it. The court noted that the unit had been constructed by builders of "requisite" capacity and after it had become part of the equipment of the vessel had been tested by competent experts in the most thorough manner and found to be perfect. The court held that the shipowner had exercised due diligence to provide a proper refrigeration unit. By implication, discovery of the washer within the unit was held to be a project beyond the ability of the ship's crew to detect. It will be observed that on these facts, there was no defect in the machinery components *per se* but rather a defect in *the manner of assembly.*

At the extreme end of the spectrum will be found such cases as *Lewis v. Aetna Ins. Co.,*[29] discussed *infra,* in connection with unexplained sinkings. There, the yacht sank at the dock from unexplained causes. The concurring justices held that an unreasonable result would be reached if the plaintiff yacht owners were denied coverage which they "reasonably assumed they had purchased because they cannot explain an inexplainable sinking."

McAuliffe concludes his penetrating analysis with language which can scarcely be improved upon. He states:

> The courts, counsel, underwriters, adjusters and shipowners should proceed with care in matters which any one of them may conceive of as involving a "latent defect." Their inquiries should be the following, and they should proceed in the sequence of inquiries here enumerated:
>
> 1. Is the defect one which could not reasonably have been detected before it manifested itself?
>
> 2. If any reasonably required inspection *might* have revealed the existence of the defect, who should have made the inspection (or test) and thus discovered the defect?
>
> 3. Had such an inspection (or test) been made, to whom would knowledge of the results be revealed?
>
> 4. Were such results in fact properly revealed to those chargeable with knowledge thereof?
>
> 5. What duty to act lay upon those who would have knowledge of the results of an inspection (or test) adequate to reveal the defect?

---

were all employed. In *Brown,* Justice Porter expressed doubt that a ship's officer is obliged on the commencement of a voyage to tap every rivet to find if it has a defect or not.

29. 264 Or. 314, 505 P.2d 914 (St.,Ore., 1973).

Latent Defect Found

There are, of course, a rather considerable number of cases in which latent defects have been found.[30]

See, also, the discussion, *infra*, with respect to those cases holding that the fact finder may conclude that a latent defect existed where a seaworthy ship sinks from unascertained causes. A typical example is *Zillah*,[31] where the court held that while the burden of proof exists upon the assured to show that the loss of the vessel was caused by some risk or hazard insured against by the policy, if seaworthiness at the inception of the risk and the beginning of the voyage is established and a loss occurs, the inference may be drawn that the loss was caused by a peril of navigation or a latent defect. See, also, *Glen Falls Ins. Co. v. Long*,[32] where a motorboat

---

30. *Oceanic S.S. Co. v. Faber*, (1907) 13 Com.Cas. 28, C.A. (shaft had a latent defect due to an imperfect weld; recovery denied, however, for replacement of the defective part itself); *Hutchins Bros. v. Royal Exchange Assur. Corp.*, (1911) 16 Com.Cas. 242, C.A.(latent defect in stern frame; however, cost of new frame held unrecoverable); *National Bulk Carriers v. American Marine Hull Ins. Synd.*, 1949 AMC 340 (Arb.) (latent defect in a spring steel washer that failed, permitting a machine screw to back out that, in turn, allowed a thermometer tube to fall into a gear train); *Thibert v. Union Ins. Soc.*, 1951 AMC 1661 (Arb.) (latent defect in a cam roller and pin); *Rensselaer*, 125 Misc. 395, 211 N.Y.S. 348, 1925 AMC 1116 (St.,N.Y.) (latent defect in a paddle shaft but recovery denied for the cost of replacing the defective part); *The Spot Pack*, 242 F.2d 385, 1957 AMC 655 (5th Cir.) (circuit breaker on board the vessel but not installed; no definitive latent defect was found but one was inferred); *Esso Manhattan*, 116 F.Supp. 814, 1953 AMC 1152 (S.D.N.Y.) (notches in defective welding of a ship's plates found to be a latent defect); *Tropical Marine Products, Inc. v. Birmingham Fire Ins. Co. of Pennsylvania (The Sea Pak)*, 247 F.2d 116, 1957 AMC 1946 (5th Cir.) (leak underneath an inaccessible refrigerated space held to be a latent defect); *Scindia Steamships (London) Ltd. v. London Assur.*, (1937) 3 All E.R. 895, 56 Ll.L.Rep. 136 (latent defect in tailshaft which then fell, damaging the propeller; damage to propeller held covered but the cost of a new shaft was not covered); *J.L. Fisheries Ltd. v. Boston Ins. Co.*, (1969) 69 D.L.R.2d 18 (N.S.,Can.) (pinion shaft broke, damaging other portions of the vessel); *Walker v. Travelers Indemnity Co.*, 289 So.2d 864 (La.App., 1974) (latent defect in "maxim silencer" on the engine of a yacht which a reasonable inspection would not have revealed); *Palmer v. Security Ins. Co.*, 263 S.W.2d 210 (St.,Mo.App., 1953) (latent defect in machinery by reason of the absence of a lock nut on a stuffing box packing nut on the drive shaft; the packing nut ran off the shaft permitting water to enter the hull and sink the vessel); *Cleveland & B. Transit Co. v. Insurance Co. of N.A.*, 115 F. 431 (S.D.N.Y., 1902) (imperfect casting of two metals created a latent defect; recovery was allowed for the defective part itself—a decision not in accord with the weight of authority); *Wills & Sons v. World Marine Ins. Ltd.* (Times, L.J., March 14, 1911; Note, (1980) 1 Lloyd's Rep. 350) (link in chain of a chain hoist gave way at the point of a bad weld; held, a latent defect); *American Shops, Inc. v. Reliance Ins. Co.*, 26 N.J. Super. 145, 97 A.2d 513 (Essex Co.Ct., 1953) (latent defect one of four possible causes upon which the court relied but without differentiating among them); *Fredericks v. American Export Lines*, 117 F.Supp. 255 (S.D.N.Y., 1953), *aff'd* 227 F.2d 450 (2d Cir., 1955) (defect existing in an iron skid by reason of it having been bent too much in the process of shaping it for use; i.e., a potential latent defect arising from a method of fabrication rather than from the makeup of the raw material from which it was made.

31. 1929 AMC 166 (St.,Minn.).

32. 1953 AMC 1841 (St.,Va.).

sank within one hour after starting on a fishing trip, by reason of a sudden and unexplained inrush of water. The owner adduced evidence of seaworthiness prior to the start of the trip; the underwriter offered no evidence. It was held that there was a presumption under these circumstances that the loss was occasioned by a peril of the sea or a latent defect.

In *Sea Pak, supra,* it will be noted that the court, in effect, held in the alternative that either the defect was latent—which presupposes that it was not discoverable by a reasonably careful inspection—or if discoverable and the master did not in fact discover it, this constituted negligence which, under the Inchmaree Clause, was covered. Thus, in the view of the court, an unexplained defect might amount to a latent defect.

Latent Defect Not Found

If a count were to be made, the cases in which latent defects have not been found would outnumber those in which such defects were found. The most common situations appear to involve pre-existing defects becoming patent and visible through wear and tear.

A typical example is *Sipowicz v. Wimble (The Green Lion).*[33] In that case, a wooden yacht in a marina foundered during clear weather and calm seas. The court found that the incursion of water in the hull resulted from a separation between the keel and keelson and the remainder of the hull, which separation was the direct and proximate consequence of the deteriorated condition of the fastenings and the frames which secured the keel and the keelson to the rest of the hull. On the owner's submission that the sinking was due to a latent defect, the court said:

> The Green Lion's defective and deteriorated metal fastenings were not, under the above definitions, latent in nature; they were clearly patent. They were observable and had been observed. . . . They were not hidden or unknown, but rather were fully revealed in the . . . condition survey report. They were not defects inherent in the metal, but were rather the result of 27 years of use.

See, also, *Presti v. Firemen's Ins. Co.,*[34] where a hole in a yacht's exhaust line was held not to be a latent defect, and *Parente v. Bayville Marine, Inc.,*[35] where the results of normal wear and tear and the corrosive effects of seawater were held not to constitute a latent defect.[36]

33. 370 F.Supp. 442, 1975 AMC 524 (D.C.N.Y.), [1974] 1 Lloyd's Rep. 593.
34. 1972 AMC 1220 (St.,Cal.).
35. 353 N.Y.S.2d 24, 1974 AMC 1399, [1975] 1 Lloyd's Rep. 333 (St.,N.Y.).
36. Other cases are: *Jarvis v. Newport News,* 312 F.Supp. 214, 1970 AMC 1697 (E.D.Va.,Sy.); *Wood v. Great American,* 289 F.Supp. 1014, 1968 AMC 1815A (E.D.,Wis.) (defect

In other decisions, the courts have simply found that no latent defect existed. For example, in *Jackson v. Mumford, supra,* the court found that a weakness in design of a connecting rod was not a latent defect. Compare, however, *Prudent Tankships Ltd., S.A. v. The Dominion Ins. Co., Ltd. (The Caribbean Sea), supra,* where the court inferentially overruled *Jackson v. Mumford* and held that a design was a latent defect.

In *Irwin v. Eagle Star Ins. (The Jomie),*[37] the insured yacht sank due to electrolysis when steel and brass pipes were improperly joined together in an air-conditioning unit. The fitting was painted black and disguised the improper joinder of brass and steel. Although the defect was hidden and the assured was not aware of the condition, the court held that there was no defect in the metal and, therefore, no latent defect in the machinery or hull but rather a "mistake" by the air-conditioning company. To the same effect was *Egan v. Washington General Ins. Corp.,*[38] where a "thru bolt" in a yacht's sea strainer was made of a ferromagnetic metal which, in combination with the bronze sea strainer, deteriorated faster than normal because of electrolysis. The court held this not to be a latent defect under an all-risk hull policy.

In *Reliance Ins. v. Brickenkamp,* discussed at length *supra,* it was held that an improperly tensioned water pump drive was not a latent defect in hull or machinery.

In *Compania Transatlantica Centro-Americana, S.A. v. Alliance Assur. Co. (The Panamanian),*[39] an automatic sea valve in a veessel at anchor opened by reason of unusual vapor pressure and jammed open, perhaps because it was old and worn; a list of the ship and small waves set up a siphon effect

---

in rubber water hose held due to ordinary wear and tear and not latent defect); *By's Chartering v. Interstate Ins.,* 524 F.2d 1045, 1976 AMC 113 (lst Cir.) (damage occasioned by defective hose the result of wear and tear and not latent defect); *Land v. Franklin,* 225 S.C. 33, 80 S.E.2d 420 (St., S.C., 1954) (opening up of hull planking not a latent defect with recovery allowed, however, under the perils clause); *Ferrante v. Detroit F. & M. Ins. Co.,* 125 F.Supp. 621, 1954 AMC 2026 (D.,Cal.) (no latent defect in broken crank shaft but recovery allowed by reason of negligence of an engineer); *McDuffie v. Old Reliable,* 1979 AMC 59 (E.D.,La.) (serious deterioration rather than a latent defect, coupled with want of due diligence on the part of the owner in failing to inspect and repair); *Larsen v. Insurance Co. of N.A.,* 252 F.Supp. 458, 1965 AMC 2576 (W.D.,Wash.) (breaking off of a suction pipe allowing water to flood a ship's hold held to be caused by gradual action of seawater, electrolysis, galvanic action or corrosion over a period of time); *Texas No. 1,* 112 F.2d 541, 1940 AMC 1106 (5th Cir.) (defects in an unseaworthy barge patent, not latent); *Reisman v. New Hampshire Fire Ins. Co.,* 312 F.2d 17, 1963 AMC 1151 (5th Cir.) (worm-eaten condition of a vessel's bottom is not a latent defect); *Oceanic S.S. v. Faber,* (1907) 13 Com.Cas. 28 (imperfect weld not becoming patent during the currency of the policy; recovery denied); *Hutchins Bros. v. Royal Exchange Assur. Corp.,* [1911] 16 Com. Cas. 242, 2 K.B. 398, C.A. (stern frame built into the vessel had a latent defect which, during the currency of the policy, became visible owing to ordinary wear and tear; recovery denied).

37. 455 F.2d 827, 1973 AMC 1184 (5th Cir.), [1973] 2 Lloyd's Rep. 541.

38. 240 So.2d 875 (Fla.App., 1970).

39. 50 F.Supp. 986, 1943 AMC 976 (S.D.N.Y.).

causing water to flow into the hot-well and flood the engine room. The engineers, being unable to find the source of the water, failed to shut a gate valve provided for that purpose and the vessel was beached to prevent her from sinking. The court held that the defective sea valve did not constitute a latent defect.[40] It would appear quite possible that the court could have held that the defective sea valve was a design defect, in which case the result reached by the court would have been consistent with *Jackson v. Mumford* but not compatible with the reasoning in *The Caribbean Sea, supra.*

In *Waterman S.S. Corp. v. U.S.S.R. & M. Co.,*[41] the court held that a true latent defect is a flaw in the metal and not a defect caused by the use of a metallic object resulting in gradual deterioration. In that case the object involved was a pelican hook which failed while being used as a lashing on deck cargo.

In *Neubros Co. v. Northwestern National Ins.,*[42] the court held that the Inchmaree Clause does not insure against patent, apparent defects or obligate the underwriters to pay the cost of repairing the latent defect. In that case, the insured barge was structurally incapable of carrying a full load and the assured failed in its affirmative duty to reveal to the underwriters that the barge was thus incapable.

In *Mayan*[43] the assured claimed under the Inchmaree Clause for damage to his yacht's diesel engine. The court observed that the assured had the burden of proof, and the evidence having failed to show any believable reason for the damage to the engine, judgment was entered for the underwriters.

Negligence of Master, Mariners, Engineers, or Pilots

The other major branch of the Inchmaree Clause which has resulted in much litigation is that which provides coverage for damage arising from the negligence of masters, officers, crews and pilots, provided such damage did not result from a want of due diligence by the assured, owner, or managers.[44]

---

40. The court held, however, that the incursion of seawater was a fortuitous sea peril; that the cause thereof was the negligence of the engineers, and that there was no want of due diligence on the part of the owners.

41. 155 F.2d 687, 1946 AMC 997 (5th Cir.), cert. den. 329 U.S. 761, 1946 AMC 1730.

42. 359 F.Supp. 310, 1972 AMC 2443 (E.D.N.Y.).

43. 1967 AMC 765 (S.D.,Fla.).

44. There are a number of cases denying recovery on the ground that the person whose negligence caused the loss was not a member of the class defined as "master, mariners, engineers or pilots." Note, however, that the American form was modified in 1955 to cover the negligence of repairmen and charterers so long as they are not assureds.

The first American case involving this branch of the clause appears to have been *New York & P.R.S.S. Co. v. Aetna Ins. Co.*[45] In that case, a vessel on its outbound voyage sustained two broken propeller blades. On the inward voyage, due to the negligence of the master, further damage to the propeller was sustained. Assuming that the further damage was due to the negligence of the master in proceeding on the inward voyage with a broken propeller, the court held that such further damage was covered by the Inchmaree Clause.

In *Chicago S.S. Lines v. U.S. Lloyd's*,[46] recovery was denied where the vessel sank because of water leaking through rivet holes left below the loaded waterline by a repairman acting under the supervision of the manager for the owner. The court held that the sinking resulted from lack of due diligence on the part of the owner.

In *Rendevous*,[47] the owner of a vessel had it reconditioned by an independent contractor boat company. The boat was launched without closing a drain valve and the vessel was damaged when it sank. The court held that the clause did not cover the negligence of a repairman who was an independent contractor, noting that there was a clear distinction between the activities of a person acting for the owner in reconditioning a vessel and the acts of a master acting professionally in handling her at sea. The court also emphasized that the Inchmaree Clause did not affect the requirement that the vessel be seaworthy at the inception of the voyage.[48]

In *Belle of Portugal*,[49] the vessel and its equipment were insured under a policy which included a form of the Inchmaree Clause. The vessel was abandoned by its crew when it caught fire and a salving vessel attempted to hoist the vessel's skiff aboard but it was lost. The underwriters denied liability on the ground that the skiff was not covered because it was lost through the negligence of the crew of the salving vessel. The court held that the action succeeded. While there was no proof that the crew of the

---

45. 192 F. 212 (D.C.N.Y., 1911), 204 F. 255 (2d Cir., 1913).
46. 12 F.2d 733, 1926 AMC 807 (7th Cir., 1926).
47. 219 Wis. 580, 265 N.W. 632, 1936 AMC 25 (St.,Wis.).
48. It should be noted again that both in *Chicago S.S. Lines* and the *Rendevous*, the decisions were rendered prior to 1955 when the American clause was amended to cover the negligence of repairmen and charterers so long as they are not assureds. Moreover, the court's emphasis in the *Rendevous* that the Inchmaree Clause does not affect the requirement that the vessel be seaworthy at the inception of the voyage may well not accord with the modern American view as to a warranty of seaworthiness in time policies. Compare, for example, *Gregoire v. Underwriters at Lloyds*, 1982 AMC 2045 (D.,Alaska), where Judge Fitzgerald held that in a time hull policy there is no implied warranty that a vessel will not break ground in an unseaworthy condition but that, where the owner of a vessel or those in privity with him send the vessel to sea knowing it to be unseaworthy, the insurer is not liable for damages proximately caused by the unseaworthiness. See, also, the excellent article by Russell W. Pritchett, "The Implied Warranty of Seaworthiness in Time Policies: The American View," *Lloyd's Maritime and Commercial Law Quarterly*, [1983] 2 LMCLQ, p. 195. See discussion, *supra*, Chapter XI, "Warranties."
49. 421 F.2d 390, 1970 AMC 30 (9th Cir.), [1970] 2 Lloyd's Rep. 386.

salving vessel was negligent, even if they had been, the clause covered losses due to the negligence of "mariners."[50]

In *The Lapwing*,[51] the policy included an Inchmaree Clause. The vessel was negligently docked by the manager of a ship repairer for the purpose of having her bottom cleaned and was damaged. The underwriters defended on the ground that the manager of the ship repairer was not a "master" within the clause. Referring to the Merchant Shipping Act, 1894, the court noted that a master was defined therein as being every person (except a pilot) having command or charge of any ship and concluded that the manager was the master of the vessel at the time the damage occurred and, therefore, the policy covered.

In *Continental Ins. Co. v. Hersent Offshore, Inc.*,[52] a construction superintendent, who was on a barge every day and made seagoing decisions for its protection, was held to be a master within the clause, and his imprudent failure in handling moorage lines, such that the barge capsized, led to recovery.

In *Lind v. Mitchell*,[53] the vessel was damaged by ice and she leaked badly; the captain, expecting a gale in which he thought the vessel would be lost, decided to abandon her and then set fire to her to prevent her from being a danger to navigation. The court held that on the facts, the abandonment was unreasonable and constituted negligence on the part of the master, thus allowing recovery.

In *Joseph H. (Stranding)*,[54] the vessel stranded. The court held that the stranding was due to grossly negligent navigation by an otherwise competent master, a risk covered by the Inchmaree Clause. Alleged violations of Liberian statutes regulating manning and watch hours were found not to have contributed to the loss.

In *McAllister Lighterage Line v. Ins. Co. of N.A.*,[55] the bargee failed to stay aboard the barge and tend the pumps as he was required to do by his duties; held, negligence of the prescribed class under the Inchmaree Clause.[56]

---

50. Arnould concludes that this result is unsound. Arnould, *Law of Marine Insurance and Average*, (16th ed.), Sec. 831, f. 71. This author agrees. It would appear that the the word "mariners" was intended to be synonymous with "crew" (of the vessel) and, as such, the crew of the salving vessel would not qualify.

51. (1940) 66 Ll.L.Rep. 174, 56 T.L.R. 520.

52. 1978 AMC 234 (2d Cir.).

53. (1928) 32 Ll.L.Rep. 70, C.A.

54. 411 F.Supp. 496, 1976 AMC 1565 (S.D.N.Y.).

55. 143 F.Supp. 697, 1957 AMC 39 (S.D.N.Y.).

56. Other cases are: *Ferrante v. Detroit F. & M. Ins. Co.*, 125 F.Supp. 621, 1954 AMC 2026 (D., Cal.); *Tropical Marine Products, Inc. v. Birmingham Fire Ins. Co. of Pennsylvania (The Sea Pak)*, 247 F.2d 116, 1957 AMC 1946 (5th Cir.); *Spot Pack*, 242 F.2d 385, 1957 AMC 655 (5th Cir.); *Adequate*, 305 F.2d 944, 1963 AMC 116 (9th Cir.); *Spooner & Son v. Connecticut Fire*, 314 F.2d 753, 1963 AMC 859 (2d Cir.) (negligence of an owner serving as a master; i.e., "operational" negligence as distinguished from a non-delegable shoreside obligation to use due

Recovery Denied—Negligence Not Found or the Failure to Exercise Due Diligence

To the contrary, in the following cases recovery was denied because: (1) no negligence was found, or (2) the negligence was that of a person not falling within the specified class, or (3) the loss resulted from a want of due diligence by the assured, the owners or managers of the vessel, or any of them.

No Negligence Found

In *Britannia Shipping Corp. v. Globe & Rutgers Fire Ins. Co.*,[57] the proximate cause of the loss of a vessel was found to be a theft although negligence may have made the theft possible.

In *Mayan*,[58] the evidence failed to show any believable reason for damage to the insured yacht's engines attributable to negligence of the master or crew.

In *Tinkerbell*,[59] a lay-up warranty required the vessel to be laid up by October 1; the vessel's loss while attempting to reach the lay-up port was attributed to mechanical difficulties rather than the negligence of the master.

Negligence Not That of One of the Specified Classes

In *Rendevous*,[60] the negligence was that of a repairman who was an independent contractor. To the same effect, see *Barbara*,[61] where the negligence was that of a mechanic employed to overhaul the diesel engine of a yacht laid up at the end of the season. As he was not an "engineer," the

---

diligence held covered); *Carter Tug Co. v. Home Insurance*, 345 F.Supp. 1193, 1972 AMC 498 (S.D.,Ill.) (negligence of a pilot and deckhand in failing to take any action to stop the flow of water into a tug which foundered and sank held covered); *Parkhill-Goodloe v. Home Ins.*, 1976 AMC 951 (M.D.,Fla.) (sinking of an otherwise seaworthy barge proximately caused by the negligence of a nighwatchman in failing to make a proper inspection of the bilges and in disconnecting a portable pump); *Continental Ins. Co. v. Hersent Offshore*, 567 F.2d 533, 1978 AMC 234 (2d Cir.) (a construction superintendent who was on a barge every day and made seagoing decisions for its protection was held to be a "master" within the clause and his imprudent failure in handling mooring lines so that the barge capsized held covered under the clause).

57. 138 Misc. 38, 244 N.Y.S. 720, 1930 AMC 1722, *aff'd* 249 N.Y.S. 908 (St.,N.Y.).
58. 1967 AMC 765 (S.D.,Fla.).
59. 533 F.2d 496, 1976 AMC 799 (9th Cir.).
60. 219 Wis. 580, 265 N.W. 632, 1936 AMC 25 (St.,Wis.).
61. 111 F.2d 134, 1940 AMC 583 (7th Cir.).

damage done by his failure to drain the water jackets which froze was held not to be covered under the clause.[62]

In *Russell Mining v. Northwestern F. & M. Ins. Co.*,[63] a barge was being kept afloat by electric pumps and was moored near a shore installation. A repairman ashore doing repairs on the shore installation inadvertently disconnected the electric power line leading to the pumps on the barge which thereupon sank. The court held that as the repairman was not engaged in repairing the barge or its equipment at the time of the loss there was no recovery.

In *Yacht Rowdy*,[64] and in *King v. Liverpool & London & Globe*,[65] the loss was negligently caused by friends of the assured-owner while aboard his vessel. In both instances, the court held that the losses were not due to persons falling within the specific classification.[66]

In *The Dalles*,[67] the clause was held not to cover the negligence of independent contractors in damaging a sternwheeler while hauling it out on a marine railway such that the hogging chains broke and the vessel was severely damaged.

Failure to Exercise Due Diligence

It is clear from an analysis of the cases that the failure to exercise due diligence may be that of the owner himself, or may arise by reason of imputation because of the negligence of the master, a member of the crew, or an independent repairman or contractor.[68]

---

62. It should be noted that this was one of the earlier forms of the clause which did not include coverage for repairmen.

63. 322 F.2d 440, 1963 AMC 2358 (6th Cir.).

64. 177 F.Supp. 932, 1959 AMC 2270 (E.D.,Mich.).

65. 37 Misc.2d 822, 238 N.Y.S.2d 799, 1964 AMC 532 (St.,N.Y.).

66. Also, in both instances, the courts found that the presence of the assured-owners aboard the vessels at the time of the casualties precluded recovery because of a failure to exercise due diligence. See discussion, *infra*, with respect to seagoing negligence versus shoreside negligence, and failure to exercise due diligence.

67. 172 Or. 91, 139 P.2d 769, 1943 AMC 1178 (St.,Ore.).

68. While it may appear anomalous that the clause covers negligence of the "master, officers, crew or pilots," yet coverage may be defeated if there is a want of due diligence, the anomaly is more apparent than real. The distinction lies in whether or not the negligence was that of the owner or that of his servants on the vessel; i.e., under the doctrine of *respondeat superior* . . . was it preparational (shoreside) or operational (seagoing)? See discussion, *infra*. Moreover, there are many different forms of Inchmaree Clauses. As the distinguished arbitrator in *Majore v. Glen Falls Ins. Co.*, 1973 AMC 1997 (Arb.), noted in his appendix, he had undertaken to compare eight various yacht policies issued locally by underwriters and found that in all eight the conventional perils clause had been displaced by all risks coverage; that two of the eight included an Inchmaree Clause which covered the negligence of an owner when acting in the capacity of a master; two had clauses which covered latent defects only and the remaining four had no Inchmaree Clauses at all. A broker's form examined contained an Inchmaree Clause but it was so worded that the owner-assured did not qualify as a member of the specified class. The precise wording of the clause is, therefore, of paramount importance.

For example, in the former category will be found such cases as *Leathem-Smith-Putnam Nav. Co. v. National U.S. Ins. Co.*,[69] where the owners of a vessel permitted holes in the hatch-leaves of the vessel without providing covers. The master negligently failed to place covers over the holes and as a result the vessel sank. The court held that the loss was due to a lack of due diligence on the part of the owners.

In *Yacht Rowdy*,[70] the owner-assured was directing some friends who negligently assisted him in laying up his yacht for the winter. Held: a lack of due diligence on the part of the owner.

In *Commercial Union v. Daniels*,[71] recovery was denied when a fishing vessel sank at a dock due to an open sea-valve not closed by reason of the negligence of the owner himself.

In *Presti v. Fireman's Fund Ins. Co.*,[72] the insured yacht sank from water entering holes in her exhaust line. The assured-owner suggested that the holes resulted from poor maintenance amounting to negligence of the owner when acting in the capacity of master and thus came within the ambit of the clause. The court agreed, in essence, but held that the negligence also consisted of a failure to exercise due diligence as it constituted a "shoreside" failure as distinguished from seagoing or operational negligence.

In *Majore v. Glens Falls Ins. Co.*,[73] the plaintiff owner had introduced into the lubricating system an oil additive which he failed to remove before departing for a trip. The parties stipulated that the plaintiff, in the exercise of due care, should have removed the additive oil before departing and that his failure to do so proximately resulted in damage to the engine. The arbitrator held that there was a want of due diligence by the owner, i.e., shoreside "preparational" negligence.

Goodman v. Fireman's Fund Ins. Co.[74] perfectly illustrates the point. In that case, the assured had an all risks policy on his 55-foot yacht, providing coverage against all risks of physical loss or damage from any external cause. Also included was a form of the Inchmaree Clause which expressly covered "negligence of masters (including owner when acting in the capacity of master)." The policy also included a lay-up warranty that the

---

69. 96 F.2d 923, 1937 AMC 925 (7th Cir.).

70. 177 F.Supp. 932, 1959 AMC 2270 (E.D.,Mich.).

71. 343 F.Supp. 674, 1972 AMC 452 (S.D.,Tex.).

72. 1972 AMC 1220 (St.,Cal.).

73. 1973 AMC 1997 (Arb.). See, also, *Holm v. Underwriters Through T.W. Rice & Co.*, [1981] 124 D.L.R.(3d) 463 (Can., B.C.), where the owner, who was also master, removed an exhaust hose but negligently failed to close the open exhaust port. The court severed the roles of master and owner and found that the negligence of the plaintiff as master in failing to close the exhaust port would be covered under the Inchmaree Clause but that the negligence of the plaintiff as owner, in leaving the vessel in the condition she was in for two weeks until she sank, was not covered under the policy.

74. 452 F.Supp. 8, 1978 AMC 846, *aff'd* 600 F.2d 1040, 1979 AMC 2534 (4th Cir.).

vessel would be laid up and out of commission between specified periods. Ice and freezing were specifically excluded from coverage.

During 1975, the owner employed professional help to lay up the yacht but in 1976 he undertook to do the work himself. Unfortunately, he omitted to drain the seawater cooling system and did not close the sea-valves which permitted seawater to enter the system. The plastic jackets broke during the course of the winter due to freezing of water in the filters and the vessel subsequently sank at the dock.

The district court held that the loss was not covered because (1) freezing was excluded from coverage; (2) the loss was not covered by the all risks clause; and (3) the provision insuring against negligence of the master did not apply. On the last point, the court held that the Inchmaree Clause did not cover shoreside negligence of the master but only his operational negligence.

On appeal, the Fourth Circuit agreed on the district court's interpretation of the Inchmaree Clause, but held that the all risks clause did provide coverage inasmuch as the assured's negligence caused the loss (an insured peril) which combined with an excluded peril (freezing), and the insured peril was the predominant efficient cause of the loss. Unfortunately for the assured, the court also held that the assured breached the lay-up warranty in failing to close the sea-valves as a part of the winterizing process, found to be a custom in the applicable waters, and his failure precluded recovery.

The obligation of the shipowner to exercise due diligence to make his vessel seaworthy is paramount and subsequently occurring negligence on the part of the master or crew does not bring the loss within the scope of the clause. In *Coast Ferries, Ltd. v. Century Ins. Co. of Canada,*[75] the vessel was improperly loaded. The court held that the shipowner was negligent in leaving the master to supervise the loading and in failing to provide him with proper data relating to the loading. There was also evidence that on prior occasions the owner had permitted the vessel to go to sea in an overloaded condition. The admitted negligence of the master in operating the vessel in an overloaded condition did not provide grounds for recovery where the owner was clearly lacking in due diligence.

Negligence of Master, Crew or Others

As noted above, if the negligence of a member of the prescribed class falls within the category of "shoreside" or "preparational" negligence, as dis-

---

75. (1974) 48 D.L.R. 2d 310, [1973] 2 Lloyd's Rep. 232.

tinguished from "operational" or "seagoing" negligence, a want of due diligence is imputed.[76]

For example, in *Chicago S.S. Lines v. U.S. Lloyd's*[77] repairers were being supervised by a company manager. The repairers were negligent in leaving open rivet holes below the waterline. It was held that the sinking resulted from a want of due diligence. In *Yacht Buccaneer*,[78] davits failed on lifting a launch; the negligence of the master was ascribed to a failure to perform the non-delegable duty of making the vessel seaworthy as distinguished from a navigational function.[79]

See, however, *Adequate*.[80] There, the yacht sank at the dock during its winter lay-up when water entered the vessel through holes in a portion of an exhaust line. The holes had apparently existed for a considerable period of time. The Ninth Circuit found that the vessel owners were "Sunday skippers" who knew literally nothing about the operation and maintenance of a yacht but instead relied almost exclusively on one who had acted as master during the summer months and who continued during the winter to look after the yacht on a voluntary basis. Clearly, the function of the volunteer former master was that of winterizing the vessel—a non-navigational function. In nonetheless allowing recovery, the court further observed that due diligence is a relative term which must be construed in light of individual cases. Perhaps the most that can be said for the decision is that a much more liberal interpretation will be given the clause where the vessel is a pleasure yacht used only sporadically during the summer months.

Interaction of the Clause with Express Warranties and the Implied Warranty of Seaworthiness

Somewhat of an anomaly is presented by the fact that the Inchmaree Clause provides coverage for loss or damage resulting from negligence or latent defect although that same negligence or latent defect might well render the vessel unseaworthy in breach of the implied warranty of seaworthiness in every voyage policy—and in the United States, in a modi-

---

76. See *Yacht Buccaneer*, 1940 AMC 1397 (Arb.); *Chicago S.S. Lines v. U.S. Lloyd's*, 12 F.2d 733, 1926 AMC 807 (7th Cir.); *Yacht Barbara*, 111 F.2d 134, 1940 AMC 583 (7th Cir.); *King v. Liverpool & London & Globe*, 37 Misc.2d 822, 238 N.Y.S.2d 799, 1964 AMC 532 (St.N.Y.).
77. 12 F.2d 733, 1926 AMC 807 (7th Cir.).
78. 1940 AMC 1397 (Arb.).
79. By comparison, see *Spot Pack*, 242 F.2d 385, 1957 AMC 655 (5th Cir.), where the master or engineers were found negligent and recovery allowed where circuit breakers, placed on board to be installed by shipboard personnel, remained uninstalled for several voyages up to the time of loss. See, also, cases cited *supra*, n. 56.
80. 305 F.2d 944, 1963 AMC 116 (9th Cir.).

fied fashion, in time policies as well.[81] While it should be emphasized that the proviso of the clause requiring due diligence of the owner relates *solely to coverages provided in the clause itself*,[82] there appears also a parallel and concomitant obligation on the part of the owner because of the implied warranty of seaworthiness. See *Tropical Marine Products, Inc. v. Birmingham Fire Ins. Co. of Pennsylvania (The Sea Pak).*[83] Stating it another way, negligence of the master, mariners, and crew is covered under the clause provided the loss or damage did not result from shoreside or preparational negligence in readying the vessel for sea. Furthermore, if the courts find that a latent defect is not discoverable by a reasonable inspection, then it necessarily follows that the assured has not breached the implied warranty of seaworthiness, and recovery is permitted under the latent defect portion of the clause.

Although the courts have not always been as precise in their language as one might wish, the rationale appears to be:

(1) If the negligence of a member of the prescribed class (whether or not he is also an owner) is seagoing or operational negligence, then recovery is permitted. If, on the other hand, the damage is due to the shoreside failure of the shipowner's managerial staff properly to prepare or equip the vessel for the voyage or service she is about to perform, then recovery is denied.

(2) If a defect exists, and the owner or his agents could or should have discovered it by a reasonable inspection, and failed to do so, then either the defect is not truly latent or the owner has breached his implied warranty of seaworthiness.

In this connection, the remarks of D. V. Moore, chairman of the British Association of Average Adjusters, at the annual meeting of the asso-

---

81. Under English law, there is no implied warranty of seaworthiness in a time policy. See Sec. 39(5), Marine Insurance Act, 1906, reading:
  In a time policy there is no implied warranty that the ship shall be seaworthy at any stage of the adventure, but where, with the privity of the assured, the ship is sent to sea in an unseaworthy state, the insurer is not liable for any loss attributable to unseaworthiness.
However, it should be noted that nearly all the American cases which purport to establish an implied warranty of seaworthiness in time policies really extend no further than holding that the owner may not recover if he fails to use all available and commercially reasonable means of repair *at the inception of the policy.* On that basis, the rules applied in America and in England are indistinguishable. See, also, *Gregoire v. Underwriters at Lloyd's,* 1982 AMC 2045 (D., Alaska), where the court reviewed all relevant cases and concluded that in a time hull policy there is no implied warranty that the vessel will not break ground in an unseaworthy condition. Where, however, the owner of the vessel or those in privity with him send the vessel to sea knowing it to be unseaworthy, the insurer is not liable for damages proximately caused by the unseaworthiness—thus applying for practical purposes the English rule.
  82. *Frederick Starr Contracting Co. v. Aetna Ins. Co.,* 285 F.2d 106, 1961 AMC 342 (2d Cir.); *Robertson v. National Insurance Co. of New Zealand Ltd.,* (1958) S.A.S.R. 143 (Aus.).
  83. 247 F.2d 116, 1957 AMC 1946 (5th Cir.).

ciation in 1956, in his address entitled "The Inchmaree Clause," are interesting and instructive.[84] Mr. Moore said, in part:

The question has been mooted as to what is the precise relationship between the provisions providing cover against the "negligence of masters, officers and crew," and the exclusion, exempting the insurers from liability for damage resulting from want of due diligence of the owners. The question arises in two ways: in the first place it might be said by some over-ingenious person, that, as the owners are legally responsible for the negligence of the master or crew, as their servants, such negligence amounts to "want of due diligence" on the part of the owners. On the other hand it may . . . and indeed has . . . been argued that the exclusion only applies to the actual personal default of the assured, the owners and managers, and if they have in fact delegated the performance of the particular duty to the master, any failure becomes "negligence of the master" and ceases to be "want of due diligence" on the part of the owner.

As far as I am aware there is no direct ruling of the Courts on the point upon the "Inchmaree" clause itself, but there are decisions on the same or similar problems in Bills of Lading cases. My own view is quite clear and is both the above extreme propositions are wrong and the position is this: (1) the provision insuring against negligence of the master, etc. provides cover against negligence by the persons named in the discharge of their duties as such, that is, the navigation and day to day running of the ship; (2) the exception excluding liability for damage due to want of due diligence by the assured owners and managers applies to negligent failure in the discharge of duties that fall within their province as such. If there is such a failure, then there is "want of due diligence" even if the performance of the duties have been entrusted to the master and ship's officers and the actual failure is theirs.

Thus, for example, the provision of proper officers and crew or sufficient bunkers for the voyage is a matter falling within the personal province of the owner or manager. Failure to exercise due diligence in this respect as, for instance, where the ship is sent to sea with a known drunkard as a captain or chief engineer[85] or with insufficient bunkers to complete the first intended stage of the voyage,[86] there would be a failure of the owners or managers and would excuse the underwriters from liability for damage resulting therefrom. This is so even if the owner or manager delegates the performance of this duty to the mas-

---

84. *From The Chair*, Addresses by Chairmen of the Association of Average Adjusters, 1873-1976, The Association of Average Adjusters and Lloyd's of London Press Ltd. (1978).
85. *Moore v. Lunn*, (1922) 15 Ll.L.Rep. 114, 155.
86. *Northumbrian Shipping Co. v. E. Timm & Son*, [1939] A.C. 397.

ter or officers of the ship, as where the master is entrusted with the task of obtaining bunkers. A failure by the master in carrying out this duty is imputed to the owner as want of due diligence on his part and does not fall within the peril "negligence of masters, etc." As Lord Porter said in *Northumbrian Shipping Co. v. E. Timm & Son,* "A failure to perform . . . cannot be excused by trusting to the discretion of the master and if he fails to act prudently, laying the blame on him." Although this was actually said in reference to the warranty of seaworthiness . . . a matter with which we are not concerned. . . . In my view the same principle is to be followed in deciding between what is want of due diligence by the owners, etc. on the one hand, and negligence of the master officers and crew on the other for the purposes of the "Inchmaree" clause.

There is thus, in my view, no conflict at all between the peril "negligence of masters, etc." and the exclusion of damage caused by want of due diligence of owners, etc.; the matters are fundamentally different although occasionally the division is not very easy to see.

Since Mr. Moore's address in 1956, several cases have arisen which tend to confirm his analysis. For example, in *Compania Maritima San Basilio S.A. v. Oceanus Mutual Underwriting Ass'n (Bermuda) Ltd. (The Eurysthenes),*[87] the vessel owner/members of a P & I association were confronted with third-party cargo claims following the vessel's stranding. The club resisted coverage on grounds that the vessel was undermanned, her charts were out of date, her echo sounder was out of order, and she did not have an operative boiler. Thus, the club contended, the vessel was unseaworthy, and the plaintiff members were privy to that unseaworthiness within the meaning of Section 39(5) of the Marine Insurance Act, 1906, providing in essence that where, with the privity of the assured, the vessel is sent to sea in an unseaworthy state, the insurer is not liable for any loss attributable to unseaworthiness.

At first instance, it was held that in principle the provisions of the Act do apply to P & I insurance as respects shipowners' liability. Consequently, Section 39(5) was applicable if the club's contentions as to unseaworthiness and privity were sustained.

The owners of the vessel argued that they were only to be deprived of their right to indemnity if they had been guilty of wilful misconduct in deliberately and recklessly sending the ship to sea knowing she was unfit. The club, on the other hand, argued that their members had no right of indemnity if their "alter ego" ought to have known the ship was not reasonably fit to be sent to sea, yet nevertheless sent her to sea.

87. [1976] 2 Lloyd's Rep. 1171, C.A.

The court of appeal held unanimously that to lose his coverage by reason of the breach of the warranty described in Section 39(5) the assured must have had not only knowledge of the facts which constituted the unseaworthiness but also knowledge that those facts rendered the vessel unseaworthy. Although acknowledging that an assured could not turn a blind eye to the recognition that certain facts constituted unseaworthiness, the court clarified its meaning in the language of Lord Denning, which warrants repeating:

> If the owner of a ship says to himself: "I think a reasonably prudent owner would send her to sea with a crew of 12. So I will send her with 12," he is not privy to unseaworthiness, even though a Judge may afterwards say that he ought to have 14. He may have been negligent in thinking so, but he would not be privy to unseaworthiness. But, if he says to himself "I think that a reasonably prudent owner would send her to sea with a crew of 12, but I have only 10 available, so I will send her with 10," then he is privy to the unseaworthiness, if a Judge afterwards says he ought to have 12. The reason being that he knew she ought to have had 12 and consciously sent her to sea with 10.[88]

Obviously, reconciling the implied warranty of seaworthiness with the Inchmaree Clause can pose difficulties. See, for example, *The Natalie*.[89] In that case, a ship repair firm repaired the assured's vessel between early March 1956 and March 29, 1956, but did so negligently by installing a defective seal ring between the propeller and the tailshaft. The ship repairers' negligence resulted in progressive corrosion of the tailshaft by seawater from the date of repairs until the damage was discovered on June 1, 1957, some 14 months later. The issue before the arbitrator was the extent of liability of the ship repairers under their port risk policy, the liability of intervening hull underwriters who insured the vessel from March 29, 1956, to March 29, 1957, and the last hull underwriters who

---

88. See, also, *Gregoire v. Underwriters' at Lloyds*, 1982 AMC 2045 (D., Alaska); *Visscher Enterprises Pty. Ltd. v. Southern Pac. Ins. Co. Ltd.*, [1981] Qd. R. 561 (1980, Aus.). See, also, "The Implied Warranty of Seaworthiness in Time Policies: The American View," by Russell W. Pritchett, [1983] 2 LMCLQ. Of considerable interest, in the context of limitation of liability actions, but bearing on whether or not the shipowner exercised due diligence, see *The Grand Champion Tankers Ltd. v. Norpipe A/S (The Marion)*, [1984] 2 W.L.R. 942, where the vessel fouled a submerged oil pipeline causing extensive damage. The incident occurred because the master was using an out-of-date and uncorrected chart which did not mark the pipeline. He had on board a more recent chart which did, but was not using it. Since the ship was, in fact, properly equipped in this respect, the owners' fault or privity consisted of a failure to exercise proper supervision. This was said to be manifested in two ways: (1) failure to operate a proper system for keeping the charts on board up to date, either by replacement or correction, and (2) failure by the managing director to ensure that an inspection report, referring to the unsatisfactory charts, was brought to his attention while he was absent from his office for a considerable period of time. The owner was denied the right to limit.

89. 1959 AMC 2379 (Arb.).

insured the vessel from March 29, 1957, to March 29, 1958. The arbitrator held that the port risk underwriters insuring the ship repairers were liable for 6/365ths (March 24 to March 29, 1956) of the cost of replacing the tailshaft plus the entire cost of a new external gland rubber seal ring and the installation thereof; that the last set of hull underwriters were liable for 64/365ths of such expenses (March 29, 1957, to June 1, 1957); and that the intervening hull underwriters during the period March 29, 1956, to March 29, 1957, were liable for nothing as the assured owner breached the implied warranty of seaworthiness as the vessel was not seaworthy when it left port on March, 29, 1956; i.e., the vessel had just left the very repair yard which had done the work negligently, and was still in port at the commencment of the policy of hull underwriters on the risk for the period March 29, 1956, to March 29, 1957.[90]

In *Pacific Queen Fisheries v. Symes (The Pacific Queen)*,[91] a wooden-hulled salvage vessel insured under a policy containing an Inchmaree Clause was lost as a result of an explosion. The court found, *inter alia*, that the vessel with the privity of her owners had been sent to sea in an unseaworthy condition. Recovery was denied on the ground that the policy was void *ab initio* because the owners had failed to disclose material increases in the risk caused by an increased gasoline carrying capacity of the vessel, as well as by reason of the breach of the implied warranty of seaworthiness.

In *Neubros Corp. v. Northwestern National Ins. Co.*,[92] the plaintiffs demise chartered barges to Levon. Levon insured under policies which contained an Inchmaree Clause. Upon being loaded, one of the barges buckled and was a constructive total loss. Both plaintiffs and Levon, in a suit against underwriters, claimed that the Inchmaree Clause modified or waived the warranty of seaworthiness, citing *Spot Pack, supra*. The court found that the barge was unseaworthy and totally incapable of carrying the loads to which it was subjected, and that the plaintiffs were aware of its unseaworthiness in this respect. The court further held that, knowing of the unseaworthiness, the plaintiffs had an affirmative duty to reveal such information to the underwriters and their failure to do so vitiated the policy.

In *Capitol Coastal Corp. v. Hartford Fire Ins. Co.*,[93] a tug sank at its dock while moored in calm water. The policy contained the usual Inchmaree Clause and, in addition, a special warranty to the effect that a named individual would be the master of the tug. In a suit on the policy, the court noted that a sinking in calm water raises a presumption that the vessel was

90. Compare *Fireman's Fund Ins. Co. v. Globe Nav. Co.*, 236 F. 618 (9th Cir., 1916) and *Ferrante v. Detroit F. & M. Ins. Co.*, 125 F.Supp. 621, 1954 AMC 2026 (D.,Cal.).
91. 307 F.2d 700, 1962 AMC 1845 (9th Cir.), [1963] 2 Lloyd's Rep. 201.
92. 359 F.Supp. 310, 1972 AMC 2443 (E.D.N.Y.).
93. 378 F.Supp. 163, 1974 AMC 2040 (E.D.,Va.), [1975] 2 Lloyd's Rep. 100.

unseaworthy and that the burden was on the assured to prove her seaworthy, or that the cause of the sinking was negligence of the master or crew
under the Inchmaree Clause. The court held that the presumption that
the vessel was unseaworthy was not rebutted by the plaintiffs, but also
noted that the acting master's negligence may have contributed substantially to the sinking. The acting master was not the individual named in
the special warranty as the person who was to act as master. On this
ground, the court held that the warranty had been breached and recovery was denied.

In *F.B. Walker & Sons, Inc. v. Valentine*,[94] the policy on a tug contained
both an Inchmaree Clause and a Watchman's Clause, the latter of which
required inspections aboard and periodic checks of the vessel. While the
tug was moored at the owner's dock, it sank by reason of water entering
through a loose rudder post stuffing box. Although holding that a want
of due diligence on the part of the assured was not proved, the court held
that non-compliance with the Watchman's Clause prevented recovery.

In *Goodman v. Fireman's Fund*,[95] discussed *supra*, although negligence
of the owner/master in laying up the vessel was held to be a covered peril
under an all risks policy, recovery was ultimately denied because the negligence of the owner/master also consisted of failing to comply with the
lay-up warranty.

In *Tinkerbell*,[96] discussed *supra*, the court avoided (in a sense) the problem by finding that the failure of the master to comply with the lay-up
warranty was not due to negligence but due simply to mechanical difficulties. Thus, the Inchmaree Clause was not applicable, and recovery was
denied because of a failure to comply with the lay-up warranty.

The language of the court in *Sea Pak*[97] is instructive and is of some aid
in resolving the apparent inconsistencies. The court said, in part:

> We cannot emphasize too strongly that, as was the purpose of the
> underwriters in making the change, the Inchmaree Clause is an ex-
> pansion of coverage of considerable magnitude. Unlike so many cases
> (citing *Union Insurance Co. of Philadelphia*, etc.), where each policy con-
> tained an express warranty of continuing seaworthiness and an exclu-
> sion of losses caused by unseaworthiness, a Time Hull Policy with no
> warranty of continuing seaworthiness but with an Inchmaree clause
> does in fact underwrite unseaworthiness of many types.

> If a vessel has become unseaworthy due to the negligence of the
> master or engineer in the maintenance of the vessel, in putting to sea
> without adequate equipment, fuel or stores, or without making re-

94. 431 F.2d 1235, 1970 AMC 2261 (5th Cir.), [1970] 2 Lloyd's Rep. 429.
95. 600 F.2d 1040, 1979 AMC 2534 (4th Cir.).
96. 533 F.2d 496, 1976 AMC 799 (9th Cir.).
97. 247 F.2d 116, 1957 AMC 1946 (5th Cir.).

quired repairs at outports where the master is the sole principal representative of the owners, the "cause" is negligence and this is expressly underwritten. If there is an undiscoverable defect in hull or machinery, the resulting unseaworthiness or the damage caused by it is nonetheless covered.

. . . For if the vessel really sank because the hull was unseaworthy, or by reason of the action of the sea alone, this no longer automatically denies recovery. Recovery is denied now only if that unseaworthiness is one not caused or brought about by the various elements of the Inchmaree Clause.

It will be observed that the court speaks in terms of unseaworthiness due to the "negligence of the master or engineer in the maintenance of the vessel," but a careful reading of the court's language will disclose that the maintenance of which the court was speaking was maintenance in an "outport" and not at the home port of the vessel where, presumably, the vessel would be under the observation and supervision of the owner.

It must be observed also that the Supreme Court in 1888 in *Union Insurance Co. of Philadelphia v. Smith*[98] laid down the rule that under American law the warranty of seaworthiness is complied with if the vessel be seaworthy *at the commencement of the risk*. However, the precedential value of that case is somewhat lessened because, there, the policy contained an express exception for losses due to unseaworthiness and courts have subsequently commented that the expression of the rule was dictum which was unnecessary to the facts then under consideration. And, as the Second Circuit observed in *Henjes v. Aetna Ins. Co.*,[99] while there is an implied warranty by the insured in a time policy that the ship is seaworthy *at the time the policy period begins*, this is true only when the vessel is in port at the time. If the vessel is on a voyage, the insurer "takes her as she may be."[100]

Clearly, then, a distinction must be drawn between negligence of the master or crew while the vessel is being prepared for sea in its home port at the commencement of the policy (shoreside or "preparational" negligence), and negligence on the part of the master or crew after the vessel has commenced its voyage and is, for example, at an outport where adequate repair facilities are not available. Want of due diligence by the assured, the owners or managers of the vessel, does not include acts of the master or crew member merely imputed on notions of *respondeat superior*.

98. 124 U.S. 405 (1888).
99. 132 F.2d 715, 1943 AMC 27 (2d Cir.), cert. denied 319 U.S. 760 (1943).
100. There is, however, authority for the proposition that if the vessel is at any port with repair and supply facilities which are sufficient in the circumstances, the warranty will apply. *New York & Puerto Rico S.S. v. Aetna Ins. Co.*, 204 F. 255 (2d Cir., 1913). See, also, *Hoxie v. Pacific Mutual Ins. Co.*, 89 Mass. 211.

Unlike the position under the Hague Rules, the proviso to the Inchmaree Clause is not concerned with a non-delegable duty to make the vessel seaworthy.[101] The proviso to the clause only comes into play in terms of shoreside or preparational negligence if the owner is the master or if the master is the "alter ego" of the owner.[102] Concomitantly, recovery may be denied if there is a breach of a separate promissory warranty even though that breach may have come about by reason of the negligence of one of the prescribed class under the Inchmaree Clause.[103]

Applicability of Cargo Cases

It must be recognized that there are many cases involving claims for cargo damage in which the shipowner has endeavored to avoid liability by claiming the existence of a latent defect not discoverable by due diligence under Cogsa or the applicable bills of lading. See 46 U.S.C. 1304(p). It is understandable that there has been a tendency to attempt to apply these cases to claims arising under the Inchmaree Clause, although the burden of persuasion is wholly different. In cargo cases, the defense of a latent defect is one which must be asserted by the shipowner who bears the burden of proving it, whereas in insurance cases arising under the Inchmaree Clause, once the assured puts on a *prima facie* case establishing the presumptive presence of a latent defect, the contract is one which will be construed most strongly against the underwriters under applicable doctrines of law.[104] As one distinguished writer has noted,[105] the U. S. Supreme Court foresaw the prospect of this diversity of result in the very year the Inchmaree Clause was first used.[106]

This essential difference was clearly recognized in a recent case, *Texaco v. Universal Marine*.[107] In that case, refusing to impute the knowledge of the master or crew to the owner, the court stated that it was not inconsistent to hold the shipowner liable to a shipper for failing in his non-delegable duty as a carrier to provide a seaworthy vessel while at the same time

---

101. See discussion, *infra*, "Applicability of Cargo Cases."
102. An example of the latter is *Chicago S.S. Lines v. U.S. Lloyd's*, 12 F.2d 733, 1926 AMC 807 (7th Cir.).
103. *Goodman v. Fireman's Fund, supra*, where the negligence of the assured/master lay in failing to lay up his vessel in accordance with custom and practice. Query: What would have been the result in *Goodman* if the failure to lay up the vessel in accordance with custom and practice had been that of a master who had been retained by the owner to accomplish the lay-up task? Compare, in this connection, *Goodman* with *Tinkerbell, supra*.
104. See *Henjes v. Aetna Ins. Co.*, 132 F.2d 715, 1943 AMC 27 (2d Cir.); *Fireman's Fund Ins. Co. v. Globe Nav. Co.*, 236 F. 618 (9th Cir., 1916).
105. Tetrault, ibid., n. 20.
106. *Liverpool & Great W. Steam Co. v. Phoenix Ins. Co., (The Montana)*, 129 U.S. 397 (1889).
107. 400 F.Supp. 311, 1976 AMC 226 (E.D.,La.).

holding that the hull underwriters did not sustain their burden of proving that the shipowner acted in bad faith or negligently in permitting his vessel to sail in an unseaworthy condition.

There are, not too surprisingly, relatively few cases involving the carriage of cargo in which the courts have sustained the defense of latent defect.[108] This is so because the obligation of a common carrier by water is an absolute, non-delegable one of making his vessel seaworthy at the commencement of the voyage.[109] As was noted by Lord Justice McKinnon in *Smith Hogg & Co. v. Black Sea & Baltic Gen. Ins. Co.*[110]:

> The limitation and qualification of the implied warranty of seaworthiness, by cutting down the duty of the shipowner to the obligation to use "due diligence . . . to make the ship seaworthy" is a limitation or qualification more apparent than real, because the exercise of due diligence involves not merely that the shipowner personally shall exercise due diligence, but that all his servants and agents shall exercise due diligence . . . ."The circumstances in which the dilemma does not arise (e.g., a defect causing unseaworthiness, but of so latent a nature that due diligence could not have discovered it) are not likely to occur often."

Unexplained Sinkings

There seems to be general agreement among English, Commonwealth, and American courts that when a vessel sinks in calm water and calm weather while in port or within a short time after sailing, there is a presumption that the vessel was unseaworthy and that the unseaworthiness was the proximate cause of the loss.[111] However, where the assured goes

---

108. See *National Sugar Refining Co. v. M/S La Villas*, 225 F. Supp. 686 (E.D.,La., 1964); *The Prussia*, 93 F. 837 (2d Cir., 1899); *The Cameronia*, 38 F.2d 522, 1930 AMC 443 (E.D.N.Y.); *The Carib Prince*, 63 F. 266 (E.D.N.Y.), *aff'd* 68 F. 254 (2d Cir., 1895), *rev'd* on other grounds, 170 U.S. 655 (1898); *The Quarrington Court*, 122 F.2d 266, 1941 AMC 1234 (2d Cir.); *Empresa Brasileira v. Lloyd Phil.*, 1978 AMC 1227 (S.D.N.Y.); *Containerschiffs v. Lloyd's*, 1981 AMC 60 (S.D.N.Y.); *Fredericks v. American Export Lines*, 117 F.Supp. 255, 1954 AMC 242 (S.D.N.Y.), *aff'd* 227 F.2d 450, 1956 AMC 57 (2d Cir.); *Brown v. Nitrate Producers S.S. Co.*, (1937) 58 Ll.L.Rep. 188; *The Dimitrios N. Rallias*, (1922) 13 Ll.L.Rep. 363. Cf., *The Bill*, 47 F. Supp. 969 (D., Md., 1942), *aff'd* 145 F.2d 470 (4th Cir., 1944).

109. See *The Muncaster Castle*, 1961 AMC 1357, (1961) A.C. 807, H.L. See, also, *The Bill*, 47 F.Supp. 969, 1942 AMC 1607 (D., Md.), *aff'd* 145 F.2d 470 (4th Cir., 1944).

110. 55 T.L.R. 766, C.A.

111. *Anderson v. Morice*, (1876) 1 A.C. 713, H.L.; *Watson v. Clark*, (1813) 3 E.R. 720, H.L.; *Pickup v. Thames & Mersey Ins. Co., Ltd.*, (1878) 3 Q.B.D. 594; *Ajum Goolam Hossen & Co. v. Union Marine Ins. Co.*, (1901) A.C. 362, P.C.; *Coons v. Aetna Ins. Co.*, (1868) 18 U.C.C.P. 305 (Can.); *Myles v. Montreal Ins. Co.*, (1870) 20 U.C.C.P. 283,(C.A., Can.); *Ewart v. Merchants' Marine Ins. Co.*, (1879) 13 N.S.R. 168 (C.A., Can.); *Rogerson v. Union Marine Ins. Co.*, (1870) 6 Nfld. L.R. 359 (Can.); *W. Langley & Sons Ltd. v. Australian Provincial Assur. Ass'n, Ltd.*, (1924)

forward with evidence showing that the vessel was seaworthy a reasonable time before the loss, the courts diverge, although the weight of authority appears to favor coverage.[112]

In *Skandia Ins. Co. Ltd. v. Skoljarev and Another*,[113] the insured vessel sank shortly after leaving port in a sea which, though subject to a considerable swell, was relatively calm. Bright, J., in the Supreme Court of South Australia, in giving judgment for the vessel owners, found that the ship was seaworthy and that there was no negligence on the part of the master and crew, applying the presumption that if a ship which is seaworthy sinks in smooth water and there is no other evidence as to the cause of loss, the casualty is attributable to a peril of the seas. The full court dismissed the appeal, and the appellant underwriter appealed to the High Court on the ground that the full court failed to recognize that the onus of proving seaworthiness lay on the vessel owners.

The High Court held that the appeal would be dismissed, stating that it is no longer the law that some extraordinary action of the wind and waves is required to constitute a fortuitous accident or casualty; that such an accident or casualty can occur even in calm seas and fair weather, and the cause of the loss need not be external to the ship.[114]

The High Court further held that the onus of proof that the loss was caused by perils of the seas is on the assured. Though the onus of proving a breach of the assured's implied warranty of seaworthiness in a voyage

24 S.R. (N.S.W.) 280 (Aus.); *Reynolds v. North Queensland Ins. Co.*, (1896) 17 L.R. (N.S.W.) 121, 13 W.N. 1 (N.S.W. Sup.Crt., F.C.,Aus.); *Massey S.S. Co. v. Importers' & Exporters' Ins. Co.*, 153 Minn. 88, 189 N.W. 415, 31 A.L.R. 1372 (1922); *Sea Pak*, 247 F.2d 116, 1957 AMC 1946 (5th Cir.); *Cary v. Home Ins. Co.*, 199 App.Div. 122, 1923 AMC 438, *aff'd* 235 N.Y. 296, 139 N.E. 274 (St.,N.Y.); *Boston Ins. Co. v. Dehydrating Process Co.*, 204 F.2d 441, 1953 AMC 1364 (lst Cir.); *Mattson v. Connecticut Fire Ins. Co.*, 80 F.Supp. 101 (D.,Minn.); *Bertie Kay*, 106 F.Supp. 244, 1952 AMC 1812 (E.D.N.C.); *Glens Falls Ins. Co. v. J.E. Long*, 195 Va. 117, 77 S.E.2d 457, 1953 AMC 1841 (St.,Va.); *Pacific Dredging v. Hurley*, 397 P.2d 819, 1965 AMC 836 (St.,Wash.); *Lewis v. Aetna Ins. Co.*, 264 Or. 314, 505 P.2d 914 (St.,Ore., 1973); *Nickerson & Sons Ltd. v. I.N.A. (The J.E. Kenny)*, (1983) C.C.L.I. 78 (Can.); *Skandia Ins. Co. Ltd. v. Skoljarev*, [1979] 26 A.L.R. 1 (H.C.,Aus.); *I.N.A. v. Lanasa Shrimp Co.*, 726 F.2d 688, 1984 AMC 2915 (llth Cir.).

112. *Anderson v. Morice*, (1876) 1 A.C. 713, H.L.; *Ajum Goolam Hossen & Co. v. Union Marine Ins. Co.*, (1901) A.C. 362, P.C.; *Ewart v. Merchants' Marine Ins. Co.*, (1879) 13 N.S.R. 168, C.A.,Can.); *Morrison v. N.S. Marine Ins. Co.*, (1896) 28 N.S.R 346 (C.A.,Can.); *W. Langley & Sons Ltd. v. Australian Provincial Assur. Ass'n Ltd.*, (1924) 24 S.R. (N.S.W.) 290 (Aus.); *Reynolds v. North Queensland Ins. Co.*, (1896) 17 L.R. (N.S.W.) 121, 3 W.N. 1 (N.S.W., Sup.Crt., F.C., Aus.); *Massey S.S. Co. v. Importers' & Exporters' Ins. Co.*, 153 Minn. 88, 189 N.W. 415, 31 A.L.R. 1372 (St.,Minn., 1922); *Sea Pak*, 247 F.2d 116, 1957 AMC 1946 (5th Cir.); *Glens Falls Ins. Co. v. Long*, 195 Va. 117, 77 S.E.2d 457, 1953 AMC 1841 (St.,Va.); *Boston Ins. Co. v. Dehydrating Process Co.*, 204 F.2d 441, 1953 AMC 1364 (lst Cir.); *Lewis v. Aetna Ins. Co.*, 264 Or. 314, 505 P.2d 914 (St.,Ore., 1973); *Capital Coastal v. Hartford Fire*, 378 F.Supp. 163, 1974 AMC 2039, [1975] 2 Lloyd's Rep. 100; *Commercial Union Ins. Co. v. Daniels*, 343 F.Supp. 674, 1973 AMC 452 (S.D.,Tex.); *Skandia Ins. Co. Ltd. v. Skoljarev and Another*, 26 A.L.R. 1 (H.C.,Aus., 1979); *I.N.A. v. Lanasa Shrimp Co.*, 726 F.2d 688, 1984 AMC 2915 (llth Cir.).

113. [1979] 26 A.L.R. 1 (H.C.,Aus.).

114. Citing *Hamilton, Fraser & Co. v. Pandorf & Co.*, (1887) 12 App. Cas. 518, and approving the statement of Lord Halsbury, L.C. at 524-5.

policy is on the insurer, and though the onus of proving that a ship insured under a time policy was sent to sea in an unseaworthy condition with the privity of the insured is on the insurer, the insurer does not bear an onus of proving unseaworthiness when it arises in relation to the issue of whether the loss was caused by perils of the seas or not; i.e.,there is no presumption of seaworthiness or unseaworthiness, unless, in the absence of other evidence as to the condition of the ship or the cause of the loss, a ship sinks in smooth water soon after the policy attaches or the ship leaves port.[115]

The High Court continued by observing that the insured will discharge his burden of proving loss by perils of the sea if he tenders evidence of sinking as a result of a fortuitous event; if there is also evidence of seaworthiness, the question of what caused the loss must be decided as a question of fact. The insured will only find it necessary to establish seaworthiness in order to prove his case if he has no direct evidence of loss due to a fortuitous event and seeks to establish by inference a case of loss due to an unascertained peril of the sea; it will be necessary for him to prove seaworthiness in order to support the necessary inference.[116]

Thus, since the trial judge had rejected the appellant's claim that the ship was unseaworthy, it was correct to infer that the loss was due to a peril of the sea even though that peril was unidentifiable.

Other courts take the position that while such proof of seaworthiness overrides a defense of breach of warranty to use diligence, the assured nonetheless has a duty of going forward with evidence to demonstrate a loss by an insured peril.[117]

As might be expected, the Inchmaree Clause has come into play with respect to cases involving unexplained sinkings. In *Bertie Kay*,[118] a shrimp boat foundered in fair weather and a calm sea. The court disapproved the cases holding that a presumption of loss from perils of the sea or latent defect arises when the assured submits proof that the vessel was seaworthy at the inception of the risk and there is no other explanation, and denied recovery. In *Glen Falls Ins. Co. v. J.E. Long*,[119] a motorboat sank within one hour after starting on a fishing trip by reason of a sudden and unexplained inrush of water. The court held that the proof sustained a finding that the boat foundered because of a peril of the sea or from a latent defect. In *Lewis v. Aetna Ins. Co.*,[120] a yacht was found sunk in its

115. Explaining *Pickup v. Thames & Mersey Marine Ins. Co., Ltd.*, (1878) 3 Q.B.D. 594.
116. Statement of L. J. Scrutton in *La Compania Martiartu v. Royal Exchange Assur. Corp.*, (1923) 1 K.B. 650 approved.
117. *Long Dock Mills, Etc. v. Mannheim Ins. Co.*, 116 F. 886 (S.D.N.Y., 1902); *Bertie Kay*, 201 F.2d 736, 1953 AMC 337 (4th Cir.); *Fine v. American Eagle Fire Ins. Co.*, 178 Misc. 27, 32 N.Y.S.2d 21, 1942 AMC 96 (1941), *aff'd* 180 Misc. 789, 46 N.Y.S.2d 512 (1943).
118. 106 F.Supp. 244, 1952 AMC 1812 (E.D.N.C.).
119. 195 Va. 117, 77 S.E.2d 457, 1953 AMC 1841 (St.,Va.).
120. 264 Or. 314, 505 P.2d 914 (St.,Ore.).

boathouse and was raised and repairs effected. In a suit on the policy for the cost of repairs, there was evidence that the yacht sank because of leaks in its hull but the cause of the leaks was unknown. The court held the jury could infer that the vessel sank because of a latent defect. In *Sea Pak*,[121] a leak inexplicably developed under a freezer in the forward part of the vessel. Recovery was allowed. To the contrary, recovery was denied in *Parente v. Bayville Marine*,[122] and in *Sipowicz v. Wimble*,[123] where the evidence tended to show that the cause of the sinking was normal wear and tear or deterioration rather than latent defect.[124]

Attention is specifically directed to *Lewis v. Aetna Ins. Co.*,[125] in which two justices in a specially concurring opinion urged a reexamination of the traditional rules of interpretation applied to the Inchmaree Clause when that clause is included in policies on pleasure craft. Citing Keeton, *Insurance Law Rights at Variance With Policy Provisions*,[126] the concurring justices urged application of the "reasonable expectations" doctrine espoused by Keeton in the following language:

> Today, when the typical owner of a pleasure craft seeks marine protection and indemnity insurance, his objective is financial protection from all or most of the risks which reasonably flow from ownership and operation of his craft. In this respect, he is not markedly different from the purchaser of automobile liability and property insurance. He bargains with the salesman about little concerning his coverage, pays his premium, and receives a printed policy. The policy itself is seldom read, and almost never understood, because the content is complicated and filled with confusing legal terminology. Nevertheless, the boat owner believes that when the contract is executed and the premiums are paid he is "covered." He may be wholly unaware of the exact type or extent of coverage, or any qualifications or exceptions to the policy coverage about which he has not been warned . . . .

> The difficulty is with the term "latent defect." In this case, the term is stretched to embrace an unknown, unexplained something that caused the *Manatee* to sink at its moorings. This interpretation does violence to the language but justice to the case. The phrase may have served a proper function in 1889 but today it only confuses courts and policyholders and frustrates the reasonable expectations of the insured, a result which courts have historically disfavored. (Citing

121. 247 F.2d 116, 1957 AMC 1946 (5th Cir.).
122. 1974 AMC 1399 (N.Y.A.D.), [1975] 1 Lloyd's Rep. 333.
123. 370 F.Supp. 442, 1975 AMC 524 (D.C.N.Y.), [1974] 1 Lloyd's Rep. 593.
124. See, also, *Reisman v. N.H. Fire Ins. Co.*, 312 F.2d 17, 1963 AMC 1151 (5th Cir.), and *Wood v. Great American*, 289 F.Supp. 1014, 1968 AMC 1815 (E.D.,Wis.) to the same effect.
125. 264 Or. 314, 505 P.2d 914 (St.,Ore., 1973).
126. 83 *Harvard Law Review* 961 (1970).

Keeton). We would reach an unreasonable result if we denied the plaintiff policyholders the coverage which they reasonably assumed they had purchased because they cannot explain an inexplainable sinking.

When members of the public purchase policies of insurance they are entitled to the broad measure of protection necessary to fulfill their reasonable expectations. . . . Where particular provisions, if read literally, would largely nullify the insurance, they will be severely restricted so as to enable fair fulfillment of the stated policy objective. . . . *Kievit v. Loyal Protect. Life Ins. Co.*, 34 N.Y. 475, 482-483, 170 A.2d 26 (1961).

In light of changed circumstances, the Inchmaree Clause should be interpreted according to the rule in *Kievit*.

Assuming the concurring justices to be correct in their interpretation, there would appear to be very valid reasons for restricting that approach to policies on pleasure craft. Certain it is that such a highly "consumerism" approach should not be applied to sophisticated assureds whose knowledge of policies may well be on a par with that of underwriters.[127]

Other Portions of the Clause

Other portions of the Clause have been involved in the following cases.[128]

In *Carter Tug*, the court held that the failure of the bilge pumps on a towboat which foundered and sank constituted a "breakdown of motor generators or other electrical machinery and electrical connections thereto" (in addition, the court found the master negligent).

In *Northwestern Mutual Life Ins. Co. v. Linard*,[129] an explosion occurred in the starboard wing tank in the vicinity of the engine room. The assured contended that the explosion fell within the scope of the clause; the underwriters contended that the ship was deliberately scuttled by the placing of an explosive device in the wing tank. The district court had held that the basic burden of persuasion lay upon the assured to show that

---

127. See, for example, *Edward A. Ryan*, 2 F.Supp. 489, 1933 AMC 350, *Ocean v. Black Sea and Baltic Gen. Ins. Co.*, [1935] 51 Ll.L.Rep. 305, C.A.; *Eagle Leasing v. Hartford Fire*, 540 F.2d 1257, 1978 AMC 604 (5th Cir.) (general rule that an insurance policy is construed against the insurer not applicable where the policy was concocted especially for the fleet of an assured which was an immense corporation managed by experienced businessmen of sophistication equal to that of the underwriters).

128. *Carter Tug v. Home Ins.*, 345 F.Supp. 1193, 1972 AMC 498 (S.D.,Ill.); *Northwestern Mutual Life Ins. Co. v. Linard*, 498 F.2d 556, 1974 AMC 877, [1974] 2 Lloyd's Rep. 398 (5th Cir.); *Antilles S.S. v. American Hull Ins.*, 733 F.2d 195, 1984 AMC 2444 (2d Cir.); *J.L. Fisheries Ltd. v. Boston Ins. Co.*, (1969) I.L.R. 1-227, 69 D.L.R. 2d 18, N.S. (Can.); and *Continental Food Products, Inc. v. Ins. Co. of N.A.*, 544 F.2d 834, 1977 AMC 2421 (5th Cir.).

129. *Supra*, n. 128.

the loss arose from a covered peril, and that the underwriters had thereupon met their burden of going forward by adducing evidence of scuttling. The court held that since the state of evidence was in equipoise, the assured had failed to meet its burden of persuasion and held for the underwriters.[129a]

On appeal, the Second Circuit agreed. The assured argued that the scuttling rule applied only when coverage was founded upon a loss from the general perils of the seas and not where there was specific coverage under the Inchmaree Clause. The appeals court held that in the end the question of coverage turned on whether the event itself was fortuitous; i.e., just as scuttling is not a peril of the sea (citing *P. Samuel & Co. v. Dumas* [1924] A.C. 431), neither is a set explosion.

In *Antilles S.S. v. American Hull Ins.*,[130] the vessel was a tanker with some of its tanks constructed of stainless steel for the carriage of liquid chemicals. Among the chemicals taken aboard were over 200 tons of glacial acrylic acid (GAA) and ethylene norbonene (ENB). These two chemicals were loaded in adjacent tanks. Enroute to destination, the GAA suddenly and explosively polymerized for reasons unknown. The resulting high pressure caused the storage tank to bulge, and the common wall between it and the tank immediately forward (which contained the ENB) to rupture, permitting material to escape into the cofferdam; i.e., the empty space between the wall of the tanks and the skin of the ship. The crew succeeded in reducing the danger of fire by hosing down the decks and pumping seawater into the cofferdam nearest the ruptured tanks.

On arrival at destination in Antwerp, Belgium, port officials refused to permit the seawater-chemical mixture to be unloaded, primarily because of the extremely noxious odor of the ENB. Later, the vessel was sailed to a tank cleaning facility near Rotterdam. The removal of the putrid cargo proved to be more arduous and costly than anticipated because GAA, a waterlike liquid in its monomer state, hardens when polymerized. This was particularly true of the bulk of the GAA in No. 6 aft tank which required over thirty days to be cleared of the hardened GAA by shoveling by hand. Near the bottom of the tank, it was necessary to use heavy-duty compressed air jackhammers to break up the granite-like mass which extended across the bottom of the tank from bulkhead to bulkhead, and adhered to them.

In the course of the work, substantial damage was done to the stainless steel skin of the tank. After the vessel was repaired, the shipowner claimed the cost of removal of all of the GAA-ENB-seawater mixture as well as the cost of repairs. The claim was made under the Inchmaree

---

129a. To the same effect, when the evidence is in equipoise, see *Compania Martiartu v. Royal Exchange Assur. Corp.*, (1923) 1 K.B. 650, 16 Asp. M.L.C. 189, *aff'd* (1924) A.C. 850, H.L.

130. *Supra,* n. 128.

Clause of the hull and machinery policy. Thirty percent of the coverage was placed in the London market which rather promptly paid its 30 percent of the claimed amount. The American hull underwriters paid for only the actual damage to the walls of both ruptured tanks, the skin or shell of the vessel, and the costs associated with the removal of the last residue of the mixture adhering to the bulkheads of the two tanks. They refused to pay for the cost of removing the bulk of the hardened mass from the cargo tanks which, it was stipulated, cost the shipowner $365,339.72.

The trial court awarded the shipowner the bulk of that amount, i.e., the sum of $271,179.01. The underwriters appealed.

On appeal, the appeal court noted that the burden was upon the shipowner to prove (1) that it was insured on a marine policy underwritten by the defendant underwriters, (2) that a loss occurred, and (3) that the loss was an event within the terms of the policy. The underwriters conceded elements (1) and (2) but contended that the loss was not within the terms of the policy; i.e., that although there was a shipboard explosion which concededly damaged the vessel, underwriters were not required to pay for the cost of removing cargo or cargo debris from the ship's cargo spaces after the vessel had reached port safely.

The appeal court noted that the seminal—and perhaps only—judicial decision on the scope of a hull policy in a damaged cargo situation was *Field v. Burr*,[131] and also cited the arbitrator's decision in *Barge J. Whitney*.[132] In the event, the appeal court reversed the trial court and held that the hull underwriters were required under the Inchmaree Clause to pay only for those expenses incurred in removal of the mixture from the cofferdam and in removing the *last residue* of material clinging to the bulkheads of the two tanks.

In *J.L. Fisheries Ltd. v. Boston Ins. Co.*,[133] the court held that a broken pinion shaft came within the term "breakage of shafts" or, alternatively, the damage flowed from a "latent defect in the machinery."

131. [1899] 1 Q.B. 579.
132. 1968 AMC 995 (Arb.). In both *Field v. Burr* and *Barge J. Whitney*, it was held that a particular average loss to a ship comprehends physical damage only to the vessel and not merely economic damage suffered by the shipowner as a carrier of cargo who is required to go to inordinate expense to clear his vessel of offending cargo in order that it might again be used to transport cargo.
133. *Supra*, n. 128. See, also, *L. & M. Electrics Pty. Ltd. v. State Gov't Ins. Office (Qld)*, (1984) 3 ANZ Ins. Cas. 60-594 (Aus.) (explosion); *Stonewall Ins. Co. v. Emerald Fisheries, Inc.*, 388 So.2d 1089 (St.,Fla., 1980) (damage to engine due to negligence of captain—insufficient lube oil supply); *Gibbar v. Calvert Fire Ins. Co.*, 471 F.Supp. 323, *aff'd* 623 F.2d 41 (7th Cir.) (failure of fuel injectors causing engine to run at excessive speed; court lumped together "breakdown of machinery, breakage of shafts, and latent defect" without distinguishing as to primary cause).

In *Continental Food Products, Inc. v. Ins. Co. of N.A.*,[134] the assured claimed that the loss occurred due to a breakdown or stoppage of the refrigeration plant for more than 24 hours—a peril specifically included in the policy although not as a part of the Inchmaree Clause. However, the assured was unable to prove that the thawing of the cargo was occasioned by that particular peril.

Liner Negligence Clause

In the early 1930s, the London market offered a broader form of Inchmaree coverage in the so-called liner negligence clause, but this coverage was restricted to vessels engaged in liner or berth service. In 1964, the American market introduced a liner negligence clause of its own. The two versions are quite similar.[135]

The American clause (May 1, 1964) reads:

The so-called Inchmaree clause of the attached Policy is deleted and in place thereof the following inserted:

This insurance also specially to cover, subject to the Average Warranty:

a. Breakdown of motor generators or other electrical connections thereto; a bursting of boilers; breakage of shafts; or any latent defect in the machinery or hull;

b. Loss of or damage to the subject matter insured directly caused by:

1. Accidents on shipboard or elsewhere, other than breakdown of or accidents to nuclear installations or reactors on board the insured Vessel;

2. Negligence, error of judgment or incompetence of any person; excluding under both a and b above only the cost of repairing, replacing or renewing any part condemned solely as a result

---

134. *Supra*, n. 128.
135. The English Liner Negligence Clause reads:
Subject to the terms and conditions of this policy, this insurance is also to cover
    Bursting of boilers and/or Breakage of Shafts.
    Damage to and/or loss of the subject matter of this insurance caused by any accident, latent defect, malicious act, negligence, error of judgment or incompetence of any person whatsoever but excluding the cost of repairing, replacing or renewing any defective part condemned solely in consequence of a latent defect or fault or error in design or construction.
    Provided that such damage or loss has not resulted from want of due diligence by the owners of the vessel or any of them or by the managers.
    Masters, Mates, Engineers, Pilots or Crew not to be considered as part owner within the meaning of this clause should they hold shares in the vessel.

of a latent defect, wear and tear, gradual deterioration or fault or error in design or construction;

provided such loss or damage (either as described in said a or b or both) has not resulted from want of due diligence by the Assured(s), the Owner(s) or Manager(s) of the Vessel, or any of them. Masters, mates, engineers, pilots or crew not to be considered as part owners within the meaning of this clause should they hold shares in the Vessel.

It will be recognized that the liner negligence clause is really a species of "all risks" policy. And, as is common with all risks policies, the burden is on the underwriter to prove that the cause of the loss was one which was excluded by the words of the policy.[136] The insured need only prove that a loss occurred, although he must furnish to the underwriter information which he has as to the cause of the loss.[137] Moreover, an all risks policy covers risks, not certainties, and purports to cover losses only from extraordinary casualties; losses occasioned by ordinary circumstances of a voyage are not indemnified. That is, only losses are covered which arise from accident or casualty attributable to an external cause.[138]

Dissecting the clause, it will be seen that subparagraph (a) covers breakdown of motor generators or other electrical connections thereto, bursting of boilers, breakage of shafts, or any latent defects in the machinery or hull *without qualification* other than the exclusion relating to the cost of repairing, replacing, or renewing any part condemned solely as a result of latent defect, wear and tear, gradual deterioration or fault or error in design or construction, and provided that the loss or damage did not result from a want of due diligence by the assured. Consequently, so long as there is an *accident* or a *failure* during the *operation* of the vessel; i.e., a fortuitous happening as distinguished from the part being condemned on inspection or survey by reason of wear and tear, deterioration, etc., then underwriters respond and this includes repairing or replacing the part which failed.[139] Mr. George Heselton explained the

136. *Goodman v. Fireman's Fund Ins. Co.*, 600 F.2d 1040, 1979 AMC 2534 (4th Cir.); *British & Foreign Marine Ins. Co. v. Gaunt*, (1921) All E.R. 447, H.L.; *Theodorus v. Chester*, [1951] 1 Lloyd's Rep. 204, K.B.D. The assured cannot, course, rest upon his laurels if the underwriter comes forward and presents theories which would account for the loss being due to normal transit risks. In that event, the plaintiff must satisfy the trier of fact that the theories advanced were neither right nor logical. *Theodorus v. Chester, supra.*
137. *Atlantic Lines v. American Motorists Ins. Co.*, 547 F.2d 11, 1976 AMC 2522 (2d Cir.).
138. *Anders v. Poland*, 181 So.2d 879, 1966 AMC 1867 (La.,App.); *British & Foreign Marine Ins. Co. v. Gaunt* (1921), *supra*, n. 136; *Berk (F.W.) & Co., Ltd. v. Style*, [1955] 3 All E.R. 625, [1955] 2 Lloyd's Rep. 382; *Greene v. Cheetham*, 293 F.2d 933, 1961 AMC 2549 (2d Cir.); *Victoria Overseas Trading Co., Pty., Ltd. v. Southern Pacific Ins. Co., Ltd.* (1965-66) N.S.W.R. 824 (Aus.); *Contractors Realty Co. v. Ins. Co. of N.A.*, 469 F.Supp. 1287, 1979 AMC 1864 (S.D.N.Y.); *Nevers v. Aetna Ins. Co.*, 546 P.2d 1240, 1977 AMC 2017 (St.,Wash.) (loss under an all risks policy does not include loss due to a defect in title to the insured subject matter).
139. As Buglass has noted (*Marine Insurance and General Average in the United States*, 2d

distinction quite well in his annual address to the Association of Average Adjusters in 1968 when he gave the following examples:[140]

> To quote two examples regarding the "Liner" Negligence Clause, I do not think it can [be] argued that the cracking of a comparatively new main engine cylinder liner is not an accident. The cause of the cracking could probably be some fault in the cooling water system (possibly covered under some other head of the Clause) but the cracking itself is an accident. On the other hand, the replacement on survey of a cylinder liner which has exceeded the acceptable limit of its weardown is clearly not an accident. It is simply a routine maintenance repair. Between these two extremes lies a No-Man's Land of incidents which may or may not be accidents dependent upon the particular circumstances. To quote another example . . . the breakage of a connecting rod when the machinery is in use. There is no doubt that the consequential damage is covered by the Clause as it is the direct result of an accident. In my view the replacement of the connecting rod is also recoverable as the breakage was directly caused by an accident. This is confirmed by the later part of the Clause which excludes the cost of repairing, replacing or renewing any defective part condemned solely (which are the material words) in consequence of a latent defect or fault or error in design or construction. The connecting rod has not been condemned from any of the foregoing causes; it has accidentally fractured whilst in service.

To the contrary, the loss or damage to the subject matter insured under subparagraph (b) must be *directly caused by* the items enumerated therein. Again, there must be an accident, a fortuitous circumstance, before there is coverage and then the insurer is liable only for *consequential damages* flowing from the accident and provided that the loss did not re-

---

ed., 1981), the exclusion with respect to the cost of repairing, replacing, or renewing any part condemned *solely* as a result of latent defect, etc., appears to have caused some difficulty to the uninitiated but it means only that the mere discovery of a latent defect, a wear or tear condition, or a fault or error in design or construction during a routine examination in port does not provide grounds for a claim under the clause. The exclusion would also apply even if, at a routine examination, the defect had manifested itself. This for the reason that, in those circumstances, there has been no accident, no actual failure in operation, but merely the condemnation of a part owing to the presence of a latent defect, wear and tear, gradual deterioration, or fault or error in design or construction. Thus, underwriters do not respond when a part is merely condemned on inspection or survey and has not been damaged due to a previous accident in operation. Conversely, underwriters are liable if the defective part failed in operation; in those circumstances the defective part has reached the breaking point and there has been an accident within the meaning of the clause. It should also be noted that the term "accident" has been given an extremely wide interpretation. See, for example, the non-marine case of *Mills v. Smith*, (1964) 1 Q.B. 30.

140. G. Heselton, "The Liner Negligence and Additional Perils Clause," *From the Chair,* Addresses by Chairmen of the Association of Average Adjusters, 1873-1976, Lloyd's of London Press, Ltd.,1978

sult from a want of due diligence on the part of the assured, owner or manager. That is, if there is an *accident*, even though it results from gradual wear and tear, deterioration, negligence of any person, etc., the underwriters are liable for the consequential damage flowing therefrom but not for the defective part itself, and provided further there is no want of due diligence.

It should also be noted that subparagraph (b) refers to the negligence, error of judgment, or incompetence of *any person;* this would include, for example, negligence of a builder, and is not limited to masters, crew, engineers, pilots, and repairers or charterers as in the ordinary Inchmaree form.

It has been said that the intent of those drafting the English liner clause was not to provide reimbursement for the defective part which failed in operation. However, the practice (following the 1934 edition of Templeman and Greenacre) is to provide for replacement of the defective part.[141]

141. 41 *Tulane Law Review*, 2 (Feb., 1967), Tetreault, "The Inchmaree Clause."

CHAPTER XV

PROXIMATE CAUSE

In General

The question of the proximate cause of a loss involves some of the most complex and troublesome considerations in marine insurance law. Stated simply, the fundamental principle underlying every contract of marine insurance is that a loss must be one which was proximately caused by a peril insured against, or as the legal maxim states: "*Causa proxima non remota spectatur*"—the proximate and not the remote cause must be looked to. This principle is contained in the first sub-section of Section 55 of the Marine Insurance Act, 1906. Section 55 reads in its entirety:

(1) Subject to the provisions of this Act, and unless the policy otherwise provides, the insurer is liable for any loss proximately caused by a peril insured against, but, subject as aforesaid, he is not liable for any loss which is not proximately caused by a peril insured against.
In particular—

(a) The insurer is not liable for any loss attributable to the wilful misconduct of the assured, but, unless the policy otherwise provides, he is liable for any loss proximately caused by a peril insured against, even though the loss would not have happened but for the misconduct or negligence of the master or crew.
(b) Unless the policy otherwise provides, the insurer on ship or goods is not liable for any loss proximately caused by delay, although the delay may be caused by a peril insured against.
(c) Unless the policy otherwise provides, the insurer is not liable for ordinary wear and tear, ordinary leakage and breakage, inherent vice or nature of the subject matter insured, or for any loss proximately caused by rats or vermin, or for any injury to machinery not proximately caused by maritime perils.

The leading American case is *Lanasa Fruit Steamship and Importing Company, Inc. v. Universal Insurance Company (The Smaragd).*[1] In that case, plaintiff was the owner of a cargo of bananas aboard the *Smaragd*. The vessel stranded and before she could be refloated, the entire cargo of bananas became overripe and rotted, causing a total loss. The general

---

1. 302 U.S. 556, 1938 AMC 1 (1938). See, also, *Norwich Union Fire Ins. Soc. v. Board of Commissioners*, 141 F.2d 600 (5th Cir. 1944).

coverage clause of the policy embraced perils of the sea. The question before the Supreme Court was, does the general perils clause cover a loss where a marine peril, viz., stranding, so delayed the voyage that the cargo became a total loss? In answering the question in the affirmative, the Court said:

> The sole question is whether in these circumstances the stranding should be regarded as the proximate cause of the loss. Respondent contends that decay or inherent vice was the proximate cause. It is true that the doctrine of proximate cause is applied strictly in cases of marine insurance. But in that class of cases, as well as in others, the proximate cause is the efficient cause and not a merely incidental cause which may be nearer in time to the result. *Insurance Company v. Boon.*[1a]

The Court then quoted from Lord Shaw's speech in *Leyland Shipping Company v. Norwich Union Fire Ins. Soc.*:[2]

> To treat *proxima causa* as the cause which is nearest in time is out of the question. Causes are spoken of as if they were as distinct from one another as beads in a row or links in a chain, but—if this metaphysical topic has to be referred to—it is not wholly so. The chain of causation is a handy expression, but the figure is inadequate. Causation is not a chain, but a net. At each point influences, forces, events, precedent and simultaneous, meet; and the radiation from each point extends infinitely. At the point where these various influences meet it is for the judgment as upon a matter of fact to declare which of the causes thus joined at the point of effect was the proximate and which was the remote cause.
>
> What does "proximate" here mean? To treat proximate cause as if it was the cause which is proximate in time is, as I have said, out of the question. The cause which is truly proximate is that which is proximate in efficiency. That efficiency may have been preserved although other causes may meantime have sprung up which have yet not destroyed it, or truly impaired it, and it may culminate in a result of which it still remains the real efficient cause to which the event can be ascribed.

In the *Leyland* case, involving a hull policy, there was an exception with repect to hostilities or warlike operations. The vessel was torpedoed and sustained severe injuries but succeeded in making the outer harbor of the port of Le Havre. Notwithstanding all efforts of pumping and otherwise, she bumped, broke her back, and sank. It was contended that she perished by a peril of the sea because the seawater entered the hole which the

1a. 95 U.S. 117.
2. [1918-1919] All E.R. 443, [1918] A.C. 350.

torpedo made. The entry of the seawater was indeed a peril of the sea and was proximate in time to the sinking. It was held, however, that the "real, efficient cause" of the sinking was that the vessel was torpedoed, and hence that the loss fell within the exception.

It will be noted that the *Smaragd* decision is directly opposed to sub-section 2(b) of Section 55 which states that the insurer is not liable for any loss proximately caused by delay, even though the delay may be caused by a peril insured against. The decision was not acceptable to the marine insurance industry and as a consequence resulted in the inclusion of a clause in American cargo policies which reaffirms the principle enunciated in sub-secion 2(b). The decision also represents one instance in which American law does not conform to English law.

Sub-section 2(b) clearly reflects the English decisions antedating the Act.[3]

Although the principle is universally admitted, no attempt has been made to work out any philosophical theory of causes and effect and, as the court in one case noted, it is probably just as well for commerce that the attempt has not been made.[4] It is simply impossible to reconcile many of the decisions. About the best that can be done in the circumstances is to acquire a "feel" for the concepts by reading all the cases. The difficulty lies in attempting to give separate and coherent treatment to the different concepts lurking within the phrase "proximate cause," because the opinions of the courts rarely, if ever, make such distinctions. Some of the concepts which appear to be indiscriminately dealt with in the decisions under the broad label proximate cause are: whether the loss is one by a peril insured against; burden of proof; presumptions; warranties, and proximate cause in the pure, or at least restricted, sense.[5]

---

3. *Pink v. Fleming*, (1890) 25 Q.B.D. 396, 6 Asp. M.L.C. 554, C.A.; *Taylor v. Dunbar*, (1869) L.R. 4 C.P. 206; *Shelbourne v. Law Investment Ins. Corp.*, (1898) 2 Q.B.D. 626, 8 Asp. M.L.C. 445; *William & Co. v. Canton Ins. Office Ltd.*, [1901] A.C. 462.

4. *Inman S.S. Co. v. Bischoff*, (1882) 7 App.Cas. 670.

5. For example, the determination of whether damage to a vessel by worms or by entry of seawater through deteriorated fastenings, hoses, etc., is covered by the policy would not appear to be a question so much of proximate cause as of whether a specific condition which allows entry of seawater is a peril of the sea. Such cases as *Northwestern Mutual Life Ins. Co. v. Linard (The Vainqueur)*, 498 F.2d 556, 1974 AMC 877, [1974] 2 Lloyd's Rep. 398 (2d Cir., 1974), and the *Lakeland*, 20 F.2d 619, 1927 AMC 1361 (6th Cir.), are, in reality, burden of proof cases. *Leathem Smith-Putnam Nav. Co. v. National U.F. Ins. Co. (The Material Service)*, 96 F.2d 923, 1927 AMC 925 (7th Cir.), principally involved a breach of warranty. *U.S. Fire v. Cavanaugh*, 732 F.2d 832, 1985 AMC 1001 (11th Cir.), involved findings that the master took the vessel beyond the geographic limits of the hull policy without the owner's knowledge and consent, where it grounded and then caught on fire. The majority held that the master had committed barratry and that it and the grounding and fire were all covered perils; the dissent took the position that the grounding was the proximate cause of the vessel's loss and, since it occurred outside the geographic limits of the policy, the assured could not recover. In *INA v. Board of Commissioners*, 733 F.2d 1161, 1985 AMC 1460 (5th Cir.), the vessel was manned by unlicensed personnel; the vessel collided with another and the question of prox-

Loss by a Combination of Causes

It must be remembered that when there are two concurrent causes of a loss, the predominating efficient one must be regarded as the proximate cause when the damage caused by each cannot be distinguished or segregated.[6] The principle applies although within the network for causation there may be found the operation of natural forces to which a disaster, within the coverage of the policy, has given play.[7] For example, in *Peters, supra*, Justice Story put the following illustration:

---

imate cause naturally arose. The court held that the proximate cause was manning the vessel with unlicensed personnel and not the collision.

6. *Hagedorn v. Whitmore*, (1816) 1 Stark. 157, N.P.; *Howard Fire Ins. Co. v. Norwich & N.Y. Transp. Co.*, 79 U.S. 194 (1870); *Yukon*, 1939 AMC 111 (Arb.); *Dole v. New England Mut. Marine Ins. Co.*, F.Cas. No. 3,966 (1st Cir., 1864).

7. *Magoun v. New England Marine Ins. Co.*, F.Cas. No. 8,961 (1st Cir., 1840); *Peters v. Warren Ins. Co.*, 39 U.S. 99 (1840). See, also, *Potter v. Ocean Ins. Co.*, F.Cas. No. 11,335 (1st Cir., 1837) where the vessel was so disabled by a storm that she became unmanageable and, subsequently, her ship's boat was lost. It was held that the loss was attributable to the storm although the loss did not occur during the actual period of the storm. In *Dole v. New England Mut. Marine Ins. Co.*, F.Cas. No. 3,966 (1st Cir., 1864), a Confederate raider boarded the insured vessel, plundered her papers, removed the crew, and set her on fire whereby she was totally destroyed. Held: the proximate cause of the loss was the taking by the raider and not fire. In *Cardwell v. Republic Fire Ins. Co.*, F.Cas. No. 2,396 (D., Ill., 1875), the vessel stranded in fair weather. Afterwards a gale came up and the vessel was lost. Held: the proximate cause was the stranding and not the gale. In *Northwestern Transp. Co. v. Boston Marine Ins. Co.*, 41 F. 793 (E.D. Mich. 1890), the vessel negligently stranded and, a storm having come up, was voluntarily scuttled to save her from total loss. The storm and not the stranding was held to be the proximate cause of the loss. In *Pennsylvania R. Co. v. Mannheim Ins. Co.*, 56 F. 301 (S.D.N.Y., 1893), a lighter owned by one carrier was directed by the employee of a second carrier into a slip. In moving into the slip, the ship grounded on a shoal and was pierced by a log, the existence of which was unknown. The proximate cause of the loss was held to be the grounding and not any negligence on the part of the carriers. In *Hagemeyer Trading Co. v. St. Paul F. & M. Ins. Co.*, 266 F. 14 (2d Cir., 1920), *cert. den.* 253 U.S. 497, fire originated in the coal bunkers of a prize vessel, which, despite all efforts to stop it, progressed until, in the judgment of the master, the vessel could not be saved. The vessel was then taken into shallow water and sunk. It was held that the fire was the proximate cause of the loss of the cargo, notwithstanding the sinking in shallow waters. In *Tyson v. Union Ins. Soc. of Canton*, 8 F.2d 356, 1924 AMC 1145 (N.D.,Cal.), cargo was damaged by rain, which could not have reached the cargo had it not been driven by the high winds. The court held that the proximate cause of the damage was the wind—an insured peril. In *Holly*, 11 F.2d 494, 1926 AMC 578 (3rd Cir.), the proximate cause of the shifting of three large boilers placed on a barge and not yet shored up was held to be due to swells of passing vessels, a peril of the sea. In *Yukon*, 1939 AMC 111 (Arb.), a fishing vessel collided with another fishing vessel. She took on water through a large hole in her bow; her crew abandoned her and took refuge on the other vessel which, however, refused to tow her to shallow water. Shortly after the collision, a fire broke out on the abandoned vessel and there appeared to be an explosion in her engine room. Four hours later, the vessel sank. In a claim by one insurer against its reinsurer, which later had insured in respect of a loss "in consequence of fire only," it was held: (1) had the fire not intervened, the vessel could have been towed to shallow water and would not have been a total loss; (2) there was no way of estimating the damage caused by the collision apart from the damage caused by the fire; (3) the dominant and efficient cause of the loss was fire; and (4) as loss by fire was the risk insured against by the reinsurer, and as the damage from the

Suppose a perishable cargo is greatly damaged by the perils of the sea, and it should, in consequence thereof, long afterwards, before arrival at the port of destination, become gradually so putrescent as to be required to be thrown overboard for the safety of the crew; the immediate cause of the loss would be the act of the master and crew, but there is no doubt that the underwriters would be liable for a total loss, upon the ground that the operative cause was the perils of the sea.[8] [Emphasis added]

Reischer v. Borwick[9] is an excellent example of the court having to select the proximate cause from two concurrent causes. In that case, a tug was insured against "risk of collision and damage received in collision with any object" but the policy did not include perils of the sea. The tug ran against a snag which did considerable damage, including breaking the cover of the condenser, leaving an opening about twenty square inches in area. The tug commenced leaking and, there being danger that the water would come into the vessel through the ejection pipes and the hole in the condenser, the pipes were plugged from the outside. While she was being towed to a place of repair, a plug came out and water rushed into the engine room through the injection pipes and the hole in the condenser cover and she began to sink. An attempt to again plug the ejection pipes failed and the vessel sank. The court held that the collision was the proximate cause of the loss although the towing of the ship through the water was a concurrent cause.

---

collision could not be distinguished from the loss by fire, the reinsurer was liable. In *Harbor Tug & Barge Co. v. Zurich Gen. Acc. & Liab. Co., Ltd.*, 24 F.Supp. 163, 1938 AMC 1197 (N.D.,Cal.), the insured vessel negligently precipitated a cargo of pipe into the water. Two days later, another vessel collided with the cargo of pipe and one of the people aboard the colliding vessel was drowned. Judgment was recovered against the owner of the insured vessel by the estate of the drowned person. In a suit by the owner of the insured vessel against his P & I underwriters, the court held that the proximate cause of the loss was the negligence of the assured in failing to mark or remove the cargo of pipe from the water, the negligence of the personnel of the insured vessel in precipitating the cargo into the water in the first place being a remote cause only. Consequently, the loss was not due to the "use" of the vessel and the claim against the P & I underwriters failed. In *Duet*, 264 F.Supp. 865, 1967 AMC 1144 (D.,Ore.), a yacht in the custody of the U. S. marshal was moved from deep water to shallow water at a time when there was a small hole in her side about 12-14 inches above the waterline. Low tides caused her to ground and lean toward the dock as a consequence of which water entered the vessel through the hole and she sank. It was held that the loss was due to a peril of the sea, being due to the grounding, and was not inevitable because of the existence of the hole.

8. Compare, however, *DeVaux v. Salvador*, (1836) 111 E.R. 845. *Peters* and *DeVaux* both involved collisions and the question of how damages should be apportioned. In the former, it was held that the loss was due to a peril of the sea; in the latter it was held that the cause was not a peril of the sea and the apportionment of damages was an arbitrary provision of the laws of nations governing damages in a collision. Subsequently, however, in *General Mut. Ins. Co. v. Sherwood*, 55 U.S. 351 (1852), the U. S. Supreme Court adopted the reasoning in *DeVaux.*

9. [1894] 2 Q.B. 548, 7 Asp. M.L.C. 493.

Leyland Shipping Company v. Norwich Union Fire Ins. Soc.[10] illustrates the same principle. There, the court had to choose between water rushing into the ship—a sea peril—through a hole made by a torpedo—a war risk. The court held the proximate cause to be the latter. Other war risk cases involve the same conscious choice of two concurrent causes.

See, for example, *Ionides v. Universal Marine Ins. Co.*,[11] where goods consisting of 6,500 bags of coffee on board the ship *Linwood* were insured for a voyage from Rio de Janeiro to New York under a policy with the following warranty: "Warranted free of capture, seizure, and detention and all the consequences thereof or of any attempt thereat, and free from all consequences of hostilities, riots or commotions." The light on Cape Hatteras had been extinguished by Confederate troops for military reasons. The master became confused about his position and went aground about ten miles south of the cape. Two days later, salvors succeeded in getting off about 150 bags of coffee and might have salved another 1,000 but for the fact that the Confederate troops appropriated the 150 bags which were salved and interrupted the salvage operations of the 1,000. The following day the ship broke up and the remaining bags aboard were lost. In a suit on the policy, the court held that the 150 bags which were salved but taken by the Confederates as well as the 1,000 bags which might have been saved were lost as a consequence of "hostilities," but the bags left aboard the ship were lost as a consequence of perils of the seas, and not the hostile act of the Confederates in extinguishing the light.[12]

Loss by a Single Cause Amounting to More Than One of the Perils Insured by the Policy

Atlantic Maritime Co., Inc. v. Gibbon[13] is an illustration of a loss by a single cause amounting to more than one of the perils insured by the policy. In

10. [1918] A.C. 350.
11. (1863) 143 E.R. 445, 1 Mar. L.C. 353.
12. See, also, *Hahn v. Corbett*, (1824) 130 E.R. 285 (due to lack of a pilot the vessel stranded and was subsequently seized and confiscated by the Spanish government); *Redman v. Wilson*, (1845) 153 E.R. 562 (ship negligently stowed later became leaky and was run ashore to prevent her from sinking and to save the cargo; held, the proximate cause of the loss was a peril of the sea although a concurring cause was the manifest unseaworthiness caused by negligence in loading); *The Lapwing*, [1940] P. 112, 66 Ll.L.Rep. 174 (yacht negligently docked by one acting as the master; held, *ejusdem generis* with stranding, a marine peril); *Walker v. Maitland*, (1821) 106 E.R. 1155 (crew went to sleep and kept no watch and the vessel ran aground; held, the loss was proximately caused by a peril of the sea and only remotely by reason of the negligence of the crew); *Techni-Chemicals Products Co. Ltd. v. South British Ins. Co. Ltd.*, [1977] 1 N.Z.L.R. 311 (contamination of oil tanks where the contamination occurred either by giving wrong instructions to a tanker driver, the tankers going to the wrong destination, or the pumping of oil into tanks in which there were other oil products; citing *Leyland Shipping Co. Ltd. v. Norwich Union Fire Ins. Soc. Ltd.*, [1918] A.C. 350, 362, and applying "common sense" principles, the court held that taking the oil to the wrong destination was the proximate cause).
13. [1953] 1 All E.R. 1086, [1953] 2 Lloyd's Rep. 294, C.A.

that case, the policy was on freight to be earned on a voyage from Taku Bar, the port for Tientsin, China, to Japan. While the vessel was at anchor, she was approached by a Chinese Nationalist destroyer and, in effect, told that there was going to be trouble and if she were present she could be hurt; if the vessel remained and was damaged, the Chinese Nationalists could not be blamed for it. At that time, the surrounding territory was controlled by the Chinese Communists. There was gunfire in the vicinity and a Chinese ship in the harbor was shelled and sunk. The master departed and later loaded a cargo of lumber in British Columbia for carriage to the east coast of the United States. After his departure, several ships arrived at Taku Bar and loaded small quantities of cargo without molestation. In a suit on the freight policy, a majority of the court held that the freight could be considered as having been lost by reason of the civil war, or by restraint of princes, or by hostile operations, but denied recovery on the ground that the "exceptions" clause in the policy prevented recovery.[14]

Loss by a Combination of Causes Where One is Excepted

Where there is a loss by a combination of causes but one of those causes is excluded by a provision in the policy, very difficult problems arise.

Clearly, the problem can be approached on two bases: (1) since there were two causes and either of them could be treated as the cause of the loss, then the exclusion of one of them should not interfere with the operation of the other, (2) since it cannot be controverted that the excluded cause was actually responsible for the loss, the exclusion clause bars any claim on the policy.

Notwithstanding the statement of the problem, there appears to be no definitive case which answers it. The courts always seem to have answered it by isolating a single peril as being the dominant "efficient" one.

For example, in *Cory v. Burr*,[15] barratry of the master was an insured peril but the policy contained a warranty of "free from capture and sei-

---

14. See, also, *Yukon*, 1939 AMC 111 (Arb.), fn. 7, *supra*, and *Carter Tug v. Home Ins. Co.*, 345 F.Supp. 1193, 1972 AMC 498 (S.D.,Ill.).

15. (1883) 8 A.C. 393. See, also, *Blaine Richards & Co. v. Marine Indemnity Ins. Co. et al*, 635 F.2d 1051, 1981 AMC 1 (2d Cir.), an action on a cargo policy after fumigated beans had been detained by the Food and Drug Administration. At first instance, the court held that the F. C. and S. Clause precluded recovery. On appeal, the case was remanded for further findings as to whether the beans had sustained physical damage, not as a result of delay but rather because of either (a) fumigation in an improper manner, or (b) use of any unacceptable fumigant. As the court noted, the plaintiff could recover by showing that either of these factors resulted in reconditioning expenses or lesser sales revenue. It will be seen that the court was faced with a conscious choice between damage due to delay during detention or damage done during the fumigation process, the former being excluded from coverage and the latter included.

zure and the consequences of any attempt thereat." The vessel was seized by the Spanish authorities because of barratrous acts of the master in engaging in smuggling. The assured was put to expense in resisting condemnation proceedings against the vessel and ultimately paid a sum of money to procure her restoration. Suit was brought against the underwriters for the recovery of the sums so expended. The House of Lords held that the loss was proximately caused by the seizure.

In *Atlantic Maritime Co., Inc. v. Gibbon,*[16] which, as pointed out above, actually involved one event constituting several different types of peril, the exception as to "frustration" was held to govern.

In *Samuel (P) v. Dumas,*[17] the final cause in the sinking of the vessel was the incursion of seawater but the dominant efficient cause was held to be an intentional scuttling—a peril not covered. Lord Sumner did not accept this view and in his dissenting speech treated the loss as one of two perils operating simultaneously. It would appear from a close reading of his speech that he came down on the side of holding that, since it could not be controverted that the excluded cause was actually responsible for the loss, the exclusion clause barred any claim on the policy.

In *Leyland Shipping Co., Ltd. v. Norwich Union Fire Ins. Co., Ltd.,*[18] as noted heretofore, the proximate cause of the loss was found to be the torpedoeing of the vessel—a war risk—and not the sinking by reason of water entering the hull.

In *Union Ins. Co. v. Smith,*[19] the policy on a tug provided that the underwriter would not be liable for loss by breaking of any part of her machinery. The tug broke her shaft and, while being towed by another tug, sprang a leak and sank. The court held that the proximate cause of the loss was the sinking. The existence of an excluded peril—breakage of the shaft—was held not to preclude recovery.

In *Naviera de Canaris (S.A.) v. Nacional Hispanica Aseguradora S.A. (Playa de Las Nieves),*[20] there was a machinery breakdown caused by a latent defect which in turn caused a stranding. This in turn resulted in a loss of time which resulted in a loss of charter hire under the charter terms. The freight policy contained an exception clause reading: "Warranted free from any claim consequent on loss of time whether arising from a peril of the sea or otherwise." The plaintiff assured contended that the proximate cause of the loss was the breakdown of machinery and

---

16. [1953] 2 All E.R. 1086, [1953] 2 Lloyd's Rep. 294, C.A.

17. [1924] A.C. 431. See, also, *France Fenwick & Co. Ltd. v. North of England Protecting and Indemnity Ass'n,* (1917) 23 Com.Cas. 37, 2 K.B. 522, where the insured vessel was damaged by running upon the wreck of a steamer which had been sunk shortly before by a German submarine. It was held that the damage was occasioned by a marine peril and not a war risk.

18. (1918) A.C. 350.

19. 124 U.S. 405 (1888).

20. [1977] 1 Lloyd's Rep. 457, H.L.

the stranding and therefore the loss of hire was consequent on that peril rather than on a loss of time. The House of Lords disagreed, holding that the loss of freight was consequent on the loss of time and therefore fell within the exceptions clause.[21]

Loss Must Relate Directly and Proximately to a Peril Insured Against

It cannot be emphasized too strongly that the loss must relate directly and proximately to a peril insured against. For example, in *Cator v. Great Western Ins. Co. of New York*,[22] part of a cargo of tea was damaged by seawater. As teas are sold in the order of the consecutive numbers marked on the packages and the consecutive numbers were broken by reason of the seawater damage to a portion, a suspicion arose as to the remainder and they sold for less than they otherwise would have brought. The assured recovered for that portion damaged by seawater but not for the diminution of value caused by mere suspicion.

In *Meyer v. Ralli*,[23] the ship met with heavy weather and a portion of the cargo was damaged. To meet expenses at the port of refuge, the master sold the cargo pursuant to an order of court which he had procured. The master could have forwarded the goods on to destination. A constructive total loss of the freight was claimed. The court held that the proximate cause of the loss was the master's act in selling the cargo and not the perils of the sea. To the same effect, see *Powell v. Gudgeon*.[24]

In *Neidlinger v. Ins. Co. of N.A.*,[25] seawater entered the vessel through a peril of the seas. The seawater permeated some sacks of cargo. The damp vapors emanating from the sacks soaked with seawater damaged sacks of barley in close proximity. The court held that the loss was not caused "by

---

21. See, also, two non-marine cases: *Wayne Tank & Pump Co. Ltd v. Employers' Liability Assur. Corp. Ltd.*, [1973] 2 Lloyd's Rep. 237 (obiter), and *Farrow (Howard) Ltd. v. Ocean Accident & Guarantee Corp. Ltd.*, (1940) 67 Ll.L.Rep. 27, both of which upheld the supremacy of an "exceptions" clause. In *Goodman v. Fireman's Fund Ins. Co.*, 600 F.2d 1040, 1979 AMC 2534 (4th Cir.), the court held that the all risk policy on a yacht provided coverage inasmuch as the assured's negligence caused the loss (an insured peril) which combined with an excluded peril (freezing) and the insured peril was the predominant efficient cause of the loss. However, the court further held that the assured breached a lay-up warranty in failing to close the sea valves as a part of the winterizing process, found to be a custom in the applicable waters, and his breach of the warranty precluded recovery. The analogy to an exceptions clause is apparent. And in *Greene v. Cheatham*, 293 F.2d 933, 1961 AMC 2549 (2d Cir.), an inherent vice clause was held to override an all risk clause.
22. (1873) L.R. 8 C.P. 552, 2 Asp. M.L.C. 90.
23. (1876) 45 L.J.Q.B. 741, 3 Asp. M.L.C. 324.
24. (1816) 105 E.R. 1108.
25. F.Cas. No. 10,086, *aff'd* 11 F. 514 (2d Cir., 1880).

actual contact of sea water with the articles damaged" within the meaning of the policy.[26]

In *Union Ins. Co. v. Smith*,[27] the policy on a tug provided that the assurer would not be liable for loss by the breaking of any part of the machinery. The tug broke her shaft and, while being towed by another tug, sprang a leak and sank. The court held that the proximate cause of the loss was a sinking. The existence of one of the excluded risks (breakage of the shaft) was held not to preclude recovery.

In *Howard Fire Ins. Co. v. Norwich & N.Y. Transp. Co.*,[28] a schooner collided with a steamer, stoving a hole in the latter, the sole effect of which would have been to sink her to the level of the upper deck. But water came in, filled the floor of the furnace whereby steam was generated, forcing the fire up to the upper deck. This loosened the housing so that the freight drifted away, lessening the floating capacity of the steamer to the point where it sank. The policy covered "against all such loss or damage . . . as should happen to the property by fire, other than fire happening by means of any invasion, insurrection, riot, or civil commotion, or of any military or usurped power." The proximate cause of the loss was the collision which, in turn, caused the fire. Since risk of fire by collision was not expressly excluded, it was held the insurer accepted the risk of all fires not expressly excepted.

In *Canada Rice Mills, Ltd. v. Union Marine & Gen. Ins. Co., Ltd.*,[29] the ship encountered heavy weather and the crew closed the ship's ventilators to prevent the incursion of seawater. As a consequence, the cargo of rice overheated. In the lower court, it was found that the proximate cause of the loss was the closing of the ventilators. On appeal, the Privy Council reversed, holding that although the damage to the rice was not caused by the incursion of seawater, it was caused by actions taken necessarily and reasonably in order to prevent such incursion and, therefore, the loss was one occurring from a peril of the sea. The court held that in any event the loss was covered by the general words of the policy, i.e., "all other perils, losses and misfortunes."

Insured Peril Concurring with Negligence of Assured

Sub-section 2(a) of Section 55 of the Act expresses one illustration wherein coverage is confirmed when the loss is proximately caused by a

---

26. See, however, *Montoya v. London Assur. Co.*, (1851) 155 E.R. 620, where hides rendered putrid by seawater contaminated tobacco nearby. Held: loss by perils of the sea.
27. 124 U.S. 405 (1888).
28. 79 U.S. 194 (1870).
29. [1940] 2 All E.R. 169, [1941] A.C. 55, 1940 AMC 1673.

peril insured against even though the loss would not have happened had it not been for the negligence of the master and crew.[30] The cases so holding are legion.[31]

30. Sub-section 2(a) of Sec. 55 expressly provides that the insurer is not liable for any loss attributable to the wilful misconduct of the assured. This sub-section must be read *in pari materia* with Sec. 78(4) imposing upon the assured and his agents the duty to take such measures as may be reasonable for the purpose of averting or minimizing the loss. For example, see *Standard Marine Ins. Co. Ltd. of Liverpool v. Nome Beach Lighterage & Transp. Co.*, 133 F. 636 (9th Cir., 1904), *cert. den.* 200 U.S. 616 (1906), where the master deliberately forced his vessel through floating ice on a voyage to Alaska, with knowledge of the dangers to be encountered and with ample time to have avoided them, in order to arrive more quickly and secure a better market for his cargo. The court held that such conduct was not mere negligence but a wilful omission to perform his duty and an intentional commission of a wrongful act. See, also, *Chicago S.S. Lines v. U.S. Lloyd's*, 12 F.2d 733, 1926 AMC 807 (7th Cir.), where the vessel sank alongside the dock, due to open rivet holes, resulting in a holding of want of due diligence on the part of the owner, thus precluding recovery under the policy. In *Astrovlanis Compania Naviera S.A. v. Linard (The Gold Sky)*, [1972] 2 Lloyd's Rep. 187, Q.B.D., Justice Mocatta held that the words "his agents" (meaning the assured's agents) in Sec. 78(4) should not be read as being applicable to the master and crew unless they were expressly instructed by the assured as to what to do or not to do in respect of suing and laboring; otherwise there would be an acute conflict between Sec. 78(4) and Sec. 55(2)(a) of the Act.

31. *Bishop v. Pentland*, (1827) 108 E.R. 705 (stranding in which the crew was negligent); *Lind v. Mitchell*, (1928) 34 Com.Cas. 81, 32 Ll.L.Rep. 70, C.A. (vessel damaged by ice negligently abandoned by master and crew; i.e., insured peril endangered the vessel and it was thereupon lost by the negligent failure of the master to take proper measures to save her); *Hahn v. Corbett, supra; Redman v. Wilson, supra, Waters v. Merchants Louisville Ins. Co.*, 36 U.S. 213 (1837) (fire negligently occasioned by the crew led to an explosion which caused the loss; policy held to cover); *The Lapwing, supra; Walker v. Maitland, supra; Orient Mutual Life Ins. Co. v. Adams*, 123 U.S. 67 (vessel swept downriver and over a falls where it sank due to the negligence of the master in casting off lines with no steam on the boilers); *Rubaiyat*, 5 F.2d 522, 1926 AMC 181 (9th Cir.) (vessel lost through capsizing; the vessel was seaworthy at the commencement of the voyage but was rendered unseaworthy by improper loading at an intermediate port); *Trinder v. Thames & Mersey Ins. Co.*, [1898] 2 Q.B. 114, 67 L.J.Q.B. 666, 8 Asp. M.L.C. 373, C.A. (negligent navigation of the master, not amounting to wilful negligence, no bar to recovery); *Rosa v. Ins. Co. of State of Pennsylvania (The Belle of Portugal)*, 421 F.2d 390, 1970 AMC 30 (9th Cir.), [1970] 2 Lloyd's Rep. 386 (fire caused by negligence of an electrician); *Astrovlanis Compania Naviera S.A. v. Linard (The Gold Sky)*, [1972] 2 Lloyd's Rep. 187, Q.B.D. (negligence of master in proceeding on voyage and declining the aid of salvors); *Patapsco Ins. Co. v. Coulter*, 28 U.S. 222 (1830) (where the policy covers risks of fire and fire is the proximate cause of the loss, the negligence of the master and crew being a remote cause, the policy covers); *General Mut. Ins. Co. v. Sherwood*, 55 U.S. 351 (1852) (proximate cause of the loss was a collision; underwriters precluded from setting up negligence of the servants of the assured as a defense); *Richelieu & O. Nav. Co. v. Boston Marine Ins. Co.*, 136 U.S. 408 (1886) (in the absence of an express stipulation in the policy, the underwriter is liable for negligence of the crew not amounting to barratry); *Earnmoor S.S. Co. v. Union Ins. Co.*, 44 F. 374 (S.D.N.Y., 1890) (ordinary negligence on the part of the ship's master not a defense for underwriters); *Morse v. St. Paul F. & M. Ins. Co.*, 122 F. 748 (1st Cir., 1903) (underwriters not discharged when master negligently left an intermediate port at which he had stopped with his vessel in an unseaworthy condition without making repairs). And see, also, *Williams v. Suffolk Ins. Co.*, F.Cas. No. 17,738 (1st Cir., 1838); *Russell Mining v. Northwestern F. & M. Ins. Co.*, 322 F.2d 440, 1963 AMC 2358 (4th Cir), and *Sorenson v. Boston Ins. Co.*, 20 F.2d 640, 1927 AMC 1288 (4th Cir.), *cert. den.* 275 U.S. 555.

Negligence of the Assured or his Agents the Sole and Proximate Cause of the Loss

Cases will be found where the proximate and sole cause of the loss was the negligence of the agents of the assured; i.e., negligence *per se* was held to be the cause of the loss.[32]

Generally speaking, the American cases denying recovery for negligence of master and crew have done so on the basis of an express exclusion contained in the policy of insurance; i.e., the policies contained warranties excepting losses caused by the negligence of the master or crew.[33] Compare, however, *Egbert v. St. Paul Fire & Marine Ins. Co.*,[34] where the policy provided that there would be no liability for damage arising from "ignorance on the part of the master or pilot as to any port or place the said steam tug may use, or from want of ordinary care or skill." It was held that the warranty referred only to the general qualifications of the master or pilot and was not a warranty against single acts of error, negligence, or mistake.

Generally speaking, it would seem that recovery should only be denied where it is found that the loss was occasioned by a breach of the implied warranty of seaworthiness—and here it should make no difference whether the breach was due to negligence or was intentional. An illustration is *Leathem Smith-Putnam Nav. Co. v. National U.F. Ins. Co., (The Material Service)*,[35] where the owners of the vessel permitted holes in the hatchleaves without providing covers; the master negligently failed to place covers over the holes and as a result the vessel sank. It was held that the loss was due to a want of due diligence on the part of the owners.

Ordinary Wear and Tear

There are a number of recent American cases denying recovery on grounds that the loss was caused by ordinary wear and tear. See *Sipowicz v.*

---

32. See, for example, *The Titania*, 19 F. 101 (S.D.N.Y., 1883) where it was held that since the damage might have been avoided by the use of ordinary care and diligence on the part of the crew, underwriters were not liable; *Tanner v. Bennett*, (1825) Ry. & M. 182, N.P., where the ship was broken up by agents of the assured after a negligent survey and a claim for total loss was denied. See, also, *Hazard's Adm'r v. New England Marine Ins. Co.*, 33 U.S. 557 (1834) (neglect of master to effect repairs held to be the sole cause of the loss); *Phoenix Ins. Co. v. Copelin*, 76 U.S. 461 (1868) (assured not excused, even though he gave the master proper directions, where the master did not observe them and the damages were thereby increased).

33. *Levi v. New Orleans Mut. Ins. Ass'n*, F.C. No. 8,290 (5th Cir., 1874); *Flint & P.M.R. Co. v. Marine Ins. Co.*, 71 F. 210 (7th Cir., 1895).

34. 71 F. 739 (D.C.N.Y., 1895).

35. 96 F.2d 923, 1937 AMC 925 (7th Cir.).

Wimble (The Green Lion)[36] (failure of metal fastenings securing keel and keelson held to be due to deterioration, not latent defect); *Parente v. Bayville Marine*[37] (results of normal wear and tear and the corrosive effects of seawater held not to be a latent defect); *Wood v. Great American*[38] (defect in rubber water hose held to be due to ordinary wear and tear); *Irwin v. Eagle Star Ins. Co. (The Jomie)*[39] (defect resulting from joining brass and iron fitting not a latent defect but mere electrolysis); *By's Chartering v. Interstate Ins.*[40] (damage occasioned by defective hose the result of gradual wear and tear); *Presti v. Firemen's Ins. Co.*[41] (hole in exhaust line resulted solely from normal wear and tear).

Wadsworth Lighterage and Coaling Co., Ltd. v. Sea Insurance Co., Ltd.,[41a] presents a classic case of wear and tear. There, a fifty-year-old barge sank while docked. No one was aboard at the time and there was no evidence of any accident which caused her loss. The court of appeal held that the loss was due to ordinary wear and tear, saying in part:

> A barge at some time or other comes to the end of its working life; it has had so much wear and tear that it is no longer able to withstand the wear and tear that is the ordinary incident of its every day work . . . .[42]

Inherent Vice

In *Blower v. Great Western Railway Co.*,[43] the court defined inherent vice as follows:

> By the expression "vice" is meant only that sort of vice which by its internal development tends to the destruction or the injury of the animal or thing to be carried.

It is a vice which is an innate or natural or normal quality of the goods. It has been defined as "any existing defects, diseases, decay or the inher-

36. 370 F.Supp. 442, 1975 AMC 524, [1974] 1 Lloyd's Rep. 593 (S.D.N.Y.).
37. 1974 AMC 1399, [1975] 1 Lloyd's Rep. 333 (St., N.Y.).
38. 289 F.Supp. 1014, 1968 AMC 1815 (E.D.,Wis.).
39. 455 F.2d 827, 1973 AMC 1184, [1973] 2 Lloyd's Rep. 489 (5th Cir.).
40. 542 F.2d 1045, 1976 AMC 113 (1st Cir.).
41. 1972 AMC 1220 (St.,Cal.).
41a. 35 Com.Cas. 1, 34 Ll.L.Rep. 285, C.A.
42. See, also, *Dudgeon v. Pembroke*, (1874) L.R. 9 Q.B. 581, *aff'd* (1877) 2 App.Cas. 284, H.L.; *Harrison v. Universal Ins. Co.*, (1862) 3 F. & F. 190, N.P.; *Patterson v. Harris*, (1861) 121 E.R. 740 (imperfect insulation on cable permitted seawater to damage the cable; held, not a peril of the sea but the inevitable consequence of the immersion of the cable in sea water); *Dodwell & Co. Ltd. v. British Dominions General Ins. Co. Ltd.*, [1955] 2 Lloyd's Rep. 391; *Wilson, Sons & Co. v. Xantho (Cargo Owners)*, (1887) 12 App.Cas. 503; and *E.D. Sassoon & Co. Ltd. v. Yorkshire Ins. Co.*, (1923) 14 Ll.L.Rep. 167, *aff'd* 16 Ll.L.Rep. 129, C.A.
43. (1872) L.R. 7 C.P. 655.

ent nature of the commodity which will cause it to deteriorate with a lapse of time,"[44] for example, meat becoming putrid,[45] or fruit becoming rotten.[46]

It is often quite difficult to differentiate whether damage to a perishable cargo resulted from (a) perils of the sea, or (b) inherent vice, or (c) neglect in the manner of stowage. For example, in *Bird's Cigarette Mfg. Co., Ltd. v. Rouse*,[47] cigarettes were found to be mildewed upon arrival at destination. Underwriters defended on the ground of inherent vice. The court found that while some of the cigarettes contained more moisture than they should have, others had been damaged by seawater and for the latter damage the underwriters were held liable.

In *E.D. Sassoon & Co. Ltd. v. Yorkshire Ins. Co.*, (1923), *supra*, cigarettes in tins arrived at destination in a mildewed condition and the tins were rusty both inside and out. The court found the loss to be due to a fortuitous risk and not inherent vice.

In *Wilson, Holgate & Co., Ltd. v. Lancashire and Cheshire Ins. Corp.*,[48] casks of palm oil were found to be damaged with a consequent leakage of oil. The underwriters denied liability on the ground that the loss was due to inherent vice, i.e., insufficiency of casks. It was held that the damage was due to bad stowage.

In *F.W. Berk & Co., Ltd. v. Style*,[49] the court held that the paper bags in which kieselguhr was packed had an inherent vice in that they were incapable of transporting the kieselguhr in the course of necessary handling.

In *Boyd v. Dubois*,[50] there was spontaneous combustion of flax put aboard the vessel in a damp condition and the underwriters were relieved of liability. But see *Greenhill v. Federal Ins. Co.*,[51] where the court expressed doubt concerning *Boyd v. Dubois* and held that the policy was vitiated where the insured had concealed the fact that the cargo of celluloid had been carried on deck and had been exposed to the elements for over two months.

In *Biddle, Sawyer & Co., Ltd. v. Peters*,[52] the policy was on cases of tinned pork. The Institute Cargo Clauses (extended cover) were attached to the

---

44. *Vana Trading Co. v. S.S. Mette Skou*, 1977 AMC 702 (2d Cir.); see, also, *Oyler v. Merriam*, [1923] 1 D.L.R. 602 (Can.).
45. *Taylor v. Dunbar*, (1869) L.R. 4 C.P. 206.
46. *Dyson v. Rowcroft*, (1803) 127 E.R. 257.
47. (1924) 19 Ll.L.Rep. 301, K.B.D.
48. (1922) 13 Ll.L.Rep. 486, K.B.D.
49. [1955] 2 Lloyd's Rep. 382, [1955] 3 All E.R. 625. See, also, *Blackshaws (Pty) Ltd. v. Constantia Ins. Co. Ltd.*, [1983] 1 AD 120 (So.Af.), 1984 AMC 637, where defective packing within a container was held to constitute inherent vice under a marine cargo policy.
50. (1811) 3 Camp. 133, N.P.
51. [1927] 1 K.B. 65, 24 Ll.L.Rep. 383, C.A.
52. [1957] 2 Lloyd's Rep. 339.

policy excluding loss or damage caused by inherent vice. The tins burst and the goods were condemned. The court held the policy did not cover.

In *Gee & Garnham Ltd. v. Whittall*,[53] there was no evidence of any transit risks which could have caused the damage, and the court held the damage must have occurred either before transit or owing to inadequate packing; accordingly, the loss came within the exception of inherent vice.

In *Teneria "El Popo" v. Home Ins. Co.*,[54] a cargo of goat skins became infested with larvae which ate up the skins. Cargo underwriters were held liable.

In *Red Top Brewing Co. v. Mazzotti*,[55] the cargo policy was upon cassava meal, as to which the risk of insect infestation is the heart of the risk. The policy contained a condition requiring inspection and a particular certificate of condition. The court held that the inspection conducted and the certificate as to condition were inadequate.

In *Greene v. Cheetham*,[56] the all risk policy contained an "inherent vice" clause. The trial court held that the inherent vice clause was rendered inoperative by the all risk clause. On appeal, the court reversed, holding that the two clauses were not inconsistent and that an all risk coverage does not include an undisclosed event existing prior to coverage or the consummation during the period of coverage of an indwelling fault in the goods existing prior to coverage.

In *Coussa v. Westchester Fire Ins. Co.*,[57] the cargo owner put in evidence of sampling six weeks before the shipment (as well as the ocean carrier's issuance of a clean bill of lading) to sustain his claim that damage found on discharge was due to an insured peril or from an external cause. The court held the loss to have been due to gradual deterioration or inherent vice.

In *Gillespie & Co. v. Continental Ins. Co.*,[58] a walnut shipment from Iran to New York was discovered damaged by insects on arrival. The consignee sued both the ocean carrier and the insurer. There being a failure of proof of the condition of the walnuts at time of shipment, the carrier was not held liable. The insurer was held liable, however, as it failed to prove that the insect eggs were present in the walnuts prior to the commencement of the shipment. The court also held that where the policy did not require cargo fumigation to repel insects during the voyage, the insurer could not belatedly assert that failure to fumigate constituted negligence by the shipper.

---

53. [1955] 2 Lloyd's Rep. 562.
54. 1955 AMC 328 (St., N.Y.).
55. 202 F.2d 481, 1953 AMC 309 (2d Cir.).
56. 293 F.2d 933, 1961 AMC 2549 (2d Cir.).
57. 1962 AMC 1805.
58. 1958 AMC 2437 (St.,N.Y.).

In *Nakasheff v. Continental Ins. Co.*,[59] an all risks policy on cargo was held to cover only a loss which might result from external causes and not from the natural and normal behavior of the fluid cargo itself, which had the characteristic of expansion with heat, causing it to force its way through and leak out of the tin containers in which it was shipped. (The policy had an F. C. & S. Clause attached. The cargo expanded and leaked due to heating while in the custody of the collector of customs who had lawfully detained it because of a wilful, knowing, and substantial under-declaration of value at the time of the entry of the shipment.)

In *Monarch Industrial v. American Motorists*,[60] packaged steel sheets were stored in the open for four months and then shipped under clean bills of lading where they were outturned badly rusted. The suit by the cargo owner against cargo underwriters under an all risks of physical loss policy from exterior causes was dismissed, where the cargo owner failed to sustain its burden of pre-shipment good order and condition and failed to adequately segregate pre-shipment and voyage damage. The court held, *inter alia*, that the clean bill of lading was only *prima facie* proof of apparent good order and condition of the exterior of the packages and said nothing of the inside of the packaged steel sheets. However, in *Bershad v. Commercial Union*,[61] summary judgment was granted against the underwriter when it failed to dispute the clean bill of lading, the mill's certificate of merchantability, and the fact of rust damage to a cargo of steel sheets.

Inherent vice in a ship has the same effect as inherent vice in cargo.[62]

---

59. 1954 AMC 986 (S.D.N.Y.).

60. 276 F.Supp. 972, 1967 AMC 2488 (S.D.N.Y.).

61. 1960 AMC 2446 (St.,N.Y.).

62. *Faucus v. Sarsfield*, (1856) 119 E.R. 836 (time policy on a vessel which was unseaworthy when it sailed even though the owner was not aware of the unseaworthiness); *Sassoon (E.D.) & Co. v. Western Assur. Co.*, (1912) A.C. 561, (1911-13) All E.R. 438, P.C. (damage due to weakness of the hull and not perils of the sea); *Ballantyne v. MacKinnon*, (1896) 2 Q.B. 455, 1 Com.Cas. 424, C.A. (time policy on a vessel which sailed with an insufficiency of coal; as a consequence, assistance from salvors was required; in a suit by owners against hull underwriters, it was held the salvage charges were rendered necessary by reason of the unfitness of the vessel and not perils of the sea); *Grant, Smith & Co. and McDonnell, Ltd. v. Seattle Construction & Dry Dock Co.*, (1920) A.C. 162, (1918-19) All E.R. 378, P.C. (drydock under charter capsized due to its inherent unfitness for the work and not to any condition of wind or sea; the charterers were to have obtained insurance for $75,000 but failed to do so; the drydock was actually worth only $34,500; the court held that the loss was not due to a marine risk and, in any event, owners could recover only its actual value of $34,500); *Pacific Dredging v. Hurley*, 1965 AMC 836 (St.,Wash.) (cause of loss an internal weakness in the vessel and not perils of the seas). Compare, however, *Potter v. Suffolk Ins. Co.*, F.Cas. No. 11,339 (1st Cir., 1835) where a stoutly built vessel having some cargo aboard and while lying at a wharf usually safe for vessels of her tonnage, took the ground and was later discovered to be leaking badly. The court held that the proximate cause of the loss was not inherent weakness in the vessel but taking the ground which was a loss within perils of the seas.

Rats or Vermin

Section 55(2)(c) of the Marine Insurance Act, 1906, makes it very clear that, unless the policy otherwise provides, the insurer is not liable for any loss proximately caused by rats or vermin. Thus, in *Hunter v. Potts* (1815) 4 Camp. 203, N.P., a loss arising from rats eating holes in the ship's bottom was held not to be within the perils insured against by the common form of marine insurance policy. See, also, *Teneria "El Popo" v. Home Ins. Co.,*[63] *Red Top Brewing Co. v. Mazzotti,*[64] *Kohl v. Parr,*[65] and *Laveroni v. Drury.*[66]

However, in *Hamilton, Fraser & Co. v. Pandorf & Co.,*[67] it was found that rats had gnawed a hole in a pipe on board the ship, whereby seawater escaped and damaged a cargo of rice, without any neglect or default on the part of the shipowner or his servants. The rice was shipped under a charter-party and bills of lading which excepted "dangers and accidents of the sea." The court held that the loss was fortuitous and unexpected and therefore fell within the ambit of dangers and accidents of the seas. Although an affreightment case, the same principles apply to marine insurance, and decisions under Article 4(2)(m) of the Hague Rules are applicable. See cases cited, Chapter 18, Tetley, *Marine Cargo Claims,* 2nd ed.

Injury to Machinery Not Proximately Caused by Maritime Perils

This exception had its genesis in *Thames & Mersey Marine Insce. Co., Ltd. v. Hamilton, Fraser & Co.*[68] In that case, a donkey engine was being used in pumping water into the main boilers of the vessel "Inchmaree" when, owing to a valve being closed which ought to have been kept open, water was forced into and split open the air-chambers of the donkey pump. The closing of the valve was either accidental or due to the negligence of an engineer and was not due to ordinary wear and tear. The assured contended that the loss was due to "other like perils" as those contained in the principal portion of the perils clause. Basically, the court held that the loss was not a type to which a maritime venture is subject.

The case led directly to the introduction of the now-famous Inchmaree Clause, in which coverage is extended for loss or damage to hull or machinery through negligence of masters, mariners, engineers, or pilots, and through any latent defect in the machinery or hull.

63. 1955 AMC 328 (St.,N.Y.).
64. 202 F.2d 481, 1953 AMC 309 (2d Cir.).
65. (1897) 1 Esp. 445, N.P.
66. (1852) 8 Exch. 166.
67. (1887) 12 App.Cas. 518, 6 Asp. M.L.C. 212, H.L.
68. (1887) 12 App.Cas. 484, 6 Asp. M.L.C. 200, H.L.

Following *Thames & Mersey v. Hamilton,* and after the introduction of
the first rudimentary Inchmaree Clause, the House of Lords had occasion to construe the clause in *Stott (Baltic) Steamers, Ltd. v. Marten.*[69] In that
case, the vessel was lying in dock and taking aboard a boiler weighing
thirty tons from a floating crane. The boiler as it descended caught upon
some coamings on the hatch. This caused the strain on the chain to be
lessened and the floating structure upon which the crane was mounted
listed away from the steamer by the operation of a counter-balance, the
boiler came free with a jerk, and the pin of the shackle attached to the
rope by which the boiler was being lifted broke and the boiler fell into the
hold and damaged the ship. The court held that the loss was not covered
by the general words in the policy as it was not due to a peril, loss, or
misfortune of a marine character nor was it covered by the then current
form of the Inchmaree Clause. It is to be doubted whether the decision
would have gone the way it did had the court had before it the modern
version of the Inchmaree Clause. In fact, it has been said that the clause
was amended to include coverage for accidents in "loading, discharging
or handling cargo" because of the *Stott* decision.

See, also, *Northwestern Mutual Life Ins. Co. v. Linard (The Vainqueur),*[70]
where an explosion mysteriously occurred in a starboard wing tank in the
vicinity of the engine room. The assured contended the loss fell within
the scope of the Inchmaree Clause; the underwriters contended the vessel had been deliberately scuttled by the placing of an explosive device in
the wing tank. The district court, holding the evidence was in equipoise,
found that the assured had failed to meet its burden of proof and held for
the underwriters. The court of appeal, in affirming, held that in the final
analysis the question of coverage turned on whether the event itself was
fortuitous; i.e., just as scuttling is not a peril of the sea (citing *P. Samuel &
Co. v. Dumas* [1924] A.C. 431) neither is a set explosion. In short, neither
scuttling nor a set explosion is a "maritime peril."

Wilful Misconduct of Assured

Section 55(2)(a) reads:

The insurer is not liable for any loss attributable to the wilful misconduct of the assured, but, unless the policy otherwise provides, he is
liable for any loss proximately caused by a peril insured against, even
though the loss would not have happened but for the misconduct or
negligence of the master or crew.

69. [1916] 1 A.C. 304.
70. 498 F.2d 556, 1974 AMC 877, [1974] 2 Lloyd's Rep. 398 (2d Cir.).

Losses attributable to the wilful misconduct of the assured have come before the courts on many occasions. As early as 1790 in *Bowring v. Elmslie*,[70a] a court denied recovery where the ship was fraudulently stranded. After World War I, and into the early 1920's, when the markets plunged dramatically ships stranded or went to the bottom in incredibly good weather and calm seas. However, scuttling is an allegation easy to make but difficult to prove. Interestingly, the courts appear to have been exceedingly reluctant to establish a rule that the burden of proof lies upon the underwriter, to the contrary contenting themselves with the assertion that the assured has the burden of proving that the loss was due to a peril covered by the policy. If the evidence is in equipoise, or if the assured fails to bring the loss within the scope of the policy, then this permits the courts to hold that the claim failed without the necessity of having to find affirmatively that the assured committed a crime.[71]

In the *Gold Sky, supra,* the underwriters failed to prove beyond a reasonable doubt that there had been in fact a scuttling. The next defense was that the assured had failed to carry out the duty imposed upon them by Section 78(4) of the Marine Insurance Act, 1906, to wit: "It is the duty of the assured and his agents, in all cases, to take such measures as may be reasonable for the purpose of averting or minimizing a loss." Justice Mocatta disposed of this contention in the following language:

I do not think that, in the absence of instructions from his owners, the master of a vessel must be taken to be included within the words "the assured or his agents," in Section 78(4), so that a failure by the master to take such measures as may be reasonable will militate against the owners' claim against the insurers. I think the words "his agents" should be in the context and to avoid an acute conflict between two subsections of the Act be read as inapplicable to the master or crew, unless expressly instructed by the assured in relation to what to do or

---

70a. 101 E.R. 939.

71. See, for example, *Pateras v. Royal Exchange Assur.,* (1934) 49 Ll.L.Rep. 400; *Issaias (Elfie E.) v. Marine Ins. Co.,* (1923) 15 Ll.L.Rep. 186, C.A.; *Anghelatos v. Northern Assur. Co. Ltd.,* (1924) 19 Ll.L.Rep. 255, H.L.; *Compania Martiartu v. Royal Exchange Assur.,* (1923) 1 K.B. 650, *aff'd* (1924) A.C. 850, H.L.; *Northwestern Mutual Life Ins. Co. v. Linard (The Vainqueur),* 498 F.2d 556, 1974 AMC 877, [1974] 2 Lloyd's Rep. 398 (2d Cir.); *Padre Island (Stranding),* 1970 AMC 600, [1971] 2 Lloyd's Rep. 431; *Samuel (P) & Co. Ltd. v. Dumas,* [1924] A.C. 431, [1924] All E.R. 66; *Astrovlanis Compania Naviera S.A. v. Linard (The Gold Sky),* [1972] 2 Lloyd's Rep. 187, 2 Q.B.D. 611; *Palmisto Enterprises S.A. v. Ocean Marine Ins. Co. Ltd. (The Diaz),* [1972] 2 Q.B. 625, [1972] 2 Lloyd's Rep. 60 (relating primarily to the question of whether or not underwriters who alleged scuttling are compelled to supply particulars where these are requested). See, also, in this connection, *Coulouras v. British Gen. Ins. Co. Ltd.,* [1922] 11 Ll.L.Rep. 100, and *Societa d'Avances Commerciales v. Merchants Marine Ins. Co.,* [1923] 16 Ll.L.Rep. 374. And, for an ancillary problem of proof, see *Probatina Shipping Co. Ltd. v. Sun Ins. Office Ltd. (The Sagegeorge),* [1974] 2 All E.R. 493, C.A., where it was held within the discretion of the court whether or not an order for production of ship's papers would be issued. In that case, the order was denied.

not to do in respect of suing and labouring. Many persons other than the master and members of the crew may be agents of the assured with the duty to act on his behalf in relation to suing and labouring. I believe this construction to be permittable and rational and to reconcile the operation of the two sub-sections in most cases in which the problem is likely to arise. It also caters for the case of barratry.[72]

Defense of Wilful Misconduct Not Sustained

There are numerous cases in which the defense of wilful misconduct has been asserted but has not been sustained.[73]

In a recent decision in British Columbia,[73a] a fishing vessel sank within three miles of a port of refuge while being towed after having broken down and taken on water in the engine room. The defense technically was a failure to take reasonable measures to avert or minimize the loss under Section 80(4) of the Canadian Marine Insurance Act (identical to Section 78(4) of the Marine Insurance Act, 1906), but the proof offered by the underwriter was tantamount to an assertion of wilful misconduct. Essentially, the underwriter urged that the assured could have beached

---

72. Contrast *Piermay Shipping Co. S.A. v. Chester (The Michael)*, [1979] 2 Lloyd's Rep. 1, C.A., where, at first instance, Kerr, J., held that to establish a loss by barratry both a deliberate sinking and the absence of owners' consent must be proved but if the court is left in doubt whether the owner consented or not the claim fails. In that case, the court held that the engineer deliberately sank the vessel but without any consent or foreknowledge on the part of the owners, and the claim for barratry thus succeeded. See, also, *Compania Maritime San Basilio S.A. v. The Oceanus Mutual Underwriting Ass'n (Bermuda) Ltd. (The Eurysthenes)*, contrasting Sec. 39(5) ("privity") with Sec. 55(2)(a) ("wilful misconduct").

73. *Communidad Naviera Baracaldo v. Norwich Union Fire Ins. Soc.*, (1923) 16 Ll.L.Rep. 45, K.B.D.; *Issaias (Elfie E.) v. Marine Ins. Co., Ltd.*, *supra* (defense asserted; court found loss to be barratry); *Lemos v. British & Foreign Marine Ins. Co., Ltd.*, (1931) 39 Ll.L.Rep. 275, K.B.D. (negligent stranding; absence of evidence of connivance, financial embarrassment of owner, and no over-insurance); *Compania Naviera Vascongada v. British & Foreign Marine Ins. Co. Ltd.*, (1935) 54 Ll.L.Rep. 35, K.B.D.; *Piper v. Royal Exchange Assur.*, (1932) 44 Ll.L.Rep. 103, K.B.D.; *Maris v. London Assurance*, (1935) 52 Ll.L.Rep. 211, C.A.; *Lind v. Mitchell, supra; Papadimitriou v. Henderson*, (1939) 64 Ll.L.Rep. 345, K.B.D., (1939) 3 All E.R. 908; *Astrovlanis Compania Naviera S.A. v. Linard (The Gold Sky)*, [1972] 2 Lloyd's Rep. 187, 2 Q.B.D. 611; *Piermay Shipping Co., S.A. v. Chester (The Michael)*, [1979] 2 Lloyd's Rep. 1, C.A.; *Orient Mut. Life Ins. Co. v. Adams*, 123 U.S. 67 (1887); *General Mut. Ins. Co. v. Sherwood*, 55 U.S. 351 (1852); *Bella*, 290 F. 992, 1923 AMC 769, 5 F.2d 570, 1925 AMC 751 (4th Cir.) (question of scuttling left undecided but libel dismissed for failure to disclose information); *Mindel v. Stewart*, 1959 AMC 1291 (St.,N.Y.); *Yacht Courageous*, 197 F.Supp. 75, 1962 AMC 1173 (D.,Mass.); *Northwestern Mut. Life Ins. Co. v. Linard (The Vainqueur)*, *supra* (although defense failed, assured failed to prove his case, the evidence being in equipoise); *Fishing Fleet v. Trident*, 598 F.2d 925, 1980 AMC 583 (5th Cir.); *Sorenson v. Boston Ins. Co. of Boston, Mass.*, 20 F.2d 640 (4th Cir., 1927); *Levi v. New Orleans Mut. Ins. Ass'n*, F.Cas. No. 8,290 (5th Cir., 1874); *New York, N.H. & H.R. Co. v. Gray*, 240 F.2d 460, 1957 AMC 616 (2d Cir.); *Franklin Ins. Co. v. Humphrey*, 65 Ind. 549 (St.,Ind., 1879); *U.S. Fire v. Cavanaugh*, 732 F.2d 832, 1985 AMC 1001 (11th Cir.) (loss found to be barratry, grounding, and fire rather than scuttling or breach of warranty).

73a. Not yet reported.

the vessel in a safe location long prior to the sinking but deliberately did not do so. The defense failed.

Defense of Wilful Misconduct Sustained

Cases in which the defense has been sustained are equally numerous.[74] For example, in *Compania Naviera Martiartu v. Royal Exchange Assur. Corp.* (1924), *supra*, the vessel was insured for £170,000 but was worth only about £14,000. The vessel was sunk while pursuing a course inside dangerous rocks, in a calm sea with little or no wind. The vessel sank hours after the crew had abandoned her, no attempt was made to attract attention or obtain assistance, and the ship's log and papers were lost.

In *Pateras v. Royal Exchange Assurance* (1934), *supra*, the evidence showed that the vessel had been navigated very unprofitably around the period of loss and that the owner's son had replaced the regular master just before the loss. The court held that the running of the vessel upon a rock was with the connivance of the assured.

In *Compania Naviera Santi, S.A. v. Indemnity Marine Assur. Co., Ltd. (The Tropaioforos)* (1960), *supra*, the evidence was incredibly overwhelming that the vessel had been deliberately scuttled. Instead of sending a distress message, the master privately telegraphed the vessel's London agents advising that water had entered the engine room and boiler room and that he had ordered the crew to abandon her. The position of the vessel was misstated and had obviously been sent deliberately to prevent an early discovery of the vessel. A later distress message also gave the ship's position incorrectly. It was not until hours later when the ship went down that the correct position was transmitted. When picked up later by another vessel, the master was clean shaven and well dressed; the crew brought

---

74. *Ansoleago Y. Cia. v. Indemnity Mut. Marine Ins. Co.*, (1922) 13 Ll.L.Rep. 231, C.A.; *Compania Naviera Martiartu v. Royal Exchange Assur. Corp.*, (1923) 1 K.B. 650, aff'd (1924) A.C. 431; *Visscherij Maatschappij Nieuwe Onderneming v. Scottish Metropolitan Assur. Co.*, (1922) 10 Ll.L.Rep. 579, C.A.; *Anghelatos v. Northern Assurance Co. Ltd.*, (1924) 19 Ll.L.Rep. 255, H.L.; *Empire S.S. Co. v. Threadneedle Ins. Co.*, (1925) 22 Ll.L.Rep. 437; *Canning v. Maritime Ins. Co. Ltd.*, (1936) 56 Ll.L.Rep. 91, K.B.D.; *Domingo Mumbru Soc. Anon. v. Laurie*, (1924) 20 Ll.L.Rep. 122, 189, K.B.D.; *Grauds v. Dearsley*, (1935) 51 Ll.L.Rep. 209; *Societe d'Avances Commerciales v. Merchants' Marine Ins. Co.*, (1924) 20 Ll.L.Rep. 74, 140, C.A.; *Pateras v. Royal Exchange Assur.*, (1934) 49 Ll.L.Rep. 400; *Compania Naviera Santi, S.A. v. Indemnity Marine Assur. Co. Ltd. (The Tropaioforos)*, [1960] 2 Lloyd's Rep. 469; *Miskofski v. Economic Ins. Co., Ltd.*, [1963] 43 D.L.R.(2d) 281 (Can.); *Rose Murphy*, 32 F.2d 87, 1929 AMC 637 (5th Cir.); *Padre Island (Stranding)*, 1970 AMC 600, [1971] 2 Lloyd's Rep. 431; *Fred v. Pacific Indemnity Co.*, 53 Haw. 384, 397, 494 P.2d 783 (St.,1972); *Fidelity Phoenix Fire Ins. Co. of New York v. Murphy*, 231 Ala. 680, 166 So. 604 (St.,Ala., 1936); *Fidelity & Cas. v. Hamill*, 1982 AMC 2094 (S.D.,Ala.) (vessel owner was privy to master's intentional scutting); *Aetna v. Hattersley*, 1984 AMC 2837 (D.,Ore.) (evidence of scuttling at least as strong as that of fortuitous loss; recovery denied); *Thomas and Maureen Doak v. Weekes and Commercial Union Assur. Co., P.L.C. & Anor.*, 4 ANZ Insurance Cas., 60-697 (S.C., Queensland, 1986) (scuttling by owner).

their luggage with them. When the master was asked for the ship's logs, he stated they had gone down with the ship.

In *Padre Island (Stranding)* (1970), *supra*, the evidence clearly established that the stranding of the vessel was an act perpetrated with the knowledge and consent of the financially hard-pressed owner.

Loss by Fear of a Peril

Loss by apprehension or expectation of loss by a peril insured against is not a loss falling under a policy of marine insurance.[75]

Thus, in *Becker, Gray & Co.* (1918), *supra*, a policy on goods covered, *inter alia*, perils of capture by men-of-war. During the voyage war was declared, and the master of the German vessel on which the goods were shipped on reaching the Mediterranean, and fearing capture by the British and French fleets, put into Messina and a month later moved to Syracuse where the voyage was abandoned. The court said in part:

> . . . To constitute a loss by capture, though actual seizure was not essential, the risk must have been so imminent as to compel the ship to take refuge in some neutral port, whereas here the ship had gone into a neutral port before she had even so much as sighted a man-of-war by the voluntary act of her master for the very purpose of avoiding the risk of capture.

75. *Becker Gray & Co. v. London Assur. Corp.*, (1918) A.C. 101, (1916-17) All E.R. 146, 14 Asp. M.L.C. 156, H.L. See, also, *Forster v. Christie*, (1809) 11 East 205, 103 E.R. 982; *Nickels & Co. v. London & Prov. Marine & Gen. Ins. Co.*, (1900) 70 L.J.Q.B. 29, 6 Com.Cas. 15; *Lubbock v. Rowcroft*, (1803) 5 Esp. 50, N.P.; *Hadkinson v. Robinson*, (1803) 3 Bos. & P. 388, 127 E.R. 212.

CHAPTER XVI

ACTUAL AND CONSTRUCTIVE TOTAL LOSS

Total loss obviously falls into two categories—actual total loss and "constructive" total loss.[1] As noted in Section 56(3), Marine Insurance Act, 1906, unless a different intention appears from the terms of the policy, an insurance against total loss includes a constructive, as well as an actual, total loss.

Either an actual or constructive total loss triggers the right to payment of the full insured or insurable value.[2]

Actual Total Loss

Section 56, Marine Insurance Act, 1906, reads:

(1) A loss may be either total or partial. Any loss other than a total loss, as hereinafter defined, is a partial loss.

(2) A total loss may be either an actual total loss, or a constructive total loss.

(3) Unless a different intention appears from the terms of the policy, an insurance against total loss includes a constructive, as well as an actual, total loss.

(4) Where the assured brings an action for a total loss and the evidence proves only a partial loss, he may, unless the policy otherwise provides, recover for a partial loss.

(5) Where goods reach their destination in specie, but by reason of obliteration of marks, or otherwise, they are incapable of identification, the loss, if any, is partial and not total.

Section 57 defines an actual total loss in very precise terms, as follows:

(1) Where the subject-matter insured is destroyed, or so damaged as to cease to be a thing of the kind insured, or where the assured is irre-

---

1. Sec. 60(1) of the Marine Insurance Act defines a constructive total loss as follows: Subject to any express provision in the policy, there is a constructive total loss where the subject matter insured is reasonably abandoned on account of its actual total loss appearing to be unavoidable, or because it could not be preserved from actual total loss without an expenditure which would exceed its value when the expenditure had been incurred.

2. The measure of indemnity is defined in Secs. 67 and 68 of the Marine Insurance Act, 1906. See discussion, Chapter IX, "Measure of Insurable Value."

trievably deprived thereof, there is an actual total loss.

(2) In the case of an actual total loss no notice of abandonment need be given.

It will be seen from the foregoing that an actual total loss may occur in three instances:

(1) Where the subject-matter is destroyed;
(2) Where the subject-matter is so damaged as to cease to be a thing of the kind insured; or
(3) Where the assured is irretrievably deprived thereof.

Simple examples of casualties which obviously constitute actual total losses are: sinking in deep water, destruction by enemy gunfire, total destruction by fire or a hurricane, running aground, and being ripped apart by heavy seas.

In oft-quoted language, Lord Watson in *Sailing Ship Blairmore Co. v. Macredie*[3] said a vessel is an actual total loss when reduced to "a mere congeries of wooden planks or pieces of iron which could not without reconstruction be restored to the form of a ship."

Another instance of an actual loss is where the ship concerned is missing, and after the lapse of a reasonable time no news of her has been received. An actual total loss may be presumed.[4]

Another illustration of the first heading is *Cambridge v. Anderson*,[5] in which a vessel was wrecked but was saved from going to pieces because her cargo was timber. The master physically abandoned; it was judged by the surveyors that the expenses of getting her off would exceed her value when repaired. Without giving notice of abandonment to underwriters, the master sold her for what she would bring. It was held she was an actual total loss and no notice of abandonment need be given.[6]

See *Cossman v. West, Cossman v. British America Assurance Co.*,[7] for an illustration, where the assured was irretrievably deprived of the insured

---

3. [1898] A.C. 593, 3 Com.Cas. 241, H.L.
4. This is the wording of Sec. 58, Marine Insurance Act, 1906.
5. (1824) 107 E.R. 540.
6. See, also, *Roux v. Salvador*, (1836) 132 E.R. 413 (a cargo of hides, being wetted with seawater, became putrescent and would have been wholly destroyed by the time they reached their destination); *Montoya v. London Assurance*, (1851) 6 Exch. 451 (hides becoming putrescent tainted tobacco stored nearby and rendered it worthless); *Bondrett v. Hentigg*, (1816) Holt N.P. 149 (ship was wrecked and some of the goods were salved and brought ashore where, however, natives seized them and destroyed part and plundered the remainder); *Asfar v. Blundell*, [1896] 1 Q.B. 123 (insurance on loss of "profit on charter"; in consequence of sea damage to the cargo, only a portion of the bill of lading freight was payable); *Berger and Light Diffusers Pty, Ltd. v. Pollock*, [1973] 2 Lloyd's Rep. 442, Q.B.D. (steel injection moulds irreparably damaged by seawater, having no value in their rusted state); *Mellish v. Andrews*, (1812) 5 Taunt. 496; *Stringer v. English and Scottish Marine Ins. Co.*, (1869) L.R. 4 Q.B. 676; *Harkley v. Prov. Ins. Co.*, (1868) 18 C.P. 335 (Can.).
7. (1887) 13 A.C. 160, P.C.

subject matter. In that case, a ship and her freight were insured, *inter alia*, against barratry of the master, and he wrongfully abandoned her. Salvors took possession, towed her into port, and instituted salvage proceedings. The ship and cargo were sold by decree of the court of admiralty but brought less than the salvage award. As the sale by the court irretrievably deprived the owners of the ship and cargo, it was held to be an actual total loss and notice of abandonment was unnecessary.

The American cases do not differ. In *Great Western Ins. Co. v. Fogarty*,[8] the Supreme Court stated it was not necessary, to constitute a total loss, that there should be an absolute extinction or destruction of the thing insured so that nothing of it could be delivered at the destination, but merely a destruction in specie, so that, while some of its component elements might remain, the thing itself in the character or description by which it was insured, was destroyed.

In *Alexander v. Baltimore Ins. Co.*,[9] the Supreme Court said that a total loss may exist where the whole of the insured property perishes or where it still exists but the voyage is lost or the expense of pursuing it exceeds the benefit arising therefrom.

In *Lenfest v. Coldwell*,[10] the court noted that a total loss occurs when the vessel no longer exists in specie or when she is absolutely or irretrievably sunk or otherwise beyond the possible control of the assured, and pointed out that the constructive total loss doctrine was designed to alleviate this "harsh requirement" and applies where the cost of repairs would exceed the vessel's repaired value.[11]

In *Edinburgh Assur. v. R.L. Burns*,[12] the court was confronted with a complex case involving a claim of actual total loss of a drilling rig off the coast of Madagascar under an "actual total loss only" policy. The placement of the coverage involved both American and London brokers. A threshold question before the court was whether American law or English applied. After determining that English law applied, the court proceeded to discuss the meaning of "actual total loss," relying wholly upon English cases.

The underwriters contended that the proper interpretation of Section 57(1) of the Marine Insurance Act compelled the court to focus on the first and third tests set forth in Section 57(1); i.e., destruction and irre-

8. 86 U.S. 640 (1873).

9. 8 U.S. 370 (1808).

10. 525 F.2d 717 (2d Cir.), 1975 AMC 2489.

11. See, also, *Robinson v. Commonwealth Ins. Co.*, F.Cas. 11,949 (1st Cir. 1838) (cargo permanently prevented from arriving at the port of destination); *Bullard v. Roger Williams Ins. Co.*, F.Cas. 2,122 (1st Cir. 1852) (vessel so injured by a sea peril as not to be repairable, except at an expense exceeding its value when repaired, is a total loss and no notice of abandonment is necessary); *Moore v. Evans*, [1918] A.C. 185.

12. 479 F.Supp. 138 (C.D. Cal.), 1980 AMC 1261.

trievable loss. This, underwriters urged, required that if an object is physically and technologically capable of being retrieved and repaired without regard to cost, then the object is not destroyed or irretrievably lost. They asserted that the drilling rig was obviously not irretrievably lost in that it was still in a known position in the channel and subject to inspection. Moreover, they argued that the parties were in agreement that the rig could be salvaged and repaired, although at considerable cost and that it therefore was not an actual total loss as a matter of law.

To the contrary, the assured interpreted English law differently. They argued that destruction meant destruction of value; that the test whether an object was still "a thing of the kind insured" applied to ships damaged in a casualty like the instant case; and that whether the subject was still a thing of the kind insured depended upon whether *as a practical business matter the thing could still be considered what it was.*

Noting that the cases made it clear that only one of the three tests mentioned in Section 57(1) need be satisfied in order to find an actual total loss, the court declined to hold that the rig met the "irretrievable deprivation" test. However, the court then proceeded to find that English law considered commercial reality in determining whether the thing insured is an actual total loss, citing *Berger and Light Diffusers Pty., Ltd. v. Pollock,* [1973] 2 Lloyd's Rep. 442, where it was found that the only way to overcome the damage to injection moulds was to recut them which was "commercially impossible." Continuing, the court said:

> . . . This court concludes that under English law the subject matter of insurance may cease to be a thing of the kind insured, or be destroyed, and hence be an actual total loss, even though there are accessible physical remains of the vessel or like entity. This court also concludes that the question whether those remains may be utilized in the reconstruction of a thing of the same kind as that insured is not dispositive of the determination whether the thing is an actual total loss. It is a matter of degree.

Observing that the underwriters argued that the test is based upon the physical possibility of salvage and repair and that the assured argued that the concept must be governed by a practical business approach, the court then applied three standards, stating:

> This court concludes that both concepts have meaning under several standards under which the trier of fact may examine the evidence. The first is the standard of reasonable salvage and/or engineering effort. The reasonable salvager must consider salvaging effort required to recover the thing insured. The reasonable engineer must consider the engineering effort required to bring the thing insured back to a functional status. If the effort required to either recover or

refurbish the thing insured is too disproportionate an effort for the resulting operational entity, then the thing insured is an actual total loss.

A second standard is whether the refurbishing effort is so extensive as not reasonably to be characterized as repair. If the refurbishing effort is so extensive as not reasonably to be characterized as repair, but rather must be considered rebuilding, then the thing insured is an actual total loss.

A third standard is whether the cost of recovering and refurbishing the thing insured is so out of proportion to the value of the resulting operational entity that the thing must reasonably be considered an actual total loss.

The court thereupon found that under all three standards, English law compelled a conclusion that the rig was an actual total loss within the term of the insurance policy.

The requirements necessary to establish an actual total loss can be rather harsh, as will be seen from the cases.[13]

---

13. *Bell v. Nixon*, (1816) Holt, N.P. 423 (ship, however damaged and maimed, still existed in specie as a ship); *Glennie v. London Assurance*, (1814) 105 E.R. 420 (arrival of goods, greatly damaged, although still existing in specie); *Gardner v. Salvador*, (1831) 1 Mood. & R. 116, N.P. (question of bona fide necessity of a forced sale); *Captain J.A. Cates Tug and Wharfage Co., Ltd. v. Franklin Ins. Co.*, [1927] A.C. 698, 28 Ll.L.Rep. 161, P.C. (tug sank in shallow water but was quickly raised); *Panamanian Oriental S.S. Corp. v. Wright*, [1970] 2 Lloyd's Rep. 365, Q.B.D. (seizure and confiscation of vessel by Vietnamese authorities; not shown that the assured had been "irretrievably deprived" of her—*reversed* on other grounds in [1971] 1 Lloyd's Rep. 487, C.A.); *George Cohen, Sons & Co. v. Standard Marine Ins. Co., Ltd.*, (1925) 21 Ll.L.Rep. 30, K.B.D. (obsolete battleship being towed went aground on Dutch coast; salvage operations would have been very expensive and there was no assurance that the Dutch authorities would permit her removal; held, not an actual total loss as the assured had not been irretrievably deprived of her); *Marstrand Fishing Co., Ltd. v. Beer*, [1937] 1 All E.R. 158, 56 Ll.L.Rep. 163, K.B.D. (loss by barratry not necessarily a total loss); *St. Margaret's Trust, Ltd. v. Navigators and Gen. Ins. Co., Ltd.*, (1949) 82 Ll.L.Rep. 752, K.B.D. (ketch listed while on a mudflat and filled up; later she was moved to another flat, where she gradually deteriorated); *Millville Mutual Marine & Fire Ins. Co. v. Driscoll*, (1884) 11 S.C.R. 183 (Can.) (vessel sustained damage; masster sold her and the purchasers had her repaired at a cost much less than the reported or estimated costs); *Church v. Marine Ins. Co.*, F.Cas. 2,711 (1st Cir. 1817) (vessel stranded but gotten off without material injury and, in the meantime, was sold by the master); *Fireman's Fund Ins. Co. v. Globe Nav. Co.*, 236 F. 618 (9th Cir. 1916) (vessel, waterlogged and abandoned by her crew, held not an actual total loss where the hull and parts of her equipment were saved and brought into port by salvors in a condition capable of being repaired at some cost); *Klein v. Globe & Rutgers Fire Ins. Co. of New York City (The Tornado)*, 2 F.2d 137 (3rd Cir.), 1925 AMC 197 (a sunken vessel held not to be an actual total loss where there was any hope of its recovery in specie at any cost).

Moreover, where cargo arrives at destination in specie although in a drastically damaged candition but nonetheless is capable of being reconditioned, and after reconditioning is sold at a reduced price, there is not a total loss but only a partial loss. *Francis v. Boulton*, (1895) 65 L.J.Q.B. 153.

Attention is also directed to Sec. 56(5) of the Marine Insurance Act, which reads:

Where goods reach their destination in specie, but by reason of obliteration of marks, or otherwise, they are incapable of identification, the loss, if any, is partial and not total.

Sale of Vessel by Master

Where, in the event of extreme necessity, such as an absence of repair facilities or lack of funds, damage cannot be repaired and an actual total loss is inevitable, the master formerly was held justified in selling the subject matter of the insurance. This was the situation in *Roux v. Salvador*.[14]

If the circumstances are such that by no means within the master's power could the subject matter be saved, it is a total loss. On the other hand, if the master, by means within his control, can by experimentation save it with a fair hope of restoring it in specie, he cannot by selling it convert it into a total loss.[15] In cargo cases, the test is not whether a prudent uninsured owner would have sold the cargo, but whether the cargo could have been sent on to its destination at less expense than its true value on arrival.[16]

In this modern era of practically instantaneous communications, it is highly unlikely that total losses of this type will be encountered with any frequency as the master can rather easily communicate with owners of vessel and cargo before selling.[17]

Total Loss of Freight

Cases involving total loss of freight are relatively numerous. Oddly enough, the courts seem to make little distinction between actual total loss of freight and constructive total loss of freight, and, interestingly, the Marine Insurance Act, 1906, makes no mention whatever of a constructive total loss of freight.[18]

See, for example, *Spence v. Union Marine Insurance Co.*, (1868) 18 L.T. 632, 16 W.R. 1010. In such cases, the proceeds of the sale of unidentifiable cargo are apportioned among the various consignees and the loss is partial, not total.

14. (1836) 132 E.R. 413. See, also, *Gordon v. Massachusetts Fire & Marine Ins. Co.*, 19 Mass. 249 (1824); *Hall v. Franklin Ins. Co.*, 26 Mass. 466 (1830); *Winn v. Columbian Ins. Co.*, 29 Mass. 286 (1831); *Bryant v. Commonwealth Ins. Co.*, 30 Mass. 543 (1833); *Pierce v. Ocean Ins. Co.*, 35 Mass. 83 (1836); *Graves v. Washington Ins. Co.*, 94 Mass. 391 (1866).

15. Compare *Doyle v. Dallas*, (1831) 1 Mood. & R. 48, N.P.; *Providence Washington Ins. Co. v. Corbett*, (1883) 9 S.C.R. 256 (Can.), and *Hall v. Franklin Ins. Co.*, 26 Mass. 466 (1830), with *Parsons v. Manufacturers Ins. Co.*, 82 Mass. 463 (1860) (freight), *Willard v. Millers' & Manufacturers' Ins. Co.*, 24 Mo. 561 (1857) (freight), and *Baker v. Brown*, (1872) 9 N.S.R. 100 (Can.) (reliance upon surveyors' advice and assured's own bona fide opinion).

16. *Watson v. Mercantile Marine Ins. Co.*, (1873) 9 N.S.R. 396 (Can.). Compare *Domett v. Young*, (1842) Car. & M. 465, N.P.

17. See, in this connection, *Australasian Steam Navigation Co. v. Morse*, (1872) L.R. 4 P.C. 222.

18. The bill introduced in Parliament contained a section dealing with freight, but it was afterwards eliminated. Thus, the general provision contained in Sec. 60(1) governs. See the remarks of the courts in *Kulukundis and Others v. Norwich Union Fire Ins. Soc., Ltd.*, (1935)

Obviously, where freight is paid in advance pursuant to a contract stipulating that freight is earned on shipment, and the vessel is lost during the voyage, the shipowner has suffered no loss of freight and there can be no recovery therefor.[19]

Regrettably, the subject of freight insurance is exceedingly complicated. At the risk of some degree of oversimplification, it is helpful to remember that the right to recover under a freight policy substantially depends upon the terms of the contract of affreightment and not upon the existence and terms of insurance policies on the vessel or its cargo.[20]

This point clearly appears in the decision in *Kulukundis and Others v. Norwich Union Fire Insurance Society, Ltd.,*[21] where the court said in part:

> . . . a shipowner, in which expression I include a charterer by demise, is entitled to claim against his freight underwriter as for a total loss of freight, if the vessel suffers such sea damage as will free the shipowner from his obligation under the contract of affreightment to carry the cargo to its destination, provided, of course, that the cargo is not in fact carried either by the shipowner himself or by abandonees of ship so as to earn the freight. There may be, perhaps, a further exception where transhipment, although optional to the shipowner, is a reasonable and practicable course . . . . The rule that a shipowner is entitled to be freed from his obligations to the freighter, if the vessel is lost in a commercial sense, is now well established, and it cannot in my judgment be treated as the same rule, or a branch of the same rule, as that which applied between owner and hull underwriter. It stands on foundations of its own, and its scope and effect must be ascertained accordingly.

---

52 Ll.L.Rep. 340, and *Yero Carras (Owners) v. London and Scottish Assur. Corp., Ltd.,* (1936) 52 Ll.L.Rep. 34, 53 Ll.L.Rep. 131, C.A.

19. See, in this connection, *Benson v. Chapman,* (1849) 5 C.B. 330, Ex.Ch.; *Scottish Marine Ins. Co. v. Turner,* (1853) 4 H.L. Cas. 312; *Allison v. Bristol Marine Ins. Co.,* (1876) 1 A.C. 209, H.L.; *Sephie,* 9 F.2d 309 (2d Cir.), 1926 AMC 446; and *Roanoke,* 298 F. 1 (9th Cir.), 1924 AMC 790. In *Sephie,* the assured took a policy on disbursements and/or profits on freight on a round trip charter. The outward freight was prepaid, ship lost or not lost. On the outward passage, the vessel became a constructive total loss. The assured was denied recovery for the outward freight but granted recovery for the inward freight. In *Roanoke,* two policies were issued on the freight, the first on freight on board or not on board on the outward voyage and the second on collect freight on the inward voyage. The vessel foundered enroute to her destination. Construing the phrase "freight on board or not on board" as meaning chartered freight as distinguished from bill of lading freight, the court held that the first policy covered the loss of freight on the inward voyage. See, also, *Santa Christina,* 1928 AMC 1074 (9th Cir.).

20. Subject always, of course, to the actual terms of the policy on freight. See, for example, the provisions of Clause 6 of the Institute Time and Voyage Clauses (freight), discussed *infra.*

21. (1935) 52 Ll.L.Rep. 340.

Phillips states the rule as follows:[22]

The interest of the owner, as well as that of the charterer in a chartered ship, depends on the terms of the charterparty. Accordingly, it must depend upon the same instrument, whether the whole, or what part, of a loss on freight falls upon the interest of the owner or charterer. Consequently, if the owner or charterer is wholly prevented, by the ship being wrecked, or by other perils insured against, from realizing the freight agreed for by a charter party or by the bills of lading for shipments by third parties to which the policy is applicable, it is an absolute total loss; and so also the loss to either will be partial, or constructively total, as in other cases.

It is apparent that several different situations may well occur, giving rise to a right to recover for a total loss of freight. That is:

(1) Both ship and cargo may become an actual total loss, in which case there is obviously an actual total loss of freight;[23]

(2) There may be a total loss of cargo only, either by reason of the cargo becoming an actual total loss or by virtue of a constructive total loss where its actual total loss is unavoidable;[24]

(3) There may be an actual total loss of ship, or a constructive total loss in a commercial sense.[25]

---

22. Sec. 1646. Phillips also notes that a constructive total loss of the cargo by capture, arrest, or detention is a constructive total loss of freight, citing *Simmonds v. Union Ins. Co.*, 1 Wash. C.C. 382, 443.

23. This is so, of course, unless freight is prepaid.

24. See *Whitney v. N.Y. Firemen's Ins. Co.*, 18 Johns. 208; *Hugg v. Augusta Ins. Co.*, 48 U.S. 595 (1849) (though the cargo is not wholly destroyed, yet if it is so damaged by perils insured against that it cannot be carried on without endangering the health or lives of the crew, or so as to arrive at the port of destination in specie, this constitutes a total loss of freight). See, however, *Rankin v. Potter*, (1873) L.R. 6 H.L. 83, where it was noted that there would not be an actual total loss of freight if, after the casualty, the vessel was capable of earning equal or some freight by carrying other cargo on the insured voyage. See, also, *Atlantic Maritime Company, Inc. v. Gibbon*, [1953] 2 Lloyd's Rep. 294, where the question whether freight earned under a substituted charter should be considered was discussed but not decided. And where perishable goods arrive in an unmerchantable condition and the consignee refuses to accept delivery, there is not only a total loss of the goods but also a total loss of the freight (assuming freight is payable at destination). *Asfar & Co. v. Blundell*, (1896) 1 Q.B. 123, C.A. The same result follows where there has been a sale of a perishable cargo. *Milles v. Fletcher*, (1779) 99 E.R. 151. But, see *Mordy v. Jones*, (1825) 107 E.R. 1106, where the vessel had to put back into port and land the whole of her cargo which had been so wetted by seawater that it could not be reshipped without danger of ignition unless dried, which would have taken about six weeks. It was held that underwriters were not liable for the loss of freight, mere delay not being sufficient. See, also, *Trinder Anderson & Co. v. Thames & Mersey Marine Insurance Co., Ltd.*, (1898) 2 Q.B. 114, 3 Com.Cas. 123, C.A., involving damage to ship and cargo where reconditioning expenses together with forwarding charges would have exceeded the value of the cargo on arrival.

25. If arrangements are made to forward the cargo to destination by another vessel, the expenses so incurred are recoverable under the Sue and Labor Clause. *Kidston v. Empire*

The last category presents by far the most interesting questions. The following cases are instructive.

In *Guthrie v. North China Ins. Co., Ltd.*,[26] the ship stranded with cargo aboard it and notices of abandonment were given to hull, cargo, and freight underwriters. The underwriters on hull and cargo paid a total loss and, thereafter, on behalf of themselves as well as the freight underwriters, entered into a contract of salvage under which a considerable part of the cargo was saved. In a suit to recover on the freight policies, the underwriters contended that there was no loss of freight by reason of perils insured against, but, rather, the loss was due to the shipowner's act in abandoning the vessel and refusing to transship the cargo. It was held that abandonment had been prudent and that freight underwriters were liable for a total loss of freight without any deduction with respect to salvage, the cargo having been carried to a port of refuge pursuant to the salvage contract and not under the original charter party.

Section 63(2) of the Marine Insurance Act, 1906, provides with respect to abandonment of a ship:

> Upon the abandonment of a ship, the insurer thereof is entitled to any freight in course of being earned, and which is earned by her subsequent to the casualty causing the loss, less the expenses of earning it incurred after the casualty; and, where the ship is carrying the owner's goods, the insurer is entitled to a reasonable remuneration for the carriage of them subsequent to the casualty causing the loss.

The sub-section quoted above merely sets forth the principle laid down in *Stewart v. Greenock Marine Ins. Co.*,[27] where the insured vessel, although damaged, successfully delivered her cargo and earned her freight but upon being drydocked was found to be a constructive total loss. Upon abandonment, underwriters paid a total loss and were held entitled to the freight earned, as it had been earned subsequent to the casualty which caused the loss.

In a subsequent suit for a total loss of the freight,[28] the House of Lords

---

Marine Ins. Co., (1866) L.R. 1 C.P. 535. Although it appears a shipowner has an implied right to transship the cargo, in the absence of an express term in a charter party or bill of lading to the contrary, this is a right and not an obligation. See *Kulukundis and Others v. Norwich Union Fire Ins. Soc., Ltd., supra.*

26. (1902) 18 T.L.R. 412, C.A. See, also, *Aakre (Charterer's Profit Risk)*, 1940 AMC 1209 (N.Y.M.), where the charterer placed the vessel on a profitable subcharter and then insured his interest in future profit. The vessel stranded and became a constructive total loss. After repairs, the vessel resumed her service but meanwhile the charter market had declined. Held: No recovery, there being no causal relation between the stranding and the loss of profit.

27. (1848) 9 E.R. 1052, H.L.

28. *Scottish Marine Ins. Co. v. Turner*, (1853) 10 E.R. 483, H.L.

held that underwriters could not be held liable for a total loss of freight where, in fact, the freight had been earned.[29]

However, it is now the invariable practice that policies on hulls contain clauses under which the hull underwriters waive claims for freight in the event of a total or constructive total loss whether notice of abandonment has been given or not.[30]

Moreover, the Institute Time and Voyage Clauses (freight), customarily attached to policies on freight, provide in Clause 6 that, in the event of actual or constructive total loss of the vessel named therein, the amount insured will be paid in full whether the vessel is wholly or partially loaded or in ballast, chartered or unchartered, and in ascertaining whether the vessel is a constructive total loss, the insured value in the hull and machinery policies shall be taken as the repaired value. No damaged or break-up value of the vessel or wreck is taken into account. However, if the vessel is a constructive total loss but the claim on the hull and machinery policy is settled on the basis of a partial loss, nothing is paid under the clauses.[31] American policies on freight are not dissimilar.

In *Carras v. London & Scottish Assur. Corp., Ltd.,*[32] the plaintiff's vessel was chartered and was to proceed to Valparaiso to load cargo. The cancelling date in the charter was November 20, 1930. Plaintiff procured a freight policy on freight and/or chartered freight and/or anticipated freight, containing clauses very similar to Clause 6 discussed above. While enroute through the Straits of Magellan, the vessel stranded and was

---

29. This rule is applicable only where the insured vessel earns the freight. If another, or substituted, vessel earns the freight, the freight underwriters and not the hull underwriters are entitled to the benefit of the freight so earned. *Hickie and Bornam v. Rodocanachi,* (1859) 157 E.R. 917.

30. See lines 140-41, AIH (June, 1977) form, and Clause 18, Institute Time Clauses (hulls). The two clauses are almost identical, the AIH form reading:

In the event of Total Loss (actual or constructive), no claim to be made by the Underwriters for freight, whether notice of abandonment has been given or not.

31. Clause 6 reads:

In the event of the total loss (actual or constructive) of the vessel named herein the amount insured shall be paid in full, whether the vessel be fully or partly loaded or in ballast, chartered or unchartered.

In ascertaining whether the vessel is a constructive total loss, the insured value in the policies on hull and machinery shall be taken as the repaired value and nothing in respect of the damaged or break-up value of the vessel or wreck shall be taken into account.

Should the vessel be a constructive total loss but the claim on the policies on hull and machinery be settled as a claim for partial loss, no payment shall be due under this Clause 6.

Similar clauses were construed in *Coker v. Bolton,* (1912) 3 K.B. 315. See, also, *Papadimitriou v. Henderson,* (1939) 64 Ll.L.Rep. 345, K.B.D.

32. [1936] 52 Ll.L.Rep. 34, 53 Ll.L.Rep. 131, C.A. See, also, *Jackson v. Union Marine Ins. Co.,* (1874) L.R. 10 C.P. 125; *Troop & Lewis v. Merchants' Marine Ins. Co.,* (1886) 13 S.C.R. 506 (Can.); *Re Jamieson & Newcastle S.S. Freight Ins. Ass'n.,* (1895) 2 Q.B. 90; and *Musgrave v. Mannheim Ins. Co.,* (1899) 32 N.S.R. (20 R. & G.) 405 (Can.).

abandoned to hull underwriters. Salvors eventually refloated her and brought her into port, where the hull underwriters surrendered the ship to the salvors in discharge of their claim. The salvors sold it and it was finally repaired in 1932. The actual value of the vessel when repaired was £13,000, but the insured value under the policy on the hull was £30,000. The cost of repairs exceeded £13,000 but was less than £30,000. It was held that since the ship could not make the cancelling date, or be tendered to the charterers according to the charter party, there was an actual total loss of the freight, the contract of affreightment clearly having been discharged because the vessel was so badly damaged she could not be repaired except at an expense in excess of her actual value. A total loss of freight having been established, there was no need to rely upon the clause with respect to the insured value being taken as the repaired value. Thus, the vessel was damaged to such an extent as to be lost in a *commercial sense.*

In *Kulukundis and Others v. Norwich Union Fire Ins. Soc.,*[33] the plaintiffs took out a policy in respect of freight on the carriage of a grain cargo. While enroute on her voyage she went aground. She was later taken off by a salvage company on terms that they should be paid £11,000 in the event of success. Hull underwriters and plaintiffs agreed to abandon the voyage upon payment by the underwriters and the ship was abandoned to the salvors. Cargo owners were notified the adventure was at an end and their underwriters paid as for a total loss. On the plaintiffs making claim, underwriters paid as for a total loss. On the plaintiffs making claim under their freight policy, it appeared that the cost of temporary repairs to the vessel, sufficient to carry her to her destination, would exceed her repaired value; that is, discharge of the salvors' lien plus temporary repairs, less the estimated general average contribution to be made by cargo, would have exceeded her value after the repairs had been carried out. It will be seen that under a freight policy the test to be used in determining whether the vessel is lost in a commercial sense is the sum necessary to complete the adventure and has no relationship to the test of what is a constructive total loss under a hull policy.

The last paragraph of Clause 6, providing that no payment shall be due under that clause if the claim on the hull policies is settled on the basis of a partial loss, came about as a result of *Petros M. Nomikos, Ltd. v. Robertson.*[34] There, freight was insured, "chartered or otherwise, in and/or over" under the provisions of the then current Institute Time Clauses (freight). The vessel was so damaged by an explosion and fire before sailing that she was technically a constructive total loss and the charter was not carried out. However, the shipowner opted not to abandon and claim

33. [1936] 55 Ll.L.Rep. 55, C.A.
34. [1939] 64 Ll.L.Rep. 45, H.L.

for a constructive total loss but instead had his ship repaired. The claim was settled on the basis of a partial loss for the insured value less the deductible franchise. It was held there had been a "conventional" constructive total loss of the vessel within the Valuation Clause and the shipowner was entitled to the full amount of the freight policy.

Time Penalty Clause. As discussed in Chapter XIII under the subheading "Loss Caused by Delay," freight policies almost invariably contain a "Time Penalty Clause" whereby the policies are warranted free from any claim consequent on loss of time whether arising from a peril of the sea or otherwise.[35]

Loss of Profits

A novel question arose in *Oscar L. Aronsen, Inc. v. Compton et al (The Megara)*.[36] In that case, the plaintiffs chartered the *Megara* and effected two anticipated charter profits policies in respect of the profits expected to be made. The underwriters agreed to pay for loss of profits if the vessel were (a) a total loss, (b) a constructive total loss, (c) a compromised total loss, or (d) an arranged total loss.[37]

The vessel stranded in the Sulu Sea. She was eventually refloated and towed to Manila for survey. The insured value was £140,000 and the owner estimated the total cost of repair at more than £142,000. He then notified underwriters he was claiming for a constructive total loss and gave notice of abandonment. The underwriters refused to accept abandonment, believing that the vessel could be repaired for approximately £79,000 in a Japanese repair yard. Eventually, the owner withdrew the claim for constructive total loss and accepted payment on a partial loss. Plaintiffs then claimed under their policy, asserting that the settlement between hull underwriters and the owner was an "arranged total loss."

The court held that the action failed because, on the evidence, the settlement had been reached on a partial loss basis and not as a compromise of a claim for a total loss.

---

35. It must be remembered that if a loss of freight is caused by a loss of time, the underwriters are not liable. *But if the vessel is a constructive total loss*, then the underwriters pay in full whether the cause of the loss of freight is loss of time or not. Compare *Petros M. Nomikos, Ltd. v. Robertson, supra,* with *Naviera de Canarias (S.A.) v. Nacional Hispanica Aseguradora S.A.,* [1977] 1 Lloyd's Rep. 457, H.L.

36. 495 F.2d 674 (2d Cir.), 1974 AMC 480, [1974] 1 Lloyd's Rep. 590.

37. "Profits" are not included in the term "goods" and, if they are to be insured, they should be specifically described as that in the policy. *Mackenzie v. Whitworth,* (1875) 45 L.J.Q.B. 233, 33 L.T. 655; *Royal Exchange Assur. v. M'Swiney,* (1850) 117 E.R. 250, Ex.Ch.; *Lucena v. Craufurd,* (1806) 127 E.R. 630, H.L.; *Anderson v. Morice,* (1876) 1 App.Cas. 713, H.L.; *Halhead v. Young,* (1856) 119 E.R. 880. In America, it appears that a loss of part of goods on which the profit is insured is a proportional loss on profits. *Loomis v. Shaw,* 2 Johns 36 (St. N.Y.).

Constructive Total Loss

Section 60, Marine Insurance Act, 1906, provides:

(1) Subject to any express provision in the policy, there is a constructive total loss where the subject-matter insured is reasonably abandoned on account of its actual total loss appearing to be unavoidable, or because it could not be preserved from actual total loss without an expenditure which would exceed its value when the expenditure had been incurred.

(2) In particular, there is a constructive total loss—

(i) Where the assured is deprived of the possession of his ship or goods by a peril insured against, and (a) it is unlikely that he can recover the ship or goods as the case may be, or (b) the cost of recovering the ship or goods, as the case may be, would exceed their value when recovered; or

(ii) In the case of damage to a ship, where she is so damaged by a peril insured against, that the cost of repairing the damage would exceed the value of the ship when repaired.

In estimating the cost of repairs, no deduction is to be made in respect of general average contributions to those repairs payable by other interests, but account is to be taken of the expenses of future salvage operations and of any future general average contributions to which the ship would be liable if repaired; or

(iii) In the case of damage to goods, where the cost of repairing the damage and forwarding the goods to their destination would exceed their value on arrival.

The AIH (June, 1977) form provides, with respect to actual and constructive total losses, as follows:

In ascertaining whether the Vessel is a constructive Total loss the Agreed Value shall be taken as the repaired value and nothing in respect of the damaged or break-up value of the Vessel or wreck shall be taken into account.

There shall be no recovery for a constructive Total Loss hereunder unless the expense of recovering and repairing the Vessel would exceed the Agreed Value. In making this determination, only expenses incurred in or to be incurred by reason of a single accident or a sequence of damages arising from the same accident shall be taken into account, but expenses incurred prior to tender of abandonment shall not be considered if such are to be claimed separately under the Sue and Labor clause.[38]

In the event of Total Loss (actual or constructive), no claim to be made by Underwriters for freight, whether notice of abandonment has been given or not.

In no case shall the Underwriters be liable for unrepaired damage in addition to a subsequent Total Loss sustained during the period covered by this Policy.

The Institute Time Clauses (hulls), paragraphs 16-19, are very similar. The Institute Time Clauses, however, use the term "insured value" rather than the AIH term "agreed value."

It is helpful in construing Section 60 and the decisions upon which it is based, to dissect the sub-sections and the component parts thereof.

Generally speaking, Section 60 defines and "circumscribes completely the conception of a constructive total loss."[39] Sub-section 2, as compared with sub-section 1, is additional and not merely illustrative.[40]

Section 60 must be construed *in pari materia* with Section 61, which details the effect of a constructive total loss and reads simply:

Where there is a constructive total loss the assured may either treat the loss as a partial loss, or abandon the subject-matter insured to the insurer and treat the loss as if it were an actual total loss.

In doing so, the following principle stands out with clarity: Notice of abandonment obviously is not an essential ingredient of a constructive total loss. To the contrary, it is a superimposed right of election where there is a constructive total loss, because even though there is a constructive total loss, the assured may nonetheless treat it as a partial loss. Stated in another fashion, it is merely a condition precedent to recovery where a constructive total loss has already occurred.[41] In fact, the vessel may be so badly damaged by a peril insured against as to entitle the owner to claim for a constructive total loss, but there is nothing to prevent the owner from electing to keep his vessel and repair her, at the same time

---

38. The last sentence of this sub-paragraph was apparently added in response to the invitation of the court in *Helmville, Ltd. v. Yorkshire Ins. Co. Ltd. (The Medina Princess)*, [1965] 1 Lloyd's Rep. 361, where the court refused to deal with the question of whether or not an assured could aggregate successive partial losses in order to claim for a constructive total loss. The court suggested that if the underwriters wished to ensure that an assured would not seek to aggregate, it would not be difficult to ensure that result by making an appropriate provision in the Institute Time Clauses to make it clear that he was not entitled to do so. The American underwriters took the hint; the English have not yet done so.

39. *Irvin v. Hine*, [1949] 2 All E.R. 1089, 83 Ll.L.Rep. 162.

40. *Richards v. Forestal Land, Timber and Railways Co.*, [1941] 3 All E.R. 62, H.L., [1942] A.C. 50; *Court Line, Ltd. v. R., (The Lavington Court)*, [1945] 2 All E.R. 357, 78 Ll.L.Rep. 390, C.A.

41. *Petros M. Nomikos, Ltd. v. Robertson*, [1939] A.C. 371, H.L.

claiming from the underwriters for the cost of repairs up to a full 100 percent.[42]

In *Disrude v. Commercial Fishermen's Ins. Exchange,*[43] the underwriters insured a fishing vessel for an "agreed valuation" of $25,000 and the amount of the insurance was $25,000. The vessel owner, subsequent to taking out the policy, made improvements to the vessel which increased its value to $44,000. Subsequently, the vessel was substantially destroyed by fire. The plaintiff assured made repairs in an agreed and reasonable amount of $25,000 (although the recitation of facts does not disclose it, the cost of repairs exceeded $25,000, but the vessel owner elected to claim for only $25,000—the face amount of the policy).[44] The vessel owner opted to claim for a partial loss and contended he was entitled to the full $25,000, less the deductible. The insurer contended, however, that its liability was to be measured by multiplying the cost of repairs by a fraction composed of the agreed value ($25,000) over $44,000, the value at the time of loss, less the deductible. The court held that Section 27(3)[45] governed and that in the absence of fraud (which was not asserted), the parties had fixed an agreed valuation of $25,000, which governed. Therefore, the formula to be used was the amount of the loss multiplied by a fraction composed of the amount of insurance over the agreed value of the vessel. (The policy provided that it was subject to English law and usage and the court decided it on that basis).[46]

Taking the respective phrases of Section 60(1) *seriatim: "Subject to any express provision in the policy."*

Keeping in mind the latter portions of Section 60(1) and 60(2)(ii) referring to the requirement that the cost of preserving or repairing must exceed the value of the subject matter, it is the "real" value which is mentioned and not the "agreed" value. Consequently, apart from a policy provision, the real value and not the policy valuation governs.[47] It is therefore not surprising that underwriters have taken steps to clarify the word "value." In the AIH (June, 1977) form, it is specially provided (lines 134-35) that "in ascertaining whether the Vessel is a constructive Total Loss the Agreed Value shall be taken as the repaired value and nothing in

---

42. *Aitchison v. Lohre,* (1879) 2 App.Cas. 755.
43. 280 Or. 245, 570 P.2d 963, 1978 AMC 261.
44. The reason the owner opted to go this route is quite patent. Had he claimed for a constructive total loss, he would have had to abandon to underwriters, who would then have received a vessel which, when repaired, would have been worth $44,000.
45. Sec. 27(3) reads:
Subject to the provisions of the Act, and in the absence of fraud, the value fixed by the policy is, as between the insurer and assured, conclusive of the insurable value of the subject intended to be insured, whether the loss be total or partial.
46. See, also, *In re Central R.R. Co. (The St. Johns),* 101 F. 469 (S.D.N.Y. 1900).
47. *Irving v. Manning,* (1847) 1 H.L. Cas. 287, 9 E.R. 766, H.L.

respect of the damaged or break-up value of the Vessel or wreck shall be taken into account." The first sentence of Clause 17, Institute Time Clauses (hulls), is essentially identical except that the term "insured value" is used instead of "agreed value."[48]

> . . . *where the subject-matter insured is reasonably abandoned* . . .

As to the meaning of the term "reasonably," see *Court Line, Ltd. v. R. (The Lavington Court)* (1945) *supra*, and *Lind v. Mitchell* (1929) *supra*. In the latter, the court said, in part:

> . . . the abandonment was unreasonable. The vessel was within 15 miles of her home port. The lifeboat into which the crew got, according to the evidence, was able to sail and row in with a north-east wind. If the lifeboat could sail, the schooner could equally have sailed with the north-east wind. The schooner was still floating high in the water seven or eight hours after she was abandoned. I assume in my judgment that the abandonment by the master was unreasonable.

In the former, the court pointed out that the word "abandonment" was used in two senses under the Act; when used in reference to a ship being abandoned, it included abandonment by the master in the exercise of his express or implied authority, as well as abandonment by the assured to the insurers.

Whether the abandonment is reasonable or not is clearly a question of fact.[49]

---

48. Essentially the same clause was contained in the policy considered in *North Atlantic S.S. Co., Ltd. v. Burr*, (1904) 20 T.L.R.. 266, 9 Com.Cas. 164. Other special clauses, varying the impact of Sec. 60, will be found in *Rowland and Marwood's S.S. Co. v. Maritime Ins. Co.*, (1901) 17 T.L.R. 516 (constructive total loss if vessel had been stranded and remained in such position for a period of six months), and *Fowler v. English and Scottish Mar. Ins. Co.*, (1865) 144 E.R. 667 (total loss to be paid thirty days after receipt of official news of capture or embargo, without waiting for condemnation). See, also, *Oscar L. Arsonsen, Inc. v. Compton, et al (The Megara)*, 495 F.2d 674, 1974 AMC 480, [1974] 1 Lloyd's Rep. 590, discussed, *supra*. See *Lenfest et al v. Coldwell*, 525 F.2d 717 (2d Cir.), 1975 AMC 2489 (policy provided that the insured value should be taken as the repaired value); *Northern Barge v. Royal Insurance*, 492 F.2d 1248, 1974 AMC 136 (no recovery for constructive total loss unless the expense of recovering and repairing the vessel exceeds the insured value); *Armar*, 1954 AMC 1674 (NYM) (repair and recovery costs must exceed insured value).

American cases are legion which establish the so-called American rule that if there is a "high probability" that the costs of repair and recovery will exceed 50% of the repaired value, the assured may claim for a constructive total loss. See, for example, *Dauntless*, 129 F.2d 582 (2d Cir.), 1942 AMC 1021. The rule has become antiquated, however, by reason of the fact that American policies universally stipulate that the expense of recovering and repairing must exceed the agreed value. That policy provisions prevail over the rule, or even countervailing state statutes, is unquestioned. *Bellingham*, 1927 AMC 11 (W.D. Wash.).

49. *Marine Ins. Co. of Alexandria v. Tucker*, 7 U.S. 357 (1806). See, also, *Providence Washington Ins. Co. v. Corbett*, (1884) 9 S.C.R. 256 (Can.), and *Cunningham v. St. Paul Fire, etc. Inc. Co.*, (1914) 16 D.L.R. 39 (Can.).

. . . on account of its actual total loss appearing to be unavoidable . . .

In *Marstrand Fishing Co., Ltd. v. Beer,*[50] the court held, in essence, that a constructive total loss of a vessel is established only when, on the *true facts* as known at the time of abandonment, and not "appearing on the facts as known to the assured," it appears to a reasonable man that the balance of probabilities is against recovery of the ship. Under English law, the facts must be such as to justify abandonment *both* at the date of notice of abandonment *and* as of the date of issuance of a "writ" (i.e., "commencement of the suit").[51]

Under American law, the facts as they exist at the time a notice of abandonment is given must be such as to justify it. If they are, then an abandonment once rightfully made is binding and conclusive as between the parties, and the rights flowing from it become vested rights, not to be divested by any subsequent events.[52] But the rule is nonetheless the same in both countries that not only must the information upon which the notice is founded prove to be true, it must also be justified by the state of facts existing at the time the notice is given. An assured cannot recover merely because he honestly believes that a total loss is inevitable; the real facts must justify such a belief.[53]

There is no impediment, of course, to an assured giving notice of abandonment upon any set of reports received by him whether or not the reports turn out to be true. In the United States, it has been held that even a newspaper report is sufficient foundation for notice of abandonment.[54] However, if it turns out that the report upon which the assured acted does not comport with the true facts as they actually existed at the time of giving the notice, the notice is a nullity.[55]

Under the English cases antedating the Marine Insurance Act, 1906, a change of circumstances between the date of notice of abandonment and filing of the writ can alter the final result; i.e., if the subject matter is restored in that interval of time, the abandonment is defeated. Although the Act contains no express provision to this effect, the cases antedating

---

50. [1937] 1 All E.R. 158, 56 Ll.L.Rep. 163.

51. Underwriters usually decline to accept notice of abandonment. If they do so, they frequently agree that the assured will be treated as if a writ had been issued as of the date of notice of abandonment. See, for example, *Barque Robert S. Besnard Co., Ltd. v. Murton,* (1909) 101 L.T. 285, where the freight had not been earned as of the date taken by consent as the date of the writ and the shipowner recovered on the freight policy although the cargo was ultimately brought to its destination.

52. *Peele v. Merchants' Ins. Co.,* F.Cas. 10,905 (1st Cir. 1822).

53. *Bainbridge v. Neilson,* (1808) 103 E.R. 800.

54. *Boseley v. Chesapeake Ins. Co.,* 3 Gill. & Johnson 450 (1831).

55. *Bainbridge v. Neilson,* (1808), *supra,* n. 53.

the Act,[56] as well as Section 91(2) of the Act,[57] would appear to establish that the rule remains unaltered.[58]

The rule in the United States is that an abandonment, when properly made, is irrevocable, and the rights of the parties are not changed by subsequent events.[59]

However, if abandonment is accepted by the underwriters it becomes irrevocable even if made on insufficient grounds.[60]

>   . . . It could not be preserved from actual total loss without an expenditure which would exceed its value when the expenditure had been incurred . . . [61]

In the United States, application of this principle can be somewhat confusing by reason of the American common law rule that the expenditure need only exceed fifty percent of the repaired value. With this basic qualification, however, the earlier American cases support the principle. The later cases, of course, reflect the almost universal policy provisions which are in harmony with the English rule.

Section 60(2)

As noted heretofore, sub-section 2 of Section 60 expands upon and is additional to Section 60(1). In one instance, however, it is probably more restrictive than was the common law prior to the adoption of the Act. As sub-section 2, paragraph (i) states, there is a constructive total loss where the assured is deprived of possession of his ship or goods by a peril insured against and it is *unlikely* that he can recover the ship or goods. In the bill as originally drafted, the word used was "uncertain"; it was changed

56. See *Ruys v. Royal Exchange Assur. Corp.*, (1897) 2 Q.B. 135.

57. Sec. 91(2) reads:
The rules of the common law, including the law merchant, save in so far as they are inconsistent with the express provisions of this Act, shall continue to apply to contracts of marine insurance.

58. *Polurrian S.S. Co., Ltd. v. Young*, [1915] 1 K.B. 922, [1914-15] All E.R. 116: *Pesquerias y Secaderos de Bacalao de Espana, S.A. v. Beer*, (1946) 79 Ll.L.Rep. 417; *Rickards v. Forestal Land, Timber & Railways Co.*, [1942] n. 40, *supra; Marstrand Fishing Co. v. Beer*, (1936) n. 50, *supra; Middows v. Robertson (and other test cases)*, [1941] 70 Ll.L.Rep. 173, H.L.

59. *Orient Ins. Co. v. Adams*, 123 U.S. 67 (1887); *Bradlie v. Maryland Ins. Co.*, 37 U.S. 378 (1838); *Royal Exchange Assur. v. Graham & Morton Transp. Co.*, 166 F. 32 (7th Cir. 1908); *Marshall v. Delaware Ins. Co.*, F.Cas. 9,127, aff'd 8 U.S. 202 (1807); *Rhinelander v. Ins. Co. of Pennsylvania*, 8 U.S. 29 (1807); *Williams v. Suffolk Ins. Co.*, F.Cas. 17,738 (1st Cir. 1838).

60. *Peele v. Merchants' Ins. Co.*, (1822) n. 52, *supra; Provincial Ins. Co. of Canada v. Leduc*, (1874) 31 L.T. 142, 2 Asp. M.L.C. 538, P.C.; *Smith v. Robertson*, (1814) 3 E.R. 936, H.L.

61. *Petros M. Nomikos, Ltd. v. Robertson*, (1939) A.C. 371, H.L.; *Navieras de Canarias, S.A. v. Nacional Hispanica Aseguradora, S.A. (The Playa da Las Nieves)*, [1977] 1 Lloyd's Rep. 457. For the American cases, see cases cited under subheading "Section 60(2)," *infra*.

in committee to "unlikely." In *Polurrian S.S. Co. v. Young*,[62] the court stated that this change altered the law to the detriment of the assured—and it clearly does, it being much more difficult to prove that recovery is "unlikely" than it would be to prove that such recovery was "uncertain."

Sub-section 2 presents four instances of a constructive total loss where loss is caused by an insured peril

(1) Deprivation of possession of ship or goods where it is:

(a) unlikely that they can be recovered; or
(b) the cost of recovery would exceed the value when recovered;

(2) In the case of damage to a ship, the cost of repairs would exceed the value of the ship when repaired;

(3) In the case of damage to goods, where the cost of repairing the damage and forwarding the goods to destination would exceed their value on arrival.

These specific instances are explored in the following discussion.

The American courts have defined the right to claim for constructive total loss in terms of the proper exercise of the right of abandonment. As Arnould has noted, the best general statement of the circumstances which confer a right to give notice of abandonment is contained in the following quotation from Justice Story's opinion in *Peele v. Merchants' Insurance Co.*:[63]

> The right of abandonment has been admitted to exist, where there is a forcible dispossession or ouster of the owner of the ship, as in cases of capture; where there is a moral restraint or detention, which deprives the owner of the free use of this ship, as in case of embargoes, blockades, and arrests by sovereign authority; where there is a present total loss of the physical possession and use of the ship, as in case of submersion; where there is a total loss of the ship for the voyage, as in case of shipwreck, so that the ship cannot be repaired for the voyage in the port where the disaster happens; and, lastly, where the injury is so extensive that by reason of it the ship is useless, and yet the necessary repairs would exceed her present value.

The American cases illustrating the principles enunciated in *Peele v. Merchants' Ins. Co.* are rather numerous.[64] Special mention should be

---

62. [1915] 1 K.B. 922, [1914-15] All E.R. 116. See, also, *Marstrand Fishing Co., Ltd. v. Beer*, (1937) 1 All E.R. 158, 56 Ll.L.Rep. 163; *Roura and Fourgas v. Townend*, (1919) 1 K.B. 189, [1918-19] All E.R. 341.

63. F.Cas. 10,905 (1st Cir.).

64. *Alexander v. Baltimore Ins. Co.*, 8 U.S. 370 (1808) (total loss occurs where the whole of the insured property perishes or where the property exists but the voyage is lost or the

made of *Armar*[65] and *Delta Supply v. Liberty Mutual.*[66] In *Armar*, the vessel had a current market value of $675,000 and was insured for $1,200,000. After a stranding, the owner estimated repair cost at $1,212,549 and gave notice of abandonment, which was refused. It was found that the reasonable costs of recovery and repair, plus 20 percent for contingencies, was $736,315. Consequently, the claim for constructive total loss failed—English conditions applied and the costs did not exceed the insured value.

In *Delta Supply v. Liberty Mutual*, it was held under an American hull policy that the policy could validly incorporate the English rule for deter-

---

expense of pursuing it exceeds the benefit arising therefrom); *Hugg v. Augusta Ins. & Banking Co.*, 48 U.S. 595 (1849) (ship carrying jerked beef put into port of distress; delay while making repairs in all probability would have occasioned a destruction of the remaining beef and there was no other vessel available in the port by which to forward the cargo; constructive total loss of cargo but no total loss of freight); *Great Western Ins. Co. v. Fogarty*, 86 U.S. 640 (1873) (vessel carrying sugar-packing machine was wrecked; half the parts of the machine were saved but they were useless and of no value except as "old iron"); *Standard Marine Ins. Co., Ltd. of Liverpool, Eng. v. Nome Beach Lighterage & Transp. Co.*, 133 F. 636 (9th Cir. 1904) (unless there is something of value to pass to underwriters, there is nothing to abandon and no case for the application of the doctrine of constructive total loss); *Klein v. Globe & Rutgers Fire Ins. Co. of New York City (The Tornado)*, 1 F.2d 137 (W.D. Pa.), 1924 AMC 452, 2 F.2d 137 (3rd Cir.), 1925 AMC 197 (actual total loss does not exist where a hope exists for the recovery of the vessel in specie at any cost; insured must determine for himself whether he has a right to abandon and is under the duty of making his determination and tendering abandonment promptly; *Fireman's Fund Ins. Co. v. Globe Nav. Co.*, 236 F. 618 (9th Cir. 1916) (high probability rule not applicable where policy contains an express provision fixing the right to abandon on certain specified terms); *Hall v. Ocean Ins. Co.*, 37 F. 371 (1st Cir. 1889) (vessel stranded and in grave danger of breaking up; held, master was justified in selling the hulk and insurers were liable for a total loss, although afterwards the vessel was saved); *Williams v. Suffolk Ins. Co.*, F.Cas. 17,739 (1st Cir. 1839) (total loss where the object of the voyage is entirely defeated by a seizure and subsequent recapture and vessel returns home); *Wallace v. Thames & Mersey Ins. Co.*, 22 F. 66 (Mich. 1884) (true basis of valuation for constructive total loss purposes is value of ship at the time of disaster; if, after damage is or might be repaired, the ship is not or would not be worth double the cost of repairs, the loss is to be treated as a "technical" total loss, the term being synonymous with a "constructive" total loss); *George W. Clyde*, 2 F.2d 767 (N.D. Ill.), 1924 AMC 1479 (underwriters could raise sunken vessel under Sue and Labor Clause without accepting abandonment); *Tashmoo*, 1937 AMC 1536 (Arb.) (upon abandonment, underwriters on payment of total loss are entitled to the subject matter of the insurance without the necessity of an acceptance of abandonment; payment of the loss being the equivalent of an acceptance); *Miss Philippine*, 188 F.2d 741 (9th Cir.) (vessel ran aground but was refloated by a salvor employed by underwriters and taken to a safe harbor by the voluntary efforts of the salvor without, however, any instructions from either the assured or the assurers; the insured failed to recover, having failed to prove either a constructive total loss or acceptance of abandonment by underwriters); *Portmar*, 209 F.2d 852 (2d Cir.), 1954 AMC 558 (a constructive total loss where the vessel was incapable of recovery or repairs within a reasonable time; mere military repairs and military emergency use of a badly damaged vessel held not to be the equivalent of restoration to the shipowner's service).

65. 1954 AMC 1674 (NYM), [1954] 2 Lloyd's Rep. 95.
66. 211 F.Supp. 429 (S.D. Tex.), 1963 AMC 1540.

mining whether or not there was a constructive total loss. There, the estimated cost of repairs was $12,700 and the insured value was $15,000. In both cases, although the claims for constructive total loss failed, the assureds recovered on the basis of a partial loss.[67] Moreover, in both decisions, it was held that the assureds were entitled to recover from the underwriters for unrepaired damages, the measure being the depreciation in value of the vessel arising from the existence of the damage. The method of arriving at the reasonable depreciation was held to be by applying the percentage of depreciation (determined by comparison of the sound and damaged values) to the insured value. See discussion, *infra*, Chapter XX, "Particular Average."

It should also be noted that where the policy covers only absolute total loss or absolute physical total loss, recovery for a constructive total loss is precluded.[68] Moreover, an unrepaired partial damage claim with respect to the insured vessel is merged into a claim for a subsequent total loss under the same policy.[69]

In computing the repair costs to be taken into account in a constructive total loss, those costs are relevant which obtain at the place of loss or where the vessel is and must of necessity make repairs.[70] Crew's wages and overtime at a port of refuge are includible as costs in determining whether the vessel is or is not a constructive total loss, and they may also be included if incurred at the port where repairs are made, provided that the crew either participated in the work or it was necessary to guard the vessel or to superintend the work.[71] The old rule of deducting one-third of the cost of repairs for replacing old material with new, known as "thirding," has no application to the computations utilized to determine whether the vessel is a constructive total loss. Such a deduction is made only when the repairs are actually effected.[72] No deduction need be made from the cost computation for repairs rendered necessary because of the decayed condition of the vessel.[73]

---

67. There is nothing to prevent this unless the policies otherwise provide; e.g., written on F.P.A. conditions. See *Tornado*, 2 F.2d 137 (3rd Cir.), 1925 AMC 197, and n. 41, *supra*. See, also, *Washburn & Moen Mfg. Co. v. Reliance Marine Ins. Co.*, 179 U.S. 1 (1897).

68. *Hampton Roads Carriers v. Boston Ins. Co.*, 150 F.Supp. 338 (D. Md.), 1958 AMC 425. However, the term "total loss," standing alone, covers a "constructive total loss." *O'Leary v. Stymest*, (1865) 11 N.B.R. 289 (Can.).

69. *Rock Transport v. Hartford F.I. Co.*, 1972 AMC 2316 (S.D.N.Y.); *The Dora Forster*, [1900] P. 241; *British and Foreign Ins. Co. v. Wilson Shipping Co., Ltd.*, [1921] A.C. 188, H.L.; and Sec. 77(2), Marine Insurance Act, 1906.

70. *Patapsco Ins. Co. v. Southgate*, 30 U.S. 604 (1831).

71. *Lenfest v. Coldwell*, 525 F.2d 717 (2d Cir.), 1975 AMC 2489.

72. *Wallace v. Thames & Mersey Ins. Co.*, 22 F. 66 (6th Cir. 1884); *Bradlie v. Maryland Ins. Co.*, 37 U.S. 378 (1838); *Henderson Bros. v. Shankland*, [1896] 1 Q.B. 525. The AIH (June, 1977) form expressly provides that general and particular average will be paid without deduction, new for old (line 111).

73. *Phillips v. Nairne*, (1847) 136 E.R. 529.

The proportionate part of salvage charged to the vessel is an includible expense.[74] In *Lenfest v. Coldwell*,[75] the court noted that although some costs are common to both, not all items allowable in general average are includible in determining whether a vessel is a constructive total loss. While a general average cost need not relate to the ship's repair, that relationship is a prerequisite to its inclusion in a constructive total loss calculation.

Amounts received in general average from other interests in payment of repairs need not be excluded from the cost computations, but general average contributions for which the ship would be liable if repaired are taken into account.[76] The value of the wreck of the vessel is not to be added to the cost of repairs,[77] nor is freight which is earned to be taken into account.[78]

Depending upon the circumstances, as a matter of common sense, those expenditures which would be reasonable in order to repair the vessel and put her back into service should be taken into consideration. These would include drydocking charges, towing expenses to bring the vessel to a port where repair facilities exist, the cost of pumps, temporary repairs to enable the vessel to be brought to a port of repair, transportation charges, communications expenses, surveyors' fees, and the like. These items are almost invariably estimates only and, if found unnecessary or exaggerated, they will either be disallowed or reduced to what is reasonable.[79]

In *Northern Barge v. Royal Insurance*,[80] the court held that the assured could defer tendering abandonment until after the vessel had been raised and the repair costs could be determined. The court also held that, in so doing, the insured was entitled to include the recovery expenses (costs of raising) incurred *prior* to the tender of abandonment in determining whether there was a constructive total loss under the policy and, on proof of such a loss, to recover the sue and labor expenses incurred (costs of raising) in addition to the stipulated policy valuation of the vessel.[81]

---

74. *Armar*, 1954 AMC 1674 (NYM), [1954] 2 Lloyd's Rep. 95; *Bradlie v. Maryland Ins. Co.*, 37 U.S. 378 (1838).
75. 525 F.2d 717 (2d Cir.), 1975 AMC 2489.
76. *Kemp v. Halliday*, (1866) 122 E.R. 1361, Ex.Ch.; Sec. 60(2)(ii), Marine Insurance Act, 1906.
77. *Hall v. Hayman*, [1912] 2 K.B. 5.
78. *Parker v. Budd*, (1896) 2 Com.Cas. 47.
79. See the discussion in *Helmville, Ltd. v. Yorkshire Ins. Co., Ltd. (The Medina Princess)*, [1965] 1 Lloyd's Rep. 361; *Hall v. Hayman*, (1912) 2 K.B. 5; *Robertson v. Royal Exchange Assur. Corp.*, (1924) 20 Ll.L.Rep. 17; *Armar*, 1954 AMC 1674 (NYM), [1954] 2 Lloyd's Rep. 95; and *Delta Supply v. Liberty Mutual*, 211 F.Supp. 429 (S.D. Tex.), 1963 AMC 1540.
80. 492 F.2d 1248 (8th Cir.), 1974 AMC 136.
81. This result may now be precluded under the AIH (June, 1977) form, which was amended to provide that expenses incurred prior to tender of abandonment shall not be

As Buglass notes,[82] as a practical matter, the change in wording quoted in footnote 81, *supra* (which is in effect an attempt to contract out of the law), achieves little, because an assured, by tendering a reasonable but early notice of abandonment when faced with a major casualty involving sue and labor expense (or, indeed, recovery expenses of any type), puts himself back in the same position he was in before the amendment; i.e., he has the right to include all recovery expenses in determining whether the vessel is a constructive total loss and to recover expenses of a sue and labor nature in addition to a total loss payment even though he may have used such expenses in the constructive loss computation. It cannot, therefore, be too strongly emphasized that prompt notice of abandonment should be tendered to underwriters *before* any substantial recovery expenses are incurred (other than salvage expenses on a "no cure—no pay" basis).

In *Parkhill-Goodloe v. Home Ins. Co.*,[83] where the insured dredge was held to be a constructive total loss, the court awarded recovery under the policy for (1) the agreed value; (2) drydocking expenses incurred for a post-salvage inspection; (3) expenses incurred subsequent to giving notice of abandonment; (4) costs for scrapping or disposing of the hulk of the vessel; and (5) attorneys' fees.[84]

Dual Valuation Clause

Occasionally, a somewhat contrived clause is utilized to arrive at a mutually acceptable insured value, as the "insured value" (or "agreed value" as the American policy forms put it) is important to both underwriters and assureds, since the reasonable costs of repair must be compared with the insured value in order to ascertain whether there has been an actual or constructive total loss.[85]

In a dual valuation clause, there are two valuations, the smaller being the basis upon which a total loss is calculated and the larger being a limit on claims other than for total loss. Usually, the smaller valuation represents the approximate market value of the vessel, while the higher valua-

considered if such are to be claimed separately under the Sue and Labor Clause (lines 138-39).

82. Buglass, *Marine Insurance and General Average in the United States*, 2d ed. (Centreville, Md.: Cornell Maritime Press, 1981).

83. 1976 AMC 951 (M.D. Fla.).

84. Attorneys' fees were awarded under the applicable Florida statute.

85. As noted earlier, sub-section 60(2)(ii) speaks in terms of there being a constructive total loss of a vessel where she is so damaged by a peril insured against that the cost of repairing the damage would exceed the *value of the ship* when repaired. The Act is silent with respect to rules for ascertaining the value of the ship; hence, the almost invariable inclusion of clauses in hull policies compelling a comparison of cost of recovery and repair with the "insured value" or "agreed value."

tion (usually arrived at by negotiation) is a sum above the assumed market value. Consequently, the assured is given a choice if his vessel is damaged to such an extent that the cost of repairs would exceed the value set for total loss purposes. He can either abandon the vessel to underwriters as a constructive total loss and be paid the smaller valuation, or he can effect repairs, in which case he can collect up to the amount of the larger valuation.

The Institute Dual Valuation Clause reads:

> (a) Insured Value for purposes of Total Loss (Actual or Constructive) . . . £
> (b) Insured Value for purposes other than Total Loss . . . £

In the event of a claim for Actual or Constructive Total Loss (a) shall be taken to be the insured value and payment by the Underwriters of their proportions of that amount shall be for all purposes payment of a Total Loss.

In ascertaining whether the vessel is a Constructive Total Loss (a) shall be taken as the repaired value and nothing in respect of the damaged or break-up value of the vessel or wreck shall be taken into account.

No claim for Constructive Total Loss based upon the cost of recovery and/or repair of the Vessel shall be recoverable hereunder unless such cost would exceed the insured value as in (a).

In no case shall Underwriters' liability in respect of a claim for unrepaired damage exceed the insured value as in (a).

Additional insurances allowed under the Disbursements Clause to be calculated on the amount of the insured value as in (a).

It will be noted that if the assured elects not to repair but claims on an unrepaired damage basis, the clause restricts the amount he can recover to the smaller valuation. Moreover, the last paragraph of the clause restricts the assured in taking out increased value, disbursements, etc. coverage to the percentage specified in the disbursements clause applied against the smaller valuation.

Damage to Goods

As sub-paragraph (iii) of Section 60(2) so clearly states, the cost of repairing the damage to goods and forwarding them on to their destination must exceed their value on arrival in order to claim for a constructive total loss. Thus, in *Rosetto v. Gurney*,[86] involving damage to a cargo of

---

86. (1851) 11 C.B. 176, 138 E.R. 438.

wheat, the court pointed out that in ascertaining whether or not it was practicable to send the cargo to destination, the jury must take into consideration the cost of unshipping the cargo, the cost of drying and warehousing it, the cost of transshipping to a new bottom, and the cost of the difference in freight (if it could be effected only at a higher rate of freight).[87]

Although the American rule is that there is a constructive total loss of cargo when the goods are damaged to more than half their value,[88] for practical purposes the rule is meaningless because it is invariably modified by express policy conditions which define a constructive total loss on cargo in the same terms used in Section 60(2)(iii) of the Marine Insurance Act, 1906.

In *Boon and Cheah Steel Pipes S. B. v. Asia Ins. Co., Ltd.*,[89] all except 12 of 668 steel pipes insured were damaged. The claim for constructive total loss failed because the assured produced no proof that the cost of reconditioning and forwarding the pipes to destination would exceed their value on arrival. The assured's claim for an actual total loss under the rule of *de minimis non curat lex* also failed because the court held that the remaining 12 pipes were not *de minimis*.

In the Institute Cargo Clauses, the Constructive Total Loss Clause reads:

> No claim for Constructive Total Loss shall be recoverable hereunder unless the goods are reasonably abandoned either on account of their actual total loss appearing to be unavoidable or because the cost of recovering, reconditioning and forwarding the goods to the destination to which they are insured would exceed their value on arrival.

It will be seen that the clause, unlike its counterpart in hull policies, tracks with the Act, as the test is the value of the goods on arrival at their destination.

Should the underwriter pay as for a constructive total loss, he is, of course, entitled to the net proceeds of the sale of the goods at the port of distress. This is a salvage recoupment. If he pays the difference between the total insured value and the proceeds of the sale, it is termed a "salvage loss."

87. See, also, *Farnworth v. Hyde*, (1866) L.R. 2 C.P. 204; *Watson v. Mercantile Marine Ins. Co.*, (1873) 9 N.S.R. 396 (Can.); *Reimer v. Ringrose*, (1851) 155 E.R. 540; and *Anderson v. Wallis*, (1813) 105 E.R. 372.

88. Phillips, Sec. 1608, citing *Gardiner v. Smith*, 1 Johns Cas. N.Y. 141, *Judah v. Randall*, 2 Caines Cas. N.Y. 324, *Ludlow v. Columbian Ins. Co.*, 1 Johns Cas. N.Y. 335, *Moses v. Columbian Ins. Co.*, 6 Johns Cas. N.Y. 219, *Marcardier v. Chesapeake Ins. Co.*, 12 U.S. 39 (1814), *Gilfert v. Hallett*, 2 Johns Cas. 296; *Mordecai v. Fireman's Ins. Co.*, 12 Rich. So.C. 512. See, also, *Washburn & Moen Mfg. Co. v. Reliance Ins. Co.*, 179 U.S. 1 (1897).

89. [1975] 1 Lloyd's Rep. 452.

Occasionally, the goods may bring a better price if sold short of destination even though the cost of reconditioning and forwarding to destination would not exceed the value on arrival. That such a sale may be commercially desirable, however, does not permit the assured to recover for a total loss by reason of the loss of the insured venture. To the contrary, if the policy excludes liability for partial loss and covers only total loss, then while the owner has the right to sell the goods, the underwriter need not respond for a loss even though the goods were sold short of destination. While a sale short of destination may well be to the underwriter's interest, he cannot be forced to agree to the sale.[90]

In *Devitt v. Providence Washington Ins. Co.,*[91] the goods insured consisted of fruits and vegetables which were shipped in a canal boat. The boat sank, and part of the cargo was recovered in a damaged condition and was sold by the assured, the proceeds being but little in excess of the expenses, and less than the sum expended by insurer in raising the canal boat and reshipping the cargo, not including the expenses of sale. The policy provided that the loss should be estimated according to the actual cash value at the place of destination on the day of the disaster; that the perishable articles should be free of particular average, and that there could be no abandonment of the subject-matter insured, nor would the acts of the insurers and their agents in saving or disposing of the property insured be considered a waiver or acceptance of abandonment, nor as affirming or denying any liability under the policy; but such acts should be considered as having been for the benefit of all concerned. The court held that the insurer was liable for the whole of the article insured.

In *Scheer v. Hanover Fire Ins. Co.,*[92] the marine cargo policy gave general coverage. The goods were placed on a dock in Manila for transshipment, and war was declared by the Japanese. Harbor facilities were unobtainable and loading and discharge of cargo impossible. All records which might have been of assistance in determining the ultimate disposition of the goods were destroyed. The court held, in the circumstances, that the assignee of the insured cargo owner could recover as for a constructive total loss.

Total Loss of an Apportionable Part

Generally speaking, there is a total loss only if the whole of the subject matter has become a total loss. However, situations can arise where there

90. See *Reimer v. Ringrose, supra,* and *Anderson v. Wallis, supra,* n. 87.
91. 70 N.Y.S. 654, *aff'd* 173 N.Y. 17, 65 N.E. 777 (1902).
92. 96 N.Y.S.2d 873, *aff'd* 100 N.Y.S.2d 1023, 277 App.Div. 1096, *appeal denied* 102 N.Y.S.2d 453, 278 App.Div. 568.

is a total loss of an apportionable part. For example, if the policy covers 1,000 tierces of salmon in bulk and 200 tierces are lost, the loss is a partial one and not a total loss of an apportionable part.[93] Suppose, however, that the policy covered 100 tierces of salmon and 50 cartons of tea, and the loss involved was all the cartons of tea; in this instance, there is a total loss of an apportionable part. Should the policy be a valued one with only a single valuation, that valuation would have to be apportioned over all the different species of goods in the shipment in order to determine the proportionate insured value of the 50 cartons of tea.

Notice of Abandonment

Section 62, Marine Insurance Act, 1906, sets forth the common law with respect to *notice* of abandonment. It reads:

(1) Subject to the provisions of this section, where the assured elects to abandon the subject-matter insured to the insurer he must give notice of abandonment. If he fails to do so the loss can only be treated as a partial loss.

(2) Notice of abandonment may be given in writing, or by word of mouth, or partly in writing and partly by word of mouth, and may be given in any terms which indicate the intention of the assured to abandon his insured interest in the subject-matter insured unconditionally to the insurer.

(3) Notice of abandonment must be given with reasonable diligence after the receipt of reliable information of the loss, but where the information is of doubtful character the assured is entitled to a reasonable time to make inquiry.

(4) Where notice of abandonment is properly given, the rights of the assured are not prejudiced by the fact that the insurer refuses to accept the abandonment.

(5) The acceptance of an abandonment may be either express or implied from the conduct of the insurer. The mere silence of the insurer after notice is not an acceptance.

(6) Where notice of abandonment is accepted the abandonment is irrevocable. The acceptance of the notice conclusively admits liability for the loss and the sufficiency of the notice.

---

93. This was the situation in *Larsen v. Ins. Co. of N.A.*, 252 F.Supp. 458, 1965 AMC 2576 (W.D. Wash.), where the free-from-particular-average warranty contained in a refrigeration rider of a marine open cargo policy was held to exempt the insurer from liability for the total loss of 11 of 21 tierces of salmon because each tierce was not a separate and "apportionable" package within the exception of the warranty.

(7) Notice of abandonment is unnecessary where at the time when the assured receives information of the loss there would be no possibility of benefit to the insurer if notice were given to him.

(8) Notice of abandonment may be waived by the insurer.

(9) Where an insurer has reinsured his risk, no notice of abandonment need be given by him.

Sub-section 1 and 7 of Section 62 must be read *in pari materia*. At first blush, they appear inconsistent. In reality they are not. Sub-section 1 absolutely requires a notice of abandonment if the assured elects to abandon. Sub-section 7 dispenses with the requirement of notice if there would be no possibility of benefit to the insurer if notice were given.[94]

Reason for the Rule Requiring Notice of Abandonment

The language of the court in *Kaltenbach v. Mackenzie*[95] is instructive with respect to the reason for the rule:

. . . That rule is founded upon two grounds, when the assured has once elected to treat the loss as a total loss, the underwriters can insist upon his abiding by the election, so as to enable them to take the benefit of any advantage which may arise from the thing insured. Therefore, the object of notice, which is entirely different from abandonment, is that he may tell the underwriters at once what he has done, and not keep it secret in his mind, to see if there will be a change of circumstances.

There is another reason: the thing in various ways may be profitably dealt with, as the ship was in this case. Therefore, the second reason for requiring notice of abandonment to be given to the underwriters is, that they may do, if they think fit, what in their option is best, and make the most they can out of that which is abandoned to them as the consequence of the election which the assured has come to.

The court in *Vacuum Oil Co. v. Union Insurance Society of Canton*[96] gave this explanation:

94. Supporting this proposition, see *Standard Marine Ins. Co., Ltd. v. Nome Beach Lighterage & Transp. Co.*, 133 F. 636 (9th Cir. 1904); *Rumsey v. Providence Washington Ins. Co.*, (1880) 13 N.S.R. 393 (C.A. Can.); *Providence Washington Ins. Co. v. Corbett*, (1884) 9 S.C.R. 256 (Can.); *Churchill v. Nova Scotia Marine Ins. Co.*, (1895) 26 S.C.R. 65 (Can.); *Kaltenbach v. MacKenzie*, (1878) 48 L.J.Q.B. 9; *Mellish v. Andrews*, (1812) 104 E.R. 749; *Farnworth v. Hyde*, (1866) L.R. 2 C.P. 204; *Associated Oil Carriers, Ltd. v. Union Ins. Soc. of Canton, Ltd.*, [1917] 2 K.B. 184; *Idle v. Royal Exchange Assur. Co.*, (1819) 129 E.R. 577; *Rankin v. Potter*, (1873) L.R. 6 H.L. 83.

95. (1878) 48 L.J.Q.B. 9. See, generally, *Singer Mfg. Co. v. Western Assur. Co.*, (1896) 10 Que. S.C. 379 (C.A. Can.).

96. (1926) 25 Ll.L.Rep. 546.

. . . The object of that is twofold. First of all, to enable the underwriters to exercise as soon as they can the care over the goods which otherwise are under the control of the assured; secondly, to prevent the assured from continuing to have an option over the underwriters, so that he may say that the goods are or are not their property in accordance with the eventual state of the goods, and sometimes in accordance with the rise or fall of the market for such goods.

The cases are rather numerous supporting the proposition set forth in sub-section 1 that the assured must give notice of abandonment if he elects to abandon.[97]

As sub-section 2 notes, no particular form of notice is required. An agent having authority from his principal to abandon needs no express formal letter or power of attorney.[98] No particular form is necessary nor is it even necessary that it be in writing.[99] It is not even necessary that the word "abandon" be used so long as the intent to give notice of abandonment is clear, although as a matter of common sense it would clearly be desirable.[100] Conduct on the part of the assured may be the equivalent of required notice.[101]

In *Insurance Co. of North America v. Johnson*,[102] the assured tendered abandonment and offered to make any further conveyance or assurance of title to the abandoned vessel which might be required. Underwriters absolutely rejected the notice of abandonment. Such absolute rejection was held to amount to a waiver of the right to object to the form of the

---

97. *Kaltenbach v. MacKenzie*, (1878) 48 L.J.Q.B. 9; *Vacuum Oil Co. v. Union Insurance Society of Canton, Ltd.*, (1926) 25 Ll.L.Rep. 546; *Green v. Royal Exchange*, (1815) 128 E.R. 958; *Western Assur. Co. of Toronto v. Poole*, (1903) 1 K.B. 376; *Harkley v. Providence Ins. Co.*, (1868) 18 U.C.C.P. 335 (Can.); *Dickie v. Merchants' Ins. Co.*, (1883) 16 N.S.R. 244 (C.A. Can.); *Phoenix Inc. Co. v. McGhee*, (1890) 18 S.C.R. 61 (Can.); *Patch v. Pittman*, (1886) 19 N.S.R. 298 (Can.); *Morton v. Patillo*, (1872) 10 N.S.R. 17 (Can.); *Woodford v. Feehan*, (1866) 5 Nfld. L.R. 148 (Can.); *Klein v. Globe & Rutgers Fire Ins. Co. of New York (The Tornado)*, 2 F.2d 137 (3rd Cir.), 1925 AMC 197; *Insurance Co. of North America v. Canada Sugar Refining Co.*, 175 U.S. 609 (1900).

98. *Chesapeake Ins. Co. v. Stark*, 10 U.S. 268 (1810).

99. *Patapsco Ins. Co. v. Southgate*, 30 U.S. 604 (1831); *Bell v. Beveridge*, 4 U.S. 272 (1803); *Currie & Co. v. Bombay Native Ins. Co.*, (1869) L.R. 3 P.C. 72, 16 E.R. 740; *King v. Walker*, (1864) 159 E.R. 509, Ex.Ch.; *Baker v. Brown*, (1872) 9 N.S.R. 100 (Can.); *Anchor Marine Ins. Co. v. Keith*, (1884) 9 S.C.R. 483 (Can.).

100. *Currie & Co. v. Bombay Native Ins. Co.*, (1869) L.R. 3 P.C. 72; *Singer Mfg. Co. v. Western Assur. Co.*, (1896) 10 Que. S.C. 379 (C.A. Can.).

101. *Portland Flouring Mills Co. v. Portland & Asiatic S.S. Co.*, 158 Fed. 113 (D. Or. 1907). So, too, may be claiming for a constructive total loss. *G. Cohen Sons & Co. v. Standard Marine Ins. Co.*, (1925) 21 Ll.L.Rep. 30.

102. 70 F. 794 (6th Cir. 1895).

notice of abandonment. Clearly, however, the notice must be unmistakable and not equivocal,[103] and must be unconditional and absolute.[104]

In *Bell v. Beveridge*,[105] the assured wrote the underwriters a letter stating "he meant to abandon" for a loss; this was held to be sufficient notice. In *Copelin v. Phoenix Ins. Co.*,[106] the insured vessel sank, and the owner notified the underwriters that he had wired the master that, if he could not raise the vessel, he should wreck her. The underwriters replied "all right." This was held not to be a notice of abandonment. In *George W. Clyde*,[107] acts of the shipowner, after the ship was raised by the underwriters, in continuing in possession and attempting a sale, were held inconsistent with an intent to abandon.

Time When Notice Must be Given

Notice of abandonment must be given within a reasonable time after intelligence of the loss has been received, but where the information is of doubtful character, the assured is entitled to a reasonable time to make inquiry.[108] What is a reasonable time is a question of fact.[109]

When a loss is well authenticated or well known, abandonment should be at once given. But if it is not certainly known, or if the extent of damage is not known, abandonment may be deferred to enable the assured to determine whether or not the circumstances are such as to entitle him to abandon.[110] An offer to abandon, made as soon as the assured obtains the

---

103. *Patapsco Ins. Co. v. Southgate*, 30 U.S. 604 (1831); *Copelin v. Phoenix Ins. Co.*, 76 U.S. 461; *Parmeter v. Hunter*, (1808) 1 Camp. 541, N.P.; *Barss v. Merchants' Marine Ins. Co.*, (1887) 26 N.B.R. 339, *aff'd*. 15 S.C.R. 185.

104. *Vacuum Oil Co. v. Union Ins. Society of Canton, Ltd.*, (1926) 25 Ll.L.Rep. 546; *Russian Bank for Foreign Trade v. Excess Ins. Co.*, (1919) 1 K.B. 39, C.A. In the latter case, the insured attempted to bargain with the underwriters, notifying them that he was agreeable to releasing them for all risks if they would pay the difference between the present value in the port of distress and the insured value. As the notice was not unconditional, it was held to be defective.

105. 4 U.S. 272 (1803).

106. 76 U.S. 461 (1868).

107. 12 F.2d 733 (7th Cir.), 1926 AMC 807.

108. Sec. 62(3) of the Act; *Chesapeake Ins. Co. v. Stark*, 10 U.S. 268 (1810); *Hurtin v. Phoenix Ins. Co.*, F.Cas. 6,941 (3rd Cir. 1806); *Currie & Co. v. Bombay Native Ins. Co.*, (1869) L.R. 3 P.C. 72, 16 E.R. 740; *Kaltenbach v. MacKenzie*, (1878) 48 L.J.Q.B. 9; *Corr v. Standard Fire & Marine Ins. Co. of New Zealand*, (1881) 7 V.L.R. 504 (Aus.).

109. Sec. 88, Marine Insurance Act, 1906; *Bell v. Beveridge*, 4 U.S. 272 (1803); *Currie & Co. v. Bombay Native Ins. Co.*, (1869) L.R. 3 P.C. 72, 16 E.R. 740.

110. *Duncan v. Koch*, F.Cas. 4,126 (3rd Cir. 1801); *Northern Barge v. Royal Insurance*, 492 F.2d 1248 (8th Cir.), 1974 AMC 136; *Currie & Co. v. Bombay Native Ins. Co.*, (1869) L.R. 3 P.C. 72, 16 E.R. 740; *Gernon v. Royal Exchange*, (1815) 128 E.R. 1083. In the United States, it has been held that it is the duty of the assured, on his vessel sinking, to make adequate investigation of the cause and the cost of raising and repairing before tendering abandonment. *George W. Clyde*, 12 F.2d 733 (7th Cir.), 1926 AMC 807.

preliminary proofs of loss, is not too late.[111] The right to abandon may be kept in suspense by agreement of the parties.[112] Where a delay in giving notice of abandonment does not prejudice the underwriter, the delay does not impair or affect the rights of the assured.[113]

The intent of the assured to suspend his option to abandon with a view toward later availing himself of some favorable contingency, should it happen, must be proved clearly and with certainty and is not to be inferred from slight circumstances or from the possibility that such would naturally be his motives.[114]

In *De Farconnet v. Western Ins. Co.*,[115] the assured wrote to the insurer inquiring "whether we must make an abandonment by judicial act, or if our present letter expressing an intent to abandon, will do?" The assurer's answer, ignoring the formal tender and denying any liability under the policy, was held to excuse a delay in making a tender.

What is a "reasonable time" in which to give notice of abandonment depends upon the facts of each case and the circumstances involved.[116]

Underwriter under No Obligation to Accept Abandonment

Sub-section 4 of Section 62 makes it perfectly clear that the underwriter is under no obligation to accept the abandonment. If the tender is properly given, but rejected by underwriters, the rights of the assured are not prejudiced.[117] In declining the notice, underwriters make it plain that they are not exercising any rights of ownership in the vessel. It is always possible, of course, that liabilities attaching to the wreck might be greater than the value of the wreck itself. The wreck, if the notice is declined, thus remains the property of the assured even though the underwriters may subsequently make payment for a constructive total loss under the policy.

111. *Gardner v. Columbia Ins. Co.*, F.Cas. 5,225 (C.A. D.C. 1825).
112. *Livingston v. Maryland Ins. Co.*, 10 U.S. 274 (1810).
113. *Young v. Union Ins. Co.*, 23 F. 279 (D. Ill. 1885).
114. *Duncan v. Koch*, F.Cas. 4,126 (3rd Cir. 1801).
115. 122 F.448 (2d Cir. 1901).
116. The following cases, in which it was held that notice was given too late, will serve as examples. Note the disparity in time. *Kelly v. Walton*, (1808) 2 Camp. 155, N.P. (four months); *Anderson v. Royal Exchange Assur. Co.*, (1805) 103 E.R. 16 (twenty-one days); *Barker v. Blakes*, (1808) 103 E.R. 581; *Aldridge v. Bell*, (1816) 1 Stark 498, N.P. (sixteen days); *Fleming v. Smith*, (1848) 1 H.L. Cas. 513, 9 E.R. 859, H.L. (six months); *Hunt v. Royal Exchange*, (1816) 105 E.R. 968; *Potter v. Campbell*, (1867) 17 L.T. 474 (nine months delay in an intermediate port before notice was given); *Kaltenbach v. MacKenzie*, (1878) 48 L.J.Q.B. 9 (thirty-one days); *Independent Transp. Co. v. Canton Ins. Office*, 173 F. 564 (D. Wash. 1909) (four months after sinking and two months after raising, cleaning, and in condition for survey).
117. *Linea Sud-Americana, Inc. v. 7295.4 Tons of Linseed*, 108 F.2d 755 (2d Cir.), 1940 AMC 476.

An abandonment, once properly made, continues notwithstanding refusal by the underwriters to accept it.[118] But the assured may withdraw the notice before it is accepted.[119]

What Is an Acceptance of Abandonment by Underwriters?

Sub-section 5 of Section 62 covers two instances in which an acceptance may be shown. The first is, of course, an express acceptance by the underwriter; the second is where acceptance can be implied from the conduct of the underwriters. However, mere silence on the part of the underwriter after notice is given is not an acceptance.

What amounts to an acceptance by underwriters is a question of fact.[120] Consequently, the cases which have been decided on this point are difficult to harmonize unless the factual situations involved are explored and clearly understood. For example, in *Washburn & Moen Mfg. Co. v. Reliance Marine Ins. Co.*,[121] the Sue and Labor Clause provided that acts of the insurer in recovery, saving, and preserving the property would not be considered an acceptance of abandonment. After a casualty, the underwriters carried the goods from a place where there was no agent of the assured, no adequate means of protection and no market, to the port of destination where there were excellent facilities for protecting and handling them, easy access to the head agency of the assured, and a good market. This was held not to be an acceptance of abandonment. By contrast, in *Provincial Ins. Co. of Canada v. Leduc*,[122] although the assured was guilty of a breach of geographic warranty, underwriters nonetheless took possession of the ship by their agent, repaired her, and kept her in their possession for an unreasonable period of time without notifying the assured that they either accepted or rejected the abandonment. This was held to be a constructive acceptance.

In *Hume v. Frenz*,[123] the insurers of a stranded vessel sent an agent to take charge of the vessel under an agreement with the owners that the agent would represent all interests. By direction of the insurers, in which the owners refused to take part, the agent contracted to salve the vessel, and after her release she was temporarily repaired, loaded with a cargo,

---

118. *The Sarah Ann*, F.Cas. 12,342 (1st Cir. Mass. 1835); *Columbian Ins. Co. v. Catlett*, 25 U.S. 383 (1827).

119. *Pasquerias v. Secaderos de Bacalao de Espana, S.A. v. Beer*, (1946) 79 Ll.L.Rep. 423, *rev'd* on the facts (1949) 82 Ll.L.Rep. 501, H.L.

120. *Shepherd v. Henderson*, (1818) 7 App.Cas. 49, H.L.

121. 179 U.S. 1 (1900).

122. (1874) L.R. 6 P.C. 244, P.C. To the same effect, see *Copelin v. Phoenix Ins. Co.*, 76 U.S. 461 (1869); *Malgor, Gonzales & Co. v. Royal Ins. Co.*, 294 F. 63 (1st Cir. Puerto Rico 1923), 1924 AMC 123.

123. 150 F. 502 (9th Cir. 1907).

and taken into port. The owners refused to give any direction respecting her employment, and on her arrival in port refused to receive her or accept her freight, claiming that she had been abandoned to the insurers, which they at all times denied. The insurers afterwards had her permanently repaired and later permitted her to be sold for the cost of such repairs. This was some five months after the stranding. It was held that the insurers' action, in retaining possession for such a length of time without permanently repairing and then permitting her to be sold, under the circumstances amounted to a constructive acceptance of the abandonment whether or not the owners originally had a right to abandon.

In *American Merchant Marine Ins. Co. of New York v. Liberty Sand & Gravel Co.*,[124] the policy provided that the insured did not have the right to abandon. Nonetheless, after casualty, the insured tendered abandonment, which the insurer rejected. Thereafter, the insurer raised the vessel, put her on drydock, and had her formally surveyed. Then, without making any repairs and without notice to the insured, the insurer bored holes in her and plugged them, and thereafter floated her to the place from which she had been raised, removed the plugs, and sank her. It was held this was a constructive acceptance of abandonment, the court noting that the clause in the policy prohibiting abandonment related only to authorized acts of the insurer and not its unauthorized acts.

In *Soelberg v. Western Assur. Co.*,[125] the insurer refused to accept an abandonment. Its agent, however, cooperated with the master in making

---

124. 282 F. 514 (2d Cir. 1922).
125. 119 F. 23 (9th Cir. 1902). See, also, *Hudson v. Harrison*, (1822) 129 E.R. 1219 (assured gave notice of abandonment and called a meeting of underwriters which three of the underwriters attended and ordered the assured to do the best he could for all parties; two months later, some of the underwriters intervened, forbidding a sale of the damaged cargo which was about to take place, and rejecting abandonment; held, an acceptance of abandonment as rejection was not made within a reasonable time); *Captain J.A. Cates Tug & Wharfage Co., Ltd. v. Franklin Ins. Co.*, [1927] A.C. 698, 28 Ll.L.Rep. 161, P.C. (tug was sunk by collision and its owners at once gave notice of abandonment; salvors employed by the insurer raised the tug in a few days, and the abandonment was not accepted; without knowledge of the assured, the salvors verbally made an offer to the insurers to purchase the tug and the offer was put into writing but withdrawn three weeks later; the assured contended that the negotiations between the insurer and the salvors constituted an acceptance of abandonment; held, no acceptance could be implied from the conduct of the insurers); *Corr v. Standard Fire & Marine Ins. Co. of New Zealand*, (1881) 7 V.L.R. 504 (Aus.) (insurers refused to accept an abandonment but took possession of the vessel for the purpose of repairing and then restoring her to her owners; held, such taking was strong evidence of acceptance of abandonment); *MacLeod v. Ins. Co. of N.A.*, (1901) 34 N.S.R. 88 (Can.) (notice of abandonment given but rejected; by direction of an agent for the insurers, the cargo was taken out and stored and the vessel was repaired; held, what was done constituted an acceptance); *George W. Clyde*, 12 F.2d 733 (7th Cir.), 1926 AMC 807 (mere raising of a vessel held not an acceptance); *Dauntless*, 129 F.2d 582 (2d Cir.), 1943 AMC 1021 (efforts of underwriters to refloat the vessel and consideration of repairs for some three months did not amount to an acceptance of abandonment, there being a Sue and Labor Clause in the policies); *Wong v. Utah Home F.I. Co.*, 1960 AMC 649 (D. Haw.) (loss paid in full and underwriters assumed control of the vessel; held, acceptance of abandonment).

temporary repairs, moving the vessel to another port, and in procuring funds with which to pay the expense of removal on a bottomry bond executed by the master. It was held that such acts did not constitute an acceptance of abandonment.

Upon acceptance of abandonment, or judgment upholding the notice of abandonment, title to the abandoned subject matter relates back to the time of loss.[126]

Abandonment Accepted is Irrevocable

Sub-section 6 of Section 62 provides that, once accepted, an abandonment is irrevocable, and such acceptance conclusively admits liability for the loss and the sufficiency of the notice.[127]

However, insurance proceeds paid by reason of a mistake of fact can be recovered by underwriters, as acceptance of abandonment based on a material mistake of fact is nullity.[128]

Underwriter May Waive Notice of Abandonment

In accordance with customary contract principles, any party to a contract may waive a requirement or condition intended for his benefit. And so it is with respect to waiver of notice of abandonment.[129] Obviously, where the assured demands payment for a total loss and the insurer complies with the request, there is no necessity for a formal notice of abandonment, and the insurer is deemed to have waived such notice.[130] Also, a disclaimer of liability being totally incompatible with acceptance of a tender of abandonment, such disclaimer renders a tender of abandonment totally futile so that a tender is not required as a prerequisite to a claim for contructive total loss.[131]

Underwriter Reinsuring Need Not Give Notice

Sub-section 9 of Section 62 expressly follows the decision in *Uzielli v. Boston Marine Ins. Co.*[132]

---

126. *Cammell v. Sewell*, (1858) 157 E.R. 615; *Chesapeake Ins. Co. v. Stark*, (1810) 10 U.S. 268; *Dederer v. Delaware Ins. Co.*, F.Cas. 3,733 (3rd Cir. 1807); *The Manitoba*, 30 F. 129 (D. Mich. 1887).

127. *Peele v. Merchants' Ins. Co.*, F.Cas. 10,905 (1st Cir. 1822); *Bradlie v. Maryland Ins. Co.*, 37 U.S. 378 (1838); *Provincial Ins. Co. of Canada v. Leduc*, (1874) L.R. 6 P.C. 244, P.C.

128. *Norwich Union Fire Ins. Soc. Ltd. v. Price*, (1934) A.C. 455, 49 Ll.L.Rep. 55, P.C.

129. Sec. 62(8), Marine Insurance Act, 1906. *Houstman v. Thornton*, (1816) Holt, N.P. 242; *Rickards v. Forestal Land, Timber & Rys. Co.*, [1941] 3 All E.R. 62, H.L.

130. *Tashmoo*, 1937 AMC 1536 (Arb.); *Wong v. Utah Home Ins. Co.*, 1960 AMC 649 (D. Haw.); *Houstman v. Thornton*, (1816) Holt, N.P. 242.

131. *Rock Transport v. Hartford Fire*, 433 F.2d 152 (2d Cir.), 1970 AMC 2185.

132. (1884) 15 Q.B.D. 11, 5 Asp. M.L.C. 405, C.A. But, see *British Dominions Gen. Ins. Co., Ltd. v. Duder*, [1915] 2 K.B. 394, C.A., criticizing *Uzielli*.

Effect of Abandonment

Section 63 accurately sets forth the common law with respect to the *effect* of abandonment. It reads:

(1) Where there is a valid abandonment, the insurer is entitled to take over the interest of the assured in whatever may remain of the subject-matter insured, and all proprietary rights incidental thereto.[133]

(2) Upon the abandonment of a ship the insurer thereof is entitled to any freight in course of being earned, and which is earned by her subsequent to the casualty causing the loss, less the expenses of earning it incurred after the casualty; and where the ship is carrying the owner's goods the insurer is entitled to a reasonable remuneration for the carriage of them subsequent to the casualty causing the loss.[134]

Millar v. Woodfall[135] clearly demonstrates the division of freight between the insured and insurer on the basis that the former takes the freight up to the time of casualty and the latter takes the freight after the casualty. In that case, the shipowner insured his vessel and his goods being carried therein by separate insurances. Enroute to destination, the vessel stranded and the owner abandoned. After abandonment, at his own expense, the assured-owner had a portion of the goods taken by lighter to port of destination and, at his own expense, procured assistance by which the ship, with the remainder of the goods on board, was brought to port of destination. Afterwards, the underwriters accepted abandon-

---

133. See *Continental Ins. Co. v. Clayton Hardtop Skiff*, 367 F.2d 230 (3rd Cir. 1966); *Chesapeake Ins. Co. v. Stark*, 10 U.S. 268 (1810); *Patapsco Ins. Co. v. Southgate*, 30 U.S. 604 (1831); *Mason v. Marine Ins. Co.*, 110 F. 452 (6th Cir. 1901); *The Falcon*, 86 U.S. 75 (1873); *The Ann C. Pratt*, F.Cas. 409, *aff'd* 59 U.S. 63 (1855); *Hurtin v. Phoenix Ins. Co.*, F.Cas. 6,941 (1806); *Symonds v. Union Ins. Co.*, 4 U.S. 417 (1806); *The Manitoba*, 30 F. 129 (D. Mich. 1887); *Cargo of the George*, F.Cas. 9,981 (D. N.Y. 1845); *Stewart v. Greenock Ins. Co.*, (1848) 2 H.L. Cas. 159, 9 E.R. 1052, and cases cited *infra* with respect to sub-section 2.

134. *Sea Ins. Co. v. Hadden*, (1884) 13 Q.B.D. 706, C.A.; *Coolidge v. Gloucester Mar. Ins. Co.*, 15 Mass. 341 (1819); *Schieffelin v. New York Ins. Co.*, 9 Johns. 21 (N.Y. 1812); *Leavenworth v. Delafield*, 1 Caines 573 (N.Y. 1804); *Rogers v. Hosack's Executors*, 18 Wend. 319 (N.Y. 1837); *Republic of China v. National Union F.I. Co.*, 163 F.Supp. 812, 1958 AMC 1529, (4th Cir.); *Alexander Maitland*, 44 F.2d 759 (6th Cir.), 1931 AMC 315; *Linea Sud-Americana v. 2,295.40 Tons of Linseed*, 108 F.2d 755 (2d Cir. 1939); *Continental Ins. Co. v. Clayton Hardtop Skiff*, 239 F.Supp. 815 (D. N.J. 1965); *Leathem v. Terry*, (1803) 127 E.R. 260; *Thompson v. Rowcroft*, (1803) 102 E.R. 742; *Sharp v. Gladstone*, (1805) 10 E.R. 10 (discussing the expenses to be apportioned between owner and underwriter); *Barclay v. Stirling*, (1816) 105 E.R. 954; *Davison v. Case*, (1820) 129 E.R. 1013 Ex.Ch.; *London Assur. Corp. v. Williams*, (1893) 9 T.L.R. 257, C.A.; *Barss v. Merchants' Marine Ins. Co.*, (1887) 26 N.B.R. 339, *aff'd*. 15 S.C.R. 185 (Can.).

135. (1857) 120 E.R. 184.

ment. On the assured claiming for the loss of the ship, the underwriters claimed credit for all the freight. The insurers were denied credit for the freight as far as the intermediate port where the owner had abandoned, but were allowed credit for the freight from the intermediate port to port of final destination, to be estimated at the current rate of freight as if brought by another ship from the intermediate port to the port of final destination.

As noted, the transfer of rights and liabilities from the assured to the assurer upon abandonment is retrospective to the date of the casualty,[136] the notice of abandonment being "validated" when it is established that, in fact, the vessel is a constructive total loss. Consequently, as a practical matter, the validity of a notice of abandonment remains in limbo so long as the underwriters are not convinced of the correctness of the figures submitted on behalf of the assured. The notice becomes operative only when the underwriters accept that the vessel is a constructive total loss. Thus, expenses incurred during this interim period of time should logically be for the underwriters' account, and this is the result which has been reached by the courts.

However, no presumption of invalidity of the notice of abandonment is created simply because underwriters decline to accept it. This was the holding in *Suart v. Merchants' Marine*.[137] In that case, the insured vessel sank and was a constructive total loss. Although notice of abandonment was given, underwriters declined to accept it. The vessel owner and the underwriters then agreed, without prejudice to their rights, to take joint action to salve the property. A tug was employed under this agreement to tow the vessel to safety, but enroute, because of the negligence of the tug's crew, another ship came into collision with the insured vessel, and both vessels sustained damage. The court held that since the underwriters were the only persons having any interest in the wreck, they were liable to pay four-fourths of the damage done, rather than three-fourths—which would have been the extent of their liability under the Running Down Clause in the policy. The court said in part:

> The truth is that the whole work was being done on terms, as between shipowners and underwriters, that it should be on account of whom it might turn out to concern, and subsequent events, viz. the subsequent ascertainment of the fact that at the time in question the vessel was a total loss, have shown that the only persons concerned were the underwriters. This, I think, is conclusive of the case and fixes the liability on the defendants [underwriters].

---

136. *Robertson v. Petros M. Nomikos*, (1931) 64 Ll.L.Rep. 45.
137. (1898) 3 Com.Cas. 312.

It would appear that, prior to the enactment of the Marine Insurance Act, once the notice of abandonment was validated the property in the subject-matter insured passed automatically to the underwriters.[138] However, Section 63 now makes it very clear that the insurer is *entitled* to take over the interest of the assured. The Act does not say that the insurer is *required* to take over that interest. Though the cases are somewhat conflicting,[139] the better view appears to be that the validation of the notice of abandonment no longer automatically passes title to the underwriters, but when the subject-matter insured is shown to be a constructive total loss in fact, or the underwriters agree to pay as for a constructive total loss, underwriters are entitled to exercise rights of ownership and, if they do so, will be deemed to have accepted the obligations which go with ownership.

This appears to be the position taken in the London market and in the United States. Customarily, the underwriters will indicate when negotiations are underway for a constructive total loss whether they or the assured will retain the wreck and the concomitant rights and obligations attaching. In some instances, underwriters will deliberately refrain from indicating a position, probably with the thought of waiting until it is clear whether the potential liabilities attaching to the wreck will exceed the likely proceeds. This is not only unfair but probably unlawful in that the underwriters, if they wish to decline the rights to which they are otherwise entitled, must advise the assured within a reasonable time.

However, as noted above, if underwriters purport to exercise an ownership interest and so conduct themselves as to take a position inconsistent with ownership still being in the shipowner, they may be held estopped to disown the wreck with all its attendant obligations.[140]

What Claims Fall upon Underwriters as a Consequence of Settling for a Constructive Total Loss

Assuming an acceptance of the notice of abandonment and the exercise of proprietary rights by underwriters, for what claims are underwriters liable?

Clearly, any claim arising out of or subsequent to a casualty giving rise to a constructive total loss, and for which a maritime lien is given against

138. *Simpson v. Thomson*, (1877) 3 App.Cas. 279, H.L.

139. Compare *A.V.G. Helvetia v. Administrator of German Property*, (1931) 1 K.B. 672, with *Court Line v. The King*, (1945) 78 Ll.L.Rep. 390. See, also, *The Republic of China, China Merchants Steam Navigation Co. Ltd. and the U.S. v. National Union Fire Ins. Co.*, 1958 AMC 1529. Cf. *Gilchrist v. Chicago Ins. Co.*, 104 F. 566 (1889), and *Rhinelander v. Ins. Co.*, 8 U.S. 29 (1807).

140. *Provincial Ins. Co. of Canada v. Leduc*, (1874) L.R. 6 P.C. 244, P.C.; *Copelin v. Phoenix Ins. Co.*, 76 U.S. 461 (1869); *Malgor, Gonzales & Co. v. Royal Ins. Co.*, 294 F. 63 (1st Cir. Puerto

the vessel, would attach to the vessel itself and thus be transferred to the underwriters as ownership obligations.[141] Thus, in the United States, any claim arising under the Federal Maritime Lien Act of 1920 would attach to the vessel. These include repairs, supplies, towage, use of drydocks or marine railways or other necessaries. In addition, maritime liens arising by general maritime law would also be cognizable, such as general average, salvage, wages of crew (for the period subsequent to the casualty until paid off or repatriated), and maritime torts such as collision, loss of life, or personal injury.

Furthermore, to the extent to which the shipowner has incurred them as a consequence of the casualty or as a part of the cost and expense of safeguarding the vessel pending underwriters' acceptance of notice of abandonment, all such expenses reasonably incurred to date would be for underwriters' account. These include, but would not be limited to, such items as general average expenditures, watchmen, port charges, mooring charges, temporary repairs if the vessel is wrecked, lighting and marking charges, and insurance premiums on hull after the expiration of the policies in force at the time of the casualty.

Obviously, the two classes of expenditure overlap each other and it would be difficult to make a definite distinction between them.

Moreover, expenses incurred by the assured to prove his claim can also be recovered to the extent that they were reasonably incurred and were necessary.[142]

By a parity of reasoning (where underwriters are entitled by exercising proprietary rights to the proceeds of the wreck), any expenses reasonably incurred to realize those proceeds will be payable by them; i.e., such expenses would be debited against any credits realized from the sale of the wreck, but only from the date of the casualty.

Interplay of Sue and Labor Clause

It is universal maritime law that an assured is duty bound, when any casualty occurs which triggers an abandonment, to exert himself to the utmost to avert or minimize the loss. In doing so, the assured is considered to be

---

Rico 1923), 1924 AMC 123; *Hudson v. Harrison,* (1822) 129 E.R. 1219; *Corr v. Standard Fire & Marine Ins. Co. of New Zealand,* (1881) 7 V.L.R. 504 (Aus.); *McLeod v. Ins. Co. of N.A.,* (1901) 34 N.S.R. 88 (Can.); *Wong v. Utah Home F.I. Co.,* 1960 AMC 649 (Haw.); *Hume v. Frenz,* 150 F. 502 (9th Cir. 1907); *American Merchant Marine Ins. Co. of New York v. Liberty Sand & Gravel Co.,* 282 F. 514 (2d Cir. 1922).

141. *Sharp v. Gladstone,* (1805) 103 E.R. 10; *Barclay v. Stirling,* (1816) 105 E.R. 954; *Gilchrist v. Chicago Ins. Co.,* 104 F. 566 (1889).

142. *Northern Barge v. Royal Insurance,* 492 F.2d 1248 (8th Cir.), 1974 AMC 136; *Parkhill-Goodloe v. Home Ins. Co.,* 1976 AMC 951 (M.D. Fla.).

the agent of the underwriters and the efforts made by him to carry out this duty do not prejudice his right to insist upon an abandonment. This duty is memorialized in the customary marine policy by the Sue and Labor Clause.[143] While the Sue and Labor Clause recites that "it shall be *lawful* to the assured . . . to sue, labor and travel . . . ," it is well settled that this is a *duty* to be exercised by the assured rather than an option which he may decline.[144] And so, Section 78(4) of the Marine Insurance Act provides:

> It is the duty of the assured and his agents, in all cases, to take such measures as may be reasonable for the purpose of averting or minimizing a loss.

Moreover, Section 78(1) clearly makes the coverage afforded by the Sue and Labor Clause supplementary to the principal coverage under the perils clause. That sub-section reads:

> Where the policy contains a suing and labouring clause, the engagement thereby entered into is deemed to be supplementary to the contract of insurance, and the assured may recover from the insurer any expenses properly incurred pursuant to the clause, notwithstanding that the insurer may have paid for a total loss, or that the subject-matter may have been warranted free from particular average, either wholly or under a certain percentage.

Keeping these principles in mind, logic dictates that the Sue and Labor Clause, as a supplementary contract, applies with respect to expenses incurred both before and after abandonment. In incurring those expenses, the master or owner is considered as having acted in good faith as the agent of the underwriter, and, with respect to expenses incurred *after* notice of abandonment (but before acceptance by underwriters), such expenses were incurred as a result of the underwriter's refusal to accept abandonment on notice being given.[145] In this connection, it must be re-

143. The Sue and Labor Clause is treated in depth in Chapter XVIII.

144. *Republic of China v. National Union Fire Ins. Co.*, 151 F.Supp. 211 (D. Md.), 1957 AMC 915, *modified* 254 F.2d 177 (4th Cir.), 1958 AMC 751.

145. Expenses incurred *prior* to notice of abandonment may well fall into a different category, depending upon policy language. Thus, the AIH (1977) form expressly provides that in ascertaining whether or not a constructive total loss has occurred, expenses incurred prior to abandonment shall not be considered if such are to be claimed separately under the Sue and Labor Clause. But, it is submitted, this applies only with respect to *ascertainment* of a constructive total loss; i.e., whether the expense of recovering and repairing the vessel exceeds the agreed value in the policy and does not relieve the underwriter of the obligation of reimbursing the assured for such prior expenses if, in fact, the master or owner acted in good faith and the expenses were reasonably and necessarily incurred. It should be emphasized, however, that the expenses must fall within the strict terms of the Sue and Labor Clause, and general average losses and salvage charges, as defined by the Marine Insurance Act, are not recoverable under the suing and laboring clause. Sec. 78(2). Since "salvage

membered that the Sue and Labor Clause is followed by the "waiver" clause reading:

And it is especially declared and agreed that no acts of the insurer or insured in recovering, saving, or preserving this property insured shall be considered as a waiver, or acceptance of abandonment.

The waiver clause would be rendered meaningless if the Sue and Labor Clause did not apply both before and after abandonment.

The basic purpose of the Sue and Labor Clause being to encourage the assured to take all reasonable steps to reduce the loss falling upon the underwriters, it is only logical that the clause should apply to expenses incurred after as well as before abandonment, regardless of whether or not the prior expenses were utilized to prove a constructive total loss.

It should also be observed that an underwriter who incurs expenses in saving or preserving the property at risk cannot offset under the suing and laboring clause those expenses against sums otherwise due the assured under the policy.[146]

Removal of Wreck

This is a most troublesome question and one which, in the United States (at least at this writing) has not been wholly resolved.

In considering constructive total losses, it becomes immediately apparent that in many instances the "constructive" total loss under consideration is a vessel which has been wrecked. The vessel having been wrecked, who bears the expenses of its removal? If the assured has given notice of abandonment to his underwriters, and those underwriters have either declined to accept the abandonment or have remained silent, upon whom does the duty lie to remove the wreck or so mark it as to avoid liabilities to third parties whose vessels may run upon it?

It is always possible, of course, that liabilities attaching to the wreck might be greater than the value of the wreck itself. Naturally, underwriters are reluctant to accept a notice of abandonment where the ultimate resolution of the question of whether or not there was a constructive total loss may not be known for some time.[147] This is so notwithstanding

---

charges" are defined by Sec. 65(2) as those charges recoverable under maritime law by a salvor *independently of contract*, salvage charges incurred when an independent salvor acts to save the vessel would not be recoverable under the suing and laboring clause, and in the case of a wrecked vessel would be a charge on the proceeds of the sale of the wreck. See *Aitchison v. Lohre*, (1879) 4 A.C. 755; *Dixon v. Whitworth*, (1880) 49 L.J.Q.B. 408; *Australian Coastal Shipping Commission v. Green*, (1971) 1 All E.R. 353, C.A.

146. *Grouan v. Stanier*, (1904) 1 K.B. 87. Compare *Commonwealth Ins. Co. v. Chase*, 20 Pick. (Mass.) 142, where the converse was held. Phillips (Sec. 1559) concluded that this doctrine was limited to Massachusetts and was unsound; that he was correct cannot be doubted.

147. If a tender of abandonment is properly given, but rejected by underwriters, the

that an abandonment, properly made, continues notwithstanding a refusal by underwriters to accept it.[148] The fact that the assured may withdraw the notice of abandonment before an acceptance by underwriters[149] does not simplify the problem.

Acceptance of a notice of abandonment by underwriters in the United States became vastly complicated following *Wyandotte Transportation Co. v. U.S.*[150] That decision actually involved two consolidated cases. In one, two barges were discovered missing. Although one barge was located, the owners reported them both sunk and then abandoned them to the United States under Title 33, U.S.C.A. In the other case, a barge loaded with liquid chlorine sank in the Mississippi River. Efforts to locate it being unsuccessful, the owner abandoned it to the United States. Some months later, the barge was discovered and the United States (at great expense because of the danger of releasing chlorine gas upon surrounding communities) succeeded in raising the barge and later sold the liquid chlorine aboard it, retaining the proceeds of the sale.

The Supreme Court held that the right given to the United States to remove the obstruction was not its only remedy and that the barge could be removed *at the owner's cost.* It is quite clear that, if a vessel is sunk through negligence, the negligent party may be compelled to remove it. Among other comments by the Court were the following:

> . . . There is no indication anywhere—in the legislative history of the Act, in the predecessor statutes, or in nonstatutory law—that Congress might have intended that a party who *negligently* sinks a vessel should be shielded from personal responsibility . . . . Applying the principles of our decision in *Republic Steel,* we conclude that other remedies, including those sought here, are available to the Government. [Emphasis supplied]

In short order, other courts began finding privity and knowledge based upon a breach of the statutory duty to remove, thus denying limitation of liability.[151] In *Chinese Maritime Trust, Ltd.,* a shipowner was denied limitation for costs assessed against it under a Panama Canal regulation providing that the canal authorities could clear a wreck from the canal at the expense of a shipowner whether or not the vessel was sunk negli-

---

rights of the assured are not thereby prejudiced. *Linea Sud-Americana, Inc. v. 7295.4 Tons of Linseed,* 108 F.2d 755 (2d Cir.), 1940 AMC 476.

148. *The Sarah Ann,* F.Cas. 12,343 (C.A. Mass. 1835); *Columbian Ins. Co. v. Catlett,* 25 U.S. 383 (1827).

149. *Pesquerias v. Sacaderos de Bacalao de Espana, S.A. v. Beer,* (1946) 79 Ll.L.Rep. 423, *rev'd* on the facts, (1949) 82 Ll.L.Rep. 501, H.L.

150. 389 U.S. 191, 1967 AMC 2553.

151. *In re Pacific Far East Line, Inc. (The Guam Bear),* 472 F.2d 1382 (9th Cir.), 1970 AMC 1592; *In re Chinese Maritime Trust, Ltd.,* 478 F.2d 1357 (2d Cir.), 1973 AMC 1110.

gently. The court, referring to the "renewed vigor" of the Rivers and Harbors Act, held that the obligation came within the privity and knowledge of the shipowner once it became aware that its vessel was obstructing navigation in the canal.[152] Nor does the Limitation of Liability Act apply to claims for damage to governmental works.[153]

The latest development in this disturbing scene is *University of Texas Medical Branch v. U.S.*,[154] in which the owner of a small research vessel sought to limit its liability for its vessel having sunk a government dredge which was later removed at government expense. The court of appeal ruled that the owner of the research vessel could not limit liability against governmental claims under the Wreck Act. The case was not decided upon the theory of an owner's knowledge of a duty to remove a wreck, as was the case in *Chinese Trust, Ltd.*, because the owner of the research vessel was not the owner of the wrecked dredge; rather, it was decided on the theory that to require the "innocent party" (the United States) to remove the wreck would conflict with the objectives *Wyandotte* sought to realize; i.e., to prevent a negligent party from shifting responsibility for the consequences of his own negligence.

Wyandotte and its progeny immediately raised, of course, the question of which policies have to respond in instances where vessels are sunk and must be removed as an obstruction. The Running Down Clause in the standard AIH policy prior to *Wyandotte* expressly excluded sums the assured might become liable to pay or did pay with respect to removal of obstructions "under statutory powers." Likewise, P & I policies routinely excluded any liabilities which would be covered by full insurance under standard forms of policies on hulls, machinery, etc. From the language in *Wyandotte*, it was not clear whether the court based its decision upon statutory powers or the common law. Consequently, the American Hull Insurance Syndicate amended the language in the Running Down Clause to add after "statutory powers" the words "or otherwise pursuant to law," and this new language has been carried forward in the new AIH (June, 1977) form. But, customary forms of P & I insurance do cover liability for costs or expenses of, or incidental to, removal of wrecks when such removal is compulsory by law.

Further compounding the problem is the fact that the Wreck Statute (33 U.S.C.A. 408-15) imposes upon an owner a personal non-delegable duty to mark the wreck. Thus, failure to mark is a breach of that personal

---

152. Compare *U.S. v. Raven*, 500 F.2d 728 (5th Cir. 1974), where the court suggested that limitation protects the owners against the consequences of a non-privity occurrence, one of which may be statutory obligations.

153. *U.S. v. Ohio Valley Co.*, 510 F.2d 1184 (7th Cir.), 1974 AMC 1477; *Hines v. U.S.*, 551 F.2d 717 (6th Cir.), 1977 AMC 380; *U.S. v. Federal Barge Lines*, 573 F.2d 993 (8th Cir.), 1978 AMC 2308.

154. 557 F.2d 438 (5th Cir.), 1977 AMC 2607.

duty, and liability arising therefrom (as by a vessel striking the sunken wreck) is not subject to limitation of liability.[155] This liability continues indefinitely, and the mere fact that the government assumes the obligation to mark the wreck does not relieve a negligent owner from the responsibility of removing the wreck.[156] Moreover, the owner's duty to locate and mark a wreck arises whether the vessel is sunk carelessly, voluntarily, or accidentally. Consequently, the government may recover from the owner the costs of locating a wreck not marked by reason of the violence of a hurricane.[157]

Wyandotte and its progeny seemingly are limited to vessels which are sunk intentionally or because of negligence. Consequently, if no negligence is involved, the non-negligent owner would appear to have no *in personam* liability for wreck removal expenses,[158] and such an innocent owner who removes his own wreck may have a right of recoupment over against others responsible for causing the wreck.[159] However, the real difficulty lies in the ease with which an owner may be found negligent. Thus, the owner's negligence can be inferred from an unexplained sinking,[160] or found to be proved under the doctrine of *res ipsa loquitur.*[161]

More alarmingly, the liability of a negligent vessel owner may not be limited to the expense of wreck removal but may be expanded to include the cost of hiring a tug to escort other vessels safely around the wreck,[162] and if the wreck causes damage to a government structure, strict liability is imposed without regard to fault.[163] Such strict liability may also result if the wreck impairs the *usefulness* of any government structure under 33 U.S.C.A. 408.[164]

In light of the foregoing, it is imperative that a non-negligent vessel owner whose vessel sinks mark it immediately and, thereafter, give prompt notification of the abandonment to the Corps of Engineers. Such a formal abandonment, assuming no negligence on the part of the owner,

---

155. *The Snug Harbor,* 53 F.2d 407, 1931 AMC 1487, *aff'd.* 59 F.2d 984 (2d Cir.), 1932 AMC 964.

156. *Humble Oil & Refining Co. v. Tug Crochet, et al,* 422 F.2d 602 (5th Cir.), 1972 AMC 1843.

157. *In re Marine Leasing Services, Inc.,* 328 F.Supp. 589 (E.D. La.), 1971 AMC 1329.

158. *United States v. Osage Co., Inc.,* 414 F.Supp. 1097 (Pa. 1976); *U.S. v. Federal Barge Lines,* 573 F.2d 993 (8th Cir.), 1978 AMC 2308.

159. *Western Transportation Co. v. Pac-Mar Services, Inc.,* 547 F.2d 97 (9th Cir. 1976).

160. *U.S. v. Osage Co., Inc.,* 414 F.Supp. 1097 (Pa. 1976); *U.S. v. Federal Barge Lines,* 573 F.2d 993 (8th Cir.), 1978 AMC 2308.

161. *United States v. Chesapeake & Delaware Shipyard, Inc.,* 369 F.Supp. 714 (D. Md.), 1974 AMC 511.

162. *United States v. Ohio Barge Lines,* 432 F.Supp. 1023 (W.D. Pa.), 1977 AMC 1200.

163. *Hines, Inc. v. United States,* 1977 AMC 380, amended on rehearing, 551 F.2d 717 (6th Cir.), 1977 AMC 1035.

164. *U.S. v. Federal Barge Lines,* 573 F.2d 993 (8th Cir.), 1978 AMC 2308.

terminates the obligation of maintaining the marking of the wreck and any liability of the innocent owner for another vessel subsequently colliding with the wreck. The owner should concurrently notify his hull and P & I underwriters, as the possibility always exists that negligence may later be inferred.

A negligent owner is in a more precarious position. Not only should his hull and P & I underwriters be immediately notified of the casualty, he should also (in conjunction with his underwriters covering wreck removal) make suitable arrangements with the Corps of Engineers or privately for the immediate marking of the wreck and eventual removal. As noted, assumption by the government of the obligation of marking and maintaining buoys at the site of the wreck does not relieve a negligent owner of the responsibility for removing the wreck.[165]

From the foregoing discussion, it can readily be seen why hull underwriters routinely decline abandonment in constructive total loss cases and refrain from taking any affirmative steps to exercise rights of ownership. The potential liabilities attaching to the vessel, generally speaking, greatly outweigh any potential value remaining in the wreck. Moreover, if any net proceeds do result from the sale of the wreck, underwriters may always avail themselves of the right to accept the proceeds, unless they have unequivocally declined to exercise rights of ownership, in which case any net proceeds resulting from a subsequent sale of the wreck would accrue to the vessel owner. Thus, the owner can abandon and be paid as for a constructive total loss and still retain rights of ownership because underwriters declined the abandonment.

In instances where the value of the wreck exceeds the removal costs, the costs of such removal may be categorized as general average, special charges, or sue and labor. The category assigned depends upon the intention of those responsible for raising and removing the vessel. This is true whether or not it is known at the time of the salvage operation if the costs will exceed the salved value. This point is well illustrated in *Seaboard Shipping Corp. v. Jocharanne Tugboat Corp. v. Sibring et al.*[166] In that case, the cost of refloating a leaking barge of gasoline materially exceeded the salved value, the barge being a constructive total loss. The work of overseeing the salvage efforts was placed in the hands of a surveyor who, in deposition, testified that he thought he was representing all the underwriters (hull, P & I, and cargo legal liability). The court held that the assured, in suing and laboring, was doing so on behalf of all the underwriters; on behalf of the hull underwriters in seeking to protect the hull of the vessel, on behalf of the P & I underwriters in seeking to prevent an explosion of

---

165. *Humble Oil Refining Co. v. Tug Crochet, et al,* 422 F.2d 602 (5th Cir.), 1972 AMC 1843.
166. 461 F.2d 500 (2d Cir.), 1972 AMC 2151. Compare, however, *Progress Marine Inc. v. Foremost Ins. Co.,* 642 F.2d 614 (5th Cir.), 1981 AMC 2315.

the leaking gasoline, and on behalf of the cargo legal liability underwriters in seeking to save as much of the cargo as possible. Indeed, some of the cargo was removed and delivered to the consignee.

The hull underwriter, having paid the salvage charges (as well as the entire hull proceeds as a constructive total loss) sued to recover the charges from the P & I underwriters and the cargo legal liability underwriters. The trial court, in essence, granted judgment for a portion of the salvage charges against the two defendant underwriters, each to bear a third.

On appeal by P & I underwriters, the court of appeal reversed, stating in part:

> . . . There was no compulsory removal of the *Val 51*. Lloyd's and Jocharanne, far from abandoning their interest in the vessel, had it towed to New York in the vain hope of salvaging the hull. No governmental order was necessary to spur the removal and the costs of the operation were therefore not chargeable to Oceanus as removal costs under its policy.
>
> The other possibility is that the benefit the lower court found Oceanus had received from the sue and labor efforts was the avoidance of explosion and potential liability for injury to persons and damage to docks or piers as well as for wreck removal. Oceanus admits that had such a disaster occurred, it might have been liable for substantial amounts, but claims that any calculation based on that possibility is extremely hypothetical and insists that the terms of its policy preclude holding it for any part of the expenses even if they tended to lessen the chance of explosion. Although we appreciate the motives of the district court in apportioning costs, we are constrained to conclude that Oceanus is correct.
>
> First we note that despite Lloyd's rhetoric, none of the expenses was incurred solely to avert those occurrences or protect those interests for which Oceanus alone was liable. All the costs were essential to any attempt to save the hull and cargo, so any benefit to Oceanus was in a sense incidental. More important, Clause 2 of the Oceanus policy excepts from coverage "claims for any loss, damage, liability or expense which would be payable under the present standard form of policy of the American Marine Insurance Syndicate on hull and machinery [identical in all essential respects to the Lloyd's policy] . . . and sufficient in amount to pay such loss, damage, liability or expense in full." As sue and labor expenses are covered by hull policies, they normally would not be recovered from the P & I policy underwriter . . . .

In addition, the appeals court held that the Oceanus policy also excluded any liability where "other insurance" also covered and that the policy expressly provided that there would be no contribution by the P & I association on the basis of double insurance or otherwise.

Rights of the Underwriters after Payment of a Constructive Total Loss

Assuming, however, that the underwriters either accept the notice of abandonment without reservations, or by their conduct are deemed to have done so, what rights do they have? Here, a clear distinction must be made between rights the underwriters might have under principles of subrogation and rights which they have after having paid as for a constructive total loss. In the former, the underwriter is limited in his recovery to what he has paid; in the latter, he may be entitled to more than he has paid if the value of the subject matter, or rights inhering in it, prove to be more than he paid. The difference is that in the former, the rights are derivative; in the latter they are direct and primary because of the *proprietary* interest which the underwriter has in the subject matter.

For example, in *North of England Iron S.S. Insurance Ass'n v. Armstrong*,[167] the vessel was valued at, and insured for, £6,000. Her real value was £9,000. She was sunk in a collision and the underwriters paid a total loss; i.e., £6,000. Eventually, the vessel owner recovered from the colliding vessel approximately £5,700. The vessel owner contended he was entitled to a proportionate part of the recovery; i.e., one-third, since the real value was £9,000 and the insured value £6,000. The court concluded that the underwriters were entitled to the whole of the £5,700 recovered.

In *Goole & Hull Steam Towing Co., Ltd. v. Ocean Marine Ins. Co., Ltd.*,[168] the same principle was followed. In that case, the vessel was valued at, and insured for, £4,000. It sustained damage in a collision with another vessel, but instead of claiming for a total loss, its owners elected to repair at a cost of £5,000. Later, they recovered £2,500 from the owners of the colliding vessel and thereupon sued their underwriters for the balance, namely £2,500. It was held that the underwriters were liable for only £1,500, i.e., the full amount for which they were liable in particular (£4,000) less the sum recovered from the colliding vessel.

Compare, however, *Standard Oil Co. of New Jersey v. Universal Insurance Co.*,[169] in which the court held that in a valued policy on cargo partially lost, the assured was a co-insurer as to the excess of actual value over in-

---

167. 39 L.J.Q.B. 81, 21 L.T. 822 (1870).
168. [1928] 1 K.B. 589, [1929] All E.R. Rep. 621, 29 Ll.L.Rep. 242.
169. 1933 AMC 675, *aff'd* without opinion, 3 F.Supp. 564, 1933 AMC 1644.

sured value and thus entitled to participate rateably in a recovery from a third party.[170]

In *Aetna Insurance Co. v. United Fruit Co. (The Almirante)*,[171] the Supreme Court expressly rejected the rationale of *North of England v. Armstrong* and held that where the real value of the vessel, lost in the collision, exceeded the agreed value in the hull policies by some $863,932, the assured was only to reimburse his hull underwriters for the sums paid to him, after deducting pro rata the legal expenses of the collision litigation. The court noted that doubt had been expressed as to *North of England* in *Burnand v. Rodocanachi*[172] and in *Thames & Mersey Marine Ins. Co. v. British & Chilean S.S. Co.*[173] The court treated the case as one of subrogation rather than as one in which the underwriter was suing by reason of a proprietary right by virtue of having paid a constructive total loss.[174]

The ultimate solution is more difficult in cases involving general average. For example, if the "contributory" value for general average purposes exceeds the agreed value in the policy, then the measure of indemnity is a comparison between the contributory and insured values in accordance with Section 73(1) of the Marine Insurance Act.[175] If the amount made good in general average and the amount of the contribution are considered separately, then under Section 73(1) the contribution recoverable from the underwriter should be reduced in proportion to any underinsurance. This would create an inequity when one considers

170. The underwriter cited several cases in support of its contention, including *North of England v. Armstrong* and *Thames & Mersey Marine Ins. Co. v. British & Chilean S.S. Co.*, [1915] 2 K.B. 214. The court, however, considered that these cases dealt with losses on hull policies and that a different rule existed between cargo and hull losses. The court relied principally on *Gulf Refining Company v. Atlantic Mutual Ins. Co.*, 279 U.S. 708 (1929), 1929 AMC 825, a case involving general average.

171. 304 U.S. 430, 1938 AMC 707.

172. (1882) L.R. 7 App.Cas. 333.

173. n. 170, *supra*.

174. It is interesting to note that the hull policies involved in the case provided for a stipulated indemnity to the owner "irrespective of the value of the vessel," and that the owner was free to effect other insurance to any amount and without disclosure of the amounts so insured. As the total of the valued policies was $582,002.25, the assured was a co-insurer to the extent of about $50,000. As protection against the risk of underinsurance, the assured procured from English underwriters additional P.P.I. insurance aggregating £65,105, partly upon hull and partly against other losses incidental to the total loss of the vessel. Both hull and P.P.I. underwriters paid off in full.

175. Sec. 73(1) reads:
Subject to any express provision in the policy, where the assured has paid, or is liable for, any general average contribution, the measure of indemnity is the full amount of such contribution if the subject matter liable to contribution is insured for its full contributory value; but if such subject matter be not insured for its full contributory value, or if only part of it be insured, the indemnity payable by the insurer must be reduced in proportion to the under-insurance, and where there has been a particular average loss which constitutes a deduction from the contributory value, and for which the insurer is liable, that amount must be deducted from the insured value in order to ascertain what the insurer is liable to contribute.

that under principles of subrogation the underwriter is entitled to the whole of the amount made good up to the amount paid by him.

Clearly, moreover, the subrogation rights of an underwriter cannot be impaired by any subsequent dealings the assured may have with other underwriters. Consequently, where the assured procures other and additional insurance, the increased value underwriters are not entitled to share pro rata in any general average balance received.[176]

Nonetheless, even where the underwriters exercise proprietary rights, their rights are measured by the subject-matter insured. This principle was established in *Attorney-General v. Glen Line Ltd.*,[177] where the Crown, as reinsuring underwriters, paid a total loss with respect to a vessel seized at the outbreak of World War I by the German government. After the war was over, the vessel was returned to her owners. Upon being sold, the vessel brought a sum much in excess of the amount paid by the Crown as a total loss. Thereafter, the vessel's owners brought suit against the German government for loss of use of the vessel and recovered a considerable sum. The Crown contended that the right of recovery was a proprietary right incidental to the ownership of the vessel to which the Crown was entitled pursuant to the provisions of Section 79 of the Marine Insurance Act. The court disagreed, holding that the sum was not paid to the vessel owners for the loss of their vessel but, instead, in respect of profits they might reasonably have been expected to earn had not the ship been seized. Lord Atkin in giving his judgment explained very clearly the difference between rights arising out of abandonment and those arising by reason of subrogation. He said, in part:

> . . . The fact is that confusion is often caused by not distinguishing the legal rights given by abandonment (s. 63) from the rights of subrogation (s. 79). No one doubts that the underwriter on hull damaged by collision and abandoned as a constructive total loss is entitled to the benefit of the right of the assured to sue the wrongdoer for the damage to the hull. But he derives his right from the provisions of s.79 whereby he is subrogated to "all rights and remedies of the assured in and in respect of the subject-matter," very different words from "all proprietary rights incidental thereto." And it is to be noted that in respect of abandonment the rights exist on a valid abandonment whereas in respect of subrogation they only arise on payment . . . .

176. *Boag v. Standard Marine Insurance Co.*, [1936] 2 K.B. 121, [1937] 1 All E.R. 714, [1937] 2 K.B. 113, C.A. Both at first instance and in the court of appeal, Phillips (Sec. 1715) was quoted with approval.

177. (1930) 37 Ll.L.Rep. 55, 46 T.L.R. 451. See, also, *Standard Marine Insurance Co. Ltd. v. Westchester Fire Insurance Co.*, 19 F.Supp. 334, 1937 AMC 363, (1937) 60 Ll.L.Rep. 202 (S.D.N.Y.), involving a denial of a right in British reinsurers to a share of out-of-pocket losses given to the U.S. underwriter by the U. S.-Germany Mixed Claims Commission, and citing *Burnand v. Rodocanachi*, (1882) 7 A.C. 333.

See discussion, *infra*, Chapter XXIII, "Subrogation, Waiver of Subrogation, Loan Receipts, and Double Insurance."

Summary

The legal and practical considerations in a constructive total loss situation may be summarized as follows:

1. Notice of abandonment should be given to underwriters at the earliest practicable time and, in any event, before substantial expenses have been incurred.[178]

2. Unless notice of abandonment has been given, no salvage contract should be entered into for a fixed sum even on a "no cure, no pay" basis. Any salvage agreement entered into should be on the basis that the amount of the salvage award would be determined after the salvage has been effected and would be based, of course, on the salved value, thus ensuring that the cost of salvage services could not exceed the salved value of the property.

3. Although it is customary for underwriters to decline to accept a tender of abandonment, the assured should nonetheless keep underwriters fully informed of the steps being taken with respect to the property at risk and financial obligation being incurred to preserve the property.

4. Care should be taken that the policies do not expire before there has been a determination as to whether or not the property is a constructive total loss. This can be done under the continuation clause, with any additional premium being recoverable by the assured if a constructive total loss is subsequently established.

5. Where the property is a wrecked vessel, underwriters have a *right* to take over ownership of whatever remains of the vessel upon payment of a constructive total loss, but no duty to do so. Consequently, instructions should be obtained from underwriters as to whether they waive all interest in the wreck. Generally speaking, the underwriters will take the position that it is premature to request that they make a decision as to waiver until their interest in the proceeds realizable upon sale (if any) and removal costs (if any) become known.

It is important to remember that where a wreck is in navigable waters, and the potential value of the wreck appears to be less than the potential liabilities arising out of wreck removal expenses, underwriters' approval of abandonment to the appropriate authorities should be requested immediately. In the absence of instructions, the owner should immediately:

---

178. Under English rules, expenses incurred *before* notice of abandonment are not includable in the calculations going to make up a constructive total loss.

(a) Abandon the wreck to, and notify, the U.S. Army Corps of Engineers;

(b) If abandonment is not possible, take steps immediately to remove it;

(c) Immediately notify P & I underwriters (or other underwriters) who may be responsible for the wreck removal; and

(d) Mark the wreck and maintain such markings.

6. It may be possible, and is highly desirable from the owner's standpoint, to arrange to sell the wreck (if it has any value) to a purchaser willing to assume any future liabilities attaching to the wreck. Approval for the sale should be obtained from anyone, such as salvors, having a lien on the wreck. In any event, underwriters having an actual or potential interest in the wreck should be kept fully informed.

7. Should there be no disposition of the wreck by the time a constructive total loss is paid (and the policies on hull are thereby cancelled), port risk insurance on the wreck should be obtained. This is desirable because P & I underwriters may take the position that their coverage ceases when the hull underwriters pay for a constructive total loss.[179]

8. Notwithstanding a waiver by the hull underwriters of any interest in the wreck, they still retain rights of subrogation. Therefore, if the assured has any rights against a third party for the loss, such rights would inure to the benefit of the hull underwriters, less the expenses incident to collection.

9. The assured should take all necessary steps under the Sue and Labor Clause to reduce the magnitude of the loss which hull underwriters would otherwise be required to bear. Coverage under the Sue and Labor Clause applies both before and after the notice of abandonment.

10. As noted earlier, under the Sue and Labor Clause all expenses necessarily and actually incurred for the preservation of the venture are recoverable from underwriters *in addition to the constructive total loss*. If, however, the assured desires to retain his vessel and claim for a partial loss (the cost of repairs not to exceed the agreed or insured value), underwriters' maximum liability would not exceed the total amount of the insured value on hull and machinery. Any loss in excess of the insured value would fall on the owner.[180]

179. The need for special insurance if the P & I insurance comes to an end should be perfectly obvious. It may well happen, for example, that other liabilities (as during a protracted salvage operation) will arise for which the original P & I may not provide cover. This does not mean that the original P & I cover must not respond for the costs arising out of the original casualty—such as wreck removal expenses or any other legal liabilities arising as a direct consequence of the original casualty—as that liability continues, but new and different liabilities are not covered. Moreover, it should be remembered that under the latest form of AIH policy, the policy is automatically terminated in the event of a payment by underwriters for a total loss.

180. The new AIH hull form authorizes additional insurances (up to 25 percent of the insured value of hull and machinery) on increased value of hull and machinery, freight,

Compromised or Arranged Total Losses

As a practical matter, it not infrequently happens that the assured will wish to retain his vessel and effect repairs, even though, technically, he could claim for a constructive total loss. At this point, it may be desirable to negotiate with underwriters for a "compromised" or "arranged" total loss. Underwriters are frequently receptive to this approach if it appears that the total cost of repairs may well equal or exceed the insured value and if, in fact, some savings may be obtained. This attitude on the part of underwriters is perfectly understandable; on the one hand, they may be forced to pay up to the insured value in terms of repairs, but, on the other, if a compromise is effected, it may well be that the compromised figure would be less than the insured value as well as reflect some credit for the value of the wreck.[181] Moreover, if a compromised settlement is reached, the full premium is payable on the policy and the policy is cancelled, thus insulating the underwriters against further risks.

---

disbursements, etc. Such additional insurances are payable in the event of a total or constructive total loss of the hull but are not payable where the assured elects to claim for a partial loss.

181. Underwriters were understandably not interested in a "compromised" total loss in *Oscar L. Aronsen, Inc. v. Compton, et al (The Megara)*, n. 36, *supra*, as they believed the vessel could be repaired for about £79,000, whereas the owner had estimated the cost of repairs at £142,000 and the insured value of the vessel was £140,000.

CHAPTER XVII

GENERAL AVERAGE

Introduction

It would be well to divest oneself of any erroneous impression that general average has any necessary connection with or is dependent upon marine insurance. To the contrary; as the late Richard Lowndes remarked in an early edition of his classic work on general average, the subject can never be as well understood as when it is studied apart from insurance, with which it is only accidentally associated.

The law of general average had its genesis in equity, and its principles were practiced long before marine insurance was developed. It applies only to shipping, and is a part of the established law of the sea, as distinguished from the law of the land.

Actually, it can be traced with confidence as far back as the Justinian Code, dating from about 540 A.D., in which the following appears:

> The Rhodian law provides that if in order to lighten a ship, merchandise is thrown overboard, that which has been given for all shall be replaced by the contribution of all.

Obviously, from the reference to Rhodian law, one must assume that general average was recognized much earlier, as Rhodes and the other Greek cities of the Aegean Sea were comparative latecomers to maritime commerce. It is most likely that it was a product of those inventive seafarers, the Phoenicians, whose ships plied the Mediterranean even before the Old Testament was written.

General average rests upon the equitable principle that whatever voluntary loss is sustained for the benefit of all parties to a common maritime adventure must be borne by all in proportion as those interested are benefited. It is a part of the maritime law of all nations and applies to government property as well as to private property. It is not dependent upon contract, although rights connected with it can be affected by contract, such as the York-Antwerp Rules.

Initially, commerce was conducted by merchants who usually accompanied their own goods, not only for the purpose of ensuring that they were not stolen or misappropriated, but also for the purpose of selling them upon arrival at destination. In the event of a disaster, such as violent seas with the vessel shipping water and liable to sink, one can readily imagine the reluctance of an owner of goods to submit voluntarily to his particular goods being thrown overboard. In such instances, the master of the vessel had to exercise his authority and direct which goods would be consigned to the briney deep. But, in turn, the unlucky merchant whose goods were sacrificed would be made at least partially whole by the contributions of the vessel owner and the other merchants whose goods were fortunately spared.[1]

It is also rather likely that the "adjustment" of general average was at one time left to the shipowner or the master of the vessel. But as vessels increased in size and the cargoes became more varied, this onerous task devolved upon experts who (presumably) were impartial and experienced.

Goodacre, in his superb text, *Marine Insurance Claims*,[2] quotes from an address which Mr. G.A. Henderson of the Commercial Union Assurance Company, Ltd. gave to the Insurance Institute of London over 50 years ago. In describing an early average adjuster, he noted:

> Hastening to the quay or wharf of Tyre or Tharsus when a vessel approached the end of her voyage, he would be ready with tablets and stilus or scroll and inkhorn to adjust the average. I forget when ink was first invented, but it was at an early date. Himself perhaps an old seaman or traveller, he would explain the ancient sea law to the inexperienced, persuade, cajole and threaten till all had paid up, and the unfortunate loser had been satisfied. Can we not see this ancient Phra the Phoenician, in his long white linen gabardine, his Semitic features glowing with satisfaction as he made up his account, balancing the matter up neatly, collecting contributions from all, including the unfortunate man who had been despoiled in order that he should be no better off than his neighbours in the long run, and finally retiring, after satisfying all, hoarse and weary, but retaining in drachmae, shekels and sesterces, a goodly recompense for his trouble and skill, and well earned it usually was! He has had many notable successors.

General average was also mentioned in the renowned Code of Oleron which Richard the Lion Heart is supposed to have taken back with him from the Crusades. Certain it is that many of the judgments contained in that Code were ultimately copied into the Black Book of Admiralty, whether or not Richard was the culprit.

English Development

The first claim for a general average contribution reported in English jurisprudence appears to have been *Whitefield v. Garrarde*.[3] The case in-

---

1. It has been said, with some degree of jocularity, that Jonah was the first case of "jettison." Fortunately, he was regurgitated by the whale. Most owners of cargoes are not so lucky.
2. *Marine Insurance Claims*, by J. Kenneth Goodacre, A.C.I.I., London, Witherby & Co. Ltd. (1981).
3. File 8, No. 54 (1540), *Select Pleas in the Court of Admiralty*, Vol. II, A.D. 1547-1602, Selden Society.

volved a claim for general average contribution for jettison of a boat and cargo from the vessel *Trinity James*. There were four reported proceedings relating to the same vessel. The various controversies appear to have been settled by arbitration; no order appears to have been made upon the claim for general average.

Birkley v. Presgrave appears to have been the first English case in which a definition of General Average was given,[4] although Lowndes states that the earliest recorded instance of a dispute concerning contribution toward a jettison was in 1285.[5] The first use of the word "average" to describe a general average contribution appears to have been in the report of *Hicks v. Palington*,[6] and again referred to in *Sheppard v. Wright*.[7] The terms "general average" do not appear until *The Copenhagen*,[8] where Lord Stowell said:

> . . . General average is for a loss incurred, towards which the whole concern is bound to contribute pro rata, because it was undergone for the general benefit and preservation of the whole. . . . General average is that loss to which contribution must be made by both ship and cargo; the loss, or expense which the loss creates, being incurred for the common benefit of both.[9]

The Marine Insurance Act, 1906, contains a definition of a general average loss and of a general average act, which was undoubtedly intended to reflect the common law decisions. Section 66 of the Act reads:

> (1) A general average loss is a loss caused by or directly consequential on a general average act. It includes a general average expenditure as well as a general average sacrifice.
>
> (2) There is a general average act where any extraordinary sacrifice or expenditure is voluntarily and reasonably made or incurred in time

---

4. (1801) 102 E.R. 86.
5. Sayles, *Select Cases in the Court of King's Bench*, Vol. 1 (Selden Society Publications, Vol. 55, 1936).
6. (1590) 72 E.R. 590.
7. (1698) 1 E.R. 13, H.L.
8. (1799) 165 E.R. 180.
9. In the *Guidon de la Mer* (1556-84), apparently a digest intended for use by the consular court of Rouen in matters of insurance, the term used is "common" or "gross" average, but from the examples given, it is clear that what was being referred to was what Lord Stowell later was to term "general average." The same terms, "common" or "gross" average, appear in the Ordonnance of Louis XIV (1681). The Ordinance of Rotterdam (1721) began its definition in almost identical terms. Clearly, Lawrence J., in his judgment in *Birkley v. Presgrave*, must have had in mind the Ordonnance of Louis XIV, for his sentence defining General Average is remarkably similar to the comparable provision in the Ordonnance. Lawrence, J. defined the term as follows:

All loss which arises in consequence of extraordinary sacrifices made or expenses incurred for the preservation of the ship and cargo comes within general average, and must be borne proportionably by all who are interested.

of peril for the purpose of preserving the property imperilled in the common venture.

As noted, general average has no necessary connection with nor is dependent upon marine insurance. However, being a risk or a liability to which participants in a maritime venture are subject, underwriters for centuries have agreed to insure in their policies the risks of general average contribution and sacrifice.

From its earlier origins, general average became more complex and began to develop in different ways in different maritime countries. Since the adjustment of a general average is customarily drawn up in accordance with the law of the port of destination, serious complications began to arise. For example, in *Simonds v. White*,[10] there was a general average loss of a cable from a vessel bound for St. Petersburg and the statement, as is common, was drawn up in accordance with Russian law. It included charges which were not allowable under English law. The court noted that although there were many variations in the laws and usages of different nations as to the losses considered to fall within the scope of general average, on one point all agree; i.e., that the place at which the average is adjusted is the place of the vessel's destination or delivery of her cargo.[11] The same rule applies where the voyage is broken up at an intermediate port and the cargo is either sold or delivered to its owners.[12]

Because the law respecting general average can differ so markedly from country to country, and the task of attempting to ascertain the law of any particular jurisdiction could be extraordinarily burdensome and intricate, efforts have been made to achieve common international agreement on the subject of general average. What uniformity has been achieved is reflected in the York-Antwerp Rules which are discussed subsequently.

American Development

While the law of general average in the United States closely parallels that of England, there are differences reflecting the Continental influences

---

10. (1824) 2 B. & C. 805, 2 L.J.O.S.K.B. 159.
11. The American law is the same. See *Peters v. Warren Ins. Co.*, F.Cas. 11,034 (1841); *Barnard v. Adams*, 51 U.S. 270 (1850); *Strong v. Fireman's Ins. Co.*, 11 Johns 323 (St., N.Y.); *Charterhague*, 281 U.S. 515, 1930 AMC 1121; *Compagnie Francaise de Navigation a Vapeur v. Bonnasse*, 15 F.2d 202, 1927 AMC 1325 (2nd Cir., 1926); *Det. For. Damp. Selskab v. Ins. Co. of N.A.*, 28 F.2d 449, *aff'd* 31 F.2d 658, *cert. den.* 280 U.S. 571, 1928 AMC 1453. The statement is subject to the qualification, of course, that wherever the statement is drawn up, it must, apart from a valid agreement to the contrary, be in accordance with the law and customs of the port of destination.
12. *National Board of Marine Underwriters v. Melchers*, 45 F. 643 (D.,Pa., 1891); *The Eliza*

that were exerted upon the American courts. In this connection, it should be observed that the term "general average" was not mentioned in an English decision until 1799 and, of course, by that time the United States was a separate and independent nation. Thus, the reported law of general average began in the United States at a time when English decisions were not available as precedents. However, as the law was derived from the same general sources, and the courts were well informed concerning the common law, it is not surprising that development has been along the same lines.

Interestingly, the first report of a case in an American court involving general average, *Brown v. Cornwell*,[13] antedated Lord Stowell's language in *The Copenhagen* by some 26 years. In that case, jettison of horses from on deck was allowed in general average.[14]

Under the federal/state system in the United States, cases involving general average can be heard either in the federal or state courts. In fact, many of the earlier cases were heard by the state courts. However, since the federal courts have exclusive jurisdiction in admiralty, and proceedings *in rem* against vessels and property and in salvage cases *in rem* must be brought before them, they have become the favored forum in cases involving general average as the parties claiming liens to enforce their rights of contribution can do so with facility.

Just as *Birkley v. Presgrave* first postulated the principles of general average in England, *Case v. Reilly*[15] performed that function in the United States. In that case, Washington, J., stated in part:

> The object is to incur a partial loss and to risk a minor or contingent danger to avoid the more certain loss of all.

In *Columbian Ins. Co. v. Ashby*,[16] Justice Story said in part with respect to contributions:

> First: That the ship and cargo should be placed in a common, imminent peril.
> Secondly: That there should be a voluntary sacrifice to property to avert that peril.

Lines, 102 F. 184 (lst Cir., 1900); see, also, *Hill v. Wilson* (1879) 48 L.J.Q.B. 764 and *Fletcher v. Alexander* (1868) 37 L.J.C.P. 193.

13. 1 Root (Conn.) 60 (1773).

14. See, also, *Campbell v. The Alknomac*, F. Cas. 2350 (1798) involving port of refuge expenses where the vessel had to put into an American port in distress; *Maggrath v. Church*, 1 Caines (N.Y.) 195 (1803); and *Whitteridge v. Norris*, 6 Mass. 125 (1809).

15. F.Cas. 2,538, 3 Wash. C.C. 298 (1814). Interestingly, nearly all the citations by counsel and the court were taken from the old Continental text writers, ordinances, and laws. *Birkley v. Presgrave* was cited in that case as well as in *Maggrath v. Church*, 1 Caines (N.Y.) 195 (1803).

16. 38 U.S. 331, 10 L.Ed. 186 (1839).

Thirdly: That by that sacrifice the safety of the other property should be presently and successfully attained.

It will be observed that the foregoing definitions involved only sacrifices and not extraordinary expenses incurred for the joint benefit of ship and cargo. The first reference to extraordinary expenses falling with the ambit of the definition appears to have been *Padelford v. Boardman*,[17] in which the court observed that general average expresses that contribution to a loss or expense voluntarily incurred for the preservation of the whole, in which all who are concerned in the ship, freight, and cargo are to bear a part proportionable to their respective interests.

The leading case in the United States on the definition of general average is *Star of Hope v. Annan*,[18] where Justice Clifford discussed the subject in exhaustive detail, and neatly characterized the two great classes of general average as follows:[19]

. . . Losses which give a claim to averages are usually divided into two great classes: (1) Those which arise from sacrifices of part of the ship or part of the cargo, purposely made in order to save the whole adventure from perishing. (2) Those which arise out of extraordinary expenses incurred for the joint benefit of ship and cargo.

It is here timely to emphasize that the last definition embracing "extraordinary expenses incurred for the joint benefit of ship and cargo" illustrates one of the fundamental differences in approach by the English and American courts. It will be seen that, while peril is a necessary element in a general average act, the American courts have extended the consequences of a general average act to include certain expenses incurred after safety has been attained. Thus, expenses incurred for the mutual benefit of ship and cargo to enable the voyage to be completed (such as temporary repairs at a port of refuge) are made good as general average.[20]

The English concept of general average limits general allowances to attainment of safety, whereas American law and practice incorporates also the common or "mutual" benefit theory and preservation of the adventure. Compare, for example, the definition of general average set

---

17. 4 Mass. 548 (1808).

18. 76 U.S. 203 (1870).

19. There are literally hundreds of American cases in which a definition of general average has been attempted. As every one of them follows the definitions laid down in *Caze v. Reilly, supra, Columbian Ins. Co. v. Ashby, supra,* and *Star of Hope v. Annan, supra,* no useful purpose would be served by citing them all. The most recent, *Eagle Term. v. Ins. Co. of USSR,* 637 F.2d 890, 1981 AMC 137 (2nd Cir.) discusses the subject in great detail, and reviews many of the preceding (and leading) decisions.

20. See, for example, *Bowring v. Thebaud,* 42 F. 799 (S.D.N.Y., 1890), 56 F. 520 (1892) and *Shoe v. Craig,* 189 F. 227 (D,Pa., 1911), 194 F. 678 (3rd Cir., 1912).

forth in Rule A, York-Antwerp Rules, which is substantially identical to the definition contained in the Marine Insurance Act, 1906, and reads:

There is a general average act when, and only when, any extraordinary sacrifice or expenditure is intentionally and reasonably made or incurred for the common safety for the purpose of preserving from peril the property involved in a common maritime adventure.

The trenchant words are, of course, "for the common safety" for the purpose of preserving from peril the "property involved" in a common maritime adventure. Consequently, under English practice, once common safety has been achieved, expenditures made thereafter are for the account of the particular parties and are not allowable in general average. As Buglass[21] puts it:

. . . It is submitted that this variance is not so much a disagreement in the definition of general average but rather a difference in putting the definition into practice.

Stating it another way, the American courts are more liberal in regarding the consequences of a general act as being a part of the original act.[22]

Nevertheless, it should be emphasized that the "mutual benefit" theory deals primarily with the question when the right of contribution in general average ceases. In no sense does it relieve the claimant to contribution of the necessity of establishing that, initially, the common venture was in "apparently imminent peril."[23] Physical peril is still the *sine quo non* of general average, under both English and American law.

Another area in which American law and practice differs from English practice is in the application of general average to vessels in ballast. English law requires that more than one interest be involved in a common adventure before a general average situation exists. Thus, under English law, "apparently imminent peril" to a vessel sailing in ballast will not suffice as only one interest is involved. By contrast, the American view is that underwriters are "parties" to the risk in the sense that they stand to lose if the venture is lost or damaged; consequently, a sacrifice or expenditure with respect to a vessel sailing in ballast is incurred as much for the benefit of the underwriters as for the shipowner.[24] Whether the American position is right or wrong is immaterial; the law and practice have become firmly established. And it makes no difference whether the vessel is a

---

21. L. Buglass, *Marine Insurance and General Average in the United States* (2d), Cornell Maritime Press, Inc., 1981.

22. See discussion, *infra*, under the heading "Consequences of General Average Act."

23. *Barge J. Whitney—Asphalt Incident*, 1968 AMC 995 (Detels, Arb.).

24. *Potter v. Ocean Ins. Co.*, F.Cas. No. 11,335 (lst Cir., 1837); *LaFonciere Compagnie v. Dollar*, 181 F. 945 (9th Cir., 1910).

yacht,[25] tugboat, lighter, barge, or other class of vessel, the important criterion being that there is insurance on the vessel.

Another area of difference between English and American law is in the treatment of reasonable temporary repairs of damage arising from excepted perils, carried out at an intermediate port where permanent repairs cannot be made, if necessary to enable the vessel to carry out her contemplated voyage. Under American law, such repairs are considered as general average, whereas under English law they are not, as the "common safety" has already been attained.[26]

The practice in England and the United States also appears to differ with respect to cutting away rigging or other appurtenances. In England, the question is phrased in terms of whether the wrecked materials, even if not cut away, would have been, in the existing circumstances, hopelessly lost; in the United States, the issue is whether the wreckage could have been saved in the hypothetical case of the peril (such as a storm) suddenly subsiding or becoming less severe.[27]

Another area of possible difference between English and American law is with respect to a voluntary stranding.[28]

The American rule appears to be that if some stranding was inevitable in any event, the loss is allowable in general average,[29] whereas if the same stranding was inevitable it is not.[30]

Effect of York-Antwerp Rules

When the York-Antwerp Rules were first introduced in 1890, they consisted of 18 numbered rules. They did not purport to deal with the whole question of general average nor to change its fundamental principles. In-

25. *Risley v. Ins. Co. of N.A.*, 189 F. 529 (S.D.N.Y, 1910); *Hahlo v. Benedict*, 216 F. 306 (1914).

26. *Bowring v. Thebaud*, 42 F. 799 (S.D.N.Y., 1890); *Star of Hope, supra*, n. 18; *Hobson v. Lord*, 92 U.S. 397 (1875); *Eagle Term. v. Ins. Co. of USSR*, 637 F.2d 890, 1981 AMC 137 (2nd Cir.).

27. See *Mary Gibbs*, 22 F. 463 (D., Mass., 1884); *Margarethe Blanca*, 12 F. 728, 14 F. 59 (3rd Cir., 1882); *May v. Keystone Yellow Pine Co.*, 117 F. 287 (D., Pa., 1902).

28. The word "possible" difference is deliberately used, as there is no English case directly in point. It was formerly the common practice of English average adjusters to exclude from general average all damage to ship or cargo resulting from a voluntary stranding, except where the damage resulted from beaching or scuttling a burning ship to extinguish a fire. This practice has been severely criticized by the leading text writers, and Rule V of the York/Antwerp Rules, 1974 now provides that when a ship is intentionally run on shore for the common safety, whether or not she might have been driven on shore, the consequent loss or damage shall be allowed in general average. Whether the change expressed in Rule V would be adopted by the English courts as expressing the correct principle under English law (in the absence of the applicability of Rule V) remains to be seen.

29. *Barnard v. Adams*, 51 U.S. 270 (1850).

30. *Shoe v. Low Moor Iron Co.*, 46 F. 125, 49 F. 252 (1891).

stead, they were designed to secure uniformity of practice, to meet some of the necessities based on modern conditions, and in order that some uncertain and disputed points might be dealt with in a particular way.

The 1890 Rules, in practice, proved to be inadequate in light of changing conditions of commerce, and in 1924, a new set of Rules was promulgated which brought them more closely in line with modern times. In addition, they contained a general declaration of the principles of general average to be applied in circumstances not otherwise provided for in the numbered rules. These principles were set forth in seven lettered rules.

A conference of "The Association for the Reform and Codification of the Law of Nations" was held at York, England in 1864 and again at Antwerp, Belgium in 1877. On the latter date, a code of Rules was adopted, known as "York and Antwerp Rules." In 1890, the conference of the association was held in Liverpool at which time the rules were revised. The new rules more closely approached the laws and usages of the United States. Successive amendments to the Rules were made in 1924, 1950 and, lastly, in 1974.

When the 1924 Rules were adopted and the new seven lettered Rules first appeared, it was clearly intended that the numbered Rules would take precedence over the lettered rules. That is, certain expenditures are recoverable under the numbered rules even in circumstances where there has been no general average act as defined in the lettered Rules. Conversely, a situation which would appear to give rise to general average under the lettered Rules can be obviated by the express provisions of the numbered Rules.

Unfortunately, the courts were not wholly aware of that intent (and it was not adequately expressed in a fashion that would be calculated to bring it to the attention of the courts). In any event, in *Vlassopoulos v. British & Foreign Marine Insurance Co. Ltd. (The Makis)*,[31] the court held that the lettered Rules constituted the general rules of general average, while the numbered Rules were to apply to specific cases. Thus, expenditures which would have been recoverable under the numbered rules were not allowed because the facts were not in accord with the general definition of general average in the lettered Rules. This was wholly unsatisfactory and an agreement was hurriedly drawn up, known as "The Makis Agreement" to nullify the court's decision.

In the 1950 revisions to the Rules, a new "Rule of Interpretation" was added, reading:

> In the adjustment of general average the following lettered and numbered Rules shall apply to the exclusion of any Law and Practice inconsistent therewith.

---

31. [1929] 1 K.B. 187, 98 L.J.K.B. 53, (1928) 31 Ll.L.Rep. 313.

Except as provided by the numbered Rules, General Average shall be adjusted according to the lettered Rules.[32]

One would have thought that this pretty well solved the problem. It came as a surprise, therefore, in 1974, in *Orient Mid-East Lines, Inc. et al v. S.S. Orient Transporter*,[33] when the Fifth Circuit held that the York/Antwerp Rules did not do away with the fundamental requirement that a ship be in a position of peril before the law of general average applies. In that case, the ship was undergoing boiler repairs at Beaumont, Texas, which were not finished when loading was completed. In order to free the berth for another vessel, the ship was intentionally grounded on the bank of an abandoned ship channel and the repairs completed. Unfortunately, the soft silt on the bottom of the channel blocked some piping and the vessel had to be moved back to the berth for boiler repairs. As the ship was pulled free of the silt by a tug, she was propelled stern first across the channel and was in danger of striking some piling. Her engines were put ahead at the last moment, whereupon she ran back across the channel and again became stuck in the silt, where she remained until the following morning at high tide when she was taken off by a tug. This unhappy chain of events resulted in almost $9,000 in expenses.

In the vessel owner's suit for contribution in general average from cargo for the expenses arising from the stranding, the Fifth Circuit held, *inter alia,* that the owner was not entitled to recovery, as the vessel and cargo, while stranded, were not in "peril." The court commented on the requirement of peril under Rules X and XI of the York-Antwerp Rules, noting that the two rules concern expenses incurred at a port of refuge entered as a general average act and were thus not applicable to the case at bar; that they were limited to action taken for the common safety, a phrase closely related to "removal from peril;" and that the plaintiff vessel owner's interpretation would run afoul of Sections 3(8) and 5 of Cogsa.

The court was clearly in error. Rules X and XI unquestionably apply not only to situations where a vessel enters a port of refuge as a general average act but also to situations where the vessel cannot leave any port or place—whether loading, call, or refuge—because of an accident happening there, and if the repairs are necessary for the safe prosecution of the voyage. As the numbered Rules prevail over the lettered Rules by virtue of the Rule Interpretation, Rule A, speaking in terms of the common safety, is overriden by the language of Rules X and XI which refer, also, to repairs necessary for the safe prosecution of the voyage.

---

32. Even here, the intent could have been made somewhat clearer. For example, the rule of interpretation could have been worded:
   General average shall be adjusted according to the principles set forth in the lettered Rules, but in case of conflict with the numbered Rules, the latter shall govern.
33. 496 F.2d 1032, 1974 AMC 2593 (5th Cir.).

In 1981, a similar situation was before the Second Circuit in *Eagle Terminal Tankers, Inc. v. Ins. Co. of USSR.*[34] In that case, while enroute on a voyage from the United States to Russia, the vessel felt a "bump" while taking on a pilot off England, but continued on its voyage to the next port of call, Rotterdam. The following day, metallic scraping noises were heard coming from the stern. Upon its safe arrival in Rotterdam, divers conducted an examination where it was found that the propeller had sustained extensive damage; among other things, the propeller's blades were bent and the propeller itself appeared to have shifted aft from the tailshaft. The damage was serious enough, as the defendant conceded, to make repairs necessary before the voyage could be resumed. Accordingly, after a portion of the cargo was unloaded and the ship placed in drydock, the propeller shaft was replaced and the ship continued on its way to Russia.

The vessel owner declared a general average, seeking contribution for expenses arising from the Rotterdam repairs from the ship's underwriters and from defendant as insurer of the cargo. The expenses covered by the statement of general average included the costs of unloading and reloading the cargo in connection with the drydocking, as well as the costs of maintaining the ship's crew and officers during the repair period. The defendant's assessed share of the expenses totalled $126,951.61. When the defendant refused to pay, the vessel owner brought suit.

At first instance, the district court granted defendant's motion for summary judgment on the ground that no general average situation existed in the circumstances of the case. Specifically, the judge found that the ship had not been threatened by any "peril," as required by traditional principles of the law of general average and under the York-Antwerp Rules which applied in accordance with the terms of the voyage charter party. Noting that the damage was discovered only after the ship was safely moored, the judge concluded that "the vessel could have remained moored indefinitely at Rotterdam without incurring the slightest peril to itself or its cargo." That the voyage could not have been completed without the repairs was deemed "irrelevant."

On appeal, the Second Circuit reversed, holding that Rules X and XI do, in fact, contemplate contribution in general average toward expenses that might not qualify under Rule A, stating, in part:

> This is particularly evident in the alternative basis of recovery set out in the numbered Rules: recovery of expenses incurred "to enable damage to the ship caused by sacrifice or accident to be repaired, if the repairs were necessary for the safe prosecution of the voyage . . . ." (the safe prosecution clause). Under this clause, repairs necessary for

---

34. 637 F.2d 890, 1981 AMC 137 (2nd Cir.).

the safe continuation of the voyage can be deemed general average acts, even if they would not be so regarded under Rule A alone . . . .

In effect, then, the safe prosecution clause is to be read not as eliminating the requirement of peril but as presuming its presence in cases where, because of accident or sacrifice, a voyage cannot safely be resumed without repairs. Such a presumption is entirely consistent with the modern interpretation of the peril requirement . . . which . . . involves only a showing of "real and substantial" danger even though ultimate catastrophe "may be distant or indeed unlikely." Lowndes and Rudolf agree that the safe prosecution clause "is a notable example of the occasions where those who supported completion of the adventure as the basis of general average prevailed over those who support the common safety."

. . . Although the ship here had not lost its propeller, the record shows that it had been seriously damaged and that its condition was deteriorating. . . . As we read these facts, the ship's condition, allegedly as the result of an accident at sea, presented a "real and substantial" danger of loss or complete incapacitation of the propeller—and consequent peril—if the ship had still been at sea or if it returned to sea with-out repairs. . . . Under these circumstances, we believe the requirements for a prima facie claim under Rules X(b) and XI(b) have been satisfied.

The court also noted its respectful disagreement with the Fifth Circuit in its decision in the *Orient Transporter, supra.*

York-Antwerp Rules—Applicable to Contracts of Affreightment

It cannot be overemphasized that the York-Antwerp Rules do not of themselves have the force of international law. To the contrary, they become effective only by express provision in the contract of affreightment. Absent as provision in the contract of affreightment that adjustment of general average will be governed according to the Rules, the adjustment may be governed by some other recognized law or code. Moreover, as already discussed, the place of adjustment in the absence of an express agreement of the parties as to some other place, is the law of the port of destination.

It should also be emphasized that the obligation to contribute in general average does not depend in the least upon any contract between the parties but, rather, upon the ancient law of the seas, i.e., as the consequence of a common danger requiring the application of natural justice.[35] However, there is nothing to prevent the parties from agreeing that

---

35. See *Burton v. English* (1883) 12 Q.B.D. 218, 53 L.J.Q.B.133; *Star of Hope v. Annan*, 76 U.S. 203 (1870); *The Roanoke*, 59 F. 163 (1893); *Simonds v. White*, (1824) 2 B. & C. 805, 811; *The Eliza Lines*, 61 F. 308, 325 (1896); *Marwick v. Rogers*, 163 Mass. 50 (1895).

the principles of general average shall not apply at all and the obligation to contribute may be limited, qualified, or even excluded by the special terms of the contract.[36]

Although the Rules do not have the force of international law, as already noted, they have gained universal acceptance in international trade and it is most unusual today to encounter a case involving affreightment of cargo to which they do not apply. For example, contracts of affreightment (bills of lading where the vessel owner or time charterer is transporting cargo of a general nature, and charters where the cargo being transported is in bulk) almost invariably contain a general average clause. A typical general average clause in a bill of lading in the United States would be worded substantially as follows:

> General Average shall be adjusted, stated and settled according to York/Antwerp Rules 1974 at the port of New York or last port of discharge at Carrier's option and as to matters not provided for in these Rules, according to the laws and usage at the Port of New York or any other place at the option of the Carrier.

In the New York Produce Exchange Time Charter (as amended October 3rd, 1946), Clause 19 provides, in part:[37]

> General Average shall be adjusted, stated and settled, according to Rule 1 to 15, inclusive, 17 to 22, inclusive, and Rule F of York/Antwerp Rules 1924, at such port or place in the United States as may be selected by the carrier, and as to matters not provided for by these Rules, according to the laws and usages at the port of New York.

In the Baltime form, the clause is relatively more simple. It reads:

> General Average to be settled according to York/ Antwerp Rules, 1974. Hire not to contribute to General Average.

Inasmuch as no international body exists to determine disputes arising over the proper interpretation of the Rules, and such disputes necessarily must be resolved by the courts of the individual countries, it will be apparent that over the course of time such interpretations may well differ. Consequently, reference will have to be made to the court decisions of those individual countries to determine the proper interpretation in the respective countries.

In any event, the effect of relatively standard general average clauses is to incorporate, by reference, the York-Antwerp Rules into nearly all

---

36. *Simonds v. White, supra*, n. 35.
37. The 1981 revision of the NYPE form substitutes the York/ Antwerp Rules 1974 for specific rules of the 1924 version.

contracts of affreightment. In the case of charter parties, which frequently contain arbitration clauses, this may cause some problems. For example, in *Alma Shipping Corp. v. Union of India*,[38] the court held that any dispute regarding general average would be subject to any arbitration clause contained in the charter.[39]

General Average Act

As has already been noted, general average losses may be either a sacrifice or an expenditure, subject, however to the numbered Rules taking precedence over the lettered Rules. Reference to the lettered Rules is only necessary when the specific circumstances set forth in the numbered Rules are not applicable.

Rule A is extremely important because it not only covers a number of actual situations which fall outside the scope of the numbered Rules, but it defines terms used in the Rules. It reads:

Rule A

There is a General Average act when, and only when, any extraordinary sacrifice or expenditure is intentionally and reasonably made or incurred for the common safety for the purpose of preserving from peril the property involved in a common maritime adventure.[40]

As a definition, however, of a general average act as envisaged under English law, it can scarcely be improved upon. If broken into its component parts, the legal precedents become more understandable.

Extraordinary Sacrifice or Expenditure. It cannot be overemphasized that one must distinguish between an "extraordinary sacrifice or expenditure" and the usual and customary measures taken in order to fulfill a carrier's obligations under the contract of affreightment. As there is a

---

38. [1971] 2 Lloyd's Rep. 393.

39. Compare, however, *The Evje* [1972] 2 Lloyd's Rep. 129, *aff'd* [1973] 1 Lloyd's Rep. 509, where it was held that an undertaking to pay any general average contribution which may be legally due is a new and independent agreement, the consideration for which is the vessel owner's agreement not to exercise his lien against cargo. Therefore, the arbitration clause in the charter was not applicable.

40. It will be observed that Rule A does not mention the "preservation of the voyage" concept which is so important under American law, although that concept is contained in Rules X and XI. The definition in Rule A is virtually identical to the English statutory definition and, of course, restricts general average to acts made or incurred for the common safety. This occasioned much concern in the United States where the 1924 Rules (which first contained the lettered Rules) were adopted with reluctance and with reservations, so much so that many general average clauses expressly omitted all lettered rules except Rule F, dealing with substituted expenses. See, for example, the general average clause in the NYPE charter (October, 1946 revision).

duty on the part of the shipowner to take reasonable care of the goods by doing all that is necessary and proper to preserve them during the ordinary circumstances of the voyage, only if the sacrifice or expense was "extraordinary". . . . or without the scope of the usual and customary services which the shipowner ought to perform in any event to comply with his duties to the cargo . . . is there a general average act. As the court stated it in *Robinson v. Price*,[41]

> . . . a shipper of cargo is entitled in time of peril to the benefit not only of the best services of the crew in order to save his goods, but of the use of all the appliances with which the ship is provided.[42]

Congdon gives as an example a steamer driven by heavy gales and seas toward a lee shore or into other positions of danger. If, to avoid the impending peril to her and the cargo, the master causes the engines to be worked to their utmost speed to take her out to the open sea and in consequence of the excessive working and racing in accomplishing this they sustain damage, the damage, although voluntary, is not the subject of contribution as such use of the engines (although at the risk of injury) is considered to be within the ordinary duty of the vessel to her cargo under the contract of affreightment. If, on the other hand, a vessel becomes disabled at sea to such an extent that it becomes necessary to work the engines in an extraordinary manner, and an extra strain is put upon them to enable her, at the risk of damage for the common benefit of vessel and cargo, to make port, the damage by such an extraordinary use, or, rather, abuse of the engines, is properly allowable in general average.

Formerly, Rule VI of the 1950 Rules provided for the allowance in general average of the extraordinary use or abuse of sails in refloating a stranded vessel. Being obsolete, it was deleted from the 1974 Rules. However, the same principle still applies, and should, in fact, a sailing

---

41. (1877) 2 Q.B.D. 295, 46 L.J.Q.B. 551.

42. See, also, *Wilson v. Bank of Victoria* (1867) 36 L.J.Q.B. 89 (use of coal to power auxiliary steam engines after vessel sustained damage not a general average expense but, rather, the performance by the shipowner of a service owed to owners of the cargo); *Harrison v. Bank of Australasia* (1872) 25 L.T. 944, 1 Asp. M.L.C. 198 (ship damaged by cyclone; used her donkey engine to pump out water; because of prolonged use, the coal supply ran out and the ship's timbers were burnt as fuel in lieu of coal; held: an extraordinary sacrifice and thus a general average sacrifice); *Navigazione Generale Italiana v. Spencer Kellogg & Sons, Inc. (The Mincio)*, 92 F.2d 41, 1937 AMC 1506 (2nd Cir.), *cert. den.* 302 U.S. 751 (1937) (excessive use of ship's engines and steering machinery to get vessel off its strand); *The Edward Rutledge*, 123 F.Supp. 318, 1954 AMC 2070 (S.D.N.Y) (vessel stranded in soft mud; no danger and hence no general average); *Van den Toorn v. Leeming*, 70 F. 251 (D.C., 1895) (exercising ordinary duty to repair not a general average act even though such temporary repairs later caused greater damage); *Willcox, Peck & Hughes v. American Smelting & Refining Co.*, 210 F. 89 (1913); *The Bona*, [1895] P. 125; *Charter S.S. Co. Ltd. v. Bowring Jones & Tidy, Ltd.*, (1930) 36 Ll.L.Rep. 272; *Walford de Baerdemaecker v. Galindez* (1897) 2 Com.Cas. 127; *Bowring v. Thebaud*, 42 F. 794 (SDNY, 1890).

vessel be involved in a general average situation, it would be appropriate to make an allowance envisaged by Rule VI of the 1950 Rules by the application of Rule A.

Rule VII of the 1974 Rules reads:

> Rule VII. Damage to Machinery and Boilers.
>
> Damage caused to any machinery and boilers of a ship which is ashore and in a position of peril, in endeavoring to refloat, shall be allowed in general average when shown to have arisen from an actual intention to float the ship for the common safety at the risk of such damage; but where a ship is afloat no loss or damage caused by working the propelling machinery and boilers shall in any circumstances be made good as general average.

The use of the term "propelling machinery and boilers" should be noted. The addition of the word "propelling" in the 1974 Rules was designed to make it clear that if auxiliary machinery and pumps are damaged as a result of a general average act while the vessel is afloat, an allowance in general average would not be prohibited. It is only the damage caused by working the propelling machinery while the vessel is afloat that is excluded. This is so because the Rule of Interpretation makes the numbered Rules paramount.[43]

Moreover, it is only the damage caused by excessive working of the main propelling machinery while afloat which is excluded by the Rule. If the damage is sustained by the machinery while the vessel is afloat by other general average acts, such as by a collision, the allowance is proper.

As Buglass notes, although the York-Antwerp Rules do not specifically deal with the point, it is the practice to allow in general average the extra fuel and engine stores consumed while working the engines in an effort to refloat the vessel (so long as the necessary peril exists). The ordinary consumption while aground, i.e., the amounts used by such auxiliaries as would have been required if the vessel were lying at her dock completely idle, is not allowable.

Navigazione Generale Italiana v. Spencer Kellogg & Sons, Inc. (The Mincio)[44] is a classic example of a ship's engines being overworked and damaged while attempting to be refloated. In that case, the vessel stranded on the muddy bottom of the Parana River in Argentina. The place of stranding was within the zone of the Pamperos or South American hurricanes and had a hurricane occurred, it would have tended to lower the depth of the water. The master testified that there was a danger

---

43. In this instance, Rule VII is more restrictive than American practice which (in the absence of the York-Antwerp Rules) permits loss or damage to machinery while afloat to be made good so long as the facts fall within the American definition of general average.

44. *Id.*, n. 42.

of opening up seams in the plating of the steamer. The second mate testified that the vessel was aground at bow and stern but not amidships where the cargo was loaded. After running her engines full speed astern on a number of occasions the vessel was finally freed. After discharging her cargo at port of destination, she was ultimately drydocked where it was discovered that she had sustained bottom damage and there was substantial damage to the ship's engines and steering machinery.

The principal issue in the case was whether or not the vessel was in peril while aground. Having concluded that the vessel was in peril, the court awarded the claim for general average against the cargo, which sum included the damages done to the ship's engines and steering machinery.[45]

Loundes & Rudolf[46] give the following practical examples of instances of damage resulting from abnormal use of engines:

A vessel on fire at sea flooded the forward compartment which put the vessel down by the head to such an extent that the propeller was largely out of water. The working of the engines in those circumstances caused considerable damage to the machinery, to which damage was fairly within the contemplation of the master and engineers. Consequently, the damage so sustained was made good as general average.

The vessel was holed when it hit a rock and the engines were worked excessively under the same conditions as the preceding example. The damage to the machinery and from the straining of the afterpart of the vessel was allowed in general average.

A vessel caught fire at sea. Large volumes of smoke entered the shaft alley and to work the engines, it was necessary to close the shaft alley door. This made it impossible for men to enter the shaft alley to oil the bearings. The engines were kept running at full speed in order to reach port, resulting in damage to the bearings by running the engines without oiling them. That damage would occur as it did was contemplated by the ship's personnel, and the damage was allowed in general average.

Intentionally and Reasonably Made or Incurred. It is axiomatic that if a sacrifice or expenditure is to be considered a general average act it must be intentional and it must be reasonably made or incurred. The following illustrative cases will be helpful:

In *Pacific Mail S.S. Co. v. New York, H. & R. Min. Co.,*[47] the vessel stranded on a reef. The master jettisoned part of the cargo, then flooded

---

45. Compare, however, *The Edward Rutledge,* n. 42, *supra.* There, the vessel stranded twice on a soft mud bottom. Each time she freed herself by using the tidal effect, her engines and lines put ashore to the dock. The court held that the vessel was not in peril.

46. *General Average and the York/Antwerp Rules* (8th Ed.), by J. Donaldson and C. Ellis.

47. 74 F. 564 (1896).

the ship to prevent a total loss from pounding. Afterwards the ship and the remaining cargo in her were salved. As the measures were intentionally taken, not for the benefit of the ship alone but also for ship and cargo, it was held to be a case for general average.

In *Lee v. Grinnell*,[48] the sails, masts and spars of a ship accidentally caught fire. They were cut away to preserve the ship and cargo. Unfortunately, one of the spars in falling pierced the deck and caused a fire in the cargo. It then became necessary to scuttle the vessel, which sank and burned to the water's edge. As a consequence of the scuttling, a part of the cargo was damaged which otherwise would have escaped, and some injury was done to the ship by reason of swelling of grain in the hold. It was held that as the cutting away of the masts and rigging and the consequence of the fire were not caused by an intent to preserve any of the property at risk, no allowance could be made for that portion of the damage in general average, but as the scuttling was a voluntary and intentional act, every loss to ship and cargo that could be distinctly traced to the scuttling as its proximate cause was to be regarded as general average.

In *May v. Keystone Yellow Pine Co.*,[49] the rudder of the ship was partly torn loose in a gale at sea. The action of the wind and sea caused it to beat violently against the hull of the vessel, and it was cut away to prevent it from beating a hole in the vessel. It was held that the value of the rudder in its damaged condition before it was cut away was a proper subject for allowance in general average.

In *The Seapool*,[50] a vessel was dragging her anchor close to a pier and in danger of going ashore or suffering heavy damage. The master was unable to turn the vessel's head toward the sea without striking the pier and damaging the propeller. He intentionally and deliberately used the face of the pier as a pivot, but both the vessel and the pier were damaged by such action. The court found that there was a general average act, an extraordinary sacrifice having been intentionally and reasonably made.

In *Austin Friars S.S. Co. Ltd. v. Spillers and Bakers, Ltd.*,[51] a vessel after having stranded was found to be leaking badly. The master and pilot concluded that the vessel would have to be docked immediately although the tide was not favorable. In doing so, they realized that the vessel would strike the pier violently as it indeed did, causing damage to both the vessel and pier. Damage to the vessel as well as liability to the harbor authorities for the damage done to the pier were allowed in general average.

The voluntary stranding cases are also excellent examples of a voluntary sacrifice, intentionally and reasonably made, for the common

---

48. 12 N.Y. Super. Ct. 400 (N.Y., 1856).
49. 117 F. 287 (D, Pa., 1902).
50. [1934] P. 53.
51. [1915] 3 K.B. 586, 84 L.J.K.B. 1958.

safety,[52] as are the cases involving deliberate scuttling of vessels on fire to put out the fire and thereby save part of the vessel and cargo.[53]

By contrast, it can scarcely be said that a voluntary sacrifice has been intentionally and reasonably made when the sacrifice occurs, not because of any conscious volition on the part of the master or those normally in control of her but, instead, because of the orders of some other paramount authority. For example, in the leading case of *Ralli v. Troop*,[54] the vessel was moored in Calcutta and near other vessels. Cargo in her holds took fire and the ship's crew and crews from neighboring vessels assisted. Afterwards, the port authorities came with fire engines, took over direction of the vessel, pumped steam and water into the holds, moved the vessel from her moorings, and put her aground. During all of this, the master arrived back aboard. The master successfully removed part of the cargo and believed it possible to remove more. However, the port authorities were fearful of the fire spreading and, acting on their own judgment, extinguished the fire by scuttling the vessel, whereby she became a wreck, not worth repairing. The court held that sacrifice was not a voluntary one on the part of the master but, rather, a compulsory sacrifice made by the paramount authority of public officials.[55]

Another case in point is *Athel Line Ltd. v. Liverpool and London War Risk Association Ltd.*[56] where two vessels in a wartime convoy were ordered back to port because the previous convoy had sustained heavy losses by an enemy raider. The order to return to port originated with the British Admiralty. The vessels lost six days on their voyage, and extra fuel and stores were consumed. The shipowners claimed for general average from their war risk underwriters. The court held that the language of Rule A did not cover mere obedience to lawful orders of a superior authority and that the acts of the masters were not "intentionally and reasonably" made by them.

It is clear, however, that while there must be an element of choice in whatever is done, that freedom of choice may, indeed, be circumscribed. The U.S. Supreme Court made this point very clearly in *Barnard v. Adams*,[57] where the court said:

> The idea that any sacrifices at sea in times of peril are voluntary in any ordinary sense of the word is quite erroneous. It is an act of the will under the sternest pressure of necessity. The alternatives are total loss if nothing is done, a lighter loss if the danger is hastened. This is all the voluntary act which remains to the master to perform. On its

52. See discussion, *infra*, under the heading "Voluntary Stranding."
53. See discussion, *infra*, under heading "Extinguishing Fire on Shipboard."
54. 157 U.S. 386, 15 Sup.Ct. 657, 39 L.Ed. 742 (1895).
55. See discussion, *infra*, "Extinguishing Fire on Shipboard."
56. (1946) 79 Ll.L.Rep. 18.
57. 51 U.S. 270, 13 L.Ed. 417 (1850).

being performed with coolness, courage and discretion the whole property and the lives of all depend. That this small amount of volition may be exercised freely and without hesitation, the policy of the law tenders to the officer the indemnity of a general contribution.

It should be observed that both the adverbs modify both verbs in the phrase "intentionally and reasonably made or incurred." Thus, the sacrifice must be made intentionally and reasonably, and the expenditure must be incurred intentionally and reasonably.[58] Moreover, a mere intention to perform an act of sacrifice is not sufficient; the intention must be to preserve from peril by making such a sacrifice.[59]

Common Safety. This is but a shorthand way of saying "for the common safety for the purpose of preserving from peril the property involved in a common maritime adventure." In this sense, Rule A adopts the English view which does not recognize as a general principle that the sacrifice or expenditure may be for the safe prosecution of the voyage, as does the American view. It should be emphasized, however, that Rules X(b) and XI(b) of the York-Antwerp Rules do recognize that the sacrifice or expenditure may relate to the safe prosecution of the voyage and, as the numbered rules prevail over the lettered rules by virtue of the Rule of Interpretation, the principle of safe prosecution of the voyage is recognized, so long as the Rules are applicable.[60]

At the risk of stating the obvious, suppose that two charter parties were executed simultaneously; one in England and one in the United States. For some inexplicable reason, in neither charter were the York-Antwerp Rules incorporated by reference. During the course of the respective voyages of the two vessels, both vessels sustained damage to their propellers and put into ports of refuge to effect repairs so that the voyages could be safely prosecuted. Under English law, absent the application of the York-Antwerp Rules (specifically Rules X(b) and XI (b)), there would be no general average act, while under American law there would be.

Both under English law and American law, the "peril" referred to need not be immediate, but it must be real and not imaginary and it must be substantial and not merely slight or nugatory. There are literally innumerable cases from both jurisdictions that define what is a "peril." For example:

---

58. *Athel Line Ltd. v. Liverpool and London War Risk Association Ltd.*, n. 56, *supra*.

59. *Daniolos v. Bunge & Co., Ltd.* (1937) 59 Ll.L.Rep. 175, *aff'd* (1938) 62 Ll.L.Rep. 65, C.A.

60. See discussion, *supra*, and *Eagle Terminal Tankers, Inc. v. Ins. Co. of USSR*, n. 34.

"Imminent peril." *Columbian Ins. Co. v. Ashby,* 38 U.S. 331;

"Danger imminent and apparently inevitable." *Barnard v. Adams,* 51 U.S. 270 ; *The Star of Hope,* 76 U.S. 203;

"Impending peril." *McAndrews v. Thatcher,* 70 U.S. 347;

"Imminent peril and impending danger." *Fowler v. Rathbones,* 79 U.S. 102;

"Imminent danger." *The Alcona,* 9 F. 172;

"Impending danger of physical injury." *Bowring v. Thebaud,* 42 F. 794;

"Imminent peril impending over the whole." *Ralli v. Troop,* 157 U.S. 386;

"Impending peril apparently imminent." *Willcox, Peck & Hughes v. American Smelting & Refining Co.,* 210 F. 89 (SDNY, 1913);

"Real and substantial, even though the advent of any catastrophe may be distant or indeed unlikely." *Navigazione Generale Italiana v. Spencer Kellogg & Sons, Inc.,* 92 F.2d 41, 1937 AMC 1506 (2nd Cir.), *cert.den.* 302 U.S. 751 (1937);

"[s]eriousness of the danger created by an accident or peril at sea rather than its immediacy." *Eagle Terminal Tankers, Inc. v. Ins. Co. of USSR,* 637 F.2d 890, 1981 AMC 137 (2nd Cir.);

"Substantial peril, either present or probable in the future." *U.S. v. Wessel, Duval & Co.,* 123 F.Supp. 318, 1954 AMC 2070 (S.D.N.Y.);

The English definition, exemplified in *Vlassopoulos v. British and Foreign Marine Insurance Co., Ltd (The Makis),*[61] is considered a classic. There, Mr. Justice Roche said:

It is not necessary that the ship should be actually in the grip, or even nearly in the grip, of the disaster that may arise from a danger. It would be a very bad thing if shipmasters had to wait until that state of things arose in order to justify them doing an act which would be a general average act. That is all, I think, which need be said with regard to that matter, unless I add this: that "peril," which means the same thing as danger, is the word used in General Rule A, just as it is the word used in the Marine Insurance Act, 1906, Section 66. The phrase is not "immediate peril or danger." It is sufficient to say that the ship must be in danger, or that the act must be done in order to preserve her from peril. It means, of course, that the peril must be real and not imaginary, that it must be substantial and merely slight or nugatory. In short, it must be a real danger.

Unquestionably, whether or not a course of action was necessary for the common safety depends upon the facts of each particular case and the

---

61. [1929] 1 K.B. 187, 98 L.J.K.B. 53, (1928) 31 Ll.L.Rep. 313.

inferences to be drawn from those facts. This is clearly demonstrated by a comparative analysis of the following cases:

In *Navigazione Generale Italiana v. Spencer Kellogg & Sons, Inc.*,[62] the vessel was aground in the Parana River in Argentina in an area susceptible of hurricanes. Moreover, she was aground fore and aft with the principal cargo weight amidships. It was held that she was in sufficient peril to warrant the acts which ultimately got her off her strand and which were allowable in general average.

By contrast, in *The Edward Rutledge*,[63] while the vessel grounded on a muddy bottom, she was twice gotten off her strand by using her engines, the action of the tides, and the use of lines put ashore to a nearby dock. It was held that the peril was insufficient to constitute a general average situation.

In *Daniolos v. Bunge and Co., Ltd.*,[64] the vessel went aground in an artificial or dredged channel leading from the Kattegat to the port of Randers. The channel was very narrow, being only some 72 feet in width and the ship occupied the greater part of the channel with its beam of 52 feet. The bottom was chalk with a certain amount of rock and, although the channel was non-tidal, the action of the wind could either increase or decrease the amount of water in the channel, thus increasing or decreasing the draft. Although tugs and the use of her engines was attempted, she could not be got off her strand until the wind changed. The vessel's owners contended that she was in danger of damaging her bottom by being thrust further up the bank or by reason of a potential collision with other vessels, and claimed in general average. The court, however, found that although she might sustain some bottom damage, it was not of such character that it could be regarded as putting the cargo in any danger. Also, the harbor authorities could have controlled traffic in the area to minimize the danger of collision. Consequently, the peril was found to be insufficient.

In *Shaver Transportation Co. v. Travelers Indemnity Co.*,[65] a barge was loaded with caustic soda and, inadvertently, the caustic soda was contaminated with tallow which had been left in the intake lines of the barge. Had not the cargo been disposed of in some fashion, eventually over the course of time the caustic soda would have eaten its way through the plates of the barge and would doubtless have caused her to sink. The vessel owner went to considerable expense to get rid of the cargo and claimed, *inter alia*, in general average. The court held that the remote danger that the caustic soda might eventually corrode the barge's plates

---

62. *Supra*, n. 42.
63. *Supra*, n. 42.
64. *Supra*, n. 59.
65. 481 F.Supp. 892, 1980 AMC 393 (D., Ore.).

and cause it to sink did not constitute the real and substantial peril required for a general average situation.

In *Soc. Nouvelle d'Armement v. Spillars and Bakers Ltd.*,[66] a tug was employed to expedite the transit of a sailing vessel from one port to another because of a fear of submarine attack. While a peril of attack did exist, and the use of the tug no doubt minimized the risk, the court found it impossible to say that both vessels and cargo had been preserved from any extra peril and therefore, in time of war, could not be considered as an extraordinary expenditure.

Interesting cases have arisen involving the question whether the peril was "real" or "imaginary." For example, in *The Wordsworth*,[67] part of a cargo of flour was damaged because the sluices were opened at sea by order of the master, under the erroneous belief that a leak which had filled the forepeak resulted from the vessel having holed itself, and that it was consequently necessary to empty the forepeak in order to discover the hole and stop the leak. The leak proved to be caused by a break in the hawse pipe and could have been reduced without opening the sluices. The court held that the damage to the cargo as a consequence of opening the sluices was a sacrifice in the interest of all concerned and was a proper charge in general average. The reasoning of the court was that a situation of imminent danger to the whole enterprise was believed to exist, and apparently did exist such as apparently required the sacrifice to be made. It was upon that judgment and belief that the sacrifice was made, and made, as supposed and understood at the time, necessarily in the interest and for the safety of all con-cerned; i.e., it is sufficient to suppose a general average charge where the judgment of the master was exercised in good faith and was formed upon reasonable grounds.

By contrast, in *Joseph Watson & Sons v. Fireman's Fund Ins. Co.*,[68] a vessel was approaching port and the hatches of No. 1 hold were opened in order to take out some mooring ropes stowed in the top part of the hold. The master noticed what he thought was smoke coming from the hold, and, believing that the vessel was on fire, caused steam to be turned into the hold with a consequent damage to some of the cargo. In the suit which followed by the cargo against their underwriters claiming for a general average loss, the court found that the evidence did not establish that there was any fire and held that the definition of general average in the Marine Insurance Act did not cover losses incurred owing to a master supposing that a common peril existed, which, as a matter of fact, did not. In rendering his decision, the judge distinguished *The Wordsworth* upon the ground

66. [1917] 1 K.B. 865, 86 L.J.K.B. 406.
67. 88 F. 313 (S.D.N.Y, 1898).
68. (1922) 12 Ll.L.Rep. 133, [1922] 2 K.B. 355.

that in that case the ship was in actual peril, although not in a way supposed by the master. The same distinction was made in *The West Imboden.*[69] In that case, the vessel was transporting, among other things, a cargo of cotton. After encountering heavy seas in which some topside damage was done, the deck above No. 2 hold was found to be hot, and when rain and heavy seas fell on the deck, it caused vapor and steam to rise. The hatches were not opened, but the officers and the master concluded that there was a fire in the hold. Steam and water were injected into the hold, and within several hours the deck was cool. Upon arrival in port, the same deck was found to be locally warm, and more steam was injected into the hold. After discharge, however, it was found that a steampipe in the hold had fractured near the deck from which steam had escaped and heated the deck plating.

The court found as a matter of fact, of course, that there was no fire, and, there having been no fire, there was no peril and hence no claim in general average. The court distinguished *The Wordsworth* by noting that in that case there was an actual peril to cargo, the master merely being mistaken as to its degree.

The peril must be one which endangers the property involved in a common maritime adventure. Mere adverse impact upon the economic interest of one of the parties to the venture will not suffice. This was the ruling in *Barge J. Whitney,*[70] where the owners of a barge laden with molten asphalt discovered on arrival at destination that the asphalt had solidified into a solid mass because of non-functioning heating coils. The barge was towed back to its home port in a warmer climate where the solidified asphalt was removed at enormous cost. A claim for the removal costs was made under the hull policy as general average disbursements. The distinguished arbitrator ruled that "peril" has reference to the possibility of physical loss or destruction of the object insured, rather than a mere loss of economic value or commercial utility, and as the barge itself was not in any physical danger, the removal costs were not recoverable as general average disbursements.

The "property" involved need not be ship and cargo. It may be the property of some third party, such as the lessor of electronics equipment—a common situation in today's shipping concerns. And, of course, in time charters, the bunkers frequently belong to the charterers although the vessel itself may be in ballast. As has already been noted, under American law there may be a general average where the vessel is in ballast, the hull underwriters being required to contribute.

69. 89 F.2d 1004, 1936 AMC 696 (E.D.N.Y), *aff'd* 1937 AMC 462.
70. 1968 AMC 995 (M. Detels, Arb.).

Consequences of General Average Act

It has already been noted that where damage is done to property of a third party by actions deliberately taken for the common safety, such as using a pier for a pivoting point to extricate a vessel from danger, the liability to the third party as a direct consequence of a general average act may be recoverable. Rule C enunciates this principle and reads:

> *Rule C*
>
> Only such losses, damages or expenses which are the direct consequence of the General Average act shall be allowed as General Average.
>
> Loss or damage sustained by the ship or cargo through delay, whether on the voyage or subsequently, such as demurrage, and any indirect loss whatever, such as loss of market, shall not be admitted in General Average.

There are, however, varying degrees of consequences. Some may be direct and immediate; others may be somewhat remote. Recovery is limited to that which is directly consequential, but troublesome problems in the nature of those involved in determining proximate causation are always present, and it is not an easy task to distinguish between loss, damage, or expense which are recoverable and those which are not.

As the second paragraph of Rule C indicates, certain specific items are excluded; i.e., loss or damage through delay or indirect losses such as loss of market. These types of losses have always been disfavored and for perfectly sound reasons. For example, in *The Leitrim (Hudson v. British and Foreign Marine Insurance Co., Ltd.)*,[71] the vessel, under time charter, was delayed at a port of refuge to undergo repairs of damage done by fire and water used to extinguish it. The charter contained a cesser clause by which the charterers were relieved of paying charter hire during the period the vessel was not working. The vessel owners claimed the loss of the charter hire in general average. The court took a common sense approach, pointing out that the loss of time was common to all parties to the venture and all suffered by the delay. Consequently, the damages from loss of time could be rightly considered as being proportionate to the interests involved and could be left out of consideration.[72]

The exclusion as to loss or damage through delay originally referred to such loss or damage on the voyage. However, in *Wetherall and Co. Ltd. v.*

---

71. (1902) P. 256.
72. However, as shown by the discussion, *supra*, relative to Rules X and XI, wages and maintenance may be recovered in general average where the vessel is detained in a port of refuge or where the voyage is prolonged.

London Assurance Corp.,[73] a contention was made that repair costs incurred through delay after the voyage were recoverable. The court, however, held that the words "on the voyage" did not imply that delay after the voyage was allowed, noting that such an allowance was inconsistent with *The Leitrim, supra.* As now worded, the Rule makes it clear that the exclusion applies to events subsequent to the voyage.

In *Anglo-Argentine Live Stock Agency v. Temperley S.S. Co.,*[74] the vessel was delayed at a port of refuge. Fodder supplied during the delay to cattle carried on board was claimed in general average. The court held that the expense was really a loss by delay for which no claim in general average could be based.

Whether or not the consequences of a general average act are direct or remote is a question of fact in every case. Congdon states the test as follows:

> Allowances in general average are not confined to the part of the vessel or cargo which was first selected to bear the voluntary sacrifice, but extend also to such other losses as are the direct consequence of the general average act, which in nearly all cases carries with it a first and a secondary loss. It is very difficult sometimes to distinguish between a direct and an indirect consequence but, generally speaking, all losses and damages which may reasonably be considered as fairly within the contemplation of the master at the time of the general average act, or are its natural and immediate result, are treated as direct consequences of the original act, and irrespective of whether the losses or damages exceeded his intention or expectation.[75]

Lowndes suggested the following test which was quoted with approval in *Anglo-Argentine Live Stock Agency v. Temperley S.S. Co., supra:*

> . . . since giving must always imply an intention to give, what we have here to ascertain must be, what loss at once has in fact occurred, and likewise must be regarded as the natural and reasonable result of the act of sacrifice. Or, in other words, what the shipmaster would naturally, or might reasonably, have intended to give for all when he resolved upon the act. If then, upon the act of sacrifice any loss ensues, which the master did not in fact bring before his mind at the time of making the sacrifice, it would have to be considered whether it were such a loss as he naturally might or reasonably ought to have taken account of.[76]

73. (1931) 2 K.B. 448, 100 L.J.K.B. 609, (1932) 39 Ll.L.Rep. 66.
74. [1899] 2 Q.B. 403, 68 L.J.Q.B. 1021.
75. See *Columbian Ins. Co. v. Ashby,* 38 U.S. 331 (1839).
76. The same test was again approved in *Austin Friars S.S. Co. v. Spillers and Bakers,* [1915] 3 K.B. 586, C.A.

With diffidence and a due deference to the learned authorities, the following test is suggested:

If the loss or damage was a natural and probable consequence of the general average act, or may reasonably be considered to have been a thing which the master contemplated would or might occur, or which, notwithstanding the exigencies of the moment, he ought reasonably to have thought about, then the loss or damage is a direct consequence of the general average act.

Only by reference to the facts in the decisions bearing on this principle can one attain a "feel" for the subject which will assist in arriving at a correct conclusion.

For example, in *McCall v. Houlder Bros.*,[77] a ship laden with perishable cargo sustained damage to her propeller which necessitated resort to a port of refuge. It being impossible to store the cargo ashore because of a lack of storage facilities, the vessel was tipped forward by the head so as to facilitate repairs to the propellers. In doing so, some of the cargo was damaged by the water. As the tipping forward was a general average act carried out for the preservation of the vessel and cargo, the incidental damage to the cargo was held to be recoverable in general average. It will be seen that the damage to the cargo by such an expedient was a direct and immediate consequence of the general average act.

Another example is *Anglo-Argentine Live Stock Agency v. Temperley S.S. Co., supra,* in which the ship involved was carrying cattle and sheep from Argentina to England. An Order in Council of the British government forbade the importation of cattle which had entered a port in Brazil. Unfortunately, the vessel was compelled to put into Bahia, Brazil after having sprung a leak in heavy weather. As a consequence, the cattle could not be discharged in England and they were sold at Antwerp for a sum much less than they would have brought had they been sold in England. The court held that putting into the port of refuge was a general average act and the loss on the sale was, therefore, allowable in general average.[78]

Other examples are *The Seapool*,[79] in which the master used a pier as a pivot in order to bring the vessel's head around so it could put to sea, and *Austin Friars Steamship Co. v. Spillers and Bakers Ltd.*,[80] in which the vessel was deliberately made to collide with a pier in order that she might be grounded to prevent a total sinking.

---

77. (1897) 66 L.J.Q.B. 408, 8 Asp. M.L.C. 252.
78. Note, however, that fodder supplied to the cattle during the enforced stay at Bahia was not allowed in general average as the expense was one which was consequent on the delay for which no claim in general average could be based.
79. [1934] P. 53, [1933] All E.R. 764, 18 Asp. M.L.C. 477.
80. [1915] 3 K.B. 586, 13 Asp. M.L.C. 162.

A classic example is *Australian Coastal Shipping Commission v. Green*,[81] which involved a claim for general average from shipowners who had been compelled to employ tugs to assist two of their vessels which were in distress. In both instances, the tugs were employed under the very stringent U.K. Standard Towage Conditions form requiring *inter alia* that the owners of the vessel assisted indemnify the tug owner for damage to the tug. During the assistance maneuvers, the tow lines broke and fouled the tugs' propellers. In the first instance, the shipowners prevailed on grounds that the tug was unseaworthy, but incurred considerable legal fees in defending. In the second instance, the tug sustained damage and had to also pay for salvage assistance provided by a third vessel. As a consequence, she was entitled to recover the sums involved from the shipowners. The shipowners contended in both instances that the expenses incurred (which they had to pay) were recoverable in general average.

A seminal issue involved was whether or not it was reasonable to enter into contracts for towage assistance which involved indemnifying the towed vessel. On this submission, the court agreed it was reasonable, as the shipowner obtained a lower rate for towage services in return for his indemnity. The court also found that there is a substantial risk in towage operations that the tow line might break and foul the tug's propeller. Thus, the court had no difficulty in finding that the hiring of the tugs under the U.K. Standard Towing Conditions was a general average act, intentionally and reasonably made for the common safety of the maritime adventure.

The principal issue before the court was whether or not the expenses were the "direct consequence" of the general average acts within the scope of Rule C. At first instance, the court held that they were. On appeal, Lord Denning (then Master of the Rolls) stated as follows:

> In both cases the master, when he engaged the tug, should have envisaged that the towline might break and foul the propeller. When it happened it did not break the chain of causation. The indemnity clause was most stringent. But did it break the chain of causation? Seeing that the clause was reasonable and was agreed to, the expenditure under it flowed directly from the general average act. It was the direct consequence of the general average act and must be accepted as general average loss.

Attention is also directed to *Van den Toorn v. Leeming*,[82] in which a crack was discovered in the shaft of a steamship while she was at sea. The shaft

81. [1971] 1 Q.B. 456, [1971] 1 All E.R. Rep. 353, [1970] 1 Lloyd's Rep. 209, [1971] 1 Lloyd's Rep. 16.
82. 79 F. 107 (2nd Cir., 1897). See, also, *Sea-Land Service, Inc. v. Aetna Ins. Co.*, 545 F.2d 1313, 1976 AMC 2164 (2nd Cir.).

was strengthened by bolts and the vessel proceeded toward port at a reduced speed. However, prior to reaching port, the shaft completely broke and greatly damaged the machinery. Contribution in general average was claimed by the shipowner from the cargo on the ground that the risk to the vessel by proceeding with the temporarily strengthened shaft was foreseen by the master and deliberately undertaken by him in full contemplation of the liability to the damage to the machinery which, in fact, subsequently occurred. That risk was incurred, according to the shipowner, in order to work the vessel into port and thus save the vessel and its cargo a greater expense in obtaining outside assistance. The evidence showed that while the master and officers recognized the possibility of a new breakdown and further damage, they confidently believed that it could be avoided. It was held, in view of such evidence, that there was no such voluntary or intentional sacrifice as to make the case one for general average.

In *Norwich & N.Y. Transp. Co. v. Ins. Co. of N.A.*,[83] the vessel struck a rock, causing a serious leak forward and danger of sinkinsg. The master, in preference to running her upon the rocks in the vicinity, took her some distance and breached her on what he supposed to be a sandy beach. Contrary to his expectation, the bottom was soft mud. The bow stuck in the mud and settled until the vessel sank and the main deck, on which was the cargo, was submerged and the cargo damaged. Had the bottom been of sand, as supposed, so as to lift and sustain the bow, the vessel would probably have remained afloat or at least with her deck above water. It was held that the loss was attributable to the attempted stranding as the proximate cause and was a subject for general average. The court discussed the doctrine of proximate cause and noted that if a maritime loss follows as a natural consequence or inevitable result of the original and involuntary cause of danger, then such original cause should be regarded as the proximate cause, but when a voluntary act intervenes, which is itself the cause of the loss, such act being substituted for the original danger of loss with a design of saving, the substituted act should be regarded as the proximate cause for general average purposes.

Rule C operates where, for example, pollution is the direct consequence of a general average act and oil pollution expenses are incurred. Thus, should a vessel be obliged to enter a port of refuge following an accident which results in the vessel leaking oil, and expenditures are incurred to avoid or minimize the pollution or liabilities arising therefrom, such expenditures should be allowable in general average. Correspondingly, pollution resulting directly from the jettison of oil, whether cargo or bunkers, for the common safety should be allowable in general average. Obviously, however, the usual rules applicable to consequential

---

83. 129 F. 1006 (2nd Cir., 1904).

damage should apply and if the pollution did not occur until some time after the general average act or was not near it in geographical terms, the pollution might be considered too remote and therefore not a direct consequence of the general average act. By the same token, if the vessel leaking oil proceeded directly to her next scheduled port, and there was no diversion into a port of refuge, there has been no general average act and any expenditure or liability resulting from the leakage would be considered the inevitable result of the accident and not the result of a general average act or the direct consequence of a general average act; i.e., the leakage would be of an accidental nature.

Rules B, E, and G

Rule B reads:

> *Rule B*
> General Average sacrifices and expenses shall be borne by the different contributing interests on the basis hereinafter provided.

This rule merely expresses the general principle that what is sacrificed or spent for the benefit of all shall be made good by all. The words "basis hereinafter provided" merely refers to the numbered rules which will be discussed subsequently.

This rule first appeared in the 1924 Rules and remains unchanged. Originally, it formed part of Rule A but was subsequently set forth as a separate rule to avoid any misunderstandings relative to the treatment of general average losses and expenditures specifically provided in the numbered rules but not falling within the Rule A definition. Nonetheless, such a misunderstanding did surface in *Vlassopoulos v. British and Foreign Marine Insurance Co. Ltd. (The Makis)*[84] and in *Orient Mid-East Lines, Inc. et al. v. S.S. Orient Transporter.*[85]

Rule E provides:

> *Rule E*
> The onus of proof is upon the party claiming in general average to show that the loss or expense claimed is properly allowable as general average.

This Rule, too, appeared for the first time in the 1924 Rules and has never been amended. It merely states the obvious under American and English jurisprudence, but may be of value in cases of general average coming before foreign courts where questions of burden of proof may

---

84. *Supra*, n. 31.
85. *Supra*, n. 33.

well differ.[86] The effect of the rule would be to express clearly where the burden of proof lies and should tend toward a desirable international uniformity.

The proper construction of Rule E was involved in *Sea-Land Service, Inc. v. Aetna Ins. Co. (The Beauregard),*[87] where the vessel involved went aground on rocks near the entrance of Rio Haina Harbor, Dominican Republic. As she had ended up fast on the rocks, the master called for tugs. After the tugs arrived and lines were put aboard, pulling commenced but just as she was beginning to move (according to some witnesses—not all), the towline broke and she ended up broadside on rocks further inshore, incurring approximately $478,000 in damages. Fortunately, several days later, she was successfully refloated and eventually made it in to harbor safely but with serious bottom damage.

At first instance, the trial court denied the vessel owner a general average contribution for the substantial bottom damage from cargo underwriters on the grounds that the bottom damage was not a general average loss, although a consent judgment for the vessel owner was entered for some $54,000, representing the costs of towing and salvage plus interest. In short, the vessel owner failed to sustain its burden under Rule E of proving that the bottom damage was "more likely" to have occurred because of the towage (admittedly, a general average act) than if no towage had been attempted. The appeals court affirmed on the ground that the trial court's findings were supported by evidence and were not clearly erroneous. The appeals court said, in part:

> We agree that the Master did or should have anticipated that the towline might part. We further agree that, if the breaking of the towline permitted a sideward movement that would not otherwise have occurred, the damage would have been general average and cases such as *Australian Coastal Shipping Commission v. Green,* [1971] 1 Ll.Rep. 16 (C.A., 1970) and *Anglo-Grecian Steam Trading Co. v. T. Beynon & Co.,* [1926] 25 Ll.L.Rep. 122 (K.B. 1926) would be in point. . . . However, the applicability of these cases here depends upon Sea-Land's ability to establish that the tow permitted the vessel to be pulled free enough to permit a sideward motion which otherwise would not have occurred. In sum, Sea-Land cannot escape the issue of fact which, as we have already indicated, it has failed to do.

Rule E appears to have been mentioned in only one English decision.[88]

---

86. In Anglo-American jurisprudence, the rule is simply that one pleading the affirmative of an issue must prove or establish that which he alleges on the balance of probabilities. Thus, one asserting or claiming an allowance in general average must prove the facts entitling him to that allowance.

87. 545 F.2d 1313, 1976 AMC 2164 (2nd Cir.).

88. *The Seapool* [1934] P. 53.

A general average statement is without legal effect and is open to question in every particular in the absence of any agreement to the contrary. In the absence of some stipulation on the subject, the average adjuster's function is only that of aiding or assisting the owner in gathering and stating data and making appropriate calculations as a suggested basis for an adjustment to be made by the owner, or under the owner's direction, and it is quite clear that an average statement under these circumstances is legally *ex parte*.[89]

However, it has been held that a general average statement prepared by an average adjuster is *prima facie* proof of (1) the losses, damages and expenses which, as factual matters, are the direct consequence of a general average act, (2) the values attaching to such losses, damages and expenses, and (3) the computations proportioning these losses, damages and expenses between the parties to the venture, but if no general average agreement has been entered into, then the party claiming the general average contribution must prove by evidence independent of a general average statement that a general average act occurred.[90] The burden of establishing that a general average act occurred and the accuracy of the computations in the general average statement is upon the party seeking the general average contribution.[91]

Rule G provides:

Rule G

General average shall be adjusted as regards both loss and contribution upon the basis of values at the time and place when and where the adventure ends. This rule shall not affect the determination of the place at which the average statement is to be made up.

Thus, although the time and place when and where the adventure ends determines the basis of values, the shipowner is at liberty to choose any adjuster.

Congdon states it as follows:

Vessel and cargo having arrived at their port of destination and the voyage terminated, the adjustment of a general average loss occurring on the voyage is usually made at that port, although not necessarily so,

89. *U.S. v. Atlantic Mut. Ins. Co.*, 298 U.S. 483, 1936 AMC 993 (1933); *Nesco*, 47 F.2d 643, 1931 AMC 657 (SDNY, 1931); *Corrado Societa Anonima D. v. L. Mundet & Son*, 91 F.2d 726, 1937 AMC 1257; *Navigazione Generale Italiana v. Spencer Kellogg & Sons*, 92 F.2d 41, 1937 AMC 1506 (2nd Cir., 1937); *Cia Atlantica Pacifica, S.A. v. Humble Oil & Ref. Company, (The M/V Clydewater)* 274 F.Supp. 884, 1967 AMC 1474 (D., Md., 1967); *Great Eastern Assoc. v. India*, 1978 AMC 1288 (SDNY, 1978); *Empire Stevedoring Co. v. Oceanic Adjusters, Ltd.*, 315 F.Supp. 921, 1971 AMC 795 (S.D.N.Y, 1970). And see discussion, *infra*, under the heading "Actions to Enforce General Average."

90. *Cia Atlantica Pacifica, S.A. v. Humble Oil & Refining Company (The M/V Clydewater)*, 274 F.Supp. 884, 1967 AMC 1474 (D., Md., 1967).

91. *Id.*, n. 90.

except that wherever it is drawn up it must, apart from a valid agreement to the contrary, be in accordance with the law, customs, and usages of the port of destination, and York/Antwerp Rules, when the latter are provided for in the contract of affreightment.

Obviously, in the case of sacrifices, the adjustment is necessarily delayed until arrival of vessel or cargo at destination, contribution being dependent upon final saving of the vessel or a substantial part of the cargo, or both.

Where the voyage is broken up at a port of refuge, and a severance of interests occurs there, the adjustment, in the absence of agreement to the contrary, should be made in accordance with the law, customs, and usages at such port.[92]

The shipowner, except when there is an agreement to the contrary in the charter party or contract of affreightment, appoints the adjuster. Although appointed by the shipowner, the adjuster's fees are borne by all the interests in proportion to their contributions.

Rule G must be read in conjunction with Rules XVI and XVII, the first of which relates to the amount to be made good for cargo lost or damaged by sacrifice, and the second of which relates to contributory values. These Rules are discussed subsequently under the appropriate headings.

It will be noted that Rule G does not define when and where the adventure ends. Logically, it should be the common maritime adventure referred to in Rule A. Thus, if the cargo is carried on to its destination, the port of destination would be where the adventure ends; correspondingly, if the voyage is abandoned, it would be the port of abandonment. Complex problems, however, can arise where cargo is carried on liner terms and the vessel's itinerary calls for her to stop at a number of successive ports. For example, suppose that a general average loss occurs between the first port of call and the second port of call, and part of the cargo is consigned to the second port of call and part to the third port of call. Obviously, the value of each part of the cargo could be determined at the third port of call, or, at the port of call to which it was consigned.[93]

Upon arrival of the vessel at the port where the adventure ends, whether that be the port of destination or the port of abandonment, at what time does the adventure end? It would seem that the only time in which this would make any difference is where there are violent fluctuations in market values. Rule XVI, however, states that it is the last day of discharge.

92. *National Board of Marine Underwriters v. Melchers,* 45 F. 643, (D., Pa., 1891); *The Eliza Lines,* 102 F. 184 (lst Cir., 1900). If the foreign law is not proved in U.S. courts, U.S. law and customs govern. *Olivari v. Thames & Mersey Marine Ins. Co.,* 45 F. 894 (S.D.N.Y, 1888).

93. See, in this connection, *Green Star Shipping Co., Ltd. v. The London Assurance* [1933] 1 K.B. 378, (1931) 39 Ll.L.Rep. 213, (1932) 43 Ll.L.Rep. 523.

Rule F is more properly discussed in a subsequent portion of this chapter in connection with Rule XIV relating to temporary repairs. It provides simply:

Rule F
Any extra expense incurred in place of another expense which would have been allowable as general average shall be deemed to be general average and so allowed without regard to the saving, if any, to other interests, but only up to the amount of the general average expense avoided.

Effect of Fault

It is a basic principle of common law in the English speaking jurisdictions that no party may claim damages or recompense for loss or damage arising from his own negligent acts. It will be seen that the right of a party to claim a general average contribution is dependent as a matter of fact upon whether or not he was free from actionable fault, but while a party at fault may not be able to claim contribution from the other parties, this does not prevent the innocent parties from claiming contributions from the other interests.[94]

It was for this reason that Rule D was inserted in the York-Antwerp Rules. The intention was that rights under contracts of affreightment should be severed from rights in general average. Stated in another fashion, rights in general average are unimpaired by any breach of the contract of affreightment, whether or not the claimant for general average contribution is the party at fault. Thus, the rights of innocent parties to the venture are not prejudiced by the fact that one of the parties to the venture was negligent or at fault, but the common law position of the party at fault is not improved. Regardless of how the general average situation arose, if in fact there is a general average sacrifice or expenditure, those parties to the venture who are innocent of fault can claim contribution from all the other interests, including the party at fault, but the party at fault is precluded from obtaining contribution unless his fault is excused by virtue of contract or law.

Rule D reads:

Rule D
Rights in contribution in General Average shall not be affected though the event which gave rise to the sacrifice or expenditure may have been due to the fault of one of the parties to the adventure; but this shall not prejudice any remedies or defenses which may be open against or to that party in respect of such fault.

---

94. *Schloss v. Heriot* (1863), 32 L.J.C.P. 211, 143 E.R. 366; *Strang, Steel v. Scott* [1889] A.C. 601; *The Irrawaddy*, 171 U.S. 187 (1898).

Congdon put it very cogently when he said:

The fact, however, that the necessity for the sacrifice or expenditure for the common benefit arose through unseaworthiness or negligence makes it none the less a general average damage or loss, viz., one incurred for the general benefit of vessel and cargo; the existence of the unseaworthiness or negligence does not change the nature of such damage or loss, but, in the absence of a valid contract to the contrary, the shipowner is precluded from claiming contribution from the cargo.

It would, of course, be grossly unfair to penalize an innocent cargo owner by denying him a right of contribution against the negligent shipowner and the other owners of cargo by holding that the fault of the shipowner precluded the application of general average principles. And this was the holding in *Pacific Mail S.S. Co. v. New York, Honduras & Rosario Mining Co.*,[94a] where the court said, in part:

. . . The appellant seeks to broaden the principle, and make it assert that no general average can exist if the shipowner or his servants created the danger to relieve from which the sacrifice was made. This proposed enlargement would turn the equities of general average into injustice, for it would compel innocent cargo, which had been sacrificed to cure the consequences of the vessel's fault, to suffer alone, although it had freed the rest of the cargo from peril. It is true that the owner of of the vessel cannot claim contribution, and is also liable for indemnity to the cargo which has been sacrificed. But the fact that the vessel was in fault presents no equitable reason for preventing the cargo owner from his right of contribution from the owners of the salved cargo, and gives them no just reason for refusing to contribute. When the calamity which was initiated by the fault of the master is imminent, it is his duty to take the measures to overcome his mistake, and, if necessary, he has the power of sacrificing a portion of the cargo to save the residue; but his previous fault does not impair the cargo owner's equitable right to receive compensation, if his sacrifice has saved the property of others.

In *Goulandris Brothers Ltd. v. B. Goldman & Sons Ltd.*,[94b] the ship was unseaworthy, but the carrier nonetheless pressed its claim for a general average contribution. Pearson, J. said:

In my view, the manifest objects of Rule D are to keep all questions of alleged fault outside the average adjustment and to preserve, unimpaired, the legal position at the stage of enforcement. The effect of the

94a. 74 F. 564.
94b. [1957] 2 Lloyd's Rep. 207.

first part of the rule is that the average adjustment is compiled on the assumption that the casualty has not been caused by anybody's fault.

The first part [of Rule D] refers to the right to contribution in general average as they will be set out in the average adjustment, and these are properly and naturally called "rights," because normally the holder of such rights is entitled to receive payment. But the second part of the Rule provides that the first part is not to prejudice remedies for faults.

The *Goulandris* decision was cited with approval in *Eisenerz v. Federal Commerce & Navigation*,[94c] where, after a grounding, cargo was discharged ashore and reloaded after the vessel had been repaired. Unfortunately, in the loading process some of the cargo was lost, damaged, or admixed. The court denied the shipowner's claim for reimbursement for the stevedoring expenses because the surveyors employed to supervise the loading were deemed to be agents of the shipowner who was thus negligent in the "care, custody and control" of the cargo.

Prior to the ratification of the Hague Rules, English law permitted wide-ranging clauses in contracts of affreightment which excused vessel owners even from their own negligence. To the contrary, under American law, common carriers were essentially "insurers" of the property carried, and clauses purporting to exempt the carrier from liability for a loss caused by the negligence of himself or his crew were considered contrary to public policy.[95]

As a consequence, American shipowners were placed at a great disadvantage compared with their foreign competitors. Although cargo interests in the United States possessed a powerful lobby, it was apparent to all that some method would have to be devised to encourage shipowning in the United States and to afford some equitable measure of protection— and competitive position—to American shipowners. The Harter Act was the result.

The first and second sections banned clauses of exoneration; the third allowed certain exemptions from liability if the shipowner used "due diligence" to make the vessel seaworthy prior to commencing the voyage; the fourth required the issuance of bills of lading showing numbers and marks; the fifth authorized the Customs service to deny clearance to vessels whose bills of lading were not in conformity with the Act; the sixth preserved the Fire Statute and Limitation of Liability Statute, and the seventh made the Act inapplicable to the transportation of live animals.

The Harter Act worked well in the United States and, subsequently, was copied in Australia, New Zealand, and Canada. The genius of the Harter Act lay in what the eminent authority, Arnould Knauth, called the

---

94c. 31 D.L.R. (3d) 209, [1970] 2 Lloyd's Rep. 332, 1970 AMC 227.
95. *Liverpool & Great Western Steamship Co. v. Phoenix Ins. Co.*, 129 U.S. 397.

"fortunate formula"; i.e., that if a shipowner exercised due diligence to make his vessel seaworthy prior to the commencement of the voyage he was entitled to exemption from liability for faults and errors in the navigation or management of his vessel, but held liable for negligence, fault or failure in the proper loading, stowage, custody, care or proper delivery of cargo entrusted to his charge.

Following enactment of the Harter Act, there were many international efforts toward achieving uniformity in bills of lading, culminating in the conference at The Hague in 1921. After intensive study, the draft of an acceptable ocean bill of lading was agreed upon. The result was known as "The Hague Rules," the intention being that the rules would be voluntarily incorporated in bills of lading much as were the well-known York-Antwerp Rules. Minor amendments were made at later conferences in 1922 and 1923. In 1924, the Convention was signed by the United States. However, it was not until 1936 that the Congress finally adopted the Hague Rules, with minor amendments, as the law of the United States.[96]

Contrasts—The Harter Act and The Carriage of Goods by Sea Act[97]

By its terms, the Harter Act covered shipments between ports of the United States and its possessions as well as shipments to and from foreign ports. The Carriage of Goods by Sea Act (herein referred to as "Cogsa") applies to contracts for carriage of goods by sea to or from ports of the United States in foreign trade. But Cogsa also provides that by express agreement, the Act may be made applicable to shipments between any port of the United States or its possessions and any other port of the United States or its possessions; this practice has been labelled the "Coastwise Option."

96. 46 U.S.C. 1300-1315.

97. In the discussion that follows, comment for the most part is restricted to the differences between the Harter Act and the United States Carriage of Goods by Sea Act, 1936. Acts comparable to the U.S. Carriage of Goods by Sea Act, 1936, incorporating the provisions of the Hague Rules, will be found in the United Kingdom (Carriage of Goods by Sea Act, 1924); Australia (Sea Carriage of Goods Act, 1925); Canada (Carriage of Goods by Water Act, R.S.C., 1970, c.C-15, 1924); New Zealand (Sea Carriage of Goods Act, 1940, as amended by the Sea Carriage of Goods Amendment Act, 1968). The essential features of those acts, as well as those of other seafaring nations, will be found summarized in Appendix "B," *Marine Cargo Claims* (2d), by William Tetley. The reader is especially directed to Professor Tetley's volume, which is international in scope and replete with decisions from nearly all jurisdictions having ratified or acceded to the Brussels Convention, 1924 or having enacted the provisions of the Hague Rules into their organic law. Attention is also directed to the new Visby Rules, which came into force on June 23, 1977 for ten nations. At that time, these Rules were already in force in the Scandanavian countries, many of the East Bloc countries and Argentina. Great Britain has ratified; at this writing, Canada, Australia, New Zealand, and the United States have not. It appears unlikely that the United States will ratify or accede in the future. The future of the new Hamburg Rules is even more bleak. For an up-to-date and exhaustive discussion of the Visby Rules, the Hamburg Rules, and their interplay with the Hague Rules, see Tetley, *Marine Cargo Claims* (2d).

A close reading of Cogsa, as compared with the Harter Act, will reveal that Cogsa applies to the parties to a shipping contract only while the cargo is being moved by water. Consequently (since Cogsa expressly preserves the Harter Act's provisions regarding the duties, responsibilities, and liabilities of the ship or carrier prior to the time when the goods are loaded on or after the time they are discharged from the ship), the Harter Act to this extent still applies.

Knauth, in his excellent text *Ocean Bills of Lading*, has so graphically described the "essential theoretical" difference between the two Acts that his comment has been extensively quoted and deserves repetition here:

> The essential theoretical difference between the Harter Act and the Hague Rules or Carriage of Goods by Sea Acts is that the negligence or exception clause of the Harter Act—Section 3—is conditional; it never operates to exonerate the carrier unless due diligence has been used to make the ship seaworthy in all respects, regardless of causal connections; whereas the exception clause of the Hague Rules—Article 4—is positive; it always operates to exonerate the carrier unless due diligence has been used in some respect proximately causing or contributing to the loss. While both the Harter Act and the Act of 1936 are statutory negligence clauses to which the shipper and carrier must conform, the Harter Act is expressed in a conditional way, whereas the Act of 1935 is expressed to declare the law.

Interestingly, the more onerous burden of the Harter Act was not judicially established until 1933 in *The Isis*.[98] In that case, a vessel left port in an unseaworthy condition because the owner failed to exercise due diligence. While proceeding up the Weser River in that unseaworthy condition, the vessel stranded through negligent navigation. There was no causal connection between the unseaworthy condition and the negligent stranding. Nevertheless, the Supreme Court held that the shipowner was not entitled to exemption under the Harter Act because he had failed to exercise due diligence to make the vessel seaworthy. Stated in another fashion, the vessel must have been seaworthy when it sailed or due diligence to make it seaworthy must have been exercised, and the burden is upon the shipowner to establish one or the other of those conditions.[99] Moreover, the exercise of due diligence to make the vessel seaworthy is unavailing, unless the shipowner is careful to claim the exemption in the contract of carriage. This was the holding in *The Carib Prince*,[100] where the carrier had inserted a provision in the bill of lading exempting him from accidents caused by latent defects in the hull, but this was held insufficient

98. 290 U.S. 333, 1933 AMC 1565, 48 Ll.L.Rep. 35 (1933).
99. *International Navigation Co. v. Farr & Bailey Mfg. Co.*, 181 U.S. 218 (1901).
100. 170 U.S. 655 (1898).

to protect him from liability for latent defects existing in the hull at the the voyage's outset. A close reading of the case reveals that had the carrier stated specifically that the exemption was to apply to latent defects existing both at and after the commencement of the voyage, he would have been insulated from liability.

Keeping in mind the fundamental difference between the Harter Act and Cogsa—that is, the Harter Act is worded in a conditional fashion, whereas Cogsa is worded in an absolute fashion—it is clear that Cogsa does not condition exemptions from liability on due diligence to make the vessel seaworthy. It is only liability for loss due to unseaworthiness that is conditioned. This is clear from a reading of Section 4(1) of Cogsa which states flatly that:

> Neither the carrier nor the ship shall be liable for the loss or damage arising or resulting from unseaworthiness unless caused by want of due diligence on the part of the carrier to make the ship seaworthy . . . [101]

The due diligence required by the Harter Act is nondelegable. The failure of independent contractors hired by the shipowner, even though of the highest repute, to use due diligence saddles the shipowner with liability just as certainly as if the negligence were that of the general manager of the shipowner or its executive Vice-President.[102] The same rule applies under the various Carriage of Goods by Sea Acts. See, in this connection, the landmark decision in *The Muncaster Castle*, decided by the House of Lords in 1961.[103] In that case, the *Muncaster Castle* was placed in the custody of one of the most reputable shipyards in England for its annual survey. In the course of the survey, the storm valves were opened. After the survey, a shipfitter negligently tightened the nuts on the covers, but such negligent tightening could not possibly have been discovered by any reasonable inspection. On the return voyage, having encountered heavy weather, the covers became loosened and seawater entered and damaged the cargo. Citing a number of American decisions, the House of Lords held that due diligence in the work itself was required and that the shipowner was liable for failing to exercise that due diligence.

The importance of exercising due diligence to provide a seaworthy vessel cannot be overemphasized. Cargo underwriters in the United States are exceptionally perceptive on the subject and quick to question the seaworthiness of the vessel and the exercise of due diligence when the facts so warrant.

---

101. See, in this connection, *The Captayannis S.*, 306 F.Supp. 866, 1969 AMC 2484 (D., Ore.).

102. *International Navigation Co. v. Farr & Bailey Mfg. Co.*, 181 U.S. 218 (1901).

103. [1961] A.C. 807, [1961] 1 Lloyd's Rep. 57, 1961 AMC 1357; see, also *American Linseed Co. v. Norfolk S.S. Co.*, 32 F.2d 291; *Norddeutscher Lloyd v. Ins. Co. of N.A.*, 110 F. 420, 427.

The terms "due diligence," "unseaworthiness," "management of the vessel," and "care, custody and control of the cargo" do not seem to differ under the Harter Act nor under Cogsa. Consequently, cases arising under the Harter Act are frequently cited interchangeably with cases arising under Cogsa.

The classic definition of "unseaworthiness" in the United States will be found in *The Silvia*[104] in which the court stated:

> The test of seaworthiness is whether the vessel is reasonably fit to carry the goods which she has undertaken to transport.

In *The Southwark*,[105] the Supreme Court also stated:

> As seaworthiness depends not only on the vessel being staunch and fit to meet the perils of the sea, but upon its character in reference to the particular cargo to be transported, it follows that the vessel must be able to transport the cargo which it is held out as fit to carry or it is not seaworthy in that respect.

Seaworthiness is a relative term, of course, and consequently must be considered in relationship to the voyage undertaken, the cargo to be carried, and its stowage. Perfection is not required.[106] In *The Sagamore*,[107] the court stated:

> A vessel may be perfectly seaworthy for cargo-carrying purposes around the harbor, and not be seaworthy for oceanic carriage; and she may be seaworthy for the carriage of a load of lumber, and not be seaworthy for a load of steel rails.

Moreover, seaworthiness is not established by the granting of classification or other inspection certificates.[108] A vessel must be able to withstand the weather to be normally expected and the generally predictable hazards; it will be presumed in such circumstances that the vessel is unseaworthy if the cause of damage to cargo is unexplained.[109]

Significantly, the Harter Act states that the obligation to exercise due diligence must be complied with up to the time of sailing of the vessel from the loading port.[110] Should the vessel be compelled to put into a port of refuge and while in that port come under the supervision or control of managing personnel of the owner, the obligation to exercise due

104. 171 U.S. 462 (1898).

105. 191 U.S. 1 (1903).

106. *The Briton*, 70 F.2d 146, 1934 AMC 667 (6th Cir.). See, also, *Standard Oil Co. v. Anglo-Mexican Petroleum*, 112 F.Supp. 630, 1953 AMC 1317 (S.D.N.Y.).

107. 300 F. 701, 1924 AMC 961 (2d Cir.).

108. *The Georgian*, 4 F.Supp. 718, 1933 AMC 1540 (S.D., Fla.) *aff'd* 76 F.2d 550 (5th Cir.).

109. *The Barge Crown*, 290 F. 733, 1923 AMC 630 (2nd Cir.).

110. *Erie & St. Lawrence Corp. v. Barnes-Ames Company*, 52 F.2d 217, 1931 AMC 1994 (W.D.N.Y., 1931).

diligence is revived and must be complied with before the vessel leaves the port of refuge.[111]

A vessel must be kept up-to-date in order to be found seaworthy.[112] Even though governmental regulations may not then require the installation of certain types of equipment, common prudence may dictate that this is necessary. This was amply demonstrated in *The T.J. Hooper*,[113] in which a tugboat not fitted with a radio was engaged in towing on the Atlantic coast. During the voyage, radio warnings were transmitted of the pendency of a storm. Had the tugboat had a radio aboard it, the warnings would have been received, and she could have headed for a port of refuge. Because of the failure of the tug to have a radio aboard, the tug lost her tow. The tug was found to be unseaworthy.

A shipowner's burden of proving due diligence includes the burden of showing that the latent defect (which in that case manifested itself during the voyage) was not discoverable prior to the commencement of the voyage.[114] It matters not that the vessel involved was a "private" ship; i.e., sailing under a charter party where the whole reach of the vessel was available for one cargo. The rule is the same, and although the vessel may be reasonably fit still breaks down under ordinary strains of the voyage, when she does so, the burden rests upon her to show her fitness. This was the case in *Societa Anonima Cantiero Olivo v. Fed. Ins. Co. (The Ettore)*,[115] where the vessel was under a private charter to transport cork from Lisbon to Philadelphia. While enroute and in relatively heavy weather, her tail shaft broke just forward of the screw which dropped off, leaving the ship helpless. The vessel was towed to a port of refuge where, after temporary repairs, she completed her voyage. Her owners claimed in general average. The principle issue was as to the seaworthiness of the vessel when she broke ground at Lisbon.

At first instance, the trial court held that the burden of proving seaworthiness was upon the shipowner and that that burden had not been

111. *The Isis*, 290 U.S. 333, 1933 AMC 1565, 48 Ll.L.Rep. 35 (1933).

112. *The Pacific Fir*, 57 F.2d 965, 1932 AMC 738 (2d Cir.).

113. 60 F.2d 737, 1932 AMC 1169 (2d Cir.). Note, also, pursuant to the Ports and Waterways Safety Act, 33 U.S.C. 1221 *et seq.* (1970), the Department of Transportation has adopted regulations requiring radar and other safety features aboard self-propelled vessels of 1,600 or more tons operating on the navigable waters of the United States. Although it was held in *The Portland Trader*, 327 F.2d 638, 1964 AMC 1500, [1963] 2 Lloyd's Rep. 278 that seaworthiness does not require a vessel to be equipped with radar, it appears that it is only a matter of time until vessels will be held unseaworthy for failure to have radar aboard and to use it. See *The Bergechief*, 274 F.2d 469, 1960 AMC 1380 (2d Cir.). More and more frequently, for example, vessels are being found at fault for failure to utilize radar properly or at all. *Gulfcoast Transit v. Anco Princess*, 1978 AMC 2471, [1978] 1 Lloyd's Rep. 293 (E.D.,La.); *Gulfcoast v. Bayou Liberty*, 1978 AMC 969 (E.D.,La.). See, also, the comment of the court in *The Chusan* [1955] 2 Lloyd's Rep. 685, where Mr. Justice Wilmer stated that one could "expect" that a modern vessel would be equipped with radar.

114. *The Caledonia*, 157 U.S. 124 (1895).

115. 62 F.2d 769, 1933 AMC 323 (2d Cir.).

carried. On appeal, the Second Circuit affirmed, noting that the right of contribution in general average is a creature of equity, and, in the absence of some reservation of the right, an unseaworthy private ship may not have contribution against the cargo when her defects occasion the sacrifice, even though those defects were not discoverable by due diligence and even though she had excused herself for breach of her contract to carry. The court noted that what determines the obligations of a vessel under a contract of affreightment is not relevant to her affirmative right to contribution in general average; i.e., an excuse for nonperformance of the contract of affreightment does not supply a fact necessary and essential to the right of contribution in general average. Thus, although a shipowner may shield himself from attack for a failure to perform the contract of affreightment, if he is to provide himself with a weapon to secure general average contributions, he must secure a stipulation that notwithstanding his failure to provide a fit ship, he may nonetheless recover contribution.

Carrier's Obligations Under Cogsa

The carrier's obligations regarding seaworthiness under the Carriage of Goods by Sea Act are set forth in Section 3(1) reading:

> The carrier shall be bound, before and at the beginning of the voyage, to exercise due diligence to:

> (a) Make the ship seaworthy; (b) Properly man, equip, and supply the ship; (c) Make the holds, refrigerating and cooling chambers, and all other parts of the ship in which goods are carried, fit and safe for their reception, carriage and preservation.

Section 4(1) of Cogsa states:
Neither the carrier nor the ship shall be liable for loss or damage arising or resulting from unseaworthiness unless caused by want of due diligence on the part of the carrier to make the ship seaworthy, and to secure that the ship is properly manned, equipped, and supplied, and to make the holds, refrigerating and cool chambers, and all other parts of the ship in which goods are carried fit and safe for their reception, carriage and preservation in accordance with the provisions of paragraph (1) of Section 3. Whenever loss or damage has resulted from unseaworthiness, the burden of proving the exercise of due diligence shall be on the carrier or other persons claiming exemption under this section.

It will be observed that under Cogsa the shipowner need only show due diligence to make the vessel seaworthy to entitle him to immunity for losses from unseaworthiness. The immunities granted to the shipowner from other classes of damage which are common to both the Harter Act and Cogsa are not conditioned on due diligence to make the vessel seaworthy. The immunities, or "exemptions" are contained in Section 4(2) and are so important that Section 4(2) is quoted in its entirety:

Neither the carrier nor the ship shall be responsible for loss or damage arising or resulting from—

(a) Act, neglect or default of the master, mariner, pilot, or the servants of the carrier in the navigation or in the management of the ship;

(b) Fire, unless caused by the actual fault or privity of the carrier;

(c) Perils, dangers, and accidents of the sea or other navigable water;

(d) Act of God;

(e) Act of war;

(f) Act of public enemies;

(g) Arrest or restraint of princes, rulers, or people or seizure under legal process;

(h) Quarantine restrictions;

(i) Act or omission of the shipper or owner of goods, his agent or representative;

(j) Strikes or lockouts or stoppage or restraint of labor from whatever cause, whether partial or general; provided that nothing herein contained shall be construed to relieve a carrier from responsibility for the carrier's own acts;

(k) Riots and civil commotions;

(l) Saving or attempting to save life or property at sea;

(m) Wastage in bulk or weight or any other loss or damage arising from inherent defect, quality or vice of the goods;

(n) Insufficiency of packing;

(o) Insufficiency or inadequacy of marks;

(p) Latent defects not discoverable by due diligence;

(q) Any other cause arising without the actual fault or privity of the carrier and without the fault or neglect of the agents or the servants of the carrier; but the burden of proof shall be on the person claiming the benefit of this exception to show that neither the actual fault or neglect of the agent or servants of the carrier contributed to the loss or damage.

Section 2 of Cogsa sets forth the carrier's duty to cargo. It reads:

The carrier shall properly and carefully load, handle, stow, carry, keep, care for and discharge the goods carried.

From the foregoing, it will be observed that while the carrier may exempt himself from fault as to the negligence of his master, crew and servants in the management or navigation of his vessel, he is precluded from exempting himself from liability for fault in respect of the care, custody and control of the cargo.

The distinction between these two categories of fault is not a very clear one; the courts generally consider all the circumstances in each situation and, in case of doubt, the issue is resolved against the vessel.[116]

Obviously, it is difficult to draw a line between conduct which constitutes a breach of the obligation of due care in respect of the cargo and conduct which constitutes a fault in the management and navigation of the vessel. As Gilmore & Black, *The Law of Admiralty*, so neatly put it:

> Few clearcut concepts have appeared for dealing with the problem; the feel of it can only be acquired by reading the cases.

Two leading cases may be helpful in elucidating the problem. In *Knott v. Botany Worsted Mills*,[117] a cargo of wool was properly stowed immediately forward of a non-watertight bulkhead. Wet sugar was loaded just aft of the bulkhead, at which time (since the vessel was trimmed by the stern) all drainage flowed aft and was carried away by the scuppers. Subsequently, after discharging cargo at an intermediate port as a consequence of which the vessel's trim was altered and she was "down by the head," the wet sugar drainage flowed forward into the cargo of wool. The Supreme Court cited the opinion of the District Court stating, in part:

> The primary cause of the damage was negligence and inattention in the loading or stowage of the cargo, either regarded as a whole, or as respects the juxtaposition of wet sugar and wool bales placed far forward. . . . There was no fault or defect in the vessel herself. . . . Since this damage arose through negligence in the particular mode of stowing and changing the loading of cargo, as the primary cause, though that cause became operative through its effect on the trim of the ship, this negligence in loading falls within the first section of the Harter Act.[118]

In *The Germanic*,[119] the vessel was discharging cargo from all hatches and, simultaneously, taking on coal in her bunkers. The vessel listed and

116. *The Vallescura*, 293 U.S. 296, 1934 AMC 1573. See, also, *Leyland Shipping Co., Ltd. v. Norwich Union Fire Ins. Soc., Ltd.* [1918] A.C. 350, [1918-1919] All E.R. Rep. 443; *R. v. Union S.S. Co. of New Zealand, Ltd.* [1940] N.Z.L.R. 754, [1940] G.L.R. 399.

117. 179 U.S. 69 (1900).

118. The first section of the Harter Act prohibits clauses of exoneration from liability for negligence in the care, custody and control of cargo; the comparable section of Cogsa is Section 3(2), together with Section 3(8).

119. 196 U.S. 589 (1905).

water entered an open coat port. The vessel sank, damaging cargo not yet unloaded. It was clear that the vessel's personnel were negligent; the question was in what respect. The Supreme Court said, in part:

> If the primary purpose is to affect the ballast of the ship, the charge is management of the vessel, but if, as in view of the findings we must take to have been the case here, the primary purpose is to get the cargo ashore the fact that it also affects the trim of the vessel does not make it the less a fault of the class which the first (of the Harter Act) removes from the operation of the third. We think it plain that a case may occur which, in different aspects, falls within both sections, and if this be true, the question which section is to govern must be determined by the primary nature and object of the acts which cause the loss.

Deviation

A deviation in English law is defined as an intentional change in the geographical route of the voyage as contracted. American courts appear to be somewhat more liberal and in some instances over-carriage and misdelivery have been found to be "deviations"[120] In essence, a deviation is a form of "fundamental breach"; i.e., a breach going to the root of the contract with the result that the cargo owners have an option not to be bound by the terms of the contract of affreightment and, therefore, are not obliged to contribute toward any losses sustained during the "new" adventure. This was the holding in *Hain Steamship Company, Ltd. v. Tate & Lyle, Ltd.*,[121] in which the House of Lords found there had been an unjustified deviation "going to the root of the contract."

Section 4(4) of Cogsa recognizes that a "reasonable" deviation is permissible. It reads:

> Any deviation in saving or attempting to save life or property at sea, or any reasonable deviation shall not be deemed to be an infringement or breach of this Act or the contract of carriage, and the carrier shall not be liable for any loss or damage resulting therefrom: Provided,

---

120. *The Silvercypress (Fire)*, 63 F.Supp. 452, 1943 AMC 510 (S.D.N.Y.) (over-carriage); *The Lafcomo*, 159 F.2d 654, 1947 AMC 284 (2d Cir.) (failure to supply tarpaulins to cover on-deck cargo, as contracted for); *Jones v. Flying Clipper*, 116 F.Supp. 387, 1954 AMC 259 (SDNY) (stowage of under-deck goods on deck); *Du Pont de Nemours International S.A. v. S.S. Mormacvega*, 493 F.2d 97, 1974 AMC 67 (2d Cir.); *St Johns Corp. v. Companhia General*, 263 U.S. 119, 1923 AMC 11 (1923) (on deck stowage of under-deck cargo); *Nemeth v. General S.S. Corp.*, 694 F.2d 609, 1983 AMC 885 (9th Cir.) (on deck stowage of under-deck cargo). Compare, however, *Iligan Integrated Steel Mills, Inc. v. S.S. John Weyerhaeuser*, 507 F.2d 68, 1975 AMC 33, where the Second Circuit refused to extend the concept of "quasi deviation," restricting it to on-deck stowage of cargo covered by underdeck bills of lading.
121. (1936) 55 Ll.L.Rep. 159 (H.L.).

however, that if the deviation is for the purpose of loading or unloading cargo or passengers it shall, prima facie, be regarded as unreasonable.[122]

Thus, under Cogsa, a deviation is acceptable if it is a reasonable one, and whether it is reasonable or not is a question of fact. Obviously, under Cogsa, a deviation in saving or attempting to save life or property at sea has been deemed to be "reasonable" whereas a deviation to load or unload cargo or passengers is *prima facie* deemed to be unreasonable. Logically, the test of what is reasonable should be, and probably is, whether both parties benefit by the deviation.[123]

For example, in *The Caspiana*,[124] the House of Lords held it was reasonable for a vessel to deviate from a port at which a strike was in progress and proceed to another port to discharge, where a "Liberties Clause" in the bill of lading permitted such action. And in *The Mormacsaga*,[125] it was held that the duty of the carrier to take care of the goods may make it imperative to deviate to an alternate port of discharge, and he could well be held at fault if he does not do so.

"Jason" Clause

Keeping in mind the basic common law principle that no party may claim damages or recompense for loss or damage arising from his own fault, it becomes important to determine when a party to a marine adventure may claim general average contributions where he has been, or may be, relieved of the consequences of that fault, either by statute or by contract.

In *The Carron Park*,[126] the question arose in England whether the negligence of a crew member in permitting water to enter the vessel, thus necessitating the unloading of the cargo, could be so excused by the terms of the bill of lading as to permit the shipowner to claim contribution in general average. The court answered in the affirmative in stating:

---

122. The proviso appears in the U.S. Carriage of Goods by Sea Act but not in the Hague Rules nor in the comparable Acts in other maritime jurisdictions.

123. See *Stag Line Ltd. v. Foscolo, Mango & Co.* [1932] A.C. 328, (1931) 41 Ll.L.Rep. 165, where the House of Lords held that a deviation in order to land engineers who were aboard to test a superheater was not reasonable because it was for the sole benefit of the shipowners.

124. [1957] A.C. 149, [1956] 2 Lloyd's Rep. 379.

125. [1968] 2 Lloyd's Rep. 184, [1969] 1 Lloyd's Rep. 515. See, also, on the effect of "Liberties" clauses and the test of reasonableness under the Hague Rules and Cogsa; *E.C.L. Sporting Goods v. U.S. Lines*, 317 F.Supp. 1245, 1970 AMC 400 (D., Mass.); *The Singapore Trader*, 540 F.2d 39, 1976 AMC 1512 (2d Cir.); *The Blandon*, 287 F. 772, 1932 AMC 242 (2d Cir.); *Surrendra (Overseas) v. S.S. Hellenic Hero*, 213 F.Supp. 97, 1963 AMC 1217 (SDNY); *The Berkshire* [1974] 1 Lloyd's Rep. 185; *Connolly Shaw, Ltd. v. A/S Det.Nordenfjeldske D/S* (1934) 49 Ll.L.Rep. 183; *Hirsh Lumber Co. v. Weyerhaeuser*, 233 F.2d 791, 1956 AMC 1294 (2nd Cir.); *Manx Fisher*, 116 F.Supp. 443, 1954 AMC 177 (N.D,Cal.); *Hellenic Lines v. Dir. Gen. India Supply Mission*, 452 F.2d 810, 1972 AMC 1035 (2d Cir.).

126. (1890) P.D. 203, 6 Asp. M.L.C. 543.

The claim for contribution as general average cannot be maintained when it arises out of any negligence for which the shipowner is responsible; but negligence for which he is not responsible is as foreign to him as the person who has suffered by it.

Therefore, such an exemption from liability under English law leaves the parties to the general average expenditures unaffected; i.e., the shipowner can claim contribution for his expenses as if they arose without his fault.

Correspondingly, although the exceptions clause may excuse the shipowner for liability for loss or damage to cargo, English law does not permit him to avoid making a contribution when cargo is sacrificed.[127]

However, it must be remembered that under American law, exculpatory clauses by carriers were frowned upon and were held invalid as being against public policy. It was not until the enactment of the Harter Act, that common carriers by water were permitted to exempt themselves from certain types of liability by express provisions in their contracts of affreightment.

It was believed by shipowners that the provisions of the Harter Act not only relieved them of liability for negligent acts of the master or crew in the navigation or management of their vessels, but also rightfully entitled them, by reason of the relief afforded them by the Act, to demand contribution in general average from cargo for sacrifices of property in successful efforts to save vessel and cargo.

The Supreme Court, however, in the case of *The Irrawaddy*,[128] disagreed and held that the intention of the Act was not to allow a shipowner to claim contribution in general average toward losses occasioned by faults in the navigation or management of the vessel, notwithstanding that such losses were incurred in saving vessel and cargo.

Shortly thereafter, the case of *The Strathdon*[129] came before the courts. There, a fire broke out in a cargo of sugar and in order to put it out, the vessel was partly filled with water. In the average adjustment, all the sacrifices were treated as general average. The cargo owners contended, however, that the fire was the result of negligence, and that the vessel's sacrifices should not be allowed but, instead, that the vessel should contribute to the sacrifices of the cargo. The court held, however, that as the cargo had claimed contribution in general average, the vessel was entitled to offset against the cargo's claim to the extent of the cargo's proportion of the shipowner's expenses and sacrifices.

The decision was commercially and logically unsatisfactory. For example, if the shipowner's contribution to the cargo's sacrifices was less than

---

127. *Crooks v. Allan* (1879) 49 L.J.Q.B. 201; *Burton v. English* (1883) 12 Q.B.D. 218, 53 L.J.Q.B. 133.
  128. 171 U.S. 187 (1898).
  129. 101 F. 600 (1900).

the cargo's contribution to the shipowner's sacrifices, the cargo owner would simply refrain from claiming in general average. The complications which could ensue where the vessel was on berth terms, and the sacrifices had arisen from negligent navigation, with the cargo of some shippers being sacrificed and others not, were horrendous.

To correct the situation, a clause (which amounted to a general average "agreement") was inserted in many bills of lading. Before it was introduced, opinions of counsel for the respective steamship lines trading out of New York, as well as of eminent independent counsel, were solicited as to its validity. The consensus was that the clause was valid. However, the legality of the clause was questioned in *The Yucatan*,[130] where the court held, in effect, that as a negligence clause, and that as respects common carriers, it was invalid as being against public policy.

The clause read at that time:

> If the owner of the ship shall have exercised due diligence to make said ship in all respects seaworthy and properly manned, equipped and supplied, it is hereby agreed that in case of danger, damage or disaster resulting from fault or negligence of the pilot, master or crew in the navigation or management of the ship, or from latent or other defects, or unseaworthiness of the ship, whether existing at time of shipment, or at the beginning of the voyage, but not discoverable by due diligence, the consignees or owners of the cargo shall not be exempted from liability for contribution in general average or for any special charges incurred, but, with the shipowner, shall contribute in general average, and shall pay such special charges as if such danger, damage or disaster had not resulted from such fault, negligence, latent or other defects or unseaworthiness.

The Yucatan was shortly followed by *The Jason*.[131] There, the bill of lading contained a clause identical with that in *The Yucatan*. The vessel, loaded with general cargo, stranded through negligence and was refloated by salvors after some of the cargo was jettisoned and after sacrifices had been made by the vessel. All of the sacrifices and expenditures were treated as general average. The shipowners claimed against the cargo for the balance due under the average statement, and the cargo claimed against the vessel for contribution for the cargo jettisoned. At first instance, the trial court, following *The Irrawaddy*, held against the shipowners' claim and, based on *The Strathdon*, held against cargo's claim. On appeal,[132] the validity of the bill of lading clause was argued for the first time. The court held that the bill of lading clause was invalid, but

---

130. 139 F. 894 (S.D.N.Y.).
131. 162 F. 56 (S.D.N.Y.).
132. 178 F. 414 (2d Cir.).

modified *The Strathdon* by holding that by virtue of the Harter Act, the ship was exempt from all claims by cargo, direct or indirect (including general average), resulting from negligent stranding. While the ship was not liable to contribute, the owners of the jettisoned cargo were allowed to claim contribution from the other interests.

The shipowner was understandably unhappy with the result as were the cargo underwriters. The shipowner considered that the court should have viewed the bill of lading clause from the standpoint of a contract which was not repugnant to the Harter Act; the cargo underwriters were disturbed that they had no rights of contribution against the shipowner. The shipowner and cargo underwriters applied jointly for a rehearing which was granted. As a consequence, the following questions of law were certified to the Supreme Court for decision:

1. Whether the general average statement above quoted from the bill of lading is valid and entitles the shipowner to collect a general average contribution from the cargo owners, under the above-stated circumstances, in respect of sacrifices made and extraordinary expenditures incurred by it subsequent to the stranding for the common benefit and safety of ship, cargo and freight.

2. Whether, in view of the provisions of the third section of the Harter Act, the cargo owners, under the circumstances above stated, have a right to contribution from the shipowner for sacrifices of cargo made subsequent to the stranding for the common benefit and safety of ship, cargo, and freight.

3. Whether the cargo owners, under the above-stated circumstances, can recover contribution from the shipowner in respect of general average sacrifices of cargo, without contributing to the general average sacrifices and expenditures of the shipowner made for the same purpose.

The petition for rehearing of the shipowner and the cargo underwriters was accompanied by a supporting petition filed by prominent shipowners, underwriters and average adjusters. All parties to the supporting petition advanced cogent reasons why the decision of the court at first instance, as well as that of the court on appeal, was not workable and resulted in injustices for one or more of the parties to the maritime adventure.

The Supreme Court rendered its decision.[133] It answered the first and second questions in the affirmative and the third question in the negative. In answering the first question, the court said, in part:

> In our opinion, so far as the Harter Act has relieved the shipowner from responsibility for the negligence of his master and crew, it is no

133. *The Jason*, 225 U.S. 32 (1912).

longer against the policy of the law for him to contract with the cargo owners for a participation in general average contribution growing out of such negligence; and since the clause contained in the bills of lading of the Jason's cargo admits the shipowner to share in the general average only under circumstances where by the act he is relieved from responsibility, the provision in question is valid, and entitles him to contribution under the circumstances stated.

With respect to the second question, the court said, in part:

Having already held that the general average clause contained in the bill of lading is valid as against the cargo owner, it follows ex necessitate that it is valid in his favor; indeed, no ground is suggested for disabling the shipowner from voluntarily subjecting himself or his ship to liability to respond to the cargo in an action or in a general average adjustment, for the consequences of the negligence of his master or crew, even though by the Harter Act he is relieved from responsibility for such negligence. Therefore we have only to determine whether by the language of the general average clause the cargo owners are entitled to contribution from the ship for sacrifices of cargo made subsequent to the stranding for the common benefit and safety. The language is that in the circumstances presented the consignee or owners of the cargo shall not be exempted from liability for contributions in general average, or for any special charges incurred, but with the shipowner shall contribute in general average, and shall pay such special charges, as if such danger, damage or disaster had not resulted from such default, negligence, etc. This language clearly imports an agreement that the shipowner shall contribute in general average. The opposite view would render the clause inconsistent with the principles of equity and reciprocity upon which the entire law of general average is founded.

On the third question, the court said:

The foregoing considerations compel a negative answer to the third question. In view of the valid stipulations contained in the bill of lading, it would be a contradiction of terms to permit the cargo owners to recover contribution from the ship in respect of general average sacrifices of cargo, without on their part contributing to the general average sacrifices and expenditures of the shipowner made for the same purpose. This would not be general average contribution, the essence of which is that extraordinary sacrifices made and expenses incurred for the common benefit and safety are to be borne proportionate by all who are interested.

With the advent of Cogsa in 1936, a "New Jason Clause" evolved which is now in common use in all shipments to which Cogsa applies, either in foreign trade or in domestic trade by virtue of the so-called "Coastwise Option." The new clause reads:

In the event of accident, danger, damage, or disaster before or after commencement of the voyage resulting from any cause whatsoever, whether due to negligence or not, for which, or for the consequences of which, the Carrier is not responsible by statute, contract or otherwise, the goods, shippers, consignees, or owners of the goods shall contribute with the Carrier in general average to the payment of any sacrifices, losses, or expenses of a general average nature that may be made or incurred, and shall pay salvage and special charges incurred in respect of the goods.

Following the passage of the Harter Act and the decision in *The Jason,* the rights of shipowner and cargo owner under American law where the disaster is due to the negligence of the shipowner or of his crew may be summarized as follows:

When sacrifices are made or extraordinary expenditures are incurred for the common benefit of vessel and cargo, and the contract of affreightment does not contain a valid general average agreement:

(1) If made and incurred by the shipowner, he cannot recover contribution in respect of his own losses.[134] If, however, he settles claims for salvage and other charges for which third parties had a lien on the cargo, it is the better view that if he can prove he exercised due diligence to make the vessel seaworthy, etc., he is entitled to recover the amounts from the cargo owner. He is, in effect, subrogated as he has advanced sums due from others.

(2) If made and incurred only by the cargo, the cargo owners recover contribution from the shipowner, as the Harter Act does not exempt the shipowner from liability for contribution to the sacrifices or expenses incurred by cargo.[135]

(3) If made or incurred by both vessel and cargo, the shipowner cannot invoke a general average adjustment but the cargo owner may do so. In that case, the shipowner is entitled to have the vessel's sacrifices and expenditures included in the adjustment. If, however, the adjustment shows a balance in his favor, he cannot collect it from the cargo owner as his own sacrifices, and losses cannot be used further than as a set-off against the vessel's contribution to sacrifices and extraordinary expenditures of the owner of cargo claiming contribution.[136]

If, on the other hand, the contract contains a valid general average agreement:

---

134. See *J. Howard Smith v. S.S. Maranon,* 501 F.2d 1275, 1974 AMC 1553 (2d Cir., 1974).
135. *The Ernestina,* 259 F. 772 (1919).
136. See *The Strathdon,* 94 F. 206, 101 F. 600 (1900).

(1) If made or incurred by the shipowner, he can recover contribution from the cargo owner if he can show that due diligence was used to make the vessel in all respects seaworthy, and properly manned, equipped and supplied.

(2) If made or incurred by cargo only, the cargo owner can recover contribution from the shipowner.

(3) If made by both vessel and cargo, either party may invoke a general average adjustment, in which all the sacrifices and expenditures are dealt with. If the adjustment shows a balance in favor of the cargo owner, he can collect it. If the balance is in favor of the shipowner, he can collect it if he can prove that due diligence was used to make the vessel in all respects seaworthy, and properly manned, equipped, and supplied.

It should be observed that the original version of the Jason Clause was formulated to meet the requirements of the Harter Act, and under that Act, the exercise by the owner of due diligence to make the vessel seaworthy on sailing is a prerequisite to claiming the protection of the Act. That is, under the Harter Act, any unseaworthiness precludes the benefits of the Act, even though the unseaworthiness may have had no causal connection with the general average act.[137]

Moreover, the courts have held that under the Harter Act, if the event giving rise to the general average occurs prior to the commencement of the voyage (such as, for example, while the vessel is loading), the shipowner is not entitled to the benefits of the Act and is thus liable for negligent acts of the master and crew. Therefore, if the general average arose as a consequence of such negligence, the cargo would not be required to contribute.[138]

Under Cogsa, however, unseaworthiness is material only if the loss or damage giving rise to general average results from it.[139] Therefore, for example, if a vessel commencing a voyage with unseaworthy pumps but with seaworthy boilers puts into a port of refuge to effect repairs because of boiler trouble, the cargo could be compelled to contribute under Cogsa but the converse would be true if the Harter Act applied.

The present-day Jason Clause was formulated to take advantage of the immunities granted by Cogsa and is both simpler and broader than the old Jason Clause formulated to take advantage of the immunities under the Harter Act.

---

137. *The Isis*, 290 U.S. 333, 1933 AMC 1565, 48 Ll.L.Rep. 35 (1933); *Panola*, 3 F.Supp. 897, 1933 AMC 1110 (S.D.N.Y.).

138. *Gilchrist v. Boston Ins.*, 223 F. 716 (6th Cir., 1915); *West Kebar*, 4 F.Supp. 515, 1933 AMC 1364 (E.D.N.Y.).

139. *The Silvercypress (Fire)*, 63 F.Supp. 452, 1943 AMC 510 (S.D.N.Y.); *Isbrandtsen Co. v. Federal Ins. Co.*, 1952 AMC 1945 (S.D.N.Y.); *Orient Trader*, [1973] 2 Lloyd's Rep. 174 (vessel deviated, but a fire which occurred thereafter was not connected with the deviation).

Prior to the decision in *The Jason*, the courts had many occasions to consider whether unseaworthiness of the vessel or negligence of the crew deprived the vessel owner of his right of contribution in general average. After the enactment of the Harter Act (followed in 1936 in the United States by the enactment of Cogsa), the decisions involving negligence have, of course, been confined to those in which the contention has been made that the shipowner/carrier was guilty of negligence in the care, custody and control of the cargo as negligence in the management and operation of the vessel is excused by the operation of statutory law. For this reason, in the discussion that follows, cases predating the Harter Act in which the courts have denied a right of contribution based on negligence of the master and crew in the navigation and management of the vessel have been excluded. However, pre-Harter Act cases in which the courts denied a right of contribution by reason of unseaworthiness or deviation are included.

The decisions rather neatly divide themselves into three categories, each of which will be discussed in the order given. They are:

(1) Unseaworthiness;
(2) Negligence in the care, custody and control of the cargo; and
(3) Deviation

Unseaworthiness

In a number of cases prior to the Harter Act, the courts found that the vessel was unseaworthy and the vessel owner was thereby deprived of his right of contribution,[140] and in probably a like number of cases, the vessels involved were found to be seaworthy.[141]

140. See, for example, *Lyon v. 56,412 Feet of Lumber*, F.Cas. No. 8,647 (sloop, laden with lumber held unseaworthy where she was manned by only three men, one of whom had lost a leg; the ship was 32 years old and had never been rebuilt and had many rotten timbers. The vessel's seams opened during a moderate storm); *Sumner v. Caswell*, 20 F. 249 (D.C., 1884) (vessel owners superintended the loading of a cargo of petroleum in 10-gallon cases from Philadelphia to Japan; upon departure, the vessel was found to be topheavy and cranky, and it was necessary to jettison 3,000 cases of the petroleum; held: the defects were within the knowledge of the owners and contribution denied); *Wilson v. Cross*, 33 Cal. 60 (St.,Cal, 1867) (vessel unseaworthy when she left port although from a latent defect); *Irving v. Glazier*, 4 N.C. 406 (St., N.C., 1816) (cargo owner not bound to contribute in general average where the vessel was unseaworthy by reason of a lack of shifting boards); *Bowring v. Thebaud*, 42 F. 794, *aff'd* 56 F. 520 (1892) (a vessel, when nearly loaded, was found to have a hole in one of her plates; for repairs, the vessel was drydocked with cargo aboard and sailed on her voyage; neither the repairs nor the expense of loading, nor any part of either were a general average charge on the cargo).

141. See, for example, *Sherwood v. Ruggles*, 4 N.Y. Super. 55 (St., N.Y., 1848) (fact that a vessel springs a leak after a few hours sailing, without any unusual stress of weather, furnishes no legal presumption of unseaworthiness in her which would authorize a court to set aside a verdict of a jury finding her seaworthy in other respects); *Fitzpatrick v. 800 Bales of Cotton*, F.Cas. No. 4,843, *aff'd* F.Cas. No. 4,319 (1877) (vessel was voluntarily stranded; the

The cases since the Harter Act and Cogsa, where the vessels were found to be unseaworthy, are quite numerous.[142] However, during the same time span, shipowners have sustained their burden of proving seaworthiness.[143] It should be observed, however, that, by implication, where the shipowner has proved that the cause of the casualty was negligence of the master or crew and has recovered, he has also successfully, at the same time, carried the burden of proof that the vessel was seaworthy, and for that reason the cases cited with respect to "Negligence," *infra*, should also be consulted.

A comparison of those cases in which the ship proved seaworthiness versus those in which courts have found unseaworthiness and denied a right of contribution will be helpful.

For example, in *Societa Anonima Cantiero Olivo v. Federal Ins. Co. et al (Ettore)*,[144] a shipowner's libel for general average contributions from cargo for port of refuge expenses was dismissed, where the shipowner was unable to prove the cause of the accident (breaking of a propeller shaft through ordinary rough weather) and that it was not the result of

---

fact that the mizzen sail of the vessel gave out in an extraordinary storm and she had no spare mizzen does not show that she was unseaworthy when she sailed).

142. *The Richmond*, 2 F.2d 903 (D., Del., 1924); *Berry Coal & Coke Co. v. Chicago, P. & St. L. Ry. Co.*, 116 Mo. App. 214, 92 S.W. 714 (St., Mo., 1906); *Pinellas*, 45 F.2d 174, 1930 AMC 1875 (4th Cir.); *Charbonnier v. U.S.*, 45 F.2d 174 (D., S.C., 1931); *The Lewis H. Goward*, 34 F.2d 791, 1924 AMC 1252 (S.D.N.Y., 1929); *U.S. v. American Trading Company (The Glymont)*, 66 F.2d 617, 1933 AMC 1293 (2d Cir.); *Societa Anonima Cantiero Olivo v. Federal Ins. Co. et al. (Ettore)*, 62 F.2d 769 (2d Cir.), *cert. den.* 289 U.S. 759 (1933); *American-West African Line, Inc. v. Socony Vacuum Corp., et al (West Kebar)*, 4 F.Supp. 515, 1933 AMC 1364 (E.D.N.Y.); *Merklen v. Johnson & Higgins et al., (The Panola)*, 3 F.Supp. 897, 1933 AMC 1110 (S.D.N.Y.); *Maria*, 20 F.Supp. 284, 1936 AMC 1307, 15 F.Supp. 745, 1936 AMC 1314 (ED,Va.); *U.S. v. Los Angeles Soap Company, et al.*, 83 F.2d 875, 1936 AMC 850 (9th Cir.); *Globe & Rutgers Fire Ins. Co. et al. v. U.S. (Zaca, Fire)*, 105 F.2d 160, 1939 AMC 912 (2d Cir.); *Petition of Kabushiki Kaisha Kawasaki Zosenjo (The Venice Maru)*, 39 F.Supp. 349, 1941 AMC 640 (S.D.N.Y.); *May v. HamburgAmerikanische etc. (The Isis)*, 290 U.S. 333, 1933 AMC 1565; *The Heddernheim*, 39 F.Supp. 558, 1941 AMC 730 (S.D.N.Y.); *The Louise*, 58 F.Supp. 445, 1945 AMC 363 (D., Md.); *Esso Providence*, 112 F.Supp. 630, 1953 AMC 1317 (S.D.N.Y.); *Schade v. National Surety*, 288 F.2d 106, 1961 AMC 1225 (2d Cir.); *Jean*, 1967 AMC 228 (ASBCA); *U.S. v. Eastmount Shipping*, 1974 AMC 1183 (S.D.N.Y.); *American Mail Line v. U.S.*, 377 F.Supp. 657, 1974 AMC 1536 (W.D.,Wash.); *Orient Mid-East v. Orient Transporter*, 496 F.2d 1032, 1974 AMC 2593 (5th Cir.); *Todd Shipyards v. U.S.*, 391 F.Supp. 588, 1975 AMC 753 (S.D.N.Y.); *Hellenic Lines v. India*, 514 F.2d 105, 1975 AMC 2457 (2d Cir.); *Master Shipping v. Farida*, 1976 AMC 91 (S.D.N.Y.); *Great Eastern v. India*, 1978 AMC 1288 (S.D.N.Y.); *Steuart Trans., STC 101*, 435 F.Supp. 798, 1978 AMC 1906 (ED,Va.); *Bubble Up v. Transpacific*, 438 F.Supp. 1100, 1978 AMC 2692 (S.D.N.Y.); *Flota Mer. Gr. Lim. Procs.*, 440 F.Supp. 704, 1979 AMC 156 (S.D.N.Y.).

143. *William J. Quillan*, 180 F. 681 (2d Cir.); *Steel Scientist*, 11 F.Supp. 175, 1935 AMC 644 (S.D.N.Y.); *Silvercypress (Fire)*, 63 F.Supp. 452, 1943 AMC 510 (S.D.N.Y.); *Army Cargo—General Average*, 1958 AMC 701 (CompGen, MSTS); *Clydewater*, 274 F.Supp. 884, 1967 AMC 1474 (D., Md.); *Esso Seattle—Guam Bear*, 314 F.Supp. 1339, 1970 AMC 1592 (N.D.,Cal.); *Eastern M. & F. Ins. v. Columbia*, 411 F.Supp. 926, 1976 AMC 931 (S.D.N.Y.); *North East Shipping—East Pakistan*, 1973 AMC 940 (Arb.); *Appeal of Columbia S.S. Co.*, 1977 AMC 1294 (ASBCA); *Containerschiffs v. Lloyds*, 1981 AMC 60 (S.D.N.Y.); *Holsatia v. Fid. & Cas.*, 535 F.Supp. 139, 1982 AMC 2505 (S.D.N.Y.).

144. 62 F.2d 769 (2d Cir.), *cert. den.* 289 U.S. 759 (1933).

seaworthiness (lack of ballast, misalignment of shaft, latent defect in shaft). In the absence of some reservation of right, an unseaworthy private vessel is denied contribution against the cargo where her defects occasioned the sacrifice, although such defects might not have been discoverable by due diligence and although she excused, by contract, herself for breach of her contract to safely carry.

The court said, in part:

> That a ship may be reasonably fit and still break down under ordinary strains, may indeed be true but when she does, it rests upon her to show her fitness. This is the well-settled law in suits upon contracts of affreightment. . . . We can see no reason for distinction in cases of contribution.

Judge Ward decided flatly that the burden was on the ship in *Lewis H. Goward*,[144a] following the analogy of suits on contracts of affreightment:

> . . . It seems to us that the rule should be the same as in suits for cargo damage, and that the burden is upon the ship, and remains so throughout. That she may start with a presumption in her favor, we need not deny. . . . If so, the failure of so vital a part of her machinery in weather which it should withstand, if staunch, is all the cargo is called upon to prove. Thereafter she must prove her general fitness, and will fail upon the issue, if the evidence is in balance. This is in accord with the rule in marine insurance . . . And in view of her exclusive command of the facts, it appears to us the reasonable doctrine. We decide the case on the assumption that the shaft and bearings were not in good order, and the ship not in ballast.

In *Globe & Rutgers Fire Ins. Co. et al v. U. S. (Zaca, Fire)*,[145] an oil burning steamer with a cargo of coal, while in a port of refuge to repair a dynamo, had a destructive fuel oil fire in a boiler room caused by a cracked supply pipe. Heat and flame made it impossible to shut off the flow of oil by the use of reach-rods. The vessel was beached and later scrapped; the coal cargo was salvaged and sold locally. The cargo sued for cargo damage and return of prepaid freight; the shipowner sued for general average contribution. The court held that the vessel was unseaworthy as to her electric generators on starting the voyage; she was also unseaworthy as to the steering engine; and the breakdown of these elements during an ordinary voyage, necessitating extended repairs at ports enroute, was not excusable. The owner was therefore not entitled to general average contribution from the cargo.

The court also held that the vessel owner was not privy to the cause of the fire, and under the Fire Statute, cargo could not recover for the loss of

---

144a. 34 F.2d 791, 1924 AMC 1251.
145. 105 F.2d 160, 1939 AMC 912 (2d Cir.).

cargo consequent on the fire but exemption from liability under the American Fire Statute (unlike the British) did not give the shipowner any right to collect general average. Moreover, deviation was held not to deprive the owner of the benefits of the Fire Statute as there was no causal connection between the deviation and the fire.

In *U. S. v. American Trading Company (The Glymont)*[146] and *U.S. v. Eastmount Shipping*,[147] the vessels were held unseaworthy by reason of failure to take on sufficient bunkers to complete the voyages. Compare, however, *Appeal of Columbia S.S. Co.*,[148] where the shipper did not prove that the carrier failed to exercise due diligence under Cogsa in sailing its vessel from California to Vietnam with a 22 percent reserve for bunkers and, on the facts, a deviation to Hong Kong during the voyage to take on additional fuel was "reasonable." The shipper was therefore held liable to contribute in general average when the vessel stranded because of a navigational error in departing from Hong Kong.

In *Esso Providence*,[149] the stern frame of a laden tanker cracked at sea so that rudder control was lost; the tanker was towed to a port of refuge and her cargo trans-shipped to destination. The crack occurred at a thermit weld at which a previous crack had been repaired six years previously. It appeared that the weld was not successful as to 20 percent of the surface, that it was porous, that its tensile strength was substantially less than that of the portions welded together. The court held that the burden of proof of due diligence was on the shipowner and, on balance, the shipowner had not carried the burden of persuasion.

In *Gemini Navigation v. Philipp Bros. (The Ionic Bay)*,[150] and in *Todd Shipyards Co. v. U.S.*,[151] the carriers failed to prove proper stowage at the loading port which rendered the vessels unseaworthy, and contribution in general average was denied.

Wirth Limited v. S.S. Acadia Forest[152] involved the sinking of a "LASH" barge while being towed in Germany for collection and eventually loading on board the *S.S. Acadia Forest* for transportation to New Orleans. The district court held that a "LASH" barge was not a vessel or ship and, alternatively, that the carrying vessel was unseaworthy by reason of a defective stern line. On appeal, the Fifth Circuit reversed, holding squarely that "LASH" barges are vessels under Cogsa and remanded for additional evidence on the unseaworthiness issue as the district court had applied the

---

146. 66 F.2d 617, 1933 AMC 1293 (2d Cir.).
147. 1974 AMC 1183 (S.D.N.Y.). See, also, *Naviera S.A. and Woodward & Dickerson*, 1969 AMC 2193 (Arb.).
148. 1977 AMC 1294 (ASBCA).
149. 112 F.Supp. 630, 1953 AMC 1317 (S.D.N.Y.).
150. 499 F.2d 745, 1974 AMC 1122 (2d Cir.).
151. 391 F.Supp. 588, 1975 AMC 753 (S.D.N.Y.).
152. 537 F.2d 1272, 1976 AMC 2178 (5th Cir.).

wrong legal standard in holding Cogsa inapplicable to "LASH" barge transportation.

Other instances where unseaworthiness has been found include those in which the shipowner failed to inspect the main crankshaft before it fractured during the voyage,[153] failed to adopt standardized procedures for ballasting deep tanks,[154] failed to provide a competent crew,[155] failed to stow and properly secure a large tractor,[156] permitted a build-up of "scale" inside the boiler tubes,[157] failed to inspect engine crankcase for missing cotter pins in the bearing bolts,[158] failed to inspect and service the vessel's electrical system after notice that it was not functioning properly prior to commencement of the voyage,[159] failed to discover and remedy badly deteriorated deck fittings;[160] failed to provide vessel with up-to-date charts and navigation books,[161] vessel repaired after a stranding but one item of repairs was overlooked,[162] vessel's condensers and boilers were not in sound condition and a long history of difficulties with condensers tubes, boiler tubes and furnaces should have given the shipowner notice that more than ordinary inspection and care was required,[163] failure to inspect the sides of the hull of the vessel,[164] negligent stowage of cargo which went adrift during the voyage,[165] vessel was equipped with outmoded, three-toggled Butterworth plates which were lost during the voyage,[166] tanker was in a generally deteriorated condition with only a makeshift cement-box repair to a "weep" in one of her tanks,[167] and recommended repairs to vessel not carried out prior to sailing.[168]

Vessel Found Seaworthy

By contrast, in *Steel Scientist*,[169] it was held that the fact that the navigator on a vessel might find it necessary to consult both charts and light books to obtain complete information did not indicate that the owner failed to

---

153. *Hellenic Lines v. Life Ins. Co. of India*, 514 F.2d 105, 1975 AMC 2457 (2d Cir.).
154. *American Mail Line v. U.S.*, 377 F.Supp. 657, 1974 AMC 1536 (W.D.,Wash.).
155. *Orient Mid-East v. Orient Transporter*, 496 F.2d 1032, 1974 AMC 2593 (5th Cir.).
156. *Master Shipping v. Farida*, 1976 AMC 91 (S.D.N.Y.).
157. *Great Eastern v. India*, 1978 AMC 1288 (S.D.N.Y.).
158. *Bubble Up v. Transpacific*, 438 F.Supp. 1100, 1978 AMC 2692 (S.D.N.Y.).
159. *Flota Mer. Gr. Lim. Procs.*, 440 F.Supp. 704, 1979 AMC 156 (S.D.N.Y.).
160. *Steuart Trans., STC 101*, 435 F.Supp. 798, 1978 AMC 1906 (ED,Va.).
161. *Maria*, 20 F.Supp. 284, 1936 AMC 1307, 15 F.Supp. 745, 1936 AMC 1314 (ED,Va.).
162. *U.S. v. Los Angeles Soap Company, et al., (West Cajoot)*, 83 F.2d 875, 1936 AMC 850 (9th Cir.).
163. *The Heddernheim*, 39 F.Supp. 558, 1941 AMC 730 (S.D.N.Y.).
164. *Schade v. National Surety*, 288 F.2d 106, 1961 AMC 1225 (2d Cir.).
165. *Jean*, 1967 AMC 228 (ASBCA).
166. *Northwest Petroleum Corp. v. Kyriakou Shipping Co., Ltd.*, 478 F.Supp. 558 (D., Mass.).
167. *Asiatic Petroleum v. American Trader*, 354 F.Supp. 389, 1973 AMC 497 (S.D.N.Y.).
168. *The Louise*, 58 F.Supp. 445, 1945 AMC 363 (D., Md.).
169. 11 F.Supp. 175, 1935 AMC 644 (S.D.N.Y.).

equip his vessel properly, although in most instances it would have been more convenient if the establishment of a new light was noted on the charts. Hence, the owner of a vessel otherwise seaworthy was exonerated from liability for cargo damage from a negligent stranding where the navigating officers failed to inform themselves by means of supplements to the navigating books on board concerning a newly established light and the owner was entitled to a general average contribution.

In *Silvercypress (Fire)*,[170] it was established at trial that the vessel was unseaworthy, but the fire aboard resulted from at least one cause not necessarily connected with the unseaworthiness. The vessel owner was therefore exonerated from liability, the contract of affreightment having been under Cogsa and the bill of lading containing a new Jason clause. Cargo conceded that the issue of a right to a general average contribution under the clause was governed by the same principles as governed the carrier's liability for physical loss of the cargo, and the owner was therefore entitled to a general average contribution.

In *Edward Rutledge*,[171] a freighter stranded on a reef, not realizing that a light on which the navigators relied had been discontinued the previous year. The necessary Notices to Mariners and other navigation data were on board the vessel, but had not been brought up to date by the second mate. It was held that the vessel was seaworthy, that the stranding was caused by negligent navigation, and under the Jason clause, cargo was required to contribute in general average.

In *Eastern M. & F. Ins. v. Columbia*,[172] the vessel's rudder fell off during a July voyage in the Indian Ocean in expectable Force 7 wind and sea conditions and without any other apparent outside cause. The rudder had been repaired, overhauled, and tested on two prior occasions and passed by independent marine surveyors, the owner's inspectors, and representatives of the American Bureau of Shipping. The captain and the chief engineer inspected the rudder and other parts of the vessel while it was light at the dock immediately prior to the voyage. The court found that the vessel owner had exercised due diligence to make the vessel seaworthy and noted, further, that it was not necessary that a ship be drydocked prior to every voyage nor was it required that the rudder and other metal parts be X-rayed to determine possible metal fatigue. Consequently, the vessel owner was entitled to general average contribution from the cargo for expenses incurred in towing the vessel to safety and for repairs put upon her.

In *North East Shipping Corp—East Pakistan*,[173] in a claim against cargo interests to recover general average contributions arising out of boiler wa-

170. 63 F.Supp. 452, 1943 AMC 510 (S.D.N.Y.).
171. 123 F.Supp. 318, 1954 AMC 2070 (S.D.N.Y.).
172. 411 F.Supp. 926, 1976 AMC 931 (S.D.N.Y.).
173. 1973 AMC 940 (Arb.).

ter contamination, the shipowner sustained its burden of proving due diligence under Cogsa by establishing that the vessel's boiler had been inspected and tested some three months before the voyage began and that the damage was occasioned by the negligence of the vessel's properly licensed personnel.

In *Appeal of Columbia S.S. Co.*,[174] the shipper failed to prove that the carrier failed to exercise due diligence under Cogsa, where the vessel was sailed on its voyage from California to Vietnam with a 22 percent reserve for bunkers, although ultimately the vessel had to deviate to Hong Kong during the voyage to take on more fuel.

In *Containerschiffs v. Lloyd's*,[175] the vessel was relatively new and built to the highest classifications. She also had had all requisite and regular inspections and certifications. While on a voyage, a connecting pipe between the lube oil gravity tank and an oil-level indicator broke, and oil sprayed onto superheated steam pipes. The fire was eventually extinguished after valiant efforts by her crew. After the fire was extinguished, the vessel's main engines could not be operated, essential switches and power cables were destroyed, and the boilers could not be started or used. Thus, there was no power to drive the ship. Towage charges in towing the vessel to a port of refuge and, thereafter, to a port of repair were incurred, as well as charges for trans-shipping the cargo. Plaintiff brought suit to recover general average contributions. The court held that the evidence established that the vessel owner had exercised due diligence to make the vessel seaworthy and that the fire had resulted from a fatigue failure in a pipe weld—a latent defect not discoverable by the usual testing procedures.

In *Holsatia Shipping Corp. v. Fidelity & Casualty Co.*,[176] it was held that the shipowner sustained its burden of proving due diligence by establishing that a breakdown at sea was caused by a defect in a lube oil pump. It was not detected, despite normal and customary maintenance and inspection procedures.

Attention is specifically directed to *Sarantex Shipping Co. v. Wilbur-Ellis Co.*,[177] involving a vessel under charter. Although bills of lading issued in connection with the voyage charter contained no Jason Clause, a provision of the charter called for settlement of general average according to the York-Antwerp Rules and obligated the cargo owner to contribute even if the expenses were necessitated through neglect or default of the owner's servants.

The vessel grounded on Clatsop Spit at the entrance of the Columbia River. In related proceedings, the court had found that the stranding oc-

---

174. 1977 AMC 1294 (ASBCA).
175. 1981 AMC 60 (S.D.N.Y.).
176. 535 F.Supp. 139, 1982 AMC 2505 (S.D.N.Y.).
177. 391 F.Supp. 884, 1975 AMC 1033 (D.Ore.).

curred by reason of the negligence of the master in attempting to proceed across the Columbia River Bar in the circumstances then existing. Although the vessel was removed from her strand and the cargo preserved largely intact, the vessel was a constructive total loss. Upon release of the cargo and in consideration thereof, the vessel owner secured a general average bond from the cargo owners. The general average clause in the charter provided that the proprietors of the cargo were to pay the cargo's share. The issues before the court were whether the carrier was entitled to general average contributions from cargo and, if so, whether the defendant purchasers of the cargo were liable under the general average bond for cargo's contributions.

On the facts of the case, the court held that the charter language relating to general average and cargo's obligations were the legal equivalent of a Jason Clause in customary form, and the cargo was thus rendered liable for contribution when the loss was occasioned by negligence of the carrier's servants.

The defendant, however, contended it was not liable under the general average bond in the absence of a Jason Clause in the bills of lading. On this submission, the court held that the defendant was privy to the entire contract of carriage set forth in the voyage charter, and was not a purchaser without notice of the terms of the contract of carriage. Thus, the court concluded, having given its general average bond, the defendant would not be permitted to escape liability under the bond on the ground that it dealt at arm's length with the shipper and relied on the bills of lading as the complete statement of the contract of carriage.

It cannot be overemphasized that in the absence of a Jason Clause or its equivalent in the contract of carriage, the shipowner/carrier cannot claim contribution in general average under American law unless the shipowner/carrier can establish that it was wholly free from fault.[178]

Moreover, a clear distinction must be drawn between the impact of the Harter Act and Cogsa. Under the Harter Act, the obligation to exercise due diligence must be complied with up to the time of sailing from the loading port,[179] and the obligation may be revived by putting into a port where managing personnel of the owner are present and supervising.[180] Under Cogsa, however, a showing of proof of seaworthiness is not necessary in order for the owner to claim the benefit of the exemptions in the

---

178. *The Albisola*, 91 F.2d 726, 1937 AMC 1257 (3rd Cir.); *The Irrawaddy*, 171 U.S. 187 (1898); *Manhattan Oil Transp. v. Salvador*, 1976 AMC 134 (S.D.N.Y.); *Clydewater*, 274 F.Supp. 884, 1967 AMC 1474 (D., Md.); *Bright Star S.S. Co. v. Industrial Molasses*, 1973 AMC 2005 (Arb.); *Sarantex Shipping v. Wilbur-Ellis*, 391 F.Supp. 884, 1975 AMC 1033 (D., Ore.); *Globe & Rutgers Fire Ins. Co. et al v. U.S. (Zaca, Fire)*, 105 F.2d 160, 1939 AMC 912 (2d Cir.); *Phipps v. Nicandor*, 44 F. 504 (S.D.N.Y., 1890); *The Strathdon*, 94 F. 206, 101 F. 600 (1899).

179. *Erie & St. Lawrence Corp. v. Barnes-Ames Co. (I.L.I. 105)*, 52 F.2d 217, 1931 AMC 1994 (W.D.N.Y.).

180. *May v. Hamburg-Amerikanische etc. (The Isis)*, 290 U.S. 333, 1933 AMC 1565.

act even though the accident occurred prior to the commencement of the voyage.[181] While Section 3(1) requires the carrier to exercise due diligence to make the vessel seaworthy "before and at the beginning of the voyage," the exemptions from liability contained in Section 4(2) of Cogsa are not conditioned upon the exercise of due diligence. Consequently, it would appear that negligence of the master or crew after loading but prior to the commencement of the voyage, in the sense of management and operation of the vessel, as distinguished from care, custody and control of the cargo, would fall within the terms of the new Jason Clause. Any general average expenditure incurred at the port of loading as a result of such negligence would give rise to a right of contribution on the part of the shipowner against cargo.

The point at which the voyage commences can, however, be very troublesome. This is illustrated clearly by comparing *The Del Sud,*[181a] and *American Mail Line v. U.S.*[182]

In *The Del Sud,* the vessel loaded, *inter alia,* coffee into No. 2 lower hold at the port of Santos, followed by calls at Montevideo and Buenos Aires for corned beef. After a call at Rio de Janeiro, she proceeded thence to New Orleans where damage was discovered for the first time to the coffee and corned beef. It was common ground that the damage occurred when seawater entered the vessel through a 12-inch fracture in the bow shell plate just below the lip of an overboard discharge soil line, which protruded about two inches outboard of the surface of the hull plates. The fracture was caused by the pressure of the ship's weight bearing upon this small protuberance by reason of a momentary contact against the concrete face of the dock while the vessel was undocking. The contact occurred when all lines had been cast off other than the bow spring line and breast line and while the vessel was being pivoted against the dock by a tug pulling on her starboard quarter.

Certainly, at the time the vessel left Santos it was, in fact, unseaworthy. The shipowner contended that the unseaworthiness was caused, and therefore excused, by a Cogsa, Section 4 act or error in the management or navigation of the vessel. Cargo, to the contrary, contended that unseaworthiness resulted from an act or error in management and navigation which existed prior to the time the voyage commenced and that, consequently, there was a failure to perform the Section 3 duty to exercise

---

181. *Isbrandtsen Co. v. Federal Ins. Co. (John W. Miller),* 113 F.Supp. 375, 1952 AMC 1945 (S.D.N.Y.), *aff'd* 1953 AMC 1033 (2d Cir.). See, also, *Mississippi Shipping Co., Inc. v. Zander & Co., Inc. (The Del Sud),* 270 F.2d 345, 1959 AMC 2143 (5th Cir.), in which the court cited with approval *Isbrandtsen, supra,* but decided the case on the basis that the voyage had already commenced when negligent navigation caused damage to the shell plating, which was later responsible for damage to the cargo during the voyage.

181a. 270 F.2d 345, 1959 AMC 2143 (5th Cir.)

182. 377 F.Supp. 657, 1974 AMC 1536 (W.D., Wash.).

due diligence "before and at the beginning of the voyage" to make the vessel seaworthy. An ingredient of this contention was, of course, that the master knew, or ought to have known, of the damage to the vessel while the vessel was yet at Santos so that a failure to inspect and repair was a want of due diligence. Thus, the owner would bear the consequences of the master's failure, since the duty to exercise due diligence rests upon all and is nondelegable.

The court held that the use of the words "before and at" did not make the commencement of the voyage—whenever that was—any less a beginning. When the voyage began, it was the voyage and not the beginning of it which continued. The dual reference was to make doubly sure that with respect to cargo then being loaded, the vessel was seaworthy at the time of the receipt of cargo and continued in that state until the ship sailed. As the court put it, the fact that the duty reached backward from commencement did not make it reach forward, as Cogsa prescribed that the latest point of performance was at the beginning. Thus, the voyage must have had some place (and time) of beginning. After that, it was not the beginning, but the voyage itself, which transpires.

The court held that in a very real sense the voyage had begun. The ship had no further purpose at the dock. She was ready for sea. She was being turned around for the purpose of leaving. The lines at the dock were fast, not to keep her there, or to continue her stay at the wharf, but were there solely for the purpose and as an essential step in her navigational maneuvering. Consequently, once it was determined that the hole in the ship's side occurred after the voyage had begun within the meaning of Cogsa, Section 3, the failure of the master to inspect and repair the damage at Santos was likewise an error in navigation and management and excused under Section 4.

In *American Mail Line v. U.S., supra,* the vessel was engaged in loading cargo in the Pacific Northwest for a voyage to various Oriental and Far East ports. After loading cargo at Portland, Oregon and Longview, Washington (on the Columbia River) she sailed for Puget Sound to load additional cargo. Puget Sound is a relatively short distance to the north of the Columbia River ports, and all the ports at which the vessel loaded in Puget Sound were relatively close to each other. At Pier 46, Seattle, the last loading point prior to her departure for sea, she was loading additional cargo. The master directed the chief mate to ballast No. 5 after starboard deep tank in order to achieve proper trim. The latter directed the carpenter to remove the gooseneck vent from the vent pipe leading into the deep tank from the main deck. The chief engineer then inserted a fire hose into the vent pipe for the purpose of filling the tank with fresh water from a shore hydrant.

The chief mate, following his usual practice of ballasting, removed the cover to the manhole access to the deep tank to allow a close inspection of the water flow until the filling was nearly completed, at which time the cover would be replaced. He did not watch over the ballasting, however, but placed the engine room personnel in charge. Unfortunately, the engine department followed a different procedure from that of the chief engineer; i.e., that of sealing the cover. Thus, when the tank cover was sealed, water would flow onto the deck through the vent pipe after it reached the top of the tank and not into the cargo compartments. The engine department erroneously assumed that the chief engineer had followed their procedure and had sealed the tank cover. Consequently, when the tank filled, it overflowed into No. 5 lower hold instead of onto deck, and moistened wood pulp stowed there. Since wood pulp expands in all directions when wet, it was necessary to discharge the cargo in No. 5 hold to relieve the pressure on the vessel's structure and to allow expansion of the cargo to its full extent, as well as to examine the various structural parts of the lower hold for possible damage. The shipowner thereupon declared a general average. The vessel owner sought to apply the "voyage by stages" doctrine, claiming that from the time of departure from the last previous port until arrival in Seattle, the vessel "broke ground" and commenced her voyage to the Oriental/Far East ports on six separate occasions. The court did not agree, holding that it was not a case of the shipowner providing transportation of cargo between Puget Sound ports. All shifts made by the vessel were merely preparatory for the ultimate voyage from Northwest ports to the Oriental/Far East ports. That is, the various shifts from ports in close proximity to each other were not "voyages" but merely steps in the process of preparing for the ultimate voyage. Accordingly, the water entered No. 5 hold "before . . . the beginning of the voyage."

So, the court said, the expenses for which contribution was sought, were necessitated by improper ballasting; i.e., a failure to stop the flow of water upon its reaching the top of the tank, and a failure to have a uniform procedure understood by the deck and engine room departments for the ballasting of tanks. The failure to have a standardized, uniform system for the ballasting of the tanks rendered the vessel unseaworthy and unfit for her intended service and created an unreasonable risk of damage to the cargo in violation of Section 3(1) of Cogsa.

The court specifically noted that even though the failure to stop the flow of water was an error in management, for which the shipowner would not have been responsible, had it occurred after the commencement of the voyage, the same error could (and was) a lack of due diligence on the part of the shipowner to make the vessel seaworthy when such conduct occurred before the beginning of the voyage. As the court said:

> . . . The existence of such an error in management does not vitiate the unseaworthiness and absolve the shipowner of responsibility. Fur-

thermore, the entry of water into No. 5 lower hold manifested plaintiff's [the shipowner's] failure to exercise due diligence before the beginning of the voyage to make the holds fit for the preservation of cargo.

The court also observed that even if the voyage had commenced at the time the shipowner contended, the claim would still fail.[183] The unseaworthiness created by the lack of a uniform ballasting procedure resulted from a want of due diligence by the shipowner which was prior to the commencement of the several stages of its intended voyage. However, as none of the parties urged this ground, the court declined to rest its decision solely upon that basis.

An eminent authority[184] has criticized the result in *American Mail Line v. U. S.*, stating that it is inequitable for a shipowner to be held responsible for the immediate results of exempted causes of damage occurring subsequent to the loading of cargo merely because the damage occurred before actually leaving the final (or even the first) loading port. It was his view, also, that the community of interest between vessel and cargo commences when cargo is loaded and, for general average purposes, the voyage begins at that time. On this interpretation (which has some legal support), any errors in navigation or management of the vessel (such as crew negligence) which occur after loading cargo but prior to sailing would come within the terms of the new Jason Clause, and contribution to any general average expenditure incurred at the port of loading as a result of excepted perils would be enforceable against the concerned cargo.

With all due respect to that learned author, it would appear that the decision in *American Mail Line v. U.S.* was predicated more upon a pre-existing failure to promulgate and enforce standardized, uniform and

---

183. The court cited the following decisions holding that the voyages had not commenced: *Bowring v. Thebaud*, 56 F. 520 (2d Cir., 1892) (vessel hauled from one dock to another within New York Harbor); *Gilchrist Transp. Co. v. Boston Ins. Co.*, 223 F. 716 (6th Cir., 1915) (after being partly loaded, vessel moved 7 miles away in the same harbor; it had not been inspected, was not made ready to sail, and the lake had not been sufficiently cleared of ice to permit safe passage); *Willowpool*, 12 F.Supp. 96, 1935 AMC 1292 (S.D.N.Y.), aff'd 86 F.2d 1002, 1936 AMC 1852 (2d Cir.) (having finished loading, vessel left wharf, but moored in harbor rather than directly putting to sea); *Isbrandtsen Co. v. Federal Ins. Co.*, 113 F.Supp. 357, 1952 AMC 1945 (S.D.N.Y.), aff'd 205 F.2d 679, 1953 AMC 1033 (2d Cir.), cert den. 346 U.S. 866 (1953) (vessel in Pearl Harbor forced to vacate its berth to a Navy vessel, moved 7 miles away to await clearance to depart the customs district); *American Agri. Chemical Co. v. O'Donnell Transp. Co.*, 62 F.Supp. 239, 1945 AMC 812 (S.D.N.Y.) (barge shifted by hand from one dock to another dock "a little further along the river" prior to the intended voyage from Buffalo to New York).

184. L. Buglass, *Marine Insurance and General Average in the United States* (2d), pp. 298–299.

workable ballasting procedures, a failure which, in the event, coupled with the negligence of the chief engineer, was the proximate cause of the damage to the cargo. Presumably, had the owner promulgated such uniform procedures, they would have embraced a requirement that the manhole cover be secured so that any overflow would go onto the deck rather than down into the cargo spaces; i.e., the same procedures that the engine room department routinely followed. Had such a procedure been established, the negligence of the chief engineer in leaving the cover off—thus violating his owner's instructions—would have been the sole cause of the cargo damage, and such crew negligence would be excused, even though it occurred after the loading of cargo but before the voyage began.

Viewed in this light, the dictum of the court that the failure to stop the flow of water was an error in management for which the shipowner would not have been responsible, had it occurred "after the commencement of the voyage" was a gratuitous observation not necessary to the decision nor precisely accurate. For example, had the shipowner promulgated such procedures, and had a crew member failed to follow them while the vessel was at sea enroute to its port of destination, such failure on the part of the crew member would clearly be excused under Section 4(2) of Cogsa. On the other hand, however, had the shipowner failed to prescribe such procedures where they were so clearly warranted, and a crew member, lacking such instructions and acting solely upon what he perceived to be an acceptable method of ballasting, left the manhole cover open, then it would be a situation where a failure of the shipowner to exercise due diligence from the outset, coupled with negligence of the crew member while at sea, proximately caused the cargo loss.

The Fire Statute

The U.S. Fire Statute,[185] enacted in 1851 as part of the Limitation of Liability Act,[186] provides a broad exemption from liability for cargo losses due to fire:

> No owner of any vessel shall be liable . . . unless such fire is caused by the design or neglect of such owner.

Where a fire gives rise to a general average situation, the shipowner is thus exempt from liability by the Fire Statute, unless the fire was caused by the actual "design or neglect" of the shipowner. The same exemption from liability also appears in Cogsa, except the words used are "fault or privity." The effect is the same, as the word "fault" corresponds generally to the word "neglect," and the word "privity" to the word "design."[187]

185. 46 U.S.C. 182.
186. 46 U.S.C. 181–189.
187. *Matter of Ta Chi Navigation (Panama) Corp., S.A.*, 677 F.2d 225, 1982 AMC 1710 (2d Cir., 1982).

Neglect, as thus used, means negligence, not the breach of a non-delegable duty.[188] The type of negligence required under the "design or neglect" standard of the Fire Statute, and the "fault or privity" standard of Cogsa, is the carrier's own negligence, not the errors of the master, or crew, or of repairmen, or other third parties.[189] If the carrier shows that the damage was caused by fire, the shipper must then prove that the carrier's negligence caused the fire.[190] The shipper can prove that the carrier caused the damage either by proving that a negligent act of the carrier caused the fire or that such an act prevented the fire's extinguishment.[191]

It should be observed that the protection afforded by the Fire Statute extends only to owners by its language, and, by extension by reason of judicial decisions to bareboat charterers; i.e., owners *pro hac vice*. On the other hand, the term used in Cogsa is "carriers," which embraces time charterers, voyage charterers, and other non-owners who issue bills of lading subject to Cogsa.[192]

Negligence

Surprisingly, there are relatively few cases in which shipowners have claimed contributions in general average but have failed when cargo interests have established that the shipowners' servants were negligent in the care, custody and control of the cargo.

For example, in *Eisenerz G.m.b. H. v. Federal Commerce*,[193] there was an error in navigation which resulted in the vessel being compelled to dis-

---

188. *Consumers Import Co. v. Kabushiki Kaisha Kawasake Zosenjo*, 320 U.S. 249, 252, 1943 AMC 1209 (1943); *Earle & Stoddart, Inc. v. Ellerman's Wilson Line, Ltd.*, 287 U.S. 420, 427, 1933 AMC 1, 5 (1932).

189. *Id.*, n. 187.

190. See *Matter of Ta Chi Navigation (Panama) Corp., S.A.*, 677 F.2d 225, 1982 AMC 1710 (2d Cir., 1982) and cases cited therein. Compare, however, *Sunkist Growers, Inc. v. Adelaide Shipping Lines, Ltd.*, 603 F.2d 1327, 1979 AMC 2787 (9th Cir.), *cert. den.* 444 U.S. 1012, 1980 AMC 2102 (1980), In *Sunkist*, which also involved a fire at sea, the Ninth Circuit held that the burden of proof is on the carrier to show that it exercised due diligence to provide a seaworthy ship in order to invoke the provisions of either section 1304(2)(b) [Cogsa] or the Fire Statute. It will be observed that *Sunkist* involves an implicit repeal of the Fire Statute by Cogsa and would render the Fire Statute of no purpose or utility. With all due respect to the Ninth Circuit court, it would appear that *Ta Chi* is correct and *Sunkist* is incorrect. Clearly, Congress did not repeal or amend the Fire Statute by the adoption of Cogsa. To the contrary, as *Ta Chi* demonstrates, Congress expressly disclaimed any intention of altering the Fire Statute and, as well, by enacting Sec. 1304(2)(b), reaffirmed the principle of law embodied in the Fire Statute.

191. *Asbestos Corp. Ltd. v. Compagnie De Navigation Fraissinet et Cyprien Fabre*, 480 F.2d 669, 1973 AMC 1683 (2d Cir.). See, also, *Lekas & Drivas, Inc. v. Goulandris*, 306 F.2d 426, 1962 AMC 2366 (2d Cir.).

192. *In re Barracuda Tanker Corp.*, 409 F.2d 1013, 1969 AMC 1442 (2d Cir.).

193. 31 D.L.R. (3d) 209, [1974] S.C.R. 1225, [1970] 2 Lloyd's Rep. 332 (Can.), 1970 AMC 227.

charge its cargo of differing grades of pig iron so that the vessel might be repaired. During the discharge, the cargo was damaged and mixed. The court held that the loss was caused by a lack of care of the cargo under Section 3(2) of the Hague Rules. As the carrier was responsible for the loss, the claim for contribution in general average was denied.

In *American Creosoting Co. v. Deutsche Petroleum Aktien Gesellschaft (The Massassoit),*[194] the vessel was chartered to transport a full cargo of creosote in bulk from Antwerp to New York, the creosote to be kept heated at 90° to 100° F. continuously during the voyage and in a fit state for ready discharge. On arrival, the cargo was short and a heavy deposit of crystals was found covering the bottom of the tanks. The vessel owner claimed that the steam heating was necessarily turned off in bad weather in order to supply additional steam for navigation purposes and that the resulting damage to the cargo was general average. It was held that the precipitation and consequent shortage resulted from the vessel's failure to keep the cargo heated to the required temperatures. As the steam was diverted to increase the vessel's speed, there was no voluntary sacrifice to avert a supposed peril, and the shipowner's claim for general contribution was denied.

In *Drew Brown Ltd. v. The Orient Trader and Owners,*[195] United States law and the new Jason Clause were applied by the Canadian courts. In that case, the vessel encountered heavy weather while carrying a cargo of tin slabs. As a consequence, a hatch beam came out of its socket. The vessel then deviated where the shipowners began discharging the cargo with the intention of forwarding it on by truck to the port of final destination. While unloading was progressing, a portion of the deck collapsed, necessitating the use of a cargo of rubber to prop it up. From unknown causes, a fire broke out, melting the rubber, which spread over the tin and damaged it. The bills of lading incorporated the new Jason Clause, Cogsa, and U.S. Fire Statute.

The cargo owners contended the vessel was unseaworthy and that the discharge of cargo at the port of refuge constituted a deviation going to the "root of the contract." Thus, the shipowners could not rely on the exemption clauses in the bills of lading nor could they claim a general average contribution.

The Exchequer Court and the Canadian Supreme Court, applying United States law, held that there was no evidence of unseaworthiness; that if the tilting of the hatch beams occurred through some fault of the shipowners, it was immaterial because it did not lead to any injury to the cargo; that there was an unreasonable deviation in the decision to forward the cargo by truck to the port of destination, but since there was no evi-

194. 28 F.2d 356, 1928 AMC 1467 (D., N.J.).
195. [1972] 1 Lloyd's Rep. 35 (Can.Ex.Ct.), [1973] 2 Lloyd's Rep. 174 (Can.Sup.Ct.).

dence that the deviation was causally connected with the fire, the shipowners were entitled to the exemption provided by the U.S. Fire Statute; and that although the deviation was unreasonable, shipowners were nonetheless entitled to a general average contribution under the new Jason Clause.

In *U.S. v. A.C. Monk Company (The Bellingham)*,[196] the cargo owner brought two libels for the same cargo damage; one alleged loss due to general average (extinguishing a fire) at the loading port, the other alleged negligent warehousing at the port of discharge. To prove the general average claim, the plaintiff produced testimony that no further damage occurred during warehousing. Nevertheless, the trial court gave a decree for negligent warehousing. On appeal, the Third Circuit reversed, noting that the plaintiff had to elect between inconsistent claims and had abandoned the claim for negligent warehousing to sustain its claim for general average. The court also pointed out that after discharge of the goods from the vessel, the carrier's liability is that of a warehouseman; i.e., to exercise ordinary care, and the burden of proving want of due care was on the owner of the goods. Thus, open air storage under tarpaulins was proper care in 1920 when all the warehouses were filled and longshoremen were on strike at the port of discharge.

Where the cargo itself causes the general average act, the cargo owner is not liable for ensuing damages and may claim in general average if he was unaware of the inherent defect in the cargo causing the damage. This was the holding in *The William J. Quillen*[196a] where the vessel had been chartered to carry a cargo of garbage tankage, which is a dry powder, the result of boiling, drying, and pressing of street garbage and packing it in bags. Because of the manufacturer's failure to cure and dry out the tankage properly, the cargo caught fire from spontaneous combustion, and the vessel's hold was flooded to put out the fire, causing damage to the remainder of the cargo not burned. The shipper had purchased the tankage from its manufacturer, and had nothing to do with its loading or stowage, and had no knowledge that it was not in proper condition. It

---

196. 180 F. 681 (2d Cir., 1910). See, also, *Greenshields Cowie and Co. v. Stephens and Sons*, [1908] A.C. 431, 1 K.B. 51, where coal being transported caught on fire from spontaneous combustion with the voyage being abandoned by reason thereof. The cargo was discharged after water had been poured into the hold. The shipowners claimed contribution in general average towards their general average expenditures; the cargo owners also claimed contribution for the damage done to their coal by the water. The court held, in part, that inherent vice of the coal did not affect the rights of contribution between the parties, so long as the cargo owner was not guilty of negligence or misconduct. (The case also involved the application of Rule III of the York-Antwerp Rules; see discussion, *infra*, under heading "Extinguishing Fire on Shipboard." See, also, *Starlight Trading, Inc. v. S.S. San Francisco*, 1974 AMC 1523 (S.D.N.Y.) involving smoke damage to cargo resulting from a deliberate closing and sealing of hatches in order to inject CO_2. Compare, however, *Boyd v. Dubois* (1811) 3 Camp. 133, N.P., where the shipper knowingly shipped wet hemp, which caught on fire.

196a. 180 F. 681 (2d Cir., 1910).

was, however, a well-known article of commerce, and both the shipowner and the shipper knew its characteristics. It was held that the shipper or his insurer (who had paid the loss) was entitled to recover from the vessel its contribution in general average to the loss caused by the water damage.

As noted heretofore, in a number of cases, shippers have contended that the damage to the cargo was caused by negligence on the part of the shipowner in the care, custody and control of the cargo. The shipowners defended on the grounds that the damage was caused by negligence of the master or crew in the navigation or management of the vessel. The cases are of interest in demonstrating the division by fault.[197]

There are innumerable cases which have been decided involving the law of carriage by sea in which the courts have been required to determine whether or not the casualty causing the damage was occasioned by negligence of the master or crew in the navigation or management of the vessel, or negligence of the master or crew in the care, custody and control of the cargo. Although these did not involve questions of general average, they could easily have done so had the damage sustained also resulted in peril to the vessel or other interests involved. Consequently, reference should be made to such decisions as aids in determining whether or not the fault involved falls in one category or the other.[198]

For example, in *Instituto Cubano de Establizacion Del Azuca v. Star Line Shipping Co., Inc. (The Capt. Theo),*[199] the vessel was chartered to carry molasses from Cuba to Louisiana. It encountered heavy swells, necessitating ballast. Cargo valve No. 6 had been carelessly left unsealed at the start of the voyage. A seaman in error ballasted tank 6 instead of tank 4 (tank 6 alone of the ballast tanks was connected to the cargo tank system). Thus, seawater entered through the unsealed valve in No. 6, spoiling the molasses therein. It was held that the unsealed cargo valve (the ultimate cause of the loss) was an error in the care and custody of the cargo outweighing the error in management in improper ballasting, and the vessel was held liable for the loss.

Although the facts did not justify a claim in general average and no such claim was made, it could be hypothesized that had the flooding of tank 6 and the connecting cargo tanks been severe enough to cause the vessel to list heavily, and had she then sought a port of refuge, a claim in general average might well have been presented. However, on the facts as presented, the "peril" would have been caused by fault on the part of the shipowner for which he would not be excused under Cogsa, and no general average contribution should be allowed.

---

197. See cases cited, *supra,* footnote 143.
198. Excellent source references are: Carver, *Carriage by Sea;* W. Tetley, *Marine Cargo Claims* (2d); *American Maritime Cases,* 5-Year Digests, under heading "Bills of Lading."
199. 1958 AMC 166 (Arb.).

Other such examples can readily be postulated from the decisions involving claims for damage to cargo.

It should also be emphasized that where damage may be the result of two concurring causes, the burden is on the carrier to prove what damage was attributable to causes excepted under the proper law of the contract of carriage. Thus, if the cause of the damage is solely, or even primarily, a neglect to take reasonable care of the cargo, the ship is liable, but if the cause of the damage is a neglect to take reasonable care of the ship, or some part of it, as distinct from the cargo, the ship would be relieved from liability. If the negligence is not towards the ship, however, but only negligent failure to use the apparatus of the ship for the protection of the cargo, the ship is not relieved.[200]

As noted heretofore, an unjustifiable deviation has the effect of "going to the root of the contract." Consequently, cargo owners have the option of no longer being bound by its terms and are not obliged to contribute toward any losses sustained during the new venture. Thus, in the event that general average expenses or losses are incurred during or after an unjustifiable or unreasonable deviation by the vessel, the cargo is not liable for contributions for the reason that when such deviation occurs, the shipowner, in essence, (at least under the common law) becomes an insurer of the cargo. So, an unjustifiable or unreasonable deviation vitiates the contract of carriage and the shipowner is liable, in personam, without the benefit of limitation, for any loss of or damage to the cargo and is deprived of all the exceptions and clauses for the carrier's benefit in the contract of carriage.[201]

Bills of lading frequently contain clauses in respect of deviation which, if construed literally, would justify the vessel in going anywhere she desired, provided she eventually reached the final ports of destination. The courts, however, have held that notwithstanding such broad and far-reaching clauses, the term "deviation" gives only a limited right of departure from the voyage and that the limits must be those of necessity and with reasonable regard for the rights of both shipper and carrier arising

---

200. *Gosse Millerd Ltd. v. Can. Gov't Merchant Marine*, 32 Ll.L. Rep. 91, [1929] A.C. 223; *Schnell v. The Vallescura*, 293 U.S. 296, 1934 AMC 1573; *Union Carbide & Carbon Corp. v. The Walter Raleigh*, 109 F.Supp. 781, 1952 AMC 618, *aff'd* 200 F.2d 908 (2d Cir.); *Sanib Corp. v. United Fruit Co.*, 74 F.Supp. 64, 1947 AMC 419 (S.D.N.Y.); *Bunge Corp. v. Alcoa S.S. Co., Inc. (The General Artigas)*, 133 F.Supp. 311, 1955 AMC 725 (S.D.N.Y.).

201. *The Sarnia*, 278 F. 459 (2d Cir., 1921); *The St. Johns N.F.*, 280 F. 553 (2d Cir., 1922); *The Balto*, 282 F. 235 (2d Cir., 1922); *The Willdomino v. Citro Chemical Co.*, 272 U.S. 718, 1927 AMC 129 (1927); *The Citta Di Messina*, 169 F. 472 (S.D.N.Y., 1909); *The Indrapura*, 171 F. 929 (D.,Ore., 1909); *Pelotas*, 43 F.2d 571, 1930 AMC 1795 (E.D., La.), *aff'd* 66 F.2d 75, 1933 AMC 1188 (5th Cir.); *World Wide S.S. Co. v. India Supply Mission*, 316 F.Supp. 190, 1971 AMC 498 (S.D.N.Y.). See, also, *Hellenic Lines v. U.S.*, 512 F.2d 1196, 1975 AMC 697 (2d Cir.), and the numerous cases cited under heading "Deviation," 5-Year Digests, American Maritime Cases.

from the nature of the contract of carriage. Consequently, the deviation (or "Liberties" Clause, as it is frequently called), must be construed with reference to the voyage contemplated by the shipowner and the shipper when the bill of lading is issued and is therefore restricted to allowing deviation to "the business and necessities of the ship pertaining to that voyage."[202]

Deviation, in a geographical sense, is a departure from the voyage contracted for. In the absence of a contrary stipulation in the bill of lading, this is the normal route of sailing between the port of loading and the port of discharge, as affected by geography and by customs of the trade, which the parties incorporate by reference.[203]

Section 4(4) of Cogsa provides:

> Any deviation in saving or attempting to save life or property at sea, or any reasonable deviation shall not be deemed to be an infringement or breach of this Act or of the contract of carriage, and the carrier shall not be liable for any loss or damage resulting therefrom; Provided, however, That if the deviation is for the purpose of loading or unloading cargo or passengers it shall, prima facie, be regarded as unreasonable.

It will be noted that the Section is totally silent with respect to the reasonable geographical scope of the voyage. But it must have been drafted with this concept in mind and, therefore, whether a deviation is "reasonable" must be determined from an analysis of whether there was a "reasonable" departure from the normal route of sailing, as modified by a reasonable interpretation of the scope of the "Liberties" Clause.

The proviso italicized above was added by Congress; it does not appear in the Hague Rules. Clearly, it makes it much more simple to prove unreasonableness where the purpose of the deviation was to load or unload cargo or passengers.[204]

The provisions of Cogsa relating to deviation clearly depart from the harsh, common law rule which made the carrier an insurer regardless of

---

202. *Austrian Union S.S. Co. v. Calafiore,* 194 F. 377 (1912). See, also, *Swift & Co. v. Furness, Withy & Co.,* 87 F. 345 (D.,Mass., 1898), and cases cited, *infra,* n. 203.

203. *Hostetter v. Park,* 137 U.S. 30 (1890). The usual "Liberties" Clause covers only "delays fairly ancillary to the prescribed voyage." *P & E Shipping Corp. v. Empresa Cubana Exportadora E. Importadora De Alimentos,* 335 F.2d 678, 1964 AMC 2006 (lst Cir., 1964); *Grace & Co. v. Toyo Kisen Kabushiki Kaisha,* 7 F.2d 889, 1925 AMC 1420 (N.D.,Cal.), *aff'd* 12 F.2d 519 (9th Cir., 1926), *cert. den.* 273 U.S. 717 (1926); *Dietrich v. U.S. Shipping Board,* 9 F.2d 733, 1925 AMC 1173 (2d Cir., 1925); *General Hide & Skin Corp. v. U.S.,* 24 F.2d 736, 1928 AMC 357 (E.D.N.Y., 1928); *Romano v. West India Fruit & S.S. Co.,* 151 F.2d 727, 1946 AMC 90 (5th Cir., 1945). See, also, *Centrosoyus-America, Inc. v. U.S.,* 31 F.2d 610, 1929 AMC 289 (S.D.N.Y., 1929); *Haroco Co. v. The Tai Shan,* 111 F.Supp. 638, 1953 AMC 887 (S.D.N.Y.), *aff'd sub nom Frederick H. Cone & Co. v. The Tai Shan,* 218 F.2d 822 (2d Cir., 1955).

204. See *Haroco Co. v. The Tai Shan,* 111 F.Supp. 638, 1953 AMC 887 (S.D.N.Y.), *aff'd sub nom Frederick H. Cone & Co. v. The Tai Shan,* 218 F.2d 822 (2d Cir., 1955).

whether or not the deviation had any causal relationship to the damage sustained. Thus, any deviation for the purpose of saving or attempting to save life or property at sea is permissible, as is any "reasonable" deviation. If a deviation is not "reasonable," then by definition it must be "unreasonable." What then, is the effect of an "unreasonable" deviation?

Those eminent authors, Gilmore & Black,[205] maintain that a case can be made out, on the face of the Act, for the proposition that Cogsa has abolished the harsh doctrine, which puts the carrier in an "insurer's" position after deviation and has substituted a liability for that damage with which the deviation has some causal connection. They point out, quite correctly, that the language of the Section is that the carrier is not to be "liable for any loss or damage resulting" from reasonable deviation, and that it is maintainable that the draftmen of that passage must have had in mind that the carrier should not be liable, even in the case of unreasonable deviation, for loss or damage other than that resulting from the deviation. They further point out that in *World Wide S.S. Co. v. India Supply Mission*,[206] the court appears to have assumed that the deviation must be causally connected with the loss sought to be averaged, if a deviation is to oust a carrier's claim to general average.

By contrast, Lowndes & Rudolf[207] state flatly that so far as deviation is concerned, the Hague Rules have made little difference, stating that the only result appears to be that so far as contracts to which the Act applies are concerned, the deviation to be justifiable must be reasonable (which in particular includes a deviation to save life or property), citing *Stag Line v. Foscolo Mango & Co.*[208]

Support for the position taken by Gilmore & Black will be found in *Drew Brown Ltd. v. The Orient Trader and Owners*,[209] a Canadian decision applying United States law and the new Jason Clause.[210]

The American courts have, thus far, demonstrated a reluctance to go so far as the position advocated by Gilmore & Black. For example, in *Hellenic Lines v. U.S.A.*,[211] the Second Circuit noted that there was a surprising dearth of post-Cogsa authority as to whether under Section 4(4) there must be a causal connection between an unreasonable deviation and the claimed loss, noting that, in any event, the burden of proving this defense should be on the deviating carrier. In that case, the Second Circuit

205. G. Gilmore and C. Black, *The Law of Admiralty* (2d), The Foundation Press, Inc., 1975, p. 180.
206. 316 F.Supp. 190, 1971 AMC 498 (S.D.N.Y.).
207. J. Donaldson, C. Ellis, C. Staughton, *The Law of General Average*, Lowndes & Rudolf, British Shipping Laws, (9th), 1964.
208. [1932] A.C. 328.
209. [1972] 1 Lloyd's Rep. 35 (Can.Ex.Ct.), [1973] 2 Lloyd's Rep. 174 (Can.Sup.Ct.).
210. Discussed, *supra*.
211. 512 F.2d 1196, 1975 AMC 697 (2d Cir.).

found that the ocean carrier had committed a voluntary unreasonable deviation when its vessel's delayed departure on a voyage from U.S. Gulf port to Red Sea ports was extended by an additional six days because the vessel proceeded to New York to load cargo in accordance with its advertised schedule, despite the carrier's promise to the shipper that the vessel would proceed directly to the Red Sea port, and the deviation precluded the carrier from relying on its bill of lading "liberties clause" to justify discharge at another port after closure of the Suez Canal by the 1967 Arab-Israeli "Six-Day War."

As late as 1981, in *Swindell-Dressler International Co. v. Hellenic Ideal*,[212] the Southern District of New York observed that the question was apparently still an open one in the Second Circuit, just as it was when discussed in *Hellenic Lines, supra*.

It will be recognized that the doctrine of deviation partakes of the doctrine—or concept—of fundamental breach, i.e. a breach so "fundamental" that it goes to the "root of the contract." Although there have been numerous cases which deal with the concept, its theoretical basis and the extent of its application remain controversial. For a time, differing views were expressed as to whether it was a rule of construction concerning the meaning and extent of exceptions clauses or whether it was a rule of law concerned with the impact of a fundamental breach on the contract as a whole.[213]

Although the term "fundamental breach" does not yet seem to be in vogue in the United States, it is very clear that the concept is alive and well in the courts of the United States. This is particularly true with respect to cases involving deviation.[214]

212. 500 F.Supp. 649, 1981 AMC 921 (S.D.N.Y.). In that case, the court found that the defendant carrier had established that (1) the risk of damage to oversize bulky construction equipment was reduced by stowing them on deck, thus eliminating the difficulty of handling them through the hatches and (2) a 29 mile detour to Crete for the purpose of switching crews did not result in any significant delay on a Houston/Jeddah voyage.

213. Compare, for example, *Suisse Atlantique Societe D'Armement Maritime S.A. v. N.V. Rotterdamsche Kolen Centrale*, [1967] 1 A.C. 361 (delays by charterers in loading and discharging cargoes preventing the vessel from performing more voyages within the time prescribed by the charter) with *Harbutt's Plasticine Ltd. v. Wayne Tank & Pump Co. Ltd.* [1970] 1 Q.B. 447, C.A. (despite the existence of an exemptions clause, a contractor held liable as a matter of law for the destruction of a factory where the pipes and heating systems of the factory were unsuitable for their purpose and caused the total destruction of the factory. In any event, in *Photo Production Ltd. v. Securicor Transport, Ltd.* [1980] 2 W.L.R. 283 (H.L.), [1980] 1 Lloyd's Rep. 545, the House of Lords expressly overruled *Harbutt's* and reiterated (or so their Lordships viewed it) the holding in *Suisse Atlantique* that whether, and to what extent, an exclusion clause is to be applied to a fundamental breach of contract, is a matter of construction of the contract. Certainly, in the view of their Lordships, there was not a rule of law by which exceptions clauses were eliminated, or deprived of effect, regardless of their terms.

214. See, for example, *Alaska Maru*, 47 F.2d 878, 1931 AMC 528 (2d Cir.); *The Silvercypress*, 63 F.Supp. 452, 1943 AMC 510; *Jones v. The Flying Clipper*, 116 F.Supp. 387, 1954 AMC 259 (S.D.N.Y.); *Atlantic Mutual Ins. Co. v. Poseidon Schiffahrrt*, 313 F.2d 872, 1963 AMC 665 (2d Cir.); *Searoad Shipping Co. v. E.I. Dupont de Nemours and Co. (The Sealane)*, 361 F.2d 833, 1966 AMC 1405 (5th Cir.), *cert. den.*, 385 U.S. 973; *De Laval Turbine, Inc. v. West India*

It will be observed that many of the cases cited involved deviation, which is, of course, a special case of fundamental breach. Unfortunately, as Tetley points out in his *Marine Cargo Claims* (2d), p. 29, United States decisions with respect to deviation should be viewed with great care for two reasons: First, American courts have often equated deck carriage, overcarriage, non-delivery, etc. with unreasonable deviation, which latter term, under the Hague Rules and in the courts of most nations, is understood to be an unreasonable and intentional change in the geographical route of the voyage as contracted. Occasionally, overcarriage will have the same effect as a deviation, but this does not make overcarriage a deviation per se. Secondly, the "intention" to breach the contract does not always seem to be a criterion in America when deciding whether a certain act was or was not a deviation under American law.

Extraordinary Sacrifice[a]

It would be well to restate the definition of a general average act, so clearly explained in Rule A, reading:

> There is a general average act when, and only when, any *extraordinary* sacrifice or expenditure is *intentionally* and reasonably made or incurred for the common safety for the purpose of preserving from peril the property involved in a common maritime adventure. [Emphasis supplied]

It must be kept in mind at all times that the risk spreading principles of traditional general average do not apply to the inherent or ordinary risks which each interest undertakes in a maritime venture. Assuming no contract provisions to the contrary, a vessel owner is always under a duty to employ any means to fulfill the contract of carriage, even though the difficulties of various sorts which may occur may result in it costing him a little more than he had hoped. Moreover, assuming no contract provisions to the contrary, a vessel owner has the obligation to provide a seaworthy vessel, that is, one which is reasonably fit at the commencement of

---

Industries, Inc., 502 F.2d 259, 1974 AMC 1619 (3rd Cir.); *The Hermosa*, 57 F.2d 20, 1932 AMC 541 (9th Cir.); *U.S. for use and benefit of Pickard v. Southern Constr. Co.*, 293 F.2d (6th Cir., 1961); *Pasquel v. Owen*, 186 F.2d 263 (8th Cir., 1950); *Knutson v. Metallic Slab Form Co.*, 128 F.2d 408 (5th Cir., 1942); *Iligan International Steel v. John Weyerhaeuser*, 507 F.2d 68, 1975 AMC 33 (2d Cir.); *Zajicek v. United Fruit Co.*, 459 F.2d 395, 1962 AMC 1746 (5th Cir.).

(a). The preliminary draft of this section of this chapter through "Contributory Values," *infra*, was prepared by Guy C. Stephenson of the firm of Schwabe, Williamson, Wyatt, Moore & Roberts, Portland, Oregon, for which the author expresses his deepest appreciation. It is indeed a tribute to the law profession that one finds so many able and experienced attorneys who are willing to contribute their time and effort to assist in producing a text which, hopefully, will be of value to the profession and to the marine insurance industry and average adjusters in general.

the voyage for the service intended. Consequently, a loss due to unseaworthiness may not be spread under general average.

For example, where a vessel fails to carry enough fuel to complete its
voyage in expectable weather, additional costs incurred by the vessel to
deviate and take on additional bunkers are not allowable in general
average.[215]

The general average sacrifice is, most likely, a creature of maritime
custom rather than legal imperative. Thus, the modern requirement that
a sacrifice be "intentional" is certainly redundant, for even in maritime
law, a sacrifice, by implication, is "intentional" and probably has been for
centuries.

A sacrifice must, however, be extraordinary. While sacrifices of cargo
or portions of the vessel are the oldest forms of a general average act, not
all such sacrifices are extraordinary. For example, a ship that is aground
in a position of peril may claim as general average damage to any ship's
machinery caused by intentional efforts to refloat the ship, but damage to
the propelling machinery of a ship which is afloat does not give rise to a
claim in general average.[216]

Extraordinary sacrifices are usually to the ship and to cargo. The most
common forms of cargo sacrifice are jettison or damage incidental to a
sacrifice of the vessel.

Jettison

Originally, the owner of jettisoned deck cargo was not entitled to the benefit of a general average contribution except where it was carried there in
pursuance of an established usage in the particular trade. If it was so carried, and was sacrificed for the general safety, the loss was allowed for in
general average, to which the under-deck cargo was required to contribute.[217] For example, in The Hettie Ellis,[218] it was held that the owner of deck
cargo could recover in general average for losses sustained by jettison
where the vessel was designed to carry a deck cargo, and was running in a
trade where it was customary and necessary to load a major part of the
cargo on deck. It was recognized early on that steamers navigating inland
waters were peculiarly adapted to carriage of deck cargo and that, in fact,
most such steamers carried the cargo on deck.[219]

215. U.S. v. Eastmount Shipping Corp. (S.S. Susquehanna), 1974 AMC 1183 (S.D.N.Y.,
1974) (York-Antwerp Rules (1950) did not excuse failure as court deemed failure to constitute unseaworthiness). See also U.S. v. Am. Trading Co.(Glymont), 56 F.2d 252, 1932 AMC
482 (S.D.N.Y, 1932), aff'd, 66 F.2d 617 (2d Cir., 1933) (costs of towage not recoverable in
general average in the circumstances involved).
216. York-Antwerp Rules (1974) Rule VII.
217. Wood v. Phoenix Ins. Co., 8 F. 27 (C.C., Pa., 1881).
218. 20 F. 507 (C.C.,Mo, 1884).
219. The William Crane, 50 F. 444 (D.,Md., 1889).

It should be emphasized, however, that a clean bill of lading presupposes a shipment under deck.[220] Lowndes & Rudolf[221] note that while the American courts followed the developing maritime practices regarding deck cargo, British courts attempted to do the same, but without similar success. In 1864, the jettison of wood cargo carried on deck "in pursuance of a general custom of the trade in which the ship was then engaged" was given the same treatment as the jettison of below-deck cargo. However, Rule I of the 1877 York-Antwerp Rules reinstituted the blanket exclusion of deck cargo from general average. At the 1890 conference, Rule I remained unchanged despite the developing British law that the jettison of deck cargo carried in accordance with the custom of the trade, and not in violation of the contract of affreightment, would be allowed in general average.

A custom or usage for the stowage of cargo other than under deck is not available to a shipowner as a defense for failure to deliver cargo lost or damaged by reason of the place and manner of stowage, unless it is clearly established and not left to conjecture. The custom must be definite, uniform, and so well known in the trade that it may be presumed that the parties considered it when making their contract.[222]

Cargo which, under agreement between shipper and master, is to be carried on deck, even though not in accordance with the usage is, as *between them*, in the absence of a valid agreement to the contrary, the subject of contribution if jettisoned for the common benefit.[223]

In *The Freda*,[224] the charterer issued a clean bill of lading to the shipper. This entitled him to have his cargo stowed below deck, but without the shipper's knowledge, it was stowed on deck and was jettisoned when the vessel stranded. The bill of lading provided that general average was to be adjusted in accordance with the 1890 York-Antwerp Rules. The court held that as between the charterer and the shipper, the cargo was to be considered as if it were stowed under deck, and the shipper was entitled to recover from the charterer the amount which would have been received in general average had the cargo been stowed under deck.

The condition of the cargo at the time it was jettisoned must be ascertained before the value to be allowed is determined, and deduction made

---

220. *The Sarnia*, 278 F. 459 (1921); *The St. Johns*, 280 F. 553 (1922). What is considered on deck or under deck can pose a problem. For example, in *The Kirkhill*, 99 F. 575 (1900) it was held that cotton stowed in the passageways of a steamer could not be considered as stowed under deck.

221. Lowndes & Rudolf, *General Average and York/Antwerp Rules*, (10th Ed., 1975), Sweet & Maxwell, London, p. 281.

222. *The Gualala*, 178 F. 405 (1910).

223. *The May and Eva*, 6 F. 628 (D.,N.J., 1881). If the bill of lading specifically exempts the shipowner from liability for loss by jettison, the shipowner is relieved from contribution to the loss occasioned by jettison for the safety of the vessel. *The Enrique*, 7 F.Supp. 490 (D.,Md., 1881).

224. 266 F. 551 (S.D.N.Y., 1918).

for the damage, if any, previously suffered as, for instance, by water entering the vessel or by shifting of cargo before it was jettisoned. If it is reasonably certain that the cargo, although sound when jettisoned must, if it had remained on board, have sustained damage before reaching its destination, the amount to be allowed is the value which it would have had on arrival in damaged condition, but the burden of proof here rests with those who refuse to contribute to the sound value, and they must show that such deterioration in value was inevitable.

Cargo may have already suffered damage before it was jettisoned, and if it can be shown that it would have sustained further damage if, instead of being jettisoned, it had remained on board, deduction must be made accordingly, the actual loss to its owner being the amount which it would have produced had it been left on board and arrived in the vessel.

Goods of a highly flammable or dangerous nature which are frequently stored on deck and are jettisoned because the packages or containers have been damaged or are adrift and thus pose a menace to the vessel and its crew, are not entitled to contribution, as the real cause for the jettison was the *vice propre* of the goods themselves.[225]

If by opening hatches to jettison cargo, other cargo is damaged, the damage is considered the direct result of the original act of opening the hatches and is just as much a voluntary sacrifice as the jettison itself and is contributed for.[225a]

When deck cargo such as logs or lumber washed adrift because of broken lashings, is jettisoned to diminish danger to the vessel and the other cargo, it is not entitled to contribution if it was impossible to secure and save it through bad weather and other conditions, as the jettison merely hastened its inevitable loss.[226]

If, after a jettison of part of the cargo for the common safety, the vessel puts into a port of refuge and the remaining cargo is necessarily disposed of by a forced sale, the value to be made good in general average is computed on the basis of the proceeds realized from the forced sale of the

---

225. *Slater v. Hayward Rubber Co.*, 26 Conn. 128 (St.,Conn., 1857). Correspondingly, goods which are on fire or become dangerously heated or worthless during the voyage, whether stowed on deck or under deck, are not allowed for in jettison, as there has been no sacrifice of anything of value.

225a. See *The Ioannis P. Goulandris*, 173 F.Supp. 140, 1959 AMC 1462 (S.D.N.Y., 1959). There, tobacco loaded in Turkey, Bulgaria, and Greece for carriage to the United States via Gibraltar was actually carried via the Suez Canal and the Cape of Good Hope because the Gibraltar route was closed by war. The tobacco heated during the long, hot voyage and actually caught on fire. At a port of refuge, water was poured into several of the holds, damaging the tobacco. Some tobacco was taken out, dried, and restowed. Upon arrival at destination, the cargo owners claimed for the damage, and the shipowner for contributions in general average. The court held that the cargo which arrived safely and/or damaged should contribute in general average to the expenses of the shipowner.

226. See *The Adele Thackera*, 24 F. 809 (S.D.N.Y., 1885).

remainder. The rationale here is that it is presumed that had such cargo not been jettisoned, it would have shared the fate of the cargo that was saved, and there being a separation of interests at the port of refuge, it is at that port that the values must be taken.

When there is a proper jettison, new cargo is sometimes loaded in the space formerly occupied by the cargo sacrificed. If the original voyage is resumed and completed, the net freight earned on the new cargo should be credited against the allowance for freight on the cargo sacrificed,[226a] but if the voyage is abandoned and a new one entered into, obviously no credit is made for the freight earned on the new voyage.

The owner of cargo jettisoned for the common benefit has a maritime lien on the vessel for the shares payable by her and her freight, enforceable by proceedings *in rem*, but the lien is limited to those shares and does not extend to the shares collected by the shipowner from the cargo saved.[227] It is important to note in this connection that if the master fails to exercise the lien, which by law he has on the goods of all shippers for their proportion of the general average contribution, and delivers the goods without requiring payment or a general average bond or other security, he and the shipowner become personally liable for the full amount of the general contribution.[228]

A shipper who asssumes by contract the risk of deck stowage is nonetheless entitled to also assume that the vessel has been loaded properly and is seaworthy. Consequently, if a jettison was rendered necessary by reason of the unseaworthiness of the vessel, the liability falls upon the shipowner notwithstanding the shipper's assumption of risk.[229]

Where cargos spontaneously combust and the vessel puts into a port of refuge in order to offload the cargo, it is frequently considered dangerous to reload the combustible cargo and carry it to its destination. In such a case, the cargo owner is not entitled to contribution in general average for any loss on the cargo by reason of its being sold or otherwise disposed of, and the vessel owner is not entitled to loss of freight. The basis for this is that the inherent heat would presumably destroy it before arrival, so that no actual sacrifice is made by leaving it at the port of refuge. By the same reasoning, the freight was lost solely because of the condition of the cargo and not by a general average act.

Rule I of the 1890 Rules specifically excluded deck cargo from general average and in this respect differed from subsequent versions of Rule I. In American courts, Rule I of the 1890 Rules caused problems for cargo.

226a. *The Rosamond,* 109 F.2d 310, 1940 AMC 195 (9th Cir.).
227. *Dupont de Nemours & Co. v. Vance,* 19 Howard 174 (1856); *The Alliance,* 64 F. 871 (S.D.N.Y., 1894), 79 F. 989 (C.C., N.Y., 1895).
228. *The Santa Anna,* 154 F. 800 (1907).
229. *The Royal Sceptre,* 187 F. 228 (S.D.N.Y., 1911).

For example, in *Geo. D. Emery Co. v. Lange (The Felix)*,[230] a deckload of lumber was jettisoned for the common safety. During jettison, the lumber damaged the vessel's propeller. Since the York-Antwerp Rules (1890) applied, the court held that the jettison itself was not allowable in general average. The consequential damage to the propeller of the vessel during the jettisoning, however, was held allowable in general average pursuant to Rule II.[231]

It was not until 1924 that the continental countries acceded to the custom of the industry, and the present rules were adopted. Rule I reads:

> No jettison of cargo shall be made good as general average, unless such cargo is carried in accordance with the recognized custom of the trade.

Rule II reads:

> Damage done to a ship and cargo, or either of them, by or in consequence of a sacrifice made for the common safety, by water which goes down a ship's hatches opened or other opening made for the purpose of making a jettison for the common safety, shall be made good as general average.

In light of modern practice, it may be said that Rule I is the exception which swallows the rule. Even where cargo is carried at "shipper's risk" under a bill of lading, if it is carried within the custom of the trade and is jettisoned, the cargo is entitled to a general average contribution, absent a *specific* contractual exclusion.[232]

Interestingly, where cargo is offloaded from a stranded vessel into a lighter which subsequently sinks and is a total loss, together with the cargo loaded aboard it, the loss of the cargo has been treated as a species of jettison and a good claim in general average. This is so because there has been an intentional exposure of the goods to an imminent and extraordinary risk with a view towards the ship's safety, and the loss of the lighter (which had been loaned to the ship but for which the shipowner had to ultimately pay) was held to be a compensable claim in general average.[233]

Extinguishing Fire on Shipboard

Cargo damaged through efforts to extinguish a shipboard fire has long been entitled to a contribution in general average. The damage includes

230. 8 F.2d 744, 1927 AMC 844 (2d Cir, 1927), *cert. den.*, 275 U.S. 540, (1927).
231. It will be observed that Rule I implicitly recognizes a jettison as a "loss" of the cargo. By contrast, Rule II speaks in terms of "damage" to the ship or cargo. Contribution for a jettison is, therefore, made pursuant to the lettered rules and not Rule II.
232. *Nicaraguan L.L.P. Lumber Co.v. Moody*, 211 F.2d 715, 1954 AMC 658 (5th Cir., 1954).
233. See *Virginia*, 1945 AMC 849 (Arb.).

water damage sustained when actually used to extinguish the fire, or water damage to cargo caused by intentionally wetting it down to contain the fire or to keep it from spreading. The right to general average contribution is not confined merely to cargo, but the shipowner may also claim in general average for damage done to the ship.[233a] This principle has been specifically memorialized in Rule III of the York-Antwerp Rules, reading:

> Damage done to a ship and cargo, or either of them, by water or otherwise, including damage by beaching or scuttling a burning ship, in extinguishing a fire on board the ship, shall be made good as general average; except that no compensation shall be made for damage by smoke or heat however caused.

There must be, however, an actual peril to the enterprise. This is determined before fire control measures are employed.[234] Where the master reasonably believes that a fire exists, and takes steps to extinguish it, cargo interests are not subject to a general average contribution if there is in fact no fire, or other peril mistakenly believed to be fire. Similarly, if the cause of the loss is related to the fault of the vessel in causing ignition, and then unreasonably delaying fire fighting measures, the vessel may not claim general average from cargo.[235]

In addition, efforts to extinguish the fire must be undertaken by one in authority over the maritime venture; efforts undertaken or initiated by a third party, such as a municipal or governmental agency, may not create a general average situation. For example, in *Ralli v. Troop*,[236] the vessel caught fire while moored in the Port of Calcutta. The fire department at the port, without suggestion or request from anyone representing the vessel, voluntarily came to the scene of the fire and assumed control of the vessel. The vessel was cut loose from its mooring and put aground, where she was scuttled and sunk. On these facts, the Supreme Court held that no general average was allowable, since the sacrifice was not made by the master or by his authority, and that the efforts of the municipal au-

---

233a. See, for example, *Nelson v. Belmont*, 12 N.Y.S. 310 (1856); *Lee v. Grinnell*, 12 N.Y.S. 400 (1856); *Nimick v. Holmes*, 25 Pa. 366 (St.,Pa., 1855); *The Roanoke*, 59 F. 161 (C.C., 1893); *Heye v. North German Lloyd*, 33 F. 60 (1887); *American Tobacco Co. v. The Katingo Hadjipatera*, 194 F.2d 449, 1951 AMC 1933 (2d Cir.); *American African Export Co., Inc. v. S.S. Export Champion*, 442 F.Supp. 715, 1978 AMC 1109 (S.D.N.Y., 1977); *The Pocone*, 1946 AMC 821 (E.D.N.Y.); *Ioannis P. Goulandris*, 1959 AMC 1462 (S.D.N.Y.); *Containerschiffs v. Lloyd's*, 1981 AMC 60 (S.D.N.Y.); cf. *Rathbone v. Fowler*, 79 U.S. 102 (1870); *Pacific Mail S.S. Co. v. New York, H. & R. Min. Co.*, 74 F. 564 (1895); *The West Imboden*, 89 F.2d 1004, 1937 AMC 462 (2d Cir.).

234. *American African Export Co. Inc. v. S.S. Export Champion*, 442 F.Supp 715, 1978 AMC 1109 (S.D.N.Y., 1977). See, also, *The Wordsworth*, 88 F. 313 (S.D.N.Y., 1898); *Joseph Watson & Sons v. Fireman's Fund Ins. Co.*, (1922) 12 Ll.L.Rep. 133, [1922] 2 K.B. 355; *The West Imboden*, 89 F.2d 1004, 1936 AMC 696 (E.D.N.Y.), aff'd 1937 AMC 462 (2d Cir.).

235. *American Mail Line v. Tokyo M. & F. Ins. Co.*, 270 F.2d 499, 1959 AMC 2220 (9th Cir., 1959).

236. 157 U.S. 386 (1895).

thorities were not for the sole benefit of the vessel and cargo, but were also for the benefit of the adjacent property.

This principle was followed in *Maloy v. Moran No. 16*,[237] where a cargo of sugar was being transferred from the steamship *Andree*, across the barge *Harrington* and onto the lighter *Moran No. 16*. During the evening a lantern aboard the *Moran No. 16* exploded, setting afire some of the transferred sugar. When the fire was discovered, the whistle of the *Andree* was blown repeatedly and the fire department was summoned by some unknown person. A hose from the *Andree* was then used in an attempt to extinguish the fire, but to no avail. The lighter was then cast adrift, soon to be recovered by municipal fire boats. These craft pushed the lighter towards a pier, where land apparatus was also employed to assist the fire boats in extinguishing the fire.

Cargo sought general average from the lighter and its owner, and the claim was allowed in the lower court. On appeal to the Second Circuit, the court reversed, with Judge Learned Hand dissenting. It held that as there was no direct evidence that the lighter called the fire department, the cargo damage was not the voluntary act of the lighter. In so doing, the court impliedly found that the lightering operation was not a common venture under which the master of the *Andree* had authority.

Where, however, the master or one authorized to act on behalf of the vessel orders municipal assistance in extinguishing a shipboard fire, it appears that general average is allowable.[238]

All damage to cargo in a general average situation is not, *per se*, allowable. Certainly, there can be no dispute that cargo actually damaged by the fire itself is not a general average sacrifice.[239]

Cargo which sustains water damage through the injection of steam or the application of water will have a claim in general average where the damage is the proximate result of the sacrifice. For example, in *Boston Insurance Co. v. Steamship Taurus*,[240] a fire in a coal bunker was extinguished with steam and water. The coal bunker was separated from the cargo holds by water tight bulkheads. On arrival at its port of destination, the cargo was found to have sustained water damage. It was found by the special commissioner that the water damage was caused by condensation, not by the efforts to extinguish the fire and, no general average was allowed.

Prior to 1974, one of the biggest problems for adjusters was in determining whether smoke damage was allowable in general average. Often, the injection of steam and the use of other fire fighting methods would

237. 40 F.2d 466, 1930 AMC 631 (2d Cir., 1930)
238. See, e.g., *Armour Fertilizer Works v. Barge Northern No. 30*, 24 F.2d 975, 1928 AMC 606 (E.D.N.C.).
239. York-Antwerp Rules (1974) Rule III.
240. 1928 AMC 1587 (S.D.N.Y. 1928).

cause additional smoke. Cargo would seek to have general average contribution for the smoke damage as an incident of the efforts to extinguish the fire.

The Second Circuit dealt with this issue in *Reliance Marine Insurance Co. v. New York & C. Mail S.S. Co.*[241] In that case, the court was asked to determine whether a cargo of tobacco damaged by smoke carried by steam used to extinguish the fire would be allowable in general average. The court denied general average stating that all parts of the cargo would have been damaged by smoke in the event that steam had not been used. Thus, it appears that the issue was one of causation.

Some courts have been successful in wrestling with the causation issue. For example, in *Starlight Trading Inc. v. S.S. San Francisco Maru et al.*,[242] the court held that cargo interests were entitled to recover in general average for smoke damage when the vessel's hatch was closed and carbon dioxide was injected to combat the fire. In allowing general average, the court noted:

> [h]ad the hatch been left open and the smoke allowed to escape, it seems to me more probable than not that the packaging of plaintiff's merchandise would have been sufficient to have protected it from the smoke . . . .[S]uch sealing [of the hatch] subjected their merchandise to smoke-filled atmosphere for a period of about 42 hours, which more probably than not caused significant penetration through the packaging which would not have otherwise have occurred.

Despite the advances in packaging and fire-fighting techniques, York-Antwerp Rule III was amended in 1974 to specifically exclude any general average compensation to cargo "for damage by smoke or heat however caused." Rule III was amended on grounds of "practical expediency."

Buglass notes that the amendment to the rule permits the allowance of *all* extinguishing damage, subject to the veto against any allowance for smoke or heat damage however caused. Under the previous version of the rule, no allowance was made in general average for damage by water or other means used to extinguish the fire if the particular part of the ship or portion of the bulk cargo or separate package of a general cargo had been touched by fire. This was based on the theory that the damage done in extinguishing the fire could not be said to have damaged any portion or package of cargo which was already on fire and therefore potentially lost. Be that as it may, the new rule stipulates that all damage caused by the extinguishing operations, except heat or smoke damage, is now to be made good in general average.

---

241. 70 F. 262 (S.D.N.Y. 1895), *aff'd*, 77 F. 317 (2d Cir., 1896), *cert. den.*, 165 US 720 (1897).

242. 1974 AMC 1523 (S.D.N.Y).

Vessel's Fuel Supply Running Short

Claims in general average may be allowable for losses or expenses incurred when a vessel's fuel supply runs short when, and only when, the vessel had a proper supply of fuel on board at the commencement of the voyage, any other unseaworthiness of the vessel did not contribute to the prolongation of the voyage, and the weather encountered was not beyond that which could be expected. Where cargo is burned for extra fuel, and the vessel owner meets these conditions precedent, cargo may have a claim in general average. Similarly, where the vessel must burn its own stores or other materials, it may have a claim allowable in general average.

In modern times, a vessel has rarely, if ever, satisfied the requirements to make such losses and expenses allowable in general average. This is particularly true given modern propulsion systems and meteorological technology. Simply put, prior to the commencement of the voyage, a vessel must have sufficient fuel to make the voyage, including an adequate surplus in the event of adverse weather conditions.

In *U.S.A. v. Eastmount Shipping Corp., (Susquehanna)*,[243] a grain ship bound for East Pakistan from Portland, Oregon, with an intermediate stop at Yokohama, was forced to divert to Midway Island to take on additional fuel. The vessel left Portland on February 2, 1971. The court did not allow the claim of the vessel owner for its expenses incurred in diverting and taking on additional fuel. Although the vessel encountered severe weather which increased fuel consumption, the court noted that such weather was "within the ambit of reasonable expectations given the direction of the ship, its plotted course, and the time of year the voyage took place." In so finding, the court took particular note of the probability of encountering Force 8 winds as between 5 to 10 percent, and then noting that "[w]hile there was less probability of encountering Force 9 and 10 winds, the prospect was not so remote that it would be discounted by a reasonably prudent voyager."

Rule IX, provides for general average for ships materials and stores burnt for fuel and reads:

> Ship's materials and stores, or any of them, necessarily burnt for fuel for the common safety at a time of peril, shall be admitted as general

---

243. 1974 AMC 1183 (S.D.N.Y. 1974). See also, *Andria Naviera S.A. as owners of S.S. Cyprinia and Woodward & Dickerson, Inc. v. American International Underwriters'Corporation,* 1969 AMC 2193 (Arb.) (where general average was denied the vessel owner from cargo for towage expense, where vessel encountered very severe weather but not beyond that which could be expected); *Hurlburt v. Turnure,* 81 F. 208 (2d Cir., 1897); *The Abbizzia,* 127 F. 495 (1904) (vessel solely liable because the failure was caused by weak or defective boilers and the condition of her bottom).

average, when and only when an ample supply of fuel had been provided; but the estimated quantity of fuel that would have been consumed, calculated at the price current at the ship's last port of departure at the date of her leaving, shall be credited to the general average.

This rule does not appear to be applicable where the cargo is burned. Thus, one claiming a general average contribution for the burning of cargo as fuel would probably seek recovery under the lettered rules. The word "cargo" was included in Rule IX of the 1890 rules, but has been absent from Rule IX since 1924.

Damage to Cargo in Discharging

Where the act of discharging cargo is a general average act, then damage or loss necessarily sustained by the cargo is allowable in general average. The usual circumstances involved may be fire, stranding, or port of refuge.

This principle is set forth in Rule XII, which provides:

> Damage to or loss of cargo, fuel or stores caused in the act of handling, discharging, storing, reloading, and stowing shall be made good as general average, when and only when the cost of those measures respectively is admitted as general average.

This rule has remained unchanged since 1924.

In other words, if the cost of moving the cargo is allowable in general average, damage sustained to the cargo as a direct result should also be allowable in general average.

The controversial issue is whether damage sustained to cargo while it is stored on shore is allowable. As Buglass puts it, a test to be used in determining whether or not damage to or loss of cargo comes within Rule XII is to ascertain whether such damage or loss would have been sustained had the cargo remained in the vessel throughout the general average detention. If it would have, there are no grounds for making an allowance in general average. It must be kept in mind that detention damages run squarely in the face of Rule C:

> Only such losses, damages, or expenses which are the direct consequence of the general average act shall be allowed as general average.
> Loss or damage sustained by the ship or cargo through delay, whether on the voyage or subsequently, such as demurrage, and any indirect loss whatsoever, such as loss of market, shall not be admitted as general average.

Accordingly, where damage to cargo is reasonably foreseeable during handling, discharge, etc., such charges are probably allowable in general average. For example, where discharge into insufficient or inadequate storage facilities is necessary, damage is "fairly within the contemplation of the master" and should be allowed as general average. This may even include some pilferage. However, damage caused by fortuitous circumstances, such as fire on the dock or in the warehouse, are probably not allowable.

This issue is made more complex when a perishable cargo is involved. If the quality of the cargo is damaged by additional handling, the damage should be allowable. However, where the damage sustained is from detention only, the cause of the loss is delay, not handling, and a claim should not be allowable in general average.

Finally, there is apparently a disagreement between American and English authorities regarding losses sustained to refrigerated cargo. Buglass takes the position that if refrigerated cargo is necessarily discharged at a port without adequate refrigeration facilities, the losses should be allowable in general average. Lowndes & Rudolf, on the other hand, state that a strict interpretation of Rule XII precludes this result, since the loss was not caused by "the active process of discharging or storing."[244]

It is submitted that the American view is in accord with the principle of general average sacrifice. Newer changes in shipping technology should not be allowed to obscure basic principles.

Sacrifices of Vessel

The principles which make loss or damage to a vessel allowable in general average are the same as those which make sacrifices of cargo allowable: there must be a peril, and there must be a sacrifice for the common good. Thus, damage done to a ship in extinguishing a shipboard fire is allowable in general average.[245] In addition, the ship's materials and stores burnt for fuel are allowable when the fuel supply was sufficient at the beginning of the voyage.[246] Similarly, vessel sacrifices of its equipment or appurtenances, such as cables, anchors, or other portions of the ship voluntarily cut away in an attempt to avoid imminent peril are allowable.[247] This does not apply, however, to portions of the ship which have been previously damaged by accident, and are subsequently cut away. "Loss or damage sustained by cutting away wreck or parts of the ship which have been previously carried away or are effectively lost by accident shall not be made good as general average."[248] This rule is apparently based upon the

244. Lowndes & Rudolf, p. 358.
245. Rule III, York-Antwerp Rules (1974).
246. Rule IX, York-Antwerp Rules (1974).
247. Rule II, York-Antwerp Rules (1974).
248. Rule IV, York-Antwerp Rules (1974).

fact that the vessel is obviously more likely than cargo to be exposed to greater risk of damage from adverse weather conditions.

A steamer may be driven by heavy gales and seas toward a lee shore or into other positions of danger. If, to avoid the impending peril to her and her cargo, the master causes the engines to be worked at their utmost speed to take her out into the open sea, and the engines are damaged, the damage (although voluntary) is not the subject of contribution because such use of the engines, albeit at the risk of injury, is considered to be within the ordinary duty of the vessel to her cargo under the contract of affreightment. On the other hand, if a vessel becomes disabled at sea to such an extent that it becomes necessary to work the engines in an extra-ordinary manner and an extra strain is put upon them to enable her to make port, damage by such extraordinary use, or rather abuse, of the engines is allowable in general average.

Stranding

Losses to the vessel and cargo may be allowable in general average in cir-cumstances of both voluntary, negligent, or unavoidable stranding. However, not all strandings constitute a general average situation. For ex-ample, in *Orient Mid-East Lines, Inc. v. S.S. Orient Transporter*,[249] the vessel underwent repairs to her starboard boiler prior to departure. It was also recommended by the surveyor that the port boiler be overhauled "at the earliest opportunity," but not later than within two months. The master hoped to accomplish the boiler repairs at the loading berth, but that was not possible as the port had scheduled another ship for loading. The mas-ter then took on a pilot and intentionally grounded the vessel in an aban-doned ship channel. The channel had a soft-silt bottom. The place of stranding proved to be unsuitable because of the silt contaminating the vessel's propulsion equipment. Accordingly, the vessel was backed off, and in moving to another anchorage, again grounded. The vessel was refloated at the next high tide and moved back to port with the aid of a tugboat. This state of affairs resulted in expenses of nearly $9,000. Later during the voyage, the turbines were rendered inoperative by the negli-gence of the crew.

In addition to other claims, the vessel owner sought a general average contribution from cargo as a result of the voluntary stranding. The court held, however, that although the stranding was indeed voluntary, the ves-sel was stranded in hopes of performing repairs which would make the vessel seaworthy, a duty which the vessel owner owed cargo in any event,

---

249. 496 F.2d 1032, 1974 AMC 2593 (5th Cir 1974), *cert. den.*, 420 U.S. 1005 (1975).

and the stranding was not performed for the common good to avoid imminent peril.[250]

Similarly, the sacrifice must be made by one in authority for the vessel. For example, in *Tampa Tugs and Towing v. M/V Sandanger*,[251] salvors successfully towed the defendant vessel to port, where it was put under arrest. Thereafter, the vessel was intentionally grounded by the tugs at the direction of the salvor and a surveyor representing cargo interest. The vessel was later de-oiled and refloated.

At trial, some of the cargo interests sought contribution from the owner of the silver cargo for these and other expenses, claiming a general average situation existed by virtue of the voluntary grounding. The court, however, did not agree, finding that, as the vessel was *in custodia legis*, those who directed the grounding were not in lawful possession and control, such as would have been the master.

Prior to 1974, there was a major difference between American law and York-Antwerp Rule V: where a vessel would have inevitably sunk or been driven ashore, general average was not allowable under Rule V. However, American law provided for general average contributions where a master, finding himself in such a situation, voluntarily stranded the vessel at a location where he reasonably believed less damage to the vessel and cargo would result. Of course, if the contract between the vessel and cargo provided for general average pursuant to the York-Antwerp Rules, the "lesser of two perils" rule would not apply.

In 1974, however, Rule V was changed to eliminate the "inevitable grounding" exception. Although Rule V mentions nothing about inevitable sinking, it is submitted that in light of the 1974 amendment, where a vessel is grounded to avoid sinking in deep water, general average would lie. Similarly, where a vessel is voluntarily driven into a dock, damage to the vessel and to the dock is allowable in general average.

It must be kept in mind that the stranding, even in a "lesser of two perils" situation, must be voluntary. Where a master unsuccessfully strands in a different location, the situation does not give rise to general average, as the agency of stranding is the force of wind and waves, not that of the master's efforts.

Involuntary or Unavoidable Stranding.. Losses or damage incurred to the vessel or cargo in refloating a stranded ship, whether voluntarily stranded or otherwise, may be allowable in general average. As explained above, damage to the vessel caused by the stranding itself, would not give

---

250. As noted heretofore, it appears the court was in error in concluding that Rule A took precedence over Rules X and XI (the exact opposite of what the drafters intended). However, the case illustrates some complexities arising out of a stranding incident.
251. 242 F.Supp. 576, 1965 AMC 1771 (S.D. Cal., 1965).

rise to a claim for general average from cargo unless the stranding was voluntary.

Of course, a vessel that is stranded or aground must be in peril before general average will lie. Most courts have taken the position that a stranded vessel is in peril, but a narrower view was taken in *U.S. v. Wessel, Duval & Co., (Edward Rutledge)*.[252] In that case the United States Government chartered the vessel from Wessel, Duval & Co. under a series of three charters, for the carriage of sugar from Caribbean ports to Germany. The charters included, *inter alia*, Cogsa and a New Jason Clause.

While under the first time charter, the vessel twice grounded in Cardenas, Cuba in attempting to leave that port. Both times, the vessel grounded in soft mud and each time was able to free herself with tug assistance and through the use of lines and her own propulsion. The vessel owner sought general average from cargo, that is the time-charter, for the expenses incurred. The court noted that cargo was required under the time-charter to contribute in general average, but found that a general average situation did not exist:

> There has been no evidence of any unusual or a perilous currents, of an abnormal or dangerous tide, of adjacent rocks, or reefs, of high winds or poor weather conditions, or of strain upon the structure of the vessel which might offer a threat of menace to the safety of the vessel or her cargo. I find that the *Edward Rutledge* on the occasion of both Cardenas strandings with proper management could have been freed by her own unaided efforts and that at no time was she or the cargo in peril. The release of the vessel may well have been delayed until a rising tide, but there is no evidence of danger—either real or substantial. The strandings of the vessel in the soft mud were mere incidents of the voyage and not events which gave rise to extraordinary common danger to the vessel or her cargo.

Assuming that the stranding puts the vessel in peril, the vessel owner cannot claim contribution from cargo for refloating damage or expenses where the stranding is caused by the vessel's unseaworthiness or negligence, absent contractual provisions to the contrary. As a general principle of law, in the absence of a valid contract to the contrary, a shipowner cannot claim contribution from the cargo if the peril to avert arose from fault or negligence on his part or on the part of his servants, notwithstanding that the sacrifice [or expenditure] was of benefit to the cargo as well as to vessel.

252. 123 F.Supp. 318, 1954 AMC 2070 (S.D.N.Y., 1954).

Where Cogsa is applicable, contribution in general average may be recovered from cargo, despite the existence of negligence where the stranding is due to one of the enumerated exceptions of the statute.[253]

Where the stranding is due to the unseaworthiness of the vessel, and the owner has failed to use due diligence to make the vessel seaworthy as of the commencement of the voyage, however, Cogsa does not excuse the owner, and he has no right to a general average contribution from cargo.[254] For example, in *A.A. Shade v. National Surety Co., et al. (Manabi)*,[255] the vessel was deliberately grounded after it was found to be in danger of sinking. The cargo was transferred to another vessel and delivered to its destination. The cause of the leak was determined to be a hole. The vessel owner failed to establish that the vessel was seaworthy at the commencement of the voyage, and general average was denied, although the bill of lading incorporated Cogsa.

Assuming that the vessel owner is excused by a contract, he may seek contribution for damage to machinery and boilers;[256] extra cost of lighting, lighter hire and reshipping and consequent damage thereby;[257] and such other claims as may be covered by Rule A.

Rule VII is quite specific in its application. It applies to damage caused to any machinery and boilers of a ship by working the propelling machinery and boilers in efforts to refloat a ship which is ashore and in a position of peril. Where the ship is afloat, no claim for general average may arise from loss or damage caused by working the propelling machinery and boilers. Where, however, the York-Antwerp Rules are not applied, Buglass suggests that such damage is recoverable under American law and practice, which permits loss or damage to machinery while afloat to be made good, provided the facts come within the American definition of general average.

In addition to the claims recoverable under Rule VII, other types of damage to the vessel may be recoverable under Rule A. Lowndes & Rudolf give these examples:

1. Extra bunkers and stores consumed while working the machinery in actual efforts to refloat;

2. Damage to hull by excessive vibration of the engines, or to cargo by leakage of water through plates started by the same vibrations;

3. Damage to the bottom of the ship caused by forcing or hauling her off or over the ground;

253. 46 USC (1304(2). See, for example, *Isbrandtsen Co. v. Federal Insurance Co.*, 113 F.Supp. 357, 1952 AMC 1945 (S.D.N.Y., 1952), *aff'd* on opinion below, 205 F.2d 679 (2d. Cir.), *cert. den.*, 346 U.S. 866 (1953).

254. 46 USC (1304)(1)

255. 186 F.Supp. 423, 1960 AMC 1105 (S.D.N.Y., 1960), *aff'd*, 288 F.2d 106 (2d.Cir.,1961).

256. York-Antwerp Rule VII.

257. York-Antwerp Rule VIII.

4. Damage caused in endeavoring to drive a ship higher up the ground, or to keep her on a rock.

The authorities generally agree that damage to the bottom of the ship caused in efforts to refloat are rarely allowed as proving causation, and the burden of proof is extremely difficult to meet. Congdon felt that there was a legal presumption in favor of cargo that bottom damage was caused accidentally, other than in situations of voluntary stranding, and the vessel owner had the burden to show which damage was caused by "getting on" and which damage was caused by "getting off."

The vessel owner in *Sealand Service, Inc. v. Aetna Insurance Co.*,[258] failed to meet his burden of proof. In that case, the vessel *Beauregard* grounded on the west breakwater of the harbor at Rio Haina, Dominican Republic. She unsuccessfully attempted to back off under her own power, and tug assistance was requested. The tug successfully put a line on board, and its efforts, combined with the ship's own power resulted in the vessel beginning to move, but the towline broke. The vessel was then forced sideways onto the rocks, and sustained bottom damage, for which the owner sought contribution from cargo. Parenthetically, the court noted that the vessel was eventually refloated approximately three days later, successfully entered the harbor, and discharged the cargo; "a happy ending for mariners, but predictably the genesis of an ascerbic dispute among underwriters and their counsel. T'was ever thus."

The court below determined that the stranding was not caused by negligence on the part of either the master or the pilot aboard. It also accepted the stipulation between the parties that the efforts of the master to free the vessel by use of the tow was a general average act. However, the court refused to allow the owners' claim in general average for bottom damage, finding that the vessel although it may have moved somewhat, never got off while under tow, and that the damage sustained would have resulted as a natural consequence of the stranding. In affirming, the court noted, with Judge Friendly in dissent, "that appellants have simply failed to sustain their burden of proof of direct damage as a result of the general average sacrifice as required by the York/Antwerp Rules."

Rule VIII is also quite specific. When a vessel is ashore, and cargo, stores, fuel, etc. are discharged as a general average act, the extra cost of "lightening, lighter, hire and reshipping . . . and the loss or damage sustained thereby, shall be admitted as general average."

General Average Expenditure—Extraordinary Expenses

A general average loss may be an expenditure as well as a sacrifice. Section 66(1) of the Marine Insurance Act, 1906, defines a general average

258. 545 F.2d 1313, 1976 AMC 2164 (2d. Cir., 1976).

loss as "a loss caused by or directly consequential on a general average act. It includes a general average expenditure as well as a general average sacrifice." Simply put, a general average expenditure is one made for the purpose of securing services or facilities necessary to save the property imperiled in a common maritime adventure.

The common examples of expenditures are "port of refuge," salvage, and substituted expenses. It must be kept in mind, however, that the expenses must be extraordinary, and incurred for the joint benefit of ship and cargo. What is or is not extraordinary expenditure must in consequence be considered in light of what has been purchased, and for the solution of this, one must look at the contract of carriage. If expenditure is incurred in carrying out the shipowner's obligations under the contract of carriage, it cannot be extraordinary expenditure. If it is otherwise incurred, it may be.

Port of Refuge Expenses

If a vessel is obliged to seek a port or place of refuge either because of damage sustained by perils of the sea, or by voluntary sacrifices, shifting of cargo, or because of sickness of crew, whereby she is rendered unseaworthy or is so disabled as to be prevented from continuing the voyage, the extra expenses of proceeding to, while at, and in leaving such port or place, *so far as they are common to vessel and cargo,* are contributed for in general average. The extra expenses include, *inter alia,* pilotage and towage into port; extra men hired to assist in pumping, wharfage; quarantine dues; discharging cargo; storing and reloading cargo; consular fees; fees of divers; pilotage and towage out of port; surveyors' fees; bill of health; restowing cargo; agency fees; wages and provisions; and fuel and engine stores.[259]

Here, Rule F must be read *in para materia* with Rules X and XI. Rule F provides:

> Any extra expense incurred in place of another expense which would have been allowable as general average shall be deemed to be general average and so allowed without regard to the saving, if any, to other interests, but only up to the amount of the general average expense avoided.

---

259. See *Padelford v. Boardman,* 4 Mass. 548 (1808); *The Star of Hope v. Annan,* 76 U.S. 203 (1870); *The Joseph Farwell,* 31 F. 844 (D., Ala., 1887); *Vowell v. Columbian Ins. Co.,* F.Cas. No. 17,019 (1827); *Hobson v. Lord,* 92 U.S. 397 (1875); *Roberts v. The Ocean Star,* F.Cas. No. 11,908 (1860); *Mitchell Transportation Co. v. Patterson,* 22 F. 49 (1884); *Barker v. Phoenix Ins. Co.,* 8 Johns. 307 (St.,N.Y., 1811); *Nelson v. Belmont,* 12 N.Y.S. 310 (St.,N.Y., 1856); *Rogers v. Murray,* 16 N.Y.S. 357 (St.,N.Y., 1858). However, estimated costs of reloading cargo is not allowable where the voyage was not resumed. *The Eliza Lines,* 102 F. 184 (2d Cir., 1900).

Rule X is entitled "Expenses at Port of Refuge, Etc." and provides:

(a) When a ship shall have entered a port or place of refuge, or shall have returned to her port or place of loading in consequence of accident, sacrifice or other extraordinary circumstances, which render that necessary for the common safety, the expenses of entering such port or place shall be admitted as general average; and when she shall have sailed thence with her original cargo, or a part of it, the corresponding expenses of leaving such port or place consequent upon such entry or return shall likewise be admitted as general average.

When a ship is at any other port or place of refuge and is necessarily removed to another port or place because repairs cannot be carried out in the first port or place, the provisions of this Rule shall be applied to the second port or place as if it were a port or place of refuge and the cost of such removal including temporary repairs and towage shall be admitted as general average. The provisions of Rule XI shall be applied to the prolongation of the voyage occasioned by such removal.

(b) The cost of handling on board or discharging cargo, fuel or stores whether at a port or place of loading, call or refuge shall be admitted as general average, when the handling or discharge was necessary for the common safety or to enable damage to the ship caused by sacrifice or accident to be repaired, if the repairs were necessary for the safe prosecution of the voyage, except in cases where the damage to the ship is discovered at a port or place of loading or call without any accident or other extraordinary circumstances connected with such damage having taken place during the voyage.

The cost of handling on board or discharging cargo, fuel, or stores shall not be admissible as general average when incurred solely for the purpose of re-stowage due to shifting during the voyage unless such re-stowage is necessary for the common safety.

(c) Whenever the cost of handling or discharging cargo, fuel or stores is admissible as general average, the costs of storage, including insurance if reasonably incurred, reloading and stowing of such cargo, fuel or stores shall likewise be admitted as general average.

But when the ship is condemned or does not proceed on her original voyage stowage expenses shall be admitted as general average only up to the date of the ship's condemnation or of the abandonment of the voyage or up to the date of completion of discharge of cargo if the condemnation or abandonment takes place before that date.

Rule XI is entitled "Wages and Maintenance of Crew and Other Expenses Bearing Up for and in a Port of Refuge, etc." and reads:

(a) Wages and maintenance of master, officers and crew reasonably incurred and fuel and stores consumed during the prolongation of the voyage occasioned by a ship entering a port or place of refuge or returning to her port or place of loading shall be admitted as general average when the expenses of entering such port or place are allowable in general average in accordance with Rule X(a).

(b) When a ship shall have entered or been detained in any port or place in consequence of accident, sacrifice or other extraordinary circumstances which render that necessary for the common safety, or to enable damage to the ship caused by sacrifice or accident to be repaired, if the repairs were necessary for the safe prosecution of the voyage, the wages and maintenance of the master, officers and crew reasonably incurred during the extra period of detention in such port or place until the ship shall or should have been ready to proceed upon her voyage, shall be admitted in general average.

Provided that when damage to the ship is discovered at a port or place of loading or call without any accident or other extraordinary circumstance connected with such damage having taken place during the voyage, then the wages and maintenance of master, officers and crew and fuel and stores consumed during the extra detention for repairs to damages so discovered shall not be admissible as general average, even if the repairs are necessary for the safe prosecution of the voyage.

When the ship is condemned or does not proceed on her original voyage, wages and maintenance of the master, officers and crew and fuel and stores consumed shall be admitted as general average only up to the date of the ship's condemnation or of the abandonment of the voyage or up to the date of completion of discharge of cargo if the condemnation or abandonment takes place before that date.

Fuel and stores consumed during the extra period of detention shall be admitted as general average, except such fuel and stores as are consumed in effecting repairs not allowable in general average.

Port charges incurred during the extra period of detention shall likewise be admitted as general average except such charges as are incurred solely by reason of repairs not allowable in general average.

(c) For the purpose of this and the other Rules wages shall include all payments made to or for the benefit of the master, officers and crew, whether such payments be imposed by law upon the shipowners or be made under the terms or articles of employment.

(d) When overtime is paid to the master, officers or crew for maintenance of the ship or repairs, the cost of which is not allowable in general average, such overtime shall be allowed in general average only up to the saving in expense which would have been incurred and admitted as general average, had such overtime not been incurred.

Under American law, the allowances for wages and provisions and for fuel and engine stores commence from the time when the vessel deviates from her voyage until she has been made ready to proceed, but (unlike the York-Antwerp Rules) no allowances are made during the time occupied in regaining the position from which she deviated.

The first question to address is under what circumstances a master's decision to put into a port of refuge will constitute a general average situation or will constitute a deviation, which is a breach of the implied covenant in every contract of afreightment that the ship shall proceed on the voyage without departure from a proper course and without unreasonable or unjustifiable delay. A vessel which is unseaworthy at the commencement of the voyage, and deviates to effect repairs during the voyage as a result of that unseaworthiness, will be precluded from seeking general average from cargo unless excused by contract.[260]

Similarly, the event which causes the master to seek a port of refuge must be an accident or other extraordinary circumstance occurring during the voyage, i.e., an event which is clearly unexpected by the vessel owner, or otherwise not ordinarily incidental to the voyage. Thus, where a vessel returns to port after encountering severe weather, which should have been anticipated given the time of year and location, the expenses involved in returning to port should not be allowable in general average.

Maritime "peril" remains part of the general average equation with respect to port of refuge expenses. The courts of the United States have recently grappled with the issue. As noted above, a vessel may be stranded, and not be in peril. On the other hand, a vessel may be at an intermediate discharge point and be "in peril." For example, in *Eagle Terminal Tankers, Inc. v. Insurance Company of USSR*, discussed *supra*, the vessel allegedly sustained propeller damage while carrying a load of grain from Port Arthur, Texas to Leningrad. At Rotterdam, her intermediate port of call, the captain decided to have an underwater examination of the vessel made after metallic scraping noises were detected. The result of the investigation indicated extensive damage to the propeller, requiring immediate repairs before proceeding on the voyage, as cargo so conceded.

Accordingly, repairs were effected at the Port of Rotterdam. A portion of the cargo was unloaded, and the ship placed on drydock where a new propeller shaft and spare propeller were installed. The cargo was then reloaded and the ship continued on to Leningrad.

The vessel owner then declared a general average and sought contribution for costs of unloading and reloading the cargo and maintaining the ship's crew and officers during the repair period. Cargo refused to make a contribution in general average, and the vessel owner filed suit.

In the district court, cargo filed a motion for summary judgment on the basis that, as the problem was discovered while the vessel was safely

---

260. *Orient Mid-East Lines v. A Shipment of Rice*, 496 F.2d 1032, 1974 AMC 2593 (5th Cir., 1974), *cert. den.* 420 US 1005 (1975).

moored in Rotterdam, the vessel was not in peril and no general average could be stated. The lower court agreed and granted summary judgment in favor of defendant.

On appeal, the Second Circuit reversed. It held that plaintiff had alleged facts sufficient to constitute a claim in general average. The contract between the parties incorporated the York-Antwerp Rules (1950), and the court gave full effect to the rules. In holding that a claim in general average had been pleaded, it noted that a peril need not be imminent, but "only real and substantial." Thus, although the vessel was not in a position of peril at the time the damage was discovered, certainly a situation of peril would have occurred had the vessel continued her voyage without undergoing repairs.

Additionally, the court noted that "the safe prosecution clause" of Rule X(b) and XI(b) bestowed upon the vessel owner a presumption that a peril exists if the vessel owner seeks contribution for expenditures made necessary "for the safe prosecution of the voyage."[261] The court said, in part:

> In effect, then, the safe prosecution clause is to be read not as eliminating the requirement of peril but as presuming its presence in cases where, because of accident or sacrifice, a voyage cannot safely be resumed without repairs . . . .
>
> Under this view of the Rules, we are satisfied that this record establishes a prima facie general average claim. Although the ship here had not lost its propeller . . . the record shows that it had been seriously damaged and that its condition was deteriorating. . . . As we read these facts, the ship's condition, allegedly as a result of an accident at sea, presented a "real and substantial" danger of loss or complete incapacitation of the propeller—and consequent peril—if the ship had been at sea or if returned to sea without repairs. Defendant implicitly recognized this threat by conceding the necessity of the repairs prior to the resumption of the voyage. Under these circumstances, we believe the requirements for a prima facie claim under Rules X(b) and XI(b) have been satisfied.

The court was quick to caution that "[o]ur holding is merely that a claim has been stated, not that it has been proved."

A difference of opinion apparently exists as to what constitutes a "port or place of refuge." The English view is that a "place of refuge" must be a locality having some or many of the characteristics of a port.[262] The American view is broader. Thus, where a vessel must undergo necessary

---

261. York-Antwerp Rules (1950), Rules X(B), XI(B).
262. *Humber Conservancy Board v. Federated Coal and Shipping Co.*, (1927) 29 Ll.L.R. 177, 179.

repairs at sea, and is detained thereby, or where it must put to sea to avoid a hurricane, it is the practice of American adjusters to allow claims for contribution, other conditions being satisfied.[263] Thus, a port or place of refuge under American law and practice is virtually anywhere where the vessel finds refuge to make necessary repairs for the common safety, or for the safe prosecution of the voyage, even including a sheltered bay or anchorage.

Allowable expenses are described fairly under Rules X and XI. The expenses allowed begin when the vessel bears off towards the port of refuge and continue until the vessel returns to her original course. As noted heretofore, American law and practice were not so generous with respect to expenses incurred in the vessel's regaining her original course.

It should be noted that neither of these rules provides a basis to allow apportionment of the actual cost of repairs. Whether the cost of repairs will be allowable in general average must be determined in light of all of the circumstances giving rise to the damage or loss.

The master is allowed a great deal of latitude in selecting a port of refuge; while he need not go to the nearest port, he does have an obligation to take the vessel to the nearest port at which she can be repaired. His selection will be viewed in light of all of the circumstances then existing. This evaluation includes considering the repair facilities available, the expense, convenience, and ultimate prosecution of the voyage, and distances involved.[264] As a matter of discretion, the master may be entitled to bring the vessel into a place of refuge where facilities are not available to effect repairs, and Rule X(a) allows as a port of refuge expenditure the cost of "necessarily removing" the vessel from that port to another port where repairs can be made.

If the York-Antwerp Rules are not applicable, and American law is applied, then as Buglass has explained it so well, if the cargo is discharged at the first port and the vessel is then taken to another port for repairs, the other expenses incurred in proceeding to the second port, such outward port charges, towage, fuel and engine stores, and the port expenses there and of re-entering the first port are considered as part of the expense of the repair of the vessel, and, in practice, are treated as a general repair expense. If the cargo is not separated from the vessel at the first port, the expenses of taking her to the other port are allowed in general average.

---

263. *May v. Keystone Yellow Pine Co.*, 117 F. 287 (D.,Pa., 1902).

264. The powers and duties of masters, and the latitude allowed them in the exercise of an honest discretion and judgment are well explained in *The Star of Hope v. Annan*, 76 U.S. 203 (1870). As the Supreme Court said there, if the master appears to have arrived at his conclusion with due deliberation, by a fair exercise of his own skill and judgment, with no unreasonable timidity, and with an honest intent to do his duty, it must be presumed, in the absence of proof to the contrary, that his decision was wisely and properly made.

However, the wages and maintenance of the crew are allowed in general average.

Rule X(b) allows the cost of handling or discharging cargo, fuel or stores "when the handling or discharge was necessary for the common safety or to enable damage to the ship caused by sacrifice or accident to be repaired, if the repairs were necessary for the safe prosecution of the voyage" where the accident or extraordinary circumstance occurred during the voyage. Mere discovery of pre-existing damage without being able to tie it to an accident or other extraordinary circumstance during the voyage does not create a general average situation.

Where cargo is discharged at a port of refuge, and is not reloaded, the charges incurred for the safekeeping of the cargo are allowable in general average up until the time when the vessel departs, the theory being that, up to the time the vessel actually sailed, the possibility of the cargo being reloaded still exists. After the vessel sails, all expenses in connection with the cargo left behind become special charges on that cargo unless the cargo is left behind because of damage caused by general average act, in which case the charges continue to be general average.

When cargo is discharged, and the cost of discharge is allowable, Rule X(c) allows the cost of insurance procured to protect the cargo while ashore "if reasonably incurred." However, American law may require more. For example, in *LW & P Armstrong, Inc. v. Mormacmar et al.*,[265] the vessel put into a port of refuge to effect repairs. The master had part of the cargo discharged to allow the vessel to proceed to a floating dock for repairs, but failed to procure fire insurance on the cargo so discharged. The court held that the carrier and its representatives were trustees of the cargo so discharged, and as such, they had a duty to place appropriate insurance on the cargo so discharged. Thus, where the storage of cargo may be allowable in general average, if the cargo is destroyed and no insurance has been placed, the vessel owner may lose its right to contribution, and may become liable for the loss of said cargo by virtue of its breach of duty.

In the event that the vessel is condemned, or the voyage abandoned, the cargo charges, allowable in general average, continue up until that point, or until the completion of the discharge of cargo, "whichever is the later."[266]

The cost of reloading and stowing discharged cargo is allowable in general average if the discharge was allowable in general average.[267]

---

265. 75 F.Supp. 520, 1947 AMC 1611 (S.D.N.Y.); *aff'd* 196 F.2d 752, 1952 AMC 1088 (2d. Cir., 1952).

266. York-Antwerp Rules (1974), Rule X(c).

267. York-Antwerp Rules (1974), Rule X(c).

However, costs of restowage during the voyage are not, unless "necessary for the common safety."[268]

As is the case with Rule X, American practice differs materially from Rule XI in several respects. For example, Rule XI allows maintenance and wage expense for the period of time when the vessel bears off to a port of refuge until it returns to its point of bearing off. As stated above, American law allows such expenses only until the time the vessel is ready to resume the voyage. The same is true with respect to allowances for fuel and engine stores. It should also be noted that where, in reaching a port of refuge, the vessel significantly advances toward her point of original destination, it is the practice to allow only those expenses attributable to the extra time involved in putting into the port of refuge.

Substituted Expenses

A substituted expense is an expenditure which is made in lieu of one which would have been allowable in general average, if made. A substituted expense is not, in and of itself, allowable in general average, but becomes recoverable insofar as it substitutes for the general average expense saved. For example, one of the earliest American cases recognizing substituted expense is *Bowring v. Thebaud*.[269] There, a vessel was dry-docked for repairs with cargo aboard. The dry-docking involved additional expenditure because of this, and this expense was allowed as it saved the cost of discharging, storing, and reloading the cargo, which would have been allowable in general average.

The York-Antwerp Rules (1974) provide for substituted expense recovery in Rule F, quoted above.

Substituted expenses are usually incurred in situations involving port of refuge and detention expenditures of the type covered by York-Antwerp Rules (1974), Rules X and XI. These situations include the cost of freight forwarding, towage to destination, temporary repairs, and overtime paid to the officers and crew in a port of refuge situation.

Whether the cost of forwarding cargo to its original destination can be claimed as a substituted expense presents several conceptual difficulties. Under the contract for carriage, the master undertakes to deliver the cargo at the port of destination in order to earn the freight. The same principle applies to the cost of towing a vessel to its port of destination rather than putting into a port of refuge; the cost of towage is chargeable to freight, being the means adopted to enable the vessel to earn it. It is the duty of the shipowner, as custodian of the cargo, to carry it to destination.

---

268. York-Antwerp Rules (1974), Rule X(b).
269. 42 F. 794, (S.D.N.Y, 1890), *aff'd,* 56 F. 520 (2d. Cir., 1892).

Consequently, if the vessel can be repaired at a reasonable cost, and in a reasonable period of time, it is the duty of the shipowner to do so.

Prior to 1974, Rule X(d) provided that where a ship was in a port of refuge where it was practicable to repair the vessel, but, in order to save expenses, the cargo was forwarded to the place of destination, or the vessel towed to the place of destination, those expenses up to the amount of the extra expenses saved were payable by the several parties of the adventure in proportion to the extraordinary expense saved. That rule was rescinded in 1974, and forwarding or towage must now fall under some other provision. As Buglass notes, as a practical matter, it had become a common practice for agreements to be prepared at the time of the general average act giving consideration to all the factors influencing the various parties to the adventure and stipulating what was, and what was not, to be allowed in general average. With the demise of Rule X(d), no doubt this practice will be even more prevalent.

These problems are often dealt with by means of a "non-separation agreement," the object of which is to obtain an extension of the treatment of forwarding expenses; to preserve the shipowner's rights to allowance for wages and maintenance of crew after the forwarding of cargo; and to insure that the cargo forwarded continues to contribute in general average. The British marine insurance market adopted a standard form of such an agreement in 1967, which provides that the transshipment or forwarding of the cargo to its original destination by another vessel does not operate to affect the "rights and liabilities in general average" of the parties affected leaving the parties in the same position they would have been in had no forwarding occurred and had the voyage continued, "for so long as justifiable under the law applicable or under the Contract of Affreightment." This form does not deal specifically with the actual cost of forwarding, and unless this is otherwise resolved by the parties, the cost of forwarding now must satisfy Rule F.[270]

In addition to a non-separation agreement, cargo underwriters usually incorporate into forwarding agreements what is known as the "Bigham Clause" which limits any potential contribution cargo might make to the cost of forwarding the cargo from the place of refuge to the point of delivery, that is, paying a second freight.[271]

Where freight has been prepaid, however, cargo may cut off its obligation to contribute in general average where it demands that the cargo be discharged at any intermediate port. In *Ellerman Lines Limited v. Gibbs, Nathanial (Canada) Limited, et al.*,[272] the vessel *City of Columbo* was bound for the City of Toronto from an unnamed port in India via Montreal. At

---

270. See, in this connection, the non-separation agreement involved in *The North Beacon*, 1960 AMC 388 (N.D.,Cal., 1959).

271. Buglass (1981), p. 260.

272. 1984 AMC 2579 (Canada, Federal Court, Trial Division, Ottawa, 1983).

Montreal, damage to the main engine was discovered, and the carrier put cargo interests on notice that repairs would take approximately 1½ months. The vessel owner offered to forward the cargo to Toronto by other means, but refused to release the cargo unless a non-separation agreement was signed. The consignees of the Toronto cargo agreed to provide general average security, but refused to sign a non-separation agreement and demanded delivery of their cargo at Montreal upon tender of the freight in full. The vessel owner refused the demand, and the court ordered release of the cargo.

The owner of the vessel then filed an action against the cargo owners and their insurers for contribution in general average. The bill of lading included a New Jason Clause and incorporated the York-Antwerp Rules. The parties stipulated that neither of these provisions were relevant.

The court first ruled that this was not a general average situation, as neither the cargo nor vessel were in peril.[273]

The court also concluded, assuming that a general average condition existed, that

> [t]he cargo owners were nevertheless fully justified in requiring their cargo be discharged forthwith in Montreal on payment of the freight charges for the entire voyage. They were not obliged to continue the voyage to Toronto nor can they be held liable at law to contribute under a general average claim for expenses subsequently incurred, whether they be engine repairs or wharfage or other damages incurred during the period of repairs.[274]

As seen above, where cargo tenders the freight for discharge at a port of refuge, no alternative exists which would allow subsequent expenses to be recoverable. This situation also arises where a question exists whether it is economically reasonable to effect repairs at a port of refuge and continue to destination or, on the other hand, to abandon the voyage at the point of destination. While the vessel certainly has the right to retain cargo aboard the vessel for a reasonable period of time, it cannot do so indefinitely. Thus, the vessel must use reasonable judgment in determin-

---

273. It can only be assumed that the parties stipulated that the damage to the ship making repairs necessary did not occur during the voyage, as required under Rule X(b). See *Eagle Terminal Tankers, Inc. v. Insurance Company of USSR, supra.*

274. In making this finding, the court relied upon the *Julia Blake*, 107 US 418, (1882); and *Wilcox, Peck & Hughes v. Alphonse Weil & Bros. (Domingo De Larrinaga)*, 24 F.2d 587, 1928 AMC 64 (S.D.N.Y, 1927). In the *Julia Blake*, the court held that where the cost of cargo's contributing in general average for port of refuge expenses exceeds the cost of taking his property at the port of refuge, cargo may choose to do the latter and not be liable in general average. It is unclear from the opinion in *Ellerman Lines* whether the court made any finding about the relative cost of contribution in general average versus tendering full freight in exchange for discharge. What is clear, however, is that a non-separation agreement or the like is the only reliable method for the vessel owner to be allowed substituted expense contribution from cargo at a port of refuge.

ing whether to incur a port of refuge and substituted expenses, or to abandon the voyage.[275]

Buglass summarizes very concisely the relevant factors to be considered as follows:

1. The length of time necessary to effect repairs;

2. The distance already covered on the charted voyage coupled with the distance from destination;

3. The cost of effecting such repairs as are necessary solely to complete the voyage;

4. The facilities for repairs at the port of refuge;

5. The freight earned or to be earned on the voyage;

6. The nature of the storage facilities available at the port of refuge, assuming cargo has to be discharged to effect repairs; and

7. The nature of the cargo itself (that is to say, whether it could survive a long delay).

It is also generally accepted that where the cost of repairing the vessel would exceed her repair value, the shipowner is allowed to abandon the voyage, as the vessel is a constructive total loss, taking into account not only the cost of repairs necessary to complete the voyage, but the freight to be earned in completing the voyage. Of course, not all items allowable in general average may be considered in determining whether the vessel is a constructive total loss.[276]

The York-Antwerp Rules specifically deal with two other types of substituted expense: overtime expense and temporary repairs. Rule XI(d) deals with overtime paid to the officers and crew of a vessel for maintenance of the ship or repairs and allows such expense "only up to the saving in expense which would have been incurred and admitted as general average, had such overtime not been incurred." Overtime worked by the repair yard is not dealt with under Rule XI(d), but it is generally agreed that it falls under Rule F, up to the amount of general average expenses saved, without regard to the saving to other interests.

When the Rules are not applicable, American practice apportions the extra cost of overtime repair expense between general and particular average savings.[277]

---

275. See *World Wide v. India Supply*, 316 F.Supp. 190, 1971 AMC 498 (S.D.N.Y.); *The Plow City*, 23 F.Supp. 548, 1938 AMC 1265 (E.D.,Pa.).

276. *Lenfest, et al. v. Coldwell*, 525 F.2d 717, 1975 AMC 2489 (2d Cir., 1975).

277. See Rule X, Association of Average Adjusters of the United States, Appendix. See, also, as another example of substituted expenses, Rule XXI of the Association of Average Adjusters of the United States, which provides for allowance in general average of the extra cost of air freight incurred in expediting the transportation of repair parts. This principle was sustained in *Western Canada S.S. Co. v. Canadian Commercial Corp.*, (1960) 2 Lloyd's Rep. 313 where a replacement tailshaft was flown from Wales to Singapore.

Temporary Repairs

Rule XIV, York-Antwerp Rules (1974) allows in general average the cost of temporary repairs made at a port of loading, call, or refuge. It reads in full:

> Where temporary repairs are effected to a ship at a port of loading, call or refuge, for the common safety, or of damage caused by general average sacrifice, the cost of such repairs shall be admitted as general average.
>
> Where temporary repairs of accidental damage are effected in order to enable the adventure to be completed, the cost of such repairs shall be admitted as general average without regard to the saving, if any, to other interests, but only up to the saving in expense which would have been incurred and allowed in general average if such repairs had not been effected there.
>
> No deductions "new for old" shall be made from the cost of temporary repairs allowable as general average.

The first paragraph simply reiterates what is already allowable in general average. Repairs effected for the common safety are allowable under Rule A, and repairs for damage caused by a general average sacrifice are allowable under Rule C as a direct consequence of a general average act.

The second paragraph of Rule XIV really speaks to the question of substituted expense, and it is only under this paragraph where a real alternative of permanent repairs must exist if temporary repairs are to be allowable. That is, if permanent repairs were not possible at the port where temporary repairs were effected, the cost of the temporary repairs is not allowable as a substituted expense under the second paragraph of Rule XIV. On the other hand, if temporary repairs are effected at the first port in order to allow the vessel to proceed to a second port for permanent repairs, the cost of the temporary repairs may be allowable pursuant to York-Antwerp Rule X(a).

The Rule itself does not define what constitutes temporary repairs. The practice is to allow the cost of temporary repairs regardless of how long the vessel continues to operate with her temporary repairs, so long as sufficient general average expenses are saved by not effecting permanent repairs at the port of refuge.

Of course, a permanent repair does not require total replacement of the damaged item. This creates a problem in adjustment where it is less expensive to repair an item rather than to replace it, and the item as repaired may have a long serviceable life. It has been suggested that such repairs should be considered as permanent unless they fail in service. If the "temporary repairs" fail and permanent repairs are therefore necessary, the rule does not allow the cost of the temporary repairs, as they effected no savings. Nor are temporary repairs effected at the conclusion of the voyage allowable under Rule XIV. They may be allowable, however, pursuant to Rule XVIII.

American law as to temporary repairs is even more generous than the York-Antwerp Rules. Under American law, reasonable temporary repairs are treated as general average if they were necessary for the safe prosecution of the voyage and it is immaterial whether or not permanent repairs could have been effected at that time and place.[278]

Salvage

Prior to 1974, there was no specific provision in the York-Antwerp Rules dealing with salvage; such expense would have to satisfy Rule A to be allowable. Thus, salvage expenses were allowable in general average only where the services were engaged or accepted by the master to save the vessel and cargo from peril.[279]

Where the services were rendered voluntarily by the salvors or were dependent upon success, the charges were assessed to the property saved and were not allowable in general average. In other words, contract salvage was generally allowable in general average, whereas pure salvage was not. Salvage undertaken on a "no cure no pay" basis was not allowable unless it otherwise met the requirements of Rule A. That is, if the services are rendered under a contract arranged by the master, if they were incurred at a time of danger, they are generally accepted as coming under Rule A.

York-Antwerp Rules (1974), Rule VI, has apparently done away with the distinction between contractual and noncontractual salvage. It reads:

> Expenditure incurred by the parties to the adventure on account of salvage, whether under contract or otherwise, shall be allowed in general average to the extent that the salvage operations were undertaken for the purpose of preserving from peril the property involved in the common maritime adventure.

Thus, where the maritime adventure has not been abandoned, and expenditure is incurred on account of salvage, those expenditures are al-

---

278. *Shoe v. Craig*, 189 F. 227 (D.,Pa., 1911).
279. *Amerada Hess Corp. v. St. Mobil Apex*, 602 F.2d 1095, 1979 AMC 2406 (2d Cir., 1979). See, also, *Gregory v. Orrall*, 8 F. 287 (1881); *Roberts v. The Ocean Star*, F. Cas. No. 11,908 (1860); *Heyliger v. New York Firemen Ins. Co.*, 11 Johns. 85 (St. N.Y., 1814); *Silent Friend*, 1943 AMC 94 (E.D.N.Y.); *Isbrandtsen Co. v. Federal Ins. Co.*, 1952 AMC 1945 (S.D.N.Y.); *Weston, Dodson & Co. v. Barge Rex*, 1959 AMC 1221 (S.D.N.Y.); *Alamo Chemical Transp. Co. v. Overseas Valdes*, 469 F.Supp. 203, 1979 AMC 2033 (E.D.,La.).

lowable in general average. Salvage of a derelict is not covered by the rule.[280]

When the salving vessel belongs to the same owner as the salved vessel, the owner may claim salvage for services rendered to the cargo.[281] The new Jason Clause usually contains a provision which provides that salvage by a sister ship shall be treated in the same manner as if the salvage had been rendered by a third party. If at the time the services are rendered, the peril has abated, the services rendered by a sister ship may constitute towage rather than salvage.[282]

The liability of cargo in general average for salvage expense depends upon the circumstances in each individual case. As a general rule, cargo is liable to contribute in general average for the total cost of the salvage operation, at least up to the point when the safety of all the property at risk has been obtained. Thus, where cargo is removed for its own benefit prior to the commencement of salvage operations, the owner of that cargo is not liable in general average, but is liable for the cost of removal. If that cargo is aboard at the time when salvage operations commence, however, cargo is liable in general average for its contribution, based upon the entire cost of the salvage operations.

Finally, before salvage charges are recoverable in general average, the salvage must be, at least in some part, successful, unless agreed otherwise by contract.[283]

It should be emphasized that the intent of Rule VI is to make the sum paid to the salvors, together with all costs and charges in connection therewith, a part of the general average expenditure, which is then to be divided between the contributing interests on the same basis as all other allowances in general average. This is to be done, of course, in accordance with the values assessed at the termination of the adventure in accordance with Rule XVII. These values are "net actual values" at the *termination of the venture*. Such values may well differ, and frequently do differ, from the values determined at the end of the salvage service. Thus, the parties' liabilities for payment of salvage differ.

For example, in the event of a reduction in the value of the vessel by the end of the voyage, as compared with the value of the vessel in the salvage determination (usually by arbitration), cargo pays more proportionately than it is required to pay in satisfying the salvage award. Such a

---

280. *Amerada Hess Corp. v. Mobil Apex, supra*, n. 54.

281. Salvage Act of 1912, 46 U.S.C. 727-731. These statutes were intended to harmonize the laws of the United States with the provisions of the Salvage Treaty adopted in Brussels in 1910.

282. *Containerschiffes v. Corp. of Lloyd's*, 1981 AMC 60 (S.D.N.Y, 1980).

283. *Complaint of Sincere Navigation Corp. (S.S. Helena)*, 327 F. Supp. 1024, 1971 AMC 2270 (E.D. La, 1971).

reduction could come about by reason of a subsequent accident on the voyage.

The solution is to arrange for insurance coverage. This is usually the amount for which salvage security has been given, plus an estimated sum for costs, plus the estimated amount of general average expenditure at risk, all of which is insured for the remainder of the voyage. Rule XX of the York-Antwerp Rules provides that the cost of such insurance is itself allowable in general average. Such insurance is generally termed "Insurance on Average Disbursements," despite the fact that a primary objective is to ensure that there is a fund available at the end of the voyage to settle the parties' liabilities for salvage. It is usually placed by the shipowner at the time when security has been given to the salvors and/or general average expenses have been incurred.

Amount to be Made Good by General Average Contribution

Once a general average sacrifice or expenditure has been made, it falls to the average adjuster to determine the value of the sacrifice or expenditure which must be "made good" through general average contribution, and to determine in what proportion each interest shall contribute to the amount to be made good. These determinations are adjusted "upon the basis of values at the time and place when and where the adventure ends."[284]

The amount to be made good requires the adjuster to determine the value of the general average sacrifice or expenditure. In addition, certain other allowances and deductions must be made, as will be seen below.

The vessel and cargo having arrived at the port of destination and the voyage having terminated, the adjustment of a general average loss occurring on the voyage is usually made at that port, although not necessarily so, except that wherever it is drawn up it must, apart from a valid agreement to the contrary, be in accordance with the law, customs and usages of the port of destination and the York-Antwerp Rules, where the latter are made applicable in the contract of affreightment.

In the case of sacrifices, the adjustment is necessarily delayed until arrival of the vessel or cargo at destination, the contribution of each being dependent upon the final saving of the vessel or a substantial part of the cargo, or both.

Where the vessel is broken up at a port of refuge, and a severance of interests occurs there, the adjustment in the absence of an agreement to the contrary, should be made in accordance with the law, customs and

---

284. York-Antwerp Rules (1974), Rule G and Rule XVII.

usages at such port.[285] For example, in *Olivari v. Thames & Mersey Marine Ins. Co.*,[286] the vessel put in at Bermuda, an intermediate port, and was condemned and sold there. Portions of the cargo were delivered to agents of the consignees in Bermuda, the cargo underwriters in New York having executed an average bond by which they agreed to pay their contribution in accordance with the established laws and usages in such cases. The adjustment was made in New York (the port of destination) in accordance with New York law, but the cargo underwriters contended it was not made in accordance with law, i.e., with Bermuda law. However, the cargo underwriters did not aver, nor did they prove, that the law and customs in Bermuda differed from those in New York, and the court held that, in the absence of such proof, they were similar, and upheld the adjustment.

Vessel

Where a vessel has suffered a general average loss, the amount to be made good depends upon whether the damage was repaired. If so, Rule XVIII of the York-Antwerp Rules (1974) provides that the amount to be made good is the "actual reasonable cost of repairing or replacing such damage or loss, subject to the deductions in accordance with Rule XIII." That rule basically deals with "new for old" deductions as well as incidental costs involved in repair such as costs of dry dock and shifting the vessel.

Where the vessel is not repaired, and the York-Antwerp Rules apply, Rule XVIII(b) sets forth the formula to be applied.

(b) When not repaired or replaced, the reasonable depreciation arising from such damage or loss, but not exceeding the estimated cost of repairs. But where the ship is an actual total loss or when the cost of repairs of the damage would exceed the value of the ship when repaired, the amount to be allowed as general average shall be the difference between the estimated sound value of the ship after deducting therefrom the estimated cost of repairing damage which is not general average and the value of the ship in her damaged state which may be measured by the net proceeds of sale, if any.

Even if the vessel is a commercial constructive total loss, if the shipowner decides to carry out repairs to the vessel, he may recover the costs of such general average repair in general average. That is, he is not required to treat the vessel as a constructive total loss if it is in his best interest to effect repairs. Obviously, if repairs are actually effected, the vessel cannot be said to have been a constructive total loss at the termina-

---

285. *National Board of Marine Underwriters v. Melchers*, 45 F. 643 (1891); *The Eliza Lines*, 102 F. 184 (1900).

286. 37 F. 894 (1888). See, also, *Bradley v. Cargo of Lumber*, 29 F. 649 (D.,Pa., 1886).

tion of the general average voyage. By effecting repairs in such an instance, the amount of the sacrifice has been determined, as the repairs necessarily equal the sacrifice.

Buglass notes a difference in American practice when the York-Antwerp Rules do not apply, and the vessel is an actual or constructive total loss:

> [The American] method is to ascertain the difference between the sound value of the vessel and the proceeds and to allow such proportion of that sum as the amount of the general average repairs bears to the amount of the entire repairs. The formula provided in the York-Antwerp Rules can result in a minus quantity and, therefore, no allowance in general average, while the American practice described above can never have such an effect.[287]

Temporary repairs are not always effected at a port of call or refuge, but may be deferred until after the completion of the voyage on which the sacrifice took place. When this occurs, Rule XIV relating to temporary repairs by its terms is not applicable. If, however, the temporary repairs are part of the reasonable cost of repairing the damage caused by the sacrifice, they are allowable under Rule XVIII. Whether the temporary repairs are part of the reasonable cost of repairs is a question of fact in each case. The principles applied in a claim for temporary repairs as particular average under a marine insurance policy would appear to be applicable in a claim under Rule XVIII.

Deductions from Cost of Repairs to Vessel. It is a universal principle that the shipowner should not benefit by any "betterments" as a result of new materials being used in effecting repairs; i.e., substituting "new for old." The York-Antwerp Rules, 1950, Rule XIII contained a complicated schedule of deductions and caused problems in interpretation. As a compromise, new language for Rule XIII was adopted in the 1974 Rules, resulting in a scale of deductions "new for old" only applicable to vessels over fifteen years old.

The new Rule XIII reads:
Repairs to be allowed in general average shall not be subject to deductions in respect of "new for old" where old material or parts are replaced by new unless the ship is over fifteen years old in which case there shall be a deduction of one-third. The deductions shall be regulated by the age of the ship from the 31st of December of the year of completion of construction to the date of the general average act, except for insulation, life- and similar boats, communications and navigational apparatus and

---

287. Buglass (1981), 212.

equipment, machinery and boilers for which deductions shall be regulated by the age of the particular parts to which they apply.

The deductions shall be made only from the cost of the new material or parts when finished and ready to be installed in the ship.

No deduction shall be made in respect of provisions, stores, anchors and chain cables.

Drydock and slipway dues and costs of shifting the ship shall be allowed in full.

The costs of cleaning, painting or coating of bottom shall not be allowed in general average unless the bottom has been painted or coated within the twelve months preceding the date of the general average act in which case one-half of such costs shall be allowed. When the 1974 Rules are not applicable and a general average is stated in accordance with American law and practice, the principle of deducting "new for old" should also be followed.[288]

The question of determining how the deductions should be calculated has caused some difficulties. This appears now to have been resolved as a matter of practice on the following basis. Deductions are limited to: (a) the cost of new material; (b) the cost of the manufacture of the new article from the material; and (c) the cost of such final preparation of the new material or the new article as may be necessary for fitting or otherwise. All other costs, including the actual fitting costs, are to be allowed in full, together with the cost of preparing any old material for the fitting of the new article and the cost of removal of the old article. Costs of transport are allowed in full except local transport costs within the premises or yard of the repairer or manufacturer, which costs are deemed to be part of the cost of manufacture or as part of the cost of preparation for fitting.

Cargo

The amount to be made good is the value of the loss which the cargo owner has sustained. Prior to 1974, the value of the cargo loss was determined on the landed value at destination. The 1974 York-Antwerp Rule XVI now provides that the value of the cargo sacrificed shall be based:

> . . . on the value at the time of discharge, ascertained from the commercial invoice rendered to the receiver or if there is no such invoice from the shipped value. The value at the time of the discharge shall include the cost of insurance and freight except insofar as such freight is at the risk of interests other than the cargo.

When cargo damaged is sold and the amount of the damage has not been otherwise agreed, the loss be made good in general average shall

---

288. Rule XIII of the Association of Average Adjusters of the United States is identical to the 1974 Rule XIII.

be the difference between the net proceeds of sale and the net sound value as computed in the first paragraph of this Rule.

It must be kept in mind that only claims for cargo which was lost or damaged as a direct consequence of a general average act are allowable. Claims for cargo which would have perished in any event, are not allowable.

Where the cargo is sold, the rule sets forth the formula for computation of the amount to be made good. In the event that the 1974 rules do not apply, the American practice, as well as the practice under the 1950 rules is that the market value at destination is used, although an exception exists where cargo sacrificed in general average is replaced at the port of loading. There, the amount to be made good is the actual cost of replacing the cargo and not the market value at destination.

Damage to undeclared or wrongfully declared cargo is not allowable in general average, but if saved, such cargo is liable to contribute. Where such cargo is declared at a value which is lower than the real value, it may be made good in general average, but at its declared value. If saved, cargo must contribute at the actual value.[289]

Freight

In a general average situation, each of the three interests involved (vessel, freight, cargo) are required to contribute their proportionate share of the expenses. Freight, as used in this context means the amount paid or to be paid for the carriage of the cargo. The freight is considered at risk of the vessel unless there is an agreement to the contrary. Payment for the carriage may be made in advance and considered earned before completion of the voyage, if an agreement to that effect has been reached by the parties; in that event the freight is deemed to be at risk of the owner of the cargo. Of course, the party whose interest is at risk must bear that interest's proportionate share of contribution in the event of a general average situation.[290]

The loss of freight is allowable in general average under Rule XV, 1974 York-Antwerp Rules "when caused by a general average act, or when the damage to or loss of cargo is so made good." Thus, claims for loss of freight arising out of damage or loss of cargo are allowable under Rule XV. Rule XV does not deal with claims for loss of freight arising out of damage to or loss of the vessel, which may be allowable under Rule A.

Rule XV is another example of the balance general average seeks to achieve. Thus, where a loss or damage to cargo is made good, that is,

289. York-Antwerp Rules (1974), Rule XIX.
290. *Waterman Steamship Corporation v. USA*, 258 F.Supp. 425, 1967 AMC 905 (S.D. Ala 1966), *rev'd* on other grounds, 397 F.2d 577 (5th Cir. 1968).

where cargo interests have recovery in general average, the vessel owner also has a recovery in general average for the freight which would have been earned on the cargo.

Although freight is usually at the risk of the carrier, as it is not earned until delivered at destination, this can be changed by contract. Such a change must be by "express words in the contract, or by words that are sufficiently intelligible to that end."[291]

Where the vessel owner takes on new cargo in the same space as the jettisoned cargo, the net freight earned is often assessed as a credit to the allowance of the freight lost by virtue of the jettison. This would also apply where cargo is discharged at a port of refuge and new cargo taken aboard. However, before any new freight can be taken into account, it is necessary to demonstrate that the space in the ship was made available by reason of the general average loss of or damage to the cargo.

Allowances

Besides requiring that a determination on the value of the general average interest lost be made, the York-Antwerp Rules provide additional, specific allowances to make good. Thus, a commission of two percent is allowable on all general average disbursements other than the wages and maintenance of master, officers and crew, and fuel and stores not replaced during the voyage.[292] The 2 percent commission is allowable where the funds have been advanced by the contributing interests, and also to any of the other parties to the maritime venture, including underwriters.

Rule XX also allows the cost of raising funds for general average disbursements, or "the loss sustained by owners of goods sold for the purpose, or the cost of insuring money advanced for general average disbursements."

In addition to the commission, York-Antwerp Rule XXI provides for seven percent interest to be allowed on all general average "expenditure, sacrifices and allowances." The interest runs in favor of the party who has sustained the general average loss or who made the disbursements.

Contributory Values

Once the amount(s) to be made good are determined, the adjuster is faced with assessing the appropriate percentage of the amount to be made good against each of the interests involved. Rule G and Rule XVII speak to the issue of contributory values. Thus, the value of the vessel is

---

291. *Waterman Steamship Corporation v. USA*, 397 F.2d 577 (5th Cir. 1968).
292. York-Antwerp Rules (1974), Rule XX.

her fair market value, ignoring any contractual obligations which the vessel may have such as any demise or time charter party to which the ship may be committed. The customary rule in the United States is that the vessel's contributory value is based on the sale prices of any similar vessels sold within a recent time period, less such adjustments as may have to be made to reflect the age and condition of the vessel being valued.[293] When no market value can be established, resort may be had to reproduction cost less depreciation.[294] Of course, any repairs effected at a port of refuge are deducted.

The contributory value of freight has been discussed generally above. It is important to recognize, however, that even if the freight is paid in advance, which is frequently the case, unless there is an express stipulation to the contrary in the contract of affreightment, such payment must nonetheless be earned by a proper delivery of the cargo. Otherwise, the freight must be repaid.[295] Where the cargo is shipped "lost or not lost," it is the same as guaranteed freight and is non-returnable even if the cargo is never delivered to destination.[296] The freight in that instance becomes part of the value of the cargo.[297]

Contracts of affreightment of bulk cargoes sometimes provide for payment of freight at a standard rate per ton on the quantity taken in, subject to a right and proper delivery of the cargo. When payable on this basis, the owner of any cargo jettisoned, notwithstanding that he is obligated to pay the entire freight even if only a portion of it is delivered, recovers the freight's value and also the freight on the jettisoned portion, the general average contribution on the freight being payable by the vessel.[298]

Rule XIV of the Association of Average Adjusters of the United States relates in part to the contributory value of freight and is rather similar to Rule XVII of the York-Antwerp Rules.

The freight should contribute on the net amount saved to the vessel by the general average act or sacrifice. To arrive at this amount, the actual expenses incurred to earn it after the general average act or sacrifice should be deducted from the gross amount at risk.

When a vessel is under charter, it is customary to state separately in the general average adjustment (for convenience in settlement) the contribution payable by the freight at the shipowner's risk and that payable by the

---

293. See *The Blanche C. Pendleton*, 295 F. 593, 1924 AMC 382 (4th Cir.) (the worth of the thing is the price it will bring).

294. *Standard Oil Co. v. Southern Pacific Co.*, 268 U.S. 146, 1925 AMC 779 (1925).

295. *The Salina Cruz*, 111 F.Supp. 227, 1953 AMC 837 (N.D.,Cal.).

296. *Allanwilde Transp. Corp. v. Vacuum Oil Co.*, 39 S.Ct. 147 (1919); *International Paper Co. v. The Gracie D. Chambers*, 39 S.Ct. 149 (1919); *Standard Varnish Works v. The Bris*, 39 S.Ct. 150 (1919).

297. *British & Foreign Marine Ins. Co. v. Maldonado & Co.*, 182 F. 744 (1910).

298. See *Christie v. Davis Coal and Coke Co.*, 110 F. 1006 (1910).

freight at the charterer's risk. Such separation, however, does not affect the liability of the vessel or cargo in any respect; i.e., the basis for ascertaining the total amount to contribute is found in the freight payable by the cargo. If, in the case of a chartered vessel, the entire freight is prepaid and at the risk of the cargo, neither the charterer nor shipowner would be called upon to contribute on the freight, irrespective of whether the charter hire was in excess of or less than the bill of lading freight. General average recognizes only the vessel, the cargo, and the freight named in the bill of lading, and is not concerned with the contractual relationship between the shipowner and charterer.

When the York-Antwerp Rules are applicable to a time charter, and the shipowner and the charterer each pay part of the expenses of the voyage in accordance with the usual charter party terms, the contributory values of the shipowner's freight are calculated on the basis of the charter hire from the date it recommences after the general average act or sacrifice until the date of discharge of cargo at destination, less expenses which would not have been incurred had the vessel and cargo been totally lost at the date of the general average act or sacrifice and not allowed in general average. The same formula applies to the contributory value of charterer's freight, but is calculated on the amount of freight due by cargo at destination according to the bills of lading, less hire of the vessel, and less such contingent expenses (port charges, costs of discharging, etc.) which would not have been incurred had the vessel been totally lost.

The contributory value of cargo set forth in Rule XVII parallels the method set forth in Rule XVI to determine the amount to be made good: the commercial invoice, plus other adjustments set forth in the Rules.

Tug, Tow, and General Average[b]

The maritime community in general and admiralty lawyers in particular are well-advised to approach the subject of general average with some caution, as has been noted earlier in this text. The subject is such that it is easy to lose one's direction, whether involved as a participant in the maritime adventure, or as an adjuster, lawyer, or a judge later asked to help sort out the consequences of a misadventure. Such confusion is especially common in applying the principles of general average to tug and tow, considering their multiple interests.

Ironically, some of the confusion may be at least partially traced to an entirely sound decision of the United States Supreme Court in 1895, a

(b). The preliminary draft from this section of the chapter through "Examples of General Average Adjustments," *infra,* was prepared by Daniel F. Knox of the firm of Schwabe, Williamson, Wyatt, Moore & Roberts, Portland, Oregon, for which the author expresses his deepest appreciation.

decision rendered in a case not involving tug and tow.[299] The case involved the voyage of a British bark from Calcutta to New York. A load of saltpeter and bales of jute butts was taken on board in Calcutta. Soon after loading and while the vessel was still in port, a fire broke out, evidently as the result of a crewman's negligence with a lantern in the chain locker. Initial fire fighting was under the direction of the master, but port authorities soon intervened. The vessel was moved away from its slip and put aground. The master removed a fraction of the jute butts during fire fighting efforts after the vessel was run aground, but was prevented from removing more by the port authorities who felt that doing so increased the risk that the fire would spread. The fire was ultimately extinguished when the port authorities scuttled the vessel. The water entering the holds caused the tightly packed bundles of jute to expand, entirely wrecking the vessel. The vessel was sold for salvage, while the master retrieved and sold the damaged jute.

Cargo promptly brought an action seeking only recovery of the proceeds of the sale of the damaged jute. The vessel counterclaimed for a general average contribution, a contribution that both the trial court and the court of appeal ordered, finding the extinguishing of the fire to have been a general average act.

The Supreme Court disagreed, holding that a general average contribution could not be compelled where the sacrifice was "made by a stranger, in no way connected with the control or care of the ship and cargo, as a distinct maritime adventure." The court went on to state that the sacrifice must be made:

> . . . for no other purpose, and by order of the owners of all the interests included in the common adventure, or the authorized representative of them all. The safety of any property on land or water, not included in that adventure, can neither be an object of the sacrifice nor a subject of the contribution.

Thus, a sacrifice in this instance was not voluntary on the part of the master, but was instead the compulsory act of the port authorities engaged in discharging their general duty to the port and all vessels in that port.[300]

Two years later, the same court decided *The J.P. Donaldson*, the first case to come before the court involving general average in a tug and tow situation.[301]

---

299. *Ralli v. Troop,* 157 U.S. 386, 15 S.Ct. 657, 39 L.Ed. 742 (1895).

300. It must be mentioned that even in 1895, the Supreme Court was compelled to mention the "diverse" (i.e., conflicting) opinions as to the application and extent of general average. The situation has not improved greatly in the intervening 92 years.

301. 167 U.S. 599, 17 S.Ct. 951 (1897).

The case involved a tug towing two barges across Lake Michigan. Both barges were manned with their own masters and crews. In a violent storm and after a long struggle, and to prevent going aground herself, the master of the tug cut the towline to the barges. While the tug was saved, both barges were lost. The tow was undertaken pursuant to a contract with the barge owners in which the tug was to receive a portion of the freight which the barges were to earn on the trip. The court noted that:

> This case presents a novel question in the law of general average, which, briefly stated, is whether a contribution in general average can be had against a steam tug for the casting off and abandonment, by her master, of her tow of barges, with the intent, and with the effect, of saving the tug.

The court began with a review of *Ralli v. Troop,* noting that it stood for the proposition that neither the object of the sacrifice nor the subject of the contribution could be the safety of property other than that included in the common adventure. In *Ralli v. Troop,* the court obviously felt the sacrifice had not been made by the master, and that the object of the sacrifice was not the safety of the vessel or cargo but of the port and other vessels in the harbor. In the case at bar, the court concluded that the issue was whether the tug and tow were so connected as to become a single maritime adventure, entrusting the master of the tug with the authority to make whatever sacrifices might be necessary for the greater good. The court concluded that the master of the tug did not have that kind of authority.

The court noted that, the barges being separately crewed, the master of the tug had no authority [and presumably no ability] to sacrifice cargo alone. That is, had a barge alone been in peril, only her master had the authority to sacrifice cargo for the preservation of the barge. Moreover, the court noted:

> If the question arises whether it is safer for one of the barges to continue in tow, or to cut loose an anchor, the decision of that question ultimately belongs to her own Master, and not to the Master of the tug. And if the question presented is either whether the barge should be run ashore for the purpose of saving her cargo, or else whether a part of the whole of the cargo of the barge should be sacrificed in order to save the rest of the cargo, or the barge herself, the decision of the question whether such stranding or jettison should or should not be made is within the exclusive control of the Master of the particular barge, and in no degree under the control of the Master of the tug; and, in either case, any right of contribution in general average cannot extend beyond that of barge and her cargo.

Thus, while the Supreme Court began its opinion in *The J.P. Donaldson* by asking the general question of whether a contribution in general average might be required in the context of the tug and tow relationship, the resolution of the case was clearly limited to the facts before the court at the time. The court did not attempt to answer the question in more general terms.

Unfortunately, however, *The J.P. Donaldson* has since been cited as standing for the proposition that "[T]he law of general average is not applicable to the relationship between the tug and her tow."[302] The case says no such thing, although it does illustrate how very difficult it may be to apply established principles of general average to a tug and tow relationship. In fact, it is clear that the court's opinion was based on more than that the mere existence of a towage contract (which under the *The White City*, 285 U.S. 195, requires a showing of negligence on the part of the tug before the tow can recover for damage). The opinion also considered that the tows were manned, and the master of the tug did not have the requisite legal control and authority over the tows to be labelled the agent of all concerned in electing to make a sacrifice of part of the common venture.

Truly, to evaluate general average cases properly, one should determine whether all units in the towing flotilla were subjected to the same common peril. As the Committee on Rules of Practice of the Association of Average Adjusters of the United States has noted, probably the only circumstance in which the entire value of a tug flotilla is brought into consideration is in cases where the tug sustains damage or a breakdown at sea so that salvage assistance must be engaged to tow the tug and its barges to a place of safety; then, the practice is to treat the cost of such salvage as a general average expenditure to be contributed to by the tug and all the barges and cargo laden thereon.

However, it may well be that a total breakdown of the tug may not be required, so long as the tug was itself in danger along with its barges. Consider this example, described by Mr. Arthur H. Platt, Chairman of the Average Adjusters Association of Canada at the annual meeting of the Association in 1973:

> A certain mill on the British Columbia coast wished to transport lumber and pulp to Vancouver Island for transshipment to Australia

---

302. *The Mohican*, 1934 AMC 112, 114 (S.D.N.Y. 1933). The case involved a barge run into a canal lock by the negligent navigation of its tug and a subsequent claim by the barge against cargo underwriters for a general average contribution. The barge was correctly held entitled to a general average contribution for certain expenditures, and likewise correctly denied a general average contribution for the negligent tug's salvage efforts (for which the barge had not paid and was not liable in any event). In deciding the case, the court made the unfortunate statement cited above as one of several grounds for denying the barge's claim for a contribution, based on alleged salvage expenses of the tug.

in a deep sea vessel. The pulp was loaded on a scow owned by the mill; a second scow was hired to carry the lumber. A tug owned by a third party was then hired to tow the two scows to destination. Shortly after leaving the loading port the tug suffered some engine trouble and, as often happens, the weather began to get dirty. Before long the scows were taking charge and pulling the tug backwards. The situation was such that the master of the tug feared his tug would turn over and be lost and so he slipped his towline, reckoning that the two scows would drift toward the shore. When the tug was out of immediate danger the master phoned the millowners who dispatched one of their own tugs to the scene. The scows were sighted, drifting and bumping together. This tug was successful in attaching a line to one of the scows and they were towed back to the loading port.

On examination it was found that each scow had received damage, later repaired at a cost of about $4,000. The pulp was badly seawater damaged and was discharged and sold, suffering a loss of approximately $20,000. The lumber was undamaged. The tug also was undamaged. Salvage expenses were agreed at about $12,000.

. . . [I]n adjusting the claim a simple principle was followed. The tug had benefitted by the sacrifice and accordingly should contribute to the various losses and expenses. The salvage charges and expenses and the physical damage to the scows and the pulp cargo were made good in general average and all the interests in the adventure, that is, the tug, the two scows and their cargoes, were brought in to contribute.

This claim was agreed without question by uninsured interests and all underwriters concerned, proving that the simple application of the ancient principle of General Average is agreeable to reasonably minded men engaged in the marine business.

Another illustration is the adjustment proposed in 1983 on a 1982 incident involving the tug *Beaver* and its tandem tow. In very heavy seas, the *Beaver*'s engine began to overheat because of the engine's malfunctioning thermostat. The very strong winds and heavy seas made it unsafe to stop the engine and attempt to replace the faulty thermostat, as would have been possible in calmer weather without danger to the tug or its tows. The tug consequently continued to tow, notwithstanding the obvious fact that to do so was causing damage to the engine. Ultimately, assistance arrived and took over the tow. On inspection, substantial damage was found to have been experienced by the tug. It appeared that no damage would have occurred had the tug been able to repair the faulty thermostat promptly.

The adjuster proposed as a general average expenditure the repair costs for the engine, to be borne by the tug and both barges (neither of which was laden with cargo). The adjuster also proposed the cost of towage as a general average expenditure. Assuming the adjuster was accurate in stating the facts, there can be little argument that the barges benefitted from the tug's sacrifice and should have contributed in general average.

It seems rather common, however, that the courts run into difficulties when confronted with a tug and tow situation involving general average. For example, in *Loveland Co., Inc. v. U.S.*,[303] the court seems to have lost sight of established general average principles. In that case, a tug and two barges were owned by the same company. The company contracted to transport cargo (five small picket boats) for the United States from Maryland to Virginia. During the voyage, the tug left the channel and grounded. When it grounded, the barges, having no means of stopping, kept moving forward. The first barge, *Loveland 33*, rammed the grounded tug and in turn was rammed by the second barge, *Loveland 32*. The collision damage to the *Loveland 33* caused her to leak, and the tug, having gotten itself ungrounded, pushed the *Loveland 33* aground to keep her from sinking.

After the accident, the tug left the *Loveland 33* aground, proceeded to tow the *Loveland 32* to its destination; after temporary repairs were made, the *Loveland 33* was towed to its destination by another tug. None of the cargo (picket boats) was damaged.

The court held that the "extraordinary" expense incurred to promote the general safety of the venture resulted from the damage caused to the barge by the grounding...not from the damage caused by the collision, which was the fact that gave rise to the need for sacrifice. In addition, for the purposes of general average contribution, the court held that the value, just before the collision, of the tug and two barges and the value of the cargo must be taken into consideration.

The court did note, correctly, that the case involved a contract of affreightment, rather than a towage contract, citing *Sacramento Navigation Co. v. Salz*.[304]

Of more recent vintage is *Northland Navigation Co. Ltd v. Patterson Boiler Works, Ltd.*, a Canadian federal case in which both counsel and court seem to have gone astray.[305] The case involved carriage of a shipment of steel buoys from Vancouver, British Columbia to Prince Rupert. Normally, these would have been carried by a self-propelled vessel, but schedule changes caused Northland (which had undertaken to carry the buoys to Prince Rupert) to engage a tug owned by a third party.

In the event, the tug and its tow encountered extraordinarily heavy seas during the voyage. With a flooded bilge and an engine about to fail,

303. 207 F.Supp. 450, 1963 AMC 260 (E.D., Pa., 1962).
304. 273 U.S. 326, 1927 AMC 397 (1927).
305. [1983] 2 F.C. 59, 1985 AMC 465 (Vanc. B.C., Trial Div., 1983).

the tug elected to set the barge and its cargo adrift. The tug consequently succeeded in extricating itself from danger, while the barge went aground. Efforts were made to salvage the barge but these proved hopeless, and the barge was abandoned. Thereafter, salvage efforts were directed solely toward saving the cargo, and those efforts ultimately succeeded.

Northland then brought suit against cargo, seeking a general average contribution of less than $2,000 as cargo's portion of the cost of the unsuccessful effort to save both barge and cargo. Northland sought an additional $7,000 (for costs of retrieving the cargo alone) as a "special charge" to cargo. No claim for general average contribution was brought against the tug, and no claim was brought for general average contribution for the loss of the barge. Under the barge owner's theory, the only general average expenditures occurred when the effort was made to save both the barge and cargo. According to cargo, the sacrifice occurred when the barge was cut adrift, and all the remainder constituted merely salvage.

The court agreed that the casting off of the towline was a general average sacrifice. The court also felt, however, that the money expended in an effort to retrieve the barge and cargo constituted extraordinary expenditure, an expenditure designed to save property imperilled in a common maritime adventure. Accordingly, the court held that at least until the barge was abandoned, both barge and cargo were in peril, and that peril was entirely restricted to the cargo and the barge. Because the tug was in no peril at the time the expenses were incurred, the court rejected cargo's argument that the tug's value ought to be taken into consideration in calculating cargo's contribution to the general average. The remaining charges, being directed to salvage of the cargo alone, had to constitute only special charges against the cargo.

If tug, barge, and cargo were indeed menaced by the same peril—the storm—then the casting off of the line was most certainly a general average sacrifice. The attendant loss of the barge should have resulted in a general average claim against the tug and cargo, and one is left to guess why no such claim was made. Under the law of the United States, costs of removing the cargo from the abandoned barge would probably constitute extraordinary expenses at a minimum.[306] Under English law, as has been seen, general average expenses are limited to expenses incurred up to the point where safety is attained, and those expenses must be for the common safety. It is quite possible that an English court would exclude all salvage costs as not involving the common safety, while a court in the United States might properly include all such expenses as extraordinary.

In any event, it is exceedingly difficult to justify limiting the general average contribution to barge and cargo alone. And having done so, it is

---

306. *Shoe v. Craig*, 189 F. 227 (D. Pa. 1911), *aff'd* 194 F. 678 (3d Cir. 1912).

even more difficult to understand why the portion of the expenses involved in the *unsuccessful* attempt to retrieve the barge were allowed as a general average expense. Success is universally accepted to be a requirement in general average. Moreover, the opinion makes no mention of any proof that the unsuccessful attempt to salve the barge benefitted cargo in any respect.

There is no reason, of course, why a tug or barge alone could not become involved in a general average situation. The United States law is that general average is payable, even though a vessel may be in ballast.[307] A mere loss, however, does not establish a right to contribution if one of the essential elements of general average is not present. This is graphically illustrated in *Barge J. Whitney—Asphalt Incident.*[308] There, a barge loaded with asphalt could not unload at its destination (Anchorage, Alaska) because the internal heating coil system used to re-melt the asphalt at destination was defective, the tubes having fractured and becoming plugged with solidified asphalt. The barge was towed back to its port of loading, primarily to avoid the hazards attendant upon Alaskan winters. The cost of cutting plates from the barge and removing the solidified asphalt was $230,000, which was claimed by the barge owner as a general average expenditure, citing *Potter* and *LaFonciere.* The arbitrator held that the mere prospect of the barge and cargo becoming total losses, in the sense of having lost all their "economic value," was not the same kind of damage comprehended in general average.

The sacrifice must, of course, be made by or on behalf of one who is a party to the common venture. This was demonstrated in *Tampa Tugs & Towing, Inc. v. Sandanger,*[309] where a vessel being salved was intentionally grounded by the salvors. The U.S. Navy extinguished the ensuing fire, and the vessel was arrested. The court held that vessel was *in custodia legis,* and no general average situation was created, as none of the parties who acted had lawful possession of the vessel, citing *Ralli v. Troop, supra.*

Particular attention is directed to *Australian Coastal Shipping Commission v. Green,*[310] where the vessel was insured under a policy incorporating the York-Antwerp Rules, 1950. The vessel was in peril and employed a tug under the U.K. Standard Towing Conditions form, requiring the shipowner to indemnify the tugowner for any damage to his tug. The tug was damaged during various maneuvers by a fouling of its propeller with the towline, whereupon the shipowner indemnified the tugowner and then claimed under the policy that the expenditure was a general average expenditure. The court agreed, holding that the underwriters were lia-

---

307. *Potter v. Ocean Assurance Co.,* 216 F. 303; *LaFonciere Co. v. Dollar,* 181 F. 945 (9th Cir. 1910).
308. 1968 AMC 995 (Arb.).
309. 242 F.Supp. 576, 1965 AMC 1771 (S.D. Cal.).
310. [1971] 1 Q.B. 456, [1971] 1 All E.R. 353.

ble, since the expenditure was a "direct consequence" of a general average act within the meaning of Rule C of the York-Antwerp Rules.

Towage vs. Salvage

A distinction must be drawn carefully between towage on the one hand and salvage on the other. For example, ordinary towage into or out of a port is an expense borne by the shipowner alone, as it is the usual incident of a voyage which the shipowner has necessarily agreed to perform. But if danger is imminent and tugs must be hired, which would under ordinary circumstances not be necessary, then the towage hire (or salvage services) would be a matter for contribution in general average.

"Salvage charges," as they are termed in the Marine Insurance Act, 1906, Section 65(2), are charges payable to a salvor under general maritime law, and do not embrace expenses for service in the nature of salvage rendered by an assured or his agents, or any person hired by them for the purpose of averting a peril. That is, technically, salvage proper cannot be general average because the shipowner never becomes liable to pay the salvors for saving cargo aboard the imperiled vessel. Of course, the salvors have a lien on the vessel for its proportion of the whole sum, to which the salvors are entitled, and, correspondingly, a separate lien on the cargo for its proportion. If the shipowner pays the whole of the salvage charge to obtain a release of the lien on cargo so that the voyage can proceed, under English law this is not a case of general average. This is because under English law, payments made merely for the benefit of the adventure are not general average. The shipowner then recovers cargo's proportion, not as general average, but as money paid for the benefit of the cargo owner. Thus, salvage charges fall on the party benefitted by the salvage and are recoverable by the owner of the interest benefitted under his policy as a loss by a peril which necessitated the salvage. Notwithstanding, it is common practice for them to be treated as general average. This practice is confirmed by Rule VI of the York-Antwerp Rules, 1974.

It has always been a troublesome question of whether, and to what extent, a vessel's master can bind cargo interests to a salvage contract. The question was litigated squarely in *China Pacific S.A. v. Food Corp. of India (The Winson)*.[311] There, the vessel stranded on a reef in the South China Sea. A salvor arrived the following day and offered to assist. The master entered into a Lloyds' Open Form Salvage Agreement on behalf of the shipowner and the cargo interests. During the salvage operation, the vessel was lightened by off-loading part of its wheat cargo into barges provided by the salvor. Approximately 15,000 tons of wheat in six separate parcels were off-loaded and carried to Manila, where they were

311. [1982] 1 Lloyd's Rep. 117, H.L.

placed in storage by the salvor to prevent deterioration. After additional efforts were unsuccessful, the salvage operation was abandoned. In the interim, the vessel owner recognized the futility of attempting to complete the voyage and tendered notice of abandonment. The vessel and cargo remaining aboard it became a total loss.

The cargo owners did not take possession of the salved wheat until some months later, by which time substantial storage and stevedoring charges had accrued for which the salvor was personally liable. These charges formed the basis for the salvor's action against the cargo owners.

The House of Lords noted that there was no direct authority and, accordingly, looked to the common law of bailment under which it was held that a bailment relationship existed between the cargo owner and a salvor, thus entitling the salvor to recover from the cargo interests all those charges advanced to preserve the cargo.

Implicit in the decision was the master's authority to bind cargo to the salvage agreement, and therefore, the shipowner's authority to turn the cargo over to the salvor in connection with the salvage service.

Under United States law, it is an accepted principle that the master has authority while acting in good faith to enter into contracts for the preservation of cargo in the vessel's care. Further, when the cargo is imperiled, the master may seek whatever means are reasonably necessary to assure the safety of the property. A contract for salvage is certainly within the master's authority, and as such, binds the vessel, her owner, and owners of the cargo.[312] However, when the vessel and cargo are in close proximity to their respective owners, such as in port, or when they can be reached easily by communication, the master is expected to consult with them. In this regard, a salvage contract entered into by the master without consulting his respective principals, when they are readily accessible to him, will be closely scrutinized by the courts.[313]

Of further importance is what happens to the lien of the shipowner on the cargo where the cargo is surrendered to a salvor. While not essential to the holding in *The Winson,* Lord Diplock took occasion to point out that on parting with possession of cargo by delivery to a salvor, the shipowner loses any possessory lien over it to which he may have been entitled for unpaid freight, demurrage, or general average. United States law is in accord, as it is clear that a lien for general average contributions, just as the lien for freight, is possessory and is lost by the unconditional surrender of the cargo.[314]

---

312. See *Andrews v. Wall*, 44 U.S. 568 (1844); *The Alert*, 56 F. 721 (S.D.N.Y. 1893); *Societa Commerciale Italiana de Navigazone v. Maru Navigation Co.*, 280 U.S. 334 (4th Cir. 1922).

313. *American Metal Co. v. M/V Belleville*, 284 F.Supp. 1002, 1970 AMC 633 (S.D.N.Y. 1968).

314. *DuPont v. Vance*, 60 U.S. 162 (1857); *N.H. Shipping Corp. v. S.S. Jackie Hause*, 1961 AMC 83 (S.D.N.Y. 1960).

Where, however, expenses in the nature of salvage are incurred by the assured, or persons employed by him under contract, such expenses may (where properly incurred for the preservation of ship and cargo) be claimed as general average.

General Average in Practice

Introduction

The precise procedure to be followed in any given general average situation is, of course, subject to the peculiarities of the voyage at hand, and the agreements between the parties to that adventure. There are, however, generally accepted rules and procedures to be followed in the commencement and processing of a general average claim. This portion of the chapter outlines the procedures to be anticipated by the parties during that process.

Generally, the adjustment is to be made at the port of destination, and in accordance with the law, customs and usages of that port. As is the case with respect to literally all legal concepts, the place (and law) of the adjustment may be varied by agreement of the parties. An attempt to initiate an adjustment prior to reaching the port of destination is premature. The right to contribution, of course, is dependent upon success in saving some part of the venture. Likewise, the participants in the venture may not be required to post security against the general average claims until the port of destination has been reached.

Should there be successive ports for the cargo, the practice (again subject to an agreement to the contrary) is to make the adjustment by applying the law and the usages of each port to that port's own cargo. Should successive ports be located in different countries with substantial differences in their laws or customs as they pertain to general average, there is a considerable potential for confusion or, at a minimum, difficulties in making the adjustment.

Occasionally, a voyage is terminated at a port of refuge. When that occurs, the interests in the voyage are severed at that point, and any general average adjustment is made not pursuant to the law and custom of the intended port of destination, but in accordance with the law, customs and usage of the port of refuge.[315] It must be stressed that when a general average incident has occurred, it is not merely the right of a vessel owner to initiate a general average adjustment, but it is also his duty to do so.[316]

---

315. *The Eliza Lines*, 102 F. 184 (2d Cir. 1900); *National Board of Marine Underwriters v. Melchers*, 45 F. 643 (D.,Pa. 1891).

316. Practitioners should recall, if faced with a general average claim to be determined under the law, customs or usages of a foreign port, that United States law requires advance

Cargo interests may often consider the law of general average as a highly inconvenient means by which contributions are unexpectedly extracted from cargo owners for mishaps occurring during the voyage. Equally likely, however, are situations where a cargo owner will be the ultimate creditor at the conclusion of a general average adjustment. Should that be the case, and the vessel owner fails to initiate a general average adjustment, the vessel owner is liable to cargo for any losses suffered by the general average creditor.[317]

The foregoing principle could presumably lead to some very interesting results. The vessel's right to general average contributions from cargo, of course, depends upon the vessel either being free from fault in bringing about the sacrifice or expense, or being exempt by contract from liability for such fault as may have existed. If the vessel was not at fault in bringing about the expenditure or sacrifice, or has an exemption from liability for whatever fault may have been involved in the loss, the vessel would ordinarily have no direct liability to the owners of cargo for cargo loss or damage. However, if the loss was occasioned by a general average sacrifice or expenditure, and the vessel entitled to seek general average contributions fails to do so, the vessel can end up liable to the cargo owners for failing to declare a general average for the benefit of the lost or damaged cargo. Even though the vessel may be a net debtor in a general average adjustment, it consequently becomes very much in the vessel's interest to declare a general average and seek contributions from all participants in the voyage. Otherwise, the vessel alone may be held liable to the owners of the lost or damaged cargo for the general average contributions of all other participants.[318]

A cargo owner, aggrieved by the vessel owner's failure to declare a general average, has a variety of remedies available. Cargo could, if so disposed, maintain *in personam* actions against other cargo owners for their

---

notice to the court of intent to rely upon foreign law and proof of the content of that law at time of trial. Fed. R. Civ. P. 44.1. In admiralty, just as in any other branch of law, failure to meet that burden will result in the court's applying the law of the forum on the assumption (however questionable) that there are no differences between the law of the forum and that of the foreign nature. See *Olivari v. Thames & Mersey Marine Ins. Co.,* 37 F. 894 (S.D.N.Y. 1888).

317. *American Tobacco Co. v. Goulandris,* 173 F.Supp.140 (S.D.N.Y.), *aff'd* 281 F.2d 179, 1962 AMC 2655 (2d Cir.). Those frustrated with the inordinate delays sometimes associated with litigation today might well take solace in reading this case. The phenomenon is not of recent origin. This complicated case arose out of the travails of a Greek-flag vessel, laden with tobacco, caught up in the outbreak of World War II. It took the vessel the better part of eight months to complete its voyage from the eastern Mediterranean to the east coast of the United States, but that delay pales into insignificance in light of the length of time required for the courts to sort out ultimate liability for the cargo damage sustained during the voyage.

318. *American Tobacco Co. v. Goulandris,* 173 F.Supp. 140 (S.D.N.Y.), *aff'd* 281 F.2d 179, 1962 AMC 2655 (2d Cir.).

proportionate contributions in general average, while simultaneously enforcing remedies against the vessel.[319] Doing so is not necessary, however, which is rather fortunate since bringing an action against the potentially numerous interests involved in a maritime adventure could be very cumbersome indeed. Instead, the cargo owner may proceed *in rem* against the vessel for its proportionate general average contribution while proceeding *in personam* against the vessel owner for the contributions the vessel owner should have exacted from the other participants in the venture.[320]

Security

When the vessel owner has determined that a general average sacrifice or expenditure has occurred, requiring contribution from the other participants to the venture, the general average adjustment must be initiated. The invariable first step, of course, is the appointment of an average adjuster. Again, the precise role of the adjuster will vary according to the law, custom and usages of the country in which the average adjustment is to be made. In the United States, average adjusters probably assume a considerably broader scope of duties than elsewhere.

In any event, the first task of the average adjuster is to determine the amount of security to be posted by the participants in the venture against the eventual resolution of the general average claims. The practice of requiring the posting of security, either in the form of a cash deposit or some sort of undertaking or guaranty, is a practical substitute for enforcement of the lien on cargo that the vessel owner enjoys for general average contributions; that is, under general maritime law, the vessel owner has a lien on cargo for *inter alia* general average contributions to be made. The lien, however, is a possessory one, and should the vessel owner make an unqualified delivery of the cargo, the lien is lost.[321]

---

319. *Id.; Motor Ship Motomar*, 1953 AMC 175 (S.D.N.Y. 1952), *aff'd* 211 F.2d 690 (2d Cir. 1954).

320. *The Emilia S. dePerez*, 22 F.2d 585, 1927 AMC 1839 (D.,Md.).

321. *The Emilia S. dePerez, supra* n. 320. In that case, the vessel owner actually did declare a general average and collected deposits from the various interests. For reasons not stated in the case, the adjustment was never completed. The owner of the sacrificed cargo consequently did not receive the contributions of the other parties to the venture. He brought suit successfully against the vessel owner for the failure to complete the adjustment. The vessel owner tried (albeit unsuccessfully) to defend on the ground that all liability should be that of the adjuster engaged by the vessel, as it was the adjuster who failed to complete the adjustment. The court rejected the argument out of hand, noting that the vessel, while able to delegate the duty to adjust to another, remained personally liable to the cargo for the completion of the adjustment. Presumably, the vessel owner was then left to pursue the adjuster who had collected (but not disbursed) the deposits. See, also, *Crooks v. Allan*, (1879) 5 Q.B.D. 38, 49 L.J.Q.B. 201. That case, involving vessel owners unwilling to go the bother of an average adjustment, is the subject of an excellent discussion in Lowndes & Rudolf, *General Average and York Antwerp Rules*, secs. 457-458 (10th Ed.).

While an unqualified delivery of cargo otherwise subject to a lien does not discharge the vessel owner's right to bring an *in personam* claim for the amount of the general average contribution which is due,[322] the (unsecured) *in personam* action is a poor substitute for the security afforded by a lien on cargo.

Theoretically, the vessel owner could retain the cargo so as to enforce the lien against the cargo once the general average adjustment is concluded. Because, however, the average adjuster will need a substantial amount of time to determine the amounts of the claims and the values of the contributing interests, it is senseless to do so. Rather, the vessel owner, through the adjuster, will seek to require the giving of security.

The security may be in the form of a cash deposit by the cargo interests or by an average bond or by an underwriters' guaranty.[323] At one time, the practice seems to have been to require cash deposits, which were generally reimbursed to cargo interests by cargo underwriters, with the underwriters taking from the assured the deposit receipt received from the adjuster or vessel owner on the posting of the cash deposit.[324] The practice of taking a bond or guarantee simply streamlines the process.[325] When cash deposits are made, interest is generally payable to the party making the deposit, where appropriate.[326]

As in the case where the vessel owner altogether neglects or refuses even to initiate the general average, the vessel owner may likewise be liable for a failure to require the posting of security for the benefit of the claimants in general average. Initiation of the general average adjustment means nothing if, at the conclusion of the process, no funds are

---

322. *DuPont de Nemours & Co. v. Vance*, 60 U.S. 162, 14 L.Ed. 584 (1856); *Cutler v. Rae*, 48 U.S. 729, 12 L.Ed. 890 (1849).

323. *Cutler v. Rae*, 48 U.S. 729, 12 L.Ed. 890 (1849). See Lowndes & Rudolf, *General Average and York Antwerp Rules*, Sec. 452 (10th Ed.). The authors include in the Appendix a typical form of bond and the typical Lloyd's form of guarantee.

324. Sec. 1114, Lowndes & Rudolf, *supra*.

325. For a good discussion of the evolution in practice regarding the taking of security, see *Corrado Societa Anonima Di Navagazione v. L. Mondet & Sons, Inc. (The Albisola)*, 18 F.Supp. 37, 1936 AMC 1740 (E.D.,Pa. 1936) and cases cited therein.

326. But, see *The West Arrow*, 10 F.Supp. 385, 1935 AMC 528 (E.D.N.Y.). In that case, the vessel owners declared a general average and collected cash deposits. Ultimately, the court determined the casualty to have been caused by the vessel's failure to make the vessel seaworthy at the commencement of the voyage. Cargo sought the return of the deposit *with interest*. The adjuster had deposited the cash in a trust account which earned no interest. The court noted that the vessel was required to give security for the benefit of the claimants in general average. Because the funds thus obtained did not earn interest in the case at hand, the court declined to require the vessel owner to pay interest to cargo. The court further held that it was not a breach of trust for the vessel owner or adjuster to fail to earn interest on the deposits. While a dissertation on the law of trusts is beyond the scope of this chapter, it would appear that the case does not represent good law at the present time. Rule XXIII of the 1974 Rules now requires the funds to be deposited so as to earn interest "where possible."

available to pay claims to the participants. Thus, a failure to obtain appropriate security for the protection of the claimants has been called a breach of the vessel's "well-recognized obligation" to care for the cargo entrusted to it for carriage.[327] The vessel's liability for failure to take security should come as no surprise. Absent the security, the cargo claimants could be left with an empty remedy. Pursuit of the other interests in the voyage may well be impractical or impossible. In short, the vessel owner has absolutely no right to place a party entitled to general average contributions in such an untenable position, and is liable for having done so.[328] The rule is the same in the United Kingdom.[329]

As a routine part of the process of obtaining security for the eventual resolution of the general average adjustment, cargo will be asked to execute a general average agreement, generally the same document as the average bond. The precise terms of the average agreement may vary from locale to locale, but in any event the vessel owner may not be unreasonable in the terms proposed in the average agreement. Generally, the vessel owner is entitled to an agreement which provides that such portion of the deposit or security as is eventually determined to be due to claimants shall be paid over at the conclusion of the adjustment (or ensuing litigation). The agreement may not prejudice cargo's right to contest the entire liability or the amount assessed by the adjuster.[330] The parties may agree, of course, to binding arbitration in the event of dispute at the conclusion of the adjustment.

Disputes over the amount of security to be posted are generally resolved by the agreement of the parties. This is not surprising, considering that cargo is unlikely to be permitted to take delivery of the goods until and unless an agreement on the amount of the deposit is reached. In the event that the dispute cannot be quickly and amicably resolved, the unhappy cargo owner has little recourse other than to tender to the vessel owner or adjuster a sum which the cargo owner believes ought to be sufficient to meet any ultimate liability.[331] If that tender is rejected, cargo may

---

327. *Dibrell Bros., Inc. v. Prince Line, Ltd.*, 52 F.2d 792 (S.D.N.Y, 1931), *aff'd* 58 F.2d 959 (2d Cir. 1932).

328. *Id.*, at 58 F.2d 94. *Accord, The Beatrice*, 35 F.2d 99, 1924 AMC 914 (S.D.N.Y.).

329. Lowndes & Rudolf, *General Average and York Antwerp Rules* (10th ed.), Sec. 455-458. The distinguished authors suggest that cargo owners, believing themselves entitled to contribution, might be able to restrain the vessel owner from delivering cargo without taking security, although there is English case law to the contrary. In the United States, there appear to be no cases dealing with an attempt to obtain injunctive relief to restrain an unqualified delivery of cargo without the taking of security. Given the duties of the vessel owner to declare the general average and to require the posting of security, there seems to be no reason why a claimant could not obtain injunctive relief on a showing of the requisite "irreparable harm."

330. E.g., *Corrado Societa Anonima Di Navagazione v. L. Mondet Sons, Inc. (The Albisola)*, 18 F.Supp. 37, 1936 AMC 1740 (E.D.,Pa.); *Huth v. Lamport*, (1886) 16 Q.B.D.442, Q.B.D.

331. Lowndes & Rudolf, *General Average and York Antwerp Rules*, Sec. 453 (10th ed.).

find itself in the unenviable dilemma of being required to choose between the posting of what it perceives to be excessive security or suffering the retention of the cargo by the vessel owner. In any event, irreconcilable differences over the amount of security to be posted are, happily, exceedingly rare.

Interest

As noted previously, if part or all of a cash deposit made by cargo owners is returned to them, the return of funds ought to be accompanied by the payment of interest for the funds so deposited. Rule XXII of the present York-Antwerp Rules, 1974, provides that cash deposits made should be paid with interest if earned. Certainly, it is now possible to earn interest on money deposited almost anywhere, so the vessel owner would be well-advised to make certain that the funds are deposited in an interest-bearing account.

As to interest on disbursements or expense incurred during the voyage in a general average situation, the practice may be very briefly summarized. If the York-Antwerp Rules apply, Rule XXI provides for the recovery of interest on the expense, sacrifice or allowance at the rate of seven percent from the date the expense, sacrifice or allowance was incurred until the date of the general average statement.[332] The payment of interest is only to be expected. Ultimately, the goal of the general average adjustment, is to ensure that all parties to the venture bear the sacrifice or expense equally, so that it does not matter who actually made the sacrifice or the expense in the first instance. If the party actually making the sacrifice or advancing the funds does not receive interest, that party is not treated in a manner equal to those more fortunate participants in the venture.

If the York-Antwerp Rules do not apply, then one is left to the law or custom of the port of destination. Practices may vary widely. In the United States, adjustments made in the absence of the York-Antwerp Rules provide for a 2½ percent commission on funds advanced and interest at the legal rate on general average disbursements and allowances.[333]

332. The 1924 Rules (in Rule XXII) allowed interest at the rate prevailing in the final port of destination, or 5% in situations where there was no prevailing rate at the port of destination. In the 1950 version of the Rules, the reference to the rate prevailing at the port of destination was omitted and a flat rate of 5% interest was mandated. Evidently, considerable practical difficulties were encountered in ascertaining prevailing rates of interest at distant ports. Moreover, the prevailing rate at such a port might well be much higher than the rate at which the money could actually be obtained elsewhere, a circumstance which would permit the party paying an expense to reap a tidy and unjustifiable profit in the adjustment. For a discussion of the historical development of the rule, see Lowndes & Rudolf, *General Average and York Antwerp Rules*, Sec. 360-363 (10th ed.).

333. *Congdon on General Average*, p. 165 (2d ed., 1923); Lowndes & Rudolf, *General Average and York Antwerp Rules*, Sec. 380 and n. 14 at p. 180 (10th ed.).

Much to the lament of the English commentators, the rule in cases decided solely on the law of the United Kingdom and not under the York/Antwerp Rules is very much different, and interest is generally not recoverable.[334]

The present York-Antwerp Rules provide that an adjustment must be made to interest allowed for any interim reimbursements made between the time the sacrifice, expense or allowance was incurred and the date of the final adjustment.[335] The requirement can lead to some rather tedious arithmetic, but the process is fairly simple. For example, assume that a vessel incurs an expense of $10,000 in a general average situation. One year later, the vessel recovers $5,000 from another vessel partially responsible for bringing about the loss, along with 10% interest, or an additional $500. One year later the adjustment is made.

To compute the actual general average loss or claim which the vessel is entitled to make, one simply calculates interest at 7 percent on the $10,000 for the first year—a total of $700 in interest. For the following year, the vessel owner would be entitled to 7 percent interest on $5,000 (since half the outlay was recovered by him), or another $350 in interest. The gross loss, then, under the 1974 Rules, is $11,050. The net general average claim is that sum less the full amount of the interim recovery, including interest. Thus, the general average claim in this example is $5,550. The vessel owner will recover such portion of that sum as is determined by the adjuster once the contributory values have been calculated.

Provision of Funds

In modern practice, the rules and laws providing for the recovery of interest in disbursements, expenses and allowances, coupled with the existence of worldwide banking networks, has virtually eliminated any need to be concerned with the very old law and practice regarding provisions for funds. Today, a master may communicate with and obtain funds from the owners, their bankers, or underwriters from virtually any port in the world. Consequently, the relatively simple rules providing for recovery of interest in the general average adjustment are sufficient to handle virtually any situation that is likely to be encountered.

Prior to the advent of modern communications and the international banking network, however, a master might well have found himself in a strange port, with little or no money, no credit, and expenses which absolutely had to be paid in order to continue the voyage. In those circum-

---

334. *Id.* at Sec. 379-380.
335. The rule (XXI) states in pertinent part:
Interest shall be allowed on expenditure, sacrifices and allowances charged to general average at the rate of 7 per cent per annum, until the date of the general average statement, due allowance being made for any reimbursement . . .

stances, the master (through the archaic bottomry bond) pledged the vessel or, if necessary, the cargo. The master was (and is) even empowered to sell portions of the cargo in order to meet general average expenses. The ultimate general average adjustment has to make good not only the sacrifices and expenses, but must also deal with the very real costs and losses associated with raising funds to contend with the misadventure and to continue to prosecute the voyage.[336]

The present version of the York-Antwerp Rules does make provision for recovery in general average of "the necessary costs of obtaining funds required by means of a bottomry bond or otherwise, or the loss sustained by owners of goods sold for the purpose."[337] In practice, this is generally limited to the recovery of any incidental (and generally insignificant) charges made by banks for wiring funds to the vessel.

In addition, the Rules still provide for the recovery in general average of a 2 percent commission on most expenses funded by any of the participants in the voyage. Wages and maintenance of the master, officers and crew, and charges for fuel and stores not replaced during the voyage are excepted from those expenditures for which a commission is payable.[338]

Insurance of Average Disbursements

Vessel owners almost invariably insure general average disbursements. The coverage afforded by that insurance and the treatment it receives in a general average adjustment require some explanation. Generally, what is insured is *not* the risk that a vessel owner may be required to make a general average disbursement in a port of refuge or an intermediate port. What *is* insured is the risk that after making such a disbursement, some further catastrophe will befall vessel and cargo which eliminates or changes the adjustment that might otherwise have been anticipated at the port of destination.

For example, assume that a vessel experiences a general average casualty and makes general average expenditures at a port of refuge. After resumption of the voyage, the seas swallow up vessel and cargo entirely. Because the contributory values are determined at the port or ports of destination when vessel and cargo actually arrive, the vessel owner's general average remedy has been extinguished by the loss of vessel and cargo. Likewise, if some less catastrophic misadventure befalls the vessel,

---

336. For an excellent discussion on the history of the treatment in general average of the cost of raising funds in years past, see Lowndes & Rudolf, *General Average and York Antwerp Rules,* Sec. 372-376 (10th ed.).

337. York-Antwerp Rules (1973), Rule XX.

338. *Id.* In the United States and in the absence of applicability of the York-Antwerp Rules, a commission of $2\frac{1}{2}\%$ is allowed on general average disbursement for advancing funds.

one could reasonably expect the contributory values, once vessel and cargo finally limp into the port of destination, to have been substantially reduced. While that would not change the quantum of the general average expense or sacrifice, it probably would change the proportions in which the parties contribute to make the sacrifice good. It is that risk—that of further mishap eliminating altogether or reducing the contributory values—against which general average disbursements coverage insures.

So, for instance, if vessel and cargo are entirely lost after a general average sacrifice or disbursement, the adjustment is made as though vessel and cargo made it from the port of refuge to the port of destination without incident. The values of vessel, cargo, and freight at risk are calculated just as though the voyage were completed without further mishap, and the general average disbursement insurance covers the entire general average benefit which would have been received at the voyage's end.

Likewise, in the event the further misadventure reduces one or more of the contributory values, an adjustment must first be made as though the subsequent mishap had not happened. The allowable general average claim must then be calculated, as well as the contributory values of ship, cargo, and freight. With these two figures, the adjuster calculates the percent of contribution to be made by the participants. For example, the adjuster may determine that had the subsequent accident not occurred, the value of ship, cargo, and freight would have totalled $1,000,000. If the allowable general average expense or sacrifice was $100,000, it will then be seen that without the intervening accident, each party to the voyage would have contributed 10 percent of their contributory values.

The adjuster then determines the *actual* values of ship, cargo and freight as they arrive in their additionally damaged state at ultimate destination. Again by way of example, assume that the vessel, cargo and freight after the intervening accident actually had a contributory value of but $700,000 at the port of destination. The claim on the general average disbursement underwriters would, therefore, be for 10 percent (the proportion of contribution which would have been exacted from each participant in the venture had the intervening mishap not occurred) of the reduction in value of the contributory values. Thus, in this example, underwriters would pay 10 percent of the $300,000 reduction in contributory value, or $30,000.

In the United States, recovery from insurance on general average disbursements (in this instance, $30,000) is credited against the actual general average expenses (here, $100,000). The balance of the claim ($70,000) is then apportioned over the final contributory values of vessel, cargo, and freight ($700,000).

In Great Britain, the amount recovered from the general average underwriters is apportioned differently. There, any *increase* in the contribution paid by vessel, cargo and freight as a result of the change in proportion in the contributory values is first made good. That is, any participant paying more money under the "as arrived" adjustment than would have been the case had there been no intervening accident, is credited with a sum sufficient to reduce the contribution to the latter level. The balance is then applied ratably between vessel, cargo, and freight.[339]

The 1974 Rules provide for recovery in general average of "the cost of insuring money advanced to pay for general average disbursements."[340] That provision permits recovery in general average of the premiums paid to obtain the average disbursements insurance, but only when the party paying that premium also funded the initial general average expense.[341] Thus, in calculating a general average claim, which includes expenditures made by the vessel owner, the cost of the premium for the average disbursements insurance should be included.

Limitation of Liability

Under the United States Limitation of Liability Act,[342] Congress extended to shipowners the ability to limit any liability arising out of a collision to the post-accident value of the vessel.[343] This limitation of liability, of course, is available to the shipowner only when the collision occurred without the privity or knowledge of the shipowner.

Because a general average situation may well arise out of the collision, the general average claimant may be forced to contend with a limitation of liability proceeding brought by the the shipowner, a proceeding that will include a variety of other claimants. Assuming that the owner is entitled to limit his liability under the Act, what rights has the general average claimant?

The first step in the limitation proceeding (again assuming the shipowner has the right to limit) is to establish the post-accident value of the vessel. Assuming the vessel survived the collision, her value is established at the port of destination (if the voyage was completed), or at the port at which the voyage was terminated.[344] To that value must be added any freight earned on the voyage, whether prepaid or not. Should the

---

339. For an excellent discussion of the manner in which recoveries from general average disbursement underwriters is apportioned in the United Kingdom, see Buglass, *Marine Insurance and General Average in the United States*, 265-267 (2d. ed.).

340. York-Antwerp Rules (1973), Rule XX.

341. Lowndes & Rudolf, *General Average and York Antwerp Rules*, Sec. 859 (10th ed.).

342. 46 U.S.C. 183 *et seq.*

343. The post-accident value, if insufficient to pay all losses, is increased to $420 per gross ton, but only insofar as it must be increased to pay for loss of life or personal injury. 46 U.S.C. 183(b). Recourse to the increased tonnage valuation is not available for general average claimants or for anyone else, for that matter.

344. *The Lara*, 1947 AMC 27, 32 (S.D.N.Y., 1946).

vessel have been repaired at an intermediate port or some port of refuge, the post-accident value is the *repaired* value with no reduction for the costs of the repairs.[345]

It is possible, of course, that the repairs at a port of refuge may themselves constitute a general average expense for which the shipowner is entitled to contribution, but that possibility is irrelevant to the task of establishing the post-accident value of the vessel. And at least one court, in the context of a limitation proceeding, gave little attention to the owner's claim of a right of contribution for repair expenses.[346]

The post-accident value of the vessel includes any tort claim the carrying vessel (this assumes the vessel seeking limitation was carrying cargo at the time of the collision) might have against other parties responsible for the collision.[347] Should another vessel share responsibility for the collision, the potential recovery for the damage to the carrying vessel—its decrease in value—becomes a portion of the limitation fund. The owner of the carrying vessel, therefore, may not limit liability to the unrepaired post-accident value of his vessel, thus retaining for himself any recovery from the other vessel for the damages done, but must include the amount of the recovery in the limitation fund for the benefit of all claimants.[348]

Having established the fund to which claimants of all types will aspire, the competing interests must then be ranged in order of priority. This is done in precisely the same manner as would be the case among competing lien claimants outside of the context of a limitation proceeding. In the United States, the priority enjoyed by the general average cargo claimant is that of a preferred maritime lien, ranking alongside salvage claims[349] and behind only "special legislative rights" (e.g., wreck removal), judicial expenses, and wages, maintenance and cure of master and crew.[350] The general average claim ranks ahead of maritime torts (including personal injury or death and non-general average cargo or property claims),

---

345. *The Lara*, 1947 AMC 27, 32-33 (S.D.N.Y., 1946).

346. *Id.* at 33. The court felt the repair expenses were motivated at least in part by the owner's wish to have the vessel continue her service at a profit after the voyage at hand, a wish which had apparently been achieved. As the expenses in the opinion of the court were thus not solely for the common adventure, little consideration was given to the owner's claim. One might well ask when, however, intermediate repairs would nearly always be a benefit to the owner beyond the voyage at hand. That the repairs might confer such an incidental benefit does not seem adequate justification to deny a claim for general average contribution.

347. *O'Brien v. Miller*, 168 U.S. 287, 47 L.Ed. 469 (1897).

348. *Id.; Accord, Oliver J. Olson & Co. v. American Steamship Marine Leopard*, 356 F.2d 728, 1966 AMC 1064 (9th Cir.).

349. There is some authority for the proposition that a lien for salvage has greater or higher priority than that for a general average claimant. *Provost v. The Selkirk*, 22 F.Cas. 888 (E.D., Mich.. 1871). As will be seen, Tetley in his 1985 work on maritime liens ranks them as co-equals. See *The Odysseus III*, 77 F.Supp. 297, 1948 AMC 608 (S.D.,Fla. 1948).

350. Tetley, *Maritime Liens and Claims*, 402 (1985).

wages of longshoremen, and all other lienable matters (including the lien of preferred ship's mortgages).[351]

It may perhaps seem unfair that the general average cargo claimant enjoys a priority superior to those killed or injured in a general average collision. It must be kept in mind, however, that the general average claimant's interest is entirely extinguished if the post-accident value of the vessel is nothing. Moreover, the funds divided by general average claimants, and those with superior claims, may not be increased by the tonnage valuation contained in the Act.[352] That increase in the limitation fund is available only for damage as a consequence of injury or death, and then only when funds sufficient to pay in full the personal injury or death claimants are not available, and the total value of the fund is less than $420 per gross ton.

General average claims, however, do not enjoy the same priority in the United Kingdom. There, the preference granted general average claims is lowly, indeed, as general average claimants are aggregated with those with *in rem* statutory rights, just behind liens for necessaries, repairmen and towage, and just prior to pilotage liens.[353] Ranking much higher are those lien claimants with special legislative rights (harbor authorities for various claims), governmental claims for wreck removal, governmental pollution claims, costs of arrest, possessory liens, salvage liens, damage liens, wage liens, liens for masters' disbursements, and preferred ship's mortgages.[354]

Rates of Exchange

On a single voyage, general average sacrifices and expenses can occur in virtually any corner of the earth's seas. As a natural consequence, expense may be incurred in the currency of any country. The value of currency in any country , of course, is in a constant state of flux when compared with the currencies of other nations. Since the rates of exchange among the various currencies will undoubtedly change between the dates on which the general average acts occur and the date of settlement, one or more of the parties to the venture is likely to experience a profit of sorts in consequence of those changes. The rates of exchange rules are therefore designed to make consistent and predictable the necessary conversions from one currency to another.

Perhaps more than any other aspect of the general average practice, the United States and the United Kingdom vary most radically with respect to the rates of exchange rules. Fortunately for practitioners in the

---

351. *Id.,* at 402-403.
352. 46 U.S.C. 183(b).
353. Tetley, *Maritime Liens and Claims,* 410.
354. *Id.,* at 408-410.

United States, the problem first arose before several courts dedicated to finding an altogether simple (if not always equitable) solution to a difficult problem.[355] The case under discussion involved a Danish vessel on a voyage from Norway to New York. The vessel twice went aground, both times incurring general average expenses. Those expenses were paid in Norwegian and Danish kroner and English pounds. The Danish owners paid the Norwegian and English expenses by purchasing the appropriate currency with Danish kroner. The average adjustment was made in New York, and the adjuster attempted to settle up by converting the expenses in Danish kroner to U.S. dollars as of the date on which the adjustment was closed. Cargo interests balked, believing that changes in the exchange rate were to their benefit to the extent of $424.66. The vessel promptly sued for that princely sum.[356]

The trial court did not quarrel at all about the owners' converting into Danish kroner all expenses at the time they were incurred. The court felt, however, that the final settlement in U.S. dollars should have been made at the termination of the voyage and not at the time of the average adjustment.[357] The court's rationale was that no other time was appropriate because the vessel owners had no right to contribution until the vessel safely arrived at its port of destination. Once that happened, the currency of the port of destination was controlled, and the rate of exchange was fixed as of the date of arrival.[358]

Aggrieved at this turn of events and the loss of their $424, the Danish owners promptly appealed to the Second Circuit. There, Judge Learned Hand had no difficulty in affirming the District Court.[359] He concluded that there was really no proper time at which to fix the exchange rate, but there was a need for consistency:" . . . some convention which will seem arbitrary to those whose interests it offends and reasonable to those whom it suits." Judge Hand fixed that arbitrary, but consistent time as the date of the termination of the voyage.[360]

Grimly determined, the owners pursued their $424 claim to the United States Supreme Court. There, an unfeeling court denied their petition for writ of *certiorari*.[361]

---

355. The U.S. District Court, Southern District of New York, and the Second Circuit Court of Appeal.

356. *The Arkansas*, 1928 AMC 1453 (S.D.N.Y.).

357. *Id.*, at 1455.

358. *Id.*, at 1457.

359. *The Arkansas*, 31 F.2d 658, 1929 AMC 585 (2d Cir.).

360. *Id.* With the perspective of time, Judge Hand's treatment of the Danish owners seems somewhat cavalier, as he noted that "[t]o the libellants whose national currency is Danish it naturally appears that exchange at the time of settlement will alone be a recoupment, but this would probably not seem true to an American owner, or indeed to any but a Dane." As is noted below, while the United Kingdom is not exactly in accord with the Danish view, it would certainly fail to share Judge Hand's view on the merits of the claim.

361. 280 U.S. 571, 74 L.Ed. 623 (1929).

Judge Hand's opinion remains the law in the United States. Generally, the date of a general average loss is held to be the date of the termination of the adventure. Losses incurred in any currency are exchanged into U.S. dollars by U.S. courts as of the date of arrival at the U.S. port. Lowndes & Rudolf express a preference for this simple rule over the practice in the United Kingdom.[362]

Lowndes and Rudolf also note that the simplest and most effective solution to the manifest rates of exchange difficulties under the law of the United Kingdom would be, as is frequently the case in the United States, to insert a clause in the bill of lading requiring that general average disbursements made in foreign currencies are to be exchanged into United States currency at the rate prevailing on the date the disbursements were made. The bills also provide for valuation of cargo claimed in foreign currency to be converted as of the last date of discharge.[363]

The rates of exchange rules in the United Kingdom are much more complicated.[364] In the absence of a simple agreement to the contrary, Rule G of the York-Antwerp Rules, 1974, requires the final adjustment to be made in the currency of the port of destination. There may be, of course, multiple ports of destination involved in a single voyage. While the adjustment itself is to be prepared in the currency of the port of destination, the exchange from the currency of loss into the currency of destination is made as of the time of the general average act or expense, unlike the American approach. Damage to cargo on arrival is calculated in the currency of destination as of the last date of discharge.[365] For cargo actually sacrificed, its value, if stated in a currency other than that of the port of termination or discharge, is exchanged into the discharge currency as of the last date of discharge.

Needless to say, whether American practice or that of the United Kingdom is followed, whenever it is necessary to have recourse to the rates of exchange rules, additional "profits" or "losses" are bound to occur. That is made inevitable simply because of the fluctuation in exchange rates. The practice in the United States, however, does have the attraction of being much more simple.

---

362. Lowndes & Rudolf, *General Average and the York Antwerp Rules*, Sec. 1152-1153 (10th ed.).

363. *Id.*, Sec. 1172.

364. *Id.*, Sec. 1141 *et seq.*, Appendix 4. Those distinguished authors devote 24 pages to an excellent thumbnail description of the rates of exchange rules in the United Kingdom. No more concise and lucid description exists.

365. Since there may be multiple ports of discharge, at all of which cargo damaged in consequence of a general average act is off-loaded, the exchange rate calculations could be enormously difficult.

Examples of General Average Adjustments

To put into context the manner in which the principles of general average actually operate, several highly oversimplified examples of general average adjustments follow. In each, the amounts to be made good in sacrifices, expenses, allowances, and interest are assumed to have been determined accurately by the adjuster. Likewise, the contributory values of vessel, cargo, and freight are assumed to be correct. Determination of the amounts to be made good, particularly the task of segregating those losses allowable in general average from those not similarly favored, and determining the sound values of the various interests to the voyage at its conclusion can be, as has been noted repeatedly, a major task. Nevertheless, these examples of the adjustments will serve to gain both an appreciation of how the allowable losses are made good and the effect of the exaction of the contributions. Moreover, they will illustrate clearly why cargo interests so frequently find general average adjustments a painful experience.

A. For the three examples set forth hereafter, it is assumed that a single general average act occurred during the voyage. Once the vessel reached its destination, the adjuster determined that the vessel was worth $1,000,000, that the single cargo interest on board had a landed sound value of $3.5 million, and the freight interest was $500,000. Thus, the total value of the adventure at its conclusion was the sum of $5 million.

(1) Assume that the only general average loss was incurred by the shipowner; expenses of $500,000. The precise nature of the general average expense is unimportant. It may have been for salvage, or, for example, extraordinary repairs at a port of refuge made necessary to prosecute the voyage successfully. The important matter is only the amount to be made good; here, $500,000 in expenses by the shipowner.

As will be noted, the $500,000 general average expense—the amount to be made good—represents precisely 10 percent of the arrived values. Each of the three interests (vessel, cargo, and freight) consequently will be called upon to contribute in general average 10 percent of their interest in the voyage. The vessel's contribution is consequently $100,000, while cargo will contribute $350,000, and freight will contribute $50,000, making up altogether the $500,000 to be made good. In this example, the entire $500,000 will be received by the shipowner to make good the general average expenses incurred during the prosecution of the voyage.

The net effect of the general average adjustment is that the vessel owner has been reimbursed $400,000 of its original $500,000 expense.

All three interests in the voyage have contributed precisely 10 percent of their respective arrived values in the general average adjustment.

Average adjustments are sometimes written in a somewhat different manner, although the outcome is precisely the same. Rather than simply dividing the amount to be made good by the total arrived, safe values of the interests in the voyage to determine the percentage contribution, the average adjuster may instead calculate a percentage of interest. That is, having determined that the total, arrived saved values of the interests total $5 million, the adjuster will then determine the percentage of ownership in the total arrived values of each of the interests. In this example, the vessel's $1,000,000 in value represents 20 percent of the total arrived value, cargo's interest represents 70 percent of the total, and the freight represents 10 percent of the total. The adjuster may then multiply those respective percentages by the amount to be made to calculate the contributions. As noted, the result is precisely the same. Here, the shipowner pays 20 percent of the $500,000 loss, or $100,000; cargo pays 70 percent ($350,000); and freight pays 10 percent ($50,000).

(2) In the second example, the arrived values are precisely as noted above. However, the general average act involved only a sacrifice of cargo, resulting in a loss to the cargo interests of $500,000. No other interest in the adventure suffered a general average loss.

In this event, the contributions to the amount to be made good by the parties to the venture are precisely the same as in the previous example. The vessel pays 10 percent of its value or $100,000; cargo pays a contribution of $350,000; and freight pays its contribution of $50,000. The cargo interests receive the full $500,000. This reduces cargo's net loss from its pre-adjustment level of $500,000 to $350,000, or precisely 10 percent of the value which was actually saved.

(3) Again assuming precisely the same landed, saved values at the port of destination, assume likewise that the vessel owner incurred allowable general average expenses of $500,000, while cargo experienced a $500,000 loss of its own. The total amount to be made good is thus $1 million, which represents a 20 percent contribution of saved values on the part of all the parties to the maritime venture.

The vessel owner subsequently contributes $200,000 in general average, cargo pays $700,000, and freight pays $100,000, altogether making up the $1 million amount to be made good. The vessel receives its $500,000 in general average expense, with the result that the vessel is a net creditor in the adjustment in the sum of $300,000. This in turn reduces the vessel's actual loss to $200,000 (applying the $300,000 net obtained in the adjustment against the $500,000 general average expense). Freight, of course, receives nothing in the adjustment and simply contributes $100,000.

Cargo, however, is a net debtor in the adjustment. Its contribution to the amount to be made good is $700,000, while it received only $500,000 for its sacrifice. Cargo is thus a net debtor in the amount of $200,000 in the adjustment, for a total loss in the voyage of $700,000. While that result may seem inequitable, the whole aim of general average is not to ensure an equal contribution among *embarked* values at the commencement of the voyage, but to ensure equal contribution among arrived, sound values at the conclusion of the voyage. At destination, cargo with a sound, arrived value of $3.5 million was landed. Absent the extraordinary sacrifices or expenses involved in the general average—which by definition saved the entire venture—cargo would have received nothing. Moreover, cargo's total loss on the voyage of $700,000 (the original $500,000 sacrifice, plus the net debt of $200,000 in the adjustment) represents precisely 20 percent of the sound, arrived value of cargo at the port of destination. Both freight and the vessel owner contributed precisely the same percentage of their arrived values.

B. For a slightly more complex problem, assume the same situation and values as stated above, but this time assume that there are three different cargo interests. On arrival at port, it is determined that the vessel's worth was $1 million; that the cargo interest of A was $1.5 million; that the cargo interest of B had a sound, arrived value of $1.75 million; that the cargo interest of C had an arrived value of $250,000; and that the freight interest was $500,000. Assume further that the vessel experienced an allowable general average expense of $100,000, while cargo interest C suffered a jettison determined to be worth $400,000. The amount to be made good is consequently $500,000. As before, the total arrived, sound values of the various parties in the maritime adventure amounts to $5 million, so the percentage of loss is 10 percent of the arrived value.

In this example, the vessel pays $100,000 in general average contribution (10 percent of the arrived value of the vessel), and receives in the adjustment $100,000 as the amount to be made good for the general average expense. The ultimate effect on the vessel owner is a "wash"—the vessel owner still suffers a $100,000 loss, which represents precisely 10 percent of the arrived sound value of the vessel.

Cargo interests A and B, along with the freight, each pay 10 percent in general average contribution, and each receives nothing in the adjustment. Cargo interest A thus pays $150,000, B pays $175,000 and freight pays $50,000.

Cargo interest C must pay in contribution $25,000 in general average, representing 10 percent of $250,000 in arrived cargo value which remains to cargo interest C. Cargo interest C also receives in the adjustment, however, the sum of $400,000, making good the jettison of $400,000. In the adjustment, cargo interest C thus becomes a net creditor for $375,000. The ultimate loss, which must be borne by cargo interest C, then, is merely $25,000, which represents precisely 10 percent of the sound arrived value of the cargo saved in the general average act.

C. Successive general average acts on a single voyage can pose additional adjustment problems. In seeking to adjust the average claims in such a situation, one must first pay close attention to what interests were aboard the vessel during each of the general average acts. In making the adjustments of the successive general average acts, it may become necessary to theoretically break a single voyage into several successive voyages, with general average acts occurring during the successive segments, and separate adjustments for each act.

Some successive general average acts need no special rules of adjustment. For example, if successive general average acts consisted solely of sacrifices, only one adjustment would be necessary, at least assuming there are no intervening ports of discharge between the successive general average acts. The landed, sound value of the cargo, vessel, and freight are computed as before, and the sacrificed values are made good. If, however, cargo sacrificed in one or more general average acts is replaced at a port of refuge, the freight earned as a consequence of the general average act will need to be factored into the adjustment of the prior average act. Moreover, if substituted cargo was aboard the vessel in a second or subsequent general average act, the value of that cargo will be the subject of a general average contribution for the interests sacrificed while the substituted cargo was aboard. Substituted cargo would have no responsibility, however, for general average consequences incurred before it was taken aboard.

A single voyage may, of course, call at several different ports in the course of a single voyage. If a general average act occurs after the discharge of some cargo, the value of that discharged cargo would not be the subject of a general average contribution, although it would be, of course, the subject of a contribution for any general average acts which preceded the discharge at the intermediate port.

Where, however, the second general average act changes the relative values of cargo, vessel and freight, it is necessary under the rules to make certain adjustments. In that event, the second (or final) general average act is adjusted first in an entirely separate general average adjustment. As would be the case in a normal adjustment, the saved values on arrival are calculated, and the losses attributable only to the second general average act would be calculated. The amounts to be paid or contributed by vessel, freight, and cargo are calculated as before.

One then turns attention to the first general average act. Again, saved values are calculated, this time adding any amounts made good in the earlier general average adjustment. The contributions of each of the parties to the adventure are then recalculated, and the result is the final general average adjustment for all parties.

The above modifications to the more routine adjustment will work to the benefit of cargo in many instances, particularly where intermediate repairs recoverable as a general average expense were incurred by the vessel at a port of refuge. Adjusting the first loss second in point of time has the effect of increasing the vessel's value in the final modification to the adjustment.

An even more complex situation occurs when a vessel experiences two general average acts; the first, before reaching an intermediate port of discharge; and the second, subsequent to the discharge of cargo at that first port, but prior to termination of the voyage. In this, thankfully, rare circumstance, there is an exception to the otherwise universally applied rule that contributions are exacted based upon the sound arrived value at the port of discharge.

In such a situation, cargo discharged at the first port has absolutely no interest in and received no benefit by virtue of the general average act that occurred following discharge at the intermediate port. As a result, the adjustment commences by adjusting first the initial general average act, calculating the values of all arrived values at the first port of discharge in order to arrive at contributions from the parties present on the voyage and to make good the sacrifices in the first general average act. The resulting adjustment is conclusive regarding all cargo discharged at the first port. As to the parties to the adventure that continued beyond the first port, the result of this initial adjustment is essentially an intermediate adjustment.

In apportioning the second general average act—the one that occurred after leaving the initial port of discharge—one begins once again with the second or final general average act. Arrived values at the second or final port are calculated, adding to the interests in the voyage any amounts which may have been made good to them in the earlier general average adjustment concerning the general average act which occurred prior to the discharge at that first port. If it happened that amounts made good in the first general average on interests continuing through the first port and onto the port of destination did not contribute to the second general average, then the owner of the affected property in the earlier general average would actually make a proportionately smaller contribution than would be the case with those who suffered no loss in the earlier general average.

After calculating the adjustment for the second of the two general averages, one then returns to the first general average incident, and calculates arrived values at the ultimate port of destination. To those values are added any amounts made good in either of the two earlier adjustments. Likewise, any contributions made in the second of the two earlier general averages are subtracted from the arrived values.

In calculating the amounts to be contributed on this final adjustment, the cargo discharged at the first port is added back in as a contributing interest upon the values established in the adjustment for the first loss (that which preceded discharge at the first port of discharge). No modification to the arrived values at the first port of that first port's cargo is made for amounts made good or amounts contributed in general average. In other words, one uses the same value for the first port's cargo as was used in determining its contribution to the first of the general average adjustments.

No collection can be made from that first cargo's interest. It did not, of course, share in the adventure in the subsequent general average situation. There will be, however, an amount calculated for a contribution on account of the first port's cargo. If the amount so calculated exceeds the amount previously calculated as due by way of contribution from that first port's cargo (and it will), the difference between the new numbers is payable by the shipowner.

The practice in the United States is to exclude passengers' baggage and personal effects from contribution to general average, even when stowed in baggage compartments, but if they are stowed there and are damaged by a general average act, the loss is a subject of contribution.[366] The 1974 Rules (Rule XVII) provide that passengers' luggage and personal effects, not shipped under bill of lading, shall not *contribute* to general average, but this does not preclude a claim for *contribution* in general average. The rule merely allows the shipowner, as between him and the cargo, to eliminate the passengers as contributors because of the difficulty in obtaining security from them and the impracticability of ascertaining correct values.

Clothes and personal effects of the master, officers, or crew which are sacrificed for the common benefit are allowed for in general average, although they are not called upon to contribute.[367]

General Average in Relation to Marine Policies

It must be remembered that, technically, general average is not part of the law of marine insurance; to the contrary, it is part of the law of carriage of goods by sea. Consequently, rights to contribution are not affected by the presence or absence of marine insurance coverage. However, as a practical matter, the various parties to the venture are almost invariably insured against liability for general average contributions. Therefore, it becomes

---

366. *Heye v. North German Lloyd*, 36 F. 705 (2d Cir., 1888).
367. *Heye v. North German Lloyd, supra*, n. 366.

important to understand what the rights and liabilities of the under-writers are where a general average situation is involved.

Generally, a policy of marine insurance provides an indemnity against general average losses and contributions, subject, of course, to the actual provisions of the policy. In general, the subject is codified in Section 66 of the Marine Insurance Act, 1906. It must be remembered, however, that the Act is not compulsory and may be varied (and frequently is) by the terms of the particular policies which are applicable.

Section 66 provides:

(1) A general average loss is a loss caused by or directly consequential on a general average act. It includes a general average expenditure as well as a general average sacrifice.[368]

(2) There is a general average act where any extraordinary sacrifice or expenditure is voluntarily and reasonably made or incurred in time of peril for the purpose of preserving the property imperilled in the common adventure.

(3) Where there is a general average loss, the party on whom it falls is entitled, subject to the conditions imposed by maritime law, to a rateable contribution from the other parties interested, and such contribution is called a general average contribution.

(4) Subject to any express provision in the policy, where the assured has incurred a general average expenditure, he may recover from the insurer in respect of the proportion of the loss which falls upon him, and in the case of a general average sacrifice he may recover from the insurer in respect of the whole loss without having enforced his right of contribution from the other parties liable to contribute.

(5) Subject to any express provision in the policy, where the assured has paid, or is liable to pay, a general average contribution in respect of the subject insured, he may recover therefor from the insurer.

(6) In the absence of express stipulation, the insurer is not liable for any general average loss or contribution where the loss was not incurred for the purpose of avoiding, or in connection with the avoidance of, a peril insured against.

(7) Where ship, freight, and cargo, or any two of those interests, are owned by the same assured, the liability of the insurer in respect of general average losses or contributions is to be determined as if those subjects were owned by different persons.

Sub-sections 1 and 2 of Section 66 are self-explanatory and do not appear to alter the principles of general average in any respect. Moreover,

---

368. See *Svensden v. Wallace*, (1884) 10 App.Cas. 404. As to the words "directly consequential," see *Atwood v. Sellar*, (1880) 5 Q.B.D. 286, C.A.

there is little or no difference between those sub-sections and Rules A and C of the York-Antwerp Rules, 1974, which, as a matter of common practice usually apply by reason of the contract of affreightment as well as by relevant policy provisions.

Clearly, the purpose of Sub-section 3 is to explain the references to contribution that follow. However, it does clarify the fact that the term "contribution" does not include losses which must be borne by the owner of the interest affected as part of his proportion of the general average.

Sub-section 4 properly draws a distinction between the rights of an insured to recover for sacrifices versus expenditures. A sacrifice, by definition, is one which is incurred to *avoid* loss by a peril insured against and, as such, is one for which insurers are liable. Thus, the owner of the sacrificed property can expect a full indemnity from his underwriters and is not obliged to give credit to underwriters for contributions which he may later receive from other parties to the venture. After payment to him by the underwriters, of course, the underwriters are entitled to subrogation rights against those contributing. The question is one of timing.

By contrast, expenditures are treated differently. There has been no "loss" of the insured subject-matter; consequently, the extent of the obligation of underwriters is only to indemnify him for the *proportion* of his expenditures which he must still bear *after taking into account contributions from others*. Stated another way, since the underwriters have not paid for a "loss" to the subject-matter insured, they have no claim by way of subrogation to such contributions.

Sub-section 5 is self-explanatory except, possibly, with respect to the measure of indemnity. It will be remembered that in the case of a sacrifice of ship, cargo or freight, the measure of indemnity is provided for in Sections 69, 70, and 71; i.e., partial losses of ship, freight, and goods, respectively. The difference between particular average claims under those sections and general average claims under Section 66(5) is that in the latter instance, interest and adjustment costs are automatically included.

Sub-section 6 is very important. Before underwriters are liable it must be determined whether the peril that threatened the venture was one which the policy insured against. The effect of the sub-section is, therefore, to exclude liability for general average loss or contribution when the general average act is for the purpose of avoiding a peril *not* insured against. For example, if the loss was occasioned by a war peril and the policy excludes war perils, there would be no liability. Nor would there be any liability if the measures taken to save the vessel were necessitated by reason of the owners attempting to cast her away, an act of wilful misconduct which is excluded by Section 55(2)(a) of the Act.[369]

---

369. Thus, general average expenditures occasioned solely and directly by unseaworthiness of the insured vessel, and not by perils of the seas or negligence of the master or crew, are not recoverable from underwriters. *The Fort Bragg*, 1924 AMC 275 (N.D.,Cal.).

What is the result, where the accident causing the general average situation comes about simply because of wear and tear? The simple answer is that it is sufficient if the venture is rescued from peril as a result of a general average sacrifice or expenditure. Thus, even when the general average situation arises from wear and tear, expenditures (such as port of refuge expenses and the like) are recoverable from hull underwriters on the grounds that the expenditures were necessary to save the vessel from a peril which might operate in the future.[370]

A good example to explain the difference in treatment where the *cause* of the loss is wear and tear (such as unseaworthiness) and where the *cause* of the loss is an insured peril is where a vessel in a debilitated state from wear and tear encounters heavy weather and either founders or runs aground. In that instance, the hull underwriters would be liable for the loss sustained.[371] By contrast, if a vessel laden with cargo sinks as the result of wear and tear, the vessel's proportion of any future salvage expenses of a general average nature would not be recoverable from hull underwriters because the salvage expenses were not incurred "in connection with the avoidance of a peril insured against." That is, *before* the salvage expenses were incurred, the vessel had already been lost from wear and tear, an uninsured peril.

It is important here to remember that the liability of underwriters to pay general average attaches *as of the date of the sacrificial act*, and not as of the date of injury or damage to the vessel. That is, the relevant time is when the decision is taken to make a sacrifice or incur an expense, rather than at the time of the accident giving rise to the necessity for the general average act.[372]

Sub-section 7 is relatively straightforward and clear. But what happens in the case of a sacrifice of part of one of the interests of the assured? Must the insurers of that interest pay in full and, if so, may they then

370. *Montgomery v. Indemnity Mutual Insurance Co.*, (1902) 1 K.B. 734.

371. This is true unless underwriters can show that the loss was caused by unseaworthiness, and under a time policy this defense will fail if there was no privity on the part of the insured. See, *Ballantyne v. Mackinnon*, (1896) 2 Q.B. 455, 65 L.J.Q.B. 616. It should be noted that the question of cargo's contribution is still the subject of contractual obligations under the contract of affreightment, but insofar as hull underwriters are concerned, liability for general average depends on whether an insured peril was avoided, although the prior circumstances might not have provided grounds for a claim.

372. *Oneida Navigation Corp. v. Alliance Assur. Co., Ltd. (The Percy R. Pyne)*, 1926 AMC 1582 (St.,N.Y.); *Norwich & N.Y. Transp. Co. v. I.N.A.*, 118 F. 307; *Wilcox, Peck & Hughes v. Am. S. & R. Co.*, 210 F. 89; *Fowler v. Rathbone*, 79 U.S. 102. In some instances, of course, the general average act and the accident will occur essentially simultaneously, but in others there may be a hiatus, such that a particular average claim may fall during one policy period, and the general average act falls within a new policy period. If so, the general average claim is payable by the policy which is operative at the time of the general average act. The general average act is, as noted above, when the decision is made which constitutes the general average act; e.g., at the time the *decision* is made to deviate rather than at the time the actual deviation takes place.

claim contribution from the assured as the owner of the other interest? The answer is that the insurers of the property sacrificed are liable only for the proportion of the property sacrificed.[373] This is so because the owner already has and retains his own contribution as to the other interest. In practice, the insurer of the property so sacrificed is treated as being entitled to credit for the contributions due from the other interests in the same ownership.

Rules as to Contribution

In the case of contributions, Section 73(1) of the Act provides:

> Subject to any express provision in the policy, where the assured has paid, or is liable for, any general average contribution, the measure of indemnity is the full amount of such contribution if the subject-matter liable to contribution is insured for its full contributory value; but if such subject-matter be not insured for its full contributory value, or if only part of it be insured, the indemnity payable by the insurer must be reduced in proportion to the under-insurance, and where there has been a particular average loss which constitutes a deduction from the contributory value, and for which the insurer is liable, that amount must be deducted from the insured value in order to ascertain what the insurer is liable to contribute.[374]

As might be expected, successive losses can create complications in adjustments, and this subject has been discussed *supra*. A peculiar problem arises, however, where a general average expenditure is followed by a total loss of the interest owned by the party incurring the expenditure, if the contributory value of the other interests is less than the amount he has spent. As noted, when general average expenditure exceeds the total arrived values of ship and cargo, cargo is liable for general average only up to its contributory value. It has been held that in such circumstances, the underwriters on ship are liable for the balance of the general average expenditure, even though it exceeds the contributory value of the ship.[375]

---

373. *Montgomery v. Indemnity Mutual Marine Ins. Co.*, (1902) 1 K.B. 734.

374. See *Balmoral Steamship Co. Ltd. v. Marten*, (1901) 2 K.B. 896, *aff'd* [1902] A.C. 711. The section is not, however, free from ambiguity, certainly with respect to the term "full contributory value." Here, Lowndes & Rudolf take the position that the term "full contributory value" means the value upon which the interest contributes, even if that is less than the sound value at the termination of the adventure. Sec. 908. To the contrary, Arnould maintains that the term means sound value at the termination of the adventure, from which the net value on which the subject-matter in fact contributes is calculated by making the appropriate deductions for damage, deterioration and expenses. Sec. 1007. The question is probably academic in light of the customary specific clauses in marine policies.

375. *Green Star Shipping Co. v. London Assurance*, [1933] 1 K.B. 378. While the point has not been litigated in the United States, it seems probable that the same result would be reached.

The rationale is that this was a proportion of the general average expenditure falling upon the shipowner and, by Sub-section 4 of Section 66 of the Act, the assured may recover from the insurer in respect of the "proportion of the loss which falls upon him."[376]

As to Vessels

American vessels are usually insured under the American Hull Institute form of policy or some derivation thereof. That form of policy contains very specific provisions with respect to general average, the most important being the paragraph at lines 128 through 133, reading:

> When the contributory value of the Vessel is greater than the Agreed Value herein, the liability of the Underwriters for General Average contribution (except in respect to amounts made good to the Vessel), or Salvage, shall not exceed the proportion of the total contribution due from the Vessel which the amount insured hereunder bears to the contributory value; and if, because of damage for which the Underwriters are liable as Particular Average, the value of the Vessel has been reduced for the purpose of contribution, the amount of such Particular Average damage recoverable under this Policy shall first be deducted from the amount insured hereunder, and the Underwriters shall then be liable only for the proportion which such net amount bears to the contributory value.

The similarity of the above provision to the language of Section 73 will be immediately apparent. Absent the provision, underwriters would be liable for the full general average contribution attaching to the vessel (both sacrifices and expenses), irrespective of any underinsurance.[377]

The new London Institute Time Clauses Hulls (1/10/83) approach the problem rather more simply. Clause 11.1 provides:

> This insurance covers the Vessel's proportion of salvage, salvage charges and/or general average, reduced in respect of any under-in-

---

376. However, when combined with any particular average claim, the entire claim cannot exceed the insured value.

377. In ascertaining the amount of underwriters' liability for general average expenses, the provision requires that the insured value must be taken into account. Thus, if the insured value of the vessel is equal to or exceeds the sound value on which the contributory value of the vessel is based, then the underwriter pays the full amount of the general average contribution. If the insured value is less than the sound value, the underwriter pays only a proportion of the expenses. General average sacrifices (i.e., amounts made good to the vessel) are not affected by the provision and are recoverable in full from underwriters without regard to underinsurance. Absent this clause, the rule derived from *International Navigation Co. v. Atlantic Mutual Ins. Co.*, 108 F. 988 would apply and the full general average contribution attaching to the vessel (both sacrifices and expenses) would be payable, regardless of any underinsurance.

surance, but in case of general average sacrifice of the Vessel the Assured may recover in respect of the whole loss without first enforcing their right of contribution from other parties.

It should also be observed that both the American Hull form and the new London Hull Clauses stipulate that general average is payable without deduction of thirds, "new for old."

Excess Liabilities Coverage. It is common practice for shipowners to procure supplementary insurance, commonly known as "increased value" or "excess liability" policies which, in the event of loss at a time when the vessel was undervalued in the hull policy, would enable them to recover in whole or in part for the excess of any general average contribution over the amount recoverable under the hull policy.[378] Again, however, even with "increased value" insurance, if the contributory value of the vessel exceeds the primary hull cover plus the increased value cover, the assured recovers for the excess only in proportion to the amount the increased value cover bears to the total excess valuation.[379]

The Question of Fault. It is again emphasized that general average is concerned with carriage by sea. Thus, hull underwriters are still liable to their assured even though he may have been in breach of the contract of affreightment; i.e., his fault under the contract of affreightment does not normally affect his right of recovery under the hull policy. The difficulty for the shipowner/assured under his hull policy as against his hull underwriters comes about if the fault on his part involves an act which is not covered under the hull policy at all, such as a deviation.

The hull underwriters are directly affected, however, in terms of their subrogation rights in the event of, for example, a sacrifice. Thus, hull underwriters, having paid the shipowner/assured for his sacrifice, may be barred from claiming contribution from cargo because of the fault of the assured under the contract of affreightment.

It should be noted, however, that P & I policies (or rules) ordinarily provide coverage for the entered member:

(a) Where the member has incurred general average expenditures, but is unable to claim contribution from cargo because of a breach of the contract of carriage; and

(b) Where the member's own proportion of general average cannot be recovered from the hull underwriters in full because the contributory value of the vessel exceeds the insured value.

---

378. In this connection, see Clause 21 (the "Disbursements Warranty" Clause) of the new London hull clauses (1/10/83) and the "Additional Insurances" Clause of the AIH (June 2, 1977) form, both of which permit additional insurances to cover excess or increased value of hull and machinery in a sum not exceeding 25% of the stated value in the hull policy.

379. *Holman and Sons v. Merchants' Marine Insurance Co.*, [1919] 1 K.B. 383.

Insurance on Cargo

Nearly all American policies on cargo include a general average clause reading substantially as follows:

> General Average and Salvage Charges payable according to United States laws and usage and/or as per Foreign Statement and/or per York/Antwerp Rules (as prescribed in whole or in part) if in accordance with the contract of affreightment.

Stated simply, cargo underwriters agree to pay for any general average contribution of their assured in accordance with the provisions of the contract of affreightment.

Regardless of the policy clauses, American law is to the effect that cargo underwriters are liable only for the full general average contribution payable by their assured, if the insured value of the cargo is equal to or exceeds the sound value on which the contributory value of the cargo was based. Thus, concerning the difference between the contributory value of the cargo and the insured value, cargo owners are co-insurers with their underwriters.[380]

The "General Average Clause" in the new London Cargo Clauses, A, B, and C is not dissimilar. In each instance, the clause reads:

> This insurance covers general average and salvage charges, adjusted or determined according to the contract of affreightment and/or the governing law and practice, incurred to avoid or in connection with the avoidance of loss from any cause except those excluded in Clauses 4, 5, 6 and 7 or elsewhere in this insurance.

Insurance on Freight

The same principles with respect to underinsurance in hull and cargo policies apply equally with respect to freight; i.e., if the sum insured is less than the gross freight at risk, the amount recoverable under the policy as respects general average contributions is reduced in proportion to the underinsurance.

---

380. See *Gulf Refining Co. v. Atlantic Mutual Ins. Co.*, 279 U.S. 708, 1929 AMC 825 (1929). It will be seen that this decision comports with the principles set forth in Sec. 73(1) of the Marine Insurance Act, 1906. However, to make assurance doubly sure, most cargo policies also contain a contributory value clause reading:

> This Company shall be liable for only such proportion of General Average and Salvage Charges as the sum hereby insured (less Particular Average for which this Company is liable hereunder, if any) bears to the Contributory Value of the Property hereby insured.

General Average Sacrifices

Unlike the rules applicable to contributions, underwriters are liable in full for general average *sacrifices* made by their assureds. In the case of a vessel, underinsurance is ignored, and underwriters are liable for the full amount of the sacrifice.[381]

Any direct claim on underwriters for general average sacrifices with respect to cargo and freight are calculated on the basis of the insured value in accordance with usual adjusting procedures.

---

381. *The St. Paul*, 100 F. 304. But, where the ship and cargo are owned by the same owner, it has been held that the assured must credit the hull underwriters with any contribution due from the cargo as general average. *Potter v. Providence & Washington Ins. Co.*, 4 Mason 298 (1826).

CHAPTER XVIII

SUE AND LABOR CLAUSE AND SALVAGE

Introduction

Considering the antiquity of the Sue and Labor Clause (it appeared as early as 1613 in the *Tiger* policy), it is rather surprising that there has been relatively little litigation concerning it. This may be due to the fact that it is rather clearly drafted.

In the old Lloyd's S.G. form, it read simply:

> . . . And in case of any loss or misfortune it shall be lawful to the assured, their factors, servants and assigns, to sue, labour and travel for, in and about the defence, safeguards, and recovery of the said goods and merchandises, and ship, etc., or any part thereof, without prejudice to this insurance; to the charges whereof we, the assurers, will contribute each one according to the rate and quantity of his sum herein insured.

In the American form (of which the AIH [June 2, 1977] is representative), it reads:

> And in case of any Loss or Misfortune, it shall be lawful and necessary for the Assured, their Factors, Servants and Assigns, to sue, labor and travel for, in, and about the defense, safeguard and recovery of the Vessel, or any part thereof, without prejudice to this insurance, to the charges whereof the Underwriters will contribute their proportion as provided below. And it is expressly declared and agreed that no acts of the Underwriters or Assured in recovering, saving or preserving the Vessel shall be considered as a waiver or acceptance of abandonment.
>
> In the event of expenditure under the Sue and Labor Clause, the Underwriters shall pay the proportion of such expenses that the amount insured hereunder bears to the Agreed Value, or that the amount insured hereunder (less loss and/or damage payable under this Policy) bears to the actual value of the salved property, whichever proportion shall be less; provided always that their liability for such expenses shall not exceed their proportionate part of the Agreed Value.
>
> If claim for Total Loss is admitted under this Policy and sue and labor expenses have been reasonably incurred in excess of any proceeds realized or value recovered, the amount payable under this Pol-

icy will be the proportion of such excess that the amount insured hereunder (without deduction for loss or damage) bears to the Agreed
Value or to the sound value of the Vessel at the time of the accident,
whichever value was greater; provided always that Underwriters' liability for such expenses shall not exceed their proportionate part of
the Agreed Value. The foregoing shall also apply to expenses reasonably incurred in salving or attempting to salve the Vessel and other
property to the extent that such expenses shall be regarded as having
been incurred in respect of the Vessel.[1]

The more important American cases are cited in *Reliance Ins. Co. v.
The Escapade*.[2] In that case, the yacht *Escapade* stranded in the Bahamas. It
was insured under a standard yacht policy at an agreed valuation of
$30,000. After the stranding, the vessel severely pounded for several days
while salvors awaited abatement of heavy seas.

The policy, under "General Conditions" provided for a private pleasure warranty reading: "Warranted by the Assured that the vessel shall be
used solely for private pleasure purposes and shall not be hired or chartered unless approved by the Assurers, and permission endorsed
hereon."

The assured learned of the stranding three days after it occurred. He
notified the agent who executed and delivered the policy for the insurer.
The agent reported to the insurer and employed a marine surveyor who
thereafter acted as the representative of the insurer. Prior to his inspection of the stranded vessel, he inquired of local salvors if they would undertake the salvage if it proved feasible. The following day the surveyor
returned and, on the same day, the agent learned from the assured that
the vessel had been chartered. That same afternoon, the agent and an
assistant called on the assured where salvage of the vessel was discussed.
Although they did not tell the assured, the agent had already discussed
the matter of the charter with the home office of the insurer and, on instructions from the home office, had called in counsel to act for the insurer because of the known breach of the private pleasure warranty.

At the afternoon meeting, the assured was insisting that the vessel was
a total loss and was therefore being abandoned to the insurer. The agent
was adamant that the insurer would not accept an abandonment and was

---

1. The new London Institute Time Clauses (Hulls), effective 1/10/83, for use with the
new Marine Policy Form recently developed, contain a much expanded Sue and Labor
Clause denominated as Clause 13. It forthrightly declares that in case of any loss or misfortune it is the *duty* of the assured and their servants and agents to take such measures as may
be reasonable for the purpose of averting or minimizing a loss which would be recoverable
under the insurance. In other respects, the new Clause 13 follows rather closely that contained in the American (AIH) form although the actual language used differs in some particulars. See Appendices 6 and 27.

2. 280 F.2d 482, 1961 AMC 2410 (5th Cir.).

equally emphatic that it was the assured's responsibility to protect his property and to salvage it if possible. Although the marine surveyor, pursuant to the insurer's directions, had made preliminary arrangements with the salvors, the agent made it plain to the assured that if he did not personally authorize the salvage, he and the surveyor, on behalf of the insurer, would call the salvors back. It was made plain to the assured that if he failed to authorize the salvage, the salvage program then underway would be stopped and the insurer would disclaim any further liability. Following such demands, the assured prepared a letter of authority along the lines demanded addressed to the salvors. This was delivered by the surveyor to the salvors who, by this time, were on the scene with their equipment.

The marine surveyor kept in constant touch with the salvage operations. When the vessel was returned to its home port, Miami, it was placed in the hands of a ship repair yard. The surveyor outlined certain work to be done but the shipyard declined to perform it. The surveyor then told the assured that he would have to authorize the work. The assured told the shipyard to do whatever the agent and the surveyor instructed them to do. It was not until almost a month after the stranding that the insurer finally disclaimed liability.

The trial court found that the insurer was estopped to deny coverage. On appeal, the fifth circuit affirmed, holding that the warranty merely provided a defense to an occurrence and loss otherwise covered by the policy but, as in the case of any other defense, it could be waived or the underwriter estopped to assert it. In doing so, this would not constitute expanding or creating a new coverage.

The insurer also raised a novel and ingenious point. It urged, in essence, that any estoppel or waiver related only to the efforts to salvage and protect the vessel from further harm, such efforts by nature being sue and labor expenditures covered separately under the Sue and Labor Clause. Thus, the estoppel and waiver ran only as to the sue and labor expenditures and not as to the loss from an insured peril.

The appeals court demolished this contention after a discussion of the history, function, and purpose of the Sue and Labor Clause, citing in the process all the more important American cases.

An analysis of the English, Commonwealth, and American cases shows conclusively that Section 78 of the Marine Insurance Act, 1906, is but a "distillation" of the principles of law embodied in those decisions. Section 78 reads:

> (1) Where the policy contains a suing and labouring clause, the engagement thereby entered into is deemed to be supplementary to the contract of insurance, and the assured may recover from the insurer any expenses properly incurred pursuant to the clause, notwithstand-

ing that the insurer may have paid for a total loss, or that the subject-matter may have been warranted free from particular average, either wholly or under a certain percentage.

(2) General average losses and contributions and salvage charges, as defined by the Act, are not recoverable under the suing and labouring clause.

(3) Expenses incurred for the purpose of averting or diminishing any loss not covered by the policy are not recoverable under the suing and labouring clause.

(4) It is the duty of the assured and his agents, in all cases, to take such measures as may be reasonable for the purpose of averting or minimizing a loss.

The clause must be read in conjunction with Sections 55(a)(2), 64(2), 65(2), 76(2), and 76(4), as well as Rule 13, Rules for Construction of Policy, of the Marine Insurance Act, 1906.

Loss Averted or Minimized Must Arise out of the Basic and Standard Perils Insured Against, and Must Be a Loss for Which the Underwriters are Liable

The cardinal principle to be kept in mind in construing the clause is that the loss averted or minimized must arise out of the basic and standard perils insured against under a marine policy and must be a loss for which the underwriters are liable.[3]

---

3. *Meyer v. Ralli*, (1876) 45 L.J.Q.B. 741, 3 Asp. M.L.C. 324; *Aitchison v. Lohre*, (1879) 4 A.C. 755, 4 Asp. M.L.C. 168, H.L., varying (1878) 3 Q.B.D. 558, C.A.; *Great American Peninsula Ry. Co. v. Saunders*, (1862) 31 L.J.Q.B. 206, 121 E.R. 1072, Ex. Ch.; *Booth v. Gair*, (1863) 143 E.R. 796; *Weissberg v. Lamb*, (1950) 84 Ll.L.Rep. 509; *Xenos v. Fox*, (1869) L.R. 4 C.P. 665, Ex. Ch.; *Uzielli v. Boston Mar. Ins. Co.*, (1884) 54 L.J.Q.B. 142, 5 Asp. M.L.C. 405, C.A.; *F.W. Berk & Co., Ltd. v. Style*, (1955) 2 Lloyd's Rep. 382, (1955) 3 All E.R. 625; *Currie & Co. v. Bombay Native Ins. Co.*, (1869) 16 E.R. 740; *Dixon v. Whitworth*, (1880) 49 L.J.Q.B. 408, 4 Asp. M.L.C. 327, C.A.; *Cunard S.S. Co. v. Marten*, (1903) 2 K.B. 511, 9 Asp. M.L.C. 452; *Western Assur. Co. of Toronto v. Poole*, (1903) 1 K.B. 376, 9 Asp. M.L.C. 390; *Biays v. Chesapeake Ins. Co.*, 11 U.S. 415 (1813); *Munson v. Standard Marine Ins. Co.*, 156 F. 44, cert. den. 208 U.S. 543 (1907); *The William Luckenbach—Powerful (Arb.)*, 1936 AMC 1796; *Barney Dumping-Boat Co. v. Niagara Fire Ins. Co.*, 67 F. 341 (2d Cir., 1895); *American Merchant Marine Ins. Co. v. Liberty Sand & Gravel Co.*, 282 F. 514 (2d Cir., 1922); *Charleston Shipbuilding & Drydocking Co. v. Atlantic Mutual Ins. Co. (Arb.)*, 1946 AMC 1611; *Magnone v. Pac. Coast F.I. Co.*, 198 Misc. 264, 97 N.Y.S.2d 663, 1950 AMC 1465 (St., N.Y.); *Connors Marine v. Northwestern Fire Ins. Co.*, 88 F.2d 637, 1937 AMC 344 (2d Cir.), companion case, 1939 AMC 447 (St.,N.Y.); *Berns & Koppstein, Inc. v. Orion Ins. Co.*, 170 F.Supp. 707, 1959 AMC 2455, 273 F.2d 415, 1960 AMC 1379 (2d Cir.); *Reliance Ins. Co. v. The Escapade*, 280 F.2d 482, 1961 AMC 2410 (5th Cir.); *Brown & Root v. American Home*, 353 F.2d 113, 1965 AMC 2689 (5th Cir.); *Haun v. Guaranty Security Ins.*, 1969 AMC 2068 (St., Tenn.); *Continental Food Products Inc. v. Ins. Co. of North America*, 1977 AMC 2421 (5th Cir.); *Australian Coastal Shipping Commission v. Green*, [1971] 1 All E.R. 353, C.A.; *Michaels v. Mutual Marine*, 472 F.Supp. 26, 1979 AMC 1673 (S.D.N.Y.); *Healy Tibbetts v.*

To illustrate the foregoing, in *Charleston Shipbuilding & Drydocking Co. v. Atlantic Mutual Ins. Co.,*[4] a marine railway was insured under a form of policy covering the marine railway itself against loss and containing the usual Sue and Labor Clause. A vessel was being launched when an accident happened and the vessel became stuck. Considerable expense was incurred in completing the launch. The policy responded for the damage to the marine railway itself but underwriters refused to pay the expense incurred in completing the launch. The arbitrator held that the steps taken by the assured to complete the launch were not in any sense directed toward averting damage to the marine railway nor to its "defense, safeguard and recovery," stating:

> The marine railway was here the subject of the insurance, but in my opinion, the steps taken by the assured to complete the launching were not in any sense directed to avert damage to the marine railway, nor directed to the "defense, safeguard and recovery" of the marine railway. They were undertaken with the sole purpose of fulfilling the assured's contract with the Department of Commerce to repair and launch the *Relief.* If those expenses be considered as sue and labor, they were necessarily incurred in order to prevent a claim by the Department of Commerce against the assured for liability . . . a subject which is not covered by the policy.

Under English law, the mere fact that the policy may contain a suing and laboring clause does not necessarily mean that recovery may be had for expenses incurred in averting a loss. For example, in *Cunard S.S. Co. v. Marten,*[5] a number of mules were shipped on the plaintiffs' vessel under a contract which contained no clause exempting plaintiffs from liability for loss of the mules through the negligence of plaintiffs and their servants. The plaintiffs effected a policy through Lloyd's to protect themselves against "liability of any kind to the owners of the mules up to £20,000 owing to the omission of the negligence clause" from the contract. The policy was in the printed S.G. form at Lloyd's and contained the usual suing and laboring clause. During the voyage, the vessel stranded through the negligence of the plaintiffs' servants and expenses were incurred by the plaintiffs in saving some of the mules and in attempting to save others which were lost. Plaintiffs sought to recover their expenses, not as a direct result of a loss under the policy but under the suing and laboring clause as expenses incurred to avert or reduce the amount of the loss. The court held that the suing and laboring clause was entirely inapplicable to the insurance contract and should be ignored; i.e., the policy

Foremost, 1980 AMC 1600 (N.D.,Cal.); *Champion Int'l v. Arkwright,* 1982 AMC 2496 (S.D.N.Y.); *Consolidated Int'l v. Falcon,* 1983 AMC 270 (S.D.N.Y.).
4. 1946 AMC 1611 (Arb.).
5. (1903) 2 K.B. 511, 9 Asp. M.L.C. 452.

was effected by a carrier of goods not upon the cargo itself but in order to protect themselves from liability which might be incurred as a carrier. Lord Justice Romer said, in part:

> . . . The Suing and Labouring Clause refers to "the said goods and merchandises and ship," and admittedly this insurance is not on any goods or merchandises or ship at all. Of course I would, if I could do so reasonably, apply that clause to the present case, but it appears to me that it cannot reasonably be applied to such a case. In my opinion, the clause was never intended to apply to such a contract of insurance; it was on the very face of it intended to apply only to an insurance on "goods, merchandises and ship."[6]

In *Xenos v. Fox*,[7] the plaintiffs were the owners of a vessel which had been sued for running down another vessel. The policy, in addition to a Sue and Labor Clause, contained a Running Down Clause providing reimbursement for damages paid by reason of the vessel damaging another vessel. The defense was successful but plaintiffs incurred costs in so defending. Asserting that had not the defense been asserted and litigation expenses incurred, the underwriters would have been held liable under the Running Down Clause, plaintiffs sought to recoup their expenses from underwriters. Holding that the Sue and Labor Clause was one of limited application, extending *only to ordinary marine perils*, and not to special risks such as those covered by the Running Down Clause, recovery was denied. On appeal, the Exchequer Chamber also held that no loss or misfortune had occurred as was comprehended within the language of the Running Down Clause.

Other illustrations of the principle that the loss averted or minimized must arise out of the basic and standard perils insured against under a marine policy will be found in *Berns & Koppstein, Inc. v. Orion Ins. Co.*,[8] *Berk (F.W.) & Co., Ltd. v. Style*,[9] and *Continental Food Products Inc. v. Ins. Co. of North America*.[10] In *Berns & Koppstein,* the court followed *Xenos v. Fox, supra,* where the policy covered perils in addition to the standard marine perils, stating:

---

6. See discussion, *infra*, however, with respect to *Emperor Goldmining Co., Ltd. v. Switzerland General Ins. Co., Ltd.*, 81 W.N. (N.S.W.) 85, 5 F.L.R. 247, (1964) N.S.W.R. 1243, (1964) 1 Lloyd's Rep. 348 (Aus.). Whereas, in *Cunard S.S. Co. v. Marten* the policy contained a suing and laboring clause but it was held inapplicable, in *Emperor Goldmining* the policy contained no suing and laboring clause yet recovery for sue and labor expenses was allowed. See, however, *Integrated Container Service, Inc. v. British Traders Ins. Co., Ltd.*, [1981] 2 Lloyd's Rep. 460, where J. Neill refused to follow *Emperor Goldmining*. Recovery was allowed but only because the policy contained a suing and laboring clause.

7. (1869) L.R. 4 C.P. 665, Ex.Ch.

8. 170 F.Supp. 707, 1959 AMC 2455, 273 F.2d 415, 1960 AMC 1379 (2d Cir.), [1960] 1 Lloyd's Rep. 276.

9. (1955) 2 Lloyd's Rep. 382, (1955) 3 All E.R. 625.

10. 1977 AMC 2421.

The rejection clause covered a special and specific risk other than and in addition to the standard marine cargo risk and is not to be circumscribed to the standard "sue and labor" clause.

The standard "sue and labor" clause covers a *voluntary* expenditure on the part of the insured to protect the goods against the *standard risks* covered by the policies. [Emphasis supplied.]

In *Berk (F.W.) & Co. v. Style,* the plaintiff had bought on an f.o.b. contract a consignment of kieselguhr to be shipped from Africa to London. The kieselguhr was packed in paper bags and the goods were insured in transit between warehouse and warehouse by two policies of marine insurance against " all risks of loss and/or damage from whatsoever cause arising." Each policy contained a suing and laboring clause binding the insurers to contribute to the charges of the assured in suing and laboring for the safeguard and recovery of the goods and also incorporated the Institute Cargo Clauses of which Clause 1 provided that the insurance would not be deemed to cover loss or damage or expense proximately caused "by . . . inherent vice or nature of the subject matter insured." When the kieselguhr was being transferred at London from the ship's hold to a lighter a number of bags burst and plaintiffs incurred expenses in rebagging and handling the cargo. The court found that the subject matter of the insurance was kieselguhr packed in paper bags and not the kieselguhr alone and that there was inherent vice in the goods because the bags in which the kieselguhr was packed were defective at the time of shipment. The court also held the expenses under the suing and laboring clause were not recoverable because the expenses could not be shown to have been due to an *accident or casualty* as the bags were in such condition at time of shipment that it was certain that they would not hold their contents in the course of necessary handling and transshipment.

In *Continental Food Products Inc. v. Insurance Co. of North America,* plaintiffs shipped frozen meat from Guatemala to Tampa, Florida. Upon arrival, it was found that some of the meat had thawed and the Department of Agriculture would not allow the thawed meat to enter the country. The entire shipment had to be repackaged and a portion of it was ultimately rejected. There was no evidence of stranding, sinking, burning, or collision. There was no evidence of refrigeration breakdown, derangement, or stoppage in excess of 24 hours. In short, there was no evidence of the loss being occasioned by a peril insured against. Plaintiffs asserted that the Sue and Labor Clause nonetheless afforded coverage for certain items of the damage. The court rejected this argument, stating in part:

> . . . The fallacy of this argument is that it ignores completely the history, function and purpose of the "sue and labor clause." . . . This clause is tied irrevocably to the insured perils coverage. Because the purpose of the clause is to reimburse the assured for expenses in-

curred in satisfying his duty to the underwriter, there is no such duty where the policy, for one reason or another, does not afford coverage. The "sue and labor clause" does not operate as an enlargement of the perils underwritten against.[11]

The form of P & I policy most widely used in the United States is the SP-23 (revised 1/56). There is a form known as SP-38 which is based essentially on SP-23 but which provides lesser coverage. Also in common use is the American Steamship Owners' Mutual Protection and Indemnity Association Inc. form of policy ("Club" policy). In none of these forms is there a Sue and Labor Clause. Like the English market, P & I (liability) policies in the United do not ordinarily contain a suing and laboring clause. This is not to say, however, that a marine liability policy may not contain a Sue and Labor Clause which will be enforced. If such a liability policy does contain a Sue and Labor Clause and it clearly was the intention of the parties that the clause would apply, it will be enforced. For example, compare *The Edward D. Ryan*[12] with *The William Luckenbach— Powerful*.[13] In the former, a tug owner recovered counsel fees and disbursements incurred in an *unsuccessful* defense of an action for damages to cargo in a barge in tow under a tower's risk clause; in the latter, the shipowner failed to recoup litigation expenses under a lighterage liability policy Sue and Labor Clause where the defense was successful and no legal liability was imposed. Both policies being liability policies, where no legal liability was imposed, there was no corresponding obligation of reimbursement, but where legal liability was imposed, expenses incurred in attempting to avert the liability were recoverable.[14] The point is well illustrated in *Munson v. Standard Marine Ins. Co.*[15] In that case, the policy was on a tug indemnifying against liability to her tows. One of the barges was

11. See, also, *Healy Tibbetts v. Foremost*, 1980 AMC 1600 (N.D.,Cal) where the court held the insurer was not obligated to indemnify the assured barge owner for its expenses in defending against liability to the United States for the cost of cleaning up an oil spill after the barge sank. The policy contained a "Pollution Exclusion Clause" and the insurer's obligation to pay reasonable defense costs was limited to "any liabilities insured hereunder," and *Shaver Transportation Co. v. Travelers Indemnity*, 481 F.Supp. 892, 1980 AMC 393 (D.,Ore.), where the insurer was held not liable for sue and labor (and other expenses) where the peril (contamination of the cargo) was not covered under a cargo policy on F.P.A. conditions. In *Biays v. Chesapeake Ins. Co.*, 11 U.S. 415 (1813), the policy covered total loss only of hides being shipped. There was a partial loss consisting of slightly less than one-third of the hides. Claim was made under the Sue and Labor Clause for the expense of saving some of the hides which had been sunk and water-damaged while being lightered. Recovery under the Sue and Labor Clause was denied because the loss which took place would not, in any event, have been covered under the policy.

12. 1933 AMC 350, *aff'd* 67 F.2d 544, 1933 AMC 1631.

13. 1936 AMC 1796 (Arb.).

14. See, also, *Scottish Metropolitan Assur. Co., Ltd. v. Groom*, (1924) 20 Ll.L.Rep. 44, C.A., where legal expenses incurred in defeating an owner's claim for a total loss were held not recoverable.

15. 156 F. 44, *cert. den.* 208 U.S. 543 (1907).

lost and the barge owner filed suit against the tug. The tug was exonerated from fault. The tug owner then brought suit against the underwriters to recoup the expenses sustained in defending the suit. The court denied recovery, stating:

> . . . The cause of the legal expenses involved here arose, not out of the fact that the policy attached but out of the fact that someone claimed that it attached when in fact it did not . . . . The underwriter is not liable . . . unless he would be liable for the loss to avert which the labor or expense is incurred.

General Average and Salvage Charges Not Recoverable under Sue and Labor Clause

It should be emphasized, as subsection (2) of Section 78 of the Act so clearly expresses, general average losses and contributions, and salvage charges, as defined in the Act, are not recoverable under the Sue and Labor Clause. This subsection merely expresses the common law on the subject prior to the adoption of the Act.[16]

Bearing in mind that Section 65(2) defines "salvage charges" as charges recoverable under maritime law by a salvor *independently of contract,* and that the customary Sue and Labor Clause itself prescribes that only expenses incurred by the assured, their "factors, servants and assigns" are recoverable, services rendered by one vessel to another vessel in distress, not as an agent of the owners of the distressed vessel upon an agreement with them, but as *independent* salvors, are salvage charges which are not recoverable under the Sue and Labor Clause as they were not incurred by the assured or its agents.[17]

For example, in *Dixon v. Whitworth,*[18] a vessel and its cargo were abandoned in a storm by the steamer towing them. Another steamer subsequently found them and towed them to destination. The owner paid the salvage award and then brought suit against the underwriters. It was held, on authority of *Aitchison v. Lohre, supra,* that the underwriters were not liable for the salvage award as it was not within the parameters of the Sue and Labor Clause.

It should be apparent that if expenses are incurred in saving property at sea, the expenses will fall into one of three categories: i.e., (1) salvage

---

16. See *Aitchison v. Lohre,* (1879) 4 A.C. 755, 4 Asp. M.L.C. 168, H.L., varying (1878) 3 Q.B.D. 558, C.A.; *Dixon v. Whitworth,* (1880) 49 L.J.O.B. 408, 4 Asp. M.L.C. 327, C.A.; *Australian Coastal Shipping Commission v. Green,* (1971) 1 All E.R. 353, C.A.

17. *Aitchison v. Lohre, supra,* n. 16.

18. *Supra,* n. 16.

charges, (2) general average expenditures, or (3) sue and labor charges. For example, if a vessel without cargo aboard strands and the master employs a tug to pull her off her strand at so much per hour, then the sums paid to the tug owner fall within the scope of sue and labor charges. If, however, the vessel has cargo aboard it and the stranding is due to negligence of the master or crew and the vessel is otherwise seaworthy, then the expense of the tug would be classified as a general average expenditure. Correspondingly, should the tug services be rendered on an emergency basis, without any prior contractual arrangement between the tug and the master of the stranded vessel, then this would be "pure" salvage and would be paid as "salvage charges."

As a practical matter, it is much more common that the the salvage services will be performed on Lloyd's Open Form (or equivalent), on the basis of "no cure, no pay." Where such a form is used, in the absence of an agreement between the parties, the salvors' remuneration would be determined by arbitration. It is somewhat of a moot point whether this constitutes charges recoverable "independently of contract" within the meaning of Section 65(2). In favor of the view that the remuneration payable to the salvors acting under a Lloyd's form constitutes salvage charges, it may be said that Section 65(2) relates merely to the quantification of the salvage claim and, since this is determined by arbitrators on general principles of maritime law, it is immaterial that the liability arises under contract. On the other hand, the Lloyd's form does form the basis of the parties' mutual rights and obligations and it is thought to be somewhat artificial to separate the liability for salvage (which clearly arises pursuant to contract) from the quantification of the claim. The better view is that the salvors' remuneration under the Lloyd's form is remuneration pursuant to contract and may therefore be recovered as sue and labor.[19] The wording of the Sue and Labor Clause in the applicable policy can, however, make a great deal of difference. For example, in *St. Margaret's Trust, Ltd. v. Navigators and General Ins. Co., Ltd.*,[20] the clause included " . . . all charges thereof including salvage charges, the cost of towing or removing the vessel to a place of safety so necessarily incurred, shall form part of the claim . . . ." The vessel lay over on her side on a mud bank at low tide and then filled up on the flood tide. The local port authority required the owner to raise her and tow her to a place of safety. This was

---

19. *N.V. Bureau Wijsmuller v. Tojo Maru (Owners)*, [1971] 1 Lloyd's Rep. 341, H.L.

20. (1949) 82 Ll.L.Rep. 752, Q.B.D. See, also, *Johnston v. New South Wales Marine Assur. Co.*, (1880) 14 S.A.L.R. 157 (Aus.), where a steamer insured under a policy containing a suing and laboring clause went ashore, was in considerable danger, and was only rescued by means of the jettison of a portion of the cargo and by aid of towage services of another steamer of the plaintiffs. It was held that the assured was entitled to recover the steamer's proportion of the towage expenses, but, as general average was not covered by the policy, there was no recovery for the loss sustained through jettison.

done and expenses were thereby incurred. It was held that the expense was recoverable under the Sue and Labor Clause quoted above. So, too, expenses incurred in indemnifying a tug owner for damage to his tug while engaged under U. K. Standard Towage Conditions were held to be general average expenditures for which the underwriters were liable. Section 78(2) excluding salvage charges was not applicable as the expenses were incurred pursuant to the contract.[21]

In *Uzielli v. Boston Marine Ins. Co.*,[22] a ship was insured by the original underwriter who, in turn, reinsured with the second underwriter who, in turn, reinsured with a third underwriter. The ship became a constructive total loss. The original underwriter settled with the assured and, at great expense, refloated the ship and sold her, his expenses amounting to 112 percent on the insured value. It was held that recovery by the first reinsurer from the second reinsurer could not exceed the face amount of the policy because the original underwriter was not the "factor, servant or assign" of the first reinsurer within the meaning of the Sue and Labor Clause.

Compare, however, *Western Assur. Co. of Toronto v. Poole*,[23] where the policy of reinsurance for constructive total loss or actual total loss excluded liability for salvage charges, but contained the usual suing and laboring clause. The owners, instead of abandoning when the vessel went aground (because the real repaired value of the vessel was in excess of the costs of salvage and repair), refloated the vessel and repaired it. They then claimed against the original underwriter who paid 107 percent of their proportion of the agreed value of the vessel. The original underwriter then claimed against the reinsurer. The court held that there being no abandonment there was no liability upon the original underwriter to pay as for a constructive total loss and the mere fact that the original underwriter had paid, in respect of a partial loss and suing and laboring charges combined upwards of 100 percent, did not entitle the original underwriter to recover as for a constructive total loss. The court further held that the clause excluding claims for salvage charges excluded the reinsurer's obligation to contribute to the sueing and laboring charges notwithstanding the omission to delete the printed clause imposing that obligation.

It must be emphasized, however, that merely because salvage charges and general average expenditures are not recoverable under the Sue and Labor Clause does not mean, of course, that they are not recoverable at all. This is so because the usual hull form also includes separate coverage for such losses. For example, the relevant portion of the AIH (1977) form reads:

21. *Australian Coastal Shipping Comm. v. Green*, (1971) 1 All E.R. 353, C.A.
22. (1884) 54 L.J.Q.B. 142, 5 Asp. M.L.C. 405, C.A.
23. (1903) 1 K.B. 376, 9 Asp. M.L.C. 390.

General Average and Salvage shall be payable as provided in the contract of affreightment, or failing such provision or there be no contract of affreightment, payable at the Assured's election either in accordance with York-Antwerp Rules 1950 or 1974 or with the Laws and Usages of the Port of San Francisco. Provided always that when an adjustment according to the laws and usages of the port of destination is properly demanded by the owners of the cargo, General Average shall be paid accordingly.

Thus, to recapitulate, salvage services rendered or expenses incurred may be recoverable as a part of suing and laboring expenses if such services were rendered under a contract between the assured and the salvor—as distinguished from "pure" or independent salvage—because the contract salvor is a "servant or assign" of the assured. Or, if rendered by an independent salvor, then the expenses may be recovered under the General Average and Salvage Clause quoted above.

The distinction between the term "salvage charges" as used in a hull policy and the loose, generic term "salvage charges" frequently used to describe the expense of salvage in the common vernacular therefore must be kept in mind. The following example may assist in clarifying the distinction:

A vessel in ballast goes aground. The owners hire a tug to pull it off. This is "contract salvage" and the expense falls under the Sue and Labor Clause because the tug owner was a servant of the assured.[24]

Same vessel but this time it is loaded with cargo. There the towage expense is a general average expense and is proportioned between vessel and cargo.

Same vessel but on this occasion no contract is entered into and the tug merely appears and engages in "pure" salvage efforts. The salvage award would fall in the category of "salvage charges" as that term is used in the General Average and Salvage Clause of the policy.

Unfortunately, the American courts have not always kept this distinction in mind and the term "salvage charges" may be—and often is—used interchangeably to refer to contract salvage, services rendered with respect to ship and cargo which are really general average expenses, and "pure" maritime salvage.[25]

24. In practice, since American law permits general average when a vessel is in ballast (while English law does not) tug hire in the first example may be claimed either as general average or under the Sue and Labor Clause, whichever is more beneficial to the assured. This is an instance where American law differs significantly from English law. See Chapter XVII, "General Average," *supra*. Of course, American law does not have the equivalent of Sec. 78(2) of the Marine Insurance Act, 1906, and developed more along the lines of the Continental system than the English system.

25. Compare *Pacific Salvage Co. v. The Feltre*, 1939 AMC 1173 (D., Ore.); *The Silent Friend*, 1943 AMC 94 (E.D.N.Y.); *MSTS Shipping Contracts—Stranding—Salvage—General*

Distinction between Towage Contracts and Salvage Contracts

Special mention must be made of the distinction between towage contracts and salvage contracts. Towage charges are, of course, frequently charges which, depending upon the circumstances, may fall within the definition of "particular charges"—and thus under the Sue and Labor Clause—or as general average expenses. A salvage service, on the other hand, must be voluntary in the sense of being solely attributable neither to a pre-existing contractual or official duty owed to the owners of the salved property. But, a towage contract, in certain circumstances, may be converted into a salvage service. For example, if the ship being towed is in imminent danger of loss, not contemplated by the parties when the towage contract was made, the contract may become converted into a salvage contract by operation of law. The determination of the existence of such peril necessary to cause such a conversion is one of fact.[26]

For example, in *Waterman S.S. Co. v. Shipowners & Merchants Towboat Co., Ltd.,*[27] a dead ship in tow broke adrift in a gale. The tug towing her and others got a new hawser aboard and resumed the tow. The court held that the towing tugs were entitled to salvage, stating in part:

> . . . Nevertheless the question whether the circumstances of a particular case are such as to turn towage into salvage is often one of much difficulty. The question, however, is essentially one of fact. The Court saw and heard the witnesses. It found that through the parting of the hawser, in a full gale, the *Herald* went adrift and into a position of grave peril solely by reason of the violence of the storm; that it was

Average (Comp.Gen., U.S.), 1958 AMC 699; *Weston, Doson & Co. v. Barge Rex*, 1959 AMC 1221 (S.D.N.Y.).

26. *Waterman S.S. Co. v. Shipowners & Merchants Towboat Co., Ltd.*, 199 F.2d 600, 1953 AMC 125 (9th Cir.). See, also, *Sinclair v. Cooper*, 108 U.S. 352 (1883); *The Josephus*, 116 F. 124 (R.I., 1902); *The Homely*, F.Cas. No. 6,661 (E.D.N.Y., 1876); *The City of Haverhill*, 66 F. 159 (S.D.N.Y., 1895); *Dumper No. 8*, 129 F. 98 (2d Cir., 1904); *Joseph F. Clinton*, 250 F. 977 (2d Cir., 1918); *Ford Motor Co. v. Manhattan Lighterage Corp.*, 97 F.2d 577, 1938 AMC 879; *The Santa Rita*, 281 F. 61 (5th Cir.); *Lafayette Shipping Corp. v. Richards*, 289 F. 27 (5th Cir., 1924); *Hendry Corp. v. Aircraft Rescue Vessels*, 113 F.Supp. 198, 1953 AMC 2115 (E.D., La.); *Santa Ana*, 107 F. 527 (W.D.,Wash., 1901); *Hme v. J.D. Spreckels & Bros.*, 115 F. 51 (9th Cir., 1902); *The Flottbek*, 118 F. 955 (9th Cir., 1902); *Kovell v. Portland Tug & Barge Co.*, 171 F.2d 748, 1948 AMC 877 (9th Cir.). For comparable English cases enunciating the same rule, see *The Minnehaha*, (1861) 15 Moo. P.C.C. 133; *The White Star*, L.R. 1 A. & E. 68; *The Pericles*, 167 E.R. 308 (1863); *The Ford*burn, (1896) 74 L.T. 200; *The Albion*, (1861) 167 E.R. 121; *The Galatea*, (1858) 32 L.T.O.S. 49; *The Saratoga*, (1861) 167 E.R. 603; *The Leon Blum*, (1915) P. 290, C.A.; *The Glenmorven*, (1913) P. 141; *The J.C. Potter*, (1870) 23 L.T. 603; *Akerblom v. Price*, (1881) 7 Q.B.D. 129; *The Homewood*, (1928) 31 Ll.L.Rep. 336; *Five Steel Barges*, (1890) 15 P. 142; *The Kingalock*, (1854) 164 E.R. 153. See, also, *Shipman v. Morrell*, (1920) 19 O.W.N. 132 (C.A.,Can.); *Fenwick v. The Glencairn*, (1898) 15 W.N. (N.S.W.) 166; *The North Goodwin No. 16*, [1980] 1 Lloyd's Rep. 71; *Texaco Southampton v. Burley*, 1983 AMC 524 (N.S.W. Ct. App., Aus.).

27. 199 F.2d 600, 1953 AMC 125 (9th Cir.).

rescued therefrom only through the efforts of the *Sea Fox* and other craft; and that the *Sea Fox* incurred risks and performed services beyond the scope of her towage contract. Contrary to the claim of appellant, it found that the danger to the tow was not occasioned or contributed to by the negligence of the tug. These findings support the award, and we are of the opinion that they are not clearly erroneous, or erroneous at all, for that matter.

In *The Saratoga*,[28] Dr. Lushington said:

The law I have laid down in more than one instance upon this point is that if, in the performance of a contract of towage, an unforeseen and extraordinary peril arise to the vessel towed, the steamer is not at liberty to abandon the vessel but is bound to render to her the necessary assistance; and thereupon is entitled to salvage reward. I am of the opinion that these rights and obligations incident to a contract of towage are implied by law, and that the law thereby secures equity to both parties and the true interest of the owners of ships. A similar law holds with respect to a pilot. On certain emergencies occurring which require extraordinary service, he is bound to stay by the ship, but becomes entitled to salvage remuneration, and not a mere pilotage fee.

A further case is *Five Steel Barges*,[29] in which Sir James Hannen said:

From the examination I have given to the decisions in point, it appears to me that it is not necessary, in order to become entitled to salvage, that the supervening danger should be of such a character as to actually put an end to the towage contract. It is sufficient if the services rendered are beyond what can be reasonably supposed to have been contemplated by the parties entering into such a contract.

Of course, a tug is obligated not to abandon her tow when it is endangered until all reasonable efforts to save her have been exhausted, but for her exertions in performing duties not within the scope of the original engagement and incurring risk, she is entitled to salvage remuneration.[30]

The rule is clear. The impact of the negligence of the towing tug upon its right to a salvage award for services subsequently rendered is determinative. If the tug is responsible for the peril in which the tow finds itself, the tug is not entitled to a salvage award.[31]

---

28. (1861) 167 E.R. 603.

29. (1890) 15 P. 142, 6 Asp. M.L.C. 580.

30. See cases cited, *supra*, n. 26. See, also, *Franklin Sears v. American Producer, et al*, 1972 AMC 1647 (N.D.,Cal.).

31. *The Mohican*, 1934 AMC 112 (S.D.N.Y.); *The Homely*, F.Cas. No. 6,661 (E.D.N.Y., 1876); *Hendry Corp. v. Aircraft Rescue Vessels*, 113 F.Supp. 198, 1953 AMC 2115 (E.D.,La.); *The Minnehaha*, (1861) 15 Moo. P.C.C. 133; *The Robert Dixon*, (1879) 5 P. 54, 4 Asp. M.L.C. 246, C.A.; *The Altair*, (1897) P. 105, 8 Asp. M.L.C. 224.

As L. J. Brett said in *The Robert Dixon:*[32]

> The plaintiffs being under a towage contract, bring this action, in which they assert that the towage service was altered into salvage; and . . . it lies on them to show that the change occurred without any want of skill on their part but by mere accident over which they had no control. The burden of proof on both the affirmative and negative issues is on the plaintiffs, that is, both that there was an inevitable accident beyond their control and that they showed no want of skill.

Salvage in General

The Supreme Court in *The Blackwall*[33] defined salvage as follows:

> Salvage is the compensation allowed persons by whose assistance a ship or her cargo have been saved, in whole or in part, from impending peril on the sea, or in recovering such property from actual loss, as in case of shipwreck, derelict, or recapture.

In the *Petition of Sun Oil Co.,*[34] the court pointed out that in its simplest form it can be described as a service voluntarily rendered in relieving property from an impending peril at sea by those having no obligation to do so.[35]

In *The Thetis,*[36] it was described as the service which those who recover property from loss or danger at sea render to the owners with the responsibility of making restitution and with a lien for their reward. In *Five Steel Barges,*[37] Sir James Hannen noted that the right to salvage may arise out of an actual contract but it does not necessarily do so; it is a legal liability arising out of the fact that property has been saved, that the owner of the property who has had the benefit of it shall make remuneration to those who have conferred the benefit upon him, notwithstanding that he has not entered into any contract on the subject.[38]

---

32. (1879) 5 P. 54, 4 Asp. M.L.C. 246, C.A.
33. 77 U.S. 1, 19 L.ed. 870 (1869).
34. 474 F.2d 1048, 1973 AMC 572 (2d Cir.).
35. See, also, *Mayflower v. The Sabine,* 101 U.S. 384 (1879); *Cope v. Vallette Dry Dock Co.,* 119 U.S. 625 (1886); *Simmons v. S.S. Jefferson,* 215 U.S. 130 (1909).
36. (1833) 166 E.R. 312.
37. (1890) 15 P. 142, 6 Asp. M.L.C. 580.
38. See, also, *The Neptune,* (1824) 1 Hagg. 227, 166 E.R. 81; *Gurney v. Mackay,* (1875) 37 U.C.Q.B. 324 (Can., C.A.); *The Keta v. The Irene M.,* [1959] Ex. C.R. 372, [1959] R.L. 280 (Can.); *The Marjorie Maude (Owners, Master and Crew) v. National Mortgage and Agency Co. of N.Z., Ltd. (The Venture),* [1959] N.Z.L.R. 969 (N.Z.).

From the foregoing definitions are deduced certain essentials. The Supreme Court in *New York Protection Co. v. The Schooner Clara*,[39] stated these essentials as follows:

> The elements necessary to constitute a valid salvage claim are as follows: (1) A marine peril to the property to be rescued. (2) Voluntary service not owed to the property as a matter of duty. (3) Success in saving the property or some portion of it from impending peril.

The right of a salvor to be rewarded for his salvage efforts under maritime law is wholly independent of marine insurance, the salvor being entitled to his reward whether or not the property is insured.

Marine Peril

The test of a marine peril, one of the essential elements in a salvage service, is not that the peril be immediate or absolute. Rather, the test is

For example, in *Fort Myers Shell and Dredging Co. v. Barge NBC 512*,[41] during a tow, the towing hawser parted and both barges in tow ran aground farther up the coast. The tug towing the barges also stranded. Two other tugs went to the rescue and after considerable effort succeeded in pulling off the barges. The court observed that the barges were stranded, that there were pilings nearby, and that sudden storms arise in the Gulf of Mexico at all times of the year.

In *DeAldaniz v. Skogland & Sons*,[42] the vessel was aground in shallow water on the beach, exposed to wind and waves in the hurricane season. In *Beach Salvage Corp. of Florida v. The Captain Tom et al*,[43] the vessel being towed broke loose during a violent storm. In *Angie & Florence*,[44] there was a breakdown of equipment. In this connection, almost any mechanical difficulty which disables a vessel results in imperiling it to some degree.

---

39. 90 U.S. 1 (1874).

40. *Fort Myers Shell and Dredging Co. v. Barge NBC 512*, 404 F.2d 137, 1969 AMC 186 (5th Cir.). In *The Freedom*, 1932 AMC 933 (S.D.N.Y.), the court stated in essence that it was not necessary that there be danger immediately impending, but if the vessel is stranded, that is, subject to the potential danger of damage or destruction, she may well be the subject of salvage services. To the same effect, see *The Phantom*, (1866) L.R. 1 A. & E. 58; *The Charlotte*, (1848) 3 Wm. Rob. 68; *The Strathnaver*, (1875) 1 A.C. 58, P.C.; *The Glaucus*, (1948) 81 Ll.L.Rep. 262; *The Troilus*, [1951] A.C. 820; *The Suevic*, [1908] P. 154 (life salvage); *Southern Cross Fisheries Ltd. v. New Zealand Fisheries Ltd. (The Newfish I)*, [1970] N.Z.L.R. 873; *Alexander v. The Gambier Isle*, [1948] Ex. C.R. 414 (Can.); *Wanganui Meat Freezing Co. Ltd. v. Hatrick*, (1911) 13 G.L.R. 617 (N.Z.); *Societe Maritime Caledonienne v. The Cythera*, [1965] 2 Lloyd's Rep. 454.

41. 404 F.2d 137, 1969 AMC 186 (5th Cir.).

42. 17 F.2d 873 (5th Cir.).

43. 201 F.Supp. 479, 1961 AMC 2244 (D., Fla.).

44. 77 F.Supp. 404 (D., Mass., 1948).

Often the salvage of the disabled vessel consists only of towing it to a port of refuge.[45]

In *The Glaucus*,[46] a ship's boilers became inoperative. The ship was towed to Aden but repairs could not be effected there. Another ship towed the vessel to Suez where repairs were effected. The court held that the fact that at all material times the vessel was a damaged ship and incapable of maneuvering under her own power put her in some degree of danger, and the second tow to Suez was held to be salvage.

In *The Troilus*,[47] the vessel lost her propeller in the Indian Ocean and she was towed to Aden. The lack of repair facilities at Aden necessitated a further tow to the United Kingdom. Although the ship and its cargo were in physical safety at Aden, both would deteriorate if not removed. The House of Lords held the service to be salvage and salvage not necessarily converted into towage merely because on the voyage the vessel was towed past ports at which she could lie in safety.[48]

Voluntary Service Not Owed as a Matter of Duty

It is necessary to show, in a proper salvage case, that the salvage service, in the absence of a contract, was voluntary and that the salvor owed no duty to the object in distress.

45. See, for example, *Lancaster v. Smith*, 330 F.Supp. 65, 1971 AMC 2560 (S.D.,Ala.) (shrimp boat developed engine trouble, necessitating a tow); *Sears v. American Producer*, 1972 AMC 1647 (N.D.,Cal.) (tug's crewmembers held entitled to salvage even though the tug owner only billed the distressed vessel for towage services); *Basic Boats v. U.S.*, 352 F.Supp. 44, 1973 AMC 522 (E.D.,Va.) (immediacy of harm not essential to salvage; tow of disabled yacht, not in immediate danger, by a U.S. Navy destroyer held to be salvage and not towage); *National Defender*, 298 F.Supp. 631, 1969 AMC 1219 (S.D.N.Y.) (stranded vessel is no immediate danger but helpless; salvage awarded); *Seaman v. Tank Barge OC601*, 325 F.Supp. 1206, 1972 AMC 2408 (S.D.,Ala.) (successful towage of a tank barge broken loose from its moorings by a hurricane and found afloat, unmanned, unlighted, and without cargo held to be salvage); *Treasure Salvors v. Atocha*, 569 F.2d 330, 1978 AMC 1404 (5th Cir.) (action of the elements in dispersing a wreck of a Spanish galleon sunk 350 years before satisfied the "marine peril" requirement of the law of salvage); *The Ella Constance*, (1864) 33 L.J.P.M. & A. 189 (want of fuel); *The Aglaia*, (1888) 13 P.D. 160 (crew suffering from frostbite).

46. (1948) 81 Ll.L.Rep. 262.

47. [1951] A.C. 58, P.C.

48. Other representative cases are: *Societe Maritime Caledonienne v. The Cythera*, [1965] 2 Lloyd's Rep. 454 (danger involved was that the ship might be stolen); *Australian United Steam Navigation Co., Ltd. v. The William E. Burnham*, (1921) 21 S.R. (N.S.W.) 224, 38 W.N. 69 (Aus.) (danger arising from the incapacity of the crew); *Brown v. The Darnholme*, (1922) 23 S.R. (N.S.W.) 195, 40 W.N. 15 (Aus.); *The Keta v. The Irena M*, [1959] Ex.C.R. 372, [1959] R.L. 280 (Can.); *Canadian Pacific Nav. Co. v. The C.F. Sargent*, (1893) 3 B.C.R. 5 (Can.); *The John Ena*, [1918] N.Z.L.R. 538, [1918] G.L.R. 326 (C.A); *Southern Cross Fisheries Ltd. v. New Zealand Fisheries Ltd (The Newfish I)*, [1970] N.Z.L.R. 873 (N.Z.). Compare, however, *Tyne Tugs Ltd. and Others v. Aldora (Owners)*, [1975] 1 Lloyd's Rep. 617, where the vessel went aground just prior to being met by a pilot and tugs already engaged to take her into port. It was held that the salvage services thereupon rendered by the pilot and the tugs ended when the danger had ceased and the parties had resumed their originally contracted roles.

In *Hobart v. Drogan*,[49] the court, after quoting from *The Neptune, supra*, to the effect that a person who without any particular relation to a ship in distress proffers useful services and gives those services as a voluntary adventurer, held that one who owed a duty to the object of salvage could not claim a salvage award. The court continued:

> And it must be admitted that, however harsh the rule may seem to be in its actual application to particular cases, it is well founded in public policy . . . .

In a subsequent case,[50] the court stated, in part:

> Suitors, in order to support such claim [to salvage] must be prepared to show that . . . the service was voluntary and that it was not rendered in pursuance of any duty owed to the owner or to the property.

Thus, Coast Guard personnel engaged in providing services to vessels in distress *ordinarily* cannot claim salvage,[51] nor can Navy personnel,[52] nor municipal firemen,[53] nor other public officials,[54] pilots,[55] master and

---

49. 35 U.S. 107 (1836).

50. *New York Harbor Protection Co. v. Schooner Clara*, 90 U.S. 1 (1874).

51. *U. S. v. Central Wharf Towboat Co.*, 3 F.2d 250, 1925 AMC 318 (1st Cir.); *The Kanawha*, 254 F. 762 (2d Cir., 1918). See, however, *The Amoco Virginia*, 417 F.2d 164, 1969 AMC 1761 (5th Cir.), where the United States was granted a salvage award commensurate with the expenses incurred by the air force, navy, and commercial sources in putting out a fire on a vessel in harbor. Apparently, personnel of the British coast guard may receive salvage remuneration where they undertake duties beyond the scope of their official and statutory duties. Admiralty Instructions, 1904, Art. 1227. Where the U. S. Coast Guard participates in a salvage operation, its services must be taken into consideration if other salvors are also involved in order to prevent the other salvors from obtaining a windfall. *Beach Salvage Corp. v. The Captain Tom*, 201 F.Supp. 479, 1961 AMC 2244.

52. Naval personnel are entitled to salvage awards where they render services beyond the scope of their normal and official duties. *The Odenwald*, 168 F.2d 47, 1948 AMC 888 (1st Cir.); *Tampa Tugs v. Sandanger*, 242 F.Supp. 576, 1965 AMC 1771 (S.D.Cal.). Naval personnel in the United Kingdom may be awarded salvage with permission of the Admiralty. Sec. 557, Merchant Shipping Act. See, also, *Page v. Admiralty Commissioners*, [1921] A.C. 137.

53. *Firemen's Charitable Ass'n v. Ross*, 60 F. 456 (5th Cir., 1893); *Davey v. The Mary Frost*, F.Cas. No. 3592 (5th Cir., 1876). Compare, however, *Fire Brigades Board v. Elderslie S.S. Co.*, (1889) 15 W.N. (N.S.W.) 320 (Aus.). Where the services are beyond the scope of their normal duties, firemen may claim salvage awards. *The Huntsville*, F.Cas. No. 6916 (D., S.C., 1890); *Bowers v. The European*, 44 F. 484 (D.,Fla., 1890); *The Wissoe*, 230 F. 318 (D., Mass., 1915).

54. Only where services rendered are beyond the scope of their normal duties may other public officials claim salvage. *The Corcrest*, (1946) 80 Ll.L.Rep. 78 (harbor master and staff); *The Mars and Other Barges*, (1948) 81 Ll.L.Rep. 452 (Port of London Authority employees); *The Citos*, (1925) 22 Ll.L.Rep. 275 (lighthouse authority employees); *The Ocean Hound*, (1950) 84 Ll.L.Rep. 5 (lifeboat crews); *The Afton*, (1873) Y.A.D. 136 (Can.) (lighthouse keeper); *Stuart v. The Columbia River*, (1921) 21 S.R. (N.S.W.) 674, 38 W.N. 185 (Aus.) (master, officers, and crew of state government steam trawler); *The Oklawaha*, 348 F.2d 627, 1966 AMC 153 (2d Cir.) (marine pilot employed by air force in Tripoli). Compare, however, *Owens v. The Alexa*, (1914) 14 S.R. (N.S.W.) 389, 31 W.N. 154 (Aus.), and *The Gregerso*, [1971] 1 All E.R. 961.

55. Only when the services of pilots are rendered by them clearly beyond the scope of their normal duties are they entitled to salvage awards. *Hobart v. Drogan*, 35 U.S. 108 (1836); *The Clarita and The Clara*, 90 U.S. 1 (1874).

crew,[56] passengers,[57] and ships' agents.[58]

Success as an Element of Salvage

The third element of salvage necessary is a successful saving of the property, in whole or in part. Unless something is saved, there is nothing that can be claimed by way of a salvage award. As the Supreme Court stated in *The Blackwall, supra:*

> Success is essential to the claim [of salvage]; as if the property is not saved, or if it perished, or in case of capture if it is not retaken, no compensation can be allowed.

The principle was reiterated in *Mayflower v. The Sabine,*[59] in which the court stated:

> Salvors who volunteer go out at their own risk for the chance of earning reward, and if not successful they are entitled to nothing, the rule being that it is success that gives them a title to salvage remuneration.[60]

However, there is an exception to the general rule which may be expressed as follows: Where a service has been rendered at the request of the persons in charge of a vessel in circumstances in which a promise to pay can be implied, a salvage award is payable for the service even though such service may not have contributed to the eventual safety and preservation of the vessel.[61]

56. A termination or dissolution of the seamen's contract of service is a condition precedent to claiming salvage. This may occur by the act of the master in discharging them or a bona fide abandonment with the master's authority. See *The Warrior*, (1862) Lush. 476; *The Georgiana*, 245 F. 321 (1st Cir., 1917); *Mason v. Blaireau*, 6 U.S. 240 (1840). See, also, with respect to abandonment, *The Le Jonet*, (1872) 27 L.T. 387, 1 Asp. M.L.C. 438; *The Victoria*, 64 F.Supp. 370, 1945 AMC 1199 (S.D.N.Y.), modified and *aff'd* 172 F.2d 434 (2d Cir.); *Smith v. Union Oil*, 1967 AMC 1097 (W.D.Wash.). Cf., *Mesner v. Suffolk Bank*, F.Cas. No. 9493 (D.,Mass., 1838); *Drevas v. U.S.*, 58 F.Supp. 1008, 1945 AMC 254 (D.,Md.,1945); *Lavall v. U.S.*, 92 F.Supp. 532, 1950 AMC 1016 (S.D.N.Y.).

57. Passengers rendering extraordinary services are entitled to salvage awards. *Newman v. Walters*, (1804) 3 Bos. & P. 612; *The Connemara*, 108 U.S. 352 (1882); *Towle v. The Great Eastern*, F.Cas. No. 14,110 (S.D.N.Y., 1864), (1864) 2 M.L.C. 148. Passengers aboard the salving vessel who assist are also entitled to share in the award. *The Calcium*, 218 F. 267 (D.,Wash., 1914).

58. Where the services are extraordinary and beyond the scope of normal duties, ships' agents may claim salvage. *Lago Oil & Transport Co., Ltd. v. U.S.*, 218 F.2d 631, 1955 AMC 697 (2d Cir.); *The Happy Return*, (1828) 2 Hagg. 198; *The Kate B. Jones*, [1892] P. 366.

59. 101 U.S. 384 (1879).

60. See, to the same effect, *The Renpor*, (1883) 8 P.D. 115 (C.A.); *The Melanie (Owners) v. The San Onofre (Owners)*, [1925] A.C. 246. Other representative cases are: *Squires v. Ionian Leader*, 100 F.Supp. 829, 1952 AMC 161; *St. Paul Marine v. Cerro Sales*, 505 F.2d 1115, 1975 AMC 503 (9th Cir.); *Dye v. U.S.*, 1977 AMC 599 (N.D.,Cal.); *The Camellia*, (1884) 9 P.D. 27; *The Kangaroo*, [1918] P. 327.

61. *Manchester Liners Ltd. v. The Scotia Trader*, [1971] F.C. 14 (Can.); *The Loch Tulla*, (1950) 84 Ll.L.Rep. 62. Compare *St. Paul Marine v. Cerro Sales, supra*, n. 60.

Subjects of Salvage

Salvage only applies to the saving of ships, their equipment, and cargo (including flotsam, jetsam, and lagan),[62] but legislation may extend the right to embrace other objects such as aircraft.[63]

Amount of the Award

There is no fixed rule by which the amount of the salvage award may be calculated. Each case is decided on its own merits.

The Supreme Court, in *The Blackwall, supra,* laid down the following criteria when it stated:

> Courts of admiralty usually consider the following circumstances as the main ingredients in determining the amount of the award to be decreed for a salvage service: (1) The labor expended by the salvors rendering the salvage service. (2) The promptitude, skill, and energy displayed in rendering the service and saving the property. (3) The value of the property employed by the salvors rendering the service and the danger to which such property was exposed. (4) The risk incurred by the salvors in securing the property from the impending peril. (5) The value of the property saved. (6) The degree of danger from which the property was rescued.[64]

The following cases are illustrative of some of the salvage awards given: *Esso Greensboro (Lim. Procs.);*[65] *Devine v. United Transportation Co.;*[66] *Barbara Lee—Invincible;*[67] *St. Paul Marine v. Cerro Sales;*[68] *The Glengyle;*[69]

62. *Cope v. Vallette Dry Dock Co.,* 119 U.S. 625 (1886); *Gas Float Whitton No. 2,* (1897) A.C. 337, 8 Asp. M.L.C. 272. But see *Flying Boat N-31235 (Salvage),* 1957 AMC 1957 (S.D., Cal.), where salvage and life salvage were awarded in the saving of a flying boat.

63. Sec. 51, Civil Aviation Act 1949, and Aircraft (Wreck and Salvage) Order 1938. Also, see *Watson v. R.C.A. Victor Co., Inc.,* (1934) 50 Ll.L.Rep. 77.

64. See, also, *The Lamington,* 86 F. 675 (2d Cir., 1898); *The Industry,* (1835) 3 Hagg. 203; *Kennedy on Civil Salvage,* (4th Ed.), p. 174.

65. 122 F.Supp. 133, 1954 AMC 734 (S.D.,Tex.) ($1,000,000 vessel which was a derelict on fire after a disastrous collision towed to port by a vessel valued at $2,000,000; high order of salvage to each crewman, officers, and mates).

66. 1957 AMC 175 (W.D.,Wash.) (barge valued at $330,000 with benzol cargo valued at $153,000 stranded in breakers when towline broke. Professional salvage vessel valued at $1,000,000 towed barge out to safety under great explosion dangers with rapid success. Held, high order of salvage and award given of $82,533 for hull and $38,850 for cargo).

67. 299 F.Supp. 241, 1964 AMC 2314 (D.,Ore.) (small fishing vessel went to the rescue of a coast guard vessel and attempted to tow her into safety in heavy weather; salving vessel finally sank but held on long enough to enable other vessels to complete the rescue. Substantial award because of the heroic efforts by a small vessel in dangerous weather).

68. 505 F.2d 1115, 1975 AMC 503 (9th Cir.) (salvage award of $200,000 for saving cargo worth $1,850,000; after saving 22 lives, a boarding party from the salving vessel boarded the salved vessel in danger of sinking, extinguished fires, closed port holes and doors, and began towing until the towline broke. The salving vessel with the permission of the coast guard then left the scene).

69. [1898] P. 97, [1898] A.C. 519 (exceptional services rendered to a vessel in imminent

The Queen Elizabeth;[70] *The Lyrma (No. 1);*[71] *The Rilland;*[72] *The Regina;*[73] *Pacific Salvage Ltd. v. C.P.R.;*[74] *Fishery Products Ltd. v. The Claudette V.;*[75] *The Ship Honolulu Maru;*[76] *N.Z. Refrigeratinq Co., Ltd. v. The Inga.*[77]

Professional Salvors

While, generally speaking, crews of professional salvage vessels are debarred from a salvage award, not because a salvage contract may not exist, but because in performing salvage services they are merely doing their duty,[78] professional salvors themselves are generally given handsome awards. This is so because such salvors maintain at considerable expense specially equipped salvage vessels in a state of readiness at all times in order to assist vessels in distress. As a matter of public policy encouragement should be given to them.[79]

Apportionment of the Award

Apportionment of an award usually comes before the courts either by a request during the course of, or shortly after, the close of an ordinary salvage action by those interested in the award, or, frequently by a sepa-

---

peril of sinking by two professional salvor tugs; award of £19,000 on a value of £76,596).

70. (1949) 82 Ll.L.Rep. 803 (vessel grounded and was gotten off by some 12 tugs; salved value of vessel was £5,983,000 and of cargo £225,000; award to the tugs of £43,500).

71. [1978] 2 Lloyd's Rep. 27 (salving tug successfully salvaged vessel which had been abandoned and was drifting, and after much difficulty brought her to safety. Subsequently, a Lloyd's agreement was signed. Value of vessel was £55,000; salvage award of 40 percent thereof or £22,000).

72. [1979] 1 Lloyd's Rep. 455 (trawler successfully salved tug and barge which had gone aground; in assessing the award, the state of the weather, degree of damage and danger to the salved vessel and her tow, the risk and peril of the salving vessel, the time employed, and the value of the property were taken into account, resulting in an award of £21,000).

73. (1871) Y.A.D. 107 (Can.) (high order salvage for very meritorius services; award of $2,500 on salved value of only $7,105).

74. [1952] Ex. C.R. 410 (Can.) (professional salvor awarded $27,500 for salving vessel and cargo worth $215,000; receipt of a subsidy from the Canadian government for maintaining the salvage vessel held not to be a factor to be taken into account in assessing the award).

75. [1960] 44 M.P.R. 391 (Nfld., Can.) (salvage of an abandoned vessel and cargo worth $56,000; award of 50 percent; matters considered in assessing the award were: fact that vessel was abandoned and a hopeless derelict, risk to salving ship, risk to personnel, damage to gear, loss of time, and availability of other help).

76. (1924) 24 S.R. (N.S.W.) 309, 41 W.N. 71 (Aus.) (salved vessel worth £87,000 and salving vessel £18,000; award of £6,000; high order of salvage calling for substantial award; principles of assessment and apportionment discussed).

77. [1918] G.L.R. 442 (N.Z.) (salved vessel stranded and was brought safely into port; salved values £21,500; salvage award of £900).

78. See *The Ocklawaha,* 348 F.2d 627, 1966 AMC 153 (2d Cir.); *The Arakan,* 283 F. 861 (D.,Cal., 1922); *The William Tell,* [1892] P. 337.

79. *Devine v. United Transportation Co.,* 1957 AMC 175 (W.D.,Wash.); *B.V. Bureau Wijsmuller v. U.S.,* 707 F.2d 1471, 1983 AMC 1471 (2d Cir.)

rate proceeding (usually by seamen dissatisfied with the award or claiming a portion of the award made to the salving vessel's owners).

The award is usually given in one amount to cover all the salved property. That amount must then be apportioned among those entitled to it.
The authority to apportion has always been inherent in the jurisdiction of
the admiralty courts.

The crews of salving vessels (except possibly the crews of professional
salving vessels) are not bound by any salvage agreement made between
the owner of the salving vessel and the salved vessel unless they have
ratified or assented to it.[80] An agreement between the salvor and the
owner of the salved vessel to arbitrate the salvage in England does not
bind the crew of the salving vessel to that forum if they are not parties to
it.[81] The rule is well stated in *Bergher v. General Petroleum Co.*,[82] where the
court stated:

> If the amount received by him [the owner of the salving vessel] un-
> der the agreement is a reasonable compensation for the full salvage
> service, including the services of the crew, he may be compelled to
> distribute to the crew their proportion of such amount. The crew,
> however, are not bound to look to him for their reward, but may look
> to the salved vessel and its owners, for neither the agreement of the
> owners nor the payment of the money is binding on them without
> their assent thereto. If it were, the owners would always have it in their
> power to defeat the rights of the crew by fixing the amount to be paid
> at such a trifling sum as to make it impossible for the crew to receive
> any commensurate reward even if the whole sum agreed upon were
> distributed among them.

The proportionate division of the award depends upon the circumstances of the case.[83] The award to the crew is usually divided according to
the ratings of the crew, with the master and senior officers usually receiving a larger percentage than the seamen.[84]

Forfeiture or Reduction of Award due To Wrongful Act, Misconduct, or Negligence of Salvors

One may ordinarily be entitled to an award of salvage but such an award
will be denied, or may be reduced, where the necessity for salvaging the
property was due to the salvor's own wrongful act, or where there was

---

80. *Squires v. The Ionian Leader*, 100 F.Supp. 829, 1951 AMC 161 (D.,N.J.).
81. *Dalmas v. Strathos*, 84 F.Supp. 828, 1949 AMC 770 (S.D.N.Y.).
82. 242 F. 967 (D.,Cal., 1917).
83. *The Gipsey Queen*, [1895] P. 176.
84. *The Spree*, [1893] P. 147; *Sears v. American Producer*, 1972 AMC 1647 (D.,Cal.).

negligence in the salvage operation, or where other improprieties exist, such as embezzlement or looting.[85]

For example, in *The Bello Corrunes*,[86] the Supreme Court said in part:

> In the case before us, it is not too much to pronounce the claim of those of the crew . . . who libel for salvage to be not only groundless but imprudent; for besides spoliation, smuggling, and the grossest irregularities, it is perfectly clear . . . that they run [sic] the vessel on shore purposely. Their subsequent conduct . . . divests them of all pretentions to compensation.

In *Bureau Wijsmuller v. The Tojo Maru*,[87] the salvors (who had negligently caused considerable damage to the vessel being salved) argued that there was a rule of law that a successful salvor cannot be liable in damages to the owner for the result of any negligence on his part; that such negligence entitles the court, or the arbitrator, to reduce or forfeit the salvage award but it cannot give rise to any claim for damages. The House of Lords rejected this argument *in toto*.

The rule in the United States as to negligence of salvors is the same.[88]

Fortunately for the salvors, however, the burden of proof as to salvors' negligence or misconduct is upon the party asserting such charge, and the evidence must be conclusive, i.e., such as leaves no doubt in the mind of the court.[89]

Right of Lien

A maritime lien accrues for salvage whether performed under contract or as a voluntary, independent service.[90] The lien arises immediately upon the rendition of the services to the vessel and attaches to the vessel, its

---

85. *The Bello Corrunes*, 19 U.S. 152 (1821); *Mason v. Blaireau*, 6 U.S. 240 (1804); *New York Harbor Protection Co. v. The Schooner Clara*, 90 U.S. 1 (1874); *The Cape Race*, 18 F.2d 79, 1927 AMC 628 (2d Cir.); *Serviss v. Ferguson*, 84 F. 202 (2d Cir., 1897); *Basic Boats, Inc. v. U.S.*, 352 F.Supp. 44, 1973 AMC 522 (D.,Va.); *The Trumpeter*, (1947) 80 Ll.L.Rep. 263; *The Delphinula*, (1946) 79 Ll.L.Rep. 611; *The Magdalen*, (1861) 31 L.J. Adm. 24; *Bureau Wijsmuller v. The Tojo Maru*, [1972] A.C. 242, [1971] 1 All E.R. 1110, [1971] 1 Lloyd's 341, H.L.; *Humphrey v. The Florence No. 2*, [1948] Ex. C.R. 426 (Can.).

86. 19 U.S. 152 (1821).

87. [1972] A.C. 242, [1971] 1 All E.R. 1110, [1971] 1 Lloyd's Rep. 341.

88. *Serviss v. Ferguson*, 84 F. 202 (2d Cir., 1897); *The Cape Race*, 18 F.2d 79, 1927 AMC 628 (2d Cir.).

89. *The Boston*, F.Cas. No. 1,673 (1st Cir., 1833); *P. Dougherty Co. v. U.S.*, 207 F.2d 626, 1953 AMC 1541 (3rd Cir.), *cert. den.* 347 U.S. 912; *The Atlas*, (1862) Lush. 518, 6 L.T. 737, 10 W.R. 850, 167 E.R. 235.

90. *The Mayflower v. The Sabine*, 101 U.S. 384 (1879); *William Leishar*, 21 F.2d 862, 1927 AMC 1770 (D., Md.); *The Snow Maiden*, 159 F.Supp. 30, 1958 AMC 272 (D.,Mass.); *Five Steel Barges*, (1890) 15 P.D. 142.

cargo and freight (where freight is saved).[91] The lien attaches to the various interests (ship, cargo and freight) severally but not jointly. Each interest thus contributes toward the salvage in proportion to its value.[92]

There is, however, no right of lien (and therefore no claim of a right *in rem*) against public vessels of a sovereign nation, nor can a sovereign be compelled to arbitrate under a Lloyd's Open Form executed by the commanding officer of one of its vessels.[93] This does not mean, however, that a sovereign nation may not be held liable *in personam* for salvage services rendered to one of its vessels.[94]

Life Salvage

As peculiar as it may sound, the saving of human life (life salvage) without the saving of property concurrently therewith or in reasonable proximity in time, does not entitle the salvor to an award. However, life salvors are entitled to a fair share of the remuneration awarded for salving the property.[95] It is possible, however, that the courts are becoming more lenient on the question.[96]

---

91. *The Mary Anne*, (1865) L.R. L A. & E. 8; *The Charlotte Wylie*, (1846) 2 Wm. Rob. 495; *Murphy v. Ship Suliote*, 5 F. 99 (5th Cir., 1880).

92. *The Charlotte Wylie*, (1846) 2 Wm. Rob. 495; *The Westminister*, (1841) 1 Wm. Rob. 229; *The Elton*, (1891) P. 265; *Richfield Oil Co. v. Georgia Co.*, 1932 AMC 287 (9th Cir.); *The Alaska*, 23 F. 597 (S.D.N.Y., 1885); *Nolan v. A.H. Basse Rederiaktieselskab*, 267 F.2d 584, 1959 AMC 1362 (3rd Cir.).

93. *B.V. Bureau Wijsmuller v. U.S. (As owner of USS Julius A. Furer)*, 1976 AMC 2514 (S.D.N.Y.).

94. *B.V. Bureau Wijsmuller v. U.S.*, 702 F.2d 333, 1983 AMC 1471 (2d Cir.). There, the second circuit affirmed a rather substantial award to a professional salvage company for removing $6.5 million government-owned cargo from a stranded merchant vessel and also held that the district court had discretion to increase the $500,000 award by a 27 percent "equitable uplift" factor to reflect inflationary decline in the value of the dollar during the pendency of the salvor's action.

95. Sec. 729 of the U. S. Salvage Act, 1912, provides that salvors of human life, who have taken part in the services rendered on the occasion of the accident giving rise to salvage, are entitled to a fair share of the vessel, her cargo, and accessories. An independent human life salvor, acting independently of the property salvors, may share in the award to the property salvors if the life salvor's efforts occur at or near the time of the accident. *Lambros v. The Batory*, 215 F.2d 228, 1954 AMC 1789 (2d Cir.); *In re Atlantic Gulf & W. Indies S.S. Lines*, 49 F.2d 263, 1931 AMC 957 (2d Cir.); *The Elkridge*, 30 F.2d 618, 1929 AMC 292 (2d Cir.); *Lykes Bros. S.S. Co. v. The Flying Boat N-31235*, 1957 AMC 1957 (S.D.,Cal.); *In re Esso Shipping Co.*, 122 F. Supp. 133, 1954 AMC 734 (S.D.,Tex.); *St. Paul Marine Transp. Corp. v. Cerro Sales Corp.*, 505 F.2d 1115, 1975 AMC 503 (9th Cir.); *Markakis v. S.S. Volendam*, 486 F. Supp. 1103, 1980 AMC 915 (S.D.N.Y.); *The Annie Lord*, 251 F. 157 (D.,Mass., 1917); *Atlantic Transp. Co. v. U.S.*, 42 F.2d 583, 1930 AMC 726 (Ct.Cl., 1930). Contrast, however, *In re Yamashita-Shinnihon Kisen*, 305 F.Supp. 796, 1969 AMC 2102 (D.,Or.) where it was held that claimants who rendered life and property salvage efforts at the time of the disaster were not entitled to share under a contract of salvage for services rendered subsequently by others in towing a disabled vessel to safety.

96. *Peninsula & Oriental Steam Nav. Co. v. Overseas Oil Carriers, Inc.*, 553 F.2d 830, 1977 AMC 283 (2d Cir.).

Salvage Charges

The liability of underwriters for salvage charges is set forth in Section 65 of the Marine Insurance Act, 1906. That section reads:

(1) Subject to any express provision in the policy, salvage charges incurred in preventing a loss by perils insured against may be recovered as a loss by those perils.

(2) "Salvage charges" means the charges recoverable under maritime law by a salvor independently of contract. They do not include the expenses of services in the nature of salvage rendered by the assured or his agents, or any person employed for hire by them, for the purpose of averting a peril insured against. Such expenses, where properly incurred, may be recovered as particular charges or as a general average loss, according to the circumstances under which they were incurred.

It will be observed that salvage charges incurred in preventing a loss by perils insured against are recoverable without there being any specific provision to this effect in the policy.[97] In fact, the old Lloyd's S.G. policy form does not mention salvage.

The Marine Insurance Act further provides, in Section 76(2):

(2) Where the subject-matter insured is warranted free from particular average, either wholly or under a certain percentage, the insurer is nevertheless liable for salvage charges, and for particular charges and other expenses properly incurred pursuant to the provisions of the suing and labouring clause in order to avert a loss insured against.

This presupposes, of course (as is the case with practically all the provisions of the Act), *that there is no express provision to the contrary in the policy.* So, where the policy on a vessel insured against the risk of "total loss only," there was no liability for salvage charges.[98]

Salvage or General Average—The York/Antwerp Rules

A comparison of the provisions of the Marine Insurance Act relating to general average (Section 66) and salvage charges (Section 65) will reveal a clear distinction between the two. However, in practice, the distinction is

---

97. *Aitchison v. Lohre*, (1879) 4 A.C. 755, at p. 765; cf. *Steamship Balmoral v. Marten*, [1901] 2 K.B. at p. 904, C.A.
98. *Dixon v. Whitworth*, (1880) 4 Asp. M.L.C. 327, C.A.

obliterated as between parties to a common adventure subject to the York/Antwerp Rules. Rule VI of the 1974 Rules provides:

> Rule VI—Salvage Remuneration
>
> Expenditures incurred by the parties to the adventure on account of salvage, whether under contract or otherwise, shall be allowed in general average to the extent that the salvage operations were undertaken for the purpose of preserving from peril the property involved in the common maritime adventure.

It will be noted, by referring to the various forms of policies set forth in the Appendix, that almost without exception they all provide that general average is payable in accordance with the law and practice at the place where the adventure ends, or in accordance with the contract of affreightment or the York/Antwerp Rules. Therefore, in practice, salvage charges incurred for the common safety are recoverable as part of general average and not as "salvage charges."

Also, as a matter of practice, when a salvage operation has been concluded, the vessel is generally in the possession of the salvor, or, if not in his possession at the time, he may have arrested it for security for his salvage claim. Thus, the shipowner will desire to have his vessel released. To accomplish this, he posts security to the salvor for all the salved property, including cargo. He will then take counter-security from the cargo interests so that he, in turn, may be paid in full on completion of the general average adjustment. If the shipowner pays the salvage award in full, he will be entitled to commission and interest thereon as allowed in the 1974 Rules, Rules XX and XXI.

Underwriters are not, of course, liable for salvage charges under their policies if the charges were incurred in preventing a loss which is otherwise not covered under the policy. For example, if the reason for the salvage services was the unseaworthiness of the vessel with the privity and knowledge of the shipowner, such as permitting the vessel to leave port with an insufficient supply of fuel, then underwriters are not liable as the services were not rendered by reason of an insured peril.[99] This principle is reiterated in Clause 11.4 of the new London Hull Clause which reads: "No claim under this Clause 11 shall in any case be allowed where the loss was not incurred to avoid or in connection with the avoidance of a peril insured against."

Interestingly, in one case, salvage charges were divided between two parties—one the government and the other an underwriter. In that case, *Pyman S.S. Co. Ltd. v. Admiralty*,[100] the vessel was insured by its owners against marine risks and the government, in turn, assumed liability for

---

99. *Ballantyne v. McKinnon*, (1897) 2 Q.B. 455, 1 Com.Cas. 424, 8 Asp. M.L.C. 173.
100. (1918) 1 K.B. 480, 14 Asp. M.L.C. 171.

war risks. Having become disabled when its propeller shaft broke, and in the midst of a gale, the ship was drifting down upon a German minefield. It was towed into a safe port and a salvage award made. The arbitrator apportioned the award between the marine risk underwriter and the government. His decision was affirmed by the courts.

Measure of Indemnity for Salvage Charges

As a matter of practice, the determination of a salvage award is tied to the salved values. The value of any one interest may, therefore, exceed its insured value. This creates a double restriction on recovery against underwriters because not only is the claim limited to 100 percent of the insured value[101] but if the property is underinsured the claim is proportionately reduced. This latter principle is demonstrated in *Balmoral Steamship Co. Ltd v. Marten*[102] where the vessel's insured value was 17.5 percent less than her salved value. As a consequence, her owner's claim under the policy was proportionately reduced. This principle is now reflected in Section 73(2) of the Marine Insurance Act which provides that where the insurer is liable for salvage charges the extent of his liability must be determined on the same principle as that applied to general average.

Recovery of Life Salvage under Policies

Keeping in mind that under American law no remuneration is payable for life salvage but that if the life salvors also salve property, they may be entitled to an enhanced award out of the salved property, it would appear that the vessel owner, having to pay such an award, could recover it from his underwriters, subject, of course, to proportioning by virtue of underinsurance. There are, thus far, no American cases on the subject. The question has arisen in England, however, in *Grand Union (Shipping), Ltd. v. London Steamship Owners' Mutual Ins. Ass'n Ltd. (The Bosworth No. 3)*[103] where it was held that the enhanced award payable by reason of life salvage was recoverable from hull underwriters.

Sister Ship Salvage

More frequently than one would surmise, salvage services are rendered to a vessel and her cargo by another vessel in the same ownership. Under both American and English law, this is termed "sister ship salvage", and the owner of the salving vessel is entitled to an award for services ren-

---

101. *Aitchison v. Lohre, supra,* n. 97.
102. (1902) A.C. 511, 9 Asp. M.L.C. 321.
103. [1962] 1 Lloyd's Rep. 483.

dered on behalf of the cargo in the salved vessel (assuming it is owned by third parties) and the master, officers, and crew of the salving vessel are entitled to an award not only against the cargo but also against the salved vessel.[104] However, in recognition that salvage efforts on the part of owners of sister vessels ought to be encouraged rather than discouraged, hull underwriters (and freight underwriters) routinely include a Sister Ship Clause in their policies.

In the new London Institute Hull Clauses, the Sister Ship Clause is Clause 9 and reads:

> Should the Vessel hereby insured come into collision with or receive salvage services from another vessel belonging wholly or in part to the same Owners or under the same management, the Assured shall have the same rights under this insurance as they would have were the other vessel entirely the property of Owners not interested in the Vessel hereby insured; but in such cases the liability for the collision or the amount payable for the services rendered shall be referred to a sole arbitrator to be agreed upon between the Underwriters and the Assured.

In the American AIH form (1977), a Sister Ship Clause appears in the General Average and Salvage Clause (lines 120-133), as well as in the collision clause (lines 158-184). The language is essentially the same as that found in the new London Institute Hull Clauses except in the method of appointing arbitrators.

Where There Is a Total Loss and There Are No Proceeds or the Expenses Exceed the Proceeds

It may well come to pass that in an emergency situation, a shipowner may incur costs in attempting to save his vessel and its cargo which fall neither within sue and labor expenses, nor salvage charges, but as general average expenses which are not fully recoverable in all circumstances—

---

104. Sec. 727 of the Salvage Act, 1912, provides: "The right to remuneration for assistance or salvage services shall not be affected by common ownership of the vessels rendering and receiving such assistance or salvage services." See *Kimes v. U.S.*, 207 F.2d 60, 1953 AMC 1335 (2d Cir.); *Spivak v. U.S.*, 203 F.2d 881, 1953 AMC 866 (3d Cir.); *Kovell v. Portland Tug & Barge Co.*, 171 F.2d 749, 1949 AMC 380 (9th Cir.); *Jacobsen v. Panama R.R. Co.*, 266 F. 344 (2d Cir., 1920); *Markakis v. S.S. Volendam*, 486 F.Supp. 1103, 1980 AMC 915 (S.D.N.Y.); *In re Esso Shipping Co.*, 122 F.Supp. 133, 1954 AMC 734 (E.D.,La.); *Hendry Corp. v. Aircraft Rescue Vessels*, 113 F.Supp. 198, 1953 AMC 2115 (E.D.,La.); *Schroeder v. U.S.*, 1951 AMC 1906 (S.D.N.Y.); *Burke v. U.S.*, 96 F.Supp. 335, 1951 AMC 1137 (S.D.N.Y.); *Hadley v. Brown*, 1949 AMC 1181 (S.D.N.Y.); *Kittelsaa v. U.S.*, 75 F.Supp. 845, 1948 AMC 500 (E.D.N.Y.); *Southern Pac. S.S. Co. v. New Orleans Coat etc.*, 43 F.2d 177, 1930 AMC 1593 (E.D.,La.); *U.S. v. Standard Oil Co.*, 258 F. 697 (D.,Md., 1919) *aff'd* 264 F. 66 (4th Cir., 1920); *Arbitration for Salvage Services Rendered by S.S. Louis McLande*, 1949 AMC 2033 (Clark, Arb., 1949).

particularly where the vessel is a total loss. Thus, although the shipowner has acted in the best interests of all parties, he may find that he is unable to recover all of his expenses. This problem has been approached by hull underwriters inserting a special clause in their policies by which any proportion of the expenses attaching to the vessel is recoverable from the hull underwriters, while the proportion attaching to the cargo is usually recoverable from the vessel owner's P & I Club. The clause in the American AIH (1977) form reads as follows:

> If claim for Total Loss is admitted under this Policy and sue and labor expenses have been reasonably incurred in excess of any proceeds realized or value recovered, the amount payable under this Policy will be the proportion of such excess that the amount insured hereunder (without deduction for loss or damage) bears to the Agreed Value or to the sound value of the Vessel at the time of the accident, whichever value was greater; provided always that Underwriters' liability for such expenses shall not exceed their proportionate part of the Agreed Value. The foregoing shall also apply to expenses reasonably incurred in salving or attempting to salve the Vessel and other property to the extent that such expenses shall be regarded as having been incurred in respect of the Vessel.

The comparable clause in the new London Institute Hull form (Clause 13.5) does not differ significantly from the clause in the AIH form.

Special Charges

Cases will be encountered in which the term "special charges" has been used. (This term appeared in the General Average and Salvage Clause of the 1941 AIH form but was deleted in the 1970 version). It is not at all clear what the term means. Presumably, it is synonymous with particular charges, i.e., expenses incurred by or on behalf of the assured for the safety and preservation of the subject matter insured, other than general average and salvage charges. Otherwise, it is an anomaly since the overall clause in which the term has appeared has reference to joint sharing of expenses in accordance with proportionate formulae, and particular average expenses are chargeable only against the specific party owning that portion of the venture which is benefitted.

The term was construed in *Western Assur. Co. v. Baden Marine Assur. Co.*[105] There, the plaintiff company insured a cargo of cattle, and reinsured a part of the risk with the defendant company, which issued a certificate containing the following clause: "Insured against absolute total

---

105. (1902) 22 Que. S.C. 374.

loss of vessel and animals, but to pay general average . . . and special charges." The ship was wrecked, and some of the cattle were jettisoned, but others were taken ashore to a place which was admittedly not safe. They were later transported to other places where, there being no shipping available to take them to their destination, they were sold. The owners assigned all rights in the cattle to the plaintiff company, which thereupon paid for them as for a total loss. In a suit against the reinsurer, it was held that the reinsurer was liable for its proportion of the costs of salvage and sale and of the expenses of feeding the cattle before sale. The court held that the words "special charges" must be taken as being synonymous with "particular charges" and, as so construed, they included all these expenses.

Sue and Labor Clause—Duty to Avert or Minimize Loss

The duty of the assured and his agents to take such measures as may be reasonable for the purpose of averting or minimizing a loss is made very clear by subsection (4) of Section 78, Marine Insurance Act, 1906, reading:

> (4) It is the duty of the assured and his agents, in all cases, to take such measures as may be reasonable for the purpose of averting or minimising a loss.

Again, this admonition is but declaratory of the common law.[106]

Note that the American form of the Sue and Labor Clause differs from the English form. In the former, the phrase is: " . . . It shall be lawful *and necessary* . . . for the assured to sue and labor"; in the latter the phrase is: "It shall be lawful to the assured", etc. In the new London Institute Hull Clauses, the draftsmen have been more forthright and the phrase now reads: "In case of any loss or misfortune it is the *duty* of the Assured . . . ." However, the courts have not construed the forms differently. For example, in *Republic of China v. National Union Fire Ins. Co.*,[107] the court said, in part:

> Although the customary form is couched in permissible terms, an assured has always been required to labor diligently for the recovery

---

106. *Benson v. Chapman*, (1849) 2 H.L. Cas. 696, 9 E.R. 1256; *Notara v. Henderson*, (1872) L.R. 7 Q.B. 225, Ex. Ch.; *Republic of China v. National Union Fire Ins. Co.*, 151 F.Supp. 211, 1957 AMC 915 (D.,Md.), modified 254 F.2d 177, 1958 AMC 751 (4th Cir.); *Kidston v. Empire Ins. Co.*, (1866) L.R. 2 P.C. 357, 16 L.T. 119, 2 Mar. L.C. 460; *Columbian Ins. Co. v. Ashby*, 29 U.S. 139 (1830); *Currie v. Bombay Native Ins. Co.*, (1869) L.R. 3 P.C. 72; *Meyer v. Ralli*, (1876) 1 C.P.D. 358; *Lind v. Mitchell*, (1928) 98 L.J.K.B. 120, 32 Ll.L.Rep. 70, C.A.

107. 151 F.Supp. 211, 1957 AMC 751 (D.,Md.), modified 254 F.2d 177, 1958 AMC 915 (4th Cir.).

of the property; he must take such action as a prudent uninsured owner would take under similar circumstances.

In light of the fact that the assured must take such action as a prudent uninsured owner would take under similar circumstances, it would seem that the failure of the assured or his agents to take appropriate action might, depending on the circumstances, have two effects:

(1) If the failure were held by the court to amount to wilful misconduct, then it would relieve the assurer from liability under subsection (2) (a) of Section 55 of the Marine Insurance Act, 1906, which reads:

> The insurer is not liable for any loss attributable to the wilful misconduct of the assured, but, unless the policy otherwise provides, he is liable for any loss proximately caused by a peril insured against, even though the loss would not have happened but for the misconduct or negligence of the master or crew.[108]

(2) Alternatively, if the failure falls short of wilful misconduct there may nevertheless be a counterclaim by underwriters for the prejudice suffered by them.

This point was discussed in *Astrovlanis Compania Naviera S.A. v. Linard (The Gold Sky).*[109] In that case a vessel struck a rock which should have been given a wide berth. Subsequently, the master continued on toward his destination, relying on his pumps rather than putting into a port of refuge. (It is an understatement to say that the circumstances involved in the case were unusual in the extreme.) The underwriters contended that the assured had breached his duty under Section 78(4) by reason of the master having refused salvage assistance to the sinking vessel. The court held that the word "agents" in Section 78(4) was capable of a wide range of different meanings dependent upon the context and circumstances in which it was used, and, in the absence of instructions from his owners, the failure of the master to take such measures as might be reasonable would not militate against his owners' claim against the insurers. The court said, in part:

> . . . I think the words "his agents" should in the context and to avoid an acute conflict between the two subsections of the Act be read as inapplicable to the master and crew, unless expressly authorized by the assured in relation to what to do or not to do in respect of suing and labouring. Many persons other than the master and members of

---

108. However, it was held prior to the Act that negligence, not amounting to wilful misconduct of the assured, does not prevent recovery. *Trinder & Co. v. Thames & Mersey Ins. Co.,* (1898) 2 Q.B.114, 8 Asp. M.L.C. 373, C.A.

109. [1972] 2 Lloyd's Rep. 187, Q.B.D.

the crew may be agents of the assured with the duty to act on his behalf in relation to suing and labouring.

The court also held that the underwriters could not raise a failure to sue and labor as a substantive defense but must assert it as a counterclaim. In *Lind v. Mitchell*,[110] Lord Justice Scrutton said on this point:

> It has been argued, therefore, that if the agents of the assured do not take all measures that are reasonable, the underwriter is not liable. Now I agree on that point—and therefore exclude it from the case— with the view taken by Lord Sumner in British & Foreign Marine Insurance Company v. Gaunt (at page 65) where he said: "The section obviously refers to Suing and Labouring. It cannot possibly be read as meaning that if the agents of the assured are not reasonably careful throughout the transit he cannot recover for anything to which the want of care contributes. The point therefore fails." I agree with this view, and therefore I shut out any argument based on section 78.

In *Fishing Fleet, Inc. v. Trident Ins. Co. Ltd.*,[110a] a fishing vessel captain fraudulently attempted to sell the vessel, lied to the owner about her shrimp catch, and disappeared after the vessel sank with a hole in her side. The boards around the hole were subsequently found to be facing outward and a hammer and crowbar were found next to the hole. The vessel was insured for $30,000.

Upon learning of difficulties with the vessel, the owner's general manager traveled to Mexico (where the vessel was last reported) to ascertain its condition. He also contacted a retired foreign service officer of the U. S. State Department and asked him to do what he could to safeguard the vessel. The retired service officer telephoned the Fisheries Attache at the U. S. embassy in Mexico City and requested him to contact the Mexican authorities, the port captain, and the local prosecutor and inform them that the captain might try to illegally dispose of the vessel. A month later, the owner sent two of its employees to investigate. By that time, the vessel was already sunk. The owner then sent a marine surveyor to ascertain the damages. The surveyor ascertained that charges of over $40,000 had accrued against the vessel from various Mexican parties.

At each stage of events, the owner kept its insurance agent informed of what was happening and, in turn, the agent was communicating with the insurer's broker. The assured did not, however, tell its agent that it suspected the vessel had been intentionally scuttled.

In due course, the vessel was seized by the Mexican authorities and sold at judicial sale.

---

110. (1928) 98 L.J.K.B. 120, 32 Ll.L.Rep. 70, C.A.
110a. 598 F.2d 925, 1980 AMC 583 (5th Cir., 1979).

The trial court held that the assured was entitled to the full insured value of $30,000 on the theory that the constructive total loss of the vessel was caused by barratry of the master. On appeal, the insurer contended that barratry was not proved; that even if proved, recovery was barred by the F. C. & S. Clause; that the assured had concealed material facts; and that the assured had failed to diligently protect its interest in the vessel.

The fifth circuit affirmed, holding that the acts of the master were barratrous; that such acts had occurred prior to seizure by the Mexican government and the vessel was thus a constructive total loss prior to the seizure; that the insurer was informed of the crucial facts surrounding the condition of the vessel and in these circumstances the insured's failure to provide the insurer with one of the possible causes of the loss (scuttling) was not grounds for avoiding the policy; and that the steps taken by the assured to protect its interest in the vessel were adequate to satisfy its duty under the Sue and Labor Clause.

In *Ope Shipping Ltd. v. Allstate Ins. Co. et al,*[110b] the facts were somewhat more convoluted. There, four ships, owned by three Panamanian corporations and one Nicaraguan corporation, all apparently under the control of General Somoza, the dictator of Nicaragua, were lost to their owners during the 1979 Nicaraguan revolution which resulted in the overthrow of the Somoza regime by Sandanista forces.

Between June 17 and June 22, 1979, all four ships were taken over by the Sandanista forces. On June 24 and 28, Somoza initiated steps to transfer title to the ships to Cayman Island corporations. Such transfer was accomplished by July 9, 1979. On or before July 10, 1979, the marine risk coverage on the ships was cancelled, either for non-payment of premiums or the change in ownership. On July 11, the war risk insurers authorized the assignment of their policy to the Cayman Island corporations and on July 13, 1979, the vessels were registered under the British flag in the Cayman Islands.

By September, 1979, all the vessels had been returned to Nicaragua and the plaintiff owners then sued to recover their insured value. In the summer of 1980, an agency of the Sandanista government commenced court actions to recover port charges for the four vessels, the vessels were attached pursuant to judicial orders and, finally, sold at public auction to the Sandanista agency. Plaintiffs claimed that their losses were covered by both the marine risk and war risk policies. The trial court held that they were covered by neither.

On appeal, the second circuit affirmed as to the marine risk issue but reversed as to the war risk. As to the marine risk policies, the court held that there was no question but that the four crews were guilty of bar-

110b. 687 F.2d 639, 1983 AMC 22 (2d Cir., 1982).

ratrous conduct. However, such acts could not be viewed in isolation without giving consideration to the causative and motivative factors. As a matter of common sense and judgment, the proximate cause of the barratrous acts was the Nicaraguan civil war. Thus, the conduct of the crews fell squarely within the F. C. & S. exclusions in the policies so as to relieve the marine risk underwriters from liability.

At trial below, the war risk underwriters were successful in persuading the trial court that they, too, were relieved of liability by reason of policy exclusions which excluded coverage for losses due to "capture, seizure, arrest, restraint, detainment, or confiscation by the Government . . . of the country in which the Vessel(s) is owned or registered . . . ." This required that the trial court pierce the corporate veils so as to place ownership of the vessels in Somoza and thus in the country of Nicaragua. The appeals court held this was error, stating that in the absence of a finding that fraud or misrepresentations were perpetrated on the war risk underwriters as would make it inequitable to hold them to the terms of their contracts, the district court should not have disregarded the corporate existence and titles. The evidence showed that the Nicaraguan registry of all four ships had been cancelled by Nicaraguan authorities as of July 9, 1979. Consequently, any confiscation or detainment by the Nicaraguan government after that date would not be excluded from coverage on the ground that Nicaragua was the country of registry.

The war risk underwriters also urged that the assureds violated their duties under the Sue and Labor Clause to exercise the care of prudent insured owners to protect their property in order to prevent or minimize loss to the underwriters. The appeals court held that although the steps taken by the assureds to regain their vessels were somewhat limited, in the circumstances where the Panamanian and Cuban governments were cooperating with the Sandinistas and Somoza and his principal aide were assassinated, such steps as were taken were all that a prudent person would have been expected to undertake.

Compare, however, *Philpott v. Swann*[111] where the master could have proceeded to a port or repair close by but did not do so; it was held that the loss by the insured was not attributable to perils of the sea as the master was not prevented by such perils from having procured repairs and earning the freight. And in *Standard Marine Ins. Co. v. Nome Beach Lighterage & Transp. Co.*,[112] it was held that a loss caused by the wilful act of the master, as agent of the assured, prevented recovery.

In *Irvin v. Hine*,[113] it was impossible to obtain an accurate estimate of the damage to the vessel without surveying her in drydock but the survey

111. 142 E.R. 800 (1861). Compare *Suo v. Openshaw Simmons Ltd. et al,* 5 B.C.L.R. 370 (1978) (Can.).
112. 133 F. 636 (9th Cir.).
113. (1949) 2 All E.R. 1089, 83 Ll.L.Rep. 162.

was never conducted. The underwriters urged that the assured had breached his duty under Section 78(4) by the failure to conduct the survey. Holding that the survey would not have averted or minimized the loss, but would merely have ascertained its extent, the court rejected the contention. And, see *Northern Barge v. Royal Insurance*,[114] where the court held that the assured could defer abandonment of the vessel until after she had been raised and the repair costs could be ascertained. The costs of raising the vessel were allowed as recoverable items under the Sue and Labor Clause.

Waiver Clause

The first paragraph of the Sue and Labor Clause in the AIH (1977) form concludes with these words: "And it is expressly declared and agreed that no acts of the Underwriters or Assured in recovering, saving or preserving the Vessel shall be considered as a waiver or acceptance of abandonment."

Similar language appears in the old Lloyd's S.G. form and has been incorporated in policies for several centuries at least. The waiver clause really complements the Sue and Labor Clause and is for the mutual benefit of both assurers and assureds. It will be remembered that it is essential if a recovery is to be made for a constructive total loss that the assured tender abandonment to the underwriter. If the underwriter declines the tender of abandonment (which almost invariably happens), then the assured should not be prejudiced if he goes forward with steps to recover, save, or preserve the vessel nor will such steps be taken to constitute a waiver of his notice of abandonment. By the same token, neither should any acts on the part of the underwriter seeking to recover, save, or preserve the vessel be deemed an acceptance of the tender of abandonment.[114a]

It should be emphasized, however, that an underwriter who incurs expenses in saving or protecting the property at risk cannot offset under the suing and laboring clause those expenses against sums otherwise due to the assured under the policy. This was the decision in *Crouan v. Stanier*.[115] In that case, the vessel had been insured against total loss and constructive total loss only. She stranded, and was abandoned to underwriters, who, in turn, declined the abandonment. Subsequently, however, the underwriters hired a firm of ship repairers to refloat the vessel, take her to a port of refuge, and repair her. As a consequence of the repairers doing so, the assured failed in his action against underwriters for a con-

---

114. 1974 AMC 136, *aff'd* 492 F.2d 1248 (N.D., Iowa).
114a. *George W. Clyde*, 12 F.2d 733, 1926 AMC 807 (7th Cir.).
115. (1904) 1 K.B. 87, 19 T.L.R. 664, 73 L.J.K.B. 102.

structive total loss. The underwriters filed a counterclaim seeking to recover from the assured, under the Sue and Labor Clause, the expenses which they had incurred on the theory that the loss averted was not one which was recoverable under the policy. The court held that the underwriters, having taken it upon themselves to incur expenses for suing and laboring, and such efforts having been successful in preventing the vessel from becoming a total loss, could not recover under any implied contract.[116]

There are a number of instances in which recovery under the policy has been denied where measures were not taken to avert or minimize the loss.[117]

For example, in *The Henry*,[118] the vessel grounded. The usual experience in groundings on that particular coast was that vessels could not be got off and the master was aware of that fact. He made no effort to get the vessel off its strand but, instead, abandoned it and sold the hulk. Recovery under the policy was denied.

In *Oswald v. Anglo-Scottish Ins. Co.*,[119] the plaintiff's vessel was stolen, beached, and then set on fire. The fire was extinguished without serious damage having been done. Plaintiff was advised to move the boat to a safer locality to avoid further damage by sudden storms. Instead, he simply tied the boat to a tree. During the night it was totally destroyed by a sudden storm. It was held that plaintiff could only recover for the damages occasioned by the fire since he had failed to take reasonable steps to avert or minimize the further loss.

Sue and Labor Expenses Recoverable even though Underwriters May Have Paid for Total Loss or the Subject Matter Was on F.P.A. Conditions

One of the most important aspects of the clause is that expenses incurred for the purpose of averting or diminishing any loss covered by the clause are recoverable even though the insurer may have paid for a total loss or

116. Logically, if underwriters recovered under an implied contract, it could only be on the theory that they acted as an agent of the assured under the Sue and Labor Clause. Thus, the assured would thereupon be entitled to recover the same amount from the underwriters under the Sue and Labor Clause. Alternatively, the underwriters' claim for salvage remuneration was denied on comparable grounds.

117. *Hugg v. Augusta Ins. & Banking Co. of City of Augusta*, 48 U.S. 595 (1849); *Howland v. Marine Ins. Co. of Alexandria*, F.Cas. No. 6,798 (D.C., 1824, C.A.); *Copeland v. Phoenix Ins. Co.*, F.Cas. No. 3,210, aff'd 76 U.S. 461 (1968); *The Henry*, F.Cas. No. 6,372 (S.D.N.Y., 1834); *Stetson v. Ins. Co. of North America*, 215 F. 186 (D., Pa., 1914); *Frank J. Fobert*, 40 F.Supp. 378, 1941 AMC 1601, 129 F.2d 319, 1942 AMC 1052 (2d Cir.); *Currie v. Bombay Ins. Co.*, (1869) L.R. 3 P.C. 72; *Oswald v. Anglo-Scottish Ins. Co.* (1961) I.L.R. 1-020 (B.C., Can.).

118. F.Cas. No. 6,372 (S.D.N.Y., 1834).

119. (1961) I.L.R. 1-020 (B.C.,Can.).

that the subject matter may have been warranted free from particular average, either wholly or under a certain percentage. The leading case is *Kidston v. Empire Marine Ins. Co.*[120] In that case, the plaintiffs insured chartered freight on a ship from the Chincha Islands to the United Kingdom. The policy contained the usual suing and laboring clause and a warranty against particular average. The ship, having been damaged in a storm, put into Rio where she became totally lost but the cargo was landed and forwarded to its destination in another vessel. The chartered freight was then paid to the shipowners. The shipowners then brought suit to recover from the underwriters a proportionate part of the sum expended in forwarding the cargo from Rio to the United Kingdom. Plaintiff shipowners contended that since the vessel had become a total loss, a total loss of freight had occurred and that inasmuch as the proportion of the homeward freight was a charge incurred in preserving the subject matter of the insurance and so relieved the underwriters from their liability for a total loss of freight, such charges were charges within the suing and laboring clause. The court said, in part:

> We are of opinion . . . that upon the ship . . . becoming a wreck at Rio, and the goods having been landed there, inasmuch as no freight *pro rata itineris* could be claimed, a total loss of freight had arisen, and that the expenses incurred in forwarding the goods to England by another ship were charges within the suing and labouring clause, incurred for the benefit of the underwriters to protect them against a claim for total loss of freight, to which they would have been liable but for the incurring of these charges, and that consequently the amount is recoverable under that clause in the policy.
>
> . . . We think, therefore, on the whole, and upon the true construction of the policy, that on the destruction of the ship and the landing of the cargo at Rio there was a total loss of the freight, unless it could be averted by the forwarding of the cargo by another ship to Great Britain; that the forwarding of the cargo by the *Caprice* was a particular charge within the true meaning of the suing and labouring clause, and not the conversion of total loss into partial loss, which brought the case within the warranty against particular average; and that the due proportion of that particular charge, that charge being within the suing and labouring clause, and incurred for the benefit of the underwriters to preserve the subject of the insurance, and to prevent a total loss, is recoverable under the policy in this action.[121]

---

120. (1866) L.R. 2 P.C. 357, 16 L.T. 119, 2 Mar. L.C. 468.
121. To the same effect, see *Lohre v. Aitchison*, (1878) 3 Q.B.D. 558, C.A., reversed on another point (1879) 4 A.C. 755; *Lee v. Southern Ins. Co.*, (1870) L.R. 5 C.P. 397; *Western Assur. Co. v. Baden Marine Assur. Co.*, (1902) 22 Que. S.C. 374 (Can.); *Glens Falls Ins. Co. v. Montreal Light, Heat, Etc.*, (1928) 45 Que. K.B. 304 (Can., C.A.); *St. Paul Fire & Marine Ins. Co. v. Pacific*

Attention is again called to the last two paragraphs of the Sue and Labor Clause in the AIH form (1977) (quoted *supra*) which apply to reduce recovery where the subject matter of the insurance is underinsured. The effect of "proportioning" under these two paragraphs may be explained as follows:[122]

A vessel is insured for its full value, i.e., $100,000. A total loss occurs during which the assured reasonably incurs sue and labor expenses in the sum of $15,000. The underwriters pay in full but realize $10,000 in selling the hulk "as is, where is." It will be seen that the sue and labor expenses exceeded the salved value by $5,000. There being no underinsurance, the assured would recover his sue and labor expenses in full. However, if the full value of the vessel were $200,000 but insured for only $100,000, then the underwriters' liability would be limited to the proportion that the insured value bears to the full value; i.e., 50 percent. Thus, the underwriters would be liable for only 50 percent of the sue and labor expenses of $15,000 or the sum of $7,500, and the assured would be a coinsurer to the extent of the remaining $7,500.
[123]

It will be observed that the 1977 AIH form differs in one significant particular from the AIH 1970 form. That is in the addition of a clause reading:

> . . . provided always that their liability for such expenses shall not exceed their proportionate part of the Agreed Value.

The explanation is quite understandable. It has happened that an assured, acting reasonably although mistakenly, has incurred expenses considerably in excess of the insured value of his vessel and recovered from the underwriters the agreed value as for a constructive total loss plus additional expenses.[124] In *Northern Barge v. Royal Insurance*,[125] for instance, the assured was held entitled to include the costs of raising his vessel prior

---

Cold Storage Co., 157 F. 625, 14 L.R.A.N.S. 1161 (9th Cir., 1907); *Leduc v. Western Assur. Co.*, (1881) 1 D.C.A. 273, 25 L.C. Jur. 280 (Can.); *Fireman's Fund Ins. Co. v. Trojan Powder Co.*, 253 F. 305 (9th Cir., 1918); *Dauntless*, 129 F.2d 582, 1942 AMC 1021 (2d Cir.); *New York Trap Rock Corp.*, 1956 AMC 469 (Arb., N.Y.); *Home Ins. Co. v. Ciconett*, 179 F.2d 892 (6th Cir., 1950); *White Star S.S. Co. v. N. British & Merc. Ins. Co. (The Tashmoo)*, 48 F. Supp. 808, 1943 AMC 399 (E.D.,Mich.).

122. Essentially the same language will be found in Clauses 13.4 and 13.5 of the New London Institute Clauses (Hull), 1/10/83.

123. Buglass notes that in practice this formula is sometimes ignored when the sue and labor charges are incurred to avert or minimize a loss which would otherwise fall on the policy, giving as an example expenses incurred in recovering or attempting to recover an anchor and cable, the loss of which would constitute a claim under the policy. If reasonably incurred by the assured, such expenses are usually paid in full without reference to the question of underinsurance.

124. *Parkhill-Goodloe v. Home Ins.*, 1976 AMC 951 (M.D.,Fla.); *Northern Barge v. Royal Insurance*, 1974 AMC 136 (N.D. Iowa), *aff'd* without opinion, 492 F.2d 1248 (8th Cir.).

125. *Supra*, n. 124.

to tendering abandonment in determining whether there was a constructive total loss and, on proof of the loss, to recover the sue and labor expenses incurred (costs of raising) in addition to the agreed value. As a consequence, the Total Loss Clause in the 1977 AIH form was amended (lines 136-139) to read:

> There shall be no recovery for a constructive Total Loss hereunder unless the expense of recovering and repairing the Vessel would exceed the Agreed Value. In making this determination, only expenses incurred or to be incurred by reason of a single accident or a sequence of damages arising from the same accident shall be taken into account, *but expenses incurred prior to tender of abandonment shall not be considered if such are to be claimed separately under the Sue and Labor Clause* [italicized portion new in the amended 1977 form].

In short, the assured cannot have his cake and eat it too.

No Loss or Damage Need Be Incurred for Sue and Labor Clause to Be Applicable

It has been argued that no recovery can be had under the Sue and Labor Clause unless actual loss or damage has first been sustained. The cases do not support this view. It is clear that the intention of the clause is to cover also expenses incurred in preventing or averting something which has not yet happened but which, if it does happen, will cause loss to the underwriters. Thus, in *Kidston v. Empire Marine Ins. Co.*,[126] Mr. Justice Willes said:

> The meaning is obvious, that if an occasion should occur in which by reason of a peril insured against unusual labour and expense are rendered necessary to prevent a loss for which the Underwriters would be answerable, and such labour and expense is incurred accordingly the Underwriters will contribute, not as part of the sum insured in case of loss or damage, because it may be that a loss or damage for which they would be liable is averted by the labour bestowed, but as a contribution on their part as persons who have avoided detriment by the result.

Again, in *Great Indian Peninsular v. Saunders*,[127] Chief Justice Earle said:

> The expense that can be recovered under the suing and labouring and travelling clause are expenses to *prevent* impending loss within the policy. [Emphasis supplied.]

126. (1866) L.R. 1 C.P. 535.
127. (1862) 2 B. & S. 266.

Lord Justice Brett's judgment in *Lohre v. Aitchison*[128] is in similar vein:

> Now the general construction of the clause has been held to be, and
> we think it is, that if by perils insured against the subject matter of the
> insurance is brought into such danger that without unusual or extra-
> ordinary labour or expense a loss will very probably fall on the Under-
> writers then each Underwriter will, whether in the result there is a
> total or partial loss, or no loss at all . . . bear his proportionate share.

It will be apparent from the foregoing cases that danger of damage to
the subject matter insured, by a peril insured against, is sufficient to bring
the Sue and Labor Clause into operation and it is not necessary to wait
until actual loss or damage has occurred.

Representative Cases Illustrative of Recovery under Sue and Labor Clause

The following cases are illustrative of those instances in which recovery
has been allowed under the Sue and Labor Clause and the circumstances
thereof.

Ship or Vessel

In *Northern Barge Line Co. v. Royal Insurance*,[129] the plaintiff's barge was
sunk by an explosion while undergoing routine repairs. Under the policy,
the defendant underwriter paid to plaintiff $167,965 for sue and labor
expenses (i.e., recovery expenses) and the stipulated cost of repairs. The
parties agreed that the defendant was liable for $39,900 recovery ex-
penses incurred in raising the barge from the river bottom. This cost was
included in the sum defendant already paid to the plaintiff. The issue
before the court was whether a constructive total loss had occurred, thus
entitling the plaintiff to collect the full agreed valuation of the barge under the policy ($163,000) or whether defendant was liable only for the
cost of repairs ($129,565). Plaintiff contended that, since a constructive
total loss is allowed under the common law where there was a high probability that the expenses of recovery and repair would exceed the policy
valuation, this was a proper case for such recovery. Clearly, the addition of
the $39,900 recovery expenses and the $129,565 stipulated repairs would
result in a sum of $169,465, exceeding the barge's policy valuation of
$163,000.

---

128. (1878) 3 Q.B.D. 558, C.A.
129. 1974 AMC 136 (N.D.,Iowa), *aff'd* without opinion, 492 F.2d 1248 (8th Cir.).

Defendant's position was that the plaintiff was precluded from adding in the recovery expenses because of its failure to tender abandonment of the barge to defendant until after they had been incurred; i.e., a determination of a constructive total loss may only be based upon the prospective expenses of recovery and repair as they appear at the time of abandonment.

Paragraph 9 of the policy read:

> No recovery for a constructive total loss shall be had hereunder unless the expense of recovering and repairing the vessel shall exceed the insured value.

The court held that the inescapable effect of this language was that an actual determination of the expenses or recovery and repair must precede allowance of a claim of constructive total loss and that a tender of abandonment prior to this determination would have been ineffective as it could only be made by raising and recovering the barge.[130]

In *The Duet*,[131] the insured yacht sank at its moorings when it grounded at low tide. The low tide caused the vessel to lean enough so that water flowed into the yacht from a hole normally above the waterline. The court held that the owner acted reasonably in arranging for the raising and repair of the yacht very shortly after its sinking and was entitled to recover the expenses of raising as well as repair.

In *Republic of China v. National Union F.I. Co.*,[132] expenses incurred by the shipowner and the United States, as mortgagee, in attempts to recover possession of vessels whose crews had defected to Communist China were held to to be recoverable under the Sue and Labor Clause; defection of the masters and crews of the vessels held to be barratry.

In *The Armar*,[133] it was held proper, in calculating recovery and repair costs, to include the expenses of salvage, drydock, and surveys, pilots and towage, and superintendence, in expenses necessary to deliver the vessel from its peril to a port of safety and thereafter make it a seaworthy vessel.

In the *Dauntless*,[134] a yacht was torn loose from its moorings by a hurricane and cast upon some submerged hulks. There having been evidence of a breaking of a mast stay during the hurricane and of a blow to the mast itself, the court held the assured was justified in unstepping the mast for an examination at underwriters' expense under the Sue and Labor Clause.

---

130. As already noted heretofore, this decision caused an amendment to the AIH (1977) form, providing that expenses incurred prior to tender of abandonment are not to be considered if such are to be claimed separately under the Sue and Labor Clause.

131. 264 F.Supp. 865, 1967 AMC 1144 (D., Ore.).

132. 151 F.Supp. 211, 1957 AMC 915 (D., Md.), modified 254 F.2d 177, 1958 AMC 751 (4th Cir.).

133. 1954 AMC 1674 (St., N.Y.).

134. 129 F.2d 582, 1942 AMC 1021 (2d Cir.).

In *Parkhill-Goodloe Co., Inc. v. Home Ins.*,[135] an otherwise seaworthy 48-year-old wooden dredge sank at her dock. After receiving a valid notice of abandonment, the underwriter refused to take over the vessel. The assured thereupon raised her, towed her to a shipyard, put her on drydock, and estimates were made of the cost of repairs. The estimate of costs of repairs exceeded the insured value and amounted to a constructive total loss. The court held that the owner was entitled to recover under the policy for (1) the agreed value, (2) drydocking for post-salvage inspection, (3) expenses incurred subsequent to giving notice of abandonment, (4) cost of scrapping the vessel, and (5) reasonable attorney's fees.[136]

Cargo

In *The Pomeranian*,[137] the policy was on live cattle against all risks, including mortality from any cause. The insurer was held liable for the extra cost of fodder supplied to the cattle while the vessel was detained in a port of refuge in order to effect necessary repairs due to perils of the sea.

In *Wilson Bros. Bobbin Co. v. Green*,[138] there was a policy on goods which also included war risks. The vessel was stopped by a German cruiser and forced to put into a Norwegian port where storage and reshipment expenses were incurred. Such expenses were held to be recoverable under the Sue and Labor Clause.

In *Francis v. Boulton*,[139] a ship containing rice collided with another vessel and was partially sunk. The rice was inundated but was eventually kiln-dried and ultimately sold at a loss. The expenses of reconditioning the rice were held recoverable under the Sue and Labor Clause.

In *St. Paul Fire & Marine Ins. Co. v. Pacific Cold Storage Co.*,[140] a vessel transporting a cargo of perishable goods up an Alaskan river was frozen in by ice. To avoid the loss of the cargo, it was shipped by land to its desti-

---

135. 1976 AMC 951 (M.D.,Fla.).

136. Other cases involving vessels are: *Reliance Ins. Co. v. The Escapade*, 280 F.2d 482, 1961 AMC 2410 (5th Cir.); *Johnston v. New South Wales Marine Assur. Co.*, (1880) 14 S.A.L.R. 157 (S.A. Sup. Ct., F.C., Aus.) (steamer pulled off strand by tugs); *Leduc v. Western Assur. Co.*, (1881) 1 D.C.A. 273, 25 L.C. Jur. 280 (Can.) (insured entitled to reimbursement for repairs in additional to full amount of the policy where the vessel became a total loss after repairs were effected); *White Star S.S. Co. v. North British & Merc. Ins. Co. Ltd. (The Tashmoo)*, 48 F. Supp. 808, 1943 AMC 399 (E.D.,Mich.) (fund derived from sale of furniture and equipment of a sunken excursion vessel [such equipment having been removed and stored ashore prior to an unsuccessful salvage operation] does not constitute salvage which may be offset against sue and labor expenses where underwriters decline abandonment).

137. (1895) P. 349.

138. (1917) 1 K.B. 860, 14 Asp. M.L.C. 119.

139. (1895) 65 L.J.Q.B. 153, 8 Asp. M.L.C. 79.

140. 157 F. 625 (9th Cir).

nation. It was held that the expenses of transshipment were within the Sue and Labor Clause.

In *Northwestern National Ins. Co. v. Chandler Leasing Corp.*,[141] the cargo policy was on an "all risks" basis, covering cargo containers "only against Total Loss and/or Constructive Total Loss due to any risks of physical loss from any external causes . . . ." The containers were leased to Pacific Far East Lines which was adjudicated a bankrupt. The lessors of the containers were additional assureds under the cargo policy. They expended various sums in locating and repairing some of the containers, and argued that the repair costs were also covered under the policy. The court held that to the extent that the lessors could prove that the repairs were made to prevent the total or constructive total loss of the containers and at a time when the containers were actively threatened by an insured peril, such losses were covered under the Sue and Labor Clause of the policy.

In *Integrated Container Service Inc. v. British Traders Ins. Co. Ltd.*,[142] the facts were remarkably similar to those involved in *Northwestern National Ins. Co. v. Chandler Leasing Corp., supra.* It, too, involved missing containers in which the assureds had expended sums in recovering some of them and claimed under the Sue and Labor Clause. Recovery was allowed under the clause. *Integrated Container* is, however, doubly interesting in that J. Neill refused to follow the New South Wales decision, *Emperior Goldmining Co. Ltd. v. The Switzerland General Ins. Co. Ltd.*[143] where J. Manning had held, in effect, that inasmuch as the Marine Insurance Act plainly imposed upon the assured the duty to take such measures as are reasonable for the purpose of averting or minimizing a loss, recovery should be allowed for expenses even in the absence of a suing and laboring clause. In the event, as the policy in *Integrated Container* did contain a suing and laboring clause, recovery was allowed thereunder.

In *Champion Int'l v. Arkwright-Boston*,[144] the ocean carrier, in essence, converted the plaintiff-assured's cargo. Ultimately, however, the plaintiff recovered its cargo in specie, virtually undamaged, and later resold it at a good price. The defendant underwriters were accordingly held liable to plaintiff under its policy of all risk of physical loss or damage to the cargo from an external source, but the question before the court was the monetary extent of defendant's liability under the policy. Correspondingly, the defendant insurer was held liable for the assured's sue and labor expenses in regaining its cargo and forwarding it on to destination as well as the assured's attorneys' fees and expenses in establishing the insurer's liability under the policy.[145]

---

141. 1982 AMC 1631 (N.D.,Cal.).
142. [1981] 2 Lloyd's Rep. 460.
143. (1964) 5 F.L.R. 247 (Aus.).
144. 1982 AMC 2496 (S.D.N.Y.).
145. Other cargo cases involving the Sue and Labor Clause are: *Fireman's Fund Ins. Co.*

Freight

In *Kidston v. Empire Ins. Co.,*[146] the policy of insurance was on chartered freight, warranted to be free from particular average. Due to a sea peril, the vessel became a constructive total loss but the cargo was landed and forwarded to destination in another vessel. The expenses of landing, warehousing, and reloading the cargo were held recoverable as particular charges under the Sue and Labor Clause.

In *Currie & Co. v. Bombay Native Ins. Co.,*[147] a ship was reduced to a wreck and totally incapable of earning its freight. The court held that there had been a total loss of freight and the freight and disbursements associated therewith were recoverable.

In *Lee v. Southern Ins. Co.,*[148] the policy covered freight. The vessel, while bound for Liverpool, stranded near Pwllheli. The cargo was landed and, in order to earn the freight, was forwarded on by rail to its destination at a cost of £200. The cargo could have been forwarded by another vessel at a cost of only £70. The insurer on the freight was held liable for £70 only rather than the full £200.

In *Tweedie Trading Co. v. Western Assur. Co. of Toronto,*[149] the policy insured the freight on a cargo of livestock. The cattlemen carried aboard the vessel refused to work and the vessel was compelled to deviate to another port for the purpose of procuring other workmen. The underwriters were held liable for the expenses of the deviation.[150]

---

v. Trojan Power Co., 253 F. 305 (9th Cir.) (cargo underwriter held liable for the extra cost of forwarding goods after the vessel stranded); *Berns & Koppstein, Inc. v. Orion Ins. Co.,* 273 F.2d 415, 1960 AMC 1379 (2d Cir.) (costs of reconditioning cargo so as to pass Food and Drug Administration inspection held recoverable under the clause); *Brown & Root v. American Home,* 353 F.2d 113, 1965 AMC 2689 (5th Cir.) (fee paid to surveyor acting solely for the underwriter held recoverable to the extent it was reasonably attributable to the action of a prudent uninsured cargo owner in the care, protection, and salvage of cargo); *Western Assur. Co. v. Baden Marine Assur. Co.,* (1902) 22 Que. S.C. 374 (Can.) (cargo of cattle; the vessel was wrecked and some cattle taken ashore where they were later transported elsewhere. There being no shipping available, they were sold. Held: underwriters liable for proportion of costs of salvage and sale and of expenses of feeding the cattle before sale); *Consolidated Int'l v. Falcon,* 1983 AMC 270 (S.D.N.Y., 1982) ("South America" clause in cargo policy terminated coverage 60 days after discharge at destination; shipper-assured had no claim for sue and labor expenses incurred after such termination. Also held: all risks policy covering "new machinery" also includes unused machinery stored in original crates); *Champion, Int'l v. Arkwright-Boston,* 1982 AMC 2496 (S.D.N.Y., 1982) (although shipper-assured was not entitled to recover from the cargo insurer for an actual total loss of cargo which was repossessed after having been converted by the shipowner, the insurer was liable for the assured's sue and labor expenses in regaining possession and forwarding the cargo to destination, and for the assured's attorneys' fees and expenses incurred in establishing the insurer's liability).

146. (1866) L.R. 2 P.C. 357, 2 Mar. L.C. 468.
147. (1869) 16 E.R. 740.
148. (1870) L.R. 5 C.P. 397, 3 Mar. L.C. 393.
149. 179 F. 193 (2d Cir., 1910).
150. See discussion of other freight policies and the applicable rules under heading of

Liability Policies

Keeping in mind at all times that the customary P & I policy does not include a Sue and Labor Clause, and that if sue and labor expenses are to be recovered under a liability policy, the policy must so provide.[151] Where the policy does so provide, such expenses are recoverable if the peril or risk involved which occasioned the expenditures is otherwise covered in the policy.

For example, in *Edward A. Ryan*,[152] a tug owner recovered his counsel fees and disbursements incurred in *unsuccessfully* defending an action for damage to cargo on a barge in tow under a tower's liability policy.

In *Pelican*,[153] the court held that the underwriters were obliged to defend claims arising out of the sinking of a charter fishing boat where the claims totalled $1,476,000 but total coverage under the policy was only $300,000, the court stating that the "duty to defend is broader than the duty to pay."

In *Narco-Lolita*,[154] legal fees incurred by the assured in defending against a claim for which the insurer was ultimately held liable were held to be recoverable under the Sue and Labor Clause in the policy.

In *Employers Mutual v. Pacific Inland*,[155] expenses of defending against a claim for damages occasioned to a dock when the assured's barge was alongside the dock were held recoverable.[156]

"Particular Average on Freight," Chapter XX, "Particular Average."

151. See discussion, Chapter XXI.

152. 67 F.2d 544, 1933 AMC 1631 (2d Cir.).

153. 1954 AMC 1446 (St., N.Y.).

154. 286 F.2d 600, 1961 AMC 1999 (5th Cir.).

155. 358 F.2d 719, 1967 AMC 1855 (9th Cir.).

156. See, also, *Charles J. King v. U.S.F. & G.*, 264 F.Supp. 703, 1967 AMC 1502 (S.D.N.Y.) (underwriters offered to defend without prejudice to their right to disclaim coverage; the insured refused and incurred expenses in unsuccessfully defending. The expenses were held recoverable); *Monari v. Surfside Boat Club*, 469 F.2d 9, 1973 AMC 56 (2d Cir.) (since liability underwriter's obligation to defend is broader than its obligation to indemnify, the insurer was held liable for legal costs incurred by the assured in defending against a claim which might reasonably have fallen within the coverage of the policy even though the court ultimately held that no coverage existed. Compare, however, *The William Luckenbach—Powerful*, 1936 AMC 1796 [Arb.]); *M.J. Rudolph v. Lumber Mutual Fire*, 371 F.Supp. 1325, 1974 AMC 1990 (E.D.N.Y.), [1975] 2 Lloyd's Rep. 108 (P and I underwriters held liable to pay the assured's expenses for removing a wreck under compulsion of law which expenses were not, of course, covered under the hull policy's Sue and Labor Clause); *The Wyoming*, 76 F.2d 759, 1935 AMC 670 (2d Cir.) (underwriters compelled to pay the fees of the assured incurred in defense of a suit wherein the liability of the assured was established); *Michaels v. Mutual Marine*, 472 F.Supp. 26, 1979 AMC 1673 (S.D.N.Y.) (even though the assured charterer did not comply with the policy requirement that it obtain the insurer's "prior written consent" before incurring legal fees and expenses, charterer entitled to indemnity where insurer breached its duty to defend. The insurer's complete (and erroneous) disavowal of liability entitled the charterer to recover its counsel fees and costs in defending a shipowner's claim for damages to the vessel during the discharge of scrap cargo); *Healy Tibbitts v. Foremost*, 1980

It is clear, however, that expenses recoverable under a Sue and Labor Clause do not include the assured's costs in suing the insurer itself. This was the holding in *Blasser Bros. v. Northern Pan-American Line et al*,[157] where the assured cargo shipper sued both the ocean carrier and its cargo underwriter for damaged cargo. The shipper recovered against both defendants and the defendant underwriter recovered on its cross-claim over against the ocean carrier. On appeal, the assured sought to recover all its costs incurred from its cargo underwriter under the Sue and Labor Clause in the policy. The court denied such recovery stating:

> . . . The purpose of the sue and labor clause is to reimburse the insured for those expenditures which are made primarily for the benefit of the insurer to reduce or eliminate a covered loss. *Continental Food Products, Inc. v. Insurance Co. of North America*, 1977 AMC 2421, 2424, 544 F.2d 834, 837 n. 1 (5 Cir. 1977), citing, *Reliance Insurance Co. v. The Escapade*, 1961 AMC 2410, 280 F.2d 482, 488-89 (5 Cir. 1960). Sue and labor expenses are sums spent by the insured in an effort to mitigate damages and loss. *Seaboard Shipping Corp. v. Jocharanne Tugboat Corp.*, 1972 AMC 2151, 2155-56, 461 F.2d 500, 503 (5 Cir. 1972). Such expenses can include salvage operations and removal of cargo to safekeeping.
>
> Expenses under a sue and labor clause do not include those which are exhausted in litigation against the insurer itself . . . .[158]

The interface between the obligation of the hull underwriters to pay sue and labor expenses under the hull policy and the correlative obligation of the P & I underwriters to respond to expenses which are not covered by a hull policy is graphically demonstrated in a quartet of cases: *M.J. Rudolph v. Lumber Mutual Fire*,[159] *Seaboard Shipping Corp. v. Jocharanne Tugboat Corp. et al*,[160] *Progress Marine, Inc. v. Foremost Insurance Company*,[161] and *Continental Oil Co. v. Bonanza Corp.*[162]

AMC 1600 (N.D.,Cal.) (P & I policy clause, giving the insurer the *right* to defend an action against the assured, does not create a *duty* to take over the defense. Held: Insurer not obligated to indemnify assured barge owner for its expenses in defending against liability to the United States for costs of cleaning up an oil spill after the barge sank. The policy contained a "Pollution Exclusion Clause," and the insurer's obligation to pay reasonable defense costs was limited to "any liabilities insured hereunder").

157. 628 F.2d 376, 1982 AMC 84 (5th Cir.).

158. By statute in many states, assureds are entitled to recover their attorneys fees and costs incurred in suits against their own underwriters if they prevail in such suits. In the instant case, such a statute existed (Fla. Stat. Ann., Sec. 627.428(1) (West 1972), but as the assured failed to comply with its procedural requirements, recovery on that basis was denied.

159. 371 F.Supp. 1325, 1974 AMC 1990 (E.D.N.Y.), [1975] 2 Lloyd's Rep. 108.

160. 461 F.2d 500, 1972 AMC 2151 (2d Cir.).

161. 642 F.2d 816, 1981 AMC 2315 (5th Cir.), *cert. den.* 454 U.S. 860, 1982 AMC 2110 (1982).

162. 706 F.2d 1365, 1983 AMC 2059 (5th Cir.).

In *M.J. Rudolph*,[163] the plaintiff bareboat chartered one of its barges to Luria International. While under tow by a third-party contractor it capsized. It was then towed to a pier on Staten Island where it later sank. Plaintiff then abandoned the barge to the Army Corps of Engineers. The City of New York then demanded that the plaintiff remove the barge as being a menace to navigation and a criminal charge for obstructing the waterfront was concurrently served on the plaintiff. The barge was thereupon removed and the plaintiff was billed $13,500 for the removal costs. Plaintiff claimed against the defendant underwriter under the P & I policy it had issued to plaintiff. Defendant refused to pay on the grounds that its policy excluded liability with respect to any loss, damage, or expense which would "be payable under the terms of the American Institute Hull Clauses (1/18/70) form of policy on hull and machinery, etc. if the vessel were fully covered by such insurance sufficient in amount to pay such loss, damage, or expense." In fact, the vessel in question was not covered by any hull insurance.

The court held that the barge was completely sunk, rendered unnavigable, and therefore a wreck; that the removal of the wreck was compulsory by law and that a standard form of AIH hull policy as referenced in the defendant's P & I policy expressly excluded wreck removal. As such liability was excluded, it would not have been covered by the Sue and Labor Clause and the defendant underwriter was therefore held liable.

In *Seaboard Shipping*,[164] a barge owned by Jocharanne, carrying 50,000 barrels of gasoline, went aground in Lake Ontario and began leaking gasoline into the water and adjacent shoreline. The Salvage Association of London appointed an independent surveyor. At the time of the grounding, the barge was covered by three policies: a $200,000 hull and machinery policy issued by Lloyd's of London; an $80,000 Open Cargo Legal Liability policy issued by Phoenix Assurance; and a $200,000 P & I policy issued by Oceanus Mutual Underwriting.

The surveyor testified that he was acting on behalf of all concerned underwriters. Lloyd's was the insurer actively engaged in the project and Oceanus was not notified of the incident until completion of the salvage work. Seaboard Shipping, the plaintiff, was hired to off-load the usable gasoline cargo; Sequin Salvage Company was engaged to refloat and work on the hull, which continued to present an explosion hazard. The surveyor urged that the vessel be towed directly to Kingston, Ontario, close by, but its owner, apparently intent on trying to save the hull, insisted that it be towed to New York, which was done. At New York, it was declared a constructive total loss.

---

163. *Supra*, n. 159.
164. *Supra*, n. 160.

The trial court found that the leaking and damaged condition of the barge threatened the separate and distinct interests of each insurer and that Jocharanne, in incurring towing and removal charges, was seeking to protect the hull, save the cargo, and prevent explosion and resultant disaster. The basis for Oceanus' obligation to reimburse Lloyd's for the expenses it incurred was found in a term of the Oceanus policy which insured against "costs or charges of raising or removing the wreck of the ship named herein when such removal is compulsory."

On appeal, the court theorized that the trial court may have held as it did based upon two theories: i.e., (1) that the barge was removed under "compulsion of law" and (2) that of a benefit Oceanus had received in the avoidance of explosion and potential liability for injury to persons and property. As to the first theory, the appeals court held that the barge was not removed under compulsion of law as its owner and Lloyd's, far from abandoning their interest in the vessel, had it towed to New York in the vain hope of salvaging it. On the second theory, even though Oceanus admitted that had such an explosion disaster occurred, it might well have been liable for substantial amounts, the court held that the Oceanus policy did not cover for loss, damage, liability, or expense which would have been payable under a standard form of hull policy, i.e., expenses normally payable under a Sue and Labor Clause. In effect, the appeals court found that the expenses involved fell under the hull policy's Sue and Labor Clause and not under the "wreck removal" provisions of the Oceanus P & I policy. Consequently, Oceanus was not liable to contribute to the sue and labor expenses.

In *Progress Marine, Inc. v. Foremost Insurance Company,*[165] the plaintiff's jackup workover barge capsized and sank, while being towed, in approximately 56 feet of water some 11 miles off the Louisiana coast. The capsizing and sinking was due to the negligence of one of the plaintiff's employees. In its submerged position, the barge was located about 1,500 feet south of a manned Shell Oil production platform and about 300 feet southeast of an Exxon Pipeline Company 10-inch high-pressure pipeline. Also in the vicinity were other offshore platforms, pipelines, and additional offshore developmental properties.

At the time of the incident, the barge was covered by a standard P & I policy, form SP-38, which obligated the insurer to reimburse the assured for such sums as it became legally liable to pay and shall have paid on account of " . . . costs or expenses of, or incidental to, the removal of the wreck of the vessel named herein when such removal is compulsory by law . . . ."

The plaintiff wasted little time in dealing with the problem. First, it rescued five crewmen trapped inside the submerged barge. It then pur-

165. *Supra,* n. 161.

sued various sue and labor activities designed to prevent the barge from becoming a total loss. Finally, the plaintiff notified the defendant insurer that the barge was a constructive total loss and abandoned it to the insurer, which, in turn, rejected the abandonment.

The plaintiff, on advice of counsel, proceeded to make arrangements for the removal of the barge. A salvage contractor succeeded in doing so, at great cost. After deduction of salvage recovery and a deductible, the plaintiff assured was out of pocket some $641,000, plus interest. Demand was made on the defendant underwriter. Although the demand was refused, the defendant conceded that the expenses incurred were reasonable.

The task before the appeals court was to construe the phrase "compulsory by law." Citing *Walter v. Marine Office of America*, 537 F.2d 89, 1977 AMC 1471 (5th Cir., 1976), the court held that the policy should be viewed in the light of the setting of the parties and the *reasonable expectations as to the risks and protection against them* so as to effectuate its purposes.[166] Declining to follow *Seaboard Shipping*, the court held that removal "compulsory by law" does not require a peremptory order by an authoritative governmental agency. Instead, it laid down a dual test; i.e., would failure to remove have reasonably exposed an insured to liability imposed by law sufficiently great to justify the expense of removal, and whether the removal was in fact "compelled by law"; that is, performed as a result of a subjective belief on the part of the assured that such was reasonably necessary to avoid legal consequences of the type contemplated by the policy.

The court did not attempt to decide the case on the basis of the tests suggested but, instead, vacated the trial court's judgment and remanded for the "dual inquiry" required.

In *Continental Oil Co. v. Bonanza Corp.*,[167] the fifth circuit *en banc* again confronted the problem. In that case, Conoco, the operator of an offshore drilling rig, chartered a vessel that, due to the negligence of its master, sank beneath the drilling rig. Conoco removed the wreck and sought to recover the cost of removal under its P & I policy. Conoco also sought a declaration that Bonanza Corporation, owner of the chartered vessel, was liable to it for the cost of removal because the vessel's sinking was caused by the negligence of the vessel's captain and deckhand, who were employees of Bonanza under Bonanza's exclusive control. Conoco, the time charterer of the vessel, was named as an additional assured under the P & I policy.

---

166. The most vocal exponent of the "reasonable expectations" doctrine is Professor Keeton (now a United States district judge). See Keeton, "Insurance Law Rights at Variance with Policy Provisions," Part I, 83 *Harvard Law Review* 961 (1970), and Part II, 83 *Harvard Law Review,* 1281 (April, 1970). See, also, *Lewis v. Aetna Ins. Co.*, 264 Or. 314, 505 P.2d 914 (St.,Ore., 1973).

167. *Supra*, n. 162.

The trial court found both Bonanza and the P & I underwriter liable on a variety of theories;[168] i.e., that the vessel's sinking was the fault of its captain and crew and therefore Bonanza, its owner, was liable; that the P & I underwriter was directly liable to Conoco on the policy; that two terms of the policy covered wreck removal expenses; and that Bonanza was not entitled to limit its liability.

On appeal, a three-judge panel affirmed the trial court,[169] holding that although Bonanza was liable to Conoco for wreck removal expenses, Conoco could not recover directly against the P & I underwriter as Bonanza's insurer because neither federal admiralty law nor Texas law permitted a direct action against an insurer.

The three-judge panel discussed the meaning of the phrase "compulsory by law" in considerable detail.[170] Relying primarily on *Progress Marine*, and although recognizing that there was no settled principle of law which would fix liability on Conoco *as the time charterer* if the sunken vessel damaged nearby properties, the panel concluded that Conoco had been compelled to remove the wreck because:

(1) The likelihood that a storm would drive the wreck onto a nearby pipeline, although difficult to estimate, nonetheless existed;

(2) The potential damages were incalculable and if the vessel damaged the nearby pipeline, oil pollution was sure to ensue; and

(3) The cost of the removal was "reasonable."

Subjectively, the court reasoned, although it was to the financial benefit of Conoco to remove the wreck as it might interfere with its oil drilling, its mixed motives for raising the wreck did not prevent it from recovering as its fear of legal liability was sufficient.

The court, although recognizing that under admiralty law Conoco could recover under the policy's wreck removal clause only if the compulsion of law arose out of Conoco's ownership of, or interest in, the vessel, and although recognizing that Conoco was only a time charterer and thus had no "ownership" interest in the vessel, nonetheless held that Conoco was "compelled by law" to raise the wreck in its capacity as "owner" of the vessel. The reasons assigned were:

(1) Conoco was responsible for the presence of the vessel in the midst of the offshore oil fields;

(2) The vessel came to rest on oil fields leased by Conoco; and

(3) Conoco knew that Bonanza, the vessel's owner, had no intention of raising the wreck.

---

168. 511 F.Supp. 62 (S.D.,Tex., 1981).

169. 677 F.2d 455, 1983 AMC 387 (5th Cir.).

170. Conoco's asserted position for removing the sunken vessel was that it posed a serious danger to other oil wells and oil pipelines in the vicinity, and that because of the potential for damage if the vessel were thrown by the seas against a nearby pipeline, and its desire to place a fixed structure on its newly drilled well, it went ahead with the removal.

Judge Dyer entered a vigorous dissent, characterizing the majority decision as "judicial legerdemain."

However, on rehearing *en banc*, Judge Dyer's views were vindicated. The majority approved the "objective" portion of the dual inquiry pronounced in *Progress Marine* but receded from the "subjective" portion. In essence, the majority held that the clause should be so construed that removal does not become compulsory by law only when a court has rendered judgment requiring it or when an official has issued a fiat. As the majority put it, there must be a compulsion, a legal duty. To be compelling, the duty must be clear and the sanctions for its violation both established and sufficiently severe to be impelling, that is, to warrant the cost of removal. Removal occasioned by a reasonable apprehension of slight consequences for inaction or by an unreasonable apprehension even of grave consequences is not "compelled."

As to Conoco's duty as a lessee of the seabed for drilling purposes, the court held that the P & I policy did not insure against removal required of an insured unless the duty was occasioned by its ownership of the insured vessel and that, in addition, neither the lease nor the regulations of the lessor government imposed the legal compulsion contemplated by the policy.

The court noted that Conoco was never the owner or even the bareboat charterer of the vessel. Thus, neither assured, Conoco or Bonanza, could recover the cost of wreck removal unless it was obliged to remove the wreck because of its status *as owner of the vessel*. As the court observed, a non-negligent owner is not personally liable for the cost of removing a sunken vessel, even if the vessel constitutes a hazard to navigation.[171]

As to Conoco's exposure to liability, the court noted that the policy extended only to a duty to remove "imposed by law." Such a duty must be present and unconditional, not remote and contingent. The possibility that, by an extension of maritime law not yet decreed, Conoco might be held liable in the future should the vessel be dislodged from the mud and propelled against other structures was not, as the court viewed it, such a legal obligation.

The court did affirm the prior holding that Bonanza was not entitled to limit its liability as the master of the vessel was sufficiently high in the hierarchy of the corporate owner to infer privity.

---

171. Citing *St. Paul Fire & Marine Ins. v. Vest Transportation*, 666 F.2d 932 (5th Cir. 1982); *Tennessee Sand and Gravel v. M/V Delta*, 598 F.2d 930 (5th Cir. 1979) modified on other grounds, 604 F.2d 13 (5th Cir. 1979); and *Agrico Chemical v. M/V Ben W. Martin*, 664 F.2d 85 (5th Cir. 1981) (a time charterer who does not control the operation or navigation of the chartered vessel is not responsible for the consequences of the vessel owner's negligence).

Must There Be a "Sue and Labor" Clause?

Section 78(4) of the Marine Insurance Act, 1906 states unequivocally:

> (4) It is the duty of the assured and his agents, in all cases, to take such measures as may be reasonable for the purpose of averting or minimizing a loss.

If, as the Act requires, an assured (or his agents) do take such measures as may be reasonable for the purpose of averting or minimizing a loss, are they entitled to be recompensed for expenses incurred in carrying out this duty?

The weight of authority seems to be in the negative unless the policy actually contains either a Sue and Labor Clause or a clause of similar import.

In this connection, attention is specifically directed to *Emperor Goldmining Co. v. Switzerland General Ins. Co.*[172] There, a valued policy was effected on cargo being carried by the ketch *Natono* from Sydney to Fiji. The policy covered all risks but excluded claims for damage proximately caused by delay. The policy did not contain a Sue and Labor Clause.

The vessel was forced to return to Sydney soon after sailing because she was leaking. She was placed in a floating dock for an examination and, in order to do so, the cargo had to be unloaded, stored, and then reloaded. Part of the cargo, being urgently needed in Fiji, was forwarded on by another vessel, the *Wiatona*. Underwriters denied liability for the expenses involved, contending that such expenses were only recoverable under a suing and laboring clause and that the policy did not contain such a clause. Citing subsection (4) of Section 84 of the Australian Marine Insurance Act, 1909 (identical with subsection (4) of Section 78 of the Marine Insurance Act, 1906), the court said, in part:

> . . . The common law is enacted in the Marine Insurance Act, 1909. Section 84 deals with the results which flow from the inclusion of a suing and labouring clause insofar as the extention of liability of the insurer is concerned. Costs described in the clause are to be recoverable notwithstanding that the insurer has paid for a total loss or that there may have been a total or partial warranty of freedom from particular average.
>
> Section 84(4) plainly imposes on the assured a duty to take such measures as are reasonable for the purpose of averting or minimising a loss. I am unable to read this provision as a duty to be carried out by

---

172. 81 W.N. (N.S.W.) 85, 5 F.L.R. 247, [1964] N.S.W.R. 1243, [1964] 1 Lloyd's Rep. 348.

the assured at his own expense, in the absence of a suing and labouring clause in the policy.

The court cited in support of its conclusion *Firemen's Fund Ins. Co. v. Trojan Powder Company*,[173] although noting that the opposing view was expressed in *Great Indian Peninsula Railway Co. v. Saunders*,[174] and *Booth v. Gair*.[175]

Continuing, the court said:

> Having regard to the conclusion at which I have arrived, substantially the whole of the plaintiff's claim succeeds. The detailed expenditure which has been satisfactorily proved, shows that the costs were incurred in unloading freight, storing it and re-loading it—the large items are in respect of the handling of explosives—and other similar expenses properly included as "particular charges."

The claim of the plaintiff for freight paid to the owners of the vessel *Wiatona* for forwarding some of the cargo on to Fiji was disallowed on the grounds that to the extent the plaintiff paid for space on the *Wiatona*, it obtained a corresponding advantage in that an equal amount of cargo space was made available for other goods on the *Natono* after she was repaired and resumed her voyage.

Ivamy, in his third edition (1979), criticizes the decision, stating in part that the decision did not appear to be in accordance with principle for if it is correct then no Sue and Labor Clause need ever be inserted in a policy. Specifically, Ivamy states:

> Again, it is submitted that since sub-ss (1),(2), and (3) of s. 84 all expressly mention the presence of the "sue and labour" clause in the policy, it would be reasonable to suppose that sub-s. (4), being part of the same section, is also intended to relate to policies containing such a clause, for it if had not been so meant, the sub-section would have expressly said so, or else there would have been a provision to this effect in a separate section so that the matter would be put beyond doubt.

Editions prior to publication of the fifteenth edition of Arnould contained language supporting the *Emperor Goldmining* decision. See, for example, Section 869, footnote 90, thirteenth edition, where it was stated:

> These [meaning expenses of warehousing and forwarding cargo] could probably also be recovered under the suing and labouring clause, at the option of the assured (see *per* Lord Ellenborough in Livie v. Janson [1810] 12 East 655); and it is at least doubtful whether even expenses incurred in order to avert a loss—such as, for instance, those

173. 253 F. 305 (9th Cir., 1918).
174. (1862) 31 L.J.Q.B. 206, 6 L.T. 297, 121 E.R. 1072.
175. (1863) 9 L.T. 386, 1 Mar. L.C. 393, 143 E.R. 796.

which were held in *Kidston v. Empire Ins. Co.* to be recoverable under the suing and labouring clause—could not also be recovered from underwriters as money paid on their behalf, apart from the clause. It is the captain's duty in an emergency to act on behalf of all concerned. Might not expenses incurred by him in doing so be recovered by his owners from the underwriters under an implied contract of agency or indemnity, such agency having been thrust upon them or their servant by perils insured against? Cf. *Le Cheminant v. Pearson* (1812) 4 Taunt. 367. Some such view appears to have been held in the American case of *White v. Republic Fire Ins. Co.* (1869) 57 Maine 91. If it were so decided the effect of the suing and labouring clause would appear to be no more than to render certain that which otherwise might have been considered doubtful.

However, in the fifteenth edition, Arnould recedes from this position stating in part: " . . . But it is submitted that particular charges are now recoverable only under the suing and labouring clause."

In the sixteenth (and latest) edition, the editors (Sir Michael J. Mustill and Jonathan C. B. Gilman) take a rather middle position, stating, in part:

> The basis of the decision in *Emperor Goldmining Co. v. Switzerland General Insurance Co.* was that it is impossible to read Section 84(4) of the Australian Marine Insurance Act 1909 (the equivalent of Section 78(4) of the Marine Insurance Act 1906) as a duty to be carried out by the assured at his own expense, in the absence of a suing and labouring clause in the policy. There is much to be said for implying a term in the policy to this effect, since the duty to sue and labour arises whether or not the suing and labouring clause is inserted, but to do so would lead to the conclusion that the clause is surplusage and that it makes no difference whether it be inserted or not.
>
> The present editors consider that a narrower view is to be preferred to that suggested by the Australian decision which has just been cited. It is submitted that the assured can recover expenses in the nature of suing and labouring expenses, in the absence of the usual clause in the policy, in those cases where it can plausibly be said that the need for the expenditure is the direct and natural result of the casualty and the Marine Insurance Act 1906 does not lay down a specific measure of indemnity which meets the case, but that the right to reimbursement is probably not one that exists in all circumstances, in the absence of the clause.[176]

---

176. As the editors also note, there are conflicting decisions on the point in the United States, citing *Fireman's Fund Ins. Co. v. Trojan Powder Co.*, 253 F. 305 (1918) (relied upon by J. Manning in *Emperor Goldmining*) and *American Merchant Mar. Ins. Co. of N.Y. v. Liberty Sand &*

The present editors also point out, as follows:

> Prior to the 15th ed., successive editors of this work stated that particular charges may be recoverable apart from the suing and labouring clause as loss occasioned by a peril insured against "when they have [been] necessarily incurred in consequence of such a peril, as for example when a peril insured against has occasioned the necessity for such expenditure." A distinction appears to have been drawn between such cases and those where expenses were incurred to prevent a peril from causing a loss. See the 14th ed., Vol. 2, at pp 790-791.

The point surfaced again in *Integrated Container Service Inc. v. British Traders Insurance Co. Ltd.*[177] In that case, the plaintiffs carried on the business of leasing containers and were insured with the defendant underwriters for marine risks. Section 2 of the policy provided, *inter alia:*

> . . . This insurance to indemnify the assured in the event of their being unable to recover from lessees or others for All Risks of loss or damage to the subject matter insured . . . .

In 1972, the plaintiffs entered into a lease agreement with Oyama Shipping Co. Ltd. for the leasing to Oyama of containers which Oyama required both for their own use and for the use of other shipping companies operating in the Far East. One of the requirements of the lease was that Oyama was to maintain insurance coverage in respect of the containers.

In 1975, the plaintiffs learned that Oyama was in financial difficulties and got in touch with Oyama's insurers with a view to submitting claims in respect of any of the containers which were recovered in a damaged condition. Oyama had, however, failed to maintain any such insurance and were adjudged bankrupt. The plaintiffs took steps to recover their containers which were scattered over the Far East at various places. Plaintiffs then made claim against their underwriters. The underwriters admitted in principle that the claim would be honored as respects lost and damaged containers but denied any claim for recovery costs since there was no question of an insured peril operating to cause the loss, and the recovery costs were solely incurred in a commercial undertaking to retrieve the containers from a bankrupt lessee.

At trial, J. Neill, relying on that portion of the insuring clause which provided that " . . . this insurance also extends to cover transits not otherwise insured by lessees or others," held that an insured peril had been operative; that the words of the policy "to indemnify the assured in the

---

Gravel Co., 282 F. 514 (1922) (where it was held that in the absence of a suing and laboring clause, particular charges were not recoverable). See Arnould, sixteenth ed., s. 914A.

177. [1981] 2 Lloyd's Rep. 460, Q.B.D.

event of their being unable to recover from lessees or others" constituted an insurance on goods and not a contract to indemnify plaintiffs against their liability to third parties up to a stipulated maximum; that there was language in the policy which constituted a Sue and Labor Clause; and that in light of the policy language the sue and labor expense incurred by plaintiffs was not to be reduced by the deductible clause in the policy.[177a]

Acknowledging that in view of his findings there was no necessity for expressing a view on the alternative claim advanced (that there was no Sue and Labor Clause in the policy) the court nonetheless in *obiter* differed with J. Manning in *Emperor Goldmining* that there was no necessity for a Sue and Labor Clause; i.e., without a Sue and Labor Clause, there would be no implied obligation on the part of the insurers to reimburse the insured for sue and labor expenses.

In a remarkably similar case, *Northwestern National Ins. Co. v. Chandler*,[178] the all risks policy insured leased containers against "total loss and constructive total loss." The insured was Pacific Far East Lines who either owned or leased them. The assured became embroiled in financial difficulties and was ultimately adjudicated a bankrupt. When the assured ceased operations, the lessors, for a variety of reasons, were unable to recover much of their equipment on lease to the assured. Some equipment was lost because the assured lacked the funds to pay for their return and the equipment was thus left scattered all over the world. Other equipment was held in various foreign countries, principally in the Middle East, by third parties who refused to relinquish possession to the lessors, or who demanded payment of debts owed by the bankrupt assured as "ransom" for the return of the equipment. Still other items could not be located due to the assured's inaccurate inventory control. The lessors made demand under the policy and the underwriters refused to pay.

The insuring clause insured against "any risks of physical loss from any external cause," but excluding risks excepted by the F. C. & S. and the S. R. C. C. warranties. The lessors contended that, as a matter of law, the policy language covered for losses due to mysterious disappearance. The underwriter urged that when supported by extrinsic evidence, the language was reasonably susceptible to an exclusion for such losses.

The court held that the insuring provisions were clear and unambiguous; that they were not reasonably susceptible to the exclusion urged; and that extrinsic evidence could not be received for the purpose of varying the terms of the policy.

177a. See *American Home Assur. Co. v. J.F. Shea Co., Inc.*, 445 F.Supp. 365 (D., D.C., 1978) where the court held that since sue and labor coverage is supplemental to the main insuring conditions, the policy deductible does not apply to sue and labor expenses unless the policy expressly so provides.

178. 1982 AMC 1631 (N.D.,Cal., 1982).

The underwriter moved for partial summary judgment that it was not liable for unpaid rentals asserted as claims under the policy; for unpaid rentals based upon reliance on a certificate of insurance or other representations as to the coverage afforded under the policy; and for repair costs amounting to less than a constructive total loss asserted under the policy as written.

The court granted summary judgment as to unpaid rentals based on the policy language; refused to grant summary judgment on the claims of misrepresentation as factual issues were presented; and denied summary judgment as to repair costs which amounted to at least one-half of the insured value of the containers. The latter ruling was based on a provision in the California Insurance Code which defined a constructive total loss as one where more than half in value of the subject matter is actually lost or more than half its value would have to be expended to recover it from the peril involved.

Some of the insureds argued that repair costs were also covered under the Sue and Labor Clause. The court held that to the extent to which it could be proved that repairs were made to prevent the total loss or constructive total loss of the containers, and at a time when the containers were immediately or actively threatened by an insured peril, such losses were covered by the clause.

Clearly, under the common law it has always been the duty of the assured to seek to minimize damages and the assured is obliged to act as if he were a prudent uninsured owner.[179] It can be argued, of course, that if the expenses incurred by the assured were incurred to minimize or avert a threatened loss for which underwriters would be liable, then to the extent to which the underwriters are insulated against greater loss, equity and good conscience would seem to require that the underwriters should at the very least share such expenses with the assured. Examples can easily be postulated whereby acts of an assured in incurring expenses to avert a loss for which underwriters would otherwise be liable would redound to underwriters' benefit to some degree even in the absence of a suing and laboring clause. In fact, an assured might well be tempted to defer incurring such expenses in order to bring pressure to bear on underwriters to respond more fully under the policy. For underwriters to discourage such expenditures would appear to be both unwise and impractical. This would appear to be true especially with respect to P & I policies, most of which do not contain suing and laboring clauses.

This point arose in *Seaboard Shipping v. Jocharanne, et al*,[180] discussed

---

179. Aside from the obligation to do so expressed in Sec. 78(4), the new London Hull Clauses, Paragraph 13.1, and the corresponding provision in the AIH (1977) form impose this obligation on the assured by contract.

180. 461 F.2d 500, 1972 AMC 2151 (2d Cir.); see, also, *Healy Tibbitts Constr. Co. v. Foremost Insurance*, 1980 AMC 1600 (N.D.,Cal.).

supra under "Liability Policies." There, even though the P & I Club admitted that had an explosion disaster occurred and it might well have been liable for substantial damages, the policy did not cover for any loss, damage, liability, or expense which would have been payable under a standard form of hull policy, i.e., expenses normally payable under a Sue and Labor Clause. Moreover, it claimed that any calculation based on the possibility of explosion was extremely hypothetical. The court agreed, noting that none of the expenses was incurred solely to avert those occurrences or protect those interests for which the club alone was liable. All the costs were essential to any attempt to save the hull and cargo, so any benefit to the club was in a sense incidental. The court continued:

> Despite the lack of coverage under the Oceanus policy, one might under these circumstances consider applying equitable principles and hold those who benefited from the services rendered for a portion of their cost, under a theory of equitable contribution or restitution. See Restatement of *Restitution,* Section 115.

However, as the court observed, the presence of a "no contribution" clause in the Oceanus policy precluded the application of such principles, as Oceanus had successfully contracted out of any liability for contribution, under any theory.

In a non-maritime context, the Oregon Supreme Court in *Gowans v. Northwestern Pacific Indemnity Co.,*[181] refused to imply the existence of a Sue and Labor Clause where the policy did not contain one. The case involved an action against an insurance company under a policy insuring for "loss by theft" to recover money paid by the assured as a reward for the return of stolen jewelry covered by the policy. The trial judge had based his decision upon a case involving the interpretation and application of the rights and duties of the insured under a sue and labor policy. Since the policy at issue in the appeal did not contain a Sue and Labor Clause and the court was unwilling to imply the existence of one, the assured did not prevail.

Attention is directed to *Slay Warehousing Co., Inc. v. Reliance Ins. Co.,*[182] which involved an inland marine policy covering loss and destruction or damage to property of others contained in the insured premises. The policy also required the assured to exercise all reasonable means to protect, safeguard, and salvage property. The assured incurred expenses in taking reasonable steps to protect chemicals stored in its warehouse from damage due to exposure following a col-

---

181. 489 P.2d 947 (Or., 1971). Compare *Einard LeBeck, Inc. v. Underwriters at Lloyd's,* 224 F.Supp. 597 (D., Or., 1963) which denied a claim under a Sue and Labor Clause for expenses in connection with the removal of a building after the building collapsed. In that instance, the assured left leased equipment in place for two months and, in addition, charged the cost of demolition to the underwriter.

182. 489 F.2d 214 (8th Cir., 1973).

lapse of the warehouse's walls. The assured recovered notwithstanding its failure to comply with another policy provision requiring it to obtain the underwriter's written consent before incurring any such expenses. The court also noted that the obligation of the underwriter to pay expenses of protecting exposed property may arise from either the insurance agreement or from an implied duty under the policy contract based upon general principles of law and equity.

Despite a diligent search, no cases can be found which have applied the principles of *Restatement of Restitution,* Section 115.

Subrogation

The subject of subrogation is treated in detail in Chapter XXIII. As applied to sue and labor claims, attention is directed to *Yorkshire Insurance Co. Ltd. v. Nisbet Shipping Co. Ltd.*[183] and *The Almirante.*[184]

In *Yorkshire Insurance,* the insured vessel was in a collision with a Canadian naval vessel. Hull underwriters paid a total loss of £72,000 on a valued policy. Her actual value was somewhat greater and, upon being paid that value by the Canadian government, the assured held a windfall or "surplus" in the nature of £55,000. The question was whether the insurer could recover from the assured the amount of such excess. The court answered in the negative.

Confusion is often caused by not distinguishing the legal rights given by abandonment from those given under principles of subrogation, i.e., the difference between having *proprietary* rights incidental to abandonment and having only the *rights and remedies* of the assured in respect of the subject-matter insured. In *Yorkshire Insurance,* the underwriters were merely subrogated to the rights of the assured.

In *The Almirante,* the facts were quite similar and the assured was required to reimburse his underwriters for all the sums paid to him by them, deducting, however, pro-rata, the expenses of the collision litigation. This point does not appear to have been decided under English law, although under American law it is quite clear.

In *Caledonia-Carinthia,*[185] the cargo insurance policy provided that it would be void to the extent of any payment made to the shipper by the carrier. After the insurer had denied liability, the shipper, at the insurer's insistence, sued the carrier and recovered, although after the expenditure of considerable sums in costs and attorneys' fees. The net recovery of the assured, after deduction of costs and fees, was less than the amount to

---

183. [1961] 1 Lloyd's Rep. 479.
184. 304 U.S. 430, 82 L.ed. 1443, 1938 AMC 707.
185. 1933 AMC 735 (NYM).

which he was entitled under the policy. In suit against the underwriters, the assured recovered the difference, together with interest and costs of the suit against the underwriters.

It should be observed that, despite the criticism of UNCTAD, the Sue and Labor Clause (Clause 13) in the new London Hull Clauses perpetuates the restriction on recoveries under the policy to that proportion which the insured or agreed value bears to the "sound" value; i.e., the assured is penalized by under-insurance even though the under-insurance may not have been his fault at all, and may have arisen by virtue of a dramatic increase in vessel values *after* the inception of the policy.